New Dictionary of Scientific Biography

Published by special arrangement with the American Council of Learned Societies

The American Council of Learned Societies, organized in 1919 for the purpose of advancing the study of the humanities and of the humanistic aspects of the social sciences, is a nonprofit federation comprising thirty-three national scholarly groups. The Council represents the humanities in the United States in the International Union of Academies, provides fellowships and grants-in-aid, supports research-and-planning conferences and symposia, and sponsers special projects and scholarly publications.

MEMBER ORGANIZATIONS

American Philosophical Society, 1743
American Academy of Arts and Sciences, 1780
American Antiquarian Society, 1812
American Oriental Society, 1842
American Numismatic Society, 1858
American Philological Association, 1869
Archaeological Institute of America, 1879
Society of Biblical Literature, 1880
Modern Language Association of America, 1883
American Historical Association, 1884
American Economic Association, 1885
American Folklore Society, 1888
American Society of Church History, 1888
American Dialect Society, 1889
American Psychological Association, 1892
Association of American Law Schools, 1900
American Philosophical Association, 1900
American Schools of Oriental Research, 1900
American Anthropological Association, 1902
American Political Science Association, 1903
Bibliographical Society of America, 1904
Association of American Geographers, 1904
Hispanic Society of America, 1904
American Sociological Association, 1905
American Society of International Law, 1906
Organization of American Historians, 1907
American Academy of Religion, 1909
College Forum of the National Council of Teachers of English, 1911
Society for the Advancement of Scandinavian Study, 1911
College Art Association, 1912
National Communication Association, 1914
History of Science Society, 1924
Linguistic Society of America, 1924
Medieval Academy of America, 1925
American Association for the History of Medicine, 1925
American Musicological Society, 1934
Economic History Association, 1940

Society of Architectural Historians, 1940
Association for Asian Studies, 1941
American Society for Aesthetics, 1942
American Association for the Advancement of Slavic Studies, 1948
American Studies Association, 1950
Metaphysical Society of America, 1950
North American Conference on British Studies, 1950
American Society of Comparative Law, 1951
Renaissance Society of America, 1954
Society for Ethnomusicology, 1955
Society for French Historical Studies, 1956
International Center of Medieval Art, 1956
American Society for Legal History, 1956
American Society for Theatre Research, 1956
African Studies Association, 1957
Society for the History of Technology, 1958
Society for Cinema and Media Studies, 1959
American Comparative Literature Association, 1960
Law and Society Association, 1964
Middle East Studies Association of North America, 1966
Latin American Studies Association, 1966
Association for the Advancement of Baltic Studies, 1968
American Society for Eighteenth Century Studies, 1969
Association for Jewish Studies, 1969
Sixteenth Century Society and Conference, 1970
Society for American Music, 1975
Dictionary Society of North America, 1975
German Studies Association, 1976
American Society for Environmental History, 1976
Society for Music Theory, 1977
National Council on Public History, 1979
Society of Dance History Scholars, 1979

New Dictionary of Scientific Biography

VOLUME 1
ABDERHALDEN–BYERS

Noretta Koertge
EDITOR IN CHIEF

CHARLES SCRIBNER'S SONS
An imprint of Thomson Gale, a part of The Thomson Corporation

THOMSON
™
GALE

Detroit • New York • San Francisco • New Haven, Conn. • Waterville, Maine • London

New Dictionary of Scientific Biography
Noretta Koertge

For permission to use material from the product, submit your request via the Web at http://www.gale-edit.com/permissions, or you may download our Permissions Request form and submit your request by fax or mail to:

Permissions Department
Gale Group
27500 Drake Rd.
Farmington Hills, MI 48331-3535
Permissions Hotline:
248-699-8006 or 800-877-4253, ext. 8006
Fax 248-699-8074 or 800-762-4058

Cover photographs reproduced by permission.

Since this page cannot legibly accommodate all copyright notices, the acknowledgements constitute an extension of the copyright notice.

LIBRARY OF CONGRESS CATALOGING-IN-PUBLICATION DATA

New dictionary of scientific biography / Noretta Koertge, editor in chief.
   p. cm.
   Includes bibliographical references and index.
   ISBN 978-0-684-31320-7 (set : alk. paper)—ISBN 978-0-684-31321-4 (vol. 1 : alk. paper)—ISBN 978-0-684-31322-1 (vol. 2 : alk. paper)—ISBN 978-0-684-31323-8 (vol. 3 : alk. paper)—ISBN 978-0-684-31324-5 (vol. 4 : alk. paper)—ISBN 978-0-684-31325-2 (vol. 5 : alk. paper)—ISBN 978-0-684-31326-9 (vol. 6 : alk. paper)—ISBN 978-0-684-31327-6 (vol. 7 : alk. paper)—ISBN 978-0-684-31328-3 (vol. 8 : alk. paper)
   1. Scientists—Biography—Dictionaries. I. Koertge, Noretta.

Q141.N45 2008
509.2'2—dc22
[B]
                         2007031384

Editorial Board

Editorial and Production Staff

PROJECT EDITOR

Angela M. Pilchak

CONTRIBUTING PROJECT EDITORS

Kristin Mallegg
Margaret Mazurkiewicz
Bridget Travers

EDITORIAL ASSISTANTS

Dana Chidiac
Emily Gruber

EDITORIAL TECHNICAL SUPPORT

Mark Droulliard
Marc Faerber
Mark Springer
Mike Weaver

MANUSCRIPT EDITORS

Rhonda K. Baird
Dorothy Bauhoff
Sylvia J. Cannizzaro
Sylvia Engdahl
Christine Kelley
John Krol
Michael L. Levine

Sarah O'Mahen
Anne Mylott
Linda Sanders

PROOFREADERS

Melodie Monahan
Amy L. Unterberger

TRANSLATORS

Erwin Fink
Louis Kibler
George Kolodziej
Donald Nicholson
Alan Thwaits

PRODUCT DESIGN

Pamela A. E. Galbreath
Linda Hubbard

IMAGING

Dean Dauphinais
Lezlie Light
Kelly Quin

GRAPHIC ART

GGS Information Services, York, PA

INDEXER

Factiva, Inc.

RIGHTS ACQUISITION AND MANAGEMENT

Scott Bragg
Jackie Jones
Sue Rudolph

TYPESETTER

Datapage Technologies International, Inc.

COMPOSITION

Evi Seoud
Mary Beth Trimper

MANUFACTURING

Dorothy Maki

PUBLISHER

Jay Flynn

EDITORIAL DIRECTOR

John Fitzpatrick

Table of Contents

Introduction

The *New Dictionary of Scientific Biography (DSB)* is a major addition to the magisterial compilation of scientific biographies edited by Charles Gillispie and published by Charles Scribner's Sons between 1970 and 1980. The original sixteen volumes of the *DSB* presented scholarly essays on the lives and careers of great scientists, mathematicians, and natural philosophers from the time of Thales, Hippocrates, and Aristotle to such twentieth-century figures as Hubble, Curie, and Einstein. In 1990, two new supplementary volumes were added to cover recently deceased figures such as Rachel Carson, Kurt Gödel, Werner Heisenberg, and Jacques Monod.

The *DSB* became an indispensable tool for a wide audience. For scholars it was a repository of authoritative biographical information and a portal to the best bibliographic sources. And for students and laypeople it provided an attractive new way to understand important scientific achievements. How better to appreciate a new concept or a new instrument than to read about the personal path that led to the innovation and to share in the excitement—and disappointments—that accompanied the scientist's discovery. The *New DSB* is committed to continuing that scholarly tradition into the twenty-first century and to extending its accessibility to a general audience through the addition of photographs of the scientists at work and images from their publications. As with the original *DSB* our goal is to identify the most noteworthy scientists and present the story of their accomplishments within the broader context of their lives in essays that reflect the best available historiographic research.

We have followed the original editorial policy of focusing on the natural and formal sciences. As the number of working scientists continues to grow, difficult decisions had to be made. The original *DSB* could undertake to cover every significant contributor to the Scientific Revolution or nineteenth-century chemistry. But we could no longer aspire to such completeness. So while not neglecting key figures in biology, chemistry, physics, and mathematics, we have endeavored to make sure that we had a crucial number of pioneers in the new sciences that are playing pivotal roles in today's society. Thus, we appointed special editors for ecology, ethology, computer science, decision theory, and space science. We also highlighted traditional disciplines that have matured and become more important, such as climatology, psychology, and physical anthropology.

The Advisory Committee wanted the *New DSB* to incorporate the very best recent scholarship in history of science studies. Thus we introduced Postscripts that update some

225 of the original articles. A striking example is the entry describing Newton's alchemy, which adds a totally new dimension to our understanding of his matter theory; the Postscript on Mendel points out a surprising connection between his famous pea experiments and earlier discussions on heredity that took place at meetings of the Moravian Sheep Breeders Society; the new commentaries on Darwin and Freud provide excellent overviews of the vast new literature on these figures. These Postscripts are intended to supplement, not supplant, the original articles.

Thanks to extensive historical research on women in science, we now have much more information available about the contributions of people such as Ada Lovelace, credited with writing the first computer program; the astronomer Caroline Herschel, discoverer of numerous comets; and Maria Agnesi, who wrote a famous pioneering book on calculus. These new entries not only tell interesting stories about our intellectual foremothers but also provide valuable information about the social structure of the scientific community. The *New DSB* fills in other gaps, including additional Arabic researchers from the medieval period, African American scientists, and important figures from a variety of Asian countries.

Our understanding of both current and past science is shaped by philosophical and sociological theories about the structure and development of science. Included in the *New DSB* are biographical essays on figures who have shaped our current ideas about science: Thomas Kuhn's notion of paradigm, Karl Popper's falsifiability criterion, and Robert K. Merton's theory of scientific norms. Many of the new entries reflect the growing interest of historians in the social conditions and disciplinary organizations in which scientists do their work. Scientific achievements emerge out of a complex interplay between the conceptual frameworks available at the time and the sometimes-idiosyncratic views of the individual scientist, all moderated by the unflagging scientific demand for empirical adequacy and the quality control mechanisms of the relevant scientific communities.

The *New DSB*, with its integral print index in volume 8, can stand as a major addition to the original work. What will amplify its value in ways that we can scarcely foresee is the simultaneous publication of a fully searchable, electronic version that combines the original *DSB* volumes, including supplements, with the new series: the *Complete Dictionary of Scientific Biography*. Because this online "e-book" version is fully searchable, users of the *Complete DSB* will be able to pose questions that would elude even the best index. Compiling a list of scientists who spent time in Leiden or Indonesia will require only a few keystrokes. What about changing understandings of terms such as *gene, infinity, symmetry,* or *reflex*? A search of the *Complete DSB* will provide a wealth of clues to the evolution of these concepts. If so moved, a curious reader could even use the e-book version to dig up multiple examples of scientists who had a strong interest in music and mountaineering—or who committed suicide! Having an electronic version of the complete 26 volumes of the world's largest collection of scientific biographies will not only facilitate research but also lead to new avenues of inquiry about how science works. Furthermore, the *Complete DSB,* when integrated into a library's collection, becomes cross-searchable with a potentially limitless array of other reference works. The user can, for example, seek different perspectives on Galileo here and in the *New Catholic Encyclopedia* and the *Encyclopedia of Philosophy* or compare the history of science perspective on Darwin with that of present-day zoologists in *Grzimek's Animal Life Encyclopedia*.

A decade passed between the completion of the *DSB* and the appearance of its first discrete supplement (vols. 17 and 18). A further seventeen years stand between that supplement and the *New DSB*. Whatever the future of information technology may hold, it seems inconceivable that our present work will stand unrevised for so long. Already, in the *Complete DSB,* new material is interleaved with old. We expect that future additions and emendations will occur on a regular basis, and we welcome suggestions and corrections to the current volumes. In that spirit, we offer this new *Dictionary* as but a step toward the goal of continuous revision and updating.

The quality of any collaborative project depends on the efforts and expertise of the Editorial Board. The *New DSB* has been especially fortunate to have such a knowledgeable and industrious group serving as editors. With the help of the Advisory Committee, twenty-three Subject Editors were selected. They played a leadership role in the selection of late-twentieth-century scientists to be included and the scholars to write the entries. To choose which of the original articles most needed new Postscripts, we solicited nominations from the history of science community and then relied heavily on the judgment of nine Editorial Consultants. We were fortunate to be able to draw on the editorial expertise of historians of science from Europe as well as North America. And we have authors from thirty-seven countries. Electronic communication made it possible for editors not only to collaborate with each other but also to interact with authors as they prepared their manuscripts. The authors were selected for their special knowledge of the scientists they were describing. The scrutiny of our academic editors and the fact checking of the copyeditors combined with the good reputations of our authors should result in biographies of the highest overall quality.

Although e-mail makes it possible to consult widely about matters both great and small, it is no substitute for being able to run down the hall to talk to a colleague. I would never have dared undertake such a project without the strong support of the historians of science and medicine at Indiana University, some of whom had been involved in the original *DSB*. Much of the scholarly work on recent scientists has been carried out by philosophers, and thus my colleagues in philosophy of biology and physics also provided valuable input. Thanks are also due to current and former graduate students in my Department, especially to Dr. Anne Mylott, whose efficiency and sage advice are reflected on every page of these eight volumes. Professional friends whose names do not appear in the roster of editors also played a crucial role—Abdelhamid Sabra and Loren Graham to name but two.

Frank Menchaca, senior vice president at Gale, took a personal interest in initiating the *New DSB* and coordinating the project with the American Council of Learned Societies, sponsor of the original *DSB* and benefactor of this continuation. John Fitzpatrick at Charles Scribner's Sons (now an imprint of Gale) facilitated the project from the outset and was an invaluable source of encouragement and solutions to seemingly intractable problems. And special thanks to Angela Pilchak at Gale. Her attention to detail, coupled with her tact and good sense, were absolutely essential to the timely and successful completion of the *New DSB*. Thanks also to Indiana University for office space and computer support.

Noretta Koertge

List of Contributors

W. Abikoff
University of Connecticut,
Department of Mathematics
Professor
  LIPMAN BERS

Pnina G. Abir-Am
Brandeis University, Women's Studies
Research Center and the Hadassah-
Brandeis Institute
Senior Research Fellow
  ERWIN CHARGAFF
  DOROTHY MOYLE NEEDHAM
  JOSEPH NEEDHAM

Charles I. Abramson
Oklahoma State University,
Laboratory of Comparative Psychology
and Behavioral Biology, Departments
of Psychology and Zoology
Professor
  CHARLES HENRY TURNER

Helmut A. Abt
Kitt Peak National Observatory
Astronomer Emeritus
  LUDWIG FRANZ BENEDIKT
  BIERMANN

Fabio Acerbi
Centre National de la Recherche
Scientifique (CNRS), UMR 8163
Savoirs, textes, langage
Researcher
  APOLLONIUS OF PERGA
  ARCHIMEDES
  DAMIANUS OF LARISSA

HERO OF ALEXANDRIA
HYPATIA

Peter Achinstein
Johns Hopkins University,
Department of Philosophy
Professor
  JOHN STUART MILL

Pascal Acot
Centre National de la Recherche
Scientifique, University of Paris 1
Researcher, Professor
  JOSIAS BRAUN-BLANQUET

Walter Wade Adams
Rice University, Richard E. Smalley
Institute for Nanoscale Science and
Technology
Director
  RICHARD ERRETT SMALLEY

George Adelman
Massachusetts Institute of Technology,
Department of Brain and Cognitive
Sciences
Research Affiliate
  FRANCIS OTTO SCHMITT

Duncan Carr Agnew
University of California San Diego,
Scripps Institution of Oceanography
Professor
  VICTOR HUGO BENIOFF
  HENRY WILLIAM MENARD
  CHARLES FRANCIS RICHTER

Marianne Gosztonyi Ainley
University of Northern British
Columbia, University of Victoria
Adjunct Professor
  CATHARINE PARR TRAILL

Kenneth Aizawa
Centenary College of Louisiana
Professor
  KORBINIAN BRODMANN
  WARREN STURGIS
  MCCULLOCH

Atsushi Akera
Rensselaer Polytechnic Institute,
Department of Science and
Technology Studies
Assistant Professor
  JOHN WILLIAM MAUCHLY

Douglas Allchin
University of Minnesota, Program in
the History of Science, Technology
and Medicine
  ALBERT LESTER LEHNINGER
  ALEX BENJAMIN NOVIKOFF
  EFRAIM RACKER
  ALBERT IMRE SZENT-GYÖRGYI

Garland E. Allen
Washington University, St. Louis,
Department of Biology
Professor
  HAMPTON LAWRENCE
  CARSON
  VIKTOR HAMBURGER

David K. Allison
Smithsonian National Museum of American History, Division of Information Technology and Communications
Chair and Curator
J. (JOHN ADAM) PRESPER ECKERT, JR.

Ralph D. Amado
University of Pennsylvania, Department of Physics
Professor Emeritus
HENRY PRIMAKOFF

Kevin Amidon
Iowa State University, Department of World Languages and Cultures
Assistant Professor
(LEOPOLD FRANZ) EUGEN FISCHER

Kirsti Andersen
University of Aarhus, Steno Department for Studies of Science and Science Education
Associate Professor
GUIDOBALDO, MARCHESE DEL MONTE
PIERO DELLA FRANCESCA

Warwick Anderson
University of Wisconsin-Madison; University of Sydney
Professor; Chair
RENÉ JULES DUBOS

Aitor Anduaga
Independent Scholar
VICENTE INGLADA

Peder Anker
University of Oslo, Forum for University History, Department of Archaeology, Conservation and Historical Studies
Researcher
JAN CHRISTIAN SMUTS

Henryk Anzulewicz
Albertus-Magnus-Institut, Bonn, Germany
Editor and scholarly collaborator
SAINT ALBETUS MAGNUS

Adam Jared Apt
Independent Scholar
Manager, Peabody River Asset Management LLC
JOHN GREAVES

Efstathios Arapostathis
Independent Scholar
VERNER EDWARD SUOMI

Mitchell Ash
University of Vienna, Department of History
Professor
KURT LEWIN

Oliver Ashford
World Meteorological Organisation
Emeritus, Jehuda Neumann Memorial Prize winner
LEWIS FRY RICHARDSON

Robert Auerbach
University of Wisconsin, Madison, Department of Zoology and Institute on Aging
Professor Emeritus
CLIFFORD GROBSTEIN

Massimiliano Badino
Max Planck Institute for the History of Science
Post-Doctoral Research Fellow
LUDWIG EDUARD BOLTZMANN

Roland Baetens
University of Antwerp, Belgium
Professor Emeritus
PAUL ADRIAAN JAN JANSSEN

Victor R. Baker
University of Arizona, Department of Hydrology and Water Resources
Professor
RALPH ALGER BAGNOLD
J. HARLAN BRETZ

Ugo Baldini
University of Padua, Faculty of Political Sciences, Department of Historical and Political Studies
Professor
GIOVANNI ALFONSO BORELLI

John Bancroft
The Kinsey Institute for Research in Sex, Gender and Reproduction
Senior Research Fellow, previously Director
ALFRED CHARLES KINSEY

Christina Helena Barboza
Museum of Astronomy and Related Sciences, Department of History of Science, Rio de Janeiro

Professor
EMMANUEL-BERNARDIN LIAIS

John Barnett
University of Oxford, Department of Atmospheric, Oceanic & Planetary Sciences, Clarendon Laboratory
Senior Academic Staff
GORDON MILLER BOURNE DOBSON

James R. Bartholomew
Ohio State University, Department of History
Professor
KEN-ICHI FUKUI

Ofer Bar-Yosef
Harvard University, Department of Anthropology
Professor
DOROTHY ANNIE ELIZABETH GARROD

Hyman Bass
University of Michigan, Department of Mathematics and School of Education
Professor
SAMUEL EILENBERG

Giovanni Battimelli
Università La Sapienza, Dipartimento di Fisica
Associate Professor
EDOARDO AMALDI

Elena Zaitseva
Moscow State University, Chemistry Department
Senior Researcher
GEORGIĬ KONSTANTINOVICH BORESKOV
GEORGIĬ NIKOLAEVICH FLEROV
NIKOLAĬ NIKOLAEVICH SEMENOV
NIKOLAY DMITRIEVICH ZELINSKIĬ

Betty M. Bayer
Hobart and William Smith Colleges, Department of Women's Studies, The Fisher Center for the Study of Women and Men
Associate Professor, Director
LEON FESTINGER

Donald deB. Beaver
Williams College, Department of
History of Science
Professor
SARAH EGLONTON WALLIS
BOWDICH LEE
DEREK JOHN DeSOLLA PRICE

Antonio Becchi
Max Planck Institute for the History
of Science, Berlin
Visiting Scholar
BERNARDINO BALDI

William Bechtel
University of California, San Diego,
Department of Philosophy and
Science Studies Program
Professor
DAVID EZRA GREEN
KEITH ROBERTS PORTER
TORBJÖRN OSKAR
CASPERSSON

Silvio A. Bedini
Smithsonian Institution
Historian Emeritus
BENJAMIN BANNEKER

Colin Beer
Rutgers University, Department of
Psychology
Professor
DANIEL SANFORD LEHRMAN
THEODORE CHRISTIAN
SCHNEIRLA

Bernadette Bensaude-Vincent
University of Paris X, Department of
Philosophy
University Professor
ROBERT COLLONGUES

Marco Beretta
Institute and Museum of History of
Science, Florence, University of
Bologna
Vice-Director, Professor
ANTOINE-LAURENT LAVOISIER

Paul Berg
Stanford University
Professor Emeritus
GEORGE WELLS BEADLE

J. Lennart Berggren
Simon Fraser University, Department
of Mathematics

Professor Emeritus
DIODORUS OF ALEXANDRIA
IBRĀHĪM IBN SINĀN IBN
THĀBIT IBN QURRA
ABŪ SAHL WAYJAN IBN
RUSTAM AL-QŪHĪ
SHARAF AL-DĪN AL-MUZAFFAR
IBN MUHAMMAD IBN AL-
MUZAFFAR AL-TŪSĪ

Carlo Bernardini
Università di Roma, La Sapienza,
Department of Physics
Professor Emeritus
BRUNO TOUSCHEK

Sylvia Berryman
University of British Columbia,
Philosophy Department
Assistant Professor
STRATO OF LAMPSACUS

Richard H. Beyler
Portland State University, History
Department
Associate Professor
WALTER MAURICE ELSASSER
ERNST PASCUAL JORDAN

John Bickle
University of Cincinnati, Department
of Philosophy and Neuroscience
Graduate Program
Head of Department, Professor
ALAN HODGKIN
ULF SVANTE VON EULER

Hinrich Biesterfeldt
University of Bochum, Seminar für
Orientalistlk
Professor
ABŪ BAKR MUHAMMAD IBN
ZAKARIYYĀ' AL-RĀZĪ

Norman Biggs
London School of Economics,
Department of Mathematics
Professor
WILLIAM THOMAS TUTTE

Ken Binmore
University College of London,
Economics Department
Emeritus Professor
JOHN FORBES NASH, JR.

Thomas Blass
University of Maryland, Baltimore
County, Department of Psychology

Professor
STANLEY MILGRAM

Birger Blombäck
Karolinska Institutet, Solna, Sweden
Professor Emeritus
PEHR VICTOR EDMAN

Marika Blondel-Mégrelis
Centre National de la Recherche
Scientifique, Paris, Institut d'Histoire
et Philosophie des Sciences et des
Techniques
Researcher (Retired)
AUGUSTE LAURENT

Arthur L. Blumenthal
Graduate Faculty, The New School
Adjunct Professor
WILHELM WUNDT

Stephen Bocking
Trent University, Environmental and
Resource Studies Program
Professor
PIERRE MACKAY DANSEREAU
CHARLES SUTHERLAND ELTON

Jim Bogen
University of Pittsburgh, Department
of HPS
Adjunct Professor
BERNARD KATZ
WILDER GRAVES PENFIELD

James J. Bohning
Lehigh University, Department of
Chemistry
Center for Emeritus Scientists in
Academic Research (CESAR) Fellow
HERMAN F. MARK

Marvin Bolt
Adler Planetarium and Astronomy
Museum
Curator
JOHN HERSCHEL

Mark Borrello
University of Minnesota, Program in
History of Science, Technology and
Medicine, Department of Ecology,
Evolution and Behavior
Assistant Professor
PETR ALEKSEYVICH
KROPOTKIN
VERO COPNER WYNNE-
EDWARDS

Soraya Boudia
Université Louis Pasteur (Strasbourg), Institut de recherches interdisciplinaires sur les sciences et la technologie
Associate Professor in History of Sciences
  MARGUERITE CATHERINE PEREY

Joanne Bourgeois
University of Washington, Seattle, Department of Earth and Space Sciences
Professor
  ROBERT SINCLAIR DIETZ

Jean-Pierre Bourguignon
Institut des Hautes Études Scientifiques, Centre National de la Recherche Scientifique
Director, Director of Research
  ANDRÉ LICHNÉROWICZ

Peter J. Bowler
Queen's University, Belfast, School of History and Anthropology
Professor
  CHARLES ROBERT DARWIN

Donald W. Boyd
University of Wyoming, Department of Geology and Geophysics
Emeritus Professor
  NORMAN DENNIS NEWELL

Michael Bradie
Bowling Green State University, Department of Philosophy
Professor
  EDMUND BRISCO FORD

Ronald Brashear
Chemical Heritage Foundation, Othmer Library
Director
  HORACE WELCOME BABCOCK

Patrice Bret
Centre National de la Recherche Scientifique, Centre Alexandre Koyré, Centre de recherché en histoire des sciences et des techniques, Paris
Associate Researcher
  MARIE GENEVIÈVE CHARLOTTE THIROUX D'ARCONVILLE
  CLAUDINE PICARDET

Willam H. Brock
University of Leicester, Department of History
Emeritus Professor
  THOMAS ARCHER HIRST
  (FRIEDRICH) AUGUST KEKULE VON STRADONITZ
  JUSTUS VON LIEBIG

Nathan Brooks
New Mexico State University, Department of History
Associate Professor
  ALEKSANDR MIKHAILOVICH BUTLEROV
  GEORGIĬ NIKOLAEVICH FLEROV
  DMITRII IVANOVICH MENDELEEV

Richard E. Brown
Dalhousie University, Department of Psychology
Professor
  DONALD HEBB

Theodore L. Brown
University of Illinois, Urbana-Champaign, Department of Chemistry and Beckman Institute
Professor Emeritus, Emeritus Director
  ARNOLD ORVILLE BECKMAN

Rod Buchanan
University of Melbourne, Department of History and Philosophy of Science
Research Associate
  HANS JÜRGEN EYSENCK

Hugh Buckingham
Louisiana State University, Department of Communication Sciences & Disorders
Professor
  ALEXANDER ROMANOVICH LURIA

Bernd Buldt
Indiana University - Purdue University Fort Wayne, Department of Philosophy
Professor, Chair
  PAUL RUDOLF CARNAP

David R. Bundle
University of Alberta, Department of Chemistry
Professor
  RAYMOND URGEL LEMIEUX

Richard W. Burkhardt
University of Illinois at Urbana-Champaign, Department of History
Professor
  WALLACE CRAIG
  HENRY ELIOT HOWARD
  JEAN-BAPTISTE LAMARCK
  KONRAD ZACHARIAS LORENZ
  MARGARET MORSE NICE

Charles Burnett
University of London, Warburg Institute
Professor
  ADELARD OF BATH

Martha Cecilia Bustamante
Université Paris 7 Denis-Diderot, Laboratoire REHSEIS UMR CNRS 7596
Associate Researcher
  GIUSEPPE OCCHIALINI

Heiderose Brandt Butscher
York University, Humanities Division, Arts Department
Lecturer
  LORENZ OKEN

Charles W. Byers
University of Wisconsin, Madison, Department of Geology & Geophysics
Professor
  LAURENCE LOUIS SLOSS

W. Malcolm Byrnes
Howard University College of Medicine, Department of Biochemistry and Molecular Biology
Assistant Professor
  ERNEST EVERETT JUST

Gerhard C. Cadée
Royal Netherlands Institute for Sea Research
Researcher
  LAMBERTUS MARIUS JOANNES URSINUS VAN STRAATEN

Joe Cain
University College London, Department of Science and Technology Studies
Senior Lecturer
  ARTHUR JAMES CAIN

Jane Callander
  DOROTHY ANNIE ELIZABETH GARROD

Werner Callebaut
Hasselt University, Belgium, Faculty of
Sciences, and Konrad Lorenz Institute
for Evolution and Cognition Research,
Austria
Professor, Scientific Manager
DONALD THOMAS CAMPBELL

Antoine Calvet
REVUE CHRYSOPIA (CNRS,
Centre d'Histoire des Sciences et des
Doctrines)
ARNALD OF VILLANOVA
(PSEUDO)
RAMON LULL

Laura Cameron
Queen's University, Ontario,
Department of Geography
Assistant Professor
SIR ARTHUR GEORGE
TANSLEY

Michele Camerota
University of Cagliari, Dipartimento
di Scienze Pedagogiche e Filosofiche
Professor
GIROLAMO BORRO
FRANCESCO BUONAMICI
GALILEO GALILEI

Martin Campbell-Kelly
University of Warwick, Department of
Computer Science
Professor
CHRISTOPHER STRACHEY

Stefano Caroti
University of Parma, Department of
Philosophy
Professor
BLASIUS OF PARMA
NICOLE ORESME

Albert V. Carozzi
University of Illinois, Urbana-
Champaign
Emeritus Professor
HORACE BÉNÉDICT DE
SAUSSURE

Alan B. Carr
Los Alamos National Laboratory
Historian
ROBERT BACHER
ROBERT SERBER

Jacqueline Carroy
École des Hautes Études en Sciences
Sociales, Centre Alexandre Koyré

d'Histoire des Sciences et des
Techniques, Paris
Director of Studies
PIERRE JANET

Cathryn Carson
University of California, Berkeley,
Department of History
Associate Professor
WOLFGANG PAULI

Christine Cole Catley
Cape Catley Ltd, Auckland, NZ
Publisher
BEATRICE TINSLEY

Marta Cavazza
University of Bologna, Department of
Philosophy
Associate Professor
LUIGI FERDINANDO MARSILI

Beate Ceranski
University of Stuttgart, Historisches
Institut, Geschichte der
Naturwissenschaften und Technik
Adjunct Professor
LAURA MARIA CATERINA
BASSI VERATI

Ku-Ming (Kevin) Chang
Academia Sinica, Institute of History
and Philology
Assistant Professor (Research Fellow)
GEORG ERNST STAHL

Michelle Chapront-Touzé
SYRTE, Observatoire de Paris, CNRS,
UPMC
Researcher
JEAN LE ROND D'ALEMBERT

François Chast
Hotel-Dieu Hospital, Paris,
Department of Toxicology, Pharmacy
and Pharmacology
Director
GERTRUDE BELLE ELION

John Robert Christianson
Luther College, Department of
History
Professor Emeritus
TYCHO BRAHE

Frederick B. Churchill
Indiana University, Bloomington,
Department of History and
Philosophy of Science

Professor Emeritus
AUGUST FRIEDRICH
WEISMANN

Eugene Cittadino
New York University, The Gallatin
School
Adjunct Professor
HENRY CHANDLER COWLES

George W. Clark
Massachusetts Institute of Technology,
Department of Physics
Professor Emeritus
BRUNO BENEDETTO ROSSI

Richard D. Clark
Millersville University, Department of
Earth Sciences
Professor, Chair
HANS ARNOLD PANOFSKY

Neil Clayton
University of Otago, Dunedin, New
Zealand
LEONARD COCKAYNE

Claudine Cohen
L'Ecole des Hautes Etudes en Sciences
Sociales, Paris
Maître de conférences
HENRI VICTOR VALLOIS

Clive Cohen
Imperial College, London, Centre for
the History of Science, Technology
and Medicine
Honorary Research Associate
WARREN KENDALL LEWIS

Alan Collins
Lancaster University, Department of
Psychology
Doctor
FREDERIC CHARLES BARTLETT

Andrew M. Colman
University of Leicester, School of
Psychology
Professor
AMOS TVERSKY

Nathaniel Comfort
Johns Hopkins University,
Department of History of Medicine
Associate Professor
BARBARA MCCLINTOCK

Roger Cooke
University of Vermont
Professor Emeritus
  SOFYA VASILYEVNA
    KOVALEVSKAYA

Edgar E. Coons
New York University, Department of
Psychology
Professor
  NEAL ELGAR MILLER

Leo Corry
Tel Aviv University, Cohn Institute for
History and Philosophy of Science and
Ideas
Director
  NICOLAS BOURBAKI

Carl F. Craver
Washington University, St. Louis,
Philosophy-Neuroscience-Psychology
Program
Associate Professor
  JULIUS AXELROD

Angela N. H. Creager
Princeton University, Department of
History
Professor
  CHRISTIAN B. ANFINSEN

Robert P. Crease
Stony Brook University, Department
of Philosophy
Professor, Chair
  MILTON STANLEY
    LIVINGSTON

Julie Roberta Cribb
UHl Millenium Institute, Learning
and Information Services Department
Development Programmes Manager
  NIKOLAY SERGEYEVICH
    SHATSKIY

Eileen Crist
Virginia Tech, Department of Science
and Technology in Society
Associate Professor
  DONALD REDFIELD GRIFFIN

Paul Croce
Stetson University, Program in
American Studies
Professor
  WILLIAM JAMES

Maurice Crosland
University of Kent, School of History
Professor Emeritus
  JEAN-BAPTISTE-ANDRE
    DUMAS
  CLAUDE LOUIS BERTHOLLET

James F. Crow
University of Wisconsin, Madison,
Laboratory of Genetics
Professor Emeritus
  MOTOO KIMURA

Mary Cubitt
University of Warwick, Department of
Computer Science
Honorary Research Fellow
  DOUGLAS RAYNER HARTREE
  JAMES HARDY WILKINSON

Gregory T. Cushman
University of Kansas, Department of
History
Assistant Professor
  JEROME NAMIAS
  BENITO VIÑES

Per Dahl
Lawrence Berkeley National
Laboratory
Retired Physicist and Visiting Scientist
  GREGORY BREIT

Gianni Dal Maso
International School for Advanced
Studies, Trieste, Functional Analysis
Sector
Research Staff
  ENNIO DE GIORGI

Andrew I. Dale
University of KwaZulu-Natal, School
of Statistics and Actuarial Science
Professor Emeritus
  THOMAS BAYES

Dane T. Daniel
Wright State University, Lake Campus
Assistant Professor
  THEOPHRASTUS PHILIPPUS
    AUREOLUS BOMBASTUS VON
    HOHENHEIM PARACELSUS

Joseph Dauben
City University of New York, Herbert
H. Lehman College, Department of
History; The Graduate Center, Ph.D.
Program in History
Professor

GEORG FERDINAND LUDWIG
  CANTOR

Keay Davidson
San Francisco Chronicle
Science Writer
  CARL EDWARD SAGAN

Martin Davis
New York University, University of
California, Berkeley
Professor Emeritus, Visiting Scholar
  JULIA BOWMAN ROBINSON

Deborah Day
University of California, San Diego,
Scripps Institution of Oceanography
Archives
Archivist
  ROGER RANDALL DOUGAN
    REVELLE

Soraya de Chadarevian
University of California, Los Angeles,
Department of History, Center for
Society and Genetics
Professor
  MAX FERDINAND PERUTZ

Alexis De Greiff A.
Universidad Nacional de Colombia,
Departmento de Sociología/Centro de
Estudios Sociales, Bogotá
Associate Professor
  MUHAMMAD ABDUS SALAM

Peter Dear
Cornell University, Departments of
History and Science and Technology
Studies
Professor
  NICCOLÒ CABEO

Jacek Dębiec
New York University, Center for
Neural Science; New York University
School of Medicine, Department of
Psychiatry
Researcher, Trainer
  JAMES WENCESLAS PAPEZ

Ute Deichmann
University of Cologne Institute for
Genetics, Leo Baeck Institute London
Research Group Leader, Research
Professor
  ERNST DAVID BERGMANN
  CARL ALEXANDER NEUBERG

Robert J. Deltete
Seattle University, Philosophy
Department
Professor
FRIEDRICH WILHELM
OSTWALD

S. Demidov
S.I. Vavilov Institute for the History of
Science and Technology of the Russian
Academy of Sciences; M. V.
Lomonosov Moscow State University
Director; Professor
LEV SEMIONOVICH
PONTRYAGIN
I. M. VINOGRADOV

Adrian Desmond
University College London,
Department of Biology
Honorary Research Fellow
THOMAS HENRY HUXLEY

David C. Devonis
Graceland University, Department of
Psychology
Professor
PAUL EVERETT MEEHL

Melanie DeVore
Georgia College & State University,
Department of Biological &
Environmental Sciences
Associate Professor
ARTHUR CRONQUIST

David H. DeVorkin
National Air and Space Museum,
Smithsonian Institution, Division of
Space History, History of Astronomy
and the Space Sciences
Senior Curator
HERBERT FRIEDMAN
DONALD HOWARD MENZEL
MARTIN SCHWARZSCHILD
LYMAN SPITZER, JR.
RICHARD TOUSEY
JAMES A. VAN ALLEN
JAMES A. WESTPHAL
FRED LAWRENCE WHIPPLE

Donald A. Dewsbury
University of Florida, Department of
Psychology
Professor Emeritus
FRANK AMBROSE BEACH, JR.

Marie A. DiBerardino
Drexel University, College of Medicine

Professor Emeritus
ROBERT W. BRIGGS

Michael R. Dietrich
Dartmouth College, Department of
Biological Sciences
Associate Professor
JOHANNES HOLTFRETER
MOTOO KIMURA

Igor S. Dmitriev
D. I. Mendeleev Museum and
Archives, St. Petersburg State
University
ALEKSANDR NIKOLAEVICH
NESMEJANOV

Ronald E. Doel
Oregon State University, Department
of History and Department of
Geosciences
Associate Professor
MARION KING HUBBERT
GERARD PETER KUIPER
MARIE THARP

Aude Doody
University College Dublin, School of
Classics
Lecturer
PLINY THE ELDER

R. H. Drent
University of Groningen, Dierecologie
Center for Ecological and
Evolutionary Studies
Professor
GERARD PIETER BAERENDS

Steffen Ducheyne
Ghent University, Centre for Logic
and Philosophy of Science, Centre for
History of Science
Member, Doctor
JOHANNES BAPTISTA VAN
HELMONT

Michael Eckert
Deutsches Museum, Munich
Researcher
ARNOLD JOHANNES WILHELM
SOMMERFELD

Matthew D. Eddy
Durham University, Department of
Philosophy
Lecturer
WILLIAM CULLEN
JOHN WALKER

Ellery Eells
University of Wisconsin, Madison
Professor Emeritus, deceased
ROBERT NOZICK

Frank N. Egerton
University of Wisconsin, Parkside,
Department of History
Professor Emeritus
ARTHUR DAVIS HASLER
AUGUST FRIEDRICH
THIENEMANN

Jean Eisenstaedt
Observatoire de Paris, Centre National
de la Recherche Scientifique
Research Director
ROBERT BLAIR

Ernest L. Eliel
University of North Carolina at
Chapel Hill, Department of
Chemistry
Professor Emeritus
VLADIMIR PRELOG

Alan C. Elms
University of California, Davis,
Psychology Department
Professor Emeritus
ERIK HOMBURGER ERIKSON

Stefan Emeis
Forschungszentrum Karlsruhe GmbH,
Institute of Meteorology and Climate
Research, Atmospheric Environmental
Research, University of Cologne
Adjunct Professor, Lecturer
RICHARD ASSMANN

Irving R. Epstein
Brandeis University, Department of
Chemistry and Volen Center for
Complex Systems
Professor
ILYA PRIGOGINE

Germana Ernst
Università di Roma Tre, Italy,
Department of Philosophy
Professor
TOMMASO CAMPANELLA

Andrea Falcon
Concordia University, Montreal,
Department of Philosophy
Assistant Professor
PLATO
XENARCHUS

İhsan Fazlioğlu
Istanbul University, Department of Philosophy
Associate Professor
ALI AL-QŪSHJĪ (ABŪ AL-QĀSIM ALĀʾ AL-DĪN ALĪ IBN MUHAMMAD QUSHJĪ-ZĀDE)

Anne Fellinger
Université Louis Pasteur (Strasbourg), Institut de recherches interdisciplinaires sur les sciences et la technologie
MARGUERITE CATHERINE PEREY

Giovanni Ferraro
University of Molise, Faculty of Mathematical, Physical and Natural Sciences
Professor
LEONHARD EULER

Paula Findlen
Stanford University, Department of History
Professor
ATHANASIUS KIRCHER

James Fleming
Colby College, Science, Technology, and Society Program
Professor
GUY STEWART CALLENDAR

Pedro Navarro Floria
Consejo Nacional de Investigaciones Científicas y Técnicas (CONICET), Argentina
HERMANN KARL KONRAD BURMEISTER

George W. Ford
University of Michigan, Department of Physics
Professor Emeritus
GEORGE UHLENBECK

John Forrester
University of Cambridge, Department of History and Philosophy of the Sciences
Professor
SIGMUND FREUD

Marye Anne Fox
University of California, San Diego, Department of Chemistry and Biochemistry

Chancellor
MICHAEL J. S. DEWAR

Tibor Frank
LEO SZILARD

Henry Frankel
University of Missouri at Kansas City, Department of Philosophy
Professor
ALLAN VERNE COX
JAN HOSPERS
JOHN TUZO WILSON

Craig Fraser
University of Toronto, Institute for the History and Philosophy of Science and Technology
Historian
AUGUSTIN-LOUIS CAUCHY

David W. Frayer
University of Kansas, Anthropology Department
Professor
DRAGUTIN (KARL) GORJANOVIĆ-KRAMBERGER
JAN JELÍNEK

Lucio Fregonese
University of Pavia, Department of Physics, Museo per la Storia
Associate Professor, Scientific Consultant
ALESSANDRO GIUSEPPE ANTONIO ANASTASIO VOLTA

Anthony P. French
Massachusetts Institute of Technology, Department of Physics
Professor Emeritus
PHILIP MORRISON

Robert Marc Friedman
University of Oslo, Department of History
Professor
TOR HAROLD PERCIVAL BERGERON
VILHELM BJERKNES

Bernhard Fritscher
University of Munich, Institute for the History of Science
Adjunct Professor
OTTO AMPFERER
ARTHUR LOUIS DAY
ALFRED FERDINAND RITTMANN

Iris Fry
Tel Aviv University, The Cohn Institute for the History and Philosophy of Science and Ideas
Doctor
STANLEY LLOYD MILLER

Yasu Furukawa
Nihon University, College of Bioresource Sciences
Professor
WALLACE HUME CAROTHERS
ICHIRO SAKURADA

Louis Galambos
Johns Hopkins University, Department of History, and the Institute for Applied Economics and the Study of Business Enterprise
Professor
KARL AUGUST FOLKERS

George Gale
University of Missouri, Kansas City, Department of Philosophy
Professor
WILLIAM HUNTER MCCREA

Enrico Gamba
GUIDOBALDO, MARCHESE DEL MONTE

Daniel Garber
Princeton University, Department of Philosophy
Professor, Chair
RENÉ DU PERRON DESCARTES

Derek Gatherer
Medical Research Council Virology Unit, Institute of Virology, University of Glasgow
Senior Computer Officer
WALTER MAURICE ELSASSER

Jean Gaudant
Comité français d'Histoire de la Géologie
Vice President, Secretary
JEAN PIVETEAU

Jean-Paul Gaudillière
CERMES, Institut National de la Santé et de la Recherche Médicale
Senior Researcher
ADOLF FRIEDRICH JOHANN BUTENANDT

Kostas Gavroglu
University of Athens, Department of
History and Philosophy of Science
Professor
  FELIX BLOCH

Clayton A. Gearhart
College of St. Benedict/St. John's
University, Department of Physics
Professor
  MAX PLANCK

Enrico R. A. Giannetto
University of Bergamo, Dipartimento
di Science della Persona
Professor
  GIORDANO BRUNO

Philip D. Gingerich
University of Michigan, Department
of Geological Sciences, Museum of
Paleontology
Professor, Director
  GEORGE GAYLORD SIMPSON

Owen Gingerich
Harvard University, Harvard-
Smithsonion Center for Astrophysics
Professor Emeritus
  CECILIA HELENA PAYNE-
  GAPOSCHKIN

Sander Gliboff
Indiana University, Department of
History and Philosophy of Science
Assistant Professor
  HEINRICH GEORG BRONN
  PAUL KAMMERER

Stephen Glickman
University of California, Berkeley,
Department of Psychology
Professor
  DONALD HEBB

André Goddu
Stonehill College, Department of
Physics and Astronomy
Professor
  NICHOLAS COPERNICUS
  WILLIAM OF OCKHAM

Hubert Goenner
Universität Göttingen, Institute for
Theoretical Physics
Professor Emeritus
  OTTO HERMANN LEOPOLD
  HECKMANN

Jan Golinski
University of New Hampshire,
Department of History
Professor, Chair
  JANE HALDIMAND MARCET

José María Gondra
University of the Basque Country,
Department of Basic Psychological
Processes
  CLARK LEONARD HULL

Gregory A. Good
West Virginia University, Department
of History
Associate Professor
  STANLEY KEITH RUNCORN

Graeme Gooday
University of Leeds, Department of
Philosophy, Division of History and
Philosophy of Science
Senior Lecturer
  GEORGE CAREY FOSTER

Matthew R. Goodrum
Virginia Tech, Department of Science
and Technology in Society
Visiting Assistant Professor
  CARLETON STEVENS COON
  JOHN DESMOND CLARK
  RAYMOND ARTHUR DART

David L. Goodstein
California Institute of Technology
Vice Provost, Professor of Physics and
Applied Physics
  CARL DAVID ANDERSON
  WILLIAM A. FOWLER

Judith Johns Goodstein
California Institute of Technology
Faculty Associate
  CARL DAVID ANDERSON
  WILLIAM A. FOWLER

Gennady Gorelik
Boston University, Center for
Philosophy and History of Science
Research Fellow
  ANDREI DMITRIYEVICH
  SAKHAROV

Leon Gortler
Brooklyn College of the City
University of New York, Department
of Chemistry
Professor Emeritus
  HERBERT CHARLES BROWN
  LOUIS PLACK HAMMETT

Constantin Goschler
Ruhr-University, Bochum
Professor
  RUDOLF CARL VIRCHOW

Jeremy Gray
The Open University, Department of
Mathematics
Professor
  LARS AHLFORS
  PAUL ERDOS
  DAVID HILBERT
  KUNIHIKO KODAIRA
  MARSTON MORSE
  ANTONI ZYGMUND

David H. Green
The Australian National University,
Research School of Earth Sciences
Professor Emeritus
  ALFRED EDWARD RINGWOOD

Mott T. Greene
University of Puget Sound, Honors
Program, Program in Science,
Technology and Society
Professor
  WLADIMIR PETER KOPPEN
  ALFRED LOTHAR WEGENER

David A. Grier
George Washington University, Elliott
School of International Affairs
Associate Professor, Associate Dean
  CHARLES BABBAGE
  ADA AUGUSTA KING,
    COUNTESS OF LOVELACE

William P. Griffith
Imperial College London, Department
of Chemistry
Senior Research Investigator
  SIR GEOFFREY WILKINSON

Tom Griffiths
Australian National University,
Canberra, Research School of Social
Sciences
Professor of History
  FRANCIS NOBLE RATCLIFFE

Shi-jie Guo
The Institute for the History of
Natural Science
  HOU TE-PANG (DEBANG
  HOU)

Jeremiah Hackett
University of South Carolina,
Department of Philosophy
Professor, Chair
ROGER BACON

Petr Hadrava
Astronomical Institute, Academy of
Sciences of the Czech Republic,
Department of Galaxies and Planetary
Systems
Researcher
CRISTANNUS DE PRACHATICZ

Alena Hadravová
Institute for Contemporary History,
Academy of Sciences of the Czech
Republic, Department for the History
of Science
Researcher
CRISTANNUS DE PRACHATICZ

Jürgen Haffer
A. Koenig Zoological Research
Institute and Zoological Museum,
Section of Biology and Phylogeny of
Tropical Birds
Research Associate
ERNST WALTER MAYR

Joel B. Hagen
Radford University, Biology
Department
Professor
WARDER CLYDE ALLEE
FREDERIC EDWARD CLEMENTS
HOWARD THOMAS ODUM
EUGENE PLEASANTS ODUM

Alan Hájek
The Australian National University,
Philosophy Program, Research School
of Social Sciences
Professor
DAVID LEWIS

Karl Hall
Central European University,
Budapest, History Department
Assistant Professor
ARKADY BENEDIKTOVICH
MIGDAL

Brian K. Hall
Dalhousie University, Department of
Biology
University Research Professor
Emeritus
CONRAD HAL WADDINGTON

Jacob Darwin Hamblin
Clemson University, Department of
History
Assistant Professor
GEORGE EDWARD RAVEN
DEACON
KONSTANTIN NIKOLAYEVICH
FEDOROV

Richard Hamblyn
University of Nottingham, School of
Geography
Postdoctoral Research Fellow
LUKE HOWARD

Thomas L. Hankins
University of Washington,
Department of History
Professor Emeritus
WILLIAM ROWAN HAMILTON

R. J. Hankinson
University of Texas at Austin,
Department of Philosophy
Professor
GALEN

Peter Hannaford
Swinburne University of Technology,
Centre for Atom Optics and Ultrafast
Spectroscopy
Professor, Director
ALAN WALSH

Valerie Gray Hardcastle
University of Cincinnati, McMicken
College of Arts and Sciences
Dean
PATRICIA SHOER GOLDMAN-
RAKIC
WALTER RUDOLF HESS
HEINRICH KLÜVER
DAVID COURTNAY MARR

Russell Hardin
New York University, Department of
Politics
Professor
MANCUR OLSON, JR.

Kristine C. Harper
New Mexico Institute of Mining and
Technology, Socorro
Assistant Professor
JULE GREGORY CHARNEY
JOSEPH SMAGORINSKY
MARIE THARP

Geoffrey Harper
Royal Botanic Garden Edinburgh
Research Associate
VLADIMIR VLADIMIROVICH
STANCHINSKIY

Ronald Harstad
University of Missouri, Columbia
J. Rhoads Foster Professor of
Economics
WILLIAM SPENCER VICKREY

Harry Heft
Denison University, Department of
Psychology
Professor of Psychology
JAMES JEROME GIBSON

Colin Hempstead
University of Teesside, Middlesbrough,
UK, School of Arts and Media
Reader (Retired)
SIR RUDOLF ERNEST PEIERLS
SIR ALAN HERRIES WILSON

Pamela M. Henson
Smithsonian Institution Archives
Institutional History Division
Director
ALFRED EDWARDS EMERSON

Klaus Hentschel
University of Stuttgart, History of
Science & Technology, Historical
Institute
Professor
ALBRECHT OTTO JOHANNES
UNSÖLD

Christine Hertler
Johann Wolfgang Goethe University,
Biosciences
Faculty
GUSTAV HEINRICH RALPH
VON KOENIGSWALD
FRANZ WEIDENREICH

Norriss Hetherington
University of California, Berkeley,
Office for History of Science and
Technology
Visiting Scholar
GEORGE CUNLIFFE MCVITTIE
IOSIF SAMUILOVICH
SHKLOVSKII

Gerhard Heywang
Bayer Industry Services, Leverkusen
OTTO GEORG WILHELM
BAYER

Ellen McNiven Hine
York University, Humanities and
Women's Studies
Professor Emerita
JEAN-JACQUES DORTOUS DE
MAIRAN

Nigel J. Hitchin
Oxford University, Mathematical
Institute
Professor
SHIING-SHEN CHERN

Lillian Hoddeson
University of Illiniois at Urbana-
Champaign, Department of History
Professor
JOHN BARDEEN
ROBERT RATHBUN WILSON

Darleane C. Hoffman
University of California, Berkeley,
Department of Chemistry and
Lawrence Berkeley National
Laboratory
Professor
GLENN THEODORE SEABORG

Dieter Hoffmann
Max Planck Institute for the History
of Science
Research Scholar
MAX PLANCK

Charles H. Holbrow
Colgate University, Department of
Physics and Astronomy
Professor Emeritus
CHARLES CHRISTIAN
LAURITSEN

Ernst Homburg
Universiteit Maastricht, Department
of History
Professor
JOHANNES MARTIN BIJVOET
JAN HENDRIK DE BOER
DIRK WILLEM VAN KREVELEN

R. W. Home
University of Melbourne
Professor Emeritus
FERDINAND JAKOB HEINRICH
VON MUELLER

Annie Hor
California State University, Stanislaus
Acquisitions Librarian
PEI WENZHONG

Michael Hoskin
Churchill College, Cambridge, St.
Edmund's College, Cambridge
Fellow, Emeritus Fellow
CAROLINE LUCRETIA
HERSCHEL
WILLIAM HERSCHEL

Richard Howarth
University College London,
Department of Earth Sciences
Honorary Professor
HAROLD JEFFREYS

Wolfgang Hübner
University of Münster, Department of
Classical Philology
Professor
VETTIUS VALENS

Karl Hufbauer
University of California, Irvine,
Department of History
Professor Emeritus
BENGT EDLÉN

David L. Hull
Northwestern University, Department
of Philosophy
Professor Emeritus
STEPHEN JAY GOULD

Paul Humphreys
University of Virginia, Department of
Philosophy
Professor
ANDREI NIKOLAEVICH
KOLMOGOROV

Michael Hunter
University of London, Birkbeck
College, School of History, Classics
and Archaeology
Professor of History
ROBERT BOYLE

Graeme K. Hunter
University of Western Ontario,
Schulich School of Medicine and
Dentistry
Professor
DOROTHY MARY CROWFOOT
HODGKIN
MICHAEL SMITH

Sarah Hutton
University of Wales, Aberystwyth,
Department of English
Professor
ANNE CONWAY

P. K. Ingle
National Chemical Laboratory, Pune,
Publication and Science
Communication Unit
Scientist
KRISHNASAMI VENKATARAMAN

Bruna Ingrao
Università di Roma, Department of
Economics
Professor
VILFREDO PARETO

Brad Inwood
University of Toronto, Departments of
Classics and Philosophy
Professor
CHRYSIPPUS

Gürol Irzik
Bogazici University, Department of
Philosophy
Professor
THOMAS SAMUEL KUHN

Konstantin Ivanov
Tula State Pedagogical University,
Russia, Department of Theoretical
Physics
Dotsent
MSTISLAV VSEVOLODOVICH
KELDYSH

Roman Jackiw
Massachusetts Institute of Technology
Professor
JOHN S. BELL

Lothar Jaenicke
University of Cologne, Institute of
Biochemistry
Professor Emeritus
FRITZ ALBERT LIPMANN

Frank A. J. L. James
The Royal Institution, London
Professor
HUMPHREY DAVY
GEORGE PORTER

Michel Janssen
University of Minnesota, School of
Physics and Astronomy
Associate Professor
HENDRIK ANTOON LORENTZ

Yang Jing-Yi
Institute for History of Natural
Sciences, Chinese Academy of Sciences
Professor
HUANG JIQING (TE-KAN)

Jeffrey Allan Johnson
Villanova University, Department of
History
Professor
FRITZ HABER

Sean F. Johnston
University of Glasgow
Reader
GERHARD HERZBERG

Alexander Jones
University of Toronto, Department of
Classics
Professor
APOLLINIARIUS
HIPPARCHUS
LEPTINES
MARINUS OF TYRE
PTOLEMY
TIMOCHARIS

Paul Josephson
Colby College, Department of History
Associate Professor
GERSH ITSKOVICH BUDKER
PETR LEONIDOVICH KAPITSA

Jim Joyce
University of Michigan, Department
of Philosophy
Professor, Chair
RICHARD CARL JEFFREY

Michael Kaasch
German Academy of Sciences
Leopoldina, Halle
Editor
EMIL ABDERHALDEN

David Kaiser
Massachusetts Institute of Technology,
Program in Science, Technology, and
Society
Associate Professor
RICHARD PHILLIPS FEYNMAN

VICTOR FREDERICK
WEISSKOPF

Masanori Kaji
Tokyo Institute of Technology,
Graduate School of Decision Science
and Technology
Associate Professor
TETSUO NOZOE

Andreas Karachalios
Mainz University, Institute for History
of Mathematics and Natural Sciences
Lecturer
ERICH ARMAND ARTHUR
HÜCKEL

Shaul Katzir
Leo Baeck Institute, London/Tel Aviv
University, The Cohn Institute for the
History and Philosophy of Science and
Ideas
Research Fellow
WOLDEMAR VOIGT

George B. Kauffman
California State University, Fresno,
Department of Chemistry
Professor Emeritus
WILLARD FRANK LIBBY
AXEL CHRISTIAN KLIXBÜLL
JØRGENSEN

Keiko Kawashima
Omohi College, Nagoya Institute of
Technology
Associate Professor
MARIE-ANNE-PIERETTE
PAULZE-LAVOISIER

Sean P. Keating
University of Cincinnati, Department
of Philosophy
ALAN HODGKIN

Brian L. Keeley
Pitzer College, Philosophy, and
Science, Technology & Society Field
Groups
Associate Professor
THEODORE HOLMES
BULLOCK

Drew Keeling
University of Zurich, Department of
History
Instructor
CHARLES DAVID KEELING

Ken Kellerman
National Radio Astronomy
Observatory; University of Virginia,
Astronomy Department
Senior Scientist, Research Professor
JOHN GATENBY BOLTON

Diana E. Kenney
Marine Biological Laboratory at
Woods Hole
Science Writer
GEORGE WALD

Michael Kessler
Museum of Pharmacy at the
University of Basel, Switzerland
TADEUS REICHSTEIN

Daniel J. Kevles
Yale University
Professor
MAX LUDWIG HENNING
DELBRÜCK

Yoshiyuki Kikuchi
The Graduate University for Advanced
Studies, Sokendai, Hayama Center for
Advanced Studies
Researcher
SAN-ICHIRO MIZUSHIMA

Helen King
University of Reading, Department of
Classics
Professor, Head of Department
HIPPOCRATES OF COS

John A. Kington
University of East Anglia, Climatic
Research Unit, School of
Environmental Sciences
Visiting Fellow
HUBERT HORACE LAMB

Chigusa Ishikawa Kita
Kansai University, Faculty of
Informatics
Associate Professor
JOSEPH CARL ROBNETT
LICKLIDER

Tinne Hoff Kjeldsen
Roskilde University, IMFUFA,
Department of Science, Systems, and
Models
Associate Professor
ALBERT WILLIAM TUCKER

Matthew Klingle
Bowdoin College, Department of
History and Environmental Studies
Program
Assistant Professor
WALLIS THOMAS
EDMONDSON

David Knight
Durham University, Department of
Philosophy
Professor
JAMES FINLAY WEIR
JOHNSTON

Charles M. Knobler
University of California, Los Angeles,
Department of Chemistry and
Biochemistry
Professor Emeritus
RICHARD BARRY BERNSTEIN

Alexei Kojevnikov
University of British Columbia,
Department of History
Associate Professor
NIKOLAI NIKOLAEVICH
BOGOLUBOV
PAVEL ALEKSEYEVICH
CHERENKOV

Adrienne W. Kolb
Fermi National Accelerator Laboratory
Archivist
ROBERT RATHBUN WILSON

Klaus Peter Köpping
University of Heidelberg, Institut für
Ethnologie
Professor Emeritus
ADOLF BASTIAN

Gerhard Kortum
Geographical Institute of the Christian
Albrechts University of Kiel
GEORG WÜST

Russell D. Kosits
Redeemer University College,
Department of Psychology
Professor
WILLIAM BENJAMIN
CARPENTER

A. J. Kox
University of Amsterdam, Institute for
Theoretical Physics
Professor

HENDRIK BRUGT GERHARD
CASIMIR
HENDRIK ANTOON LORENTZ

Helge Kragh
University of Aarhus, Steno
Department for Studies of Science and
Science Education
Professor
HERMANN BONDI
WILLEM DE SITTER

Regina A. Kressley
Johann Wolfgang Goethe-University,
Department of Developmental
Psychology
Scientific Staff
MATHILDE CARMEN HERTZ

Henri Krop
Erasmus University, Rotterdam
Tenured Lecturer
FRANK PIETERSZOON
BURGERSDIJK

Hans Kruuk
University of Aberdeen, School of
Biological Sciences
Honorary Professor
NIKOLAAS TINBERGEN

Radha Kumar
Jamia Millia Islamia, New Delhi,
Nelson Mandela Centre for Peace and
Conflict Resolution
Professor, Director
KRISHNASAMI VENKATARAMAN

Jan Lacki
University of Geneva, School of
Physics, History and Philosophy of
Science
Lecturer, Researcher
LOUIS (VICTOR PIERRE
RAYMOND) BROGLIE

James T. Lamiell
Georgetown University, Department
of Psychology
Professor
LOUIS WILLIAM STERN

Hannah Landecker
Rice University, Department of
Anthropology
Assistant Professor
EDMUND VINCENT COWDRY

Y. Tzvi Langermann
Bar-Ilan University, Department of
Arabic
Professor
RABBI MOSES BEN MAIMON
MAIMONIDES

Pierre Laszlo
University of Liège and École
Polytechnique, Palaiseau
Professor Emeritus
EDGAR LEDERER
DONALD J. CRAM

James M. Lattis
University of Wisconsin, Madison,
Department of Astronomy
Director, UW Space Place
CHRISTOPH CLAVIUS

Roger D. Launius
National Air and Space Museum,
Smithsonian Institution
Curator
HOMER EDWARD NEWELL JR.
GERALD ALAN SOFFEN

Goulven Laurent
Comité Français d'Histoire de la
Géologie; l'Académie Internationale
d'Histoire des Sciences et des
Techniques
Science Historian, Vice President
ETIENNE GEOFFROY SAINT-
HILAIRE

F. W. Lawvere
University at Buffalo, Department of
Mathematics
Professor Emeritus
SAUNDERS MAC LANE

Homer E. Le Grand
Monash University, Department of
Philosophy and Bioethics
Professor
SAMUEL WARREN CAREY

David E. Leary
University of Richmond
Professor
ERNEST ROPIEQUET HILGARD

Joseph LeDoux
New York University, Center for
Neural Science
Professor, Director
JAMES WENCESLAS PAPEZ

William H. K. Lee
U. S. Geological Survey
Emeritus Scientist
 KEIITI AKI

G. Jeffery Leigh
University of Sussex, Department of
Chemistry
Professor Emeritus
 JOSEPH CHATT

James Lennox
University of Pittsburgh, Department
of History and Philosophy of Science
Professor
 ARISTOTLE

Walter Lenz
University of Hamburg, Institute of
Oceanography
Oceanographer
 PAUL GERHARD SCHOTT

Mark Lepper
Stanford University, Department of
Psychology
Professor
 ROBERT PAUL ABELSON

Elena S. Levina
Russian Academy of Sciences, S.I.
Vavilov Institute for the History of
Science & Technology
Professor
 YURY ANATOLYEVICH
 OVCHINNIKOV

Raphael D. Levine
University of California, Los Angeles,
Department of Chemistry and
Biochemistry
Professor
 RICHARD BARRY BERNSTEIN

David H. Levy
Jarnac Observatory
Astronomer
 BARTHOLOMEUS (BART) JAN
 BOK
 EUGENE MERLE SHOEMAKER

Ruth Prelowski Liebowitz
U.S. Air Force Electronic Systems
Center, Hanscom Air Force Base,
Massachusetts
Chief, ESC History Office
 HELMUT ERICH LANDSBERG

Mary Susan Lindee
University of Pennsylvania,
Department of History and Sociology
of Science
Professor
 JAMES VAN GUNDIA NEEL

Richard A. Littman
University of Oregon, Department of
Psychology
Professor Emeritus
 JOHN BROADUS WATSON

Maiken Lykke Lolck
University of Aarhus, Steno
Department for Studies of Science and
Science Education
PhD Student
 INGE LEHMANN

Malcolm S. Longair
University of Cambridge, Astrophysics
Group, Cavendish Laboratory
Professor
 MARTIN RYLE

Pierre Lory
Sorbonne, École Pratique des Hautes
Etudes, Section des Sciences
Religieuses
Director of Studies
 JĀBIR IBN HAYYĀN

Cornelia Lüdecke
University of Hamburg, Centre for
History of Natural Sciences,
Mathematics, and Technology
Privatdozent
 SOPHIE C(H)ARLOTTE
 JULIANE MOELLER

A. J. Lustig
University of Texas, Austin,
Department of History
Assistant Professor
 WILLIAM DONALD HAMILTON

Christoph Lüthy
Radboud University Nijmegen,
Faculty of Philosophy and Faculty of
the Sciences
Professor
 SÉBASTIEN BASSON (BASSO)
 DAVID GORLAEUS

John M. Lynch
Arizona State University, Barrett
Honors College

Honors Faculty Fellow
 PETER BRIAN MEDAWAR

Kirk Allen Maasch
University of Maine, Climate Change
Institute and Department of Earth
Sciences
Professor
 BARRY SALTZMAN

Ian Maclean
University of Oxford, All Souls
College, Faculty of History
Professor
 GIROLAMO CARDANO
 PETER RAMUS

Brenda Maddox
Journalist
 ROSALIND ELSIE FRANKLIN

Kazuaki Maenaka
Hanazono University, Faculty of
Letters
Professor
 MATUYAMA MOTONORI

Jane Maienschein
Arizona State University, School of
Life Sciences, Center for Biology and
Society
Professor
 THOMAS HUNT MORGAN

Patrick S. Market
University of Missouri, Columbia,
Department of Soil, Environmental
and Atmospheric Sciences
Associate Professor
 BERNHARD HAURWITZ

Gerald Markowitz
City University of New York, John Jay
College, Interdisciplinary Studies
Program
Professor
 KENNETH AND MAMIE CLARK

Ben Marsden
University of Aberdeen, Department
of History
Lecturer
 JOHN AITKEN

Ursula B. Marvin
Harvard-Smithsonian Center for
Astrophysics

Senior Geologist Emeritus
DIMITRI SERGEYEVICH KORZHINSKII

J. N. Mather
Princeton University, Department of Mathematics
Professor
JÜRGEN K. MOSER

Christina Matta
University of Wisconsin, Madison, Department of the History of Science
SIMON SCHWENDENER

Jean Mawhin
University of Louvain, Department of Mathematics
Professor
JEAN LERAY

J. P. May
University of Chicago, Department of Mathematics
Professor
JOHN FRANK ADAMS

Innocenzo Mazzini
University of Macerata
CORNELIUS CELSUS

Massimo Mazzotti
University of Exeter, Department of Sociology and Philosophy
Lecturer
MARIA GAETANA AGNESI

Charles McCarty
Indiana University, The Logic Program
Professor
ALFRED TARSKI

John McCleary
Vassar College, Department of Mathematics
Professor
HASSLER WHITNEY

W. Patrick McCray
University of California, Santa Barbara, Department of History
Professor
LEO GOLDBERG
JESSE LEONARD GREENSTEIN

Robert McCutcheon
Independent Scholar
VIKTOR AMAZASPOVICH AMBARTSUMIAN

Colin McLarty
Case Western Reserve University, Department of Philosophy
Chair
GARRETT BIRKHOFF
CLAUDE CHEVALLEY
JEAN DIEUDONNÉ
SAUNDERS MAC LANE
ANDRÉ WEIL

Michael McVaugh
University of North Carolina, Department of History
Professor Emeritus
ARNALD OF VILLANOVA

Roger Meade
Los Alamos National Laboratory
Archivist
ROBERT SERBER

Christoph Meinel
University of Regensburg, Institute of Philosophy
Professor
JOACHIM JUNGIUS

Michèle Mertens
University of Liège, Département des Sciences de l'Antiquité
Conservator
ZOSIMOS OF PANOPOLIS

Ad Meskens
Departement Bedrijfskunde, Lerarenopleiding en Sociaal Werk
MICHIEL COIGNET

Josef Michl
University of Colorado, Department of Chemistry and Biochemistry
Professor
MICHAEL J. S. DEWAR

Ronald Mickens
Clark Atlanta University, Physics Department
Professor
ELMER SAMUEL IMES

Heikki Mikkeli
University of Helsinki, Renvall Institute for European Area and Cultural Studies
Docent, Researcher
JACOPO (GIACOMO) ZABARELLA

Hans Mikosch
Technical University Vienna, Institut für Chemische Technologien und Analytik
Assistant Professor
ERIKA CREMER

Sara Joan Miles
Eastern University, Esperanza College
Dean Emeritus
CLÉMENCE-AUGUSTE ROYER

Sari Miller-Antonio
California State University, Stanislaus, Department of Anthropology and Geography
Professor, Chair
PEI WENZHONG

Eric Mills
Dalhousie University, Department of Oceanography
Professor Emeritus
HILDEBRAND WOLFE HARVEY
GORDON ARTHUR RILEY

Peter Milne
University of Stirling, Department of Philosophy
Professor
KARL RAIMUND POPPER

Henry L. Minton
University of Windsor, Department of Psychology
Professor Emeritus
LEWIS MADISON TERMAN

Simon Mitton
University of Cambridge, St Edmund's College
Fellow
FRED HOYLE

Amirouche Moktefi
University of Strasbourg, IRIST; University of Nancy 2, LPHS-AHP
CHARLES LUTWIDGE DODGSON

Georgina M. Montgomery
Montana State University, Department of History
Visiting Assistant Professor
CLARENCE RAY CARPENTER
DIAN FOSSEY

Michel Morange
École Normale Supérieure, Centre
Cavaillès
Professor
ROBERT WILLIAM HOLLEY

Cathleen Synge Morawetz
New York University, Courant
Institute of Mathematical Sciences
Professor Emerita
OLGA ALEXANDROVNA
LADYZHENSKAYA
OLGA ARSENIEVNA OLEINIK

Edward K. Morris
University of Kansas, Department of
Applied Behavioral Science
Professor
BURRHUS FREDERIC (B. F.)
SKINNER

Peter J. T. Morris
Science Museum, London
Manager
DEREK HAROLD RICHARD
BARTON
PAUL JOHN FLORY
ARCHER JOHN PORTER
MARTIN
WALTER JULIUS REPPE

Vivian Moses
Queen Mary University London;
King's College London; University
College London
Professor Emeritus
MELVIN CALVIN

Ken Mowbray
American Museum of Natural History,
Department of Anthropology
Research Associate
MARY DOUGLAS NICOL
LEAKEY

Douglas J. Mudgway
National Aeronautics and Space
Administration: Jet Propulsion
Laboratory (retired)
Tracking and Data Systems Manager
WILLIAM HAYWARD
PICKERING

Axel Mueller
Northwestern University, Department
of Philosophy
Assistant Professor
NELSON HENRY GOODMAN

Staffan Müller-Wille
University of Exeter, Department of
Sociology and Philosophy
Research Fellow
CARL LINNAEUS
GREGOR MENDEL

Shawn Mullet
Harvard University, Department of
the History of Science
PhD Student
DAVID JOSEPH BOHM
EDWARD TELLER

Walter Munk
University of California, San Diego,
Scripps Institution of Oceanography
Research Professor
ROGER RANDALL DOUGAN
REVELLE

Anne Mylott
Indiana University, Department of
History and Philosophy of Science
MATTHIAS JACOB SCHLEIDEN

Christine Nawa
University of Regensburg, Lehrstuhl
für Wissenschaftsgeschichte
ROBERT WILHELM EBERHARD
BUNSEN

Paul Needham
Stockholm University, Department of
Philosophy
Professor
PIERRE-MAURICE-MARIE
DUHEM

Clifford M. Nelson
U.S. Geological Survey
Geologist
CLARENCE RIVERS KING
JOHN WESLEY POWELL

Gareth Nelson
University of Melbourne, School of
Botany
Research Fellow
COLIN PATTERSON

Michael J. Neufeld
Smithsonian Institution, National Air
and Space Museum
Chair and Museum Curator
WERNHER VON BRAUN

Peter M. Neumann
The Queen's College, Oxford, and the
University of Oxford Mathematical
Institute
Fellow
WALTER FEIT
DANIEL GORENSTEIN
PHILIP HALL

William Newman
Indiana University, Department of
History and Philosophy of Science
Professor
ISAAC NEWTON
DANIEL SENNERT

Ian A. M. Nicholson
St. Thomas University, Department of
Psychology
Professor
GORDON WILLARD ALLPORT
ABRAHAM MASLOW

Richard G. Niemi
University of Rochester, Department
of Political Science
Professor
WILLIAM HARRISON RIKER

Alfred Nordmann
Technische Universität Darmstadt,
Institut für Philosophie
Professor
HEINRICH RUDOLF HERTZ

David Norman
University of Cambridge, Department
of Earth Sciences, Sedgwick Museum
Director
YANG ZHONGJIAN

Joseph A. November
University of South Carolina,
Department of History
Assistant Professor
GEORGE ELMER FORSYTHE

Igor Novikov
Niels Bohr Institute for Astronomy,
Physics, and Geophysics
Professor Emeritus
YAKOV BORISOVICH
ZELDOVICH

Vivian Nutton
University College London, Wellcome
Trust Centre for the History of
Medicine
Academic Staff
RUFUS OF EPHESUS

Mary Jo Nye
Oregon State University, Department
of History
Professor
  PATRICK MAYNARD STUART
    BLACKETT
  LINUS CARL PAULING
  MIHÁLY (MICHAEL) POLÁNYI

Lynn K. Nyhart
University of Wisconsin, Madison,
Department of the History of Science
Professor
  ERNST HAECKEL
  MORITZ WAGNER

Gerhard Oberkofler
Universität Innsbruck,
Universitätsarchiv
Professor
  ERIKA CREMER

Roderick O'Donnell
Macquarie University, Department of
Economics
Professor
  JOHN MAYNARD KEYNES

Robert C. Olby
University of Pittsburgh, Department
of History and Philosophy of Science
Research Professor
  WILLIAM BATESON
  FRANCIS HARRY COMPTON
    CRICK
  GREGOR MENDEL

David Oldroyd
University of New South Wales,
School of History and Philosophy
Honorary Visiting Professor
  JAMES HUTTON
  DARASHAW NOSHERWAN
    WADIA

Lennart Olsson
Friedrich-Schiller-Universität Jena,
Institut für Spezielle Zoologie und
Evolutionsbiologie
Professor
  SVEN OTTO HÖRSTADIUS

Donald L. Opitz
DePaul University, School for New
Learning
Assistant Professor
  EDGAR DOUGLAS ADRIAN

ANDREW CROSSE
JOHN WILLIAM STRUTT

Wayne Orchiston
James Cook University, Centre for
Astronomy
Senior Lecturer
  JOHN GATENBY BOLTON

Vítězslav Orel
Mendelianum in the Moravian
Museum, Brno
Director Emeritus
  GREGOR MENDEL

Naomi Oreskes
University of California, San Diego,
Department of History
Professor
  HENRY MELSON STOMMEL

Eduardo L. Ortiz
Imperial College, Department of
Mathematics
Professor Emeritus
  JOSÉ MARÍA DE LANZ
  ANTÓNIO A. MONTEIRO

Michael A. Osborne
University of California, Santa
Barbara, Program in History of
Science, Technology, and Medicine
Associate Professor
  ISIDORE GEOFFROY SAINT-
    HILAIRE
  ÉDOUARD-MARIE HECKEL

Carla Rita Palmerino
Radboud University Nijmegen,
Faculty of Philosophy
Professor
  PIERRE GASSENDI

Maria K. Papathanassiou
National and Kapodistrian University
of Athens, Faculty of Mathematics
Assistant Professor
  STEPHANUS OF ALEXANDRIA

Hyung Wook Park
University of Minnesota, Program in
History of Science, Technology, and
Medicine
PhD Student
  FRANK MACFARLANE BURNET

Armando J. Parodi
Fundación Instituto Leloir

President
  LUIS FEDERICO LELOIR

Karen Hunger Parshall
University of Virginia, Departments of
Mathematics and History
Professor
  JAMES JOSEPH SYLVESTER

Cesare Pastorino
Indiana University, Department of
History and Philosophy of Science
PhD Student
  FRANCIS BACON

J. M. S. Pearce
Department of Neurobiology, Hull
Royal Infirmary, East Yorkshire
Emeritus Consultant Neurologist
  GORDON MORGAN HOLMES

Carl Pearson
Indiana University, Department of
History and Philosophy of Science
Visiting Professor
  JOHN PHILOPONUS

Volker Peckhaus
University of Paderborn, Institut für
Humanwissenschaften: Philosophie
Professor
  FRIEDRICH LUDWIG GOTTLOB
    FREGE

Phillip James Edwin Peebles
Princeton University, Department of
Physics
Professor Emeritus
  ROBERT HENRY DICKE

S. George Pemberton
University of Alberta, Department of
Earth & Atmospheric Sciences
Professor, Research Chair
  RUDOLF RICHTER

Jon V. Pepper
University College London,
Department of Mathematics
Honorary Research Fellow
  THOMAS HARRIOT

Anthony L. Peratt
Los Alamos National Laboratory,
Applied Physics Division
Guest Scientist
  HANNES OLOF GOSTA
    ALFVÉN

Stefano Perfetti
University of Pisa, Department of
Philosophy
Professor
AGOSTINO NIFO

Anders Persson
Swedish Meteorological and
Hydrological Institute, Meteorological
Analysis and Prediction Section
Researcher
ERIK HERBERT PALMÉN
SVERRE PETTERSSEN
REGINALD COCKCROFT
SUTCLIFFE

Aleksandar Petrovic
Serbian Academy of Science and Arts
MILUTIN MILANKOVIĆ

Steve Philips
Ghent University, Centre for History
of Science, Department of Early
Modern History
PhD Student
JODOCUS HONDIUS
PETRUS PLANCIUS

Gualtiero Piccinini
University of Missouri, St. Louis,
Department of Philosophy
Assistant Professor
ALLEN NEWELL

Anne D. Pick
University of Minnesota, Institute of
Child Development
Professor Emerita
ELEANOR JACK GIBSON

Herbert L. Pick
University of Minnesota, Institute of
Child Development
Professor
ELEANOR JACK GIBSON

Kathleen E. Pigg
Arizona State University, School of
Life Sciences
Associate Professor
KATHERINE ESAU

Brian Pippard
University of Cambridge, Department
of Physics, Cavendish Laboratory
Professor Emeritus
NEVILL FRANCIS MOTT

Régine Plas
Université Paris V René Descartes,
Centre de Recherces Psychotropes,
Santé Mentale, Société
Professor
PIERRE JANET

Irina Podgorny
Universidad Nacional de La Plata,
Facultad de Ciencias Naturales y
Museo de La Plata, Archivo Histórico
CONICET Investigadora
ROBERT LEHMANN-NITSCHE
FRANCISCO PASCASIO
MORENO

John A. Pojman
The University of Southern
Mississippi, Department of Chemistry
& Biochemistry
Professor
ILYA PRIGOGINE

Theodore M. Porter
University of California, Los Angeles,
Department of History
Professor
KARL PEARSON

Lawrence M. Principe
Johns Hopkins University,
Department of the History of Science
and Technology and Department of
Chemistry
Professor
WILHELM HOMBERG

Gregory Radick
University of Leeds, Department of
Philosophy, Division of History and
Philosophy of Science
Senior Lecturer, Chair
WILLIAM HOMAN THORPE

Leo Radom
University of Sydney, School of
Chemistry
Professor
JOHN ANTHONY POPLE

Jakov Radovčić
Croatian Natural History Museum,
Krapina Collection
Curator
DRAGUTIN (KARL)
GORJANOVIĆ-KRAMBERGER

F. Jamil Ragep
McGill University, Institute of Islamic
Studies
Research Chair
QUṬB AL-DĪN MAḤMŪD IBN
MASʿŪD IBN AL-MUṢLIḤ AL-
SHĪRĀZĪ

Sally Ragep
McGill University, Institute of Islamic
Studies
Senior Researcher
SHARAF AL-DĪN MAḤMŪD IBN
MUḤAMMAD IBN ʿUMAR AL-
JAGHMĪNĪ

Peter J. Ramberg
Truman State University, Division of
Science
Associate Professor
JAMES MASON CRAFTS

Pierre Rat
University of Burgundy
Honorary Professor
HENRI TINTANT

Simon Olling Rebsdorf
University of Aarhus, Steno
Department for Studies of Science and
Science Education
Associate Professor
BENGT GEORG DANIEL
STRÖMGREN

Brian Regal
Kean University, Department of
History
Assistant Professor
HENRY FAIRFIELD OSBORN

Karin Reich
University of Hamburg, Department
of Mathematics
Professor
MARCEL GROSSMANN

Carsten Reinhardt
University of Bielefeld, Institute for
Science and Technology Studies
Professor
HERBERT SANDER GUTOWSKY

Maria Rentetzi
National Technical University of
Athens, School of Applied
Mathematics and Physics
Assistant Professor
MARIETTA BLAU

Martin Reuss
U. S. Army Corps of Engineers, Office
of History
Senior Historian (retired)
ROBERT ELMER HORTON

Hans-Jörg Rheinberger
Max Planck Institute for the History
of Science, Berlin Director
ALBERT CLAUDE

Robert C. Richardson
University of Cincinnati, Department
of Philosophy
Professor
BORIS EPHRUSSI
EDWARD LAWRIE TATUM

Olivier Rieppel
The Field Museum, Department of
Geology
Curator and Chair
OTTO HEINRICH
SCHINDEWOLF

John S. Rigden
Washington University in St. Louis,
Department of Physics
Professor
EDWARD MILLS PURCELL
ISIDOR ISAAC RABI

Michael Riordan
University of California, Santa Cruz,
Department of Physics
Adjunct Professor
WILLIAM BRADFORD
SHOCKLEY

Gerrylynn K. Roberts
The Open University, Faculty of Arts,
Department of History of Science,
Technology & Medicine
Senior Lecturer
CHISTOPHER KELK INGOLD

Libby Robin
Australian National University, Fenner
School of Environment and Society;
National Museum of Australia
Senior Fellow; Senior Research Fellow
FRANCIS NOBLE RATCLIFFE

Eleonora Rocconi
University of Pavia, Faculty of
Musicology
Researcher
DIDYMUS

PORPHYRY
PTOLEMAIS OF CYRENE

Michel Rochas
Conseil Général des Ponts et
Chaussées
Ingénieur général
LÉON PHILIPPE TEISSERENC
DE BORT

Alan Rocke
Case Western Reserve University,
Department of History
Professor
JONS JACOB BERZELIUS
ADOLF WILHELM HERMANN
KOLBE
ADOLPHE WURTZ

Raul Rojas
Freie Universität Berlin, Fachbereich
Mathematik und Informatik, Institut
für Informatik
Professor
KONRAD ZUSE

Nils D. Roll-Hansen
University of Oslo, Department of
Philosophy, Classics, History of Art
and Ideas
Professor Emeritus
LOUIS PASTEUR

Joandomènec Ros
University of Barcelona, Faculty of
Biology, Department of Ecology
Professor
RAMON MARGALEF

Rachael Rosner
Independent Scholar
CARL RANSOM ROGERS

Donald K. Routh
University of Miami, Department of
Psychology
Professor Emeritus
ROGER WOLCOTT SPERRY

David Rowe
Johannes Gutenberg Universitat
Mainz, Geschichte der Mathematik
und der Naturwissenschaften
Professor
SOPHUS LIE

David Rudge
Western Michigan University,
Department of Biological Sciences,

Mallinson Institute for Science
Education
Associate Professor
HENRY BERNARD DAVIS
KETTLEWELL

Martin J. S. Rudwick
University of Cambridge, Department
of History and Philosophy of Science
Affiliated Research Scholar
GEORGES CUVIER

William McKinley Runyan
University of California, Berkeley,
School of Social Welfare
Professor
HENRY ALEXANDER MURRAY

Nicolaas A. Rupke
Göttingen University, Institute for the
History of Science
Professor and Director
RICHARD OWEN

Colin A. Russell
The Open University, Department of
History of Science, Technology and
Medicine
Professor Emeritus
EDWARD FRANKLAND
ROBERT ROBINSON
ALEXANDER ROBERTUS TODD

Klaus Ruthenberg
Coburg University of Applied
Sciences, Faculty of Science and
Technology
Professor
FRIEDRICH ADOLF PANETH

Abdelhamid I. Sabra
Harvard University, Department of
the History of Science
Professor Emeritus
ABU ʿALI AL-HASAN IBN AL-
HASAN IBN al-HAYTHAM

Dorothy Sack
Ohio University, Department of
Geography
Professor
ARTHUR NEWELL STRAHLER

Cihan Saclioglu
Sabanci University, Istanbul, Faculty
of Engineering and Natural Science
Professor
FEZA GÜRSEY

Cora Sadosky
Howard University, Department of
Mathematics
Professor
  ALBERTO PEDRO CALDERÓN

Klaus Sander
University of Freiburg, Faculty of
Biology
Professor
  HILDE MANGOLD

Lisa T. Sarasohn
Oregon State University, Department
of History
Professor
  MARGARET CAVENDISH

Helga Satzinger
University College London, Wellcome
Trust Centre for the History of
Medicine
Reader
  CÉCILE AND OSKAR VOGT

Wolfgang Scherer
Universidad Central de Venezuela,
Department of Geology
Professor
  WILLIAM CHRISTIAN
    KRUMBEIN

Londa Schiebinger
Stanford University, Department of
History and the Clayman Institute for
Gender Research
Professor
  MARIA SIBYLLA MERIAN
  MARIA MARGARETHA
    WINKELMANN

Judith Johns Schloegel
Independent Scholar
  HERBERT SPENCER JENNINGS
  TRACY SONNEBORN

Wolfgang Schlote
Johann Wolfgang Goethe-University
Frankfurt Main, Edinger Institute
Professor Emeritus
  LUDWIG EDINGER

Florian Schmaltz
Johann Wolfgang Goethe University
Frankfurt am Main, History of
Science Working Group
  RICHARD KUHN

Warren Schmaus
Illinois Institute of Technology, Lewis
Department of Humanities
Professor
  ROBERT K. MERTON

Gail K. Schmitt
Princeton University, Department of
History, Program in the History of
Science
PhD Student
  RUTH SAGER

Erhard Scholz
University of Wuppertal, Department
C - Mathematics
Professor
  FELIX HAUSDORFF
  HERMANN CLAUS HUGO
    WEYL

Jay Schulkin
Georgetown University, Department
of Physiology and Biophysics
Research Professor
  CURT P. RICHTER

David M. Schultz
University of Helsinki, Division of
Atmospheric Sciences; Finnish
Meteorological Institute
  TOR HAROLD PERCIVAL
    BERGERON

Hans-Werner Schütt
Technical University Berlin, Institute
of Philosophy and History of Science
Professor
  EILHARD MITSCHERLICH

Vera Schwach
Norwegian Institute for Studies in
Research and Higher Education,
Center for Innovation
Senior Researcher
  SVEN OTTO PETTERSSON

Joel S. Schwartz
City University of New York, College
of Staten Island, Department of
Biology
Professor Emeritus
  ROBERT CHAMBERS

Silvan S. Schweber
Brandeis University, Martin A. Fisher
School of Physics
Professor
  HANS ALBRECHT BETHE

  J. ROBERT OPPENHEIMER
  JULIAN SCHWINGER

Jérôme Segal
École Normale Supérieure de Paris,
Centre Cavaillès
Assistant Professor
  CLAUDE SHANNON

Gino Segrè
University of Pennsylvania,
Department of Physics
Professor
  HENRY PRIMAKOFF

Robert Seidel
University of Minnesota, Department
of History of Science, Technology and
Medicine
Professor
  LUIS WALTER ALVAREZ
  EMILIO GINO SEGRÈ

Rena Selya
University of California, Los Angeles,
Department of History
Lecturer
  SALVADOR EDWARD LURIA
  MAURICE HUGH FREDERICK
    WILKINS

Dennis L. Sepper
University of Dallas, Department of
Philosophy
Professor
  JOHANN WOLFGANG VON
    GOETHE

Reinhard W. Serchinger
SePhys, Consultant in Applied Physics
Owner
  WALTER HANS SCHOTTKY

Eldar Shafir
Princeton University, Department of
Psychology and the Woodrow Wilson
School of Public and International
Affairs
Professor
  AMOS TVERSKY

Sonu Shamdasani
University College London, Wellcome
Trust Centre for the History of
Medicine
Reader
  CARL GUSTAV JUNG

Michael H. Shank
University of Wisconsin, Madison,
Department of the History of Science
Professor
JOHANNES REGIOMONTANUS

Gordon M. Shepherd
Yale University School of Medicine,
Department of Neurobiology
Professor
JOHN CAREW ECCLES

Abner Shimony
Boston University, Departments of
Philosophy and Physics
Professor Emeritus
JOHN S. BELL

Martin Shubik
Yale University, Department of
Economics
Professor
OSKAR MORGENSTERN

Gerold Siedler
Kiel University, Leibniz Institute for
Marine Sciences
Professor
ALBERT JOSEPH MARIA
DEFANT

Ruth Lewin Sime
Sacramento City College, Department
of Chemistry
Professor Emeritus
OTTO HAHN

Ana Simões
Universidade de Lisboa, Centro de
História das Ciências
Professor
ROBERT SANDERSON
MULLIKEN

Maxine Singer
Carnegie Institution of Washington;
National Institutes of Health
President Emeritus; Scientist Emeritus
GEORGE WELLS BEADLE

Rivers Singleton
University of Delaware, Departments
of Biological Sciences and English
Associate Professor
HERMAN MORITZ KALCKAR
SEVERO OCHOA
HARLAND GOFF WOOD

S. Sivaram
National Chemical Laboratory, Pune
Director
KRISHNASAMI VENKATARAMAN

Robert A. Skipper
University of Cincinnati, Department
of Philosophy
Professor
RONALD AYLMER FISHER
SEWALL WRIGHT

Nancy Slack
The Sage Colleges, Department of
Biology
Professor Emeritus
G. EVELYN HUTCHINSON

Leo B. Slater
Johns Hopkins University, Institute for
Applied Economics and the Study of
Business Enterprise
Fellow
ROBERT BURNS WOODWARD

Phillip R. Sloan
University of Notre Dame,
Department of History
Professor
GEORGE-LOUIS LE CLERC,
COMTE DE BUFFON

Chris Smeenk
University of California, Los Angeles,
Department of Philosophy
Assistant Professor
DENNIS WILLIAM SCIAMA

Barry H. Smith
Weill Medical College of Cornell
University, Department of
Neuroscience
Professor, Attending Surgeon
FRANCIS OTTO SCHMITT

Charles H. Smith
Western Kentucky University,
Department of Library Public Services
Professor, Science Librarian
ALFRED RUSSEL WALLACE

John K. Smith
Lehigh University, Department of
History
Associate Professor
PAUL HUGH EMMETT
EUGÈNE JULES HOUDRY

Justin E. H. Smith
Concordia University, Department of
Philosophy
Associate Professor
GOTTFRIED WILHELM
LEIBNIZ

Pamela H. Smith
Columbia University, Department of
History
Professor
JOHANN JOACHIM BECHER

Robert W. Smith
University of Alberta, Department of
History and Classics
Professor
JAN HENDRIK OORT

Vassiliki Betty Smocovitis
University of Florida, Departments of
Zoology and History
Professor
I. MICHAEL LERNER
GEORGE LEDYARD STEBBINS,
JR.

Walter Sneader
University of Strathclyde, Institute of
Biomedical Sciences
Honorary Lecturer
ARTHUR EICHENGRÜN

Thomas Söderqvist
University of Copenhagen
Professor, Director
NIELS KAJ JERNE

Michael M. Sokal
Worcester Polytechnic Institute,
Department of Humanities and Arts
Professor Emeritus
JAMES MCKEEN CATTELL

Marianne Sommer
Eidgenössische Technische Hochschule
Zürich, Chair of Science Studies
Privatdozentin
WILFRID EDWARD LE GROS
CLARK
KENNETH PAGE OAKLEY

Henrik Kragh Sørensen
University of Aarhus, Steno
Department for Studies of Science and
Science Education
Post Doc
NIELS HENRIK ABEL

Sverker Sörlin
Royal Institute of Technology,
Stockholm, Division for History of
Science and Technology
Professor
  SVANTE AUGUST ARRHENIUS

Theodore L. Sourkes
McGill University, Department of
Psychiatry
Professor Emeritus
  JOHANN LUDWIG WILHELM
    THUDICHUM

P. E. Spargo
University of Cape Town, Department
of Physics
Associate Professor Emeritus
  JAMES LEONARD BRIERLY
    SMITH

T. A. Springer
Utrecht University, Mathematics
Institute
Professor
  ARMAND BOREL

John Stachel
Boston University, Department of
Physics, Center for Einstein Studies
Professor Emeritus
  ALBERT EINSTEIN

Ida H. Stamhuis
Vrye University, Faculty of Exact
Sciences
Professor
  JANTINA TAMMES
  HUGO DE VRIES

Matthew Stanley
Michigan State University,
Department of History
Professor
  ARTHUR STANLEY
    EDDINGTON

Richard Stanley
Massachusetts Institute of Technology,
Department of Mathematics
Professor
  GIAN-CARLO ROTA

Carlos Steel
University of Leuven, Institute of
Philosophy
Professor
  JOHANNES SCOTTUS
    ERIUGENA

Hubert Steinke
University of Bern, Institute for the
History of Medicine
Research Associate
  ALBRECHT VON HALLER

Friedrich Steinle
Bergische Universität Wuppertal,
Faculty of Humanities
Professor
  MICHAEL FARADAY

Lester D. Stephens
University of Georgia, Department of
History
Professor Emeritus
  JOHN EDWARDS HOLBROOK
  JOSEPH LeCONTE
  ALFRED GOLDSBOROUGH
    MAYOR

Thomas F. Stocker
University of Bern, Physics Institute
Professor
  HANS OESCHGER

Soňa Štrbáňová
Academy of Sciences of the Czech
Republic, Institute for Contemporary
History
Associate Professor
  MARJORY STEPHENSON

James E. Strick
Franklin and Marshall College,
Department of Earth and
Environment
Assistant Professor
  HENRY CHARLTON BASTIAN
  NORMAN HAROLD HOROWITZ
  HAROLD P. KLEIN

Jeffrey L. Sturchio
Merck & Co., Inc.
Vice President
  KARL AUGUST FOLKERS

Yasumoto Suzuki
Geological Survey of Japan, Geological
Information Center
Retired Member
  KIYOO WADATI

Edith Dudley Sylla
North Carolina State University,
Department of History
Professor
  JAKOB BERNOULLI
  THOMAS BRAWARDINE

WALTER BURLEY
JOHN DUMBLETON
RICHARD SWINESHEAD AND
  ROGER SWYNESHED

Scott Tanona
Kansas State University, Department
of Philosophy
Assistant Professor
  NIELS HENRIK DAVID BOHR

Ian Tattersall
American Museum of Natural History,
Division of Anthropology
Curator
  MARY DOUGLAS NICOL
    LEAKEY

Pierre Teissier
University of Paris X, Nanterre,
Centre d'histoire et de philosophie des
sciences
PhD Student
  ROBERT COLLONGUES

Joachim Telle
University of Heidelberg and
University of Freiburg/Breisgau,
Germanistische Seminare
Professor
  ADAM OF BODENSTEIN
  ALEXANDER VON SUCHTEN

Roger Temam
Indiana University, Bloomington,
Institute for Scientific Computing and
Applied Mathematics
Professor
  JACQUES-LOUIS LIONS

Mary Terrall
University of California, Los Angeles,
Department of History
Associate Professor
  PIERRE LOUIS MOREAU DE
    MAUPERTUIS

Tosun Terzioğlu
Sabanci University
President
  CAHIT ARF

Bert Theunissen
Utrecht University, Institute for the
History and Foundations of Science
Professor
  MARIE EUGÈNE FRANÇOIS
    THOMAS DUBOIS

Denis Thieffry
Université de la Méditerranée, Faculté des Sciences de Luminy, Département de Biologie
Professor
JEAN LOUIS BRACHET

Jacques Thierry
University of Burgundy, Laboratory of Biogeosciences
Professor Emeritus
HENRI TINTANT

Johannes M. M. H. Thijssen
Radboud University Nijmegen, Faculty of Philosophy
Professor
ALBERT OF SAXONY
JOHN BURIDAN

Anne Tihon
Université Catholique de Louvain, Department of Greek, Latin and Oriental Studies, Institut Orientaliste
Professor
GEORGE CHIONIADES
THEODORE MELITENIOTES
MANUEL MOSCHOPOULOS
GEORGES PACHYMERES
ISAAC ARGYRUS

Werner Tochtermann
Christian-Albrechts-Universität zu Kiel, Institut für Organische Chemie
Professor Emeritus
GEORG WITTIG

Daniel P. Todes
Johns Hopkins University, School of Medicine, Department of the History of Medicine
Professor
IVAN PETROVICH PAVLOV

Hugh Torrens
Keele University, United Kingdom, School of Earth Sciences and Geography
Professor Emeritus
JOHN FAREY

Alain Touwaide
Smithsonian Institution, National Museum of Natural History, Department of Botany
Historian of Sciences
NICOLÒ LEONICENO
GUILLAUME PELLICIER

Anthony S. Travis
The Hebrew University of Jerusalem, Sidney M. Edelstein Center
Professor
ERNST DAVID BERGMANN
CHARLES BLACHFORD MANSFIELD

Simon Trépanier
University of Edinburgh, School of History, Classics, and Archaeology
Lecturer
EMPEDOCLES OF ACRAGAS

François Treves
Rutgers University, Department of Mathematics
Professor
LAURENT SCHWARTZ

Virginia Trimble
University of California, Irvine, Department of Physics and Astronomy
Professor
JOHN NORRIS BAHCALL
THOMAS GOLD

Roger Turner
University of Pennsylvania, History and Sociology of Science Department
PhD student
HORACE ROBERT BYERS
FRANCIS WILTON REICHELDERFER

Susan Turner
Monash University, Department of Geosciences, and Queensland Museum, Paleontology and Geology Section
Honorary Senior Research Associate
DOROTHY HILL

Ryan D. Tweney
Bowling Green State University, Department of Psychology
Professor Emeritus
DONALD ERIC BROADBENT

Monica Ugaglia
LEONARDO GARZONI, S.J.

Peter Ullrich
Universität Koblenz-Landau, Campus Koblenz, Mathematisches Institut
Professor
GEORG FRIEDRICH BERNHARD RIEMANN

Melvyn C. Usselman
University of Western Ontario, Department of Chemistry
Professor
WILLIAM HYDE WOLLASTON

Ezio Vaccari
Università dell'Insubria (Varese, Italy), Dipartimento di Informatica e Comunicazione
Professor
GIOVANNI ARDUINO

Adrienne van den Bogaard
Delft University of Technology, Faculty of Technology, Policy and Management, Department of Philosophy
Assistant Professor
WYBE EDSGER DIJKSTRA

Philip van der Eijk
Newcastle University, School of Historical Studies
Professor
DIOCLES OF CARYSTUS

René van der Veer
Leiden University, Department of Education and Child Studies
Professor
LEV SEMYONOVICH VYGOTSKY

Ton van Helvoort
Independent Scholar, The Netherlands
A. HUGO T. THEORELL

David Van Reybrouck
Independent Scholar and Author, Brussels
SHERWOOD LARNED WASHBURN

Hugo van Woerden
University of Groningen, Kapteyn Astronomical Institute
Professor
HENDRIK CHRISTOFFEL VAN DE HULST

Veeravalli Varadarajan
University of California, Los Angeles, Department of Mathematics
Professor
HARISH-CHANDRA

Hemmo J. Veenstra
LAMBERTUS MARIUS JOANNES URSINUS VAN STRAATEN

Cristina Viano
Centre National de la Recherche
Scientifique, Université de Paris-
Sorbonne
Senior Research Fellow
OLYMPIODORUS OF
ALEXANDRIA
OLYMPIODORUS OF THEBES

Fernando Vidal
Max Planck Institute for the History
of Science
Senior Research Scholar
JEAN PIAGET

Bernard Vitrac
Centre National de la Recherche
Scientifique, UMR 8667, Centre
Louis Gernet, Paris
Director of Research
EUCLID

James R. Voelkel
Massachusetts Institute of Technology
Senior Fellow
JOHANNES KEPLER

Annette B. Vogt
Max Planck Institute for the History
of Science, Berlin Research Scholar
TATIANA A. EHRENFEST-
AFANAS'EVA
LINA SOLOMONOVNA SHTERN

Hans Volkert
Deutsches Zentrum fur Luft und
Raumfahrt (DLR), Institut fur Physik
der Atmosphare (IPA)
Staff Scientist
FELIX MARIA VON EXNER-
EWARTEN

Craig B. Waff
Air Force Research Laboratory,
History Office
Historian
GEORGE BIDDELL AIRY

Kameshwar C. Wali
Syracuse University, Department of
Physics
Professor Emeritus
SUBRAHMANYAN
CHANDRASEKHAR

Scott Walter
University of Nancy, Department of
Philosophy

Maître de conférences
JULES HENRI POINCARÉ

Jessica Wang
University of British Columbia
Associate Professor
EDWARD UHLER CONDON

Zuoyue Wang
California State Polytechnic
University, Pomona, Department of
History
Associate Professor
WU CHIEN-SHIUNG
ZHONGYAO ZHAO
ZHU KEZHEN

Walter Warwick
Micro Analysis & Design Principal
Research Analyst
ALAN MATHISON TURING

A. M. C. Waterman
University of Manitoba; St. John's
College, Winnipeg
Professor Emeritus; Retired Fellow
THOMAS ROBERT MALTHUS

C. Kenneth Waters
University of Minnesota, Department
of Philosophy, Minnesota Center for
Philosophy of Science
Professor, Director
JULIAN HUXLEY

Bruce H. Weber
California State University Fullerton,
Bennington College
Professor Emeritus
PETER DENNIS MITCHELL

Nadine M. Weidman
Harvard University, History of Science
Lecturer
KARL SPENCER LASHLEY

Stephen J. Weininger
Worcester Polytechnic Institute,
Department of Chemistry &
Biochemistry
Professor Emeritus
PAUL DOUGHTY BARTLETT

Paul Weirich
University of Missouri-Columbia,
Department of Philosophy
Professor
BRUNO DE FINETTI
FRANK PLUMPTON RAMSEY

LEONARD JAMES SAVAGE
HERBERT ALEXANDER SIMON

Rainer Weiss
Massachusetts Institute of Technology,
Department of Physics
Professor Emeritus
DAVID TODD WILKINSON

Kathleen Wellman
Southern Methodist University,
Department of History
Professor
JULIEN OFFRAY DE LA
METTRIE

Simone Wenkel
Universität zu Köln, Institut für
Genetik
PhD Candidate
CARL ALEXANDER NEUBERG

Catherine Westfall
Michigan State University, Lyman
Briggs College
Visiting Associate Professor
EUGENE WIGNER

John A. Weymark
Vanderbilt University, Department of
Economics
Professor
JOHN CHARLES HARSANYI

E. O. Wiley
University of Kansas, Department of
Ecology and Evolutionary Biology;
Biodiversity Research Center
Professor, Senior Curator
(EMIL HANS) WILLI HENNIG

Alan F. Williams
University of Geneva, Department of
Inorganic Chemistry
Professor
AXEL CHRISTIAN KLIXBÜLL
JØRGENSEN

Kathleen Broome Williams
Cogswell Polytechnical College,
General Education Program
Director and Professor
GRACE HOPPER

David B. Wilson
Iowa State University, Department of
History
Professor
WILLIAM WHEWELL

Richard Wilson
Harvard University, Department of
Physics
Professor
  KENNETH (KEN) TOMPKINS
    BAINBRIDGE

Andrew S. Winston
University of Guelph, Department of
Psychology
Professor
  EDWIN GARRIGUES BORING

Judith E. Winston
Virginia Museum of Natural History,
Marine Biology
Curator
  LIBBIE HENRIETTA HYMAN

Rega Wood
Stanford University, Department of
Philosophy
Research Professor
  RICHARD RUFUS OF
    CORNWALL

Walter W. Woodward
University of Connecticut,
Department of History

Assistant Professor
  JOHN WINTHROP, JR.

Robert H. Wozniak
Bryn Mawr College, Department of
Psychology
Professor
  JOHN BROADUS WATSON

Franz M. Wuketits
University of Vienna, Institute for
Philosophy of Science
Professor
  OTTO KOEHLER
  ERICH VON HOLST

Sepideh Yalda
Millersville University, Department of
Earth Sciences
Professor
  TETSUYA THEODORE FUJITA
  CHARLES WARREN
    THORNTHWAITE
  GILBERT THOMAS WALKER
  HARRY WEXLER

Ellis Yochelson
National Museum of Natural History,
Department of Paleobiology
Research Associate, deceased

HARRY STEPHEN LADD
CURT TEICHERT

Zhendong You
China University of Geosciences,
Faculty of Earth Sciences
Professor
  DING WENJIANG (V. K.
    TING)
  YIN ZANGXUN

Christian C. Young
Alverno College, Division of Natural
Sciences, Mathematics & Technology
Professor
  ALDO LEOPOLD

Palle Yourgrau
Brandeis University, Department of
Philosophy
Professor
  KURT FRIEDRICH GÖDEL

Li Zhang
Chinese Academy of Sciences,
Institute for the History of Natural
Science
Professor
  PETER P. T. SAH

List of Scientists by Field

MATHEMATICS

Abel, Niels Henrik
Adams, John Frank
Agnesi, Maria Gaetana
Ahlfors, Lars
Albert of Saxony
Apollonius of Perga
Archimedes
Arf, Cahit
Argyrus, Isaac
Babbage, Charles
Bacon, Roger
Baldi, Bernardino
Bernoulli, Jakob (Jacob, Jacques, James) I
Bers, Lipmann
Birkhoff, Garrett
Bogolubov, Nikolai Nikolaevich
Borel, Armand
Borelli, Giovanni Alfonso
Bourbaki, Nicolas
Bradwardine, Thomas
Calderón, Alberto Pedro
Cantor, Georg Ferdinand Ludwig
Cardano, Girolamo
Cauchy, Augustin-Louis
Chandrasekhar, Subrahmanyan
Chern, Shiing-Shen
Chevalley, Claude
Clavius, Christoph
Coignet, Michiel

d'Alembert (Dalembert, D'Alembert), Jean Le Rond
de Finetti, Bruno
De Giorgi, Ennio
Descartes, René Du Perron
Didymus
Dieudonné, Jean
Dijkstra, Wybe Edsger
Dodgson, Charles Lutwidge
Ehrenfest-Afanas'eva, Tatiana A.
Eilenberg, Samuel
Erdos, Paul
Euclid
Euler, Leonhard
Farey, John
Feit, Walter
Fisher, Ronald Aylmer
Forsythe, George Elmer
Frege, Friedrich Ludwig Gottlob
Gödel, Kurt Friedrich
Gorenstein, Daniel
Grossmann, Marcel
Hall, Philip
Hamilton, William Rowan
Harish-Chandra
Harriot (or Hariot), Thomas
Hartree, Douglas Rayner
Hausdorff, Felix
Hero of Alexandria
Hilbert, David
Hipparchus

Hirst, Thomas Archer
Hondius, Jodocus
Hypatia
Ibn al-Haytham, Abu 'Ali al-hasan Ibn al-hasan
Ibrāhīm Ibn Sinān Ibn Thābit Ibn Qurra
Inglada, Vicente
Jeffreys, Harold
Jungius, Joachim
Keldysh, Mstislav Vsevolodovich
Kepler, Johannes
King, Ada Augusta, the Countess of Lovelace
Kodaira, Kunihiko
Kolmogorov, Andrei Nikolaevich
Kovalevskaya, Sofya Vasilyevna (Sonya)
Ladyzhenskaya, Olga Alexandrovna
Lanz, José María de
Leibniz, Gottfried Wilhelm
Leray, Jean
Lichnérowicz, André
Lie, Sophus
Lions, Jacques-Louis
Mac Lane, Saunders
Mauchly, John William
Maupertuis, Pierre Louis Moreau de
McCrea, William Hunter
McVittie, George Cunliffe
Milanković, Milutin

Monte, Guidobaldo, Marchese del
Monteiro, António A.
Morse, Marston
Moschopoulos, Manuel
Moser, Jürgen K.
Nash, John Forbes, Jr.
Newell, Homer Edward, Jr.
Newton, Isaac
Oleinik, Olga Arsenievna
Oresme, Nicole
Pachymeres, Georges
Pearson, Karl
Piero della Francesca
Poincare, Jules Henri
Pontryagin, Lev Semionovich
Prachaticz, Cristannus de

Ptolemais of Cyrene
Ptolemy
Qūhī (or al-Kūhī), Abū Sahl Wayjan Ibn Rustam al-
Ramsey, Frank Plumpton
Ramus, Peter, also known as Pierre de la Ramee
Regiomontanus, Johannes
Richardson, Lewis Fry
Robinson, Julia Bowman
Rota, Gian-Carlo
Savage, Leonard James
Schwartz, Laurent
Seaborg, Glenn Theodore
Stephanus of Alexandria
Sylvester, James Joseph

Tarski, Alfred
Tucker, Albert William
Turing, Alan Mathison
Tūsī, Sharaf al-Dīn al-Muzaffar Ibn Muhammad Ibn al-Muzaffar al-
Tutte, William (Bill) Thomas
Tversky, Amos
Valens, Vettius
Vinogradov, I. M.
Walker, Gilbert Thomas
Weil, André
Weyl, Hermann Claus Hugo
Whitney, Hassler
Wigner, Eugene
Wilkinson, James Hardy
Zygmund, Antoni

PROBABILITY/DECISION AND GAME THEORY

Bayes, Thomas
Bernoulli, Jakob
Broadbent, Donald Eric
Buffon, George-Louis Le Clerc, Comte de
Carnap, Paul Rudolf
de Finetti, Bruno
Dodgson, Charles Lutwidge
Fisher, Ronald Aylmer
Gödel, Kurt Friedrich
Goodman, Nelson Henry
Harsanyi, John Charles

Jeffrey, Richard Carl
Jeffreys, Harold
Keynes, John Maynard
Kolmogorov, Andrei Nikolaevich
Kuhn, Thomas Samuel
Lewis, David
Mill, John Stuart
Morgenstern, Oskar
Nash, John Forbes, Jr.
Nozick, Robert
Olson, Mancur, Jr.
Pareto, Vilfredo

Pearson, Karl
Popper, Karl Raimund
Ramsey, Frank Plumpton
Riker, William Harrison
Savage, Leonard James
Schwartz, Laurent
Simon, Herbert Alexander
Tarski, Alfred
Tucker, Albert William
Tversky, Amos
Vickrey, William Spencer

LOGIC

Albert of Saxony
Buridan, John (Jean)
Burley, Walter
Carnap, Paul Rudolf
Chrysippius
Dijkstra, Wybe Edsger
Dodgson, Charles Lutwidge
Frege, Friedrich Ludwig Gottlob

Galen
Gödel, Kurt Friedrich
Goodman, Nelson Henry
Jungius, Joachim
Lewis, David
Ockham, William of
Popper, Karl Raimund
Ramsey, Frank Plumpton

Ramus, Peter, also known as Pierre de la Ramee
Rāzī, Abū Bakr Muḥammad Ibn Zakariyyā', Al-
Robinson, Julia Bowman
Tarski, Alfred
Turing, Alan Mathison
Zuse, Konrad

COMPUTER SCIENCE

Babbage, Charles
Dijkstra, Wybe Edsger
Eckert, J. (John Adam) Presper, Jr.
Forsythe, George Elmer
Hopper, Grace

King, Ada Augusta, the Countess of Lovelace
Licklider, Joseph Carl Robnett
Newell, Allen
Mauchly, John William

Shannon, Claude
Strachey, Christopher
Turing, Alan Mathison
Wilkinson, James Hardy
Zuse, Konrad

NATURAL PHILOSOPHY

Adelard of Bath
Albertus Magnus, Saint
Ali al-Qūshjī, Abū al-Qāsim Alā' al-
Dīn Alī ibn Muhammad Qushjī-
zāde
Bacon, Francis
Bacon, Roger
Basson (Basso), Sébastien (Sebastian,
Sebastiano)
Blasius of Parma
Borro, Girolamo
Boyle, Robert
Bradwardine, Thomas
Bruno, Giordano
Buffon, George-Louis Le Clerc,
Comte de
Buonamici, Francesco
Burgersdijk, Frank Pieterszoon

Buridan, John (Jean)
Burley, Walter
Cabeo, Niccolò
Campanella, Tommaso
Cavendish, Margaret, Duchess of
Newcastle
Conway, Anne
Descartes, Rene Du Perron
Dumbleton, John
Empedocles of Acragas
Eriugena, Johannes Scottus
Gassendi, Pierre
Gorlaeus (van Goorle, van Gooirle),
David
Helmont, Johannes (Joan) Baptista
Van
John Philoponus
Jungius, Joachim

Leibniz, Gottfried Wilhelm
Maupertuis, Pierre Louis Moreau de
Newton, Isaac
Nifo, Agostino
Olympiodorus of Alexandria
Oresme, Nicole
Paracelsus
Plato
Rufus, Richard of Cornwall
Stephanus of Alexandria
Strato of Lampsacus
Volta, Alessandro Giuseppe Antonio
Anastasio
Winthrop, John, Jr.
Xenarchus
Zabarella, Jacopo (Giacomo)

COSMOLOGY

Alfvén, Hannes Olof Gosta
Aristotle
Bacon, Francis
Bondi, Hermann
Brahe, Tycho
Bruno, Giordano
Chrysippus
Clavius, Christoph
Copernicus, Nicholas
Dicke, Robert Henry

Eddington, Arthur Stanley
Gold, Thomas
Heckmann, Otto Hermann Leopold
Herschel, William
Hoyle, Fred
Jordan, Ernst Pascual
Kuiper, Gerard Peter
McCrea, William Hunter
McVittie, George Cunliffe
Morrison, Philip

Newton, Isaac
Ptolemy
Ryle, Martin
Sakharov, Andrei Dmitriyevich
Sciama, Dennis William
Sitter, Willem de
Tinsley, Beatrice
Wilkinson, David Todd
Zeldovich, Yakov Borisovich

ASTRONOMY

Airy, George Biddell
Ali al-Qūshjī, Abū al-Qāsim Alā' al-
Dīn Alī ibn Muhammad Qushjī-
zāde
Ambartsumian Amazaspovich, Viktor
Apolliniarius
Argyrus, Isaac
Babcock, Horace Welcome
Bacon, Roger
Bahcall, John Norris
Banneker, Benjamin
Bernoulli, Jakob (Jacob, Jacques,
James) I
Biermann, Ludwig Franz Benedikt
Bok, Bartholomeus (Bart) Jan
Bolton, John Gatenby

Borelli, Giovanni Alfonso
Brahe, Tycho
Chandrasekhar, Subrahmanyan
Chioniades, George (or Gregory)
Clavius, Christoph
Copernicus, Nicholas
d'Alembert (Dalembert, D'Alembert),
Jean Le Rond
Diodorus of Alexandria
Eddington, Arthur Stanley
Edlén, Bengt
Euler, Leonhard
Galilei, Galileo
Gassendi, Pierre
Gold, Thomas
Greaves, John

Greenstein, Jesse Leonard
Harriot (or Hariot), Thomas
Heckmann, Otto Hermann Leopold
Herschel, Caroline Lucretia
Herschel, John
Herschel, William
Hipparchus
Hoyle, Fred
Ibn al-Haytham, Abu 'Ali al-hasan
Ibn al-hasan
Ibrāhīm Ibn Sinān Ibn Thābit Ibn
Qurra
Jaghmīnī, Sharaf al-Dīn Mahmūd ibn
Muhammad ibn 'Umar al-
Kuiper, Gerard
Leptines

Liais, Emmanuel-Bernardin
McCrea, William Hunter
McVittie, George Cunliffe
Meliteniotes, Theodore
Menzel, Donald Howard
Monte, Guidobaldo, Marchese del
Newton, Isaac
Oort, Jan Hendrik
Payne-Gaposchkin, Cecilia Helena
Prachaticz, Cristannus de
Ptolemy
Purcell, Edward Mills
Runcorn, Stanley Keith

Qūhī (or al-Kūhī), Abū Sahl Wayjan
    Ibn Rustam al-
Quṭb al-Dīn Maḥmūd ibn Masʿūd
    ibn al-Muṣliḥ al-Shīrāzī
Ramus, Peter
Regiomontanus, Johannes
Ryle, Martin
Sagan, Carl
Schwarzschild, Martin
Shklovskii, Iosif Samuilovich
Sitter, Willem de
Spitzer, Lyman
Stephanus of Alexandria

Strömgren, Bengt Georg Daniel
Timocharis
Tinsley, Beatrice
Ṭūsī, Sharaf al-Dīn al-Muzaffar Ibn
    Muḥammad Ibn al-Muẓaffar al-
Unsöld, Albrecht Otto Johannes
Valens, Vettius
Van de Hulst, Hendrik Christoffel
Westphal, James A.
Whewell, William
Whipple, Fred Lawrence
Winkelmann, Maria Margaretha
Xenarchus

ASTROPHYSICS

Ambartsumian, Viktor Amazaspovich
Babcock, Horace Welcome
Bahcall, John Norris
Biermann, Ludwig
Bok, Bartholomeus (Bart) Jan
Bolton, John
Bondi, Hermann
Chandrasekhar, Subrahmanyan
Eddington, Arthur Stanley
Edlén, Bengt
Fowler, William A.
Friedman, Herbert
Gold, Thomas
Greenstein, Jesse Leonard

Heckmann, Otto Hermann Leopold
Herzberg, Gerhard
Hoyle, Fred
Jeffreys, Harold
Kuiper, Gerard Peter
Lauritsen, Charles Christian
McCrea, William Hunter
Menzel, Donald Howard
Morrison, Philip
Newell, Homer Edward, Jr.
Oort, Jan Hendrik
Payne-Gaposchkin, Cecilia Helena
Purcell, Edward Mills
Ryle, Martin

Sagan, Carl
Schwarzschild, Martin
Sciama, Dennis William
Shklovskii, Iosif Samuilovich
Spitzer, Lyman, Jr.
Strömgren, Bengt Georg Daniel
Tinsley, Beatrice
Unsöld, Albrecht Otto Johannes
Van de Hulst, Hendrik Christoffel
Westphal, James
Whipple, Fred
Wilkinson, David Todd
Zeldovich, Yakov Borisovich

SPACE SCIENCE

Bahcall, John Norris
Friedman, Herbert
Goldberg, Leo
Horowitz, Norman Harold
Keldysh, Mstislav Vsevolodovich
Klein, Harold P.
Kuiper, Gerard Peter

Miller, Stanley Lloyd
Newell, Homer Edward, Jr.
Pickering, William Hayward
Rossi, Bruno Benedetto
Sagan, Carl Edward
Shoemaker, Eugene Merle
Soffen, Gerald Alan

Spitzer, Lyman, Jr.
Tousey, Richard
Van Allen, James A.
von Braun, Wernher
Westphal, James A.
Whipple, Fred Lawrence

CLASSICAL PHYSICS

Archimedes
Baldi, Bernardino
Bassi Verati (Veratti), Laura Maria
    Caterina
Bernoulli, Jakob (Jacob, Jacques,
    James) I
Blair, Robert

Borelli, Giovanni Alfonso
Cabeo, Niccolò
Cauchy, Augustin-Louis
Crosse, Andrew
d'Alembert (Dalembert, D'Alembert),
    Jean Le Rond
Damianus of Larissa

Descartes, René Du Perron
Duhem, Pierre-Maurice-Marie
Euler, Leonhard
Faraday, Michael
Foster, George Carey
Galilei, Galileo
Garzoni, Leonardo S. J.

Gassendi, Pierre
Hamilton, William Rowan
Hero of Alexandria
Hertz, Heinrich Rudolf
Ibn al-Haytham, Abu 'Ali al-hasan
  Ibn al-hasan
Keldysh, Mstislav Vsevolodovich

Kepler, Johannes
Leibniz, Gottfried Wilhelm
Mairan, Jean-Jacques Dortous de
Maupertuis, Pierre Louis Moreau de
Milanković, Milutin
Monte, Guidobaldo, Marchese del
Moser, Jürgen K.

Newton, Isaac
Poincaré, Jules Henri
Ramus, Peter
Voigt, Woldemar
Volta, Alessandro Giuseppe Antonio
  Anastasio
Wollaston, William Hyde

THERMODYNAMICS/STATISTICAL MECHANICS

Boltzmann, Ludwig Eduard
Ehrenfest-Afanas'eva, Tatiana A.
Flory, Paul John
Korzhinskii, Dimitri Sergeyevich

Odum, Howard Thomas

Prigogine, Ilya

Schottky, Walter Hans

Touschek, Bruno

Uhlenbeck, George

Voigt, Woldemar

THEORETICAL PHYSICS

Bell, John Stewart
Bethe, Hans Albrecht
Bloch, Felix
Bogolubov, Nikolai Nikolaevich
Bohm, David Joseph
Boltzmann, Ludwig Eduard
Bondi, Hermann
Broglie, Louis (Victor Pierre
  Raymond)
Casimir, Hendrik Brugt Gerhard
Condon, Edward Uhler
Dicke, Robert Henry
Eddington, Arthur Stanley
Einstein, Albert
Feynman, Richard Phillips
Gödel, Kurt Friedrich
Gursey, Feza

Hartree, Douglas Rayner
Hückel, Erich Armand Arthur
Jordan, Ernst Pascual
Lichnérowicz, André
Lorentz, Hendrik Antoon
Mairan, Jean-Jacques Dortous de
Menzel, Donald Howard
Morrison, Philip
Oppenheimer, J. Robert
Pauli, Wolfgang
Pauling, Linus Carl
Poincaré, Jules Henri
Popper, Karl Raimund
Sakharov, Andrei Dmitriyevich
Salam, Muhammad Abdus
  (Abdussalam)
Schwinger, Julian

Sciama, Dennis William
Shklovskii, Iosif Samuilovich
Sommerfeld, Arnold Johannes
  Wilhelm
Spitzer, Lyman, Jr.
Strutt, John William, third Baron
  Rayleigh
Teller, Edward
Touschek, Bruno
Uhlenbeck, George
Voigt, Woldemar
Weisskopf, Victor Frederick
Weyl, Hermann Claus Hugo
Wigner, Eugene
Zeldovich, Yakov Borisovich

NUCLEAR SCIENCE/RADIOACTIVITY

Amaldi, Edoardo
Bacher, Robert
Blackett, Patrick Maynard Stuart
Blau, Marietta
Bohr, Niels Henrik David
Cherenkov, Pavel Alekseyevich
Flerov, Georgiĭ Nikolaevich
Fowler, William A.

Hahn, Otto
Lauritsen, Charles Christian
Libby, Willard Frank
Livingston, Milton Stanley
Oppenheimer, J. Robert
Perey, Marguerite Catherine
Primakoff, Henry
Rabi, Isidor Isaac

Segrè, Emilio Gino
Serber, Robert
Szilard, Leo
Uhlenbeck, George
Weisskopf, Victor Frederick
Wilkinson, Sir Geoffrey
Wu Chien-Shiung
Zhao, Zhongyao

PARTICLE/HIGH-ENERGY PHYSICS

Alfvén, Hannes Olof Gosta
Alvarez, Luis Walter

Bell, John Stewart
Breit, Gregory

Budker, Gersh Itskovich
Cherenkov, Pavel Alekseyevich

Feynman, Richard Phillips
Goldberg, Leo
Hoyle, Fred
Migdal, Arkady Benediktovich
Morrison, Philip

Occhialini, Giuseppe
Primakoff, Henry
Salam, Muhammad Abdus
   (Abdussalam)
Schwinger, Julian

Seaborg, Glenn (Glen) Theodore
Spitzer, Lyman, Jr.
Touschek, Bruno
Wilson, Robert Rathbun

CONDENSED MATTER/SOLID STATE

Bardeen, John
Bloch, Felix
Collongues, Robert
Condon, Edward Uhler

Friedman, Herbert
Kapitsa (or Kapitza), Petr Leonidovich
Migdal, Arkady Benediktovich
Mott, Nevill Francis

Primakoff, Henry
Schottky, Walter Hans
Shockley, William Bradford
Wilson, Sir Alan Herries

ALCHEMY/CHYMISTRY

Arconville, Marie Geneviève Charlotte
   Thiroux d'
Arnald of Villanova (Pseudo)
Becher, Johann Joachim
Bodenstein, Adam of
Boyle, Robert
Helmont, Johannes (Joan) Baptista
   Van
Homberg, Wilhelm

Jābir ibn Hayyān
Jungius, Joachim
Lull, Ramon
Newton, Isaac
Olympiodorus of Alexandria
Paracelsus, Theophrastus Philippus
   Aureolus Bombastus von
   Hohenheim

Rāzī, Abū Bakr Muḥammad Ibn
   Zakariyyāʾ, al-
Stahl, Georg Ernst
Suchten, Alexander von
Stephanus of Alexandria
Winthrop, John, Jr.
Zosimos of Panopolis

GENERAL CHEMISTRY

Arconville, Marie Geneviève Charlotte
   Thiroux d'
Becher, Johann Joachim
Berzelius, Jons Jacob
Cullen, William
Crosse, Andrew
Davy, Humphrey
Foster, George Carey

Frankland, Edward
Helmont, Johannes (Joan) Baptista
   Van
Homberg, Wilhelm
Lavoisier, Antoine-Laurent
Mitscherlich, Eilhard
Picardet, Claudine
Paulze-Lavoisier, Marie-Anne-Pierette

Porter, George
Sennert, Daniel
Stahl, Georg Ernst
Suchten, Alexander von
Volta, Alessandro Giuseppe Antonio
   Anastasio
Walker, John
Winthrop, John, Jr.

THEORETICAL CHEMISTRY

Dewar, Michael J. S.
Fukui, Ken-ichi
Hahn, Otto
Hartree, Douglas Rayner
Hückel, Erich Armand Arthur
Ingold, Chistopher Kelk

Kekule von Stradonitz (Kekulé),
   (Friedrich) August
Mendeleev, Dmitrii Ivanovich
Mulliken, Robert Sanderson
Paneth, Friedrich Adolf
Pauling, Linus Carl

Pople, John Anthony
Prelog, Vladimir
Prigogine, Ilya
Smalley, Richard Errett
Wigner, Eugene

PHYSICAL CHEMISTRY

Arrhenius, Svante August
Bartlett, Paul Doughty
Bernstein, Richard Barry

Bijvoet, Johannes Martin
Boer, Jan Hendrik de
Boreskov, Georgiĭ Konstantinovich

Cremer, Erika
Dewar, Michael J. S.
Duhem, Pierre-Maurice-Marie

Flory, Paul John
Franklin, Rosalind Elsie
Gutowsky, Herbert Sander
Hammett, Louis Planck
Herzberg, Gerhard
Hückel, Erich Armand Arthur
Jørgensen, Axel Christian Klixbüll

Mark, Herman F.
Mizushima, San-ichiro
Mulliken, Robert Sanderson
Ostwald, Friedrich Wilhelm
Pauling, Linus Carl
Polányi, Mihály (Michael)

Pople, John Anthony
Porter, George
Prigogine, Ilya
Semenov, Nikolaï Nikolaevich
Smalley, Richard Errett
Theorell, A. Hugo T.

ANALYSIS/SPECTROSCOPY

Bainbridge, Kenneth Tompkins
Barton, Derek Harold Richard
Beckman, Arnold Orville
Condon, Edward Uhler
Cremer, Erika
Edlén, Bengt
Frankland, Edward

Franklin, Rosalind Elsie
Gutowsky, Herbert Sander
Harvey, Hildebrand Wolfe
Herzberg, Gerhard
Hodgkin, Dorothy Mary Crowfoot
Imes, Samuel Elmer

Jørgensen, Axel Christian Klixbüll
Lemieux, Raymond Urgel
Liebig, Justus von
Martin, Archer John Porter
Polányi, Mihály (Michael)
Walsh, Alan

INORGANIC CHEMISTRY

Boer, Jan Hendrik de
Brown (Brovarnik), Herbert Charles
Chatt, Joseph
Emmett, Paul Hugh
Frankland, Edward

Haber, Fritz
Jørgensen, Axel Christian Klixbüll
Libby, Willard Frank
Nesmejanov, Aleksandr Nikolaevich
Paneth, Friedrich Adolf

Perey, Marguerite Catherine
Pettersson, Sven Otto
Wilkinson, Sir Geoffrey
Wittig, Georg

ORGANIC CHEMISTRY

Bartlett, Paul Doughty
Barton, Derek Harold Richard
Bayer, Otto Georg Wilhelm
Beckman, Arnold Orville
Bergmann, Ernst David
Brown (Brovarnik), Herbert Charles
Bunsen, Robert Wilhelm Eberhard
Butlerov, Aleksandr Mikhailovich
Carothers, Wallace Hume
Crafts, James Mason
Cram, Donald J.
Dewar, Michael J. S.
Edman, Pehr Victor
Eichengrün, Arthur
Flory, Paul John
Folkers, Karl August
Frankland, Edward
Fukui, Ken-ichi

Gutowsky, Herbert Sander
Haber, Fritz
Hammett, Louis Plack
Holley, Robert William
Houdry, Eugéne Jules
Ingold, Chistopher Kelk
Kekule von Stradonitz (Kekulé),
    (Friedrich) August
Kolbe, Adolf Wilhelm Hermann
Kuhn, Richard
Laurent, Auguste
Lemieux, Raymond Urgel
Liebig, Justus von
Mansfield, Charles Blachford
Mark, Herman F.
Nozoe, Tetsuo
Ovchinnikov, Yuri Anatolyevich

Pasteur, Louis
Prelog, Vladimir
Reichstein, Tadeus
Reppe, Walter Julius
Robinson, Robert
Sah, Peter P.T.
Sakurada, Ichiro
Smalley, Richard Errett
Smith, Michael
Todd, Alexander Robertus (Baron
    Todd)
Van Krevelen, Dirk Willem
Venkataraman, Krishnasami
Wittig, Georg
Woodward, Robert Burns
Wurtz, Adolphe
Zelinskiĭ, Nikolay Dmitrievich

BIOCHEMISTRY

Abderhalden, Emil
Anfinsen, Christian B.
Axelrod, Julius

Bijvoet, Johannes Martin
Butenandt, Adolf Friedrich Johann
Calvin, Melvin

Caspersson, Torbjörn Oskar
Chatt, Joseph
Delbrück, Max Ludwig Henning

Edman, Pehr Victor
Elion, Gertrude Belle
Hodgkin, Alan
Hodgkin, Dorothy Mary Crowfoot
Folkers, Karl August
Green, David Ezra
Holley, Robert William
Horowitz, Norman Harold
Kalckar, Herman Moritz
Klein, Harold P.
Kuhn, Richard
Lederer, Edgar
Lehninger, Albert Lester
Leloir, Luis Federico

Lemieux, Raymond Urgel
Lipmann, Fritz Albert
Martin, Archer John Porter
Miller, Stanley
Mitchell, Peter Dennis
Needham, Dorothy
Neuberg, Carl Alexander
Novikoff, Alex Benjamin
Ochoa, Severo
Ovchinnikov, Yuri Anatolyevich
Pauling, Linus Carl
Racker, Efraim
Reichstein, Tadeus

Sah, Peter T. T.
Schmitt, Francis Otto
Shtern, Lina Solomonovna
Smith, Michael
Soffen, Gerald Alan
Stephenson, Marjory
Szent-Györgyi, Albert Imre
Tatum, Edward Lawrie
Theorell, A. Hugo T.
Todd, Alexander Robertus
Wald, George
Wood, Harland Goff
Zelinskiĭ, Nikolay Dmitrievich

GEOLOGY

Arduino (or Arduini), Giovanni
Bretz, J Harlan
Chambers, Robert
Crosse, Andrew
Darwin, Charles Robert
Ding Wenjiang (V. K. Ting)
Farey, John

Goethe, Johann Wolfgang von
Hutton, James
King, Clarence Rivers
Lavoisier, Antoine-Laurent
LeConte, Joseph
Linnaeus, Carl
Menard, Henry William

Mitscherlich, Eilhard
Powell, John Wesley
Richter, Rudolf
Rittmann, Alfred (Alfredo) Ferdinand
Van Straaten, Lambertus Marius
    Joannes Ursinus
Walker, John

GEOPHYSICS/PLATE TECTONICS

Aki, Keiiti
Alvarez, Luis Walter
Ampferer, Otto
Benioff, Victor Hugo
Blackett, Patrick Maynard Stuart
Carey, Samuel Warren
Cox, Allan Verne
Day, Arthur Louis
Dietz, Robert Sinclair
Elsasser, Walter Maurice
Gold, Thomas

Hospers, Jan
Huang Jiqing (Te-Kan)
Hubbert, Marion King
Inglada, Vicente
Jeffreys, Harold
Krumbein, William Christian
Landsberg, Helmut Erich
Lehmann, Inge
Matuyama Motonori
Milanković, Milutin
Richter, Charles Francis

Ringwood, Alfred Edward
Runcorn, Stanley Keith
Shatskiy, Nikolay Sergeyevich
Sloss, Laurence Louis
Strahler, Arthur Newell
Van Allen, James A.
Wadati, Kiyoo
Wadia, Darashaw Nosherwan
Wegener, Alfred Lothar
Westphal, James A.
Wilson, John Tuzo

OCEANOGRAPHY

Baerends, Gerard Pieter
Deacon, George Edward Raven
Defant, Albert Joseph Maria
Dietz, Robert Sinclair
Edmondson, Wallis Thomas
Fedorov, Konstantin Nikolayevich
Harvey, Hildebrand Wolfe
Margalef, Ramon

Marsili (or Marsigli), Luigi Ferdinando
Mayor (formerly Mayer), Alfred
    Goldsborough
Moeller, Sophie C(h)arlotte Juliane
Namias, Jerome
Palmén, Erik Herbert
Pettersson, Sven Otto

Revelle, Roger Randall Dougan
Riley, Gordon Arthur
Schott, Paul Gerhard
Stommel, Henry Melson
Tharp, Marie
Wüst, Georg

METEOROLOGY

Aitken, John
Aristotle
Assmann, Richard
Bergeron, Tor Harold Percival
Bjerknes, Vilhelm
Byers, Horace Robert
Charney, Jule Gregory
Defant, Albert Joseph Maria
Dobson, Gordon Miller Bourne
Exner-Ewarten, Felix Maria von
Fujita, Tetsuya Theodore
Haurwitz, Bernhard
Herschel, John

Horton, Robert Elmer
Howard, Luke
Köppen, Wladimir Peter
Lamb, Hubert Horace
Liais, Emmanuel-Bernardin
Mauchly, John William
Mendel, Johann Gregor
Namias, Jerome
Palmén, Erik Herbert
Panofsky, Hans Arnold
Petterssen, Sverre
Picardet, Claudine

Reichelderfer, Francis Wilton
Richardson, Lewis Fry
Saltzman, Barry
Saussure, Horace Bénédict de
Smagorinsky, Joseph
Suomi, Verner Edward
Sutcliffe, Reginald Cockcroft
Teisserenc de Bort, Léon Philippe
Viñes, Benito
Walker, Gilbert Thomas
Wexler, Harry
Zhu Kezhen

CLIMATOLOGY

Arrhenius, Svante August
Callendar, Guy Stewart
Keeling, Charles David
Köppen, Wladimir Peter

Lamb, Hubert Horace
Landsberg, Helmut Erich
Milanković, Milutin
Namias, Jerome

Saltzman, Barry

Thornthwaite, Charles Warren

Zhu Kezhen

PALEONTOLOGY

Bronn, Heinrich Georg
Burmeister, Hermann Karl Konrad
Cuvier, Georges
Dubois, Marie Eugène François
  Thomas
Gorjanović-Kramberger, Dragutin
  (Karl)
Gould, Stephen Jay
Hill, Dorothy
Huxley, Thomas Henry
Jelínek, Jan

Koenigswald, Gustav Heinrich Ralph
  von
Ladd, Harry Stephen
Lamarck, Jean-Baptiste
Moreno, Francisco Pascasio
Newell, Norman Dennis
Oakley, Kenneth Page
Osborn, Henry Fairfield
Owen, Richard
Patterson, Colin

Pei Wenzhong
Piveteau, Jean
Richter, Rudolf
Schindewolf, Otto Heinrich
Simpson, George Gaylord
Teichert, Curt
Tintant, Henri
Wadia, Darashaw Nosherwan
Yang Zhongjian
Yin Zanxun

PALEOANTHROPOLOGY/PHYSICAL ANTHROPOLOGY

Bartlett, Frederic Charles
Bastian, Adolf
Callendar, Guy Stewart
Campbell, Donald Thomas
Clark, John Desmond
Clark, Wilfrid Edward Le Gros
Coon, Carleton Stevens
Dart, Raymond Arthur
Dubois, Marie Eugène François
  Thomas

Fischer, (Leopold Franz) Eugen
Garrod, Dorothy Annie Elizabeth
Gorjanović-Kramberger, Dragutin
  (Karl)
Jelínek, Jan
Koenigswald, Gustav Heinrich Ralph
  von
Leakey, Mary Douglas Nicol
Lehmann-Nitsche, Robert
Libby, Willard Frank

Moreno, Francisco Pascasio
Oakley, Kenneth Page
Pei Wenzhong
Piveteau, Jean
Vallois, Henri Victor
Virchow, Rudolf Carl
Walker, John
Washburn, Sherwood Larned
Weidenreich, Franz

NATURAL HISTORY

Arduino (or Arduini), Giovanni
Aristotle
Bodenstein, Adam of
Buffon, George-Louis Le Clerc,
    Comte de
Burmeister, Hermann Karl Konrad
Cronquist, Arthur
Cullen, William
Geoffroy Saint-Hilaire, Étienne
Geoffroy Saint-Hilaire, Isidore
Goethe, Johann Wolfgang von
Haller, [Victor] Albrecht von

Heckel, Édouard-Marie
Holbrook, John Edwards
Hutton, James
Hyman, Libbie Henrietta
Kinsey, Alfred
LeConte, Joseph
Lee, Sarah Eglonton Wallis Bowdich
Linnaeus, Carl
Marsili (or Marsigli), Luigi Ferdinando
Mayr, Ernst Walter
Merian, Maria Sibylla

Mueller, Ferdinand Jakob Heinrich
    von
Oken (or Okenfuss), Lorenz
Piaget, Jean
Pliny the Elder (Gaius Plinius
    Secundus)
Ratcliffe, Francis Noble
Saussure, Horace Bénédict de
Smith, James Leonard Brierly
Traill, Catharine Parr
Walker, John

EVOLUTIONARY BIOLOGY

Anfinsen, Christian B.
Baldwin, James Mark
Bronn, Heinrich Georg
Cain, Arthur James
Campbell, Donald Thomas
Carson, Hampton Lawrence
Chambers, Robert
Darwin, Charles Robert
Emerson, Alfred Edwards
Fisher, Ronald Aylmer
Geoffroy Saint-Hilaire, Isidore
Gould, Stephen Jay
Haeckel, Ernst
Hamilton, William Donald
Hennig, (Emil Hans) Willi
Huxley, Julian

Huxley, Thomas Henry
Kammerer, Paul
Kettlewell, Henry Bernard Davis
Kimura, Motoo
Kinsey, Alfred
Koenigswald, Gustav Heinrich Ralph
    von
Kropotkin, Petr Alekseyvich
Ladd, Harry Stephen
Lamarck, Jean-Baptiste
Lerner, I(sadore) Michael
Mayr, Ernst Walter
Osborn, Henry Fairfield
Owen, Richard
Patterson, Colin
Piaget, Jean

Popper, Karl Raimund
Royer, Clémence-Auguste
Schindewolf, Otto Heinrich
Simpson, George Gaylord
Smuts, Jan Christian
Sonneborn, Tracy Morton
Stebbins, George Ledyard, Jr.
Tintant, Henri
Waddington, Conrad Hal
Wagner, Moritz
Wallace, Alfred Russel
Washburn, Sherwood Larned
Weidenreich, Franz
Weismann, August Friedrich Leopold
Wright, Sewall
Wynne-Edwards, Vero Copner

ECOLOGY

Allee, Warder Clyde
Braun-Blanquet, Josias
Clements, Frederic Edward
Cockayne, Leonard
Cowles, Henry Chandler
Dansereau, Pierre Mackay
Dubos, René Jules
Edmondson, Wallis Thomas
Elton, Charles Sutherland
Emerson, Alfred Edwards

Harvey, Hildebrand Wolfe
Hasler, Arthur Davis
Heckel, Édouard-Marie
Hutchinson, G. Evelyn
Ladd, Harry Stephen
Lee, Sarah Eglonton Wallis Bowdich
Leopold, Aldo
Margalef, Ramon
Mayor (formerly Mayer), Alfred
    Goldsborough

Nice, Margaret Morse
Odum, Eugene Pleasants
Odum, Howard Thomas
Oeschger, Hans
Ratcliffe, Francis Noble
Riley, Gordon Arthur
Stanchinskiy, Vladimir Vladimirovich
Tansley, Sir Arthur George
Thienemann, August Friedrich
Wynne-Edwards, Vero Copner

PHYSIOLOGY

Abderhalden, Emil
Adrian, Edgar Douglas, first Baron
    Adrian of Cambridge

Aristotle
Bastian, Henry Charlton
Borelli, Giovanni Alfonso

Carpenter, William Benjamin
Cullen, William
de Vries, Hugo

Descartes, René Du Perron
Eccles, John Carew
Elsasser, Walter Maurice
Ephrussi, Boris
Galen
Gold, Thomas
Goldman-Rakic, Patricia Shoer
Haller, [Victor] Albrecht von
Hasler, Arthur Davis
Hertz, Mathilde Carmen
Hess, Walter Rudolf
Hodgkin, Alan
Holmes, Gordon Morgan
Jennings, Herbert Spencer

Katz, Bernard
Koehler, Otto
La Mettrie, Julien Offray de
Lashley, Karl Spencer
Lavoisier, Antoine-Laurent
LeConte, Joseph
Luria, Alexander Romanovich
McCulloch, Warren Sturgis
Paracelsus, Theophrastus Philippus
   Aureolus Bombastus von
   Hohenheim
Pavlov, Ivan Petrovich
Richter, Curt P.
Sah, Peter P. T.

Schleiden, Matthias Jacob
Schwendener, Simon
Shtern, Lina Solomonovna
Suchten, Alexander von
Tatum, Edward Lawrie
Volta, Alessandro Giuseppe Antonio
   Anastasio
Von Euler, Ulf Svante
von Holst, Erich
Winthrop, John, Jr.
Wollaston, William Hyde
Wundt, Wilhelm

CELLULAR/DEVELOPMENTAL BIOLOGY

Aristotle
Baldwin, James Mark
Bastian, Henry Charlton
Bateson, William
Brachet, Jean Louis
Briggs, Robert W.
Carson, Hampton Lawrence
Caspersson, Torbjörn Oskar
Claude, Albert
Cowdry, Edmund Vincent
Dubos, René Jules
Ephrussi, Boris
Esau, Katherine
Grobstein, Clifford

Haeckel, Ernst
Haller, [Victor] Albrecht von
Hamburger, Viktor
Holley, Robert William
Holtfreter, Johannes
Hörstadius, Sven Otto
Huxley, Julian
Just, Ernest Everett
Klein, Harold P.
Luria, Salvador Edward
Mangold, Hilde
Maupertuis
McClintock, Barbara

Morgan, Thomas Hunt
Novikoff, Alex Benjamin
Oken, Lorenz
Pasteur, Louis
Porter, Keith Roberts
Purcell, Edward Mills
Sager, Ruth
Schleiden, Matthias Jacob
Schwendener, Simon
Sonneborn, Tracy Morton
Stephenson, Marjory
Tatum, Edward Lawrie
Waddington, Conrad Hal

GENETICS

Bateson, William
Beadle, George Wells
Briggs, Robert W.
Caspersson, Torbjörn Oskar
Delbrück, Max Ludwig Henning
de Vries, Hugo
Ephrussi, Boris
Fischer, (Leopold Franz) Eugen
Ford, Edmund Brisco
Hamilton, William Donald
Horowitz, Norman Harold

Huxley, Julian
Jennings, Herbert Spencer
Kettlewell, Henry Bernard Davis
Kimura, Motoo
Lerner, I(sadore) Michael
Luria, Salvador Edward (Salvatore)
McClintock, Barbara
Mendel, Johannes Gregor
Morgan, Thomas Hunt
Neel, James Van Gundia

Pearson, Karl
Sager, Ruth
Schmitt, Francis Otto
Shockley, William Bradford
Sonneborn
Tammes, Jantina
Tatum, Edward Lawrie
Weismann, August Friedrich Leopold
Wright, Sewall
Waddington, Conrad Hal

MOLECULAR BIOLOGY

Anfinsen, Christian B.
Brachet, Jean Louis
Chargaff, Erwin

Crick, Francis Harry Compton
Delbrück, Max Ludwig Henning
Franklin, Rosalind Elsie

Holley, Robert William
Jerne, Niels Kaj
Jordan, Ernst Pascual

Kalckar, Herman Moritz
Luria, Salvador
Ochoa, Severo

Pauling, Linus Carl
Perutz, Max Ferdinand
Sagan, Carl Edward

Schmitt, Francis Otto
Smith, Michael
Wilkins, Maurice Hugh Frederick

ETHOLOGY/ANIMAL BEHAVIOR

Allee, Warder Clyde
Nice, Margaret Morse
Baerends, Gerard Pieter
Beach, Frank Ambrose Jr.
Carpenter, Clarence Ray
Craig, Wallace
Fossey, Dian
Griffin, Donald Redfield

Hertz, Mathilde Carmen
Howard, Henry Eliot
Huxley, Julian
Jennings, Herbert Spencer
Koehler, Otto
Lehrman, Daniel Sanford
Lorenz, Konrad Zacharias

Schneirla, Theodore Christian
Thorpe, William Homan
Tinbergen, Nikolaas
Turner, Charles Henry
von Holst, Erich
Watson, John Broadus
Wynne-Edwards, Vero Copner

PSYCHOLOGY

Abelson, Robert Paul
Allport, Gordon Willard
Aristotle
Baldwin, James Mark
Bartlett, Frederic Charles
Bastian, Adolf
Beach, Frank Ambrose Jr.
Boring, Edwin Garrigues
Broadbent, Donald Eric
Campbell, Donald Thomas
Carpenter, William Benjamin
Cattell, James McKeen
Chrysippius
Clark, Kenneth and Mamie
Cullen, William
Erikson, Erik Homburger
Eysenck, Hans Jürgen
Festinger, Leon
Freud, Sigmund
Galen

Gibson, Eleanor Jack
Gibson, James Jerome
Hebb, Donald
Hertz, Mathilde Carmen
Hilgard, Ernest Ropiequet
Hull, Clark Leonhard
James, William
Janet, Pierre
Jung, Carl Gustav
Klüver, Heinrich
Kinsey, Alfred
La Mettrie, Julien Offray de
Lashley, Karl Spencer
Lehrman, Daniel Sanford
Lewin, Kurt
Luria, Alexander Romanovich
Maslow, Abraham
Meehl, Paul Everett
Milgram, Stanley
Miller, Neal Elgar

Murry, Henry Alexander
Nifo, Agostino
Pavlov, Ivan Petrovich
Piaget, Jean
Richardson, Lewis Fry
Richter, Curt P.
Rogers, Carl Ransom
Rufus, Richard of Cornwall
Schneirla, Theodore Christian
Simon, Herbert Alexander
Skinner, Burrhus Frederic
Sperry, Roger Wolcott
Stern, Louis William
Tansley, Arthur George
Terman, Louis Madison
Tversky, Amos
Vogt, Cécile and Oskar
Vygotsky, Lev Semyonovich
Watson, John Broadus
Wundt, Wilhelm

COGNITIVE SCIENCE

Abelson, Robert Paul
Babbage, Charles
Bartlett, Frederic Charles
Festinger, Leon
Hebb, Donald
Hull, Clark Leonard
James, William
Kuhn, Thomas Samuel

Lashley, Karl Spencer
Luria, Alexander Romanovich
Marr, David Courtnay
McCulloch, Warren Sturgis
Newell, Allen
Penfield, Wilder Graves
Piaget, Jean

Shannon, Claude
Simon, Herb
Sperry, Roger Wolcott
Turing, Alan Mathison
Tversky, Amos
Vygotsky, Lev Semyonovich
Wundt, Wilhelm

NEUROSCIENCE

Adrian, Edgar Douglas, first Baron
   Adrian of Cambridge

Axelrod, Julius
Bastian, Henry Charlton

Brodmann, Korbinian
Bullock, Theodore Holmes

Clark, Wilfrid Edward Le Gros
Crick, Francis Harry Compton
Eccles, John Carew
Edinger, Ludwig
Goldman-Rakic, Patricia Shoer
Hamburger, Viktor
Hebb, Donald

Holmes, Gordon Morgan
Katz, Bernard
Klüver, Heinrich
Lashley, Karl Spencer
Luria, Alexander Romanovich
Marr, David Courtnay
McCulloch, Warren Sturgis

Papez, James Wenceslas
Penfield, Wilder Graves
Schmitt, Francis Otto
Sperry, Roger Wolcott
Thudichum, Johann Ludwig Wilhelm
Vogt, Cécile and Oskar
Vygotsky, Lev Semyonovich

MEDICAL SCIENCE

Abderhalden, Emil
Arconville, Marie Geneviève Charlotte
 Thiroux d'
Arnald of Villanova
Assmann, Richard
Axelrod, Julius
Bacon, Francis
Bodenstein, Adam of
Borelli, Giovanni Alfonso
Borro, Girolamo
Buonamici, Francesco
Burnet, Frank Macfarlane
Cardano, Girolamo
Carpenter, William Benjamin
Claude, Albert
Cowdry, Edmund Vincent
Diocles of Carystus
Dubos, René Jules
Edinger, Ludwig
Eichengrün, Arthur

Elion, Gertrude Belle
Elsasser, Walter Maurice
Galen
Helmont, Johannes (Joan) Baptista
 Van
Hippocrates of Cos
Howard, Luke
Janssen, Paul Adriaan Jan
La Mettrie, Julien Offray de
Leoniceno, Nicolò
Linnaeus, Carl
Luria, Salvador Edward (Salvatore)
Maimonides, Rabbi Moses Ben
 Maimon
Medawar, Peter Brian
Nifo, Agostino
Paracelsus, Theophrastus Philippus
 Aureolus Bombastus von
 Hohenheim
Pasteur, Louis

Pellicier, Guillaume
Prachaticz, Cristannus de
Purcell, Edward Mills
Quṭb al-Dīn Maḥmūd ibn Masʿūd
 ibn al-Muṣliḥ al-Shīrāzī
Rāzī, Abū Bakr Muḥammad Ibn
 Zakariyyāʾ, al-
Reichstein, Tadeus
Rufus of Ephesus
Sah, Peter P. T.
Sennert, Daniel
Stahl, Georg Ernst
Starkey, George
Stephanus of Alexandria
Suchten, Alexander von
Virchow, Rudolf Carl
Von Euler, Ulf Svante
Wilson, Alan Herries

TECHNOLOGY/ENGINEERING

Aitken, John
Blau, Marietta
Boer, Jan Hendrik de
Boreskov, Georgiĭ Konstantinovich
Butenandt, Adolf Friedrich Johann
Callendar, Guy Stewart
Condon, Edward Uhler
Cremer, Erika
Eckert, J. (John Adam) Presper, Jr.
Frankland, Edward

Horton, Robert Elmer
Hou Te-pang (Debang Hou)
Houdry, Eugéne Jules
Kapitsa, Petr Leonidovich
Lewis, Warren Kendall
Licklider, Joseph Carl Robnett
Milanković, Milutin
Pickering, William Hayward
Reichstein, Tadeus
Reppe, Walter Julius

Sakharov, Andrei Dmitriyevich
Schottky, Walter Hans
Shannon, Claude
Smalley, Richard Errett
Smith, Michael
Turing, Alan Mathison
Van Krevelen, Dirk Willem
von Braun, Wernher
Wigner, Eugene
Wilson, Sir Alan Herries

NATURE OF SCIENTIFIC INQUIRY

Aristotle
Babbage, Charles
Bacon, Francis
Bohr, Niels Henrik David
Boring, Edwin Garrigues

Borro, Girolamo
Descartes, René Du Perron
Duhem, Pierre-Maurice-Marie
Galilei, Galileo
Goethe, Johann Wolfgang von

Goodman, Nelson Henry
Gould, Stephen Jay
Herschel, John
Jennings, Herbert Spencer
Kuhn, Thomas Samuel

La Mettrie, Julien Offray de
Lewin, Kurt
Liais, Emmanuel-Bernardin
Meehl, Paul Everett
Merton, Robert K.
Mill, John Stuart

Paneth, Friedrich Adolf
Poincaré, Jules Henri
Polányi, Mihály (Michael)
Price, Derek John DeSolla
Royer, Clémence-Auguste
Sagan, Carl Edward

Schindewolf, Otto Heinrich
Schleiden, Matthias Jacob
Weyl, Hermann Claus Hugo
Whewell, William
Zabarella, Jacopo (Giacomo)

SCIENCE PEDAGOGY/POPULARIZATION

Bastian, Adolf
Bergmann, Ernst David
Bretz, J Harlan
Campbell, Donald Thomas
Cattell, James McKeen
Chambers, Robert
Clavius, Christoph
Ding Wenjiang (V. K. Ting)
Ehrenfest-Afanas'eva, Tatiana A.
Eysenck, Hans Jürgen
Forsythe, George Elmer
Foster, George Carey
Frankland, Edward
Gould, Stephen Jay
Hennig, (Emil Hans) Willi
Hilgard, Ernest Ropiequet

Hirst, Thomas Archer
Huxley, Julian
Huxley, Thomas Henry
Imes, Elmer Samuel
Jelínek, Jan
Johnston, James Finlay Weir
Mac Lane, Saunders
Marcet, Jane Haldimand
Mark, Herman F.
Morrison, Philip
Namias, Jerome
Needham, Joseph
Newell, Norman Dennis
Odum, Eugene Pleasants
Oken (or Okenfuss), Lorenz
Prachaticz, Cristannus de

Purcell, Edward Mills
Sagan, Carl Edward
Saussure, Horace Bénédict de
Seaborg, Glenn Theodore
Sonneborn, Tracy Morton
Terman, Lewis Madison
Tinbergen, Nikolaas
Tinsley, Beatrice
Turner, Charles Henry
Vygotsky, Lev Semyonovich
Whewell, William
Wilson, Alan Herries
Yin Zanxun
Zhu Kezhen

SCIENCE POLICY

Abderhalden, Emil
Amaldi, Edoardo
Bacher, Robert
Bahcall, John Norris
Bergmann, Ernst David
Bondi, Hermann
Fossey, Dian

Grobstein, Clifford
King, Clarence Rivers
Marsili (or Marsigli), Luigi Ferdinando
Neel, James Van Gundia
Pickering, William Hayward
Price, Derek John DeSolla

Rabi, Isidor Isaac
Revelle, Roger Randall Dougan
Seaborg, Glenn (Glen) Theodore
Teller, Edward
Vickrey, William Spencer
Zhu Kezhen

List of Nobel Prize Winners

NOBEL PRIZE IN PHYSICS

Hendrik Antoon Lorentz, 1902
Max Planck, 1918
Albert Einstein, 1921
Isidor Isaac Rabi, 1944
Wolfgang Pauli, 1945
Edward Mills Purcell, 1952
William Bradford Shockley, 1956
Pavel Alekseyevich Cherenkov, 1958
Emilio Gino Segrè, 1959
Eugene Wigner, 1963
Richard Phillips Feynman, 1965
Julian Schwinger, 1965
Martin Ryle, 1974
Nevill Francis Mott, 1975
Muhammad Abdus Salam, 1979
Ken-ichi Fukui, 1981
Subrahmanyan Chandrasekhar, 1983
William A. Fowler, 1983

NOBEL PRIZE IN MEDICINE

Ivan Petrovich Pavlov, 1904
Thomas Hunt Morgan, 1933
Albert Imre Szent-Györgyi, 1937
Walter Rudolf Hess, 1949
Tadeus Reichstein, 1950
Fritz Albert Lipmann, 1953
A. Hugo T. Theorell, 1955
Edward Lawrie Tatum, 1958
Severo Ochoa, 1959

Peter Brian Medawar, 1960
Francis Harry Compton Crick, 1962
Maurice Hugh Frederick Wilkins, 1962
John Carew Eccles, 1963
Alan Hodgkin, 1963
George Wald, 1967
Robert William Holley, 1968
Max Ludwig Henning Delbrück, 1969
Salvador Edward Luria, 1969
Bernard Katz, 1970
Ulf Svante Von Euler, 1970
Konrad Zacharias Lorenz, 1973
Nikolaas Tinbergen, 1973
Albert Claude, 1974
Roger Wolcott Sperry, 1981
Barbara McClintock, 1983
Niels Kaj Jerne, 1984
Gertrude Belle Elion, 1988

NOBEL PRIZE IN CHEMISTRY

Friedrich Wilhelm Ostwald, 1909
Fritz Haber, 1918
Richard Kuhn, 1938
Otto Hahn, 1944
Robert Robinson, 1947
Glenn Theodore Seaborg, 1951
Archer John Porter Martin, 1952
Linus Carl Pauling, 1954
Nikolaï Nikolaevich Semenov, 1956
Willard Frank Libby, 1960

Max Ferdinand Perutz, 1962
Dorothy Mary Crowfoot Hodgkin, 1964
Robert Burns Woodward, 1965
Robert Sanderson Mulliken, 1966
George Porter, 1967
Luis Federico Leloir, 1970
Gerhard Herzberg, 1971
Geoffrey Wilkinson, 1973
Paul John Flory, 1974
Vladimir Prelog, 1975
Ilya Prigogine, 1977
Peter Dennis Mitchell, 1978
Georg Wittig, 1979
Donald J. Cram, 1987
Michael Smith, 1993
Richard Errett Smalley, 1996
John Walker, 1997
John Anthony Pople, 1998

NOBEL PRIZE IN ECONOMICS

Herbert Alexander Simon, 1978
John Charles Harsanyi, 1994
John Forbes Nash, Jr., 1994
William Spencer Vickrey, 1996

NOBEL PEACE PRIZE

Andrei Dmitriyevich Sakharov, 1975

A

ABDERHALDEN, EMIL (*b.* Oberuzwil [canton St. Gallen], Switzerland, 9 March 1877; *d.* Zürich, Switzerland, 5 August 1950), *physiology, biochemistry, medical ethics.*

Abderhalden was a leading figure in the early development of modern biochemistry. He made important contributions to protein chemistry, in particular to the clarification of the composition of peptides, and to nutritional research. The detection of what he believed were specific proteases (*Abwehrfermente,* defense enzymes) proved a mistake, however. He was a controversial protagonist in matters of medical ethics and eugenics and involved himself in social and political affairs to an extraordinary degree. He was the president of the oldest German academy, the German Academy of Natural Scientists Leopoldina (now German Academy of Sciences Leopoldina), during the years of the National Socialist (NS) regime.

Abderhalden, son of the primary school teacher Nikolaus (also known as Niklaus) Abderhalden and his wife Anna Barbara (née Stamm), studied medicine in Basel (medical examination in 1901, doctor's degree in 1902). Already as a student, Abderhalden was mentored by the professor for physiological chemistry, Gustav von Bunge. Abderhalden also followed Bunge's example of active engagement in social matters and in his fight against the abuse of alcohol.

While studying issues of digestion and the resorption of iron, Abderhalden began to study the composition of proteins. To continue his studies, he went to Berlin. Here he worked in the laboratory of the famous chemist Emil Hermann Fischer. In Fischer's laboratory, Abderhalden was introduced to his future principal field of work, protein biochemistry, and started his career (1904 *habilitation* in physiology, 1908 title professor). In 1908 he succeeded the sensory physiologist Hermann Munk as ordinary professor for physiology at the Berlin Veterinary College. After he had refused to go to Tübingen, he accepted the appointment as ordinary professor for physiology at Halle University (succeeding Julius Bernstein) in 1911.

Initially, Abderhalden regarded Halle as a waiting place. The Kaiser Wilhelm Society (Kaiser Wilhelm Gesellschaft, or KWG) had earlier promised him a new research institute in Berlin or Cologne. The plans, at first postponed because of World War I and the difficult postwar years, never materialized, although Abderhalden did occasionally receive financial support for his research work from the KWG. Despite attractive offers, for example from the universities of Vienna and Basel, and various lamentations about his outdated institute (since he initially did not promote a planned new university institute because of the KWG prospect, and later the opportunity disappeared for lack of money and then the beginning of World War II), Abderhalden remained in Halle until 1945. There he could teach both physiology and physiological chemistry, whereas the other institutions generally offered him teaching possibilities for only one discipline. The expansion of biochemistry, which Abderhalden also promoted, tended more and more toward a total (also organizational) separation of biochemistry from physiology. Abderhalden also remained in Halle in order to manage several social activities set up according to his ideas. This engagement meant a lot to him, and he dedicated to it much time and effort—quite uncommon for the work of an experimenting academic teacher.

Research. Under the supervision of his teacher Bunge, Abderhalden began his research activities doing comparative analytical work on blood and milk from different species. Knowing the differences between food proteins and functional proteins in the body, Abderhalden was convinced that the current understanding of digestion was wrong. Many physiologists, including Bunge, believed that proteins taken in with food would only be disintegrated during digestion for exploitation in the body but largely remain structurally unchanged or be decomposed only to a small extent so that less energy should be required to build endogenous proteins. Abderhalden argued that during digestion in the intestines, food proteins are disintegrated as far as into the free amino acids, which are then resorbed and transported by the blood. In Fischer's laboratory, he worked on the degradation of proteins and the synthesis of short-chain "polypeptides" and contributed to the understanding of the structure of peptides (or proteins as understood at that time; since the macromolecular structure was discovered later, this "understanding of proteins" could only be fragmentary). Later Abderhalden showed that, in nutrition, proteins can be represented by free amino acids; developed solutions for a substitution therapy (also in connection with industry); and looked at the different biological value of amino acids, as some had to be taken in with food whereas others were synthesized by the body. He also dealt with issues of hormone and vitamin research. He also discovered a cystine storage disease, Abderhalden-Fanconi (-Kaufmann-Lignac) syndrome.

In his research, Abderhalden always attempted to derive practical benefit for medical therapy. His *Abwehrfermente* gained Abderhalden scientific fame for a short while. (These were first called *Schutzfermente,* or protective ferments, in the original edition of *Schutzfermente des tierischen Organismus* [1912].) He developed and constantly improved the so-called Abderhalden Reaction (AR), a complicated method for verifying the assumedly highly specific defensive ferments against "foreign" proteins. The concept of defensive ferments, simply stated, meant that any "foreign" proteins (e.g., foreign to blood, like cancer cells, or exogenous, like parts of bacteria) that go into blood should prompt specific ferments (enzymes) that did not occur there previously and that now decompose these "foreign" substances. These defensive ferments were thought to be verifiable in blood through reaction with certain substrates (obtained from substances either foreign to blood or exogenous) by means of two processes, namely the optical method and the dialysis method. Abderhalden developed a multitude of possible applications—from the detection of pregnancy to tumor diagnosis. The AR was supposed to be a useful diagnostic tool for dysfunctions of internal organs, several infectious diseases, and even psychiatric states.

Emil Abderhalden. *Portrait of Emil Abderhalden.* SCIENCE PHOTO LIBRARY/PHOTO RESEARCHERS, INC.

Initially, Abderhalden's methods met with wide interest in medical circles, but the concept as a whole failed to stand the acid test of science. The ongoing controversies damaged Abderhalden's reputation as scientist; but despite a multitude of counterarguments from well-known researchers, he insisted on his misconceptions. Despite a loss of public interest in the subject matter in the 1920s, Abderhalden's methods had a renaissance during the Third Reich. It has been proved that Abderhalden's methods were used by coworkers of some National Socialist researchers (for example, Otmar Freiherr von Verschuer and Claus Schilling) who were charged with Nazi crimes.

The complexity of the method, with its failure-prone steps (for example, substrate preparation) and difficulties in handling, and vulnerable statements or mistakes in the arguments of his opponents often allowed Abderhalden to reject falsifications. He always tried to invalidate objections by putative improvements of his method, but he failed to take the important step from a qualitative (coloration) evaluation to a quantitative (exact measured) one (even though he himself regarded measurement as necessary). Furthermore, he tested new (clinical) applications in several very different fields with questionable results instead of elucidating the fundamentals of his putative discovery by basic research.

During World War II, Abderhalden was prevented by a heavy workload of applied research from adapting his methods to the up-to-date standards of biochemistry. He also lacked opportunities for international comparison. After World War II, he had hardly any opportunity to work experimentally at his last place of activity in Zürich. Therefore he was able to adhere to his incorrect principles. Thus his defense enzymes are now mentioned in connection with scientific errors, occasionally even fraud, in the natural sciences. Although it has to be kept in mind that neither immunology nor enzymology in a modern sense existed when Abderhalden conducted his experiments, the question as to the causes of his persistence in error while confronting strong contemporary evidence is largely unsolved. The complexity of the experiments certainly played an important role. Unquestionably, Abderhalden contradicted his own standards in neglecting the need for quantitative measurements and in his emphasis on applications instead of fundamental research. Nevertheless, Abderhalden's importance should not be limited to the *Abwehrfermente* question.

Abderhalden was a gifted and strict university teacher with a large circle of students (for example, Hans Brockmann, Horst Hanson, Kurt Heyns). He authored sought-after textbooks on physiological chemistry and physiology and edited multivolume method manuals. From the early1930s he came into conflict with the emerging National Socialists at the university; they defamed his institute as an "El Dorado of Jews and aliens" ("Der Kampf," No. 136, p. 9, Thu 18.8.1932). Indeed, Abderhalden had a number of students, among them Andor Fodor, Ernst Gellhorn, and Ernst Wertheimer, who were deemed "Jews" in National Socialist terminology and had already left Germany during the Weimar Republic or were expelled from Germany after 1933. On the one hand, Abderhalden, who was known as a democrat at the University of Halle, was the focus of attention of some Nazi students who demanded his dismissal and opposed the international orientation of his Leopoldina management. On the other hand, Abderhalden welcomed important parts of National Socialist policy, especially the image of physicians as "guardians" of national health, and the eugenic actions, including the sterilization law. Throughout his life, Abderhalden regarded social questions in the light of his eugenic convictions.

Since Abderhalden was a Swiss as well as a German national, he was not conscripted to the German armed forces in World War I. So he organized the transport of the wounded in Halle and equipped several mobile army hospitals with money donated by citizens. In 1915 he founded an alliance for the preservation and augmentation of German national power; one of its activities was to ensure the supply of food to the people of Halle by leasing land for growing potatoes. Abderhalden set up an infant nursery, and after the war he organized holidays in Switzerland for more than sixty thousand weak German children.

In his book *Das Recht auf Gesundheit* (1921), Abderhalden detailed his eugenic opinion and advocated the sterilization of persons with genetic diseases. In the 1920s, he tried to set up a physicians' and popular alliance for sexual ethics and founded a journal (*Ethik*) that dealt with matters of ethics (for example, experiments involving humans, eugenics) and controversially discussed questions of medical ethics. *Ethik*—although later sympathetic to the National Socialist zeitgeist—sometimes harbored views in contradiction to the official NS line. *Ethik* demanded very outspoken "positive eugenics" and emphasized that sterilization of people suffering from a hereditary disease was by no means sufficient, but should be complemented by advancement of families, provision of universal healthy housing , and the fight against alcohol. Also, the euthanasia of incurably ill people was already discussed and rejected in the mid-1930s, at a time when the NS leadership explicitly refused to have this issue on the agenda. These discussions were held before the NS instituted its euthanasia program and were not conducted in the same spirit. The journal ceased publication after serious controversies in 1938 without, however, having been banned.

Abderhalden's ethical maxims always valued the people (*Volk*) over the individual. Here there is a clear link to the National Socialist "ethic without humanity." As a social ethicist, Abderhalden viewed himself as a "physician" for the "Volkskörper" (body of the people). According to his ethical views, individual rights had to be curtailed if it seemed necessary for the "advancement of the Volk." Important elements of his ethics, such as eugenic convictions, related to the advancement of future generations.

Abderhalden's ethical and eugenic concepts must be considered in their historical context. Abderhalden formed his ethical and eugenic views in the crisis years after World War I. He not only established theoretical principles, he also rendered practical help to cope with a major crisis. He rescued many German children from hunger and tuberculosis by accommodating them in Switzerland. This cannot be explained without reference to his strong eugenic convictions. Abderhalden absolutely shared the opinions voiced by many eugenists at that time: While the best men had fallen at the fronts and were unavailable to manage economic recovery, many handicapped who, had been unfit for military service, had survived in institutions and now had to be supported by an impoverished state. Abderhalden demanded that the scarce funds should not be spent on those people suffering from hereditary diseases because they were of "less value" for the continued existence of the nation, but should be concentrated to ill children (who could be cured with "reasonable" spending of funds) as guarantors of future generations and thus a successful future.

But Abderhalden's point of view is by no means identical with the National Socialist ethic. It would be incorrect and unhistorical to regard Abderhalden's convictions as convenient justification for the Nazi crimes. However, the fact of a serious and far-reaching entanglement, for example, his approval of the Nazi sterilization law, has to be recognized.

Abderhalden had been a member of the German Academy of Natural Scientists Leopoldina (Leopoldina) since 1912 and chairman of the medical section from 1926 to 1931. In 1931, he was elected president of this oldest German academy, founded as the Academia Naturae Curiosorum in 1652. When he assumed office in 1932, he supported the membership of many well-known foreign scientists, reorganized the academy's structures, and expanded its range of activities. While advocating high scientific standards, Abderhalden was also ready to make concessions to the National Socialist state policy and the "NS-Zeitgeist." Abderhalden prevented the election to the academy of National Socialist exponents whose scientific achievements he considered as being insufficient and he refused to accept foreigners proposed for political reasons. But under his leadership nearly all important champions of race hygiene were listed in the academy register, and he celebrated the so-called achievements of the Führer (Adolf Hitler) at the annual festive academy sessions. The most serious breach of academic integrity was the cancellation of membership of many Jewish academy members (among them Albert Einstein), mainly in the years 1937–1938. Abderhalden reported the cancellation to the local National Socialist authority, the Gauleiter, but he did not inform either the members whose membership had been canceled or the public.

After World War II, on the order of the American occupation forces, Abderhalden was deported on 24 June 1945 from Halle, later to be a part of the Soviet-occupied zone, to a place near Darmstadt in the American zone. Abderhalden was the head of a trek of about 750 people (the "Abderhalden-Transport"). In September 1945 Abderhalden returned to Switzerland. He worked as a professor of physiological chemistry at the University of Zürich before he finally retired in 1947. With his book *Gedanken eines Biologen* (1947), Abderhalden reviewed his

life convictions without, however, admitting to his association with the National Socialist regime. Although living in Zürich, Abderhalden remained president of the Leopoldina until his death; the difficult daily business in the Soviet-occupied zone/German Democratic Republic was managed by his deputy, the geographer Otto Schlüter, in Halle. Abderhalden was married to Margarete Barth; they had five children.

BIBLIOGRAPHY

WORKS BY ABDERHALDEN

Editor. *Bibliographie der gesamten wissenschaftlichen Literatur über den Alkohol und den Alkoholismus.* Berlin and Vienna: Urban & Schwarzenberg, 1904.

Lehrbuch der physiologischen Chemie in dreissig Vorlesungen. Berlin and Vienna: Urban & Schwarzenberg 1906.

Editor. *Biochemisches Handlexikon.* 14 vols. Berlin: Springer, 1911–1933.

Schutzfermente des tierischen Organismus: Ein Beitrag zur Kenntnis der Abwehrmaßregeln des tierischen Organismus gegen körper-, blut- und zellfremde Stoffe. Berlin: Springer, 1912.

Editor. *Handbuch der biologischen Arbeitsmethoden.* 106 vols. and register volume. Berlin and Vienna: Urban & Schwarzenberg, 1920–1939.

Das Recht auf Gesundheit und die Pflicht, sie zu erhalten: Die Grundbedingungen für das Wohlergehen von Person, Volk, Staat und der gesamten Nationen. Leipzig, Germany: Hirzel, 1921.

Editor. *Ethik, Pädagogik und Hygiene des Geschlechtslebens* (1922), later: *Sexualethik* (1925), *Ethik: Sexual- und Gesellschafts-Ethik* (1926–1933), *Ethik* (1933–1938). A journal.

Lehrbuch der Physiologie in Vorlesungen. 4 vols. Berlin: Urban & Schwarzenberg, 1925–1927.

Gedanken eines Biologen zur Schaffung einer Völkergemeinschaft und eines dauerhaften Friedens. Zürich: Rascher, 1947.

OTHER SOURCES

Deichmann, Ute, and Benno Müller-Hill. "The Fraud of Abderhalden's Enzymes." *Nature* 393 (1998): 109–111. Presents an extreme point of view.

Frewer, Andreas. *Medizin und Moral in Weimarer Republik und Nationalsozialismus: Die Zeitschrift "Ethik" unter Emil Abderhalden.* Frankfurt, Germany, and New York: Campus Verlag, 2000.

Gabathuler, Jakob. *Emil Abderhalden: Sein Leben und Werk.* Wattwil, Switzerland: Abderhalden-Vereinigung, 1991.

Kaasch, Michael. "Sensation, Irrtum, Betrug?—Emil Abderhalden und die Geschichte der Abwehrfermente." *Acta Historica Leopoldina* 36 (2000): 145–210.

Kaasch, Michael, and Joachim Kaasch. "Wissenschaftler und Leopoldina-Präsident im Dritten Reich: Emil Abderhalden und die Auseinandersetzung mit dem Nationalsozialismus." *Acta Historica Leopoldina* 22 (1995): 213–250.

———. "Emil Abderhalden: Ethik und Moral in Werk und Wirken eines Naturforschers." In *Medizingeschichte und Medizinethik: Kontroversen und Begründungsansätze, 1900–1950,* edited by Andreas Frewer and Josef N.

Neumann, 204–246. Frankfurt, Germany, and New York: Campus Verlag, 2001.

Kessler, Stanley, and Gustav J. Martin. "The Abderhalden Reaction: A Review of the Literature on the Defense Proteinases (Abwehrfermente)." *Experimental Medicine and Surgery* 16, nos. 2–3 (1958): 190–212.

Wolf, George. "Emil Abderhalden: His Contribution to the Nutritional Biochemistry of Protein." *Journal of Nutrition* 126 (1996): 794–799.

Michael Kaasch

ABEL, NIELS HENRIK

(*b.* Finnöy, an island near Stavanger, Norway, 5 August 1802; *d.* Froland, Norway, 6 April 1829), *mathematics.* For the original article on Abel see *DSB,* vol. 1.

Since the first volume of the original *Dictionary of Scientific Biography* appeared in 1970, relatively few new biographical facts have been discovered concerning Niels Henrik Abel. Øystein Ore, who wrote the biography for the *DSB,* was a distinguished Norwegian-American mathematician and had written one of the most comprehensive biographies of Abel (1954, English 1957). Subsequent research has contextualized Abel's life and work, either within contemporary Norwegian culture—as in the biography by Arild Stubhaug (Norwegian 1996, English 2000)—or within the rich mathematical developments of the nineteenth century. The present article discusses some of these new trends in understanding Abel's work.

Early Career. Abel was initially taught by his father, and his mathematical productivity commenced after he moved to Oslo (Christiania) to attend the cathedral school. When Bernt Michael Holmboe became Abel's mathematics teacher, he realized and nurtured Abel's mathematical potential. Together they studied the most important mathematical works of the eighteenth century, and Holmboe remained Abel's friend, exerting an influence on his mathematics.

In 1825 Abel embarked on a European tour sponsored by the Norwegian government. The two important mathematical stops on the tour were Berlin and Paris with a third in Copenhagen. However, Abel never went to meet Carl Friedrich Gauss in Göttingen. Instead, the second great influence—beside Holmboe—on Abel's mathematical life was August Leopold Crelle, the German official, organizer, and mathematics enthusiast, whom Abel met in Berlin.

Crelle's major project in the first part of the 1820s was the creation of a German mathematical journal. When Abel passed through Berlin, Crelle finally realized the project, gathering a group of young mathematicians around him and launching the *Journal für die reine und angewandte Mathematik* in 1826. During the first four years of the *Journal,* Abel was its main contributor, responsible for more than 375 pages—about 25 percent—of the papers published. Together, Crelle's organization and Abel's extensive mathematical production quickly led the *Journal* to become one of the major mathematical outlets of the nineteenth century.

Abel's mathematical production was devoted to three main topics, namely the theory of equations, the study of elliptic functions, and the foundations of analysis. Of these, the first two are intimately related, as much of Abel's interest in elliptic functions was of an algebraic nature for instance motivated by the division problem for the lemniscate.

Theory of Equations. In 1826, in the first volume of the *Journal für die reine und angewandte Mathematik* to which Abel contributed substantially during its first years, Abel presented a proof that the general equation of the fifth degree could not be solved by radicals. After first believing to have found a solution, Abel soon realized his mistake and published what was the first widely circulated comprehensive proof of the algebraic insolubility of the quintic equation. A few years later, in 1828 and 1829, Abel published another result—derived from researches into elliptic functions (see below)—of an extensive class of algebraically solvable equations. These equations generalized the construction by ruler and compass of the division of the lemniscate arc (see below), and they were characterized by a property of their roots: If the roots were expressible by rational functions as x, $\theta_1(x)$, $\theta_2(x), \ldots, \theta_k(x)$ and the functions commuted, $\theta_j \theta_k = \theta_k \theta_j$, the equation would be algebraically solvable. Later such equations were called *Abelian,* and after the study of equations was associated with the study of permutation groups, such groups too came to be called *Abelian* when they were commutative.

Abel's third work on the theory of equations dealt with the question of determining and delineating the concept of algebraic solvability. In a notebook manuscript of 1828 (first published in Abel's collected works, 1839, vol. II), Abel discussed the failed search for a solution formula throughout the eighteenth century and formulated an agenda for asking the right questions:

> In fact, one proposed to solve the equations without knowing if that was possible. In this case, one might come to the solution although that was not certain at all; but if by misfortune the solution was impossible, one might search an eternity without finding it. To infallibly reach anything in this matter, it is necessary to follow another route. One should give the problem such a form that it will

always be possible to solve it, which can always be done for any problem. Instead of demanding a relation, of which the existence is unknown, one should ask whether such a relation is possible at all. (Abel, 1881, vol. II, p. 217)

This manuscript was never completed for publication because other interests came to occupy Abel's time. A few years later, in a couple of famous manuscripts, Evariste Galois outlined the answer that would eventually solve Abel's question of characterising the equations that can be solved algebraically by transforming it into a question concerning groups.

Theory of Elliptic Functions. Abel's first encounters with the theory of equations had a lasting impact on his mathematical production: The questions, tools, and inspirations that he developed and used in this algebraic context permeated his approach to other areas. Most importantly, Abel's main field of interest, the theory of elliptic functions, can be seen as deriving from essentially algebraic questions and methods.

In 1827, in the *Journal,* Abel published a remarkable paper simply titled "Recherches sur les fonctions elliptiques" that opened a new set of ideas to mathematicians interested in the theory of functions. This paper dealt with the inverse functions of the elliptic integrals that had been studied in the eighteenth century by Adrien-Marie Legendre and others. Abel's inversion was a bold step: It consisted of a formal inversion followed by an extension to the entire complex plane based on another formal trick. Thus, from the elliptic integral of the simplest kind,

$$\alpha(x) = \int_0^x \frac{dx}{\sqrt{(1 - c^2 x^2)(1 + e^2 x^2)}},$$

Abel proposed to study the inverse function

$$\Phi(\alpha) = \mathbf{x}$$

and extend it to a function of a complex variable by formally substituting $x + iy$ for x as the upper limit of integration. In the 1820s rigorous theories of complex integration were being developed by, for example, Augustin-Louis Cauchy, but Abel's extension was carried out in a purely formal way. A central step in the deductions was the realization that the function $\Phi(\alpha)$ had two independent complex periods. Because of the formal nature of the inversion, the function $\Phi(\alpha)$ was to be subsequently studied and made accessible to the powerful machinery of analysis developed in the eighteenth century, and Abel derived series expansions to this end.

A major result in Abel's paper was the solution of the division of the lemniscate curve (mentioned above) whose arc length was known to be expressible by the integral

$$\int \frac{dx}{\sqrt{1 - x^4}}.$$

By extending the methods used by Carl Friedrich Gauss for the division of the circle, Abel found that the division of the lemniscate was intimately linked to the division of the circle. In particular, the lemniscate arc can be divided into n equal parts by ruler and compass precisely when n is the product of a power of 2 and distinct primes of the form $1 + 2^{2^k}$ (so-called Fermat primes).

Despite his important contributions to the theory of equations and his creation of the theory of elliptic functions, the part of Abel's work that exerted the greatest influence on nineteenth-century mathematics was a vast generalization of the theory of elliptic functions. Abel studied integrals of algebraic differentials, namely, $\int f(x, y) dx$, where f was a rational function and x and y were related by a polynomial equation $\chi(x, y) = 0$. Such integrals were the topic of Abel's so-called Paris Memoir, which he handed in to the Académie des Sciences in October 1826 but did not live to see published—later, such integrals were named "Abelian integrals" in his honor. When the Paris Memoir was finally published in 1841 it was too late for it to be included in the first edition of Abel's collected works. Subsequently the manuscript was lost, but was partially recovered in the twentieth century (portions were found in 1952 and 2002).

Abel's interest in integrals of algebraic differentials actually predates both his algebraic breakthroughs and his invention of elliptic functions. For the very general class of Abelian integrals of algebraic differentials, Abel found the remarkable property that any sum of similar integrals could be reduced to a definite number (only depending on χ) of integrals and logarithmic and rational terms,

$$\int^{x_1} f(x, y) dx + \ldots + \int^{x_k} f(x, y) dx =$$
$$\int^{z_1} f(x, y) dx + \ldots + \int^{z_m} f(x, y) dx + V,$$

where V designates the logarithmic and rational terms. The limits of integration $z_1, \ldots, z_m$ would be given by an algebraic equation in the original limits $x_1, \ldots, x_k$. The number of independent integrals (m) would later be developed into the concept of *genus* by subsequent generations of mathematicians as the theory matured and became conceptualized. This astonishing result generalized the addition formulas for elliptic integrals that Abel had used in his introduction of the elliptic functions.

Foundations of Analysis. One of the major transitions that took place in the 1820s concerned the notion of rigor in analysis. Abel became an ardent follower of Augustin-

Louis Cauchy's new program, and he contributed an improved proof of the binomial theorem. Abel's letters from his European tour to Holmboe include remarkable observations on the state of analysis that have provided historians with a fresh look at the reception of Cauchy's program. Despite his critical attitude toward unfounded reasoning, however, Abel employed Eulerian arguments and tricks in other fields of research, in particular in the theory of Abelian integrals.

Influence. During the nineteenth century the theory of the so-called Abelian integrals (see above) attracted the attention of many great mathematicians, most importantly Carl Jacobi, and Abel's idea of inverting elliptic integrals into elliptic functions was generalized as well. In working with the Abelian integrals, Abel employed the algebraic techniques that he had learned and developed in his algebraic researches. Therefore, Abel's theory of Abelian integrals was primarily an algebraic theory. Later, when questions of assigning meaning to the integration with complex limits became paramount, this theory gradually shifted its focus to analytic and geometric methods with the works of Karl Weierstrass and Bernhard Riemann.

Abel's research was anchored within its contemporary mathematical traditions. He drew heavily on his inspiration from Leonhard Euler, Gauss, and Legendre, and his research interests were motivated by some of the open questions of his time. However, Abel did much more than answer a few isolated questions. His research opened up new paths of inquiry, and his technique of asking the right questions was admired by his contemporaries, as illustrated by an 1829 letter from Jacobi to Legendre:

> The vast problems which he [Abel] had proposed to himself—i.e. to establish sufficient and necessary criteria for any algebraic equation to be solvable, for any integral to be expressible in finite terms, his admirable discovery of the theorem encompassing all the functions which are the integrals of algebraic functions, etc.— characterize a very special type of questions which nobody before him had dared to imagine. He has gone but he has left a grand example. ("Correspondance mathématique entre Legendre et Jacobi," *Journal für die reine und angewandte Mathematik* 80 [1875], pp. 265–266)

Thus, Abel was rightly seen as a mathematician asking new questions, employing new techniques and reaching new conclusions, some of which were quite unsuspected. Viewed in the context of the dramatic changes that occurred in mathematics during the nineteenth century, Abel was at the same time deeply entangled in the formal techniques of eighteenth century and

Niels Henrik Abel. © CORBIS

an instigator who stimulated new lines of thinking for the nineteenth century: new questions, new techniques, and new types of answers. Because of the lasting impression that Abel exerted on nineteenth-century mathematics, Weierstrass called him "Abel the Fortunate" despite the fact that Abel died at age twenty-six.

Abel's research was both situated within and contributed to an international mathematical literature. Although international in his own times, Abel subsequently came to play a particularly important role in Norwegian intellectual life. His life, work, and the neglect of the Norwegian government to take care of its brightest son played into the agenda of Norwegian independence from Sweden at the turn of the twentieth century: The centenary celebrations of Abel's birth became a showpiece of Norwegian culture only three years before the dissolution of the union with Sweden in 1905. Similarly, the bicentennial of his birth was celebrated in style and became the occasion for the institution of the Abel Prize for outstanding research in mathematics, which has been awarded annually since 2003. In the early twenty-first century, the life and work of Niels Henrik Abel, widely publicized throughout Norway, is used as an example in promoting mathematics.

SUPPLEMENTARY BIBLIOGRAPHY

WORKS BY ABEL

Oeuvres Complètes de N. H. Abel, mathématicien, avec des notes et développements. Edited by B. M. Holmboe. 2 vols. Christiania, Norway: Chr. Gröndahl, 1839.

Oeuvres Complètes de Niels Henrik Abel, new ed. Edited by L. Sylow and S. Lie. 2 vols. Christiania: Grøndahl, 1881. Reprinted, New York: Johnson Reprint, 1973.

OTHER SOURCES

Houzel, Christian. "The Work of Niels Henrik Abel." In *The Legacy of Niels Henrik Abel: The Abel Bicentennial, Oslo, 2002,* edited by Olaf Arnfinn Laudal and Ragni Piene. Berlin: Springer, 2004.

Ore, Øystein. *Niels Henrik Abel: Mathematician Extraordinary.* Minneapolis: University of Minnesota Press, 1957. Reprinted, New York: Chelsea, 1974.

Sørensen, Henrik Kragh. "Abel and His Mathematics in Contexts." *NTM: International Journal of History and Ethics of Natural Sciences, Technology, and Medicine* 10 (2002): 137–155. Includes further references.

Stubhaug, Arild. *Niels Henrik Abel and His Times: Called Too Soon by Flames Afar.* Translated by Richard H. Daly. Berlin: Springer, 2000.

Henrik Kragh Sørensen

ABEL, NILS
SEE **Abel, Niels**.

ABELSON, ROBERT PAUL (*b.* Brooklyn, New York, 12 September 1928; *d.* New Haven, Connecticut, 13 July 2005), *social and political psychology, cognitive science.*

Abelson was a major figure in social psychology during the last half of the twentieth century, a man whose ideas both helped to shape the agenda of social psychology, and contributed to the emerging fields of political psychology and cognitive science. Trained in part as a mathematical statistician, Abelson was a very early champion of mathematical models and computer simulations within these fields, applying these techniques to study the development of social attitudes and networks, the structure of political ideologies, the forecasting of electoral outcomes, and the representation of people's everyday generic knowledge of the dynamics of recurrent social situations. Among his many specific contributions were his formal models and empirical studies of cognitive consistency, his detailed analyses of the frequently irrational "psycho-logic" underlying people's social and political attitudes, his

computer simulations of both political ideologies and electoral outcomes, and his introduction of "social scripts" as a method for analyzing the acquisition and organization of people's everyday knowledge about the expected goals and actions of individuals in familiar social settings.

Early Life and Career. Born in Brooklyn, New York, to Miles and Margaret Abelson in 1928, Abelson attended an experimental grammar school created to serve highly gifted students, and then moved after graduation to the widely acclaimed Bronx High School of Science. He received his BSc in mathematical statistics from the Massachusetts Institute of Technology (MIT), staying there to pursue an MSc in mathematics. As a student, Abelson served as a participant in a study of communication networks being conducted by Alex Bavelas, a student of Kurt Lewin. He became fascinated with this topic and eventually wrote his master's thesis on the mathematics of such networks. From MIT he went to Princeton University, from which he received his PhD in psychology in 1953. There, in addition to his formal training in psychometrics, he met two important mentors. One was the legendary statistician John Tukey, who helped to sustain Abelson's lifelong interest in statistical issues and in political forecasting, and the other the irrepressible personality theorist, Sylvan Tomkins, whose creatively idiosyncratic ideas on emotions proved an important stimulus to Abelson's later work on social attitudes and political psychology.

Abelson taught at Yale University for the next forty years in the psychology and political science departments. First recruited there to serve as a research assistant by Carl Hovland in 1952, he progressed rapidly through the ranks to become a full professor in 1963. It was also there that he met his wife and muse for more than fifty years, the former Willa Dinwoodie, a psychologist who had trained at Radcliffe College. It was there as well that their two children, William and John, were born. Sadly, it was in New Haven, as well, that he was first diagnosed with the Parkinson's disease that so crippled his body for the last fifteen years of his life.

Work on Social Attitudes and Political Attitudes. At the time Abelson first arrived at Yale, Hovland's famed Communication and Attitude Change Program was just starting to make the study of social attitudes and attitude change into the central and most distinctive topic in social psychology, as it would remain for the next quarter of a century. Surrounded by an exceptional collection of talented young researchers from different backgrounds, all recruited by Hovland and all focused on the topic of how to change people's attitudes, Abelson, in a characteristically maverick move, chose to address the reverse side of the problem, focusing on the question of why, in the real world, social attitudes seemed so often and so apparently irrationally resistant to change.

Abelson's answer to this question involved the study of what he called "psycho-logic"—those pressures within an individual's larger belief system that might constrain that person's willingness to change individual beliefs within that system, even in the face of potentially probative and persuasive new evidence. This analysis, explicitly designed to be contrasted with a purely logical analysis, emphasized the array of emotional and motivational factors that often seemed to be stronger determinants of social attitudes than more purely rational factors. With Milton Rosenberg (1958), Abelson examined the way in which the organization of attitudes and the pressures toward affective and cognitive consistency, in particular, made real-world persuasion difficult. Their mathematical generalization and extension of Fritz Heider's early qualitative consistency model, balance theory, explicitly quantified these consistency pressures and suggested how one could predict which of an individual's beliefs should be most likely to change in the face of new information or persuasive communications of different sorts. In addition, Abelson himself (1959) elegantly elaborated a number of more specific psychological mechanisms that people often use to resist persuasive attempts, especially when those attempts were directed toward challenging attitudes or beliefs that they hold with conviction (1988).

These concerns with cognitive consistency also led to Abelson's first forays into the then-novel domain of computer simulations. Most famous among these was his "Goldwater machine" (early 1960s), which sought to model the ideology of a then-current candidate for the U.S. presidency during the height of the Cold War era. In particular in this work, Abelson sought to show how "hot" affective or motivational processes might be incorporated into an otherwise "cool" and rational computer-based model of political attitudes. The resulting simulation proved quite successful in generating responses, which despite their endearingly clumsy syntax, seemed to contain enough real-world knowledge to capture the gist of at least one simple and consistent political worldview. Thus, told that the John F. Kennedy administration had been too soft on the Berlin Wall, the simulation might reply that: "Yes, I would not hesitate to say that recent administrations not make trouble for Communist schemes." At the same time, the program's failings were equally manifest in its inability to reject similarly ideologically consistent, but practically absurd, statements like "Castro throws eggs at Taiwan," to which the program blithely responded "That's just the sort of provocation you would expect from a Communist."

This intersection of Abelson's interests in political attitudes and computer modeling also led to his contributions, with Ithiel de Sola Pool, to the art and science of political forecasting. Pool, Abelson, and Samuel Popkin, for example, published an early and influential illustrative simulation of the 1960 U.S. presidential elections, titled *Candidates, Issues, and Strategies* (1964). In this study, traditional sociodemographic variables and reported party identification were combined in an innovative but historically informed manner to generate an extensive and detailed typology of literally hundreds of potential voting blocks that could later be used to explain actual election outcomes. This work, in turn, led to Abelson's extended involvement, with John Tukey, in some of the very first voter forecasting models used by the major American television networks to predict election outcomes in real time, in the face of only early and fragmentary returns. Indeed, from 1962 to 1972, Abelson worked behind the scenes for the National Broadcasting Company, deciding when to "call" major state and national races.

Modeling Belief Systems. Searching for a way to incorporate more of the types of mundane real-world knowledge that went into the political forecasting work into his ideology simulations, Abelson encountered the work of the computer scientist Roger Schank at Stanford University. After helping to lure Schank to Yale's own computer science department, Abelson began a long-term collaboration on the problem of how to represent, in programmable terms, people's generic everyday knowledge of human motives and actions. Certainly, the most prominent result of this collaboration was Schank and Abelson's landmark book, *Scripts, Plans, Goals, and Understanding* (1977). Even for those psychologists who had little personal interest in computer simulations, the mere introduction and elaboration of the concept of generic social "scripts" as descriptions of the way in which people analyze, encode, and understand actions in everyday life (as well as the political domain) proved a major theoretical contribution (1981). Such scripts, consisting of sequences of expected interactions coupled with lists of plausible alternatives to specified default options, allowed psychologists to understand and represent people's knowledge of how individuals in their culture typically behave in various recurring everyday settings, such as dining at a restaurant, going to the beach, or interviewing for a new job.

Perhaps more than most academics, however, Abelson's considerable influence derived not only from his own published work, but also from his legendary efforts as a classroom teacher. For four decades, he taught the graduate statistics courses in the psychology department at Yale, in a fashion as unusual as it was compelling. Even in this frequently dry subject, he was able to generate interest and enthusiasm, and promote understanding, through the use of anecdotes, quips, and stories that his students would later routinely wish that they could duplicate. Indeed, many of his former students have testified to consulting their carefully preserved notes from his courses even some thirty or forty years later. Fortunately for the field, many of his insights and at least some of the charm and eloquence embedded in these courses was eventually published as *Statistics as Principled Argument* (1995).

A charismatic teacher and inveterate storyteller, Abelson also conveyed to his students a distinctive appreciation of so-called high impact experiments, at least in the domain of social psychology. Classic studies (such as those of Solomon Asch, Stanley Milgram, Muzafer Sherif, and others), he suggested, could best be thought of as empirical parables, designed to bring slices of the real-world into the laboratory, in the form of otherwise carefully staged dramas, in which the only unscripted element was the actual reactions of subjects placed in these staged settings but unaware of the artifice involved. These arguments were later illustrated and elaborated in Abelson's last book, with Kurt Frey and Aiden Gregg, titled *Experiments with People* and published shortly before his death (2004).

Running through Abelson's manifold contributions to fields as diverse as social psychology, political forecasting, and cognitive science were several prominent threads. The first was his obviously prodigious intelligence and exceptional originality. Always known for his way with words, on the one hand, Abelson was the father of many concepts and terms, and especially contrasts, now a part of the standard lexicon in psychology: logical versus "psychological," "hot" versus "cold" cognition, "scripts" versus schemas, and "neat" versus "scruffy" (i.e., more top-down and linear versus more interactive and emergent) styles of writing computer code. He was equally at home, on the other hand, with mathematics and proved just as creative in inventing new statistical methods and contrasts more closely tailored to fit particular data sets and specific theoretical questions that he and his students encountered.

The second thread was his penchant for theatrical metaphors. Whether discussing the characteristics of classic psychology experiments, the centrality of scripts to our everyday understanding of social interactions, the importance of familiar metaphors and prototypes as determinants of political attitudes and actions, or perhaps the best way to present a difficult concept to his students, Abelson was prone to think in terms of stories. A dedicated amateur thespian and director, a talented singer, and a renowned charades maven, he had not only a keen sense of drama but also the ability to take on half a dozen or more roles himself in the space of a single tale.

Finally, there was Abelson's famed sense of humor. Whether titling a course in social cognition "Things That Go Bump in the Mind," coining deep but entertaining "laws" of statistics such as "Chance is lumpy," and "There is no such thing as a free hunch," or penning papers with titles such as "On the Surprising Longevity of Flogged Horses," Abelson always managed to capture his audience's attention and pique their curiosity. Indeed, in his final years, his body increasingly racked by the advance of his Parkinson's disease, he was still able to author a heartbreakingly sad, yet funny, account of his struggles with the disease in a paper titled, "Like a Hole in the Head—Pallidotomy Surgery for Parkinson's Disease: A Patient's Journal." Abelson brought to the study of social psychology a statistician's rigor, an artist's eye, and a playwright's ear, inspiring countless students and colleagues with his uncanny ability to turn work into play.

Abelson was twice a Fellow at the Center for Advanced Study in the Behavioral Sciences and was an elected Fellow of the American Psychological Association, the American Statistical Association, and the American Academy of Arts and Sciences. He was also named a William James Fellow of the American Psychological Society and received Distinguished Scientific Contribution awards from the American Psychological Association and the Society of Experimental Social Psychology.

BIBLIOGRAPHY

WORKS BY ABELSON

With Milton J. Rosenberg. "Symbolic Psycho-logic: A Model of Attitudinal Cognition." *Behavioral Science* 3 (1958): 1–12.

"Modes of Resolution of Belief Dilemmas." *Journal of Conflict Resolution* 3 (1959): 343–352.

"Computer Simulation of 'Hot' Cognition." In *Computer Simulation of Personality: Frontier of Psychological Theory*, edited by Silvan Tomkins and Samuel Messick. New York: Wiley, 1963.

With Ithiel de Sola Pool and Samuel Popkin. *Candidates, Issues, and Strategies: A Computer Simulation of the 1960 Presidential Election.* Cambridge, MA: MIT Press, 1964.

With Elliot Aronson, William J. McGuire, et al., eds. *Theories of Cognitive Consistency: A Sourcebook.* Chicago: Rand-McNally, 1968.

"Social Psychology's Rational Man." In *Rationality and the Social Sciences: Contributions to the Philosophy and Methodology of the Social Sciences*, edited by Stanley I. Benn and Geoffrey W. Mortimore. London: Routledge and Kegan Paul, 1976.

With Roger C. Schank. *Scripts, Plans, Goals, and Understanding: An Inquiry into Human Knowledge Structures.* Hillsdale, NJ: Erlbaum, 1977.

"The Psychological Status of the Script Concept." *American Psychologist* 36 (1981): 715–729.

"Conviction." *American Psychologist* 43 (1988): 267–275.

Statistics as Principled Argument. Hillsdale, NJ: Erlbaum, 1995.

With Kurt Frey and Aiden Gregg. *Experiments with People: Revelations from Social Psychology.* Mahwah, NJ: Erlbaum, 2004.

OTHER SOURCES

Read, Stephen J., Ira J. Roseman, Mark R. Lepper, et al. "In Memoriam: Robert P. Abelson (1928–2005)." *Association for Psychological Science Observer* 19 (December 2006): 19–25. A collection of short tributes by a dozen contemporaries and collaborators.

Roseman, Ira J., and Stephen J. Read. "Psychologist at Play: Robert P. Abelson's Life and Contributions to Psychological Science." *Perspectives on Psychological Sciences* 2 (2007): 86–97. A thoughtful, short biography introducing Abelson and his contributions.

Schank, Roger C., and Ellen Langer, eds. *Beliefs, Reasoning, and Decision Making: Psycho-logic in Honor of Bob Abelson.* Hillsdale, NJ: Erlbaum, 1994. A Festschrift by former students and collaborators in honor of Abelson's retirement from Yale.

Mark R. Lepper

John Frank Adams. CERN/SCIENCE PHOTO LIBRARY/PHOTO RESEARCHERS, INC.

ADAMS, JOHN FRANK (*b.* Woolwich, United Kingdom, 5 November 1930; *d.* near Brampton, United Kingdom, 7 January 1989), *mathematics, algebraic topology, stable homotopy theory.*

Adams was a leading figure in algebraic topology. His work was the first to systematize the branch of algebraic topology that became known as stable homotopy theory. He solved several of the outstanding problems in algebraic topology by stable methods, which he pioneered. His name is attached to the Adams spectral sequence, the Adams operations, and the Adams conjecture. Adams was a problem solver, and each of these named contributions came from Adams's work on a particularly important specific problem, namely the Hopf invariant one problem, the vector fields on spheres problem, and the problem of computing certain groups $J(X)$. His work on each of these problems led to substantial advances in mathematics that reached far beyond the specific problem at hand. The development of stable homotopy theory as a subject, the development of topological K theory as an effective calculational tool, and the development of guiding principles and goals in the study of stable homotopy theory derive from his work on these problems.

Life and Career. Adams's mother was Jean Mary Baines, a biologist; his father, William Frank Adams, was a civil engineer. His early education was somewhat disrupted by the events of World War II, but occurred mainly at Bedford School. Adams served in the Royal Engineers during 1948 and 1949 before beginning his university education. He entered Trinity College, Cambridge, in 1949, taking Part II of the Mathematical Tripos in 1951 and Part III in 1952. He married Grace Rhoda Cathy in 1953; their fam-

ily eventually included one son and three daughters (one adopted).

Adams obtained his PhD at Cambridge in 1955. His thesis advisor was Shaun Wylie and his thesis examiners were Peter Hilton and Henry (J. H. C.) Whitehead, who was at the time the dominant figure in algebraic topology in England. It is surely Whitehead's influence that led Adams to this subject. Roughly speaking, algebraic topology assigns discrete algebraic invariants to continuous phenomena, giving an algebraic picture of topological shapes. At the time, the subject was in its infancy, and Adams was to become one of its leading pioneers.

From 1955 to 1958, Adams was a Research Fellow at Trinity College, and he succeeded Wylie as a Fellow and College Lecturer at Trinity Hall, Cambridge, in 1958. He moved to Manchester University in 1962 and returned to Cambridge as a Fellow of Trinity College and Lowndean Professor of Astronomy and Geometry in 1970. He spent the rest of his career there. He made many trips to the United States, visiting Princeton in 1957–1958 and 1961 and making frequent visits to the University of Chicago from 1957 to 1985. He was killed in a car crash on

7 January 1989 while driving from London to his home in Hemingford Gray.

Stable Homotopy Theory. In algebraic topology, one obtains conclusions about spaces by studying algebraic invariants. The simplest such invariants are the homotopy groups $\pi_n(X)$ of a space with base point. These are obtained by dividing the base-point preserving continuous maps $S^n \to X$, where S^n is the *n*-sphere, into equivalence classes, where two maps are equivalent if one can be continuously deformed into the other. There is a way of suspending a space, creating a new space ΣX. For example, ΣS^n is S^{n+1}. There is a homomorphism $\pi_n(X) \to \pi_{n+1}(\Sigma X)$, and Hans Freudenthal proved in 1937 that if *n* is large relative to the dimension of *X*, then this homomorphism is an isomorphism. For example $\pi_{n+q}(S^n)$ is isomorphic to $\pi_{n+q+1}(S^{n+1})$ if $q < n - 1$. The common value is called the *q*th stable homotopy group of spheres. Algebraic invariants of spaces that are independent of dimension, in the sense that this illustrates, are said to be stable. Adams was among the first to articulate the notion of stable phenomena and to articulate the principle that translation of a seemingly unstable problem into a stable one can be the first step towards its solution.

For example, one can ask for which *n* the sphere S^n admits a multiplication with a two-sided identity element. This is an unstable problem, called the Hopf invariant one problem. Adams solved it, showing that only *n* = 0, 1, 3, and 7 are possible, by first translating it into a stable problem. In the course of his work on this problem, he introduced an algebraic tool, later called the Adams spectral sequence, for the calculation of stable homotopy groups. This tool gave a powerful method for tackling stable problems calculationally. His work led to a changed point of view on algebraic topology as a whole, and it is now understood that stable homotopy theory, although typically dealing with infinite dimensional objects, is by far the most calculationally accessible part of the subject as a whole. Adams is rightly viewed as the creator of the subfield of stable homotopy theory.

K Theory. Stable homotopy theory is the natural home of homology and cohomology theories, which are pairs of sequences k_q and k^q of abelian groups satisfying certain axioms, among them the stability axiom that $k^q(X)$ is isomorphic to $k^{q+1}(\Sigma X)$. The earliest homology theories to be developed were ordinary ones, which are characterized by the dimension axiom $k^q S^0 = 0$ if $q \neq 0$, where S^0 is the zero sphere. The first "extraordinary theory" to be introduced was *K* theory, which was defined around 1960 by Michael Atiyah and Friedrich Hirzebruch. A theorem of Raoul Bott states that *K* theory is periodic, so that $K^q(X)$ is isomorphic to $K^{q+2}(X)$ for all *X*. This theory starts from a group $K^0(X)$ defined in terms of complex vector bundles over the space *X*. There is a variant, $KO^*(X)$, defined in terms of real vector bundles over *X*, that is periodic of period eight rather than two and carries more information. A second main stream of Adams's work was the use of *K* theory to solve problems in algebraic topology.

For example, one can ask how many linearly independent vector fields there are on an *n*-sphere. This is again an unstable problem that can be translated into a stable problem. However, while Adams solved the Hopf invariant one problem by use of secondary cohomology operations in ordinary cohomology, he solved the vector fields on spheres problem by use of "primary cohomology operations" in real *K* theory. Adams introduced the appropriate operations, and they are now called the Adams operations. Adams and Atiyah later showed that these primary operations in complex *K* theory can be used to obtain a simplified solution of the Hopf invariant one problem.

The *J*-homomorphism. There is a connection between *K* theory and stable homotopy theory. It is given by the *J*-homomorphism, which is a general construction that starts from the groups $KO_*(X)$ and constructs quotient groups $J_*(X)$. When *X* is a point, the *J*-homomorphism connects the *K* theory of a point to the stable homotopy groups of spheres. Adams studied the groups $J_*(X)$ in a fundamentally important series of papers. He arrived at a conjectural relationship between the Adams operations and the question of when vector bundles become equivalent under a weaker equivalence relation than that used to defined *K* theory, namely fiber homotopy equivalence, and he showed how to compute $J(X)$ assuming the truth of this conjecture, which was later called the Adams conjecture. Although he himself did not prove the conjecture, he proved special cases to which the general case was reduced by later work of Daniel G. Quillen and, independently, Dennis Sullivan. Their solutions opened up vast new areas of algebraic topology, leading Quillen to introduce algebraic *K* theory and Sullivan to introduce localizations and completions of topological spaces.

The original importance of the *J*-homomorphism was its role in differential topology. One can ask how many different differential structures there are on an *n*-sphere, for example. The answer, in dimensions above four, is directly related to the *J*-homomorphism, as John Milnor and Michel A. Kervaire showed. However, Adams's work led to a quite different perspective. The *J*-homomorphism gives a way of seeing a small part of stable homotopy theory, which is very far from being periodic, in terms of periodic *K* theory. Adams was convinced that this was only a starting point, and that there should be higher periodicities that reveal more of the structure of stable homotopy theory. That point of view has guided the development of stable homotopy theory ever since his original *J(X)* papers.

Later Work. These contributions all date from the first decade of Adams's mathematical work. His later work, although less spectacular, was also of considerable influence. His early work included a substantial amount of homological algebra related to the understanding and calculation of the Adams spectral sequence, and later homological work played a key role in the proof of the Segal conjecture, a problem that greatly interested Adams in later years. A series of papers on maps between classifying spaces turned out to be prescient precursors of substantial later work in that direction. His many other contributions pale only in comparison with the extraordinary level of his early work.

Adams was the leading figure in the algebraic topology community for close to thirty years. He had voluminous correspondence, took the refereeing of papers very seriously, and wrote a great many reviews of papers for publication in *Mathematical Reviews*. His vibrant personality and great erudition, together with his intolerance of slovenly work and his competitiveness, made him a somewhat feared but wholly revered person. He was awarded the Berwick Prize of the London Mathematical Society in 1963 and the Sylvester Medal of the Royal Society of London in 1982. He was elected a Fellow of the Royal Society in 1964.

BIBLIOGRAPHY

A complete bibliography of Adams's work may be found in N. Ray and G. Walker, eds. Adams Memorial Symposium on Algebraic Topology, *London Mathematical Society lecture note series 175–176, 2 vols., Cambridge, U.K., and New York: Cambridge University Press, 1992.*

WORKS BY ADAMS

"On the Structure and Applications of the Steenrod Algebra." *Commentarii Mathematici Helvetici* 32 (1958): 180–214.

"On the Non-Existence of Elements of Hopf Invariant One." *Annals of Mathematics* Second Series 72, no. 1 (1960): 20–104.

"Vector Fields on Spheres." *Annals of Mathematics* Second Series 75, no. 3 (1962): 603–632.

"On the Groups J(X)." I–IV. *Topology* 2 (1963): 181–195; 3 (1965): 137–171; 3 (1965): 193–222; 5 (1966): 21–71.

The Selected Works of J. Frank Adams. Edited by J. P. May and Charles B. Thomas. 2 vols. Cambridge, U.K.; New York: Cambridge University Press, 1992. Most of Adams's published work has been collected here.

OTHER SOURCES

James, I. M. "John Frank Adams." *Biographical Memoirs of Fellows of the Royal Society of London* 36 (1990), 1–16.

May, J. P. "Memorial Address for J. Frank Adams." *Mathematical Intelligencer* 12, no. 1 (1990): 40–44.

———. "Reminiscences on the Life and Mathematics of J. Frank Adams." *Mathematical Intelligencer* 12, no. 1 (1990): 45–48.

Ray, Nigel, and Grant Walker, eds. *Adams Memorial Symposium on Algebraic Topology.* London Mathematical Society lecture note series 175–176. 2 vols. Cambridge, U.K.; New York: Cambridge University Press, 1992. Includes a paper describing Adams's work.

J. P. May

ADELARD OF BATH

ADELARD OF BATH (*b.* England, c. 1080; *d.* c. 1150), *natural philosophy, translations.* For the original article on Adelard of Bath see *DSB,* vol. 1.

Adelard belonged to a group of scholars in the West country of England who involved themselves in mathematics and astronomy in the early twelfth century. He is best known as a translator of Euclid's *Elements*.

Life. In his writings Adelard calls himself "a man of Bath," and uses Bath in examples in astronomical and magical texts, while documents from Bath Priory in 1100, 1106 and 1120 appear to refer to the same Adelard as a steward and knight of the bishop, John de Villula of Tours. He was educated, however, in the French schools, both in Tour, where a famous, but unnamed, wise man elucidated the science of astronomy for him, and in Laon, from which he departed for a seven-year period of travel devoted to the "studies of the Arabs." His journey included Salerno, Magna Graecia (where he met a Greek philosopher who was an expert in medicine and the nature of things), and Syracuse in Sicily (to whose bishop, William, he dedicated the *De eodem et diverso*), as well as parts of the Norman Principality of Antioch: he mentions experiencing an earthquake at Mamistra (Misis) and hearing a scholar talk about the sinews of the body in Tarsus. There is no evidence that he visited Spain, and the transcriptions of Arabic terms in his translations, which reflect Spanish pronunciation, may rather be due to collaboration with Arabic speakers of Hispanic origin in England. It seems that, on his return from his seven-year trip, he spent the rest of his life in England or in Normandy, where he wrote most of his works. The last evidence for his life is from early 1150 when he dedicated his *De opere astrolapsus* to the young Henry Plantagenet, who was to become Henry II in 1154.

Original Works. Adelard wrote two kinds of work: original texts written in a polished and elegant Latin, intended for a wide audience; and mathematical works translated or adapted from Arabic texts, written presumably for fellow scientists. The earliest of the first group is probably the *De eodem et diverso*, which is an exhortation to the study of philosophy, following the model of Boethius's *De consolatione philosophiae*. His aim is to show how the epistemology of Plato and Aristotle can be reconciled in a theory of universals which is very similar to what was later called the indifference theory. He already shows himself, however, particularly interested in geometry (for which he gives practical examples from the agrimensorial tradition) and astronomy, on which he promises to write more.

The *Quaestiones naturales* was the most popular of his literary works, and often accompanies Seneca's *Natural Questions* in the manuscripts. It takes the form of a lively dialogue between Adelard, who champions the studies of the Arabs and his nephew, a student of "Gallic studies." The dialogue is built on a framework of apparently pre-existing "natural questions" that probably formed the basis of debate in the medical school of Salerno, which Adelard had visited. As such, the topics are on natural science, arranged from lowest parts of the universe (the roots of plants) to the highest (the stars and unmoving sphere). No direct Arabic sources can be recognized; literal quotations rather come from Plato's *Timaeus* and Cicero's *On the Nature of the Gods*. Nevertheless, the tenor of the discussions could reflect the conversations that he engaged in on his sojourn in Sicily and the Middle East. The aim of the *Quaestiones naturales* is to show how one should work out problems rationally, on the basis of observation, rather than depend on the writings of authorities.

Other texts combine a literary style with practical instructions: on using the abacus (a text based on the tradition of the late eleventh-century abacist, Gerbert d'Aurillac), on hawking (largely devoted to the care of hunting birds and the treatment of their diseases), and on using the astrolabe (this text combines a summary of Ptolemaic astronomy, with instructions on use, and refers to the help of an Arabic teacher).

Translations. In his translations from Arabic Adelard seems to have been following a program in mathematical studies. This program began with the study of Euclid's *Elements*, of which there is one translation (known as "Adelard I") clearly in Adelard's style, and continued through the study of spherical geometry (Adelard may have worked on Theodosius's *Spherics*) to that of astronomy. Adelard translated the canons (rules) and tables of al-Khwarizmi, probably in 1126, a date mentioned in the manuscripts. With these tables, from which one could work out the positions of the planets, the Sun, and the

Moon, at any time, an astronomer could then apply himself to the practical aspect of his art, namely astrology. Adelard translated a convenient handbook on the subject (Abu Ma'shar's *Abbreviation of the Introduction to Astrology*), a set of astrological aphorisms (Pseudo-Ptolemy's *Centiloquium*), and texts on how to make astrological talismans (Thabit ibn Qurra's *Liber prestigiorum*) and perform ceremonial magic (the *Liber Lunae de scientia Abel*). In two manuscripts Adelard's canons to the tables of al-Khwarizmi are interspersed with chapters by Petrus Alfonsi, a converted Jew from Huesca in Aragon, and followed by a version of the tables calculated from 1 October 1116. Since Petrus Alfonsi is also attested as instructing Walcher, prior of Great Malvern (d. 1135), in Arabic astronomy, he could well have been a conduit by which Arabic mathematical texts from Spain reached the West Midlands. Although a Spanish origin for the other texts is not provable, the tables of al-Khwarizmi are clearly from al-Andalus, since they are in the revision made for Cordova by Maslama al-Majriti (d. 1070), and had already been replaced in the Middle East by more up-to-date tables. The tables of al-Khwarizmi (composed between 813 and 833) are based on Indian and Persian planetary models, rather than on those of Ptolemy.

Transmission of Euclid. Adelard's reputation as a scientist is based on his involvement in the transmission of Euclid's *Elements*. While the literal translation ("Adelard I") was not widely diffused, a version ("Adelard II") based on this, on the fragmentary translation of Boethius, and on an Arabic-Latin version by Hermann of Carinthia, but giving "directions for proof" rather than Euclid's proofs themselves, became the standard text of the *Elements* and remained so until it was gradually replaced by the version of Campanus of Novara (c. 1259). Although the manuscripts consistently attribute the work to Adelard himself and there are references in them to "Adelard's ingenuity," Adelard II may have been written by one of his pupils (Robert of Chester is the most likely candidate), as was the introduction to *Helcep Saracenicum* (Saracen calculation)—written calculations with numerals having place value—composed for "his master Adelard" by a certain Ocreatus. A third version of the *Elements*, attributed to Adelard ("Adelard III"), represents yet another stage in the teaching of geometry (perhaps due to John of Tinemue), in which the full proofs were restored, but directional comments on the lines of Adelard II were included.

Adelard's reputation in geometry in particular is further attested by his name appearing in a list of three "modern" geometers in a late-twelfth-century introduction to arithmetic in Cambridge, Trinity College, MS R.15.16. Adelard's translation of the tables of al-Khwarizmi and an early version of Adelard II were included in Thierry of Chartres's collection of basic texts on the liberal arts, the

Heptateuchon, but it was primarily in England that Adelard left his mark as a pioneer in the scientific tradition which culminated in the work of Robert Grosseteste (d. 1253) in the early thirteenth century.

SUPPLEMENTARY BIBLIOGRAPHY

WORKS BY ADELARD OF BATH

Boncompagni, B. "Intorno ad uno scritto inedito di Adelardo di Bath intitolato 'Regule abaci.'" *Bulletino di bibliografia e di storia delle scienze matematiche e fisiche* 14 (1881): 1–134.

Suter, Heinrich, Axel A. Bjørnbo, and Rasmus O. Besthorn, eds. *Die astronomischen Tafeln des Muhammad ibn Mūsā al-Khwārizmī in der Bearbeitung des Maslama ibn Ahmed al-Madjrīrī und der latein. Übersetzung des Athelhard von Bath.* Copenhagen: A.F. Høst, 1914.

Dickey, Bruce G. *Adelard of Bath: An Examination Based on Heretofore Unexamined Manuscripts.* PhD diss., University of Toronto, 1982. Includes an edition of *De opere astrolapsus.*

The First Latin Translation of Euclid's Elements *Commonly Ascribed to Adelard of Bath.* Edited by Hubert L. L. Busard. Toronto: Pontifical Institute of Mediaeval Studies, 1983. ("Adelard I.")

Robert of Chester's (?) Redaction of Euclid's Elements, *the So-called Adelard II Version.* 2 vols. Edited by Hubert L. L. Busard and Menso Folkerts. Basel, Switzerland: Birkhäuser, 1992.

Adelard of Bath: Conversations with His Nephew: On the Same and the Different [De eodem et diverso], *Questions on Natural science* [Quaestiones naturales], *and On Birds* [De avibus]. Edited and translated by Charles Burnett, et al. Cambridge, U.K.: Cambridge University Press, 1998.

Johannes de Tinemue's Redaction of Euclid's Elements, *the So-Called Adelard III Version.* Edited by Hubert L. L. Busard. Stuttgart, Germany: Steiner, 2001.

OTHER SOURCES

Burnett, Charles, ed. *Adelard of Bath: An English Scientist and Arabist of the Early Twelfth Century.* London: Warburg Institute, University of London, 1987. Includes articles on the tables of al-Khwarizmi by R. Mercier, on the Euclid versions by R. Lorch and M. Folkerts and on the astrolabe by E. Poulle.

———. "*Algorismi vel helcep decentior est diligentia:* The Arithmetic of Adelard of Bath and His Circle." In *Mathematische Probleme im Mittelalter: der lateinische und arabische Sprachbereich,* edited by Menso Folkerts, 221–331. Wiesbaden, Germany: Harrassowitz, 1996.

———. "The Latin and Arabic Influences on the Vocabulary Concerning Demonstrative Argument in the Versions of Euclid's *Elements* Associated with Adelard of Bath." In *Aux origines du lexique philosophique européen,* edited by Jacqueline Hamesse, 117–135. Louvain-la-Neuve, Belgium: Fédéracion internationale des instituts d'études médiévales, 1997.

Busard, Hubert L. L. *Campanus of Novara and Euclid's* Elements. 2 vols. Stuttgart, Germany: Steiner, 2005. Includes a detailed account of the transmission of Euclid's *Elements* before Campanus.

Cochrane, Louise. *Adelard of Bath: The First English Scientist.* London: British Museum Press, 1994.

Compagni, Vittoria Perrone. "Studiosus incantationibus. Adelardo di Bath, Ermete e Thabit." *Giornale critico della filosofia italiana* 80/81 (2001): 36–61. On *Liber Lunae de scientia Abel.*

Speer, Andreas. *Die entdeckte Natur.* Leiden, Netherlands, and New York: E.J. Brill, 1995, pp. 18–75. On the *Quaestiones naturales.*

Charles Burnett

ADRIAN, EDGAR DOUGLAS, FIRST BARON ADRIAN OF CAMBRIDGE (*b.* London, England, 30 November 1889, *d.* Cambridge, England, 4 August 1977), *physiology, neurophysiology, electroencephalography.*

Adrian is noted for extending the all-or-none principle of skeletal muscle action to motor and sensory nerve fibers and advancing experimental electrophysiology through use of the thermionic, triode valve amplifier. With Sir Charles Sherrington, he was awarded the Nobel Prize in 1932 for discoveries on the functions of the neurons.

Family Background and Education. Adrian was the third and youngest son of Alfred Douglas Adrian, C.B., K.C. (1845–1922), a legal advisor to the British Local Government Board in London, and Flora Lavinia Barton (1858–1935), daughter of Charles Howard Barton (c. 1815–1898), a mathematics master at the Royal Military College, Sandhurst. Adrian's oldest brother, John, died within a few days of his birth in 1886. The second oldest brother, Harold Douglas Adrian (1887–1910), was a gifted classics scholar. The Adrians lived in relative prosperity in London, opposite the entrance to Primrose Hill and near Regent's Park, where the family often visited the zoo and botanical gardens. In 1903, Edgar Adrian entered Westminster School as a King's Scholar. In his studies, he benefited from Westminster's modernized science curriculum and Henry Robert Robertson's drawing lessons. Adrian entered Trinity College, Cambridge, as a major scholar in natural science in 1908.

At Cambridge, Adrian came under the influence of Keith Lucas, a fellow of Trinity College and a noted physiologist. Lucas directed Adrian's undergraduate studies, in which Adrian read physics, chemistry, physiology, anatomy, and botany for the Natural Science Tripos, Part I. After taking a First Class in the examination for 1910, he continued to read physiology for Part II, in which he again took a First Class in 1911.

At the end of his first year as an undergraduate, Adrian became a member of Cambridge's Natural Science Club, where he befriended other distinguished scientists, including surgeon Geoffrey Langdon Keynes and physicist Geoffrey Ingram Taylor (the latter also serving as Adrian's tutor in physics). Stimulated by papers read in the club, Adrian developed his early ideas about the relevance of new electronic instrumentation for experimental studies of nerve action. Between 1909 and 1914, in 1919, and in 1921, Adrian read various papers to the club, and in 1921, he was elected an honorary member.

Through the influence of Lucas, Adrian entered a circle of eminent physiologists, especially Joseph Barcroft, Walter Morley Fletcher, William Bate Hardy, and Archibald Vivian Hill, all of whom held appointments in Cambridge's noted Physiological Laboratory, established by Michael Foster in 1883. Most significantly, Adrian learned about Lucas's experimental work on muscular contraction and nerve impulses, performed in a basement room at the foundation of the Babbage Lecture Theatre. By 1905, Lucas had shown that skeletal muscle fibers obeyed the "all-or-none" principle first established for heart muscle contractions by U.S. physiologist Henry Pickering Bowditch in 1871. This principle holds that, within a single fiber, a threshold exists above which the intensity of a stimulus produces a full-sized mechanical response, but below which it produces no response at all. Although Lucas amassed evidence suggesting that the law might be true for nerve fibers, he failed to demonstrate this definitively and did not explicitly extend the principle to nerves. Adrian's collaboration with Lucas, begun as early as 1911, encouraged him to deepen this line of research as a postgraduate. Between 1912 and 1914, he published a series of papers in which he provided a generalized statement of the all-or-none principle in motor nerves and reported on a series of experiments concerning the conduction of nerve impulses under a variety of conditions, including periods of enhanced excitability and refractory periods. The merit of his work won Cambridge's Walsingham Gold Medal for Physiology and a fellowship at Trinity College, which he commenced in 1913.

In addition to his studies, Adrian found recreation in hiking, mountain climbing, fencing, and membership in Trinity's Lake Hunt, which organized manhunt games in the Lakes District. He was conversant in a broad range of subjects ancillary to his scientific interests, including hypnotism, psychoanalysis, and philosophy. He continued to exercise the artistic skill he developed as a youth and contributed paintings to the Cambridge Post-Impressionist Exhibition of 1913, a well-received showing that Adrian and his friends had actually intended as a hoax.

Having previously met Lucas and Adrian during a visit to Cambridge, the noted Harvard physiologist

Edgar Adrian. *Edgar Douglas Adrian, first Baron Adrian of Cambridge.* © HULTON-DEUTSCH COLLECTION/CORBIS.

Alexander Forbes invited Adrian to spend some time at his laboratory in 1914, but Adrian declined the offer in order to devote himself full-time to completing the requirements for a medical degree. He began his clinical training at Addenbrooke's Hospital, Cambridge, in the summer of 1914, and within a few weeks he transferred to St. Bartholomew's Hospital, London, where he completed his studies. Cambridge granted him the M.B. in 1915.

Adrian's medical degree enabled him to contribute to war-related work in hospitals for the duration of World War I. In this work, he developed techniques of case study from two particularly influential physicians: Sir Francis Martin Rouse Walshe, at the National Hospital, Queen Square, London; and Sir Adolph Abrahams, at the Connaught Military Hospital, Aldershot. Adrian's caseloads consisted primarily of patients suffering from neurological injuries and shell shock. From his firsthand experience in treating a variety of such illnesses, he furthered his ideas relating the physiological and psychological bases of neuroses. Lucas, meanwhile, lent his engineering skill to the research staff of the Royal Aircraft Factory at nearby Farnborough, where Adrian was living. Unfortunately, in

October 1916, while carrying out flight tests over the Salisbury Plain, Lucas died in a midair collision. Adrian inherited his teacher's laboratory, where he utilized the extant apparatus in new experiments that he commenced almost immediately after the war.

Research on Nerve Action through Valve Amplification, 1919–1927. In early 1919, Trinity College appointed Adrian as lecturer in natural science and demonstrator in the Physiological Laboratory. With the war's conclusion in the summer, he returned to Cambridge to carry out his newly appointed duties—for which an influx of postwar medical undergraduates created a high demand. Students such as Bryan Harold Cabot Matthews and Rachel Eckhard (who later married), two important collaborators in Adrian's later research, remembered him as an especially effective lecturer. Within a busy schedule that included heavy teaching and advising loads, a seat on the Trinity College Council (1920–1924), and service in the Physiological Society of London—as secretary (1923–1926), temporary editor (1925), and member of the editorial board (1926–1936)—Adrian furthered his earlier, pre-war research and forged ahead in new areas of inquiry.

Initially, Adrian investigated the character of nerve and muscle fiber responses to excitation, resulting in a series of publications that showed interesting correlations between levels of acidity, the time course of electric charge, and refractory periods. His measurements relied on Lucas's electrical instruments, but limitations in the technology hampered Adrian's ability to detect and interpret minute electrical impulses. He thus turned to improving the amplification of recording circuits, a problem of considerable interest to the entire physiological field. In 1921, the Cambridge Scientific Instruments Company (CSI) designed a new string galvanometer, and Adrian then invited Forbes to collaborate with him in research employing the new recording device. Upon Forbes's arrival in the summer, the team utilized a single-stage triode amplifier with the CSI string galvanometer to record sensory nerve impulses. Their observations enabled them to extend the all-or-none principle to the sensory nerves. Forbes's visit initiated a close friendship with Adrian that lasted until Forbes's death in 1965.

Following the success of the 1921 research, Adrian desired even higher amplification than was possible with the single-stage valve. By early 1925, he wrote to Herbert Spencer Gasser and H. S. Newcomer to request details about a three-stage, thermionic valve amplifier, a device they used to amplify electrical impulses in order to record action potentials in the phrenic nerve. A redesign of the amplifier by W. G. Pye and Company of Cambridge enabled Adrian to amplify natural impulses by 1,850 times, as opposed to the mere 560 times that the one-stage amplifier had achieved. He used his design of the three-stage valve with Lucas's capillary electrometer to record impulses in frog-leg nerve-muscle preparations. While attempting to establish a stable baseline, he unexpectedly encountered oscillating signals that he initially regarded as aberrations. In the process of making adjustments, he noted that the preparation produced oscillations when the muscle was allowed to hang from the frog's knee joint but that, when supported on a glass plate, it produced a stable baseline. This detection of neural signals sent by the muscle spindles through the nerve fibers represented a major breakthrough in amplification and opened up entirely new lines of electrophysiological research.

In 1925 and 1926, with initial assistance from Sybil Cooper and then critical assistance from Yngve Zotterman, a recent medical graduate visiting from Switzerland, Adrian succeeded in isolating a single nerve spindle and showed that electrical impulses do not vary regardless of their stimuli, that their frequency conveys the intensity of sensation, and that the type of nerves in action convey the quality. Physiologists have come to understand the so-called frequency code of sensation as an essential characteristic of nerve action that is fundamentally important to the scientific understanding of the functioning of nervous systems. In collaboration with Detlev Wulf Bronk, an American biophysicist, in 1928 Adrian showed similar features to motor nerve action: only one kind of nerve impulse is present, and the force of contraction—like the intensity of sensation—varies by the frequency of the nerve impulses and the number of fibers present.

Research on the Brain, Limb Movement, and Sensory Organs, 1926–1959. As with Bronk, from 1926 onward, Adrian often collaborated with other researchers in illuminating further physiological facts. His most important collaborations involved work on the optic nerve with Rachel Eckhard Matthews, electrical waves in the brain's sensory cortex with Bryan Matthews, and nerve action in the pyramidal tracts (between the motor cortex and spinal cord) responsible for the movement of the limbs. He summarized the main conclusions of his investigations regarding sensation, nerve action, and perception in three important monographs that are based on lectures: *The Basis of Sensation* (1928), *The Mechanism of Nervous Action* (1932), and *The Physical Background of Perception* (1946). These are short summaries of his research appearing in articles presented for more general audiences, with comments on the state of each field.

Adrian continued to favor his three-stage triode amplifier and capillary electrometer system until Bryan Matthews designed a moving-iron oscillograph that proved more effective in recording small electrical impulses occurring rapidly in succession of each other. A couple of Matthews's innovations in electrical recording equipment enabled Adrian—in collaboration with Matthews and, later, with Katsusaburo Yamagiwa—to expand upon Hans Berger's observations of rhythmic electrical oscillations emanating from the human head. In the mid-1930s, Adrian and his colleagues showed that the rhythm of 10 oscillations per second was developed in the occipital and parietal regions of the cortex and that the overriding condition for its production is the subject's visual inattentiveness. Their expansion upon Berger's work helped to found electroencephalography (EEG) as a clinical specialty. Although use of the electroencephalograph in diagnoses of brain conditions was received with some controversy, it has served as an important diagnostic tool for epilepsy and several kinds of encephalitis.

From the late 1930s onward, Adrian attacked a wide range of topics in his research that treated various aspects of the nervous system as a whole. He made pioneering advances in research on the sense of smell, particularly the contributions of specific receptors in stimulating mitral units of the olfactory organ. Moreover, he argued that smells could be categorized based on spatial and temporal maps of excitation and specific receptor contributions, a schematic that has guided posthumous research on the subject.

Adrian's research career effectively ended in 1958 after a disastrous flood, caused by a water leak in an upstairs room, ruined his laboratory. In his seventieth year, he was not inclined to start over with new equipment. He continued, however, to lecture and publish on topics in neurophysiology, science education and policy, and science biography until his death.

Appointments and Family Life. Adrian was elected a Fellow of the Royal Society of London in 1923; he was later appointed Foulerton Research Professor (1929–1937), foreign secretary (1946–1950), and president (1950–1955). He received the society's Royal Medal in 1934 and Copley Medal in 1946. He was also president of the British Association for the Advancement of Science in 1954 and of the Royal Society of Medicine (1960–1962), receiving that society's Gold Medal in 1950. He was elected to Britain's prestigious Order of Merit in 1942.

At Cambridge, he was appointed to a university lectureship in 1920. In 1937, he succeeded Sir Joseph Barcroft as professor of physiology, a chair he retained until 1951. In that year, he became master of Trinity College, a post he held until 1965. Near the conclusion of his research career, he accepted further administrative posts, including president (1955) and chancellor (1957–1971) of the University of Leicester and vice-chancellor (1957–1967) and chancellor (1968–1975) of the University of Cambridge. He also served as trustee of the Rock-

efeller Institute (later Rockefeller University) in New York (1962–1965) and, for many years, as the governor of his elementary school, Westminster School.

Early in his Cambridge career, at a gathering hosted by CSI chairman Horace Darwin, Adrian met Hester Agnes Pinsent, daughter of Hume Chancellor Pinsent, a solicitor, and Dame Ellen Frances Parker Pinsent, a pioneer and promoter of mental health services. The couple married on 14 June 1923. Like her mother, Hester Adrian advanced the mental health field, and she led penal reform efforts. She was made a dame of the British Empire (D.B.E.) in 1965. She enjoyed hiking with her husband during the holidays, until a climbing accident in the Lake District in 1942 required her right leg to be amputated above the knee. The Adrians had two daughters, Jennet and Anne, and a son, Richard Hume, who shared in his father's interests and enjoyed a noted career in physiology. In 1955, Edgar was created Baron Adrian of Cambridge, one of the last hereditary titles granted in England. Because his son Richard's marriage produced no heir, the title became extinct in 1995. The motto on the family's coat of arms was derived from a quote by Quintus Cicero, *Non temere credere* ("Do not believe rashly").

Adrian's international acclaim was accompanied by many awards and memberships in foreign academies. With Charles Sherrington he won the Nobel Prize in Physiology or Medicine in 1932 for cumulative research clarifying the function of the neuron. He received the Chevalier de la Legion d'Honneur in 1956. He was part of a scientific delegation to visit Russia in 1945; nearly a decade later (1953–1954) he was Banting Lecturer at the University of Toronto, where he participated in the opening of the Charles H. Best Institute of Physiology in September 1953. He was elected to fellowships, honorary memberships, and foreign, corresponding, or associate memberships in dozens of academies that included prestigious societies in Europe, North America, and Latin America. He received no fewer than twenty-nine honorary doctoral degrees from universities around the world.

Adrian's Nobel Prize banquet speech established his reputation as an eloquent ceremonial speaker. His professional colleagues particularly remembered the many impressive speeches he delivered while holding leadership offices of scientific societies. After being raised to the peerage, he regularly sat in the House of Lords and spoke effectively on scientific policy concerns, nuclear disarmament, and use of chemical and biological weapons.

Following his wife's sudden death in 1965, Adrian moved back into Trinity College, where he lived in a set of corner rooms in Nevile's Court. His own health began to decline in 1975. He spent his final two weeks under the care of the Evelyn Nursing Home in Cambridge, where he died.

BIBLIOGRAPHY

A complete bibliography of Adrian's works may be found in Hodgkin, Biographical Memoirs of Fellow of the Royal Society *(1979), pp. 68–73. Major collections of Adrian's scientific, personal, and administrative papers are at Trinity College Library, Cambridge. Significant collections of Adrian's correspondence may be found in archives at the Medical Research Council, London; Francis A. Countway Library of Medicine, Boston; Woodson Research Center, Rice University; Nuffield College Library, Oxford; Churchill Archives Center, Cambridge; Department of Manuscripts and University Archives, Cambridge University Library; and Trinity College Library, Cambridge.*

WORKS BY ADRIAN

The Basis of Sensation: The Action of the Sense Organs. New York: W. W. Norton, 1928.

The Mechanism of Nervous Action: Electrical Studies of the Neurone. Philadelphia: University of Pennsylvania Press, 1932.

The Physical Background of Perception, Being the Waynflete Lectures Delivered in the College of St. Mary Magdalen, Oxford, in the Hilary Term, 1946. Oxford: Clarendon Press, 1946.

"Memorable Experiences in Research." *Diabetes* 3, no. 1 (1954): 17–18.

OTHER SOURCES

Bradley, John Kirkham, and Elizabeth M. Tansey. "The Coming of the Electronic Age to the Cambridge Physiological Laboratory: E. D. Adrian's Valve Amplifier in 1921." *Notes and Records of the Royal Society of London* 50, no. 2 (1996): 217–228.

Brazier, Mary. "The Historical Development of Neurophysiology." In *Handbook of Physiology.* Section 1: *Neurophysiology,* edited by John Field, H. W. Magoun, and Victor E. Hall, pp. 1–58. Washington, DC: American Physiological Society, 1959.

Frank, Robert Gregg, Jr. "Instruments, Nerve Action, and the All-or-None Principle." *Osiris* 9 (1994): 208–235.

Fulton, John Farquhar. "Historical Reflections on the Backgrounds of Neurophysiology: Inhibition, Excitation, and Integration of Activity." In *The Historical Development of Physiological Thought,* edited by Chandler M. Brooks and P. F. Cranefield. New York: Hafner, 1959.

Hill, Archibald Vivian. *The Ethical Dilemma of Science and Other Writings.* New York: Rockefeller Institute Press, 1960.

Hodgkin, Sir Alan Lloyd. "Chance and Design in Electrophysiology: An Informal Account of Certain Experiments on Nerve Carried Out between 1934 and 1952." In *The Pursuit of Nature,* edited by Alan L. Hodgkin. Cambridge, U.K.: Cambridge University Press, 1977.

———. "Edgar Douglas Adrian, Baron Adrian of Cambridge." *Biographical Memoirs of Fellows of the Royal Society* 25 (1979): 1–79.

Keynes, S. "A Cambridge Hoax: The Post-Impressionist Exhibition of 1913." *Cambridge Review* 109 (1987): 116–124.

O'Connor, W. J. *Founders of British Physiology: A Biographical Dictionary, 1820–1885.* Manchester, U.K.: Manchester University Press, 1988.

Shepherd, G. M., and Janice Brown. "The Peak of Electrochemical Experiments in Physiology: A Unique View through Walter Miles' 'Report of a Visit to Foreign Laboratories' in 1920." *Caduceus* 5 (1989): 1–84.

Tansey, Elizabeth M. "Charles Sherrington, E. D. Adrian, and Henry Dale: The Cambridge Physiological Laboratory and the Physiology of the Nervous System." In *Cambridge Scientific Minds,* edited by Peter Harman and Simon Mitton, pp. 187–201. Cambridge, U.K.: Cambridge University Press, 2002.

Tasaki, Ichiji. "Conduction of the Nerve Impulse." In *Handbook of Physiology.* Section 1: *Neurophysiology,* edited by John Field, H. W. Magoun and Victor E. Hall, pp. 75–121. Washington, DC: American Physiological Society, 1959.

Zotterman, Yngve. "Neurophysiology in the Nineteen Twenties." *The Rockefeller Institute Review* 2, no. 4 (1964): 1–4.

Donald L. Opitz

ADRIAN, FIRST BARON
SEE **Adrian, Edgar Douglas, first Baron Adrian of Cambridge**.

ADRIAN, LORD
SEE **Adrian, Edgar Douglas, first Baron Adrian of Cambridge**.

AGNESI, MARIA GAETANA (*b.* Milan, Italy, 16 May 1718; *d.* Milan, 9 January 1799), *mathematics.* For the original article on Agnesi see *DSB,* vol. 1.

Agnesi was the first woman ever to publish a book of mathematics in her own name. The book, titled *Instituzioni analitiche ad uso della gioventù italiana,* appeared in Milan in 1748. In its two volumes Agnesi presented the principles and methods of algebra, Cartesian geometry, and calculus. Hers was among the first textbooks to offer such a complete introductory survey—and certainly the most accessible to beginners. The only other text published by Agnesi in her life was *Propositiones philosophicae* (1738), a collection of theses that, when she was twenty years old, signed the completion of her philosophical studies. This kind of publication was routinely expected from college students at the end of their course. Being a woman, Agnesi was prevented from accessing college; however, she carried out her training privately, under the supervision of eminent tutors. Agnesi also authored some writings of religious character, including a mystical treatise that remained unpublished. From 1752 onward she devoted her life to teaching young girls and to the assistance of the old and sick of her city, first at the Ospedale Maggiore and then, from 1771, at the Pio Albergo Trivulzio, a charitable institution she directed for almost thirty years.

Maria Gaetana Agnesi was born into a prominent Milanese family, which had accumulated remarkable wealth with the trade of wool and silk textiles. Pietro, her father, abandoned the trading activities of his ancestors and, by the time of Gaetana's birth, was engaged in a difficult attempt to bring his family into the city's aristocracy. Contrary to what was stated in the original entry, Pietro was not a university lecturer, nor had he any significant connection to the academic world. Gaetana's exceptional education was entrusted entirely to private tutors, mainly local ecclesiastics, and should be understood within Pietro's overall strategy of social enhancement. In the periodical gatherings at Palazzo Agnesi—or *conversazioni,* as these soirées were called—Gaetana performed in front of prestigious guests from all over Europe. Mainly she engaged in disputations with university lecturers over topics in natural philosophy and mathematics. On these occasions she defended the positions of the "moderns"—Isaac Newton, the Dutch experimental philosophers, and Italian natural philosophers such as Antonio Vallisneri—against the criticisms of scholastic and Cartesian philosophers. Together with her sister Maria Teresa, who was to become a renowned harpsichord player and composer, Gaetana provided Pietro with remarkable social visibility through the 1730s, just as he was pursuing a royal title and a coat of arms for his family.

Agnesi's precocious talent for the study of languages, philosophy, and mathematics was always coupled with an intense religious piety. In fact her religiosity was nurtured by those same tutors who were supervising her philosophical and mathematical studies. These learned ecclesiastics were actively involved in an attempt to reform the theological, liturgical, and social features of contemporary Catholicism. Essentially they supported an antibaroque devotion, characterized by a more sober and rational set of practices. In opposition to contemporary Jesuit teaching, these reformers deemed necessary the introduction of the experimental sciences and modern mathematics in universities and religious institutions of higher education.

Agnesi herself would contribute importantly to this reformist current with her textbook, the first to be expressly designed to help young students to learn algebra and calculus. The distinguishing features of the book depend largely on its didactic purpose. Thus, for example, unlike the authors of other contemporary treatises and

Maria Agnesi. © CORBIS.

articles on the techniques of calculus, Agnesi gave priority to the systematization of this diverse literature and to the clarification of the concepts she used, which was often achieved by relating them to the student's most familiar intuitions. The *Instituzioni* were also shaped by Agnesi's belief that the study of mathematics had particular relevance in the context of a truly Christian upbringing. The truths of geometry were exemplary in their certainty and assumed metaphysical relevance in the framework of a Malebranchian theory of knowledge of the sort she embraced. Agnesi was very clear about the priority of geometrical evidence over algebraic manipulation of symbols, hence her choice to present the most recent developments in calculus in purely geometrical terms and her emphasis on techniques such as the geometrical construction of equations. Throughout the book she keeps analytical formalism detached from mechanical and empirical considerations in order to preserve the simplicity, rigor, and evidence she held to be distinctive of the classical tradition in geometry. Unique among the texts on calculus that appeared in those years, Agnesi's does not contain a single example of the application of its techniques to the solution of problems in experimental physics and rational

20

mechanics. Analytic methods are presented as significant for the solution of geometrical problems and the study of curves interesting exclusively for their metric properties, such as the *versiera*, the curve most commonly associated with Agnesi's name.

Following the publication of her book Agnesi reached the apex of her fame, and in 1750 she was offered a lectureship in mathematics at the University of Bologna through the personal intervention of the pontiff, Benedict XIV. Agnesi, however, never went to Bologna, convinced that her contribution to the pedagogy of mathematics was now concluded. Rather, she began devoting most of her time to teaching young girls from poor backgrounds to read, write, and count and to deepen her knowledge of religious literature. Agnesi also began volunteering at the great public hospital of Milan and soon opened the gates of her family palace to sick and infirm women who could not be assisted at the hospital. In 1752 the sudden death of her father freed her from her last commitments to the *conversazione* at the family palazzo. In 1771 Agnesi was nominated director of the female section of the Pio Albergo Trivulzio, a major charitable institution for the care of the sick and old in Milan. She ran it through the troubled years of the end of the century with her usual passion and determination. After bequeathing her inheritance to the city's charitable institutions and to her relatives, Agnesi spent the last part of her life in poverty. She died in 1799 and was buried in a common grave off the city walls.

SUPPLEMENTARY BIBLIOGRAPHY

Findlen, Paula. "Maria Gaetana Agnesi." In *The Contest for Knowledge: Debates over Women's Learning in Eighteenth-Century Italy*, edited and translated by Rebecca Messbarger and Paula Findlen. Chicago: Chicago University Press, 2005.

Mazzotti, Massimo. "Maria Gaetana Agnesi: Mathematics and the Making of the Catholic Enlightenment." *Isis* 92 (2001): 657–683.

Truesdell, Clifford. "Maria Gaetana Agnesi." *Archive for History of Exact Sciences* 40 (1989): 113–142.

Massimo Mazzotti

AHLFORS, LARS
(*b.* Helsigfors, Finland, 18 April 1907; *d.* Pittsfield, Massachusetts, 11 October 1996), *mathematics, complex function theory, Riemann surface theory, conformal geometry, quasiconformal mappings, theory of Kleinian groups.*

Ahlfors was one of the leaders in the field of complex function theory for more than fifty years. Among his earliest successes was a geometric reformulation and deepening of Rolf Nevanlinna's profound study of the values of complex functions. Later he was instrumental in the revival of interest in the topic of Kleinian groups, and he enriched function theory with the techniques in the theory of quasiconformal mappings. He was also an influential teacher and textbook writer.

Life and Career. Ahlfors's mother, Sievä Helander, died giving birth to him, and his father, Axel Ahlfors, an engineer, sent him to two aunts for his early upbringing. He soon showed an aptitude for mathematics, doing his older sisters' homework for them and quickly outstripping his teachers at the local school. He also read mathematics books on clandestine trips to his father's library, which is how he came to learn the calculus. When Lars went to Helsinki University in 1924, he studied mathematics under Ernst Lindelöf and Rolf Nevanlinna, two of the major figures in the field of complex function theory, a branch of mathematics that was particularly cherished in Finland at the time. At age twenty-one, Ahlfors followed Nevanlinna to the Eidgenösische Technische Hochschule (ETH, also known as the Zürich Polytechnic School) in Zürich, Switzerland, where he began to do original work on his own, and he was awarded his PhD in 1930 from Helsinki University for the work he did in Zürich. In 1933 he returned from Zurich to Helsinki and married Erna Lehnert; the marriage proved to be a happy one and ended only with his death.

In 1935 Ahlfors took up a three-year teaching position at Harvard University in Cambridge, Massachusetts, and in 1936 he was awarded one of the first two Fields Medals at the International Congress of Mathematicians in Oslo, Norway, for his work on complex function theory. But he became homesick and returned to Helsinki in 1938, where he spent most of the World War II as a professor at Helsinki University before being appointed to a professorship at the University of Zürich in 1944. He had to pawn his Fields Medal to get enough money to make the trip; later, some Swiss mathematicians helped him retrieve it.

In 1946 Ahlfors returned to Harvard, becoming the William Caspar Graustein Professor in 1964, a position he held until his retirement in 1977. The first edition of his book *Complex Analysis* came out in 1953; it ran to three editions and was for decades the incontestable standard introduction to the subject. Students attending his lectures, delivered in a thundering basso and in a strong Scandinavian accent, recalled them as stunningly beautiful. In 1981 he was awarded a prestigious Wolf Prize in mathematics "for seminal discoveries and the creation of powerful new methods in geometric function theory."

Lars Ahlfors. WOLF FOUNDATION. REPRODUCED BY
PERMISSION.

Complex Function Theory. A striking result of Émile
Picard's in 1880 shows that a meromorphic function that
fails to take three values in the extended complex plane is
in fact constant. Much energy was expended over the next
forty years in finding elementary proofs of this result and
exploring its implications, and the definitive account was
given only in 1925 by Rolf Nevanlinna. The theory, called
value distribution theory, is both profound and technically very difficult. Ahlfors earned his Fields Medal in
1936 in part because of the way his use of geometric ideas
greatly simplified it. In presenting him with the medal,
Constantin Carathéodory said it was hard to say if it was
more surprising that Nevanlinna could develop his theory
without the aid of geometry or that Ahlfors could con-
dense the whole theory to a mere fourteen pages.

In his 1935 account, "Zur Theorie der Überlagerungsflächen," Ahlfors introduced geometry by
regarding the image of a meromorphic function as a covering surface of the Riemann sphere. He then interpreted
the fundamental concepts of Nevanlinna theory as properties of the covering surface. For example, Nevanlinna's
counting function says how many times the meromorphic
function on a disc of a given radius takes a given value.
Geometrically, this says how many points on the image
surface lie over a given point of the Riemann sphere.
Ahlfors then derived the main results in what became a

characteristic method of his: exploiting a combination of
metrical and topological arguments. But he did more,
because his formulation of the theory extended it to a
much wider class of functions than the meromorphic
ones, namely the quasiconformal mappings. A further
reworking of the Nevanlinna theory made greater use of
the methods of differential geometry in the hope that a
generalization to higher dimensions could be found. But
that had to wait almost thirty years, with the work of
Raoul Bott and Shiing-Shen Chern in 1965 and then the
work of Phillip Griffiths.

Quasiconformal Mappings. Quasiconformal mappings
were introduced by Herbert Grötzsch and Oswald Teichmüller in the mid-1930s and applied very successfully by
Teichmüller to the study of the moduli space of a Riemann surface, the space of all complex structures on the
surface. Teichmüller, a committed Nazi, died on the Russian front in World War II, and after the war Ahlfors and
his close colleague Lipman Bers, at Columbia University
in New York, decided to rescue the theory from the
shadow cast upon it by its creator. As Bers, quoting
Plutarch, noted in 1960 in his paper "Quasiconformal
Mappings and Teichmüller's Theorem," "it does not of
necessity follow that, if the work delights you with its
grace, the one who wrought it is worthy of your esteem"
(p. 90).

Informally, a map between two Riemann surfaces is
quasiconformal if it maps infinitesimal circles to infinitesimal ellipses (a conformal map will map infinitesimal circles to infinitesimal circles); and if the eccentricity of the
resulting ellipses is bounded, the quasiconformal map is
said to be of bounded distortion. Teichmüller showed that
among quasiconformal mappings from one Riemann surface to another of the same genus, there is a unique one
with a maximal degree of distortion, modulo a certain
equivalence relation that involves a homotopy consideration. Furthermore, these equivalence classes form a space
T_p that describes all the complex structures on a Riemann
surface of the given genus. The description is, however,
redundant, and a certain group intervenes that acts on the
space T_p. This group is called the mapping class group, the
corresponding quotient space is the space M_p of complex
structures on the Riemann surface, and Teichmüller's
space is the universal covering space of M_p. Teichmüller
also gave another description of his space in terms of
quadratic differentials on the Riemann surface, and this
connected it with a rich seam of technical mathematics.

One of Ahlfors's first contributions to Teichmüller
theory after the war was to simplify and generalize the definition of a quasiconformal mapping. He then gave clear
new proofs of Teichmüller's main results. In this way he
made the theory accessible for the first time to a whole

generation of mathematicians, and the theory blossomed. It was extended to mappings between spaces of higher dimension, and in many areas of mathematics, quasiconformal mappings proved the right generalization of the much more restricted class of conformal mappings. For example, a classical theorem of Marcel and Frigyes Riesz states that a map between Jordan domains induces a map between their boundaries that is absolutely continuous with respect to a linear measure if the boundaries are rectifiable and the map is conformal. In 1956 Ahlfors and Arne Beurling showed in the joint paper "The Boundary Correspondence under Quasiconformal Mappings" that if the map is only quasiconformal, the induced map in the boundaries can be completely singular.

Ahlfors also found results concerning the existence of quasiconformal mappings with prescribed distortion, and these have had profound implications elsewhere, for example, in Dennis Sullivan's solution of the Fatou-Julia problem on wandering domains in complex iteration theory. Iteration theory is also a source of geometric objects called quasi-circles, the image of a circle under a quasiconformal map of the extended complex plane to itself. These can be very complicated objects; they may, for example, have any Hausdorff measure m in the range $0 < m < 2$. Even so, Ahlfors was able to give a very simple characterization of quasi-circles that has become fundamental in the study of these objects.

Kleinian Groups. Ahlfors, Bers, and their students also did major work in the 1950s and 1960s on Kleinian groups. Fuchsian and Kleinian groups had been introduced by Henri Poincaré in the 1880s as discrete groups of transformations of, respectively, non-Euclidean two-dimensional and non-Euclidean three-dimensional space. Neither theory is simple, but it is fair to say that the Kleinian theory more or less languished from the point when Poincaré abandoned it until Ahlfors came along. He took a different approach to Poincaré and revived the subject. Bers had shown in 1965 that Fuchsian groups obey a finiteness condition, which says (to oversimplify) that the quotient of the upper half plane by a finitely generated Fuchsian group is an orbifold of finite type. More accurately, the set of nonsingular points in the quotient has that property. Indeed, as Bers knew, this was an old result; the significance of his work was that it derived the result by modern methods, specifically, Eichler cohomology and the use of analytic potentials. This was the stepping-stone for Ahlfors to come up with the generalization to Kleinian groups, but this was no trivial advance. Ahlfors had to replace the analytic potentials with the much larger class of smooth potentials and so to rebuild Eichler cohomology on new foundations.

Ahlfors, Bers, and their students also went back to the original suggestion of Poincaré that the behavior of a Kleinian group can be studied by what it does on the boundary of non-Euclidean space. The action of the Kleinian group shunts various points out to the boundary, and Ahlfors conjectured that this limit set would necessarily have two-dimensional Lebesgue measure zero. This result is still unproved, but it reopened the connection to three-dimensional topology that Poincaré had stressed, and in the 1970s this approach was developed extensively by William Thurston in a series of papers that have shaped the field ever since.

A number of Ahlfors's other ideas deserve mention. The uniformization theorem of Poincaré and Paul Koebe, dating from 1907, says that every Riemann surface is covered either by the sphere, the Euclidean plane, or the non-Euclidean plane. The last two are topologically indistinguishable, so the question of determining whether the Riemann surface of a given complex function is covered by the Euclidean or the non-Euclidean plane is delicate. The first case is called, for reasons that go back to the work of Felix Klein in the 1880s, the parabolic case, the second the hyperbolic case, and distinguishing between the two is called the type problem. Very early in his career, Ahlfors was able to give a sufficient criterion for a function to be of parabolic type. The criterion makes fundamental use of the different ways the circumference of a circle depends on the radius in the two cases.

Bloch's Constant. In 1936 and 1937, Ahlfors and Helmut Grunsky gave a striking estimate of what is called Bloch's constant. Given an analytic map defined on the unit disc and normalized so that its derivative at the origin has modulus 1, Bloch had proved that there is a subdomain of the disc that is mapped one-to-one and conformally onto a disc of a certain radius that is independent of the function studied. Bloch's constant is the maximum such radius. Ahlfors found a lower bound of $\sqrt{3}/4$ for this constant, which has scarcely been improved to this day. More importantly, the way Ahlfors came to this result was a novel reinterpretation of Schwarz's lemma, which says that an analytic function mapping the unit disc to itself and fixing the origin satisfies $|f'(0)| < 1$ unless the map is a rotation, in which case $|f'(0)| = 1$. In 1916 George Pick observed that this implies that any analytic map of the disc to itself decreases hyperbolic (non-Euclidean) lengths unless it is a hyperbolic isometry. Ahlfors reinterpreted this as a statement about two metrics in the disc and then found new results by varying the metric. This idea has since proved its worth in many areas on the complex function theory of one and several variables.

Bloch's Principle. Bloch himself had proclaimed a heuristic principle of considerable depth, that any qualitative principle known to be exact in a certain domain remains correct in a new setting if one modifies its statement in a continuous way. Ahlfors triumphantly vindicated this principle in his work on value distribution theory. It is one of the main results of value distribution theory that given five distinct points in the complex plane, a_1, a_2, ... , a_5, and a meromorphic function f, at least one of the equations $f(z) = a_i$ has a unique solution. This is a considerable generalization of Picard's theorem that a meromorphic function on the complex plane cannot omit three values without being constant. To make this statement amenable to Bloch's principle, it can be reformulated it this way: given three disjoint domains and a nonconstant meromorphic function, the pre-image of at least one of these domains has at least one bounded component. This invites the claim that given five disjoint domains in the complex plane whose boundaries are Jordan curves and a nonconstant meromorphic function f, there is a domain D that is mapped homeomorphically onto exactly one of these domains. This is called, for obvious reasons, the Five Islands Theorem. It was conjectured by Bloch and proved by Ahlfors in 1932, using his method of mixing topological considerations with metric distortion theorems.

BIBLIOGRAPHY

Ahlfors's papers, and a complete bibliography of his work, can be found in the two volumes of his Collected Papers, *edited by Lars Valerian Ahlfors (Boston: Birkhäuser, 1982).*

WORKS BY AHLFORS

"Zur Theorie der Überlagerungsflächen." *Acta Mathematica* 65 (1935): 157–194.

Complex Analysis: An Introduction to the Theory of Analytic Functions of One Complex Variable. New York: McGraw-Hill, 1953.

With Arne Beurling. "The Boundary Correspondence under Quasiconformal Mappings." *Acta Mathematica* 96 (1956): 125–142.

Lectures on Quasiconformal Mappings. Princeton, NJ: Van Nostrand, 1966.

OTHER SOURCES

Bers, Lipman. "Quasiconformal Mappings and Teichmüller's Theorem." In his *Analytic Functions,* 89–119. Princeton, NJ: Princeton University Press, 1960.

Bott, Raoul, Clifford Earle, Dennis Hejhal, et al. "Lars Valerian Ahlfors." *Notices of the American Mathematical Society* 45, no. 2 (1998): 248–255.

Eremenko, Alexandre. "Ahlfors' Contribution to the Theory of Meromorphic Functions." Available from http://www.math.purdue.edu.

Gehring, Frederick, Irwin Kra, Steven G. Krantz, et al. "The Mathematics of Lars Valerian Ahlfors." *Notices of the American Mathematical Society* 45, no. 2 (1998): 233–242.

Gleason, Andrew, George Mackey, and Raoul Bott. "Faculty of Arts and Sciences—Memorial Minute: Lars Valerian Ahlfors." *Harvard University Gazette* 25 (January 2001): 16.

Lehto, Olli. "On the Life and Works of Lars Ahlfors." *Mathematical Intelligencer* 20, no. 3 (1998): 4–8.

Jeremy Gray

AIRY, GEORGE BIDDELL (*b.* Alnwick, Northumberland, England, 27 July 1801; *d.* Greenwich, England, 2 January 1892), *astronomy.* For the original article on Airy see *DSB*, vol. 1.

The original *DSB* article on Airy was written by Olin J. Eggen, an astrophysicist who argued that Airy's talents as an organizer (particularly the "sense of order" he brought to the directorship of the Royal Observatory) were the sole justification for his inclusion in the *DSB*. Eggen, taking a somewhat Whiggish view of the history of astronomy, concluded that Airy was "not a great scientist, but made great science possible," and he identified that "great science" as occurring not during Airy's tenure at the national observatory, but rather when the Greenwich stellar observations, made to provide a framework within which planetary motions could be measured, were used in the twentieth century for understanding the origin and evolution of the stars. As a result, Eggen wrote an essay that provided few details of the accomplishments that earned Airy high respect in his own lifetime.

Focusing narrowly on Airy's formal duties as superintendent of the Royal Observatory, Greenwich, Eggen failed to comprehend why certain contemporaries considered him the astronomer *par excellence* of his day. Writing from the vantage point of 1903, the great American astronomer Simon Newcomb, for example, saw Airy as the most commanding figure in the astronomy of his time, and as the person who had introduced large-scale production into astronomy. Later historians have also emphasized Airy's factory-like approach to astronomical work at Greenwich.

Early Achievements. Even while still at Cambridge as director of the University observatory, Airy demonstrated a characteristic innovativeness in his work. Perceiving that the routine reduction of positional observations could be most accurately carried out by human computers working on preprinted skeleton sheets that were easily checkable by a supervising computer, he introduced such sheets not only for the reduction of Cambridge observations, but also the solar, lunar, and planetary observations of former Astronomer Royal James Bradley (made at Greenwich) and the circumpolar star observations of English astronomer Stephen Groombridge (made at Blackheath). (Airy likewise introduced use of the skeleton sheets at Greenwich upon becoming Astronomer Royal.)

But beyond such organizational innovations, Airy made lasting scientific and technical contributions to several fields. One was optics. Although the circular "bulls-eye diffraction pattern around a point source of light (such as a star) as seen through a refracting telescope had earlier attracted the notice of William Herschel and Thomas Young, Airy, in an 1834 article published in the Transactions of the Cambridge Philosophical Society, was the first to analyze the pattern mathematically according to the size of the circular aperture and the wavelength of the light. The pattern still bears his name in the early twenty-first century (the Airy disk). At Cambridge, Airy designed and supervised the erection of a large equatorial refractor with an 11.75-inch Cauchoix objective whose construction was made possible with funds provided by the Duke of Northumberland. It became known as the largest and best-mounted instrument in Great Britain, and his version of the English yoke mount was later used for an even larger equatorial installed at Greenwich in 1859. After arriving at Greenwich and eventually perceiving the need for replacement instruments there, Airy designed three new positional instruments—an altitude and azimuth instrument (1847), a transit circle (1851), and a reflex zenith tube (1851)—and an associated barrel chronograph (1854).

Career and Prestige. At the Royal Observatory Airy established its magnetic, meteorological, and astrophotographic and spectroscopic departments. He pioneered within England the transmission of telegraphic time signals for railway and Post Office use and arranged for the use of submarine telegraphy to determine longitude differences between Greenwich and numerous foreign observatories. He also made notable contributions to geodesy. For example, in 1854 Airy conducted an experiment of swinging a single pendulum from both the top and bottom of a deep mine, which enabled him to measure gravity and compute the density of the earth. A year later he theorized that the presence of root structures of lower density were necessary under mountains in order to maintain isostatic equilibrium.

As the senior "scientific" civil servant, Airy became the de facto government scientist to be called upon by government leaders. A significant portion of his time was devoted to so-called "extraneous government business," that is, his participation in numerous commissions of state and other government bodies. Barely noted by Eggen,

Sir George Biddell Airy. © HULTON-DEUTSCH COLLECTION/CORBIS.

these bodies included commissions on such wide-ranging matters as the standards of measurements, harbors, railway gauges, sewers, coinage, ordnance surveys, sale of town gas, and meteorology. Airy was also consulted concerning the Australian universities of Sydney and Melbourne, the Great Exhibition of 1851 at Hyde Park, London, and the Paris Exhibition of 1855. He provided advice regarding such topics as steam-engine propellers and ship building, compass correction in iron ships, railways, sawmills for ship's timbers, construction of the Westminster Clock, navigation on the River Dee, the Atlantic submarine cable, and the compilation of a Gold Standard Table for the Bank of England.

The Neptune Controversies. For better or worse, Airy's reputation, both among contemporaries and later commentators, has been highly influenced by his perceived role in the controversies surrounding the mathematical predictions and optical discovery of the planet Neptune in the mid-1840s. One has to be puzzled, however, by Eggen's claim that commentators prior to him had almost universally blamed Airy for withholding planetary observations from John Couch Adams, one of the two mathematicians (Urbain Le Verrier was the other) engaged at this time in determining the orbit and current position of a hypothetical transuranian planet that might be causing the observed erratic motion of the planet Uranus. Quite the contrary, the controversies (too detailed to be discussed at length here) concerned whether Airy and James Challis had properly encouraged Adams's researches (including the publication of them) in late 1845, whether these astronomers had unjustifiably delayed searching for Adams's hypothetical planet, and whether Airy had acted properly in withholding information about Adams's researches not only from Le Verrier (when the latter corresponded with Airy in late June 1846), but also from other British astronomers (who might have conducted planet searches independent of the one carried out by Challis, with Airy's encouragement, in the summer of 1846). The French scientific community also questioned whether Adams and Challis deserved any share of the credit for either the mathematical or optical discovery of Neptune.

Airy himself had hoped to provide a definitive account justifying his actions through the presentation of a selection of relevant letters at the Royal Astronomical Society (RAS) meeting of 13 November 1846 and their appearance in the *Monthly Notices of the RAS* 7 (1846, pp. 121–144) and other publications, but these letters instead provoked interpretations unintended by and unflattering to Airy. The printed letters, however, form only a small portion of a file of Neptune-related correspondence and other documents that was maintained by Airy. For over thirty years, beginning in the late 1960s, historians were eager to consult this file, but were prevented from doing so by its removal from the Greenwich Archives by none other than Eggen himself, who secretly held onto it until his death. Fortunately it was recovered and is now available for researchers.

SUPPLEMENTARY BIBLIOGRAPHY

Airy's Neptune file was returned in 1999 to England, where it is now a part (vol. 96a) of the Royal Greenwich Observatory Archives, Papers of George Airy, RGO 6, in the Cambridge University Library. A detailed catalogue of the entire collection, comprising 848 volumes and occupying 12 cubic meters, is available online from http://janus.lib.cam.ac.uk/db/node.xsp?id=EAD%2FGBR%2F0180%2FRGO%206. The collection includes not only incoming letters, but also press copies (many unfortunately faded) of outgoing letters. Numerous letters of Airy may also be found in the papers of his contemporaries, including John Couch Adams (St. John's College Library, Cambridge University), Charles Babbage (British Library), James Challis (Cambridge University Library), Augustus De Morgan (University College London), James Glaisher (Royal Astronomical Society Library), Sir John Herschel (Royal Society Library), Sir John Lubbock (Royal Society Library), Sir Charles Lyell (Edinburgh University Library), several Earls of Rosse (Birr Castle Archives), Sir Edward Sabine (National Archives),

Richard Sheepshanks (Royal Astronomical Library), Sir George Stokes (Cambridge University Library), John Tyndall (Royal Institution of Great Britain), and William Whewell (Trinity College Library, University of Cambridge).

Ashworth, William J. "John Herschel, George Airy and the Roaming Eye of the State." *History of Science*, 36 (1998): 151–178.

Bennett, J. A. "George Biddell Airy and Horology." *Annals of Science* 27 (1980): 269–285.

Chapman, Allan. "Private Research and Public Duty: George Biddell Airy and the Search for Neptune." *Journal for the History of Astronomy* 9 (May 1988): 121–139.

———. "Science and the Public Good: George Biddell Airy (1801–92) and the Concept of a Public Servant." In *Science, Politics, and the Public Good,* edited by Nicolaas A. Rupke. London: Macmillan, 1988.

Howse, Derek. *Greenwich Time and the Discovery of Longitude.* Oxford, U.K.: Oxford University Press, 1980.

Kollerstrom, Nicholas. "Recovering the Neptune Files." *Astronomy and Geophysics* 44 (5, 2003): 5.23–5.24.

———. "An Hiatus in History: The British Claim for Neptune's Co-Prediction, 1845–1846." *History of Science* 44 (2006): 1–28 and 349–371.

Meadows, A. J. *Greenwich Observatory,* Vol. 2: *Recent History (1836–1975).* London: Taylor & Francis, 1975.

Perkins, Adam. "'Extraneous Government Business': The Astronomer Royal as Government Scientist: George Airy and his Work on the Commissions of State and Other Bodies, 1838–1880." *Journal of Astronomical History and Heritage* 4 (2001): 143–154.

Rawlins, Dennis. "British Neptune-Disaster File Recovered." *DIO* 9 (1, 1999): 3–25.

Satterthwaite, Gilbert E. "Airy and Positional Astronomy." *Journal of Astronomical History and Heritage* 4 (2001a): 101–113.

———. "Airy's Transit Circle." *Journal of Astronomical History and Heritage* 4 (2001b): 115–141.

Schaffer, Simon. "Astronomers Mark Time. Discipline and the Personal Equation." *Science in Context* 2 (1988): 115–145.

Sheehan, William, et al. "The Case of the Pilfered Planet: Did the British Steal Neptune?" *Scientific American* 291 (6, 2004): 92–99. Available from http://www.sciam.com.

Smith, Robert W. "The Cambridge Network in Action: The Discovery of Neptune." *Isis* 80 (1989): 395–422.

———. "A National Observatory Transformed: Greenwich in the Nineteenth Century." *Journal for the History of Astronomy* 22 (1991): 5–20.

Standage, Tom. *The Neptune File: A Story of Astronomical Rivalry and the Pioneers of Planet Hunting.* New York: Walker, 2000.

Craig B. Waff

AITKEN, JOHN (*b*. Falkirk, Stirlingshire, Scotland, 18 September 1839; *d*. Falkirk, 13 November 1919), *engineering, dust, condensation, dew, meteorology.*

Aitken was a physicist and meteorologist who worked as a gentleman amateur outside academia. His research, which was experimentally virtuosic but eschewed mathematical formulations, clarified the origins of dew and, most importantly, the role of dust in the formation of cloudy condensations. One of the scientific instruments he invented, the Aitken dust counter, inspired Charles T. R. Wilson's work on cloud chamber detectors.

Early Years. John Aitken was born on 18 September 1839 in Falkirk, Stirlingshire, the fourth son of Margaret Russel and Henry Aitken, businessman and head of the legal firm Russel & Aitken. As a young boy, despite persistent ill health, John studied at the Falkirk Grammar School. Like his father and brothers, he then attended the University of Glasgow, taking classes in logic, chemistry, and mathematics in his first year (1855–1856). The following session, while continuing his study of mathematics, Aitken graduated at the top of William J. M. Rankine's revived class of civil engineering and mechanics—thus preparing himself to support his father, who had a wide portfolio of mining, railway, and shipping interests. That year he also was at the head of William Thomson's natural philosophy class, establishing a friendship with the professor that endured throughout his life.

After leaving the university in the summer of 1857, Aitken was an apprentice engineer for two years in Dundee, and then for three years (and certainly by 1861) he was in Glasgow as a student with Robert Napier & Sons, prominent Clyde shipbuilders and marine engineers who were closely linked, through James Robert Napier, to both Rankine and Thomson. Surviving drawings of marine steam engines, screw propellers, and paddle wheels (1863–1864) show that Aitken was a consummate draftsman, but a further breakdown in his health forced him to abandon an engineering career. Thus, even though his notes on new safety valves and on an arrangement using two cranks to produce variable motion (supplementing Robert Willis's science of mechanism) went to the journal *Engineering* in 1867 and 1868, these were but an amateur's hints and suggestions, not patented innovations. After the death of both his father and mother (1860) Aitken had become financially secure on inherited wealth, despite having no profession, and by 1867 he had retired to Falkirk, where he lived for many years, unmarried, with his brothers James, Henry, and Robert, lawyer, ironmaster, and clerk, respectively.

Life as a Gentleman Philosopher. Back in Falkirk, Aitken dedicated himself to pursuits suited to a retiring though not reclusive gentlemanly invalid who was permitted only a few hours of work each day: reading, photography, gardening, ornithology, and angling. As he was an intensely religious man, for him such activities, with their emphasis on the divine power present in the everyday phenomena of the natural environment, dovetailed perfectly with painstaking experimental natural philosophy. The latter kept him busy indoors at the family home of Darroch and, from 1897, in his own home Ardenlea: a purpose-built residence with workshop *cum* laboratory provided with turning lathe, carpenter's bench, glassware, delicate instruments, and other apparatus Aitken himself had constructed. Although garden and workshop provided flowers for the Falkirk Infirmary and bric-a-brac for charitable re-sale, fulfilling Aitken's local obligations, nature and laboratory together also represented the merger of outdoor observation and hands-on experimental skill that would become Aitken's public scientific hallmark.

From 1870 Aitken began to publish extensively, first in professional photographic journals. From 1871 he was a regular contributor to Norman Lockyer's *Nature*, over the years sending in papers on sundry topics ranging from butterflies to the economies of the heat-engine regenerator. At the 1871 meeting of the British Association for the Advancement of Science, Aitken met James Clerk Maxwell and discussed color sensation; shortly afterward Aitken's first major paper, describing experiments that supported a modified form of Young's three-color theory, appeared before the Royal Scottish Society of Arts (1872). In this work, Aitken had emphasized physiological considerations—such as retinal fatigue—in color perception. The important work that was to follow concerned ever more precise investigations of the everyday phenomena of nature.

Research in Meteorology. First, Aitken showed how dust was needed for cloudy condensation to take place in naturally occurring circumstances. This work reflected his training by Rankine and Thomson, two founders of classical thermodynamics, and a consequent fascination with the practical conditions of changes of state (notably the melting and freezing of ice (1873). In his "On Dust, Fogs, and Clouds" (December 1880), Aitken showed a rapt audience of Royal Society of Edinburgh Fellows that the condensation of water vapor to form mist, fog, and cloud required the presence of invisible dust particles. *Nature* publicized Aitken's results to acclaim: by 1882 they had won the sanction of Lord Rayleigh and, with their extension in a paper "On the Formation of Small Clear Spaces in Dusty Air" (1884), Aitken won the Keith Prize (for 1883–1885) from the Royal Society of Edinburgh. Later he broadened his studies in the production and condensing effects of dust to include the influence of locality, altitude, wind conditions, pressure, time of day, and industry.

A second series of experimental researches settled a centuries-old controversy about the origin of dew: Did it rise from the soil by evaporation, fall from the atmosphere by condensation, or have some other source? In 1885 Aitken reevaluated William Charles Wells's *Essay on Dew* (1814), a work praised by John Herschel, the ultimate methodological judge, as a beautiful specimen of inductive experimental inquiry. Through typically minute observations, Aitken concluded that, according to prevailing conditions that he precisely specified, the vapor which condenses as dew on cold surfaces comes mainly from the ground below, not from the air above; thanks to his experiments on broccoli, Aitken could announce, *contra* Wells, that the so-called dewdrop on leaves of plants is actually exuded sap. Despite vehement criticism from authorities such as Charles Tomlinson, dew—and garden vegetables—helped cement Aitken's position as a natural philosopher.

Although Aitken was involved in many other areas of scientific study, it was these two pieces of work especially that won him an international reputation as an experimental physicist, even at a time when his lack of enthusiasm for mathematical formulations placed him well outside the British academic mainstream, at least as it was represented by the Cambridge wrangler. Two characteristics of Aitken's work illustrate this. The first is the use of instruments that he designed and often made himself. The chromomictor (1885) recalled his earliest significant work, using lenses and a camera obscura rather than conventional rotating disks to mix lights of different colors for experiments in physiological optics.

Most famous, however, were his various dust counters. Because condensation normally required dust, the number of droplets of water falling onto a silvered surface as saturated air was slightly expanded would indicate the number of particles. By 1889 Aitken had created a heavy-duty form, requiring a complex housing, suitable for a first-class laboratory; a simple pocket dust counter was available by 1890. The koniscope, or dust detective, (1892) used an optical technique to gauge the concentration of dust in air. Aitken regularly exhibited both koniscope and pocket dust counter (for example, at the British Association meeting at Nottingham in 1893), and it was left to the Edinburgh instrument maker William Hume, a man active in the Royal Scottish Society of Arts and in the distribution of kits for experimental physics classes and public health laboratories, to manufacture, market, and further develop the apparatus into the early twentieth century.

Aitken made wide use of the portable counter himself: partly for his health and partly to gather data. He made excursions within Scotland (often to the holiday resort of Kingairloch), ascended Swiss peaks, and, even

before its public opening in 1889, sampled the air at the top of the Eiffel Tower in Paris. During 1894–1895 Fridlander had carried Aitken's dust counters around the globe, charting prevalence of dust particles in the great oceans far from land. Others were stationed in the Sahara (1897) to correlate dust with precipitation.

The second characteristic was best illustrated in Aitken's discussions of the dynamics of cyclones and anticyclones, begun in 1900 but still causing a stir as late as 1916. Rather than deploy the abstruse mathematical models that were likely beyond him, Aitken simply imitated on a large experimental scale within his laboratory the production and movement of the cyclone itself. His apparatus deployed a large vertical metal tube standing on three legs above a disk three times the tube's diameter. Gas burners mounted inside the tube created an up-draught; vanes, or chemical fumes, showed the direction of the circulation of the affected air. This process of mimicry, reducing macroscopic phenomena to manageable laboratory scale, was adopted by many contemporary British physicists. Conscious of British neo-Baconian traditions, Aitken developed strategies to avoid mathematical theorizing when he conceived it to be merely fashionable, premature, or downright dubious. He prided himself on the fact that his "test tube kind of work" could discredit the assumptions of "mathematical workers" (Aitken to Smithells [14 July 1917].] Significantly, his library lacked Newton's *Principia Mathematica* but contained works by the archetypical experimenters Robert Boyle and Michael Faraday: well read in his chosen fields, his indifference to scientific orthodoxy when close observation (or effective laboratory mimicry) challenged it allied him to the early Royal Society's motto: "nullius in verba," ironically, Newton's motto.

Perhaps this was the reason that Aitken's enthusiasms centered increasingly on meteorological questions. From 1884 until his death he took a particular interest in the accurate measurement of air temperature, criticizing in particular the use of Thomas Stevenson's thermometer screen, a standard piece of apparatus despite its unreliability in hot climates. He recorded weather data at home systematically and with precision for many years. From 1890 two Aitken dust counters—one self-acting, one portable—could be found alongside the other recording instruments central to the observational regime of the permanently staffed Ben Nevis Meteorological Observatory. Designed by Stevenson and opened in 1883, the observatory at the summit of Britain's highest mountain was the prestige project of the Scottish Meteorological Society (founded in 1855), and as both founding donor and one of a team of directors (through the 1890s) Aitken served beside elite scientific representatives of the Royal Societies of Edinburgh and London.

Intriguingly, the talented student Charles Thomas Rees Wilson, who was trained at Cambridge University and the Cavendish Laboratory, took a summer job at the observatory in 1894, witnessed Aitken's instruments, and went on to extend the original dust counters to create an apparatus, later known as a cloud chamber, capable of tracking not dust particles but ions. Wilson (and Aitken before him) had seen that in more extreme circumstances than those normally occurring in nature (with considerable rates of expansion and cooling of saturated air), cloudy condensation formed in dustless air around electric ions. Wilson published his work in 1895, ultimately receiving the Hughes Medal of the Royal Society of London (1911). J. J. Thomson's classical experiments of the late 1890s on the mass and charge of the electron (later so called) effectively extended Aitken's technique: Thomson deployed Wilson's idea to detect and count charged particles in dust-free air. Thus the dust counter had a new life in the world of particle physics.

Aitken's work won widespread recognition from individuals and institutions alike. He gravitated from the Royal Scottish Society of Arts, which he had joined in December 1871, to become a Fellow of the Royal Society of Edinburgh (RSE) in April 1875, supported by three reform-minded Glasgow University professors: Allen Thomson (anatomy), James Thomson (engineering), and William Thomson (Lord Kelvin; natural philosophy). The work of the last of these, on vortex atoms, received indirect support soon after from Aitken's experiments (December 1875) on the rigidity produced by centrifugal force. Thereafter the RSE became Aitken's chief outlet for his many publications. But in June 1889 he became a Fellow of the Royal Society of London, again with the support of James and William Thomson, and with his reputation as a philosopher of dust, profound observer, and ingenious instrument designer running high Although Aitken was happy to discourse upon the romance of dust before the ladies at a Royal Society of London *conversazione* shortly after his election, he shied away from senior office in these scientific institutions on health grounds (although, characteristically, he did hold the office of honorary president in the local Falkirk Natural History and Archaeological Society).

Aitken also received numerous distinctions, including the Gunning Victoria Jubilee Prize of the Royal Society of Edinburgh for his work in the physics of meteorology (for the period 1893–1896, awarded 1897), an honorary LLD from the University of Glasgow (1902), and a prestigious Royal Medal from the Royal Society of London in recognition of his lifelong researches on the nuclei of cloudy condensations (1917). Appropriately, he was awarded Gold Medals for his instruments, including the portable and pocket dust counters and the koniscope, when they were exhibited at the Franco-British Exhibition of 1908.

Aitken died at Ardenlea on 13 November 1919, at the age of eighty, and was buried in the Falkirk Cemetery five days later. His scientific investigations had left him unconvinced by spiritualism, impervious to T. H. Huxley's agnosticism, and religiously devout to the end. As one of Falkirk's richest citizens and a constant philanthropist and humanitarian, he left half of his estate of nearly £100,000 to his local community, establishing a "temperance café" to promote the moral improvement of local workers, and the rest as a fund for the poor of Falkirk. The Universities in Edinburgh and Glasgow shared the scientific apparatus he offered them jointly in his will. The Royal Society of Edinburgh accepted the money he left for a posthumous monument (to himself) in the form of a collection of his papers. The editor and meteorologist C. G. Knott knew well that Aitken had labored long and hard to "elucidate the workings of Nature in her everyday moods" (*Nature* [27 November 1919]: 338).

BIBLIOGRAPHY

Falkirk Council Archives has Aitken's papers, including engineering drawings, experimental notebooks, draft articles, meteorological records, and domestic records (c. 1863 until his death) in the Russel & Aitken WS Papers supplemented by Dep. 240 (formerly National Library of Scotland). Correspondence with James Clerk Maxwell, George Gabriel Stokes, Sir Joseph John Thomson, and William Thomson (Lord Kelvin) is in Add. 7655, Add. 7656, Add. 7654 and Add. 7342, respectively, in Cambridge University Library. There is an additional letter to William Thomson (Lord Kelvin) in MS Kelvin A4, Glasgow University Library. Material relating to Aitken and the Royal Scottish Society of Arts (Acc. 4534) and the Royal Society of Edinburgh are in the National Library of Scotland. The Brotherton Library at the University of Leeds has letters from Aitken and Arthur Smithells (MS 416). There is a letter to William Fletcher Barrett in Barrett's papers at the Royal Society of London. Original instruments can be found in the Royal Museum of Scotland (NMS T1983.125) and in the Science Museum, London (1908-193).

WORKS BY AITKEN

Collected Scientific Papers of John Aitken, LL.D., F.R.S. Edited by Cargill G. Knott. Cambridge, U.K.: Cambridge University Press for the Royal Society of Edinburgh, 1923. This is the key collection, with an introductory memoir superseding or synthesizing the contemporary obituaries (many of which Knott had provided). There is an extended, if incomplete and not wholly reliable, bibliography. Since Knott edited the papers extensively, it is advisable to check the originals.

OTHER SOURCES

Clarke, Tristram N., Alison D. Morrison-Low, and Allen D. C. Simpson. *Brass and Glass: Scientific Instrument Making Workshops in Scotland.* Edinburgh: National Museums of Scotland, 1989. For information on Aitken's association with

Edinburgh instrument maker William Hume, see pp. 133–137.

Galison, Peter. *Image and Logic: A Material Culture of Microphysics.* Chicago: University of Chicago Press, 1997 (esp. pp. 81–96). On cloud formation experiments, the dust chamber, mimetic experiments, meteorology and relationship with C. T. R. Wilson.

————, and Alexi Assmus. "Artificial Clouds, Real Particles." In *The Uses of Experiment: Studies in the Natural Sciences*, edited by David Gooding, Trevor Pinch, and Simon Schaffer. Cambridge, U.K., and New York: Cambridge University Press, 1989. Aitken's mimetic experiments in physics and, especially, C. T. R. Wilson.

Podzimek, Josef. "John Aitken's Contribution to Atmospheric and Aerosol Sciences: One Hundred Years of Condensation Nuclei Counting." *Bulletin of the American Meteorological Society* 70 (1989): 1538–1545.

Roy, Marjory. *The Weathermen of Ben Nevis, 1883–1904.* London: Royal Meteorological Society, 2004. On the Aitken dust counter as a meteorological instrument.

Ben Marsden

AKI, KEIITI

AKI, KEIITI (*b.* Yokohama, Japan, 3 March 1930; *d.* La Plaine des Cafres, La Réunion, France, 17 May 2005), *seismology.*

Aki was a pioneer in almost all fields of seismology. He established scaling laws for a broad range of phenomena in seismology and seismotectonics. He initiated new seismological analyses of earthquake sources and the structure and dynamics of the Earth. Linking geodynamic models and nonlinear dynamics models, he greatly furthered predictive understanding of earthquakes. His leadership in developing new research programs in seismology and his vision for integrating seismological research has been felt around the world. Aki was the "dean of the world's seismologists," in the words of Frank Press given at a party honoring Keiiti Aki in 2004.

Keiiti Aki, known as Kei, was born on 3 March 1930 in Yokohama, Japan, to a family of engineers with a hundred-year tradition of education and openness to the West. When Aki was nineteen years old, he was among the twelve students admitted to the Geophysics Department of Tokyo University. There he was taught by world-class professors, including Chuji Tsuboi, Takeshi Nagata, Takeo Matuzawa, and Koji Hidaka, and obtained his BSc and PhD degrees in geophysics in 1952 and 1958, respectively.

From 1952 to 1966 Aki was mostly at Tokyo University, though he also visited the California Institute of Technology as a research fellow. In 1966 Frank Press recruited Aki to the United States to join the faculty of the Massachusetts Institute of Technology (MIT) as a professor of geophysics. Aki became a mentor to a large number of graduate and postdoctoral students. He also spent summers working with colleagues all over the world. Thinking that students should get their hands dirty with seismic data, Aki sent many of his students to the United States Geological Survey in Menlo Park in the summers, and Aki himself also visited frequently. To be close to California earthquakes, Aki in 1984 moved to the University of Southern California, where he became that university's first W. M. Keck Foundation Professor of Geophysics. He was responsible for establishing the Southern California Earthquake Center, where his vision for integrated research on earthquakes has been practiced by scientists and engineers in many disciplines working together.

In 1995 Aki moved to La Réunion (a French island in the Indian Ocean) so that he could study its volcano firsthand. After making excellent progress in predicting volcanic eruptions, Aki returned to the problem of earthquake prediction and wrote a book-length manuscript on it in 2004. During the last five years of his life, Aki lectured annually in Japan as an advisor to the Japanese Association for the Development of Earthquake Prediction. His last project was promoting the Coda Club for collaborative research on using coda waves, which make up the late part of seismic signals, to predict earthquakes worldwide.

Aki died from a brain hemorrhage on 17 May 2005 at La Réunion, following an accidental fall. Aki had four children: sons Shota of Weare, New Hampshire, and Zenta of Redondo Beach, California, from his marriage to Haruko Uyeda; and daughters Kajika and Uka of La Réunion, with Valerie Ferrazzini.

Aki's Own View of His Work. In 2004 Kei Aki was awarded the Bowie Medal, the highest honor bestowed annually by the American Geophysical Union. At the scientific symposium celebrating this honor, Aki, in a speech introducing the symposium, presented a brief summary of his work, a summary that started and ended with earthquake prediction. He said that his first paper in 1954 employed a statistical approach and was motivated by Norbert Wiener's *Cybernetics*, published in 1948. After applying Wiener's prediction method to earthquake-catalog data (a list of origin time, hypocenter, and magnitude of earthquakes), Aki realized that the data then available were poor and that Wiener's method for a stationary linear system was too simplistic to model the physics of earthquakes. Turning to a physical approach, Aki followed two paths: deterministic modeling and stochastic modeling. The deterministic approach required simple models of earth structures and earthquake processes and was only possible for long-period waves, which averaged the complex details of structures and processes. This research started out as long-period seismology, producing useful concepts such as the seismic moment, and has grown to broad-band seismology, in which the upper limit of the applicable frequency range has been steadily extended. The stochastic-modeling approach accepts the existence of small-scale heterogeneities and tries to determine their statistical properties. While this approach cannot delimit heterogeneities in time and space, it can demonstrate their existence. Aki used this approach to study many aspects of short-period seismology.

After a career of fifty years in deterministic and stochastic modeling, Aki sought to encourage others to take a multipronged approach toward the goal of earthquake prediction. Aki took the general position that one's success in predicting a phenomenon was a measure of how well one understands it. If one can successfully predict a natural phenomenon such as earthquakes, then mitigating its hazards and saving lives becomes effective and practical.

Contributions to Seismology. Aki said that his main contribution to seismology was to have "developed a variety of interpretation methods of seismological data for delineating earth structures and dynamic processes in tectonically active regions." Realizing the inadequacy of earthquake-catalog data available in 1954 (consisting mostly of data from earthquakes with magnitude greater than 5), Aki proposed monitoring the more numerous micro-earthquakes (those with magnitude less than 3) as an important element in earthquake-prediction research. The frequency distribution of earthquakes occurring in a given area and time interval had been established by Beno Gutenberg and Charles Richter in the 1940s:

$$\log N(M) = a - bM$$

where M is the earthquake magnitude, $N(M)$ is the number of earthquakes with magnitude greater than or equal to M, and a and b are constants. Because the value of b is about 1, magnitude 2 earthquakes are about 1,000 times more frequent than magnitude 5 earthquakes. Aki's idea was subsequently incorporated into the Japanese program for earthquake prediction in the early 1960s, and hundreds of micro-earthquake networks (consisting of many closely spaced and highly sensitive seismometers), which followed the Japanese program, were established around the world. The vast amounts of data from these micro-earthquake networks led to numerous advances in seismology, many of them pioneered by Aki and his students and colleagues.

Earthquake Sources. Aki's contributions to seismology cover source, path, and site effects over the entire frequency range of seismic waves. In 1966 Aki introduced the concept of seismic moment, which quantifies earthquake size on a physical basis. This was the most significant advance since earthquake magnitude scales were introduced by Charles Richter and Beno Gutenberg in the 1930s as an empirical basis for the earthquake size. Aki realized that because a double-couple earthquake source is equivalent to a fault slip in an isotropic elastic body, the scalar value of its component is equal to the shear modulus times the fault slip integrated over the fault plane:

$$M_0 = \text{shear modulus} \times \text{average slip} \times \text{slipped area}$$

The seismic moment can be estimated from the far-field seismic spectrum, and also from the average slip and the area of the slipped surface inferred from the near-field seismic, geologic, and geodetic data. Aki demonstrated the consistency of estimating seismic moments from two separate sets of data from the 1964 earthquake in Niigata, Japan.

In 1967 Aki discovered the fundamental scaling laws for seismic spectra of earthquakes and proceeded to interpret these laws in terms of physical models. He made the first calculation of the ground motion produced by an earthquake fault, independently from Norman Haskell, and he was able to infer the characteristics of slip on the fault.

In 1977 Aki introduced the barrier model of earthquakes and, with Shamita Das, made the first theoretical and numerical investigations of dynamic earthquake rupture on heterogeneous faults. In 1972 he and Yoshiaki Ida introduced the first seismological model of what later became known as slip weakening. In 1977 he and Michel Bouchon developed the discrete-wave-number method (which allowed the full calculation of strong ground motion for kinematic models of faulting). And in 1983 he and A. S. Papageorgiou proposed a specific barrier model for quantitatively describing inhomogeneous faulting and predicting strong ground motion.

Effects of Lateral Heterogeneities on Seismic Waves. In collaboration with some of his early students, Ken L. Larner and David M. Boore, in the late 1960s and early 1970s Aki developed powerful numerical methods for computing the response of realistic earth structures to seismic shaking. These methods were subsequently expanded on by others and applied to a number of important problems in engineering seismology. With these same students, in 1971 he published one of the first papers describing the effects of soft sedimentary basins on seismic waves, demonstrating that the basin response is dominated by surface waves scattered by wave conversion at the basin margins and showing that the motion in the center of a basin can be many times larger than that expected for flat-lying layers.

Seismic Tomography from Travel Times. Realizing a dense seismic array recorded large amounts of data containing important information about the Earth, Aki pioneered travel-time tomography as a means of studying lithospheric structure beneath dense seismic arrays, and he and his collaborators published seminal papers almost a decade ahead of its widespread application to global seismology.

In the summer of 1974 Aki visited the Norwegian Seismic Array (NORSAR) at Kjeller, Norway. From his initial random-media studies, Aki expected that deterministic mapping of the Earth's heterogeneities should be feasible. The NORSAR data were an inspiration in this regard: Changes in time and amplitude across the array were clearly visible in the records. Aki synthesized many diverse developments in inverse problems (see below) and array data to produce three-dimensional imaging through ray tracing of a block model of the lithosphere and asthenosphere. Anders Christoffersson and Eystein Husebye happily joined Aki in developing this concept of tomographic imaging into a research tool (the ACH method), and they used the P-travel-time residuals of the NORSAR data and the Large Aperture Seismic Array (LASA) data as a test.

At the fall meeting of the American Geophysical Union in San Francisco in 1974, Aki related the exciting work with the NORSAR data to William H. K. Lee. Aki and Lee realized that the inversion of arrival times of local earthquakes was unique (unlike the teleseismic inversion), because the studied volume of the Earth contained both the sources (earthquake hypocenters) and receivers (stations). Therefore, they could use arrival times of local earthquakes to calculate simultaneously both earthquake hypocenters and the velocity structure beneath the seismic network. Aki then spent the summer of 1975 with Lee at the U.S. Geological Survey in Menlo Park, and they completed the extension of the ACH method of teleseismic tomography to local earthquake tomography. Several of Aki's students, notably Cliff Thurber, subsequently further advanced the ACH method. Since Aki and colleagues initiated its use in 1974–1975, seismic tomography has been further developed and/or applied by many seismologists all over the world. It has become the principal tool for mapping and understanding the structure of earth's crust and mantle.

Coda and Scattering. Aki elucidated the scattering and attenuation processes that govern the propagation of high-frequency seismic waves. In his pioneering work in 1969, Aki interpreted coda waves of local earthquakes as waves scattered by randomly distributed heterogeneities in the lithosphere. In 1975 Aki and Bernard Chouet made the first attempt to predict the explicit form of the time-dependent power spectrum of coda waves for a mathemat-

ical model of earthquake source and earth medium. In 1980 Aki developed a method for normalizing coda on the basis of the uniform spatial distribution of coda energy.

Beginning in the 1980s, measurements of coda Q and scattering coefficients were made worldwide. Aki and his colleagues (Mike Fehler, Mitsuyuki Hoshiba, Haruo Sato, Ru-shan Wu, Yuehua Zeng) developed theoretical models for the synthesis of seismogram envelopes over short periods based on radiative transfer theory. Working principally with Anshu Jin, Aki also focused on spatiotemporal changes in coda Q. In his 2004 paper, Aki proposed using coda waves for monitoring temporal changes in parameters of the medium to predict earthquake occurrence and volcanic eruption.

Quantitative Seismology. In his original research Aki covered an extremely broad range of problems in seismology. His creativity in approaching topics at the forefront of seismology was based on his skill at devising new experiments and his superb mastery of the theoretical background. This creativity is best exemplified by his two-volume treatise *Quantitative Seismology* (1980), coauthored with Paul Richards. It has set the standard for teaching seismology and doing advanced research in the field since 1980 and has been the most frequently cited book in seismology since its publication. Even as of 2006 it is required reading for advanced classes in seismology and geophysics. A second edition appeared in 2002 and was translated into Japanese by Kōji Uenishi, Nobuki Kame, and Hideo Aochi.

Fault-zone-guided Waves. In the 1990s Aki, with Yehuda Ben-Zion and Yong-gang Li, theoretically and observationally analyzed fault-zone-guided waves that result from constructive interference of critically reflected waves within low-velocity fault-zone layers. These waves can be used to obtain high-resolution information on the internal structure of fault zones, and have since been recorded and modeled in various fault zones around the world.

Volcanic Seismology. Aki also developed quantitative theory and methods for interpreting seismic signals originating from volcanoes. In 1977 Aki (with Mike Fehler and Shamita Das) proposed the first fluid-filled-crack model to explain the characteristics of volcanic tremors in Hawaii and introduced the seismic-moment rate to express the intensity of volcanic tremors at their source. In 1981 Aki and Bob Koyanagi applied this model to deep tremors at Kilauea Volcano and proposed that Kilauea receives a steady supply of magma from the mantle. Using a method of statistical analysis that Aki designed in 1957 for microseisms, Valerie Ferrazzini, Kei Aki, and Bernard Chouet in 1991 analyzed the wave field generated by the eruption of Pu'u 'Ō'ō in Hawaii and showed that the shallow eruption tremors consist primarily of fundamental modes of Rayleigh and Love waves. Since then, this method has been used on numerous volcanoes. Aki and Valerie Ferrazzini in 2000 presented a model for predicting eruptions of the Piton de la Fournaise (La Réunion Island) by integrating geological, petrological, and seismic data (such as the occurrence, duration, and dominant frequency of long-period events).

Legacy. Aki published more than 200 papers (see "Publication List of Keiiti Aki," compiled by Takashi Miyatake, in Ben-Zion and Lee, 2006), supervised more than fifty doctoral dissertations, and received many honors. Among those honors were election to the U.S. National Academy of Sciences (1979), the Medal of the Seismological Society of America (1986), the Thorarinsson Medal from the International Association of Volcanology and Chemistry of the Earth's Interior (2000), the Bowie Medal of the American Geophysical Union (2004), and the Gutenberg Medal of the European Geosciences Union (2005).

Kei Aki will be remembered not only as a brilliant seismologist and teacher but also as a cheerful friend and colleague in collaborative research. Aki was optimistic and firmly believed that if people work together, any problem can be solved. Frank Press recognized that though Aki "could have been a leader of any scientific discipline he chose to engage in, Kei selected seismology for its humanitarian potential—or simply stated, for its promise (as yet only partially fulfilled) of saving lives and mitigating tragedy" (Tributes to Kei Aki, 2004).

BIBLIOGRAPHY

The 1964 Niigata Earthquake Archive at the IRIS Data Management Center (USA) was established in honor of Kei Aki in 2004 (available from http://www.iris.edu/seismo/quakes/1964niigata/). This archive serves as an online Web site for Aki, so that his many contributions and related materials can be posted for free access. The Web site includes a collection of personal tributes to Kei in 2004 and reveals aspects of Kei that are not captured in more formal publications. A list of these formal publications has been compiled by Takashi Miyatake, "Publication List of Keiiti Aki," in Advances on Studies of Heterogeneities in the Earth's Lithosphere, *edited by Yehuda Ben-Zion and William H. K. Lee (Boston: Birkhäuser: 2006).*

WORKS BY AKI

"Generation and Propagation of G Waves from the Niigata Earthquake of June 16, 1964, Part 2: Estimation of Earthquake Moment, Released Energy, and Stress-Strain Drop from the G Wave Spectrum." *Bulletin of Earthquake Research. Institute* 44 (1966): 73–88.

"Scaling Law of Seismic Spectrum." *Journal of Geophysical Research* 72 (1967): 1217–1231.

With David M. Boore and Ken L. Larner. "Comparison of Two Independent Methods for the Solution of Wave-Scattering Problems: Response of a Sedimentary Basin to Vertically Incident *SH* Waves." *Journal of Geophysical Research* 76 (1971): 558–569.

With Yoshiaki Ida. "Seismic Source Time Function of Propagating Longitudinal Shear Cracks." *Journal of Geophysical Research* 77 (1972): 2034–2044.

With Bernard Chouet. "Origin of Coda Waves: Source, Attenuation, and Scattering Effects." *Journal of Geophysical Research* 80 (1975): 3322–3342.

With William H. K. Lee. "Determination of Three-Dimensional Velocity Anomalies under a Seismic Array using First P Arrival Times from Local Earthquakes, 1. A Homogeneous Initial Model." *Journal of Geophysical Research* 81 (1976): 4381–4399.

With Michel Bouchon. "Near-Field of a Seismic Source in a Layered Medium with Irregular Interface." *Geophysical Journal of Royal Astronomical Society* 50 (1977): 669–684.

With Anders Christoffersson and Eystein S. Husebye. "Determination of the Three-Dimensional Seismic Structure of the Lithosphere." *Journal of Geophysical Research* 82 (1977): 277–296.

With Shamita Das. "Fault Plane with Barriers: A Versatile Earthquake Model." *Journal of Geophysical Research* 82 (1977): 565–570.

With Paul G. Richards. *Quantitative Seismology: Theory and Methods.* 2 vols. San Francisco: Freeman, 1980. 2nd ed., Sausalito: University of Science Books, 2002.

With Robert Koyanagi. "Deep Volcanic Tremor and Magma Ascent Mechanism under Kilauea, Hawaii." *Journal of Geophysical Research* 86 (1981): 7095–7109.

With Apostolos S. Papageorgiou. "A Specific Barrier Model for the Quantitative Description of Inhomogeneous Faulting and Prediction of Strong Ground Motion, Part I and II." *Bulletin, Seismological Society of America* 73 (1983): 693–722, and 953–978.

With Valerie Ferrazzini and Bernard Chouet. "Characteristics of Seismic Waves Composing Hawaiian Volcanic Tremors and Gas Piston Events Observed by a Near-Source Array." *Journal of Geophysical Research* 96 (1991): 6199–6214.

With Valerie Ferrazzini. "Seismic Monitoring and Modeling of an Active Volcano for Prediction." *Journal of Geophysical Research* 105 (2000): 16,617–16,640.

"Synthesis of Earthquake Science Information and Its Public Transfer: A History of the Southern California Earthquake Center." In *International Handbook of Earthquake and Engineering Seismology,* edited by William H. K. Lee, Hiroo Kanamori, Paul C. Jennings, and Carl Kisslinger, Part A. San Diego, CA: Academic Press, 2002.

"A New View of Earthquake and Volcano Precursors." *Earth Planetary Space* 56, no. 8 (2004): 689–713.

OTHER SOURCES

Ben-Zion, Yehuda, ed. *Seismic Motions, Lithospheric Structures, Earthquake and Volcanic Sources.* Boston: Birkhäuser, 2003.

———, and William H. K. Lee, eds. *Advances on Studies of Heterogeneities in the Earth's Lithosphere.* Boston: Birkhäuser, 2006.

Lee, William H. K., comp. "A Collection of Tributes to Kei Aki, December 16, 2004, San Francisco." Available from http://www.iris.edu/seismo/quakes/1964niigata/, 2004.

Richards, Paul G. "In Memoriam—Keiiti Aki (1930–2005)." *Seismological Research Letters* 76 (2005): 551–553.

William H. K. Lee

AL-SHĪRĀZĪ, QUṬB AL-DĪN

SEE **Quṭb al-Dīn Maḥmūd ibn Masʿūd ibn al-Muṣliḥ al-Shīrāzī**.

ALBERT OF SAXONY

ALBERT OF SAXONY (*b.* Helmstedt, Lower Saxony, c. 1320; *d.* Halberstadt, Saxony, 8 July 1390), *physics, logic, mathematics.* For the original article on Albert of Saxony see *DSB,* vol. 1.

Recent research has revealed more information about Albert's life and writings. For example, although his contributions to natural philosophy reflected his reading of John Buridan and Nicole Oresme, they also contained many original elements.

Biographical Information. Albert of Saxony's name appears for the first time in the records in 1351, when he obtained the degree of master of arts at the University of Paris under master Albert of Bohemia. This date implies that he must have been in Paris at the end of 1350. He was probably born in 1320 (not in 1316, as has been traditionally assumed). It is very unlikely that Albert studied at the University of Prague before moving to Paris. The university in Prague was only founded in 1349, and the curricular requirements at Prague and at Paris exclude such a transition. Although there are no records, it is more likely that Albert would have received his early training at schools in his diocese, at Halberstadt or Magdeburg, and then moved to the *studium generale* of Erfurt. Only one work, if it is authentic, dates from the pre-Paris period, the *Philosophia pauperum,* which has references to Erfurt.

Once in Paris, Albert became involved in administrative duties for the English-German nation to which he belonged, and for the entire arts faculty. He was proctor, examiner, receptor, and in 1353 rector. In 1352 and 1355, he was one of the members of the committee who prepared the list of applications for papal benefices for university masters (*rotulus*).

In addition to these administrative duties, Albert was chiefly concerned with teaching and writing. The univer-

King Albert of Saxony. *King Albert of Saxony in full military regalia. Circa 1892.* **HULTON ARCHIVE/GETTY IMAGES.**

sity records show the names of approximately forty students who obtained their master's degree under Albert. His more than twenty writings, which cover logic and natural philosophy, but also ethics, are usually in the literary format of commentaries on Aristotle, and all originated at Paris. In addition, he started his study in theology as early as 1353 but he never finished, and there are no writings in this discipline.

Probably in 1361 Albert left Paris. The period 1362–1364 in Albert's career is blank, but the two letters that bind this period indicate that he was busy at Avignon for Pope Urban V and in Vienna at the court of Duke Rudolph IV. He was involved in the founding of the University of Vienna in 1365, and became its first rector. Because of the death of Duke Rudolph IV, and the ensuing rivalry between his two brothers, the university did not flourish and had only a faculty of arts. The university was reestablished in 1383–1384. Albert of Saxony left Vienna within a year, to become bishop of Halberstadt in 1366. He remained bishop until his death on 8 July 1390.

Writings on Natural Philosophy. Although several works by Albert of Saxony have been edited since the original *DSB* article, it is not possible yet to place his thought within its fourteenth-century context. It seems clear, however, that the assessment in the original *DSB* article that Albert of Saxony depended heavily on the works by Buridan, and lacked originality, needs to be revised. In the past, Albert of Saxony, together with Oresme and a few other Parsian thinkers, has been perceived as a proponent of the Buridan school, with all the connotations that this label may have, such as that of student-teacher relationships, and a unified homogeneous school of thought. Closer examination of the doctrines and dating of texts has replaced this picture of the Buridan school with that of a small intellectual network of nearly contemporary masters of arts, who were familiar with each others' work and at times responded to one another.

Albert of Saxony's most important work in logic is his *Perutilis logica* (Very useful logic), written around 1356. It is a handbook in logic, organized into six treatises. It covers all the basics of medieval logic, such as propositions, properties of terms, consequences, fallacies, insolubles, and obligations. Although the influence of William of Ockham is discernible, it is an independent treatise with its own original twists. Albert distances himself in many respects from Buridan's logic. Another logical work from about the same period is the *Quaestiones circa logicam* (Questions on Logic). This is a set of disputed questions about the signification of terms, reference, and truth. The *Sophismata*, a set of propositions whose interpretation raises semantic problems because of the presence of certain logical terms, shows the influence of William of Heytesbury. Albert's solutions to the semantic difficulties rely on Heytesbury's theory of *sensus divisus* and *compositus*, that is, the position and scope of modal operators in propositions.

One of Albert's most important works in natural philosophy is his *Quaestiones super libros Physicorum*, a question-commentary on Aristotle's *Physics*. It raises many of the problems that are also raised in Buridan's question-commentary. The relation between the two works, however, is more complex than was initially thought. It is clear in the early 2000s that Albert of Saxony had access to a previous version of Buridan's question-commentary on the *Physics*, the so-called *tertia lectura*. In his final version of the question-commentary on the *Physics*, Buridan responded to Albert of Saxony. In other words, Albert's *Quaestiones* on the *Physics* are chronologically located between Buridan's *tertia lectura* and his *ultima lectura*. Albert of Saxony's *Quaestiones super libros Physicorum* are usually dated shortly after 1351. This date is suggested by one of its copies, whose introductory remarks tie the text to Albert's opening lecture (*principium*) on Aristotle's *Physics*, which was held in 1351. This does not imply, however, that the entire commentary was finished by that time. The most plausible conclusion is that the work must

have been finished sometime between 1352 and 1357, before Buridan's ultimate question-commentary.

Buridan and Albert of Saxony held opposing views about the ontological status of spatial extension. In general, medieval thinkers believed that spatial extension belonged in the category of quantity, and that some substances, such as bodies, have extension as their most important feature. However, not only the substance of body, but also many of its qualities were considered to be extended. The dimensions of Socrates's whiteness, for instance, were believed to coincide with Socrates himself, that is, with substance. But is it really accurate to equate quantity with substance and quality, respectively, or should quantity be considered a separate entity? Buridan held the latter view. One of the many arguments in support of this position hinges on the phenomenon of condensation and rarefaction. Experience teaches that the extension or quantity of a given substance can vary, whereas the amount; of substance and its quality remain constant: no new parts of substance are added, nor any destroyed (in contrast to the phenomena of growth and diminution). Albert of Saxony defended the position that extension or quantity coincides with substance. He attributes condensation and rarefaction to the local motion of the parts, which supposedly have some kind of elasticity.

On the question of the ontological status of motion, Albert follows the view of Ockham that motion is not something different from the moving body. However, on the basis of an argument involving God's supernatural interference, he concludes that motion is an inherent flux in a moving body. In other words, motion is a distinct property of a body, a position Buridan also defended.

In his discussion of projectile motion, Albert qualifies Buridan's view as the truest view (*quam pro nunc reputo veriorem*). It attributes the projectile's motion to a certain motive force, a *virtus motiva* or *virtus impressa*, an impressed power. Albert does not use the term *impetus*. Buridan introduced this new term only in his last version of his question-commentary on the *Physics*, which Albert did not know. Albert interprets Aristotle's views with respect to motion and velocity, in *Physics* book 7, in accordance with Bradwardine's rules. In an effort to solve the apparent contradictions between Bradwardine's approach and Aristotle's text, Albert states that Aristotle's text has probably been mistranslated.

Albert's discussion of the void shows striking similarities to that by Oresme. He must have known Oresme's *Physics*. Albert's well-organized question-commentary on Aristotle's *De caelo* provides further evidence of his thoughtful and independent approach to contemporary issues in natural philosophy. Albert includes many questions that had been raised by both Oresme and Buridan, but approximately one-third of Albert's fifty-six questions do not appear in the *De caelo* questions of Oresme and Buridan. Also noteworthy is that, unlike almost all other scholastic natural philosophers, Albert grouped related questions together under three major themes. This broke with the traditional way of organizing questions by simply following Aristotle's text.

What emerges from these varied examples is that Albert of Saxony was not a plagiarizer, but rather that he was well versed in the works of some of his contemporaries and used them in his own philosophical endeavors.

SUPPLEMENTARY BIBLIOGRAPHY

A survey of all of Albert of Saxony's works and the known manuscript sources is provided in Jürgen Sarnowsky, Die aristotelisch-scholastische Theorie der Bewegung *(see below). See further Olga Weijers,* Le travail intellectuel à la faculté des arts de Paris: Textes et maîtres (ca. 1200–1250), *vol. 1 (Turnhout, Belgium: Brepols, 1994); also the extremely useful bibliographical guide by Harald Berger, "Albert von Sachsen (1316?–1390): Bibliographie der Sekundärliteratur" and its supplements (see below).*

WORKS BY ALBERT OF SAXONY

Muñoz García, Angel. *Perutilis logica, o, Lógica muy útil (o utilísima).* México: Universidad Nacional Autónoma de México, 1988. Provides a transcription (and a Spanish translation) of the incunabular edition (Venice 1522) of Albert's logical handbook.

Kann, Christoph. *Die Eigenschaften der Termini: Eine Untersuchung zur "Perutilis Logica" des Alberts von Sachsen.* New York: Brill, 1994. Includes an edition of treatise two of the *Perutilis logica.*

Patar, Benoît. *Expositio et Quaestiones in Aristotelis libros Physicorum ad Albertum de Saxonia attributae.* 3 vols. Louvain: Editions Peeters, 1999. The authenticity of this question-commentary by Albert of Saxony has never been doubted, except by this editor. He believes that the text is the first version of the commentary by John Buridan, but his thesis is not supported by textual or paleographical evidence.

Fitzgerald, Michael J. *Albert of Saxony's Twenty-Five Disputed Questions on Logic.* Leiden: Brill, 2002. Provides a critical edition of a set of logical disputations, the so-called *Quaestiones circa logicam.*

OTHER SOURCES

Berger, Harald. "Albert von Sachsen (1316?–1390): Bibliographie der Sekundärliteratur." *Bulletin de Philosophie Médiévale* 36 (1994): 148–185.

———. "Fortsetzung und Ergänzungen zur Bibliographie der Sekundärliteratur." *Bulletin de Philosophie Médiévale* 37 (1995): 175–186.

———. "Albert von Sachsen (+1390): 2. Fortsetzung und Ergänzungen zur Bibliographie der Sekundärliteratur." *Bulletin de Philosophie Médiévale* 38 (1996): 143–152.

———. "Albert von Sachsen (+1390): 3. Fortsetzung und Ergänzungen zur Bibliographie der Sekundärliteratur." *Bulletin de Philosophie Médiévale* 40 (1998): 103–116.

———. "Albert von Sachsen (+1390): 4. Fortsetzung und Ergänzungen zur Bibliographie der Sekundärliteratur" *Acta Mediaevalia* 17 (2004): 253–279.

Biard, Joël. "Les sophismes du savoir: Albert de Saxe entre Jean Buridan et Guillaume Heytesbury." *Vivarium* 27 (1989): 36–50.

———, ed. *Itinéraires d'Albert de Saxe, Paris-Vienne au XIVe siècle: Actes du colloque organisé le 19–22 juin 1990 dans le cadre des activités de l'URA 1085 du CNRS à l'occasion du 600e anniversaire de la mort d'Albert de Saxe.* Paris: Vrin, 1991.

Grant, Edward. "The Unusual Structure and Organization of Albert of Saxony's *Questions on De caelo.*" In *Itinéraires d'Albert de Saxe, Paris-Vienne au XIVe siècle,* edited by Joël Biard. Paris: Vrin, 1991.

Sarnowsky, Jürgen. *Die aristotelisch-scholastische Theorie der Bewegung: Studien zum Kommentar Alberts von Sachsen zur Physik des Aristoteles.* Münster: Aschendorff, 1989. The most fundamental monograph on Albert of Saxony's physics to date.

———. "Place and Space in Albert of Saxony's Commentaries on the *Physics.*" *Arabic Sciences and Philosophy* 9 (1999): 25–45.

———. "Nicole Oresme and Albert of Saxony's Commentary on the Physics: The Problems of Vacuum and Motion in a Void." In *Quia inter doctores est magna dissensio: Les débats de philosophie naturelle à Paris au XIVe siècle,* edited by Stefano Caroti and J. Celeyerette. Florence, Italy: Olschki, 2004.

Thijssen, J. M. M. H. "The Buridan School Reassessed: John Buridan and Albert of Saxony." *Vivarium* 42, no. 1 (2004): 18–42.

Johannes M. M. H. Thijssen

ALBERT THE GREAT
SEE **Albertus Magnus, Saint**.

ALBERTUS MAGNUS, SAINT (also known as Albert the Great, A. de Lauging, A. Teutonicus, A. Coloniensis, Doctor Universalis) (*b.* Lauingen, Bavaria, c. 1200; *d.* Cologne, Prussia, 15 November 1280), *theology, moral philosophy, natural philosophy.*

For some time now, historical research has underestimated Albertus Magnus's originality and significance in terms of intellectual history. He has not been considered an independent thinker, but rather has been viewed as a precursor of his disciple, Thomas Aquinas. More recent research challenges this antiquated stereotype, proving that he was a rigorously systematic thinker and the originator of a theologically based system of scientific explication that covers the entire scope of reality as conceived conceptually and experienced empirically. His outstanding contribution to the history of science was the introduction of Aristotelian philosophy into scientific reflection throughout the Latin West, as well as the delimitation of secular science from theology. He was one of the first medieval thinkers to justify both philosophy and the nontheological scientific disciplines on the one hand, and theology on the other hand, with a view to the conception of science contained in Aristotle's *Posterior Analytics*. In doing so, he treated each of them with respect to their subjects, principles, methods, as well as objectives and identified them as autonomous sciences in the strict sense of the word.

Life. Albertus Magnus was born around 1200 in the Swabian town of Lauingen on the Danube, the son of a family of knights or *ministeriales*. His childhood remains obscure, with the exception of a few reminiscences in his works dating from this time. From about 1222 onward, he was studying in North Italy, probably Padua, where he acquired his initial basic knowledge of Aristotle's writings on the philosophy of nature. There he met Jordan of Saxony in 1223, the master-general of the Dominican order, who recruited him to join the Order of Preachers. Following the novitiate and the basic studies in theology at Cologne, in the late 1220s or early 1230s, he was entrusted with teaching duties at houses of study run by the Teutonia, the Dominicans' German province, in Hildesheim, Freiburg in Breisgau, Regensburg, and Strasbourg. In the early 1240s, the order's master-general, Johannes of Wildeshausen, sent him to Paris to obtain a doctorate in theology. From 1245 until the summer of 1248, he held one of the Dominican chairs at the University of Paris. Commissioned in 1248 with the establishment and operation of the Dominicans' *studium generale* (general house of studies) in Cologne by the order's general chapter, he traveled there together with his student, Thomas Aquinas. From 1254 to 1257, he was provincial of the order's province of Teutonia. In 1256 he spent time at the Papal Curia in Anagni, where he defended the mendicant orders against the attacks of the secular clergy and took a position on the heterodox teachings of monopsychism and astral determinism.

The years 1257 to 1260 saw him once again teaching at the *studium generale* in Cologne. On 5 January 1260, Pope Alexander IV installed him as bishop of Regensburg. Despite the objection raised by the Dominican master-general, Humbert of Roman, Albert obeyed the pope's will and assumed the bishopric, though resigning the episcopal see one year later—after the death of Alexander IV in 1261. From 1261 to 1263, he was working as a private tutor at the papal curia in Viterbo and Orvieto. Pope Urban IV appointed him papal legate, preaching the crusade in Germany, Bohemia, and throughout the German-

Saint Albertus Magnus. © BETTMANN/CORBIS.

speaking area. Supported by the Franciscan preacher Berthold of Regensburg, he carried this assignment out only until Urban IV's death on 2 October 1264. From 1264 to 1269, he lectured at the Dominican houses of study in Würzburg and Strasbourg.

Following the wish of the master-general, Johannes of Vercelli, he proceeded to Cologne, arbitrating between the archbishop, Engelbert of Falkenburg (1261–1274), and the citizenry of Cologne. He remained loyal to the city until his death. Despite diminishing strength and progressively deteriorating eyesight, he continued to be active in a variety of fields, among other things on behalf of the pope and King Rudolf of Habsburg. His alleged participation in the Council of Lyons in 1274 and a journey to Paris for the purpose of defending the teachings of his student, Thomas Aquinas, against condemnation are not historically documented and are rather doubtful, not least of all due to his advanced age. He passed away on 15 November 1280 at the Dominican convent in Cologne and was interred in the convent church. Because of the abolition of the monastery under Napoléon Bonaparte and the closure of the church in 1802, his grave was relocated to St. Andreas Church where it remains to this day. In 1931 Albert was canonized and made *doctor ecclesiae* (teacher of the church) by Pope Pius XI. In 1941 Pope Pius XII declared him the patron saint of those pursuing the natural sciences.

Work. Albert was involved in almost all areas of contemporary science and left to posterity an extensive literary work. This oeuvre may be classified in three groups: (1) the theological works, (2) the philosophical treatises, and (3) occasional writings.

The writings included in first category cover the entire sphere of systematic, biblical, and practical theology. Among them—apart from the moral-theological first work, *De natura boni,* the first three-part draft of the commentary on the sentences (*De sacramentis, De incarnatione,* and *De resurrectione*), the two-part *Summa de creaturis,* and the *Summa de bono*—are, above all, the commentary on the sentences itself and the commentary on the *Corpus Dionysiacum,* that is, on the mystical theology of the Christian Neoplatonist, Pseudo-Dionysius Areopagita. The last-mentioned theological work, characterized by Neoplatonic thought, stands out by virtue of its richness in content and originality, as well as the systematic significance it occupies within Albert's complete works and the thinking of the *Doctor Universalis.* In addition, close to thirty theological treatises (*Quaestiones*) have come down, written in Paris and Cologne. From his creative period in Paris, four university sermons are extant. A major part of Albertus Magnus's theological writings is composed of the commentaries on the Holy Scriptures of the Old and New Testaments. His late writings include two works on theological systematics and one exegetic commentary, the *Summa theologiae sive de mirabili scientia dei* I–II, a two-part explanation of the mass liturgy and the sacrament of the Eucharist, *Super missam* and *De corpore domini,* as well as the *Commentary on Job.*

The second class of writings encompasses the philosophical works, whose core elements are considered the commentaries on the *Corpus Aristotelicum,* that is, on all of Aristotle's writings available in Latin translation at the time, in addition to other works attributed to Aristotle. Apart from the commentaries, this category also encompasses original works of Albert himself that close any gaps in Aristotle's scientific edifice. Even prior to introducing at Cologne's *studium generale,* his philosophical project of commentating all of Aristotle's writings and subsequently putting it into practice, he was holding lectures there on the *Nicomachean Ethics* from 1250 to 1252. These lectures comprise the first of Albert's two *Ethics* commentaries and the first commentary ever composed in the Latin West on the entirety of this Aristotelian work. In this work, Albert presents his interpretation of Aristotle's philosophical

ethics in the form of a literal exposition with questions. Making a strict methodical distinction between philosophical ethics and theological moral doctrine and between the philosophical and theological order of science and understanding, the tract appeared in print for the first time in the years 1968 to 1972 (Books I–V) and 1987 (Books VI–X).

After interpreting the *Nicomachean Ethics,* Albert set about working on his large-scale philosophical project of commentating (and supplementing) the Aristotelian body of writings, including some pseudepigraphic works that were attributed to Aristotle. He introduced his program at the beginning of the commentary on the *Physics,* justifying it on the one hand with the demands of a solid study of the natural sciences based on a secure foundation, and on the other hand with the request on this score made repeatedly over many years to him by his cobrethren. As a guiding principle for the planning and realization of his project, he used the Platonic-Aristotelian division of philosophy that he had adapted, which distinguishes *philosophia realis* (natural philosophy, mathematics, and metaphysics) from *philosophia moralis* (moral philosophy) and *philosophia rationalis* (logic).

Achievements. In carrying out his Aristotle project, Albert on the one hand rendered the philosophical and scientific teachings in the Stagirite's works intelligible to Latin speakers, demonstrating that they did not pose a threat to the Christian-oriented worldview and way of thinking but instead offered great benefits. On the other hand, he considerably extended the Aristotelian system of science and the knowledge potential it freed. He accomplished this by critical examination, constructive combination, and the assimilation of previous insights in the field of the philosophical and exact sciences as derived from various sources, namely from the Greek, Islamic-Arabian, Jewish, and Latin cultural regions, and as characterized by different philosophical systematics. Particularly noteworthy are the field of anthropology—especially the theory of intellect, in which he expounds his doctrine of the possibility of an intellectual and moral perfection of human beings—and the disciplines relating to the philosophy of nature and natural sciences such as mineralogy, botany, and zoology; the mathematical area including geometrical perspective and geometry; and, not least, metaphysics as the philosophy of being and *first* philosophy, in other words, the philosophical fundamental science par excellence. In all of the fields mentioned, Albert critically consolidated the previous knowledge he encountered and used it for the benefit of both contemporaries and subsequent generations.

The last section of Albert's works is composed of occasional writings, by means of which he expressed his opinion on urgent topical issues relating to the doctrine as well as questions of legal practice and everyday life. He authored them by order or request of superiors or friends, revealing Albert virtually in the role of a consultant. Among these tracts are the short works "On the Unity of the Intellect" (*De unitate intellectus*) and "On Fate" (*De fato*), representing the written reports of Albert's public statements at the Papal Curia in Anagni about the heterodox teachings of the Arabic philosophers on monopsychism and determinism.

The peculiarity of Albert's thinking stems from its ontotheological foundation and holistic approach. His work and thinking, founded on theology, are univeralist in character and limited neither to one particular aspect of reality nor to one specific mode of its examination and explanation. Their significance cannot be attributed merely to their relevance in terms of the history of philosophy, as most researchers still assume, for they exceed the field of philosophy and theoretical sciences by far and display a more comprehensive, theologically based dimension of intellectual history. Any acknowledgment of Albert's life's work has to take into consideration this specific way of thinking and his way of life as well, with the latter indeed helping to explain this way of thinking. The theological foundation and structure of his thinking prove to be the hermeneutic key to the Albertan system of a holistic interpretation that confronts the demands of scientific investigation in its fullest form and consequence and lives up to these demands; it constitutes an interpretation of the whole of reality, both as it is understood conceptually and as it is experienced. If one were to reduce this system to its philosophical content, it would be, in terms of philosophical systematics, eclectic, inconsistent, and in the final analysis incomprehensible.

BIBLIOGRAPHY

WORKS BY ALBERTUS MAGNUS

Alberti Magni Opera Omnia. Edited by Albertus-Magnus-Institut. Münster, Germany: Aschendorff Verlag, 1951–. Many recent volumes.

Die Werke des Albertus in ihrer handschriftlichen Überlieferung. Teil I: *Die echten Werke.* Edited by Winfried Fauser. *Alberti Magni Opera Omnia.* Tomus subsidiarius, vol. 1. Münster, Germany: Aschendorff, 1982. Works transmitted in manuscript form.

"Albertus-Magnus-Handschriften. 1.(–4.) Fortsetzung." Edited by Winfried Fauser. *Bulletin de Philosophie Médiévale* 24 (1982): 115–129; 25 (1983): 100–120; 26 (1984): 127–151; 27 (1985): 110–151. Works transmitted in manuscript form.

De animalibus, XXII–XXVI. Translated by James J. Scanlan. *Albert the Great. Man and the Beasts. (De animalibus, Books 22–26).* Medieval & Renaissance Texts & Studies, vol. 47. Binghamton, NY: Center for Medieval and Early Renaissance Studies, 1987.

Commentary on Dionysius' Mystical Theology. Translated, edited, and introduced by Simon Tugwell. *Albert & Thomas: Selected Writings.* New York: Paulist Press, 1988. 1–129 (Preface); 131–198 (Transl.).

De animalibus. Translated and annotated by Kenneth F. Kitchell and Irven M. Resnick. *On Animals: A Medieval Summa Zoologica.* 2 vols. Baltimore, MD, and London: Johns Hopkins University Press, 1999.

Super Euclidem, Lib. I, translated by Anthony Lo Bello. *The Commentary of Albertus Magnus on Book 1 of Euclid's Elements of Geometry.* Ancient Mediterranean and Medieval Texts and Contexts. Medieval Philosophy, Mathematics, and Science, vol. 3. Boston and Leiden, Netherlands: Brill, 2003.

OTHER SOURCES

Anzulewicz, Henryk. "Neuere Forschung zu Albertus Magnus. Bestandsaufnahme und Problemstellungen." *Recherches de Théologie et Philosophie médiévales* 66 (1999): 163–206. An overview of research.

———. "Die Denkstruktur des Albertus Magnus. Ihre Dekodierung und ihre Relevanz für die Begrifflichkeit und Terminologie." In *L'élaboration du vocabulaire philosophique au Moyen Âge,* edited by Jacqueline Hamesse and Carlos Steel, 369–396. Rencontres de Philosophie Médiévale, vol. 8. Turnhout, Belgium: Brepols, 2000.

———. "Zur kritischen Ausgabe der Werke des Albertus Magnus." *Anuario de Historia de la Iglesia* 11 (2002): 417–422. A report on the editorial project.

———. "Albertus Magnus (um 1200–1280) im Licht der neueren Forschung." *Archiv für mittelalterliche Philosophie und Kultur* 10 (2004): 52–96.

Craemer-Ruegenberg, Ingrid. *Albertus Magnus.* Dominikanische Quellen und Zeugnisse, vol. 7, edited by Henryk Anzulewicz, Leipzig, Germany: Benno Verlag, 2005. Bibliography, pp. 188–215.

Honnefelder, Ludger, and Mechthild Dreyer, eds. *Albertus Magnus und die Editio Coloniensis.* Lectio Albertina, vol. 1. Münster, Germany: Aschendorff, 1999.

———, et al., eds. *Albertus Magnus und die Anfänge der Aristoteles-Rezeption im lateinischen Mittelalter* [Albertus Magnus and the beginnings of the medieval reception of Aristotle in the Latin West]. Subsidia Albertina, vol. 1. Münster, Germany: Aschendorff, 2005.

Hossfed, Paul. "Albertus Magnus." In *Klassiker der Naturphilosophie. Von den Vorsokratikern bis zur Kopenhagener Schule,* edited by Gernot Böhme, 74–85. Munich, Germany: Verlag C. H. Beck, 1989.

Libera, Alain de. *Métaphysique et noétique: Albert le Grand.* Paris: J. Vrin, 2005.

Meyer, Gerbert, Albert Zimmermann, and Paul-Bernd Lütringhausen, eds. *Albertus Magnus Doctor universalis 1280/1980.* Walberberger Studien. Philosophische Reihe, vol. 6. Mainz, Germany: Matthias-Grünewald-Verlag, 1980.

Resnick, Irven M., and Kenneth F. Kitchell Jr. *Albert the Great: A Selectively Annotated Bibliography (1900–2000).* Medieval and Renaissance Texts and Studies, vol. 269. Tempe: Arizona Center for Medieval and Renaissance Studies, 2004.

Senner, Walter, et al., eds. *Albertus Magnus. Zum Gedenken nach 800 Jahren: Neue Zugänge, Aspekte und Perspektiven.* Quellen und Forschungen zur Geschichte des Dominikanerordens, NF vol. 10. Berlin: Akademie Verlag, 2001.

Weisheipl, James A., ed. *Albertus Magnus and the Sciences: Commemorative Essays 1980.* Studies and Texts, vol. 49. Toronto: Pontifical Institute of Mediaeval Studies, 1980.

Henryk Anzulewicz

ALEMBERT, JEAN LE ROND D'

SEE **d'Alembert, Jean**.

ALFVÉN, HANNES OLOF GOSTA (*b.* Norrkorping, Sweden, 30 May 1908; *d.* Stockholm, Sweden, 2 April 1995), *physics, plasma state of matter, magnetohydrodynamics, plasma cosmogony, plasma cosmology.*

Alfvén, winner of the 1970 Nobel Prize in Physics, is acknowledged as one of the greatest creative and intuitive intellects of the twentieth century. Alfvén made contributions to physics that are being applied in the early twenty-first century in the development of particle beam accelerators, controlled thermonuclear fusion, hypersonic flight, rocket propulsion, and the braking of reentering space vehicles. Applications of his research in space science include explanations of the Van Allen radiation belt, the reduction of Earth's magnetic field during magnetic storms, the magnetosphere (a protective plasma envelope surrounding Earth), the formation of comet tails, the formation of the solar system, the dynamics of plasmas in the Earth's galaxy, and the fundamental nature of the universe itself.

Alfvén played a central role in the development of several modern fields of physics, including plasma physics, the physics of charged particle beams, and interplanetary and magnetospheric physics. He is also regarded as the founder of the branch of plasma physics known as magnetohydrodynamics. The number of concepts bearing his name indicates the significance of his contributions to science: Alfvén waves, Alfvén number, Alfvén layer, Alfvén velocity, and so on. He also made important contributions in which his role as originator was not widely known for many years. In 1963, for example, he was the first to assert the large-scale filamentary structure of the universe.

Early Life and Education. Alfvén came from a family of high achievers. His father, Johannes Alfvén, was a physician, as was his mother, Anna-Clara Romanus Alfvén (a pioneer in her own right, being one of the first female physicians in Sweden), and his uncle, Hugo Alfvén, was a famous composer. Two childhood experiences had a significant influence on his intellectual development and scientific career. One was the gift of a popular book on astronomy by Camille Flammarion, which kindled his lifetime fascination with astronomy and astrophysics. The other was the school's radio club, in which he was an active member, building radio receivers and learning first-hand how radio waves behave within Earth's varying ionospheric plasma. These interests led to his study at the University of Uppsala, where he specialized in mathematics and experimental and theoretical physics, and where he received his doctor's degree in 1934. His thesis was titled "Investigations of the Ultra-short Electromagnetic Waves."

Royal Institute of Technology. In 1934 Alfvén became a member of the Nobel Institute for Physics in Stockholm, and in 1940, at age thirty-two, he became professor of electromagnetic theory and electrical measurements at the Royal Institute of Technology in Stockholm. There in 1945 he was elected to a newly created chair of electronics, which became chair of plasma physics in 1963. At this time Alfvén's research dealt with the properties of high-voltage phenomena.

Sweden utilized long-distance, high-voltage direct current (DC) electrical power lines in order to increase its power capacity and minimize transmission losses from its hydroelectric generators in the north to the industrial south. One attribute of the DC system is the reduced cost of construction. However, a shortcoming of high-voltage DC lines occurs at the substation, where corona discharges cause the porcelain insulators to break down. By chance, such a substation was clearly visible from the window of Alfvén's laboratory. Alfvén set his energies to the task of resolving this problem and, in the process proposed what was to become a much studied phenomenon of plasma physics: "double layers," regions of strong electric fields parallel to the local magnetic field in the rarefied plasma of space. Earlier, the Nobel chemist Irving Langmuir had discovered the tendency for plasmas to set barriers, or "cells," within itself which Langmuir called cathode or double sheaths. It was the application of this new particle-accelerating mechanism and the t____ for plasma to form sheaths, cells, and current filaments that led Alfvén into the world that came to be called space and cosmic plasmas, the environmental space surrounding planetary probes and Earth orbiting satellites.

Alfvén's approach to physics was based on insight and intuition. He was quick to understand how nature works and was able to place new observations into a framework larger than that required for merely explaining the observations themselves. For example, in the early 1930s it was commonly thought that the cosmic rays filling the universe were gamma rays. However, when it was discovered in 1937 that they were charged particles, Alfvén offered the unique suggestion that the galaxy contained a large-scale magnetic field and that the cosmic rays moved in spiral orbits within the galaxy because of the forces brought to bear by the magnetic field. He stated that if plasma was spread throughout the galaxy, the latter could be completely permeated by a magnetic field. This plasma could carry the electrical currents that would then generate the galactic magnetic field.

Such a hypothesis, based on a great leap of creative intuition but without grounding in apparent rational thought or inference, left Alfvén's proposal open to much criticism because, at the time, interstellar space was thought to be a vacuum incapable of supporting the electrical currents and particle beams he was proposing. But Alfvén had got the scientific community thinking about an idea that would be very much in vogue in the 1980s and 1990s.

Alfvén Waves. Alfvén's discovery of hydromagnetic waves in 1942 is another instance of an original idea having a far-reaching impact on multidisciplinary science. On strictly physical grounds, Alfvén concluded that an electromagnetic wave could spread through a highly conducting medium, such as the ionized gas of the sun, or in plasmas anywhere. Generally, it was thought that electromagnetic waves could penetrate only a very short distance into a conductor and that, as the resistance of a conductor became smaller and smaller, the depth of penetration by an electromagnetic wave would go to zero. Thus, with an ideal electrical conductor, there could be no penetration of electromagnetic radiation. But Alfvén was proposing a form of electromagnetic wave that could propagate in a perfect conductor with no attenuation or reflection.

His work was not acknowledged as both correct and important until 1948, when he gave lectures on hydrodynamic waves while on his first trip to the United States. Alex Dessler, professor at the University of Arizona and former editor of the esteemed journal, *Geophysical Research Letters,* provided an oversimplified statement of what happened: "During Alfvén's visit he gave a lecture at the University of Chicago, which was attended by [Enrico] Fermi," Dessler reported. As Alfvén described his work, the Arizona professor continued, Fermi nodded his head and said, "Of course." The next day the entire world of physics said, "Oh, of course" (Alfvén 1988b, p. 250).

Contributions to Science. Alfvén's contributions were primarily in electrical engineering, space plasma science, physics, and astrophysics. In 1937 he postulated a galactic magnetic field, a postulate that forms the basis for one of today's fastest-growing areas of research in astrophysics—cosmic magnetism. With his colleague, Nicolai Herlofson, Alfvén in 1950 became the first to identify nonthermal radiation from astronomical synchrotron radiation, which is produced by fast-moving electrons in the presence of magnetic fields. The realization that the synchrotron mechanism of radiation is important in celestial objects has been one of the most fruitful developments in astrophysics because almost all the radiation recorded by radio telescopes derives from this mechanism.

His prediction of the existence of the phenomenon called critical ionization velocity—which is crucial to understanding how accelerating matter to extreme velocities leads to its changes of state, as well as being the primary mechanism for the formation of planets—was verified to exist in interstellar space only in 1997, two years after his death.

Conflicts with Prevailing Views. Alfvén became active in interplanetary and magnetospheric physics at a time when his viewpoint in this field was a minority opinion. Alfvén's opinions were consistent with those of the founder of magnetospheric physics, the great Norwegian scientist Kristian Birkeland, who went on to found the Norwegian industrial energy megagiant, *Norsk Hydro.* By the end of the nineteenth century, Birkeland had presented a strong case backed by theory, laboratory experiments, polar expeditions, and a chain of magnetic-field observatories throughout the world—that electric currents flowing down along Earth's magnetic fields into the atmosphere were the cause of aurora and polar magnetic disturbances.

However, in the decades after Birkeland's death in 1917, Sydney Chapman, the highly regarded British geophysicist, became the recognized leader in interplanetary and magnetospheric physics. Chapman proposed, in opposition to Birkeland's ideas, that currents flowed only in the ionosphere, with no downflowing currents. Chapman's theory was so mathematically elegant that it won wide acceptance. Based on Chapman's ideas, algebraic expressions of the ionospheric current system could, with absolute mathematical rigor, be derived by any student of the subject. Birkeland's work might have disappeared completely except for Alfvén, who became involved long after Chapman's ideas had gained predominance. Alfvén insisted that Birkeland's current system made more sense because downflowing currents that followed Earth's magnetic field lines were necessary for driving most of the ionospheric currents. The dispute was finally settled in 1974, four years after Chapman's death, when Earth satellites measured downflowing currents for the first time.

This account illustrates problems that were typical of the those Alfvén faced in his scientific career. Interplanetary space was generally regarded to be a good vacuum, disturbed only by occasional comets. This opinion was broadly accepted because space appeared to be that way, having been viewed only with telescopes at optical wavelengths. The electrical currents offered by Alfvén, however, created a telltale signature only in the radio portions of the electromagnetic spectrum, so they had not yet been observed at the time he stated his view that such currents existed in space. Therefore, Alfvén's proposition met with great skepticism.

In 1939 Alfvén proposed an extraordinary hypothesis of magnetic storms and auroras that has broadly influenced contemporary theories of plasma dynamics in Earth's magnetosphere. He used the idea of electric charges spiraling in magnetic fields to compute the movement of electrons and ions. This approach came to be universally adopted by plasma physicists and was used until the boring task was consigned to computers in the mid-1970s. Yet in 1939, when Alfvén offered his paper on the subject to the leading American geophysical journal, *Terrestrial Magnetism and Atmospheric Electricity,* the paper was turned down because it did not correspond with the theoretical calculations of Chapman and his colleagues. As a result, Alfvén had to publish this seminal paper, "A Theory of Magnetic Storms and of the Aurorae" (1939) in a Swedish-language journal not readily accessible to the worldwide scientific community, *Kungliga Svenska Vetenskapsakademiens Handlingar, Tredje Serien.* Several of Alfvén's other key articles faced similar difficulties.

It is common in science that one or two major discoveries locate their author in the rank of leading authorities, with enormous influence and continuous funding usually ensuing. This, however, did not happen to Alfvén. At no time during his scientific career before winning the Nobel Prize did those scientists who were using his work generally recognize Alfvén as a leading innovator.

Dessler has written of his recognition that Alfvén's contributions were going unnoticed:

> When I entered the field of space physics in 1956, I recall that I fell in with the crowd believing, for example, that electric fields could not exist in the highly conducting plasma of space. It was three years later that I was shamed by S. Chandrasekhar into investigating Alfvén's work objectively. My degree of shock and surprise in finding Alfvén right and his critics wrong can hardly be described. I learned that a cosmic ray acceleration mechanism basically identical to the famous mechanism suggested by Fermi in 1949 had [previously] been put forth by Alfvén. (Dessler, 1970, p. 605)

Alfvén and Nuclear Energy. In 1967 Alfvén issued a scathing denunciation of Sweden's nuclear research program, objecting to what he thought was the insufficient provision of funds for projects on peaceful uses of thermonuclear energy, and he left his homeland saying, "My work is no longer desired in this country" (Weinraub, 1970, p. 2708).

Part of his antinuclear rational derived from the granite found in Scandinavia, which—because of its strength and hardness—was proposed for the storage of nuclear waste. Alfvén had an interest in geophysics, primarily for reasons related to problems of planetary evolution. Taking visitors through the Swedish countryside on their way to a morning breakfast of *pannkakor* (Swedish pancakes), he frequently stopped along the way to point out the cracks in the granite rocks and remark on their inadequacy as a nuclear waste depository.

After Alfvén announced his intention to leave Sweden, he was immediately offered professorships in both the Soviet Union and the United States. Following two months in the Soviet Union, he moved to the United States, where he tested the professorial waters in the departments of electrical engineering at the University of Southern California in Los Angeles and then the University of California at San Diego in La Jolla. Reconciled with the Swedish government in the end, Alfvén for the rest of his life alternated between California and Sweden, from October to March in La Jolla and April to September in Stockholm.

Alfvén and Astrophysics. Because his ideas frequently were at odds with generally accepted or standard theories, Alfvén always had difficulty with the peer review system, especially as practiced by Anglo-American astrophysical journals. "I have no trouble publishing in Soviet astrophysical journals," Alfvén once disclosed, "but my work is unacceptable to the American astrophysical journals" (Peratt, 1988, p. 197).

Alfvén never gained the nearly automatic acceptance generally given senior scientists in scientific journals. "The peer review system is satisfactory during quiescent times, but not during revolutionary or catastrophic times in a discipline such as astrophysics, when the establishment seeks to preserve the status quo," he remarked (Peratt, 1988, p. 197).

One reason that Alfvén's work in astrophysics was ignored may be that he regarded himself, first and foremost, as an electrical power engineer; in fact, he rather enjoyed the accusation of encroachment into astrophysics leveled by other cosmologists and theoreticians. Alfvén claimed that plasma physics had traditionally been neglected in astrophysics:

> Students using astrophysical textbooks remain essentially ignorant of even the existence of plasma concepts, despite the fact that some of them have been known for half a century. The

conclusion is that astrophysics is too important to be left in the hands of astrophysicists who have gotten their main knowledge from these textbooks. Earthbound and space telescope data must be treated by scientists who are familiar with laboratory and magnetospheric physics and circuit theory, and of course with modern plasma theory. (Alfvén, 1986b, p. 790)

Based on plasma physics, Alfvén and his colleagues for decades proposed an alternative cosmology to both the steady state and the big bang cosmologies. While the big bang theory was preferred by most astrophysicists for almost fifty years, it has been challenged by new observations, especially over the last few decades. In particular, the discovery of coherent structures of galaxies hundreds of millions of light years in length and the large-scale streaming of superclusters of galaxies at velocities that may approach 1,000 kilometers (620 miles) per second presents problems that are hard, if not impossible, to square with the big bang theory.

To Alfvén, the problems being raised were not surprising: "I have never thought that you could obtain the extremely clumpy, heterogeneous universe we have today, strongly affected by plasma processes, from the smooth, homogeneous one of the big bang, dominated by gravitation" (Peratt, 1988, p. 197).

The difficulty with the big bang, Alfvén thought, resembled the flaws in Chapman's theories, which the scientific community erroneously accepted for decades. Astrophysicists, he felt, tried too hard to extrapolate the origin of the universe from mathematical theories worked out on the blackboard. "The appeal of the big bang," said Alfvén, "has been more ideological than scientific. When men think about the universe, there is always a conflict between a fabled approach and the empirical scientific approach. In fable, one tries to deduce how the gods must have created the world—what perfect principles must have been used" (Peratt, 1988, p. 196).

To Alfvén, the big bang was a myth conceived to explain creation. "I was there when Abbé Georges Lemaître first proposed this theory," he recalled (Peratt, 1988, p. 196). Lemaître was, at the time, both a member of the Catholic hierarchy and an accomplished scientist. Privately, Lemaître acknowledged that this theory was a way to square science with St. Thomas Aquinas's theological dictum of *creatio ex nihilo*, or creation out of nothing.

But if the big bang is a myth, how and when did the universe begin? "There is no rational reason to doubt that the universe has existed indefinitely, for an infinite time," Alfvén explained. "It is only fable that attempts to say how the universe came to be, either five thousand or twenty billion years ago" (Peratt, 1988, p. 196).

"Since religion intrinsically rejects empirical methods, there should never be any attempt to reconcile scientific theories with religion," Alfvén said.

An infinitely old universe, always evolving, may not be compatible with the Book of Genesis. However, religions such as Buddhism get along without having any explicit creation fables and are in no way contradicted by a universe without a beginning or end. *Creatio ex nihilo*, even as religious doctrine, only dates to around AD 200. The key is not to confuse fable and empirical results, or religion and science. (Peratt, 1988, p. 196)

Alfvén acknowledged that his plasma universe theory might take a long while to pierce the popular consciousness. "After all," he asserted to a group of physicists, "most people today still believe, perhaps unconsciously, in the heliocentric universe." The group, at first disbelieving, quickly nodded in agreement as Alfvén continued: "Every newspaper in the land has a section on astrology, yet few have anything at all on astronomy" (Peratt, 1988, p. 196).

Awards, Honors, and Writings. Alfvén achieved worldwide recognition in his lifetime. He received the Nobel Prize in Physics (1970), the Gold Medal of the Royal Astronomical Society (1967), the Gold Medal of the Franklin Institute (1971), the Lomonosov Medal of the USSR Academy of Sciences (1971), and the Bowie Medal of the American Geophysical Union (1988), among other awards. Several academies and institutes placed his name on their membership lists: the Institute of Electrical and Electronics Engineers, the European Physical Society, the Royal Swedish Academy of Sciences, the Royal Swedish Academy of Engineering Sciences, the American Academy of Arts and Sciences, and the Yugoslav Academy of Sciences. Alfvén also was one of the very few scientists who held foreign memberships in both the U.S. and Soviet academies of sciences.

Besides his scientific papers, Alfvén wrote popular science books. These include *Worlds-Antiworlds: Antimatter in Cosmology* (1966) and *The Great Computer: A Vision* (1968). The latter book was written under the pen name Olof Johannesson. Other popular books include *Atom, Man, and the Universe: The Long Chain of Complications* (1969) and (with his wife, Kerstin Alfvén) *Living on the Third Planet* (1972).

Career Pattern. Regardless of his basic contributions to physics and astrophysics, Alfvén—who in 1991 retired from his posts of professor of electrical engineering at the University of California at San Diego and professor of

Hannes Olof Gosta Alfvén. *Hannes Alfven receiving the Nobel Prize from King Gustaf Adolf of Sweden.* AP IMAGES.

plasma physics at the Royal Institute of Technology in Stockholm—was still regarded as a heretic by many in those very fields. Alfvén's theories in astrophysics and plasma physics have usually won acceptance only twenty or thirty years after their publication. Typically, and also concomitant with his eightieth birthday in 1988, Alfvén was granted the most esteemed prize of the American Geophysical Union, the Bowie Medal, for his work three decades earlier on comets and plasmas in the solar system. Controversial for fifty years, many of his theories about the solar system were vindicated only as late as the 1980s through measurements of cometary and planetary magnetospheres by artificial satellites and space probes.

Although Alfvén received the coveted Nobel Prize and other distinguished honors from around the world— and while a rash of scientific journals published special issues in honor of his eightieth birthday—for much of his career, Alfvén's ideas were initially dismissed or met with great skepticism. Even in the early twentieth century, physicists are little aware of Alfvén's many contributions to fields of physics, where his ideas are employed without knowledge of who conceived them.

Personal Life. Alfvén supported many social causes. He was, for example, active in the worldwide disarmament movement, having been president of the Pugwash Conference on Science and World Affairs, Leningrad, May 1970, special Board on Atmospheric Sciences and Climate, Amnesty International, Energy, Food and Disarmament International. He had significant correspondence with groups connected with nuclear disarmament as well as with people such as Ralph Nader (interestingly, one of his seminal papers was written with Edward Teller), Energy Resources Conservation and Development Commission Hearings, "Plasma Astrophysics International Conference on Conflict Resolution and Peace Studies, USSR Academy of Sciences, Committee for Soviet Scientists for Peace, 1986," Scientific Research Council on Peace and Disarmament." In addition, his son was the Swedish secretary of the Physicians for Social Responsibility. Alfvén was fond of studying the history of science and Eastern philosophy and religion.

He was known for his humor and for having an anecdote for all occasions. Alfvén enjoyed traveling to places that do not have tour guides or are not normally listed in travel guide books, especially to places such as Sri Lanka, the Fiji Islands, and the Amazon River. His residence depended on the seasons: from spring to autumn in Europe and from autumn to spring in North America. Alfvén could speak fluently in English, German, and French, and nearly so in Russian; he also spoke some Spanish and some Chinese. He stayed physically active until the last four years of his life. Even when he was eighty-two years old, he entertained guests with wine at his La Jolla apartment, hurrying them to the beach at sunset, hoping to catch a glimpse of the "green flash," the phenomenon that sometimes occurs as the sun sinks below the ocean horizon.

BIBLIOGRAPHY

The Register of Hannes Alfvén Papers, comprising 1,200 linear feet (thirty archives boxes) of biographical materials. correspondence, writings (including drafts), photographs, meetings and grants records, and other materials is maintained by the Mandeville Special Collections Library, Geisel Library, University of California, San Diego. A comprehensive description is available from http://orpheus.ucsd.edu/speccoll/testing/html/mss0225a.html.

WORKS BY ALFVÉN

"A Theory of Magnetic Storms and of the Aurorae." *Kungliga Svenska Vetenskapsakademiens Handlingar, Tredje Serien* [Royal Swede Vetenskapsakademiens documents, third series] 18 (1939): 1–39, partial reprint in *Eos Transactions of the American Geophysical Union* 51 (1970): 181–193.

With R. D. Richtmyer and Edward Teller. "On the Origin of Cosmic Rays." *Physical Review* 75 (1949): 892–893.

With Carl-Gunne Fälthammar. *Cosmical Electrodynamics.* 2nd ed. Oxford: Clarendon Press, 1963.

Worlds-Antiworlds: Antimatter in Cosmology. San Francisco: W.H. Freeman, 1966.

"Antimatter and Cosmology." *Scientific American* 216 (April 1967): 106–114.

The Great Computer: A Vision. London: Gollancz, 1968. This book was written under the pen name Olof Johannesson.

Atom, Man, and the Universe: The Long Chain of Complications. San Francisco: W.H. Freeman, 1969.

"Plasma Physics, Space Research, and the Origin of the Solar System: Nobel Lecture." In *Les Prix Nobel en 1970.* Stockholm: Nobel Foundation, 1971.

With Kerstin Alfvén. *Living on the Third Planet.* San Francisco: W.H. Freeman, 1972.

With Gustaf Arrhenius. *Evolution of the Solar System.* Washington, DC: Scientific and Technical Information Office, National Aeronautics and Space Administration, U.S. Government Printing Office, 1976.

With Carl-Gunne Falthammar and Syun-Ichi Akasofu. "The Significance of Magnetospheric Research for Progress in Astrophysics." *Nature* 275 (1978): 185–188.

Cosmic Plasma. Dordrecht, Netherlands: Reidel, 1981.

"Model of the Plasma Universe." *IEEE Transactions on Plasma Science* PS-14 (1986a): 629–660.

"Double Layers and Circuits in Astrophysics." *IEEE Transactions on Plasma Science* PS-14 (1986b): 779–793.

"The Plasma Universe." *Physics Today* (September 1986c): 2–7.

"Cosmology in the Plasma Universe." *Laser and Particle Beams* 6, pt. 3 (1988a): 389–398.

"Memoirs of a Dissident Scientist." *American Scientist* 76 (1988b): 250–251.

"Cosmology in the Plasma Universe: An Introductory Exposition." *IEEE Transactions on Plasma Science* 18, no. 1, (1990): 5–10.

"Cosmology: Myth or Science?" *IEEE Transactions on Plasma Science* 20, no. 6 (1992): 590–600.

OTHER SOURCES

Dessler, Alexander J. "Swedish Iconoclast Recognized after Many Years of Rejection and Obscurity." *Science* 170 (1970): 604–606.

Fälthammar, Carl-Gunne. "Plasma Physics from Laboratory to Cosmos—The Life and Achievements of Hannes Alfvén." *IEEE Transactions on Plasma Science* 25 (1997): 409–414.

———, and Dessler, Alexander J. "Biographical Memoirs, Hannes Alfven." *Proceedings of the American Philosophical Society* 150 (2006): 649–662.

Peratt, Anthony L. "Dean of the Plasma Dissidents." *World & I* (May 1988): 190–197.

Potemra, Thomas A., and Anthony L. Peratt. "The Golden Anniversary of Magnetic Storms and the Aurorae." *IEEE Transactions on Plasma Science* 17 (1989): 65–68.

Weinraub, B. "Three Scientists Win Nobel Prizes." *New York Times Biographical Edition* 28 October 1970.

Anthony L. Peratt

ALĪ AL-QŪSHJĪ (ABŪ AL-QĀSIM ALĀ' AL-DĪN ALĪ IBN MUHAMMAD QUSHJĪ-ZĀDE)

(*b.* probably Samarqand, early fifteenth century; *d.* Istanbul, Turkey, 1474), *astronomy, natural philosophy.*

Alī al-Qūshjī was a philosopher-theologian, mathematician, astronomer, and linguist who produced original studies in both observational and theoretical astronomy within fifteenth-century Islamic and Ottoman astronomy. He contributed to the preparation of Ulugh Beg's *Zīj* at the Samarqand Observatory, insisted on the possibility of the Earth's motion, and asserted the need for the purification of all the scientific disciplines from the principles of Aristotelian physics and metaphysics.

Life. Qūshjī was the son of Ulugh Beg's falconer, whence his Turkish name Qushči-zāde. He took courses in the linguistic sciences, mathematics, and astronomy as well as other sciences taught by scholars in the circle of Ulugh Beg. These included Jamshīd al-Kāshī, Qādīzāde al-Rūmī, and Ulugh Beg himself.

In 1420 Qūshjī secretly moved to Kirmān, where he studied astronomy (c. 1423–1427) with Mollā Jāmī the mathematical sciences. Upon his return to Samarqand around 1428, Qūshjī presented Ulugh Beg with a monograph (*Hall ishkāl al-qamar*) in which he solved a variety of problems; Ulugh Beg was reported to have been quite pleased. Sources say that Ulugh Beg referred to Qūshjī as "my virtuous son" ("ferzend-i ercümend," Nuruosmaniye MS 2932, f. 2b). Indeed, after the death of Qādīzāde, it was Qūshjī whom Ulugh Beg commissioned to administer the observational work at the Samarqand Observatory that was required for his *Zīj* (astronomical handbook). Qūshjī, often referred to as "Sāhib-i rasad" (head of observation), contributed to the preparation and correction of the *Zīj*, but it is unclear to what extent and at what stage. This question becomes especially problematic in view of Qūshjī's criticisms of it and his pointing out of mistakes, in his *Sharh-i Zīj Ulugh Beg* (Commentary on Ulugh Beg's *Zīj*).

Upon Ulugh Beg's death in 1449, Qūshjī, together with his family and students, spent a considerable time in Herat, where he wrote his theological work *Sharh al-Tajrīd*, a commentary to Nasīr al-Dīn al-Tūsī's (d. 1274) work *al-Tajrīd fī ilm al-kalām*, which he presented to the Timurid Sultan Abū Saīd. After Abū Saīd's defeat by Uzun Hasan in 1469, Qūshjī moved to Tabrīz, where he was welcomed by the latter. It is said that Qūshjī was sent to Istanbul to settle a dispute between Uzan Hasan and Mehmed the Conqueror; after accomplishing the mission, he returned to Tabrīz. However, around 1472 Qūshī, together with his family and students, left permanently for Istanbul either on his own or because of an invitation from Sultan Mehmed.

When Qūshjī and his entourage approached Istanbul, Sultan Mehmed sent a group of scholars to welcome them. Sources say that in crossing the Bosporus to Istanbul, a discussion ensued about the causes of its ebb and flow. Upon arrival in Istanbul, Qūshjī presented his mathematical work *al-Muhammadiyya fī al-hisāb* to the sultan, which was named in his honor.

Qūshjī spent the remaining two to three years of his life in Istanbul. He first taught in the Sahn-i Thamān Madrassa (founded by Sultan Mehmed); then he was made head of the Ayasofya Madrassa. In this brief period Qūshjī educated and influenced a large number of students, who, along with his writings, were to have an enormous impact on future generations. He died in 1474 and was buried in the cemetery of the Eyyūb mosque.

Prolific Writer. Qūshjī, especially when compared with his contemporaries such as Kāshī and Qādīzāde, was a remarkable polymath who excelled in a variety of disciplines including language and literature, philosophy, theology, mathematics, and astronomy. He wrote works in all these fields, producing books, textbooks, and short monographs dealing with specific problems. His commentaries often became more popular than the original texts and themselves became the subject of numerous commentaries. Thousands of copies of Qūshjī's works are extant and many were taught in the madrassas.

Qūshjī's philosophy of science, which had important repercussions for the history of astronomy, is contained in his commentary to Tūsī's *Sharh al-Tajrīd*. Besides being one of the most important theological works in Islam, this commentary lays down the philosophical principles of Qūshjī's conception of existence, existents, nature, knowledge, and language. As for the mathematical sciences, Qūshjī in general tried to free them from Hermetic-Pythagorean mysticism and to provide an alternative to Aristotelian physics as the basis for astronomy and optics. He sought to define body (*jism*) as being predominantly mathematical in character. Qūshjī claimed that the essence of a body is composed of discontinuous (atomic) quantity while its form consists of continuous (geometrical) quantity. When a body is a subject of the senses, it then gains its natural properties (qualifications).

One consequence of Qūshjī's anti-Aristotelian views was his striking assertion that it might well be possible that the Earth is in motion. Here Qūshjī followed a long line of Islamic astronomers who rejected Ptolemy's observational proofs for a stationary Earth; Qūshjī, though, refused to follow them in depending on Aristotle's philosophical proofs, thus opening up the possibility for a new physics in which the Earth was in motion. Qūshjī's views were debated for centuries after his death, and he exerted a profound influence on Ottoman-Turkish thought and scientific inquiry, in particular through the madrassa and its curriculum. His influence also extended to Central Asia and Iran, and it has been argued that he may well have had an influence, either directly or indirectly, upon early modern European science, to which his ideas bear a striking resemblance.

Qūshjī wrote five mathematics books, one in Persian and four in Arabic. His *Risāla dar ilm al-hisāb* (Persian), written during his stay in Central Asia (along with his enlarged Arabic version of this work, *al-Risāla al-Muhammadiyya fī al-hisāb*), were taught as a mid-level textbooks in Ottoman madrassas. In these works, in accordance with the principles he laid down in the *Sharh al-Tajrīd*, he tried to free mathematics from Hermetic-Pythagorean mysticism. As a result, Ottoman mathematics took on a practical character, which hindered traditional studies such as the theory of numbers.

Astronomy. In the field of astronomy, one of Qūshjī's most important contributions is in the observational program for the *Zīj-i Ulugh Beg* and in his corrections to the work, both before and after publication. In addition, he produced nine works on astronomy, two in Persian and seven in Arabic. Some of them are original contributions while others are pedagogical. In his theoretical monograph entitled *Fāʾida fī ishkāl uṭārid*, Qūshjī criticizes and corrects opinions and ideas pertaining to Mercury's motions mentioned in Ptolemy's *Almagest*. Another work is his *Risāla fī asl al-khārijī yumkinu fī al-sufliyayn*, which deals with an eccentric model instead of epicyclical models for both inner and outer planets; it has vital importance for a sun-centered cosmology-astronomy, on the path to Copernicus through Regiomontanus.

Qūshjī's *Risāla dar ilm al-hayʾa* (Persian), written in Samarqand in 1458, was commonly used as a teaching text; there exist more than eighty manuscript copies of it in libraries throughout the world. It was also translated into Turkish. Two commentaries were written on it, one by Muslih al-Dīn al-Lārī (d. 1571), the other by an anonymous author. Lārī's commentary was widely taught in Ottoman madrassas. Qūshjī's *Risāla* was also translated into Sanskrit and thus represents the transmission of Islamic astronomy to the Indian subcontinent. Qūshjī wrote an enlarged version of the work in Arabic under the name *al-Fathiyya fī ilm al-hayʾa*, which was presented to Sultan Mehmed in 1473. This work, taught as a middle-level textbook, was commented on by Gulām Sinān (d. 1506) and Qūshjī's famous mathematician-astronomer great-grandson Mīram Çelebī (d. 1525). It was also translated into Persian by Muīn al-Dīn al-Husaynī and into Turkish by Seydî Ali Reîs (d. 1563). In the *Risāla* and the *Fathiyya*, Qūshjī followed the principles he had laid down in his *Sharh al-Tajrīd* by excluding an introductory section on Aristotelian physics, which customarily had introduced almost all previous works of this kind.

BIBLIOGRAPHY

Brockelmann, Carl. *Geschichte der arabischen Litteratur.* 2nd ed. Vol. 2 (1949), 235; Supp. 2 (1938), 329–330. Leiden: E. J. Brill.

Fazlıoğlu, İhsan. "Ali Kuşçu." In *Yaşamları ve yapıtlarıyla Osmanlılar ansiklopedisi*, edited by Ekrem Çakıroğlu, vol. 1, 216–219. Istanbul: YKY, 1999.

———. "Qushji." In *Biographical Encyclopaedia of Astronomers*, edited by Thomas Hockey. Springer/Kluwer, forthcoming.

İhsanoğlu, Ekmeleddin, et al. *Osmanlı astronomi literatürü tarihi* (*OALT*) [History of astronomy literature during the Ottoman period]. Vol. 1, 27–38 (no. 11). Istanbul: IRCICA, 1997.

———. *Osmanlı matematik literatürü tarihi* (*OMLT*) [History of mathematical literature during the Ottoman period]. Vol. 1, 20–27 (no. 3). Istanbul: IRCICA, 1999.

Pingree, David. "Indian Reception of Muslim Versions of Ptolemaic Astronomy." In *Tradition, Transmission, Transformation: Proceedings of Two Conferences on Pre-modern Science Held at the University of Oklahoma*, edited by F. Jamil Ragep and Sally P. Ragep, with Steven Livesey, 471–485. Leiden: E. J. Brill, 1996.

Ragep, F. Jamil. "Tūsī and Copernicus: The Earth's Motion in Context." *Science in Context* 14 (2001): 145–163.

———. "Freeing Astronomy from Philosophy: An Aspect of Islamic Influence on Science." *Osiris* 16 (2001): 66–71.

———. "Ali Qushji and Regiomontanus: Eccentric Transformations and Copernican Revolutions." *Journal History of Astronomy* 36 (2005): 359–371.

Saliba, George. "Al-Qūshjī's Reform of the Ptolemaic Model for Mercury." *Arabic Sciences and Philosophy* 3 (1993): 161–203.

Tashköprüzāde. *Al-Shaqāʾq al-numāniyya fī ulamāʾ al-dawlat al-uthmāniyya.* Edited by Ahmed Subhi Furat, 159–162. Istanbul, 1985.

Ünver, A. Süheyl. *Astronom Ali Kuşçu, Hayatı ve Eserleri.* Istanbul: Kenan Matbaası, 1948.

Zeki, Salih. *Asar-i bakiye.* Vol. 1, 195–199. Istanbul: 1329 [1913/1914].

İhsan Fazlıoğlu

ALLEE, WARDER CLYDE (*b.* near Bloomingdale, Indiana, 5 June 1885; *d.* Gainesville, Florida, 18 March 1955), *ecology, animal behavior.* For the original article on Allee see *DSB*, vol. 17, Supplement II.

Allee was a central figure in the development of a distinctive school of ecology that flourished at the University of Chicago during the first half of the twentieth century. According to historian Gregg Mitman, ecology at Chicago developed quite independently of Darwinian evolution and Mendelian genetics, being much more heavily influenced by ideas drawn from developmental biology, physiology, and animal behavior. Victor Shelford, Allee's mentor at the University of Chicago, argued that the study of ecological communities should be conducted without regard to evolutionary problems, focusing instead on the physiological responses of animals to their environments. Allee's dissertation on the behavior of aquatic isopods (*Asellus communis*) investigated the effects of dissolved oxygen, carbon dioxide, and other environmental stimuli on the orientation behavior of these small invertebrates in ponds and flowing streams. Populations living in ponds oriented differently from those living in streams with strong currents. Allee discovered that by manipulating environmental conditions he could make isopods collected from ponds behave like those taken from streams, and vise versa. This seemed to rule out hereditary differences between populations and suggested that orientation behavior was a direct response to environmental factors.

Later Research. When he returned to the University of Chicago as an assistant professor after World War I, Allee broadened this experimental, physiological approach to study the causes of animal aggregations. Allee sometimes referred to this approach to the study of populations as "mass physiology," and he argued that the unconscious cooperation or "proto-cooperation" found in loose aggregations of isopods and other simple animals was the starting point for the complex, cooperative behaviors found in truly social animals, including humans. Understanding and improving human society became a powerful motivation for Allee's ecological and behavioral research.

Allee's physiological approach to ecology and behavior was partially transformed by his later interactions with his colleague Alfred Emerson during the 1930s. Emerson, who studied termites and other social insects, brought an evolutionary perspective that had been absent in Allee's earlier research. According to Mitman, Allee did not abandon his earlier commitments to physiology and development, but assimilated aspects of Emerson's evolutionary thinking. What unified Allee, Emerson, and other University of Chicago ecologists was a deep commitment to the population as a fundamental evolutionary unit. During the late 1930s, Allee increasingly emphasized natural selection as a causal factor in the evolution of behavior, but he believed that it acted primarily on groups of individuals rather than on the individuals themselves. Allee was able to argue that cooperation was a group adaptation that evolved because more cooperative groups had greater success than less cooperative groups. This commitment to group selection allowed Allee to view even phenomena such as dominance and social hierarchies in cooperative terms. In both cases he argued that these social interactions reduced conflict, which had survival value for the population as a whole. This perspective on social behavior was later widely abandoned by evolutionary biologists, particularly during the late 1960s and 1970s.

Social Implications and Legacy. Throughout his career Allee emphasized the implications of biology for understanding human social behavior. His studies of animal aggregations and the evolution of cooperation meshed neatly with his social activism and his political and religious opposition to war. Raised as a Quaker, Allee remained a strict pacifist throughout his life. His renunciation of war and vocal support for conscientious objectors during World War I made him a target of criticism and some public persecution. During the 1940s Allee argued

that his behavioral research provided evidence against a biological basis for war and strongly supported a theory of sociality based upon cooperation among individuals. According to Mitman, Allee viewed ecologists as "social healers" whose research could provide a naturalistic basis for ethics. Mitman argues that after World War II, this idea of ecologists as social healers was swept aside by Eugene Odum and other ecosystem ecologists who embraced an engineering perspective and were more interested in environmental issues than social ones. During the 1950s Odum's textbook, *Fundamentals of Ecology*, rapidly eclipsed *Principles of Animal Ecology* (1949), which Allee had written with his colleagues at the University of Chicago. Despite their striking differences in perspective, Odum agreed with Allee about the importance of group selection and the evolutionary prevalence of cooperation even among very simple organisms.

Both historians and biologists agree that Allee's reputation was diminished by George C. Williams's *Adaptation and Natural Selection* (1966). In this highly influential work Williams championed individual selection and effectively discredited purported examples of group selection. Allee was one of the major targets of Williams's critique. As a result, Allee left a somewhat contradictory legacy. In 1973 the Animal Behavior Society instituted an annual student research award in his name, but Edwin Banks later complained that many younger animal behaviorists were unaware of Allee's important contributions to the field. Some ecologists remain interested in the eponymous "Allee Effect" (that undercrowding can be as deleterious to organisms as overcrowding), and they acknowledge Allee's pioneering work on this phenomenon. But although Allee viewed aggregations as an example of unconscious cooperation leading to group adaptation, most ecologists in the early twenty-first century explain them in terms of individual fitness. Ironically, Elliot Sober, David Sloan Wilson, and other evolutionary theorists who have attempted to revive interest in group selection strongly disassociate their ideas from what they characterize as naive group selection arguments used by Allee.

SUPPLEMENTARY BIBLIOGRAPHY

Allee's papers are archived in the Special Collections Research Center of the University of Chicago Library. A complete bibliography of Allee's published work appears in Karl P. Schmidt's "Warder Clyde Allee, 1885-1955," in Biographical Memoirs, *published by the National Academy of Sciences.*

WORKS BY ALLEE

Animal Aggregations: A Study in General Sociology. Chicago: University of Chicago Press, 1931.

The Social Life of Animals. New York: Norton, 1938.

With Alfred E. Emerson, Orlando Park, Thomas Park, et al. *Principles of Animal Ecology.* Philadelphia: Saunders, 1949.

Cooperation among Animals, with Human Implications. New York: Schuman, 1951.

OTHER SOURCES

Banks, Edwin M. "Warder Clyde Allee and the Chicago School of Animal Behavior." *Journal of the History of the Behavioral Sciences* 21 (1985): 345–353.

Mitman, Gregg. "Dominance, Leadership, and Aggression: Animal Behavior Studies During the Second World War." *Journal of the History of the Behavioral Sciences* 26 (1990): 3–6.

———. *The State of Nature: Ecology, Community, and American Social Thought, 1900–1950.* Chicago: University of Chicago Press, 1992.

Schmidt, Karl P. "Warder Clyde Allee, 1885-1955." *Biographical Memoirs* 30 (1957): 2-40.

Sober, Elliot, and David Sloan Wilson. *Unto Others: The Evolution and Psychology of Unselfish Behavior.* Cambridge, MA: Harvard University Press, 1998.

Stephens, Philip A., W. J. Sutherland, and Robert P. Freckleton. "What Is the Allee Effect?" *Oikos* 87 (1999): 185–190.

Williams, George C. *Adaptation and Natural Selection: A Critique of Some Current Evolutionary Thought.* Princeton, NJ: Princeton University Press, 1966.

Joel B. Hagen

ALLPORT, GORDON WILLARD (*b.* Montezuma, Indiana, 11 November 1897; *d.* Cambridge, Massachusetts, 9 October 1967), *psychology, psychology of personality, social psychology.*

Known as the "patron saint" of personality psychologists (Eysenck, 1990, p. 3), Allport was a major figure in American "personality" psychology. His 1937 textbook *Personality: A Psychological Interpretation* is widely viewed as an important landmark in the establishment of "personality" as a legitimate subdiscipline in psychology. Intellectually wide ranging, Allport also wrote extensively on the topic of social psychology, and his work on the history of social psychology, prejudice, and religion were widely cited. A critic of both psychoanalysis and behaviorism, Allport championed an eclectic psychology that would respect the scientific method while simultaneously honoring human potential and individual uniqueness—an approach that contributed to the development of humanistic psychology in the 1960s. Although he never established his own "school" of psychology, Allport exercised considerable influence within the field and in a 1951 survey of clinical psychologists he placed second only to Sigmund Freud as the theorist of most direct value in day-to-day clinical work.

Origins and Education. Allport was born in Montezuma, Indiana, in 1897, the youngest son of John Allport, a physician, and Nellie Wise, a homemaker and temperance activist. The Allports were an extraordinarily hardworking and high-achieving family, and both parents became prominent members of the local community. The family were devout Methodists, and Allport grew up in a world of piety and morally based service. Foreign missionaries were regular visitors in the home, as were members of the Woman's Christian Temperance Union (WCTU). The Christian, service-oriented temper of the Allport home is evident in Allport's middle name, Willard. The name was in honor of Frances Willard, a leading advocate of higher education for women and a national president of the WCTU.

For much of Allport's boyhood, the family home doubled as a hospital, an arrangement that made his physician father's life (and that of his family) a continuous form of service to others. John Allport boasted of never having taken a vacation, and he demanded a similar devotion to work among his family. This uncompromising work ethic generated some resentment within the family, but it left a lasting imprint on Allport, who in his career as a psychologist became renowned for his productivity and extraordinary devotion to work.

Most of Allport's youth was spent in Cleveland, Ohio, where the family settled at the turn of the twentieth century. Although Allport respected his father's work ethic, his mother was the more influential figure. Consciously avoiding outdoor "boyish" pursuits, Allport excelled in school and academically oriented extracurricular activities. At the time of his graduation from high school in 1915, he was second in a class of one hundred, editor of the student newspaper, and the faculty choice to read the commencement address.

At the suggestion of his brother Floyd, Allport enrolled at Harvard University in the fall of 1915. Although he had come to reject the Methodist evangelicism of his youth, Allport retained a keen moral earnestness, and he was drawn to academic fields that echoed the themes of morally based social service that his parents had practiced. The Department of Social Ethics was a particular interest. According to the Harvard social ethicist James Ford, social ethics endeavored to "determine what constitutes goodness" and to study the "adoption of social method to the achievement of moral purpose" (1923, p. 1). Inspired by his social ethics studies, Allport undertook an extensive program of social work as a student, including stints at the Boston Juvenile Court, the Bureau of Industrial Housing and Transportation, and the YMCA.

As an undergraduate, Allport was intrigued by another field with moral potential: psychology. He was introduced to the topic by the famous German psychologist Hugo

Münsterberg, but it was Allport's own brother Floyd who was the more important influence. Seven years older than Gordon, Floyd was a graduate student in psychology at Harvard and Münsterberg's assistant. Allport regarded Floyd as an inspirational figure and he listened attentively to his brother's personal advice and scholarly observations on psychological issues. A key question that emerged out of their discussions was to dominate much of Gordon Allport's subsequent work in psychology: could human nature be completely understood through the methods of natural science? Münsterberg thought not, arguing that there was a "purposive" dimension of human experience that transcended the determinism of natural science and could thus only be examined philosophically. In contrast, Floyd Allport argued that all human experience could be grounded in the physical world and ultimately subject to scientific scrutiny. Floyd had little regard for philosophical discussions and he called for the reworking of psychology "in terms of the behavior complex" (Münsterberg, 1914, p. 300).

Allport graduated from Harvard in 1919, lacking professional direction but with his moral idealism still largely intact. In search of a challenging outlet for his benevolent aspirations, he accepted a position as a missionary and lecturer at Robert College in Constantinople (now Istanbul), Turkey. Allport emerged from the experience more worldly and less optimistic about the potential for the moral regeneration of society. "People here [in Turkey] are so hopelessly dishonest, indifferent and fatalistic, that all endeavors seem wasted," Allport remarked in his diary, "Why should one waste his life in addition to the lives of the wretches who will perish ignominiously in spite of all efforts for their improvement?" (1919–1920, p. 137). Increasingly aware of the limitations of social service, Allport developed a clearer sense of his professional ambitions. Academia was to be his calling, and in 1920 he returned to Harvard as a graduate student in the social ethics and psychology departments.

Before returning to Cambridge, Allport visited Vienna, where he met Sigmund Freud in his famous home, 19 Berggasse. The story of Allport's meeting with Freud is one of the best-known anecdotes in the history of psychology, and the meeting was a decisive event in Allport's life as a psychologist. Having some understanding of psychoanalysis from his undergraduate studies, Allport told Freud about something he had seen on the tram: "A small boy about four years of age had displayed a conspicuous dirt phobia. He kept saying to his mother, 'I don't want to sit there … don't let that dirty man sit beside me.'" Since the boy's mother was a "well starched Hausfrau" with a "dominant and purposive" look, Allport expected Freud to make a connection between the mother's manner and the boy's phobia. However, to Allport's surprise, Freud interpreted the story as an expres-

sion of Allport's own character. "When I finished my story," Allport recalled, "Freud fixed his kindly therapeutic eyes upon me and said, 'And was that little boy you?'" (1967, p. 8).

Freud may have been quite astute in his observation, but in Allport's mind the interpretation demonstrated a limitation of psychoanalysis. Freud was too anxious to search for a "deep" unconscious motive and thus apt to go astray in his interpretations. Allport came back to this story repeatedly in his later career, and he developed a reputation as a forceful critic of psychoanalysis and a proponent of a psychology that emphasized the human potential to transcend sexual and environmental forces.

Early Career. Allport's contributions to the psychological study of personality are second to none. Widely revered as one of the subdiscipline's founders, he has been described as the "chief pioneer in the development of a psychology of personality" (Jennes, 1979, p. 12). His 1921 literature review on the topic was the first of its kind, and his 1922 dissertation is widely viewed as the first psychology dissertation on personality. He taught one of the first courses on personality in 1924, coauthored one of the first psychometric studies of personality (1928), and authored the first major textbook in the field (1937). Despite all these "firsts," Allport viewed the field he helped establish with considerable unease, and he developed into a forceful critic of methodological approaches and assumptions that he had himself helped initiate. At the heart of Allport's discomfort lay the still unresolved question about human nature. Was there an aspect of human nature that transcended natural science? In his earliest work as a psychologist, Allport followed his brother Floyd and answered this question with a resounding no, but as his career unfolded he became increasingly convinced that there remained a fundamental and scientifically uncapturable mystery at the heart of human experience. For all his skepticism, Allport remained enamored with the possibility of scientific mastery over personality. Hoping to strike a balance between the ideals of mystery and mastery, Allport advocated both the quantitative measurement of personality and a qualitative reverence for the unique, individual person.

"Personality" was Allport's first and enduring love in psychology. He came to the topic fresh from his experience in Turkey, where his idealism had been tempered but not completely destroyed. Indeed, the challenges he experienced in Turkey lent force to the central idea of social ethics. Moral enthusiasm alone was not enough to bring about effective change in an increasingly urban, industrial age. Scientifically based tools and systems of understanding were needed if humanity's prosperity was to be secured. Within this context, psychology—the science of mind and behavior—clearly had an important role to play.

The choice of "personality" as a PhD dissertation topic was grounded in the logic of scientifically informed social service. Titled "An Experimental Study of the Traits of Personality with Application to the Problems of Social Diagnosis" (1922), the dissertation reflected a growing scholarly fascination with the category. In the 1910s, social workers had written extensively of the need to develop a new, more professional sounding discourse. Older categories—most notably "character"—had begun to sound dated and had associations with Victorian moralism and preachiness. In contrast, "personality" sounded fresh, modern, and scientific; it seemed to connote the person as they actually were and not as they appeared through the lens of Christian ethics. The category had a similar appeal in psychiatric, sociological, and legal circles. Within psychology, "personality" had also come to signal the idea of an "objective self." The famous behaviorist psychologist John Watson used the term *personality* to refer to an "individual's total assets and liabilities on the reaction side" (Watson, 1919, p. 417).

Allport's early approach to "personality" was informed by Watson's definition and by the ambitions of social workers for scientific instruments that could objectively measure human nature. Personality was envisioned as a product of the interaction between the environment and a set of simple reflexes rooted in the "innate systems of nervous organization" (Allport, 1922, p. 24). For his dissertation, Allport produced an "instrument of individual measurement" that foreshadowed the methodological trajectory of American personality psychology. After experimenting with both electric shock and word-association tests as possible measures of personality, Allport tested and subsequently endorsed what he termed the "method of represented situations" (Allport, 1922, p. 103). In this now familiar technique, participants were asked to respond to a series of questions not by "subjectively worded replies," but by checking one of several possible answers attached to each question. By the mid-1920s most personality trait tests used a similar paper and pencil procedure.

Two Approaches to "Personality." In 1922–1923, Allport undertook a postdoctoral fellowship in Germany that was to have a decisive impact on his thinking. In Germany, he came under the influence of the Hamburg psychologist William Stern, a scholar renowned for his development of the intelligence quotient (IQ) concept. Although much of Stern's fame rested on his work in quantitative, natural science–oriented psychology, he was in fact a sharp critic of the trend in psychology to limit the study of human nature to the mechanistic language and methods of the natural sciences. Informing Stern's critique was a distinction between two types of individuality: relational and real. Relational individuality was defined statistically in terms of

Gordon Allport. © BETTMANN/CORBIS.

deviations from corresponding norms. In contrast, real, or pure individuality referred to a kind of unique, "spiritual" unity that defied scientific capture. According to Stern, psychological measurements of the sort devised by Allport targeted relational individuality, while leaving "real" individuality unaddressed and unappreciated. Stern's project, known as "personalism," made the person ontologically fundamental and aimed to show that human experience was characterized by a "synthesizing higher unity. Not a complex of differential forms of psychical phenomena, but a genuine individuality, something indivisibly singular, a personality" (Stern, 1930, p. 348).

"Personalistic" psychology resonated strongly with Allport, and he soon published "The Study of the Undivided Personality," a paper that highlighted the shortcomings of a psychology based solely on "relational individuality." In the paper, Allport argued that personality was not the sum of measurable traits, but a "unique quality" that had its "origin in the form in which the traits are combined, and in the manner in which they function together" (1924, p. 132). Allport continued to advance this argument for the remainder of his career, even while continuing his earlier, psychometric study of personality traits.

Allport returned to Harvard in 1924 as an instructor in the Department of Social Ethics. It was here and not in the psychology department that he launched Personality and Social Adjustment, one of the first courses in the United States on personality. In the summer of 1925, Allport married the social worker Ada Gould, and in 1926 the two moved to Dartmouth College, where Allport took up a position in the Department of Psychology. Still interested in the measurement of relational individuality, in 1928 Allport and his brother Floyd published the *A-S Reaction Study*, a personality scale that measured the traits of ascendance-submission. Allport returned in 1928 to Harvard's Department of Psychology and Philosophy, where he remained for the rest of his career.

At Harvard, Allport was obliged to operate in a scholarly environment dominated by the kind of mechanistic psychology that he had criticized so forcefully while in Germany. Harvard psychologists such as Edwin G. Boring, Karl Lashley, and Stanley Smith Stevens embraced a hard-nosed empiricism and they regarded Allport's interest in the qualitative veneration of the unique "real" individual with a suspicion bordering on hostility. Allport's ability to survive and indeed thrive in this environment is a testament to his people skills as much as it is a tribute to the intellectual force of his arguments. Graceful, diplomatic, and unfailingly courteous, Allport had a talent for befriending people and an ability to fit in. Over the years, these skills helped propel Allport to a number of positions of institutional and disciplinary leadership. In 1936 he was elected to a three-year term on the Council of Directors of the American Psychological Association (APA). He was appointed chair of the Harvard psychology department in 1937, and from 1938 to 1949 he served as editor of the *Journal of Abnormal and Social Psychology*. Rounding out this cavalcade of honors, in 1938 he was elected president of the APA—the first "personality" psychologist ever to hold the office.

The professional success that Allport enjoyed is all the more remarkable given his ongoing commitment to the unique real individual. This interest brought Allport to topics such as *Verstehen* (intuition; 1929) and graphology (1933)—subjects that lay well outside the domain of mainstream, laboratory psychology. In both of these projects, Allport hoped to follow in the footsteps of Stern by cultivating an appreciation of the "unity and congruence" of the individual person (Allport, 1930, p. 124). Unfortunately for Allport, neither of these interests resonated in a disciplinary environment dominated by positivism and relational individuality. In the 1930s Allport enjoyed greater scholarly success with his psychometrically oriented work. In 1931 he published with Philip E. Vernon

A Study of Values: A Scale for the Measuring the Dominant Interests in Personality, a paper-and-pencil test designed to assess an individual's belief system across six value types. In 1936 Allport and Henry Sebastian Odbert published a study that would ultimately lead to one of the most influential of all the psychometric approaches to personality: the Five Factor Model. Titled "Trait-Names: A Psycho-Lexical Study," the study was designed to uncover the "underlying structural units of personality" through an analysis of eighteen thousand personality related terms from *Webster's New International Dictionary* (Allport, 1937, p. 353).

Allport endeavored to synthesize his scholarly interests in his magnum opus: *Personality: A Psychological Interpretation* (1937). In this influential text, Allport envisioned the field as the study of both "real" and "relational" individuality. Borrowing a pair of philosophical terms from the German philosopher Wilhelm Windelband (1848–1915), Allport described personality psychology as both an idiographic and a nomothetic discipline. The idiographic approach, aimed at understanding the unique particulars of an individual case, contrasted with the nomothetic approach, which sought general laws using the procedures of the natural sciences. Though some of Allport's German mentors believed that these two approaches were antagonistic, Allport saw them as "overlapping and as contributing to one another" (1937, p. 22). The nomothetic search for general laws, he argued, may yield a "law that tells how uniqueness comes about" (p. 558). Allport endeavored to develop such a "law" himself, focusing on the contentious topic of human motivation. Psychoanalysis held that the behavior of adults was rooted in biological needs and early childhood experiences. While acknowledging the importance of these factors, Allport argued that adult motives grew out of earlier systems and eventually became independent of them. Known as the "functional autonomy of motives," the theory held that adult action was contemporary and not determined by "infantile or archaic" causes. "The life of a tree is continuous with that of its seed, but the seed no longer sustains and nourishes the full grown tree" (p. 194). Described by one pair of commentators as the "best known and most controversial" of Allport concepts (Hall & Lindzey, 1970, p. 269), functional autonomy reflected his religiously inspired belief in the power of the individual personality to become something greater than the sum of its past—a theme that he would later expand on in his book *Becoming* (1955).

Social and Religious Interests. Although missionary work had tempered Allport's social idealism, he remained committed to the ideal of scientifically informed social reform. In the 1930s he helped establish the Society for the Psychological Study of Social Issues (SPSSI) and he was chairman of the APA Committee on Displaced Foreign Psychologists, which assisted European psychologists who had been persecuted by the Nazis. During World War II, Allport contributed to the war effort through research on scapegoating, rumors, and prejudice, some of which later appeared in *The Psychology of Rumor* (1947), coauthored with Leo Joseph Postman. Allport also helped author the "Psychologists Manifesto," a policy document of humanitarian principles for the postwar world (Murphy, 1945). The most notable reflection of Allport's commitment to social reform was his 1954 *The Nature of Prejudice,* a highly influential text, which in its abridged paperback edition became one of the "best selling social psychological books in publishing history" (Pettigrew, 1999, p. 420). Despite the book's great success, Allport later concluded following a trip to South Africa that his "psychological bias" had led him to "underestimate the forces of history and of traditional social structure" in the development of prejudice (1967, p. 20).

Ever sensitive to current events, Allport's work on prejudice and indeed his entire approach to psychology was ultimately grounded in a deeply felt religious commitment. A practicing Episcopalian, he brought to psychology an ecumenical concern about the corrosive impact of science and technology on the human condition, and like his mentor Stern he feared that the theories and methods of mechanistic psychology underestimated human potential and individual uniqueness. Sensing a divine presence in his work, Allport confided to his wife that *Personality* "isn't my book, never have I felt possessive of it. I believe I was appointed by Providence to add a bit of push backward to the rising tide of barbarism and ignorance in psychology" (quoted in Nicholson, 2003, p. 205). Allport's ongoing spiritual commitments are most apparent in *The Individual and His Religion* (1950) and in *Waiting for the Lord* (1978), a posthumously published collection of thirty-three meditations delivered at the Appleton Chapel at Harvard over twenty-nine years.

Allport's criticisms of mechanistic psychology were influential in the establishment of humanistic psychology in the 1960s. Although he attended the 1962 Old Saybrook conference that helped establish humanistic psychology, Allport was reluctant to take on the label, preferring instead to continue his advocacy for an "open system"—a psychology that was both idiographic and nomothetic. In the postwar period his research interests reflected this duality. Allport continued to revise his nomothetic-type personality while simultaneously working on *Letters from Jenny* (1965)—a detailed analysis of a "unique life" (1967, p. 21).

Allport died of cancer in 1967. Over the years, his scholarly output and personal charm inspired a number of able students including well-known psychologists such as

Stanley Milgram, M. Brewster Smith, and Thomas Pettigrew. Devoted to a humane, socially relevant, and methodologically eclectic psychology, Allport remains an influential figure in modern psychology.

BIBLIOGRAPHY

WORKS BY ALLPORT

"The Journal of Gordon Allport." 1919–1920. Unpublished manuscript in possession of Robert Allport.

"Personality and Character." *Psychological Bulletin* 18, no. 9 (1921): 441–455.

"An Experimental Study of the Traits of Personality with Application to the Problems of Social Diagnosis." PhD diss., Harvard University, 1922.

"The Study of Undivided Personality." *Journal of Abnormal and Social Psychology* 19 (1924): 132–141.

With Floyd H. Allport. *A-S Reaction Study: A Scale for Measuring Ascendance-Submission in Personality; Manual for Directions, Scoring Values, and Norms.* Boston: Houghton Mifflin, 1928.

"The Study of Personality by the Intuitive Method: An Experiment in Teaching from the Locomotive God." *Journal of Abnormal and Social Psychology* 24 (1929): 14–27.

"Some Guiding Principles in Understanding Personality." *Family* (1930): 124–128.

With Philip E. Vernon. *A Study of Values: A Scale for Measuring the Dominant Interests in Personality.* Boston: Houghton Mifflin, 1931.

———. *Studies in Expressive Movement.* New York: Macmillan, 1933.

With Henry S. Odbert. "Trait-Names: A Psycho-Lexical Study." *Psychological Monographs: General and Applied* 47, no. 1 (1936): 171–220. Also published as a book: *Trait-Names: A Psycho-Lexical Study.* Albany, NY: Psychological Review, 1936.

Personality: A Psychological Interpretation. New York: Holt, 1937. The textbook that helped establish personality as a subdiscipline of psychology.

The Appeal of Anglican Catholicism to an Average Man. Advent Papers no. 3, pp. 1–19. Boston: Advent Press, 1944.

With Leo Joseph Postman. *The Psychology of Rumor.* New York: Holt, 1947.

The Individual and His Religion: A Psychological Interpretation. New York: Macmillan, 1950.

The Nature of Prejudice. Cambridge, MA: Addison-Wesley, 1954.

Becoming: Basic Considerations for a Psychology of Personality. New Haven, CT: Yale University Press, 1955.

Pattern and Growth in Personality. New York: Holt, Rinehart and Winston, 1961. A revision of Allport's classic 1937 textbook on personality.

Masterson, Jenny Gove, pseud. *Letters from Jenny.* Edited and interpreted by Gordon W. Allport. New York: Harcourt, Brace & World, 1965.

"Gordon Allport." In *A History of Psychology in Autobiography,* vol. 5, edited by Edwin Boring and Gardner Lindzey, 3–25. New York: Appleton Century, 1967.

With Peter Anthony Bertocci. *Waiting for the Lord: 33 Meditations on God and Man.* New York: Macmillan, 1978.

OTHER SOURCES

Allport, Floyd. "Behavior and Experiment in Social Psychology." *Journal of Abnormal Psychology* 14 (1919): 297–306.

Barenbaum, Nicole B. "How Social Was Personality? The Allports' 'Connection' of Social and Personality Psychology." *Journal of the History of the Behavioral Sciences* 36 (2000): 471–487.

———. "Four, Two, or One? Gordon Allport and the Unique Personality." In *Handbook of Psychobiography,* edited by William Todd Schultz. New York: Oxford University Press, 2005.

Elms, A. "Allport's Personality and Allport's Personality." In *Fifty Years of Personality Psychology,* edited by Kenneth H. Craik, Robert Hogan, and Raymond N. Wolfe. New York: Plenum, 1993.

Eysenck, Hans. *Rebel with a Cause: The Autobiography of Hans Eysenck.* London: Allen, 1990.

Ford, James. "Introduction." In *Social Problems and Social Policy,* edited by James Ford, 1–7. Boston: Ginn, 1923.

Hall, Calvin S., and Gardner Lindzey. *Theories of Personality.* New York: Wiley, 1970.

Jennes, A. "Gordon W. Allport." In *International Encyclopedia of the Social Sciences: Biographical Supplement,* edited by David Sills, vol. 18. New York: Free Press, 1979.

John, O., and R. Robins. "Gordon Allport: Father and Critic of the Five-Factor Model." In *Fifty Years of Personality Psychology,* edited by Kenneth H. Craik, Robert Hogan, and Raymond N. Wolfe, 215–236. New York: Plenum, 1993.

Lamiell, James, and Werner Deutsch. "In the Light of a Star: An Introduction to William Stern's Critical Personalism." *Theory & Psychology* 10 (2000): 715–730.

Lunbeck, Elizabeth. *The Psychiatric Persuasion: Knowledge, Gender, and Power in Modern America.* Princeton, NJ: Princeton University Press, 1994.

Münsterberg, Hugo. *Psychology: General and Applied.* New York: Appleton, 1914.

Murphy, Gardner. *Human Nature and Enduring Peace.* Boston: Houghton Mifflin, 1945.

Nicholson, I. "To 'Correlate Psychology and Social Ethics': Gordon Allport and the First Course in American Personality Psychology." *Journal of Personality* 65 (1997a): 733–742.

———. "Humanistic Psychology and Intellectual Identity: The 'Open' System of Gordon Allport." *Journal of Humanistic Psychology* 37 (1997b): 60–78.

———. *Inventing Personality: Gordon Allport and the Science of Selfhood.* Washington, DC: American Psychological Association, 2003. A detailed biography of the first half of Allport's career.

———. "From the Book of Mormon to the Operational Definition: The Existential Project of S. S. Stevens." In *Handbook of Psychobiography,* edited by William Todd Schultz, 285–298. New York: Oxford University Press, 2005.

Pettigrew, T. "Gordon Willard Allport: A Tribute." *Journal of Social Issues* 55, no. 3 (1999): 415–427.

Schafer, R., I. Berg, and B. McCandless. "Report on Survey of Current Psychological Testing Practices." *Supplement to Newsletter, Division of Clinical & Abnormal Psychology,* American Psychological Association 4, no. 5 (1951).

Stern, William. "William Stern." In *A History of Psychology in Autobiography,* vol. 1, edited by Carl Murchison, 335–388. New York: Russell & Russell, 1930.

Watson, John B. *Psychology from the Standpoint of the Behaviorist.* Philadelphia: Lippencott, 1919.

Ian Nicholson

ALVAREZ, LUIS WALTER (*b.* San Francisco, California, 13 June 1911; *d.* Berkeley, California, 1 September 1988), *physics, particles and detectors, geophysics.*

Alvarez was among the talented physicists who shaped the course of high-energy particle physics in the twentieth century. He was responsible for advances in instrumentation, organization, and application in that field, and invented scores of devices that made radar, nuclear weapons, and ground-controlled aviation feasible, as well as solving many mundane problems. His ingenuity made him a national resource in matters ranging from the Oppenheimer trial to the investigation of the Kennedy assassination. Among his greatest discoveries was a theory that accounted for the extinctions of dinosaurs and thousands of other species in the Cretaceous-Tertiary transition. He was a charismatic leader of large projects and an ingenious experimenter and inventor.

Luie, as his friends called him, was the son of the well-known physician and newspaper columnist Walter C. Alvarez, and the grandson of Luis F. Alvarez, a Spanish immigrant to the United States who was trained in medicine at Cooper Union Medical School and practiced in Hawaii. Luie's aptitude for invention was stimulated by the mechanical and electrical instruments in his father's laboratories at the Hooper Foundation in San Francisco and the Mayo Clinic in Rochester, Minnesota. Alvarez chose to study at the University of Chicago, where he received his BSc, MS, and PhD in physics. During his first years at Chicago, he developed a method of teaching the technique of grazing incidence spectroscopy using a broken phonograph record, a method he subsequently published in *School Science and Mathematics.* His first scientific paper, written with his advisor, Arthur Compton, the leading American researcher in cosmic-ray physics, reported Alvarez's experimental verification of what came to be called the east-west effect in cosmic radiation. This was the result of the effect of the magnetic field of the earth on charged particles that make up cosmic rays. The effect had been predicted by Bruno Rossi, who replicated the discovery two months later in Eritrea.

Although he graduated in 1936, when academic jobs were difficult to find, he was asked to become a research assistant at the Radiation Laboratory of the University of California in Berkeley, which became a formal research unit in the same year. Berkeley's Ernest Lawrence knew Luie well from his visit to the Century of Progress Exhibition in Chicago in 1933, when Lawrence spent a day impressing the young graduate student with his enthusiasm and camaraderie. Luie's sister had been Lawrence's secretary and his father sat on the board of the Macy Foundation, which funded Lawrence's research. Two years after Luie's arrival, he was appointed assistant professor in Berkeley's physics department, and he retained his association with the university for the rest of his life.

Always a quick study, Alvarez soon mastered the literature of the field and the operation of the cyclotron, a notoriously difficult particle accelerator. He collaborated with Edwin M. McMillan in the design of the sixty-inch cyclotron and in the development of a means for extracting the beam from the cyclotron, making it unnecessary to shut it down to insert targets, thus greatly increasing the productivity of the machine in the manufacture of radioisotopes. The cut-and-try methods employed in the construction and use of the cyclotron transcended the theoretical understanding of its operation and accustomed Alvarez to the kind of bold leaps that marked the career of his mentor Lawrence. In addition, Alvarez carefully and thoroughly designed and executed his experiments with the cyclotron and prized physics before production of isotopes.

For example, in 1939 Alvarez used the newly completed Crocker medical cyclotron to discover helium-3, an important isotope of helium that, instead of the usual two protons and two neutrons, contains two protons and only one neutron. After Ernest Rutherford's discovery of tritium in 1934 (an isotope of hydrogen containing one proton and two neutrons), Hans Bethe and others believed that tritium was stable and produced by helium-3's radioactive decay. In setting up his experiment, Alvarez observed the acceleration of particles of mass three by tuning the radio-frequency field of the cyclotron. Because his source material was extracted from natural gas in Oklahoma, he concluded that helium-3, like its isotope helium-4, must be stable, because the deposits of gas were thousands of years old. With his graduate student Robert Cornog, he went on to find that tritium produced by deuteron bombardment of heavy water was actually radioactive.

Attracted by the work of the Fermi group, Alvarez succeeded in extracting a slow neutron beam from the cyclotron that facilitated his measurement of neutron scattering in hydrogen. With Felix Bloch, he determined the magnetic moment of the neutron, a key step in the development of nuclear magnetic resonance imaging (MRI).

Enrico Fermi's postulation of nuclear decay through the emission of an electron afforded another avenue to knowledge of particles interacting inside the atomic nucleus, including positron emission and orbital electron capture. Gian-Carlo Wick provided theoretical insight into these processes, but it was Alvarez who first observed the capture of electrons from the innermost energy level, the K level. He accomplished this by interpreting the x-rays given off by the electrons as they were captured. Alvarez suggested to his student Phillip Abelson that Abelson might use the same techniques to determine the atomic numbers of the so-called "transuranium elements," which Enrico Fermi had postulated would result from slow-neutron bombardment of uranium and other heavy elements, but which had defied traditional physical and chemical methods of identification.

When fission was discovered by Otto Hahn, Fritz Strassman, and Lise Meitner in late 1938, Abelson was planning to examine the x-ray spectra of elements below uranium, having failed to find any of atomic numbers exceeding the known ninety-two elements. Alvarez read of the discovery while having his hair cut in the Berkeley campus barber shop, and immediately informed Abelson, who was quickly able to duplicate the German results on neutron bombardment of uranium. Abelson and McMillan soon found evidence of elements heavier than uranium in cyclotron-bombarded uranium foils, resulting in the discovery of neptunium and of plutonium (by Glenn Seaborg working with Emilio Segrè), for which McMillan and Seaborg received the Nobel Prize in Chemistry in 1951.

Radar. A number of military agencies had sought to develop means of detecting enemy aircraft after World War I demonstrated the menace of aerial bombardment, using radio detection and ranging (radar). Because the size of the target that could be located by radio waves was proportional to their wavelengths, development pushed from shortwave radio to smaller and smaller wavelengths. The limits on this development were the magnitude of the electron tubes that generated the waves. A solution to this problem was the substitution of a solid-state device, the cavity magnetron, for the electron tube. This discovery, made by John T. Boot and Herman Randall at Marcus Oliphant's cyclotron in Birmingham, England, made possible the development of microwave radar.

In the year after World War II began in 1939, President Franklin Delano Roosevelt approved the formation of the National Defense Research Committee (NDRC) under the leadership of Vannevar Bush, president of the Carnegie Institution, to augment military scientific

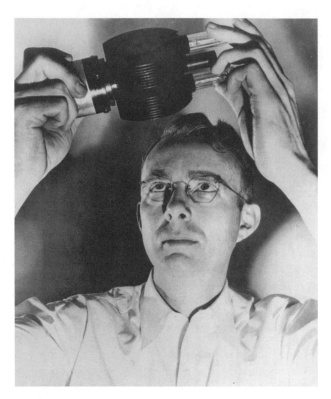

Luis Walter Alvarez. *Luis Walter Alvarez examining a radio transmitter used in radar ground control.* **AP IMAGES.**

research. Alfred Lee Loomis, an amateur physicist and philanthropist who had supported Lawrence's development of a giant cyclotron at the Radiation Laboratory in Berkeley, chaired the Microwave Committee of the NRDC. When Loomis learned of the cavity magnetron from the British, he asked committee member Lawrence to recruit a staff for a new laboratory at MIT to develop it. To cloak the effort, the name "Radiation Laboratory" was adopted. Lawrence recruited Alvarez and sent both Alvarez and McMillan to the MIT laboratory, which was headed by another cyclotron builder, Lee A. DuBridge of the University of Rochester. Alvarez took charge of expediting the development of the first successful radar sets that detected surfaced submarines as well as aircraft. He also devised a means to land aircraft under difficult conditions through Ground-Controlled Approach radar (GCA).

Nuclear Weapons. Alvarez was subsequently summoned to the Metallurgical Laboratory at the University of Chicago, where his former advisor, Arthur Compton, had centralized war work on plutonium, including Fermi's experimental nuclear reactors (piles) from Columbia University and Seaborg's plutonium chemistry from the University of California, over Lawrence's vehement objections that his laboratory could do the job and Compton's could not in a meeting Alvarez attended. Lawrence, however,

continued to develop a means of separating fissile uranium-235 isotopes from uranium-238 using a modified cyclotron as a giant mass spectrometer. Although Alvarez intended to join this effort, illness delayed his transfer, and Robert Oppenheimer recruited him to work at the new Los Alamos laboratory building the atomic bomb.

Alvarez's achievements at Los Alamos played a large part in making the implosion bomb possible. The designers thought at first to make a plutonium bomb achieve criticality through firing one fraction of a critical mass into another fraction, as was done with their uranium weapon. However, Emilio Segrè discovered that their reactor-made plutonium contained an isotope with a high probability of spontaneous fission. Thus, two separated fractions would not be stable long enough to allow the shotgun design. An alternative suggestion explored by Seth Neddermeyer and Ed McMillan, who had preceded Alvarez at Los Alamos, was implosion of a subcritical mass of plutonium by a sphere of high explosives. Working with Harvard chemist George Kistiakowsky, who developed the high-explosive lenses that focused the inward-moving wave of the high-explosive blast, Alvarez devised a system that simultaneously ignited thirty-six detonators regularly spaced on the outside of the high explosive to successfully compress the nuclear fuel to criticality. In order to determine the effectiveness of this system, Alvarez detonated spheres of highly radioactive radium-lanthanum with high explosives inside modified Army tanks; the resulting gamma-radiation showed the regularity of the implosion.

The final test of this system was made at an Army bombing range north of Alamogordo, New Mexico, in the Jornada del Muerto, which Oppenheimer had designated Trinity site. Alvarez, who had been asked to design a means of measuring the force of the blast, observed the test from a B-29 flying twenty-five miles away. He convinced Oppenheimer that he should be allowed to use the blast detectors he had created in combat. Hence, Alvarez flew with the mission that dropped the first atomic bomb—which was of the original uranium shotgun design—on Hiroshima, releasing his parachute-borne detectors from an accompanying B-29. He was thus present at the explosions of both the first uranium and the first plutonium bombs.

Alvarez returned to accelerator work at the Radiation Laboratory in Berkeley after the war. The Manhattan Engineer District provided Alvarez and his colleagues with generous funding to complete a 184-inch synchrocyclotron and an electron synchrotron based upon McMillan's newly discovered principle of phase stability, and a proton linear accelerator designed by Alvarez based on his experience with microwave power generators in the radar program. Alvarez's group included both his former graduate students and a number of talented individuals he had encountered during the war, most notably Wolfgang Panofsky, who subsequently led the effort to create the Stanford Linear Accelerator (linac). Alvarez's machine made modest contributions to studies of nuclear scattering but was soon abandoned for higher-energy machines. The design, however, was incorporated as an injector of protons and heavier ions in many postwar synchrotrons.

After the first Soviet atomic bomb was detected in September 1949, Lawrence again mobilized Alvarez for nuclear weapons development. With Edward Teller, the two men successfully advocated the development of the "Super," or hydrogen bomb, over the opposition of the General Advisory Committee (GAC) of the Atomic Energy Commission, chaired by their former University of California colleague, Robert Oppenheimer. Lawrence had proposed to build a heavy-water reactor to provide tritium for the Super, but when the GAC rejected the project, turned to the manufacture of fissile materials by electronuclear means. The Oak Ridge and Argonne National Laboratories retained their reactor responsibilities.

At a formal Naval Air Station in Livermore, California, Alvarez's linac was scaled up some four hundred times to produce deuterium ions that could be turned on various targets, depending on the material desired. Although the prototype was made to work with great difficulty, discovery of uranium on the Colorado plateau made such an expensive alternative unnecessary.

The crash program to develop the hydrogen bomb interfered with Alvarez's scientific career, as had World War II. Although developments in liquid-hydrogen technology associated with the first thermonuclear tests bore fruit in his later development of the bubble chamber, he paid a price in terms of his career as a research scientist. He also lost the esteem of his fellow physicists when he sided against Oppenheimer in the advocacy of the Super. When Oppenheimer was called to account by political enemies in the Eisenhower administration in 1954, Alvarez testified, along with Edward Teller, in support of the interpretation of Oppenheimer's obstruction to this development as unwise. He did not go so far as Teller in suggesting Oppenheimer's disloyalty, but helped to give the hearing panel a reason to terminate Oppenheimer's clearance.

Bubble Chambers and Big Science. Alvarez returned to Berkeley and began a new career in particle physics in 1954 just as the Bevatron, a 6.2-billion-electron-volt proton accelerator, was being completed by the Radiation Laboratory. He recognized that traditional nuclear detectors would not work well with the output of the new machine, which would be the highest-energy machine in existence. Learning of the invention of the bubble cham-

ber by Donald Glaser of the University of Michigan, he undertook to build a series of such chambers at the Radiation Laboratory. As he had done with the MTA, Alvarez scaled up the chambers rapidly with generous subsidies from the Atomic Energy Commission, from 1.5 inches to 72 inches between 1955 and 1959. He recognized the need for automated analysis of the resulting photographs, which were produced at a rate of several million per year, and organized a group of physicist-programmers to provide it. He also encouraged the development of mechanized means of scanning the photographs for interesting events, leading to the development of a series of track-following devices such as the Franckenstein, invented by James Franck. These ancillary devices made the bubble-chamber system an effective and productive means of detecting many new particles and particle resonances. This work resulted in the award of the Nobel Prize in Physics to Alvarez in 1968.

The virtue of the liquid-hydrogen bubble chamber lay in the simplicity of the target—the hydrogen atom. Unlike earlier bubble chambers, which used hydrocarbon compounds, interactions with hydrogen atoms by particles from the Bevatron were simple to interpret. A significant event was more easily identified, permitting semiautomated and automated techniques to be employed. Alvarez's group introduced techniques comparable to those of the assembly line in automotive manufacture, including division of labor, continuous processing, and quality control. The "industrialization" of particle detectors exemplified in the liquid-hydrogen bubble chamber similarly enhanced productivity.

Alvarez and his group pursued their particles in much the same way Lawrence had sought new radioisotopes in the 1930s. By focusing on one subatomic particle at a time and thoroughly charting its interactions, they were able to resolve important questions in particle physics as well as to suggest new ones. Unencumbered by theoretical constraints, they demolished existing theory and forced new interpretations on the particle physics community. The bubble chamber, like the cyclotron for accelerators, became the detector of choice in high-energy physics laboratories in the 1960s, and, like his mentor Lawrence, Alvarez was generous with help to would-be emulators of his system, supplying bubble-chamber film to those who did not have the means to produce it at their own laboratories.

Public Scientist. After Lawrence died at the age of fifty-seven in 1958, however, Alvarez chose not to follow Lawrence's example in laboratory administration. Offered the directorship of the Lawrence Radiation Laboratory by University of California President Clark Kerr, Alvarez elected to remain head of his bubble-chamber group. McMillan, who succeeded Lawrence as director, did not succeed in winning Alvarez's loyalty, and this led to Alvarez's resignation as associate director and, eventually, his decision to pursue new activities.

Alvarez enjoyed the role of Cold War scientist and turned increasingly to service on panels of scientific advisors to the Atomic Energy Commission and the Department of Defense, as well as other government and private agencies interested in radar, aviation, and nuclear weapons. He was an advisor to the Central Intelligence Agency, National Security Agency, and Federal Aviation Administration, among others. Science policy was largely shaped by physicists of his generation. This branch of science in particular enjoyed substantial federal research funding and, as a part of the elite military-industrial complex, played a crucial role in directing that expenditure. Alvarez was able to acquire funding for his group from the National Aeronautics and Space Administration when he decided to resign from the administration of the Lawrence Radiation Laboratory, for example, to make a search for the magnetic monopoles that physical theory predicted, but which his team failed to find either in meteorites or in lunar rock samples, where long-term cosmic-ray bombardment should have made them.

Return to Cosmic Rays. Alvarez simultaneously searched cosmic rays for evidence of the antimatter that Hannes Alfven had predicted should enter the earth's galaxy from galaxies made of it and separated from this galaxy by an electron plasma. He used a five-ton superconducting magnet borne aloft by balloons to detect them and, when that failed, undertook a survey with smaller superconducting magnets. As with the magneton, this search served to establish that these visitors were undetectable.

Alvarez also found an archaeological use for cosmic rays. The pyramid of Chephren at Giza had only one subterranean chamber, unlike the two constructed by his predecessors, and Alvarez believed that there might be other chambers that could be revealed by "x-raying" the pyramid with cosmic-ray muons, whose passage through the stone would be less attenuated by such voids in the pyramid's structure. Despite the Arab-Israeli War of 1967, which forced his team of American and Egyptian physicists to postpone their work, the spark-chamber detectors he placed in the subterranean chamber made an extensive survey of incoming muons and found no hidden chambers. The method is still used in the early twenty-first century to investigate massive structures.

Nobel Prize. In 1968, Alvarez was awarded the Nobel Prize in Physics for his bubble-chamber work and the resulting discoveries. Although he had been disappointed when he did not receive the prize jointly with Donald Glaser in 1961 and trailed his other Radiation Laboratory

colleagues Lawrence, McMillan, Seaborg, Segrè, and Owen Chamberlain to Stockholm, he made the most of his undivided funds by inviting the senior members of his group to join him there for the award ceremonies and took some condolence that while not the earliest, his was the longest prize citation for the award. Unlike many Nobel laureates, he resolved not to accept the social liabilities that usually come with the prize, and refused to sign petitions and attend other celebrations, including the Lawrence Radiation Laboratory party held in his honor by McMillan.

Alvarez did enjoy the liberation from his quotidian duties at the laboratory to investigate unusual phenomena. His attention was drawn to the ongoing controversy surrounding the assassination of John F. Kennedy when he was given access to the only visual recording of that incident, the Zapruder film made by an amateur photographer in Dallas at the time. Many critics of the Warren Commission, which conducted an investigation of the assassination and concluded that a lone gunman, Lee Harvey Oswald, perpetrated it, believed the film belied that conclusion. Alvarez systematically tackled the analysis of the film and found that it supported the commission's conclusion, particularly with respect to Kennedy's physical response to the fatal shot and with respect to the timing of the three shots. As an example of forensic science, his study was a tour de force that undermined alternative scenarios that had become a leitmotif of the 1970s.

His last experiment in forensic science dealt with the mass extinction of dinosaurs and other species. His son, Walter, who had become a geologist, detected a thin layer of clay laid down at approximately the same period as the dinosaurs' disappearance, and brought a sample of it to Luis Alvarez's attention. Intrigued by the association, Luis suggested that they measure the length of time that had been required to make the deposit. In order to determine the age of the clay, Luis thought first to use as tracers radioactive elements produced in the Earth's atmosphere by cosmic rays (e.g., carbon-14). However, their lifetimes proved an order of magnitude too small, so Luis elected to search for elements that were more abundant in meteorite debris than in normal soil. Iridium was detected by Radiation Laboratory nuclear chemists using neutron activation analysis and proved three hundred times more abundant in the clay layer than in the surrounding limestone layers.

Subsequent investigation revealed that the layer also did not have elements associated with supernovae, thought by some to have caused the mass extinction, and through a process of elimination Alvarez concluded that a ten-kilometer meteor had struck the earth and created a dust cloud that orbited it long enough to cause the extinctions by cooling and interfering with plant growth.

Alvarez's explanation of the Cretaceous-Tertiary mass extinction has won increasing acceptance among paleontologists, especially since a candidate impact site was discovered in the Yucatan peninsula of Mexico. Although there are competing theories that seek to account for the extinction in terms of terrestrial causes, the Alvarez hypothesis has not been refuted, and he believed it would be the scientific accomplishment for which he would be longest remembered.

Alvarez's discoveries and inventions made him one of the most remarkable and versatile scientists of the twentieth century, and his technological accomplishments were both abundant and profitable, giving rise to a variety of spin-off firms from which he drew profit as well as pride. In addition to his many radar patents, he also held patents for electronuclear machines, x-ray detectors for explosives in airline baggage, optical systems, and range detectors for golf carts. For these accomplishments he was elected to the Inventors' Hall of Fame, and won numerous awards, including the Collier Trophy of the National Aeronautical Association, the National Medal of Science, and the Pioneer Medal of the American Institute of Electrical and Electronic Engineers.

On 1 September 1988, a year after he completed his autobiography, Alvarez died of cancer in Berkeley, California. His work in high-energy physics had transformed experimental practice by importing collaborative research into the laboratory, as historian Peter Galison has shown, and contributed to the triumph of "big science" in the twentieth century.

BIBLIOGRAPHY

WORKS BY ALVAREZ

With Arthur H. Compton. "A Positively Charged Component of Cosmic Rays." *Physical Review* 43 (1933): 835–836. An account of the discovery of the east-west effect in cosmic radiation.

"Capture of Orbital Electrons by Nuclei." *Physical Review* 54 (1938): 486–497.

With Robert Cornog. "Helium and Hydrogen of Mass 3." *Physical Review* 56 (1939): 613.

With Felix Bloch. "A Quantitative Determination of the Neutron Moment in Absolute Nuclear Magnetons." *Physical Review* 57 (1940): 111–122.

With Hugh Bradner, James V. Franck, Hayden Gordon, et al. "Berkeley Proton Linear Accelerator." *Review of Scientific Instruments* 26 (1955): 111–133.

With Frank S. Crawford, Myron L. Good, and M. Lynn Stevenson. "Lifetime of K-Mesons." *Physical Review* 101 (1956): 503–505.

With Hugh Bradner, Frank S. Crawford Jr., J. A. Crawford, et al. "Catalysis of Nuclear Reactions by μ-Mesons." *Physical Review* 105 (1957): 1127–1128.

"High-Energy Physics with Hydrogen Bubble Chambers." In *Proceedings of the Second United Nations International Conference on Peaceful Uses of Atomic Energy,* vol. 30, *Fundamental Physics.* Geneva: United Nations, 1958.

With Phillipe Eberhard, M. L. Good, William Graziano, et al. "Neutral Cascade Hyperon Event." *Physical Review Letters* 2 (1959): 215–219.

With Margaret Alston, Phillipe Eberhard, M. L. Good, et al. "Resonance in the Λ-Π System." *Physical Review Letters* 5 (1960): 520–524.

With Margaret Alston, William Graziano, M. L. Good, et al. "Resonance in the K-Π System." *Physical Review Letters* 6 (1961): 300–302.

With D. O. Huwe, G. R. Kalbfleisch, Margaret Alston, et al. "The 1660 MeV Y^*_1 Hyperon." *Physical Review Letters* 10 (1963): 184–188.

"A Physicist Examines the Kennedy Assassination Film." *American Journal of Physics* 44 (1976): 813.

With Walter Alvarez, Frank Asaro, and Helen V. Michel. "Extraterrestrial Cause for the Cretaceous-Tertiary Extinction." *Science* 208 (1980): 1095.

Alvarez: Adventures of a Physicist. New York: Basic Books, 1987.

OTHER SOURCES

Galison, Peter. *Image and Logic: A Material Culture of Microphysics.* Chicago: University of Chicago Press, 1997.

Garwin, Richard L. "Memorial Tribute for Luis W. Alvarez." *Memorial Tributes,* National Academy of Engineering, vol. 5. Washington, DC: National Academy Press, 1992.

Trower, W. Peter, ed. *Discovering Alvarez: Selected Works of Luis W. Alvarez with Commentary by His Students and Colleagues.* Chicago: University of Chicago Press, 1987.

Heilbron, John, and Robert Seidel. *Lawrence and His Laboratory,* vol. 1, *A History of the Lawrence Berkeley Laboratory.* Berkeley: University of California Press, 1989.

Robert W. Seidel

AMALDI, EDOARDO

(*b.* Carpaneto Piacentino, Italy, 5 September 1908; *d.* Rome, Italy, 5 December 1989), *nuclear physics, cosmic ray physics, science policy, international collaboration, arms control.*

One of the leading figures of twentieth-century Italian science in the field of fundamental experimental physics, Amaldi contributed to nuclear physics in the 1930s and 1940s and to cosmic ray and particle physics in the postwar years; he also became one of the pioneers in the experimental search for gravitational waves in the early 1970s. Far more important than his direct contributions to knowledge, however, was his role as a true statesman of science. It is largely thanks to his drive and initiative that Italian physics was able to emerge from the collapse following World War II; he was instrumental in finding adequate support and building solid institutions in the postwar years. He was also one of the main actors in the process that turned the dreams of large transnational scientific projects among European countries into realities, first and foremost the Conseil Européen pour la recherche nucléaire (CERN; European Organization for Nuclear Research).

In Rome with Fermi. As a boy, Amaldi lived in a scientific and academic environment. His parents were Laura Basini and Ugo Amaldi, the latter a distinguished mathematician and university professor. Ugo's academic career led him from Modena to Padua, where young Edoardo went to secondary school, and finally, in 1924, to the University of Rome. There, Ugo became colleagues with some of the outstanding Italian mathematicians of the time, such as Vito Volterra, Tullio Levi-Civita, Guido Castelnuovo, and Federigo Enriques. Edoardo enrolled at the University of Rome in 1925 as a student of engineering. Two years later, however, he switched to physics, attracted—as were a few other brilliant students, such as Emilio Segrè and Ettore Majorana—by the presence of Enrico Fermi, who had just been called upon by the director of the Istituto fisico (Physics Institute), Orso Mario Corbino, to occupy the first chair of theoretical physics ever established in Italy. Amaldi took his degree in physics in July 1929 with a dissertation on the Raman spectrum of the molecule of benzene; his thesis advisor was Franco Rasetti, who had joined Fermi in moving from Florence to Rome, first as Corbino's assistant and, beginning in 1930, as professor of spectroscopy.

By the end of the 1920s, a strong group of young physicists was established at the Physics Institute on Rome's via Panisperna (Panisperna Street), and research efforts were slowly but deliberately shifted from the original concern with spectroscopic problems to the new frontier of nuclear physics. Under Fermi's leadership, it became common practice to send young people to leading research centers abroad for extended periods to improve their skills. In 1931 Amaldi spent ten months working in Leipzig, Germany, in Peter Debye's laboratory, learning X-ray diffraction techniques in liquids; he also spent time at the Cavendish Laboratory in Cambridge, England, during the summer of 1934 and at Columbia University in New York City and the Department of Terrestrial Magnetism of the Carnegie Institution in Washington, D.C., in the summer of 1936.

Following the discovery of artificially induced radioactivity in January 1934, Fermi, soon joined by the whole team, began a methodical search of the effects produced by neutron bombardment on every element known. Rather than use positively charged alpha particles as projectiles—as had been done in the previous experi-

ments by Frédéric Joliot and Iréne Curie—Fermi chose to utilize neutrons emitted by a radon-berillium source, reasoning that the uncharged particles would have greater ability to penetrate the atomic nucleus. The very expensive radon needed to build this source was available to him through the generosity of Corbino's former assistant, Giulio Cesare Trabacchi, then director of the Public Health Institute's Physics Laboratory.

The long series of experiments were of paramount importance for the understanding of nuclear properties, and they culminated in October 1934 with the discovery of the greater efficiency of slowed-down neutrons in activating nuclear transformations. It was a truly new way of doing group work in experimental physics; the published papers carried the signature of all team members (Fermi, Rasetti, Amaldi, Segrè, the chemist Oscar D'Agostino, and later on the younger Bruno Pontecorvo). Clearly, Fermi was the intellectual leader and the driving force, and for the results of these experiments he would receive in 1938 the Nobel Prize in Physics.

Most of the work in the following couple of years was done by Fermi and Amaldi. (Rasetti and Pontecorvo were mostly absent from Rome, and Segrè had moved to a professorship in Palermo.) During this period Amaldi acquired a competence in nuclear physics, particularly on the subject of neutron properties, that turned him into one of the leading authorities in the field. In 1937 he won a professorship at the University of Cagliari in Sardinia, but was instead immediately called on to occupy the chair of experimental physics in Rome left vacant by the sudden death of Corbino, a position that Amaldi kept until retirement. Amaldi kept working on nuclear physics with Fermi and Rasetti; together they designed and began to build a Cockroft-Walton accelerator, which was completed in 1939 and installed in the building of the Istituto di sanità pubblica (Public Health Institute).

By the late 1930s, however, the general situation in Italy was rapidly deteriorating; lack of funds and support to keep research competitive, the emergence of a clear alignment of Italian fascism with Hitler's Germany, and the racial laws promulgated in 1938 led to the forced or voluntary emigration of a great number of Italian physicists. This included Fermi, who left for the United States at the end of 1938. When the war began, Amaldi was the only member of the original via Panisperna group remaining in the country.

The War Years. Left alone in Rome with a small group of younger people, Amaldi for a while concentrated his research efforts on nuclear fission, working with a mixed group of physicists from the Physics Institute and the Public Health Institue, while the theoretical work was done in collaboration with Gian-Carlo Wick, who had replaced Fermi. This activity was interrupted in 1940, when Amaldi was sent to the African front for a few months. Back in Rome, research on fission continued briefly, but by 1941 the suspicion had arisen that working on fission exposed the group to the danger of being recruited to do war-related research. It was thus decided to abandon research on fission and instead direct experimental work toward the problems of proton-neutron scattering, while some of the younger group members began promising research activity on cosmic rays. Though research conditions during the war were difficult, Rome was in a better situation than centers in the north, especially after liberation in June 1944. Most of what had been left of active research in Italy, both in terms of expertise and people, was concentrated in Rome at the end of the war. In collaboration with Wick and Gilberto Bernardini, who had grown in the research tradigion inaugurated in Florence by Bruno Rossi, Amaldi deliberately took upon himself the task of the reconstructing physics in his country, starting from the vantage point offered by his location in the capital. The first move, successfully completed in October 1945, was to secure the establishment of a research center for nuclear and elementary particle physics from the reconstituted Consiglio nazionale delle ricerche (National Research Council, CNR) at the Physics Institute in Rome.

The Years of Reconstruction. During a trip by Amaldi to the United States in 1946, Fermi offered him a chair at the University of Chicago. Amaldi declined, having by now resolved that his duty was to take care of scientific development in his homeland. On the occasion of his trip, Amaldi was confronted with the sensitive character that his research interests had acquired during the war. For example, restrictions were imposed for security reasons on discussion of some matters of real or supposed military interest; thus, beyond a certain limit it was impossible for him to talk freely even with Fermi about nuclear problems. He found that disturbing on ethical grounds and harmful to scientific progress. That experience strenghtened in him the conviction, already matured during the war years, that any genuine scientific collaboration should be planned in total freedom from military control, a general policy that he strictly adhered to in the following years.

Direct contact with the new level of financial support given to nuclear and particle physics in the United States after the war convinced Amaldi that the best course of action for Italian physics would be to abandon ambitious programs in fields requiring expensive instrumentation, such as the postwar generation of particle accelerators, and to concentrate on those research sectors where good results could reasonably be obtained with the modest means at his country's disposal. As a consequence, focus was placed on research in cosmic rays, a relatively inexpen-

sive field where Italian physicists could rely on a solid tradition. A first significant step was the construction of a high-altitude laboratory in the Alps in 1947, while new research centers followed in the footsteps of the Rome center, namely, Padua in 1948, Turin in 1951, and Milan in 1952.

Meanwhile, Amaldi was also giving support to the first initiatives aimed at the development of applied nuclear research, training young engineers and physicists and finding support among politicians interested in the exploitation of nuclear energy for civilian purposes, a program that led a few years later to the construction of Italy's first power reactors. Relying on the strength of this active network and on the support of CNR's president Gustavo Colonnetti, Amaldi and Bernardini could then take a significant step in reshaping the institutional panorama of Italian physics with the establishment in 1951 of the Istituto nazionale di fisica nucleare (National Institute of Nuclear Physics, INFN), financed by CNR through the channel of the Comitato nazionale per le ricerche nucleari (National committee for nuclear research, CNRN), a body in charge of both fundamental and applied nuclear research. Bernardini was the first president of INFN. Amaldi followed him, serving from March 1960 to January 1966.

The INFN physicists' first important set of activities was their participation in three different international collaborations between 1952 and 1954 that launched high-altitude balloons carrying photographic emulsions for the study of cosmic rays. The Rome group led by Amaldi was actively present in the first and second collaborations. Soon after, a more ambitious program was initiated for the creation of a national laboratory for high-energy physics, equipped with a competitive accelerator. Formulated in 1954, the project became reality in less than five years. The electrosynchrotron of the Laboratori nazionali in Frascati, near Rome, started operating in February 1959. Amaldi's extremely active role, both in the physics community and with politicians and administrators in Rome, was in the end decisive in winning a site close to Rome as the location for the new laboratory. This was in accordance with a general design that left the development of nuclear facilities for civilian purposes to the northern areas of the country and concentrated fundamental research near the capital.

Building European Science. Soon after the end of the war, physicists throughout Europe came to realize that only a collaborative effort between several countries could keep Europe competitive under the new conditions of the postwar years. Plans for a great European laboratory for fundamental physics were first explicitly advanced around 1950 on several occasions. Amaldi was one of the strongest advocates of the idea from the very beginning, an idea he could effectively push in his capacity as vice president (from 1948 to 1954) of the International Union of Pure and Applied Physics (IUPAP). The ambitious plan quickly took form with the institutional support offered by the United Nations Economic, Social, and Cultural Organization (UNESCO). Amaldi and the French physicist Pierre Auger, director of the scientific section of UNESCO, were the driving force for a project that had a great power of attraction for the younger generations of European physicists but that also had to face difficulties and opposition, on both the scientific and governmental levels.

By May 1951, however, a detailed plan was approved by a selected team of experts from eight countries, and early in 1952 an intergovernmental conference established a provisional organization, which took the name of Conseil Européen pour la recherche nucléaire. Amaldi was elected general secretary of the provisional CERN; in that temporary post he supervised all the crucial phases of the new institution's infancy, including the early stage of the work on the site of the laboratory, which was finally built on grounds allocated by the city of Geneva in Switzerland. He left his position when CERN entered into official existence in September 1954, refusing the offer to become the first general director, inspired among other considerations by his desire to return to more active research in physics. Paralleling the development of the laboratory in Frascati, CERN's large proton synchrotron was successfully completed in 1959, reaching a record-setting energy of 28 GeV. Amaldi kept strong ties with CERN, maintaining a position on the scientific bodies shaping its policy.

In 1963 Amaldi created the European Committee for Future Accelerators (ECFA), an independent body charged with the design of the new machines to be built in Europe at CERN and beyond; he was its president until 1969. In the late 1960s he was president of the group that planned the new 300 GeV proton synchrotron for CERN, a project that was finally approved by the CERN member states in 1971, when Amaldi was in charge as president of the CERN council. Occupying important positions both at INFN and at CERN simultaneously often put Amaldi in the delicate position of balancing resources between domestic developments and international cooperation, as when a choice had to be made between giving Italy's support to the 300 GeV machine project in Geneva or launching a great effort towards a new Italian proton synchrotron. On that occasion he was strongly in favor of keeping the CERN project alive, even if that meant giving up an interesting program at home. He was convinced that priority had to be granted to Europe, both because Europe would ultimately always have access to much larger resources and because of his strong conviction concerning the importance of transnational cultural and scientific collaboration.

A network of scientists and politicians similar to the one that had contributed to the success of CERN arose in the early 1960s, when a joint European effort in space science was discussed. Again, Amaldi took a leading role in launching the idea and pushing it through scientific and political circles. As a result, in 1964 the European Space Research Organization was established; ten years later it gave birth to the European Space Agency. One distinctive feature of the new institution, on which Amaldi insisted repeatedly, was its lack of any connection with military interests; in his view, such projects had to blend a genuine international character with a total independence from any military-oriented goals, which, he believed, would endanger freedom of research by imposing secrecy and preventing a genuine transnational collaboration.

Cosmic Rays and Particle Physics. In the time left over from academic and administrative duties and frantic activity as an organizer and planner of science, Amaldi continued to do active research and lead groups of younger collaborators, moving his interest toward the field of cosmic ray physics. An exciting discovery came during the collaborative high-altitude balloon flights in 1953: A track was found in one of the emulsions exposed to cosmic radiation that could be interpreted as evidence of the annihilation process of an antiproton, a particle whose existence was taken for granted on a theoretical basis but that had never been observed. To gain better support for the scant evidence offered by that single track, Amaldi turned to his former friend Emilio Segrè, now at the University of California at Berkeley, proposing a joint research program aimed at the detection of similar events in emulsions exposed to the beam of protons produced by Berkeley's Bevatron, at the time the most powerful accelerator in the world and the only one reaching an energy high enough to produce proton-antiproton pairs. The Rome-Berkeley collaboration lasted for a couple of years, giving a number of important results on antiprotons and their annihilation properties. The first confirmation of such a process clearly visible in emulsion tracks, however, did not come until a few weeks after Segrè and his group had independently detected the antiproton by a different experiment that relied on counters instead of emulsions. For this discovery, Segrè and Owen Chamberlain were awarded the Nobel Prize in Physics in 1959. The Rome group just missed receiving that recognition. It was further confirmation for Amaldi of the absolute need for European physicists to push hard on the CERN program and to invest in large-scale, competitive experimental facilities.

The Late Years. A completely new research field was opened to Italian physicists by Amaldi in the 1970s. His interest in the problem of the experimental detection of gravitational waves went back to a course on that subject given by Joseph Weber, the pioneer of that kind of instrumentation, at a summer school in Varenna in 1962. In 1970 a group under Amaldi's leadership was formed in Rome with the aim of designing and building cryogenic detectors for gravitational waves. In the beginning, small-scale antennae were planned and put into operation. A number of constructive problems connected with the design and proper working of these instruments were tackled and solved in the course of years, which resulted in a better understanding of the underlying physics. Larger detectors were built in succession, in Rome and Frascati and then at CERN: There the cryogenic antenna Explorer was installed in the 1980s, which in 1989 attained the highest sensitivity ever reached. Throughout this period Amaldi, while leaving to others the responsibilty for the actual direction of research, played an active role both in the planning and execution of experiments and in recruiting young students to the field. The detection of gravitational waves remained an open problem at the beginning of the twenty-first century; huge facilities have been built for the purpose in large international collaborations with an important presence of active Italian physicists, a legacy of a tradition that goes back to Amaldi's initial foresight.

Along with active scientific research, in his mature years Amaldi increasingly devoted time to collecting his memories and putting on paper those moments in the history of physics to which he had been a personal witness. Starting with commemorations of friends and colleagues and recollections of relevant events, this reconstruction of a personal and collective memory slowly evolved into the production of more profound writings, characterized by growing insight into the more general historical context and a care for sources and documentation not usually found in similar works by scientists. In his writing he was helped by a habit, developed during his early days as leader of the Italian physics community, of keeping every relevant document related to his work and to the institutions with which he was involved. His personal archive helped him to produce works halfway between the traditional scientist's recollection and the scholarly research of the independent historian, which will be an invaluable source for further studies in the history of twentieth-century science for some time to come.

Peace and Arms Control. A concern for peace and a strong feeling of the responsible role the scientific community should play in achieving it had always been a natural complement to Amaldi's unshakable belief in the open character of science and the need for international cooperation. Together with his colleagues who, like him, stayed in Italy during the war, he was spared the difficult decision of whether to take part in projects related to the possible military use of nuclear physics—although he

honestly admitted later that, had this not been the case, he would in the end have put his competence in the service of the Allies, who looked to him, beyond any doubt, the right side on which to fight. After the war he followed with interest the first attempts of American physicists to establish some sort of organization aimed at the control of the arms race. When the Pugwash movement for the control of nuclear weapons was created in 1957, following a 1955 appeal by Bertrand Russell and Albert Einstein, he was asked at the beginning to participate. He attended the second Pugwash meeting in 1958 and was a member of the Continuing Committee, the governing body of the movement, from 1962 to 1972.

Together with his physicist colleague Carlo Schaerf, Amaldi was the founder of the International School on Disarmament and Research on Conflicts (ISODARCO) and acted as its president from its inception in 1966 to his death. In 1982 he led a delegation of Italian physicists to the president of Italy to present a resolution of concern with the ongoing arms race and the danger to Europe created by the installation in Europe and Italy of Cruise missiles. As a follow-on to this document, the Unione scienziati per il disarmo (Italian Union of Scientists for Disarmament, USPID) was founded. This organization has kept the discussion of disarmament issues alive in Italy by organizing international meetings and spreading documented scientific information on these issues. One of Amaldi's last official public speeches was in 1987, when he led a delegation of Italian scientists to the International Forum organized in Moscow by Soviet general secretary Mikhail Gorbachev, in the new distension scenario that was opening at the time.

Amaldi was married to Ginestra Giovene, one of the very few women among the physics students in Rome during the 1930s. They had three children: Ugo, Francesco, and Daniela. Ugo followed in his father's footsteps and became a high-energy physicist.

Amaldi was a member of a number of academies and learned societies. In 1988 and 1989 he was the president of the Accademia dei Lincei, Italy's national academy. Amaldi retained his full capacities until dying suddenly of a stroke at age eighty-one.

BIBLIOGRAPHY

Amaldi's papers are deposited in the library of the Physics Department at the University La Sapienza in Rome. They consist of a large collection (more than 650 boxes) of correspondence, notebooks, documents, drawings, and photos. A full list of Amaldi's approximately two hundred scientific publications can be found in Carlo Rubbia Piero Angela, Edoardo Amaldi scienziato e cittadino d'Europa (Milan, Italy: Leonardo Periodici, 1992).

WORKS BY AMALDI

The Production and Slowing Down of Neutrons. Handbuch der Physik series, 38. Berlin: Springer-Verlag, 1959. A fundamental review of neutron physics.

"From the Discovery of the Neutron to the Discovery of Nuclear Fission." *Physics Report* 111, nos. 1–4 (1984): 1–331. An excellent blend of technical competence and historical accuracy.

Da via Panisperna all'America: I fisici italiani nella seconda guerra mondiale. Edited by Giovanni Battimelli and Michelangelo De Maria. Rome, Italy: Editori Riuniti, 1997. Includes an unpublished manuscript by Amaldi and a selection of correspondence covering the years 1938–1946.

20th Century Physics: Essays and Recollections, a Selection of Historical Writings. Edited by Giovanni Battimelli and Giovanni Paoloni. Singapore; River Edge, NJ: World Scientific, 1998. A large selection of historical writings by Amaldi, with English translation of those originally published in Italian.

OTHER SOURCES

Battimelli, Giovanni, Michelangelo De Maria, and Giovanni Paoloni. *L'istituto nazionale di fisica nucleare: Storia di una comunità di ricerca.* Rome: Laterza, 2002. Amaldi is the key figure throughout the volume.

Hermann, Armin, John Krige, Dominique Pestre, et al. *History of CERN.* 3 vols. Amsterdam, New York: North-Holland Physics Publications, 1987–1996. Of particular interest is the discussion in the first volume of Amaldi's role in the early stages of CERN.

Rubbia, Carlo, and Piero Angela. *Edoardo Amaldi scienziato e cittadino d'Europa.* Milan: Leonardo Periodici, 1992. Includes a biography by Rubbia and a long interview conducted by Angela in 1980.

University of Roma la Sapienzem Department of Physics. *Proceedings of the Conference "Edoardo Amaldi. Physics, Politics of Research and Civil Commitment,"* Rome, 20–21 December 1999. Giornale di Fisica, Quaderni di Storia della Fisica N. 7, 2000.

Giovanni Battimelli

AMBARTSUMIAN, VIKTOR AMA-ZASPOVICH

(*b.* Tbilisi, Georgia [Russian Empire], 18 September 1908; *d.* Byurakan, Armenia, 12 August 1996), *astrophysics, radiative transfer, principle of invariance, stellar dynamics, interstellar absorption, active galactic nuclei.*

Recognized as one of the giants of twentieth-century astrophysics, Ambartsumian is best known for his pioneering work in three areas: (1) invariance principles as applied to the theory of radiative transfer; (2) inverse problems of astrophysics; and (3) the empirical approach to problems of the origin and evolution of stars and galax-

ies. An honorary or foreign member of twenty-eight national academies of sciences, Ambartsumian served as both vice president (1948–1955) and president (1961–1964) of the International Astronomical Union (IAU) and as president of the International Council of Scientific Unions (ICSU). Arguably Armenia's greatest scientist of modern times, Ambartsumian was born in the waning days of the Russian Empire. Coming of age after the 1917 Bolshevik Revolution, Ambartsumian would—as he created his own revolution in astrophysics—live a life that was shaped and directed by the Soviet system in which he lived. Reflecting this dichotomy, the present article is divided into discussions of the scientific and political aspects of Ambartsumian's life.

Early Years. Ambartsumian was born in Tbilisi, Georgia, which at the start of the twentieth century was the cosmopolitan hub of the Russian Empire's Transcaucasian territories. His father Amazasp Asaturovich Ambartsumian graduated from the Institute of Oriental Languages in Moscow and received a law degree from St. Petersburg University. A linguist who translated classic Greek literature into Armenian, Ambartsumian's father encouraged him from an early age to show an interest in knowledge in general and in science in particular. Viktor Ambartsumian displayed an aptitude for mathematics by age four and had become captivated by astronomy by age eleven. He gave talks on astronomy while still a student in secondary school and worked in the school observatory.

Following in his father's footsteps, Ambartsumian went to St. Petersburg (which had been renamed Leningrad) in 1924 and enrolled in the Department of Physics and Mathematics at Leningrad State University (LSU). There he met fellow student Nikolai Kozyrev, who quickly became Ambartsumian's close friend and professional collaborator. As Ambartsumian described in a 1987 interview, in Kozyrev he "found a comrade with whom I became friends because we had absolutely identical goals." By 1925, Ambartsumian and Kozyrev were working together on problems of radiative transfer and were publishing papers in the *Astronomische Nachrichten, Zeitschrift für Physik, Monthly Notices of the Royal Astronomical Society,* and other major international journals of the day. The relationship between Ambartsumian and Kozyrev became so close that they were known by a single nickname: "the Ambars."

Ambartsumian and Kozyrev also had a close friendship with fellow astronomy student Dmitrii Eropkin. In addition, this astronomical trio maintained a friendship with a group of LSU physics "musketeers" that included Dmitrii Ivanenko, George Gamow, Lev Landau, and Matvei Bronshtein. Ambartsumian and Kozyrev completed their studies at LSU in 1928 and went to Pulkovo

Observatory on the outskirts of Leningrad for graduate study under the astrophysicist Aristarkh A. Belopolskii.

Like Kozyrev, the physicist Ivanenko figured as a coauthor in Ambartsumian's early works. In particular, in the late 1920s, Ambartsumian and Ivanenko tackled the widespread assumption that atomic nuclei consist of protons and electrons. At a time when the neutron had yet to be discovered, most physicists presumed that the weight of a nucleus came entirely from protons. Moreover, if the charge of a nucleus was something other than would be expected from the number of protons, the nucleus must contain negatively charged electrons to offset the positively charged protons. In studying β decay, however, Ambartsumian and Ivanenko came to the conclusion that an electron is created spontaneously at the time it is ejected from an atom and could not, therefore, have been in the atom's nucleus. The 1930 paper by Ivanenko and Ambartsumian anticipated the discovery of the neutron by two years.

In 1929, Ambartsumian ventured into mathematics. Werner Heisenberg and Erwin Schrödinger had just published works in which questions of atomic spectra and atomic energy levels were posed as problems of the eigenvalues of several operators—that is, given an operator, find the eigenvalues and eigenfunctions. Ambartsumian turned this around to ask to what extent an atom's spectrum determines its structure. If the eigenvalues are known, is it not possible to first find the operator and then see how unambiguously the operator determines the functions and parameters entering into that operator? Ambartsumian could not answer this question completely, but he did solve a special case in which he proved that among all vibrating strings only the homogeneous vibrating string has eigenvalues that are specific to it—that is, homogeneous vibrating strings have a spectrum of eigenvalues. Ambartsumian's paper on this, the theory of inverse spectral problems associated with Sturm-Liouville operators, was published in 1929 in the physics journal *Zeitschrift für Physik,* where it went largely unnoticed until it was discovered by mathematicians in the mid-1940s and became a significant research topic in the ensuing decades.

After completing his graduate work in 1931, Ambartsumian served as Pulkovo's Scientific Secretary in 1931 and 1932 while simultaneously working as a lecturer at LSU. During this time Ambartsumian traveled to Pulkovo's southern station in Simeis, Crimea, where he met and married Vera Fyodorovna, the niece of observatory director Grigorii Shain, with whom he would have four children.

In 1932, Ambartsumian published a paper in the *Monthly Notices of the Royal Astronomical Society* on the radiative equilibrium of planetary nebulae that would become a cornerstone of the modern theory of gaseous nebulae. In the following year Ambartsumian and Kozyrev published a work in which the masses of gas clouds ejected by novae were estimated for the first time.

Leaving Pulkovo in 1934, Ambartsumian returned to LSU and organized the Soviet Union's first university department of astrophysics. (His first graduate student was Viktor V. Sobolev.) In 1935, when academic degrees were reintroduced into the educational system for the first time since the establishment of the Soviet state, Ambartsumian was awarded a doctoral degree based on his scientific work through that date.

In the mid-1930s, Ambartsumian turned his attention to inverse problems of astrophysics. English astrophysicist Arthur Eddington had posed the question of whether it is possible to determine the distribution of the space velocities of stars based on the distribution of radial velocities. Ambartsumian showed how this can be done, in the process carrying out the first ever numerical inversion of the Radon transform that today is the basis of tomography, the reconstruction of two-dimensional images from a set of one-dimensional projections and angles. The paper containing Ambartsumian's solution was submitted to the *Monthly Notices of the Royal Astronomical Society* by Eddington himself.

In 1938, Ambartsumian and his student Sh. G. Gordeladze studied bright dusty nebulae and the stars illuminating them. They concluded that such nebulae are illuminated only as a by-product of their accidental placement between the Earth and a bright star. Moreover, Ambartsumian and Gordeladze carried out computations showing that only about 0.05 percent of the galaxy's dust nebulae are illuminated in this manner by bright stars. From this they concluded that interstellar absorption has a patchy structure and that interstellar matter is in the form of clouds. Subrahmanyan Chandrasekhar later described Ambartsumian's approach to studying fluctuations in the brightness of the Milky Way as "marvelously elegant" (p. 3). In 1939, at the age of 31, Ambartsumian was elected a corresponding member of the Academy of Sciences of the USSR.

World War II and Beyond. World War II brought an abrupt change in Ambartsumian's career. With German forces approaching Leningrad in 1941, Ambartsumian organized the evacuation of much of Leningrad State University to a safe location beyond the Ural Mountains in Elabuga. There Ambartsumian established and headed the Elabuga branch of LSU, for which he was subsequently awarded an Order of Lenin.

Even during the war years, Ambartsumian continued his pioneering work in astrophysics, in 1943 developing and applying the invariance principle to the problem of isotropic scattering in a semi-infinite, plane-parallel atmosphere. According to this principle, the reflective capability of a medium consisting of infinitesimally thin, parallel layers of nearly infinite optical depth does not change if a new layer with the same optical properties is added. Applying this principle, Ambartsumian developed a system of simple functional equations describing light scattering in a turbid medium. These equations found immediate application to problems of radiative transfer in the Sun and other stars, and they have since been applied in optics, mathematical physics, and a number of other fields. Chandrasekhar described the principle of invariance as "a theoretical innovation that is of the greatest significance" (1988, p. 3) and did much to develop Ambartsumian's innovation further.

As the war moved towards its end, in 1944 Ambartsumian moved his family to Yerevan, Armenia, where he helped to found the Armenian Academy of Sciences, serving first as vice president (1944–1947) and then as president (1947–1993). From that point forward, science in Armenia was synonymous with the name Ambartsumian.

In 1946, he founded Byurakan Observatory, Armenia's first major and as of 2007 still most important observatory for astrophysical research. He directed Byurakan through 1988 and continued as its honorary director thereafter. He simultaneously served as chairman of the Department of Astrophysics at Yerevan State University. In 1964 Ambartsumian founded the Armenian journal *Astrofizika,* serving as its editor in chief through 1987.

In 1947, he turned his attention to hot giant and supergiant stars (spectral classes O and B) and T Tauri variable stars, which were known to have a tendency to be found in groups. Ambartsumian studied the spatial velocities of these groups and discovered that they occupy limited spatial volume—that is, they are physical systems. He introduced the term stellar associations to describe these groupings. Analyzing the physical forces at work in these associations, Ambartsumian determined that they are highly unstable and therefore will dissipate with time. Given that this dissipation has not yet occurred, the stars in these associations must be quite young—on the order of tens of millions of years. From this he concluded that star formation in the galaxy is an ongoing process and that stellar associations are the regions in which star formation is taking place. His discovery of stellar formations opened an entirely new field of astrophysical research.

In the 1950s, following the discovery of strong radio sources in external galaxies, Ambartsumian began studying clusters of galaxies and discovered that these too are unstable, thereby implying that galactic formation also is an ongoing process. In 1958, he gave a report to the Solvay Conference on Physics in Brussels in which he said that explosions in galactic nuclei cause large amounts of

mass to be expelled. For these explosions to occur, galactic nuclei must contain bodies of huge mass and unknown nature. From this point forward Active Galactic Nuclei (AGN) became a key component in theories of galactic evolution. In the later twentieth century, AGNs came under direct observational study with the advent of space-borne x-ray observatories such as *Chandra.*

Teoreticheskaia Astrofizika, edited by Ambartsumian, was published in Russian in 1952 and became a bible for a generation of astrophysicists. It appeared in English translation in 1958 and epitomized to the world the high level of development that astrophysics had achieved in the Soviet Union—with much of the credit attributed to Ambartsumian. A member of the IAU from 1946 on, he served as its vice president from 1948 through 1955 and as its president from 1961 through 1964. He had become the most widely known and respected Soviet astrophysicist in the world. Between 1956 and 1960, he was awarded the Janssen Medal of the French Academy of Sciences, the Bruce Medal of the Astronomical Society of the Pacific, and the Gold Medal of the Royal Astronomical Society.

He remained active as an astrophysicist well into the 1990s as he continued to develop his work on inverse problems of astrophysics, the invariance principle, and stellar and galactic evolution. He raised the stature of the search for extraterrestrial intelligence (SETI) by hosting two SETI conferences, and Armenia became a magnet for foreign astrophysicists traveling to conferences and seminars organized by Ambartsumian at Byurakan. Internationally, he served two terms as president of the ICSU (1968–1972) and was a frequent speaker at IAU and other international seminars. He died on 12 August 1996, in Byurakan.

A Soviet Astrophysicist. Ambartsumian grew up through the turbulent years of World War I, the Bolshevik Revolution, civil war, Lenin's New Economic Policy of the 1920s, and the rise of Joseph Stalin. Like many if not most young educated Soviet men of his day, Ambartsumian was a patriot who believed his country was at the forefront of a great movement that would transform the world and improve the lot of mankind everywhere. Whereas his close friend and collaborator Nikolai Kozyrev would be rudely disabused of this notion in the late 1930s, all evidence indicates that Ambartsumian remained committed to the Soviet system to the end. His scientific genius combined with his political loyalty took him to the heights of the Soviet scientific establishment.

Ambartsumian was elected a corresponding member of the USSR Academy of Sciences in 1939 and joined the Communist Party in 1940. During those same years he published newspaper articles at LSU with titles such as "We

Will Help the Finnish People Again Obtain Independence" and "We Will Fight for a Genuinely Scientific, Materialistic, World View." In 1948, he was a member of the Central Committee of the Communist Party of the Armenian SSR, and beginning in 1950, he served as a deputy in the USSR Supreme Soviet. He was also a delegate to Communist Party congresses in the 1960s and 1970s. In 1953, he was elected a full member of the Academy of Sciences, and by 1955, he was a member of the Academy's presidium. A recipient of Lenin and Stalin prizes in 1946 and 1950, Ambartsumian himself served on the committee for Lenin and USSR State prizes in the period 1947 through 1972. He served as chairman of the Academy of Sciences' Astronomical Commission from 1944 to 1946 and chairman of the Commission on Cosmogony from 1952 through 1964. He was also a member of the editorial board of the Soviet Union's main astronomy journal, the *Astronomicheskii zhurnal,* from 1944 through 1979.

Ambartsumian was an ardent proponent of dialectical materialism, that component of Marxist-Leninist ideology that concerns the philosophy of science, and he directly connected this philosophical view to his astrophysical interpretations. For example, Ambartsumian wrote that he was guided by the principles of dialectical materialism when he did his work that led to the determination that galactic nuclei contain bodies of huge mass. Indeed, his views on dialectical materialism as a guiding principle in scientific research spawned a school of followers that included the philosopher Vadim V. Kaziutinskii. Sometimes working together, Ambartsumian and Kaziutinskii wrote frequently on the subject of dialectical processes at work in the history and evolution of the universe.

Ambartsumian's towering authority as an astrophysicist combined with his position in the Soviet establishment made him arguably the most powerful Soviet astronomer of his day. He used his power to advance the cause of astrophysics throughout the Soviet Union in the postwar years when major new observatories with astrophysical capabilities were established. He also worked to advance the careers of V. V. Sobolev and other talented young Soviet astrophysicists. For his work to advance science in Armenia, a grateful nation proclaimed Ambartsumian a National Hero of Armenia in 1994.

The hierarchical nature of the Soviet system and, in particular, the Academy of Sciences meant that not all of Ambartsumian's colleagues were happy with his power and influence. Iosif Shklovskii, an astrophysicist no less talented than Ambartsumian, wrote with sad irony that the support of one or more of the "mafias" was needed for an otherwise outstanding scientist to be elected a member of the academy. In astronomy and astrophysics it was Ambartsumian who had the power to promote or block the election of individual candidates.

Finally, shadows from the 1930s followed Ambartsumian in hushed whispers throughout his career. While he was being elected a corresponding member of the Academy of Sciences in 1939, his close friend Kozyrev was languishing in an NKVD prison, on his way to serve a ten-year sentence in the labor camps of the Soviet Gulag. The Great Purges of 1936 through 1938 took a tremendous toll among astronomers and physicists. Although Kozyrev survived his imprisonment, Eropkin, Bronshtein, and many other of Ambartsumian's friends and colleagues from the early 1930s were executed outright or perished in the camps. Both within the Soviet Union and abroad, there were those who asked why these scientists perished while Ambartsumian flourished. Kozyrev's relations with Ambartsumian were strained for the remainder of his life, and in the West there were those who questioned whether Ambartsumian had played a role in unleashing the terror that swept away much of Pulkovo Observatory, including its director Boris Gerasimovich, in the late 1930s. A number of Gerasimovich's colleagues outside the Soviet Union were aware that his relations with Ambartsumian had been strained beyond the breaking point, and there were some who believed Ambartsumian had personally fanned the flames that led ultimately to Gerasimovich's execution in 1937.

Even after the fall of the Soviet Union and into the early 2000s, historians differ regarding Ambartsumian's role during the purges of the 1930s. Although some continue to see his role as negative, at least one has pointed to archival letters showing that Ambartsumian was himself terrified that he too was about to be arrested, and another historian has suggested that Gerasimovich's dislike of Ambartsumian may in fact have saved him. Whereas Ambartsumian's friends Kozyrev and Eropkin were still at Pulkovo when arrests began there in 1936, Ambartsumian had been dismissed by Gerasimovich two years earlier and was at LSU. This alone may have been sufficient to save Ambartsumian from the fate that befell his colleagues. Although his role from 1936 through 1938 may have been less than heroic, there is no hard evidence to suggest that he was guilty of anything more serious than surviving at a time when others did not.

Scientific Legacy. Viktor Ambartsumian left a legacy of personal scientific achievement that places him at the top ranks of twentieth-century astrophysics. Working within the Soviet system, he almost single-handedly created an infrastructure for astronomy and astrophysics in Armenia and kept the Soviet Union at the forefront of theoretical astrophysics. In the words of Chandrasekhar, "There can be no more than two or three astronomers in this century who can look back on a life so worthily devoted to the progress of astronomy."

BIBLIOGRAPHY

WORKS BY AMBARTSUMIAN

With Dmitrii Ivanenko. "Über eine Folgerung der Diracschen Theorie der Protonen und Elektronen." *Doklady Akademii Nauk SSSR-A* 6 (1930): 153–155.

With Nikolai Kozyrev. "Über die Massen der von den neuen Sternen ausgestossenen Gashüllen." *Zeitschrift fürAstrophysik* 7 (1933): 320–325.

With Sh. G. Gordeladze. "Problem of Diffuse Nebulae and Cosmic Absorption." *Biulleten' Abastumanskoi astrofizicheskoi observatorii* (1938): 37-68. In English and Georgian.

Teoreticheskaia Astrofizika. Moscow: GTTI, 1952. In Russian. Translated by J. B. Sykes as *Theoretical Astrophysics.* London and New York: Pergamon Press, 1958.

"On the Evolution of Galaxies." In *La Structure et l'Evolution de l'Univers,* edited by R. Stoops. Brussels: Coudenberg, 1958. A translation of part of this paper, with commentary, appears in *A Source Book in Astronomy & Astrophysics 1900-1975,* edited by Kenneth R. Lang and Owen Gingerich. Cambridge, MA: Harvard University Press, 1979.

With V. V. Kaziutinskii. "Dialektika poznaniia evoliutsionnykh protsessov vo Vselennoi" [Dialectical perception of evolutionary processes in the universe]. In *Materialy III Vsesoiuznogo soveshchaniia po filosofskim voprosam sovremennogo estestvoznaniia, vyp. III [Materials of the third all-Union conference on philosophical questions of modern natural science].* Moscow: Nauka, 1981. An example of Ambartsumian's views on the role of dialectical materialism in scientific research.

A Life in Astrophysics: Selected Papers of Viktor A. Ambartsumian, edited by R.V. Ambartzumian. New York: Allerton Press, 1998. A compendium of his most important papers as selected by Ambartsumian prior to his death and edited by his son Rouben.

OTHER SOURCES

Arp, H. C. "Ambartsumian's Greatest Insight—The Origin of Galaxies." In *Active Galactic Nuclei and Related Phenomena : Proceedings of the 194th Symposium of the International Astronomical Union held in Byurakan, Armenia, 17-22 August 1998,* edited by Yervant Terzian, E. Khachikian, and Daniel Weedman. San Francisco: Astronomical Society of the Pacific, 1999.

Arzumanyan, Ashot. *Envoy of the Stars.* Moscow: Progress Publishers, 1987.

Blaauw, Adriaan. *History of the IAU: The Birth and First Half-Century of the IAU.* Boston: Kluwer, 1994.

———. "In Memoriam: V. A. Ambartsumian." *Journal of Astrophysics and Astronomy* 18 (March 1997): 1–2.

Boyarchuk, A. "Influence of V. A. Ambartsumian on the Development of Astronomy." In *Active Galactic Nuclei and Related Phenomena : Proceedings of the 194th Symposium of the International Astronomical Union held in Byurakan, Armenia, 17-22 August 1998,* edited by Yervant Terzian, E. Khachikian, and Daniel Weedman. San Francisco: Astronomical Society of the Pacific, 1999.

Chandrasekhar, Subrahmanyan. "To Victor Ambartsumian on his 80th Birthday." *Astrofizika* 29 (1988): 7–8. Reprinted in *Journal of Astrophysics and Astronomy* 18 (March 1997): 3–4.

Dadaev, A. N. "Biografiia N. A. Kozyreva." Available from http://www.univer.omsk.su/omsk/Sci/Kozyrev/index.win.htm.

———. "Nikolai Aleksandrovich Kozyrev." In *Kozyrev N. A. Izbrannye trudy.* Leningrad: Izd-vo.Leningradskogo universiteta, 1999.

Eremeeva, A. I. "Political Repression and Personality: The History of Political Repression against Soviet Astronomers." *Journal for the History of Astronomy* 26 (1995): 297–324.

Finashina, G. N. *Viktor Amazaspovich Ambartsumian.* Biobibliografiia uchenykh SSSR [Biographic bibliography of scientists of the USSR], no. 3, edited by A. N. Nesmeianov. Moscow: Izd. Nauka, 1975. Contains a detailed bibliography of Ambartsumian's publications.

Graham, Loren. *Science, Philosophy, and Human Behavior in the Soviet Union.* New York: Columbia University Press, 1987. Includes a discussion of the role dialectical materialism played in Ambartsumian's astrophysical research.

Israelian, Garik. "Victor Amazasp Ambartsumian, 1912-1996." *Bulletin of the American Astronomical Society* 29 (1997): 1466–1467. Obituary prepared by the Historical Astronomy Division of the AAS.

McCutcheon, Robert A. "The Early Career of Viktor Amazaspovich Ambartsumian: An Interview (YEREVAN, October 1987)." *The Astronomy Quarterly* 7 (1990): 143–176.

Mirozoian, L. V. *Viktor Ambartsumian.* YEREVAN: Izd. Aiastan, 1985.

Pecker, Jean-Claude. "Viktor Ambartsumian and the IAU." *Astrofizika* 29 (1989): 409.

Shklovskii, Iosif Samuilovich. *Eshelon (nevydumannye rasskazy)* [Echelon: true stories]. Moscow: Izd-vo Novosti, 1991. Shklovskii's reminiscences about astronomy and astrophysics under the Soviet system, with several references to Ambartsumian.

———. *Five Billion Vodka Bottles to the Moon: Tales of a Soviet Scientist.* New York: W. W. Norton, 1991. This English-language version of Shklovskii's reminiscences contains many of the stories included in *Eshelon* as well as others that did not appear there.

"Victor Amazasp Ambartsumian (1908–1996)." *Active Galactic Nuclei and Related Phenomenan: Proceedings of the 194th Symposium of the International Astronomical Union held in Byurakan, Armenia, 17-22 August 1998,* edited by Yervant Terzian, E. Khachikian, and Daniel Weedman. San Francisco: Astronomical Society of the Pacific, 1999.

"Victor Ambartsumian (1908–1996)." Armenian Astronomical Society. Available from http://www.aras.am/Ambartsumian.html.

Robert A. McCutcheon

AMPFERER, OTTO (*b.* Hötting, near Innsbruck, Austria, 1 December 1875; *d.* Innsbruck, 9 July 1947), *geology, tectonics.*

Ampferer was an outstanding authority on the geology of the Eastern Alps, where he introduced the new ideas of folding and nappe tectonics. His field mapping of large areas of the Northern Calcareous Alps is still the most comprehensive one ever done by a single Alpine geologist. And his theory of understreaming currents as the moving force of orogeny ranked him among the pioneers of the modern theory of plate movement.

Beginnings and Scientific Career. Ampferer's parents both came from Tyrolian farmer families. His father, Nikolaus Ampferer, was a post office clerk. His father was born not far from the Karwendelgebirge. His mother, Gertraud Zangerl, grew up near the Lechtal Alps. These two areas were the later domains of study by their son. During his school days his teachers acquainted Ampferer with the sciences. In 1895 he began to study physics and mathematics at Innsbruck—especially geology with the Austrian geologist Josef Blaas. In 1899 he earned his PhD with a study of the geology of the southern parts of the Karwendelgebirge.

In 1901 Ampferer joined the Austrian Geological Survey (k.-k. Geologische Reichsanstalt, which became the Geologische Bundesanstalt) in Vienna. One year later, on 20 November 1902, Ampferer married Olga Sander (d. 1952), a sister of the Austrian mineralogist Bruno Sander. She became his lifelong companion and assistant in most of his fieldwork.

Despite several later offers to change to a university career, Ampferer never left the Austrian Geological Survey. After nearly twenty years he became chief geologist in 1919, and in 1925 he was appointed its vice-director. Finally, from 1935 to 1937, Ampferer served as director of the Geologische Staatsanstalt (its official name between the two world wars).

As an authority on the geology of the Austrian Alps, Ampferer became the favored expert for engineering projects there, especially the construction of new hydroelectric generating stations in the Alps. Ampferer delivered about one hundred expert reports during his scientific career starting in 1908. Examples include reports on the Achensee and Ybbs valley hydroelectric generating stations and on the water supply of his home town, Innsbruck.

To his contemporaries, the young Ampferer was also known as a mountaineer. He did about 2,000 climbing tours, among them some difficult first ascents. The most famous one was the ascent of the Guglia di Brenta in the Dolomites. On 18 August 1899, together with the Innsbruck mountaineer Karl Berger, Ampferer succeeded in climbing its difficult north wall—now called Ampferer wall (Ampfererwand)—thus improving the scale of mountaineering techniques by one more degree.

Field Mapping, Stratigraphy, and Glacial Geology. Geological field mapping was the centerpiece of Ampferer's scientific work. In its extent it has hardly any counterpart in Alpine geology. His areas of research were the Northern Calcareous (limestone) Alps before World War I, and among them, the Karwendelgebirge, the Sonnwendgebirge (a more common name is Rofan Mountains), and the Lechtal Alps. After the war Ampferer continued his work in the Kaisergebirge, and in Vorarlberg as far as the Rhätikon Mountains, and the Rhine transverse valley in Liechtenstein.

The result of nearly four decades of research—including about 4,000 days in the field—was an impressive series of geological maps. Without overlooking his collaborators, especially the Austrian geologist Wilhelm Hammer, the geological maps with annotations of Tyrol and Vorarlberg published between 1912 and 1937, were mostly his work. There might be no other area of such dimensions within the Alps that has been mapped in such a unified manner as the twelve sheets of the geological map 1:75,000 of the Austrian part of the Eastern Alps. In addition Ampferer prepared geological maps of the Lechtal Alps, the Karwendelgebirge, and other areas for the German and Austrian Alpine Club (Deutscher und Österreichischer Alpenverein).

Geological mapping supplied Ampferer with the materials for the elaboration of new ideas on Alpine stratigraphy, glacial geology, and tectonics. In the upper Lech valley he discovered the (up to then) largest deposit of volcanic or melaphyric rocks within the Northern Calcareous Alps. For the hornstone breccia (*Hornsteinbreccien*) of the Rofan Mountains, Ampferer first discussed its sedimentary origin that was later confirmed by his brother-in-law Bruno Sander using sedimentographical methods. And before 1914 he proved the Cretaceous age of the thin, dark strata of marlstones and sandstones (*Kreideschiefer* or Lechtal shales), which are widely distributed in the Western Lechtal Alps.

In glacial geology Ampferer was particularly engaged in the study of the sediments of the Inn valley terraces. He found it to be of much greater extent than hitherto known and frequently covered by morainal material. Thus, he proposed an interglacial origin in 1908. The hypothesis was objected to strongly, because it contradicted the famous section of the *Höttingen breccia (Höttinger Breccie)*, a locus classicus of Alpine glacial geology. In 1921 Albrecht Penck, the leading German glacial geologist, joined Ampferer's position. Nevertheless, Ampferer himself called it into question in 1939 when he discovered large angular erratics within fine-sandy sediments of the lower Inn valley, whose existence, he thought, required a former nearby glacier.

Tectonics. Tectonics were the second main concern of Ampferer's scientific work. Following his background in physics and engineering geology, he was particularly interested in the mechanical problems of alpinotype tectonics. He became the main advocate of the doctrine of nappes for the Eastern Alps.

He first demonstrated respective structures in 1902 at the Inntal nappe (which he originally called Karwendel overthrust). This was one year before Pierre Termier used the theory of nappes to produce the first unified geological interpretation of the European Alps. By his discovery of the Karwendel overthrust, a large-scale flat upthrow of Triassic layers on Jurassic ones, Ampferer pioneered the idea of flat, onlapping thrust sheets—that is, of disconnected sedimentary mantles without any trace of a reversed middle limb. This contrasted with the large fold nappes known from the Western Alps. In 1911, together Wilhelm Hammer, he presented a comprehensive discussion of the tectonics of the Eastern Alps in his "Geologischer Querschnitt durch die Ostalpen vom Allgäu zum Gardasee."

The tectonic idea, however, for which Ampferer became best known, is his hypothesis of understreaming currents as the moving force of mountain building. As early as 1906, Ampferer had published his comprehensive paper "Ueber das Bewegungsbild der Faltengebirge" (Moving patterns of fold mountains). Contrary to the then prevailing contraction hypothesis, he unfolded the idea that the structures of Earth's crust are due to movements caused by subcrustal currents, that is, within the liquid zone beneath Earth's crust, understreaming currents and decreases of volume take place upon which Earth's outer skin is patterned.

It might be questionable to what extent this idea was completely new, and also how far it actually anticipated the idea of convection currents, compared for instance, to the work of the English geologist Arthur Holmes. Nevertheless, Ampferer made a causal link between subcrustal currents, large-scale crustal dislocations, and the detachment of the upper from the lower crust in orogenic belts. Furthermore he appreciated a concept similar to subduction by his notion of zones of downsucking (Verschluckungszonen). He first used this notion in 1911 to refer to the process in which one section of the crust slides below another (see Figure 1).

The elaboration of Ampferer's hypotheses fell to other geologists—such as his Austrian colleague Robert Schwinner or the German geologist Ernst Kraus. Nevertheless, in 1924 Ampferer pleaded for his idea of understreaming currents as the best available moving force for continental drift. And in 1941, in a paper on the geological history of the Atlantic Ocean, he anticipated the idea of seafloor spreading by stating that continents can be

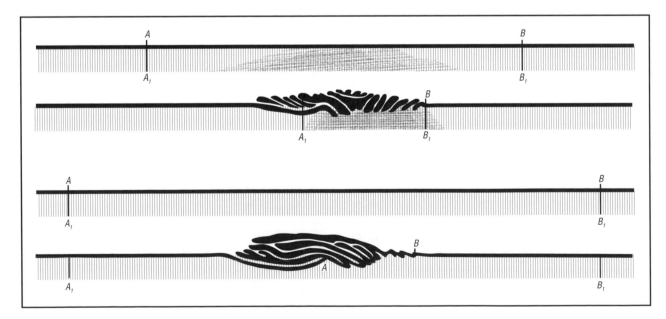

Figure 1. *Ampferer's first visual representation of his idea of mountain building by downsucking of crustal masses, compared to the classical contraction theory. The upper sketches illustrate the situation for the presumption of a strong downsucking: for example, of the immersion of crustal masses into the substratum. The two lower sketches illustrate the situation for the contraction theory.*

70

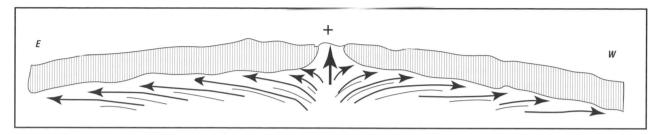

Figure 2. *Separation of a continental block by a rising understreaming current (convection current), pushing the two parts aside. (+) indicates the position, where the mid-oceanic ridge emerges, thus, recording the bisection of the separation.*

split by understreaming currents rising from Earth's interior (see Figure 2).

Reception of Ampferer's Work. Ampferer's ideas on global tectonics and mountain building were little known outside German speaking countries during his lifetime. This might have been due to the fact that he hardly ever left his well-defined area of research. Apart from a geological expedition—partly by military order—to Albania, Montenegro, and Western Serbia in 1917 and 1918; some studies with the Scottish female geologist Maria Matilda Ogilvie Gordon in the Dolomites in 1926, 1928, and 1935; and a few expert reports for foreign engineering projects—Ampferer never left his Austrian Alpine home.

Nevertheless, his geological work found high recognition. Among others, in 1936, he was appointed a member of the Deutsche Akademie der Naturforscher Leopoldina, and—although he never taught at a university—corresponding member of the Austrian Academy of Sciences in 1925 (ordinary member in 1940). The Austrian Geological Society honored him by originating an Otto Ampferer Award in 1983, to be awarded annually for outstanding achievements by young scientists in the earth sciences.

BIBLIOGRAPHY

Ampferer's papers (manuscript maps and correspondence) are in part located in the Library of the Geologische Bundesanstalt in Vienna and partly in the Natural History Department of the Tyrol States Museum (Tiroler Landesmuseum Ferdinandeum) at Innsbruck, Austria.

WORKS BY AMPFERER

With Wilhelm Hammer. "Geologische Beschreibung des südlichen Teiles des Karwendelgebirges." *Jahrbuch der k.k. geologischen Reichsanstalt* 48 (1898 [published 1899]): 289–374.

"Über den geologischen Zusammenhang des Karwendel- und Sonnwendjochgebirges." *Verhandlungen der geologischen Reichsanstalt* [no volume number] (1902): 104–113.

"Geologische Beschreibung des nördlichen Teiles des Karwendelgebirges." *Jahrbuch der k.k. geologischen Reichsanstalt* 53 (1903): 169–252.

"Studien über die Inntal-Terrassen." *Jahrbuch der k.k. geologischen Reichsanstalt* 54 (1904 [published 1905]): 91–160.

"Ueber das Bewegungsbild von Faltengebirgen." *Jahrbuch der k.k. geologischen Reichsanstalt* 56 (1906): 539–622.

"Studien über die Tektonik des Sonnwendgebirges." *Jahrbuch der k.k. geologischen Reichsanstalt* 58 (1908): 281–304.

"Geologischer Querschnitt durch die Ostalpen vom Allgäu zum Gardasee." *Jahrbuch der k.k. geologischen Reichsanstalt* 61 (1911): 531–710.

"Ueber die Tektonik der Alpen." *Die Naturwissenschaften* 12 (1924): 1007–1014.

"Ueber Kontinentalverschiebungen." *Die Naturwissenschaften* 13 (1925): 669–675.

Über die geologischen Verhältnisse des Achensees und die beim Bau des Achenseewerkes geschaffenen neuen Aufschlüsse. Innsbruck, Austria: Tiroler Wasserkraftwerke, 1926.

"Beiträge zur Glazialgeologie der westlichen Südtiroler Dolomiten." *Zeitschrift für Gletscherkunde* 16 (1928): 242–260.

"Ergebnisse der geologischen Forschungsreisen in Westserbien. Part 3: Zur Tektonik und Morphologie des Zlatibormassivs." *Denkschriften der mathematisch-naturwissenschaftliche Klasse der Akademie der Wissenschaften in Wien* 101 (1928): 361–424.

Bergtage: Gewalt und Glück der Höhen. Große Bergsteiger 4. Munich, Germany: Rother, 1930.

"Über einige Grundfragen der Gebirgsbildung." *Jahrbuch der k.k. geologischen Reichsanstalt* 87 (1937): 375–384.

"Gegen den Nappismus und für die Deckenlehre." *Zeitschrift der Deutschen Geologischen Gesellschaft* 92 (1940): 313–327.

"Gedanken über das Bewegungsbild des atlantischen Raumes." *Sitzungsberichte der mathematisch-naturwissenschaftlichen Klasse der Akademie der Wissenschaften in Wien*, Part 1, 150 (1941): 19–35.

"Über die Bedeutung von Gleitvorgängen für den Bau der Alpen." *Sitzungsberichte der mathematisch-naturwissenschaftlichen Klasse der Akademie der Wissenschaften in Wien*, Part 1, 151 (1942): 9–26.

OTHER SOURCES

Flügel, Helmut W. "A. Wegener—O. Ampferer—R. Schwinner: The First Chapter of the 'New Global Tectonics.'" *Earth Sciences History* 3 (1984): 178–186. The paper is a modified version of Helmut W. Flügel. "Wegener—Ampferer—Schwinner: Ein Beitrag zur Geschichte der Geologie in Österreich." *Mitteilungen der österreichischen geologischen Gesellschaft* 73 (1980): 237–254.

Klebelsberg zu Thumburg, Raimund von. "Otto Ampferers geologisches Lebenswerk." *Jahrbuch der Geologischen Bundesanstalt* 92 (1947 [published 1949]): 93–116. The most complete available bibliography, the text includes a list of Ampferer's geological maps as published by the Austrian Geological Service and the German and Austrian Alpine Club. Ampferer's available geological maps are to be found on the homepage of the Geologische Bundesanstalt in Vienna, available from http://www.geologie.ac.at.

Leutner, Manfred. *Wissenschaftstheoretische Fallstudien zur Entwicklung der erdwissenschaftlichen Forschung in Österreich: Wilhelm Haidinger, Franz von Hauer, Otto Ampferer.* Abhandlungen der Geologischen Bundesanstalt in Wien, 55. Vienna: Geologische Bundesanstalt, 1999.

Sander, Bruno. "Otto Ampferer." *Almanach der Österreichischen Akademie der Wissenschaften* 98 (1948): 227–233. With selected bibliography and portrait.

Seibold, Ilse, and Eugen Seibold. "Neues aus dem Geologen-Archiv (1991). Mit Erinnerungen an Alfred Wegener und Otto Ampferer: Warten auf Anerkennung." *Geologische Rundschau* 81/82 (1992): 267–273.

Thenius, Erich. "Otto Ampferer—Begründer der Theorie der Ozeanbodenspreizung." *Die Geowissenschaften* 6 (1988): 103–105.

Bernhard Fritscher

ANDERSON, CARL DAVID (*b.* New York, New York, 3 September 1905; *d.* San Marino, California, 11 January 1991), *antimatter, physics, positron.*

Anderson was awarded the Nobel Prize in Physics in 1936 for the discovery of antimatter, in particular the positive electron, or positron. Just one year later, he was promoted to associate professor of physics at the California Institute of Technology (Caltech), in Pasadena, California, and in 1939 he became a full professor.

Winning the Nobel Prize came as a considerable surprise to Anderson. Unbeknownst to him he had been nominated for it by Caltech's chief administrative officer and unofficial president Robert A. Millikan (himself a physics laureate in 1923), and Anderson had to borrow $500 from Millikan just to be able to go to Stockholm and get his share of the award, which amounted to $20,000. He shared the prize with Victor Franz Hess of the University of Innsbruck, who was honored for his work in cosmic rays.

Anderson was a quiet, unassuming man. As a graduate student at Caltech, he signed up to take a course in quantum theory from the theoretical physicist J. Robert Oppenheimer, who was then dividing his time between the physics departments at Caltech and the University of California, Berkeley. About forty people were following the course. Oppenheimer, who was not yet the eloquent speaker he would later become, would mumble his way through lectures, writing a squiggle, or part of an equation, on whatever part of the board happened to be handy. It was all too much for Anderson, who went to see Oppenheimer to tell him he was dropping the course. Anderson later recalled the incident in his autobiography, reporting that Oppenheimer urged him to stay, promising that by the end of the term "everything will be all right" (Anderson, 1999, p. 18). When he asked why it was so important that he not drop the course, he was told it was because he was the only registered student.

Anderson was born in New York City in 1905, the only child of Carl David Anderson, a chef, and Emma Adolfina Ajaxson, both of whom grew up on farms near Stockholm and came to America around 1900, in their late teens. (Their son, Carl, learned Swedish at home, and was able to converse with the king of Sweden comfortably in that language when he accepted his Nobel Prize in Stockholm at the age of thirty-one.) In 1912 the family moved to Los Angeles, where Anderson attended grade school and Los Angeles Polytechnic High School, from which he graduated in 1923. By then his parents had separated and he continued to live at home with his mother for many years. In 1923 he enrolled at Caltech, hoping to become an electrical engineer, but in his sophomore year a course in modern physics with Ira Bowen turned him into physics major.

Discovery of the Positron. After receiving his BS in 1927, Anderson remained on campus as a graduate student, working under Millikan on the emission of electrons induced by bombarding various gases with x-rays. He received his PhD magna cum laude in 1930 and stayed on at Caltech as a research fellow, working with Millikan on cosmic rays. Initially, Millikan had urged him to go elsewhere to broaden his research experience, and, accordingly, Anderson had applied for and won a National Research Council fellowship to work under Arthur H. Compton at the University of Chicago. But Millikan then had a change of heart and convinced Anderson to stay on at Caltech, where Anderson spent his entire career.

Millikan's newfound interest in the study of cosmic rays accounted for his sudden determination to hang on to the talented Anderson. Millikan was convinced (inaccurately, as it turned out) that cosmic rays, a term that he himself coined in 1925 for the penetrating radiation bombarding Earth from all directions, were the birth pangs of new elements being formed out in space. In order to prove this hypothesis, he needed accurate measurements of their energies. He established three research efforts at Caltech in the new field, each using a different type of detector: one under Victor Neher using electroscopes, one under William Pickering using Geiger counters, and one under Anderson using cloud chambers in a magnetic field. Anderson's investigations paid off almost immediately, but not exactly as Millikan had foreseen.

Anderson built his magnetic cloud chamber (designed entirely by him) in the Guggenheim Aeronautical Laboratory on the Caltech campus, where the generator that powered the wind tunnel provided enough electricity to handle 600 kilowatts. The giant magnet, which took Anderson many months to build, consisted of eight hundred turns of copper tubing laboriously wound into two coils welded together to carry electrical current and cooling water. In a cloud chamber, a supersaturated vapor is caused, by a sudden change in pressure, to form visible droplets on the track left behind by a fast moving charged particle. A handmade camera inserted in a square hole at one end of the magnetic pole piece allowed Anderson to record the curved tracks of condensation left by an electron or any other charged particle. Incoming cosmic-ray particles entering the field would curve to the left if they were negatively charged or to the right if they were positive. In the very first experiments in 1931 and 1932, Anderson saw the deflected tracks of as many positive as negative cosmic-ray particles. At this time, scientists had identified two elementary particles of matter: negatively charged electrons, and positively charged nuclei. Anderson and Millikan initially disagreed over whether the vivid tracks they observed in Anderson's much-improved cloud chamber were actually negative charges moving downward (Millikan's view) or positives moving upward (Anderson's view), but Anderson finally settled the question by placing a lead plate in the path of the particles. They would have more energy and therefore less curvature before passing through the plate than after, when they would be slower and therefore curve more. On 2 August 1932, these efforts were rewarded by a clear track left by a particle moving upward through the plate and curving to the left, meaning it was positively charged, but with a degree of ionization in the cloud chamber gas that indicated that the particle had the mass of an electron. This event marked the entirely unexpected discovery of the positive electron.

One month later, pushed by Millikan to establish the priority of his findings quickly, Anderson published a brief report on "The Apparent Existence of Easily Deflectable Positives," in *Science;* the definitive results and famous photograph ("it's got to be a positive electron," Anderson later recalled thinking) appeared in *Physical Review* in 1933. The physics world expressed skepticism. However, a relativistic theory by the Cambridge University theorist Paul A. M. Dirac, published in 1930, had predicted the existence of a positive electron, and the evidence on Anderson's photographic plate was unimpeachable. Anderson's result was soon confirmed by Dirac's Cambridge colleagues Paul M. S. Blackett and Giuseppe P. S. Occhialini, who in a March 1933 paper in the *Proceedings of the Royal Society* reported similar results and proposed the mechanism of pair production to account for their existence. They postulated that when an energetic gamma ray was converted into matter, it would emit a negatively charged electron, balanced by Dirac's positively charged positron (as the positive electron came to be called). Asked once by an interviewer if Dirac's theory had influenced the direction of his research, Anderson replied, "I don't know whether the existence of Dirac's work had any effect at all on the work I was doing. I was looking at the cloud chamber data and going by that."

James Chadwick reported the discovery of the neutron in 1932. With the neutron and the positron as two new fundamental particles of matter, the physics world suddenly looked considerably more complicated than it had previously seemed, a trend that has continued to the present day.

Mu Meson Research. Anderson, together with his first graduate student, Seth Henry Neddermeyer, went on to discover two more elementary particles, which came to be called the positive and negative mu-mesons, or muons. Unlike his discovery of the positron, these discoveries were not due to mere chance, but were rather the result of much hard work, a great deal of it carried out at the summit of Pikes Peak in Colorado, where the cosmic-ray flux was considerably stronger than at sea level. The research also had to be done on a shoestring budget. It was the height of the Depression and funds were scarce. Anderson and Neddermeyer started by buying a 1930 flatbed truck for $400. They mounted the cloud chamber on it and transported it with great difficulty to the top of Pikes Peak (in point of fact they had to be towed up the mountain—the ancient truck just could not make it). They also brought along a Cadillac motor generator, but it would not produce adequate power at 4,300 meters (14,000 feet). When they took the generator to Colorado Springs to be fixed, the old truck broke down.

Fortunately, at this dismal point in the story, a savior appeared in the form of a General Motors vice president accompanying the test-drive of a new truck to the top of Pikes Peak. Hearing the two scientists' tale of woe, he kindly arranged for their truck to be towed back up the mountain, and had the engine replaced. That did not end their difficulties, but it was certainly a timely intervention.

Carl D. Anderson. *Dr. Carl D. Anderson at Inyokern Proving Grounds doing scientific research.* JR EYERMAN/TIME LIFE PICTURES/GETTY IMAGES.

Anderson and Neddermeyer subsequently took thousands of pictures and discovered among them the clear tracks of both positively and negatively charged particles that were too heavy to be electrons and too light to be protons. In fact they had found the mu-meson, whose discovery was first presented by Anderson at a physics colloquium at Caltech on 12 November 1936, followed by a short note in

Science ("we hemmed and hawed about it in the '36 publication," Anderson told an interviewer in 1966). In the absence of a theoretical framework that could explain the existence of two new elementary particles of intermediate mass, Anderson and Neddermeyer adopted a cautious and conservative approach. The formal announcement followed in the 15 May 1937 issue of *Physical Review,* but only after Anderson and Neddermeyer had taken an additional six thousand photographs of cosmic-ray particles in Anderson's cloud chamber as additional proof that the pair of new particles really existed. Anderson later recalled that he provided the first reference in the physics literature to the new particles in the closing line of his 12 December 1936 Nobel lecture in Stockholm, where he said, "These highly penetrating particles, although not free positive and negative electrons, will provide interesting material for future study." Unfortunately, the world of physics had no place for these new particles, and their precise nature and significance remained a mystery until after World War II.

World War II ushered in a change in Anderson's activities. According to Anderson's autobiography, when Arthur H. Compton approached him informally in May 1942 concerning his possible availability to head the Manhattan Project—which produced the atomic bomb—Anderson replied that he did not wish to be considered, largely because he could not afford to support two households, one for his ailing mother in Pasadena, and another for himself in a distant city. In February 1943, that job went to his former teacher, Oppenheimer, while Anderson joined the solid-propellant rocket project headed by Charles C. Lauritsen, another Caltech professor. In 1941 Caltech had contracted with President Franklin Roosevelt's new National Defense Research Committee for the development and testing of land and aircraft rocket projectiles for the U.S. Navy. In particular, Anderson worked on how to fire various types of Caltech artillery rockets from military aircraft, and he was successful enough to be flown to Europe in June 1944 to supervise the installation of rockets on Allied fighter planes.

When the war came to an end, so did Anderson's bachelorhood. In 1946 he married Lorraine Bergman, who had been married once before and had a three-year-old son, Marshall David, whom Anderson adopted. The couple settled in San Marino, not far from Caltech, and had a son, David Anderson, born in 1949.

With the war over, Anderson resumed his studies of cosmic rays. His research group included Robert Leighton and Eugene Cowan, both of whom would become Caltech professors, and Donald Glaser, who would win the Nobel Prize in 1960 for his 1952 invention of the bubble chamber, a novel type of particle detector. The team's work turned up a variety of baffling new elementary particles, which would collectively be dubbed the "strange" particles by Anderson's Caltech colleague Murray Gell-Mann, but by the late 1950s particle accelerators had begun to replace cosmic rays as the preferred source of these high energy phenomena, and Anderson moved increasingly into administrative work. In 1962 he became head of Caltech's Division of Physics, Mathematics, and Astronomy, a job he held until 1970. During his chair-

manship, two Caltech faculty won Nobel Prizes in physics: Richard Feynman in 1965, and Gell-Mann in 1969. Anderson himself won numerous honors in addition to his Nobel, including the Gold Medal of the American Institute of the City of New York (1935), the Presidential Certificate of Merit (1945), the Elliott Cresson Medal of the Franklin Institute (1937), and the John Ericsson Medal of the American Society of Swedish Engineers (1960).

In 1979, Anderson recorded an oral history for the Caltech archives. Asked about his research activities in later life, Anderson replied, "I did try to do some research, even after retiring as division chairman … under some difficulties because I was near enough at that time to retirement so I could not expect to take on graduate students…. So I did some minor work that had nothing to do with particle physics, but it did have to do with things that I had thought about for many, many years but were less important than what I was doing at that time, namely working with cosmic rays and particles." These last experiments, he added, did not provide the same psychic enjoyment as his earlier work and he stopped doing research completely in 1976 when he became Board of Trustees Professor of Physics, Emeritus. A fan of auto racing and automobiles from a very early age, Anderson drove a sporty convertible long after he retired. He was also a ham radio operator (call sign W6KGR), dabbled in real estate, and belonged to the Twilight Club, an exclusive private club to which Millikan and other prominent Pasadena men belonged. Anderson was nearly 80 when he started to write an account of his life. The manuscript, finished in 1991, shortly before his death, was published in 1999, eight years later.

BIBLIOGRAPHY

The Archives of the California Institute of Technology holds a selection of Anderson's papers, including lecture and technical notes, plates and prints of cloud-chamber photographs, and portions of the apparatus used by Anderson in his discoveries of the positron and the mu-meson. The Archives also contains a 1979 oral history interview in eight sessions with Anderson by Harriett Lyle and a transcript of a more technically focused interview by Charles Weiner in 1966.

WORKS BY ANDERSON

"The Apparent Existence of Easily Deflectable Positives." *Science* 76, no. 1967 (1932): 238–239.

With Robert Andrews Millikan. "Cosmic-Ray Energies and Their Bearing on the Photon and Neutron Hypotheses." *Physical Review* 40 (1932): 325–328.

"The Positive Electron." *Physical Review* 43 (1933): 491–494.

"The Production and Properties of Positrons." In *Les Prix Nobel*, vol. 9, *Les Prix Nobel en 1936*. Stockholm: Imprimerie Royale, 1937.

With Seth H. Neddermeyer. "Nature of Cosmic-Ray Particles." *Reviews of Modern Physics* 11 (1939): 191–207.

"Early Work on the Positron and Muon." *American Journal of Physics* 29 (1961): 825–830.

The Discovery of Anti-Matter: The Autobiography of Carl David Anderson, the Youngest Man to Win the Nobel Prize. Edited by Richard J. Weiss. Singapore: World Scientific, 1999.

OTHER SOURCES

Brown, Laurie M. "Nuclear Forces, Mesons, and Isospin Symmetry." In *Twentieth Century Physics,* vol. 1, edited by Laurie M. Brown, Abraham Pais, and Brian Pippard. Bristol, U.K., and Philadelphia: Institute of Physics Publishing; New York: American Institute of Physics, 1995.

Brown, Laurie M., and Lillian Hoddeson, eds. *The Birth of Particle Physics.* Cambridge, U.K.: Cambridge University Press, 1983.

Goodstein, Judith R. *Millikan's School: A History of the California Institute of Technology.* New York: W. W. Norton, 1991.

Kevles, Daniel J. *The Physicists: The History of a Scientific Community in Modern America.* Cambridge, MA: Harvard University Press, 1995. First issued in 1978 and still a very readable account of Anderson's research program.

New York Times. "Carl Anderson, 85, Nobelist, Dies; Discovered the Positive Electron." 12 January 1991.

Pickering, William H. "Carl David Anderson, September 3, 1905–January 11, 1991." *Biographical Memoirs of the National Academy of Sciences* 73 (1998): 25–38. Includes a selected bibliography.

Schwarz, John. "Fifty Years of Antimatter." *Engineering & Science* 46, no. 2 (1982): 24–25. A special issue of the Caltech magazine on the fiftieth anniversary of the discovery of the positron.

Stuewer, Roger H., ed. *Nuclear Physics in Retrospect: Proceedings of a Symposium on the 1930s.* Minneapolis: University of Minnesota Press, 1979.

David L. Goodstein
Judith R. Goodstein

ANFINSEN, CHRISTIAN B. (*b.* Monessen, Pennsylvania, 26 March 1916; *d.* Pikesville, Maryland, 14 May 1995), *biochemistry, protein structure, molecular biology, evolution.*

Anfinsen received the Nobel Prize in Chemistry in 1972 for his biochemical investigations of protein structure. Proteins catalyze essential chemical reactions in living cells as well as performing many other vital regulatory and structural functions. Proteins are made of amino acids in long linear sequences; they are functional only when these chains (called polypeptides) are folded into specific three-dimensional shapes. Anfinsen studied how a protein molecule acquires and maintains this specific shape by exposing one well-characterized protein, the enzyme ribonuclease, to conditions in which it became unfolded and structurally disordered. He and his coworkers demonstrated that the completely unfolded, or denatured, ribonuclease could spontaneously regain its fully native, functional state, including reforming the correct covalent chemical links between non-adjacent amino acids, the disulfide bonds. In conjunction with these findings, he developed the "thermodynamic hypothesis," the notion that a protein in solution acquires its three-dimensional native structure because it is the most stable, i.e., the Gibbs free energy of that state is lowest. Anfinsen perceived in his thermodynamic theory a biological implication, that all of the information needed for the correct folding of a protein is contained in the linear polypeptide chain, and hence in the genetic sequence specifying the string of amino acids. This notion became a central part of the conceptual framework of molecular biology, and put into relief the "protein folding problem"—understanding how a particular amino acid sequence specifies the three-dimensional configuration—that has occupied protein chemists and structural biologists since the 1960s.

Youth and Early Career. Anfinsen was born in Menossen, a mill town south of Pittsburgh in which half of the 1910 population was foreign-born, and spent part of his childhood in nearby Charleroi. He was the child of Norwegian immigrants, Christian Boehmer Anfinsen Sr., a mechanical engineer, and Sophie Rasmussen Anfinsen, Lutherans who raised their children with the Norwegian language and cultural heritage. The family moved to Philadelphia in the 1920s. In 1933 Anfinsen was admitted to Swarthmore College, where he played on the school's football team while studying chemistry. After graduating in 1937, he went on to the University of Pennsylvania to pursue a Ph.D. in organic chemistry. During the next two years, however, his interests shifted towards biochemistry. He applied for and was awarded a fellowship from the American Scandinavian Foundation to study enzymes at the Carlsberg Laboratory in Copenhagen, and left the University of Pennsylvania with a master's degree in 1939. In a memoir he wrote for his fiftieth college reunion, Anfinsen referred to this year in Copenhagen as "perhaps the most formative and exciting year of my life" (p. 2).

The Carlsberg Laboratory had been founded in 1876 through the philanthropy of brewer J. C. Jacobsen to investigate scientific problems associated with brewing. In the early twentieth century it became a leading center for microbiology (in its Department of Physiology) and biochemistry (in the Department of Chemistry). In 1937, Kaj Ulrik Linderstrøm-Lang became head of the Chemistry Department, succeeding S. P. L. Sørenson, known for his work on the importance of pH to enzyme function. Linderstrøm-Lang focused on the ionization of

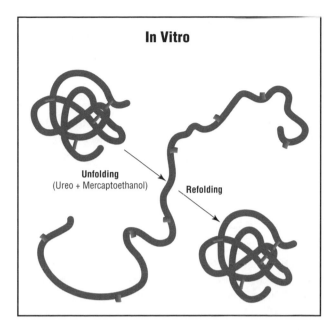

In Vitro

Unfolding
(Ureo + Mercaptoethanol)

Refolding

Figure 1. *Schematic diagram of a protein model system for studying how a linear polypeptide chain folds into a functional protein. A native protein, with intramolecular disulfide bonds linking nonadjacent amino acid residues (there are four depicted in this protein), is reduced and unfolded with b-mercaptoethanol and 8 M urea. After these reagents are removed, the reduced protein is allowed to undergo spontaneous refolding and reoxidation, through which the original disulfide bonds re-form. Anfinsen and his colleagues performed experiments of this sort using the protein ribonuclease*

enzymes, deriving equations for the titration curve of a protein. During his months in Copenhagen Anfinsen became familiar with the problems and techniques of protein chemistry. The growing war—which extended the Nazi occupation into Denmark in April 1940—prompted Anfinsen to return early, with a first-hand sense of the crisis gripping Europe. His immigrant family was directly touched by the horrors of war; according to his second wife, Anfinsen's Jewish maternal grandmother's family disappeared after the Germans invaded Bergen, Norway.

Anfinsen applied to Harvard University for graduate work in biological chemistry, having been encouraged to do so by visiting scientists from Harvard at the Carlsberg Laboratory. He began his Ph.D. at Harvard in 1941, investigating the histochemistry of the retina for his dissertation with A. Baird Hastings. That same year he married his first wife, Florence Bernice Kenenger, with whom he had three children (Carol Craft, Margot Britton, and Christian B. Anfinsen III). Anfinsen completed his doctoral degree in 1943, at which point he became an instructor, teaching Harvard Medical School students at a time of accelerated medical training during the war. From 1944 to 1946, Anfinsen also participated as a civilian scientist

in war-related research on malaria sponsored by the Office of Scientific Research and Development. Anfinsen's biochemical research on the metabolism of blood in healthy monkeys and in monkeys infected with *Plasmodium knowlesi* resulted in four publications.

From 1945 to 1948 Anfinsen was an associate in biological chemistry at Harvard Medical School. There he collaborated with Arthur K. Solomon in applying radioactive isotopes, newly available from the U.S. Atomic Energy Commission's nuclear reactors, as tracers to investigate metabolism. He spent the 1947–1948 period as an American Cancer Society Visiting Investigator at Hugo Theorell's laboratory at the Medical Nobel Institute in Sweden. Anfinsen returned to Harvard Medical School in 1948 as an assistant professor of biological chemistry and a Markle Scholar.

Laboratory at the National Institutes of Health. In 1950, James Shannon, associate director of research at the newly created National Heart Institute, approached Anfinsen about becoming chief of the Laboratory of Cellular Physiology. Anfinsen surprised many of his Harvard colleagues by accepting Shannon's offer. In part, he attributed the decision to the fact that the move doubled his salary overnight. However, he was not the only prominent biochemist of his generation who went to work for the federal government in Bethesda. In the 1950s and 1960s, laboratories at the National Institutes of Health (NIH) were headed by Arthur Kornberg (Nobel Prize, 1959), Bernard Horecker, Earl Stadtman, Leon Heppel, Bruce Ames, Marshall Nirenberg (Nobel Prize, 1968), and Martin Rodbell (Nobel Prize, 1994). Shannon became director of the NIH in 1955, and until 1968 he presided over not only the rapidly expanding extramural grants system but also a prominent program of intramural research. It was during his years at NIH (1950–1981) that Anfinsen made the scientific contributions that defined his career.

Anfinsen did spend sabbaticals during this period away from the NIH, including two years abroad in his first decade there. In 1954, he received a Rockefeller Foundation Fellowship to return to the Carlsberg Laboratory. He went to Copenhagen by way of Cambridge, England, to advance his knowledge of protein sequencing techniques. In Copenhagen during the 1954–1955 period, he worked with Linderstrøm-Lang and members of his group on the structure of ribonuclease. In addition, the award of a Guggenheim Foundation Fellowship enabled Anfinsen to spend a year at the Weizmann Institute of Science in Rehovot, Israel, in 1958–1959. In 1962, Anfinsen returned to Harvard Medical School as a professor in the Department of Biological Chemistry. He was invited to become chair of that department, but instead went back to the NIH in 1963, having been offered the opportunity to head a new laboratory at the National Institute of Arthritis and Metabolic Diseases. Anfinsen named this new unit the Laboratory of Chemical Biology; he was its chief until 1981.

At the beginning of 1950s, Anfinsen employed radioisotopically labeled amino acid precursors to investigate how proteins are synthesized in the cell—whether they are built up from individual amino acids, sequentially, on a template, or whether short peptides serve as intermediates, combined to make complete proteins. Results from radiolabeling chick ovalbumin during biosynthesis inclined him to favor the second mechanism. Other projects in his laboratory concerned the behavior and metabolism of various lipoproteins and cholesterol as well as the purification and characterization of L-glutamic acid dehydrogenase. Whereas some of Anfinsen's work addressed heart disease, especially biochemical aspects of atherosclerosis, the position at NIH gave him sufficient freedom to pursue basic protein chemistry.

Work on Ribonuclease. During his early years at the NIH, Anfinsen began analyzing the effects of proteolytic enzymes on ribonuclease, an enzyme that digests ribonucleic acid (RNA). The susceptibility of proteins to proteolytic (peptide-cleaving) enzymes, which were first purified in the 1920s and 1930s, provided early evidence that proteins have a polypeptide structure. But these enzymes, such as pepsin, trypsin, and chymotrypsin, could also be used as probes of protein structure. In the late 1940s, Linderstrøm-Lang and his colleagues demonstrated that for B-lactoglobulin, enzymatic digestion with trypsin occurred in two phases, the second of which seemed to result from denaturation of the polypeptide chain, exposing new sites for cleavage. Anfinsen's analysis of ribonuclease digestion by pepsin offered a similar picture, in which the main initial cleavage product seemed little changed in size and shape from intact ribonuclease. His subsequent study indicated that four disulfide bonds bridged different segments of the single polypeptide. Proteolysis produced protein fragments small enough to be sequenced, and in 1954 Anfinsen published the sequence of the four N-terminal residues. This effort was inspired by Frederick Sanger's pioneering elucidation of the amino acid sequence of insulin, another pancreatic protein.

Anfinsen's choice of ribonuclease for intensive investigation reflected not only the enzyme's small size and stability, but also the availability to researchers of large amounts of this protein, which had been purified from bovine pancreas by the Armour Company. Anfinsen took his "precious bottle of ribonuclease" (Richards, 1972, p. 493) with him when he went to the Carlsberg Laboratory in 1954. That year in Linderstrøm-Lang's laboratory,

Anfinsen continued his work on ribonuclease with several other protein chemists there, including Bill Harrington, Aase Hvidt, Martin Otteson, John Schellman, and Fred Richards. In a short communication to *Biochimica et Biophysica Acta*, six of these scientists reported the surprising result that ribonuclease retained full activity even when in a solution of eight molar urea, which denatures proteins by disrupting hydrogen bonds. In light of this, they claimed that only a small portion of the ribonuclease molecule was responsible for catalysis, and that an ordered secondary structure was not required for the enzyme's activity. As Anfinsen noted in 1989, he spent the next fifteen years after this paper's appearance disproving that last conclusion.

In other respects, however, this publication laid the groundwork for Anfinsen's continuing investigations of ribonuclease structure. When Anfinsen returned to the United States, Stanford Moore and William H. Stein were already making headway on determining the complete 124-amino acid sequence of ribonuclease. Rather than merely entering into a sequencing race, Anfinsen focused his efforts on understanding the relationship between biological function and chemical structure. He used limited proteolysis to show that an aspartic acid residue, the fourth amino acid from the C-terminal end, was essential for catalytic activity. A derivative of ribonuclease missing just those four amino acids was completely inactive. This finding supported the assertion of the 1955 multi-author paper that the active center was a small part of the whole protein, though Anfinsen recognized that amino acids elsewhere on the linear polypeptide chain, brought into proximity in the folded structure, participated in binding and catalysis.

Anfinsen's laboratory also investigated the role of enzyme's four disulfide bonds (which covalently link the protein's eight cysteine residues). Whereas Moore and Stein disrupted these bonds irreversibly, treating the protein with performic acid, Anfinsen cleaved them by simply reducing the disulfide bonds to free (or chemically protected) sulfhydryl groups. This cleavage of disulfide linkages by reduction could only be achieved under conditions—eight molar urea—that also denatured the protein. The activity of ribonuclease was completely lost when all four disulfide bonds were broken, although not all of the disulfide bonds were essential for activity. More intriguingly, in 1957 Anfinsen reported that denatured enzyme with completely reduced sulfydryl residues could recover activity spontaneously, after removal of the denaturant and re-oxidation of some of the disulfide bonds through exposure to air. This provided the core observation underlying Anfinsen's subsequent experiments.

Christian B. Anfinsen. *Christian Anfinsen accepting the Nobel Prize from Swedish Crown Prince Carl XVI Gustaf.* AP IMAGES.

The Nobel Prize. Over the next five years, members of Anfinsen's laboratory, particularly Michael Sela, Edgar Haber, and Frederick H. White Jr., characterized the process by which denatured ribonuclease re-acquired its native structure in solution. Under suitable conditions, the eight reduced cysteine sulfhydryls oxidized to produce the four original disulfide bonds, among 105 possible combinations. As these four researchers stated in their 1961 paper, "From chemical and physical studies of the reformed enzyme, it may be concluded that the information for the correct pairing of half-cystine residues in disulfide linkage, and for the assumption of the native secondary and tertiary structures, is contained in the amino acid sequence itself" (p. 1309). The authors obtained evidence that some of the first disulfide linkages re-formed were not the native bonds, but that, over time, rearrangement of the disulfide bridges produced the original linkages. In the course of these continuing studies, ribonuclease became a leading model system for investigating the kinetics of protein folding.

For his work on ribonuclease, Anfinsen was awarded the Nobel Prize for Chemistry in 1972. He received half of the monetary award, the other half being shared by Moore and Stein for their determination of the enzyme's amino acid sequence and their investigation of its catalytic mechanism. By this time, Anfinsen's renaturation of ribonuclease emblematized the primacy of the genetic sequence in determining protein folding and function. Like other landmark experiments in molecular biology, Anfinsen's experimental work gave older genetic concepts new molecular meaning. His thermodynamic hypothesis postulated that the "linear information of the genotype" resulted in the spontaneous formation of phenotypically functional proteins (Anfinsen, 1968, p. 17). But in contrast to a younger generation of molecular biologists, Anfinsen did not want to see protein biochemistry become secondary in significance to work on molecular genetics. The idea that the sequence of amino acids carried the instructions for protein folding helped to include proteins as well as nucleic acids in the new world of informational agents.

From Anfinsen's first articulation of the thermodynamic hypothesis, he recognized that even if the "folding process is thermodynamically guided" (1961, p. 447), other factors in the cell may affect the kinetics of the process. In the case of ribonuclease, Anfinsen contended, the process of rearrangement of disulfide bonds was too slow in vitro to account for its rapid, efficient biosynthesis in vivo. Consequently, he embarked on a search for an enzyme in beef liver that catalyzed sulfhydryl-disulfide interchanges. In 1966, members of his laboratory identified and purified this enzyme, protein disulfide isomerase. Since the 1970s, biologists have uncovered a host of other cellular agents that facilitate correct protein folding and assembly in vivo. The scientists who investigate these "molecular chaperones" in the early 2000s continue to cite Anfinsen's work on ribonuclease as canonical to the study of protein folding, even as they qualify its significance.

Other Scientific Contributions and Honors. Anfinsen published his sole monograph, *The Molecular Basis of Evolution*, in 1959, the centennial of the appearance of Darwin's *On the Origin of Species*. Anfinsen's book offered an up-to-date survey of discoveries in genetics and protein chemistry, arguing that a convergence of these fields could enable "a greater understanding of the fundamental forces underlying evolutionary process" (p. vii). Anfinsen contended that biological molecules such as proteins and nucleic acids, no less than fossils, are historical records of species variation for evolutionary interpretation. He emphasized the primacy of proteins in evolutionary selection: "The phenotypic picture present by an organism is the summation of the effects, physical and catalytic, produced by the complement of protein molecules characterizing the species in question" (p. 185). In addition to arguing for the salience of molecular evidence to evolutionary biology, Anfinsen sought to preserve a central place for protein chemistry alongside molecular genetics in the emerging field of molecular evolution.

Over the course of the 1960s Anfinsen's laboratory worked on several proteins, including B-galactosidase and staphylococcal nuclease. Staphylococcal nuclease provided a simpler model for protein folding than ribonuclease because it lacked disulfide bonds. In their work on this enzyme, Anfinsen, Meir Wilchek, and Pedro Cuatrecasas applied the technique of affinity chromatography to protein purification. Their method involved coupling a ligand or inhibitor of the desired protein to a Sepharose column, so that the protein was bound—while other cellular proteins passed through—before being selectively eluted. Their joint paper announcing the effectiveness of this method for protein purification remains, after the 1972 Nobel Lecture, Anfinsen's most-cited publication. Anfinsen also selected staphylococcoal nuclease in his attempt to chemically synthesize a catalytically active enzyme from scratch. In the end, he and his coworkers achieved a semi-synthesis by coupling peptide fragments prepared by solid phase synthesis. In the 1970s, Anfinsen

turned his attention to the study of interferon, an antiviral agent of great medical promise that was available only in miniscule quantities. His group used affinity chromatography to purify this protein, and in collaboration with scientists at the California Institute of Technology, they published its amino acid composition and the N-terminal sequence of one of the two components in 1980.

In the 1960s through the 1990s, Anfinsen received numerous honors beyond the 1972 Nobel Prize. His alma mater, Swarthmore College, awarded him an honorary doctorate in 1965, the first of eleven such degrees he received. He was a member of the American Philosophical Society, the National Academy of Sciences, serving on its Council from 1974 to 1977, and the American Society of Biological Chemistry (later the American Society of Biochemistry and Molecular Biology), for which he served as president in 1971–1972. Anfinsen also received recognition beyond the United States, being selected for membership in the Royal Danish Academy and the Vatican's Pontifical Academy of Science, and receiving medals from the State of Israel and from universities in Naples and Jerusalem.

Political Activities and Other Interests. Anfinsen involved himself in political action from the 1950s, particularly through letter-writing campaigns. He was among more than eleven thousand scientists who signed Linus Pauling's 1957 petition calling for a ban on the atmospheric testing of nuclear weapons. He opposed the Vietnam War, participating in a vigil held on the NIH Bethesda campus in 1964 after the U.S. Congress passed the Gulf of Tonkin resolution. In 1969 he and his NIH colleague Marshall Nirenberg protested the Brazilian government's removal of prominent scientists from their university positions. After receiving the Nobel Prize in 1972, Anfinsen made use of his public status to make appeals on behalf of foreign scientists mistreated by their governments and advocate for stronger federal funding of biomedical research.

In 1973, Anfinsen and several other distinguished scientists co-authored a letter to President Nixon, expressing concern about the denial of exit visas to scientists in the Soviet Union and calling for greater scientific exchange between the two countries. That same year, he allied himself with prominent NIH scientists to oppose Nixon's Conquest of Cancer Agency, on the grounds that it would draw funding away from basic research; the petition they circulated was signed by more than 3,000 biomedical scientists. Along similar lines, in 1983 Anfinsen, Julius Axelrod, Nirenberg, and D. Carleton Gajdusek, all Nobel prize-winning NIH scientists, coauthored a letter protesting Reagan's budget cuts to intramural research programs at the NIH. From 1981 to 1989, Anfinsen served as chairperson of the National Academy of Science's Committee for Human Rights. He was especially concerned about the plight of "Refuseniks" and other dissident scientists in the Soviet Union and Latin America. In the late 1980s, Anfinsen was among the prominent scientists who questioned the scientific value of the Human Genome Project.

In obituaries and reminiscences, his colleagues recall Anfinsen's down-to-earth nature (everyone in the laboratory called him "Chris") and emphasize that his dedication to science did not exclude other passions. He played both viola and piano, and when at the Carlsberg Laboratory in 1954–1955, he and his wife formed a chamber music ensemble with other scientists and spouses. The other avocation to which Anfinsen devoted himself was ocean sailing. During the last part of his life, religion also occupied a central place. Anfinsen and his first wife divorced in 1978. The following year he married Libby Esther Shulman Ely, and he converted to Orthodox Judaism. As Anfinsen wrote in 1987, "Although my feelings about religion still very strongly reflect a fifty-year period of orthodox agnosticism, I must say that I do find the history, practice, and intensity of Judaism an extremely interesting, philosophical package" (p. 2).

By the time that Anfinsen converted, he had developed strong connections to the Weizmann Institute in Israel, having served on its Board of Governors since 1962 and chaired its Scientific Advisory Board for many years. Anfinsen's first point of contact to the Weizmann Institute, where he eventually spent three sabbatical years, was Michael Sela, who came to Anfinsen's laboratory as a postdoctoral fellow in 1956 and spent two more periods at the NIH working with Anfinsen. Sela was associated with the Weizmann Institute for his entire five-decade career and served as its director from 1975 to 1985. In 1981 Anfinsen retired from the NIH to accept a job at as chief scientist for Taglit, a research company being formed by the research arm of the Weizmann Institute (Yeda) and the investment firm E. F. Hutton. However, just two weeks after he and his wife moved to Israel, E. F. Hutton withdrew its funding, leaving Anfinsen in limbo.

In 1982, Anfinsen returned to Maryland to accept an appointment as a professor of biology at Johns Hopkins University. There he launched his last major research effort, a study of the proteins of thermophilic bacteria—microbes that thrive at temperatures high enough to denature the proteins of other organisms, presenting a puzzle to protein chemists. Anfinsen was working on a project, funded by the National Science Foundation, to develop thermostable enzymes to aid in the remediation of environmental contamination and nuclear waste in the oceans, when he suffered a heart attack and died in May 1995.

BIBLIOGRAPHY

The Christian B. Anfinsen Papers are archived in the National Library of Medicine. A finding aid and selected papers are available through the Profiles in Science *series at profiles.nlm.nih.gov. The online collection includes copies of short reminiscences by Anfinsen, including the 1987 profile he wrote for the* 50th Reunion Yearbook of the Swarthmore College Class of 1937 *(quoted above), as well as his curriculum vitae, a full list of his publications, a selection of his correspondence, and a wide range of other primary sources.*

WORKS BY ANFINSEN

With Robert R. Redfield, Warren L. Choate, et al. "Studies on the Gross Structure, Cross-Linkages, and Terminal Sequences in Ribonuclease." *Journal of Biological Chemistry* 207 (1954): 201–210.

With W. F. Harrington, Aase Hvidt, et al. "Studies on the Structural Basis of Ribonuclease Activity." *Biochimica et Biophysica Acta* 17 (1955): 141–142.

"The Limited Digestion of Ribonuclease with Pepsin." *Journal of Biological Chemistry* 221 (1956): 405–412. This publication implicated the C-terminal end, particularly a specific aspartic acid residue, in the activity of ribonuclease.

With Michael Sela and Frederick H. White Jr. "Reductive Cleavage of Disulfide Bridges in Ribonuclease." *Science* 125 (1957): 691–692.

With Frederick H. White Jr. "Some Relationships of Structure to Function in Ribonuclease." *Annals of the New York Academy of Sciences* 81 (1959): 515–523.

The Molecular Basis of Evolution. New York: Wiley, 1959.

With Edgar Haber, Michael Sela, and Frederick H. White Jr. "The Kinetics of Formation of Native Ribonuclease During Oxidation of the Reduced Polypeptide Chain." *Proceedings of the National Academy of Sciences, USA* 47 (1961): 1309–1314.

With Charles J. Epstein and Robert F. Goldberger. "The Genetic Control of Tertiary Protein Structure: Studies with Model Systems." *Cold Spring Harbor Symposia on Quantitative Biology* 28 (1963): 439–449. This contribution introduced the term "thermodynamic hypothesis" to refer to the notion that Gibbs free energy drives protein folding.

With Francesco DeLorenzo, Robert F. Goldberger, et al. "Purification and Properties of an Enzyme from Beef Liver which Catalyzes Sulfhydryl-Disulfide Interchange in Proteins." *Journal of Biological Chemistry* 241 (1966): 1562–1567.

"Spontaneous Formation of the Three-Dimensional Structure of Proteins." *Developmental Biology Supplement* 2 (1968): 1–20.

With Pedro Cuatrecasas and Meir Wilchek. "Selective Enzyme Purification by Affinity Chromatography." *Proceedings of the National Academy of Sciences, USA* 61 (1968): 636–643.

"Studies on the Principles that Govern the Folding of Protein Chains." Nobel Lecture, December 11, 1972, available at http://nobelprize.org. Also published as "Principles that Govern the Folding of Protein Chains." *Science* 181 (1973): 223–230.

"One Hundred Years of Originality, Quality and Style." *Carlsberg Research Communications* 41 (1976): 293–298. This retrospective essay and the one from 1986 (below) recount Linderstrøm-Lang's charismatic and intellectual influence on protein science, and also give a sense of the fraternity of scientists that emerged from his laboratory.

With Kathryn C. Zoon, Mark E. Smith, et al. "Amino Terminal Sequence of the Major Component of Human Lymphoblastoid Interferon." *Science* 207 (1980): 527–528.

"The International Influence of the Carlsberg Laboratory on Protein Chemistry." *Perspectives in Biology and Medicine* 29 (1986): S87–S89.

"Commentary on 'Studies on the Structural Basis of Ribonuclease Activity.'" *Biochimica et Biophysica Acta* 1000 (1989): 197–199. This article comments on the erroneous conclusion of the 1955 paper on ribonuclease published from the Carlsberg Laboratory.

OTHER SOURCES

Kresge, Nicole, Robert D. Simoni, and Robert L. Hill, "The Thermodynamic Hypothesis of Protein Folding: The Work of Christian Anfinsen." *Journal of Biological Chemistry* 281 (2006): e11–e13.

Michaelis, Anthony R. "Obituary: Christian B. Anfinsen." *Interdisciplinary Science Reviews* 20 (1995): 96.

Moudrianakis, Evangelos N. "From Protein Coagulation and Reversible Denaturation to the Protein Folding Problem: Chris Anfinsen Defining the Tradition." *The FASEB Journal* 10 (1996): 179–183.

Richards, Frederic M. "The 1972 Nobel Prize for Chemistry." *Science* 178 (1972): 492–493.

———. "Linderstrøm-Lang and the Carlsberg Laboratory: The View of a Postdoctoral Fellow in 1954." *Protein Science* 1 (1992): 1721–1730.

Young, Michael. "Christian B. Anfinsen (1916–1995): Remembering His Life and His Science." *Protein Science* 4 (1995): 2237–2239.

Angela N. H. Creager

ANICETO MONTEIRO, ANTÓNIO

SEE **Monteiro, António**.

APOLLINARIUS (Aizanoi, Phrygia, *fl.* first or early second century CE), *astronomy*.

Apollinarius was among the most prominent Greek astronomers of the time immediately preceding Ptolemy, a period in the history of Greek astronomy about which scholars are very poorly informed. His chief contributions were apparently in lunar theory.

In his second century CE commentary on Hippocrates's *Airs, Waters, Places* (c. 400 BCE), a work extant only in Arabic translation, Galen found occasion to attack intellectuals of his time living at Rome for their ignorance of the writings of the most important astronomers. Among them he lists Apollinarius of Aizanoi (a city in Phrygia) along with Hipparchus (second century BCE), two other men otherwise unknown, and—if the name is not an interpolation in the Arabic text—Ptolemy (second century CE). Like Galen's catalogue of astronomers as a whole, Apollinarius is emblematic of the tenuous knowledge of Greco-Roman science, for though he is frequently mentioned in sources, none of his works has survived or is even known by title.

One specimen of Apollinarius's writings survives, a passage of about five hundred words quoted in a fragment of an anonymous commentary on Ptolemy's *Handy Tables*, composed in the early third century CE and fortuitously preserved in a medieval astrological manuscript. Apollinarius begins by defining terms for the various periodicities associated with the Moon—the synodic month and the sidereal, anomalistic, and dracontic months—and he explains how the Moon's anomalistic motion, characterized by its varying distance from the Earth, affects the length of the synodic month. The bulk of the passage, however, sets out Apollinarius's correct contention that the Moon's motion in latitude, reckoned as its progress in the plane of its orbit relative to the nodal line, is also affected by the anomaly, contrary, he says, to what the "Chaldeans" (Babylonian astronomers) believed. Hence, if one seeks a precise value for the dracontic month by comparing pairs of observed lunar eclipses widely spaced in time, ideally one ought to look for eclipses such that the Sun and Moon are in the same situations with respect to their anomalies as well as at precisely the same locations in the zodiac; these conditions, however, cannot be fulfilled within a span shorter than "many myriads of years." The fragment breaks off at this point, but it is enough to show that Apollinarius was criticizing the kind of approach to measuring lunar periodicities that Ptolemy attributes to Hipparchus in Book IV of the *Almagest*.

The late-second-century astrologer Vettius Valens claims to have used Apollinarius's tables for computing positions of the Sun and Moon, and that these tables employed the Babylonian convention according to which the vernal equinoctial point is at the eighth degree in Aries, not the beginning of the sign as Hipparchus and Ptolemy assumed. From numerical details given elsewhere in Valens's work, it appears that Apollinarius's lunar tables were of a type well-known from Greco-Egyptian papyri, using Babylonian-style zigzag functions to represent the Moon's daily motion in longitude and argument of latitude. By contrast, Paul of Alexandria (fourth century CE) and Porphyry (third century CE) both group Apollinarius with Ptolemy as astronomers who computed ascensional arcs by means of spherical trigonometry rather than the Babylonian arithmetical methods in common use.

BIBLIOGRAPHY

Jones, Alexander. *Ptolemy's First Commentator.* Philadelphia: American Philosophical Society, 1990. The testimonia concerning Apollinarius are listed and discussed here.

Neugebauer, Otto. *A History of Ancient Mathematical Astronomy.* Vol. 2. Berlin; New York: Springer-Verlag, 1975. The testimonia regarding Apollinarius are presented and considered.

Toomer, Gerald J. "Galen on the Astronomers and Astrologers." *Archive for History of Exact Sciences* 32 (1985): 193–206. Contains Galen's Hippocratic commentary.

Alexander Jones

APOLLONIUS OF PERGA

APOLLONIUS OF PERGA (*b.* Perga, Asia Minor, second half of third century BCE.; *d.* early second century BCE) *mathematical sciences, geometry.* For the original article on Apollonius see *DSB,* vol. 1.

The main advances in Apollonian scholarship since the original article come from the edition of texts extant only in Arabic translation. This article describes the recent researches, in the perspective of a new edition of the Greek text on the transmission of the *Conics* and a short account of Apollonius's foundational endeavors.

A mistaken claim contained in the original article on Apollonius, namely, that in the pre-Apollonian approach to conic sections only the parabola could be represented by the method of "application of areas" (p. 184), was corrected by Gerald Toomer in his edition of Diocles's *On Burning Mirrors* (1976).

Works and Fragments Extant in Arabic Translation. The masterly edition of the Arabic translation of books V–VII of the *Conics* provides scholars with an invaluable working tool. However, no relevant changes in the contents emerge when compared with Edmund Halley's Latin translation.

Fragments recovered from Arabic sources, most notably Ibrâhîm ibn Sinân's *Selected Problems* (*SP*) and al–Sijzî's *Geometrical Annotations* (*GA*), can be related to proofs contained in Apollonius' minor works, most of which were apparently translated into Arabic:

- Apollonius's method of solution for two of the four problems treated in the *Inclinations* can be recovered from extensive fragments in *GA*.

- A proposition in *SP* solves a case of a particular locus problem. The proof is a synthesis and is similar to that of the lemma to *Plane Loci* II.1 given

in Pappus's *Collectio* VII.187. Therefore, the latter appears to rework original Apollonian material.

- An analysis (*SP*) and fragments related to the synthesis (*GA*) are reported to pertain to the locus problem known as the Circles of Apollonius (*Plane Loci* II.1). These texts confirm that the proof of the same proposition given by Eutocius in his commentary to the *Conics* was completely rewritten by him.

- Two lemmas to the *Tangencies* (*GA*), in form of an analysis followed by a very sketchy synthesis, coincide with lemmas to the same work in Pappus's *Collectio* VII.167–174. The latter's proofs are slightly different, more detailed, and contain also a complete synthesis. Al-Sijzî found the lemmas in his text of the *Tangencies,* but it is not said that they were contained in the original as well.

The Textual Tradition of the Conics. The Greek text of the *Conics* is available in the commented edition that the Neoplatonic scholar Eutocius prepared in the sixth century CE. Recent studies have thoroughly investigated aims and methods of this edition, trying to sift out possible additions to the original Apollonian text. Eutocius declares that he had found several divergent editions of the treatise; he chose the proofs to be retained in the main text following a criterion of mathematical clarity, and transcribed the others in his commentary. Eutocius's criterion inclined him to give prominence in the constitution of his text to reworked propositions, coming from the preceding scholarly tradition. Secondary Arabic sources can be brought to bear on the subject, as well as the series of lemmas to the *Conics* that the fourth-century geometer Pappus proves in *Collectio* VII.233–311: It appears that the text of the *Conics* underwent conspicuous modifications both before and after Eutocius's edition. Such modifications and those introduced by Eutocius's editing, as can be reconstructed by a careful assessment of the available sources, include: the addition of some problems to book II; the addition of missing cases in single propositions; the rearrangement of the order of the propositions of the initial segments of books I and II; the partition of a single proposition into consecutive theorems or, inversely, fusion of several results into one single proposition, possibly with suppression of some of them; and the redrawing of some diagrams. A rather puzzling point is that some of the lemmas presented by Pappus do not find any application in the received text of the *Conics.*

Apollonius's Foundational Endeavors. These endeavors are mainly attested by the fourth-century Neoplatonist Proclus, who ascribes to Apollonius a few arguments aiming at explaining or modifying notions and proofs in the *Elements.* They include:

- A clarification of the conception of line; an anonymous clarification of the conception of surface, very similar in structure to the clarification of the conception of line, also should be ascribed to Apollonius.

- A general definition of angle as "contraction of a surface or of a solid into one single point under an inflected line or surface."

- A proof of *Common Notion* 1, resorting to the transitivity of the relation "occupying the same place as."

- Alternative proofs of *Elements* I.10 (to find the midpoint of a segment), and of I.11, (to draw the perpendicular to a straight from a point on it). These proofs avoid resorting to I.1, as is done instead in the *Elements.* The alternative proof of *Elements* I.23 (to construct on a given straight an angle equal to a given one) applies III.27 and avoids resorting to I.22.

Two more proofs reported by Proclus are very likely Apollonian. They are an anonymous alternative proof of I.2 (to place a given segment at a given point as its extreme), that does not use I.1 and entails a less restrictive interpretation of *Elements* I.post.3; and the alternative proof to *Elements* I.5 (the angles at the basis of an isosceles triangle are equal) ascribed to Pappus. The latter proof cleverly employs superposition of the isosceles triangle with its mirror image; in his *Prolegomena* to Euclid's *Data,* Marinus of Neapolis relates that in the *General Treatise* Apollonius introduced the term *tetagmenon* as a substitute for *dedomenon.*

Such interventions are guided by a concern with deductive economy, and aim at minimizing the number of notions and basic propositions employed. The rationale behind the alternative constructions appears to have been to avoid using *Elements* I.1 or, more generally, constructions of triangles; the proof of I.5 reduces to zero the number of auxiliary geometrical objects introduced. The proof of *Common Notion* 1 can be read as an attempt at coordinating the *Elements* and the *Data,* since in the latter the notion of "occupying a place" is the one to which the notion of "given in position" is reduced. Assuming the same notion as a basic one entails such a wider interpretation of *Elements* I.post.3 as permits to drastically simplify the proof of I.2, thereby greatly reducing the interest in a construction like I.1. The related notion of "superposition" is pivotal in the study of homeomeric lines, whose thorough study is very likely among Apollonius's achievements. This was the only class of lines in Greek mathematics directly defined as a whole in terms of a characteristic property.

SUPPLEMENTARY BIBLIOGRAPHY

WORKS BY APOLLONIUS OF PERGA

Conics, Books V to VII: The Arabic Translation of the Lost Greek Original in the Version of the Banû Mûsâ, 2 vols. Edited, translated, and with commentary by Gerald J. Toomer. Berlin: Springer-Verlag, 1990. The first critical edition of the books of the *Conics* which are extant only in Arabic.

Hogendijk, Jan P. "Arabic Traces of Lost Works of Apollonius." *Archive for History of Exact Sciences* 35 (1986): 187–253. This fundamental contribution to the reconstruction of the lost analytical works of Apollonius contains a commented edition of the fragments extant in Arabic sources.

OTHER SOURCES

Decorps-Foulquier, Micheline. "Eutocius d'Ascalon éditeur du traité des *Coniques* d'Apollonios de Pergé et l'exigence de 'clarté': un exemple des pratiques exégétiques et critiques des héritiers de la science alexandrine." In *Sciences exactes et sciences appliquées à Alexandrie,* edited by Gilbert Argoud and Jean-Yves Guillaumin. Saint-Étienne, France: Publications de l'Université de Saint-Étienne, 1998. The article discusses aims and methods of Eutocius's commentary to the *Conics.*

———. "Sur les figures du traité des *Coniques* d'Apollonios de Pergé édité par Eutocius d'Ascalon." *Revue d'histoire des mathématiques* 5 (1999): 61–82.

———. *Recherches sur les* Coniques *d'Apollonios de Pergé et leurs commentateurs grecs.* Paris: Klincksieck, 2000. This fundamental book is a detailed investigation of the modifications the Apollonian text has undergone during its transmission through late Antiquity and the Middle Ages.

———. "La tradition manuscrite du texte grec des *Coniques* d'Apollonios de Pergé (livres I–IV)." *Revue d'Histoire des Textes* 31 (2001): 61–116. The article reconsiders the whole manuscript tradition of the extant Greek text of the *Conics.* It confirms that the manuscript *Vaticanus graecus* 206 is the sole independent witness of the text. However, the relationships between its descendants are established on firmer basis than was made by the first editor, Johan L. Heiberg.

Diocles. *Diocles On Burning Mirrors: The Arabic Translation of the Lost Greek Original.* Edited, translated, and with commentary by G. J. Toomer. Berlin: Springer-Verlag, 1976. On pp. 3–17, a fuller treatment can be found of the pre-Apollonian theory of conic sections than the one offered on pp. 180–182 of the original article.

Euclide. *Les Éléments: Traduction et commentaires par Bernard Vitrac,* 4 vols. Vol. 3: *Livre X.* Paris: Presses Universitaires de France, 1998. On pp. 399–411, a compact reconstruction is presented of Apollonius' work on irrational lines.

Federspiel, Michel. "Notes critiques sur le Livre I des *Coniques* d'Apollonius de Pergè." *Revue des Études Grecques* 107 (1994): 203–218. This and the following articles by the same author throw considerable light on the peculiar mathematical language employed by Apollonius and, more generally, in Greek mathematics.

. "Notes linguistiques et critiques sur le Livre II des *Coniques* d'Apollonius de Pergè (Première partie)." *Revue des Études Grecques* 112 (1999): 409–443.

———. "Notes linguistiques et critiques sur le Livre II des *Coniques* d'Apollonius de Pergè (Deuxième partie)." *Revue des Études Grecques* 113 (2000): 359–391.

———. "Notes linguistiques et critiques sur le Livre III des *Coniques* d'Apollonius de Pergè (Première partie)." *Revue des Études Grecques* 115 (2002): 110–148.

Fried, Michael N., and Sabetai Unguru. *Apollonius of Perga's Conica: Text, Context, Subtext.* Leiden: Brill, 2001. An overall assessment of the *Conics* that tries to explain and interpret the text without resorting to modern conceptions and notation. The book offers a remarkable overview of Apollonius' masterly mathematical insight, pinpoints features of his geometrical approach to conic sections that were completely neglected by previous scholars, and firmly places his work in the Euclidean tradition.

Knorr, Wilbur R. "The Hyperbola-Construction in the *Conics*, Book II: Ancient Variations on a Theorem of Apollonius." *Centaurus* 25 (1982): 253–291. The article shows that a theorem in the extant version of the *Conics* is a later addition.

———. *The Ancient Tradition of Geometric Problems.* Cambridge, MA: Birkhäuser, 1985. On pp. 293–338 of this book, a thorough analysis is developed of some among Apollonius' most remarkable achievements.

Pappus of Alexandria. *Book 7 of the Collection,* 2 vols. Edited, translated, and with commentary by Alexander Jones. New York: Springer-Verlag, 1986. On pp. 510–546, an account is offered of Apollonius's lost works. A translation of a part of the Arabic text of Apollonius's *Cutting off of a Ratio* is given on pp. 606–619.

Saito, Ken. "Compounded Ratio in Euclid and Apollonius." *Historia Scientiarum* 31 (1986): 25–59. A study of a mathematical tool widely employed by Apollonius.

Unguru, S. "A Very Early Acquaintance with Apollonius of Perga's Treatise on Conic Sections in the Latin West." *Centaurus* 20 (1976): 112–128. The author shows that a detailed knowledge of the *Conics* is exhibited in Witelo's *Perspectiva,* surmising that this derives from a very early, otherwise unattested, Latin translation of the Apollonian treatise.

Fabio Acerbi

ARCHIMEDES (*b.* Syracuse, 287 BCE, *d.* Syracuse, 212 BCE), *mathematics, physics, pneumatics, mechanics.* For the original article on Archimedes see *DSB,* vol. 1.

The major contribution to Archimedean studies in the second half of the twentieth century is M. Clagett's *Archimedes in the Middle Ages.* Other contributions have touched on partial or minor points, and the overall picture presented in the original article is by and large unchanged. The points emphasized in the present post-

script are the alleged formation of Archimedes in Alexandria, his concern with astronomical matters, recent advances concerning transmission and authenticity of some of his treatises, the additional information gained by a new reading of the Archimedean palimpsest, a more satisfactory edition of the Arabic tract containing the construction of the regular heptagon ascribed to Archimedes, the edited tract *On mutually tangent circles*, and finally, the approximation for (3.

Archimedes and Alexandria. It is usually assumed that Archimedes studied in Alexandria. However, no source asserts this and a critical assessment of the evidence commonly adduced suggests the contrary. Diodorus Siculus (*Bibliotheca Historica, V.37.3*) wrote that Archimedes invented the *cochlias* when he was in Egypt. As Archimedes wrote a treatise *On spirals* and the device was in fact extensively used in Egypt, the Diodorean claim is more likely his or others' inference conflating two well-known facts, and at any rate it entails nothing about Archimedes's studies in Alexandria. It is positively known that Archimedes addressed some of his works to Alexandrian scholars: Eratosthenes, Conon, and Dositheus. Eratosthenes was born in Cyrene, studied in Athens, and went to Alexandria not before 246 BCE. As a consequence, Archimedes could not have met him during his alleged Alexandrian formation: He simply addressed him as a personality of high institutional and scientific rank. Conon was very likely older than Archimedes and performed astrometeorological observations in Sicily, as Ptolemy's *Phaseis* attests. Because Archimedes's father was an astronomer, as noted in the prefatory letter of the *Sand-reckoner*, it is more likely that Conon and Archimedes were personally acquainted, if this ever happened, on the occasion of Conon's stay in Sicily than during a hypothetical Alexandrian sojourn of Archimedes. Dositheus, whose observations too are recorded in Ptolemy's *Phaseis*, was merely a substitute addressee after Conon's death, and Archimedes's prefatory letters appear to imply that he never met Dositheus. Finally, no sources at all support the commonly held view that some form of public or private teaching was established in Alexandria in connection with the activities of the museum.

Archimedes and Astronomical Matters. Archimedes's use in the *Sand-reckoner* of Aristarchus's model is well known, as well as his attested interest in constructing a model planetarium. In the *Sand-reckoner* a remarkable feature is the estimate of the change in the apparent solar diameter when the observer shifts from the center to the surface of Earth. Two other items deserve mention. In *Almagest III.1* Ptolemy quoted Hipparchus's references to solstice observation reports by him and Archimedes that were supposedly accurate to the quarter-day. In the context it is clear

Archimedes. *Engraving of Archimedes.* © BETTMANN/CORBIS.

that Hipparchus was talking about multiple observations. This would make Archimedes the first known Greek to have recorded solstice dates and times in successive years, not just in one particular calendrically significant epoch year as Meton and Aristarchus did. In Hippolytus's *Refutation of all Heresies*, numbers are ascribed to Archimedes for the following:

1. intervals between successive cosmic bodies, from Earth to the zodiac;

2. the circumference of the zodiac;

3. the radius of Earth;

4. distances of cosmic bodies from the surface of Earth, the Moon and the zodiac being excluded.

The numerals in the text are fairly corrupted and do not match, and the issue is complicated by the fact that the ordering of the series of cosmic bodies in (1) and (4) do not agree; Hippolytus surely drew from earlier epitomes. In fact, after suitable emendations, the two sequences of numbers in (1) and (4) can be made to agree and (1) has the form $ma + nb$, where m, n are integers and a, b are fixed lengths. The actual values of n suggest that Archimedes took up a pre-existing model, presumably of late Pythagorean origin, of cosmic distances arranged according to a musical scale, and adapted it to his own purposes, about which only conjectures can be made. A mark of Archimedean origin is that the numbers are named in accordance with the system of octads developed in the *Sand-reckoner*.

Textual Tradition and Authenticity. Refined criteria suited to establish a chronological ordering of the Archimedean works have been proposed by Wilbur R. Knorr. The criteria are:

1. The form of exhaustion procedure employed: The passage from the "approximation" form (allegedly the one at work in *Elements XII*) to the "difference" form and finally to the "ratio" form are successive refinements. This is the main criterion.

2. The proportion theory employed: A pre-Euclidean proportion theory is at work in early works, whereas in *Spiral lines* the theory of *Elements V* is applied.

3. The so-called lemma of Archimedes: It is introduced only in later works, whereas juvenile essays rest on the bisection principle implicit in *Elements XII* and later justified by *Elements X.1*.

4. Resorting to mechanical methods as an heuristic background: This is typical of later works.

5. The degree of formal precision in a proof: This increases after Conon's death.

Knorr's main underlying assumption is that variations in the above usages should receive an historical and not a technical explanation. Terminological arguments have been developed by Tohru Sato supporting to some extent Knorr's reconstruction. A distinction between an early and a mature group of works results. The former includes, in this order, *Measurement of the Circle, Sand-reckoner, Quadrature of Parabola* Props. 18 to 24, and *Plane Equilibria I* and *II*. Most of the mature treatises are ordered by internal references; the first and the last work in the series, which escape cross-referencing, would be respectively *Quadrature of Parabola*, Props. 4 to 17, and the *Method*. No one of the above criteria is conclusive, and the number of ad hoc assumptions and adjustments necessary to make the proposal a coherent whole reduces it merely to a plausible guess.

Other scholarly contribution to problems of authenticity and transmission of the Archimedean corpus include:

1. Knorr's tentative reconstruction of the original text of the *Measurement of the Circle*, with particular emphasis on Alexandrian and late ancient editions and epitomes, and on the transmission of the resulting corpus of writings through antiquity and the Middle Ages;

2. John Berggren's analysis, based on internal consistency and mathematical relevance, of the spurious theorems in the *Equilibria of Planes*;

3. Knorr's reconstruction of a lost Archimedean treatise on the center of gravity of solids, with reduction to Archimedean sources of the whole extant tradition on the balance;

4. by the same author, an assessment in the negative of the evidence about an Archimedean *Catoptrics*.

The Archimedean Palimpsest. The Archimedean palimpsest reappeared in 1998 after it was stolen in the years around World War I. The considerable gain offered by the digital techniques employed in reading the underlying writing is balanced, at times overbalanced, by the dramatic decay of the material conditions of the manuscript. The very good photographic plates taken at the time of the discovery of the palimpsest, preserved at the Royal Danish Library in Copenhagen, *Ms. Phot. 38*, and covering about two thirds of the relevant *folia*, are still an indispensable piece of evidence, as they portray the manuscript in a decidedly more acceptable state of conservation. It appears that the transcription of the first editor was fairly accurate: It is in principle to be expected that the text he procured will need only marginal corrections. Real advances can be hoped for only for those portions of text that were left unread by the first transcription.

Only two, very short, fragments from the palimpsest have been edited so far, Proposition 14 of the *Method* and what remains of the *Stomachion*, and these provisional texts do not clearly distinguish the parts coming from a really new reading of the manuscripts from those in which resort to the photographs or to Johan Ludvig Heiberg's text was necessary. A new edition of the Arabic fragment of the *Stomachion* is a desideratum. What remains of this work appears to refer to a square *ADGB* divided into 14 parts (see Figure 1, taken from the Arabic fragment), where *E, H, M, N, C* are middle points of *BG, BE, AL, DG, ZG,* respectively, *EZ* and *HT* are drawn perpendicular, *A* belongs to *HK* produced and *O* to *BC* produced. The Arabic fragment simply gives the values of the areas of the fourteen parts as fractions of the area of the whole square. Such areas turn out to be unit fractions of the whole; the only exception, the area of *HEFLT*, is written as a sum of unit fractions. The Greek fragment amounts to a short, initial introduction and to a partial construction of the diagram (the one implied by the Greek text actually makes *AZEB* a square). As a preliminary result it is proved that *AB >BL*, and as a consequence ∠*AMB* > ∠*LMB*, but then the text breaks off. The aim, stated by Archimedes in the introduction, is "finding out the fitting-together of the arising figures." Just after that, Archimedes asserts that

> there is not a small multitude of figures made of them, because of it being possible to take them (*the text is here hardly readable*) into another place

of an equal and equiangular figure, transposed to hold another position; and again also with two figures, taken together, being equal and similar to a single figure, and two figures taken together being equal and similar to two figures taken together-[then], out of the transposition, many figures are put together. (Netx, Acerbi, and Wilson, 2004, p. 93)

One speculative possibility is that the *Stomachion* contained a first application of combinatorial techniques: to count in how many ways the initial configuration can be broken off into its constituent pieces and then recomposed, with the pieces arranged in a different way.

In *Method 14*, a passage unread by Heiberg, within a column of text that requires extensive restoration, reveals that Archimedes handles infinite multitudes of mathematical entities by setting them in one-to-one correspondence. One should not attach too much importance to this move as if it was an anticipation of modern set-theoretic treatment of infinities. The move adds nothing to the explicit character of *Method 14*, and in any case analogous features can be found outside Archimedes, for instance in Pappus, *Collectio IV.34*.

The Regular Heptagon and Other Arabic Sources. A new edition of the Arabic treatise makes it possible to write in a correct form some passages in the construction of the regular heptagon ascribed to Archimedes. What follows should replace the text from "*HD = DB*" to "arc *AH* = 2 arc *HB*" in Proposition 17 (lines 14–33 of the second column on p. 225 of the original *DSB* article):

> Since ∠*CHD* = ∠*DBT*, and ∠*CDH* = ∠*TDB*, and *HD = DB*, then *CD = DT*, *CH = TB* and one circle contains the four points *B, H, C, T*. [Actually the equality *CH = TB* is of no subsequent use and the last statement follows directly from the equality of angles *CHD* and *DBT*.] Since *CB·DB = AC²* = *HC²*, and *CB = TH*, while *DB = DH*, *TH·HD* = *HC²*, and Δ *THC* ∼ Δ *CHD*. So ∠*DCH* = ∠*HTC*. But ∠*DCH* = 2∠*CAH*, so ∠*CTH* = 2∠*CAH*. But ∠*CTD* = ∠*DBH*, so ∠*DBH* = 2∠*CAH*, and arc *AH* = 2 arc *HB*.

It may be added that the *neusis* involved in the construction of the heptagon can be solved in a straightforward way by a simple adaptation of the solution of the *neusis* reported in Pappus, *Collectio IV.60*, as a preliminary to the angle trisection. It turns out that the construction, by intersection of two hyperbolas, is identical with the one proposed by the Arabic mathematician al-Saghânî. The proof, if framed in analogy with Pappus, that the construction really solves the *neusis* is considerably simpler than that in al- Saghânî.

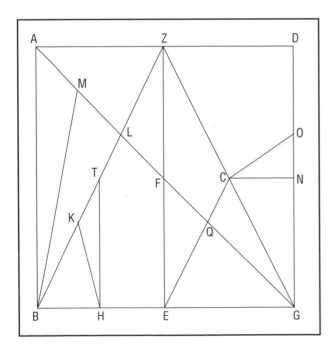

Figure 1.

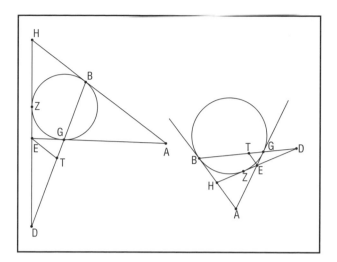

Figure 2.

The short Arabic treatise *On mutually tangent circles*, ascribed to Archimedes in the title, is a collection of fifteen lemmas concerning circles rather than a work with a discernible aim; only seven lemmas out of fifteen involve mutually tangent circles. If the original really dates back to Archimedes, what is read is most likely an epitome, possibly containing some accretions. A similar assessment should be extended to other compilations ascribed to Archimedes and redacted in the format of "Books of Lemmas," such as the *Liber assumptorum* or the shorter version of the so-called *Book of Lemmas* whose longer version is credited to a certain Aqâtun in the transmitted Arabic version Two propositions of some interest can be singled out from *On mutually tangent circles*. The first is lemma 12 (see Fig. 2, representing one possible configuration). Two tangents *AB* and *AG* are drawn to the same circle, and the points of tangency *B* and *G* are joined by a straight line. From point *D* on that line another tangent is drawn, touching the circle at *Z* and intersecting the other two tangents at *E* and *H*. To prove that *HD* : *DE* = *HZ* : *ZE*. The easy proof draws the parallel *ET* to *AB* and argues by similar triangles and from the equality of tangents to a circle drawn from the same point.

One interesting feature is that the lemma holds also when the two initial tangents are parallel: In this case the text displays two letters *A* denoting different points. The fact that Apollonius proposed similar theorems for conic sections in *Conics III* might be taken as supporting the Archimedean origin of lemma 12, because Apollonius shaped his *Conics* as a system of scholarly references to preceding authors. The second result is lemma 15, quoted also by al-Bīrūnī and assigned by him to "Archimedes in the Book of Circles." A broken line *AGB*, with *AG >BG*, is inscribed in a segment of circle (see Figure 3); bisect arc

AB at *D* and drop perpendicular *DE* from *D* on to *AG*. To prove that *AE* = *EG* + *GB* three proofs are given, the first of which runs as follows. Take arc *HD* = arc *DG* and *EZ* = *EG*; join *DG, DZ, DA, DH, HA*. A rather involved but elementary argument shows that Δ *AZD* = Δ *AHD*. Hence *AZ* = (*AH* =) *BG*. Summing *EZ* = *EG* to this equality, what is required is obtained.

A very similar theorem is proven by Ptolemy in *Almagest I.10* in order to calculate the chord of the half-angle. Because the latter result can be easily derived from the so-called Ptolemy's theorem, the fact that Ptolemy himself does not do that suggests that the alternative approach he reports was the basis of earlier chord tables. Simplified variants of the same theorem as in *Almagest I.10* are Prop. 14 of the treatise, ascribed to Archimedes, having the above-mentioned construction of the regular heptagon as Prop. 17, and lemma 3 of the *Liber assumptorum*. It is likely that both the theorem in the *Almagest* and lemma 15 were different cases of a more comprehensive Archimedean proposition; however, it is not said that he devised such a proposition for trigonometric purposes.

Approximation for √3. The approximation 1351-780 >√3 >265/153 found in *Measurement of the Circle*, Prop. 3, appears to have received a fairly satisfactory explanation in the remark that the successive convergent fractions of the development in continued fraction of √27, when divided by 3, are 5/3, 26/15, 265/153, 1351/780. The approximated value ascribed to Archimedes in *Diophanes 20a* (Diophantus, p. 22.16 Tannery) and implied for instance in Hero's calculations in *Metrica I.17* is 26-15. As these values can be obtained by a procedure of successive reciprocal subtractions, traces of which can be found in the Greek mathematical corpus, it is likely that the approximations at issue were obtained in that way.

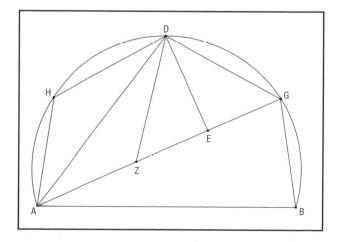

Figure 3.

SUPPLEMENTARY BIBLIOGRAPHY

WORKS BY ARCHIMEDES

"On mutually tangent circles." In *Archimedis Opera Omnia, cum Commentariis Eutocii:* vol. IV: *Über einander berührende Kreise.* Edited by I.L. Heiberg. Translated from the Arabic into German and with notes by Y. Dold-Samplonius, H. Hermelink und M. Schramm. Stuttgart, Germany: B.G. Teubner, 1975. The Arabic translation of the a tract ascribed to Archimedes. The edition proposes a German translation and a facsimile reproduction of the unique manuscript Bankipore 2468 rather than a critical text and apparatus.

Dold-Samplonius, Yvonne, ed. "Book of Lemmas." In *Book of Assumptions by Aqâtun.* Ph.D. diss., University of Amsterdam, 1977.

Netz, Reviel, Fabio Acerbi, and Nigel Wilson. "Towards a Reconstruction of Archimedes's *Stomachion,*" *SCIAMVS* 5 (2004): 67–99.

New editions of fragments from the Palimpsest are available in the following articles.

Netz, Reviel, Ken Saito, and Natalie Tchernetska. "A New Reading of *Method* Proposition 14: Preliminary Evidence from the Archimedes Palimpsest (Part 1)." *SCIAMVS* 2 (2001): 9–29.

———. "A New Reading of *Method* Proposition 14: Preliminary Evidence from the Archimedes Palimpsest (Part 2)." *SCIAMVS* 3 (2002): 109–125.

OTHER SOURCES

Berggren, John L. "A Lacuna in Book I of Archimedes' *Sphere and Cylinder.*" *Historia Mathematica* 4 (1977): 1–5. A discussion of a specific problem in Archimedes's writings is found here.

———. "Spurious Theorems in Archimedes' *Equilibria of Planes.*" *Archive for History of Exact Sciences* 16 (1977): 87–103. See this text about some problems of authenticity in the Archimedean corpus.

Clagett, Marshall. *Archimedes in the Middle Ages.* Vol. 1. *The Arabo-Latin Tradition.* Madison: The University of Wisconsin Press, 1964; Vol. 2. *The Translations from the Greek by William of Moerbeke.* Memoirs 117. 2 tomes; Vol. 3. *The Fate of the Medieval Archimedes 1300–1565.* Memoirs 125. 3 tomes; Vol. 4. *A Supplement on the Medieval Latin Traditions of Conic Sections (1150–1566).* Memoirs 137. 2 tomes; Vol. 5. *Quasi-Archimedean Geometry in the Thirteenth Century.* Memoirs 157. 2 tomes. Philadelphia: American Philosophical Society, 1976–1984. The entire mediaeval Archimedean tradition is now available in this masterful edition.

Hogendijk, Jan P. "Greek and Arabic Constructions of the Regular Heptagon." *Archive for History of Exact Sciences* 30 (1984): 197–330. The Archimedean tract on the regular heptagon is best read in this edition. The proposed translation is from p. 289.

Knorr, Wilbur R. "Archimedes and the *Elements*: Proposal for a revised Chronological Ordering of the Archimedean Corpus." *Archive for History of Exact Sciences* 19 (1978): 211–290. The new chronological ordering of Archimedes's works was proposed here.

———. "Archimedes' Lost Treatise on the Centers of Gravity of Solids." *Mathematical Intelligencer* 1 (1978): 102–109.

———. "Archimedes' Neusis-Constructions in Spiral Lines." *Centaurus* 22 (1978): 77–98.

———. "Archimedes and the Pre-Euclidean Proportion Theory." *Archives internationales d'histoire des sciences* 28 (1978): 183–244. This article corrects in fact "Archimedes and the *Elements,*" which mainly focused on exhaustion procedures, so that what in the latter paper is adherence to Euclidean methods becomes in the present one a mark of pre-Euclidean provenance. Such a move is possible once entire portions of the *Elements,* for instance book XII, are regarded as simply reporting Eudoxean elaborations.

———. "Archimedes and the Spirals: The Heuristic Background." *Historia Mathematica* 5 (1978): 43–75.

———. *Ancient Sources of the Medieval Tradition of Mechanics. Greek, Arabic and Latin Studies on the Balance.* Supplemento agli *Annali dell'Istituto e Museo di Storia della Scienza,* 1982, Fasc. 2. The reduction to non-extant Archimedean sources of the whole extant tradition on the balance is argued at length here.

———. "Archimedes and the Pseudo-Euclidean *Catoptrics*: Early Stages. In the Ancient Geometric Theory of Mirrors." *Archives internationales d'histoire des sciences* 35 (1985): 28–105. The nonexistence of an Archimedean *Catoptrics,* although attested by a number of sources, is argued in detail in this work.

———. "Archimedes after Dijksterhuis: A Guide to Recent Studies." In *Archimedes.* Princeton, NJ: Princeton University Press, 1987. A complete bibliography updated to 1987 can be found here.

———. "On Archimedes' Construction of the Regular Heptagon." *Centaurus* 32 (1989): 257–271.

———. *Textual Studies in Ancient and Medieval Geometry.* Boston, MA: Birkhäuser, 1989. Part III of this book presents a very ambitious reconstruction of the textual tradition of the Archimedean text *Measurement of the Circle.*

———. "On an Alleged Error in Archimedes' *Conoids*, Prop. 1." *Historia Mathematica* 20 (1993): 193–197. A discussions of a very specific problem in Archimedes' writings is found here.

———. *The Ancient Tradition of Geometric Problems.* Boston, MA: Birkhäuser 1986. Reprint, New York: Dover 1993. Knorr offers a very good account of Archimedes' mathematical techniques.

Netz, Reviel. *The Works of Archimedes: Translated into English, together with Eutocius' Commentaries, with Commentary, and Critical Edition of the Diagrams.* Vol. 1: *The Two Books On the Sphere and the Cylinder.* Cambridge, U.K.: Cambridge University Press, 2004. This is the first volume of a new English translation of Archimedes's works.

Neugebauer, Otto. *A History of Ancient Mathematical Astronomy.* 3 vols. Berlin: Springer, 1975. Neugebauer offered the first discussion of the problem of the numbers for the distances of the cosmic bodies.

Osborne, Catherine. "Archimedes on the Dimensions of the Cosmos." *Isis* 74 (1983): 234–242. The difficult problem of the numbers for the distances of the cosmic bodies is tackled here.

Schneider, Ivo. *Archimedes: Ingenieur, Naturwissenschaftler und Mathematiker.* Darmstadt, Germany: Wissenschaftliche Buchgesellschaft, 1979. The best overall account of Archimedes's life and works after Dijksterhuis's book.

Sezgin, Fuat. *Geschichte des Arabischen Schrifttums. Band V, Mathematik bis c. 430 H.* Leiden: E.J. Brill, 1974. A fairly complete account of the Arabic Archimedes with detailed list of manuscripts is available here.

Taisbak, Christian M. "An Archimedean Proof of Heron's Formula for the Area of a Triangle; Reconstructed." *Centaurus* 24 (1980): 110–116.

———. "Analysis of the So-called "Lemma of Archimedes" for Constructing a Regular Heptagon." *Centaurus* 36 (1993): 191–199. This analysis of the Archimedean tract on the regular heptagon is very helpful.

Tohru Sato. "Archimedes' *On the Measurement of a Circle* Proposition 1: An Attempt at a Reconstruction." *Japanese Studies in the History of Science* 18 (1979): 83–99. It is argued that the extant Latin translation by Gerard of Cremona was based on a better text than the extant Greek.

———. "Archimedes' Lost Works on the Center of Gravity of Solids, Plane Figures, and Magnitudes." *Historia Scientiarum* 20 (1981): 1–41. Sato presents a different view from Knorr on reduction to non-extant Archimedean sources of the extant tradition on the balance.

———. "A Reconstruction of *The Method* 17, and the Development of Archimedes' Thought on Quadrature. Part One." *Historia Scientiarum* 31 (1986): 61–86. Linguistic arguments supporting the ordering proposed by Knorr are offered here and in the following article.

———. "A Reconstruction of *The Method* 17, and the Development of Archimedes' Thought on Quadrature. Part Two." *Historia Scientiarum* 32 (1987): 75–142. The article also contains a reconstruction of a lost Archimedean proposition.

Vitrac, Bernard. "A propos de la chronologie des œuvres d'Archimède." In *Mathématiques dans l'Antiquité*, edited by J.Y. Guillaumin. Saint-Étienne, France: Publications de l'Université de Saint-Étienne 1992. Knorr's unstated presuppositions and methods in establishing the Archimedean chronology are criticized in this work.

Fabio Acerbi

ARCONVILLE, MARIE GENEVIÈVE CHARLOTTE THIROUX D'

(*b.* Paris [?], France, 17 October 1720; *d.* Paris [?], 23 December 1805), *chemistry, anatomy, translation.*

Madame d'Arconville was one of the very few eighteenth-century women who not only undertook translations of scientific works, but also carried out her own long-lasting program of experiments. A prolific author, she wrote or translated anonymously dozens of texts on scientific matters, as well as literature, morality, and history.

Life and Education. Marie Geneviève was daughter of André Guillaume d'Arlus or Darlus, a wealthy farmer-general. When she was only fourteen years old, she married Louis Lazare Thiroux d'Arconville, a councillor—later a president—at the Paris parliament, and brought him a 350,000-French-pound endowment. The eldest of their three sons, Louis Thiroux de Crosne, became an *intendant*—a royal administrator in the province—then the Paris lieutenant general of the police; he was eventually beheaded during the Terror (in 1794), while his mother spent a few months in jail.

Being disfigured by smallpox at age twenty-two, Madame d'Arconville chose an austere life thereafter and professed Jansenist morals. She also founded a charitable institution close to her country house at Meudon, near Paris on the road to Versailles. But she mainly devoted her time to reading—including Voltaire and Jean-Jacques Rousseau—and attending courses, as well as to writing and conducting experiments in botany and chemistry. Not only was she able to translate English and Italian, she also learned several sciences, notably those taught in public courses at the Jardin du Roi (King's Garden), and she practiced botany, agriculture, and chemistry. In her thirties, she took up the pen and started publishing translations; from the 1760s, she produced original works as well. She translated numerous novels, plays, and poems, and she wrote essays on morals, then biographies of late-sixteenth- and early seventeenth-century French figures, including Cardinal Arnaud d'Ossat, King Francis II, and Queen Marie de Médicis. She is even said to have written the *Essai sur l'amour-propre envisagé comme principe de morale (Essay on Self-respect as Principle of Morals)*, which King Frederick II read at the Berlin Academy in 1770. At her death, she left a twelve-volume manuscript of *miscellanea,* which was lost and then rediscovered at the end of the twentieth century. Although she avoided Parisian society, she received into her home and met many of the great authors and scientists of her time, including Voltaire, Denis Diderot, Bernard de Jussieu, Guillaume-Chrétien Lamoignon de Malesherbes, Pierre-Joseph Macquer, and Antoine-Laurent Lavoisier.

Scientific Writings. In 1759 Madame d'Arconville, in collaboration with anatomist Jean-Joseph Süe, published a French edition of Alexander Monro's *Anatomy of the Human Bones* (1726). She added a few personal observations in footnotes and a preface, which reveals a profound admiration for Jacques Bénigne Winslow, and, most significantly, a volume of plates (Monro's original was not illustrated, and the author stated that illustrations gave a wrong idea of reality). One of her illustrations is the first published engraving of the female skeleton: the figure showed a smaller rib cage than the male skeleton, due to the long-term use of a corset, and a smaller head-to-body ratio, which the legend of the plate connected with the inferior capacity of women. Sixteen years later, she published a new volume of *Mélanges* (Miscellanea), including two other papers by Monro, in addition to fifteen texts of anatomy, medicine, and botany that she translated from the *Philosophical Translations of the Royal Society of London* for 1720.

Despite her extensive writings in other fields, Madame d'Arconville's keenest interest was chemistry. In 1759 she also translated Peter Shaw's *Courses of Chemistry* into French. In addition to correcting his errors, she added an original 94-page preliminary discourse on the origin and progress of chemistry, which stressed the "revolution" carried out by Joachim Becher, Hermann Boerhaave, Georg Ernst Stahl, Wilhelm Homberg, Nicolas Lemery, Étienne-François Geoffroy, and others. For the first time, she referred to her own experiments—some of which were replications, some original—which she published seven years later, in *Essai pour servir à l'histoire de la putréfaction* (Essay for the History of Putrefaction; Paris, 1766).

Her researches had been supervised by Macquer, who became her mentor in chemistry and a close friend as she followed his chemical courses. A few years after Émilie du Châtelet had worked on combustion and fire (1737–1744), Madame d'Arconville equipped laboratories in Paris and Meudon, where she conducted various experiments on gums and resins and above all on putrefaction, which she saw as the key of "physical sciences" and the basis of natural history. She carried out a ten-year series of some three hundred meticulous experiments on human bile and on the conservation of meat, using thirty-two classes of preservatives, including mineral acids and bases (1754–1764). For every observation of the state of decay of her samples, she carefully recorded a few variables, such as time, temperature, and weather. Her results were eventually published in a detailed manner, and she also displayed them through ten elaborate charts in descending order of the preservatives' effectiveness. Daring to differ with Boerhaave and John Pringle, she showed that putrefaction was involved in animal life as well as in plants. Like Pringle, whose work she often referenced in both her translation from Shaw and her own book, she recognized the good effect of *quinquina* (cinchona), but contrary to him, she proved that *camomilla* (chamomile) was not better. At the very moment the book was being printed, she added a brief notice reporting on the recent French translation of David Macbride's *Experimental Essays*, which also dealt with this matter.

Madame d'Arconville never signed either her own works or her translations, as she apparently considered the various pitfalls of authorship for women: "Do they display science or pretty wit? If their works are bad, they get a bird; if they are good, one robbed them; they keep merely the ridiculousness of having presented themselves as the authoresses" (Briquet, 1804, p. 13). Nonetheless, her writing did circulate in the 1770s literary reviews, and her secretary Rossel collected her works in a seven-volume *Mélanges de littérature, de morale et de physique* (Miscellanea of literature, morals, and physics) in 1775. The single volume devoted to scientific and medical matters included her previous three prefaces and several previously unpublished shorter translations in medicine and science.

Despite their anonymity, Madame d'Arconville's works were referred to by chemists dealing with the chemistry of life, like Macbride (as soon as 1767, in the second edition of his *Experimental Essays*) and William Higgins in Britain, Macquer and Antoine-François de Fourcroy in France. Fourcroy even referred repeatedly to her work in his publications, ranging from *Eléments d'histoire naturelle et de chimie* (Elements of natural history and chemistry; Paris, 1786) to his dictionary of chemistry for the *Encyclopédie méthodique* (Methodical encyclopedia, vol. IV; Paris, 1806).

BIBLIOGRAPHY

WORKS BY ARCONVILLE

Translator. *Leçons de chymie propres à perfectionner la physique, le commerce et les arts* [Peter Shaw, *Courses of Chemistry*]. Paris: Jean Thomas Herissant, 1759.

Translator. *Traité d'ostéologie* [Alexander Munro, *Anatomy of the Human Bones*]. 2 vols. Paris: Didot le jeune, 1759.

Essai pour servir à l'histoire de la putréfaction. Par le traducteur des Leçons de Chymie de M. Shaw, premier Médecin du Roi d'Angleterre. Paris: P. Fr. Didot le jeune [and Théophile Barrois], 1766.

Mélanges de littérature, de morale et de physique. 7 vols. Vol. 4, *Discours sur différents objets de physique; Mémoires... tirés des Transactions philosophiques.* Amsterdam: Aux dépens de la compagnie, 1775.

OTHER SOURCES

Arnault, Antoine-Vincent, et al. *Biographie nouvelle des contemporains.* 20 vols. Paris: Colas, 1820–1829.

Briquet, Fortunee B. *Dictionnaire historique, litteraire, et bibliographique Françaises et des etrangeres naturalisees en France.* Paris: Treuttel et Würtz, 1804.

Girou Swiderski, Marie-Laure. "Écrire à tout prix. La présidente Thiroux d'Arconville, polygraphe (1720–1805)." Available from http://aix1.uottawa.ca/~margirou/Perspectives/XVIIIe/arconvil.htm.

Poirier, Jean-Pierre. *Histoire des femmes de science en France. Du Moyen-Âge à la Révolution.* Paris: Pygmalion/Gérard Watelet, 2002.

Rayner-Canham, Marelene, and Geoffrey Rayner-Canham. *Women in Chemistry: Their Changing Roles from Alchemical Times to the Mid-twentieth Century.* Washington, DC: American Chemical Society and Chemical Heritage Foundation, 1998.

Patrice Bret

ARDUINI, GIOVANNI

SEE **Arduino, Giovanni**.

ARDUINO, GIOVANNI (*b.* Caprino Veronese, Italy, 16 October 1714; *d.* Venice, Italy, 21 March 1795), *geology, mineralogy, mining.* For the original article on Arduino see *DSB,* vol. 1.

In the second half of the eighteenth century, the work of Arduino contributed decisively to ideas about basic lithostratigraphic classification of rocks and mountain building. Arduino's classification of mountains is widely regarded by twenty-first-century historians of geology as the basis for the modern chronological subdivisions of Earth's geological history. Since the early 1990s, some new historical studies revealed in detail the multidisciplinarity of Arduino's scientific and technical works as well as the extent of his correspondence, unpublished manuscripts, and part of his geo-mineralogical collection.

Classification System. The lithological studies carried out by Arduino as a result of twenty years of fieldwork in the mountain areas of central and northern Italy (the hills of Tuscany, the Modenese Apennines, the Alps, and the pre-Alps of the Italian regions of Veneto and Lombardy) were supported by a specialized knowledge of mining. After his technical apprenticeship in the iron mines of Chiusa/Klausen in the region of Tyrol, Arduino became supervisory assistant and later director of the lead and silver mines of Tretto (near Vicenza) in the Venetian Republic from 1740 until the mines were closed by the government in1747. Between 1748 and 1752 Arduino worked as land surveyor in Vicenza drawing detailed maps for the local land register and in 1754 he was also nominated public engineer in the same city. Meanwhile, Arduino spent about two months at the end of 1753 (not 1773, as stated in the original *DSB* article), exploiting some copper mines near Montieri in Tuscany. He returned there in January 1756 for a longer period of work including an evaluation of a mercury mining operation in Silvena, nearby Monte Amiata, during the summer of 1757.

From 1740 to 1757 Arduino obtained his metallurgical knowledge and was self-taught in mineralogy and chemistry. During this period Arduino's interest in the study of Earth's strata and in the interpretation of different kinds of rocks grew together with his advanced experience in mining. This practical knowledge and the capacity to observe the structure of the mountains with the aim of obtaining a precise idea of their potential for mineral exploitation clearly formed the basis of Arduino's geological studies in the 1760s and above all of the lithostratigraphical subdivision of rocks and mountains into four units.

The theory of lithostratigraphical subdivision was outlined for the first time in the *Due Lettere sopra varie osservazioni naturali* (Two letters on various natural observations, 1760) and refined in the *Saggio Fisico-Mineralogico di Lythogonia e Orognosia* (Physical-Mineralogical essay of lithogony and orognosy," 1774). The decisive turning point toward a broader reflection on the classification of rocks and mountains can clearly be linked to a journey that Arduino undertook at the end of October 1758 in the Agno Valley of the upper Vicentine area. Here the geological and geomorphological characteristics observed in the approximately 20 kilometer journey up the valley (explored in different excursions to the reliefs on both sides) definitively convinced Arduino to elaborate a general theory that also capitalized upon his observations up to that point in various Alpine, pre-Alpine, and Apennine regions.

The classification into four units or orders (*ordini*) was based mainly on lithology without using precise paleontological indicators—apart from the indicated difference between primary mountains without fossils and secondary mountains with fossils—and included different rock types that formed three kinds of mountains and one kind of plain in the regular chronological order of their formation. According to Arduino, the primary mountains were underlain by a primeval rock type (*roccia primigenia*), later identified as schist, that had been found at the base of all the reliefs examined and therefore was considered of older origin with respect to the others. This rock is now known as metamorphic crystalline rock made essentially of quartz and mica. Moreover, the fourth and youngest chronolithological unit (called *quarto ordine*), including only alluvial deposits and remaining the least treated of all the lithostratigraphical units, was never defined by Arduino with the term *quaternary* or *quaternario*.

The system elaborated by Arduino—still regarded by the geological world as one of the starting points for modern stratigraphy—was much more complex and better articulated than all other analagous attempts previously expressed within the European scientific milieu, such as, for example, those by Carolus Linnaeus, Anton Lazzaro Moro, Giovanni Targioni Tozzetti, and Johann Gottlob Lehmann. However, the classification model proposed by Arduino received diverse responses in Italy by the end of the eighteenth century: Arduino's model was favored by several Venetian naturalists, but criticized by other Piedmontese and Lombard scientists working in the central and western Alps. These latter scholars, following the opinion of the majority of the European geologists at that time, rejected the supposed position of the schist below the granite as a sign of an older age, supporting instead the granite as the only real primeval rock.

Work on Formation of Strata. In an unpublished work—the incomplete manuscript *Risposta Allegorico Romanzesca* (Allegorical fictional reply) on the genesis of Earth's surface, begun at the end of 1771 and directed to the Swedish scientist Johann Jakob Ferber—Arduino tried to realize a general subdivision of the history of Earth into four epochs. He intended to correlate them with the orogenetic and lithological processes first outlined in his classification of 1760. In this manuscript, edited and published in 1991 by Ezio Vaccari, Arduino outlined various lithogenetic and orogenetic scenarios (linked to the isolated or combined action of fire, water, or wind) and he distinguished them into two different levels of intensity: first, catastrophic events during volcanic eruptions and also in the fast process of consolidation with fractures of Earth's crust following the violent downpour of rain on the fluid incandescent surface; and, second, slower and uniform events during the sedimentary deposition which occurred within the waters of the ancient sea.

Arduino's position with regard to the different physical causes of the formation of his four lithostratigraphic orders (and therefore of the three classes of mountains) emerged clearly in "Saggio Fisico-Mineralogico" (1774). This text represented the more mature expression of his geological thinking. Fire alone was responsible for the formation of the oldest primary mountains of the first subdivision, as well as for the primeval rocks placed at the base of all the visible rock formations. Water was the only geological agent that determined the deposition of the alluvial and coastal terrains respectively in the planes and marine coasts, composing the fourth order which was of more recent formation with respect to the others. Between these two lithogenetic stages (respectively oldest and latest) of Arduino's classification were placed the second subdivision of primary reliefs—the secondary mountains (produced by water and partially modified by fire) and the tertiary mountains (of analogous origin to the secondary, but sometimes also only volcanic). Therefore, according to Arduino, water and fire had acted alternatively on all these orographic units that had formed successively within a complex chronological and orogenetic scheme.

In the early twenty-first century geologists recognize the importance of Arduino's term *tertiary*, which takes its place in the modern standard stratigraphic column. Moreover, Arduino's reflections on the alternate action of fire and water during the long geological history of Earth's surface opened up the possibility of an actual third way between the catastrophist and uniformitarian hypotheses, beyond the too-rigid historiographical division between "Neptunism" and "Vulcanism" or "Plutonism."

Arduino's geological researches during the second half of the eighteenth century concerned mostly the stratigraphy of the Venetian Alps and pre-Alps, but also included the possible volcanic nature of some rocks of the same area. These studies gave him a huge reputation in the European scientific community. His printed works, above all the "Due lettere" (1759) and the "Saggio Fisico-Mineralogico," were widely known outside of Italy. The anthological *Raccolta di memorie chimico-mineralogiche* (Collection of Chemical-mineralogical Memoirs, 1775) contained these two previous works as well as other significant writings mainly published in the Venetian scientific journal *Giornale d'Italia* such as the letters on the remains of some extinct volcanoes in Veneto ("Alcune osservazioni Orittologiche," 1769; "Effetti di antichissimi Vulcani," 1775). In the German-speaking states the main works of Arduino were part of private and academic scientific libraries. They were included in the German edition of the *Raccolta* (*Sammlung*, 1778), promoted by the Austrian mineralogist Ignaz von Born, and translated by the mining officer August Constantin von Ferber, companion in studies of the distinguished mineralogist Abraham Gottlob Werner in the Mining Academy of Freiberg in Saxony.

Arduino had a large correspondence with several European scientists, especially in Germany and in Sweden. Some letters were printed, mostly in the *Giornale d'Italia*, which was published in Venice from 1764 to 1796. However, a considerable amount of his correspondence was never published, including some of his scientific writings. Arduino cataloged all his papers—even the rough copies of his letters: every note, letter, or drawing was ordered in files according to subject. He also kept all the correspondence he received in the relevant subject files. Some of the original labeled folders are still preserved in the Giovanni Arduino manuscript collection kept in the Municipal Library of Verona in northern Italy and reordered from 1987 to 1988 (the catalog is published in Ezio Vaccari, *I manoscritti di uno scienziato veneto*, 1994). In the previous years only a few scholars had examined the papers of Arduino because of their disorganized state. Currently the whole collection, more than one thousand papers, is divided in new thematic folders, distributed inside five boxes (location numbers: 757–761) according to the different subjects of their contents.

The correspondence of Arduino from 1758 to 1793 (sent and received letters) includes distinguished European scientists such as Ignaz von Born, Johann Jakob Ferber, Alberto Fortis, Anton Maria Lorgna, Anders Jahan Retzius, and John Strange. Many handwritten papers, notes, and drawings concern the different fields of the scientific work of Arduino: his researches concerning the geology, mineralogy, and mining of the Venetian area; his reports of chemical and metallurgical experiments and also documents about the scientific controversies on the process of the fusion of iron and about the project for a new furnace for the evaporation of the vitriol; his agricultural and hydraulic writings for the Venetian government; his geological sketches, mining drawings, and bibliographical summaries, together with pieces of information received from various people concerning his main scientific interests. Among these papers some original writings stand out: the *Risposta Allegorico-Romanzesca;* rough notes on fieldwork such as the description of the volcanic rocks (among them is listed basalt) in San Giovanni Ilarione in the Alpone Valley near Verona; sketches concerning the mines of the Tretto hills; and the stratigraphy of the Agno Valley in the territory of Vicenza.

Like many other eighteenth-century geologists, Arduino had a large collection of minerals, rocks, and fossils. He collected them mainly during his fieldwork in the Venetian area during the 1760s, but also before this time when he was director of mines in Tuscany and Veneto. He collected fossils and precious stones at the request of noble Venetians for enriching their naturalistic cabinets. Many specimens were also given to Arduino by various correspondents in Italy and abroad. In return he often sent to them small collections of Italian material. Between 1779 and 1782 he sent two boxes of minerals and volcanic rocks, mostly from northern Italy and Vesuvius, to the German scientists Franz Karl Achard and to Nathanael Gottfried Leske. The sixty-five specimens sent to Leske in Leipzig were included in his large collection, which was bought in 1792 by the Dublin Society and is now kept in the National Museum of Ireland. Some specimens from the Leskean collection kept in Dublin have been identified by Ezio Vaccari and Nigel Monaghan ("I minerali di Giovanni Arduino," 1993) as those sent from Arduino to Leske. The collection owned by Arduino in Venice was purchased after his death by the marquis Giovan Battista Gazola in Verona, but this collection was taken in 1797 by the French army and probably was brought to Paris where, to date, it has been not possible to trace Arduino's specimens.

SUPPLEMENTARY BIBLIOGRAPHY

WORKS BY ARDUINO

"Due lettere del sig. Giovanni Arduino sopra varie sue osservazioni naturali." 30 January and 30 March 1759. In *Nuova Raccolta di Opuscoli Scientifici e Filologici* 6 (1760): xcix–clxxx.

"Alcune osservazioni Orittologiche fatte nei Monti del Vicentino." 21 March 1769. In *Giornale d'Italia* 5 (1769): 409–411.

"Saggio Fisico-Mineralogico di Lythogonia e Orognosia." *Atti dell'Accademia delle Scienze di Siena, detta de' Fisiocritici* 5 (1774): 228–300.

Raccolta di memorie chimico-mineralogiche, metallurgiche e orittografiche del Signor Giovanni Arduino, e di alcuni suoi Amici, Tratte dal Giornale d'Italia. Venice: Milocco, 1775.

Sammlung einiger mineralogisch-chymisch-metallurgisch und oryktographischer Abhandlungen, des Herr Johann Arduino, und einiger Freunde desselben. Aus dem italienischen übersetzt, durch A.C.v.F.C.S.B.C.R. [August Constantin von Ferber]. Dresden, Germany: In der Waltherischen Hofbuchhandlung, 1778.

"Descrizione epistolare, con osservazioni chimiche, di alcuni prodotti fossili inviati al Sig. Achard." 23 April 1779. In *Nuovo Giornale d'Italia* 4 (1780): 2–5, 9–12, 17–20, 25–28, 33–37.

"Al Celebre Signor Nathanael Godofredo Leske … Lettera Orittologica del Ch. Sign. Giovanni Arduino … con Indice di Saggi di alcune produzioni Vulcaniche, Minerali e Fossili da esso al medesimo professore dirette." 2 July 1782. In *Nuovo Giornale d'Italia* 7 (1783): 9–14, 17–23.

"Effetti di antichissimi Vulcani osservati dal Sig. Giovanni Arduino, nel mese di Marzo dell'anno 1769, nei monti della Villa di Chiampo, e di altri Luoghi vicini del Territorio di Vicenza." March 1769. In *Raccolta di memorie chimico-mineralogiche, metallurgiche e orittografiche.* Venice: Milocco, 1775. Reprinted in *Nuovo Giornale d'Italia* 7 (1783): 161–167.

"Primo contributo all'inventario del carteggio di Giovanni Arduino." Edited and translated by Ezio Vaccari. *Nuncius. Annali di Storia della Scienza* 5 (1990): 79–126. The first inventory of Arduino's correspondence in the period 1753 to 1795 is provided in this text.

Risposta Allegorico Romanzesca di Voniangi Riduano, Osservatore Longobardo, al Celebre Orittologo viaggiatore Signor Giovanni-Giacomo Ferber del Collegio Metallico di Svezia, sopra la Genesi della presente faccia della Terra. Manuscript in Biblioteca Civica, Verona, Italy, "Fondo G. Arduino," b. 758, II.a.1–3, cc.19. This text was published as "Storia della Terra e tempi geologici in uno scritto inedito di Giovanni Arduino: la 'Risposta Allegorico-Romanzesca' a Ferber." Annotated by Ezio Vaccari. *Nuncius. Annali di Storia della Scienza* 6 (1991): 171–211.

"I manoscritti di uno scienziato veneto del Settecento: notizie storiche e catalogo del fondo 'Giovanni Arduino' della Biblioteca Civica di Verona." In *Atti dell'Istituto Veneto di Scienze, Lettere ed Arti,* edited by Ezio Vaccari. *Classe di Scienze fisiche, matematiche e naturali* 151 (1992–1993): 271–373. The catalog of Arduino's collection of manuscripts in the Municipal Library (Biblioteca Civica) of Verona is published here.

OTHER SOURCES

Arrigoni, Tiziano. "Geologia e ricerca mineraria nel Settecento: Giovanni Arduino e le miniere di Toscana." *Ricerche storiche* (Piombino) 15 (1985): 275–297. A useful study on Arduino's mining activity in Tuscany.

Bassani, Angelo. "Una perizia di Giovani Arduino: l'analisi chimico-merceologica del natro." *Rendiconti della Accademia Nazionale delle Scienze detta dei XL, Memorie di Scienze Fisiche e naturali* 5, no. 16 (1992): 453–462. Short study of one of the many unpublished chemical reports written by Arduino for the Venetian government.

Curi, Ettore, ed. *Scienza, tecnica e "pubblico bene" nell'opera di Giovanni Arduino (1714–1795). Convegno di Studi-Verona, 9–10 febbraio 1996.* Verona, Italy: Accademia di Agricoltura, Scienze e Lettere, 1999. Proceedings of the main symposium on Arduino, including significant papers on his diverse scientific researches and technical skills.

Fumi, Gianpiero. "Giovanni Arduino." In *Scritti teorici e tecnici di agricoltura, II. Dal Settecento agli inizi dell'Ottocento,* edited by Sergio Zaninelli, 131–144. Milan, Italy: Il Polifilo, 1989. This is a biographical sketch based on Arduino's agricultural activities.

Giormani,Virgilio. "Giovanni Arduino e il problema del salnitro nella Repubblica Veneta." *Rendiconti della Accademia Nazionale delle Scienze detta dei XL, Memorie di Scienze Fisiche e naturali* 5, no. 16 (1992): 447–452. An examination of Arduino's proposals for the production of saltpeter in the Republic of Venice.

Lazzari, Corrado, and Fabrizio Bizzarini, eds. *Atti del Seminario "Giovanni Arduino e i geologi veneti del Settecento" (Venezia, 1 giugno 1995).* Venice: Società Veneziana di Scienze Naturali-Museo Civico di Storia Naturale, 1996. These proceedings of a workshop include the presentation of new archival documents by Giorgio Zoccoletto on the nomination of Arduino as supervisor of agriculture in the ministry for the improvement of uncultivated land of the Republic of Venice.

Vaccari, Ezio. "L'attività agronomica di Pietro e Giovanni Arduino." In *Scienze e tecniche agrarie nel Veneto dell'Ottocento,* 129–167. Venice: Istituto Veneto di Scienze, Lettere ed Arti, 1992. A comparative study of the agronomical works of the brothers Pietro e Giovanni Arduino.

———. *Giovanni Arduino (1714–1795). Il contributo di uno scienziato veneto al dibattito settecentesco sulle scienze della Terra.* Florence, Italy: Olschki, 1993. A complete and detailed biography on Arduino, based on published and unpublished sources with particular attention to his geological studies within the eighteenth century European scientific context. Includes the complete bibliography of Arduino's works.

———. "Cultura scientifico-naturalistica ed esplorazione del territorio: Giovanni Arduino e Giovanni Targioni Tozzetti." In *La politica della scienz: Toscana e Stati italiani nel tardo Settecento,* edited by Giulio Barsanti, Vieri Becagli, and Renato Pasta, 243–263. Florence, Italy: Olschki, 1996. A comparative study of the scientific methods and the geological theories of Arduino and the Tuscan naturalist Giovanni Targioni Tozzetti.

———. "The 'Classification' of Mountains in Eighteenth Century Italy and the Lithostratigraphic Theory of Giovanni Arduino (1714–1795)." In *The Origins of Geology in Italy,* edited by Gian Battista Vai and W. Glen E. Caldwell, 155–175. Geological Society Special Paper 411. Boulder, CO: Geological Society of America, 2006. A detailed analysis of Arduino's most influential geological theory.

———. "From Tyrol to Venice: The Papers of Giovanni Arduino (1714–1795) as Valuable Sources for the History of Mining and Geology." *Geo.Alp* (Innsbruck) *Sonderband* 1 (2007): 155–164. A presentation of Arduino's collection of manuscripts in the Municipal Library (Biblioteca Civica) of Verona.

———, and Nigel T. Monaghan. "I minerali di Giovanni Arduino nella collezione geo-mineralogica di Nathanael Gottfried Leske: Verifica di un caso di comunicazione scientifica nell'Europa del tardo Settecento." *Geologica Romana* 29 (1993): 547–565. A study on the exchange of rocks and minerals between Arduino and the German naturalist Nathanael Gottfried Leske is the focus of this text.

Ezio Vaccari

ARF, CAHIT

ARF, CAHIT (*b.* Selanik, Ottoman Empire [later Thessaloníki, Greece], 11 October 1910; *d.* İstanbul, Turkey, 26 December 1997), *mathematics, algebra, algebraic number theory.*

Arf was the leading Turkish mathematician of the twentieth century. His research was mainly in algebraic number theory and related fields, although he also contributed to elasticity theory and analysis. An invariant for quadratic forms over a field of characteristic 2 introduced by Arf in his early works has, as it turned out, important applications in algebraic and differential topology. This invariant appears in mathematics literature as the Arf invariant. Concepts such as Arf rings, Arf closure, and Arf characters also carry his name. Arf was one of the founding members of the Turkish Mathematical Society in 1948 and played a major role in the establishment of the Scientific and Technical Research Council of Turkey (TÜBİTAK) in 1963.

The story of Arf's childhood runs parallel to the history of the turbulent final years of the Ottoman Empire. With the outbreak of the Balkan War in 1912, his middle-class family had to migrate from Selanik to İstanbul. The Ottoman Empire entered World War I as one of the Central Powers, which lost the war. İstanbul was occupied by an Entente force, and a Greek army landed in İzmir in 1919. The Ottoman government was compelled to sign the Treaty of Sèvres in 1920. Immediately afterwards a national assembly convened in Ankara, led by Mustafa

Kemal, refused to accept the terms of the Sèvres treaty. Arf's family went from İstanbul to Ankara, via Kastamonu. The Ankara government assigned his father to reorganize the postal services in Adana after this southern city was retaken from the French. From Adana, Arf's family came back to Ankara and returned to İstanbul after the war between Turkey and Greece (May 1919–August 1922) ended. Finally, the family settled in İzmir. The Ottoman Empire was dissolved and Turkey was declared a republic in 1923.

Arf's extraordinary gift for mathematics was discovered by his schoolteacher in İzmir. The teacher encouraged Arf by regularly asking him to produce his own proofs of classical theorems in geometry without consulting books. His father bought French francs when that currency was devalued in order to send his son to France. Arf went to Paris and graduated from the Lycée St.-Louis. With a scholarship he continued his education in that city at the École Normale Supérieure. After his graduation, he refused offers to continue towards a doctorate, because he wanted above all to return to Turkey and be a schoolteacher.

Although Arf asked to be assigned as a mathematics teacher to a school in the provincial city of Kastamonu, the Ministry of Education instead appointed him to a prominent school, Galatasaray, in İstanbul. In 1933 he entered İstanbul University and decided to pursue an academic career in mathematics as an assistant professor. In 1937 he went to Göttingen University in Germany for his doctorate. His supervisor was Helmut Hasse. Because Arf was already mathematically mature, he completed his doctoral studies in 1938. The main result of his thesis was later known as the Hasse-Arf theorem. Upon advice of Hasse, he stayed in Göttingen during the difficult period leading to World War II, studying quadratic forms over a field of characteristic 2. He introduced a complete invariant for such forms, which is known as the Arf invariant in the literature. This invariant turned out to be very important in algebraic and differential topology.

From Göttingen, Arf returned to İstanbul University in 1939, where he worked until 1962. He continued his research on invariants of certain algebraic structures over fields of characteristic 2, worked on multiplicity sequences of algebraic branches, and published a series of papers on elasticity theory. Arf was promoted to professor in 1943 and to ordinarius professor in 1955. He spent a year (1951) at the University of Maryland and was elected a corresponding member of the Mainz Academy in Germany.

After leaving İstanbul University in 1962, he taught at Robert College in İstanbul, spent two years (1964–1966) at the Institute for Advanced Study in Princeton, New Jersey, and then one year at the University of California at Berkeley. Upon his final return to Turkey in 1967, he entered the recently established Middle East Technical University in Ankara, where he worked until retiring in 1980.

Arf generally avoided administrative duties in his academic career, although he served as the president of TÜBİTAK from 1967 until 1971 and was the president of the Turkish Mathematical Society from 1985 until 1989. When the government tried to impose stricter control over Middle East Technical University in 1977, Arf—who believed in autonomy for Turkish universities—led a group of professors in opposition. His influence on Turkish mathematics was profound. He was a constant source of inspiration and encouragement, especially for younger mathematicians.

Robert Langlands was a young mathematician when he was visiting Middle East Technical University from 1967–1968. Langlands' year at Ankara was quite decisive for his own research, in particular through his contact with Cahit Arf. Arf had pointed out to him a paper by Helmut Hasse who had proved the first results in the direction that Langlands was working at that time.

Arf received numerous awards for his contributions to mathematics and for his stance in support of scientific excellence and academic freedom. Among them are the İnönü Award (1948), the TÜBİTAK Science Award (1974), and the Commandeur des Palmes Académiques (1994). He was an honorary member of the Turkish Academy of Sciences and received honorary doctorates from Black Sea Technical University, Middle East Technical University, and İstanbul Technical University. To commemorate his legacy, Middle East Technical University instituted the Cahit Arf Lectures in 2001.

BIBLIOGRAPHY

A complete bibliography of Arf's works is included in The Collected Papers of Cahit Arf, *cited below.*

WORKS BY ARF

"Untersuchungen über quadratische Formen in Körpern der Charakteristik 2" (Research on quadratic forms over fields of characteristic 2). *Journal für die reine und angewante Mathematik* 183 (1941): 148–167.

"Une interprétation algébrique de la suite des ordres de multiplicité d'une branche algébrique" (An algebraic interpretation of the multiplicity orders of an algebraic branch). *Proceedings of the London Mathematical Society* (2) 50 (1948): 256–287.

"On the Determination of Multiply Connected Domains of an Elastic Plane Body, Bounded by Free Boundaries with Constant Tangential Stresses." *American Journal of Mathematics* 74 (1952): 797–820.

The Collected Papers of Cahit Arf. Edited by Tosun Terzioğlu. Ankara: Turkish Mathematical Society, 1990.

OTHER SOURCES

Ikeda, Masatoshi G. "Cahit Arf's Contribution to Algebraic Number Theory and Related Fields." *Turkish Journal of Mathematics* 22 (1998): 1–14.

Langlands, Robert. "Benim tanidiğim Cahit Arf" (Recollections of a year in Turkey with Cahit Arf). 2004. Available from http://www.sunsite.ubc.ca/DigitalMathArchive/Langlands/intro.html.

Middle East Technical University. Department of Mathematics. "Cahit Arf Lectures." Available from http://www.math.metu.edu.tr/~arflectures.

O'Connor, John J., and E. F. Robertson. "Cahit Arf." *MacTutor History of Mathematics.* September 1998. Available from http://www-history.mcs.st-andrews.ac.uk/biographies/arf.html.

Roquette, Peter J. "Introduction of Langlands at the Arf Lecture." 2004. Available from http://www.rzuser.uni-heidelberg.de/~ci3.

Terzioğlu, Tosun. *Cahit Arf.* Ankara: Middle East Technical University, 1981.

———, and Akin Yilmaz, eds. *"Anlamak" Tutkunu Bir Matemakçi Cahit Arf* (Life story of Cahit Arf). Ankara: Türkiye Bilimler Akademisi, 2005.

Tosun Terzioğlu

ARGYRUS, ISAAC (*b.* c. 1300 or 1310, Thrace; *d.* c. 1375), *astronomy, mathematics, theology.*

Born in Thrace around 1300 or 1310, Argyrus lived in Constantinople, where he pursued his scientific activity around 1367 to 1373. As a monk he participated in the religious disputes (Hesychasm), writing anti-Palamite tracts, directed especially against John Cantacuzenus (Emperor John VI, r. 1341–1355). The latter wrote a long tract against Argyrus. His scientific work was in astronomy, arithmetic, and geometry. A scholium presents him as a pupil of Nicephorus Gregoras, but his name is never cited by the latter.

Argyrus wrote two treatises on the *New Tables*, both based on Ptolemy, with the date of origin 1 September 1367, and for the meridian of Byzantium. The former treatise was an adaptation of Ptolemy's *Handy Tables* of the Sun and Moon, arranged in periods of twenty-four years and for the Roman (i.e., Julian) calendar. The cycle of twenty-four years was adopted because it allowed the easy insertion of bissextile (leap year) years. No explanation was given for the choice of the initial year, but one may think that it was intended to begin with a leap year (1368). The difference between the meridians of Alexandria and Byzantium was, according to Ptolemy, 4°50'/15° = 18^m, that must be subtracted from the time at Alexandria, but Argyrus erred in adding the values corresponding to the 18^m.

The second treatise was based on the tables of syzygies in the *Almagest,* starting with the conjunction of 23 September 1367. The correction of the 18^m was correctly applied. These two treatises concern only the Sun and Moon, and were intended especially to facilitate the calculation of syzygies, of importance for finding the date of Easter. At the end of the first treatise, Argyrus declared that he also adapted the tables of the five planets for the period of twenty-four Julian years and Roman months, but these tables were not preserved.

Another of his works is a *Treatise on the Date of Easter.* This treatise, which begins with an account of the solar and lunar cycles, was composed in 1372 to 1373 and was dedicated to Andronicus Oinaiotes. This account was followed by explanations about the beginning of the year. He then considered the date of Easter and the correction of the traditional calculation. These three texts have sometimes been considered as separate treatises, but the Paschal method was a continuation from the preceding chapters, at least in the manuscript *Marcianus gr.* 328 (fifteenth century), that included a collection of the scientific works of Argyrus. As for the traditional fixing of the date of Easter, Argyrus mentioned two sources of error, the lunar cycle of nineteen years and the length of the solar year. The inexactness of the nineteen-year cycle was an argument that goes back to Barlaam (c. 1332) and was based on Ptolemy. Ptolemy's value (365¼–1/300) was inexact for the length of the solar year. Alluding to the *Persian Tables* and using his own observation of the summer solstice, Argyros proposed to replace the fraction 1/300 by "a fraction greater than 1/200" (Migne, 1857, p. 19, col. 1312). He found, as a result, that the spring equinox was "before March 15." He did not cite Barlaam, but referred explicitly to Nicephorus Gregoras who, he said, proposed this reform in the presence of the emperor; in consequence of which, again according to Argyrus, it was decided to apply this reform. This formally contradicts the account of Nicephorus Gregoras himself, who declared that the emperor decided not to apply this reform for fear of troubles in the church.

The astronomical work of Argyrus also included a *Treatise on the Astrolabe,* based on that of Nicephorus Gregoras and dated 1367 to 1368. He assumed Ptolemy's value of precession, 1° in 100 years.

A treatise titled *Paradosis tōn Persikōn Kanonōn* is sometimes attributed to Argyrus, but this treatise was in fact Book Three of the *Tribiblos* of Theodore Meliteniotes, which was widely diffused in the manuscripts. It is not impossible that Argyrus inserted some alterations, but this matter is unsettled. According to the Jewish scholar Mordecai Comtino, Argyrus and his students criticized the *Persian Tables,* but that is not evident from the extant work. The manuscripts have contradictory remarks on this matter.

Argyrus is the author of a *Treatise on the Square Root,* in which he perfected the method of Hero of Alexandria. He developed a method of approximation that he presented as his own, but which is close to that developed by Nicolas Rhabdas (c. 1340). At the end of the treatise he gave a table of roots of 1 to 102, expressed in the sexagesimal system. We also owe to him a *Treatise on Geodesy* (also called *On the Reduction of Triangles*), which is probably the same text as the *Letter to Colybas of Mitylene* on the same subject. This short treatise corrects the crude errors of the land surveyors. The text was followed in many manuscripts by a note, probably due also to Argyrus, on Bryson's method of the *Squaring of the Circle.*

A number of astronomical scholia (on Cleomedes, Theon of Alexandria) and also geographical scholia were attributed to Argyrus, as well as an edition of the *Harmonics* of Ptolemy. Apart from the theological works mentioned above, and his scientific output, he wrote a treatise on poetic meters, and commentaries on Aristotle.

It is difficult to make a judgment of the work of Argyrus. There exists no critical edition of his astronomical work, and in the manuscripts it is not easy to distinguish original work from revisions or later additions. His works were very extensively used by his immediate successors, but they very much confused the manuscript tradition. Conservative, he remained true to the Ptolemaic tradition, even though one finds a mention of the Persians in his Paschal treatise. The only trace of innovation—if it is not indeed an interpolation—is a correction to the length of the tropical year, but this does not appear in his astronomical tables. Argyrus emerges as the perfect Byzantine savant, trained in all the scientific disciplines of the ancients, as well as theology and philology, editing, and commenting the texts in the manuscripts. However, his interventions have not yet been precisely cataloged.

BIBLIOGRAPHY

Allard, André. "Le petit traité d'Isaac Argyre sur la racine carrée." *Centaurus* 22 (1978): 1–43. Treatise on the square root.

Delatte, Armand. *Anecdota Atheniensia et alia: Tome II, Textes grecs relatifs à l'histoire des sciences.* Paris: Faculté de Philosophie et Lettres, Liège and Librairie E. Droz, 1939.

Lefort, Jacques, René-Claude Bondoux, Jean-Claude Cheynet, et al., with the collaboration of J.-M. Martin. *Géométries du fisc byzantin.* Paris: Réalités Byzantines, 1991. On geodesy.

Migne, J.-P. *Patrologia graeca,* t.19, Paris, n.p., 1857: col. 1279–1316. Reproduction of Denys Petau, *Uranologion sive systema variorum authorum* …, Paris, n.p., 1630, pp. 359–383. Easter treatise.

Petau, Denis. *Uranologion sive systema variorum authorum....* Paris. 1630, pp. 359–383. A reproduction edited by J. Migne. *Patrologia graeca* t. 19: col. 1279–1316. city1857.

Pingree, David. "The Astrological School of John Abramius." *Dumbarton Oaks Papers* 25 (1971): 191–215.

Schissel, Otmar. "Die Österrechnung des Nikolaos Artabasdos Rhabdas." *Byzantinisch-Neugriechische Jahbücher* 14 (1937–1938): 43–59.

Tihon, Anne. "L'astronomie byzantine à l'aube de la Renaissance (de 1352 à la fin du XVe siècle)." *Byzantion* 64 (1996): 244–280.

Anne Tihon

ARISTOTLE (*b.* Stagira in Chalcidice, 384 BCE; *d.* Chalcis, 322 BCE), *theory of science, physics, cosmology, meteorology, psychology, biology.* For the original article on Aristotle see *DSB,* vol. 1.

The original *DSB* entry on Aristotle was penned by four notable scholars with different backgrounds and areas of expertise, who wrote autonomous essays on:

1. his scientific method, physics, and cosmology (G. E. L. Owen),

2. his natural history and zoology (David M. Balme),

3. his anatomy and physiology (Leonard G. Wilson), and

4. the Aristotelian tradition and its influence on the history of science (L. Minio-Paluello).

Since these entries were written, Aristotle's investigations of the natural world have been the object of a great deal of high-quality scholarship. One of the lessons of that scholarship, to which Balme was a major contributor, is that the above division of topics obscures more about Aristotle's natural science than it clarifies. The distinctions marked in the early twenty-first century by *zoology, natural history, anatomy,* and *physiology* map poorly on to Aristotle's investigation of animals; and the work that conventionally bears the English title *Physics* will be badly misunderstood by anyone who imagines it is Aristotle's attempt to do what is today called physics.

In this postscript, Aristotle's general theory of scientific knowledge (as presented primarily in his *Posterior Analytics*) will be discussed separately from his contributions to natural science. Within this latter group, those texts that present and defend Aristotle's distinctive *principles* for natural science (especially *Physica, Generatione et Corruptione,* and *De Partibus Animalium I*) will be distinguished from the application of these principles to investigations of distinctive domains of the natural world (*Meteorologica, De Partibus Animalium II–IV, De Generatione Animalium I–V, Historia Animalium I–X, De Motu Animalium, De Incessu Animalium, Parva Naturalia, De Caelo I–IV*). The majority of Aristotle's contributions to natural science are devoted to the study of animals; and this reflects Aristotle's view that the study of living things is central to the investigation of nature. Therefore this postscript will focus on what is conventionally referred to as Aristotle's *biology*. Ideally, because Aristotle claimed that knowledge about the soul contributes greatly to the study of nature (402a4), this should also include his *De Anima* (*On the Soul*), but there will be only passing references to it.

Theory of Science. Beginning with the eighth "Symposium Aristotelicum," in 1978, the *Posterior Analytics* (*APo.*) has been studied more intensely than at any time since the Renaissance. That research led to revaluations of three assumptions of the previous *DSB* entry: (1) that there is a serious conflict between Aristotle's theory of science and his practice; (2) that this may be due to the theory taking mathematics, rather than natural science, as its model; and (3) that the *APo.* has little to say about scientific inquiry. Each of these views has now been seriously challenged.

To develop systematic views about scientific investigation, one first needs a concept of the goal to be achieved, and recent research suggests *APo. I* be thought of as Aristotle's articulation of that goal. The goal is a system of concepts and propositions organized hierarchically, ultimately resting on knowledge of the essential natures of the objects of an established kind and certain other necessary first principles. These definitions and principles form the basis of causal explanations of propositions identifying attributes that belong to the objects being investigated per se, in virtue of their natures. A system of formal proof and validity is outlined in the *Prior Analytics,* providing logical standards for scientific explanation. It should be possible to display scientific explanations as syllogisms in which the "middle term" identifies the cause in virtue of which an attribute belongs necessarily to its subject. For example, having interior angles equal to two right angles belongs to all triangles in virtue of something essential to being a triangle (*APo. I.* 4, 5). It belongs necessarily to all equilateral triangles as well—but only because they are triangles. The middle term of a scientific demonstration of this property will refer to that essential property of triangles in virtue of which it belongs to all triangles.

Aristotle, in *APo. II,* discussed how to achieve this goal: how to achieve knowledge of essences (expressed in definitions) and how the search for essences is related to the search for causal explanations (expressed in the form

of demonstrations). Perceptual experience gives us a grasp of the target of inquiry that is not yet scientific knowledge as characterized in book I, but does provide a sufficient grasp on the subject to direct further inquiry. We may begin by asking whether there really is an object of inquiry with a nature and a stable set of properties to be explained (*APo. II.* 1, 89b23–25). Once we have grounds for believing that "thunder" signifies a single, recurrent natural phenomenon, for example, we may go on to inquire into its cause, which is precisely to find out what thunder really is (*APo. II.* 1, 89b29–31). The result can be expressed as a definition or as a demonstration. Thunder, which signifies a certain kind of noise in the clouds is, in essence, the noise caused by fire being extinguished in clouds. Such a noise is present whenever extinction of fire is present; thus when extinction of fire is present in the clouds, thunder is present in the clouds (*APo. II.* 10, 94a4–8).

In this discussion, thunder and eclipses are his primary examples of natural inquiry, but Aristotle also provided an extended biological example, the seasonal loss of leaves in broad-leaved plants. From experience, one learns that certain trees lose their leaves seasonally. The first step toward scientific understanding will be to determine whether this is a single phenomenon. Aristotle suggested that to determine this one must search for other properties shared by plants that lose their leaves, being broad-leaved, for example. Such correlations provide good reason to think that there is a kind to which leaf loss belongs as such. He closed chapter 16 of Book II with the following summary:

> Hence in these cases the middle term and what it is explanatory of must be equal and must convert. For example, why do trees shed their leaves? If it is because of solidification of the moisture, then if a tree sheds it leaves solidification must hold, and if solidification holds—not of anything whatever but of a tree—then the tree must shed its leaves. (98b35–39)

Since the whole point of the example is that not all trees shed their leaves but only those with broad leaves, "tree" here must stand in for "trees with broad leaves." Something essential to being broad-leaved causes loss of leaves—Aristotle here suggested that there is a seasonal solidification of moisture at the leaf juncture (presumably cutting off nutrition to the leaves). As with thunder, a causal explanation of leaf loss is also an account of its essence (*APo. II.* 17, 99a22–23).

There is, then, a sophisticated theory of inquiry here, and research done since the publication of the *DSB* suggests that it accords rather well with the practices revealed in Aristotle's scientific investigation of animals. This research will now be briefly summarized.

Aristotle. *Engraving of Greek philosopher Aristotle.* TIME LIFE PICTURES/MANSELL/GETTY IMAGES.

Foundations of Natural Science. Four works in particular are devoted to the articulation and defense of Aristotle's distinctive set of principles for investigating the natural world: *Physics, On the Parts of Animals I, Generation and Corruption I,* and *On the Soul I–II.* Aristotle was at great pains to distinguish the science of nature from two other theoretical disciplines, mathematics and first philosophy (metaphysics). The work typically referred to as *Physics* is a collection of books aimed at articulating and defending a unique set of first principles and causes for the science of nature. In the original *DSB* entry, G. E. L. Owen stressed Aristotle's method of reviewing "the common convictions and common linguistic usage of his contemporaries, supplemented by the views of other thinkers." Because, Aristotle claimed, these common convictions were "storehouses of experience," this "dialectical" methodology (which he also saw at work in *De Caelo* and *Generation and Corruption*) was aimed at "saving the phenomena."

There is no doubt that when Aristotle enters a domain that is well trodden, previous views on the topic being investigated are critically reviewed; but typically these views create impediments to progress, *aporiai*, not phenomena to be saved. The *Physics* is an extended argument aimed at overcoming those impediments and providing a new foundation for the science of nature. Consider in outline the first four books of *Physics* (*Ph.*). The chief concerns of Book I are first to defend the assumption that natural things are subject to change against the Eleatics and then to articulate the number and kind of principles required to properly characterize any kind of change. This involves a critical review of the assumptions of previous thinkers, but Aristotle's final position was profoundly different from those he rejected. It must be, because Aristotle aimed to defend a kind of change rejected by virtually all his predecessors, the unqualified coming to be of a substantial being, such as the development of an animal or plant. In such cases, the stable subject underlying qualitative, quantitative or spatial change is now the outcome of a change, raising profound questions about what underlies the change. Aristotle introduced his concepts of potentiality and actuality and matter and form in order to deal with this problem. (A full defense of unqualified generation comes in *Generation and Corruption I,* and in book *II* he applied the results to the transformation of the elements.)

With the general principles of change delineated, *Ph. II* chapter 1 argues that the distinctive mark of natural beings is that they have their own inherent sources and causes of change—indeed this is their nature (*physis*). The remainder of book *II* explores the implications of that account of nature. Chapter 2: What are the inherent sources in a natural being? (Answer: matter and form.) Chapter 3: How many causes are there and of what sort? (Answer: four: matter, form, moving cause, end.) Chapters 4–6: Is chance to be included among the causes, as some have claimed? (Answer: no; but causality is involved in chance events). Chapter 7: Because there are only two natures, are all four of these causes involved in nature? (Answer: yes; but three of the four involve form and the fourth matter.) Chapter 8: In particular, how can either of these natures act for the sake of an end? (Answer: "Since nature is twofold, nature as matter and nature as form, and the latter is an end, and everything else is for the end, the cause as that for the sake of which must be form" [199a31–33].) Chapter 9: But can that view be compatible with things happening of necessity? (Answer: yes, because beside the necessity associated with matter there is a necessity associated with natural ends.) Once more, the entire book is an exploration of the presuppositions of Aristotle's unique and unprecedented views about what it is to have and to be a nature.

The introduction to *Ph. III–IV* (200b12–25) again stresses the foundational nature of this work. Because nature is a source of change, Aristotle explained, we need to be clear on exactly what change is. And because it will turn out that it is continuous, and the continuous is argued by some to be infinite, we must determine whether the infinite exists and if so in what sense. And because some hold that change requires place, time, and void, we must investigate these as well. This is, indeed, the program for the remainder of books *III–IV.*

In sum: the *Physics* has the character of what, in the early twenty-first century, would be called philosophy of science—explorations of concepts such as change, nature, causality, explanation, teleology, necessity, chance, space, time, and infinity. The exploration of nature requires that we be secure about our starting points; these books aim at establishing the proper starting points for any natural investigation. And while a preliminary step in each investigation is to review previous views on the subject, Aristotle's final position rarely saved the opinions of his predecessors or of common sense. Invariably Aristotle used innovative philosophical tools to forge an unprecedented position on the foundations of natural science.

On the Parts of Animals I (*PA I*) was yet another foundational work, in this case a philosophical exploration of the standards required for a successful scientific study of living things. Its continuity with *Ph. II* is often correctly noted. To cite just one example, the discussions of teleology and conditional necessity in these two works are the only theoretical discussions of these topics in the corpus, and they complement one another in detail. It is less commonly noted that this book is also the bridge between the account of scientific knowledge in the *Analytics* and Aristotle's actual presentation of the results of his investigations of animals. For example, he argued for the priority of goal causation to efficient causation on grounds it is by stating the goal that one identifies the defining nature in things that are generated (639b13–21). And during his defense of conditional necessity—the idea that certain materials and processes are necessary for the realization of an end—he noted that this implies a different manner of demonstration than in other theoretical sciences (639b22–640a9).

The form of an organism is assumed to be its soul (in the sense defended in the *De Anima,* the functional capacities for nutrition, reproduction, perception, locomotion, and thought). But after noting this, a model for biological explanation emerges that applies the general ideals of the *Analytics* to this domain: a small number of explanatorily basic features are present simply because that is what it is to be that sort of animal; one does not further explain why birds are flyers or fish swimmers. In all other cases an attribute (such as a part or some feature of a part) must be shown to belong to the animals it belongs to either because its life requires or is made better by it, or because it is necessitated by the material nature of the animal.

On the Parts of Animals I, 2–3 follows with an attack on dichotomous division (as found in late Platonic dialogues and in fragments of Speusippus) as inadequate for organizing the biological world. Out of this attack emerges a new method of division, whereby general kinds (e.g., bird, fish, insect, soft-shelled animal) with many correlated differentiae are taken as the starting point of division. Division proceeds from these general differentiae (wing, leg) and articulates increasingly specific forms of each difference. If all birds have beaks, "beak" will stand at the head of a division into increasingly specific forms of beak. Division appears to play the same limited role of properly ordering and relating differences that it is given in *APo.,* yet there are numerous innovations intended for biological application. One can see division of this kind in practice in the *Historia Animalium* (*HA*) *I–X.*

How are the general kinds assumed by division identified? Aristotle turned to this question in *PA I.* 4. By attending to what led people to formulate the concepts of *bird* and *fish*, we can identify the principles to be deployed. *Bird* refers to a collection of organisms sharing a set of perceptually apparent features (beak, a peculiar form of bipedalism, feathers, wings, flight, etc.) each of which vary along a number of perceptual continua (dimensions, texture, color, density, etc.). With respect to these shared features, birds differ only in degree from each other, while they differ in kind from, say, fish—lung and gill, or feather and scale differ in kind, not merely in degree. Thus division under each of these general features remains within a determinate range and it is by attending to these general, correlated features that the "great kinds" (*megista gene*) of animals are identified. Further study will uncover their natures, the living functions for the sake of which the parts are structured and arranged as they are.

PA I. 5 first provides a stirring defense of the value of the scientific study of life when carried out in the proper, philosophical spirit (644b22-645a36). Then (645b1–36) it integrates its results, showing how a division of biological functions, paralleling that of the system of animal parts: "So the body is in a way for the sake of the soul, and the parts are for the sake of the functions in relation to which each of them developed by nature" (645b18–20).

Theory in Practice. Recent work on the model of science in the *APo.* and on the theoretical foundations of natural science developed in *Physics* and *PA I* helps us better to understand the way Aristotle's scientific investigations are organized. The theory of inquiry in *APo. II* is explicitly invoked at the very beginning of a number of Aristotle's animal studies. *HA*, for example, opens by introducing the kinds of differences among animals to be studied, and then states the purpose of the investigation to come and where it fits in the entire scientific study of animals. We must, he said,

> first grasp the differences and the attributes belonging to all animals. After this, we must attempt to discover the causes. For it is natural to carry out the investigation in this way, beginning with the inquiry into each thing; for from these inquiries it becomes clear both about which things the demonstration should be and from which things it should proceed. (*HA I.* 6, 491a7–14)

The term *inquiry* in this quote (and in what follows) translates *historia,* and throughout the biological works it is used to refer to the precausal stage of inquiry discussed in *APo.* That, rather than what we would call a natural history, is the purpose of the inquiry reported in *HA.* If "History of Animals" were not so entrenched as its title, it would be far better to refer to it as "Inquiries into Animals."

Understanding *HA* in light of *APo.* and *PA I* helps to explain a number of the puzzling features, some of which Balme pointed to in his contribution to the *DSB* entry: its organization around multiple, correlated differentiae rather than animal kinds; the virtual absence of the language of causal investigation, vocabulary that is pervasive in the other (causal) treatises; its interest in identifying great kinds (*megista gene*) and widest class generalizations (e.g., "all that breathe in and out as many as take in air all these have a lung, windpipe and esophagus" (*HA II.* 15, 506a2–3). A number of scholars in the nineteenth and twentieth centuries had argued that most or all of *HA* was written after Aristotle's death, and in his *DSB* entry Balme endorsed this claim. By the time he had prepared the introduction to the Loeb edition of *HA VII–X* (Balme, 1991), however, he had rejected these arguments, at least in part because of the realization that many of them depended on a misunderstanding of *HA's* structure and purpose.

Conversely, looking back to what is reported in *HA,* the beginnings of *On Animal Locomotion* (704b7–10) and *PA II* (646a8–12) identify themselves as reporting the results of causal investigations, referring back to the "inquiries" (*historiai*) as accounts of the data in need of explanation. This is not mere window dressing. *PA II–IV* and *HA* are focused intently on giving accounts of the essential natures of the parts, specifying the functional differences for the sake of which the structural and material differences are present. *On the Generation of Animals* (*GA*) begins by explaining the differences among the parts related to generation in the first half of book *I,* and proceeds to a causal explanation of animal generation, organized according to the appropriate differentiae: live-bearing, egg-laying, or spontaneously generated. Approaching Aristotle's science through his own theory of

science, rather than through our modern categories of natural history versus anatomy and physiology, has provided a better understanding of its goals and organization.

The discussion of anatomy and physiology contributed to *DSB* by L. G. Wilson focused on Aristotle's discussion of the vasculature and heart in *HA.* It provides valuable insights into Aristotle's likely method of dissection and its limitations. There is, however, little said about cardiac function, or about Aristotle's general approach to the parts of animals. An analysis of Aristotle's causal theory of the heart illustrates his general method of causal investigation of animal parts.

Aristotle began by discussing what is true of all hearts as such, and then moves on to explain the differentiation of hearts in different kinds of blooded animals. Aristotle's general account of the heart concludes (1) that the heart is present for the sake of originating blood, (2) that it is also the primary perceptive part, and (3) that it is thus the primary organ of the perceptive capacity of soul, the capacity essential to being an animal (*PA III.* 4, 666a34–36). It is part of Aristotle's explicit theory that many animals that perceive lack hearts. *PA III.* 4, however, is part of the discussion of the internal organic parts of blooded animals. Aristotle turned to the bloodless animals in book *IV,* and when he did so he noted that they must have an analogue of the heart and blood (cf. *PA IV.* 5 678b1–7).

The definition of a heart and the explanation of why animals with hearts have hearts are intertwined in just the way *APo.* would lead us to expect. Once this general explanation for why all blooded animals have a heart was in place, he went on to explain differences in its location (666b1–12), sinews (666b13–20), number of cavities (666b21–35), "articulation" (667a6–11), size (667a11–22), and even the relation of these differences to the animal's character (667a12–22). Just before concluding, he discussed the critical status of the heart for life and death (667a32–667b12).

As in his study of the heart, Aristotle's method of finding the widest class to which an attribute belongs per se in order to focus causal investigation can also be illustrated by his account of why certain animals have multiple stomachs (ruminants). Aristotle began by noting that this trait is correlated with cloven hoofs, horns, and a dearth of upper teeth, and this level of similarity is sufficient for Aristotle to seek a single explanation for it. Aristotle typically identified the animals with this complex of structures in common by a nominal phrase that literally translates as "the ones that do not have both rows of teeth (*ta mē amphôdonta*)" (cf. *PA III.* 2, 663b29–664a3, *III.* 14, 674a32–b18; *APo. II.* 14, 98a13–19). As with the *APo.* example of broad-leaved trees, this group is identified as a result of the search for that demonstration. The lack of teeth is due to the diversion of material suitable for teeth to make hoofs and horns. Because of the resulting lack of teeth, food enters the digestive track in a relatively unprocessed state, requiring a more complex system of stomachs to fully digest it.

Another grouping that Aristotle investigated that does not constitute a previously identified kind is the group of animals that possess lungs and also share a number of correlated features—windpipe, esophagus, neck, epiglottis (or equivalent)—all of which can be explained by reference to breathing. Aristotle concluded his discussion of the lung by claiming that, even though animals with a lung do not constitute an identified kind, the lung is nevertheless part of their being (*ousia*)—as much, he insisted, as having feathered wings is part of the being of birds (*PA III.* 6, 669b8-12).

Tradition and Influence. The entry of Minio-Paluello for the original *DSB* entry was comprehensive through 1970. However, between 1970 and the early twenty-first century there has been a revolution in our understanding of the Aristotelian tradition. Theophrastus, Aristotle's younger coworker and successor as head of the Lyceum, has been the subject of systematic and comprehensive investigation of primary sources and a related series of conferences, under the general guidance of William Fortenbaugh, during the past twenty-five years. Similarly, under the general guidance of Richard Sorabji, the Greek commentaries on Aristotle are being translated with annotation into English, introducing them to a new audience and leading to a significant scholarly reappraisal of their role in transmitting and reshaping Aristotle's ideas. Moreover, the systematic study of the Syriac-Arabic tradition reported on by Minio-Paluello, which not only transmitted Aristotelianism but transformed it in a variety of ways, has expanded. The Aristoteles Latinus and Aristoteles Semitico-Latinus Projects aim to publish editions of all the Latin, Syriac, Arabic, and Hebrew translations of Aristotle from Greek (as well as Latin translations of Syriac, Arabic, and Hebrew translations) and has already published many volumes of his scientific treatises. An annotated English translation of Albertus Magnus, *De Animalibus* has made this great work more widely available. These projects are only part of the transformation of the field of medieval philosophy due both to a wealth of newly edited texts and a deepening understanding of the historical influences on it and of the complexity of its relationship with Renaissance Aristotelianism.

Under the influence of scholars such as Charles Schmitt, Charles Lohr, and William Wallace, there has been an unprecedented growth in our understanding of the Aristotelian tradition in the Renaissance. This point is exemplified by briefly discussing what has happened during these intervening years in our understanding of the tradition and influence of Aristotle's "biological" works, many of them referred to collectively during the medieval period as *De Animalibus*.

The first chapter of Schmitt's groundbreaking *Aristotle and the Renaissance* bore the title "Renaissance Aristotelianisms." His work targeted the widespread tendency to, as he later put it, "lump all Aristotelian traditions together as part of the old medieval world" (p. 91) and to seek the roots of modernity in an eclectic mix of reactions against it. In the fourth chapter, on "Eclectic Aristotelianism," he spent a great deal of time discussing the many distinct ways, in various cultures, that Aristotelianism was comfortably infused with all sorts of other currents. In discussing Italy, for example, he mentioned the very different approaches of Pietro Pomponazzi and Agostino Nifo. During the past decade, Stefano Perfetti, of Pisa, has done a meticulous study of their respective commentaries on Aristotle's *De Partibus Animalium* (as well as that of Niccolò Tomeo), giving rich and concrete meaning to Schmitt's point. Though all three would claim to be part of an Aristotelian tradition, they brought to their studies differences in methods and philosophical assumptions that belie the uniformity that, even in 1983, historians of science took for granted.

Those works, which were based on the printed Latin translation of the biological works by Theodorus Gaza that first appeared in 1476, form part of the background to a broad and eclectic Aristotelian reaction to the Galenism that had dominated the theory and practice of medicine. Gradually, practitioners of human dissection became the sources of empirical challenges to Galenic orthodoxy. In Aristotle's animal studies they found a radically different justification for dissection. The study of animals was a central part of natural philosophy, not a practice ancillary to medicine. It was a universal and comparative study of parts in whatever animals had them, not an art restricted to the investigation of health and disease in humans. Those who taught it, then, had the right to be considered professors of natural philosophy, and not merely "demonstrators."

This movement gained enormously from the assistance of artists and printers in the production of dramatically presented anatomical drawings and could point to texts in Aristotle to indicate an ancient origin for this practice. By the time William Harvey entered Padua (perhaps already prepared by reading the eclectic Aristotelianism of John Case in England) for his medical training in 1599, the likes of Andreas Vesalius and Realdo Colombo had transformed the subject. His own mentor, Fabricius ab'Aquapendente, was teaching and practicing philosophical anatomy—an anatomy that was universal in scope, comparative in method, and theoretical in its aims. It was the philosophical and theoretical basis for the art of medicine. Under an unmistakable Aristotelian influence, the places of the two disciplines had been reversed.

Schmitt saw Harvey, whose work on the movement of the heart and on animal generation is a high point of the new "experimental philosophy," as an exemplar of an eclecticism that integrated new developments within an Aristotelian framework. Another example of the same tendency is found in Aristotelians such as Christoph Clavius and Christopher Scheiner who, during the sixteenth and seventeenth centuries, drawing on Aristotle's discussions of the "more natural of the mathematical sciences" (optics, harmonics, astronomy, mechanics), embraced the application of mathematics to the study of nature.

In light of the scholarship on every aspect of the Aristotelian tradition since the 1970s, Minio-Paluello's statement in the original *DSB* entry that "Aristotle's influence [in the province of science] is very limited, or effective only in the sense that mistakes, eliciting opposition, criticism, and new solutions to old and new problems, are the starting point of scientific progress," (p. 267) needs to be seriously reconsidered.

SUPPLEMENTARY BIBLIOGRAPHY

For texts, translations, and secondary literature published before 1970, consult the original DSB *bibliographies compiled by Owen, Balme, Wilson, and Minio-Paluello. The following bibliography is restricted to works published since then and is highly selective. Many of the works referenced, however, have extensive bibliographies on their subjects. A reasonably comprehensive bibliography of recent primary and secondary literature (through 1995) on Aristotle can be found in* The Cambridge Companion to Aristotle *edited by Jonathan Barnes. The following bibliography is subdivided according to the subdivisions in the text. At the end of the bibliography, a number of valuable entries are noted related to these topics in the online scholarly resource,* Stanford Encyclopedia of Philosophy. *Each is a commendable introduction to these topics and each contains a helpful bibliography and links to related cites.*

ARISTOTLE

Theory of Science: Works by Aristotle: Texts, Translations, and Commentaries

Analytica Posteriora. Translated and edited by Wolfgang Detel. 2 vols. Berlin: Akademie-Verlag, 1993.

Posterior Analytics. Edited by Jonathan Barnes. 2nd ed. Oxford: Oxford University Press, 1994.

Topics I and VIII: With Excerpts from Related Texts. Translated and edited by Robin Smith. Oxford: Oxford University Press, 1997.

Theory of Science: Other Sources

Berti, Enrico, ed. *Aristotle on Science: "The Posterior Analytics": Proceedings of the Eighth Symposium Aristotelicum Held in Padua from September 7 to 15, 1978.* Padua, Italy: Editrice Antenore, 1981.

Charles, David. *Aristotle on Meaning and Essence.* Oxford: Oxford University Press, 2000.

Ferejohn, Michael. *The Origins of Aristotelian Science.* New Haven, CT: Yale University Press, 1991.

Kullmann, W. *Wissenschaft und Methode.* Berlin: De Gruyter, 1974.

Lear, Jonathon. *Aristotle and Logical Theory.* Cambridge, U.K.: Cambridge University Press, 1980.

Lloyd, G. E. R. *Aristotelian Explorations.* Cambridge, U.K.: Cambridge University Press, 1996.

McKirihan, Richard, Jr. *Principles and Proofs: Aristotle's Theory of Demonstrative Science.* Princeton, NJ: Princeton University Press, 1992.

Foundations of Natural Science: Works by Aristotle: Texts, Translations, and Commentaries

Physique. Translated and edited by Pierre Pellegrin. Paris: G.F. Flammarion, 2000.

Physics: Books I and II. Translated and edited by William Charlton. Oxford: Oxford University Press, 1992.

Physics: Books III–IV. Translated and edited by Edward Hussey. Oxford: Oxford University Press, 1983.

Physics: Book VIII. Translated and edited by Daniel Graham. Oxford: Oxford University Press, 1999.

Foundations of Natural Science: Other Sources

Bostock, David. *Space, Time, Matter, and Form: Essays on Aristotle's "Physics."* Oxford: Oxford University Press, 2006.

Coope, Ursula. *Time for Aristotle: "Physics IV." 10–14.* Oxford: Oxford University Press, 2005.

De Grandt, F., and P. Souffrin, eds. *La Physique d'Aristote et les conditions d'une science de la nature.* Paris: Vrin, 1991.

Falcon, Andrea. *Aristotle and the Science of Nature: Unity without Uniformity.* Cambridge, U.K.: Cambridge University Press, 2005.

Gill, Mary Louise. *Aristotle on Substance: The Paradox of Unity.* Princeton, NJ: Princeton University Press, 1989.

Haas, Frans A. J. de, and Jaap Mansfeld, eds. 2004. *Aristotle's On Generation and Corruption Book I.* Symposium Aristotelicum XV Deurne, Netherlands 1999. Oxford: Oxford University Press, 2004.

Johnson, Monte Ransome. *Aristotle on Teleology.* Oxford: Oxford University Press, 2005.

Judson, Lindsay, ed. *Aristotle's Physics: A Collection of Essays.* Oxford: Oxford University Press, 1991.

Quarantotto, Diana. *Causa Finale, Sostanza, Essenza in Aristotele: Saggio sulla struttura dei processi teleologici naturali e sulla funzione del telos.* Elenchos: 46. Naples, Italy: Bibliopolis, 2005.

Wardy, Robert. *The Chain of Change: A Study of Aristotle's "Physics" VII.* Cambridge, U.K.: Cambridge University Press, 1990.

Waterlow [Broadie], Sarah. *Nature, Change, and Agency in Aristotle's "Physics": A Philosophical Study.* Oxford: Oxford University Press, 1982.

Natural Science/Biology: Works by Aristotle: Texts, Translations, and Commentaries

Balme, David M. *Historia Animalium, Volume I (Books I–X: Text)*. Prepared for publication by Allan Gotthelf. Cambridge, U.K.: Cambridge University Press, 2002.

———. *De Partibus Animalium I and De Generatione Animalium I with passages from II.1–3*. Prepared for publication by Allan Gotthelf. Clarendon Aristotle Series. Oxford: Oxford University Press, 1992.

———. *History of Animals VII–X*. Prepared for publication by Allan Gotthelf. Loeb Classical Library. London and Cambridge, MA: Harvard University Press, 1991.

Lanza, Diego, and Mario Vegetti. *Opere biologiche*. Turin, Italy: Unione tipografico-editrice torinese, 1971.

Lennox, James G. *Aristotle. On the Parts of Animals* I–IV. Oxford: Oxford University Press, 2001.

Louis, Pierre. *Météorologiques*. Collection des universities de France. Paris: Société d'édition "Les Belles lettres," 1982.

Migliori, Maurizio. *La generazione e la corruzione*. Filosophi anitichi. Naples, Italy: L. Loffredo, 1976.

Pepe, Lucio. Aristotele. *Meteorologia: Testo Greco a fronte*. Bompiani testi a fronte: 81. Milan, Italy: Edizione Bompiani, 2003.

Natural Science/Biology: Other Sources

Gotthelf, Allan, and James G. Lennox, eds. *Philosophical Issues in Aristotle's Biology*. Cambridge, U.K.: Cambridge University Press, 1987.

Kullmann, Wolfgang, and Sabine Föllinger, eds. *Aristotelishche Biologie: Intentionen, Methoden, Ergbnisse; Akten des Symposions über Aristoteles' Biologie vom 24.–28 Juli 1995 in der Werner-Reimers-Stiftung in Bad Hamburg*. Philosophie der Antike, vol. 6. Stuttgart, Germany: Franz Steiner Verlag, 1997.

Lennox, James G. *Aristotle's Philosophy of Biology: Studies in the Origins of Life Science*. Cambridge, U.K.: Cambridge University Press, 2001.

Pellegrin, Pierre. *Aristotle's Classification of Animals: Biology and the Conceptual Unity of the Aristotelian Corpus*. Translated by Anthony Preus, rev. ed. Berkeley: University of California Press, 1986.

THE ARISTOTELIAN TRADITION

Even a selective bibliography on this topic is impossible. The edited texts alone that have been produced in since 1970 would run for many pages. Below are some valuable collections of essays and some monographs that provide an overview of some aspects of the topic. But for those who are seriously interested, consulting the various Web sites listed at the end of the bibliography is advised.

Di Liscia, Daniel, Eckhard Kessler, and Charlotte Methuen, eds. *Method and Order in Renaissance Philosophy of Nature: The Aristotelian Commentary Tradition*. Aldershot, U.K.: Ashgate, 1997.

Gill, Mary Louise, and James G. Lennox, eds. *Self-Motion from Aristotle to Newton*. Princeton, NJ: Princeton University Press, 1994.

Kithcell, Kenneth F., Jr., and Ireven Michael Resnick. *Albertus Magnus on Animals: A Medieval Summa Zoologica*. 2 vols. Baltimore and London: Johns Hopkins University Press, 1999.

Lohr, C. H. *Latin Aristotelian Commentators II*. Florence, Italy: Corpus Philosophorum Medii Aevi, 1988.

Schmitt, Charles D. *Aristotle and the Renaissance*. Martin Classical Lectures, vol. 27. Cambridge, MA: Oberlin College by Harvard University Press, 1983.

———, Eckhard Kessler, and Quentin Skinner, eds. *The Cambridge History of Renaissance Philosophy*. Cambridge, U.K.: Cambridge University Press, 1988.

Sharples, R. W., ed. *Whose Aristotle? Whose Aristotelianism?* Ashgate Keeling Series in Ancient Philosophy. Aldershot, U.K.: Ashgate, 2001.

Steel, Carlos, Guy Guldentops, and Pieter Beullens, eds. *Aristotle's Animals in the Middle Ages and Renaissance*. Mediaevalia Loveniensia: ser. 1, studia 27. Leuven, Belgium: Leuven University Press, 1999.

Wildberg, Christian. *Philoponus: Against Aristotle, on the Eternity of the World*. London: Duckworth, 1987.

Revival of Aristotelianism in the Renaissance

Bylebyl, Jerome. "The School of Padua: Humanistic Medicine in the Sixteenth Century." In *Health, Medicine and Morality in the Sixteenth Century*, edited by Charles Webster. Cambridge, U.K.: Cambridge University Press, 1979.

Cunningham, Andrew. "Fabricius and the 'Aristotle project' in Anatomical Teaching and Research at Padua." In *The Medical Renaissance of the Sixteenth Century*, edited by Andrew Wear, Roger K. French, and I. M. Lonie. Cambridge, U.K.: Cambridge University Press, 1985.

Frank, Robert G., Jr. *Harvey and the Oxford Physiologists: Scientific Ideas and Social Interaction*. Berkeley: University of California Press, 1980.

French, Roger K. *William Harvey's Natural Philosophy*. Cambridge, U.K.: Cambridge University Press, 1994.

Schmitt, Charles B. *Reappraisals in Renaissance Thought*. London: Variorum Reprints, 1989.

Wear, Andrew, Roger K. French, and I. M. Lonie, eds. *The Medical Renaissance of the Sixteenth Century*. Cambridge, U.K.: Cambridge University Press, 1985.

STANFORD ENCYCLOPEDIA OF PHILOSOPHY SITES ON ARISTOTLE AND THE ARISTOTELIAN TRADITION

Aristotle

http://plato.stanford.edu/entries/aristotle-natphil/

http://plato.stanford.edu/entries/aristotle-mathematics/

http://plato.stanford.edu/entries/aristotle-biology/

http://plato.stanford.edu/entries/aristotle-causality/

Commentators on Aristotle

http://plato.stanford.edu/entries/aristotle-commentators/

http://plato.stanford.edu/entries/alexander-aphrodisias/

http://plato.stanford.edu/entries/philoponus/

Medieval Aristotelianism
http://plato.stanford.edu/entries/medieval-philosophy/
http://plato.stanford.edu/entries/albert-great/

Renaissance Aristotelianism
http://plato.stanford.edu/entries/aristotelianism-renaissance/
http://plato.stanford.edu/entries/pomponazzi/
http://plato.stanford.edu/entries/zabarella/

James G. Lennox

Arnald of Villanova. SCIENCE PHOTO LIBRARY/PHOTO RESEARCHERS, INC.

ARNALD OF VILLANOVA (*b.* Aragon, Spain, c. 1240; *d.* at sea off Genoa, Italy, 6 September 1311), *medical sciences.* For the original article on Arnald of Villanova see *DSB,* vol. 1.

The continuing publication of Arnald's medical works, a series not even begun when the original *DSB* was published, has thrown much new light on the details of his thought and its relation to developments in medicine at the end of the thirteenth century, as well as on the sequence and dating of his writings. *De intentione medicorum,* composed at the beginning of his Montpellier teaching, put forward a consistent medical philosophy, derived from Avicenna, that Arnald maintained to the end of his career, a medical instrumentalism that distinguished between absolute philosophical truth and a medical "truth" whose only test was its sufficiency to bring about a patient's health. And by the end of the 1290s Arnald had become an active figure in the European assimilation of what has been called the "new Galen"; he was particularly enthusiastic about the promise of Galen's *De interioribus* to orient the practitioner in diagnostics and pathology, and he prepared an epitome of its first two books for his students to master.

Finally, his *Aphorismi de gradibus, Medicationis parabole,* and commentary on the first Hippocratic aphorism, all as of 2007 datable to the years around 1300, reveal his enthusiasm for another new pedagogical technique of the day, the presentation of medical knowledge in aphoristic and tabular form. While this period of scientific maturity coincides with Arnald's growing commitment to theological investigation, it remains an open question whether he kept these two aspects of his thought separate or whether they formed an integrated whole.

Arnald's mission to Paris in 1300 (not 1299, as stated in the earlier *DSB* article) brought his teaching career to an end, but his medical writing continued, now, however, intended to win the support of patrons rather than to educate students and colleagues. Works from this period include the *Regimen sanitatis,* which he composed for Jaume II of Aragon; the *Speculum medicine,* which the

same king was avidly seeking in 1308; the military *Regimen,* which Arnald prepared for the king's army during its attack on Almeria in 1309; and the *Practica summaria,* which he seems to have drawn up for Pope Clement V. Two other works ascribed to Arnald, an *Antidotarium* and a work on poisons, may have been assembled from notes after his death by a medical disciple, Petrus Cellerarius. In combination with other evidence, they hint at Arnald's possible activity at the court of Robert of Naples in the last two years of his life and at his interest in the new chemical medicine of the day, which could perhaps have encouraged the attribution of alchemical works to him after his death, but there is now little doubt that all the "Arnaldian" alchemical work is apocryphal.

SUPPLEMENTARY BIBLIOGRAPHY

WORKS BY ARNALD OF VILLANOVA

Arnaldi de Villanova Opera medica omnia. Vol. 2, *Aphorismi de gradibus,* edited by M. R. McVaugh (1975); Vol. 3, *Tractatus de amore heroico; Epistola de dosi tyriacalium medicinarum,* edited by M. R. McVaugh (1985); Vol. 4, *Tractatus de consideracionibus operis medicine sive de flebotomia,* edited by

P. Gil-Sotres and L. Demaitre (1988); Vol. 5.1, *Tractatus de intentione medicorum*, edited by M. R. McVaugh (2000); Vol. 6.1, *Medicationis parabole*, edited by J. A. Paniagua; *Pirqé Arnau de Vilanova*, edited by L. Ferre and E. Feliu (1990); Vol. 6.2, *Commentum in quasdam parabolas et alias aphorismorum series: Aphorismi particulares, Aphorismi de memoria, Aphorismi extravaganates*, edited by J. A. Paniagua and P. Gil-Sotres (1993); Vol. 7.1, *Epistola de reprobacione nigromantice ficcionis (De improbatione maleficiorum)*, edited by S. Giralt (2005); Vol. 10.1, *Regimen sanitatis ad regem Aragonum*, edited by L. García-Ballester and M. R. McVaugh (1996); Vol. 10.2, *Regimen Almarie (Regimen castra sequentium)*, edited by L. Cifuentes and M. R. McVaugh (1998); Vol. 11, *De esu carnium*, edited by D. M. Bazell (1999); Vo.l. 15, *Commentum supra tractatum Galieni de malicia complexionis diverse*, edited by L. García Ballester and E. Sánchez Salor; *Doctrina Galieni de interioribus*, edited by R. J. Durling (1985); Vol. 16, *Translatio libri Galieni de rigore et tremore et iectigatione et spasmo*, edited by M. R. McVaugh (1981); Vol. 17, *Translatio libri Albuzale de medicinis simplicibus*, edited by J. Martínez Gázquez and M. R. McVaugh; *Abū-l- Ṣalt Umayya, Kitāb al-adwiya al-mufrada*, edited by A. Labarta; *Llibre d'Albumesar de simples medecines*, edited by L. Cifuentes (2004). Barcelona: University of Barcelona Press. A continuing series of critical editions with historical introductions.

Opera theologica omnia. Vol. 3. Barcelona, 2004. Contains editions of Arnald's commentary on *De semine scripturarum* and his *Allocutio super tetragrammaton*.

OTHER SOURCES

Garcia-Ballester, Luis. "The 'new Galen': A challenge to Latin Galenism in Thirteenth-Century Montpellier." In *Text and Tradition: Studies in Ancient Medicine and Its Transmission: Presented to Jutta Kollesch*, edited by Klaus-Dietrich Fischer, Diethard Nickel, and Paul Potter. Leiden, Netherlands: Brill, 1998. A seminal study that discusses the new appreciation of Galen in medical faculties c. 1300.

Giralt, Sebastià. *Arnau de Vilanova en la impremta renaixentista.* Manresa, Spain: Publicacions de l'Arxiu Històric de Ciències de la Salut, 2002.

McVaugh, Michael. "Further Documents for the Biography of Arnau de Vilanova." *Dynamis* 2 (1982): 363–372.

———. *Medicine Before the Plague: Patients and Practitioners in the Crown of Aragon, 1285–1335.* Cambridge, U.K.: Cambridge University Press, 1993. Attempts in part to situate Arnald in the wider social context of western European medical practice.

Mensa i Valls, Jaume, and Sebastià Giralt. "Bibliografia Arnaldiana (1994–2003)." *Arxiu de Textos Catalans Antics* 22 (2003): 665–734. Annual bibliographies in this journal continue to cover scholarship having to do with both Arnald's scientific and theological interests.

Perarnau, Josep, ed. *Actes de la I trobada internacional d'estudis sobre Arnau de Vilanova,* in *Arxiu de Textos Catalans Antics* 14 (1995); *Actes de la II trobada internacional d'estudis sobre Arnau de Vilanova,* in *Arxiu de Textos Catalans Antics* 23–24 (2004–2005). Collections of fundamental papers laying out the state of current scholarship and directions for research.

Ziegler, Joseph. *Medicine and Religion, c. 1300: The Case of Arnau de Vilanova.* Oxford: Oxford University Press, 1998.

Michael McVaugh

ARNALD OF VILLANOVA (PSEUDO)

(fourteenth through sixteenth centuries), *alchemy*.

The Pseudo-Arnald of Villanova corpus is a set of alchemical works which, from the fourteenth to the sixteenth centuries, were usually attributed to the celebrated physician Arnald of Villanova (c. 1240–1311). The present article aims to summarize the history, theoretical content, and influence on science of this group of works.

The conception of an Arnald of Villanova at once physician and alchemist had such staying power that it was still accepted in 1934 by Lynn Thorndike, whose *History of Magic and Experimental Science* set forth a first account of Arnald's supposed alchemical writings. After Juan A. Paniagua's pathbreaking article of 1959, however, the apocryphal character of the whole corpus was accepted as the most persuasive hypothesis, based as it was on the work (later lost) of Jacques Payen who concluded from a scientific examination of one of the main works in the corpus, the *Rosarius philosophorum*, that its attribution to Arnald was meritless. Subsequent research initiated by Michela Pereira and William R. Newman succeeded in situating the corpus in its historical context. These authors pointed up the relationship between the Pseudo-Arnald corpus and such other alchemical texts as those of Pseudo-Raymond Lull and Pseudo-Geber (Paul de Tarente). These contributions, along with the work of Michael McVaugh, would seem to have established the apocryphal nature of the Pseudo-Arnald corpus beyond doubt.

Formation of the Pseudo-Arnald Corpus. The earliest attributions to Arnald of Villanova date from the mid-fourteenth century (the very first was made after 1323, as the Palermo, *Biblioteca Comunale*, 4 Qq A 10 attests. They were apparently linked to a legend retailed by the canonist John Andrea (1346), according to which an Arnald of Villanova successfully demonstrated alchemical transmutation to the Roman Curia in 1301. This legend presumably stemmed from the interest of certain cardinals in a distillation process reputed to bestow long life and from their concern with scientific investigation and experiment in general. Furthermore, the claim that Arnald of Villanova had cured Pope Boniface VIII of stones by applying a gold astrological seal did much to reinforce his extraordinary prestige.

The Pseudo-Arnald corpus was built up little by little on the basis of alchemical compilations and correspondence addressed to various princes, including Robert of Anjou, king of Naples; Philip IV the Fair of France; and James II of Aragon, with whom Arnald had connections. Many such texts, initially either anonymous or attributed to other, less celebrated individuals, had by the end of the fourteenth century been firmly ascribed to Arnald of Villanova. This is true of the main works of the corpus: the *Rosarius philosophorum*, the *Flos florum*, the *Epistola super alchimia ad regem Neapolitanum*, and the *Novum Testamentum*. A number of indications suggest that the corpus was formed and developed in places and circles associated with the Catalan physician himself (Sicily, Catalonia, Naples). In sharp contrast to the relationship between the Pseudo-Lull corpus and the actual Ramon Lull (c. 1232–1316), however, no common ground is discernible between the scientific work of Arnald of Villanova and the alchemical texts of which he was said to be the author.

The fifteenth century was the heyday of the Pseudo-Arnald corpus, which expanded continually throughout the period, so that by the next century it comprised no less than twenty-four works (see Vatican Barberini collection, MS 273). Caution is required here, however, for some references correspond either to mere extracts or to abridged versions, even though the title given may suggest a complete work. A careful review of the various titles and texts results in a revision downward to a total of nineteen works, along with approximately ten recipes.

Composition of the Pseudo-Arnald Corpus. The corpus is made up, first, of purely alchemical works promoting the "mercury alone" thesis, according to which the transmutation of base metal into gold presupposes the prior elimination of all substances other than the "primal metal," which is a constituent of all metals. This thesis is related to the "mercury-sulfur theory" of the generation of metals, which posits an ideal mercury containing a pure, red sulfur that gives the alchemical product its gold color. This notion, prevalent in the fourteenth and fifteenth centuries, had its origins in the *Summa perfectionis*, part of the Pseudo-Geber corpus (late thirteenth century). It was justified in terms of the imitation of nature: the alchemist was said to be reproducing in the laboratory a process of metallic generation that might take as much as a thousand years in nature. The *Summa perfectionis* also disseminated the idea that the elements and metals were composed of small particles of variable size. Thus impure metal exposed to heat was said to be purified by particles of fire that penetrated it, expelling the bad sulfur and leaving only pure metal. This corpuscular theory, so characteristic of Pseudo-Geber, owes a debt to concepts of medieval physics passed down by scholastic medicine and ultimately derived from Aristotle's *Physics and Meteorologica*.

Reference is made in many parts of the corpus to the "mercury alone" thesis, including (to name only the most important) *Flos florum*, *Rosarius philosophorum*, *De secretis naturae*, *Quaestiones tam essentiales quam accidentales ad Bonifacium VIII*, *Epistola super alchimia ad regem Neapolitanum*, *Phoenix*, *Speculum alchimiae*, and *Novum lumen*. Among these works, the *Speculum alchimiae* and above all the *Rosarius philosophorum* are seemingly the most consistent with the *Summa perfectionis* of Pseudo-Geber, for they rehearse its most typical themes: "mercury alone," corpuscularism, the concept of "three medicines," and the arguments of the *Summa*'s didactic preface.

Medico-alchemical texts are the second component of the Pseudo-Arnald corpus. They are three in number, namely *Liber de vita philosophorum*, *Epistola ad Jacobum de Toleto de distillatione sanguinis humani,* and *De aqua vitae simplici et composita*. These texts belong to a tradition distinct from that of Pseudo-Geber. Placed under the supposed patronage of Arnald of Villanova, friend and physician to Pope Boniface VIII, they outlined an alchemy of the elixir of life—bound up with the art of medicine—which excluded such artificial and corrosive materials from its distillations and manipulations and claimed rather to start only from such noble and natural substances as human blood (*Epistola ad Jacobum de Toleto de distillatione sanguinis humani*), gold (*Liber de vita philosophorum*), or wine (*De aqua vitae simplici et composita*). The charge of incoherence leveled at Pseudo-Arnald by Michela Pereira is based in large part on the fact that the corpus contains both texts of a medical nature on distillatory alchemy and texts on the alchemy of transmutation. Only one work in the corpus, the *Rosarius philosophorum*, may be said to touch on both spheres (after the fashion of Pseudo-Lull's *Testamentum*), for it deals not only with alchemical research directly inspired by the *Summa perfectionis* but also with the definition of the elixir as a sovereign medicine, just as applicable to metals as to the human body.

Although the much greater part of the Pseudo-Arnald of Villanova corpus comprises learned texts dealing in the scholastic manner with both technical and theoretical aspects of alchemy, at least one treatise, certainly of Franciscan origin, is entirely allegorical, namely the *Tractatus parabolicus*, which had the good fortune to be cited by John of Rupescissa in his *Liber lucis* (1350). It is possible, furthermore, to discern traces of religious prophesying and Christianity in *De secretis naturae* and even in some alchemical recipes. One may also cite *Defloratio philosophorum*, which includes an alchemical tale and various recipes. Such allegorical, even exegetical alchemical texts, which compare the philosopher's stone to Christ, are harbingers of the spiritual alchemy of the modern period.

This account of the composition of the Pseudo-Arnaldian corpus would be incomplete if no mention were made of translations into the vernacular (into French, Catalan, or Provençal). These emerged very soon, beginning in 1360 (cf. the copy of *Rosaire des philosophes* in the Bibliothèque de l'Arsenal, Paris, MS 2872) and reflect the success quickly encountered by these works and their rapid spread beyond the narrow confines of the academic world.

Posterity of the Pseudo-Arnald Corpus. As noted, the allegorical *Tractatus parabolicus* was invoked by John of Rupescissa, author of *De quinta essentia* (1351–1352), a work of medical chemistry dealing with the distilling of alcohol in order to produce an elixir of life or quintessence. The *Rosarius philosophorum*, composed before 1343, may be one of the sources of the Pseudo-Lullian *Testamentum* (1332), for the close relationship between the two texts is evident; the same may be said of John Dastin's Rosarius (fourteenth century): both of these treatises invoke the *Summa perfectionis* of Pseudo-Geber. This gives some measure too of the importance taken on by the *Rosarius philosophorum* among predominantly medical manuscripts of the fourteenth and fifteenth centuries. Similarly, the fact that the work was copied as a scientific manuscript—as witness the one in the Bibliothèque de l'Arsenal in Paris as of the early 2000s (MS 2872), which was no doubt commissioned by Charles V—stamps it (like the *Testamentum*) as a treatise as significant as Aldebrandin de Sienne's thirteenth-century French work *Régime du Corps* or as the pseudo-Aristotelian *Secret of Secrets*. Responding in 1385 to Thomas of Bologna, a partisan of a diversified alchemy (concerned with potable gold, connections with astrology, plants, the quintessence, and so on), Bernard of Trier invoked the *Rosarius philosophorum* to buttress his defense of an orthodox alchemy of transmutation, roundly reprimanding Thomas for endorsing an alchemical medicine that was nothing but nostrums, unlike the true medicine of metals, as described in the *Rosarius*. As for Geoffrey Chaucer (1390), Pseudo-Arnald—or specifically the author of the *Rosarius*—supplied him with a model of the alchemist (see the "Canon's Yeoman's Tale" in *The Canterbury Tales*). Lastly, pseudo-Arnaldian writings exercised a real influence on the search for remedies in times of plague.

During the Renaissance, the transmutational alchemy of Pseudo-Geber at first dominated the publication of medieval alchemical texts in printed form. Its promotion was usually backed up by the works of Pseudo-Arnald and Pseudo-Lull, the latter holding open the door to many possible combinations between transmutational concerns and the medico-alchemical tradition stemming from John of Rupescissa. Subsequently the division in the Pseudo-Arnald corpus between more specifically medico-alchem-

ical works and works of pure alchemy was radically reinforced. Thus the publisher Tommaso Murchi's edition of Arnald's *Opera omnia* (1504) comprised just four works, described as "true alchemy," or in other words the alchemy of mercury, concerned solely with isolating "primal matter," or mercury-sulfur. In draconian fashion, Murchi excluded many alchemical texts attributed to the famous physician and retained only those that he deemed the most authentic: *Rosarius philosophorum*, *Novum lumen*, *Epistola super alchimia ad regem Neapolitanum*, and *Flos florum*. Other works were later included in such large collections as those of Lazarus Zetzner (Strasbourg, 1613) and Jean-Jacques Manget (Geneva, 1702), but the editorial line barely changed, for the new choices too dealt solely with the "truly alchemical" theory of "mercury alone." Meanwhile such medico-alchemical works of Pseudo-Arnald as that dealing with the distillation of blood—*Epistola ad Jacobum de Toleto de distillatione sanguinis humani*—were far less widely circulated.

However, the compiler Philipp Ulstad, whose book *Coelum philosophorum* (1525) introduced Europe to alchemical theories of distillation based on the idea of quintessence, was able to draw a very clear distinction, invoking the authority of Arnald of Villanova, between a noxious alchemy of mercury and a medical alchemy based on natural gold. Moreover, for all those with a passion for alchemy, metallurgy, and miraculous cures, the reference to Pseudo-Arnald remained inevitable. One need only mention Georgius Agricola (Georg Bauer, 1494–1555), who, though critical of what he considered a suspect science, nevertheless, in the preface to his *De re metallica* (1550), placed Arnald of Villanova, along with Lull (and Merlin), among the very few medieval alchemists of real significance. While Andreas Libavius (c.1540–1616), though doubtful about its ascription to Arnald, continued to look upon the *Rosarius philosophorum* as an essential work of practical alchemy that only a seasoned natural philosopher could understand, followers of Paracelsus such as Adam of Bodenstein (1528–1577) viewed Pseudo-Arnald, and notably the *Rosarius*, as a foreshadowing of the medical chemistry that they sought to advance under the banner of their master.

BIBLIOGRAPHY

Most manuscripts containing pseudo-Arnaldian texts are listed in Lynn Thorndike and Pearl Kibre's Catalogue of Incipits of Mediaeval Scientific Writings in Latin *(Cambridge, MA: Mediaeval Academy of America, 1937; rev. ed., 1963) and in volume 3 of Thorndike's* History of Magic and Experimental Science *(see below), pp. 654–676. See also Dorothea Waley Singer's* Catalogue of Latin and Vernacular Alchemical Manuscripts in Great Britain and Ireland, Dating from before the Sixteenth Century *(Brussels: Union Académique Internationale, 1928), no. 228, which indicates English translations where they exist; and James Corbett's* Catalogue des manuscrits alchimiques latins: Manuscrits des bibliothèques publiques de Paris antérieurs au XVIIe siècle *(Brussels: Union Académique Internationale, 1939) and* Catalogue des manuscrits alchimiques latins: Manuscrits des bibliothèques publiques des départements français antérieurs au XVIIe siècle *(Brussels: Union Académique Internationale, 1951). Note the importance of manuscripts such as those at the Palermo Biblioteca Comunale: 4 Qq A 10 and at the University Library of Bologna: 104 (Latin 138).*

MODERN PUBLISHED VERSIONS OF THE PSEUDO-ARNALD CORPUS

Manget, Jean-Jacques. *Bibliotheca chemica curiosa seu rerum ad alchemiam pertinentium thesaurus instructissimus.* 2 vols. Geneva: Choet, G. de Tournes, Cramer, Perachon, Ritter, and S. de Tournes, 1702; reprint, Bologna: Arnaldo Forni, 1976. Collects major works of the Pseudo-Arnald corpus, including *Rosarius philosophorum, Novum lumen, Flos florum, Epistola super alchimia ad regem Neapolitanum, Quaestiones tam essentiales quam accidentales ad Bonifacium VIII, Novum Testamentum, Speculum alchimiae.* For the most part these texts are merely versions extracted either from a single manuscript or from an earlier printed publication itself derived from a manuscript; this explains the significant variations between Manget's printed texts and those of the oldest manuscripts. Any serious study of the texts therefore requires that their content be verified by reference to the original manuscripts.

Calvet, Antoine. "Le De vita philosophorum du pseudo-Arnaud de Villeneuve, texte du manuscrit de Paris, BnF ms. latin 7817." *Chrysopoeia* 4 (1990–1991): 35–79.

———. "Le Tractatus parabolicus du pseudo-Arnaud de Villeneuve, présentation, édition et traduction." *Chrysopoeia* 5 (1997): 145–171.

———. "Le De secretis naturae du pseudo-Arnaud de Villeneuve, présentation, édition et traduction." *Chrysopoeia* 6 (1997–1999): 155–206.

———. "Quelques versions du Flos florum du pseudo-Arnaud de Villeneuve, textes présentés par A. Calvet et édités par S. Matton." *Chrysopoeia* 6 (1997–1999): 207–271.

OTHER SOURCES

Calvet, Antoine. "Les alchimica d'Arnaud de Villeneuve à travers la tradition imprimée (XVIe–XVIIe)." In *Alchimie: Art, Histoire et Mythes,* edited by Didier Kahn and Sylvain Matton, 157–190. Paris: Société d'Étude de l'Histoire de l'Alchimie, 1995. Includes a list of imprints from the Renaissance to the eighteenth century containing pseudo-Arnaldian alchemical works.

Crisciani, Chiara. "Alchemy and Medicine in the Middle Ages: Recent Studies and Projects for Research." *Bulletin de Philosophie Médiévale* 38 (1996): 9–21.

———, and Michela Pereira. "Black Death and Golden Remedies: Some Remarks on Alchemy and the Plague." In *The Regulation of Evil: Social and Cultural Attitudes to Epidemics in the Late Middle Ages,* edited by Agostino Paravicini Bagliani and Francesco Santi, 7–39. Florence: Sismel Edizioni del Galluzo, 1998.

McVaugh, Michael. "Chemical Medicine in the Medical Writings of Arnau de Vilanova." II *Trobada Internacional d'Estudis sobre Arnau de Vilanova. Arxiu de Textos Catalans Antics* 23–24: (2004–2005): 239–264. The author explains why it has become difficult to authenticate the medico-alchemical texts attributed to Arnald of Villanova.

Newman, William R. *The Summa Perfectionis of Pseudo-Geber.* Leyden, Netherlands: E. J. Brill, 1991. Newman provides a critical edition and an English translation of the *Summa perfectionis,* an important source for the pseudo-Arnaldian alchemical corpus. His introduction offers a detailed study of the questions raised by the text and a discussion of the Pseudo-Geber theory of matter, the historical and philosophical context of the Summa, and its influence.

Paniagua, Juan A. "Notas en torno a los escritos de alquimia atribuidos a Arnau de Vilanova." In *Studia Arnaldiana: Trabajos en torno a la obra médica de Arnau de Vilanova, c. 1240–1311.* Barcelona: Fundación Uriach 1838, 1994: 451–464 (XIV: 406–419).

Pereira, Michela. "Arnaldo da Vilanova e l'alchimia. Un'indagine preliminare." In *Actes de la I trobada internacional d'estudis sobre Arnau de Vilanova,* vol. 2, edited by Josep Perarnau, 165–174. Barcelona: Institut d'Estudis Catalans, 1995. The author surveys the whole issue, emphasizing the relationship between the quest for longevity and pseudo-Arnaldian alchemy. She appends a list, as exhaustive as possible, of alchemical texts invoking the authority of Arnald of Villanova (pp. 135–149); the bibliography from Latin manuscript 273 in the Vatican's Barberini collection (pp. 149–151); and transcriptions of the *Defloratio philosophorum,* the *Exempla* or *Liber prophetiarum* (Tractatus parabolicus), and the letter on blood (Epistola ad Jacobum de Toleto de distillatione sanguinis humani) (pp. 152–171).

Thorndike, Lynn. *A History of Magic and Experimental Science.* Vol. 3. New York: Columbia University Press, 1934. See pp. 52–84 and 654–676 for a list of works and manuscripts.

Antoine Calvet

ARNAU DE VILANOVA

SEE **Arnald of Villanova**.

ARRHENIUS, SVANTE AUGUST (*b.*

Vik, near Uppsala, Sweden, 19 February 1859; *d.* Stockholm, Sweden, 2 October 1927), *physical chemistry.* For the original article on Arrhenius see *DSB,* vol. 1.

There was no major biography of Arrhenius in English until the Swedish-born sociologist Elisabeth Crawford (1937–2004), née Tjerneld, published her widely acclaimed *Arrhenius: From Ionic Theory to the Greenhouse Effect* (1996). It remains the central authority on Arrhenius, although there has since emerged growing literature on many aspects of Arrhenius's career, in particular his theory of the greenhouse effect. In modern research Arrhenius has emerged as a more complicated personality than H. A. M. Snelders's original *DSB* entry suggests. As a young man Arrhenius worried about his career prospects, and he was personally hard pressed by his Uppsala colleagues and by their very modest assessment of his dissertation. European colleagues, in particular Wilhelm Ostwald and to some extent Jacobus Henricus van't Hoff, rescued his career. With time and success he himself created a countermyth, touted in interviews in the popular media, of his early undiscovered genius, of which the Nobel Prize (1903) served as the ultimate evidence.

Overview. Arrhenius's life was full of difficult decisions regarding where he actually belonged. He was understood in the German and Continental centers of science, but he wanted to pursue science in Sweden, where his repertoire was wider and his influence outside science deeper. At the same time he was ambivalent about Uppsala, which is why he was happy to be called to the Stockholm Högskola (not the Royal Institute of Technology) after his successful *Wanderjahre* in Germany, Riga (Ostwald), and Amsterdam (van't Hoff). In 1891 he started his teaching at the Högskola, became full professor in 1895 and rector for three consecutive terms. The Högskola was a private institution, free of the complicated regulations that marked the public universities, and he cherished that freedom of thought and action. It suited his personality, which was expansive and convivial, and he thrived under these favorable circumstances.

The position also suited his deep-rooted materialism, which was both scientific (commitment to atomism) and political. He had been at Uppsala during the radical 1880s, when some of his closest friends and colleagues became members of the newly founded Verdandi association. He embraced secession of Norway from the union with Sweden, and he had many Norwegian friends. Essentially an optimist, he believed in science's active contribution to industry and social progress; however, he held reservations with respect to Ostwald's monistic energeticism, which he found idealist and improbable.

Arrhenius's outlook was liberal and reformist, resulting in a degree of scepticism toward Uppsala, which he considered snobbish, introspective, and conservative. By contrast, he had a very favorable view of Stockholm, a much bigger city with many ties with industrial, commercial, and political circles, of which he would himself become part, particularly during his years as rector. He used his scientific position to promote industry and made calculations of Sweden's future energy resources. Reinforced by the Nobel Prizes and adorned with an increasing number of scientific societies, Stockholm was

Svante Arrhenius. © HULTON-DEUTSCH COLLECTION/CORBIS.

becoming a center of European science, and Arrhenius predicted that Uppsala would soon be outdistanced by the capital. He did what he could to spur that development by taking students and junior colleagues and building a European network. After his Nobel Prize his network even extended to the United States, where he did a comprehensive tour in 1904 and lectured on immunochemistry at Berkeley.

Research Style. Arrhenius's research style was as expansive as his personality and after his protracted controversies around the ionic theory he cast his net even wider. He was easily diverted by new inspirations or apparently random contacts or proposals. Much of this newer work was in cosmic physics, a field where already in 1903 he was able to publish a thousand-page *Lehrbuch der kosmischen Physik*. He was inspired by his Stockholm colleagues, including Otto Pettersson, Vilhelm Bjerknes, and numerous other scientists who contributed to the development of inventories of natural resources in northern Sweden, and also by a series of research expeditions to the Arctic. He was himself a member, as a hydrographer, of an expedition to Spitsbergen in 1896. In this way Arrhenius was presented with topics on which he could bring his own skills to bear and provide new scientific ideas. Some of these ideas, on volcanoes, physiology, serology, and a multitude of other interests, proved short-lived, and some proved marginal or even considered whimsical, such as his belief in the transportation of living spores (*panspermy*) from outer space to Earth.

Greenhouse Effect. The same was said for a long time about his theory of the greenhouse effect, which was revived in the second half of the twentieth century. Arrhenius's work on this problem in 1895–1896 was not driven by any attempt to understand global climatic warming, but rather the opposite, namely to understand the mechanisms behind ice ages, a central concern of Scandinavian geophysicists. The reception of Arrhenius's greenhouse paper was almost nil until 1938, when the British engineer Guy Stewart Callendar published a paper on human climate forcing, using the greenhouse connection as a point of departure. Callendar's ideas were also marginalized, and not until the 1970s did there emerge a common understanding that the greenhouse theory was of great significance. The latter career of Arrhenius's theory has been less about whether the theory is correct, and more about the size of the contribution of anthropogenic greenhouse gases on measured increases in global temperatures, which could be caused by other factors whose contributions are hard to determine.

Since the late 1980s Arrhenius has become more famous as the founding figure of an understanding of global warming than for the discovery of electrolytic dissociation, for which he was awarded the Nobel Prize in 1903. A common feature of the two theories, however, is that they have been surrounded by controversy, ionic theory during his lifetime, the greenhouse effect long after his death. Indeed, almost all important work that Arrhenius did, and some of his less important work as well, drew attention and controversy. He fell out with his erstwhile friend Walther Nernst and continued to contest Nernst's Nobel Prize, awarded 1920 and handed over in 1921, until that was no longer possible. He quarreled incessantly with the Frankfurt immunologist Paul Ehrlich, who was not able to follow Arrhenius's mathematical method and was more interested in therapy than in theory. That so many came to question and even to dislike Arrhenius had something to do with his easy moves between chemistry, biology, and physiology, always using the tools of physical chemistry. But on another level it was partly his fame and standing as a central figure in the expanding power centers of Stockholm that made him a local and national celebrity even before the Nobel Prize. He was a man who seemed to thrive in battle; it released his energies, it lent eloquence to his vitriolic polemics, and it provided him stamina for his fourteen-hour workdays over months and years.

Work was also a cure when human relations were a strain. Sofia Rudbeck, his first wife, started as a graduate student at the Högskola in 1892 and became his private assistant; they married in 1894. She left him the following year, revealing unusual independence and radical tendencies perhaps tinted by her emerging contacts with the theosophist movement—incompatible with the earthy materialism of her husband. The divorce was granted in July 1896. Sofia retained custody of their son, Olof Wilhelm, the divorce agreement stipulating that the father would not see his son until he was five. Briefly sustained by Alfred Nobel, Sofia endured financial hardships and later earned her living as a photographer.

Arrhenius was as popular as he was controversial. He easily made friends and kept them through his good spirits and a flood of letters. He ate and drank with the same gusto as he devoured any new topic that came his way. He was a storyteller and a witty and good-humored speaker. He also was adept at coining phrases and metaphors, sometimes at the cost of precision but with a significant effect on his career as an author of popular science, a genre he transformed. He has sometimes been disparaged as a scientist who did not like experiments. The opposite is true: He was an ardent and competent experimentalist, but he always put his ideas first, carrying out deeper investigations to test what started as intuition but could prove to be an important hypothesis.

SUPPLEMENTARY BIBLIOGRAPHY

Bensaude-Vincent, Bernadette. "Myths about a Polymath." *Nature* 384 (1996): 36–37. A review of Elisabeth Crawford's *Arrhenius: From Ionic Theory to the Greenhouse Effect*.

Crawford, Elisabeth. *Arrhenius: From Ionic Theory to the Greenhouse Effect*. Canton, MA: Science History, 1996.

Servos, John W. "A Scientific Venturer: *Arrhenius*, reviewed by J. W. Servos." *Science* 273 (1996): 1512–1513. A review of Elisabeth Crawford's *Arrhenius: From Ionic Theory to the Greenhouse Effect*.

Sörlin, Sverker. "Rituals and Resources of Natural History: The North and the Arctic in Swedish Scientific Nationalism." In *Narrating the Arctic: A Cultural History of Nordic Scientific Practices*, edited by Michael T. Bravo and Sverker Sörlin, 73–122. Canton, MA: Science History, 2002.

Weart, Spencer. *The Discovery of Global Warming*. Cambridge, MA: Harvard University Press, 2003.

Sverker Sörlin

ASSMANN, RICHARD (*b.* Magdeburg, Germany, 13 April 1845; *d.* Giessen, Germany, 28 May 1918), *medicine, meteorology, aerological measurements, discovery of the stratosphere.*

Assmann contributed significantly to the exploration of the free (high altitude) atmosphere and to observational techniques in meteorology between 1880 and 1910. He conducted human scientific ascents with balloons for about ten years and became one of the discoverers of the stratosphere in 1902. His cloud observations on mountaintops led to the clarification of the nature of cloud droplets. He invented the aspirated psychrometer, a radiation-shielded instrument to measure simultaneously the temperature and humidity of air. Following his suggestion, sounding balloons continued to be made from rubber in the early 2000s. The summit of his career was the 1905 inauguration of the meteorological observatory at Lindenberg, southeast of Berlin, whose first director he became.

From Medicine to Meteorology. Assmann was the first of three children of the leather maker and town councillor Adolph Assmann and Dorothea, née Burkhard. Having finished school in his native town, Assmann matriculated for medicine at the University of Breslau in 1865 and continued these studies in Berlin, interrupted by two years of military service. In 1869, he took his doctor's degree in medicine with a thesis titled Hemophilia. A year later he received his license to practice medicine and served as a sergeant first class and surgeon in the Prussian army in the Franco-Prussian War (1870–1871). Directly after the war he settled as a physician in the small town of Freienwalde on the river Oder. In 1871, he married Johanna Andrée, and six years later their only child was born. Here in his spare time he started to study meteorological phenomena and set up a small private observatory in the tower of a war memorial. The observatory was equipped with self-registering instruments built by Assmann. During this period he visited established meteorological offices including the Deutsche Seewarte (German Hydrographical Institute) in Hamburg, where he was introduced to the noted climatologist Wladimir Köppen, with whom he corresponded nearly his whole life.

In 1879, Assmann moved back to his native town of Magdeburg, hoping to become medical superintendent of the municipal hospital. Failing to receive this appointment, he happened to meet a former classmate, Alexander Faber, the owner and editor of the local newspaper *Magdeburgische Zeitung,* who wanted to establish a meteorological station in order to supply weather reports for his newspaper. Assmann agreed to become head of this station, which was situated in a 34-meter-high tower specially built for this purpose on the grounds of the newspaper print shop. The station opened on 1 November 1880 and issued its first daily weather map on 12 December, just a few days after the publication of the world's first newspaper weather map in London. Financial support provided by Faber enabled Assmann to leave the medical

practice and become a full-time meteorologist. In 1881, he founded the Society for Agricultural Meteorology in Magdeburg, which soon established a network of more than 250 observing stations in central Germany. In the following year he founded *Monatsschrift für praktische Witterungskunde* (Monthly Paper for Practical Meteorology). Renamed *Das Wetter* (The Weather) two years later, the journal turned into a publication for popular meteorology. The journal was intended to promote widespread interest in meteorology among people whose livelihood depended on the weather, including farmers, gardeners, and foresters. With this, Assmann hoped to increase the number of diligent weather observers. Assmann served as its chief editor until the end of his life. In 1904, he founded and thereafter edited together with Hugo Hergesell the scientific journal *Beiträge zur Physik der freien Atmosphäre* (Contributions to the Physics of the Free Atmosphere). In contrast to *Das Wetter,* the *Beiträge* was established to serve for the exchange of information among scientists working on the exploration of the free atmosphere (i.e., the upper troposphere and the stratosphere). It was devoted especially to the physical processes occurring in these atmospheric layers.

Cloud Physics and Aspirated Psychrometer. In November 1884, Assmann made investigations in cloud physics on top of the Brocken, the highest peak (1,141 meters) of the Harz Mountains in central Germany. Using a microscope he definitively settled the question of whether cloud particles are droplets or bubbles in favor of the first. In the following years he also investigated rime, hoarfrost, and snow crystals. In 1885, he earned an additional degree (*Habilitation*), this time from Halle University, by presenting a thesis on the thunderstorms in Central Germany. On 30 October of that year he gave his inaugural lecture at Halle as an unpaid university lecturer (*Privatdozent*).

In 1886, Assmann became a civil servant at the Prussian Royal Meteorological Institute in Grünau, near Berlin, and headed the department on thunderstorms and extraordinary phenomena. The director of this institute was Wilhelm von Bezold, who also was the first professor of meteorology at Berlin University beginning in 1885. Here Assmann made his famous instrumental invention: the aspirated psychrometer. Aiming to construct a thermometer that was not influenced by shortwave radiation from the sun, he suspended two mercury-in-glass thermometers in a chromium-plated, highly polished frame. The bulbs of the thermometers were surrounded by two coaxial metal tubes through which the air was drawn by means of a clockwork-driven fan at the top of the central hollow column. The bulb of one of the thermometers was covered by wet muslin. The evaporating moisture from the muslin kept this thermometer at a lower temperature than the other one. As evaporation increases in proportion to the

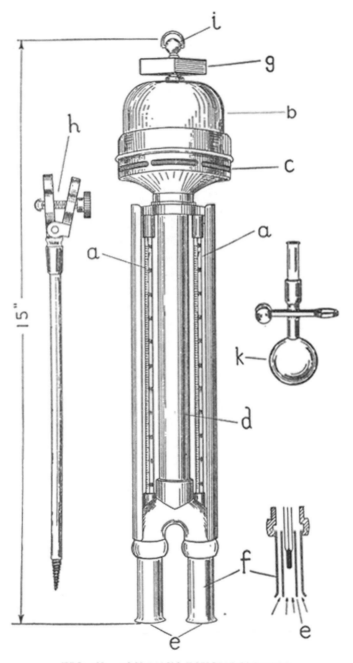

FIG. 62—ASSMANN PSYCHROMETER

a—Thermometers
b—Dome containing clockwork
c—Fan and air outlets
d—Main air duct
e—Air inlets
f—Polished tubes protecting thermometers

g—Key for winding clockwork
h—Clamp for supporting the instrument
i—Point of support of the instrument; the clamp holds the ball securely but allows the instrument to hang vertically
k—Injector for wetting muslin of wet bulb

The Assmann Psychrometer. *Drawing of the Assmann Psychrometer from the Handbook of Meteorological Instruments.* **CROWN COPYRIGHT (2007), DATA SUPPLIED BY THE MET OFFICE.**

dryness of the air, the temperature difference between the two thermometers could be converted into values for air humidity. The principle of Assmann's psychrometer is still used today, with platinum resistance thermometers substituting for the older mercury thermometers.

Aerology. In 1892, Assmann's department at the meteorological institute was expanded to include measuring devices. In 1886, he also joined the Deutscher Verein zur Förderung der Luftschiffahrt zu Berlin (German Association for the Advancement of Airship Aeronautics in Berlin), which had been founded in 1881. He took over the planning of balloon ascents for scientific purposes promoted by this association. Human scientific aviation began on 1 March 1893 with the ascent of the balloon *Humboldt* in the presence of the German emperor. During the following six years the association carried out sixty-five ascents. The balloons were filled with a mixture of hydrogen and methane and carried open baskets for the passengers. For higher ascents oxygen was available for the passengers through pipes from steel bottles. The instrumentation consisted of a mercury barometer, a hair hygrometer, Assmann's aspirated psychrometer, and a simple radiation measurement device (black bulb thermometer). Different observers conducted the ascents; the most frequent traveler was the meteorologist Reinhard Süring. During the forty-fourth ascent on 4 December 1894 the record height of 9,155 meters was reached by the balloon *Phönix* during a courageous solo voyage by Arthur Berson, Assmann's closest coworker. Assmann himself was on board during three ascents. In addition to the manned balloons Assmann also operated unmanned registration balloons, some of which reached heights well above 10,000 meters during their ten ascents. The aerological program was completed by twenty-one ascents of tethered balloons, two of them carrying human aeronauts.

Initially, balloon ascents were conducted from different places in and around Berlin. Following Assmann's strong suggestions, an aeronautical observatory was established in 1899 as a fourth department of the Meteorological Institute, with Assmann as head. The following year balloon operations were centralized on an army target range near Tegel, northwest of Berlin. Assmann promoted regular launches of instrumented kites and kite-balloons—means of meteorological observation equal or even superior to free-floating balloons. The results of these soundings were published daily in newspapers and, from 1903, in the official weather bulletin of the Deutsche Seewarte in Hamburg.

The Discovery of the Stratosphere. By 1894, several unmanned balloons carrying self-registering instruments had reached—as became obvious later—the stably strati-

fied air layer above the troposphere that is now named the stratosphere. Since no one had anticipated the existence of such a layer, Assmann had always been very cautious with respect to the temperature readings which indicated the presence of a so-called upper inversion. On 7 July 1894, the registering balloon *Cirrus* reached an isothermal layer, later called the tropopause. This ascent was one of ten made by Assmann between 1894 and 1897. Five ascents supplied readings from heights between 11.7 and 21.8 kilometers. The thermometer readings showed a cessation of the usual temperature decrease with height at about fifteen kilometers. Assmann, however, suspected that his instruments had been adversely affected by radiation. His doubts were finally removed by the measurements made during a balloon ascent up to 10.5 kilometers conducted by Arthur Berson and Reinhard Süring on 31 July 1901. The results confirmed the readings of the unmanned balloon missions. From 1896 on, similar registration balloon ascents were organized by the French meteorologist Teisserenc de Bort in Trappes near Versailles. In 1902, both scientists, who were friends and had long exchanged scientific results, made public their results nearly simultaneously and made their common, though independent, discoveries public. Teisserenc de Bort spoke to the Paris Academy of Science on 28 April and Assmann to the Berlin Academy of Science on 1 May.

The most important contribution by Assmann to high altitude exploration was the introduction of the closed balloon of india rubber in place of the open-mouthed balloon of varnished paper, that Teisserenc de Bort had employed. Rigid paper balloons lost their lifting force with increasing height, while elastic rubber balloons expanded with increasing height and decreasing pressure and thus guaranteed a more or less constant lifting force, upward velocity, and—very important—a constant ventilation of the meteorological instruments. The introduction of rubber balloons made possible ascents to over 20 kilometers. When a balloon burst and fell to the ground, the instrument registers could be evaluated if the balloon was recovered. From 1900 to 1913, a total of 317 rubber balloons were launched under the guidance of Assmann, of which only 16 could not be recovered.

In 1908 (most probably at the 29 September meeting of the German Meteorological Society in Hamburg), Teisserenc de Bort coined the terms *troposphere* and *stratosphere*. The intermediate layer, the *tropopause,* was named in 1926 by the English meteorologist Sir William Napier Shaw in his *Manual of Meteorology.* Shaw called the identification of the tropopause and the stratosphere the "most surprising discovery in the whole history of meteorology."

The Aeronautical Observatory at Lindenberg. The aeronautical observatory in Tegel proved to be too close to the expanding city of Berlin. Occasionally, broken ropes from failed kite ascents fell on electric and telephone lines and on the cables of the streetcar lines that extended into the outskirts of Berlin. By 1902, the army gave notice that the observatory in Tegel would be closed. A more suitable location for the observatory was found about one hundred kilometers southeast of Berlin on a little hill near the village of Lindenberg. New buildings were erected, and on 16 October 1905, the observatory was inaugurated by the Prussian king and German emperor Wilhelm II. The ceremony was also attended by Prince Albert I of Monaco, who had made his yacht available for balloon ascents to explore the free atmosphere over the sea and who took part in the data evaluation. Assmann's work was deemed important enough that the observatory became an independent scientific institution instead of part of the Prussian Meteorological Institute.

The observatory conducted systematic monitoring of the vertical distribution of wind, temperature, and humidity in the free atmosphere. Such information was necessary—apart from scientific needs—for the rapidly evolving field of aeronautics. In the first thirty years of the observatory, more than 25,000 vertical soundings of the troposphere and the lower stratosphere were performed with specially designed instruments. In 1910, based on the experience from such measurements, Assmann wrote a memorandum, "On the establishment of an aeronautical weather service relying on aerological observations," in which he proposed a network of pilot balloon stations for Germany and an alert service for aeronauts. This network, organized by Assmann and having its central office in Lindenberg, started its operations in 1911 with twenty-five pilot balloon stations and six hundred thunderstorm reporting points at post and telegraph offices.

On 1 October 1914, Assmann retired and was succeeded by Hugo Hergesell, the former president of the International Commission for Scientific Aeronautics (founded 1896) and professor in Strassburg since 1900. The observatory continue to exist in the early 2000s, one of two remaining observatories of the German Weather Service, still devoted to the monitoring of vertical profiles of atmospheric parameters. That the observatory kept its tasks nearly unchanged for over a century demonstrates the essential soundness of Assmann's scientific vision. After retirement, Assmann moved to Giessen and lectured at the university there. In 1915, he published a book on the Royal Prussian Aeronautical Observatory Lindenberg, in which he summarized his scientific achievements. He died in Giessen sixteen months after his wife.

Awards. In 1903, Assmann, together with Berson, was awarded the second Buys-Ballot medal by the Royal Netherlands Academy of Arts and Sciences. This prize is given once every ten years to the scientist who has made outstanding contributions to the development of meteorology. On 16 October 2005, during the centennial ceremony, the name of the Meteorological Observatory in Lindenberg was supplemented by the term "Richard Assmann Observatory."

BIBLIOGRAPHY

Personal notes on Richard Assmann's life written by his daughter, Helene Assmann, are kept in the private ownership of the Assmann family. A large collection of letters written between Assmann and Wladimir Köppen from 1882 to 1914 is in the archives of the University Library in Graz, Austria.

WORKS BY ASSMANN

"Mikroskopische Beobachtung der Wolken-Elemente auf dem Brocken." *Meteorologische Zeitschrift* 2 (1885): 41–47. On the nature of cloud droplets.

"Eine neue Methode zur Ermittlung der wahren Lufttemperatur." *Sitzungsberichte der Königlich Preussischen Akademie der Wissenschaften zu Berlin* 46 (1887): 505–515. First publication on the invention of the aspired psychrometer.

Das Aspirations-Psychrometer: Ein Apparat zur Bestimmung der wahren Temperatur und Feuchtigkeit der Luft. Abhandlungen des Preussischen Meteorologischen Instituts Vol. 1, No. 5, 117–270. Berlin: A. Ascher, 1892. Complete description of Assmann's aspiration psychrometer.

With Arthur Joseph Stanislaus Berson. *Wissenschaftliche Luftfahrten.* 3 vols. Braunschweig: F. Vieweg und Sohn, 1899–1900. Covers the scientific balloon ascents between 1893 and 1899.

"Über die Existenz eines wärmeren Luftstromes in der Höhe von 10 bis 15 km." *Sitzungsberichte der Königlich Preussischen Akademie der Wissenschaften zu Berlin* 24 (1902): 495–504. Minutes of the session at the Berlin Academy of Sciences in which Assmann reported on the discovery of the stratosphere.

Das Königlich Preussische Aeronautische Observatorium Lindenberg. Braunschweig: Vieweg, 1915.

OTHER SOURCES

Bernhardt, Karl-Heinz. "Zur Erforschung der Atmosphäre mit dem Freiballon—die Berliner wissenschaftlichen Luftfahrten (1888–1899)." *Dahlemer Archivgespräche* 6 (2000): 52–82. Overview of scientific balloon ascents in Berlin from 1888 to 1899.

Hoinka, Klaus P. "The Tropopause: Discovery, Definition, and Demarcation." *Meteorologische Zeitschrift* 6, n.s., (1997): 281–303. Extensive discussion of the role of Teisserenc de Bort and Assmann in the discovery of the stratosphere.

Labitzke, Karin G., and Harry van Loon. *The Stratosphere: Phenomena, History, and Relevance.* Berlin: Springer-Verlag, 1999. First chapter on the history of the discovery of the stratosphere.

Peppler, A. "Richard Assmann." *Das Wetter* 35 (1918): 70–79. Obituary giving a detailed portrayal of his life, in the popular magazine he edited.

Steinhagen, Hans. *Der Wettermann.* Neuenhagen: Findling Verlag, 2005. An extensive biography of Assmann, partly based on letters written by Assmann to Wladimir Köppen between 1882 and 1913. The book was written on the occasion of the centennial of the Lindenberg observatory.

Stefan Emeis

AXELROD, JULIUS (*b.* New York, New York, 30 May 1912, *d.* Bethesda, Maryland, 29 December 2004), *pharmacology, neurochemistry neurotransmitters, metabolism.*

Axelrod made fundamental contributions to understanding the mechanisms of chemical neurotransmission and drug metabolism. His discoveries contributed directly to the design of drugs to treat psychiatric disorders, to control physiological systems, and to relieve pain. He won the Nobel Prize for Physiology or Medicine in 1970 for his work on the reuptake and deactivation of neurotransmitters such as norepinephrine and serotonin.

Early Education and Training. Julius ("Julie") Axelrod was born and raised in a poor Jewish neighborhood on the Lower East Side of Manhattan. His parents, Isadore and Molly, immigrated to the United States from Poland. His father was a basket maker, and his mother worked in the home. Neither was functionally literate in English.

Upon graduation from Seward Park High School, Axelrod studied at New York University (NYU). He exhausted his family's savings after one year and transferred to the tuition-free College of the City of New York. His grades in chemistry were poor, especially in qualitative analysis, the area in which he would later build his reputation. He graduated in 1933, at the height of the Great Depression, with a BS in biology. In the same year, he lost sight in his left eye in a laboratory accident. As a result, he was deferred from the World War II draft and was free to pursue his dream of becoming a doctor.

Axelrod's applications to medical school were rejected, however, and he was hired as a laboratory technician at the Harriman Research Institute at NYU. He worked for K. G. Falk, preparing buffer solutions and assisting with research on enzymes in malignant tumors. When funding for the laboratory ran out in 1935, Axelrod turned down work with the U.S. Postal Service for a less lucrative position working for George B. Wallace, a retired pharmacology professor, in the Laboratory of Industrial Hygiene at the New York City Department of Health. Axelrod's job was to assay the levels of vitamins in fortified food products. He had to learn the available techniques for measuring vitamins and to modify them for application to food products. This work gave him early experience as an experimentalist. The lab also exposed him to the *Journal of Biological Chemistry*.

While working with Wallace, Axelrod married Sally Taub, who had a degree in chemistry from Hunter College. With the birth of their sons Paul (1946) and Alfred (1949), Taub quit her job in an insurance agency to work in the home. She later earned a teaching certificate from the University of Maryland and became an elementary school teacher. Until 1949, Axelrod and his family lived within blocks of his parents and his two sisters (Gertrude and Pearl) in Brooklyn, New York.

During this period Axelrod studied chemistry in postgraduate night courses at NYU. He wrote a thesis, "The Ester-Hydrolyzing Actions of the Tissues of Polyneuritic, Normal, 'Cured,' and Thiamin-Fed Rats." Rats deprived of thiamin (vitamin B1) develop polyneuritis, a general swelling of nerve tissues, which is one of the symptoms of beriberi. As part of an investigation of the mechanism producing this symptom, Axelrod ground the organs of rats, exposed them to different kinds of esters (an organic compound), and measured the ability of these tissues to hydrolyze the esters. For this research, he received his Master's of Science degree in chemistry in 1942. He continued to work with Wallace until he was thirty-four years old.

Bernard Brodie and Non-Aspirin Pain-Relievers. In 1946, Wallace gave Axelrod a funded project to determine why protracted use of non-aspirin pain relievers (such as acetanilide, an ingredient in the then-popular pain reliever Bromoseltzer) produce an abundance of methemoglobin, the oxidized form of hemoglobin, which fails to bind oxygen. Bernard B. Brodie, a pharmacologist, invited Axelrod to perform these studies at Goldwater Memorial Hospital (Welfare Island, later Roosevelt Island, New York). Brodie was part of a research group, headed by James A. Shannon, that was charged in part with running clinical trials on anti-malarial vaccines during the Japanese embargo on quinine during World War II. Shannon recruited a number of gifted scientists for this purpose, including Robert Berliner, Robert Bowman, Thomas Kennedy, and Sidney Udenfriend, all of whom made significant contributions to biochemistry. As Axelrod later wrote, "It was in this atmosphere that, in a period of a few years, I became a researcher" (1988, p. 4).

Brodie taught Axelrod that the body metabolizes drugs and that metabolites can have both beneficial and harmful consequences. It was known at the time that the acetanilide in Bromoseltzer can be metabolized into

N-acetyl-p-aminophenol and analine, and it was known that analine can produce methemoglobin. It was not known whether acetanilide metabolizes into analine in the human body. Axelrod developed a sensitive assay for analine levels in blood and urine. He and Brodie showed that analine levels rise after doses of acetanilide and that analine and methemoglobin levels are correlated. This finding led them to suggest that N-acetyl-p-aminophenol, later commonly known as acetaminophen, could replace acetanilide as a pain reliever without this potentially deadly side effect (Brodie and Axelrod, 1948). Amid worries in the 1970s that aspirin causes gastric ulcers, acetaminophen (marketed as Tylenol) became, and remained in the early 2000s, one of the best-selling pain relievers in history.

Metabolism of the Sympathomimetic Amines. In 1949, Shannon was appointed director of intramural research at the National Heart Institute (NHI), part of the National Institutes of Health (NIH) in Bethesda, Maryland. Axelrod, Brodie, and many of the other Goldwater scientists soon followed. Initially, Axelrod worked with Brodie in the Laboratory of Chemical Pharmacology, investigating analgesics and the effects of ascorbic acid (vitamin C) on drug metabolism. Again, Axelrod found himself in a stimulating environment: "Among the scientists working in Building 3 in the 1950's, more than half became members of the National Academy of Science, five became Nobel laureates, and three were appointed directors of NIH" (2003, p. 3).

By 1952, Axelrod was doing independent research in Brodie's lab. His first project was to describe the metabolism of caffeine. This work soon broadened to include the metabolism of a class of drugs that George Barker and Henry Hallett Dale named the "sympathomimetic" amines. These drugs, which include amphetamine, ephedrine, and methamphetamine, produce effects similar to the activation of the sympathetic nervous system. The sympathetic nervous system can be activated to produce a set of coordinated responses that enable the body to deal with stresses and threats. For example, activation of the sympathetic nervous system increases blood pressure and heart rate, accelerates breathing, constricts the arteries, and dilates the pupils. Axelrod found that the sympathomimetic amines are metabolized by a variety of pathways, including conjugation (by joining with other molecules), deamination (the removal of an amino group, NH_2), and hydroxylation (the addition of a radical hydroxyl group, OH). He also showed that the precise metabolic pathways vary across species (1953; 1954a).

Axelrod's work on the sympathomimetic amines led him to discover and localize a new class of liver enzymes. To study amine metabolism *in vitro*, Axelrod exposed liv-

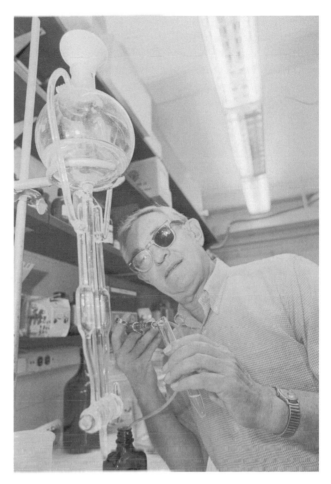

Julius Axelrod. *Julius Axelrod in the laboratory.*
© BETTMANN/CORBIS.

ers from different species to sympathomimetic amines, measured the rate at which the drugs are metabolized, determined the metabolic end products, and inferred the pathways by which those end products are produced. His study of amphetamine metabolism was the centerpiece of this project (1954b; 1955a). When Axelrod applied amphetamine to sliced or homogenized rabbit liver, the drug was rapidly metabolized. He found that he could speed up the metabolism by adding triphosphopyridine nucleotide (TPN, later known as NADP, for nicotinamide adenine dinucleotide phosphate), which was already known to be a coenzyme in many biochemical pathways. Axelrod concluded that the metabolic pathway involves TPN as a coenzyme.

To determine which parts of liver cells metabolize the amphetamine, he centrifuged the cells, separating them into different cell fractions containing different cellular components. He then applied amphetamine and TPN to the different cell fractions. None of them metabolized the drug by itself. When he added amphetamine and TPN to a mixture of the cytosolic fraction (the intracellular fluid) and the fraction containing microsomes, the drug rapidly disappeared, leaving ammonia and phenylacetone as end products. This reaction led him to conclude that in rabbit liver, amphetamine is deaminated by an oxidative enzyme that uses TPN as a coenzyme.

Axelrod did not know whether the necessary enzyme was in the cytosol or in the microsomes. To decide, he heated the cell fractions to denature the heat-labile enzymes. When he heated the cytosolic fraction to 55°C and then added unheated microsomes, amphetamine, and TPN, the amphetamine was metabolized. When he heated the microsomal fraction to 55°C and added unheated cytosol, amphetamine, and TPN, the amphetamine was not metabolized. The crucial enzyme, he concluded, was in the microsomes, but the cytosol must contain a necessary coenzyme; amphetamine is not metabolized by the microsomal fraction and TPN alone.

To identify the coenzyme, Axelrod exposed the microsomal fraction to amphetamine, TPN, and to three different substrates (glucose 6-phosphate, isocitric acid, and phosphogluconate). The single quality that these substrates have in common is that they all reduce TPN to TPNH (or reduced TPN, later known as NADPH). The amphetamine disappeared. Perhaps, then, the coenzyme in the cytosol is necessary to reduce TPN to TPNH. When he added TPNH to the microsomal fraction alone in the presence of oxygen, the amphetamine was again metabolized, convincing Axelrod that he had discovered an enzyme in rabbit liver that deaminates amphetamine in the presence of oxygen and TPNH. The structure of amphetamine, and the necessity of TPNH for its metabolism, suggested that this was a new kind of enzyme. Similar enzymes were subsequently discovered for the metabolism of ephedrine and other drugs as well. These findings amounted to the discovery of a new class of liver enzymes, later known as cytochrome P450 enzymes. These enzymes, which are found in all lineages of life, metabolize most organic chemicals (such as bilirubin) and many drugs and pollutants. They are also involved in the synthesis, activation, and inactivation of a number of regulatory molecules.

Axelrod's Conversion to Neurochemistry. The work on sympathomimetic amines gave rise to an authorship dispute between Axelrod and Brodie, and Axelrod left Brodie's lab. Despite his already substantial contributions to science and his post as a senior chemist at NIH, Axelrod recognized that his chances for advancement were limited without a PhD. He took a leave of absence to do graduate work at George Washington University. His advisor, pharmacologist George Mandel, arranged for him to submit some of his work on the sympathomimetic

amines as a dissertation, "The Fate of Sympathomimetic Phenylisopropylamines." In 1955, at the age of forty-two, Axelrod earned his PhD.

While Axelrod was working on his dissertation, Seymour Kety, scientific director of the joint intramural program of the National Institute of Mental Health (NIMH; established 1949), and Edward Evarts, director of the Laboratory of Clinical Sciences, invited Axelrod to set up a section in their laboratory. Kety became head of that laboratory in 1956. The explicit mission of the NIMH was to integrate basic and clinical research on psychiatric disorders. Although Kety allowed Axelrod considerable intellectual freedom, Axelrod felt obliged to do work relevant to mental health. His first project was to characterize the distribution and metabolism of lysergic acid diethylamide (LSD), an experimental psychiatric drug that would become widely used as a recreational drug (Axelrod et al., 1956). Axelrod did not take this drug himself.

Methyl Transferase Enzymes. Early in 1957, Axelrod attended a seminar in which Kety recounted evidence that epinephrine, a neurotransmitter and hormone (also known as adrenalin) is rapidly converted to adrenochrome when it is exposed to air. Kety also reported that ingestion of adrenochrome produces hallucinations like those experienced by people with schizophrenia, which suggested that schizophrenia might result from abnormal metabolism of epinephrine. Axelrod decided to study the metabolism of epinephrine and norepinephrine (also known as noradrenalin), using the same tools he had used to study other sympathomimetic amines.

At the time, it was widely believed that epinephrine and other catecholamines are metabolized in the body by the enzyme monoamine oxidase (MAO). This hypothesis conflicted with the fact that pharmacological inhibitors of MAO have no effect on the rapid recovery of the sympathetic nervous system from the effects of an injection of epinephrine. Axelrod surmised that a different enzyme was implicated. In March 1957, the biochemist Marvin Armstrong and Armand McMillan reported that patients with norepinephrine-producing tumors excrete large quantities of 3-methoxy-4-hydroxymandelic acid (VMA), a product that could be produced by the O-methylation (the addition of a methyl group, CH_3) and deamination of epinephrine and norepinephrine. Guessing that the donor of the methyl group in the methylation reaction might be S-adenosylmethionine, Axelrod added S-adenosylmethionine and epinephrine to a rat liver homogenate. He observed that the epinephrine was rapidly metabolized and that the product was an O-methylated form of adrenaline (which he called metanephrine), indicating the presence of an O-methylating enzyme. Axelrod purified this enzyme and then demonstrated that it could O-methylate catechols but could not O-methylate monophenols. The enzyme, which he named catechol-O-methyltransferase (COMT), was soon found to be ubiquitous in the brain. (Axelrod and Tomchick, 1958). The discovery of this enzyme furthered the understanding of catecholamine metabolism, led to the development of drugs to inhibit COMT in the treatment of Parkinson's disease with L-dopa, and led to the development of new biological markers in biopharmacological studies. Axelrod later wrote, "As a result of these findings, I then considered myself a neurochemist" (1988, p. 13).

Regulation of Neurotransmitters at Synapses. Between 1958 and 1961, Axelrod carried out the experiments on the inactivation of neurotransmitters that earned him the Nobel Prize. His work focused on the inactivation of epinephrine and norepinephrine at synapses in the sympathetic nervous system. At the time it was known that acetylcholine, the neurotransmitter at the neuromuscular junction, is inactivated when it is rapidly metabolized by the enzyme acetylcholinesterase. Many suspected that all neurotransmitters are deactivated through enzymatic transformation.

Two preliminary findings set the stage for Axelrod's discoveries. First, Axelrod showed that inhibitors of COMT did not prolong the effects of norepinephrine on blood pressure, suggesting that something else must be responsible for its inactivation at sympathetic synapses. Second, Kety commissioned the New England Nuclear Corporation to manufacture tritiated epinephrine (epinephrine labeled with tritium, or [3H]epinephrine) and norepinephrine ([3H]norepinephrine). He used these to show that schizophrenics do not metabolize catecholamines differently from controls.

Axelrod borrowed the tritiated epinephrine and norepinephrine from Kety and developed sensitive methods for measuring their concentrations in tissues and blood. When he injected cats with large doses epinephrine or norepinephrine, he found that the drugs failed to cross the blood-brain barrier (which prevents some substances from entering the brain's circulatory system) and that they tended to concentrate in organs richly innervated by the sympathetic nervous system (such as the heart and the salivary glands). This result suggested to Axelrod that epinephrine and norepinephrine might be taken up by sympathetic nerves. To test this hypothesis, he and Georg Hertting (a visitor in the laboratory) made unilateral lesions to the superior cervical ganglia of cats, causing the nerves innervating the eyes and the salivary glands to die. They then injected the cats with [3H]norepinephrine. They found that the radiolabeled neurotransmitter concentrated on the intact (innervated) side and not on the lesioned side (Hertting et al., 1961a), that it is released

from nerves when they are stimulated (Hertting and Axelrod, 1961), and that drugs such as cocaine block its reuptake (Hertting et al., 1961b). Research quickly revealed that other transmitters, such as dopamine and serotonin, are also taken up into nerve terminals and that their use could also be regulated with drugs.

Axelrod's work on the synthesis, metabolism, and regulation of drugs and neurotransmitters provided lasting insights into the mechanisms of the chemical synapse. These insights had direct implications for the use of drugs to change the activities of the central and peripheral nervous systems. By the end of the millennium, drugs that inhibit serotonin reuptake, such as fluoxetine (brand name, Prozac), were widely used to treat depression. Axelrod predicted that in the new millennium, drugs would be available to cure mental illness, eliminate prejudice, enhance intelligence, suppress unwanted memories, and make all psychedelic trips pleasant. Asked if Freud was "dead," he replied, "Not for people who want to spend their money on psychoanalysis, but for the treatment of severe mental illness, yes, he is."

Melatonin and the Pineal Gland. A final major component of Axelrod's career as a neurochemist involved work on the synthesis of melatonin (5-methoxy-N-acetyltryptamine) and its regulation in the pineal gland in accordance with circadian rhythms. In 1958, Aaron Lerner isolated melatonin from the pineal gland of cows. Axelrod was attracted to melatonin because it has a methoxy group, as do many other catecholamine metabolites, and because it has a nucleus that resembles serotonin, which is structurally similar to LSD and was then believed to be involved in psychosis.

In 1958 and 1959, Axelrod and the biochemist Herbert Weissbach used radiolabeled enzymes to establish that melatonin is synthesized in the pineal gland from tryptophan and serotonin. The synthesis required the essential enzyme hydroxyindole-O-methyltransferase (HIOMT), which was soon found to be highly localized to the pineal gland in mammals.

When Richard J. Wurtman joined Axelrod's laboratory in 1962, he reawakened Axelrod's interest in the pineal. Wurtman had shown that rats in constant illumination enter a persistent state of estrus (commonly known as heat) and that this state can be reversed with injections of bovine pineal extract. Axelrod surmised that environmental lighting (that is, the light/dark cycle) might control HIOMT activity. In 1963, he and Wurtman found that rats raised in constant light have reduced HIOMT activity in the pineal gland relative to those raised in constant dark. Given that injections of melatonin also prevent the effects of light on the estrus cycle, Axelrod concluded that the effect of illumination on estrus is mediated by the pathway for the synthesis of melatonin. Knowing that norepinephrine-containing sympathetic nerves innervate the pineal gland, Axelrod and his colleagues killed these nerves by removing the superior cervical ganglia. The effect of light on HIOMT activity (and so melatonin synthesis) was eliminated.

In 1963, W. B. Quay showed that serotonin and melatonin levels have regular daily fluctuations; they are high during daylight and low at night. Axelrod and his postdoctoral fellow, Solomon H. Snyder, found that the circadian rhythm in serotonin and melatonin persisted even when animals were placed in continuous darkness; there is an internal clock (Axelrod, Wurtman, and Snyder, 1965). Constant illumination, however, abolished the serotonin rhythm, as did destroying the nerves that connect the brain to the superior cervical ganglia. This result indicated that the internal clock is in the brain. Subsequent work identified regions in the hypothalamus (particularly, the suprachiasmatic nucleus) as plausible locations for the biological clock. Axelrod developed a theoretical perspective according to which the pineal gland is a transducer of information about the day/light cycle into hormonal signals for the control of bodily functions.

Nobel Prize and Axelrod's Political Turn. Axelrod shared the 1970 Nobel Prize with Bernard Katz and Ulf von Euler for "fundamental research into the nature of the chemical neurotransmission process." He recognized that this award gave him political clout, and he used it to promote several causes. Axelrod repeatedly made and joined public statements against governmental attempts to target biomedical research funding to specific large-scale projects, such as finding a cure for cancer. In this domain, and in his laboratory, Axelrod stressed the importance of knowing what problems can and cannot be solved with the tools available at the time. He also stressed the importance of intellectual freedom in the development of science as a whole and in the development of individual scientific careers.

Although he became an atheist early in life and resented the strict upbringing of his parents' religion, he identified with Jewish culture and joined several international fights against anti-Semitism. Alexandr Solzhenitsyn won the Nobel Prize for Literature in the same year that Axelrod won his own, but Solzhenitsyn was not allowed to attend the ceremony. After returning home, Axelrod repeatedly called on the Soviet Union to free such Jewish scholars as Benjamin G. Levich, Ilye Glezer, and Andrei D. Sakharov, who were imprisoned and had been refused the right of emigration and/or imprisoned on grounds that Axelrod and many others believed to be based in an anti-Semitic Soviet policy. (These Soviet scientists came to be known as "Refuseniks.")

Axelrod also fought political battles on behalf of Israel. In 1975, he joined an international group of scientists who threatened to resign from the International Brain Research Organization, which is affiliated with UNESCO, until UNESCO resolutions banning Israeli participation in the organization were lifted. In 1979, he was among those who advocated pulling the United States out of the World Health Organization (WHO) if the WHO failed to allow Israel a vote in its decision-making process.

Learning of these pursuits, however, should not cause one to lose sight of the fact that Axelrod was first and foremost a researcher who believed that long hours of free inquiry using the right tools with the right colleagues can result in fundamental discoveries that have the power to shape the future of humankind. Although he officially retired in 1984, he continued to work in a small lab at NIMH until he died of a heart attack in his home in Rockville, Maryland, in 2004.

BIBLIOGRAPHY

Many of Axelrod's papers are available online at Profiles in Science *at the national Library of Medicine http://profiles. nlm.nih.gov/HH/. The Julius Axelrod Papers (1910–2004) are housed at the National Library of Medicine.*

WORKS BY AXELROD

With Bernard B. Brodie. "The Fate of Acetanilide in Man." *Journal of Pharmacology and Experimental Therapeutics* 94 (1948): 29–38.

"Studies on Sympathomimetic Amines. I. The Biotransformation and Physiological Disposition of l-ephedrine and l-norephedrine." *Journal of Pharmacology and Experimental Therapeutics* 109 (1953): 62–73.

"An Enzyme for the Deamination of Sympathomimetic Amines." *Journal of Pharmacology and Experimental Therapeutics* 110 (1954a): 2.

"Studies on Sympathomimetic Amines. II. The Biotransformation and Physiological Disposition of d-amphetamine and d-methamphetamine." *Journal of Pharmacology and Experimental Therapeutics* 110 (1954b): 62–73.

"The Enzymatic Deamination of Amphetamine (Benzedrine)." *The Journal of Biological Chemistry* 214 (1955): 753–763.

"The Enzymatic N-demethylation of Narcotic Drugs." *Journal of Pharmacology and Experimental Therapeutics* 117 (1956): 322–330.

With Robert Tomchick. "Enzymatic O-methylation of Epinephrine and Other Catechols." *Journal of Biological Chemistry* 233 (1958): 702–705.

With Georg Hertting, Irwin Kopin, and L. G. Whitby. "Lack of Uptake of Catecholamines after Chronic Denervation of Sympathetic Nerves." *Nature* 189 (1961): 66–68.

With Georg Hertting. "The Fate of Tritiated Noradrenalin at the Sympathetic Nerve Ending." *Nature* 192 (1961): 172–173.

With Georg Hertting and L. Gordon Whitby. "Effect of Drugs on the Uptake and Metabolism of ³H-norepinephrine." *Journal of Pharmacology and Experimental Therapeutics* 134 (1961): 146–153.

With Richard J. Wurtman and Solomon H. Snyder. "Control of Hydroxyindole O-methyltransferase Activity in the Rat Pineal Gland by Environmental Lighting." *Journal of Biological Chemistry* 240 (1965): 949–954.

"An Unexpected Life in Research." *Annual Reviews of Pharmacology* 28 (1988):1–23. Axelrod's career review.

"Journey of a Late Blooming Biochemical Neuroscientist." *Journal of Biological Chemistry* 278 (2003): 1–13. Axelrod's career review, emphasizing neurochemistry.

OTHER SOURCES

Kanigel, Robert. *Apprentice to Genius: The Making of a Scientific Dynasty.* Baltimore, MD: Johns Hopkins University Press, 1981. Depicts Axelrod as student and mentor.

Carl F. Craver

B

BABBAGE, CHARLES (*b.* Walworth, Surrey, England, 26 December 1791; *d.* London, England, 18 October 1871), *mathematics, computing, statistics, economics, philosophy of science.* For the original article on Babbage see *DSB*, vol. 1.

Babbage is generally remembered as the nineteenth-century prophet of the modern computer. He was a mathematician who designed two distinct types of mechanical computing devices that were rediscovered in the late 1930s, a time when American and European engineers were building electronic computing machines. Since that period, the story of Babbage served as a starting point for the computer age, the distant founder of a modern discipline. Many a discussion of the field began with a brief treatment of Babbage's computing engines. The London Science Museum constructed one of his computing machines from the original plans in order to demonstrate the validity of Babbage's ideas.

After the first major biography of Babbage appeared in 1982, scholars developed a broader understanding of Babbage that places his computing machines in the context of his other scientific work. Babbage explored a number of fields, including geology, chemistry, economics, electricity, actuarial mathematics, astronomy, statistics, and mechanical engineering. In probing these different areas, he developed three basic themes that served as his foundation stones for the practice of science. The first was the importance of analysis, the dissection of ideas into their fundamental components. The second was the value of symbolism, the tool for recording and manipulating ideas. The last is need for well, democratic institutions to support scientific research. These themes are best seen in his efforts to reform the English scientific community and his writings on industrial management but they are also found in his work on computing machines.

Education and Early Career. Babbage was born into a middle-class family with rising fortunes. His father was a London banker, who made enough money to be able to purchase an estate in the country. Though he was educated at minor regional schools, Babbage was prepared for the Cambridge University entrance exam by a scholar from Oxford. In this preparatory work Babbage demonstrated a substantial skill in mathematics and a firm interest in the mathematical writings of continental mathematicians represented by Leonhard Euler, Joseph-Louis Lagrange, and Pierre-Simon Laplace, a group that was often identified as the "analytical school."

Babbage entered Trinity College, Cambridge, in the fall of 1810. His first months at college were awkward as he struggled to find a place among the aristocratic students who had studied at England's public schools. He shunned the ordinary course of study at Cambridge, which was focused on the mathematical ideas of Isaac Newton, and spent hours studying the analytical mathematicians. In the spring of 1812 he fell into a group of like-minded students and formed an organization known as the Analytical Society. The leader of this group was John Herschel, son of the astronomer William Herschel. For the rest of Babbage's life Herschel would be his best friend and closest confidant.

Over the next eighteen months Babbage and Herschel prepared a small volume of mathematical papers called the *Memoirs of the Analytical Society* (1813). After

The first computer. *A section of the "Difference Engine," the first computer, designed by Charles Babbage.* **AP IMAGES.**

Herschel graduated from college in May 1813, Babbage turned his attention from mathematics to chemistry. He created a small laboratory in his college rooms and started a program of experiments. Most of these experiments consisted of subjecting different substances to extremely high temperatures. His study was guided by England's premier chemist of the time, Smithson Tennant, who had just taken an appointment at Cambridge. Babbage's interest in the subject faded when his time at college came to an end, but he would later write that "I have never regretted the time I bestowed upon [chemistry] at the commencement of my career" (1864, p. 27).

In June 1814 Babbage left Cambridge with a bachelor's degree, married Georgiana Whitmore, and moved to London. For the next seven years he returned to mathematical work and published more than a dozen papers. Though he is usually associated with the traditional ideas of calculus—the analysis of motions and forces—Babbage actually devoted most of his energies to a branch of algebra called the calculus of functions. This branch looks at broad classes of mathematical functions and tries to determine the properties of those functions.

During his time in London, Babbage became interested in geology and astronomy. He also traveled to France in search of scientific books. While in Paris he was likely introduced to the work of Gaspard de Prony, who had completed a large set of logarithm and trigonometry tables. De Prony had been able to divide the labor of computing these tables among ninety assistants. This work impressed Babbage, and he would draw upon it when he returned to England.

The Difference Engine. In 1820 he became a founding member of the Astronomical Society, a group of businessmen who were interested in revising the *Royal Nautical Almanac,* the annual volume that was used by navigators and surveyors. This book gave lengthy tables that showed the positions of the heavenly bodies on every night of the year. It needed to be prepared years in advance and required a substantial amount of calculation.

In preparing some ancillary tables for the *Almanac,* Babbage conceived of a machine that might assist with the calculation. The machine would calculate polynomial interpolations; it would draw curves through points on a graph. Babbage called this machine the Difference Engine, because it used the method of finite differences to compute the interpolations. For this idea he received a gold medal from the Astronomical Society and a grant of funds from the British government to complete the machine.

Though Babbage was quickly able to complete a prototype of his Difference Engine, he found that the full machine was considerably more complicated than he had anticipated. He spent seven years refining the design and developing new machining techniques. During this time he visited different English companies in order to learn how they engineered complicated machinery. He also became engaged in other activities. He became interested, for a time, in the new insurance industry. He wrote a treatise on the construction of mathematical tables. He experimented with electricity. He wrote papers on machinery and mechanical engineering. And he lobbied for an academic appointment at the new University of London.

In 1827 Babbage was confronted, in less than six months' time, by the deaths of a son, his father, and his wife. Abandoning his Difference Engine, still unfinished, he retreated to Europe. During his travels he was introduced to many of Europe's leading scientists and learned that he had been appointed to the Lucasian chair at Cambridge, the professorship that had once been held by Newton.

Babbage returned to England invigorated and filled with new ideas. He first became involved in the reform movement and stood for election to Parliament twice as a Liberal or Whig. He lost both times and turned from politics back to scientific projects. From the notes he made while visiting machine shops and factories he wrote a book titled *On the Economy of Machinery and Manufactures* (1832), which was probably his most influential work during his lifetime. It took the economic ideas of Adam Smith and updated them to the machinery age. The book showed not only how machines might be used in industry but how they might be used most economically.

Most of Babbage's economics ideas were based upon the division of labor. He recognized that the division of labor could be applied not only to physical tasks such as manufacturing but also to mental tasks such as the computation of a trigonometry table. Furthermore, he recognized that the division of labor allowed factory owners to reduce the cost of manufacturing by assigning each individual task to the least expensive laborer capable of handling that task. This insight became one of the foundations of industrial management.

As one of the country's leading experts on computation, Babbage was appointed to a committee reviewing the *Royal Nautical Almanac.* This group met in the offices of the Royal Astronomical Society and considered both the contents and means of producing the almanac. They recommended adding a substantial number of tables to the volume. They also urged that the British government use a more systematic form of management to compute the tables, though they stopped short of recommending that Babbage's machine be used for the calculations.

During this period Babbage also became interested in the organization of scientific societies. In particular he became a champion of the modern, self-organized scientific institution. In an 1830 pamphlet, *Reflections on the Decline of Science,* he argued that "science has long been neglected and declining in England" (p. i). England's major scientific society of the time, the Royal Society, was not entirely self-governed and had many members who were not scientists. Babbage, who had been a member of the Royal Society since his graduation from Cambridge, attempted to reform the society but found little assistance. Frustrated by the work, he and a small group of friends decided to found a new society, the British Association for the Advancement of Science, based on the principles of self-organization by scientists.

The Analytical Engine. In 1834, with his Difference Engine still unfinished, Babbage conceived a new, more general machine for the evaluation of functions. This machine resembled the modern computer in that it read operations from a string of punched cards and performed those operations on individual numbers. It also had a means of storing and retrieving numbers. He would name the new device the Analytical Engine after his interest in analytical mathematics. It was far more complicated than his Difference Engine, which could calculate only polynomials. It required him to prepare new designs, new plans, and new descriptions.

In his work on the Analytical Engine, Babbage was briefly assisted by Ada Lovelace, the daughter of the poet Lord Byron (George Gordon Byron). Lovelace played a

Charles Babbage. © HULTON-DEUTSCH COLLECTION/CORBIS.

key role that moved Babbage's idea beyond its inventor into the larger world: She translated and annotated a description of the Analytical Engine and wrote the instructions that would compute a set of values called Bernoulli numbers. In modern terminology the term *program* would be used to identify this set of instructions.

While Babbage was working on his design for his Analytical Engine he was also continuing to organize scientific institutions. He was a founding officer of the Royal Statistical Society. At the time, statistical science included most of the fields that have since devolved into social sciences: economics, sociology, psychology, and anthropology. Babbage was interested in the mathematical foundations of these fields and corresponded with most of the leading statisticians of the day, including the Belgian Adolphe Quetelet.

Though he worked on many different projects during the late 1830s, Babbage devoted most of his attention to his Analytical Engine. "My coach house was now converted to a forge," he wrote, "whilst my stables were transformed into a workshop" (1864, p. 27). He refined the design of the machine, carefully describing the motion of each part in a notation that he had devised. Through these years his ideas about calculation drew the attention of

individuals both in England and in Europe. In 1840 Babbage discussed his Analytical Engine at a scientific conference in Turin, Italy, which proved to be one of the more gratifying moments in his life. Two years later his workshop was visited by Prince Albert, the husband of Queen Victoria.

Through 1842 the British government had supported the development of Babbage's computing machines and had given him fifteen thousand pounds to help pay for materials and the salary of a skilled machinist. However, the government had become impatient with Babbage's progress. In twenty years of work he had failed to complete a full, working machine. In the fall of that year the chancellor of the exchequer informed him that the government would no longer provide him with funds. Babbage appealed to the prime minister, but he was unable to change the decision.

Babbage was angered by the action of the British government and was particularly stung by a report from the astronomer royal, George Airy, who wrote, "I believe the machine to be useless, and that the sooner it is abandoned, the better it will be for all parties" (George Airy to Henry Goulburn, September 16, 1842, Papers of the Royal Greenwich Observatory, Cambridge University). For the next twenty-five years Babbage would devote himself to erasing that verdict and establishing the value of his ideas. However, Airy probably made the correct judgment for the time. Babbage's calculators would have had limited application. Within the nineteenth-century scientific community only astronomers might regularly have found a use for one of Babbage's machines, and none of them could have kept it fully occupied.

In 1854 Babbage's ideas came to the attention of George and Edvard Scheutz, a father and son from Sweden. After reading a description of the Difference Engine, they designed and built their own version. This machine was smaller and lighter than the engine conceived by Babbage. They used gears and levers that would have been suitable for the mechanism of a clock. In contrast, Babbage used technology that would have been appropriate for a steam engine. Babbage's engine, if completed, would have filled a room. The Scheutz engine sat nicely on a table and looked like a complicated music box.

Babbage was pleased with Scheutz engine and praised it publicly. The machine was purchased by the Dudley Observatory in Albany, New York, and was given its test, in 1858, by the staff of the *American Nautical Almanac.* The Americans used it to compute part of an astronomical table that showed the position of the planet Mars. Though they ultimately completed the task, they found the machine difficult to set up and more trouble than it was worth. "The result thus far," wrote one member of the staff, "has not been such as to demonstrate to my satisfaction that any considerable portion of the *Almanac* can be computed more economically by this machine" (*U.S. Naval Observatory Annual Report for 1858*, p. 7).

Later Years. At this time Babbage began to withdraw from scientific work. One author speculates that Babbage had a problem with his eyes that made it hard for him to work and exacerbated his difficult personality. Increasingly he turned to problems that were trivial and not worthy of his talents. He designed a system for coastal navigation and worked on minor problems of machining. However, he did complete a new, refined design for his Difference Engine and continued to promote his ideas on computation.

Babbage remained a key member of the scientific community. He knew Charles Darwin and had a brief correspondence with George Boole. Yet during the last years of his life he continued to return to his computing engines. In 1861 he wrote an autobiography, which is largely a defense of his ideas on computing machines. He also returned to his Analytical Engine, looking at calculations and seeing how he might do them with his machine. For the most part he went over old ground. He looked at different mathematical expressions and tried to write code for them. Only a few times did he begin to wander into fields that would really show the power of the computer, but he never pursued these ideas very far. He died in 1871 with his machines still unfinished.

In 1879 the British Association for the Advancement of Science considered the possibility of building an Analytical Engine from Babbage's plans but concluded that such a project was beyond their ability and resources. A decade later Babbage's son, Henry Prevost Babbage, constructed part of the machine, the section involved with the actual computation. The younger Babbage also collected and published his father's papers on calculating machines.

A practical Difference Engine was demonstrated by the *Royal Nautical Almanac* in the 1920s. The superintendent of the *Almanac*, L. J. Comrie, discovered a commercial bookkeeping machine that had a structure similar to that of Babbage's original computing machine. It can "be called a modern Babbage machine," Comrie wrote, for "it does all that Babbage intended his difference engine to do and more" (Comrie, 1936, p. 94). Comrie showed how this machine could be used to compute some of the *Almanac*'s tables. The *Almanac* staff made regular use of this machine until it was replaced with an electronic computer in the 1950s.

Babbage is connected to the modern computer through the work of Howard Aiken, a Harvard University graduate student who built a computing machine in the early 1940s. Aiken discovered Babbage's papers and a model of his computing machine while he was designing his own device. Aiken quickly grasped what Babbage had accomplished and identified him as one of the founders of the field of computation, "a radical inventor," according to Aiken's biographer, "who was not fully appreciated by his contemporaries" (quoted in Cohen, 1999, p. 72).

SUPPLEMENTARY BIBLIOGRAPHY

The major collections of Babbage's papers are found at the British Library and at the Beinecke Library at Yale University.

WORKS BY BABBAGE

Reflections on the Decline of Science in England, and on Some of Its Causes. London: B. Fellowes, 1830.

On the Economy of Machinery and Manufactures. London: Charles Knight, 1832; New York: New York University Press, 1989.

Passages from the Life of a Philosopher. London: Longman, Green, Longman, Roberts and Green, 1864; New York: New York University Press, 1989. An autobiography largely devoted to defending his reputation as the designer of computing machines.

Memoirs of the Analytical Society. In *Aspects of the Life and Thought of Sir John Frederick Herschel,* edited by S. S. Schweber. Vol. 1. New York: Arno Press, 1981. The complete text of Babbage and Herschel's mathematics volume.

Works of Charles Babbage. Edited by Martin Campbell-Kelly. New York: New York University Press, 1989. Most of his papers but not quite all.

OTHER SOURCES

Ashworth, William T. "The Calculating Eye: Baily, Herschel, Babbage, and the Business of Astronomy." *British Journal of the History of Science* 27 (1994). 409–441.

Bromley, Alan. "Charles Babbage's Analytical Engine, 1838." *IEEE Annals of the History of Computing* 4 (1982): 196–217. This paper and the three that follow are the definitive technical analyses of Babbage's machines.

———. "The Evolution of Babbage's Calculating Engines." *IEEE Annals of the History of Computing* 9 (1987): 113–136.

———. "Charles Babbage's Analytical Engine, 1838." *IEEE Annals of the History of Computing* 20 (1998): 29–45.

———. "Babbage's Analytical Engine Plans 28 and 29A: The Programmer's Interface." *IEEE Annals of the History of Computing* 22 (2000): 5–19.

Campbell-Kelly, Martin. "Charles Babbage and the Assurance of Lives." *IEEE Annals of the History of Computing* 16 (1994): 5–14.

Cohen, I. Bernard. *Howard Aiken, Portrait of a Computer Pioneer.* Cambridge, MA: MIT University Press, 1999.

Comrie, Leslie J. "Inverse Interpolation and Scientific Applications of the National Accounting Machine." *Supplement to the Journal of the Royal Statistical Society* 3, no. 2 (1936): 87–114.

Enros, Philip C. "The Analytical Society (1812–1813): Precursor of the Revival of Cambridge Mathematics." *Historica Mathematica* 10 (1983): 24–27.

Grier, David A. "Biographies and Writings by Charles Babbage (1791–1870)." *Communications Book Notes Quarterly* 37 (2006): 7–13. Complete bibliography of biographies and other books about Charles Babbage.

Hyman, Anthony. *Charles Babbage, Pioneer of the Computer.* Princeton, NJ: Princeton University Press, 1982. The canonical biography. Largely based on Babbage's autobiography.

IEEE Annals of the History of Computing. Including those articles listed here, this journal has published more than thirty papers on Charles Babbage and his machines.

Keller, C. R. "Babbage the Unfortunate." *British Journal of Ophthalmology* 88 (2004): 730–732.

Swade, Doron. *The Cogwheel Brain: Charles Babbage and the Quest to Build the First Computer.* London: Little, Brown, 2000. Published in the United States as *The Difference Engine.* New York: Viking, 2001.

Van Sinderen, Alfred W. "Printed Papers of Charles Babbage." *IEEE Annals of the History of Computing* 2 (1980): 169–185. Contains a complete list of Babbage's published works.

Williams, Michael M. "Babbage and Bowditch: A Transatlantic Connection." *IEEE Annals of the History of Computing* 9 (1988): 283–290.

David Alan Grier

Horace Babcock. SCIENCE PHOTO LIBRARY/PHOTO RESEARCHERS, INC.

BABCOCK, HORACE WELCOME (*b.* Pasadena, California, 13 September 1912; *d.* Santa Barbara, California, 29 August 2003), *astrophysics, solar physics, science administration, instrumentation.*

Babcock is best known as a pioneer in the study of solar and stellar magnetic fields and for his ability to produce innovative instruments that enabled him to break new ground in astronomical research. His scientific career was no less important for his tenure as director of one of the leading astronomical centers of the world as he saw it through a period of tremendous expansion.

Origins. Babcock was born in Pasadena, California, to the astronomer Harold Delos Babcock and Mary Eliza Babcock. Harold Babcock had joined the staff of the Carnegie Institution of Washington's new Mount Wilson Observatory three years earlier in 1909, coming from the National Bureau of Standards in Washington, DC. Harold Babcock became a renowned solar astronomer at the Mount Wilson Observatory and remained on the staff there until his retirement in 1948. During his early years Horace Babcock came to know the Mount Wilson Observatory and its staff quite well and naturally became interested in astronomy. With his father, the young Babcock visited the mountain observatory several times as a youth and he always remembered the noise and activity surrounding the construction of the great 2.5-meter (8.2-foot) Hooker Telescope. In 1928 Babcock apprenticed in the observatory's optical shop in Pasadena and learned the craft of instrument design and production. He entered the California Institute of Technology (Caltech) in 1930 and during his time there he assisted his father with his solar observations using the 45.72-meter (150-foot) solar tower telescope on Mount Wilson. After graduating with a BS in physics in 1934, Babcock decided to pursue his astronomical interests as a graduate student at the University of California at Berkeley.

Early Career. Babcock received his PhD in 1938 with the dissertation "On the Rotation of the Andromeda Nebula." In his research Babcock, using the 0.9-meter (36-inch) Crossley reflecting telescope at Berkeley's Lick Observatory on Mount Hamilton, California, measured the rotation of the nebula, now known as the Andromeda Galaxy (or M31), at various distances from its center in order to determine the distribution of mass throughout the galaxy. An interesting result of his research was the realization that the mass-to-luminosity ratio of M31 actually increases as one moves away from the bright central region of the galaxy. In the early 2000s some astronomers pointed to Babcock's research as the first observational evidence of dark matter, though it was overlooked by many at first.

Babcock remained at the Lick Observatory for one more year after his graduation as a research assistant. In 1939 he presented a paper on his M31 research at a conference marking the dedication of the 2.1-meter (84-inch) telescope of the new McDonald Observatory in Texas. Primarily on the basis of his presentation, Babcock was hired immediately as an instructor and staff member of the McDonald Observatory by the University of Chicago (which operated the observatory for the University of Texas). Having learned the shortcomings of doing galactic spectroscopy with the Mayall nebular spectrograph at the Lick Observatory, Babcock designed a much faster spectrograph for galactic spectrum analysis at the McDonald telescope; the instrument proved to be a great success for many astronomers in the coming years.

When the United States entered World War II, the University of Chicago allowed Babcock to do war work on radar development at the Radiation Laboratory of the Massachusetts Institute of Technology. In 1942 he transferred back home, joining the rocket project at Caltech.

Research at the Mount Wilson Observatory. With the end of the war, Babcock planned to return to his normal duties for the University of Chicago but before he left Caltech he was offered a job on the staff of the Mount Wilson Observatory by its new incoming director, Ira S. Bowen, who had also been with the Caltech rocket project during the war. At Mount Wilson (which would soon become the Mount Wilson and Palomar Observatories in 1948), Babcock split his duties between research in solar and stellar magnetism and the development of new astronomical instruments. His first significant instrument design was a microdensitometer that was to be used to study the spectrographs produced by both the 2.5-meter (8.2-foot) Hooker Telescope and the soon-to-be-completed 5-meter (16.4-foot) Hale Telescope on Mount Palomar. The device produced excellent results but proved difficult to work with except by the most resolute observers and Babcock thus considered it a failure.

His researches in solar magnetism were initially carried out in collaboration with his father Harold, who still worked at the Mount Wilson Observatory. Even after the latter retired in 1948, they continued their joint investigations at the observatory's Hale Solar Laboratory in Pasadena. Astronomers had measured strong magnetic fields in sunspots early in the twentieth century (up to a few thousand gauss). In the Babcocks' work, Horace

invented and developed the first solar magnetograph, which enabled the pair to detect weak magnetic fields on the sun's surface. Using an early version of the magnetograph, by the mid-1950s the Babcocks showed that the general magnetic field of the sun was about one gauss, much weaker than the spurious results reported by George Ellery Hale earlier in the century. In 1961 Horace Babcock proposed a magnetohydrodynamic model to explain sunspots and their magnetism through the differential rotation of the Sun (where the equatorial region of the Sun rotates faster than the poles).

Babcock extended his magnetic work to the distant stars as well as the Sun. While the Sun's magnetic field is too weak to be detected at stellar distances, it was believed that some stars might have stronger fields that could be detected. Babcock's work was quickly rewarded as he discovered the first example of a stellar magnetic field on the star 78 Virginis in 1946. By studying the Zeeman effect—that is, the splitting of a spectral line into a number of components due to the presence of a magnetic field—in the lines of that star's spectrum, he found a general magnetic field of 1,500 gauss at the pole. Babcock subsequently discovered over 150 stars with measurable magnetic fields and this led to the publication in 1958 of his important article "A Catalog of Magnetic Stars."

Babcock's gift for designing instruments led him to the development and refinement, with his father at first, of the ruling engines at the Mount Wilson Observatory for the production of reflection diffraction gratings. Babcock implemented a number of design improvements, including using interferometric control of the diamond that would rule the lines in the gratings. His greatest achievement here was probably his production of the four optically matched gratings that would be used for the 5-meter (200-inch) Hale Telescope's spectrograph. The gratings produced by Babcock and his technicians in the 1950s were the best available and many were liberally loaned to observatories all over the world. It would not be overstating the case to say that the Mount Wilson and Palomar Observatories, through its use and loan of diffraction gratings, was involved in most of the astronomical spectroscopy being carried out in the 1940s and 1950s.

Babcock also designed monitors to test atmospheric seeing conditions; these were used by the Mount Wilson and Palomar staff and other observatories to determine the best locations for new telescopes. As he pursued this line of work, he proposed in 1953 a new method of compensating for atmospheric effects in optical observations. His research led to the development of what was later called adaptive optics, a technology that allows telescopes to quickly modify their optical components to cancel out the effects of turbulence in the atmosphere.

Observatory Director. On 1 July 1964, Babcock became the director of the Mount Wilson and Palomar Observatories (soon to be renamed the Hale Observatories). His administrative abilities had come to the fore when he had been appointed assistant director in 1957. Eventually, with his scientific, technical, and administrative experience, he became the logical successor to Bowen as director when the latter retired in 1964. Although Babcock's interests lay far removed from administrative duties, he saw the directorship as an opportunity to seriously pursue his desire to establish a large telescope in the Southern Hemisphere. As director, Bowen had been able to successfully complete the Hale Telescope, get it into operational condition, and integrate it nicely into the astronomical research milieu, so the time was right for Babcock to take the next step in the observatory's development.

Thanks to Babcock's urgings to start planning for a southern telescope soon after he became assistant director, preparations in the form of site surveys for the new Southern Observatory of the Carnegie Institution of Washington, or CARSO, had already begun when he became director. The initial plan was to have a 5-meter (16.4-foot) telescope as the new observatory's centerpiece with smaller supporting instruments, including a 1.2-meter (48-inch) Schmidt camera. Babcock oversaw a complex operation, which involved site testing in Australia, South Africa, and Chile, followed by intricate efforts to obtain the land for CARSO in Chile. Babcock was the chief negotiator with the Chilean president Eduardo Frei Montalva, in the successful bid to obtain a parcel of land on the ridge of the Las Campanas peaks at an altitude of 2,400 meters (7,874 feet) on the western range of the Andes. In order to gain help with funding for construction and operation, the Carnegie Institution had discussions with Canada, Great Britain, and Australia in order to see if these countries were interested in a joint southern venture. These plans did not reach fruition, and CARSO had to be diminished in scope from its original concept. The program was rewarded with the official opening of what became the Las Campanas Observatory in 1972, first with the 1-meter (40-inch) Henrietta Swope Telescope and later with the Irénée du Pont Telescope, a 2.5-meter (100-inch) instrument (reduced in size from the planned 5-meter telescope) that became operational in 1977.

Other administrative issues during Babcock's tenure as director included: the unsuccessful attempt to move the Mount Wilson and Palomar Observatories headquarters onto a site on the Caltech campus; the start of the observatories' pursuing federal funds, including the attempt to obtain general operating support from the National Science Foundation, and the competition for these funds from Kitt Peak National Observatory; the construction and dedication in 1970 of the 1.5-meter (4.9-foot) telescope on Palomar Mountain to take some of the lighter duties away from the 5-meter (16.4-foot) telescope; Babcock's personal involvement in the failed efforts to build a science museum in Pasadena; Babcock's involvement in the National Academy of Science's efforts to define the future needs of American astronomy, in talks with Harvard about constructing a Shapley Memorial Telescope at Las Campanas, and in discussions with the Massachusetts Institute of Technology on their becoming a part of the Hale Observatories (which they did not).

Retirement. Babcock retired from the Hale Observatories in 1978, having successfully established the observatories in the Southern Hemisphere. He continued to work at the observatories' headquarters in Pasadena for another twenty years on various projects mostly related to adaptive optics and telescope mountings. In 1998 he moved to a retirement community in Santa Barbara, California, where he continued to concentrate on astronomical instrumentation until a few months before his death in 2003.

Babcock's awards from his peers include the Draper Medal of the National Academy of Sciences (1957), the Eddington Medal (1958) and the Gold Medal (1970) of the Royal Astronomical Society, and the Bruce Gold Medal of the Astronomical Society of the Pacific (1969). Because of Babcock's natural reticence, little is known of his private life except that he did have two children from a first wife and one child from his second wife, Elizabeth M. Jackson. Both marriages ended in divorce. One of his true enjoyments was sailing, and for several years he owned a sailboat that he could retreat to along with an occasional colleague. The boat was equipped with a number of homemade electronic gadgets made by Babcock, including one that enabled the ship to steer itself by sensing the Earth's magnetic field relative to the course he set.

BIBLIOGRAPHY

An important archival resource is Babcock's collection of papers as director of the Mount Wilson and Palomar Observatories (later Hale Observatories). These are on permanent deposit at the Henry E. Huntington Library in San Marino, California, as part of the archives of the Observatories of the Carnegie Institution of Washington. There is an oral history interview with Babcock available at the AIP's Center for the History of Physics.

WORKS BY BABCOCK

"On the Rotation of the Andromeda Nebula." PhD diss., University of California, Berkeley, 1938. A work that continued into the early 2000s to be cited in reviews about "dark matter."

"Zeeman Effect in Stellar Spectra." *Astrophysical Journal* 105 (1947): 105–119. The initial discovery of large magnetic fields in stars.

"The Possibility of Compensating Astronomical Seeing." *Publications of the Astronomical Society of the Pacific* 65 (1953): 229–236. A paper that is generally regarded as being the first to discuss adaptive optics.

"A Catalog of Magnetic Stars." *Astrophysical Journal Supplement Series* 3 (1958): 141–210. The culmination of Babcock's research on magnetic stars.

"The Topology of the Sun's Magnetic Field and the 22-Year Cycle." *Astrophysical Journal.* 133 (1961): 572–587. The model proposed here continues to be the basis of current models of solar magnetism.

"Diffraction Gratings at the Mount Wilson Observatory." *Vistas in Astronomy* 29 (1986): 153–174. A helpful memoir that includes details about the Babcocks' work with diffraction gratings.

With T. G. Cowling. "General Magnetic Fields in the Sun and Stars (Report on Progress of Astronomy)." *Monthly Notices of the Royal Astronomical Society* 113 (1953): 357–381. A magisterial summary of the state of the new field of magnetohydrodynamics.

OTHER SOURCES

Abell, George Osgood. "Award of the Bruce Gold Medal to Dr. Horace W. Babcock." *Publications of the Astronomical Society of the Pacific* 81 (1969): 179–183.

Lovell, Sir Bernard. "Award of Gold Medal to Dr. Horace Welcome Babcock (address)." *Quarterly Journal of the Royal Astronomical Society* 11 (1970): 85–87.

Preston, George W. "Horace Welcome Babcock (1912–2003)." *Publications of the Astronomical Society of the Pacific* 116 (2004): 290–294.

Sandage, Allan. "Horace Welcome Babcock." *Proceedings of the American Philosophical Society* 150 (2006): 152–160. Some of the dates mentioned in this paper do not match those reflected in Babcock's own papers.

Vaughan, Arthur H. "Horace Welcome Babcock, 1912–2003." *Bulletin of the American Astronomical Society* 35 (2003): 1454–1455.

Ronald Brashear

BACHER, ROBERT FOX (*b.* Loudonville, Ohio, 31 August 1905; *d.* Montecito, California, 18 November 2004), *atomic spectra, nuclear physics, scientific administration.*

Bacher will be remembered for his significant contributions to physics, education, and, as a public servant, to his country. In the 1930s he coauthored a standard work on atomic spectra, and went on to help Hans Bethe redefine the field of nuclear physics. During World War II, Bacher served as a leader in the effort to develop radar at the Massachusetts Institute of Technology (MIT) Radiation Laboratory, and went on to play a critical role in building the atomic bombs at Los Alamos, New Mexico.

In the decades following the war, Bacher held a number of federal posts before turning his attention to the California Institute of Technology (Caltech), an institution he helped restructure and modernize. Though history has often overlooked Bacher, he clearly remains one of the most talented, versatile, and influential physicists of his generation.

Early Life and Career. Bacher was born to Harry and Byrl Fox Bacher in Loudonville, Ohio, on 31 August 1905. The family moved to Ann Arbor, Michigan, during Bacher's early childhood. He first became acquainted with physics in high school, but initially had little enthusiasm for the field, as he recalled in a 1980 oral history interview: "Actually, I was more interested in chemistry than physics because the physics course I took, while very thorough, was really very dull." In his senior year, Bacher's vague interest in the sciences found a catalyst. During the 1980 interview, he shared an anecdote regarding his first trip to the University of Michigan chemistry library: "I went and was absolutely floored. I saw the first things I'd ever seen about the atom." Bacher instantly developed a passion for science, and upon graduating in 1922 he enrolled at the University of Michigan to pursue his new dream of becoming a physicist.

Bacher obtained his bachelor of science degree in physics from Michigan in 1926. Having distinguished himself as an outstanding student during his years at Michigan, he gained acceptance into Harvard's prestigious physics program. Bacher spent his first year of graduate school at Harvard before returning home to Ann Arbor to study at his alma mater. The high cost of tuition at Harvard, coupled with his father's rapidly deteriorating physical condition, necessitated his return to Michigan. In 1928 the university awarded Bacher the Charles Coffin Fellowship, which helped ease his financial burden. It was the first of several such awards.

The same year Bacher returned to Michigan, Samuel Goudsmit joined the physics department's staff. Goudsmit, a Dutch theorist, soon became Bacher's mentor. In fact, Bacher later stated in a 1981 oral history interview: "He had more influence on my education than anyone else." Only a few years later, the pair would publish *Atomic Energy States, as Derived from the Analyses of Optical Spectra* (1932), a seminal work that is still referenced in the early twenty-first century.

The year 1930 proved to be a momentous one for Bacher. He completed work for his doctorate, joined the research society Sigma Xi and the American Physical Society, and won his second fellowship, this time from Caltech. He also married Jean Dow, whose family had been longtime neighbors of the Bachers. When his fellowship at Caltech ran out, Bacher was named a National Resident

Fellow at MIT. Eager to return home, he accepted the Lloyd Fellowship from Michigan in 1932.

When his fellowship expired in 1933, Bacher found himself unemployed in Depression-battered Michigan. During the year that followed, Bacher had time to ponder the mysteries of the atom in depth. In doing so, he began to develop a new interest, as he related in his 1980 interview: "It turned me more toward doing research and turned my interests toward nuclear physics—I had worked in atomic spectra up until then—and this was a sort of fateful time for me."

Bacher's sojourn came to an end in 1934, when he accepted a position with Columbia University as an instructor. He stayed there for a year before moving on to Cornell University in 1935. While at Cornell, Bacher worked closely with the future Nobel laureate Bethe, who had undertaken the task of standardizing the field of nuclear physics. In a series of articles Bethe, along with Bacher and M. Stanley Livingston, reevaluated the existing literature, filled research gaps, and attempted to resolve standing research problems. These articles, which soon became collectively known as "Bethe's Bible," served as the standard text for generations of nuclear physicists to come.

World War II. Bacher remained on Cornell's faculty through the end of World War II, enjoying a series of promotions: to assistant professor in 1937, to associate professor in 1940, and finally to professor in 1945. He became adept at performing cross-section measurements, and worked with Cornell colleagues Charles P. Baker and Boyce McDaniel to correct the boron absorption method that the Nobel laureate Enrico Fermi had popularized. In a 1984 interview, Bacher explained that upon learning of the team's results, his friend Fermi said: "You're right. You publish it. It's good physics." Bacher's work with Goudsmit a decade earlier had established his credentials as a theorist. His ongoing collaborative relationship with Fermi would solidify his standing as an experimentalist. This near-unique combination would soon draw the attention of two critical wartime projects.

With the Japanese attack on Pearl Harbor just months away, Lee DuBridge recruited Bacher to serve as a leader at the MIT Radiation Laboratory (Rad Lab). Rad Lab scientists performed research on the new technology of radar, and Bacher led the division responsible for the development of equipment that could translate incoming signals. The Rad Lab employed Bacher until early 1943, when an acquaintance, J. Robert Oppenheimer, recruited him to work on the secret atomic bomb project at Los Alamos. Bacher, who had been working on problems in nuclear physics for the previous decade, hesitantly accepted.

Bacher and Manhattan Project consultant Isidor I. Rabi, who had been associate director of the Rad Lab

since 1940, shared a serious concern: would the lab at Los Alamos fall under military control? The Manhattan Project's director, General Leslie R. Groves, originally planned for all the scientists to become commissioned army officers. Bacher and Rabi flatly refused to accept their commissions. At first, this created somewhat of a crisis. General Kenneth D. Nichols, Groves's deputy, relates in his memoir, *The Road to Trinity*:

> In February 1943, [James] Conant, [Vannevar] Bush, Groves, [Col. J. C.] Marshall, and I met with Rabi and Bacher … and spent the better part of the day trying to convince them that a military laboratory was essential. However, they were adamant and made it clear that even if the initial research activities were conducted as a civilian organization, they would tender their resignations if it were later militarized, war or no war. (1987, p. 152)

Because Oppenheimer regarded the two MIT physicists as essential, their protests carried considerable weight. Thus, Los Alamos and other Manhattan Project installations remained under civilian control, although the threat of a military conversion loomed during the war.

While at Los Alamos, Bacher remained at the very core of the project. His first assignment was to head the Experimental Physics (P) Division, one of the laboratory's four original technical divisions. Bacher's division carried out a variety of experiments to demonstrate the viability of a nuclear bomb. During this period, Oppenheimer entrusted Bacher with additional responsibilities as well: Bacher was asked to serve on the governing board, and he chaired the coordinating council. These advisory committees created policy and coordinated research activities across the new laboratory. Over time Bacher, by then a close friend of Oppenheimer's, came to serve as the laboratory's de facto deputy director.

By spring 1944, P Division scientists discovered that plutonium, unlike its fissionable counterpart uranium, would fizzle in a simple, gun assembly–type bomb. In order to use plutonium, the physicists would have to pursue a second method of ignition: implosion. Implosion was much more complicated than the gun method, but if it worked it would salvage the plutonium production program and probably yield a much more efficient weapon. Oppenheimer reorganized the laboratory in August 1944 in order to achieve maximum efficiency for the implosion effort. The P Division was disbanded and Bacher was made head of the new Weapons Physics, or "Gadget" (G) Division. The primary function of Bacher's division was to propose and build an implosion bomb. To do this, Bacher assembled one of the most talented scientific teams in history. His group leaders included two future Nobel laureates, Luis Alvarez and Edwin McMillan, as well as Bruno Rossi, Otto Frisch, and several other internationally recognized physicists.

As 1945 began, Bacher's division grew in confidence. Implosion appeared to be feasible, and a test date was scheduled for July. For the final push, Oppenheimer established the Cowpuncher Committee to drive implosion development through to completion. Bacher, along with five others, "rode herd" on the committee, their efforts eventually culminating in the 16 July Trinity test. An implosion bomb was successfully detonated early that morning, achieving a yield equivalent to twenty-one thousand tons of TNT. Bacher related his first thoughts after Trinity in his 1980 interview: "It was indeed an enormous relief. Everybody's first reaction was a mixture of many things but everybody was terribly tired by the time that bomb went off." The next implosion bomb would fall on Nagasaki, Japan, less than a month later, helping bring World War II to a close.

Bacher's taxing work at Los Alamos left him exhausted. In January 1946, he returned to a full professorship at Cornell. Though he was happy to return to Ithaca, he could not avoid continued federal service. The previous November, he had already joined Dr. Richard Tolman's Declassification Committee, which cleared thousands of Manhattan Project documents for release to the general public. Bacher also served on the Manhattan Project's Advisory Committee on Research and Development as well as the Technical Committee on Inspection and Control. Additionally, he was a technical advisor to the United Nations (UN). As a member of Bernard Baruch's UN mission, he helped develop policy to control atomic energy. Perhaps Bacher's most enjoyable assignment came in conjunction with his work at the UN. He was selected to chair the planning committee for the new Brookhaven National Laboratory, a UN Atomic Energy Commission project.

AEC Commissioner. Bacher enjoyed much of his postwar work, welcoming the challenges of organizing the new Brookhaven Laboratory and the physics lab at Cornell. But unfortunately, duty called once again. In 1946, in order to address the unprecedented issues surrounding atomic energy, Congress established the U.S. Atomic Energy Commission (AEC). David E. Lilienthal, the Tennessee Valley Authority's first chairman, was selected to chair the commission and recommended Bacher as a charter member. Bacher, who had already settled into his postwar life, was not excited about the prospect. Yet, Lilienthal was determined to acquire Bacher's services, penning in his journal, "He has just what we need—a feeling for the subject, an understanding of how important the Atomic Energy Commission's work is and can be, and a clear recognition of the central importance of an adjustment of the international impasse" (1964, p. 100). Working

Robert Bacher. © CORBIS.

behind the scenes, Lilienthal also secured the aid of Bacher's good friend Oppenheimer. With Oppenheimer, Lilienthal, and his sense of duty urging him, Bacher decided to take the position. His knowledge, experience, and status as the only scientist on the commission prompted Lilienthal to exclaim, "He will make all the difference in the world" (p. 102).

Bacher's selection was welcomed with almost universal acclaim. In fact, the most negative critique came from Edward Teller, who wrote in a letter to Maria Goeppert-Mayer, "Scientifically, we may have done worse by getting someone else," conceding, "Bacher is a great administrator" (2001, pp. 263–264). Bacher began his term on 1 November 1946, and quickly developed friendships with the other commissioners. These friendships made his work bearable, but he never found the work appealing, despite its importance.

As the end of his first term approached, fatigue began to set in. Bacher desperately wanted to return to academia. However, it was becoming apparent, especially to

Lilienthal, that Bacher would be extremely difficult to replace. Therefore, a compromise was reached: when the commissioners came up for reconfirmation, Bacher would accept only a one-year term. During his second term, Bacher continued to serve effectively. He educated his fellow commissioners on atomic energy and played a critical role in formulating early nuclear-weapons policy. On 10 May 1949, Bacher's term came to a close.

Caltech and Scientific Advising. After leaving the AEC, Bacher immediately accepted the position of leader for the reeling Physics, Mathematics, and Astronomy Division at Caltech, where he had studied as a Fellow almost two decades before. Caltech's president, Lee DuBridge, knew Bacher was the perfect man for the job. As Bacher's former supervisor at the Rad Lab, DuBridge fully appreciated Bacher's skills as a scientist and administrator. Now, DuBridge would count on his friend to help him restructure and modernize the small institution. Together, the team would gradually bring Caltech into a new era of prominence, returning it to the fore of the nation's leading universities.

Though Bacher had left Washington, he did not refrain from engaging in nuclear-policy discussions. In 1950 he publicly questioned the usefulness of the hydrogen bomb in a *Scientific American* article, arguing that it would be of limited strategic value: "While it is a terrible weapon, its military importance seems to have been grossly overrated in the mind of the laymen.... The most tragic part is that the hydrogen bomb will not save us and is not even a very good addition to our military potential" (p. 14). In the same article, Bacher also called for openness on the part of the government. He remained true to this stance decades later, stating in an oral history interview: "I think it's very important for people to be given as many facts as possible and to try and get them information which is both correct and non-inflammatory, whether this is pro or anti on the nuclear end of things."

Throughout the 1950s Bacher worked on several projects and served on many committees. In 1951 he joined the Vista Project, which was led by DuBridge. The project identified specific military problems that the North Atlantic Treaty Organization would encounter in the event of a Soviet attack on Western Europe. Two years later, in 1953, he joined the Science Advisory Committee (SAC) for the Office of Defense Mobilization.

Bacher left the SAC in 1955, but in 1957 was asked to serve on the President's Science Advisory Committee (PSAC), a higher level, expanded version of the SAC, which reported directly to the president. He accepted the new challenge at the urging of its chair, James R. Killian. As a member of the committee, Bacher actively engaged in the 1958 test-ban negotiations with the Soviets. The

talks led to a temporary test moratorium but more importantly paved the way for the formal Limited Test Ban Treaty of 1963. Killian relates in his memoir, *Sputnik, Scientists, and Eisenhower,* Bacher "made important contributions to helping the policy makers to understand the complexities of the problem." Killian continues, "In all of his work, he was deliberate, thorough, and judicial" (1977, p. 162). Bacher continued to serve the Eisenhower administration under the president's second chief science advisor, Manhattan Project veteran George Kistiakowsky, until 1959, when he left the PSAC to spend more time at Caltech.

With DuBridge's blessing, Bacher transformed Caltech into a center for research in the new field of high-energy particle physics as head of the Mathematics, Physics, and Astronomy Division. He brought in leading theorists, including the Nobel laureates Richard Feynman and Murray Gell-Mann, and constructed state-of-the-art tools such as the electron synchrotron, a high-energy accelerator. Throughout the 1950s and into the 1960s, Bacher carefully groomed the division, elevating it to one of the nation's finest. For his outstanding efforts, he was made the university's first provost in January 1962. In that capacity, he worked very closely with DuBridge and inherited many functions from the president's office.

Despite his new role at Caltech, Bacher made time to participate in prominent professional societies. He was president of the American Physical Society for 1964, and served as president of the International Union of Pure and Applied Physics from 1969 to 1972. During his final years at Caltech he helped hire DuBridge's successor, Harold Brown, and facilitated a seamless transition. Bacher retired from his duties as provost on 31 August 1970, his sixty-fifth birthday. He retained a faculty position and was immediately elected to the academic policy committee by his colleagues. Six years later, Bacher retired from the Caltech faculty and was awarded the title professor emeritus.

Retirement and Death. Even in retirement, Bacher remained active in the scientific community. He spent much of his time working on energy-related matters at the National Aeronautics and Space Administration and at Caltech's Jet Propulsion Laboratory and often visited his colleagues back at the Physics, Mathematics, and Astronomy Division. In 1983, the fortieth anniversary of Los Alamos National Laboratory's founding, Bacher served as master of ceremonies for the celebration. Many old friends, including Rabi, Bethe, and Alvarez, attended the celebration as well.

Robert Fox Bacher died in Montecito, California, on 18 November 2004. He lived a long life, and accomplished much during it. His work as a scientist and administrator with the Manhattan Project will probably remain his defining achievement, although this marked only the beginning of a remarkable career in science and public service. As an AEC commissioner, he tackled the international problems presented by atomic energy, remaining an active proponent of its responsible use throughout his life. He advised several luminaries, including Oppenheimer, Baruch, and President Dwight Eisenhower. Bacher also played a major role in transforming Caltech into one of the world's premier institutions of higher learning. Despite the complex nature of his work and his impressive list of accomplishments, Robert Bacher remained a kind, modest gentleman. Perhaps Killian described him best in his memoir: "Those who knew him as a leading physicist and science administrator at Cal Tech and those who have sailed with him off the Pacific Coast can only think of him as a shining, gifted figure, friendly, thoughtful, and deeply devoted to his country" (1977, p. 163).

BIBLIOGRAPHY

WORKS BY BACHER

With Samuel A. Goudsmit. *Atomic Energy States, as Derived from the Analyses of Optical Spectra.* New York: McGraw-Hill, 1932.

———. "Atomic Energy Relations. I." *Physical Review* 46 (1934): 948–969.

With Charles P. Baker and Boyce D. McDaniel. "Experiments with a Slow Neutron Velocity Spectrometer II." *Physical Review* 69 (1946): 443–451.

With David Lilienthal et al. "First Report of the U.S. Atomic Energy Commission." *Science* 105 (1947): 199–204.

"The Physicist and the Future Development of Atomic Energy." *Bulletin of the Atomic Scientists* 4 (1948): 99–102.

"Research and the Development of Atomic Energy." *Science* 109 (1949): 2–7.

"The Hydrogen Bomb: III." *Scientific American* 182 (1950): 11–15.

Interview by Mario Balibrera. Transcript, 1980. Los Alamos National Laboratory Archives. The Los Alamos National Laboratory Archives include multiple oral histories of Bacher, as well as his classified and unclassified wartime papers.

Interview by Mary Terrall. Transcript, 19 June 1981. California Institute of Technology Archives. The Caltech Archives include multiple oral histories of Bacher, as well as an extensive collection of Bacher's papers.

Interview by Lillian Hoddeson and Allison Kerr. Transcript, 30 July 1984. Los Alamos National Laboratory Archives.

With Hans A. Bethe and M. Stanley Livingston. *Basic Bethe: Seminal Articles on Nuclear Physics, 1936–1937.* Los Angeles: Tomash; New York: American Institute of Physics, 1986.

Robert Oppenheimer, 1904–1967. Los Alamos, NM: Los Alamos Historical Society Press, 1999.

OTHER SOURCES

Carr, Alan B. *Robert Bacher: The Forgotten Physicist.* Los Alamos, NM: Los Alamos Historical Society Press, 2007.

Goodstein, Judith R. *Millikan's School: A History of the California Institute of Technology.* New York: Norton, 1991.

Hoddeson, Lillian, Paul W. Henriksen, Roger A. Meade, et al. *Critical Assembly: A Technical History of Los Alamos during the Oppenheimer Years, 1943–1945.* Cambridge, U.K.: Cambridge University Press, 1993. Recognized by Los Alamos National Laboratory as an official wartime history of Project Y.

Killian, James R. *Sputnik, Scientists, and Eisenhower: A Memoir of the First Special Assistant to the President for Science and Technology.* Cambridge, MA: MIT Press, 1977.

Lilienthal, David E. *The Journals of David E. Lilienthal.* Vol. 2, *The Atomic Energy Years, 1945–1950.* New York: Harper and Row, 1964.

Nichols, Kenneth D. *The Road to Trinity.* New York: William Morrow, 1987.

Teller, Edward, with Judith L. Shoolery. *Memoirs: A Twentieth-Century Journey in Science and Politics.* Cambridge, MA: Perseus, 2001.

Alan B. Carr

BACON, FRANCIS (*b.* London, England, 22 January 1561; *d.* London, 9 April 1626), *philosophy of science, cosmology, theory of matter, life sciences, medicine.* For the original article on Bacon see *DSB,* vol. 1.

Baconian studies have seen many major developments since publication of the original *DSB* article in 1970. In particular, it is now clear that, in parallel to the methodological reflections culminating in the *Novum organum,* Bacon developed a complex and coherent system of positive natural philosophy. This key Baconian scientific interest remained in large part unrecognized until the research of Graham Rees. Both through the reinterpretation of well-known texts and the use of newly discovered sources, Rees identified and delineated what he called Bacon's "Semi-Paracelsian Cosmology," a "highly speculative system of the world," with its natural background in a complex theory of matter and spirits (Rees 1975a–b; Bacon, 1984). Conceived as early as 1592, the system's cosmological features were mainly sketched in the works *Thema coeli* (c. 1612; *Theory of the Heaven*) and *De fluxu et refluxu maris* (c. 1611; *On the Ebb and Flow of the Sea*); however, Bacon's theory soon after developed to include a sophisticated and elaborate analysis of life and living processes, which culminated in the late *Historia vitae et mortis* (1623; *History of Life and Death*). New, striking evidence for these interests emerged with the discovery and publication, in the early 1980s, of a hitherto unknown

	Sulfur Quaternion	Mercury Quaternion
Tangible Matter	Sulfur (subterranean)	Mercury (subterranean)
	Oil and oily, inflammable substances	Water and "crude," noninflammable substances
Pneumatic Matter	Terrestrial fire (sublunar)	Air (sublunar)
	Sidereal fire (matter of heavenly bodies)	Ether (medium of heavenly bodies)

Figure 1. *Quaternion theory.*

lengthy Baconian treatise on biological and medical matters, *De vijs mortis* (1610s, *The Ways of Death;* see Bacon, 1984 and 1996).

In the past, many readings of the Baconian project have accentuated the weight of Bacon's methodology and philosophy of science, while assigning an ancillary and peripheral role to his interests in natural philosophy; Mary Hesse's original *DSB* entry was a fine example of this type of analysis. However, the new and reinforced evidence of Bacon's dedicated commitment to the study of nature decisively renders this type of interpretation dated and calls for a better integration between Bacon's scientific concerns and the other areas of his philosophy.

Theory of Matter and Cosmology. Bacon's interest in astronomy and cosmology predated the formulation of his theory of matter. Nevertheless, these two areas became strongly associated in his mature reflection, and he developed his matter theory by integrating it with and fitting it to his cosmological ideas: for this reason, it is worthwhile to treat them jointly.

For Bacon, matter existed in both *tangible* and *pneumatic* forms. Tangible matter is concentrated on Earth and is inert and passive. By contrast, highly active pneumatic matter, or spirit, constitutes the source of any change in the Baconian universe. For instance, tangible matter confines very active *attached* spirits, which are interspersed in different proportion in any terrestrial body and naturally tend to escape from their bounds. This tendency produces many of the macroscopic transformations taking place on Earth and in the subterranean regions. Spirits can also be found *free,* outside of tangible matter: the sublunary and celestial regions are mainly occupied by spirits in this form.

Both tangible and pneumatic matter can also be classified through what Rees has called Bacon's "quaternion theory." According to this idea, all entities belong to a family or, to use a Baconian expression, "tribe," possessing four constituents (a "quaternion"). Bacon identified two

principal groups, respectively the *mercury* and *sulfur* quaternions. The division between mercurial and sulfuric components pertains to the entire universe: in the subterranean realm, it mainly consists in the division between the two constituents of sulfur and mercury proper, while on the surface of Earth it takes the form of the opposition between oily, inflammable substances (sulfuric in nature), and watery, noninflammable ones (mercurial).

Moving from Earth toward the heavens, four different types of free spirits can be found. Air and ether belong to the mercury quaternion, while terrestrial and sidereal fires are situated in the sulfur quaternion. Because of their constitutions, these opposite groups engage in a mutual struggle, and each zone of the heavens is dominated by a specific component (see Table 1).

Thus, the sublunary region is dominated by air, while fire is present in a weak and gross form. With an increase of distance from Earth, the influence of fire becomes stronger, balancing that of ether, a rarified and purer form of air. In the region of the fixed stars, sidereal fire is dominant, pure, and strong. In general, the various components become purer with the increase of their distance from Earth.

Bacon adjusted his theories of matter and quaternions to his idiosyncratic model of the universe. As early as 1592 he had adopted the cosmological system of the medieval Arab astronomer Alpetragius (al-Bitrūjī). Though little studied today, Alpetragius's work was translated into Latin in 1217 by Michael Scot with the title *De motibus celorum* and was fairly well known during the Middle Ages and Renaissance.

Alpetragius's work was an attempt to replace the Ptolemaic model with an astronomical system more conformable to Aristotelian physics. The Alpetragian model was geocentric and required nine celestial spheres. According to Alpetragius, the primum mobile completed its rotation in about a sidereal day and transferred its motion beneath, to the sphere of the fixed stars. However, during this process the motion of this sphere was slightly attenuated, so that the sphere would take exactly twenty-four hours to complete its rotation. This attenuation also occurred within the spheres of the planets, with a progressive delay of their motion. This progressive abatement of the spheres' motion in relation to the primum mobile and the daily rotation of the heavens accounted for the periodic motion of a planet.

Bacon did not assign any role to the celestial spheres but adapted his quaternions theory to the Alpetragian model. In this way he explained the progressive attenuation to the motion of the planets: having a fiery nature, they find greater resistance to their motion when closer to Earth because of the opposition of the mercurial principles of ether and air. Bacon's matter theory also accounted for the planets' deviation from circular orbits, which intensified the closer the planet was to Earth:

> for just as substances degenerate in purity and explication, so too do their motions degenerate. Now it happens that, as in their speed the higher planets move faster, and the lower more slowly, so also do the higher make closer spirals, and ones which come nearer to the circles, but the lower make spirals more distinct and open. For as they descend they always depart more and more both from that splendour of velocity and perfection of circular motion, ever in regular order. (*The Oxford Francis Bacon* [*OFB*], vol. 6, p. 183)

Bacon encountered more difficulties, however, when he tried to analyze the retrograde motion of the planets. In this case he had to turn to ad hoc explanations, using the differences and fluctuations in the physical properties of the ethereal medium in which the planets move. Also, Bacon could not accommodate Galileo Galilei's discoveries of Jupiter's satellites within his strongly geocentric system (*OFB*, vol. 6, pp. 187–193).

A further implication of Bacon's quaternion theory when applied to celestial matters regarded tides and winds. Because of the "conformity" of their internal configurations, elements of the same quaternion are driven by "consent" (or consensus), that is to say, they possess similar inclinations and related behaviors. This general rule is particularly true in the case of the mercury quaternion: The daily westward motion of the ethereal heavens, even though "enormously weakened," extends by consent to sublunary air and water. This correspondence sets a constant westward wind, tending to decrease with altitude. Also, the wind is "more observable in the tropics, because it moves there in larger circles" (*The Works of Francis Bacon* [*WFB*], vol. 2, pp. 26–27; vol. 5, p. 147). Tides are set in motion by the same mechanism: "I am entirely of the opinion that this same motion belongs to the mass of waters and exists in it, but that is slower than in the air" (*OFB*, vol. 6, p. 79). Bacon subsequently argued that the presence of two ebbs and flows per day was because of the presence of the "Old and New World":

> I think it necessarily follows that these two obstacles communicate and insinuate the nature of a double reciprocation to the whole mass of the waters, and from this arises that quarter of the diurnal motion; as, that is, with the waters checked on both sides, the ebb and flow of the sea unfolds itself twice a day over a six-hour period, since there is a double advance and likewise a double retreat. (*OFB*, vol. 6, p. 87)

Biological and Medical Ideas. Biological and medical matters have received particular attention in Baconian studies since the 1980s (Bacon [edited by Rees], 1984, 1996; Gemelli, 2004; Giglioni, 2005). In part this interest was sparked by the publication in 1984 of the newly discovered Baconian treatise on the prolongation of life titled *De vijs mortis* (*The Ways of Death*). The discovery and publication of this work were remarkable in that this treatise is Bacon's longest Latin manuscript to be published after the seventeenth century (Bacon [edited by Rees], 1984).

Bacon's interest in medical subjects was strong and manifest throughout his career. *De vijs mortis,* written sometime during the 1610s, was Bacon's first extensive writing on biological and medical issues, subsequently elaborated and developed in his *Historia vitae et mortis,* published in 1623. As in the case of his cosmology, Bacon's biological ideas had strong foundations in his theory of matter. In particular, Bacon's biology was based on the fundamental distinction between inanimate and vital spirits. According to Bacon, when it comes to the action of the attached inanimate spirits inside them, the tangible parts of living beings are not different from those of inanimate bodies. The tripartite activity of the inanimate spirits, or *actio triplex,* respectively corresponds to the attenuation of the moist parts of the body and their conversion in pneumatic matter; the escape of the spirit from the body; and the consequent "Contraction of the Grosser Parts after the Emission of the Spirit" (*WFB*, vol. 2, pp. 119–120; vol. 5, pp. 231–232). These steps lead to the decay of the body, the final effect of the *actio triplex.*

By contrast, vital spirits are unconstrained and diffused continuously all over the organism. In plants, the spirit is "merely branched, and permeating through small thread-like channels." In animals, spirit congregates and collects in "some hollow space," or cell, mainly "the ventricles of the brain." Furthermore, vital spirits possess a "degree of inflammation," which supplies motion and vital faculties, "gentler by many degrees than the softest flame" but still requiring continuous nourishment. All the functions of the organisms are dependent on the activity of the vital spirits: "Attraction, retention, digestion, assimilation, separation, excretion, perspiration, and even the sense itself, depend upon the properties of the several organs, as the stomach, liver, heart, spleen, gall, brain, eye, ear, and the rest. But yet none of these actions would ever be set in motion without the vigour, presence, and heat of the vital spirit" (*WFB*, vol. 2, p. 215; vol. 5, pp. 323–324). The vital spirit is then like "the master-wheel which turns the other wheels in the body of man" (*WFB*, vol. 2, p. 221; vol. 5, p. 330). The activity of the vital spirit ends when the spirit is "deprived either of motion, or of refrigeration, or of aliment." Any of these causes produces the death of the organism (*WFB*, vol. 2, p. 225; vol. 5, pp. 334–335).

Francis Bacon. LIBRARY OF CONGRESS.

The major motivations for Bacon's biological interests were medical: in the appendix to the *New Atlantis,* while enumerating the *magnalia naturae* (wondrous works) to be achieved for the use and benefit of humankind, "prolongation of life," "restitution of youth in some degree," and "retardation of age" figured at the top of Bacon's list (*WFB,* vol. 3, p. 167). But it was only through the knowledge of the activity of the spirits in the organism that these wonders could be achieved: As Bacon stated in *The Advancement of Learning,*

> It is more probable, that he that knoweth the nature of arefaction, the nature of assimilation of nourishment to the thing nourished, the manner of increase and clearing of the spirits, the manner of the depredations which spirits make upon the humors and solid parts, shall by ambages of diets, bathings, anointings, medicines, motions, and the like, prolong life or restore some degree of youth

or vivacity, than that it can be done with the use of a few drops or scruples of a liquor or receit. (*WFB,* vol. 3, p. 362)

Moreover, the *Historia vitae et mortis* and his posthumous *Medical Remains* (1679) testify to Bacon's technical interests in medical remedies, dietary directions, and pharmacology. During the seventeenth and eighteenth centuries Bacon's research on longevity was quoted and admired by medical authors like Johannes Antonides Van der Linden, Martin Lister, Hermann Boerhaave, and Albrecht von Haller (Gemelli, 2005).

The Role of the Speculative Philosophy. The various features of Bacon's system of speculative philosophy well show the eclecticism of his intellectual construction. Bacon employed a variety of sources from very different traditions. Several characteristics of his system were certainly Paracelsian: in particular, like the Paracelsians, Bacon associated air and water with the mercurial aspect, and fire with the sulfuric one. Moreover, Bacon's chemical theory of the world bears a strong resemblance to similar ideas developed by Paracelsians like Petrus Severinus, Oswald Croll, and, in particular, the French chemical author Joseph Duchesne (Quercetanus). However, other characteristics of his system clearly diverged from Paracelsianism. For instance, Bacon did not assign any special role to salt, the third of Paracelsus's *tria prima*. Moreover, Bacon's very atypical merging of chemical ideas with the astronomical doctrine of Alpetragius is original and not reflected in the work of other authors. Also, Bacon never tried to reinterpret scripture (and in particular the account of the creation in Genesis) in light of his chemical notions, as in the case of the Mosaic chemical cosmogonies of the Paracelsians. It is clear, then, that Bacon's appropriation of Paracelsian concepts was far from uncritical. Another tradition that clearly informs Bacon's conceptions of spirits is Renaissance pneumatism, very likely mediated by such figures as Bernardino Telesio and Agostino Doni (Bacon [edited by Rees], 1996). All of these sources show Bacon's close association with many intellectual trends of Renaissance natural philosophy, and warn us against anachronistic readings and interpretations of Bacon's enterprise.

Several issues have been raised regarding the new picture of the Baconian project emerging from this impressive body of works and speculative theories. Was Bacon's speculative philosophy a radically different enterprise from his project for the reform of knowledge in the *Great Instauration*? And, more specifically, what was the precise philosophical significance of these speculative doctrines?

In her *DSB* entry on Bacon, Hesse suggested that the role of Bacon's natural reflections inside his more general philosophical system was merely ancillary and preparatory. According to Hesse, "unlike [René] Descartes, Bacon was not attempting to reach theoretical conclusions but, rather, to lay the necessary foundations for his inductive method" (p. 374). This interpretation is questionable, both in light of Bacon's speculative philosophy and also in terms of some of the clues that Bacon himself left regarding his general intentions and the value to be assigned to this work. As he explained in the "Distributio operis" ("Plan of the Work"), Bacon divided the project of his *Great Instauration* into six parts. *De augmentis scientiarum* and the *Novum organum* constituted the first and second sections, while a third was reserved for *Natural Histories* (including the *Historia vitae et mortis*). If the sixth and final part of the *Instauration* was to be occupied by the ultimate fruits of Bacon's new induction, the fourth and the fifth ones were likely to be devoted to examples and expositions of the speculative philosophy. Bacon explicitly stated the provisional character of this latter material. This

was not yet a "universal or systematic theory," he said (*OFB*, vol. 11, p. 175). Instead, he compared it to "interest payable until the principal can be had" and the true philosophy established. Certainly this provisional research was going to be presented by way of "examples of investigating and discovering according to my plan and way" (this being the purpose of the fourth part). However, at the same time, Bacon also suggested that one assign considerable value and significance to these investigations. For instance, with some false modesty, he stated that he hoped that his speculations "from my unceasing acquaintance with nature … may be greater than the measure of my mind leads me to expect" (*OFB*, vol. 11, p. 43). In fact, as he more bluntly affirmed in the *Novum organum*, he thought that his work on natural philosophy was greatly superior to anything thus far produced: "here and there I have in some special subjects conclusions … which are far truer, more certain and also (I think) more fruitful than those that men have employed hitherto" (*OFB*, vol. 11, p. 175). He even suggested that some of this material, once properly confirmed by his method, could directly become part of the sixth and final part of the *Instauration* (*WFB*, vol. 3, p. 547). Thus, Bacon's aims were not simply methodological but implied the achievement of a body of positive knowledge.

Still, the more general question regarding the exact role and significance of the speculative philosophy inside Bacon's work considered as a whole remains open to interpretation, and charting this precise degree of integration is one of the important tasks with which Baconian scholars are now confronted. For instance, in what ways do the speculative doctrines conform to the more "traditional" elements of Bacon's philosophy, such as his theory of forms, or the new induction? These and other problems, still to be thoroughly examined, nevertheless confirm the fact that the study of Bacon's philosophy and science remains a lively and stimulating area of research.

SUPPLEMENTARY BIBLIOGRAPHY

Historically, the primary source for Baconian scholarship has been the Victorian edition of Bacon's works by Spedding, Ellis, and Heath (abbreviated as WFB). *This edition is commonly referred to in two parts: Volumes one through seven comprehend Bacon's works, while volumes eight through fourteen cover Bacon's correspondence. At this writing a new edition comprising both is being prepared by Oxford University Press,* The Oxford Francis Bacon *(abbreviated as* OFB), *with Graham Rees and Lisa Jardine as general editors. This edition includes new material plus new facing-page translations of all Bacon's Latin works. The volumes also contain comprehensive introductory essays. To date, five volumes have been edited (vols. 4, 6, 11, 13, and 15). In addition, 1984 saw the first edition and annotated translation of the newly discovered Baconian treatise* De vijs mortis. *The same treatise has been published with improved typographical standards and readings in the* OFB, *vol. 6.*

WORKS BY BACON

The Works of Francis Bacon. Edited by James Spedding, Robert Leslie Ellis, and Douglas Denon Heath. 14 vols. London: Longman, 1857–1874.

Francis Bacon's Natural Philosophy: A New Source. A Transcription of Manuscript Hardwick 72A. Edited, translated, and with commentary by Graham Rees, assisted by Christopher Upton. Chalfont St. Giles, U.K.: British Society for the History of Science, 1984.

Philosophical Studies c. 1611–c. 1619. Edited by Graham Rees. Vol. 6 of *The Oxford Francis Bacon.* Oxford: Clarendon Press, 1996.

The Advancement of Learning. Edited by Michael Kiernan. Vol. 4 of *The Oxford Francis Bacon.* Oxford: Clarendon Press, 2000.

The Instauratio Magna: Last Writings. Edited by Graham Rees. Vol. 13 of *The Oxford Francis Bacon.* Oxford: Clarendon Press, 2000.

The Essayes or Counsels, Civill and Morall. Edited by Michael Kiernan. Vol. 15 of *The Oxford Francis Bacon.* Oxford: Clarendon Press, 2000.

The Instauratio Magna. Part 2: Novum Organum and Associated Texts. Edited by Graham Rees. Vol. 11 of *The Oxford Francis Bacon.* Oxford: Clarendon Press, 2004.

OTHER SOURCES

Gaukroger, Stephen. *Francis Bacon and the Transformation of Early-Modern Philosophy.* Cambridge, U.K.: Cambridge University Press, 2001.

Gemelli, Benedino. *Aspetti dell'atomismo classico nella filosofia di Francis Bacon e nel Seicento.* Florence, Italy: Leo S. Olschki, 1996. An excellent analysis of Bacon's debt to classic atomism and Lucretius.

———. "Francis Bacon: Un riformatore del sapere tra filosofia e medicina." *Cronos* 7, no. 2 (2004): 227–276.

Giglioni, Guido. "The Hidden Life of Matter: Techniques for Prolonging of Life in the Writings of Francis Bacon." In *Francis Bacon and the Refiguring of Early Modern Thought: Essays to Commemorate The Advancement of Learning (1605–2005).* Edited by Julie Robin Solomon and Catherine Gimelli Martin. Aldershot, U.K., and Burlington, VT: Ashgate, 2005.

Jardine, Lisa. *Francis Bacon: Discovery and the Art of Discourse.* Cambridge, U.K.: Cambridge University Press, 1974.

Jardine, Lisa, and Alan Stewart. *Hostage to Fortune: The Troubled Life of Francis Bacon.* New York: Hill and Wang, 1999. An authoritative modern biography.

Martin, Julian. *Francis Bacon, the State, and the Reform of Natural Philosophy.* Cambridge, U.K.: Cambridge University Press 1992.

Peltonen, Markku, ed. *The Cambridge Companion to Bacon.* Cambridge, U.K.: Cambridge University Press, 1996. A useful collection of introductory essays by leading Baconian scholars.

———. "Bacon, Francis, Viscount St Alban (1561–1626)." In *Oxford Dictionary of National Biography.* Oxford University Press, September 2004. Available from http://www.oxforddnb.com. A useful short biography.

Pérez-Ramos, Antonio. "Essay Review: Bacon in the Right Spirit." *Annals of Science* 42, no. 6 (1985): 603–611.

———. *Francis Bacon's Idea of Science and the Maker's Knowledge Tradition.* Oxford: Oxford University Press, 1988. An important philosophical analysis of Bacon's project.

Rees, Graham. "Francis Bacon's Semi-Paracelsian Cosmology." *Ambix* 22 (1975a): 81–101.

———. "Francis Bacon's Semi-Paracelsian Cosmology and the Great Instauration." *Ambix* 22 (1975b): 161–173.

Urbach, Peter. *Francis Bacon's Philosophy of Science: An Account and a Reappraisal.* La Salle, IL: Open Court, 1987.

Vickers, Brian. Review of *The Oxford Francis Bacon* Volume VI: *Philosophical Studies c. 1611–c. 1619,* edited by Graham Rees. *Isis* 90 (1999): 117–119.

Zagorin, Perez. *Francis Bacon.* Princeton, NJ: Princeton University Press, 1998. A good introductory survey of Bacon's life and philosophy.

Cesare Pastorino

BACON, ROGER (*b.* England, c. 1214 or 1220; *d.* Oxford, England, c. 1292), *mathematics, astronomy, natural philosophy.* For the original article on Bacon see *DSB,* vol. 1.

Bacon has long been recognized as a key intellectual figure in the Middle Ages, but interpretations of his role have varied. The previous *DSB* article on Roger Bacon by A. C. Crombie and John North will remain a classic and should be consulted. It is particularly important for the account of Bacon's mathematics and astronomy. Since 1970, however, there have been significant new editions and studies of Bacon's works on grammar, logic, natural philosophy, astrology, experimental science, and moral philosophy. There has been a real advance in the production of good quality Latin texts with accurate matching geometric diagrams. And so, step by step, scholarship is on the way toward a more critical appreciation of all of the achievements of Bacon as a philosopher, scientist, and moral philosopher/theologian. The only major alteration to the chronology of Bacon is the realization that he returned from Paris to Oxford around 1280.

In 1859, William Whewell set the tone for modern accounts of "Roger Bacon and the Sciences" (Whewell, 1859). He viewed Bacon as an advocate of experiment ahead of his time. Robert Adamson in 1876 considered Bacon a philosopher of science. In the 1900s, Lynn Thorndike (1914, 1916) and Pierre Duhem (Bacon, 1909) asserted that the role of observation in Bacon's science was minimal and added nothing to the science. A. C. Crombie in his *Robert Grosseteste and the Origins of Modern Science* (1953) argued that the qualitative aspects of modern science originated at Oxford in the early thirteenth century. This interpretation was not universally accepted.

The present entry brings the scholarship up to date and gives an overview of Bacon's program of research especially in the light of new textual discoveries and new studies. Much of the recent scholarship has emphasized that Bacon must be seen in the context of his own times and the scientific concerns of those times. To avoid anachronism one should interpret Bacon as a medieval scientist and not as an early modern or modern scientist.

The most significant advances in Bacon scholarship since 1970 have been the following: the discovery of the missing section of *Opus maius* on signs (*De signis*). The study of this and related logical texts has led to a better understanding of Bacon's philosophy of language and semiotics. One has also gained a better understanding of his applications of learning to theology, a more precise knowledge of his understanding of mathematics, the first reliable text of his major work on natural philosophy, *De multiplicatione specierum* (On the multiplication of species), the first reliable text of the *Perspectiva*, a better understanding of the sources of the *scientia experimentalis*, a better knowledge of his moral philosophy.

Life and Works. Bacon remarks in the *Opus tertium* that around 1267 to 1268 he had devoted forty years to study since he had first learned the alphabet and that no other scholar worked some much in the arts and sciences as he had done. Some scholars use this text to argue that Bacon was speaking about his elementary education and was born c. 1220. Others hold that he was born c. 1214.

With the exception of the logical works, the Aristotelian *Quaestiones* are found in manuscript, Amiens MS Bibl. Mun. 406. They include two sets of questions on the *Physica* and the questions on the *Metaphysica* of Aristotle, the questions on the *Liber de causis*, the pseudo-Aristotelian *De vegetabilibus*. A second version of the questions on the *Physica* has recently been found in Philadelphia MS Free Library, Lewis Europe, ff. 77ra-85rb. It led to new critical research.

The early logical works consist of the *Summa grammatica, Summa de sophismatibus et distinctionibus* and the *Summulae dialectics* (=*Summulae super totam logicam*). These works show that Bacon was indebted to the teaching of logic at Oxford and Paris in the 1230s and 1240s, especially to Robert Kilwardby. They received much critical study in recent years and show that Bacon was a mature philosopher of logic who was representative of terminist and premodist grammar.

Scholars have long held that Bacon was a pioneer in introducing the study of Aristotle as interpreted by Averroës and Avicenna to the University of Paris c. 1240. Recent research has shown that two Erfurt manuscripts

Roger Bacon. © HULTON-DEUTSCH COLLECTION/CORBIS.

(Stadtbibliothek Q. 290 and Q. 312) once ascribed to Walter Burley (fourteenth century) belong to the first half of the thirteenth century. The editor of the questions on the *Physica* attributed these to Richard Rufus of Cornwall, a contemporary and opponent of Bacon. This research alters the accepted view of Bacon as the first to teach Aristotle at Paris (see Richard Rufus of Cornwall, 2003).

It has been demonstrated that already in the 1240s, Bacon confronted and reviewed some of the major issues concerning Latin Averroism that would become a vital part of philosophical discussion at Paris in the 1260s and 1270s. One can conclude that by 1248 Bacon ceased being a master of arts at Paris, became an independent scholar, and returned to England. He was back in Paris in 1251.

When Bacon joined the Franciscan order about 1256, he expected that it would support his scholarly work. Instead, he entered a ten-year period of enforced absence from teaching. He had been attracted to the order by the philosophical, theological and scientific example of Robert Grosseteste and Adam Marsh. He had personally known Adam Marsh and may have seen Robert Grosseteste.

Roger Bacon and Science. The *Opus minus, minus, tertium,* the related foundational work in philosophy of nature, *De multiplictione specierum,* and the work on burning mirrors, *De speculum comburentibus,* together with an optical lens, were sent to the pope c. 1267 to 1268. They were seen as a preamble to a major work on philosophy. Together with these in the 1260s, he produced the *Communia naturalium, Communia mathematica, Epistola de secretis operibus naturae et the nullitate magiae.* The *Compendium studii philosophiae* can be dated to about 1271. This is largely a work of polemic on the state of studies in Paris. The edition of the important work in medieval politics and statecraft in Latin translation from the Arabic, the *Secretum secretorum,* was completed at Oxford about 1280. The *Compendium studii theologiae* is usually dated to c. 1292.

One must bear in mind that Bacon in the 1260s is writing as an individual author for a patron, Pope Clement IV. Although a onetime master of arts, he was no longer a teaching master at the university. Still, much of his polemic is centered on the struggles in the arts and theology at Paris. The pope instructed Bacon in 1266 to ignore the rules of his order and to send him his remedies about a matter of some importance. What does this mean?

Bacon offered a structural critique of the scholastic practice in the universities. He favored language study and science over *Sentence Method,* and advocated training in mathematics and the sciences as requirements for students in theology. Bacon's later works on languages and sciences were written in the specific historical and political context of the Mongol invasion of Europe, the sack of Baghdad in 1258, and the geopolitical situation of a Europe hemmed in by both the Mongols and Islam. His sense of world geography was aided by the travel reports of William of Roebruck. Bacon offered a criticism of the Latin Averroism/radical Aristotelianism of the schools.

The overall division of the *Opus maius* is Stoic: language study, natural philosophy/mathematics, and morals. The general context is theological: the arts and sciences leading to human well-being in this world and the next. Part One examines the causes of error in education and is critical of some theological limits on science. These causes are: belief in unworthy authority, long custom, uncritical popular opinion, and concealment of academic ignorance in a display of rhetorical wisdom. Part Two contains the pre-Cartesian view of truth and wisdom as a result of a universal revelation to the Hebrews that was transmitted through the Greeks, Romans, and Islam to medieval Christianity. Part Three deals with language study, grammar, semantics, and semiotics. Bacon's semi-

otics is now seen as very important for medieval logic. His account of semiotics, *De Signis,* was discovered in 1978 (Fredborg, Nielsen, Pinborg, 1978). Bacon's proposals were radical. He advocated language training in Hebrew and Greek. He wrote Hebrew and Greek grammars. Bacon's ontology pointed toward the priority of the individual and the realist/nominalist issues in medieval thought.

Parts Four, Five, and Six of the *Opus maius* present the main themes of Bacon's contribution to scientific education. In addition, one should add the scientific works mentioned above. It is important to see Bacon's main contribution to science as one who advocated scientific education in an arts faculty that was dedicated to the linguistic arts. Bacon had a very wide reading knowledge of most of the newly translated work from Greek, Jewish, and Islamic philosophy and science. His major claim to fame in science is that he was the first Latin thinker to comprehend and write on most of the ancient sources of Optics. In brief, he initiated the tradition of Optics/*Perspectiva* in the Latin world. This tradition would be formulated as teaching text by both John Pecham and Witelo of Silesia, his contemporaries, and would be taken up by the tradition leading to both Johannes Kepler and René Descartes. In his *Perspectiva* (*Opus maius,* Part Five) and *De scientia experimentali* (*Opus maius,* Part Six), he outlined a sketch for a scientific method, one that takes Optics as the model for an experimental science. In fact, Bacon and his contemporaries succeeded in the endeavor to have *Perspectiva* added to the four traditional *quadrivium* university subjects: arithmetic, geometry, astronomy, and music.

Opus maius, Part Four, deals with mathematics and the applications of mathematics. Bacon presented reasons for a reduction of logic to mathematics and saw mathematics as the key to an understanding of nature. Clearly, he was proclaiming the usefulness of mathematics for knowledge. He was not doing mathematical theory. Following his abbreviation of the *De multiplicatione specierum* which shows how mathematics might be applied to physics, he dealt with the application of astronomy/astrology to human affairs, the uses of mathematics in religious rites as in chronology, music, symbolism, calendar reform, geographical knowledge, and a resume of astrology. It used to be thought that Bacon was a Platonist in his view of the absolute priority of mathematics. That view has been seriously qualified. He did not reduce physics to mathematics. His explicit work on mathematics, the *Communia mathematica,* was not an exercise in mathematics: it was a presentation of the common notions that are important for a variety of mathematical practices. Bacon himself acknowledged those who were better mathematicians, namely, John of London, Pierre de Maricourt, and Campanus of Novara (Molland in Bacon, 1997). In general, Bacon was more interested in what mathematics can provide about knowledge of the world as an aid to missionary activity. He sent a map of the world to the pope.

Bacon was very interested in the applications of astronomy/astrology to human events. Although committed to a doctrine of freedom of the will, he held to a deterministic notion of causation in nature based on the Islamic authority on astrology, Abu Ma' Shar (Albumassar) and on the *De radiis* of al-Kindi. And because he held to a doctrine of universal radiation in nature, he had to account for the influence of the heavens on the human body and hence on the human mind. Much of the polemic in his later works consisted of a justification of this interest in the face of traditional theological objections. He was also interested in alchemy. It was his determined interest in both of these areas that led to disagreement with his superiors in the Franciscan order, specifically, Bonaventure.

The Philosophy of Nature. Bacon's treatise *De multiplicatione specierum* written before 1267 is closely related to the study of light, vision and perception in the *Perspectiva*. David C. Lindberg (1983a) noted that Bacon took Grosseteste's physics of light, a development of al-Kindi's universal radiation of force, out of its metaphysical background. He developed a universal doctrine of physical causation.

The use of species in this account is not that of Porphyry's logic or the perceptual notion of likeness. It is "the force or power by which any object acts on its surroundings" (Lindberg, 1983a, p. Lv). It denotes "al-Kindi's universal force, radiating from everything in the world to produce effects" (Lindberg, 1983a, p. Lv). As Bacon himself noted, "species [force, power] is the first effect of an agent. ... the agent sends forth a species into the matter of the recipient, so that, through the species first produced, it can bring forth out of the potentiality of matter [of the recipient] the complete effect that it intends" (Lindberg, 1983a, pp. 6–7). This was a universal theory of natural causation as the background for Bacon's philosophy of vision and perception. Most importantly, species is a univocal product of the agent. The first immediate effect of any natural action is definite, specific, and uniform. This production is not the imparting of an external form. The species is educed from the active potency of the matter (Lindberg, 1983a, p. 13).

This was a first attempt in the Latin world to provide separate domains for material and spiritual being. Natural causation occurs naturally according to regular processes or laws of nature. There is no spiritual being in the medium as was commonly taught by other Scholastic philosophers. No, for Bacon, universal causation was cor-

poreal and material, and matter itself in not just pure potentiality but was rather something positive in itself. Hence, the general philosophy of nature prepared the theoretical ground for the specific application of mathematics to matters of vision and perception.

Perspectiva. Bacon, in his *Perspectiva* and related works, presented his model for a careful and detailed application of mathematics to the study of nature and mind. In imitation of the *De aspectibus* of Alhacen (Ibn al-Haytham), he provided an application of geometry to vision that within the terms of reference of his times was partly successful.

Bacon's approach to vision and perception, however, was not an exercise in contemporary mathematical optics. It should be seen as the sketch of a philosophy of perception and mind. These topics constitute Part One and a section of Part Two. The text then opens onto a consideration of direct, reflected and refracted vision, and ends with the application of geometrical models for moral and religious considerations.

Part One and Part Two, distinction one and two deal with the structure of the eye, problems of vision and visual errors. The aim is psychological and epistemological, that is, to set out the conditions for certifiable or verifiable and certain perception. The theory of the eye is taken from the Galenic tradition handed on by Constantine the African's translation of Hunyan ibn Isaq and from Avicenna and Ibn al-Haytham. For this tradition, vision occurs when the crystalline humor is altered by the intromission of visual species from the object. Vision is completed when the species proceeds through the vitreous humor to the optic nerve and through this to the common nerve. It is here that a common visual judgment is made. Bacon followed Ibn al-Haytham and imposed a geometrical model on the eye. Using this model, Bacon was able to give a geometrical account of radiation through the eye. How then does one avoid confusion in vision and gain verifiable clarity? For Bacon, the perpendicular ray was primary; the other rays were treated as cases of indirect vision. Yet, the rays were refracted in the rear surface of the crystalline humor.

Bacon was concerned with optical illusions, whether inverted images, magnification, vision of distant objects, the moon illusion, and such matters. He attempted to solve in a rational and experimental manner the puzzles found in Ptolemy, Ibn al-Haytham, and others. Still, he was a child of his sources. These do not provide him with the more advanced data and mathematical method that would be characteristic of the seventeenth century. Rather, Bacon provided a functional qualitative geometry of the eye and vision. He was committed to an intromission theory of vision but he combined it with an extramission theory of vision that avoided the anthropomorphisms of earlier theories. He used the extramission theory mainly to emphasize the active role of the eye in vision.

In Parts Two and Three, he was to a certain extent successful in applying geometry to problems of direct, reflected, and refracted vision. He moved the study of these matters to a new level. The geometrical arguments were worked out with careful diagrams and various appeals are made to experimental conditions. What are these conditions? Some of them are simple thought experiments or even reports of experiments (actual or imaginary) from earlier writers. It seems clear, however, that Bacon himself did experimental work with pinhole images, lenses, and discrete observations. This did not lead to a pure geometrization of nature and he inevitably fell back on physical, perceptual, and metaphysical arguments. One might argue that he lacked the notion of infinity that is present in modern geometry.

Bacon introduced another important item for science. He refers to the laws of reflection and refraction as *leges communes nature.* For Bacon in his account of nature in *Communia naturalium* and the later works in general, a general law of nature governed universal force. This universal law of nature is imposed on a world of Aristotelian natures. This notion would have a significant future in experimental science.

Bacon ended Part Three with an account of how a better understanding of the phenomena of nature could lead to a more accurate knowledge of natural phenomena mentioned in scripture. He found in visual phenomena significant metaphors and analogies for use in moral and religious teaching. Direct evidence of Bacon's influence here in making science available for an educated public is seen in the use of his work by Pierre de Limoges in his influential work *De oculo morali* (On the moral eye), written in Paris between 1275 and 1289. MS Paris, BN Lat. 7434 owned by Pierre de Limoges contains an early copy of Bacon's *Perspectiva.* All of this suggests Pierre de Limoges as a very early reader of Bacon's works.

De scientia experimentali. Presupposing the *Perspectiva,* Bacon in *De scientia experimentali* and in related works on the halo and on burning mirrors situated this new scientific practice as a desired area of study in the medieval university. Starting from Aristotle's account of *empeiria* (*experience*), Bacon argued that logical argument alone is not sufficient for the verification of things. Even arguments that have their origins in experience will need to be verified by means of an intuition of the things in the world. He distinguished natural scientific argument from moral and religious mystical intuition, although he did allow for the notion of a revealed intuition in science.

His aim was to provide a method for science, one that was analogous to the use of logic to test validity in arguments. This new practical method consisted of a combination of mathematics and detailed experiential descriptions of discrete phenomena in nature. It would be distinguished from the conjurations of magic and from religious belief. It would also be different from philosophy of nature and from broad optical knowledge. These two areas are important for broad theory, but according to Bacon, they do not provide access to minute, detailed experiments. Nevertheless, for his description of the first example of an experimental science, the study of the rainbow, Bacon was dependent on Aristotle, Seneca, and Avicenna.

His own important contribution is to be found in his calculation of the measured value of forty-two degrees for the maximum elevation of the rainbow. This was probably done with an astrolabe, and in this, Bacon advocated the skillful mathematical use of instruments for an experimental science. That Bacon had mathematical competence in this field can be seen in his account of the *Halo* (Duhem edition of *Opus tertium*) and in his complex arguments in *De speculis comburentibus.* Bacon took up Grosseteste's theory of refraction and tried to work out the difficulties. Important here is his emphasis on the role of individual drops of water for the process of reflection and refraction. A correct account of the rainbow would appear some forty years after Bacon in the *De iride* of Theodoric of Freiberg.

A second task for experimental science was the discovery by experience alone of instruments (armillary sphere), new medical cures, chemical discovery, and military technologies. An important item here is the discovery of magnetism. It would seem that Bacon was reporting on the actual experimental work of Magister Petrus Peregrinus, author of *De magnete,* who is lauded in the *Opus tertium* as the only worthwhile experimentalist at Paris. Bacon has been lauded down the centuries for his medical learning, but recent scholarship limited the number of works attributed to Bacon. Still, it is important here to note that he did draw on medical practice to set out rules and procedures that, in a nonscholastic manner, would lead to a more experimental approach to nature. The third task was that of the prognostication of the future on the basis of astronomical or astrological knowledge.

The conclusion to the *De scientia experimentali* is important. Bacon presented the ideal of the philosophical chancellor who will organize science and its technological products for the benefit of the *Res publica Christiana.* In this, he was influenced by the important *Mirror of Princes* from the Islamic World, the *Sirr-al-'asrar* (*Secretum secretorum,* Steele ed. [1909–1940, Vol. 5]). Stewart C. Easton proposed that this work was the guiding vision for Bacon's reform of science. Steven Williams argued (1994) that Bacon completed the edition of this work after his return to Oxford c. 1280. Still, there is much cross-reference between this work and Bacon's writings in the 1260s.

David C. Lindberg has given a succinct summary of Bacon's model for an experimental science (Bacon, 1997). He saw four main aspects. First, Bacon's theories of *perspectiva* were not his own creation. He took the best available materials from Greek and Islamic scholars and produced his own synthesis. Second, there is much evidence that Bacon himself did mathematical work and experiments with visual phenomena such as pinhole images and the measurement of the visual field. Third, as seen above, Bacon correctly calculated the maximum degree of elevation for the rainbow. Fourth, the experiments in Bacon, especially in the *Perspectiva,* served theoretically significant functions. It supplied observational data that required explanation in terms of a given optical theory. The usual role of experiment in Bacon is to "confirm, refute or challenge theoretical claims" (Bacon, 1997, p. 271).

One might have expected Bacon to have given equal treatment to astronomy, but in this field he was a child of his time. He reported on the accounts of Aristotle, Ptolemy, and Alfraganus (Steele ed., Vol. 4). He discussed the pros and cons in a scholastic manner but did not advance the field in the manner that he did for *Perspectiva.* Bacon's *Moralis philosophia (Opus maius, VII)* concerns philosophy of religion, social philosophy, a theory of the virtues, an astrological sociology of religion and cultures, and an account of argument and rhetoric.

Roger Bacon had an immediate influence on early fourteenth-century philosophers such as John Duns Scotus and William of Ockham especially in terms of the role of the doctrine of species in epistemology, and in matters relating to semantics and semiotics (see Tachau, 1998). He would also seem to have been read by members of the Merton School. It was in the late Middle Ages that Roger Bacon came to be seen as a hero for English medicine. Reduced to a figure of comedy in the late sixteenth century, his manuscripts were recovered by John Dee and Sir Kenelm Digby. His scientific works were first published in the early seventeenth century as a result of the Rosicrucian interest in science. The *Opus maius* was first published in 1733. Roger Bacon's works began to be studied with the new historical interest in medieval texts in the nineteenth and early twentieth centuries.

SUPPLEMENTARY BIBLIOGRAPHY

WORKS BY BACON

Opera quaedam hactenus inedita (=*Opus tertium, Opus minus, Compendium studii philosophiae, Epistola de secretis operibus Artis et Naturae, et de nullitate Magiae*). Edited by John S.

Brewer. London, 1859. Reprint, Nendeln, Lichtenstein: Kraus Reprint, 1965.

The Greek Grammar of Roger Bacon and a Fragment of His Hebrew Grammar. Edited by Edmund Nolan and Samuel A. Hirsch. Cambridge, U.K.: Cambridge University Press, 1902.

Un fragment inédit de l'Opus tertium de Roger Bacon. Edited by Pierre Duhem. Florence, Italy: Quarrachi, 1909.

Opera hactenus inedita Rogeri Baconi (Vols. 1–16). Edited by Robert Steele, Ferdinand M. Delorme, Andrew Little, et al. Oxford: Clarendon Press, 1909–1940.

Fr. Rogeri Bacon Compendium Studii Theologiae. Edited by Hastings Rashdall. Aberdeen, U.K.: Aberdeen University Press, 1911.

Roger Bacon Essays. Collected and edited by A. G. Little. Oxford: Clarendon Press, 1914. These essays, some on Bacon's science, are still valuable.

"*Les Summulae dialectics de Roger Bacon.*" *Archives d'Histoire Doctrinale et Litteraire du Moyen Age* 53. Edited by Alain de Libera (1986): 139–289; 54 (1987): 171–278.

Roger Bacon and the Sciences: Commemorative Essays. Edited by Jeremiah Hackett. New York: Brill, 1997. (Studien und Texte zur Geistesgeschichte des Mittelalters, Band LVII): Woodward & Howe on Geography/Cartography; Van Deusen on Music; Molland on Mathematics; Hackett on Astrology; Lindberg on Light, Vision and Universal Radiation of Force; Newman on Alchemy; Hackett on *scientia* experimentalis; Getz on Roger Bacon and Medicine; Williams on the *Secretum secretorum.*

Roger Bacon and Aristotelianism. Edited by Jeremiah Hackett. *Vivarium* 35 (September 1997): 129–320. This special edition of the journal is a study of the place of Bacon in the reception of Aristotle. See papers by Marmo, Trifogli, Donati, Wood, Noone, Long, Hackett.

OTHER SOURCES

Adamson, Robert. *Roger Bacon: The Philosophy of Science in the Middle Ages.* Manchester, U.K.: J.E. Cornish, 1876.

Bagliani, A. Paravicini. "Ruggero Bacone, autore del *De ratardatione accidentium senectutis?*" in *Studi Medievali,* 3rd ser., 28 (1987): 707–728.

Ebbesen, Sten. "The Dead Man Is Alive." *Synthese* 40 (January 1979): 43–70.

Fredborg, K. M., Lauge Nielsen, and Jan Pinborg, eds. "An Unedited Part of Roger Bacon's *Opus Maius: De signis.*" *Traditio* 34 (1978): 75–136.

Hedwig, Klaus. "Roger Bacon's *Scientia experimentalis.*" In *Philosophen des Mittelalters,* edited by Theo Kobush. Darmstadt, Germany: Primus, 2000.

Lindberg, David C. *Theories of Vision from Al-Kindi to Kepler.* Chicago: University of Chicago Press, 1978.

———, ed. *De multiplicatione specierum* and *De speculis comburentibus.* Oxford: Clarendon Press, 1983a.

———. *Studies in the History of Medieval Optics,* London: Variorum Reprints, 1983b.

———. *Perspectiva.* Oxford: Clarendon Press, 1996.

"Lines of Influence in Thirteenth Century Optics: Bacon, Witelo, and Pecham." *Speculum* 46 (January 1971): 66–83.

Maloney, Thomas S. "The Semiotics of Roger Bacon," *Medieval Studies* 45 (1983): 120–154.

———. "The Extreme Realism of Roger Bacon." *Review of Metaphysics* 38 (June 1985): 807–837.

———, ed. *Compendium studii theologiae.* Leiden, Netherlands: Brill, 1988.

Massa, Eugenio, ed. *Rogeri Baconis Moralis Philosophia.* Zürich: Thesaurus Mundi, 1953.

Matthews, Gareth B. "A Medieval Theory of Vision." In *Studies in Perception: Interrelations in the History of Philosophy and Science,* edited by Peter K. Machamer and Robert G. Turnbull. Columbus: Ohio State University Press, 1978.

Molland, A. G. "Roger Bacon as Magician." *Traditio* 50 (1974): 445–460.

———. "Roger Bacon and the Hermetic Tradition in Medieval Science." *Vivarium* 31 (1983): 140–160.

———. "Roger Bacon's Appropriation of Past Mathematics." In *Tradition, Transmission, Transformation: Proceedings of Two Conferences on Pre-Modern Science Held at the University of Oklahoma,* edited by F. Jamil Ragep, Sally P. Ragep, and Steven Livesey. Leiden, Netherlands: Brill, 1996.

———. "Roger Bacon's *De laudibus mathematicae:* A Preliminary Study." In *Texts and Contexts in Ancient and Medieval Science: Studies on the Occasion of John E. Murdoch's Seventieth Birthday,* edited by E. Sylla and M. McVaugh. Leiden, Netherlands: Brill, 1997.

Newman, William R. "The Alchemy of Roger Bacon and the *Tres espistolae* Attributed to Him," in *Comprendre et maitriser la nature au moyen age: mélanges d'hisgtoire offerts a Guy Beaujouan,* Geneva: Droz, 1994.

Richard Rufus of Cornwall, *In Physicam Aristotelis,* edited by Rega Wood. Auctores Britannici medii aevi, 16. Oxford: Oxford University Press for The British Academy, 2003.

"Roger Bacon and the Reception of Aristotle in the Thirteenth Century: An Introduction to His Criticism of Averroes." In *Albertus Magnus and the Beginnings of the Medieval Reception of Aristotle in the Latin West,* edited by Ludger Honnefelder, Rega Wood, Mechthild Dreyer, et al. Münster, Germany: Aschendorff Verlag, 2005.

Tachau, Katherine H. *Vision and Certitude in the Age of Ockham: Optics, Epistemology and the Foundations of Semantics 1250–1350.* Leiden, Netherlands: Brill, 1988.

Thorndike, Lynn. "Roger Bacon and Experimental Method in the Middle Ages." *Philosophical Review* 23 (1914): 271–298.

———. "The True Roger Bacon I," and "The True Roger Bacon II." *The American Historical Review* 21 (1916): 237–257, 468–480.

Whewell, William. *History of the Inductive Sciences from the Earliest Times to the Present Times,* Vol. 1. New York, 1859.

Williams, Steven J. "Roger Bacon and His Edition of the Pseudo-Aristotelian." *Secretum secretorum, Speculum* 69 (1994): 57–73.

Jeremiah Hackett

BAERENDS, GERARD PIETER (*b.* The Hague, Netherlands, 30 March 1916; *d.* Groningen, Netherlands, 1 September 1999), *ethology, innate releasing mechanism (IRM), heterogeneous summation of stimuli, supernormality, hierarchical structure of behavior, organismic zoology, marine science, overfishing.*

Baerends, arguably the most influential pupil of biologist Nikolaas (Niko) Tinbergen, is counted among the founders of ethology. He built a world-renowned research laboratory at Groningen, Netherlands, integrating ecological and physiological themes centered on the behavior of intact organisms in their natural surroundings. Equally important, he was a major mover behind the postwar expansion of marine science in the Netherlands.

Growing Up in The Hague. Gerard Baerends, the only child of Pieter Gerardus Baerends and Adriana Johanna Baerends, née Hulstkamp, grew up in The Hague, where his father was a civil servant. As a youngster, Gerard roamed the countryside and nearby beach, at that time an ideal setting for nature study. As a high school boy he was enthralled by a lecture of Nikolaas Tinbergen from Leiden University, as a result joining a youth movement for nature study and becoming imprinted on biology for life. As an active member of this Nederlandse Jeugdbond voor Natuurstudie (NJN; Netherlands youth association for nature study), he also underwent the intensive coaching of his peers, particularly Luuk Tinbergen. Nikolaas's younger brother and one year older than Baerends, Luuk was a budding scientist gifted with artistic abilities. This remarkable, emancipatory Dutch youth movement (founded in 1920) encouraged excursions and field studies for young people, including write-ups in their journals. Barring membership to all above the age of twenty-three, it thus broke free from interference by the older generation. As Baerends assessed it in his "Early Ethology" (1991), the NJN had a profound influence on the upcoming scientific generation by promoting independence of thought.

Formative Years in Leiden. An assiduous student at Leiden University, Baerends quickly came under the spell of Nikolaas Tinbergen and in his first year in 1934 was already helping as a "slave" (as volunteers were then called) during his holidays in the field experiments then just starting in the herring gull colony in the nearby dunes. Tinbergen, a brilliant and charismatic teacher, had returned the year before from his 1932–1933 Greenland expedition to take up his duties lecturing on animal behavior and had just initiated intensive six-week ethology practicals. As one of the pioneer generation, Baerends later described the hallmarks of these famous experimental courses for third year students, the first ethology courses in the world:

> At the beginning of the course the students were asked just to observe the behaviour of their animals and record it as carefully as possible, with pencil and paper. Following this introductory period, they were encouraged to start asking questions, and thus to wonder about the behavior they had observed. These questions were then critically discussed and where necessary corrected and refined. Finally, the students were invited to design and carry out experiments for testing their own hypotheses. (1991, p. 11)

Aside from research projects at the Leiden laboratory and local coastal dunes, Tinbergen instituted major studies of behavior by observing insects in the pinewoods and sands of Hulshorst. Staff and students camped out, and in this informal setting of self-discovery, Baerends undertook his PhD study on the provisioning behavior of the digger wasp *Ammophila campestris*. At the early age of twenty-five, Baerends defended his thesis (published in full in 1941), remarkable for its wealth of detail on case histories and field experiments amassed during seven summers. (He had the help of another of Tinbergen's students, Jos van Roon, in this enterprise, and the couple married in 1942.) In Tinbergen's autobiographical *Curious Naturalists* (1958), he devoted a whole chapter to Baerends's study, stressing its originality. Conceived as an extension of his own preoccupation with homing, Tinbergen wrote that "the Baerendses went their own way … and discovered many very remarkable things" (p. 84), somewhat to his initial discomfiture as he had intended the project to concentrate on orientation. Luckily Tinbergen gave his pupil full freedom. In his thesis, Baerends contributed the insight that the organization of behavior could best be conceived as hierarchical in structure. This conception, molded in close collaboration with Tinbergen, became one of the unifying principles of the developing field of ethology and provided a framework for the study of motivation and of the conflicts between opposing tendencies that were to take center stage in the next few decades.

Growing up in The Hague with easy access to the coast, Baerends had an early fascination for the sea, and as a young student was recruited as a volunteer during coastal cruises by Jan Verwey, the director of the Zoological Station at Den Helder. These days at sea made a profound impression and led to a lifelong friendship between the two men. Baerends developed this interest by doing part of his master's research at the Plymouth Marine Biology Laboratory in England, also undertaking theoretical work in oceanography. Upon completion of his thesis he was promised a position at an oceanographic research institution in the Dutch East Indies. The German occu-

pation of the Netherlands in May 1940 prevented him from taking up this job in the tropics (and indeed delayed the formal defense of his thesis, as Leiden University was closed), but fortunately, Baerends was able to undertake fisheries research near home instead, joining the government research institute at IJmuiden in 1942. During the remainder of the war years, he achieved mastery of the archives and reports bearing on the overfishing problem of North Sea fish stocks. At war's end Baerends accompanied the fishermen at sea and learned at firsthand their problems. In 1946 he had the opportunity of verifying his opinions with colleagues in the United Kingdom, where the youthful duo of Ray Beverton and Sidney J. Holt had made great analytical strides. His official government report outlining how sustainable yields could be obtained from the North Sea fishery was judged to deserve a wider audience and was republished in translation in the United States.

A New Laboratory. In the immediate postwar years, an optimistic wave of recovery swept over the Netherlands, and the universities too tried hard to make up for the lost years. The professorship in zoology at the University of Groningen had fallen vacant due to the sudden death of the respiratory physiologist Engel Hendrik Hazelhoff in 1945, and when Baerends was approached to fill the post, he jumped at the chance. Baerends stipulated that he would make fieldwork the primary source of inspiration: academic biologists would go outdoors again. Baerends foresaw that despite all their fascination, career opportunities for scientists trained as ethologists would remain limited, and inspired by his taste for applied research in fisheries, he determined to develop both ecological and ethological themes in restructuring the Zoology Laboratory around its tradition of experimental work. His inaugural lecture was thus drawn from his work on the North Sea fisheries, and about half of the forty-three PhD students he eventually trained (ten of them in turn holding professorships) chose ecological themes.

This auspicious start (Baerends was only thirty and achieved his professorship a year before Nikolaas Tinbergen did at Leiden) should not blind one to the fact that Groningen, despite its glorious past, had little to offer at the time. Only five or six students enrolled in biology annually, the staff was tiny, the equipment was antiquated, and his laboratory was an odd amalgamation of decrepit buildings downtown. Baerends rose to the challenge and with characteristic vigor prepared for expansion. The university authorities were impressed and a new laboratory was situated in the botanic gardens in the suburb of Haren, tailored to the new concepts of teaching and research. Innovations included facilities for maintaining birds in captivity, a generous aquarium building for holding and observing fish, and a vibration-free wing designed for sophisticated neurophysiological work. As Baerends stated in his "Field Studies" entry (1981), "a full understanding of the causation, development, function, and evolution of behaviour requires studies of animals living freely in their natural environment, studies of captive animals under semi-natural conditions, and studies of animals and even parts of them in the laboratory" (p. 189). Supporting staff included a professional artist and taxidermist; carpentry shop; glass blower; photographer; instrument makers, later supplemented with an electronics team; and, of course, animal caretakers. The new teaching labs were spacious and light, and when the laboratory was opened in 1953, it was by far the best in the country.

In these early years Baerends recruited staff by enlisting friends from Leiden. Foremost among them was Luuk Tinbergen (the younger brother of Nikolaas), chosen to fill the first chair in ecology in the country specifically to develop field-based animal ecology. At Leiden in 1946, Luuk had defended his thesis on the ecology of the sparrow hawk in interaction with its avian prey. Observational work in the laboratory was closely bound up with fieldwork of unparalleled intensity, done with the help of a growing body of enthusiastic students captivated by Baerends's flair as lecturer. The field teams camped together at Hulshorst with Luuk (a direct continuation of the famous prewar camps of Nikolaas and his circle) or on the island Terschelling, where Baerends was able to use a World War II bunker in the dunes as his base of operations in the Herring Gull colony, starting in 1950.

Undertaking the gull work was a watershed event for Baerends and was to occupy him for the rest of his life. Nikolaas Tinbergen accepted a position at Oxford University starting in September 1949, and in a sense Baerends inherited the project he had already been associated with in his student days. Aside from the fact that he was intrinsically interested in the problem of how nesting gulls recognize their eggs, the techniques of field experimentation with dummy eggs appealed to him as a wonderful introduction to ethology for his students. With his more quantitative mind, Baerends felt he could take the study further than Tinbergen had done. The stickleback program that was the hallmark of the original ethology laboratory remained in the capable hands of Jan van Iersel, who became Tinbergen's successor at Leiden.

International Consolidation of Ethology. Just before Tinbergen's move to Oxford, an important symposium titled Physiological Mechanisms in Animal Behaviour was convened by the Society for Experimental Biology in Cambridge, England, in 1949. This meeting, initiated by William H. Thorpe and Tinbergen, heralded the emergence of ethology as a discipline and united observation on intact animals; sophisticated physiological laboratory

work aimed at revealing central steering mechanisms; and, of course, the emerging theory.

This gathering brought the main prewar proponents of ethology together again for the first time. Konrad Z. Lorenz, only recently returned as a prisoner of war from Russia, met his colleagues again after an absence of ten momentous years. In his contribution (nearly fifty pages but now for the first time in English and available for a broader readership and including his famous "water closet model" for motivation), Lorenz reiterated his approach to the study of innate behavior by the comparative method. By contrast Baerends called into question the Lorenzian view that reactions in the form of "innate motor patterns" in reaction to "releasers" were really free from the influence of learning, thus foreshadowing his later contribution from the gull experiments. Nikolaas Tinbergen expanded on the concept of the hierarchical organization underlying instinctive behavior that he and Baerends had originated, seeking to bridge the gap with the Cambridge neurophysiologists participating at the meeting by drawing in their own work at the lower levels of coordination.

Erich von Holst, a German neurophysiologist of great originality, was prevented by illness from attending. However, he sent a letter (in German), which in its arrogant and assertive tone shocked Baerends and Tinbergen, treading deeply on their sensitivities after the long years of occupation. This dismay threatened to block communication with the group at Wilhelmshaven, where von Holst had assembled a team of brilliant young scientists (under the auspices of the Max Planck Gesellschaft). Baerends therefore persuaded Otto Koehler, the diplomatic doyen of German ethology, to visit von Holst personally on the way home after the Cambridge conference. The resulting invitation by von Holst to meet together in Wilhelmshaven in 1950 led to a reconciliation (von Holst turned out to be a charming host of open disposition) and marked the initiation of regular international ethology conferences. As one of the prime movers behind these conferences in the coming years, Baerends made a major contribution on the international scene.

The new laboratory in Haren was the venue for the International Ethology Conference in 1955, which was notable for bringing participants from North America. Chief among them was Daniel Lehrman, who as enfant terrible had published in 1953 a fundamental critique of the Lorenz theory on instinctive behavior. Baerends (together with van Iersel) had met Lehrman in Montreal in 1954 at the 14th International Congress on Psychology and quickly discovered common ground in highlighting weaknesses of the concepts as originally formulated by Lorenz. (A common interest in bird-watching surfaced as well.) The 1955 meeting at Baerends's laboratory brought some seventy ethologists together, and appropriately,

Lehrman was pictured between Lorenz and Baerends (with Tinbergen immediately behind them) in the official conference photograph. In a conversation many years later, Lehrman emphasized how vital the early contacts fostered by the rather informal ethology conferences had been in leading to a rapprochement and a new synthesis, giving equal emphasis to learned and innate components of behavior.

With his tact, linguistic abilities (fluent German, English, and French, in addition to his native Dutch), and reputation, Baerends was heavily involved in organizing these international gatherings until the early 1970s, when due to the increasing number of "converts" to ethology, they could no longer be convened by invitation. For many in the younger generation, these conferences were testing grounds for new methods and ideas and provided fascinating glimpses into how the leaders of ethology and their disciples interacted. Baerends's international dimension was strengthened by the meticulous care he devoted to the journal *Behaviour*—which he founded in 1948, together with Thorpe and Tinbergen—serving as executive editor through more than one hundred volumes; he retired from the board in 1991.

Typically, it was also Baerends who took the lead in assembling seventeen essays in a book titled *Function and Evolution in Behaviour* (1975), issued to mark the retirement symposium of his teacher. In December 1973 Tinbergen had just been awarded the Nobel Prize, together with Karl von Frisch and Lorenz, "for their discoveries concerning the organization and elicitation of individual and social behaviour patterns." Baerends contributed to the book an evaluation of the conflict hypothesis originated by Tinbergen to explain the evolution of displays that was much appreciated by Tinbergen himself, and documented by some reviewers as the most important chapter.

By the early 1950s the teaching of ethology and related subjects at Groningen was far ahead of that at any other university, and new techniques of electrostimulation with miniaturized electrodes augured well for integration with neurophysiology. A major disaster overtook the team at this time, however, with the sudden death of Luuk Tinbergen in September 1955 (at the age of only thirty-nine and recently promoted to a full professorship). This dynamic ecologist was a behavioral ecologist before the term was coined and was at the time deeply involved in defining his ethological concept of *search image* on the basis of observing dietary choice in free-living tits feeding their nestlings. Luuk's colleagues and students at Groningen worked through his unpublished notes and papers, and the result was a two-hundred-page monograph, "The Dynamics of Insect and Bird Populations in Pine Woods" (1960). Although Baerends did his best to replace him, it would take decades to build a new ecology group working with birds in the field and thus linking with the ethologists.

Lasting Contributions to Ethology. Baerends made his mark with a series of papers in the 1950s. Together with his wife Jos, he assembled "An Introduction to the Study of the Ethology of Cichlid Fishes" (1950), a well-illustrated monograph on the behavior of cichlid fish based on aquarium observation and experiment; it inspired research the world over on these tropical fish and their complex parental care. With several of his new students Baerends produced a monumental study, "Ethological Studies on *Lebistes reticulatus*" (1955), on the guppy, another aquarium study quantifying the interaction between perception (the external stimulus situation) and motivational factors in eliciting behavioral reactions. The insights encapsulated in one of the figures have made this a classic that found its way into many textbooks. In those early years, a colony of black terns nested on a lake behind his house, and together with another student team, Baerends observed pair formation and egg care. In "Observations on the Behaviour of the Black Tern" (1956), Baerends and his collaborators speculated on the phylogenetic origins of the displays, thus complementing Nikolaas Tinbergen's program on larids, then gathering momentum at Oxford.

Meanwhile, data from the annual campaigns in the herring gull colonies were accumulating at an alarming rate. In the 1960s Baerends faced the dilemma that his duties as director of what had become a large institute (its scientific staff numbered eighteen) with a visiting rate from North America (postdoctorals and PhD students) even exceeding that of Oxford left him little time for reflection. Temporarily, he had also taken on directorship of the Netherlands Institute for Sea Research, with its new quarters on the island of Texel, to guide this legacy of his old friend Verwey through a difficult interim phase. The invitation to spend the academic year 1964–1965 in the congenial setting of the Center for the Advanced Study of the Behavioral Sciences at Stanford University in Stanford, California, came in the nick of time. That year of unremitting analysis laid the basis for "The Herring Gull and Its Egg. Part I" (1970), by Baerends and Rudi H. Drent, the first of two monographs drawing the gull work together. In a book chapter titled "Stimulus Selection" (1973), Baerends and Jaap Pieter Kruijt also presented the essence of the finding that the external features of the egg combined in a quantitative manner to provide a compound stimulus value, thereby substantiating the concept of "heterogeneous summation."

Alfred Seitz had pioneered this concept, contending that the animal reacted to the sum total of stimuli, and he reasoned that it must be feasible to measure the stimulus

Gerard Baerends with gull eggs. *Various sizes and shapes of false gull eggs used by Dutch researcher Gerard Baerends during hatching behavior studies.* THOMAS D. MCAVOY/TIME LIFE PICTURES/GETTY IMAGES.

NEW DICTIONARY OF SCIENTIFIC BIOGRAPHY

value of an object in all possible sensory modalities (such as shape, color, texture, and size) to discover how these were combined by the animal. The challenge was to find a method to measure the contribution of each of these features of the stimulus, and Baerends perfected the technique of quantifying the response of a parent gull when presented with two competing egg models on the nest rim. Which would be rolled in first? This work, drawing on nearly one thousand field trials integrated in a gigantic titration exercise, elucidated why under certain circumstances the parent gull returning to the nest might prefer to retrieve an egg deviating strongly from normal, with exaggerated features (in color, stippling, and size) representing the "super-normal" stimulus (i.e., the stimulus value surpassing the value for the real egg).

A distraction, albeit a rewarding one, was posed by an invitation to provide scientific backing to the talented cinematographer Bert Haanstra to produce a film illustrating the status of ethological understanding at that time. The finished product, *Bij de Beesten af* (1972; with the English-language version, *Ape and Superape,* aptly following in 1973 when the Nobel Prize awarded to von Frisch, Lorenz, and Tinbergen had drawn attention to the subject), reflected Baerends's conviction that by juxtaposition, the viewer would readily appreciate that human behavior, despite all the trappings of modern society, was but a step away from that of the wild creatures depicted. The film, viewed by millions the world over, sensitized the public to the sociobiology debate that followed, leading to a growing awareness to consider the message ethology conveyed for the human sciences. Baerends wrote a richly illustrated chapter, "De mens als produkt van de evolutie" (1972; Mankind as a product of evolution), in the popular book, *Bij de Beesten af,* that appeared simultaneously with the film. He also supervised the editing of excerpts of the movie for educational purposes, garnishing the many lectures he gave to students enrolled in psychology with the motto "see for yourself."

In the late 1960s a wave of democratization swept over Dutch universities. Although very much a believer in decisions by consensus, Baerends felt frustrated by the new layers of bureaucratic interference from above. In this depressing atmosphere Baerends received an unexpected offer from the Max Planck Gesellschaft, asking if he would succeed Lorenz (who was due to retire) at the Seewiesen Institute near Munich. On the one hand, this was a tempting offer, as Baerends had a high regard for not only the scientists at Seewiesen, but also for Jürgen Aschoff's group at nearby Erling-Andechs. On the other hand, he feared that acceptance would put him still further away from hands-on research. Opportunely, a counterproposal was launched by the Royal Netherlands Academy of Arts Sciences, Groningen University, and the Ministry of Education and Sciences. This alternative

offered a personal chair, allowing Baerends to continue his work in his own surroundings abetted by a small research group, completely free of bureaucratic interference. Accepting the latter offer, Baerends devoted the years from 1973 until his official retirement in 1986 to publishing the remainder of his backlog of unfinished manuscripts, which would amount to nearly half of his lifetime writing output. Most notably, it included "The Herring Gull and Its Egg. Part 2" (1982), the second monograph on the herring gull work, coauthored with Rudi Drent. During this time he also supervised an additional seventeen PhD students. Furthermore, Baerends headed out into the gull colony again, engaging in research that incorporated the insights generated by game theory made tangible by Maynard Smith and his group in England. Baerends also found the time to put the finishing touches on a monograph, "The Morphogenesis of the Behaviour of the Domestic Cat" (1979). It concerned the development of play behavior in domestic kittens, which had been a long-term project of his wife, Jos, the coauthor.

Baerends had an enormous impact on the rise of ethology worldwide and for decades was "Mr. Ethology" in the Netherlands. It is no coincidence that the four chair holders in animal behavior in the country in 2006 were all trained in Groningen. Elected to the Royal Netherlands Academy of Sciences (1958), the Hollandsche Maatschappij van Wetenschappen In Haarlem (1968), knighted by Queen Juliana, and receiving an honorary doctorate in 1965 from the University of Rennes in France, many honors came his way. Baerends was gratified by elevation to Fellow of the American Association for the Advancement of Science in 1980, the citation reading "for foremost work in ethology and for development of the world famous institute at Groningen." Perhaps the most fitting epitaph is a quote from the closing pages of his monumental "The Herring Gull and Its Egg," where the determined empiricist surfaces: "Properly documented descriptions will be of more use for bridging the gap between ethological analysis and behavioural physiology than attempts at neat classifications in theoretically based categories" (Baerends and Drent, 1982, p. 357).

BIBLIOGRAPHY

A bibliography of Baerends's published writings is in "Proceedings of the G. P. Baerends Symposium." Netherlands Journal of Zoology 35 (1982): 1–376. *A significant quantity of unpublished documents related to Baerends is held at the University of Groningen, Central Archives, Groningen.*

WORKS BY BAERENDS

"Fortpflanzungsverhalten und Orientierung der Grabwespe *Ammophila campestris* Jur." *Tijdschrift voor Entomologie* 84 (1941): 68–275. His PhD thesis.

"De rationele exploitatie van den zeevischstand." *Ministerie van Landbouw Visserij & Voedsel, Mededelingen* 36 (1947): 1–99. Translated into English as "The Rational Exploitation of the Sea Fisheries with Particular Reference to the Fish Stock of the North Sea." *U.S. Department of the Interior Fish and Wildlife Service, Special Science Report: Fisheries* 13 (1950): 1–102.

"Specialization in Organs and Movements with a Releasing Function." *Symposium Society for Experimental Biology* 4 (1950): 337–360.

With Jos M. Baerends-van Roon. "An Introduction to the Study of the Ethology of Cichlid Fishes." *Behaviour Supplement* 1 (1950): 1–242.

With R. Brouwer and H. T. Waterbolk. "Ethological Studies on *Lebistes reticulatus* (Peters). I. An Analysis of the Male Courtship Pattern." *Behaviour* 8 (1955): 249–334.

With B. Baggerman, H. S. Heikens, and J. H. Mook. "Observations on the Behaviour of the Black Tern, *Chlidonias n. niger* (L.) in the Breeding Area." *Ardea* 44 (1956): 1–71.

With Rudi H. Drent, et al., eds. "The Herring Gull and Its Egg. Part I." *Behaviour Supplement* 17 (1970): 1–312.

"De mens als produkt van de evolutie." In *Bij de Beesten Af,* edited by Anton Koolhaas, et al. Amsterdam: Uitgeverij Ploegsma, 1972.

With Jaap Pieter Kruijt. "Stimulus Selection." In *Constraints of Learning,* edited by Robert A. Hinde and J. Stevenson-Hinde. London and New York: Academic Press, 1973.

"An Evaluation of the Conflict Hypothesis as an Explanatory Principle for the Evolution of Displays." In *Function and Evolution of Behaviour,* edited by Gerard P. Baerends, Colin Beer, and Aubrey Manning. Oxford: Clarendon Press, 1975.

With Colin Beer and Aubrey Manning, eds. *Function and Evolution in Behaviour.* Oxford: Clarendon Press, 1975.

With Jos M. Baerends-van Roon. *The Morphogenesis of the Behaviour of the Domestic Cat, with a Special Emphasis on the Development of Prey-Catching.* Verhandelingen Koninklijke Nederlandse Akademie van Wetenschappen. Amsterdam and New York: North-Holland Publishing, 1979.

"Field Studies." In *The Oxford Companion to Animal Behaviour,* edited by David McFarland. Oxford: Oxford University Press, 1981.

With Rudi H. Drent. "The Herring Gull and Its Egg. Part II." *Behaviour* 82 (1982): 1–415.

"Two Pillars of Wisdom." In *Studying Animal Behaviour: Autobiographies of the Founders,* edited by David A. Dewsbury. Chicago: University of Chicago Press, 1985.

"Early Ethology: Growing from Dutch Roots." In *The Tinbergen Legacy,* edited by Marian S. Dawkins, Tim R. Halliday, and Richard Dawkins. London and New York: Chapman and Hall, 1991.

OTHER SOURCES

Dewsbury, Donald A. "Americans in Europe: The Role of Travel in the Spread of European Ethology after World War II." *Animal Behaviour* 49 (1995): 1649–1663.

Drent, Rudi H. "Dropping the Pilot: Gerard Baerends, 1916–1999." *Ardea* 88 (2000): 113–118.

Hinde, Robert A. *Animal Behaviour: A Synthesis of Ethology and Comparative Psychology.* New York: McGraw-Hill, 1966.

———. *Ethology, Its Nature and Relations with Other Sciences.* Oxford and New York: Oxford University Press, 1982.

Kruuk, Hans. *Niko's Nature, a Life of Niko Tinbergen and His Science of Animal Behaviour.* Oxford and New York: Oxford University Press, 2003.

Lehrman, Daniel S. "A Critique of Konrad Lorenz's Theory of Instinctive Behavior." *Quarterly Review of Biology* 28 (1953): 337–363.

Lorenz, Konrad Z. "The Comparative Method in Studying Innate Behaviour Patterns." *Symposium of the Society for Experimental Biology* 4 (1950): 221–268.

"Proceedings of the G. P. Baerends Symposium." *Netherlands Journal of Zoology* 35 (1982): 1–376. Includes a biographical sketch.

Slater, Peter J. B. Review of *Function and Evolution in Behaviour,* edited by Gerard P. Baerends, Colin Beer, and Aubrey Manning. *Animal Behaviour* 24 (1976): 720.

Thorpe, William H. *The Origins and Rise of Ethology: The Science of the Natural Behavior of Animals.* London: Heinemann Educational, 1979.

Tinbergen, Luuk. "The Dynamics of Insect and Bird Populations in Pine Woods." *Archives neérlandaises de Zoologie* 13 (1960): 259–473.

Tinbergen, Nikolaas. "The Hierarchical Organization of Nervous Mechanisms underlying Instinctive Behaviour." *Symposium of the Society for Experimental Biology* 4 (1950): 305–312.

———. *Curious Naturalists.* London: Country Life, 1958. Baerends's PhD dissertation is discussed in chapter 6.

Van Hooff, Jan A. R. A. M. "Levensbericht Gerard Pieter Baerends." In *Levensberichten en Herdenkingen 2005.* Amsterdam: Koninklijke Nederlandse Akademie van Wetenschappen, 2005.

Verwey, Jan. "In Memoriam Luuk Tinbergen." *Ardea* 43 (1955): 293–308. A necrology of the younger brother of Nikolaas, with a bibliography.

Voous, Karel H. "Baerends, Gerardus Pieter." In *In de ban van Vogels, Ornithologisch Biografisch Woordenboek van Nederland.* Utrecht, Netherlands: Scheffers, 1995.

R. H. Drent

BAGNOLD, RALPH ALGER (*b.* Devonport, England, 3 April 1896; *d.* probably in Blackheath, England, 28 May 1990), *physics of transport of natural materials by wind and water.*

Brigadier Ralph Bagnold is best known for his pioneering work on the wind-blown sands of deserts. He was also a professional soldier and desert explorer of considerable accomplishment. Bagnold authored many of the most fundamental and oft-cited papers on the physical nature of sediment transport in rivers, on beaches, and in the ocean.

Early Life. Bagnold was born at the Manor House, Stoke, Devonport, England, on 3 April 1896. His father, Colonel Arthur Henry Bagnold, was a contemporary officer with Hebert Kitchener, and he saw active service with the Royal Engineers in Cyprus, Egypt, South Africa, and the Sudan. His paternal grandfather, Major General Michael Edward Bagnold, served more than thirty years in India and its dependencies. Ralph Bagnold himself received a regular army commission in 1915, serving in France and Flanders during World War I. He subsequently took an honors degree in engineering from Cambridge University in 1921 and served thereafter in various military postings until retiring from the British army in 1935.

Ralph Bagnold's lifelong scientific interest in the physical mechanisms for the natural transport of granular materials by wind and water was kindled at an early age. As a five-year-old, living in a converted coffee mill in the highlands of Jamaica in the Caribbean, he diverted part of the mill's stream through a rock channel, built a working model of the household drainage system, and observed a flood event. These interests later overlapped with wide-ranging explorations, particularly when the army posted him to Egypt in 1926. There, Bagnold joined a small group of fellow officers who enjoyed traversing remote areas by cross country expeditions in light cars. His many challenges included driving a Model-T the entire length of the Sinai Desert and driving a Ford truck from India to Egypt. However, it was in the sand seas of the Libyan Desert that science and adventure merged. A 10,000-kilometer (6,200-mile) trip, much of it in uninhabited northwestern Sudan, was organized in 1932 using Model-A Fords. These travels are described in Bagnold's book *Libyan Sands: Travel in a Dead World* (1943), written in Hong Kong shortly before his first retirement from military service.

Research on Sand Dunes. During his expeditions Bagnold became fascinated with the geometrical order and regular spacing of the great desert dunes. He found that during violent sandstorms, the dense, moving clouds of sand, in contrast to the associated dust, extended no more than a meter or so (just over three feet) above the ground. This led to physical questions as to the forces that could lift relatively dense sand grains up into thin, moving air or how the mass rate of sand movement might be related to wind strength. With his retirement from military service at the rank of major in 1935, Bagnold was able to pursue the science that was necessary to answer these questions.

At the hydraulics laboratory of Imperial College, University of London, Bagnold constructed a wind tunnel

Ralph Bagnold. *Major Ralph Bagnold of the Royal Signal Corps sitting on a specially modified Model-T Ford used for exploring the deserts of North Africa.* HULTON ARCHIVE/GETTY IMAGES.

of his own design, much of it from salvaged materials. The resulting experiments and field measurements from return trips to Egypt were described in several papers and in his important book *The Physics of Blown Sand and Desert Dunes*, published in 1941. For his work on various projects, he conceived and produced instruments that were appropriate for measuring the parameters that he deemed to be of interest. These included the desert sun compass, the instant-reading, multi-tube manometer, and the piezometric pressure gauge. In 1938, he turned his attention to problems in the water transport of sediments, a theme to which he returned after World War II.

With the outbreak of war in 1939, Bagnold was recalled to military service. His return to Egypt was accidental, resulting from a convoy collision at sea that interrupted his posting to East Africa. Nevertheless, his unique knowledge of the remote areas of the Libyan Desert was eventually appreciated by the British command in Cairo. Bagnold was entrusted with the urgent raising and subsequent command of the Long Range Desert Group (LRDG). He assembled this special unit within a mere six weeks. Operating essentially as a private army, it was assigned missions of reconnaissance and raiding behind the Italian lines throughout the interior of Libya. Promoted to colonel, Bagnold led the LRDG on trips as far as eight hundred miles behind enemy lines. One daring trip to Chad resulted in that French province joining the Allied cause, becoming the only French overseas dependency to do so voluntarily. When Erwin Rommel's Afrika Corps entered the war, the LRDG observation posts reported all movements along its supply routes to the front lines in northern Africa.

Sediment Transport. In 1944, Ralph Bagnold retired for a second time from the British army, having reached the ultimate rank of brigadier. He accepted the position of director of the Shell Research Laboratory near Chester, England. After two years, however, he resigned to continue his private studies of granular transport by water and air. His experiments were performed at Imperial College and also at his home office-workshop at Rickwoods in Kent. Around this time his sister, Enid Bagnold, reintroduced Bagnold to his future wife, Dorothy Plank, and the marriage took place in 1946. Enid was quite a famous author: Her novels include *National Velvet* (1935) and among her plays was *The Chalk Garden* (1956).

In 1958, Luna B. Leopold invited Bagnold to Washington, D.C., to be a consultant to the United States Geological Survey (USGS) on matters of sediment transport in rivers. He spent one month per year for the next several years in this capacity. This period generated several of the classical papers on sediment transport mechanics, many of which he published as professional papers of the USGS. One of these, a 1966 study titled *An Approach to the Sediment Transport Problem from General Physics*, treats the transport of grains by fluid as the work of a machine. As such, sediment movement depended on rates of energy supply and of transport work done against friction. The machine analogy led immediately to the concept of stream power, which controls the transport rate of the solids that are immersed in a fluid.

Bagnold's approach to problems of sediment transport contrasted sharply with that of the hydraulic engineers of his day. The engineers followed a tradition of seeking to account for sediment movement in kinematic terms. Their approach derived from studies that simplified the complex dynamics of fluid flow by eliminating the fluid density. The result of this tradition was a lack of attention to the very important density differences between the moving grains and the transporting fluid. This density disparity is exactly what piqued Bagnold's curiosity about wind transport of sand during his earliest

desert explorations. Bagnold realized that the engineering approach was inevitably self-defeating. Thus, his most important contributions derive from looking at a very basic problem in a completely different way and in developing the insights, theory, and experiments to resolve the physical elements of that problem.

For his Libyan Desert explorations, Bagnold was awarded the 1933 Founder's Gold Medal of the Royal Geographical Society. His scientific research accomplishments were recognized by a Fellowship in the Royal Society of London in 1944, the G. K. Warren Prize of the U.S. National Academy of Sciences in 1969, the Penrose Medal of the Geological Society of America in 1970, the Wollaston Medal of the Geological Society of London in 1971, the Sorby Medal of the International Association of Sedimentologists in 1978, and the David Linton Award of the British Geomorphological Research Group in 1981.

Brigadier Ralph Bagnold continued to work productively right up to his death in 1990, at age ninety-four. He disliked anything pompous or stuffy. He would often characterize himself as "a mere amateur" in science. Once he even registered for a major international symposium by listing his profession as "farmer" (in reference to his estate at Rickwoods). In commenting on his scientific research in 1988, he described his role in science to be "to stir the pool of complaisant tradition with the stick of fact."

BIBLIOGRAPHY

A complete bibliography of Bagnold's published works can be found in Thorne, MacArthur, and Bradley, 1988, cited below.

WORKS BY BAGNOLD

Libyan Sands: Travel in a Dead World. London: Hodder and Stoughton, 1935. A popular account of Bagnold's desert expeditions of 1927, 1929, 1930, and 1932.

"The Movement of Desert Sand." *Proceedings of the Royal Society of London* Series A, 157 (1936): 594–620.

"The Size-Grading of Sand by Wind." *Proceedings of the Royal Society of London* Series A, 163 (1937): 250–264.

The Physics of Blown Sand and Desert Dunes. London: Metheun, 1941. Reprint, London: Chapman and Hall, 1971.

"Early Days of the Long Range Desert Group." *Geographical Journal* 105 (1945): 30–46. Bagnold's account of his famous World War II military unit.

"Motion of Waves in Shallow Water. Interaction between Waves and Sand Bottoms." *Proceedings of the Royal Society of London* Series A, 187 (1946): 1–18.

"Experiments on a Gravity-Free Dispersion of Large Solid Spheres in a Newtonian Fluid under Shear." *Proceedings of the Royal Society of London* Series A, 225 (1954): 49–63.

"The Flow of Cohesionless Grains in Fluids." *Philosophical Transactions of the Royal Society of London* Series A, 249 (1956): 235–297.

Some Aspects of the Shape of River Meanders. Washington, DC: U.S. Government Printing Office, 1960.

An Approach to the Sediment Transport Problem from General Physics. Washington, DC: U.S. Government Printing Office, 1966.

"The Nature of Saltation and of 'Bed-Load' Transport in Water." *Proceedings of the Royal Society of London* Series A, 332 (1973): 473–504.

Sand, Wind, and War: Memoirs of a Desert Explorer. Tucson: University of Arizona Press, 1990. Bagnold's autobiography.

OTHER SOURCES

Greene, Jay E., ed. "Bagnold, Ralph Alger." In *McGraw-Hill Modern Scientists and Engineers,* vol. 1. New York: McGraw-Hill, 1980. Brigadier Bagnold himself contributed to this short biography.

Kenn, M. J. "Memorial to Ralph Alger Bagnold, 1896–1990." *Geological Society of America Memorials* 8 (1992): 91–93. A brief biography researched and written by the former head of hydraulics at Imperial College, University of London.

Thorne, Colin R., Robert C. MacArthur, and Jeffery B. Bradley, eds. *The Physics of Sediment Transport by Wind and Water: A Collection of Papers by R. A. Bagnold.* New York: American Society of Civil Engineers, 1988. Includes a brief biography, a bibliography, and reprints of many of the Bagnold's published works.

Victor R. Baker

BAHCALL, JOHN NORRIS

(*b.* Shreveport, Louisiana, 30 December 1934; *d.* New York, New York, 17 August 2005), *astrophysics, solar physics, x-ray astronomy, gravitational lensing, active galaxies, solar neutrino problem, weak interaction physics, observations from space, science policy.*

An American astrophysicist, Bahcall was both a hedgehog and a fox (in Isaiah Berlin's sense). Best known for more than forty years of engagement with what became "the solar neutrino problem," he also made important contributions to the understanding of the structure of the Milky Way galaxy, the significance of absorption lines in the optical spectra of quasars, and astronomical constraints on fundamental physics, and to science policy issues, including the championing of the Hubble Space Telescope (HST) and setting of priorities for the 1990s among major ground- and space-based astronomical initiatives.

Background and Family. Bahcall was the son of Mildred (who held degrees in music and social work) and Malcolm (a successful salesman, born a few months after his parents arrived in the United States from Russia) Bahcall. The family name was originally Bachalor. Brother Robert Bah-

call followed his father into sales, while John Bahcall, after high school years devoted largely to tennis and debate, entered Louisiana State University thinking of a degree in philosophy and, perhaps, a career in the reform rabbinate. Summer courses at the University of California, Berkeley, and financial support from a cousin, led to his remaining there, where the fulfillment of a science requirement with a standard introductory physics course led to a switch in direction and degrees in physics (AB 1956, UC Berkeley; MS 1957, University of Chicago; PhD 1961, Harvard). The PhD dissertation, directed by David Layzer, concerned the calculation of energy levels of highly ionized atoms for comparison with recent measurements by Bengt Edlén.

During a research fellowship at Indiana University, Bahcall studied theory of the weak interaction (responsible, for instance, for neutron decays) under Emil Konopinski and calculated rates of nuclear decay under conditions different from laboratory ones. Thinking that the effects could never be measured, he was drawn to consideration of nuclear reactions in stars by a conversation with astronomer Marshall Wrubel and by a classic paper on formation of the elements in stars by E. Margaret Burbidge, Geoffrey R. Burbidge, William A. Fowler, and Fred Hoyle (1957, known to astrophysicists as B^{2}FH). Bahcall published a short paper pointing out that certain nuclear reaction rates in stars would be quite different from laboratory ones, which led Fowler to invite him to the California Institute of Technology in 1962 to work on related problems in physics and astrophysics.

Bahcall rose from research fellow to assistant to associate professor of physics at Caltech, but meanwhile had also spent parts of 1968 to 1970 at the Institute for Advanced Study, where he became professor of natural sciences (1971–2000) and the Richard Black Professor of Natural Sciences (1997 until his death), simultaneously holding a visiting position at Princeton University.

In 1965, Bahcall gave lectures on nuclear astrophysics in Israel at the invitation of Yuval Ne'eman (coinventor of a standard model of elementary particle physics). There he met nuclear physics student Neta Assaf (MS 1965, Weizmann Institute; PhD 1970, Tel Aviv University). After an extended, largely long-distance courtship, Neta was persuaded to come to California, and they were married in September 1966. Their three children, Safi, Dan, and Orli, all earned PhDs in technical subjects.

Neta and John Bahcall appear as coauthors on more than twenty papers, including studies of quasars, x-ray sources, and globular clusters, as well as some of the early solar neutrino papers, though their interests later diverged: she focusing on large-scale structure in the universe and he on the topics in the following sections. Safi is also a Bahcall coauthor on one paper.

John N. Bahcall. *John N. Bahcall, The Richard Black Professor of Astrophysics, Institute for Advanced Study, Princeton, N.J.* COURTESY OF NETA BAHCALL, PROFESSOR OF ASTROPHYSICS, PRINCETON UNIVERSITY.

Solar Neutrinos. Raymond Davis Jr., at Brookhaven National Laboratory, had begun development of a radiochemical detector for reactor neutrinos in the 1950s, based on ideas from Luis Alvarez and the Italian-American-Russian physicist Bruno Pontecorvo. The key reaction is one in which chlorine-37 captures a neutrino, producing argon-37 and an electron. The ^{37}Ar has a half-life near thirty-five days for decaying back to ^{37}Cl, during which time the argon atoms can be swept out of the C_2Cl_4 (perchloroethylene) detector liquid and counted by standard radiochemical techniques. Extension to the solar neutrino regime would require a much larger detector than Davis's original 1,000 gallons and also a location in a deep mine to provide shielding from cosmic-ray noise. William Fowler, who had been interested in the solar case from the beginning, brought Bahcall into the program in 1962, because of the differences in reaction rates in stars versus in the lab that Bahcall had begun to calculate. Detection of neutrinos

from the Sun was, and is, important because the light comes from the surface and has scattered its way out over about 100,000 years since it was made by central nuclear reactions, while the neutrinos stream straight out—apart, it turns out, from rotating from electron neutrinos to one or both of the other species, muon and tau neutrinos.

Instrumentation and predictions developed in parallel. A critical pair of papers in 1964 from Davis and Bahcall made clear that the expected neutrino flux was, just barely, within experimental grasp and that the largest uncertainties appeared to be in rates for certain nuclear reactions, both for production in the Sun and for capture by chlorine nuclei. Construction of the 100,000-gallon detector tank, in the Homestake Mine in Lead, South Dakota, began in 1966 and data collection in 1968. The 1968 prediction was 7.5 ± 3 SNU, where SNU, or solar neutrino unit, means 10^{-36} captures per chlorine-37 atom per second. But the data were setting, at first, only upper limits around 3 SNU and, eventually, a measured value of 2.6 SNU—about one-third of expectations.

At this point, Bahcall the hedgehog came into his own. Sometimes alone, sometimes with collaborators, he continued to refine the physics in the calculations of expected capture rate. The result never varied outside the 7.5 ± 3 SNU range of 1968, though the error bars shrank with better numbers for nuclear reaction rates, solar composition, and other contributing physics. About twenty possible explanations for the discrepancy were published between 1969 and 1977. A few said Davis was somehow not getting all the argon-37 atoms out of his tank (only about 1.5 per day were expected). Most proposed models of the Sun that were different from Bahcall's standard one. And Bruno Pontecorvo put forward the idea of oscillations between the one sort of neutrino (electron) the Davis detector could see and another species (the mu neutrino) as early as 1969.

But it took more than thirty years and a succession of additional experiments to show this was the right answer. Davis's experiment was working just fine, the nuclear numbers were OK, and Bahcall's calculation was right. But weak-interaction physics was different from the standard model (in ways that were still being incorporated into early twenty-first-century theories of elementary particle physics). Over the years, additional detectors were built to look at the Sun, especially ones using gallium-71, which can capture the low energy solar neutrinos from the main hydrogen-fusion process. These too were deficient.

A Japanese group, headed by Masatoshi Koshiba, built a succession of ever-better experiments at Kamioka, originally intended to look for proton decay. These confirmed the deficiency of high-energy solar neutrinos and, later, showed that neutrinos produced by cosmic rays hitting the Earth's upper atmosphere oscillate between species (mostly mu neutrinos to the third kind, the tau neutrino). In the 1990s, the Sudbury Neutrino Observatory (SNO) in Canada, using heavy (deutcrated) water as the detector, began also seeing fewer electron neutrinos than were expected, and, finally, early in the twenty-first century confirmed that the missing ones were arriving from the Sun as mu neutrinos.

Bahcall continued to improve the calculations throughout these decades, and his last papers dealt with reconciling the solar neutrino flux (at last well understood!) with the best numbers for solar composition and measurements of the deep interior structure that come from the frequencies of subtle quivering of the gaseous body of the Sun (helioseismology).

Other Scientific Contributions. Quasars were discovered in 1963, soon after Bahcall arrived at Caltech, by astronomy faculty member Maarten Schmidt. Debate quickly arose between a majority of astronomers (including Schmidt) who concluded that these bright, compact sources of radio and visible radiation were at the large distances implied by their redshifts and Hubble's law, and the sources therefore very bright, and a minority who thought that the sources were nearby and the redshifts due to some new physical principle. In 1965, Bahcall and Edwin E. Salpeter (a nuclear physicist at Cornell who had suggested a model for quasars involving black holes the previous year) pointed out that distant quasars would surely have gas clouds between Earth and them, which would absorb some of the light in a recognizable pattern. Such absorption lines turned up about two years later in many observations (some with Bahcall as a collaborator), and Bahcall was in the forefront of developing the mathematical tools to demonstrate that many (not all) of the absorption clouds were in deep intergalactic space, and the sources themselves therefore as distant as their redshifts indicate.

Bahcall continued to work on aspects of quasar astronomy right through to the Hubble Space Telescope era, heading the key project team working on absorption lines in QSOs (the radio-quiet equivalent of quasars). Less happily, Bahcall attempted HST imaging of the galaxies of which QSOs are the bright centers. He set worrisomely small upper limits to how big and how bright some of these galaxies could be, but other groups soon found the expected host galaxies.

In 1972, the Bahcalls were in Israel, with access to a one-meter telescope at Wise Observatory. X-ray astronomy was an exciting, relatively new field, and the Uhuru satellite had just produced a better position for the bright source called Hercules X-1. Stellar astronomer William Liller, looking at catalogued objects in the right part of the sky, had suggested that the known variable star HZ Herculis and Her X-1 might be the same object. The Bahcalls were able to confirm this by showing that the light varies with the same period and phase as the x-rays, because the source consists of a normal star orbiting and periodically eclipsing a neutron star. In 1975, Bahcall and Jeremiah P. Ostriker (then at Princeton University) were among the first to suggest that some other x-ray sources, those in old globular clusters of stars, might not be binary systems but single black holes of 100–10,000 solar masses accreting gas from the clusters. This issue was again under consideration thirty years later.

In the lead-up to the launch of what became the Hubble Space Telescope, Bahcall was concerned both about aspects of the operations process, particularly the availability of sufficient guide stars to keep the telescope correctly aimed, and about using resulting data to learn about the various populations of stars in the Milky Way. With postdoc Raymond Soneira, he showed that guide stars would sometimes be in short supply, and the planned

John Bahcall. COURTESY OF NETA BAHCALL, PROFESSOR OF
ASTROPHYSICS, PRINCETON UNIVERSITY.

operation procedure was modified accordingly. Their
model of galactic structure was subsequently widely used
in dark-matter searches and other studies. Information on
the numbers and stability of binary stars with very wide
separations was one of many byproducts of the Bahcall
group's observations and calculations.

Both solar neutrino and quasar data can be used to
address problems in fundamental physics. Among those
considered by Bahcall were possible changes with time in
the strength of the electromagnetic force (below
detectability in 1967 and still so in a 2004 paper), limits
on the extent to which electric charge might not be conserved (a 1996 collaboration with Maurice Goldhaber,
who had been director of Brookhaven National Laboratory when Davis and Bahcall first started working
together on solar-neutrino detection), and tests of the
combined conservation of charge, parity, and time reversal (again, only limits—very tight ones).

The cooling of neutron stars, the gravitational lensing
of quasar images by galaxies between us and them, the
structure of globular clusters, limits on dark matter in the

disk of the Milky Way, neutrinos from supernovae, and
sources of the highest-energy cosmic rays and their implications for neutrino astrophysics of the future were among
the other topics on which Bahcall the fox said something
important.

Public Policy Issues. Bahcall was the first astrophysicist
on the staff of the Institute for Advanced Study, and it was
expected that he would build up a group there. This happened, and it flourished, with a few additional permanent
staff members and some interaction with Princeton University and its students, but largely on the basis of outstanding postdoctoral researchers, who arrived, were often
mentored by Bahcall, and then went on to permanent
positions elsewhere. He was also instrumental in building
the astrophysics groups at the Weizmann Institute and Tel
Aviv University in Israel.

The idea of a large optical telescope in space, having
originally been championed by Lyman Spitzer, was in the
air at Princeton in the 1970s. In addition, in 1973, when
Robert O'Dell (of Marshall Space Flight Center,
Huntsville, Alabama) and Nancy Roman (then at NASA
headquarters) began canvassing the astronomical community for ideas and support for a Large Space Telescope,
Bahcall responded with both enthusiasm for what might
be done and an offer to help. By the end of 1973, he was
part of the working group. In the second phase of development, he became head of the photometry team and
then a proponent of the idea of taking many short-
duration exposures that could be used for serendipitous searches and perhaps education. This eventually
happened.

Over the next few years, the Space Telescope was several times in trouble and at risk of being removed completely from the NASA program. In response, Bahcall,
together with Spitzer and a few others, orchestrated one of
the first and most successful campaigns of congressional
visits, letters to members of Congress from the community, and lobbying by potential contractors for the telescope.

By 1977, when a NASA advisory panel helped select
the first instrument package and associated science working group, it was inevitable that Bahcall would be part of
it. He championed charge-coupled devices as light detectors and the retention of spectroscopic capability when
cost-saving efforts threatened these. When HST finally
flew, though the effort to bring its science center to
Princeton had failed (in favor of a proposal from Johns
Hopkins University), Bahcall became head of the key-
project team studying quasar absorption lines, which produced something like fifteen papers over the next decade.
Neta Bahcall commuted by train between Princeton
and Baltimore to serve as head of the science program

160　　　　　　　　　　　　　　　　　　　NEW DICTIONARY OF SCIENTIFIC BIOGRAPHY

selection office and chief of the general observer support branch at Space Telescope Science Institute for about six years under director Riccardo Giacconi.

Since 1960, the astronomical community has produced decadal reports recording past progress and prioritizing its equipment needs for the next ten years. The published products have inevitably been named for the scientists who chaired the panels: the (Albert) Whitford Report for the 1960s, the (Jesse) Greenstein report for the 1970s (which did not really advocate an optical telescope in space), and the (George) Field report for the 1980s. In about 1988, geophysicist Frank Press, then president of the U.S. National Academy of Sciences, suggested that the next one should be the Bahcall Report for the 1990s. With great interest but some misgivings, Bahcall took this on.

The process involved a larger number of astronomers than had ever been directly concerned before (or since), with fifteen disciplinary panels of twenty members each, as well as the main panel of fifteen chaired directly by Bahcall. There were also numerous town meetings and presentations to groups of astronomers. The final recommendations prioritized ground- and space-based initiatives in a single list, and most of the highest-ranked programs had been accomplished or were underway by the time the next panel reported, including U.S. owned 8-meter telescopes in Hawaii and Chile (operational from the late 1990s), the Space Infrared Telescope Facility (launched in August 2003 and then renamed the Spitzer Space Telescope), and a large array for millimeter radio astronomy, construction of which began in the Atacama Desert of Chile in 2005. A characteristic moment in Bahcall chairing had him responding to two panel members who had disagreed at length, and somewhat obscurely, with "I agree with you both; now let's go on."

Prizes and Recognition. Over the years, Bahcall received the Warner Prize (for young astronomers, in 1970), the Heineman (a mid-career award, in 1995, the same year Davis won the Tinsley prize), and the Russell Lecturership (a lifetime award, in 1999) from the American Astronomical Society. Additional major recognition included membership in the U.S. National Academy of Sciences and the Academia Europaea, the Hans Bethe Prize of the American Physical Society, the U.S. National Medal of Science (1998), the Benjamin Franklin Medal and the Fermi Award of the Department of Energy (both shared with Davis in 2003), the million-dollar Dan David Prize (2003) from Israel, and the Comstock Prize of the U.S. National Academy of Sciences (2004). When the 2002 Nobel Prize in Physics was announced as going half to Raymond Davis and Masatoshi Koshiba for the development of neutrino astrophysics and half to Riccardo Giacconi (for contributions to the establishment of x-ray

astronomy), there was considerable feeling in the physics community that it should have been a three-way award, entirely in neutrino astrophysics, with Bahcall as the third winner. His public stance was that he was proud to have been considered.

BIBLIOGRAPHY

WORKS BY BAHCALL

"Beta Decay in Stellar Interiors." *Physical Review* 126, no. 3 (1962): 1143–1149.

"Solar Neutrinos. 1. Theoretical." *Physical Review Letters* 12, no. 11 (1964): 300–302.

With R. A. Wolf. "An Observational Test of Theories of Neutron-Star Cooling." *Astrophysical Journal* 142, no. 3 (1965): 1254–1256.

With Edwin E. Salpeter. "On the Interaction of Radiation from Distant Sources with the Intervening Medium." *Astrophysical Journal* 142, no. 4 (1965): 1677–1681.

With Maarten Schmidt. "Does the Fine-Structure Constant Vary with Cosmic Time?" *Physical Review Letters* 19, no. 22 (1967): 1294–1295.

With Giora Shaviv. "Solar Models and Neutrino Fluxes." *Astrophysical Journal* 153 (1968): 113–125.

"A Systematic Method for Identifying Absorption Lines as Applied to PKS 0237–23" *Astrophysical Journal* 153 (1968): 679–688.

With P. James E. Peebles. "Statistical Tests for the Origin of Absorption Lines Observed in Quasi-Stellar Sources." *Astrophysical Journal* 156 (1969): L7–L10.

With Ron D. Ekers. "On the Possibility of Detecting Redshifted 21-cm Absorption Lines in the Spectra of Quasi-Stellar Sources." *Astrophysical Journal* 157 (1969): 1055–1064.

With Maarten Schmidt and James E. Gunn. "Are Some Quasi-Stellar Objects Associated with Clusters of Galaxies?" *Astrophysical Journal* 157 (1969): L77–L79.

With Neta Bahcall and Geoffrey Burbidge. "Relative Correlation of Large- and Small-Redshift Quasi-Stellar Objects with Clusters of Galaxies." *Astrophysical Journal* 166 (1971): L77–L80.

With Neta Bahcall. "The Period and Light Curve of HZ Herculis." *Astrophysical Journal* 178, no. 1 (1972): L1–L4.

With Richard Hills. "The Hubble Diagram for the Brightest Quasars." *Astrophysical Journal* 179, no. 3 (1973): 699–703.

With Paul C. Joss and Roger Lynds. "On the Temperature of the Microwave Background Radiation at a Large Redshift." *Astrophysical Journal* 182, no. 3 (1973): L95–L98.

With Jeremiah Ostriker. "Massive Black Holes in Globular Clusters?" *Nature* 256, no. 5512 (1975): 23–24.

With Henry Primakoff. "Neutrino-Antineutrino Oscillations." *Physical Review D* 18, no. 9 (1978): 3463–3466.

With Raymond Soneira. "The Universe at Faint Magnitudes. I. Models for the Galaxy and the Predicted Star Counts." *Astrophysical Journal Supplement Series* 44, no. 1 (1980): 73–110.

With Raymond Soneira. "The Distribution of Stars to V=16th Magnitude near the North Galactic Pole: Normalization,

Clustering Properties, and Counts in Various Bands." *Astrophysical Journal* 246 (1981): 122–135.

With Raymond Soneira. "Predicted Star Counts in Selected Fields and Photometric Bands: Applications to Galactic Structure, the Disk Luminosity Function, and the Detection of a Massive Halo." *Astrophysical Journal Supplement Series* 47, no. 1 (1981): 357–401.

Oral History Program Interviews conducted by P. Hanle, primarily about Hubble Space Telescope. 3 January 1983, 20 December 1983, 22 March 1984, 29 March 1984. National Air and Space Museum, Washington DC.

With Piet Hut and Scott Tremaine. "Maximum Mass of the Objects that Constitute the Unseen Disk Material." *Astrophysical Journal* 290 (1985): 15–20.

With Neta Bahcall and Donald P. Schneider. "Multiple Quasars for Multiple Images." *Nature* 323, no. 6088 (1986): 515–516.

With Sheldon Glashow. "Upper Limit on the Mass of the Electron Neutrino." *Nature* 326 (1987): 476–477.

With Roger Ulrich. "Solar Models, Neutrino Experiments, and Helioseismology." *Reviews of Modern Physics* 60, no. 2 (1988): 297–372.

With Buell Jannuzi, Donald P. Schneider, et al. "The Ultraviolet Absorption Spectrum of 3C 273." *Astrophysical Journal* 377 (1991): L5–L8.

With Dan Maoz, Roger Doxsey, et al. "The Snapshot Survey: A Search for Gravitationally Lensed Quasars with the Hubble Space Telescope 1." *Astrophysical Journal* 387 (1992): 56–68.

Interview conducted by Robert Smith, primarily about the Decadal Survey. 26 August 1992.

With Jacqueline Bergeron, Alec Boksenberg, et al. "The HST Quasar Absorption Line Key Project I: First Observational Results, Including Lyman-(and Lyman-Limit Systems." *Astrophysical Journal Supplement Series* 87 (1993): 1–43.

With Sofia Kirhakos and Donald P. Schneider. "*HST* Images of Nearby Luminous Quasars." HST Special issue, *Astrophysical Journal Letters* 435, no. 1, pt. 2 (1 November 1994): L11–L14.

With Sofia Kirhakos and Donald P. Schneider. "HST Images of Twenty Nearby Luminous Quasars." In *Quasar Hosts: Proceedings of the ESO-IAC Conference Held on Tenerife, Spain, 24–27 September 1996.* Heidelberg: Springer Verlag, 1997.

With Eli Waxman. "Ultrahigh Energy Cosmic Rays May Come from Clustered Sources." *Astrophysical Journal* 542 (2000): 542–547.

With Peter Mészáros. "5–10 GeV Neutrinos from Gamma-Ray Burst Fireballs?" *Physical Review Letters* 85 (2000): 1362–1365.

With Vernon Barger and Danny Marfatia. "How Accurately Can One Test CPT Conservation with Reactor and Solar Neutrino Experiments?" *Physics Letters B* 534, nos. 1–4 (2002): 120–123. Available from http://xxx.arxiv.org/abs/hep-ph?papernum=0201211.

With Eli Waxman. "Has the GZK Suppression Been Discovered?" *Physics Letters B* 556, nos. 1–2 (2003): 1–6. Available from http://xxx.arxiv.org/abs/hep-ph?papernum=0206217.

With Charles L. Steinhardt and David Schlegel. "Does the Fine-Structure Constant Vary with Cosmological Epoch?" *Astrophysical Journal* 600 (2004): 520.

With Hitoshi Murayama and Carlos Pena-Garay. "What Can We Learn from Neutrinoless Double Beta Decay Experiments?" *Physical Review D* 70 (2004): art. no. 033012. Available from http://xxx.arxiv.org/abs/hep-ph?papernum=0403167.

With Aldo M. Serenelli and Sarbani Basu. "New Solar Opacities, Abundances, Helioseismology, and Neutrino Fluxes." *Astrophysical Journal* 621 (2005): L85. Available from http://xxx.arxiv.org/abs/astro-ph?papernum=0412441.

With Eric B. Norman. "Improved Limit on Charge Conservation Derived from ^{71}Ga Solar Neutrino Experiments." *Physical Review D* 53, no. 7 (1996): 4086–4088.

With Ray J. Weymann, Buell Jannuzi, et al. "The *Hubble Space Telescope* Quasar Absorption Line Key Project. XIV. The Evolution of Ly(Absorption Lines in the Redshift Interval *z* = 0–1.5." *Astrophysical Journal* 506 (1998): 1–18.

OTHER SOURCES

Burbidge, E. Margaret, Geoffrey R. Burbidge, William A. Fowler, and Fred Hoyle. "Synthesis of the Elements in Stars." *Reviews of Modern Physics* 29 (1957): 547–650. Known to astrophysicists as B^{2}FH.

Hargittai, Magdolna, and Hargittai, Istvan. "Interview with John Bahcall." *Candid Science IV: Conversations with Famous Physicists.* London: Imperial College Press, 2004.

Ostriker, Jeremiah. "John Norris Bahcall 1935–2005." *Nature* 437 (1 September 2005): 43.

Virginia Trimble

BAINBRIDGE, KENNETH (KEN) TOMPKINS

(*b.* Cooperstown, New York, 27 July 1904; *d.* Lexington, Massachusetts, 14 July 1996), *experimental physics, mass spectography, microwave radar.*

Many people remember Bainbridge for his famous remark to J. Robert Oppenheimer on the morning of 16 July 1945, immediately after the first atomic bomb test at Alamogordo, New Mexico: "Now we are all sons of bitches." This contrasted with Oppenheimer's sophisticated reference to the line from the *Bhagavad Gita*: "I have become Death; the Destroyer of Worlds." But Bainbridge, an outstanding experimenter, was always more direct in his approach. Bainbridge was recognized early in his scientific career for his precise measurements of mass differences between nuclear isotopes, using the mass spectrograph he had designed. When compared to the energies of decay radiations, these confirmed Albert Einstein's mass-energy equivalency. In collaboration with the late Jabez Curry Street, he designed and built a small cyclotron at Harvard University that was later sent to Los Alamos National Laboratory in New Mexico. Even before the United States entered World War II Bainbridge joined the Radiation Laboratory at the Massachusetts Institute of Technology (MIT) spending 2 1/2 years there developing microwave radar, particularly high-powered systems. In the spring of 1943 he transferred to the nuclear weapons project at Los Alamos. Starting in 1945, he built a new, more precise mass spectrograph, began the construction of a new cyclotron, and was able to measure changes in the decay rates of some radioactive nuclei resulting from differing molecular bonding and from physical compression.

Early Years 1904–1929. Bainbridge was born on 27 July 1904, in Cooperstown, New York. He grew up in New York City, attending the Horace Mann School and the Horace Mann High School. The Bainbridge family lived on Riverside Drive near 158th Street and the Hudson River, where just after World War I returning naval vessels docked. Bainbridge, interested in radio in high school, put an antenna on the family's rooftop. Ship radio operators would knock on his door to investigate. Ken bought 5-watt vacuum tubes from his callers for a couple of dollars. Thereby he set up a radiotelephone, obtained a radio amateur license, and operated a "ham" station with the call letters 2WN.

In 1921 Ken entered MIT to study electrical engineering in a five-year cooperative program with the General Electric Company (GE). In the summers he worked at one of the General Electric facilities, first in Lynn, Massachusetts, and then mostly at the Research Laboratories in Schenectady, New York. As an outgrowth of his work there, Ken obtained a couple of patents on photocells. After completion, with both an MS and a BS degree, he changed his direction to physics. Karl T. Compton, a consultant to GE, recognized Bainbridge's quality, and recruited him for graduate work at Princeton, where he was head of the physics department. Bainbridge remembered, with pleasant amusement, his interview with Dean Andrew Fleming West and quoted him as saying, "You're nice boys, but it's too bad you never went to college."

It was at Princeton that Bainbridge began his lifelong interest in mass spectroscopy. He first searched for the then undetected element 87 of the periodic table, an element that should behave chemically as a heavy alkali. But his search was unfruitful and it was left to Marguerite Perey at the Radium Institute of Paris to find element 87 and call it "francium." This disappointment discouraged Bainbridge but did not stop him.

Postdoctoral Appointments, 1929–1934. After completing his PhD program at Princeton, Bainbridge spent four years at the Franklin Institute's Bartol Research Founda-

tion, first as a National Research Council fellow and then as a Bartol Research Foundation fellow. The "Bartol" was directed by William Francis Gray Swann, who was especially interested in research on cosmic rays and nuclear physics. Bainbridge continued to develop his mass spectrographs at Bartol and undertook precise nuclear mass measurements to confirm the mass-energy equivalence, $E = Mc^2$. While at Bartol, in September 1931 Bainbridge married Margaret ("Peg") Pitkin, then a member of the Swarthmore teaching faculty.

In the summer of 1933 Bainbridge joined the Cavendish Laboratory of Lord Ernest Rutherford, a world leader in experimental nuclear physics. In a later year Bainbridge described how Rutherford stopped him in passing in a corridor to ridicule as obviously impractical a suggestion just made to him by a visitor, Leo Szilard, for a nuclear chain reaction based on protons. Szilard went on to envisage a much more practical process involving neutrons, which, of course, only became reality after neutron-induced uranium fission was discovered. Bainbridge began a continuing close friendship with John D. Cockroft (later Sir John) at Cambridge, which became important later. Peg had also traveled to Cambridge, and their first child, Martin K. Bainbridge, was born there in 1933.

Prewar Academia, 1934–1939. In September of 1934 Bainbridge returned to the United States and joined the faculty of the physics department at Harvard University, where he later became the first George Vasmer Leverett Professor of Physics. He built and employed an improved mass spectrograph that he had designed during his sojourn at the Cavendish Laboratory and proposed a method of modifying isotopic abundance using gaseous counterflow in a Holweck molecular vacuum pump. In 1935 Bainbridge led the construction of a cyclotron as a joint project between the Harvard Graduate School of Engineering, represented by Professor Harry Mimno, and the physics department, represented by with Bainbridge and Street. Bainbridge and Street were the primary workers. The cyclotron was complete in 1938, and the report of the physics department in 1939 states that radioactive materials were supplied to Harvard Medical School, Massachusetts General Hospital, and Memorial Hospital in New York, and in addition to uses for physics at Woods Hole Meteorological Station, MIT physics department, and members of Williams College and Purdue University. It supported the work of fourteen researchers in Harvard departments. According to the late Roger Hickman, who as a graduate student assisted in the construction, the cost was about $40,000, of which about $20,000 came from the Rockefeller Foundation, which then funded medical research. The Bainbridge's two daughters Joan Bainbridge Safford and Margaret Tomkins (Bainbridge) Robinson were born in Cambridge, Massachusetts.

Kenneth Bainbridge. © CORBIS.

The War Years, 1939–1945. In 1939 Bainbridge became concerned about the rise of Nazism in 1939 as Europe became embroiled in World War II. When Britain sent the Tizard Mission in September of 1940, sharing their military secrets, Bainbridge took a leave of absence from Harvard and joined Ernest Orlando Lawrence in the newly formed Radiation Laboratory at MIT to develop microwave "radar." While there Bainbridge interacted with the local Raytheon company. Bainbridge's friendship with British physicists, especially with Cockroft, who had been a scientist member of the Tizard Mission, became an invaluable asset. In 1941 he was selected to go on a visit to England in 1941 to gain information about the radar program, but he also learned of British progress toward releasing nuclear energy while attending a meeting of the Maud Committee, which was overseeing that effort in Britain. Bainbridge's particular project at the Radiation Laboratory was the push toward higher-powered radars, especially for the navy. He found the navy at that time the most technically oriented of the U.S. military services and the least handicapped by protocols related to military rank. This experience was reflected in his concern about

the organization of Los Alamos, where he was recruited in May of 1943, which operated under the Manhattan District of the U.S. Army and General Leslie R. Groves.

At Los Alamos it became clear that a cyclotron was needed to measure various nuclear reaction cross sections of interest, and to supplement the work already being ably carried out at the Princeton cyclotron. Bainbridge knew where one was to be found—at Harvard. Discussions began at a high administrative and top secret level, between Harvard president James B. Conant (then away from Cambridge) and Groves, and it was agreed that Harvard would sell the cyclotron to the U.S. government for $1 with an informal promise of a cyclotron to replace it when the war was over. Because the atomic bomb project was top secret, the purpose of the purchase had to be disguised from those not cleared for secret information. A medical physicist, Dr. Hymer Friedell, and a nuclear physics expert Robert Wilson accompanied the cyclotron. The "cover story" was that the cyclotron was needed for medical treatment of military personnel, and it was sent to St. Louis to be forwarded to an "unknown destination."

At Los Alamos early in 1944, at the request of George Kistiakowsky and Oppenheimer, who had been named director of the National Laboratory in 1942, Bainbridge undertook the oversight of the design of high explosive assemblies and the preparations for a full-scale test of a nuclear bomb. In articles in the *Bulletin of the Atomic Scientists* in 1975, Bainbridge lucidly described the search for an appropriate site, the preparations, and the successful carrying out of the test early in the morning of 16 July 1945. The second of those stories was entitled: "A Foul and Awesome Display." His immediate thought on witnessing the first explosion was relief that the test was successful; for if not, he would have had to find out what had gone wrong. His famous remark, noted in the introduction above, marked the beginning of his dedication to ending the testing of nuclear weapons and to maintaining civilian control of future developments in that field.

Return to Academic Life, 1945–1969. In the fall of 1945 Bainbridge returned to academic science at Harvard. He undertook construction of a large mass spectrograph, designed for high resolution of masses. The prewar cyclotron was replaced by a much more powerful one utilizing the then newly invented concept of synchronous acceleration. He handed over the task first to Wilson, who had joined the physics department at Harvard after the end of the war, and then to Norman F. Ramsey, who joined Harvard in 1947. Unfortunately, the cyclotron design had been completed before discovery of the pi meson, and the energy of the new synchrocyclotron turned out to be just less than that required for pion production. For about a dozen years the new Harvard cyclotron was employed for many scattering experiments and other studies of nucleon-nucleon forces and of nuclear structure. During construction, Bainbridge insisted to his students that it was for nuclear research and not for medical work. One of the students, David Bodansky, recalls his saying, "There will be no rats running around this cyclotron." He was shortly contradicted when one of the first experiments was, in fact, irradiation of animals! The operating life of the cyclotron was greatly extended when it became a facility for research on the use and clinical applications of the highly focused proton beam in collaborative projects with staff members from the Massachusetts General Hospital. It was shut down finally on 2 June 2002, when its role was taken over by an even more powerful and flexible dedicated machine at the hospital, enabling further expansion of the important clinical applications developed using the physics cyclotron.

Bainbridge devoted much of his energy just after the war to designing for the Harvard physics department an advanced laboratory in nuclear physics intended as a course of study for graduate students. Because of the many new students underwritten by the GI Bill, the number of graduate students in physics was far greater than had been the norm before the war. Nuclear physics had gained new visibility and popularity from its contributions to winning the war. Students gained their first experience in activities preparing them for research in experimental physics in Bainbridge's meticulously designed and documented laboratory. The experiments ranged from a replication of Joseph John Thompson's positive ray apparatus (a precursor of mass spectrographs) to a bent crystal x-ray spectrograph, a 180-degree beta-ray spectrograph using the then new technique of nuclear magnetic resonance (NMR) for field calibration, and an analysis of tracks in photographic emulsions to identify muons. Demonstrating his dislike of the development and testing of nuclear weapons, he also set up an associated facility to collect and measure radioactive fallout. It is noteworthy that he measured fallout from the first Chinese bomb test as soon as the radioactive particles arrived in Massachusetts, two weeks after the explosion. In his fundamental research he built balanced ionization chambers with which he was able to determine changes in lifetimes of several long-lived isomers, which decay by internal electron conversion when their atoms are differently bonded chemically or are subjected to physical compression. In addition to constructing his large mass spectrograph to make precise measurements of mass differences among pairs, he built an elegant double-focusing electron spectrograph. In the years before his retirement in 1975, Bainbridge devoted much of his time to improving the facilities in his graduate student advanced laboratory, which was later integrated with the laboratory for advanced undergraduates.

From 1950 to 1954 Bainbridge served as chairman of the physics department at Harvard. This was a time marked by the vicious attacks on certain members of academia, and especially at Harvard, by the House Un-American Activities Committee and a committee of the Senate dominated by Senator Joseph McCarthy. Bainbridge gave generously of his time and energy overseeing the relationship between the university administration and one of his colleagues, who became a prime target of these attacks. In this he had the unanimous support of the department. Bainbridge was as precise in his administrative dealings as in his physics. In January 1955, he wrote to this author (RW) that the department, the dean, and the president had voted to appoint me as assistant professor, but the appointment still had to be approved by the Harvard Corporation. But, he added, "the last time the Corporation rejected such a recommendation was in 1847" (or some similar date). Such careful precision, which included the details of possible promotion to tenure, was most helpful to young faculty.

Later Years and Retirement. In the late 1950s Bainbridge was one of the first members of the Harvard faculty to participate in a new academic exchange program with the Soviet Union. The University of Leningrad was designated as Harvard's sister university. In June 1975 in his last year before his retirement, Bainbridge was enlisted to serve on a joint Iran-Harvard planning commission to design Reza Shah Kabir University for Iran. Bainbridge and his Harvard colleagues made several visits to Iran; however, this project was short-lived because of the political upheaval and expulsion of the shah from Iran.

Bainbridge never forgot the awful problems that the world faces because of the knowledge of how to make an atomic bomb. He constantly discussed them, stimulated no doubt by his wife, Peg, who was a member of the Society of Friends (Quakers) and an antiwar activist. He was most proud of his articles in the *Bulletin of the Atomic Scientists,* one on the use of the bomb; and another on the importance of civilian control of atomic energy. He opposed the May-Johnson bill, which kept military control, whereas the MacMahon bill set up the Atomic Energy Commission of five civilian commissioners. He was proud of his membership in the Federation of Atomic Scientists. He would discuss some of the major actors: Compton, Henry D. Smyth, Szilard, Oppenheimer, and somewhat reluctantly, Edward Teller.

In 1966 Bainbridge and his family finished a summer house in Chilmark, Martha's Vineyard, designed and constructed with the same careful attention to detail that exemplified all of Bainbridge's activities. Then in January

1967 Bainbridge suffered a tragic loss when his wife Margaret (Pitkin) Bainbridge, the mother of his three children, died suddenly at their home in Watertown, Massachusetts, from a blood clot associated with a recently fractured wrist. In October 1969 Bainbridge married Helen Brinkley King, an old friend then serving as an editor for the William Morrow publishing house in New York City. She, as well as his son, Martin, predeceased him. His two daughters, Joan and Margaret, led successful professional lives.

Bainbridge was awarded the Levy Medal of the Franklin Institute in 1934. He was elected a fellow of the American Academy of Arts and Sciences in 1937 and a member of the National Academy of Sciences in 1946. He was the recipient of two letters of commendation from General Groves for his work on the Manhattan Project and the Presidential Certificate of Merit for his services as staff member of the MIT Radiation Laboratory.

BIBLIOGRAPHY

The primary source for this memoir is the memoir for the National Academy of Sciences by Robert V. Pound and Norman F. Ramsey, both colleagues of Bainbridge and colleagues and close friends of this author. With their permission, I quote and paraphrase liberally excerpts from their fine memoir.

WORKS BY BAINBRIDGE

"The Harvard Cyclotron." *Harvard Alumni Bulletin* 17 (May 1940): 1010–1015.

"The Reminiscences of Kenneth T. Bainbridge." Transcript of an oral history interview conducted by Joan Safford. Columbia University Oral History Research Office, New York, 1964.

"Prelude to Trinity." *The Bulletin of Atomic Scientists* 31 (April 1975): 42–46.

"A Foul and Awesome Display." *The Bulletin of Atomic Scientists* 31 (May 1975): 40–46.

"Electrical Engineer." Transcript of an oral history interview conducted by John Bryant. IEEE History Center, Rutgers University, New Brunswick, NJ, 1991.

OTHER SOURCES

Pound, Robert V., and Norman F. Ramsey. "Kenneth Tompkins Bainbridge, July 27, 1904–July 14, 1996." In *Biographical Memoirs*, Vol. 76. Washington, DC: National Academy Press, 1999.

Pound, Robert, Richard Wilson, and Norman Ramsey. "Memorial Minute: Kenneth Tompkins Bainbridge." *Harvard University Gazette* (7 May 1998): 8.

Sopka, Katherine R. "Physics at Harvard during the Past Half-Century: A Brief Departmental History." Harvard University, Department of Physics, 1978.

Wilson, Richard. *A Brief History of the Harvard University Cyclotrons.* Cambridge, MA: Harvard University Press, 2004.

Richard Wilson

BALDI, BERNARDINO (*b.* Urbino, Italy, 5 June 1553; *d.* Urbino, Italy, 10 October 1617); *mechanics, mathematics.* For the original article on Baldi see *DSB,* vol. 1.

Baldi is one of the most illustrious representatives of the circle of scientists that formed in Urbino in the second half of the sixteenth century. Polyglot, polygraph, and poet, as well as scientist, expert on architecture, and skilled draftsman, Baldi is the author of numerous works that were still in manuscript form at the time of his death; many of them remained unpublished as of 2007. In the corpus of his manuscripts of particular interest is the *Vite de' matematici* (Lives of the mathematicians; almost two thousand manuscript pages), which in part constitutes the base for the brief summary collected in the *Cronica de' matematici* (posthumous, 1707; Chronicle of mathematicians). His major contribution to the field of mechanics is his commentary on the pseudo-Aristotelian *Mechanical Problems,* published posthumously in the work *In mechanica Aristotelis problemata exercitationes* (1621; Exercises in the mechanical problems of Aristotle). Among the literary works that reflect the scientific formation of the author are the *Cento apologi* (1590; One hundred apologues) and two poems, the *Invenzione del bossolo da navigare* (manuscript dated 1579; The invention of the navigational compass) and *La nautica* (1590; Navigation).

Among his contemporaries Baldi was famous for his extraordinary mastery of languages (his biographers report that he knew at least a dozen). In this respect the decisive factors were his early studies at Urbino under the guidance of Giovanni Antonio Turoneo and his later acquaintance in Rome with Giovanni Battista Raimondi, the inspiration and promoter of the Tipografia Medicea Orientale. From him he learned Arabic, which permitted him to pursue in depth his meticulous work in scientific and literary sources.

History of Mathematics. The *Vite de' matematici* constitutes a kind of history of the mathematical sciences, the first example of its genre in the modern era. With it Baldi intended to fill a historiographic gap and to accord to mathematicians the same dignity that up to that time had been reserved for artists, philosophers, and orators. The work was begun after the death of the mathematician Federico Commandino (1575), and most of it was completed around 1590. The idea of presenting mathematics in its historical context was not new to the Renaissance, but the encyclopedic scope that Baldi gave to his work made it exemplary. He took a similar all-encompassing approach in the *De verborum Vitruvianorum significatione* (1612; On the meaning of Vitruvius's terms), a meticulous analysis of the obscure passages in Vitruvius's *De architectura* (On architecture; first century BCE).

Mechanical Problems. Baldi's *In Mechanica Aristotelis Problemata Exercitationes* offers the same compositional originality, which in this case directly involves the scientific content. The *Mechanical Problems* of the Pseudo-Aristotle (Baldi agrees with the attribution of the work to Aristotle, although doubts about its authorship had already been raised) was the object of numerous editions and commentaries during the sixteenth and seventeenth centuries, but the *Exercitationes* show a singular independence from previous publications. The thirty-five problems become the pretext for long digressions on the topic, in which the influence of Archimedes's work is evident and openly acknowledged: "Considerantes enim Aristotelem aliis principijs usum, ac probatissimi post eum fecerint Mechanici, demonstrasse, morem huiusce facultatis studiosis gesturos nos fore arbitrati sumus, si easdem illas quaestiones Mechanicis, hoc est, Archimedeis probationibus confirmaremus" (*Praefatio* [Preface], n.p. [Considering that Aristotle in his demonstrations relied on principles that were different from those adopted by the best mechanicians coming after him, we have judged that it would have been possible to explain the method of this investigation treating these same questions in accordance with the criteria of mechanics, that is in agreement with those adopted by Archimedes]). Baldi's commentaries offer original considerations that impart a distinctly innovative character to the treatment. This is what occurs, for example, in the commentary to Quaestio XVI (problem sixteen). Taking as his point of departure the problem enunciated by the Pseudo-Aristotle ("Dubitatur, quare, quo longiora sunt ligna, tanto imbecilliora fiant, & si tolluntur, inflectuntur magis: tametsi quod breve est ceu bicubitum fuerit, tenue, quod vero cubitorum centum crassum"; *Mechanica Aristotelis* … , p. 95 [We ask why the pieces of wood become weaker the longer they become; and, if they are raised, they bend more, even though the short piece of wood, which may measure two cubits for example, is thin, and that one hundred cubits long is very thick]), Baldi undertakes a careful analysis of certain themes of mechanics as applied to architecture, and he anticipates the interpretation of the mechanism of the fracture of a beam that will later be described by Galileo in the *Discorsi e dimostrazioni matematiche intorno a due nuove scienze* (1638; Dialogues … concerning two new sciences). This treatment has no parallel in any previously published text. The *resistentia solidorum* (resistance of solids) is placed at the center of a study that compares the static-constructive experience with the principles of mechanics. Baldi's interest in this field of research, situated on the boundary between mechanics and architecture, is further confirmed by his studies on Vitruvius and by his consulting work as an expert in architecture in Urbino, Guastalla, and Rome (in Cardinal Cinzio Aldo-

brandini's circle). Moreover, Baldi numbers Vitruvius and Leon Battista Alberti among the mathematicians.

The originality of the *Exercitationes* poses the problem of identifying possible links with earlier unpublished sources. Pierre Duhem takes for granted that certain ideas found in Leonardo da Vinci's manuscripts exerted an influence on Baldi. Knowledge of some of those manuscripts cannot be excluded a priori, for the greatest dispersion of Leonardo's papers occurred at the end of the sixteenth century in Milan, a city that Baldi knew well from his having frequented the circle of Carlo Borromeo. Nevertheless, there is no proof confirming the hypothesis advanced by Duhem, who on other points of Baldian bibliography as well gives evidence of conducting an overly hasty analysis of the sources. In the case of the Quaestio XVI, moreover, one can note how the approach chosen by Baldi to the problem of structural mechanics differs in both substance and method from the one that Leonardo adopts on several occasions in his manuscripts (for example, as regards the mechanism of the fracture of arches).

Possible Influence on Galileo. Another important historiographic problem regards Galileo Galilei's knowledge of the *Exercitationes*. Numerous testimonies demonstrate that Baldi's work was immediately discussed by several scientists of the age (for example, Isaak Beeckman and Marin Mersenne). In the work of Daniel Mögling *Mechanischer Kunst-Kammer Erster Theil* … (1629), one can even find a translation of the *Exercitationes*, with the addition of an iconographic apparatus that corrects many of the printing errors of the original edition. The same Quaestio XVI, moreover, becomes the base of explicit inspiration for the five theorems on vaults described by Henry Wotton in his *Elements of Architecture* (1624). Similar attention to Baldi's commentaries can be found in Giovanni de Guevara's *In Aristotelis Mechanicas Commentarij* (1627, Commentaries on problems of mechanics). See Giovanni de Guevara, *Ioannis de Guevara Cler. Reg. Min. in Aristotelis Mechanicas Commentarij: una cum additionibus quibusdam ad eandem materiam pertinentibus*, Iacobum Mascardum, Roma 1627, cited by Galileo in his *Discorsi*. It is known that Guevara corresponded with Galileo and asked him on several occasions for his opinion on the commentaries to the *Mechanical Problems*. Despite this wide knowledge of Baldi's work throughout Europe, Galileo never cites him in his *Discorsi*, and his name does not appear in the extensive correspondence of the Pisan scientist. It seems nevertheless very unlikely that he was not familiar with the content of Baldi's work, at least indirectly and through mutual interlocutors.

There has been much discussion about the dating of the manuscript of the *Exercitationes*, and historians have usually settled on a date around 1590. To formulate credible hypotheses one must keep in mind that the principal biographers (Giovan Mario Crescimbeni and Ireneo Affò) refer to at least two manuscripts devoted to the *Mechanical Problems*. Certainly Baldi's interest in the subject goes back to his formative years in Urbino under the tutelage of Commandino and during his friendship with Guidobaldo del Monte, and to the time of his studies at the University of Padua. Nevertheless, the first manuscripts dedicated to the subject were to be reworked many times in subsequent years, and what was eventually given to the press was certainly revised during the author's final years. On the basis of these considerations we can affirm that the *Exercitationes*, like many other Baldian works, were reexamined, refined, and reorganized in the 1609–1617 period, when Baldi returned to live permanently in Urbino after the long stay in Guastalla.

SUPPLEMENTARY BIBLIOGRAPHY

WORKS BY BALDI

Bernardino Baldi, Le vite de' matematici: Edizione annotata e commentata della parte medievale e rinascimentale [Bernardino Baldi, The lives of mathematicians: annotated edition of the medieval and Renaissance parts, with commentary]. Edited by Elio Nenci. Milan: FrancoAngeli, 1998.

"*In mechanica Aristotelis problemata exercitationes.*" Mainz: Viduae Ioannis Albini, 1621. As part of the Archimedes project, available from http://archimedes2.mpiwg-berlin.mpg.de/archimedes/archimedes_templates.

OTHER SOURCES

Battiferri, Marc'Antonio Vergilii. *Oratione funebre in lode di monsignor Bernardino Baldi d'Urbino Abbate di Guastalla* [Funerary oration in praise of Monsignor Bernardino Baldi of Urbino, Abbot of Guastalla]. Urbino: A. Corvini, 1617. The first biographical profile of Baldi. Reprinted in *Seminario di studi su Bernardino Baldi Urbinate (1553–1617)* [Seminar of studies on Bernardino Baldi of Urbino], edited by Giorgio Cerboni Baiardi. Urbino: Accademia Raffaello, 2006.

Becchi, Antonio. *Q. XVI. Leonardo, Galileo, e il caso Baldi: Magonza, 26 marzo 1621. Traduzione dei testi latini, note e glossario a cura di Sergio Aprosio* [Q. XVI: Leonardo, Galileo, and the Baldi Case: Magonza, 26 March 1621. Translation of Latin texts, notes, and glossary prepared by Sergio Aprosio]. Venice: Marsilio, 2004.

Crescimbeni, Giovan Mario. *La vita di Bernardino Baldi, abate di Guastalla* [The life of Bernardino Baldi, abbot of Guastalla]. Edited by Ilaria Filograsso. Urbino: Quattro Venti, 2001. Transcription of the manuscript *La vita di Bernardino Baldi* (1703–1704).

Gamba, Enrico. "Saggio bibliografico sull'ambiente scientifico del ducato di Urbino" [Bibliographic essay on the scientific environment of the duchy of Urbino]. *Studia Oliveriana*, nos. 8–9 (1988–1989): 35–67.

Gamba, Enrico, and Vico Montebelli. *Le scienze a Urbino nel tardo Rinascimento* [The sciences in Urbino in the high Renaissance]. Urbino: QuattroVenti, 1988.

Nenci, Elio, ed. *Bernardino Baldi (1553–1617) studioso rinascimentale: Poesia, storia, linguistica, meccanica, architettura; Atti del convegno di studi di Milano, 19–21 Novembre 2003.* [Bernardino Baldi, 1553–1617, Renaissance scholar: poetry, history, linguistics, mechanics, architecture]. Milan: FrancoAngeli, 2005.

Rose, Paul Lawrence. *The Italian Renaissance of Mathematics: Studies on Humanists and Mathematicians from Petrarch to Galileo.* Geneva: Droz, 1975.

Serrai, Alfredo. *Bernardino Baldi. La vita, le opere, la biblioteca* [Bernardino Baldi: his life, his works, his library]. Milan: Bonnard, 2002.

Antonio Becchi

BALDWIN, JAMES MARK (*b*. Columbia, South Carolina, 12 January 1861; *d*. Paris, France, 9 November 1934), *psychology, philosophy, biology, mental development, social development, evolutionary mechanisms.*

Baldwin carried out psychology's first systematic, experimental studies of infant behavior and introduced a biosocial theory of individual adaptation—its evolutionary origins, ontogenetic development, and sociocultural formation—that helped shape the direction of modern developmental psychology. He contributed an evolutionary principle, now known as the Baldwin effect, which, though still controversial in evolutionary theory, has come to occupy an important place in evolutionary computation.

Childhood and Education. Baldwin was the son of Cyrus Hull Baldwin, a merchant, and Lydia Eunice Ford Baldwin. After attending private schools and working for two years in the city of his birth, Baldwin traveled to New Jersey in 1878 to enter the Salem Collegiate Institute. Three years later he enrolled as a sophomore at Princeton University.

At Princeton, his most important mentor was President James McCosh. Arguably the last great exponent of Scottish realism in the tradition of Thomas Reid, McCosh viewed the God-created human mind as possessing innate, universal tendencies to perceive the world as it actually is. Mind and reality exist in a preestablished harmony whereby perception of the world is guaranteed a general validity. From this perspective, scientific progress cannot contradict religious truth since both reflect the operation of God-given mental operations. This principle allowed McCosh to foster the teaching of science at

Princeton without regard to religion and introduce biological evolution and the then new experimental psychology of Wilhelm Wundt to his undergraduates. Both of these exerted a powerful influence on the young Baldwin.

On 18 June 1884 Baldwin graduated from Princeton. Awarded the Chancellor Green Mental Science Fellowship for a year's study abroad, he spent a semester in Leipzig, Germany, attending lectures by Wundt and serving as an experimental subject in the recently established psychological laboratory.

Academic Positions and Accomplishments. In September 1885 Baldwin returned to Princeton to enroll in the Princeton Theological Seminary and to assist in modern languages in the college. His enthusiasm, however, had been captured by the new psychology, and much of his time was devoted to translating Theódule Ribot's *German Psychology of To-day* (1886), a history of recent trends in scientific psychology.

After two years at Princeton, by which time he had abandoned all thought of a theological career, Baldwin accepted a professorship in logic and philosophy at Lake Forest University in Illinois. He remained there until 1889. During this period he taught psychology and wrote a dissertation opposing materialism, for which he received a Princeton doctorate under McCosh in 1888. On 22 November in that same year, he married Helen Hayes Green, daughter of a prominent professor at Princeton Theological Seminary. They had two daughters, Helen, born in 1889, and Elizabeth, born in 1891.

At Lake Forest, Baldwin also published his *Handbook of Psychology: Senses and Intellect* (1889), which drew for its inspiration on both the new experimental psychology and the old Scottish mental philosophy. The generally positive reception accorded to *Senses and Intellect* figured prominently in his receiving an offer of the chair of logic and metaphysics at the University of Toronto, to which he moved in November 1889.

Baldwin remained at Toronto until 1893, a period of transition in which he ended his reliance on the old mental philosophy tradition and became an experimental psychologist. At Toronto he founded the first psychological laboratory in Canada, completed work on the second volume of his *Handbook*, subtitled *Feeling and Will* (1891), and initiated a classic series of experimental studies of infant behavior. These observations, to be described below, marked the beginning of Baldwin's shift toward the evolutionary, developmental perspective on mind for which he is best remembered.

In the fall of 1893, while the infancy work was still in progress, Baldwin returned to Princeton to occupy the Stuart Chair in Psychology and establish a new psychological laboratory. Upon arrival he began rereading the literature on biological and mental evolution. This led to his two most important theoretical contributions, both having to do with the conceptualization of related evolutionary mechanisms, one ontogenetic, the other phylogenetic.

In *Mental Development in the Child and the Race*, published in 1895, and *Social and Ethical Interpretations in Mental Development*, which appeared in 1897, Baldwin articulated a biosocial theory of individual adaptation that is his primary claim to fame within psychology. In 1896, in an article titled "A New Factor in Evolution," Baldwin described a mechanism by which acquired accommodations might influence the course of phylogenetic evolution by natural selection. This mechanism has become known in evolutionary theory and evolutionary computation as the Baldwin effect. Both Baldwin's biosocial theory of individual adaptation and the Baldwin effect will be described below.

The years at Princeton also saw the cofounding, with the Columbia University psychologist James McKeen Cattell, of the *Psychological Review* and Baldwin's election, in 1897, to the presidency of the American Psychological Association. His presidential address, "On Selective Thinking" (1898), which applied principles of variation and selection to the process of intellectual discovery, is often cited as a landmark in evolutionary epistemology. In that same year, Baldwin began recruiting authors for the monumental *Dictionary of Philosophy and Psychology*. Published under his editorship between 1901 and 1905, "Baldwin's Dictionary" recruited many of the world's great minds to the Herculean task of providing systematic definitions for the major concepts of philosophy and psychology. In recognition of this effort and his many other contributions, Baldwin was awarded honorary degrees by the universities of Oxford, Glasgow, South Carolina, and Geneva.

In December 1903, motivated by a resurgent interest in philosophy occasioned by his editing the *Dictionary*, declining interest in laboratory work, and growing dissatisfaction with administrative developments at Princeton, Baldwin accepted a professorship in philosophy and psychology at Johns Hopkins University in Baltimore. There, in addition to founding another major journal, the *Psychological Bulletin*, he drew on philosophical insights derived from work on the *Dictionary* to examine the nature and development of thought in relation to reality. This led to four books published between 1906 and 1915 (three under the general title *Thought and Things: A Study of the Development and Meaning of Thought or Genetic Logic* and a fourth titled *Genetic Theory of Reality, Being the Outcome of Genetic Logic as Issuing in the Aesthetic Theory of Reality Called Pancalism*) that traced the evolution of intelligence—from early prelogical, pre-reflective thought and the rise of meaning through the emergence of

James Mark Baldwin. ARCHIVES OF THE HISTORY OF AMERICAN PSYCHOLOGY - THE UNIVERSITY OF AKRON.

reflection, logic, and higher-order synthetic cognition to an ultimate transcendence of intellectual dichotomies in aesthetic experience. Unfortunately this work was difficult conceptually, neologistic in the extreme, and out of step with trends in both philosophy and psychology. It was then and continued to be largely ignored.

In 1908, at the peak of his academic career, Baldwin was arrested in a Baltimore bordello. In the aftermath of his arrest, he was forced to resign his position at Hopkins and generally ostracized by his American colleagues. In 1909 he moved with his family to Paris. Between 1909 and 1912 Baldwin traveled periodically between Paris and Mexico City, where he delivered lectures at the School of Higher Studies in the National University. These resulted in two publications: *The Individual and Society* (1911) and *History of Psychology: A Sketch and an Interpretation* (1913). His history lectures, which focused on parallels between the development of psychological thought from the Greeks to the moderns and that of the individual mind in ontogenesis, constitute the first genetic epistemological history of a science. In 1911 he was elected correspondent of the Academy of Moral and Political Sciences, Institute of France, to fill a vacancy created by the death of William James.

Later Years in Paris. From 1912 until his death at age seventy-three, Baldwin involved himself in American affairs in France and in lobbying for French causes in the United States. After the outbreak of World War I, in the face of what he perceived as German military aggression, he became quite critical of American isolationism. In 1915 he published *La France et la guerre: Opinions d'un américain*, a defense of French participation in the war, and in 1916 he issued *American Neutrality: Its Cause and Cure*, urging U.S. entrance into the war on behalf of the Allies.

In March 1916 Baldwin journeyed to Oxford to deliver the Herbert Spencer Lecture, "The Super-State and the 'Eternal Values'"—a focused attack on German political ideology. On his return voyage, the unarmed passenger ship *Sussex* on which he was traveling was hit by a German torpedo as it was crossing the English Channel. Baldwin and his wife survived with only minor injuries, but their younger daughter, Elizabeth, was left permanently crippled by the attack.

In 1917, in honor of his dedication to the French cause, Baldwin was awarded the Legion of Honor. Following the Armistice, he worked on his memoirs. These were privately published in 1926 as *Between Two Wars (1861–1921)*.

Studies of Infant Behavior. Baldwin's interest in developmental psychology began with the birth of his first daughter, Helen, in 1889. At the time, the study of children's behavior relied exclusively on two methods, naturalistic observation and questionnaires, neither of which was experimental. Familiar with the laboratory methods of Leipzig, Baldwin introduced experimental method into the study of infant behavior. Described in a series of papers in *Science* beginning in 1890, his first systematic experiments were designed to explore the conditions under which reaching with one or two hands occurs between the baby's fourth and tenth months. The objects and colors toward which the baby was allowed to reach, their distance and direction from her body, and the child's position at the table were all systematically manipulated. To quantify and record variation in reaching distance precisely, the stimuli were placed in position by means of a set of sliding rods, and experiments were always carried out at the same time of day. Although Baldwin's results—optimal reaching distance at 9–10 inches, a preponderance of two-handed reaching, and right-hand preference first emerging only when the child was presented with brightly colored objects at distances slightly beyond her reach—are interesting, the real value of Baldwin's work for an emerging scientific psychology lay in his use of methods that were experimental, controlled, quantitative, adopted with an explicit concern for research design, and focused on a specific type of behavior.

Biosocial Theory of Individual Adaptation. Baldwin's infant observations also bore fruit in another direction. From the mental philosophy perspective of McCosh, human perception was assumed to be governed by fixed, natively given principles existing in God-given harmony with reality. Humans perceive the world as it is because God has created them to do so. Even cursory observation of his infant daughters, however, made it clear to Baldwin that this view required modification. Because infant perception is blind to aspects of reality obvious to the perception of an adult, human perception cannot exist in preestablished harmony with reality. Furthermore, the mind of the infant, far from being governed by fixed principles, is undergoing rapid intellectual change. Having come to this realization, Baldwin set out to describe a mechanism by which the direction of development toward a progressively more adequate adaptation to reality could be explained.

Although Baldwin's theory was only fully worked out between 1894 and 1897, its beginnings can be found in concepts already present in his work at Toronto. There, borrowing in part from Herbert Spencer and Alexander Bain and with a clear debt to Charles Darwin, George John Romanes, and William James, Baldwin began for the first time to conceive of mental development as a process involving both the repetition and conservation of useful reactions (habit) and the adaptation of the individual to changing conditions so that new and progressively more useful reactions are acquired (accommodation). In addition, he became increasingly impressed with the extent to which infants cognize the environment through direct and immediate action on it (see especially "Infant Psychology," 1890, and "Suggestion in Infancy," 1891). Baldwin termed this idea the "principle of dynamogenesis."

It was only with the publication of *Mental Development* and *Social and Ethical Interpretations,* however, that Baldwin brought these concepts together in a developed biosocial theory. In its most general form, this theory argues that all organisms are characterized by a *dynamogenic tendency* to relate to stimuli by acting on them. In any adaptive action, both habit and accommodation are operative. *Habit* is a tendency to action, the ability to repeat what has been successful in the past. It begins with a congenital susceptibility to act in defined ways in relation to certain stimuli and, as it changes over time through accommodation, becomes the conserver of the organism's life history. *Accommodation* is the adaptive process by which habit is altered to incorporate new possibilities for action.

What, then, is the adaptive goal of accommodation? How are actions modified in relation to environmental change? And by what criteria are modified reactions selected for retention? Baldwin's most general answer to these questions is that accommodation serves to maintain contact with desirable stimulations (those vital to the organism and producing pleasure) and minimize contact with those that are undesirable (deadly and painful). The modification of action takes place through a "circular" process that he terms "organic selection." In *organic selection*, vital stimuli trigger pleasure or pain leading to an excess discharge of varied movements, some of which are successful in bringing about repetition of the pleasurable or inhibiting repetition of the painful stimulus. Pleasure and pain, in other words, serve as the criteria by which successful movements are selected for retention so as better to adapt the organism. This circular process of adaptation is congenitally given (i.e., selected for in the evolutionary history of the species) and serves as a prototype for all higher forms of accommodation, even those that take place mentally through the mediation of consciousness.

When Baldwin addressed the issue of conscious accommodation, he focused on a particular type of circular reaction that he termed "conscious imitation." In *conscious imitation*, movement elicited dynamogenically by a stimulus not only tends to maintain contact with the stimulus but to reproduce it by virtue of the fact that imitative action more or less mirrors the stimulus. This reproduction of the stimulus then enters consciousness as part of the next stimulus for the succeeding act. Conscious imitation, in other words, tends in circular fashion to perpetuate itself. It is easily observed in its purest form in very young children; moreover, in Baldwin's view, it underlies, albeit in a more obscure fashion, even the complex conscious accommodations of the adult.

As accommodation proceeds on the basis of circular reactions, three additional factors—memory, association, and voluntary attention—come into play, and with the participation of these factors individual adaptation reaches its highest level in accommodations that are volitional in nature. *Memory* involves the reinstatement of a perception as an internal stimulus in the absence of the original. *Association* links external stimuli to internal stimuli, so that habit becomes elaborated into a complex network of associated processes and the relevant dynamogenically elicited reactions tend to realize themselves in concert. Because of this complexity, actions may eventually lose the imitative or stimulus-reproducing character from which they originated and take on a purely mental form. It is in *voluntary attention* that Baldwin finds the most highly developed form of mental accommodation. Through voluntary attention, consciousness deliberately selects that to which the habit system will be accommodated, and new elements of reality are assimilated to the old (the habit system) and given their meaning.

In this theory of the process by which action, consciousness, reality, and an underlying dispositional cognitive system (habit) change in an adaptive fashion, Baldwin had proposed a biologically given functional mechanism by which the mind gradually develops toward a progressively more adequate adjustment to the real world as a function of experience. Baldwin's interest, however, also lay in the development of the social mind, and no sooner had he elaborated his biologically based concept of organic selection than he extended it to the social domain.

Like all consciousness, *social consciousness* (e.g., the infant's perception of a parental smile) is a joint function of habit and social stimuli (termed *social suggestions* to emphasize the dynamogenic nature of social consciousness) and tends to realize itself in social action. *Social action*, in turn, may *imitatively* mirror social suggestion (e.g., the infant smiles in return) or *inventively* vary from it (e.g., the infant sticks out her tongue). In either case, social action changes the social stimulus (e.g., the baby feels herself smile or stick out her tongue and sees the parent's answering response). This changed stimulus contains elements that are relatively novel as well as those that are familiar. Assimilation of this combination of novel and familiar to habit forces an accommodation with concomitant change in social consciousness expressing itself in new social action which again changes the social stimulus, leads to ever newer accommodations, social consciousnesses, social actions, and so on—in a circular process of social adaptation that continues throughout life.

The criterion for success by which social actions are selected for incorporation into the habit system Baldwin terms "social confirmation." *Social confirmation* is a change in social stimuli that results from and reflects the nature of social action (e.g., the parent's returning the infant's smile). Over the course of development, as novel social actions receive social confirmation and are selected as part of the child's own social habit repertoire, they become available to give meaning to the actions of others. The child's consciousness of the other, therefore, comes to reflect consciousness of self. Baldwin refers to this aspect of the process of social adaptation as "the dialectic of the social self." Finally, social stimuli, social actions, and social confirmations all exist in a broader social context from which they receive cultural meaning. In *Social and Ethical Interpretations*, Baldwin labels this context "social heredity," describing it as "the mass of organized tradition, custom, usage, social habit, etc., which is already embodied in the institutions and ways of acting, thinking, etc., of a given social group, considered as the normal heritage of the individual social child" (1895, p. 301). *Social heredity* is, in effect, the system of social meanings into which the child is born and to which the child must become enculturated.

The Baldwin Effect. As Baldwin was elaborating the social implications of his principle of organic selection as a mechanism of acquired adaptation in the individual, he was also engaged in extending these ideas to account for the influence of individual adaptation on species evolution. Although Baldwin's view was not yet fully worked out in *Mental Development*, it is clear that he was already aware of the issue. "No theory of development is complete," he wrote in 1895, "which does not account for the transmission in some way, from one generation to another, of the gains of the earlier generations, turning individual gains into race gains" (p. 204).

As a confirmed Darwinian, Baldwin knew that any mechanism he might propose to link individual adaptation to phylogenetic evolution had to be consistent with the principle of natural selection. In discussions with C. Lloyd Morgan, a British psychologist and zoologist, and Henry Fairfield Osborn, a Columbia University biologist, Baldwin developed a hypothesis that he thought met these criteria. This hypothesis was announced in the *American Naturalist* of June–July 1896 and extensively discussed, together with issues of heredity and instinct, physical and social heredity, determinate evolution, and isolation and selection, in *Development and Evolution* (1902).

To emphasize what he saw as the close relationship between individual adaptation and evolutionary change, Baldwin borrowed the term "organic selection," already introduced for individual adaptation, for his new factor. In its most developed form, his argument goes as follows: Congenital variations that are "coincident with" and therefore lend themselves to the successful acquisition of new adaptations (accommodations) will influence individual survival and be subject to natural selection. Over evolutionary time these variations will be accumulated and support ever better accommodations in the same direction. Individual adaptations, in other words, while not physically inherited, screen congenital variations in the direction of a developing function (i.e., favoring both convergent and correlated adaptations), thereby providing the opportunity for natural selection to exert an effect along determinate lines. On this basis, as he put it in *Development and Evolution*, "it is the accommodations which set the pace, lay out the direction, and prophesy the actual course of evolution" (1902, p. 39).

Although the Baldwin effect was once largely dismissed as a minor factor in evolutionary change (see, for example, Simpson, 1953), interest in it renewed between 1975 and 2005. This reflects a growing concern with the relationship between behavior and evolution in both evolutionary biology and evolutionary computation and increased recognition of the possibility that selection is carried out not by the environment alone but by the organism and environment in constructive interaction (see Sánchez and Loredo, 2007, for an excellent discussion of these issues).

BIBLIOGRAPHY

Only a few Baldwin papers are known to be extant. These are in the Princeton University Library. Additional correspondence can be found in the papers of William James, Hugo Münsterberg, George M. Stratton, Edward B. Titchener, and Robert M. Wenley. Letters received from William James are at the Bodleian.

WORKS BY BALDWIN

As translator. *German Psychology of To-day*, by Th. Ribot. New York: Scribners, 1886.

Handbook of Psychology: Senses and Intellect. New York: Holt, 1889.

"Infant Psychology." *Science* 16 (1890): 351–353.

"Origin of Right or Left-Handedness." *Science* 16 (1890): 247–248.

"Recognition by Young Children." *Science* 15 (1890): 274.

Handbook of Psychology: Feeling and Will. New York: Holt, 1891.

"Suggestion in Infancy." *Science* 17 (1891): 113–117.

"Distance and Color Perception by Infants." *Science* 21 (1893): 231–232.

Mental Development in the Child and the Race: Methods and Processes. New York: Macmillan, 1895.

"Heredity and Instinct." *Science* n.s. 3 (1896): 438–441, 558–561.

"A New Factor in Evolution." *American Naturalist* 30 (1896): 441–451, 536–553.

"Determinate Evolution." *Psychological Review* 4 (1897): 393–401.

Social and Ethical Interpretations in Mental Development. New York: Macmillan, 1897.

"On Selective Thinking." *Psychological Review* 5 (1898): 1–24.

Dictionary of Philosophy and Psychology. Vols. 1–3. New York: Macmillan, 1901–1905.

Development and Evolution. New York: Macmillan, 1902.

Thought and Things: A Study of the Development and Meaning of Thought or Genetic Logic. 3 vols. New York: Macmillan, 1906–1911.

The Individual and Society. Boston: Badger, 1911.

History of Psychology: A Sketch and an Interpretation. London: Watts, 1913.

Genetic Theory of Reality, Being the Outcome of Genetic Logic as Issuing in the Aesthetic Theory of Reality Called Pancalism. New York: Putnam, 1915.

La France et la guerre: Opinions d'un américain. Paris: Alcan, 1915.

American Neutrality: Its Cause and Cure. New York: Putnam, 1916.

The Super-State and the "Eternal Values." Being the Herbert Spencer Lecture. London: Oxford University Press, 1916.

Between Two Wars, 1861–1921; Being Memories, Opinions, and Letters Received by James Mark Baldwin. Boston: Stratford, 1926.

"James Mark Baldwin." In *A History of Psychology in Autobiography*, vol. 1, edited by Carl Murchison. Worcester, MA: Clark University Press, 1930.

OTHER SOURCES

Broughton, John M., and D. John Freeman-Moir, eds. *The Cognitive-Developmental Psychology of James Mark Baldwin*. Norwood, NJ: Ablex, 1982.

Cairns, Robert B. "The Making of a Developmental Science: The Contributions and Intellectual Heritage of James Mark Baldwin." *Developmental Psychology* 28 (1992): 17–24.

Hoff, Tory L. "Psychology in Canada One Hundred Years Ago: James Mark Baldwin at the University of Toronto." *Canadian Psychology* 33 (1992): 683–694.

Holmes, Eugene Clay. *Social Philosophy and the Social Mind: A Study of the Genetic Methods of J. M. Baldwin, G. H. Mead, and J. E. Boodin*. New York: n.p., 1942.

Noble, David W. *The Paradox of Progressive Thought*. Chap. 4, "James Mark Baldwin: The Social Psychology of the Natural Man." Minneapolis: University of Minnesota Press, 1958.

Richards, Robert J. *Darwin and the Emergence of Evolutionary Theories of Mind and Behavior*. Chap. 10, "James Mark Baldwin: Evolutionary Biopsychology and the Politics of Scientific Ideas." Chicago: University of Chicago Press, 1987.

Russell, James. *The Acquisition of Knowledge*. Sect. 1.2, "James Mark Baldwin and Genetic Epistemology." New York: St. Martin's Press, 1978.

Sánchez, José Carlos, and José Carlos Loredo. "In Circles We Go: Baldwin's Theory of Organic Selection and Its Current Uses: A Constructivist View." *Theory and Psychology* 17 (2007): 33–58.

Sewny, Vahan D. *The Social Theory of James Mark Baldwin*. New York: King's Crown Press, 1945.

Simpson, George G. "The Baldwin Effect." *Evolution* 7 (1953): 110–117.

Weber, Bruce H., and David J. Depew, eds. *Evolution and Learning: The Baldwin Effect Reconsidered*. Cambridge, MA: MIT Press, 2003.

Wilson, R. Jackson. *In Quest of Community: Social Philosophy in the United States, 1860–1920*. Chap. 3, "James Mark Baldwin: Conservator of Moral Community." New York: Wiley, 1968.

Wozniak, Robert H. "Thought and Things: James Mark Baldwin and the Biosocial Origins of Mind." In *Psychology: Theoretical-Historical Perspectives*, edited by Robert W. Rieber and Kurt Salzinger. 2nd ed. Washington, DC: American Psychological Association, 1998.

———. "Lost Classics and Forgotten Contributors: James Mark Baldwin as a Case Study in the Disappearance and Rediscovery of Ideas." In *The Life Cycle of Psychological Ideas: Understanding Prominence and the Dynamics of Intellectual Change*, edited by Thomas C. Dalton and Rand B. Evans. New York: Kluwer Academic/Plenum, 2004.

Robert H. Wozniak

BANNEKER, BENJAMIN (*b.* Baltimore County, Maryland, 9 November 1731; *d.* Baltimore

County, 9 October 1806), *observational astronomy, ephemerides, almanacs.*

A tobacco farmer, and amateur astronomer, Benjamin Banneker was an inspiration for his mathematical achievements. He is frequently described as the first African American man of science.

Early Life. Banneker was born free in Baltimore County, Maryland, on 9 November 1731. He was the son of a freed slave from Guinea named Robert and of Mary Banneky, daughter of a formerly indentured English servant named Molly Welsh and her husband, Bannka, a slave whom she freed and who claimed to be the son of a Gold Coast tribal chief.

Banneker's early years were spent with his family, including three sisters, growing tobacco on his parents' 100-acre farm near the banks of the Patapsco River. In his early years he had been trained to read and write by his grandmother by means of a Bible she had purchased from England, but his only formal schooling was attendance for a week or two in a nearby Quaker one-room schoolhouse. Benjamin became a voracious reader, borrowing books from wherever he could, and developed considerable skill in mathematics. He enjoyed devising mathematical puzzles and solving those brought to him by others. At about the age of twenty-one he constructed a striking wall clock, without ever having seen one. It is said that it was based on his recollections of the mechanism of a pocket watch. Apparently, he visualized it as a mathematical puzzle, relating the numerous toothed wheels and gears, carving each carefully from seasoned hardwood with a pocket knife. For a bell, he utilized either part of a glass bottle or metal container. The timepiece appears to have been the first clock in the region and brought those who had heard about it to his cabin to observe it and listen to it strike. The clock continued to function successfully for more than fifty years, until his death.

Inheriting the family farm at his father's death, Banneker lived with his mother until her demise. Then living alone, he continued to grow and sell tobacco until about the age of fifty-nine, when rheumatism forced him to retire. His farm made him virtually self-sufficient, with a productive vegetable garden, thriving fruit orchards, and several hives of bees that he maintained. Banneker and his family had been among the first clients of the newly established Ellicott Store, in nearby Ellicott's Lower Mills, and during his leisure he continued to visit it frequently, purchasing small items he required, perusing the wealth of imported merchandise, occasionally purchasing an inexpensive book for his own small library. Most of all he enjoyed the opportunity to read newspapers from other cities that the store sold and that provided him with a link to the outer world.

Now, with the freedom of retirement from work, Banneker turned with new vigor to his astronomical studies, often whiling away the hours until dawn scanning the night skies with his telescope and recording notations for an ephemeris for an almanac he was compiling for the following year.

Work in Observational Astronomy. It was just at this time that fate sought him out for an important role to play in the nation's history. The surveyor Andrew Ellicott had recently been appointed by President George Washington to produce a survey of selected lands on which to establish a national capital. Ellicott urgently required an assistant with some knowledge of astronomy to work in the field observation tent during the night hours. He traveled to Ellicott's Lower Mills hoping to hire his cousin George Ellicott, Banneker's neighbor, who was an amateur astronomer. However, his cousin, being unable to leave his own work, instead recommended Banneker, whom he felt had become sufficiently informed on the subject to fulfill the position. Banneker was hired and, overwhelmed by the opportunity, he traveled together with Andrew Ellicott to the site that was to become the national capital, arriving early in the new year of 1791.

Banneker worked in the observatory tent for more than four months, from the beginning of February until the end of April 1791. It was grueling work, for he was forced to spend the long hours of the night lying on his back in order to use an instrument called a zenith sector. His assignment was to observe through the instrument's telescope as stars transited over the zenith, noting the exact moment of each star's transit and recording it for Ellicott's use when he arrived the next morning.

It was extremely tiring work for a man of Banneker's advanced years, but despite the discomfort, he derived considerable pleasure and pride from the knowledge that he was contributing to such an important project. Also, after taking a nap during the early daylight hours, Banneker had the privilege of using Ellicott's astronomical textbooks, which were maintained in the observatory tent. This enabled him to complete the ephemeris he was compiling for an almanac for the following year, 1792. For his participation on the survey, including travel, Banneker was paid a total of $60.

Correspondence with Jefferson. Soon after returning home, Banneker sent a handwritten copy of his completed ephemeris to Secretary of State Thomas Jefferson because, as he wrote, Jefferson was considered to be "measurably friendly and well disposed towards us," referring to the African American race, "who have long laboured under the abuse and censure of the world. … And have long been looked upon with an eye of contempt, and … long have been considered rather as brutish than human, and scarcely able of mental endowments (1792)."

Submitting his calculations as evidence to the contrary, Banneker urged Jefferson to work toward bringing an end to slavery. Jefferson answered promptly:

No body wishes more than I do to see such proofs as you exhibit, that nature has given our black brethren, talents equal to those of other colors of men, and that the appearance of a want of them is owed merely to the degraded condition of their existence, both in Africa & in America. ... No body wishes more ardently to see a good system commenced for raising the condition of both their body & mind to what it ought to be, as fast as the imbecility of their present existence, and other circumstances which cannot be neglected, will admit. (Payne, 1862, pp. 168–171)

Jefferson was so impressed with Banneker's calculations that he sent a copy to the Marquis de Condorcet, secretary of the French Academy of Sciences in Paris, with an enthusiastic cover letter. No reply was forthcoming from Condorcet, however, because at just the time of the arrival of Jefferson's letter, the French diplomat had been forced to go into hiding for opposing the monarchy and for having supported a republican form of government. During the following year, the two letters, the one from Banneker to Jefferson and the statesman's reply, were published in the United States in a widely distributed pamphlet and in at least one periodical.

Publication of the Almanac. James McHenry, a senator from Maryland, had been so impressed with Banneker's almanac manuscript that he wrote an endorsement for it that was published together with the almanac by the Baltimore printer Goddard & Angell. The almanac bore the title *Benjamin Banneker's Pennsylvania, Delaware, Maryland, and Virginia Almanack and Ephemeris for the Year of Our Lord 1792.* In addition to its sales in Baltimore, the almanac was made available also by printers in Alexandria, Virginia, and in Philadelphia. It proved an immediate success, and Banneker's lifestyle soon changed somewhat, as he became acknowledged by neighbors and occasionally by others visiting the region.

During the next five years, Banneker continued to calculate ephemerides, which he sold and which were published in almanacs bearing his name in the title. Promoted by the abolitionist societies of both Pennsylvania and Maryland, Banneker's almanacs were published by several printers and sold widely in the United States and also in England. Twenty-eight separate editions of his almanacs are known to have been published.

Generally, in the production of an almanac, the astronomer provided only the ephemeris, and the remaining content was selected and furnished by the printer, who often selected random prose and poetry taken from the published press or journals. Frequently included were useful tables of weights and measures, coinages, interest rates and scales of depreciation, measurements of roads, and distances of cities from the place of publication, a calendar of meetings of courts of law holding sessions where the almanacs would be sold, and so forth.

The remainder of the pages of these inexpensive and poorly printed pamphlets generally were filled with moral elevating scriptural quotations, proverbs, allegorical stories, and puritanical essays. By the beginning of the eighteenth century, however, the almanac's content changed distinctly in tone from its earlier religious bias to one of more practical considerations, with emphasis on education and literary and historical content. As a consequence, in time the almanac became more entertaining, with homely wisdom cast in contemporary language. By the end of the eighteenth century, the publication had become the most common printed item in the American republic, printed in every state, each vying with others in developing a new marketable item. In the period that Banneker was undertaking the preparation of an ephemeris, the century was drawing to a close and once more the almanac content was undergoing a change, with new emphasis on local causes and national events.

In a period when clocks and watches were luxuries and common timepieces consisted primarily of time glasses and sundials, information about the times of sunrise, noon, and sunset were of considerable importance to the prospective purchaser, as well as the phases of the moon, eclipses, and conjunction. Among the most desirable and useful features of Banneker's almanacs proved to be a tide table for the Chesapeake Bay region, which made his almanacs particularly desirable for river pilots, fishermen, and others living near and making their living on the water. It listed times for high water or high tide at Cape Charles, Point Lookout, Annapolis, and Baltimore. Why Banneker's competitors ignored this feature is hard to understand, because it was simple enough to calculate the high tide at Annapolis, for instance, which was two hours later than at Point Lookout, while at Baltimore and Head-of-the-Bay the high tide was five hours later than at Point Lookout. The tide table was simplified considerably in Banneker's almanacs for the years 1795 and 1796, which provided data for determining tides in ports as distant north as Halifax and Boston. This feature was titled "Rule to find the Time of High Water in the following Places" and consisted simply of an additive for each of the places listed, to be combined with the day of the Moon's age.

It was Banneker himself and not his printer who compiled the tide tables for his almanacs. It was a simple matter to acquire the data, and no mathematical

Benjamin Banneker. *Benjamin Banneker, 1791.* HULTON ARCHIVE/GETTY IMAGES.

achievement was involved. The changing of the tides had been associated with the motion of the Moon for centuries. Once the time of the highest or spring tide was known at a particular point at the age of the full or new moon, it was a simple matter to derive a table for each day of the month at the same place. Banneker applied the standard daily retardation of forty-eight minutes, or four-fifths of an hour. This determination of the highest tide waters or spring tides on the days of the full or new moon was known as "the establishment of the port" and generally was marked on the charts for the port in question.

From data in his published almanacs, it is evident that Banneker made his observations from a point of latitude 39°30' north and a longitude of 4 hours, 59 minutes west. In addition to recording in his manuscript astronomical journal the ephemerides for each of the years for which he calculated them, Banneker also included miscellaneous exercises in mathematics and astronomy.

In the pages of his manuscript astronomical journal as well as in his commonplace book, Banneker occasion-

ally recorded miscellaneous items about unusual atmospheric phenomena he had observed. Typical of these random notes was an entry on the very first page of the journal, under the date of 23 December 1790. He noted, "About 3 o'clock A.M. I heard a Sound and felt the Shock like heavy thunder I went out but could not observe any Cloud above the Horizon. I therefore Conclude it must be a great Earth Quake in some part of the Globe." Another item, recorded on 4 May 1792, described how "In a Squall from the N.W. I observed the Lower regions of the Clouds to move Swiftly before the wind, and the upper region Slowly against it."

Even in his later years the weather continued to preoccupy him. On 2 February 1803, he noted,

> in the morning part of the day, there arose a very dark Cloud, followed by Snow and haile a flash of lightning and loud thunder crack, and then the Storm abated untill after noon, when another cloud arose the Same point, viz, Northwest with a beautiful Shower of Snow but what beautyfyed the Snow was the brightness of the Sun, which was near Setting at the time.

A comparison of the contents of Banneker's published ephemerides made with those calculated and published by his contemporaries Ellicott, William Waring, and Mary Katherine Goddard, has revealed that Banneker's calculations consistently reflected an overall high degree of comparative accuracy. An error analysis of the astronomical data in Banneker's almanacs revealed that his data compared very favorably with that published by his contemporaries. There was no significant difference between Banneker's star data and that published by the two contemporary almanac makers. Although Banneker's planetary data may have appeared to be somewhat less accurate than that of Ellicott or Goddard, it was still quite usable by the ordinary purchaser of the almanac. Considering that the length and complexity of the calculations involved in determining the rising and setting of certain stars and planets, and realizing that this was only a small segment of the mathematics required for one year's almanac, one can have only the greatest respect for this self-taught man of science.

Although Banneker continued to calculate ephemerides every year through the year 1802, those after 1797 remained unpublished, but were carefully recorded in his manuscript journal and commonplace book, which survive as unique records of an eighteenth-century almanac maker.

Character. Banneker espoused no particular religion, but as an early biographer noted, "His life was one of constant worship in the great temples of nature and science." (Allen, 1921) As places of worship in his vicinity grew in number, Banneker visited each of them, but gave preference to the meetings of the Society of Friends, where "he presented a most dignified aspect as he leaned in quiet contemplation on a long staff, which he always carried after passing his seventieth year. And he worshipped, leaning on the top of his staff." (Allen, 1921)

A description of Banneker was provided by Martha Tyson, daughter of George Ellicott, who had seen him when she was a young woman. "The countenance of Banneker," she wrote,

> had a most benign and thoughtful expression. A fine head of white hair surmounted his unusually broad and ample forehead, whilst the lower part of his face was slender and sloping towards the chin. His figure was perfectly erect, showing no inclination to stoop as he advanced in years. His raiment was always scrupulously neat; that for summer wear, being of unbleached linen, was beautifully washed and ironed by his sisters. … In cold weather he dressed in light colored cloth, a fine drab broadcloth constituting his attire when he designed appearing in his best style.

No known portrait of Banneker exists. Lacking such, an image frequently used is a woodcut portrait bust of a young black man, imaginary and not based on life, wearing the typical Quaker garb of the period. Purported to be of Banneker, this image illustrated the cover of a 1797 edition of one of his almanacs. The most accurate representation known may be found on a modern mural painting by the late William H. Smith of the survey of the federal territory. It hangs in the Maryland House on the John F. Kennedy Highway in Aberdeen, Maryland. In 1980 the U.S. Postal Service issued a commemorative stamp honoring Banneker based on imagined features.

On 9 October 1806, during a nap following his usual morning walk, Banneker quietly died in his sleep, just one month short of his seventy-fifth birthday. In accordance with instructions he had left, immediately following his death all the items that had been borrowed from his neighbor George Ellicott, including the worktable, instruments, and books, had been returned to him by Banneker's nephew. Included also was Banneker's astronomical journal.

Banneker was buried two days later, on Tuesday, 11 October, in the family burial ground within sight of his house, a few yards away. During the services, as his body was being lowered into his grave, the mourners were startled as they looked up to see his house, a wooden building, suddenly burst into flame. Before help could be summoned, the entire structure burned to the ground. All its contents were totally destroyed, including Banneker's clothing and other personal possessions, a few bits of furniture, a sparse collection of books and printed copies of his almanacs, as well as the fabled well-worn striking

clock. The only item known to have escaped destruction was his quarto Bible, which had been removed from his house after his death and before the funeral, probably by one of his sisters. The cause of the conflagration was never determined.

Banneker's death did not pass totally unnoticed. An obituary announcement appeared in the *Federal Gazette* on 28 October 1806, almost three weeks after his death. It provided a description of Banneker's way of life and concluded, "Mr. Banneker is a prominent instance to prove that a descendant of Africa is susceptible of as great mental improvement and deep knowledge into the mysteries of nature as that of any other nation."

BIBLIOGRAPHY

WORK BY BANNEKER

Copy of a Letter from Benjamin Banneker to the Secretary of State, with His Answer. Philadelphia: Printed and Sold by Daniel Lawrence, 1792.

OTHER SOURCES

Allen, Will W. *Banneker, the Afro-American Astronomer.* Washington, DC, 1921.

Bedini, Silvio A. *Early American Scientific Instruments and Their Makers.* Washington, DC: U.S. Museum of History and Technology, Smithsonian Institution, 1964. See pages 22–25.

———. *The Life of Benjamin Banneker: The First African-American Man of Science.* 2nd ed., revised and expanded. Baltimore: Maryland Historical Society, 1999.

Conway, Moncure D. "Benjamin Banneker, the Negro Astronomer." *Atlantic Monthly* (January 1863): 79–84.

Kurtz, Benjamin. "The Learned Negro." *Lutheran Observer* 16, no. 31 (25 August 1848): 134–345.

Latrobe, John H. B. "Memoir of Benjamin Banneker: Read before the Historical Society of Maryland." *Maryland Colonization Journal*, n.s., 2, no. 23 (May 1845): 353–364.

LePhillips, Phillip. "The Negro, Benjamin Banneker; Astronomer and Mathematician, Plea for Universal Peace." *Records of the Columbia Historical Society* 20 (1917): 114–120.

McHenry, James. "Account of Benjamin Banneker, a Free Negro." *Universal Asylum* (November 1791).

Payne, Daniel Alexander. "A Literary Curiosity—Letter from Benjamin Banneker to Hon. Thos. Jefferson." *Repository of Religion and Learning and of Science and Art* 4, no. 7 (July 1862): 168–171.

Tyson, Martha E. *A Brief Account of the Settlement of Ellicott's Mills, with Fragments of History therewith Connected, Written at the Request of Evan T Ellicott, Baltimore, 1865.* Baltimore, MD: Printed by J. Murphy, 1871.

———. *Banneker, the Afro-American Astronomer from the Posthumous Papers of Martha E. Tyson.* Edited by Her Daughter. Philadelphia: Friends' Book Association, 1884.

Silvio A. Bedini

BARDEEN, JOHN (*b.* Madison, Wisconsin, 23 May 1908; *d.* Boston, Massachusetts, 30 January 1991), *condensed-matter physics, superconductors, superconductivity, many-body theory, transistor.*

Bardeen worked on developing the quantum mechanical theory of solids throughout his entire physics career. He was among the handful of American physicists who first applied this theory to real (rather than ideal) materials. He was the first person ever to win two Nobel Prizes in the same field—the first, in 1956 with Walter Brattain and William Shockley for the invention of the transistor; the second, in 1972 with Leon Cooper and J. Robert Schrieffer for the theory of superconductivity.

Early Years. Bardeen's highly educated family, whose American roots trace back to the Plymouth Colony, placed a strong value on frugality, hard work, learning, and service to society and nation. His grandfather Charles William Bardeen, who had enlisted as an abolitionist in the Civil War at age fourteen, established *School Bulletin Publications,* in which for fifty years he expressed his progressive views on quality education. John Bardeen's father Charles Russell Bardeen, a graduate in the first class of the Johns Hopkins University medical school, founded and served as dean of the University of Wisconsin's medical school. John's mother Althea Harmer had studied art in New York and Chicago and taught home economics at the University of Chicago's progressive laboratory high school established by John Dewey. At the time she met and married Charles Russell, she ran a small interior decorating business in Chicago. John Bardeen and all his siblings, his older brother William, his younger brother Thomas, his younger sister Helen, and his even younger half-sister Ann, grew up in Madison.

To keep John from being bored in school, Althea had him skipped so often that he finished eighth grade before he was nine. At that age he entered the University of Wisconsin's University High School, whose progressive philosophy resembled that of the Dewey School, where Althea had taught. Charles Russell encouraged John's science education by working mathematics problems with him during the great flu epidemic of 1918 and by purchasing organic dyes and other chemicals for him to experiment with in his basement laboratory. An unusually quiet boy, John relied on his extroverted older brother Bill to help him communicate. He would recreate this pattern in later years with a few of his closest friends and colleagues, including his wife Jane, his Bell Laboratories partner Walter Brattain, and his first graduate student, Nick Holonyak.

In April 1920, when John was not yet twelve, Althea died of breast cancer. Less than six months later, Charles Russell married his secretary, Ruth Hames. John nevertheless completed his University High coursework by age

John Bardeen. AP IMAGES.

thirteen. Given his youth, he postponed entering the freshman class at the University of Wisconsin for two years, taking extra courses, mainly in mathematics, at Madison Central High School.

Training and First Positions. At the University of Wisconsin Bardeen majored in electrical engineering. He responded with excitement to quantum mechanics, as presented by John Van Vleck in his Wisconsin course on quantum physics and in Van Vleck's research seminar, but Bardeen was not yet ready to become a physicist. The engineer Leo J. Peters supervised Bardeen's master's thesis on electrical prospecting for oil. When Peters left

Wisconsin to take a position at Gulf Research Laboratories in Pittsburgh, Bardeen worked on a problem in antenna theory, which did not inspire him. In 1930, he followed Peters to Gulf Labs and returned to the geophysics of electromagnetic prospecting. Although Bardeen initially enjoyed his work at Gulf, geophysics never fully captured his interest. He so much enjoyed participating in a research seminar in modern physics at the University of Pittsburgh that in the Depression year of 1933 he gave up his secure position at Gulf to enter Princeton's graduate program in mathematics. The night before he left Pittsburgh he met Jane Maxwell, his future wife. Their courtship would solidify over the next five years and result in a marriage of fifty-three years.

Bardeen's Princeton studies laid the foundation for his career in physics. Following the example of his friend Frederick Seitz, who was Eugene Wigner's first graduate student, Bardeen became Wigner's second graduate student. Seitz and Bardeen, along with Conyers Herring, Wigner's third graduate student, and a small group of John Slater's graduate students at MIT, comprised the first generation of American theoretical physicists who were trained to apply quantum mechanics to real solids. In 1933, focusing on sodium, Wigner and Seitz developed a seminal approximate method for calculating real band structures. To this evolving framework Bardeen contributed his thesis calculation of the work function of metals, a measure of the energy required to remove an electron from the surface of a metal. He used a wave function describing each electron with its own single-electron wave function and in approximating the distribution of electrons at the surface of the metal, included higher contributions arising from the forces which were correlating electrons with each other. In later life, Bardeen claimed that Wigner taught him how to attack problems by reducing them to their bare essentials.

In the spring of 1935, Bardeen was invited to become a Junior Fellow in Harvard's Society of Fellows despite the uncomfortable tongue-tied interview he had with a group of Senior Fellows. During his three years of research at Harvard, Bardeen focused on "many-body" problems where the interactions between electrons, or between electrons and the lattice, play a significant role. He was often frustrated because physics was not yet equipped with adequate theoretical tools for treating such interactions; these tools would evolve after World War II. In Bardeen's first year at Harvard, he became acquainted with William Shockley, then completing his doctoral thesis at MIT under Slater. During Bardeen's second semester, Shockley accepted a position at Bell Telephone Laboratories, the research and development arm of the American Telephone and Telegraph Company. From that position, Shockley would later help bring Bardeen to Bell Laboratories. An important influence on Bardeen during his Harvard period was the experimental physicist Percy Bridgman, widely recognized for his pioneering studies of the physics of materials under high pressure (and sometimes credited with developing the philosophy of operationalism, often associated with Einstein's development of the special theory of relativity). Bardeen found applying quantum theory to Bridgman's data so fulfilling that in later years he would try to recreate the model of working closely with an experimentalist whenever possible.

One of the problems Bardeen struggled with unsuccessfully at Harvard was explaining superconductivity, the complete loss of electrical resistance in certain metals and alloys when their temperature falls below a critical transition temperature. Numerous theories of superconductivity had been proposed in the 1920s and early 1930s following the development of quantum mechanics, but they all failed. In 1935, a breakthrough occurred when the brothers Fritz and Heinz London published a speculative empirical theory of superconductivity designed to explain the observed Meissner effect, the expulsion of magnetic field by superconductors. Bardeen was among those who immediately sensed the importance of the Londons' suggestion of a "rigidity" of the ground-state wave function (rigid, because it is not much altered by a magnetic field) as a consequence of the proposed gap in energy between the ground state and the low-lying exited states. But he could not yet use this clue to develop a theory of superconductivity from first principles.

Bardeen married Jane Maxwell in June 1938, shortly after the Department of Physics of the University of Minnesota offered him his first teaching position. At Minnesota Bardeen continued to pursue superconductivity with a theory that assumed the only electrons that count are those near the edge of the Fermi surface. These, Bardeen believed, might create a field oriented opposite to the applied field, shielding the electrons inside from the applied field and causing the observed diamagnetism. In favorable circumstances, he argued, small displacements of the ions inside superconductors would cause the electrons to gain a small amount of energy that more than compensated for the energy spent on ionic displacement, causing gaps to form in the electronic structure. As the experimental numbers this theory predicted disagreed with the observed values by more than a factor of ten, Bardeen did not commit his calculation to print.

In Minnesota, the Bardeens' first child, James Maxwell Bardeen, was born on 9 May 1939. By the time their second child, William Allan Bardeen, was born, on 15 September 1941, Bardeen had begun to move the family to Washington, DC, so that he could serve his country by researching the influence fields of ships at the Naval Ordnance Laboratory (NOL) to help allied troops defend against German magnetic firing mechanisms. The

Bardeens' third child, Elizabeth Ann Bardeen (called Betsy), was born on 25 April 1944, in the period when the family lived in Washington. All three children subsequently entered scientific careers: James and William studied physics and Betsy computing.

Bell Laboratories and the Transistor. Bardeen soon grew restless at NOL, unhappy both with his military engineering work, which diverted him from his physics research, and with the inflexible and chaotic military bureaucracy. He returned to fundamental physics as soon as the war ended, accepting an offer to work on basic solid-state physics in a new semiconductor group at Bell Laboratories headed by Shockley. The group Bardeen joined was a section of the laboratory's recently established solid-state research department, modeled by the executive vice president Mervin Kelly on the successful multidisciplinary wartime laboratories. In the new semiconductor group, besides the two theorists Bardeen and Shockley, were two experimental physicists, Walter Brattain and Gerald Pearson, a chemist, Robert Gibney, and a circuit expert, Hilbert Moore. One goal was to replace vacuum tube systems, which had been the basis of the telephone system's growth during the 1920s and 1930s, with semiconductor technology. Bardeen studied the wartime reports on silicon and germanium, which had been produced during the war because of the use of semiconductors in radar detectors.

Bardeen's work leading to the transistor began soon after he arrived in October 1941, when Shockley asked him to examine a design that he had sketched about six months earlier for a silicon field-effect amplifier. The device did not work. Five months later, Bardeen had a theory to explain this failure. It assumed that a substantial number of electrons were trapped in surface states and thus could not contribute to conduction. Shockley's interest in this research flagged over the course of the group's two-year study of surface states.

The "magic month" culminating in the transistor began in November 1947 during the group's study of surface states. On encountering a magnetic problem caused by droplets of water condensing on his apparatus, Brattain immersed the apparatus in various liquids and found that the photovoltaic effect he was studying increased whenever the liquid used was an electrolyte. After Bardeen suggested that ions in the electrolytes might be creating an electric field large enough to overcome the surface states, the team noticed that when water or an electrolyte was used they could vary the photo EMF (electromotive force) over a large range, indicating a possible way to build a field-effect semiconductor amplifier. Bardeen's close interplay with Brattain, in which he served as "the brain" and

Brattain as "the hands," resembled his earlier collaboration with Bridgman (del Guercio et al., 1998).

Bardeen offered many suggestions for variations to try in the group's evolving work aimed at inventing a semiconductor amplifier, for instance, to try different electrolytes and to use a slab of p-type silicon with an n-type "inversion layer," in which the sign of charge carriers was opposite to that of carriers in the bulk material and where the carriers had higher mobility than in deposited thin films. One crucial suggestion was to replace the silicon altogether with a piece of the "high-back-voltage germanium" developed during World War II by the Purdue University group working under Karl Lark-Horowitz. Another was to substitute for the electrolyte an oxide film Brattain had seen growing on the germanium. With these changes, their experiment on 11 December 1947 showed amplification. But the current was flowing in the opposite direction than expected. Only gradually did Bardeen and Brattain realize that their oxide had washed off, allowing holes, empty electron states near the top of an otherwise filled energy band acting like positive particles, to flow into the germanium. Owing to this contact, the device they had built amplified on a different principle than by the field effect. To increase the signal, Bardeen now suggested their classic geometry, in which two narrowly separated metallic line contacts were pushed down on the germanium to allow the holes to flow closer to the input signal. This experiment worked the first time they tried it, on 16 December 1947. The device, later named the transistor, was born. Bardeen's soft murmur to his wife Jane that evening, "We discovered something today," was almost inaudible, but since he typically said nothing about his work she knew it had been a special day (Jane Bardeen, 1991c).

The invention of the transistor would in time change the world by making possible the microchip and all the devices that followed from it, but the discovery ruined the spirit of the Bell Laboratories semiconductor group. Shockley, who had been uninvolved in the invention of the original transistor, stunned Bardeen and Brattain when he tried to patent the invention in *his* name, hoping to base it on his suggestion of the field-effect amplifier. Shockley's plan failed because the patent attorneys discovered that Julius E. Lilienfeld, a Polish-American inventor, had already patented the field-effect notion in 1930. Shockley further antagonized Brattain and Bardeen by preventing them from working on the consequences of their historic invention, a second transistor, known as the junction device, which could better be used commercially. The work at this stage was already tense, because Bardeen and Brattain, occupied with the tedious process of drafting patent applications, were anxious that physicists elsewhere, for instance, those working at Purdue, might scoop them. Indeed, in Paris, Heinrich Welker and Herbert

Mataré would soon file a patent on a device similar to their invention. Meanwhile, Shockley continued to work secretly on his design for the junction device. But when John Shive demonstrated that holes could travel through the bulk of a semiconductor, Shockley suddenly announced his work, fearing that Bardeen would instantly apply the new clue and invent the junction transistor before he could take credit for it. Brattain and Bardeen were appalled when they learned that Shockley had hidden his work from the group (Riordan and Hoddeson, 1977, 163–186).

Bardeen considered taking a position at Oak Ridge National Laboratory directing the solid-state work of the reactor program. James Fisk, then at Harvard but scheduled to return to Bell Laboratories as the director of Physical Research, advised Bardeen to wait the crisis out. Bardeen returned to the work on superconductivity he had started at Minnesota. Unfortunately, while superconductivity was still the outstanding unsolved riddle of solid-state physics, in this period it was of little interest at Bell Laboratories. Bardeen worked on the problem alone. What soon riveted him to this work was a phone call he received on 15 May 1950 from Bernard Serin, an experimental physicist at Rutgers. In studying pure isotopes of mercury, Serin's group found an *isotope effect*: the lighter the mass, the higher the temperature at which the material turns superconducting. Emanuel Maxwell at the National Bureau of Standards had found the same effect independently. Bardeen realized this meant "that electron-lattice interactions are important in determining superconductivity" (Handwritten notes, 15 May 1950. Bardeen papers, University of Illinois). In his Minnesota work, Bardeen had tried to explain the energy gap in the electronic structure of superconductors using a single-electron quantum mechanical model. He explored whether applying a small periodic distortion to the lattice could lower the energy and introduce band gaps near the Fermi surface. Although his initial attempt to use the new clue about the electron-lattice interactions failed to rescue his earlier theory, he felt quite sure he was on the right track and secured his priority in a letter to the *Physical Review*. He did so at roughly the same time that a colleague, Herbert Fröhlich, came to similar conclusions about the electron-lattice interactions. At this point, neither Bardeen nor Fröhlich could show how these interactions could actually lower the energy as was necessary to achieve superconductivity.

Bardeen continued to feel isolated in his work on superconductivity at Bell Laboratories. In October 1950, when he encountered Seitz at a physics conference, he asked whether Seitz knew of any jobs in academia. Seitz, who had recently moved to the University of Illinois, went directly to his dean and to the head of the Department of Physics who soon pieced together an offer for Bardeen

jointly in physics and electrical engineering. Bardeen accepted in April 1951, and the family moved to Illinois during the summer of 1951.

University of Illinois and Theory of Superconductivity. Bardeen and his first graduate student, Nick Holonyak, became instant and unlikely friends. The bond that developed between the soft-spoken, mature, and meditative Bardeen and the talkative, young, and exuberant Holonyak resembled the relationship Bardeen had had with his extroverted Bell Labs partner Brattain, and earlier with his older brother William. Holonyak worked in the semiconductor laboratory, which was created in the fall of 1952 in the space that previously had housed the university's historic ILLIAC computer. According to Holonyak, Bardeen never "picked up a pair of pliers," but would come by the laboratory almost daily to encourage the students to learn for themselves how to conduct an experiment (Holonyak, 1991).

Although he was now back in academia, Bardeen maintained a number of industrial ties, the longest-lasting one with Xerox Corporation (initially called the Haloid Company), and others with General Electric and Supertex, an electronics firm founded by Henry Pao, one of Bardeen's students. Bardeen also participated in creating the Midwest Electronics Research Center, which helped industries develop their research capability in cooperation with research universities.

Once settled at Illinois, Bardeen immersed himself fully in the problem of superconductivity. Seeking new tools for dealing with the electron interactions in superconductors, he explored David Bohm's recently developed theory of electron-electron interactions in plasmas. Bardeen invited Bohm's graduate student David Pines to work with him at Illinois as his postdoctoral assistant. Based on Pines's study of the interactions in the simpler case of the polaron, Bardeen and Pines developed a formalism for treating the coupling of electrons to the lattice vibrations. They found that in cases where the energy transfer is small, the attractive interaction is stronger, suggesting a possible mechanism for superconductivity. In the meantime, Bardeen examined all the work that had been done on superconductivity, while preparing a long review article on the topic published in 1956 in the *Handbuch der Physik*.

In the fall of 1953, J. Robert Schrieffer, who had written an undergraduate thesis at MIT under Slater, joined the graduate physics program at Illinois. Schrieffer chose Bardeen as his thesis advisor and, by the spring of 1955, had selected the theory of superconductivity as his thesis topic. As Pines had accepted a teaching post at Princeton, Bardeen invited Leon Cooper, a young theorist with a field theory background, to join him as a postdoctoral associate. In the last months of 1955, Cooper showed that if the net force between two electrons just outside the Fermi surface is attractive they would form a bound state lying below the normal continuum of states and separated from the continuum by an energy gap. It appeared clear that if the entire ground state of a superconductor was composed of such pairs, the state would have properties that were qualitatively different from those of the normal state and would be separated from the excited states by an energy gap. The solution to the long-standing riddle looked near, but a major hurdle remained: how to cope theoretically with the large number of overlapping electron pairs in a superconductor.

In the middle of this work, Bardeen was surprised to learn that along with Brattain and Shockley he had won the 1956 Nobel Prize for the invention of the transistor. Encouraging Cooper and Schrieffer to keep working on superconductivity, Bardeen traveled to Stockholm to accept his prize. He was ambivalent about doing so, not only because he did not wish to leave his work on superconductivity hanging at this point, but because he was not quite sure the transistor deserved a Nobel Prize. He also felt embarrassed to be awarded a Nobel Prize before his teachers Wigner and Van Vleck had received theirs.

The turn in the team's work on superconductivity came in the last days of January 1957, soon after Bardeen returned from Stockholm. While riding on a subway in New Jersey, Schrieffer wrote down a promising expression for the superconducting ground state wave function. Recognizing the implications, Bardeen moved the team into an intense period of work in which the three feverishly computed all the relevant experimental quantities, including the energy gap and the second-order phase transition. The Bardeen-Cooper-Schrieffer theory (BCS), published in July 1957, proved to be the triumphant solution of the problem which for four and a half decades had stumped all the best theorists in the world.

After steering his team to the discovery of BCS, Bardeen fell into the role of the guru of the Illinois Physics Department; he spent most days answering questions posed by his colleagues and students. Because of his experience and detailed knowledge of physics, he could often point directly to the heart of a problem or even to its solution. But there were the times when Bardeen's colleagues could not grasp the master's meaning and simply accepted his judgment. The fact that they sometimes accepted his intuition blindly caused a few embarrassments. His initial resistance to Brian Josephson's 1962 theory predicting that electron pairs in superconductors can tunnel quantum mechanically through a thin barrier separating two superconductors became the subject of a famous debate staged between Bardeen and Josephson at a major conference in 1962. Josephson won the debate.

In 1965, President Lyndon Johnson honored Bardeen with the National Medal of Science, the nation's highest award for scientific achievement. Bardeen worried that the Swedish Academy of Sciences would hold to its tradition of never awarding a person a Nobel Prize twice in the same field, and thus rob Schrieffer and Cooper of their well-deserved honor. But in 1972, the Nobel Committee broke precedent and awarded Bardeen, Cooper, and Schrieffer the Nobel Prize for their theory of superconductivity. Less than two years later Bardeen retired from teaching at the age of 65. He nevertheless continued to work on research most days, with his office door open to colleagues and students. Among the few changes colleagues observed was that Bardeen stopped wearing a tie when he came to the university.

Throughout his time at Illinois, Bardeen occasionally served on national advisory panels, for example, in 1951 for the Office of Naval Research (ONR), and from 1959 through 1962 on the President's Science Advisory Committee (PSAC) under Dwight D. Eisenhower and then John F. Kennedy. In 1968, he began a term as president of the American Physical Society (APS), which unfortunately included the violence that erupted during the 1968 Democratic National Convention in Chicago as a consequence of protest against the war in Vietnam. Bardeen found himself mediating a conflict between those who wished to cancel the Chicago APS meeting to protest the brutality of police actions and those who felt that canceling the meeting to make a political comment was an inappropriate use of the APS organization.

Bardeen initially resisted the invitation in 1981 to serve on President Ronald Reagan's White House Science Council (WHSC), the replacement for PSAC, which President Richard Nixon had abolished in 1973. Bardeen reluctantly agreed to serve when his colleagues argued that a man of his knowledge and convictions was needed on the committee. Bardeen stepped down from the WHSC shortly after Reagan and his science advisor George Keyworth committed the United States, without consulting the WHSC, to the space-based missile defense program known as the Strategic Defense Initiative (SDI) (or popularly, as Star Wars). The SDI program so worried Bardeen that he wrote several articles about its dangers, including a *New York Times* editorial on the subject in May 1986, coauthored with Hans Bethe, although it was largely written by Kurt Gottfried.

Last Years. During the 1980s, Bardeen's scientific work was largely focused on a novel quantum mechanical theory of charge density waves (CDWs), a phenomenon he believed could be explained in similar terms as superconductivity. The many-body physics community was initially intrigued by Bardeen's theory of CDWs, but as time progressed, more and more physicists preferred the competing classical model, which predicted measurable relationships between the amount of impurities in the materials and the threshold voltage at which the CDWs begin to slide. As Bardeen's theory lost ground, he felt increasingly bitter about the opposition; his own confidence in the theory persisted to the end of his life. Bardeen described the CDWs in 1989 as "a beautiful example of macroscopic quantum mechanics, with many analogies to superconductivity," and he insisted that all the evidence "indicates that it is necessary to treat CDW metals as macroscopic quantum systems with quantum tunneling as an essential feature" (Bardeen, 1989).

Bardeen's friendship with Holonyak offered a partial antidote for the unhappiness he experienced from the mid-1980s on. For a time he was able to relax and take Holonyak's advice: "Look, if it's a good day and you have such an inclination, go play golf" (Holonyak, 1998a). But by the end of the 1980s, Bardeen's health was failing seriously. With his vision impaired by macular degeneration and with gout in his legs, golf became extremely difficult. Yet when the physics community was shaken by the excitement arising from the 1987 discovery of high temperature superconductivity, Bardeen, like many other theorists, jumped on the bandwagon and tried to develop a theory for this phenomenon.

In December 1990, the month in which Bardeen's last article about the CDWs appeared in *Physics Today*, physicians in Urbana aspirated nearly a liter of fluid from his chest. X-rays revealed a mass in his lungs. A bronchoscopy and a mediastinoscopy at Boston's Brigham and Women's Hospital showed that his cancer had spread, thus surgery was out of the question. The surgeon, Dr. David Sugarbaker, marveled at Bardeen's calm dignity in the face of his own mortality and suggested radiation, but on 30 January 1991, before any radiation could be administered, Bardeen died of a massive heart attack. Jane brought her husband's ashes home to Champaign-Urbana. In May, the family buried them in Madison. On 31 March 1997, Jane also died, seven days short of her ninetieth birthday. Their son William designed a single low stone monument for the graves of both his parents, with a pattern referring to his mother's interest in the natural world and his father's two Nobel Prizes.

BIBLIOGRAPHY

The largest collection of Bardeen's personal and family papers is held by William and Marjorie Bardeen in Warrenville, Illinois. Many of Bardeen's scientific papers can be found in the University of Illinois Archives in Urbana, Illinois. Bardeen's Bell Laboratories notebooks belong to Lucent Technologies. The interviews with John Bardeen, David Bohm, J. Robert Schrieffer, and William Shockley, as well as the 1991 interviews with Frederick Seitz cited here, can be found at the Center for History of Physics of the American Physical Society. All other interviews cited here can be found at the University of Illinois.

WORKS BY BARDEEN

With Eugene Wigner. "Theory of the Work Function of Monovalent Metals." *Physical Review,* series 2, 48 (1935): 84–87.

With Walter Brattain. "The Transistor: A Semi-Conductor Triode." Letter. *Physical Review,* series 2, 74 (1948): 230–231.

With Walter Brattain. "Physical Principles Involved in Transistor Action." *Physical Review,* series 2, 75 (1949): 1208–1225.

"Theory of Superconductivity. Theoretical Part." In *Handbuch der Physik,* vol. 15. Berlin: Springer, 1956.

With Leon N. Coooper and J. Robert Schrieffer. "Theory of Superconductivity." *Physical Review,* series 2, 108 (1957): 1175–1204.

Interviews: By Lillian Hoddeson. 12 and 16 May 1977, 1 and 22 December 1977, and 13 February 1980. By Hoddeson and Gordon Baym. 14 April 1980a.

"Reminiscences of the Early Days in Solid State Physics." *Proceedings of the Royal Society of London* A 371 (1980b): 77–83.

With Hans A. Bethe. "Back to Science Advisors." *New York Times,* 17 May 1986.

"Classical versus Quantum Models of Charge-Density-Wave Depinning in Quasi-One-Dimensional Metals." *Physical Review B* 39 (15 February 1989): 3528–3532.

"Superconductivity and Other Macroscopic Quantum Phenomena." *Physics Today* 43, no. 12 (1990): 25–31.

OTHER SOURCES

Bardeen, Jane. Interviews: By Lillian Hoddeson and Irving Elichirigoity. 6 June 1991a. By Vicki Daitch. 29 September 1991b. By Brian Pippard, David Pines, Lev Gor'kov, Ansel Anderson, Gordon Baym, Lillian Hoddeson, and Charles Slichter. 9 October 1991c. By Vicki Daitch. 23 November 1993. By Vicki Daitch. 2 December 1994.

del Guercio, G., et al. *Transistorized!* Documentatary film. KTCA-ScienCentral, PBS, 1998.

Hoddeson, Lillian. "The Discovery of the Point-Contact Transistor." *Historical Studies in the Physical Sciences* 12, no.1 (1981a): 41–76.

———. "The Emergence of Basic Research in the Bell Telephone System, 1875–1915." *Technology and Culture* 22 (1981b): 512–544.

Hoddeson, Lillian, Ernest Braun, Jurgen Teichmann, and Spencer Weart, eds. *Out of the Crystal Maze: Chapters from the History of Solid-State Physics.* New York: Oxford University Press, 1991.

Hoddeson, Lillian, and Vicki Daitch. *True Genius: The Life and Science of John Bardeen.* Washington, DC: Joseph Henry Press, 2002.

Holonyak, Nick. Interviews: By Lillian Hoddeson and Fernando Irving Elichirigoity. 29 May 1991. By Vicki Daitch, 21 January 1993. By Hoddeson and Riordan. 30 July 1993. By

Hoddeson. 12 June 1998a. By Hoddeson and Daitch. 6 August 1998b. By Daitch. 6 December 2000.

Riordan, Michael, and Lillian Hoddeson. *Crystal Fire: The Birth of the Information Age.* New York: W. W. Norton, 1997.

Lillian Hoddeson

BARTLETT, FREDERIC CHARLES

(*b.* Stow-on-the-Wold, Gloucestershire, England, 22 October 1886; *d.* Cambridge, England, 30 September 1969), *anthropology, cognitive psychology, experimental psychology, social psychology.*

Bartlett produced one of the most original and provocative psychological theories of remembering while also exercising an unprecedented influence over the shape of British academic psychology. Two intellectual contributions stand out: his early emphasis on psychological processes as constituted in and constitutive of social interaction, and his development of an account of remembering that emphasized its reconstructive nature. A number of his ideas have become repeated points of reference in psychology: effort after meaning, remembering as reconstruction, and the schema as a means of ensuring order in mental life. At an institutional level, Bartlett was made the founding Professor of Experimental Psychology at Cambridge University in 1931. Through his activities within the academic discipline and his involvement in agencies concerned with psychology as an applied discipline, Bartlett played a key role in the way in which British psychology developed in the mid-twentieth century. His contributions to psychology and to bodies such as the Royal Air Force and the National Institute for Industrial Psychology led to a host of honors, including Fellow of the Royal Society (1932), the Royal Medal of the Royal Society (1952), honorary degrees from many universities, and a knighthood (1948).

Entering Psychology. Frederic Charles Bartlett was born in Stow-on-the-Wold, Gloucestershire, England, in 1886. He was the second son of William Bartlett, a boot maker, and Temperance Howman. He suffered from pleurisy in his teenage years and consequently received much of his schooling at home. When Bartlett began his studies through the University of London in 1909, psychology as an independent academic discipline and as a profession was hardly extant in Britain. As a consequence, like many of his contemporaries in British psychology, Bartlett's education was not in psychology. Instead, he first took an honors degree in philosophy, and then a master's degree in sociology and ethics in 1911. Apparently still hungry for learning, he went to Cambridge to pursue a degree in

moral sciences. On graduation in 1914 he replaced Cyril Burt as an assistant in Cambridge's recently founded psychological laboratory. Thereafter, Bartlett never left Cambridge for any extended period, and he died there in 1969.

At Cambridge, Bartlett considered pursuing a career in philosophy, and his first publication was a book on logic. However, he became disenchanted with the idea of a career in philosophy after an encounter with Bertrand Russell and G. E. Moore and an attempt to defend Henri Bergson's ideas at the Moral Sciences Club. Russell and Moore were arguably the two most eminent philosophers in Britain at the time, and Russell in particular had a reputation for intellectual pyrotechnics. After such a meeting, Bartlett's decision not to pursue philosophy is hardly difficult to understand. Nevertheless, the influence of philosophy, especially the work of the Cambridge philosopher James Ward, was to be discernible in all of his most important psychological work prior to World War II.

Fortunately, Cambridge held intellectual attractions other than philosophy, most importantly anthropology and the presence of W. H. R. Rivers. Rivers was the university's first lecturer in experimental psychology; however, as part anthropologist, part psychoanalyst, part psychologist, part physiologist, and part medical doctor, he defies easy classification. He had been important in developing the notion of diffusionism in British anthropology (broadly speaking, the claim that cultural developments occurred through one culture borrowing and adapting entities from another culture). The importance of diffusionism was apparent in Bartlett's fellowship thesis for St. John's College, which he completed in 1916: "Transformation Arising from Repeated Representation: A Contribution towards an Experimental Study of the Process of Conventionalisation." In it, he used loosely controlled experiments to examine the idea that as items are repeatedly remembered, their form becomes more conventional. The thesis contained themes, methods, and data that were to feature in his later works: effort after meaning, the method of description, the method of repeated reproduction, and the notion of conventionalization.

Unable to serve in World War I because of health problems, Bartlett conducted research of potential relevance to the war effort. Prompted by the unlikely sounding Lancashire Anti-Submarine Committee, Bartlett, together with his future wife Emily Mary Smith, performed experiments on the detection of sounds of weak intensity. The aim of these experiments was to produce a means whereby the Navy could select those people best able to detect the sound of submarines. Their work represented the beginnings of an aspect of Bartlett's career that was to endure until his retirement: a concern to introduce psychologists into applied research, including that relevant to military needs. During World War I, Bartlett also

184

did some work with shell-shocked soldiers at the Eastern General Hospital near Cambridge. However, unlike several of the key figures in early British psychology, his encounters with these soldiers do not appear to have profoundly affected his work in psychology.

From the Psychology of Primitive Culture to Remembering. At the end of World War I, Bartlett stayed on in the laboratory in Cambridge. Rivers had impressed on him the importance of experimental work in psychology for progress in anthropology. In the 1920s this aspect was apparent in Bartlett's experiments on the reproduction of folk stories, in his discussions of the psychology of contact between cultures, and in his reflections on group organization, leadership, and the social function of symbols. These publications reflected his interest in producing a psychology that acknowledged the importance of biological factors but which was grounded in social and cultural processes, an interest that was most fully articulated in his book *Psychology and Primitive Culture* (1923).

In *Psychology and Primitive Culture*, Bartlett addressed central issues in diffusionist anthropology: How were elements transferred from one culture to another? And what happened to them when they were? By "elements" Bartlett meant cultural forms such as artifacts, folk stories, and institutions. As in his fellowship thesis, he argued that psychological processes were integral to understanding transfer and change, but conversely, one could only truly understand psychological processes as embedded in these wider sociocultural conditions. Thus, what was psychological and what was cultural were interdependent, and neither could be reduced to the other. The key psychological concept in understanding this interdependence was that of tendencies. Tendencies were promptings to action (bodily movements, thoughts, or emotions) that were highly sensitive to all aspects of a situation, including cognitive, affective, and reactive factors. He argued that different tendencies underpinned fundamental forms of social relationship, such as tendencies toward conservation and constructiveness, individual tendencies, and group difference tendencies. Some tendencies were universal, while others differentiated individuals; some were innate, while others were derived, that is, socially acquired. Bartlett believed that interactions between different tendencies were important psychologically. For example, a conflict of tendencies led to affective reactions. The concept attempted to bridge the biological, the psychological, and the sociocultural in a manner that was reminiscent of Rivers's work.

Bartlett's account of tendencies was not widely taken up, and psychologists largely ignored *Psychology and Primitive Culture*; in obituaries of Bartlett, it often received only passing mention. However, reading Bartlett's work in

Frederic Bartlett. *Bartlett, right, receives the Queen's Medal from Royal Society president Edgar Douglas Adrian, 1 December 1952.* HULTON ARCHIVE/GETTY IMAGES.

the round and in its historical context, it is difficult to sustain the claim that the book was the least noteworthy of his major publications. As some scholars have pointed out, it was an early if unsuccessful attempt to produce an account of psychological processes as fundamentally grounded in sociocultural conditions. According to this view, his later work, which tended to treat the individual as less social, was a retreat from this earlier insight—the implication being that had he persisted with his earlier views, he would have helped to produce a radically social psychology.

In 1922, the year before *Psychology and Primitive Culture* was published, Rivers died unexpectedly in his rooms in St. John's College. It was a severe blow, not only to Bartlett but, it would seem, to all those who had known Rivers, a man whose influence on people at a personal level appears to have been profound. Although Bartlett retained his interests in anthropological matters and published on them for many years after Rivers's death, they were never again such a prominent part of his research.

Bartlett wrote on a wide range of issues in the 1920s, but his next important book was *Remembering: A Study in Experimental and Social Psychology* in 1932. While it was not as radically social in its orientation as his earlier book, *Remembering* was nevertheless regarded as an original and unconventional work. Two sets of experiments reported in the book have deservedly received particular attention. The first set was based on a method known as repeated reproduction, which he had used in his thesis studies. Here a person was presented with some kind of stimulus and was then asked to recall it on several subsequent occasions. The second set was based on a method known as serial reproduction—a method recommended to him by the mathematician and later cybernetician, Norbert Wiener—in which a person was presented with a stimulus and was then asked to recall what he or she could in writing before passing that recollection on to a second person, who was then asked to repeat the process. Bartlett used several types of stimuli, most famously stories based on indigenous folk stories. He regarded the practice, common in many memory experiments, of using meaningless materials (such as invented nonwords) as stimuli to be a mistake. For Bartlett, the essence of perceiving and remembering was the effort to make sense of the world, what he called "effort after meaning." Consequently, he argued that stimuli in memory experiments should carry meaning because materials in real life did so (and even if stimuli were designed not to carry meaning, people would impose meaning upon them).

From his data, Bartlett concluded that people's recollections typically differed from the original stimulus. For example, people's recollections usually retained the basic form of the story but simplified it, unfamiliar features were frequently transformed into more familiar ones or omitted altogether, and recollections included material that was not in the original stimulus but that could have reasonably been inferred from it, a process Bartlett termed "rationalization." Bartlett's main conclusion was that remembering was fundamentally a reconstructive activity rather than a reproductive one. This was radical in two main ways. First, it departed somewhat from the two most dominant metaphors of memory: storage and inscription. For Bartlett, neither of these metaphors sufficiently captured the changing and adaptive characteristics of memory. Second, partly as a result of the storage metaphor, most psychological theories of memory until then had been concerned with how much people remember and had explained forgetting through processes such as decay. Bartlett was not so much concerned with memory as an amount of material as with the idea that when remembering, one reconstructs a memory, and thus what one remembers is rarely a literal reproduction of what was encountered. That is, he was interested in the qualitative nature of changes. For him, the reconstructive nature of remembering had adaptive and functional value because, he argued, situations in nature are rarely repeated exactly. Sometimes Bartlett has been interpreted as saying that lit-

eral recall cannot occur, but this is to go too far; he argued that perfect recall could occur but required particular and exceptional conditions to do so.

Bartlett's choice of the gerundive form for his book's title reflected his belief that remembering was an act. Its reconstructive nature arose from it being influenced by what had been encountered, the circumstances at recall, and an actively organized and changing mass of past experiences. Remembering was not a faculty for reflection or for straightforward reproduction of things previously encountered. Instead, it was a set of complex, active processes that enabled the person to engage with the world. One of the most novel elements of this account was the role assigned to the mental representation of the past as an organized yet constantly changing mass of experiences into which new experiences were integrated and transformed, and by which the memories of those experiences could be altered. Though he preferred the phrase "organized setting," Bartlett settled on the term *schema* to describe this fluid yet structured mass. The term had been used by his friend, the neurologist Henry Head, to explain how previous and current body positions could have an effect on the maintenance of position and on movement to new positions (clearly, the term also owes something to Kant). Bartlett realized that the idea provided him with a theoretical framework for his data. He treated schemata as unconscious mental entities and, even more than Head, he stressed their dynamic nature. A schema operated as a mass rather than as a collection of individual elements, but this made it difficult to understand how individual episodes could ever be recalled or recalled with any degree of accuracy. Although he attempted to solve this problem through the notion of the schema turning back on itself, Bartlett never clarified what such a process might entail.

Bartlett's view of mind as active in constructing an interpretation of the world owed much to one of his teachers, James Ward. Ward is relatively obscure in the early twenty-first century, but Bertrand Russell described him as his "chief teacher," and William James held him in high esteem. Throughout his writings, Ward consistently emphasized the active constructive nature of mind. This treatment of mind as shaping people's interpretation of stimuli is frequently depicted as one of the qualities that differentiated Bartlett's work from that of the behaviorists, who were beginning to dominate American academic psychology at the time. However, in following Ward, what Bartlett was opposing was a strictly associationist and empiricist view of mind.

The more neglected part of *Remembering* was concerned with the social psychology of remembering. Drawing on experimental and anthropological data, most of which had been collected by others, Bartlett examined how social influences modified what people recall. He

186

resisted notions such as collective unconscious and the idea that a social group could itself have a memory. However, he echoed his earlier claim that one could only understand individuals as individuals in a particular social milieu. In particular, he stressed remembering as something done in a social setting. Again, the importance of Bartlett's text lay not in its particulars but in his emphasis on remembering as an activity that was something firmly embedded in social conditions. This aspect of Bartlett's message was subsequently ignored in the vast majority of experimental studies of memory.

Bartlett's theory of remembering has received criticism as well as praise. The criticisms have taken three general forms. First, though influential, his notion of schema has been attacked as being inadequate as the sole means of mentally representing human knowledge. Bartlett's solution to the problem of retrieving individual items from schemata has also been considered underspecified and obscure. Second, Bartlett's experiments have been criticized for being too loosely controlled and analyzed. Third, in general his theories have been regarded as too vague to guide a program of experimental research. As academic psychology became increasingly dominated by experimentation, statistical analyses, and the rhetoric (if not the practice) of falsification, these flaws were regarded as serious. Nevertheless, Bartlett's account of remembering remains one of the few truly original, radical theories of memory, and schema theory had a major impact on computational accounts of cognitive processes.

World War II. The final major shift in Bartlett's thinking and writing came during World War II. Bartlett argued that the war changed psychologists' thinking and practices because of two main factors: the increased military reliance on complex machines and the way in which psychologists were required to work on problems in collaboration with mathematicians, physicists, and engineers. For Bartlett, these circumstances required a psychology that concentrated on sequences of behavior and on behavior with machines. He was further influenced in this by a postgraduate student, Kenneth Craik, who arrived in Cambridge in 1936. Because of the war, Craik and Bartlett concentrated on practical problems; it was Craik's general approach, however, that had a lasting effect on him. Craik speculated that aspects of human cognition, such as recognition, memory, and prediction, were characteristics shared by machines. He also argued that human thought operated by creating an internal model of the external world. It is difficult to ascertain what role Bartlett may have had in the development of these ideas, but he appears to have believed that they promised a new direction for psychological research. Tragically, Craik was killed in a road accident in 1945; like the death of Rivers more than twenty years earlier, his death was a heavy personal and professional blow to Bartlett.

Though Bartlett continued to publish occasional papers on anthropological or social psychological matters, his output after the war became more concerned with understanding the perceptual and cognitive processes of the individual. The most prominent concept in these later publications was that of skill. He developed the idea most thoroughly in his last book, *Thinking: An Experimental and Social Study*, published in 1958, some six years after he had retired. Drawing on analogies from performance in cricket and tennis, two of his favorite interests, he argued that thinking could be conceived of as a high-level skill. In the book, he also made much of the division between thinking in closed systems and adventurous thinking (by which he meant something akin to thinking that tested or refused constraints). The psychological theories proposed in *Thinking* were more individualistic in orientation than in his earlier books. Subsequently, Bartlett's concern to understand topics such as the thinking of scientists, everyday reasoning, and the thinking of artists all became areas of interest in the field of cognitive psychology.

Bartlett's three books, *Psychology and Primitive Culture*, *Remembering*, and *Thinking*, represent the major academic publications of his career. However, he also contributed to many university and government committees, and wrote numerous reports for government, industry, and the military. For example, for the Flying Personnel Research Committee alone he produced twenty-nine reports or commentaries during World War II, covering topics such as pilot selection, the kinds of skills required by pilots, the different types of fatigue experienced by air crews, and the design of instruments. The exact significance of these contributions remains to be fully assessed, but they are testament to a growing tendency of a variety of bodies to treat psychologists as able to provide expert advice. How that advice was received is another matter.

Bartlett died in Cambridge on 30 September 1969 after a short illness. He was survived by Lady Bartlett (née Emily Mary Smith) and their two sons, Hugh and Denis.

Bartlett and the Shape of British Psychology. When Bartlett started work at the laboratory in Cambridge in 1914, psychology was a tiny and barely independent discipline in the United Kingdom. By the time he retired in 1952, psychology was firmly established in British universities and in a variety of social practices. Of course, these developments are not attributable to Bartlett, as there were much larger forces at play, but Bartlett did play a unique and powerful role in shaping the direction of what he described as the "upstart discipline."

When Charles Myers left Cambridge in 1922 to develop the National Institute of Industrial Psychology (NIIP), Bartlett became the new director of the laboratory and expended considerable effort on consolidating and expanding psychology within Cambridge. In 1931, the year before he published *Remembering*, he was appointed Cambridge's first Professor of Experimental Psychology. He had the political skill and acumen to take advantage of the situation, and the Cambridge department grew considerably under his leadership. But his influence was wider; by 1957 ten of the sixteen chairs of psychology in the United Kingdom had a direct link of some kind to Bartlett. While his own approach to the means of knowledge production did not rely on strictly controlled experiments, during these years he fostered experimental psychology as the approach to the subject. For some, this was simply Bartlett's recognition of the necessities of establishing psychology as a science, understanding the means of doing so, and exercising his abilities to achieve it. For others, however, his efforts encouraged an unnecessarily narrow discipline.

Bartlett did not confine himself to building up psychology as a purely academic discipline. At Myers's invitation he joined the Council and Advisory Board of the NIIP in 1922. Though the NIIP was short-lived, for a time between the two world wars it was the most important psychological organization in Britain. It attracted industrialists and eminent academics, and it was sufficiently prominent to be addressed by the British prime minister, J. Ramsay MacDonald, in 1929. Bartlett was also involved with the Medical Research Council (the MRC was a major source of state funding of research); as another example of his efforts to create a discipline with an applied dimension, in 1943 Bartlett instigated moves to set up an MRC-funded Applied Psychology Research Unit, and the plans came to fruition the following year. Bartlett argued that the unit should not conduct research on vocational guidance, and although social psychology was mentioned in the early discussions, it never formed a large part of the unit's research activities. Bartlett ensured that Craik got the directorship of the unit rather than Eric Farmer, a reader in industrial psychology at Cambridge who might reasonably have expected the appointment. The unit became dominated by experimental work and grew to be one of the most important research institutions in British psychology. Bartlett's role in helping to found and shape it is another example of the powerful place he occupied in British psychology.

Bartlett's Legacy. It is rarely disputed that Bartlett produced a challenging and original theory of remembering and that he profoundly shaped British psychology. Beyond that, however, there is considerable dispute. He has been fêted by cognitive psychologists as a founding father of

their subdiscipline, and as someone who was ahead of his time in realizing that psychologists must renew their willingness to develop theories of mental processes. For others, his emphasis on cognition was admirable, but his cognitive theories were hopelessly underspecified, and his empirical work was so loosely controlled as to be nearly worthless. Some have praised the radical nature of his early concern to relate psychological processes to sociocultural conditions but have lamented his later retreat from this position to a more individualistic psychology. He has been regarded as a visionary who was right to promote an academic psychology based on experimentation. Others have seen him as someone who missed opportunities to create a broader-based and more diverse academic psychology, and some have claimed that he himself had grave doubts over the value of much experimental psychology. For many, he was brilliant and shrewd; yet one member of a government committee regarded his advice as a mix of the impractical and mere common sense. Perhaps what Bartlett's career best highlights is how psychology became increasingly identifiable as a separate discipline, and how it promised a scientific expertise that would be relevant to domains as different as the maintenance of morale and the design of aircraft cockpits.

BIBLIOGRAPHY

There is no archive of Bartlett's personal papers. However, Cambridge University Library holds a small archive of papers relating to his scientific and professional work. The library also holds a copy of his fellowship thesis and a draft of an autobiography covering his life and career up to 1914.

WORKS BY BARTLETT

Exercises in Logic. London: University Tutorial Press, 1914.

"Transformation Arising from Repeated Representation: A Contribution towards an Experimental Study of the Process of Conventionalisation." Fellowship thesis, St. John's College, Cambridge, 1916.

With Emily Mary Smith. "On Listening to Sounds of Weak Intensity." *British Journal of Psychology* 10 (1919): 101–129.

"Some Experiments on the Reproduction of Folk-Stories." *Folk-Lore* 31 (1920): 30–47.

"Psychology in Relation to the Popular Story." *Folk-Lore* 31 (1920): 264–293.

Psychology and Primitive Culture. London: Cambridge University Press, 1923.

"Feeling, Imaging and Thinking." *British Journal of Psychology* 16 (1925): 16–28.

"The Social Psychology of Leadership." *Journal of the National Institute of Industrial Psychology* 3 (1926): 188–193.

Psychology and the Soldier. Cambridge: Cambridge University Press, 1927.

"An Experiment upon Repeated Reproduction." *Journal of General Psychology* 1 (1928): 54–63.

Remembering: A Study in Experimental and Social Psychology. London: Cambridge University Press, 1932.

The Problem of Noise. Cambridge: Cambridge University Press, 1934.

History of Psychology in Autobiography, vol. 3, edited by Carl Murchison. Worcester, MA: Clark University Press, 1936.

Political Propaganda. Cambridge: Cambridge University Press, 1940.

"Current Problems in Visual Function and Visual Perception." *Proceedings of the Physiological Society* 55 (1943): 417–425.

"The Measurement of Human Skill." *Occupational Psychology* 22 (1948): 31–38.

With Norman H. Mackworth. "Planned Seeing: Some Psychological Experiments." *Air Ministry Air Publication,* 1950, no. 3139B.

"The Bearing of Experimental Psychology upon Human Skilled Performance." *British Journal of Industrial Medicine* 8 (1951): 209–217.

Thinking: An Experimental and Social Study. London: Allen & Unwin, 1958.

OTHER SOURCES

Brewer, William F., and Glenn V. Nakamura. "The Nature and Functions of Schemas." In *Handbook of Social Cognition*, vol. 1, edited by Robert S. Wyer and Thomas. K. Srull. Hillsdale, NJ: Lawrence Erlbaum Associates, 1984. A scholarly review of schema theories in psychology that gives a central place to Bartlett's work.

Broadbent, Donald E. "Frederic Charles Bartlett, 1886–1969." *Biographical Memoirs of Fellows of the Royal Society* 16 (1970): 1–13.

Collins, Alan F. "The Embodiment of Reconciliation: Order and Change in the Works of Frederic Bartlett." *History of Psychology* 9 (2006): 290–312. Argues that the themes of order and change provide a unifying thread in Bartlett's key academic writings.

Costall, Alan. "Why British Psychology Is Not Social: Frederic Bartlett's Promotion of the New Academic Discipline." *Canadian Psychology* 33 (1992): 633–639. One of the main papers arguing that Bartlett promoted experimental psychology at the expense of a more social psychology.

Harris, A. D., and Oliver L. Zangwill. "The Writings of Sir Frederic Bartlett, CBE, FRS: An Annotated Handlist." *British Journal of Psychology* 64 (1973): 493–510.

Jenkins, J. G. "Review of F. C. Bartlett, *Remembering.*" *American Journal of Psychology* 47 (1935): 712–715.

Kashima, Yoshihisa. "Recovering Bartlett's Social Psychology of Cultural Dynamics." *European Journal of Social Psychology* 30 (2000): 383–403. An argument for reinstating the project outlined in Bartlett's early writings.

Neisser, Ulric. *Cognitive Psychology.* New York: Appleton-Century-Crofts, 1967. A seminal text in cognitive psychology that treats Bartlett as a key figure in founding the subdiscipline.

Northway, Mary L. "The Concept of the Schema: Part 1." *British Journal of Psychology* 30 (1940): 316–325.

Oldfield, R. C., and Oliver L. Zangwill. "Head's Concept of the Schema and Its Application in Contemporary British Psychology: Part III. Bartlett's Theory of Memory." *British Journal of Psychology* 33 (1943): 113–129.

Ost, James, and Alan Costal. "Misremembering Bartlett: A Study in Serial Reproduction." *British Journal of Psychology* 93 (2002): 243–255. An account of the different ways in which Bartlett's theories have been described.

Saito, Akiko, ed. *Bartlett, Culture and Cognition.* Hove, UK: Psychology Press, 2000. The best single volume collection of expositions and assessments of Bartlett's work.

Shotter, John. "The Social Construction of Remembering and Forgetting." In *Collective Remembering,* edited by David Middleton and Derek Edwards. London: Sage, 1990. An attempt to highlight the neglected social aspects of Bartlett's theories of remembering.

Zangwill, Oliver L. "*Remembering* Revisited." *Quarterly Journal of Experimental Psychology* 24 (1972): 123–138. A not entirely positive review of Bartlett's seminal work by one of his postgraduates and his successor as Professor of Experimental Psychology at Cambridge.

Alan F. Collins

BARTLETT, PAUL DOUGHTY (*b.* Ann Arbor, Michigan, 14 August 1907; *d.* Lexington, Massachusetts, 11 October 1997), *physical organic chemistry, free radical polymerization.*

Bartlett was the outstanding American physical organic chemist of the twentieth century and a world leader in the field. Physical organic chemistry focuses on the mechanisms of organic reactions, and its mainly British founders were bent on upholding its status as a "proper" science and were little concerned with applications. When Bartlett's career began in the early 1930s, the great majority of reactions under study were polar, involving ionic reactants and/or intermediates. Within a decade he had begun studying free radical as well as polar reactions and had turned his attention to free radical polymerization, thereby demonstrating the relevance of mechanistic investigations to processes of industrial and even military importance. Bartlett notably took advantage of organic chemistry's synthetic powers to synthesize compounds specifically tailored to test mechanistic hypotheses. He promoted mechanistic organic chemistry in both the academy and industry, and a sizable number of Bartlett's graduate students and postdoctoral fellows secured important posts in both spheres, accounting in large part for the U.S. dominance of physical organic chemistry after World War II.

Early Years. Paul Doughty Bartlett was born on 14 August 1907 in Ann Arbor, Michigan, the only child of George

M. Bartlett and Mary Louise (Doughty) Bartlett. Mary Louise Bartlett was a piano teacher, and Paul imbibed from her a lifelong love of music. His technical prowess can be traced to his father, who possessed unusual mechanical aptitude and inventiveness. George Bartlett had been forced to leave school by the age of ten due to his father's early death, but at the urging of a prescient teacher he returned to high school at age twenty-one. After receiving his diploma, George enrolled at Amherst College, an elite liberal arts institution in Massachusetts. Upon graduation in 1901, he obtained a teaching position at the Case School of Applied Science in Cleveland, Ohio. Two years later George was appointed an instructor at the University of Michigan in Ann Arbor, where Paul was born. In 1910, George Bartlett took a position with the Diamond Chain Company of Indianapolis, Indiana. After seventeen years there he was appointed to a professorship in the school of mechanical engineering of Purdue University in West Lafayette, Indiana, despite his lack of formal training in engineering.

By his own account, Paul Bartlett received an exceptionally good primary and secondary education in Indianapolis, where he became fluent in German and fascinated by chemistry, both of which were to be formative occurrences. An exceptional student even during his early years in Indianapolis, in 1924 Bartlett followed his father to Amherst, from which he graduated summa cum laude in 1928. Guided by his professors, Bartlett entered Harvard University that fall specifically to take his PhD with James Bryant Conant. Conant was a leader in applying physical techniques to the study of organic reactions, the defining methodology of physical organic chemistry. Bartlett's combination of a strong interest in organic chemistry with a marked aptitude for physics and mathematics made him an ideal collaborator in Conant's research. The aim of that research was to understand reaction mechanisms—the entire progression of energetic and geometric changes that molecules undergo in their journey from reactants to products. Such studies were the core of the new subdiscipline eventually termed physical organic chemistry.

Postdoctoral and Academic Appointments. After obtaining his PhD in 1931 for work on the kinetically complex reaction of semicarbazide with carbonyl compounds, Bartlett received a National Research Council (NRC) Fellowship. At Conant's urging, he went to the Rockefeller Institute in New York City and worked in the laboratory of Phoebus A. Levene during 1931–1932. Conant was convinced that the future of organic chemistry lay in its applications to biology, and Levene's research encompassed stereochemistry and nucleic acids. Although influenced by Conant's views in many ways, Bartlett did not share his mentor's enthusiasm for biochemistry. So, on nights and Sundays, he went to Columbia University where he tied up some "loose ends" from his thesis. The end of his NRC Fellowship marked the end of Bartlett's brief foray into biochemistry.

In 1932, Bartlett accepted an assistant professorship at the University of Minnesota during the depths of the Depression. The salary could barely support himself and his wife, Mary Lula Court, whom he had married in 1931, and with whom he subsequently had three children: Joanna, Geoffrey, and Sarah. Bartlett's research program in reaction mechanisms had just gotten under way in Minnesota when he was called back to Harvard as an instructor in 1934 to continue Conant's initiative in reaction mechanisms, because Conant had accepted the university's presidency in 1933. Bartlett would remain at Harvard for forty years, becoming Erving Professor of Chemistry in 1948. There he would carry out most of the work that established his renown. Following his mandatory retirement in 1972, Bartlett remained at Harvard for an two additional years while his coworkers completed their projects. During that period Bartlett accepted the Welch Research Professorship of Chemistry at Texas Christian University (TCU), a post he took up in 1974 and held for the next eleven years, retiring completely from academic life in 1985.

Pursing Organic Reaction Mechanisms. Several American contemporaries of Conant's were also doing significant studies of reaction mechanisms, a pursuit that held out the eventual promise of allowing chemists to predict and control the course of reactions a priori. However, the

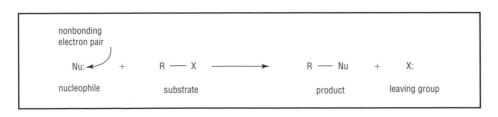

Figure 1.

dominant figure in the field was a Briton, Christopher K. Ingold of University College London, whose 1934 article, "Principles of an Electronic Theory of Organic Reactions," in *Chemical Reviews*, was a landmark in establishing the new subdiscipline. Indeed, some of Bartlett's first research problems built upon the prior investigations of major European figures such as Ingold. The genuine admiration that Bartlett and his American colleagues felt for Ingold's great accomplishments was tempered by what many saw as the latter's imperious ways. In 1936, Bartlett wrote, "In the electronic interpretation of organic reactions, certain English chemists have been pioneers. Their views might originally have been more cordially received in this country, if presented inductively and in terms whose meanings are well known" (1938b, p. 2278).

Ingold had been studying nucleophilic substitution, an important class of reactions both chemically and biologically (Figure 1). Based on extensive experimentation, he asserted that there were only two fundamental mechanisms operative in nucleophilic substitution: a two-step mechanism in which the leaving group departs first and the remaining carbocation subsequently combines with the nucleophile, and a one-step mechanism in which bonding of the nucleophile and departure of the leaving group, which take place on opposite faces of the molecule, are coordinated (Figure 2). Bartlett carried out a classic experiment by designing a molecule, 1-chloroapocamphane, whose structure prevented it from reacting by either mechanism. This compound proved to be remarkably inert to substitution even under strenuous conditions, providing very convincing support for Ingold's mechanistic hypotheses. Bartlett's approach—designing a molecule specifically to test a theory—was a hallmark that eventually became characteristic of American physical organic chemistry.

Even before he conceived of the apocamphane experiment, Bartlett had taken a keen interest in the role of carbocations as reaction intermediates. A number of his earliest papers as an independent investigator concerned several rearrangements in which carbocations had been shown by the German chemist Hans Meerwein to play a

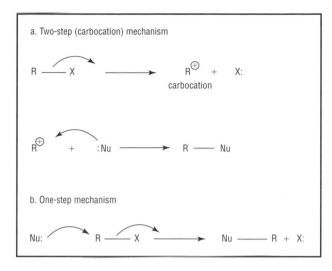

Figure 2.

crucial role. In common with many others, including Ingold, Bartlett was a great admirer of Meerwein's work and his approach to mechanistic problems. Yet Meerwein was never able to nurture physical organic chemistry in Germany to anywhere near the extent that Ingold and Bartlett did in the United Kingdom and the United States, respectively. That failure can be traced largely to differences in reception among the national chemical communities, an issue that is explored at greater length below.

The apocamphane investigation also sheds light on Bartlett's human qualities. The student who carried it out, Lawrence Knox, was one of a miniscule number of African Americans studying for a PhD in the sciences in the late 1930s. Although Knox got off to a rocky start—he was thirty years old when he entered Harvard and had health problems his first year—Bartlett supported his request for funds, describing him as having conducted outstanding research. Bartlett's laboratory was also unusually hospitable to female and Jewish students at a time when they were not very welcome in graduate science programs.

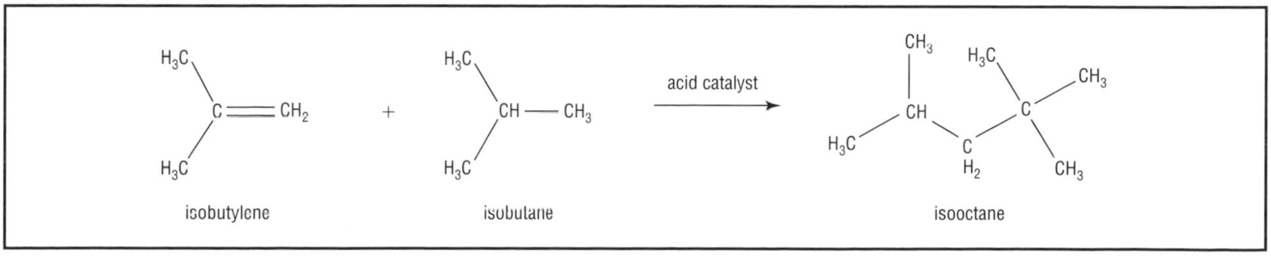

Figure 3.

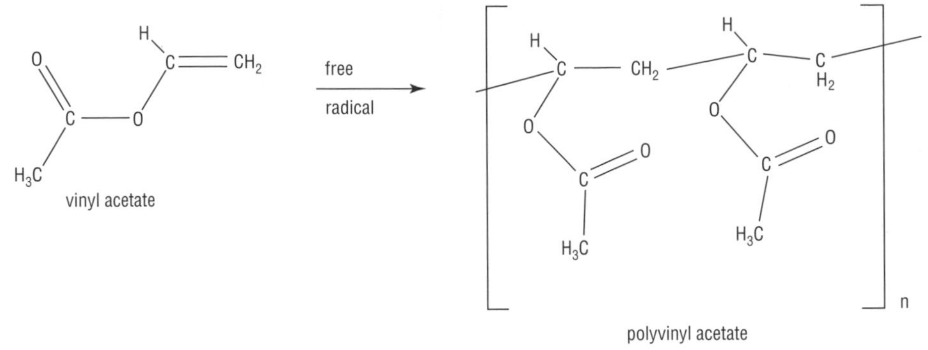

Figure 4.

Industry, War, and Mechanistic Chemistry. In 1938, after receiving the American Chemical Society's Award in Pure Chemistry, Bartlett declared during an interview that his work had no practical application. The following years were to completely disprove that claim. During the mid-1930s, as war clouds gathered over Europe, Universal Oil Products (UOP) discovered a one-step process for synthesizing isooctane, a major component of high performance aviation fuel (Figure 3), that was quickly scaled up for production. This counterintuitive paraffin alkylation reaction intrigued Bartlett, and by 1940, he had conceived a mechanism for it involving a carbocation (the type of intermediate involved in two-step nucleophilic substitutions; see Figure 2). In the summer of 1941, he became a consultant to UOP and received a grant to test his mechanism. The experimental results strongly supported a carbocation mechanism in which the crucial step took place in milliseconds, and Bartlett's work made it possible to improve the yield.

After the United States entered World War II in December 1941, Bartlett's involvement in war-related research grew much more intense. For example, his group expended considerable effort synthesizing antimalarials and insect repellents. Those projects were almost completely empirical, but Bartlett's investigations of vinyl and allyl acetate polymerization (Figure 4) were decidedly more fundamental in nature. His professional interest in polymers was first engaged in 1940 by a small consulting contract. Then, a year later, Pittsburgh Plate Glass (PPG), which was exploring glasslike polymers, established two graduate fellowships at Harvard to support polymer research under Bartlett's direction. These investigations were scientifically challenging as well as commercially and militarily important. In 1943, Bartlett remarked that the work was the most interesting that he had ever been involved in, because it was pure research in support of a synthetic resin that was of great concern to the Army.

At first glance, paraffin alkylation and vinyl acetate polymerization seem to have little in common. However, they are both chain reactions that take place by way of *reaction intermediates*, transient species with short lifetimes. In paraffin alkylation, the intermediate is a carbocation, in vinyl polymerization a *free radical*. The general types of intermediate are small in number (Figure 5), and identifying their presence is a principal focus of mechanistic investigations and a key to understanding and controlling a wide variety of organic reactions.

Free Radicals and Funding. Bartlett's continuing involvement with polymerization led to several new research areas. His interests focused on oxygen (O_2), sulfur (S_8), and a number of their derivatives, all of which have

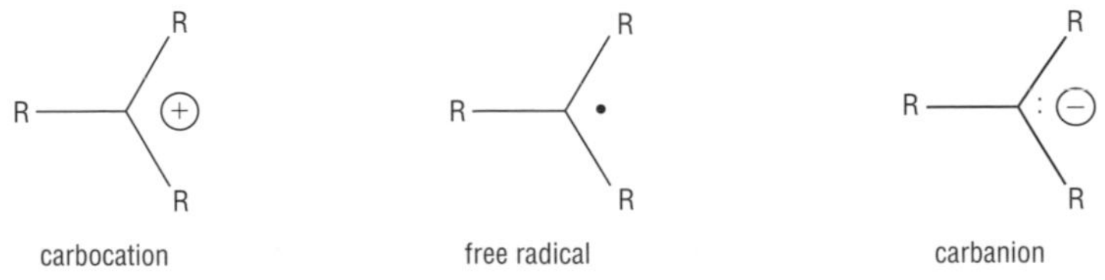

Figure 5.

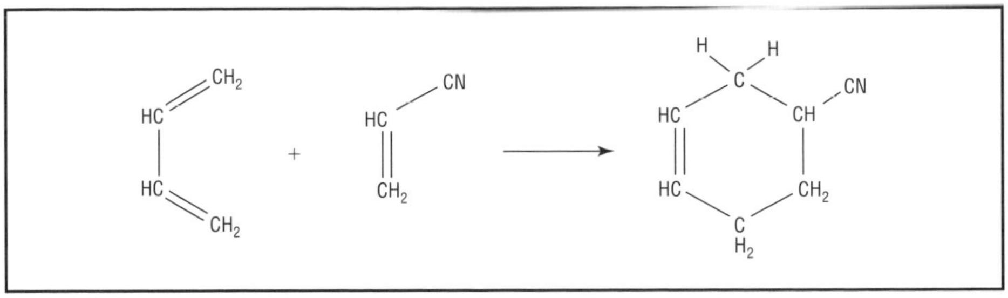

Figure 6.

marked accelerating or inhibiting effects, or both, on free radical polymerization. His group's examination of S_6 and S_8 and their reactions with organic substrates opened an entirely new research field. Bartlett's exploration of organic peroxides and peroxyesters, widely used as polymerization initiators, brought clarity to a previously clouded subject. In the 1960s, Bartlett also became very interested in singlet oxygen, an electronically excited state of ordinary O_2, and pursued its chemistry at both Harvard and TCU.

Important insights into molecular behavior can often be gleaned from cases in which reactions do not follow the expected course. The enormously useful Diels-Alder reaction is a thermal cycloaddition that creates a new six-membered ring and usually takes place in one step, without an intermediate (Figure 6). Bartlett studied a series of thermal cycloadditions that yielded mainly four-membered rings and showed that biradical intermediates intervened (Figure 7). These results were important for the theory of cycloadditions, which were enshrined in the subsequent Woodward-Hoffmann rules.

Before World War II, support for fundamental research was in short supply in the United States, but the war changed that dramatically. In 1941, both UOP and PPG made graduate fellowships and material support available for Bartlett's work, and he later became a consultant to PPG and several other firms. These consultancies brought major benefits to both parties. Bartlett grappled with challenging problems that blossomed into major research topics for him, while his sponsors obtained valuable research data as well as access to talented graduate students and postdoctoral fellows looking for industrial rather than academic positions. Because of Bartlett's success in applying a mechanistic approach to commercially important chemistry, his students were increasingly sought after. Many found places in industry, where they altered the focus of much industrial research, while Bartlett himself had a major impact by conducting minicourses in physical organic chemistry at the research laboratories where he consulted.

Although much of Bartlett's wartime research was routine, some projects demanded just the kind of skills and insight he cultivated. An outstanding example was the mechanistic investigation of mustard gas and the related nitrogen mustards (which found commercial applications and chemotherapeutic uses). When the war ended, military research contracts immediately dried up. Fearing that the pool of scientific talent and innovation that played a decisive role in the war would be lost, several military agencies stepped into the breach. First and foremost was the Office of Naval Research (ONR). In 1946, Bartlett submitted a proposal to the ONR, and the following year he received a contract for a research proposal, titled "General Theory of Structure and Mechanism of Reaction of Free Radicals," which reflected the ONR's commitment to fundamental research. In late 1947, Bartlett joined the ONR's Advisory Panel on Organic Chemistry and assumed a major role in distributing ONR research funds for the next two and a half years. In spite of the many burdens they imposed, World War II and the Cold War advanced Bartlett's research, and the dicipline of physical organic chemistry, in significant ways.

Honors and Internationalism. Given his scientific prowess and strategic position at the intersection of influential academic, industrial, and government-military networks, Bartlett was the generally acknowledged dean of American physical organic chemistry. His stature may be inferred from the various honors he acquired. In addition to the Award in Pure Chemistry, recognition from the American Chemical Society included the Gibbs, Richards, and Nichols Medals, while the Gesellschaft Deutscher Chemiker gave him its August Wilhelm von Hofmann Medal. In 1968, Bartlett received the highest scientific honor in the United States, the National Medal of Science. He also held a number of honorary degrees, fellowships, and lectureships, along with honorary memberships in numerous chemical and scientific societies. As much in the forefront ethically as professionally, Bartlett was a committed scientific internationalist. During the war he took on a Japanese-American graduate student shortly

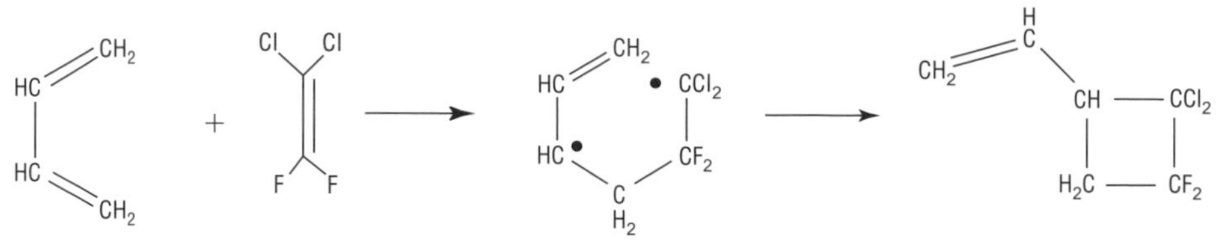

Figure 7.

after the student's release from an internment camp, and after the war's end, he established contact with several of the German chemists he had long valued.

Bartlett's reputation for fairness and probity landed him in the middle of a seething controversy between Herbert C. Brown, on the one hand, and virtually the entire physical organic establishment, on the other, over the existence of so-called nonclassical ions (a term Bartlett deprecated). Asked to adjudicate the controversy, Bartlett put together an annotated collection of most of the principal papers through 1964 (*Nonclassical Icons*, 1965). The selection and annotations were as scrupulous as Bartlett's experimental work.

Fluent in German, Bartlett admired German culture and especially German science. He was intent on reestablishing contact with those German chemists whom he still respected. In 1951, Bartlett hosted Rudolf Criegee from the University of Karlsruhe and the following year took on one of Criegee's students as a postdoctoral fellow. In 1954, under the auspices the Amerika Häuser (America Houses), Bartlett went on a two-month tour of West Germany, giving thirty lectures and seminars in German and encountering enthusiastic receptions everywhere. In Marburg, he met one of his heroes, Meerwein, whose pathbreaking studies had inspired some of Bartlett's earliest independent research efforts.

Bartlett and Meerwein. A cadre of German chemists that included Meerwein, Criegee, Walter Hückel, and Fritz Arndt had been carrying out first-rate mechanistic work in the 1920s and 1930s, yet Germany played but a minor role in the initial development of physical organic chemistry. A comparison of Bartlett and Meerwein's careers illustrates the different trajectories of physical organic chemistry in Germany and the United States and how those trajectories were shaped by cognitive, institutional, personal, and historical factors.

A major institutional factor working against the establishment of the new subdiscipline in Germany was the geographic separation of the organic and physical chemistry institutes in German universities. Each institute was self-contained, and there was often little interchange between their reigning professors. The situation in American universities was entirely different, allowing and even encouraging cross-disciplinary interaction. The presence of serious cognitive barriers is illustrated by Meerwein's mechanistic investigations related to terpenes, naturally occurring plant substances. Camphor and borneol were important terpenes of commerce whose derivatives exhibited confusing chemical behavior. Building on the work of the Russian chemist Egor Egorovich Vagner, Meerwein made sense of this behavior with the revolutionary proposal that the compounds were undergoing carbon-skeleton rearrangement via carbocation-type intermediates (Meerwein and van Emster, 1922). The notion that organic compounds (in contradistinction to inorganic ones) could dissociate into ions flew in the face of the conventional wisdom that was strongly embedded in German organic circles.

In 1923, Meerwein submitted a manuscript proposing a completely dissociated, stable carbanion as a reaction intermediate. This was too much for the editors of the *Berichte*, which had published Meerwein's previous articles; they returned the manuscript and asked Meerwein to shorten it by leaving out the "speculative" material. Highly offended, Meerwein withdrew the paper and began directing his future publications to other journals. This incident reveals much about the contemporaneous climate in German organic chemistry, in which outmoded notions about the distinction between organic and inorganic chemistry still held sway.

From 1900 to 1939, German organic chemists were, on the one hand, enormously successful in classical research; on the other hand, they were very conservative theoretically: The Lewis electron pair bond took hold very slowly in their ranks. Their work in synthesis and natural products, which required little knowledge of bonding or mechanisms, earned them more Nobel Prizes than organic chemists of any other nation. (The Americans garnered none in organic chemistry.) The research stars in the fields of synthesis and natural products attracted a majority of the best students, and published copiously. By comparison with those stars, Meerwein's output was rather modest— seventy-six papers over a fifty-seven-year period (which included the war years, in which students and material resources were scarce). In the United States, the Bartlett groups published 270 papers over a fifty-one-year period. The personal and national import of comparisons like these was captured by a 1966 obituary of Meerwein in *Angewandte Chemie*, which noted that "his work has only been fully appreciated in Germany after World War II, and then largely as a result of the high regard in which he was held by the Americans." Chief among them was Paul Bartlett.

BIBLIOGRAPHY

The majority of Bartlett's correspondence is in the Harvard University archives. A substantial minority, including mainly but not exclusively material from his post-Harvard years, is in the Chemical Heritage Foundation Archives, Philadelphia. P.D. and the Bartlett Group at Harvard, 1934–1974 *(1975) and A. A. M. Roof, ed.,* P.D. and the Bartlett Group at TCU, 1974–1985 *(1985) together contain a complete list of Bartlett's publications.*

WORKS BY BARTLETT

With Irving Pöckel. "The Wagner-Meerwein Rearrangement: A Kinetic Reinvestigation of the Isomerization of Camphene Hydrochloride." *Journal of the American Chemical Society* 60 (1938a): 1585–1590. This reevaluation of seminal work by Meerwein exhibits Bartlett's acumen in identifying underappreciated results of his peers and predecessors.

Review of H. B. Watson, "Modern Theories of Organic Chemistry." Journal of the American Chemical Society 60 (1938b): 2278.

With Lawrence H. Knox. "Bicyclic Structures Prohibiting the Walden Inversion: Replacement Reactions in 1-Substituted 1-Apocamphanes." *Journal of the American Chemical Society* 61 (1939): 3184–3192. Presents Bartlett's highly original work with Knox on substitution reactions.

With Francis E. Condon and Abraham Schneider. "Exchanges of Halogen and H between Organic Halides and Isoparaffins in the Presence of Al Halides." *Journal of the American Chemical Society* 66 (1944): 1531–1539. The investigation that nailed down the mechanism of paraffin alkylation.

With C. Gardner Swain. "The Absolute Rate Constants in the Polymerization of Vinyl Acetate." *Journal of the American Chemical Society* 67 (1945): 2273–2274. Bartlett's first major paper on the kinetics of free radical polymerization.

With C. Gardner Swain. "Kinetics of Hydrolysis and Displacement Reactions of B, B-Dichlorodiethyl Sulfide (Mustard Gas) and of B -Chloro- B' -Hydroxydiethyl Sulfide (Mustard Chlorohydrin)." *Journal of the American Chemical Society* 71 (1949): 1406–1415. A direct application of mechanistic organic chemistry to an important military problem.

Ed. *Nonclassical Icons: Reprints and Commentary.* New York: W. A. Benjamin, 1965. The selection and annotations are as scrupulous as Bartlett's experimental work

With David Mendenhall and Dana L. Durham. "Controlled Generation of Singlet Oxygen at Low Temperatures from

Triphenyl Phosphite Ozonide." *Journal of Organic Chemistry* 45 (1980): 4269-4271. Based on his continuing studies at Texas Christian University of peroxides, ozonides, and the highly reactive singlet oxygen, which he, Mendenhall, and Durham were able to generate under mild conditions.

"James Bryant Conant." *Biographical Memoirs of the National Academy of Sciences* 54 (1983): 91–124. This obituary is revealing about both author and subject.

OTHER SOURCES

Dimroth, K. "Hans Meerwein als Mensch und Lehrer." *Angewandte Chemie* 78 (1966): 353–355; "Hans Meerwein, the Teacher and the Man." *Angewandte Chemie International Edition in English* 5 (1966): 338–341.

Ingold, Christopher K. "Principles of an Electronic Theory of Organic Reactions." *Chemical Reviews* 15 (1934): 225–274. One of the principal documents in the founding of physical organic chemistry, in which Ingold introduces his much contested but generally triumphant nomenclature.

McBride, J. Michael, ed. *P.D. and the Bartlett Group at Harvard, 1934–1974.* New Haven, CT: privately published, 1975. A collection of speeches, encomia, research histories, and letters from co-workers during Bartlett's Harvard years. This volume and the Roof publication cited below give a good deal of insight into Bartlett's character as a person and research supervisor.

Meerwein, Hans, and Konrad Van Emster. "Über Die Gleichgewichtsisomerie Zwischen Bornylchlorid, Isobornylchlorid und Camphenchlorhydrat." *Berichte der Deutschen Chemischen Gesellschaft* 55 (1922): 2500–2528.

Roof, A. A. M., ed. *P.D. and the Bartlett Group at TCU, 1974–1985.* Fort Worth, TX: privately published, 1985. Similar to *P.D. and the Bartlett Group at Harvard, 1934–1974* (1975) but much smaller, it covers his years at Texas Christian University.

Westheimer, Frank. "Paul Doughty Bartlett, August 14, 1907–October 11, 1997." *Biographical Memoirs of the National Academy of Sciences* 75 (1998): 25–37. This the "official" obituary, by Bartlett's Harvard colleague and close personal friend.

                                 Stephen J. Weininger

BARTON, DEREK HAROLD RICHARD

(*b.* Gravesend, Kent, England, 8 September 1918; *d.* College Station, Texas, 16 March 1998), *organic chemistry, conformational analysis, free radical synthetic chemistry.*

Between 1940 and 1970 organic chemistry experienced a complete transformation, which affected what organic chemists did and how they did it. In a nutshell, organic chemistry in 1980 retained only its self-imposed limitation to carbon-based compounds and its commitment to organic synthesis. This revolution was characterized by the adoption of organic reaction mechanisms and theoretical chemistry to explain the course of reactions, the use of physical instrumentation to determine chemical structure, and more generally the employment of techniques derived from physical chemistry. In undergraduate teaching, the rote learning of chemical properties and preparations was replaced by a problem-solving approach based on mechanistic chemistry. On the negative side, the determination of structure using degradation reactions—hitherto a major branch of organic chemistry—was completely swept away. During the transition period, however, the traditional and new methods of structure determination interacted in a fruitful manner. Difficult structures that had tormented chemists for decades were solved in the space of a few years, and insights obtained from mechanistic chemistry as well as biosynthetic reasoning led to the development of new reactions.

An informal cadre of brilliant chemists was at the heart of this revolution. Derek Barton was one of its most active members and exemplified the transformation of the revolution in organic chemistry better than anyone else, not least because he moved right across the whole field, rather than choosing to specialize in one area. Barton had the gift of drawing out the general implications of work initiated by other more specialized chemists (a trait he shared with Robert Burns Woodward and Paul Flory) and the ability to bridge the boundaries of different fields of chemistry. He also had the ability (and confidence) to use his intuition to realize a hitherto incomplete chain of reasoning (in contrast to Woodward's insistence on the use of deductive logic). Barton called this use of intuition "gap jumping," which is also the title of his autobiography. This intellectual role was balanced by a strong interest in inventing new reactions—a surprisingly rare phenomenon among modern organic chemists—that were of great value to the rapidly expanding pharmaceutical and petrochemical industries.

Education and Early Research. Barton was born on 8 September 1918, in Gravesend, Kent, England, the son of William Thomas Barton, a carpenter and timber merchant, and Maude Henrietta (née Lukes) Barton. The timber business prospered, and Barton became a boarder at Tonbridge, a leading public school in Kent, in 1932. When his father died in 1935, Barton left school and prepared to take on the family business. Within a couple of years, however, he decided to study chemistry. After a year's preparation at the local technical college, he enrolled at Imperial College, and completed his BSc in two years.

For his PhD, Barton took up a research fellowship sponsored by the Distillers' Company, investigating the pyrolysis (chemical decomposition or change brought about by heat) of the dichloroethanes. He was supervised

by Martin Mugdan (1869–1949), who had been a leading industrial researcher in Munich before he was forced by the Nazis to leave Germany in 1939. As a result of his experiments, Barton was able to show that the thermal decomposition of 1,2-dichloroethane (ethylene dichloride) could occur through two different pathways, the intramolecular elimination of hydrogen chloride or a more rapid free-radical chain reaction.

After he completed his PhD in 1942, Barton was recruited for military intelligence. World War II was at its height, and he had been declared unfit for military service because of a weak heart. He spent two years developing water-free invisible inks, which could not be detected with the iodine spray method. Barton married Jeanne Kate Wilkins, a clerk, on 20 December 1944. Their only child, William Godfrey Lukes Barton, was born on 8 March 1947, and they were divorced in the early 1960s. Toward the end of the war, Barton went into industry and worked on organophosphorus chemistry for Albright & Wilson, a major phosphorus producer, at its Oldbury factory in the English Midlands.

Imperial College and Harvard. After a year at Albright & Wilson, Barton returned to Imperial College as a teaching assistant. The teaching itself was mundane, but the move back to academia enabled Barton to devote himself to steroid chemistry. Steroids were a rapidly growing field of interest to the pharmaceutical industry and had already attracted the attention of many leading academic and industrial chemists. Having already annoyed Sir Ian Heilbron, the professor of organic chemistry at Imperial College, Barton was fortunate that Tim Jones (later Sir Ewart Jones) took him under his wing. A young upcoming lecturer at Imperial with an interest in steroid chemistry, Jones suggested that Barton investigate the relationship between optical rotation and the structure of the triterpenoids. This was a period when chemists tried to use the optical properties of complex molecules, in particular the steroids and terpenoids, to determine their absolute chemical structure without the need for lengthy and tedious chemical studies. Woodward had introduced his empirical rules for the ultraviolet spectra of ketones with a conjugated double bond in 1941. When a relationship between a given optical property and a structural feature had been established, the existing literature could then be trawled for other examples. Barton was able to correlate the structures of several triterpenoids using differences in molecular rotation. He then extended this approach to steroids, for which there was more data.

A shared interest in the chemistry of the steroids brought Barton to the attention of Louis Fieser at Harvard University. When Woodward took a sabbatical in 1949–1950, Fieser—as head of the chemistry

Derek H. R. Barton. AP IMAGES.

department—offered Barton a temporary position for a year. This was a turning point in Barton's career because it introduced him into Woodward's circle and to his rigorous mechanistic analysis of chemical problems. Even in 1986, Barton wrote with awe of Woodward's legendary seminars, in which, following a talk from a visitor, Woodward would lead a thorough discussion and then present, and usually solve, a chemical problem.

During his stay at Harvard, Barton developed conformational analysis. After Henry van't Hoff and Achille Le Bel had independently explained the optical activity of certain organic compounds in terms of a tetrahedral carbon atom in 1874, chemists had begun to visualize chemistry in three dimensions rather than two. Taking up the tetrahedral carbon hypothesis, Hermann Sachse showed in 1890 that, contra Adolf von Baeyer, strainless six-membered rings (cyclohexane rings) were possible if they were not planar. Sachse identified two potentially stable forms, or *conformers*—what are now called the chair and the boat. Sachse's mathematics were beyond any contemporary organic chemists, so his proposal lay fallow until 1918, when Ernst Mohr showed by x-ray crystallography that diamond consisted of an unbounded network of chair cyclohexanes. This finding revived Sachse's hypothesis but left open the question of which, if any, conformation would predominate in the gas and liquid phases. In

occupied Norway, in 1943, the physical chemist Odd Hassel had shown that cyclohexane itself preferred the chair conformation. Furthermore he had shown that decalin (two fused cyclohexane rings) favored the chair-chair conformation. This was an important finding, as two heavily researched groups of natural products—steroids and triterpenoids—contained fused cyclohexane rings. Although Barton had already used Hassel's conformations in his research on abietic acid (a major constituent of rosin) at Imperial in 1948, it was only when Fieser presented a seminar on steric effects in the chemistry of the steroids at Harvard that Barton realized the immense value of the conformational approach for steroid chemistry. Drawing on the findings of Hassel and others, Barton showed that there were two different positions for substituents attached to a cyclohexane ring: polar (now called axial) and equatorial. Barton used this "conformational analysis" to explain the sometimes unexpected behavior of different substituents in ring compounds and to predict the relative stability of one conformation over another. He thus arrived at different conclusions from Fieser, and the older chemist generously suggested they both publish papers on the subject in *Experientia*. The subsequent short paper established Barton as the founder of conformational analysis, for which he received the Nobel Prize in 1969. During his sabbatical at Harvard, Barton also met Ernest Eliel at Notre

Dame University in Indiana, and converted him to the cause of conformational analysis. As a leading stereochemist, Eliel became one of the major proponents of this new approach in the United States. Subsequently, molecular models played an important role in conformational analysis, especially the type introduced by the Swiss chemist André Dreiding in 1958.

Birkbeck College and Glasgow. On his return to Britain in 1950, Barton became a reader (equivalent to associate professor) at Birkbeck College. Part of the University of London, Birkbeck catered to part-time students; the teaching was done in the evening, leaving the rest of the day free for research. Barton continued his development of conformational analysis, using it, for example, to establish the chemical structure of ß-amyrin (a triterpenoid found in rubber latex) and "artostenone," a supposed sterol obtained from the jackfruit. He showed that artostenone was a terpenoid with an unusual cyclopropane ring, and it was subsequently given the more appropriate name of cycloartenone. Barton also synthesized the important steroid lanosterol with Woodward and Arthur Patchett (working in relay across the Atlantic), using Woodward's cholesterol synthesis as a starting point. It was during the Birkbeck period that Barton became a member of the elite group of organic chemists, and his growing stature was confirmed by his election to the Royal Society in 1954.

Although Barton was now a professor at Birkbeck, he was clearly in the running (and believed himself to be destined) for one of the major chemistry chairs. Hoping for Oxford, Barton agreed to go to Glasgow if he was not appointed. With hindsight—as Tim Jones's forthcoming appointment to the Oxford chair was an open secret—it is perhaps surprising that he did not plan to succeed Jones in Manchester, which had hitherto been a stepping-stone to a chair at Oxford or Cambridge. However, having committed himself to Glasgow, Barton missed out on Manchester and also Imperial, where Patrick Linstead had been unexpectedly appointed rector of the college in October 1954. Barton's stay in Glasgow as the Regius Professor of Chemistry was brief (1955–1957), but it was productive and marked a shift in his research. He worked closely with Monteath Robertson, the famous x-ray crystallographer, using traditional degradation methods to study the structure of several phytochemicals, such as limonin, while Robertson's group obtained the structure using x-ray crystallography. This overlap of techniques (which also occurred in the case of ß-amyrin, where the structure had been determined by Harry Carlisle using x-ray crystallography) was fruitful but short-lived—the traditional chemical methods were abandoned, mainly because of the introduction of computers into x-ray crystallography and the growing use of nuclear magnetic resonance for structure determination. In this period, Barton also applied himself to the study of phenolic coupling, a free radical reaction that linked two phenol molecules. In collaboration with Theodore Cohen, he used the concept of phenolic coupling to predict the biosynthesis of the morphine alkaloids. Barton had already become interested in organic photochemistry as a way of carrying out chemical reactions—another example of boundary bridging—and in Glasgow he studied the photochemical rearrangement of α-santonin (a compound found in Levant wormwood).

Return to Imperial College. Despite his success in Glasgow—the university authorities always agreed to his requests for funds and he formed a strong partnership with Ian Scott—Barton was keen to go back to his alma mater, Imperial College, when the chair became vacant again after the sudden death of Ernest Braude. Soon after his return to Imperial, Barton was invited to collaborate with the newly established Research Institute for Medicine and Chemistry in Cambridge, Massachusetts, funded by the Schering Corporation. The director, Maurice Pechet, a steroid chemist who had taken his PhD with Fieser, asked Barton to synthesize aldosterone acetate, a hormone that controls the electrolyte balance in the body. Drawing on his prior knowledge of free radical pyrolysis, Barton proposed a simple but hitherto unknown reaction. An alkyl nitrite could be photolyzed to establish an oxime group on a neighboring carbon. Fortunately Schering had hired an excellent Glasgow-trained chemist, John Beaton, who was able to carry out the proposed reaction (now known as the Barton reaction or the Barton nitrite photolysis) and thereby produced a large amount (60g) of hitherto scarce aldosterone acetate in 1960. Inspired by this successful industry-academia collaboration, the Ciba pharmaceutical company set up the Woodward Research Institute in Basel, Switzerland.

In the late 1950s and 1960s Barton continued to develop his ideas on the biosynthesis of morphine and related alkaloids involving phenolic coupling. He made extensive use of the radioactive tracers tritium (^{3}H) and carbon-14, which had just become commercially available from the Radiochemical Centre at Amersham, England. Barton was able to show the basic soundness of his ideas, sometimes forming an unexpected intermediate along the way. This work was then extended to the biosynthesis of other phenolic alkaloids, notably the alkaloids derived from the coral tree.

After 1970 Barton concentrated on the development of new reactions for use in organic synthesis. His first major success in this period arose from his collaboration with Schering, which was looking for a good way of removing hydroxyl groups from aminoglycoside antibiotics (such as gentamicin, discovered by Schering in 1963)

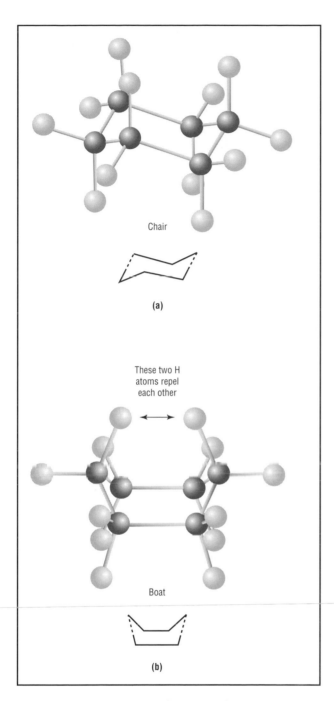

Figure 1. The two possible conformations of cyclohexane.

ful reaction is usually known as the Barton-McCombie deoxygenation reaction. Subsequently, Barton's group developed a whole series of free radical reactions based on thiohydroxamic esters.

The ideal intermediate in free radical synthetic chemistry is the "well-behaved" radical, one that follows the desired pathway and does not attack the solvent or produce excess by-products through side-reactions. In the mid-1980s, Barton developed the concept of the "disciplined radical," which would be held in check by the "disciplinary group," for example, the thiocarbonyl group. This approach arose from his attempt to create an effective free radical decarboxylation reaction. Free radical decarboxylation had been known since Hermann Kolbe electrolyzed the salts of carboxylic acids in 1846, but the reaction had hitherto been unsuitable for complex compounds. By reacting the mixed anhydride of a thiohydroxamic acid and a carboxylic acid with tributyltin hydride, the corresponding decarboxylated hydrocarbon was formed. This reaction, first carried out with William Motherwell and David Crich in 1983, is now known as the Barton decarboxylation.

In the early 1960s Barton suffered from nervous exhaustion after his divorce from Kate and threw himself into the reading of French classics. His reading made him wish to improve his French and he took French lessons at the Institut Français in South Kensington. Barton's teacher, Christiane Cognet, soon realized she had a star pupil in her class and they were married in 1969. In the same year Barton was awarded the Nobel Prize jointly with Odd Hassel "for their contributions to the development of the concept of conformation and its application in chemistry." The Hofmann Chair of Organic Chemistry was created for him by Imperial College in 1970, and two years later, he was knighted in Britain and enrolled into the Legion d'Honneur as a chevalier (he became an officer in 1985). He was president of the Royal Institute of Chemistry (now the Royal Society of Chemistry) in 1973–1974.

Barton was invited to join the editorial board of *Tetrahedron* soon after it was founded by Robert Maxwell in 1957. The board was initially chaired by Sir Robert Robinson and R. B. Woodward. Barton became co-chairman of the editorial board on Robinson's death in February 1975 and the sole chairman when Woodward died in July 1979. Just before Robinson's death, Maxwell also appointed Barton as the editor-in-chief of *Comprehensive Organic Chemistry.* He published this impressive and useful six-volume work in collaboration with David Ollis of Sheffield University (another member of the Woodward circle) in 1979. Nearly two decades later, Barton was joint editor in chief of *Comprehensive Natural Products Chemistry* with Koji Nakanishi of Columbia

to increase their resistance to bacterial degradation. On the basis of another reaction, which involved the elimination of a thiocarbonyl group from a steroid, Barton suggested the free radical deoxygenation of a thiocarbonyl derivative of the aminoglycoside using tributyltin hydride as the hydrogen donor. The experimental work was carried out by Stuart McCombie in 1975, and this very use-

University, supported by Otto Meth-Cohn of Sunderland University. This impressive nine-volume work was published shortly after Barton's death in 1998. Meanwhile *Tetrahedron* had expanded under Barton's leadership from 3,137 pages in 1975 to 16,003 pages in 1998 and had spawned another journal, *Tetrahedron: Asymmetry,* in 1990.

France and Texas. In 1977, in a characteristic change of direction, Barton became one of the codirectors of the Institut de Chimie des Substances Naturelles (ICSN) at Gif-sur-Yvette, in the southwestern suburbs of Paris. He took early retirement (at sixty) from Imperial College a year later to become sole director of the institute following the amalgamation of its two departments with the agreement of the other codirector Pierre Potier. This was partly in the expectation that he would retire at seventy, but also because Christiane was keen to return home. During his time at Gif-sur-Yvette, Barton insisted that all meetings be held in French even if there were no French chemists present; this led to the introduction of neologisms such as "obvieusement," "éléphant-blanc," and "hareng rouge."

Soon after Barton arrived at Gif-sur-Yvette, in 1980, John Cadogan, the new director of research at British Petroleum (BP) and a leading free radical chemist, offered him funds for a blue-skies project. Barton decided to examine the oxidation of hydrocarbons using iron chemistry, a field of obvious interest to BP. This research stemmed from his earlier work on biosynthetic pathways and perhaps from the Barton reaction, which led to the oxidation of previously unfunctionalized carbon atoms. His starting point was the oxidation of adamantane by Iwao Tabushi (a student of Paul von Ragué Schleyer) using an iron complex, B-mercaptoethanol, and oxygen. The initial experiments were failures, but Barton had the idea of adding metallic iron and acetic acid to the reaction, which had a positive effect on the yield of the reaction. His group eventually developed "Gif systems" for the oxidation of hydrocarbons with oxygen, which contained iron, acetic acid, and pyridine.

Barton had originally gone to France with the expectation of retiring at seventy, but the incoming Socialist government introduced a uniform retirement age of sixty-five in 1984. Hearing that Barton would have to retire soon, and knowing that he would want to continue his research, Scott, his friend from Glasgow days, and Albert Cotton—who knew Barton through Geoffrey Wilkinson, another Nobel laureate at Imperial College—decided to create a post for him at Texas A&M University. In 1986 they offered him a full professorship, and at the age of sixty-eight Barton moved to College Station, Texas, as the Dow Professor of Chemical Invention. At Texas A&M,

Barton continued to develop "Gif chemistry," and the Gif systems were followed by the GoAgg systems—which employed potassium or organic peroxides instead of oxygen. ("*Go Aggies!*" is the war cry of the supporters of the A&M football team, but it has been claimed that GoAgg is short for "Gif Oxidation in Aggie Land.")

Christiane died of ovarian cancer in 1992, despite being one of the first patients to be given taxotere, and Barton lost the great love of his life. In the following year he married Judith Cobb, a neighbor in College Station who had been a great support to Barton in his bereavement. His colleagues and former students were determined to make the most of Barton's forthcoming eightieth birthday, and in early 1998, celebratory conferences were held in the Maldives and at the Scripps Research Institute in La Jolla, California. Back home in College Station, Barton died suddenly of a heart attack on 16 March 1998.

Barton's Place in History. Barton was one of the leaders in the revolution that took place in organic chemistry in the 1950s and 1960s. This was not because he was a pioneer in the use of physical instrumentation or even, despite his work on conformational analysis, in the discovery of organic reaction mechanisms, but because he introduced—with others such as Robinson, Woodward, and Elias James Corey—a new way of thinking about organic chemistry, which converted it from a practical—if also intellectual—exercise into a series of problems that had to be assessed and solved using organic reaction mechanistic theory and conformational analysis. He gained the ability to generate new insights by deliberately working at the boundaries between different fields, something that occurred accidentally early in his career, and by constantly moving to emerging areas of research. Late in his career, Barton became one of the few modern academic chemists to be a single-minded creator of new reactions, which perhaps harked back to his family craft traditions. His influence was strengthened by his social connections with other leading chemists, including Woodward, Sir Robert Robinson, Carl Djerassi, Vladimir Prelog, and Gilbert Stork, partly through frequent meetings at international conferences and partly through his editorial work for *Tetrahedron*. Whereas Woodward failed to produce many leading organic chemists to succeed him, Barton saw himself as the "kingmaker" of organic chemistry and he put considerable effort into making arrangements for the future of his best students. By 2005 these included the professors of organic chemistry at Cambridge (Steven Ley), University College London (Motherwell), Imperial College, London (Anthony Barrett), and Oxford (Sir Jack Baldwin).

The chemist Tony Barrett has noted (probably tongue-in-cheek) that many chemists considered Barton to be "aloof, demanding and taking pleasure in over-whelming any scientist he disagreed with," but that he personally found him to be "kind, considerate, supportive and generous." Certainly Barton's perceived aloofness was mainly shyness. Barton kept a close watch on his students and liked to push them, but he was kind and generous in many different ways to those students who responded well to this pressure. As one of the "high priests" of organic chemistry (to use Stork's revealing phrase), Barton felt a moral obligation to maintain rigorous standards, and to prevent any possible sloppiness or fraud. He habitually asked any student claiming they had made a new compound to show him the crystals. There was always a robust discussion of the latest results in his group's weekly meetings, and his researchers sometimes held back a piece of good news, to be used when there was nothing else positive to report. Barton's personality also mellowed as he grew older, partly as result of Christiane's influence.

The most striking aspect of Barton's character was his boundless passion for doing chemistry; he had published more than a thousand papers by the time of his death. He had an incredible work ethic and in his autobiography he remarked that he preferred chemistry to spare time. Even at Texas A&M University, when he was in his seventies, Barton worked long hours. Judy Barton recalls that: "Derek would get up around 4 a.m., read his journal while he drank a pot of tea, and be at work by 7 a.m. His only real meal of the day was a leisurely lunch at 11:30 a.m. for at least 90 minutes at home. He returned to the laboratory until at least 7 p.m. when he came home to tie up professional loose ends. He and I shared a social conversation every night when his work was completed" (Barton, personal communication). Like Woodward, he often worked on Christmas Day. The sources of his enthusiasm for chemistry and his work ethic are not clear. Barton considered becoming a priest in his early teens, with his father's encouragement, and he remarked in his autobiography that he felt the need from an early age to devote himself "to some noble cause." Barton never gave any explanation for his passion for chemistry beyond the fact he enjoyed reading science books when he was home on sick leave from Tonbridge School. Perhaps his work ethic arose partly from his need to justify his premature departure from the family business. It certainly stemmed from his strong sense of competition with his chemical peers and his desire to leave his imprint on organic chemistry. Although Barton realized that this could often be best achieved by collaborating with other chemists and supporting the careers of his students, he also "wished to be remembered for all time" for his contribution to organic chemistry (William Motherwell in Scott and Potier, 2000, p. 61).

There was another side to Barton's nature that few outside his close circle ever saw. He claimed that he could

have become a concert pianist instead of a chemist. He saw a similarity between chemical and musical notation, saying, "if I had not been a great chemist, I would have chosen to be a great composer," for both music and chemistry were a matter of "orchestrating your own signature of creativity" (Motherwell, personal communication). Barton was certainly fond of music, especially the work of Gustav Mahler.

Barton was one of the great organic chemists of the twentieth century, yielding in significance only to Woodward and H. Emil Fischer. It is a measure of his greatness—as Motherwell has pointed out—that he was one of only two organic chemists in that century to give his name to an adjective: Bartonian (the other of course was Woodward).

BIBLIOGRAPHY

WORKS BY BARTON

With David Ollis, eds. *Comprehensive Organic Chemistry*. 6 vols. Oxford: Pergamon Press, 1979.

Some Recollections of Gap Jumping. Washington, DC: American Chemical Society, 1991. This autobiography is by far the best source about Barton. The main text is short (the series editor, Jeffrey Seeman, had to coax three codas from him to flesh it out), and the amount of detail about his personal life is minimal. Like any other autobiography, *Gap Jumping* has to be treated with caution. Nonetheless, it is an useful source of information, not least because it shows what Barton himself considered to be important in his extensive body of research, and in one of his codas he sketches his personal philosophy.

With Shyamal I. Parekh. *Half a Century of Free Radical Chemistry*. Cambridge, U.K.: Cambridge University Press, 1993. This slim survey of his work on free radical chemistry provides a good introduction to the development of the "disciplined free radical."

Reason and Imagination: Reflections on Research in Organic Chemistry; Selected Papers of Derek H. R. Barton. Singapore and River Edge, NJ: World Scientific/Imperial College Press, 1996. A collection of his most important papers (137 out of 1,041). The subtitle reflects Barton's willingness to use his intuition as opposed to Woodward's insistence on the rigorous employment of logic.

With Koji Nakanishi and Otto Meth-Cohn, eds. *Comprehensive Natural Products Chemistry*. 9 vols. New York: Elsevier, 1999.

OTHER SOURCES

Coley, Noel G. "Barton, Sir Derek Harold Richard (1918–1998)." *Oxford Dictionary of National Biography*. Oxford: Oxford University Press, 2004. A good summary of his life, based largely on *Gap Jumping*.

Cotton, F. Albert. "Derek H. R. Barton, 8 September 1918–16 March 1998." *Proceedings of the American Philosophical Society* 144 (2000): 292–296. Provides the only detailed account of Barton's American period.

Ley, Steven V., and Rebecca M. Myers. "Barton, Sir Derek Harold Richard." *Biographical Memoirs of the Royal Society of*

London 48 (2002): 1–23. Useful for the personal details lacking in *Gap Jumping*.

Scott, A. Ian, and Pierre Potier, eds. *The Bartonian Legacy.* London: Imperial College Press, 2000. A posthumous volume of recollections by his coworkers that nicely complements *Gap Jumping*.

Peter J. T. Morris

BASSI VERATI (VERATTI), LAURA MARIA CATERINA (*b*. Bologna, Italy, 29 October 1711; *d*. Bologna, 20 February 1778), *physics*.

In the eighteenth century, a period comparatively rich with opportunities for women's participation in scientific activities, Europe's first female university professor Laura Bassi Verati (or Bassi Veratti) is most remarkable for the unique institutional success she was able to achieve. Her biography and career path is intimately linked to the learned culture of her home town Bologna, where she became the central personality teaching, practicing, and representing the newly emerging field of experimental physics.

Biography. Bassi, the only surviving child of the Bolognese jurist Giuseppe Bassi and his wife Rosa Cesarei, received her early instruction in the Latin language by male relatives and her further education by the family physician Gaetano Tacconi, who was a professor of medicine at the University of Bologna. Teaching her the classics and training her to hold philosophical disputations in Latin about any conceivable subject, Tacconi developed his gifted pupil on the humanist model of the learned prodigy. In 1732, Bassi was ready to be presented to the public. The city's social elite and learned public as well as the municipal authorities and the Bolognese archbishop Prospero Lambertini were all equally delighted with this prodigiously learned and eloquent young woman. They decided to crown her achievements by a doctoral degree, thus highlighting Bologna's identity as "la dotta," the learned city. Within months, Bassi gained fame throughout Europe as the "Bolognese Minerva." By the end of the year, she found herself not only a doctor but also a professor of the Bolognese University—and a highly paid one, indeed.

Apart from its old and famous university, Bologna boasted another scientific institution, the Institute of Science (Istituto delle Scienze). It had been created in 1711 to provide a home for the teaching of the experimental sciences and had an academy to further original research attached to it. Under the influence of such advisors as the chemist Jacopo Bartolomeo Beccari, the discoverer of

gluten and Bolognese limestone, and the astronomer Eustachio Manfredi, who was one of the first to disseminate Newton's work in Italy, Bassi changed the focus of her scholarly activities and turned to the sciences. She took lessons in mathematics and, among others, read Newton, whose optical experiments she repeated for herself.

While not abandoning her role as the "Bolognese Minerva," Bassi increasingly devoted herself to physics. This gradual change was confirmed by her marriage to Giuseppe Verati (1707–1793), a young professor of medicine at the Bolognese university, who had also studied physics and later became known for his researches on medical electricity. Though she also met with severe criticism for abandoning her virginity, Bassi now had the possibility of entertaining a scientific salon and offering private lectures in experimental physics.

When Pope Benedict XIV (papacy 1740–1758), who knew her from his time as Bolognese archbishop, initiated a major reform of the Bolognese academy of sciences in 1745, Bassi managed to get one of the newly created paid positions, albeit a supernumerary one (*sopra numero*) which left her status somewhat contested. From 1745 on, Bassi regularly participated in academy life. Like the other members of the core group of paid academicians—the "Benedettini"—she read a paper on her own original research once a year and published papers in the academy's transactions, the *Commentarii*. In 1772, Bassi also obtained the professorship of physics at the Bolognese Institute of Sciences and, accordingly, held three paid positions at three different scientific institutions at the same time.

Bassi had eight children and was actively involved in Bolognese scientific life until she died from heart failure at the age of sixty-six. Though she had no female disciples, she provided a role model for many scientifically minded women, including Dorothea Erxleben, the first woman to obtain a medical degree in Germany in 1754.

Scientific Work. Like the work of many eighteenth-century scientists, Bassi's research does not easily relate to a single subject. Judging from her few publications and the unpublished talks she gave at the academy, her research activities comprehended hydromechanics, electricity, and optics as well as pneumatics and the study of gases. Her most notable research was concerned with the bubbles produced in gases.

Bassi explained her observations by using the Newtonian concept of attraction as interpretative framework, and by analogies to electricity which reveal how closely she followed the developments in this new field. Together with her husband, Bassi advocated Franklin's theory of one electric fluidum (as opposed to the rival two-fluida theory) and became its main Bolognese defender. Because of the differing results she obtained in her own experiments, she doubted the exact validity of the Boyle-Mariotte law on the reciprocity of the volume and pressure of a gas. Like the work on the origins of bubbles, however, the further research which she had announced never came to a tangible result. Her research work as a whole—which was also hampered by representational as well as family duties—therefore gives the impression of being broad to some extent.

As a teacher of physics, Bassi was of supreme importance not only for Bologna but for the whole of northern Italy. She acted as a mentor and patron for such younger scientists as Lazzaro Spallanzani and Alessandro Volta and also was sought after by those who wanted to become members of the Bolognese academy, Voltaire being the most prominent among her clients. At Bologna, her private lectures on experimental physics gave virtually the only opportunity for instruction, let alone experimental demonstrations in physics. As suggested by her academy talks and the scientific instruments she bought, during her whole career Bassi kept abreast of current developments. Her prominence in the learned culture of northern Italy brought attention to experimental physics. Through her work, physics formed as a discipline integrating experimental *and* mathematical traditions.

Laura Maria Caterina Bassi Verati. SCIENCE PHOTO LIBRARY/PHOTO RESEARCHERS, INC.

BIBLIOGRAPHY

Bassi published only two papers. Her unpublished papers have been reproduced in Ceranski, 1996.

WORKS BY BASSI

"De Problemate Quodam Hydrometrico." *De Bononiensi Scientiarum et Artium Instituto atque Academia Commentarii* 4 (1757): 61–73.

"De Problemate Quodam Mechanico." *De Bononiensi Scientiarum et Artium Instituto atque Academia Commentarii* 4 (1757): 74–79.

Bassi–Verati, Laura. Fondo speciale. Biblioteca Comunale dell'Archiginnasio, Bologna. Important collection pertaining to Bassi's biography and contemporary perception. For a description cf. Tommasi, Raffaella. "Documenti riguardanti Laura Bassi conservati presso l'Archiginnasio." *L'Archiginnasio* 57 (1962): 319–324.

Melli, Elio, ed. "Epistolario di Laura Bassi Verati. Edizione critica, introduzione e note." In *Studi e inediti per il primo centenario dell'Istituto Magistrale Laura Bassi.* Bologna: STE, 1960. Collection of letters by Bassi.

OTHER SOURCES

Berti Logan, Gabriella. "The Desire to Contribute: An Eighteenth-Century Italian Woman of Science." *American Historical Review* 99 (1994): 785–812. Contains minor errors; otherwise a comprehensive article concentrating on Bassi's scientific work.

Cavazza, Marta. "Laura Bassi e il suo gabinetto di fiscia sperimentale: Realta e mito." *Nuncius* 10 (1995): 715–753. Tells the fascinating story of the collection of Bassi's scientific instruments.

———. "Laura Bassi 'maestra' di Spallanzani." In *Il cerchio della vita: Materiali di ricerca del Centro Studi Lazzaro Spallanzani di Scandiano sulla storia della scienza del settecento,* edited by Walter Bernardi and Paola Manzini. Florence: L. S. Olschki, 1999. Discusses Bassi's role as teacher of the naturalist Spallanzani, probably her most important pupil.

Cenerelli, G., ed. *Lettere inedite alla celebre Laura Bassi scritte da illustri italiani e stranieri con biografia.* Bologna: Tipografia di G. Cenerelli, 1885. Collection of letters to Bassi.

Ceranski, Beate. "Il carteggio tra Giovanni Bianchi e Laura Bassi, 1733–1745." *Nuncius* 9 (1994): 207–231.

———. *"Und sie fürchtet sich vor niemandem": Die Physikerin Laura Bassi (1711–1778).* Frankfurt: Campus Verlag, 1996. Comprehensive book-length biography of Laura Bassi, covering both scientific and social historical aspects.

Elena, Alberto. "'In lode della filosofessa di Bologna': An introduction to Laura Bassi." *Isis* 82 (1991): 510–518. Concise review of older literature on Bassi.

Findlen, Paula. "Science as a Career in Enlightenment Italy: The Strategies of Laura Bassi." *Isis* 84 (1993): 441–469. Discusses Bassi's career in terms of the patronage system.

———. "The Scientist's Body: The Nature of a Woman Philosopher in Enlightenment Italy." In *The Faces of Nature in Enlightenment Europe*, edited by Lorraine Daston and Gianna Pomata. Berlin: Berliner Wissenschafts-Verlag, 2003. Intriguing cultural historical reading of the discourses about Bassi as sexual being and sexual object.

Beate Ceranski

BASSON (BASSO), SÉBASTIEN (SEBASTIAN, SEBASTIANO) (*b.* near Metz, c. 1580; *d.* after 1625), *natural philosophy.* For the original article on Basso see *DSB,* vol. 1.

Basson has been famous since the seventeenth century for his fairly aggressive attempt to replace Aristotelian natural philosophy with his own system, which relied on a unique combination of atoms and other material and spiritual entities. Scholarship in the early twenty-first century presents a fuller understanding of his life and work.

Basson's Life. Basson was a stranger to the Republic of Letters and moreover tried hard to conceal his identity. On the title page of his only known publication, the *Philosophia naturalis,* he described himself only as a doctor of medicine. As a consequence, since the mid-seventeenth century a variety of erroneous biographical assumptions have sprung up. Of these his identification as a Parisian doctor and as a sixteenth-century Italian philosopher have been the most tenacious. As to his nationality, the question is still not settled. In the *Philosophia naturalis,* he identified as his birthplace a region called Le Saulnois, near Metz, in the Duchy of Lorraine. However, there is some circumstantial evidence that he may have been the scion of an Italian family by the name of Basso, who were courtiers in the service of Christina of Denmark, duchess dowager of Lorraine. But because in the only known autograph signature, he wrote his name as Basson, this spelling must at this stage be considered the only legitimate one.

Basson received his college education at the Jesuit Academy of Pont-à-Mousson, also in Lorraine. Pierre Sinson, the only professor he mentioned in the *Philosophia naturalis,* taught there between 1593 and 1599, which provides the only clue as to Basson's approximate date of birth. About the period between his graduation from Pont-à-Mousson and the year 1611, it may be inferred

that he obtained a medical degree somewhere, visited Rome, converted to Calvinism, and got engaged to his later wife in the Swiss town of Lausanne. A university professor in that town recommended him in 1611 to the Academy of Die, a minuscule and poor Calvinist college in the French Alps. There, Basson served from 1611 to 1625 in the double capacity of first regent, responsible for the graduating class of schoolboys, and of professor of eloquence. At various moments, he unsuccessfully tried to be promoted to one of the vacant professorships in theology, Hebrew, or philosophy. Judging by the archival record, Basson became increasingly frustrated in the litigious and precarious atmosphere of the little city of Die, whose Jesuits tried hard to squeeze the Protestant academy out of existence. After a series of clashes with his superiors. Basson threatened before the academic senate in September 1625 to publish an atheist tract, was thereupon expelled from the academy, and disappeared from Die, and from the historical record. Where he went and when he died is not known.

While Basson's *Philosophia naturalis* was being printed at Geneva, representatives of the Company of Ministers and Professors caught sight of the manuscript and found that it was not only "full of peculiar opinions and directly contrary to Aristotle as taught and accepted" at Calvinist Geneva, but more in particular that "many dangerous things were proposed in it, be it against the Deity, the Providence of God, and the truth of the divine nature of the Son or of the eternal word of God" (*Registres de la Compagnie des Pasteurs,* 20 October 1620 [Archives de l'État et de la République de Genève, R.Cp.Past.7, fol. 14v]). The printing was stopped, and only after Basson's personal appearance before the company in January 1621 was it resumed. What portions of his text were changed, if any, to satisfy the theological censors is not known.

Basson's Natural Philosophy. The worries of the Genevan theologians are not hard to understand, for Basson's philosophical treatise is above all a polemical text. In fact, his irately anti-Aristotelian epistle "To the Reader," which is the most eloquent and lively part of his book, was reprinted as an independent chapter in the third, 1662 edition of Jean de Launoy's history of Aristotle's changing *fortuna* at the University of Paris. Basson there attacked the authority of Aristotle by arguing that he was a lonely voice dissenting from a venerable chorus of ancient authorities, that included not only the pre-Socratics and Plato, but also Hippocrates and later representatives of Greek medicine. Basson's main objective was to abolish the principles of prime matter and of substantial forms. His sustained attempt to explain away all Aristotelian forms may have influenced René Descartes, who was acquainted with it. Nevertheless, the frequently heard description of Basson as a precursor of Descartes's mechanical philosophy is quite misleading. In fact, as a substitute for the active Aristotelian forms, Basson offered a plethora of entities that were neither mechanical nor, as it turns out, easily reconciled with one another. Most famously, he offered atoms as the ultimate components of matter, and equally famously, he allowed for atomic clusters of various orders, of which each is a bearer of a distinct set of properties. For this proposal, Basson has repeatedly been celebrated as one of the inventors of the molecule. What Aristotle had described as the generation and corruption of higher forms, Basson explained away as the aggregation and resolution of such complex atomic aggregates.

However, only one type of atom was described in detail, namely the wedge-shaped fire atoms of Platonic extraction and naturally endowed with dissecting power. Basson believed these to be responsible for a whole range of natural phenomena, including rarefaction, heat, distillation, and light. Inflammation, explosion, and evaporation, in turn, must be viewed as the effects of the liberation of fire particles that had been locked up in a tight nexus of other particles. But because atoms are inert, Basson needed additional entities as causal agents, so as to explain natural processes. He was, however, torn between a variety of explanatory models. The most radical was presented in book four of his *Philosophia naturalis,* where Basson presented God as the only cause *tout court* and dismissed all secondary causal agents. His proposal that God personally "does all things continuously, and moves them himself, and leads them singly to their sundry destinations" (*Philosophia naturalis,* 1621, p. 197) is retraceable, albeit somewhat indirectly, to the Islamic atomists of the Kalām. Fire burns, Basson wrote, because "in the presence" of fire particles, God causes burning—a view that not only echoed the atomism of the Kalām, but also anticipated the doctrines of such seventeenth-century occasionalists as Arnold Geulincx or Nicolas de Malebranche. Using the same line of reasoning, Basson rejected the existence of the vegetative and sentient souls, attributing to God the functions that had traditionally been attributed to these higher forms. Of equally Islamic origin and equally rife with post-Cartesian adumbrations is Basson's claim that "the conservation of things by God is their continuous creation" in each atom of time (*Philosophia naturalis,* p. 304).

The divine absolutism of books four and five of the *Philosophia naturalis* is, however, absent from all other parts of this work. Basson's frequently heard nominalist battle cry that redundant entities ought to be rejected from the explanatory tool kit becomes almost inaudible from book six onward, where a plethora of agencies of Neoplatonic, Stoic, and Pythagorean extraction were introduced so as to mitigate between God's omnipotence and particular physical phenomena. Among them, a certain type of material spirit, ether or pneuma was the most prominent. Basson, like Giordano Bruno (whom he did not seem to have known), took this spirit from the Stoics. Ether is said to fill the pores between the atoms and activates each of them according to their preordained aptitude, but it also fills the roles of a Neoplatonic world soul and motor of all things and that as a medium, and mediator, between God and the physical world.

For early Catholic readers, including Marin Mersenne, it was beyond doubt that Basson's doctrines were not only false, but outright heretical. But even Protestant readers such as Isaac Beeckman and Daniel Sennert, who nurtured sympathies for atomism, found much of it incoherent and absurd. The causal setup of the world was indeed explained by Basson in mutually incompatible ways, and the same was true for his atoms, which are sometimes depicted as possessing independent agency and causally efficient properties (such as the fire particles' lacerating wedge shape), but at others as mere instruments in God's hands. But whereas some of Basson's atomist explanations did have a traceable impact on the evolution of seventeenth-century matter theory, most of his technical explanations in such diverse fields as meteorology, astronomy, mechanics, or (Paracelsian-style) pharmacology were so aberrant and ad hoc that few appear to have taken them seriously. If one takes into account that Basson, in the isolated Alpine town of Die (which moreover had a pitiful university library), had even in 1621 not yet heard of Galileo Galilei's celestial discoveries of 1610 (that had become common knowledge in all major European cities by the end of that same year) his lack of sophistication in the less philosophical and more applied scientific disciplines becomes explicable. Still, Basson's reputation as an anti-Aristotelian and atomist was such that in 1649, his treatise went through a second edition, in the hands of no lesser a publisher than the Elsevier's Amsterdam press.

SUPPLEMENTARY BIBLIOGRAPHY

WORK BY BASSON

Philosophiae naturalis adversus Aristotelem libri XII, in quibus abstrusa veterum physiologia restauratur et Aristotelis errores solidis rationibus refelluntur. Geneva: Pierre de la Rouière, 1621. 2nd ed. Amsterdam: Ludovicus Elsevier, 1649. The editions earmarked for exportation to Catholic lands carry the deceitful place name "Aureliana," instead of "Geneva."

OTHER SOURCES

Brugger, Walter. "Sebastian Basso. Ein Vorläufer des Okkasionalismus (1621)." In *Kleine Schriften zur Philosophie und Theologie.* Munich, Germany: Johann Bachmann Verlag, 1984, pp. 118–138. The first author to have noticed the occasionalist elements in Basson.

Gregory, Tullio. "Studi sull'atomismo del Seicento. I. Sebastiano Basson." *Giornale critico della filosofia italiana* 43 (1964):

38–65. An erudite article that places Basson in the context of late Renaissance criticism of Aristotle; although Basson comes out looking like a humanist scholar.

Kubbinga, H. H. "Les premières théories 'moléculaires': Isaac Beeckman (1620) and Sébastien Basson (1621)." *Revue d'Historie des Sciences* 37 (1984): 215–233. This is a reliable, though somewhat celebrative, analysis of Basson's multilevel atomism.

Lasswitz, Kurd. *Geschichte der Atomistik vom Mittelalter bis Newton.* 2 vols. Hamburg, Germany: Leopold Voss, 1890. Reprinted. Hildesheim, Germany: Georg Olms, 1984, pp. 467–481. Still an excellent doctrinal starting point.

Lüthy, Christoph. "Thoughts and Circumstances of Sébastien Basson. Analysis, Micro-History, Questions." *Early Science and Medicine* 2 (1997): 1–73. This work reconstructs Basson's biography and doctrine on the basis of archival sources.

Nielsen, Lauge Olaf. "A Seventeenth-Century Physician on God and Atoms: Sebastian Basso." In *Meaning and Inference in Medieval Philosophy: Studies in Memory of Jan Pinborg,* edited by Norman Kretzmann, 297–369. Dordrecht, Netherlands: Kluwer Academic Publishing, 1988. A good analysis of Basson's atomism in the framework of Protestant theological thought.

Christoph Lüthy

BASTIAN, ADOLF

BASTIAN, ADOLF (*b.* Bremen, 26 June 1826; *d.* Port-of-Spain, Trinidad, 3 February 1905), *ethnography, cultural anthropology, comparative psychology, museums.*

Though rarely mentioned in the early twenty-first century, Bastian was undoubtedly one of the preeminent German scientists of the nineteenth century trying to forge the new discipline of ethnology or socio-cultural anthropology, which still considers him a founding father, though the scope of his undertaking was closer to that of a polymath than of a disciplinary specialist. He endeavored to lay the foundations for an epistemology as well as for the empirical range of a science of culture by combining individual psychology with collective manifestations of the whole of human cultural productions (material as well as ideational), first outlined in his massive three volume publication of 1860, *Man in History.*

Overview of Career. Bastian may have inherited from his merchant father his administrative skills, as well as his love of encountering peoples all over the world. Adolf studied at five universities, including law at Heidelberg, and life sciences at Berlin and Jena. Before obtaining the MD from Prague in 1850 he read for medicine under the tutelage of Rudolph Virchow (Würzburg). In 1851 he signed onto a trip to Australia as a ship's doctor; this and other voyages would occupy twenty-five of his remaining fifty-five years. He conducted fieldwork in almost every inhabited part of the globe, collecting material for a scientific study of comparative psychology.

He devoted 1865 to 1873 to helping organize ethnography in Germany. Beginning as an assistant director in the royal museums in Berlin; he reorganized and enlarged the ethnographic collection. For two years he and Robert Hartmann edited the *Zeitschrift für Ethnologie,* which became the official journal of the Berlin Society for Anthropology, Ethnology, and Prehistory, which Bastian established in 1869 (together with Virchow). In 1873 he became a director and an honorary professor at the university. In 1886 the Museum für Volkerkunde was inaugurated in a new building rivaling similar institutions in London and Paris; he continued to expand its holdings with results of his and others' collecting expeditions. He also co-founded the German Society for Exploring Equatorial Africa (often just called the "African Society") during his presidency of the Berlin Geographical Society (1871–1873).

Geography and Folk Ideas. Bastian drew upon the rapid advances of the natural sciences—from Fechner to Helmholtz—and combined the theories of plant physiology, plant ecology, cellular biology as well as psychophysics and research in sense perception with notions taken from the history of ideas on man's place in nature, drawing upon pre-Socratic thinkers and church fathers as much as on Giambattista Vico, Johann Gottfried Herder, and neo-Kantianism. However he thought that a new, universal "science of mankind", required the collection of evidence from concrete social life in all possible or existing (past and present) ethnic diversity. Of particular importance were for him those ethnic groups which were in his time labeled "primitive societies" as they would yield the "simplest" kinds of thought processes. His insight into the dire results of colonialism, which destroyed traditional cultures like a "forest fire," as he put it (Bastian, 1881, pp.179–181; translated in Köpping, p. 107), was one of the driving forces behind his ceaseless and at times seemingly obsessive travels (seven times around the globe!). His intellectual mentor Alexander von Humboldt provided the other inspiration for collecting field data. Humboldt's *Kosmos* of 1844 challenged the next generation of scholars to tackle organic and cultural phenomena and interdependencies in cultures all over the world.

Bastian took up this challenge (see Bastian, 1869; Köpping, pp. 157–162). Ethnographers had to accumulate as many examples as possible of collective representations (*Gesellschaftsgedanken*), which however had to be analyzed into folk ideas (*Völkergedanken*), the distinctive way a particular group looked at the world, which depended on environmental conditions as well as historical contingencies. In order to correlate the different folk ideas to geography, Bastian developed his arrangement of geographic culture areas where a range of ethnic groups (*Völkerkreis*) shared a range of folk ideas (*Gedankenkreise, Vorstellungskreise*). This aspect of his work resembled that of the anthropogeographer Friedrich Ratzel, with whom he engaged in long public polemical debates.

Only when the impact of geography and the historical development of ethnic idea systems had been sufficiently accounted for, could the uniformity behind them could be deduced and arranged into a set of elementary ideas (*Elementargedanken*) shared by all humanity. He believed that the psychic unity of humankind was responsible for elementary ideas. For Bastian, elementary ideas were an artificially post hoc abstracted notion, whereas folk ideas were the concrete expressions of ethnic groups.

Bastian used a variety of scientific metaphors to express his notion of elementary ideas, sometimes comparing them to cells, sometimes to the most simple forms of plants such as the cryptogams (ferns, mosses and lichens), sometimes to crystals. Inherent in these comparisons is the notion of laws of cultural evolution. Just as the isolated smallest unit contained the potential for the growth of an adult individual, elementary ideas developed. But without further stimuli (geographical or historical changes) folk ideas would not develop further but stagnate. Many of these concepts Bastian took over from the psychophysics of Fechner as well as from the research of Helmholtz.

Besides material cultural productions being the repository of elementary ideas, the collective representations of a whole group, the folk ideas, are to be found specifically in myths and oral traditions, an area to which Bastian contributed extensively in his many works on a diversity of religious systems from the Hawaiian foundation myth of the Kumulipo to treatises on shamanism, Buddhism, and Hinduism. He attributed mental processes not only to the organic structure of the brain but also (decades before Freud) postulated that any disturbances (excitation or deprivation) of the genital system led to what he called delusional or religious aberrations (such as trances, vertigo, hallucinations, or mass hysteria). On the other hand he considered some of the manifestations of religious systems such as shamanism appropriate responses to specific environmental contingencies and correlated in several cases the appearance of new charismatic religious movements to sociohistorical disturbances.

Without doubt his demanding and often cumbersome style of writing hindered the adoption of his ideas, though twentieth-century anthropology has selectively picked up such notions as culture as superorganic, the culture area, diffusionism and cultural hybridity, or ethnicity as collective social formations. His ceaseless effort collecting evidence from all possible cultural repertoires led to some concrete foundations of anthropology as a university

Adolf Bastian. *Adolf Bastian, circa 1900.* HULTON ARCHIVE/GETTY IMAGES.

discipline and of ethnographic collections in national institutions in Germany.

Bastian died—appropriately on his eighth world trip—while swimming off the coast of Trinidad in 1905.

BIBLIOGRAPHY

WORKS BY BASTIAN

Der Mensch in der Geschichte: Zur Begründung einer Psychologischen Weltanschauung. Leipzig: O. Wigand, 1860.

Festrede bei der von den Naturwissenschaftlichen Vereinen Berlins veranstalteten Humboldt-Feier: Gesprochen am Säkurlatage. Berlin: Wiegandt & Hempel, 1869. Memorial oration.

Der Völkergedanke im Aufbau einer Wissenschaft vom Menschen: und seine Begründung auf ethnologische Sammlungen. Berlin: F. Dümmlers, 1881.

Der Buddhismus in seiner Psychologie. Berlin: F. Dümmler, 1882.

Zur Kenntnis Hawaii's. Berlin: F. Dümmler. 1883.

Controversen in der Ethnologie. 4 vols. Berlin: Weidmann, 1893–1894.

OTHER SOURCES

Humboldt, Alexander von. *Kosmos: Entwurf einer physischen Weltbeschreibung.* 4 vols. in 2. Stuttgart: J. G. Cotta, 1844. Translated by Elise C. Otté as *Cosmos: A Sketch of a Physical Description of the Universe.* New York: Harper, 1859.

Köpping, Klaus-Peter. *Adolf Bastian and the Psychic Unity of Mankind: The Foundations of Anthropology in Nineteenth Century Germany.* Münster: Lit Verlag, 2005. Re-edition of original edition with University of Queensland Press of 1983.

Penny, H. Glenn. *Objects of Culture: Ethnology and Ethnographic Museums in Imperial Germany.* Chapel Hill: University of North Carolina Press, 2002.

Tylor, Edward B. "Professor Adolf Bastian: Born June 26, 1826; Died February 3, 1905." *Man* 5 (1905): 138–143. Lists his various journeys abroad and activities in Germany. Refers readers to other obituaries and a 16-page, "practically complete list" of Bastian's writings.

Klaus-Peter Köpping

BASTIAN, CHARLTON

SEE **Bastian, Henry Charlton**.

BASTIAN, HENRY CHARLTON (*b.* Truro, Cornwall, England, 26 April 1837; *d.* Chesham Bois, Buckinghamshire, England, 17 November 1915), *neurology, microbiology and origin of life, physiology, pathology.* For the original article on Bastian see *DSB,* vol. 1.

Much new secondary literature has appeared, including Stephen Jacyna's detailed study of Bastian's theory of aphasia and other neurological disorders, but most of which has overthrown the older caricature of Bastian (largely created by Thomas Henry Huxley and John Tyndall) as an isolated figure in his support for spontaneous generation.

Relation to Darwin. Bastian was one of the most talented of the young Darwinian evolutionists in the 1860s, under Huxley's mentorship. His interest in the origin of life and experiments in spontaneous generation were the direct result of his commitment to Charles Darwin's and Herbert Spencer's evolutionary ideas; Bastian, like many others, felt that evolution implied and required a naturalistic origin of the first living things. His work was supported by Richard Owen and Alfred Russel Wallace. Darwin, too, took great interest in Bastian's logic and experiments on

spontaneous generation. Darwin had, after all, assiduously avoided the topic throughout most of *On the Origin of Species* (1859), only to put in some ambivalent-sounding language in the last few pages of the book (speaking of one or a few original living forms "into which life was first breathed"). And Darwin's few private remarks on the subject also reveal an ambivalence over spontaneous generation up until about 1877. He did feel that an explanation of life's beginning in concert with scientific naturalism would help the cause. Yet the earlier associations of spontaneous generation with materialism and political radicalism, and with Robert Chambers's model of evolution in *Vestiges of the Natural History of Creation* (1844)—widely criticized by professional scientists as amateurish—all those were associations Darwin and Huxley very much wished to avoid. Before Huxley, Robert Grant of University College, London, had been an earlier scientific mentor to Bastian. Grant's radical, materialistic versions of spontaneous generation linked to evolution were infamous among the professional scientific circles appealing to the middle class where Darwin and his chief supporters operated.

Nonetheless, Huxley's famous 1869 essay "The Physical Basis of Life" and his support for Ernst Haeckel—even championing the supposedly living organism *Bathybius haeckelii* spontaneously generated on the sea floor—led many to believe, like Bastian, that Huxley and Darwin actually believed in spontaneous generation and thought it integral to evolutionary science. So when Bastian argued in favor of the possibility of spontaneous generation in an anonymous 1869 series in the *British Medical Journal,* then publicly beginning in 1870, a sizable fraction of Darwinian supporters agreed with this logic. Huxley soon concluded that Bastian was too eager to publish and not sufficiently cautious experimentally, which persuaded him to use his September 1870 presidential address at the British Association for the Advancement of Science to head off a possible debacle for Darwinism should Bastian turn out to be wrong because of experimental error. "Darwin's bulldog" used his famous "Biogenesis and Abiogenesis" address to outflank Bastian and declare an official Darwinian position on the origin of life. Huxley now argued that life probably had emerged from nonlife by naturalistic means, but that this "abiogenesis," as he called it, must have taken millions of years and was possible only under the very different conditions of the Earth's distant past. All experiments claiming to prove that spontaneous generation could occur rapidly under current conditions were deeply flawed, argued Huxley, siding with Louis Pasteur. Not least among those mistaken, Huxley said, was Bastian. Huxley was trying to put the inflammatory, materialistic, origin of life question safely to rest by claiming that it was simply beyond the reach of science.

Critique of Germ Theory. Even after Huxley's frontal attack, so formidable was Bastian as a rhetorician, and so skilled as an experimentalist, particularly in microscopy, that a sizable minority of Darwinians still supported his view over Huxley's, especially in medical circles, where support for spontaneous generation was widespread because of opposition to early versions of the germ theory of disease. Most scientific doctors subscribed to Justus von Liebig's zymotic theory of disease, in which germs were seen as at most the spontaneously generated by-products of a chemically catalyzed disease process, rather than as its cause. Bastian, like Charles Murchison, became a new spokesman for many of their long-standing critiques of overly simplistic germ theories: If germ = disease, for instance, then in epidemics why does not everybody in the village, or even in the same household, get sick? Only when incorporating the later discoveries of immunology could more sophisticated germ theories satisfy doctors on such counts. Furthermore, the Edinburgh physiology professor John Hughes Bennett influentially came out in support of spontaneous generation in 1868, and he linked it with his well-known "molecular theory" of disease. Bennett's "molecules" (also described by Georges-Louis Leclerc de Buffon, Robert Brown, and by Matthias Jakob Schleiden and Theodor Schwann) were among many microscopic particles, from colloids to the "gemmules" of Darwin's pangenesis hypothesis, Haeckel's "plastidules," and other basic "life units" in theories popular during the 1860s and 1870s. Pleomorphist theory, of the easy transformation among microbial forms of bacteria and fungi, even interconversion between the two, was also widespread at this time, championed especially by Karl Wilhelm von Nägeli. All of these theories created more theoretical space for belief in spontaneous generation of very simple cells from smaller "living units" during this time. Pleomorphist theory also specifically undercut germ theories, such as that of Robert Koch, that presumed fixed, unchanging bacterial species, each of which caused a specific disease. Only when these theories gradually fell out of vogue (for example, Bennett's theory after his death in 1875) or were disproven experimentally did support for spontaneous generation begin to decline.

The physicist Tyndall was an early and zealous convert to oversimplistic germ theories of disease, so he joined Huxley in attacking Bastian and suggesting that Bastian's experimental technique must be sloppy. Tyndall (soon joined by Edwin Ray Lankester) included in his critique many remarks gratuitously insulting doctors for being too obdurate, set in their ways, unscientific, or just plain dull, to appreciate the merits of Joseph Lister and William Budd's germ theories. As a result, a rift opened between doctors (especially scientific doctors and those sympathetic to Darwinian evolution) and nonmedical scientists, and it deepened considerably because of the heated debate

Henry Bastian. *Henry Bastian, circa 1875.* HULTON ARCHIVE/GETTY IMAGES.

over Bastian's theories that continued from 1870 to 1878. Medical forums such as the Pathological Society of London were long supportive of Bastian's case. The Royal Society, dominated in the 1870s by X Club Darwinians such as Tyndall, Huxley, and Joseph Dalton Hooker, became a hostile place for Bastian and a sympathetic one for Tyndall—the two men's papers received unequal treatment in the publication process.

In the end, the debate was as much a power struggle among Darwinian factions as it was about the outcome of experiments. Tyndall's discovery in 1877 of heat-resistant bacterial endospores is often taken as an *experimentum crucis*, but this is at least partly retrospective. Tyndall had to blatantly contradict some of his own experiments from 1875–1876 to promote the new discovery; this was passed over easily by his allies, but few of Bastian's supporters found the new spores convincing. Similarly, William Henry Dallinger and John Drysdale's 1873–1875 observations on spore-formation by protists under continuous microscopic observation changed relatively few minds at the time. The outcome of the experimental debate was underdetermined by the experiments alone. Bastian has come to be seen as a serious Darwinian scientist who led the minority faction in one of the most outstanding schisms in evolutionary science during the first twenty years after *On the Origin of Species.* The restoration of this portrait involves reclaiming the existence of a large camp within Darwinism, even in Britain, that saw spontaneous generation and evolution as inseparably linked doctrines from 1859 until 1878 or so. The declining fortunes of spontaneous generation had quite as much to do with defeat of that camp in the power struggle by Huxley and Tyndall's camp, as well as with numerous broad theoretical and technical changes in biology and medical science during this period, as it had to do with any particular experiment or even the sum of all the experimental data.

SUPPLEMENTARY BIBLIOGRAPHY

Adam, Alison E. *Spontaneous Generation in the 1870s: Victorian Scientific Naturalism and Its Relation to Medicine.* PhD diss., Sheffield Hallam University. Sheffield, U.K., 1988.

Barton, Ruth. "'An Influential Set of Chaps': The X Club and Royal Society Politics, 1864–1885." *British Journal for the History of Science* 23 (1990): 53–81.

Desmond, Adrian, and James R. Moore. *Darwin.* London: Michael Joseph, 1991.

Geison, Gerald. *The Private Science of Louis Pasteur.* Princeton, NJ: Princeton University Press, 1995.

Huxley, Thomas Henry. "Biogenesis and Abiogenesis" (1870). In *The Scientific Memoirs of Thomas Henry Huxley*, Vol. 3. London: Macmillan, 1901.

Jacyna, L. Stephen. *Lost Words: Narratives of Language and the Brain, 1825–1926.* Princeton, NJ: Princeton University Press, 2000.

Kamminga, Harmke. *Studies in the History of Ideas on the Origin of Life from 1860.* PhD diss., University of London, 1980.

Strick, James E. "Darwinism and the Origin of Life: The Role of H. C. Bastian in the British Spontaneous Generation Debates, 1868–1873." *Journal of the History of Biology* 32 (1999): 51–92.

———. *Sparks of Life: Darwinism and the Victorian Debates over Spontaneous Generation.* Cambridge, MA: Harvard University Press, 2000.

———, ed. *Evolution and the Spontaneous Generation Debate.* 6 vols. Bristol, U.K.: Thoemmes, 2001. This set reprints most of Bastian's major works on the origin of life, as well as many important reviews of his books.

———, ed. *The Origin of Life Debate: Molecules, Cells, and Generation.* 6 vols. Bristol, U.K.: Thoemmes, 2004. This set reprints many primary articles in the spontaneous generation debates, "molecular theories," and so forth, from 1748 to 1890.

Worboys, Michael. *Spreading Germs: Disease Theories and Medical Practice in Britain, 1865–1900.* Cambridge, U.K.: Cambridge University Press, 2000.

James E. Strick

BATESON, WILLIAM (b. Whitby, England, 8 August 1861; d. Merton, London, 8 February 1926), *embryology, genetics.* For the original article on Bateson see *DSB*, vol. 1.

Since the mid-1970s the increasing attention given to the history of genetics has brought fresh studies on Bateson. A growing interest in the history of scientific institutions and the funding of research has also led to further studies of Bateson's unusual career. A detailed account is now available of his efforts to gain financial and institutional support in Cambridge and to harness the willing hands of the young women of Newnham College, and of his role as the first director of the John Innes Horticultural Institute at Merton. The discovery in 1983 of homeobox genes that control body plans, and the abrupt alterations to those plans caused by mutations among these genes, is a reminder of the examples of just such mutants described by Bateson in 1894. The manner in which genetics and embryology come together in the homeobox helps us to appreciate the undercurrent of embryological thinking in Bateson's conception of variability and genetics.

Variations. The first phase of Bateson's research—using embryology to reveal phylogeny—formed a part of the research program pursued in Cambridge University's zoology department. His decision to terminate such work can be viewed within the broad context of what Peter Bowler has called the period of "The Eclipse of Darwinism." Skepticism concerning the role of natural selection had been opening the way to suggestions of the internal source of adaptive variation, a scenario in which natural selection seemed unlikely to have played a creative role. Bateson next turned to variation, calling it "the essential phenomenon of evolution" (*Materials*, 1894, p. 6). To this new agenda he brought what embryology had taught him: the importance of symmetry in the organization of living things, and the repetition of parts, or "meristic" variation, as he called it, and the substitution of parts, or "homeotic" variation. Then there were variations in "the substance of the parts themselves"; he called these "substantive" variations. The first class of variations invited analysis in terms of patterns of cell division leading to radial and bilateral symmetries. The second suggested the appeal to chemistry—ferments producing pigments that color eyes, flowers, and skin.

Bateson's enthusiastic study of these variations led to the 600-page *Materials for the Study of Variation* (1894). The subtitle *Treated with Especial Regard to Discontinuity in the Origin of Species* announced the message of the book. It was diametrically opposed to the continuity of variation assumed by the Darwinians. But his travels to Russia and Egypt in search of discontinuities in the environment that match discontinuities between species proved fruitless. Henceforth he decided that the distinctiveness of species—their discontinuity—was not to be attributed to natural selection having eliminated intermediate forms from a continuously varying population, but to the discontinuity of the variations themselves. Therefore he set out to establish the extent of discontinuity in variation, compiling a long catalog of examples that fill the twenty-one chapters of *Materials,* from extra antennae, legs, and palpi in insects to supernumerary digits, hands, feet, teeth, and teats in humans. He even reported one case of an insect with an extra antenna issuing from one of its eyes (*Materials,* fig. 19, p. 151). The discontinuity of such variations, he reasoned, should be manifest in their non-blending character when crossbred. Accordingly, he concluded the book with an appeal for "the organization of systematic experiments in breeding, a class of research that, he judged, calls for more patience and more resources than any other form of biological inquiry" (p. 574).

In 1895 he began such a program, and was soon able to draw on assistance from the women of Newnham College. Here Marsha Richmond's account of their assistance to Bateson has filled a gap in accounts of Bateson's informal network of Cambridge researchers. Bateson suggested or assigned breeding experiments: *Veronica* to Dora Pertz; Mendel's peas to Hilda Blanch Kilby; *Lathyrus* to Mary Hart-Davis; *Antirrhinum* to Muriel Wheldale; mice to his sister-in-law, Florence Durham; and canaries to her and Dorothea Charlotte Edith Marryat. Two events that encouraged this support were the failure of the campaign for degrees for women in 1897 and the ensuing exclusion of women from the Morphological Laboratory and from beginning courses in biology (Richmond, 2001, p. 64). Richmond has also described the important role played by Edith Rebecca Saunders as Bateson's first and longest-serving collaborator from 1895 until 1910. Only when Bateson began to deputize for Professor Alfred Newton in 1899 did he gain followers among the male students, starting with Reginald Crundell Punnett in 1904, followed by Leonard Doncaster, Robert Lock, and Reginald Philip Gregory.

Promotion of the Mendelian Program. Bateson's experience in crossbreeding prepared him to take the lead in 1900 in promoting in the English-speaking world the work of Gregor Mendel and his rediscoverers. Bateson first read about what became known as Mendelian segregation in the offspring of hybrids (F_2) when Hugo de Vries sent him his first paper on the subject, published in the *Comptes rendus de l'Académie des Science.* Here de Vries made no mention of Mendel. Evidence has been presented to claim that this was the paper that Bateson read while traveling to London to give his lecture "Problems of Heredity." The report of this lecture written by the

respected Dr. Maxwell Masters and published in the *Gardeners' Chronicle* four days later also makes no mention of Mendel. Indeed, it appears that Bateson presented Hugo de Vries's results as modifications of Galton's law because he was incorporating De Vries's results into the Galtonian framework of the talk he had prepared (Olby, 1987). This is hardly surprising, for as early as 1897 Galton had suggested how his ancestral law could be applied to non-blending characters, using data from the pedigree of basset hounds. Instead of considering ancestral contributions to offspring to be blended in each individual, he pictured them as being *distributed* in pure form to members of the offspring, in proportions conforming to the ancestral law, not unlike the effects of Mendelian segregation (Galton, 1897; see also Pearson, 1900). Only on his return to Cambridge did Bateson see De Vries's second, more detailed paper in which Mendel's work is acknowledged. Only then did he possess the information leading him to the 1865 volume of the *Verhandlungen der Naturforschenden Vereines in Brünn* in the Cambridge University Library.

Bateson had turned to crossbreeding experiments in order to establish that new variations, providing they were of a discontinuous character, would not be swamped by crossing with the normal form. Mendel's paper then provided him with an explanation of the underlying stochastic process at the level of the germ cells. For Bateson, Mendel's essential discovery was "the purity of the gametes." Bateson's insistence on the significance for evolution of discontinuous variations thus became attached to the Mendelian theory, a situation that guaranteed opposition to Mendelism from Darwinians. The infamous controversy between Mendelians and Darwinian biometricians that followed has been the subject of much interest, especially because Donald Mackenzie and S. Barry Barnes attempted a sociological analysis of the controversy. Bateson's success in taking control of the Royal Society Evolution Committee in 1897—and hence gaining access to Royal Society grants for his research—undoubtedly embittered the biometricians, but it gave Bateson the resources to continue and expand his breeding studies.

Meanwhile, during the fourteen years in which Bateson carried out breeding experiments in Cambridge, apart from the award of the Balfour studentship to his collaborator, Reginald Crundall Punnett, he received no research funds from the university or from any of its associated funding bodies. In 1903, however, Bateson's friend, Christina J. Herringham, the well-known copyist of Italian masters and wife of the Wimpole Street consultant Sir Wilmot Parker Herringham, offered to furnish the funds needed so that Bateson would be able to pay a salary for an assistant. Two years later Francis Darwin and his brothers supplied funds, enabling Bateson to have a greenhouse

William Bateson. SPL/PHOTO RESEARCHERS, INC.

constructed for the hybridization of tender plants. Any other financial support came from outside Cambridge.

In 1907 Bateson spent three months in the United States and gave the Silliman Lectures at Yale University that October. The warm reception that greeted him there raised his self-esteem, but he was not prepared when, on his return to Cambridge, the University offered him not a chair but a readership, and in zoology, not genetics. Although he was persuaded to accept, shortly thereafter a member of the University offered the funds to establish and support for five years a chair of biology that was clearly intended for Bateson. In June 1908 he was elected. The duty of the professor would be to "teach and make researches in that branch of biology now entitled Genetics (Heredity and Variation)" (B. Bateson, p. 112). Bateson now had the status and salary worthy of his achievements and international reputation, but the chair carried no funds for research, and its future after the five years was not assured. A year later, when Bateson learned of the plans for a Horticultural Institution funded by the late John Innes and of the appeal for applications for the post

of director, he did not apply. On the twelve-member advisory Council for the Trust, however, were five of Bateson's friends. Passing over two of Bateson's excellent former coworkers—Gregory and Lock—they opened negotiations with him. Responding positively, he substantially modified the Council's plan for the Institute, and on these terms he accepted the position. In 1910, after forty-nine years in Cambridge, he left to begin a new life.

Move to Merton. During the early years at Merton, Bateson was occupied with establishing his staff and instituting his research program. Across the ocean, Thomas Hunt Morgan, Arthur H. Sturtevant, Calvin B. Bridges, and Herman J. Muller were breeding fruit flies (*Drosophila*) and exploring the relation between heredity and the chromosomes. Their book, *The Mechanism of Mendelian Heredity* (1915), established the chromosomes as the bearers of the Mendelian factors or genes. As William Coleman has already explained, Bateson vigorously opposed it. For him the fundamental process underlying heredity and development was cell division, not chromosomes. The association of particular Mendelian factors he attributed to differential rates of "reduplication" of the gametes carrying those factors, rather than to the position of the factors close together on the same chromosome. Mechanistic theory he did support, but not the conjectured *structural* complexities of cell organelles, which at the time were only clearly distinguished with the magic of staining techniques. Nor could he ignore the problems posed by the theory. How can the chromosomes control differentiation if each cell has the same complement? Should not the chromosomes of cells in different tissues differ? And why did the number of chromosomes in different species not vary in accordance with the degree of complexity of the species?

Seven years after the publication of *The Mechanism of Mendelian Heredity,* Bateson visited Morgan's laboratory at Columbia University and withdrew his opposition to their theory. Addressing the American Association for the Advancement of Science in Toronto, Bateson declared: "I come at this Christmas season to lay my respectful homage before the stars that have arisen in the west ... The arguments of Morgan and his colleagues, and especially the demonstrations of Bridges, must allay all skepticism as to the direct association of particular chromosomes with particular features of the zygote" (B. Bateson, p. 392).

When Bateson retired from the John Innes Horticultural Institute (JIHI) in 1926 he could take special credit for the new knowledge gained concerning compatibility and incompatibility between varieties of apples, pears, plums, and cherries; his work, however, could easily give the impression of a piecemeal collection of studies lacking a clear focus. Actually, Bateson's several projects—on double flowers, rogue peas, and plant chimeras—were aimed at demonstrating segregation without meiosis. He was following his own advice to "treasure your exceptions." Such a strategy during his early years of working on Mendel's laws had revealed one exception after another. Pursuing them had led to his discovery of gene interaction: epistasis and hypostasis, "coupling" (i.e., linkage), differing expressions of dominance, as in sex determination, and much else. Many of these research topics were natural choices for a horticultural institute and arose out of Bateson's close connections with the Royal Horticultural Society and with prominent members of the trade.

Bateson had succeeded in transferring his researches from Cambridge to Merton, but unlike Morgan, he had neither built up a team of researchers at Merton, nor had he attracted colleagues of the caliber of Bridges and Muller. In altering the Council's plan, he had abolished the four well-paid positions recommended by Council, choosing instead to offer minor grants to students, some at £50 per year, intended chiefly for "women students who wish to devote themselves to research in various fields but can scarcely afford to earn nothing at all" (Olby, 1989, p. 506). Cyril Dean Darlington, a future director of the JIHI, began working there without pay, as did the mycologist Dorothy Cayley. On his retirement, Bateson expressed his regret that he had not achieved more at the JIHI. "When the centre of chief interest in genetics shifted away from work of my type to that of the American group," he wrote, "I was already too old and too much fixed in my ideas to become master of so very new and intricate a development" (p. 507).

Shortly after he became established at the JIHI, Bateson was surprised to be invited back to Cambridge. This invitation resulted from the concern of former prime minister Arthur Balfour, who wished to see genetics properly established at Cambridge and thus took the lead in seeking funds for a chair of genetics there. Aided by Lord Esher and encouraged by Prime Minister Herbert Henry Asquith, a benefactor was found: William George Watson, of the Maypole Dairy company (Opitz, 2005). In 1912, at Balfour's instigation, the chair was offered to Bateson; by this time, however, he felt well settled at Merton and declined. The call from Cambridge, supported by two prime ministers, speaks to the reputation Bateson had acquired since the early years when the Cambridge Darwinians viewed him as a dissident member of their community who sniped at their work, often in a scornful tone.

Honors. Bateson's work was recognized by the Royal Society with the award of the Darwin Medal in 1904, the Royal Medal in 1923, and he was the Society's Croonian lecturer in 1920. The Royal Horticultural Society awarded him the Victoria Medal in 1911 and the Royal

Institution elected him Fullerian Professor (1912-1915). At a national level he served in 1912 as chairman of Lloyd George's important Development Commission and ten years later he was offered a Knighthood which he declined. In 1910 he received an honorary degree from Sheffield University and became an Honorary Fellow of his Cambridge College, St. John's.

SUPPLEMENTARY BIBLIOGRAPHY

Originals and copies of Bateson's correspondence and papers (1883-1929) are preserved and cataloged at the John Innes Archive, The John Innes Center, Norwich, United Kingdom (Originally the John Innes Horticultural Institution). The originals of part of this large collection are held in the archives of the American Philosophical Society, Philadelphia, and at Cambridge University Library. A small collection of Bateson Family Papers 1829–1921 is held at the American Philosophical Society .

WORKS BY BATESON

Materials for the Study of Variation, Treated with Especial Regard for the Study of Variation. London and New York: Macmillan, 1894. Cited as *Materials.*

Problems of Genetics. New Haven, CT: Yale University Press, 1913. Reprinted in the Silliman Milestones in Science series, New Haven, CT: Yale University Press, 1979.

OTHER SOURCES

Bateson, Beatrice. *William Bateson, F.R.S.. His Essays and Addresses together with a Short Account of His Life.* Cambridge: Cambridge University Press, 1928. Cited as "B. Bateson."

Bowler, Peter. *The Eclipse of Darwinism: AntiDarwinian Evolution Theories in the Decades around 1900.* Baltimore, MD: Johns Hopkins University Press, 1983.

Cock, Alan. "William Bateson's Rejection and Eventual Acceptance of Chromosome Theory." *Annals of Science* 40 (1983): 19–59.

Galton, Francis. "The Average Contribution of Each Several Ancestor to the Total Heritage of the Offspring." *Proceedings of the Royal Society* 61 (1897): 403.

Henig, Robin M. *The Monk in the Garden: The Lost and Found Genius of Gregor Mendel, the Father of Genetics.* Boston and New York: Houghton Mifflin, 2000.

Lipset, David. *Gregory Bateson: The Legacy of a Scientist.* Englewood Cliffs, NJ: Prentice Hall, 1980.

Mackenzie, Donald, and S. Barry Barnes. "Biometriker versus Mendelianer. Eine Kontroverse und ihre Erklarung." *Kölner Zeitschrift für Soziologie und Sozialpsychologie* (1975) Sonderheft 13, section iv, pp. 165–196, and an abbreviated account: "Scientific Judgement: The Biometry-Mendelism Controversy," in *Natural Order: Historical Studies of Scientific Culture,* edited by S. B. Barnes and Steven Shapin. Beverly Hills and London: Sage Publications, 1979.

Morgan, Thomas Hunt; A. H. Sturtevant; H. J. Muller; and C. B. Bridges. *The Mechanism of Mendelian Heredity.* New York: Henry Holt, 1915.

Olby, Robert. "William Bateson's Introduction of Mendelism to England: A Reassessment." *British Journal for the History of Science* 20 (1987): 399–420.

———. "Scientists and Bureaucrats in the Establishment of the John Innes Horticultural Institution under William Bateson." *Annals of Science* 46 (1989): 497–510.

———. "The Dimensions of Scientific Controversy: The Biometric-Mendelian Debate." *British Journal for the History of Science* 22 (1988): 299–320. Critiques Mackenzie and Barnes.

———. "Horticulture: The Font for the Baptism of Genetics." *Nature Reviews Genetics* 1 (2000): 65–70.

———. "The Monk in the Garden" by Robert Henig. *Perspectives in Biology and Medicine* 45 (2002): 142–145. Book review.

Opitz, Donald L. "'No Doubtful or Uncertain Enterprise': Balfour, Bateson, and Britain's First Chair of Genetics at Cambridge, 1894–1914." History of Science Society Meeting, Minneapolis, MN, 3–6 November 2005.

Pearson, Karl. "Mathematical Contributions to the Theory of Evolution—on the Law of Reversion." *Proceedings of the Royal Society* 66 (1900): 141.

Richmond, Marsha L. "Women in the Early History of Genetics: William Bateson and the Newnham College Mendelians, 1900–1910." *Isis* 92 (2001): 55–90.

———. "The 'Domestication' of Heredity: The Familial Organization of Geneticists at Cambridge, 1895–1910." *Journal of the History of Biology* 37 (2004): 1–41.

Robert C. Olby

BAYER, OTTO GEORG WILHELM

(*b.* Frankfurt am Main, Germany, 4 November 1902; *d.* Burscheid [near Cologne], Germany, 1 August 1982), *organic chemistry, macromolecular chemistry.*

Bayer's greatest achievement was ultimately the invention of polyurethane chemistry. Using the polyaddition of diisocyanates and polyoles was a very new principle of making polymers, yet at first, his closest colleagues were very skeptical. Until his death Otto Bayer influenced the development of this versatile family of plastics. He received about 400 patents and won numerous honors from universities, industry, and professional associations. He headed Bayer research for more than three decades, and served with distinction on the company's board of management and as chairman of its supervisory board in the crowning work of his career.

The success of his invention is shown in the fact that as of 2005 about 7 million tonnes of polyurethanes were produced worldwide. This is about 5 percent of the total polymer production.

Childhood and Education. Bayer's parents were descendants of an old southwest German farmer's family, and it is really not surprising that he himself had a lot of features characteristic of his ancestors, such as his traits of being economical, open-minded, and hard-working. At the age of twelve, Bayer established a laboratory in the attic of his parents' house; from that time onward he wanted to become a chemist. After his final exam at the Klinger-Oberrealschule in Frankfurt, he began his chemistry studies at Frankfurt University in 1921. In only three and a half years, he finished his studies with excellent grades. His research advisor was Julius von Braun, who was known to conduct research in many different areas. After obtaining his PhD in January 1925, with a dissertation on the synthesis of talose from galactose via enzymatic separation techniques (title: *I. Die Darstellung einiger seltener Monosacharide mittels Diphenylmethandimethyldihydrazin; II. Zur Kenntnis der katalytischen Hydrierung des Indolkomplexes*), he worked an additional two and half years in von Braun's group as a postdoctoral assistant. A dozen publications from this time demonstrate that the young Bayer was able to develop many interesting results in different fields. In 1927, he married Lonny Stellisch. The marriage was childless.

Dyestuff Chemistry at Mainkur. On 1 May 1927, Bayer, at age twenty-four, started his industrial career in a research laboratory of the IG Farben works at Mainkur, near Frankfurt (formally named Leopold Cassella & Co), in the group of Georg Kalischer, who introduced him to dyestuff chemistry. As this chemistry is mainly based on new intermediates, Bayer synthesized many new aldehydes by oxidation of aromatic methyl or methylene compounds. These aldehydes were important intermediates for vat dyestuffs and could be easily prepared on a large scale.

In the early 1930s, vat dyestuffs on the basis of anthraquinones were of particular interest. Bayer developed a commercial product, Anthrasole Yellow V, which was easily prepared by acylation of 1-aminoanthraquinone with 4-biphenylcarboxylic acid chloride and which had very high light fastness.

As early as September 1927, he filed his first patent (D.R.P. 496321) concerning "Verfahren zur Herstellung von Effektfäden aus Baumwollenen oder Anderen Pflanzlichen Fasern" (Method for the preparation of fancy yarns made of cotton or other natural plant fibers). The reaction of aromatic sulfonic acid chlorides with basic groups conducted on alkaline pre-treated fibers results in yarns that can no longer be dyed by certain dyestuffs and have been used in mixed textile fabrics with special effects.

During these years at Mainkur, Bayer not only did research but also gained management experience. As a result, in 1931 he was appointed head of a department there.

Research Director at Leverkusen. In 1934, Bayer, who was not quite thirty-two years old, became the head of the central scientific research laboratory (*Wissenschaftliche Hauptlaboratorium*) of the IG Farben works at Leverkusen, near Cologne, with a staff of some sixty chemists. He held this post until 1951, when he was appointed a member of the board of directors of the newly created Bayer AG, Leverkusen, a result of the splitting up of IG Farben into three different companies: BASF, Hoechst, and Bayer. The company name "Bayer" refers to the dyestuffs firm of Friedrich Bayer & Co., founded in 1863. (Otto Bayer was not related to Friedrich Bayer.) Otto Bayer was accepted by everyone due to his thorough knowledge in chemistry and due to his creative ideas in all fields of chemistry. He was a man of quick decisions and he knew that his coworkers could achieve good results if not too tightly controlled. Bayer was confident in the abilities of his scientists and able to correctly assign the scientists to topics where they would be able to achieve results. In cases in which the researchers felt there would be no solution of a given problem, he had ideas and suggestions. He was helpful, had direct contact with his scientists, and was often seen in the lab as he always was curious to learn the newest results.

In his new role as research director at Leverkusen, Bayer became involved in many new areas of research. Apart from dyestuffs, his original field, he was engaged, for instance, in rubber chemistry, plastics, fibers, pharmaceutical research, and crop protection. In 1939 he became a member of the Board of Directors of IG Farben.

In 1944, Bayer became honorary professor of the technical organic chemistry department at the University of Cologne. Over the course of two decades he gave lectures on special aspects of organic chemistry. Bayer enjoyed familiarizing the students with new technical processes and giving them insight into the problems of industrial chemistry. He had close contact with nearly all universities in Germany and friendly relationships with many of their chemistry professors.

Bayer's life-long commitment to chemical literature supported the continuation of important scientific work. An example is his support of the Gmelin database. He also played an important part in establishing the Studiengesellschaft zur Förderung der Chemischen Dokumentation mbH, from which the "Internationale Dokumentationsgesellschaft für Chemie mbH" for the chemical industry evolved. He rendered outstanding service to the new edition of the Houben-Weyl reference series for preparative methods in organic chemistry that was published beginning in 1952. Without his intense and constant effort as

Otto Georg Wilhelm Bayer. COURTESY OF BAYER AG.

co-editor, the publication of the Houben-Weyl series would not have been accomplished. The volumes on aldehydes and anthraquinones were written entirely by him.

In the very difficult postwar years in Germany, Bayer promoted the revival of academic research in that country. Otto Bayer promoted university research with his initiative in 1950 to create the Fonds des Verbands der Chemischen Industrie (Fund of the chemistry industry). Companies that are members of this association of the chemical industry are committed to pay a specific amount to this fund per year.

In the mid-1930s, polymerization and co-polymerization of vinyl compounds and dienes for making synthetic rubber and important polymers such as polystyrene and polyvinylchloride were used technically. At that time the researchers in Leverkusen had experience in making cellulose triacetate fibers and in the field of synthetic rubber. IG Farben produced the thermoplastics polystyrene and polyvinyl chloride. A real breakthrough came when Wallace Carothers started his research on polymers via the polycondensation process in 1932 at Du Pont. Finally in 1935, he invented nylon (polyamide 66) in reacting adipic acid with hexamethylene diamine. This polymer quickly became very important for fibers. From the very beginning Otto Bayer had believed that polyamides excellent textile market value. Since polyamides were patented

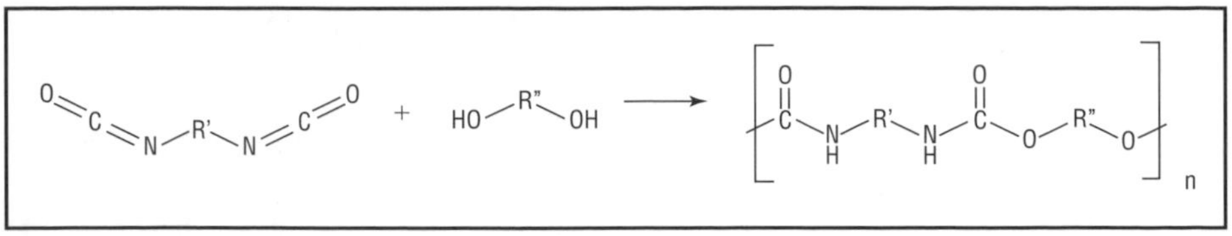

Figure 1.

by Du Pont, and being convinced that the future belonged to plastics, Bayer looked for new ways and new structures (polymer backbones) to enter this field. He had the idea of preparing polymers similar to polyamides by replacing the methylene group adjacent to the carbonyl-group by oxygen and hoped for polymers with properties that are better than those of Carother's polyamides. In developing the diisocyanate polyaddition process, Bayer became a pioneer who gained worldwide recognition through the founding of the very complex industrial branch of polyurethanes (PUR)

The basic idea of making polyurethanes is rather simple: Isocyanates react with alcohols quantitatively in an exothermic reaction to yield a urethane. Consequently, diisocyanates and dialcohols should form new long-chain macromolecules by a polyaddition reaction. Similarly, polyureas could be expected if diisocyanates and polyamines were used as the starting materials. Perhaps both polyadditions would yield usable plastics, and in contrast to Carothers's polycondensation reaction, this polyaddition reaction had the advantage of occurring exothermically at room temperature and without any splitting off of by-products.

Bayer needed diisocyanates as starting materials. Prior to 1936 just seven diisocyanates had been described in chemistry literature. Their yields were poor, their purity was low, and it was impossible to use the methods for their preparation on a large scale. Werner Siefken, reporting to Otto Bayer, had experience in making monoisocyanates from amines with phosgene since 1934. Bayer asked him to try applying his method to the synthesis of diisocyanates. The result was that Siefken became the first to prepare diisocyanates via the phosgene route in 1936. He was able to generate starting materials in a large variety with high yield and high purity, and scaling up was easy. The reaction of phosgene with diamines remains the most important base for the polyaddition reaction in the early twenty-first century.

Bayer gained support for his idea of preparing polymers by the reaction of isocyanates and polyoles through the authority of his personality and his demonstration of competence. His innovative power and ability to motivate his co-workers are as admirable as the basic idea itself.

A few examples will illustrate the dynamic development of this new class of polymers. The first trials in 1936 with 1,6-hexamethylenediisocyanate and simple linear dialcohols reacted to yield fibers and thermoplastic polymer intermediates, but the properties of polyamide could not be achieved. In 1937, Bayer succeeded in producing a polymer by reacting 1,8 octane diisocyanate with 1,4 butanediol, creating a tough plastic. Fibers made of this new polyurethane had higher stiffness and lower uptake of water than polyamide 66. It was later used to manufacture high-quality brush bristles. The first basic patent in the field of polyaddition, which laid the foundation for all subsequent work on polyurethanes and polyureas, was filed on 13 November 1937. It was the result of Bayer's research, along with that of his coworkers Werner Siefken, Heinrich Rinke, Ludwig Orthner, and Heinz Schild.

In 1938–1939, when hydroxyl group-bearing polyesters were substituted for low molecular weight dialcohols, a breakthrough was achieved. Coatings of previously unachievable high molecular weight could be obtained, and it was even possible to cross-link them on the substrate that was coated. Adhesion, elasticity, gloss, water resistance, and thermal stability were drastically improved.

Due to the fact that the polyaddition started directly after mixing the isocyanates with the hydroxy end groups containing co-reactants, these coatings could only be used as two component coatings. Nevertheless, this was the beginning of a development in polyurethane chemistry that led to light stable coating types that came to be used worldwide, for example, for coatings of railroad cars and airplanes.

Bayer also wanted to prepare cast elastomers, not only fibers or coatings. In 1941, liquid polyesters with hydroxylic endgroups and diisocyanates were poured into molds and then mixed; however, the resulting products were full of bubbles. These bubbles consisted of carbon dioxide coming from the reaction of isocyanates with traces of water and the ensuing decomposition of the generated carbamic acids and the reaction with free carboxy groups in the polyesters. His coworkers were not convinced of the need to continue research in this field. One of them gave an internal report in which he noticed that the polyurethanes were "only suitable as imitation of emmentaler cheese." This report also came to the headquarters in

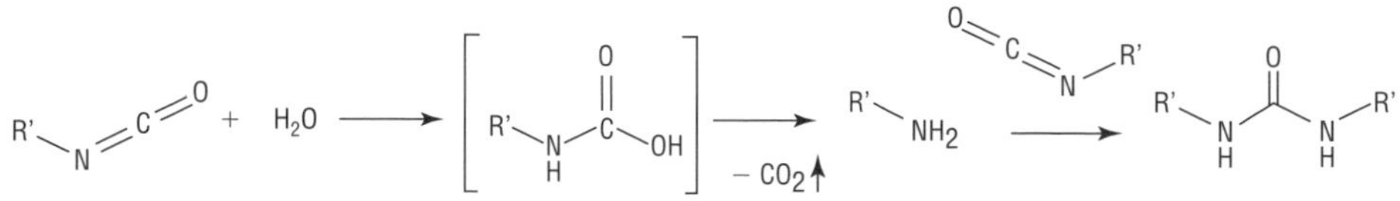

Figure 2.

Frankfurt, where the board of directors were in doubt whether it was a good decision to charge Bayer with the direction of the laboratory in Leverkusen. In addition Paul Schlack invented in 1938 the polymerisation of caprolactam to yield polyamide 6 at IG Farben. The development of this polymer was by far more promising than the polyurethanes. But Bayer's insistence and patience was crowned with success: The disadvantage of generating bubbles in cast elastomers was converted into an advantage of making foams that resulted in the triumph of polyurethanes of the twenty-first century.

Water adds to the isocyanate group yielding an instable carbamic acid. The reaction of the resulting amine with excess isocyanate leads to the positive effect of increasing the molecular weights. Therefore, it was just a matter of dosing the components correctly to prepare polyurethane foams. The final product is a polyurethane with urea groups in the backbone.

Consequently the first PUR-foam products were produced in 1943–1944. Prototypes made from PUR-foam under the external skin of phenolic-resin impregnated paper—the so-called "parts of a sandwich" were used as propeller blades, landing flaps, snow-skids for military equipment, and soles of soldiers' boots.

The higher prices of the products when compared with a rubber mixture or rubber latex were compensated for by better mechanical properties and a very fast method of preparation without heating.

This completely new family of polyurethane foams succeeded in the mattress as well as in the upholstery market, and closed-cell rigid foams entered the market in application areas like refrigerators and insulation. The real breakthrough of this new chemistry came in the 1950s when tailor-made machines and processing technology became industrially available. The variety made the principle of the isocyanate polyaddition reaction surpass the possibilities offered by the polymerization of vinyl monomers and dienes.

Surprisingly, much better products were obtained when exclusively bifunctional building blocks such as polyesterdiol, 1,4-butanediol, and diisocyanates were used. These new polyurethane elastomers, known as Vulkollan, were unusual in their preparation as well as in

their properties: They were prepared directly from the starting components by pouring them into molds, and they had a high tensile strength, a high modulus, and a high resistance to tear and abrasion that had never been observed before. Also, they were unusually resistant to ozone, oxygen, gasoline, oil, and solvents.

Polyurethanes are also used to protect and design surfaces, as with textile coatings and leather finishes. For a long time, solvents were necessary for applications where low viscosities were essential, but Bayer suggested, during the early 1960s, the development of aqueous polyurethane systems by the incorporation of ionic groups. Because of this suggestion, polyurethane ionomers were generated, and a new class of aqueous dispersions was established that could be prepared without the use of emulsifiers and high sheer forces. Together with powders and high solids products (solutions polymers with more than 60 percent of a polymer), aqueous polyurethanes are used as anti-shrink treatments of wool, glue, coatings for paper, glass fiber sizings, plasticizers for gelatin used in photographic applications, thin-walled materials through dip coagulation, tanning agents, and dyestuff additives.

In 1947, Bayer wrote the first review on his research in polyurethane chemistry, "Das Di-Isocyanat-Polyadditionsverfahren (Polyurethane)," in *Angewandte Chemie*. It covered the results from 1937 to 1945.

Acrylonitril Fibers and Other Products. Otto Bayer had other notable accomplishments besides inventing the polyurethane chemistry and many di- and polyisocyanates and the corresponding diols and polyols. He also was engaged in other fields of polymers research. Of great economic importance was the direct synthesis of acrylonitrile from acetylene and hydrocyanic acid, a synthesis discovered by Bayer and Peter Kurtz at Leverkusen about 1940. This was important for the production of polyacrylnitril (PAN) fibers. In 1941, Herbert Reim of the IG Farben works at Wolfen found a solvent from which acrylnitril could be spun to PAN fibers. As a result, the direct synthesis of acrylnitril was begun on a large scale in Leverkusen during 1942. It resulted in a substantial reduction in the price of acrylonitrile. Subsequently, acrylonitrile was considered for a wide variety of polymer synthesis. Without it, the inexpensive technical production of the oil-resistant acrylonitrile butadiene rubber Perbunan since 1942, and later, in 1954, the polyacrylonitrile fiber Dralon would not have been possible.

Bayer was also engaged in research on active ingredients for pharmaceuticals, pesticides, and other final products. Under his leadership the central research laboratory evolved into a research institution that began step-by-step to cover all areas of technical organic chemistry. Under Bayer's leadership, his laboratory developed several new drugs against tuberculosis, a particular typeof cancer, and infections.

In the 1930s, Bayer proposed the phosphoric acid esters as a new class of insecticides. As hydrofluoric acid became readily available, he asked his co-worker Gerhard Schrader to synthesize acid fluorides. Alkylsulfonyl fluorides proved to be highly active but too volatile. Phosphoric acid difluorides were recognized as insecticides. In December 1936, phosphoric acid ester amide cyanides, the first widely effective compounds, were introduced into the market. General use in agriculture, however, was questionable due to the high toxicity for warm-blooded animals. Schrader was able to make a breakthrough for the insecticidal phosphoric compounds that resulted in worldwide applications and great commercial success, as with E 605.

Promotions, Honors, and Awards. In 1951, Otto Bayer became a member of the Board of Management of the newly created Farbenfabriken Bayer AG. He held this post until 1961, when he was appointed a member of the Supervisory Board. From 1964 to 1967, he acted as a chairman of the Supervisory Board. In these different roles his influence on decisions of the Board of Management was great, and he played a decisive part in shaping the fate of Bayer AG for decades to come.

Especially during the years when Bayer was a captain of industry, he received many honors and awards. Four universities and two technical universities presented him with an honorary doctorate, and many highly regarded scientific committees named him as a member, including the Gesellschaft Deutscher Chemiker, Frankfurt/Main, of which he was a co-founder in 1950; the Deutsche Forschungsrat, Bonn, the Akademie der Wissenschaften und der Literatur, Mainz, the Rheinisch-Westfälische Akademie der Wissenschaften, Düsseldorf; the Chemists' Club of New York; and the Max Planck Gesellschaft, Munich, to which he belonged as senator for ten years.

He received many medals and prizes. They include the Adolf von Baeyer Memorial Medal of the Gesellschaft Deutscher Chemiker (1951); the Gauss-Weber Medal of the University of Göttingen (1952); the Siemens Ring of the Werner von Siemens Foundation (1960), along with Walter Reppe and Karl Ziegler; the Hermann-Staudinger Prize of the Gesellschaft Deutscher Chemiker (1973); the Carl Dietrich Harries Plaque of the Deutsche Kautschuk Gesellschaft (German Rubber Society); and the Charles Goodyear Medal of the American Chemical Society (1975).

After Otto Bayer's death, the family fortune of Otto and Lonny Bayer became the capital stock of two foundations. The Otto Bayer Foundation awards outstanding university professors with the Otto Bayer Prize. The Otto and Lonny Bayer Foundation helps those facing social hardships.

Bayer believed in the synergy between basic research in chemistry and industrial development; he wanted to help again with as little bureaucracy as possible. The grant for assistant professors (Dozentenstipendium) of the Fonds des Verbands der Chemischen Industrie created by his recommendation became one of the most valued distinctions among young professionals.

BIBLIOGRAPHY

Some unpublished documents are stored in the Bayer Archive, 51368 Leverkusen, Germany, Building C 302. The best bibliographical source is the paper by Büchel et al, cited below.

WORKS BY BAYER

With Julius von Braun and Georg Blessing. "Katalytische Hydrierungen unter Druck bei Gegenwart von Nickelsalzen, VIII: Verbindungen der Indol-Reihe." *Berichte der Deutschen Chemischen Gesellschaft* 57 (1924): 392–403.

With Julius von Braun. "Zur Kenntnis der katalytischen Hydrierung von Indolbasen." *Berichte der Deutschen Chemischen Gesellschaft* 58 (1925): 387–393

With Georg Kalischer. " Verfahren Zur Herstellung Von Effektfäden Aus Baumwollenen Oder Anderen Pflanzlichen Fasern." (*Deutsches Reichspatent 496321* [6 Sept 1927]) [Chem. Zentralbl. 1931, Ii 2223 R].

"Polyurethanes." *Modern Plastics* 24, no. 10 (1947): 149–152, 250, 252, 254, 256, 260, 262.

"Das Di-Isocyanat-Polyadditionsverfahren (Polyurethane)." *Angewandte Chemie* 59 (1947): 257–288.

With Otto Hecht, Hugo Kroeper, Otto Roelen, et al. "Aliphatic Compounds." *FIAT Reviews of German Science, 1939–1946,* Volume on Preparative Organic Chemistry, Part I, 1948, 1–209. Published by the Office of Military Government for Germany, Wiesbaden.

With Wilhelm Becker, Georg Jayme, Walter Kern, et al. "Organic Compounds of High Molecular Weight." *FIAT Reviews of German Science, 1939–1946*, Volume on Preparative Organic Chemistry, Part III, 1948, 1–352. Published by the Office of Military Government For Germany, Wiesbaden.

"Die Chemie des Acrylnitrils." *Angewandte Chemie* 61 (1949): 229–241.

With Erwin Mueller, Siegfried Petersen, Hans-Frank
Piepenbrink, et al. "New Types of Highly Elastic Substances.
Vulcollans." *Angewandte Chemie* 62 (1950): 57–66.

With Erwin Mueller, Siegfried Petersen, Hans-Frank
Piepenbrink et al. "Polyurethans. IX. New Types of Highly
Elastic Products: Vulcollans (2)." *Angewandte Chemie* 64
(1952): 523–531.

"Neuere Entwicklungen des Diisocyanat-Polyadditions-
Verfahrens (Polyurethane)." *Farbe und Lack* 64 (1958):
235–241.

"Zur Entwicklung und Problematik des organischen
Makromolekuels." *Angewandte Chemie* 71 (1959): 145–152.

With Erwin Mueller. "Das Aufbauprinzip der Urethan-
Elastomeren 'Vulkollan.'" *Angewandte Chemie* 72 (1960):
934–939.

With Heinrich Gold and Siegfried Petersen. "Fluorescent
Brightening Agents of the Triazole Series." In *Recent Progress
in the Chemistry of Natural, and Synthetic Colouring Matters
and Related Fields*, edited by T. S. Gore et al. New York:
Academic Press, 1962.

Das Diisocyanat-Polyadditionsverfahren. Munich, Germany: Carl
Hanser Verlag, 1963.

*Die Rolle des Zufalls in der organischen Chemie: Ansprache des
Ministerpräsidenten Dr. Franz Meyers.* Cologne, Germany:
Westdeutscher Verlag, 1964.

OTHER SOURCES

Buechel, Karl Heinz, Hanna Soell, Dieter Arlt et al. "Otto Bayer
1902–1982." *Chemische Berichte* 120 (1987): xxi–xxxv.

Morawetz, Herbert. *Polymers: The Origins and Growth of a
Science.* 1985. Repr., New York: Dover, 1995.

Tschimmel, Udo. *Die Zehntausend-Dollar-Idee: Kunststoff-
Geschichte vom Zelluloid zum Superchip.* Düsseldorf,
Germany: Econ Verlag, 1989.

Vieweg, Richard, and A. Höchtlen, eds. *Kunststoff-Handbuch.*
Vol. 7, *Polyurethane.* Munich, Germany: Hanser, 1966.

Gerhard Heywang

BAYES, THOMAS (*b.* Bovingdon, Hertford-
shire[?], England, 1702; *d.* Tunbridge Wells, Kent, England, 7 April 1761), *probability.* For the original article on
Bayes see *DSB,* vol. 1.

Bayes is rightly remembered chiefly for his work on
the determination of the support for a statistical hypothesis provided by experimental data (or, on the determination of the probability of a cause from knowledge of an
observed occurrence). However, he also provided results
concerning the approximation of the skew beta distribution, the series expansion of log *z!*, and (with Richard
Price) a series expansion of the Normal probability
integral.

Genealogy. The eldest of the seven children of Joshua
(who was *not* a Fellow of the Royal Society) and Anne (née
Carpenter) Bayes, Thomas might well have been born in
Bovingdon, near Hemel Hempstead in Hertfordshire.
William Urwick (1884, p. 390) states that Joshua Bayes
ministered at the Box Lane Chapel, in Bovingdon, after
his ordination (in 1694), and remained there for about
eleven years before returning to London. There he became
an assistant to John Sheffield at St. Thomas's, Southwark,
and he subsequently officiated at the dissenting chapel in
Leather Lane in Hatton Gardens. Here Thomas later
assisted him, before moving to Tunbridge Wells in the
early 1730s.

Education. While it is uncertain where Thomas received
his early education, there is no doubt that he later studied
at Edinburgh University. The records of that institution
for 1719 (Scottish style) show that Thomas was admitted
on the nineteenth of February, and his name is also
recorded in the *List of Theologues in the College of Edinburgh since October 1711.* Like many intending to become
Nonconformist ministers, he did not take the MA degree,
and returned to London licensed but not ordained.

The certificate detailing Bayes's admission to the university library was signed by James Gregory, brother of the
Scottish mathematician and astronomer David Gregory,
his immediate predecessor in the chair of mathematics,
and nephew of the illustrious James Gregory
(1638–1675). David Gregory has been credited with the
introduction of Isaac Newton's *Principia* to Edinburgh
students, and it is possible that his brother James continued with this practice. Thus Bayes might have been
exposed to the fluxionary calculus, and this could well
have accounted for the precision and understanding
evinced in his *Introduction to the Doctrine of Fluxions.*

Works. In his *Divine Benevolence* Bayes argued that the
works of God are inspired and motivated by benevolence,
contra the view expressed in John Balguy's earlier tract
that rectitude was the guiding principle. Subsequently
Henry Grove saw wisdom as God's most fundamental
attribute. All three of these tracts were studied at dissenting academies of that period.

In addition to *An Essay towards Solving a Problem in
the Doctrine of Chances,* volume 53 of the *Philosophical
Transactions of the Royal Society* contains a *Letter* from
Bayes on a semiconvergent series. Here he showed that the
well-known James Stirling–Abraham de Moivre series
"for" log *z!* in fact diverges for any *z* (the divergence for
z = 1 had been shown by the Swiss mathematician Leonhard Euler some six years before Bayes's death).

On the matter of the scholium in the *Essay,* Stephen
M. Stigler interprets Bayes as showing that, for the

balls-and-table example, $Prob(M=p)=1/(n+1)$ for $p=0,$ $1, \ldots ,n,$ a characterization of the uniform distribution on $[0,1]$ due to Bayes. Suppose next that we have an event (say E) of whose probability (say 0) we are ignorant. Because the probability that E occurs p times in n trials is also $1/(n+1)$, 0 must again be uniformly distributed. That is, that 0 has a uniform distribution is implied by the constancy of $Prob(E=p)$. When the scholium is viewed in this way, the problems sometimes thought to arise from the apparently arbitrary choice of a uniform prior disappear.

The *Essay* was followed by a *Supplement*, partly by Richard Price, published in volume 54 of the *Philosophical Transactions*. In addition to Bayes's famous result, these two papers contain, in the rules, an approximation to the two-sided beta probability integral that is considerably better than the Normal approximation (in essence, the skew beta probability density function, obtained by Bayes as a posterior density, is approximated by a symmetric beta probability function multiplied by a factor tending in the limit to 1, the two betas having the same maximum and points of inflexion). Also to be found in the *Supplement* is a series expansion, by Price, of the Normal approximation to the posterior distribution derived in the *Essay*.

In the library of the Royal Society of London is a letter from Bayes to John Canton commenting on work by Thomas Simpson on errors in observations. Bayes's view was that an increase in the number of observations will not cause a decrease in the probability of error if the measuring device is inaccurate. With this is connected Simpson's assumption that errors in excess and in defect of the true value are equally probable.

A serendipitous find by David R. Bellhouse in the Kent County Archives in Maidstone, U.K., suggests that Bayes might well have been used by Philip Stanhope, 2nd Earl Stanhope, as a mathematical critic and commentator. Bellhouse discovered several items in the Stanhope Collection: (1) preliminary drafts of Bayes's paper on series; (2) a derivation, in Bayes's hand, of the series for log z! that does not use the semiconvergent series; and (3) letters between Bayes and Stanhope, supportive of the above suggestion, referring to some observations by Patrick Murdoch. There is also a note, in Stanhope's writing, headed "The Reverend Mr Bayes's Paper concerning Trinomial divisors."

The Equitable Life Assurance Society in London holds a notebook by Bayes. With passages in French, Latin, English, and an obscure seventeenth-century shorthand, the notebook contains notes on matters as diverse as mathematics, electricity, optics, and music.

Death. Although giving up his ministry in 1752, Bayes probably remained in Tunbridge Wells, where he died in 1761, being interred in the family vault in the Bunhill

Fields Burial Ground, near Moorgate, London. Despite frequent restorations of the vault, the inscriptions have at times been difficult to decipher. This is perhaps the reason for the Canadian philosopher Ian Hacking's recording of Thomas's death as the seventeenth, rather than the seventh, of April.

SUPPLEMENTARY BIBLIOGRAPHY

Bellhouse, David R. "On Some Recently Discovered Manuscripts of Thomas Bayes." *Historia Mathematica* 29, no. 4 (2002): 383–394.

———. "The Reverend Thomas Bayes, F.R.S.: A Biography to Celebrate the Tercentenary of His Birth." *Statistical Science* 19, no. 1 (2004): 3–43.

Dale, Andrew I. *Most Honourable Remembrance: The Life and Work of Thomas Bayes.* New York: Springer-Verlag, 2003. Reprints of and commentaries on Bayes's works.

Grant, Alexander. *The Story of the University of Edinburgh during Its First Three Hundred Years.* 2 vols. London: Longmans, Green, 1884.

Hald, Anders. *A History of Mathematical Statistics from 1750 to 1930.* New York: Wiley, 1998.

Stigler, Stephen M. "Thomas Bayes's Bayesian Inference." *Journal of the Royal Statistical Society*, ser. A, 145, pt. 2 (1982): 250–258.

Urwick, William. *Nonconformity in Herts: Being Lectures upon the Nonconforming Worthies of St. Albans, and Memorials of Puritanism and Nonconformity in all the Parishes of the County of Hertford.* London: Hazell, Watson, and Viney, 1884.

Andrew I. Dale

BEACH, FRANK AMBROSE, JR. (*b.* Emporia, Kansas, 13 April 1911; *d.* Berkeley, California, 15 June 1988), *psychology, behavioral endocrinology, animal behavior, ethology.*

Beach was a comparative and physiological psychologist of the first order. Along with William C. Young, he was responsible for establishing the field of behavioral endocrinology—the study of hormones and behavior. He has been called the "conscience of comparative psychology" because of his influence in directing those psychologists studying animals toward working on a wide variety of behavioral patterns in a wide variety of species. Further, he worked to establish the study of sexual behavior as a valid, scientific enterprise.

Biographical Information. Frank Beach's father was a professor and head of the music department at the Kansas State Teachers College in Emporia, later Emporia State University. Young Frank, who rarely used the "Jr.," attended both the Teachers College and Antioch College, receiving his BS degree in education from the former in 1932. Unable to find a job during the Depression, he stayed on to complete an MS degree in psychology with a thesis on the question of color vision in rats. He continued graduate study at the University of Chicago, where he was influenced by such scientists as Harvey Carr, Karl Lashley, Paul Weiss, and C. Judson Herrick. Beach found Lashley's disciplined, yet nondirective, approach appealing. Financial difficulties led him to leave Chicago for a year to teach high school English at Yates Center, Kansas. On his return to Chicago, he found that Lashley had moved on to Harvard University, but Carr was receptive to a dissertation on the effects of lesions to the cerebral cortex on the maternal behavior of rats. Beach completed his dissertation work in one additional year but a difficulty in completing the requirement in German delayed his PhD degree until 1940.

For 1936 and 1937, Lashley hired him as an assistant in neuropsychology at Harvard, where he studied the effects of brain lesions on copulatory behavior in rats. Beach then moved to the Department of Experimental Biology at the American Museum of Natural History in New York City. Upon the death of his department chair, G. Kingsley Noble, in 1940, Beach took the lead in saving the department from extinction. He became a full curator and renamed his unit the Department of Animal Behavior.

In 1946, Beach moved on to the psychology department at Yale University; he was named a Sterling Professor in 1952. He spent 1957 and 1958 as a fellow at the Center for Advanced Study in the Behavioral Sciences at Stanford University. He then became a professor of psychology at the University of California, Berkeley in 1958, retiring to the status as professor emeritus twenty years later. He continued active in the field during his retirement.

After a failed first marriage, Beach married Anna Beth Odenweller, a theater student in Chicago, in March 1936. They had two children: Frank A. Beach III, born in 1937, and Susan Elizabeth, born in 1942. Anna Beth died in 1971, and Beach later married Noel Gaustad.

Beach was elected president of the Eastern Psychological Association in 1951, the Western Psychological Association in 1968, the Division of Experimental Psychology of the American Psychological Association in 1949, and the International Academy of Sex Research in 1977. He served as a charter member of the psychobiology panel of the National Science Foundation. In 1955, he joined the National Research Council Committee for the Study of Problems of Sex; he became the committee's chair two years later. He also served on the Publications Board and Policy and Planning Board of the American Psychological Association, the Advisory Board of the Marine Studios

and Marine Research Laboratory in St. Augustine, Florida, and on the Board of Scientific Directions of the Roscoe B. Jackson Memorial Laboratory in Bar Harbor, Maine.

He was elected a member of the American Philosophical Society, the American Academy of Arts and Sciences, and the National Academy of Sciences, the latter at the age of 38. Beach received the Warren Medal of the Society of Experimental Psychologists, the Distinguished Scientific Contribution Award of the American Psychological Association, and honorary doctorates from McGill University, Williams College, and Emporia State University. The Frank A. Beach Award and Lectureship, designed to reward and encourage young scientists in behavioral endocrinology, was established in 1990. The lectures are published annually in the journal *Hormones and Behavior.*

Development of Scientific Contributions. Late in life, Beach could not recall how he first got interested in animal research. Because there was no relevant instruction at the Teachers College, he believed that it must have been through reading. As the department could offer neither instruction nor facilities, he had to develop apparatus and techniques on his own. In his research he concluded that rats are color blind.

At Chicago, Lashley's permissive style allowed Beach the freedom he needed to explore problems of interest to him. Further, Lashley's areas of primary interest coincided well with Beach's. With Lashley gone when he returned to Chicago, Beach again had to rely on his own skills, and those of fellow students, to complete his dissertation research. In his halcyon year at Harvard, Beach was able to mature his skills under Lashley's tutorage.

At Harvard, Beach found that cortical lesions led to a loss of copulatory behavior in rats. A colleague there suggested that the deficit might be secondary to damage to the endocrine system. While at the American Museum, Beach audited a course in endocrinology at New York University. This was an important event. Finding that there was little information on endocrinological influences on behavior, Beach decided to gather what information he could find and published his first book, *Hormones and Behavior* (1948). This was the first comprehensive review of information on this important topic. He began active research on the effects of hormones on mating behavior during this period. His interest in the interaction of hormones and behavior remained with him the rest of his life; he conducted many experiments and wrote many papers. These included a 1975 article on the status of the field and a historical review of the field (1981). In 1979, Beach, along with Julian Davidson and Richard Whalen, founded the field's first, and foremost, journal, *Hormones and Behavior.*

Exposure to the biologists at the museum helped to direct Beach's interest toward an evolutionarily based animal psychology. He became an early supporter of the research of the European ethologists and helped to promote in the United States the ethological approach toward naturally occurring behavioral patterns and their evolutionary significance. He served on the first editorial board of the ethological journal, *Behaviour.*

In New York and New Haven, Beach began to expand his comparative base. In 1948, having already worked on rats, hamsters, cats, alligators, pigeons, and pouchless marsupials, *Marmosa cinera,* he instituted a research program on dogs, an emphasis that would occupy him for much of the rest of his career. He further expanded his horizons into human sexuality, collaborating on a 1951 book, *Patterns of Sexual Behavior,* with anthropologist Clellan S. Ford. The book dealt with both the evolution of mammalian behavior and cultural variations in humans.

The warm climate and sympathetic atmosphere of Berkeley appealed to Beach and he flourished there. He founded the Field Research Station for Behavioral Research there, which allowed him to continue and expand his interest in hormones and social and sexual behavior in dogs. From 1985 into the early 2000s, the facility was used for a major research program on hormones and behavior in spotted hyenas, a program in which Beach participated during his last years.

As his interest in sexual behavior continued to develop, Beach hosted two important conferences in which he brought together scholars from a variety of disciplines in 1961 and 1962. The edited volume *Sex and Behavior* resulted from these conferences. He was able to facilitate communication among researchers interested in sexual behavior from a variety of disciplinary perspectives. On the occasion of his sixty-fifth birthday, former students and postdoctoral fellows held an honorary conference in Berkeley. This event resulted in a sequel, *Sex and Behavior: Status and Prospectus.*

Having eschewed major teaching commitments during much of his career, Beach increased his undergraduate teaching in his later years. In addition to courses in comparative psychology, he taught an experimentally oriented class in human sexuality. He was so highly regarded that he was awarded the American Psychological Association's Award for Distinguished Teaching in Biopsychology in 1985. As a result of his experience teaching courses in human sexuality, he published yet another book, *Human Sexuality in Four Perspectives* (1976).

Characteristics of His Work. Beach remained a Midwestern, hard-nosed empiricist throughout his career. His studies were conducted without elaborate equipment or complex mathematical analyses. Following in Lashley's footsteps, he believed in simple, straightforward experiments that would uncover significant phenomena that would be apparent to the naked eye. By early twenty-first century standards, some of the methodology was a bit crude. Nevertheless, he was able to make some important findings.

As important as were his empirical studies, his integrative articles were even more significant. Beach had a knack for sensing either cutting-edge trends in his field or the need to bring together information that could alter the course of research. He not only wrote timely and insightful articles, but titled them in such a way as to make them stand out and have impact. His contributions in this area are remarkable.

His early integrative papers were reviews of material primarily on the brain mechanisms of reproductive behavior. Beach proposed that both the hormonal milieu and proper stimulus input were essential for the display of mating behavior. He believed that hormones played a greater role in the so-called lower vertebrates than in mammals and in females of most species than in males. He thought that stimuli in the various modalities summed to facilitate the occurrence of sexual activity.

A classic integrative article was his 1950 "The Snark Was a Boojum." Beach believed that comparative psychology had begun early in the twentieth century as the study of a broad range of behavioral patterns in a wide range of species but had lost this breadth. He presented data to suggest this trend and emphasized his point with a cartoon of a white rat as the Pied Piper of Hamelin leading animal psychologists down an unproductive path. He advocated a return to the earlier breadth. Beach followed this up with "Experimental Investigations of Species-Specific Behavior" (1960), in which he made the case for a decreased emphasis on the study of learning in animal psychology.

In "The Descent of Instinct" (1955), he traced the history of the instinct concept and delineated the difficulties of applying it to animal behavior and discussed the difficulties with the nature-nurture dichotomy. He believed that the development of behavior reflected the interactive influences of both genes and environment. Beach thought that once behavioral patterns had been carefully analyzed, there would be no need for a category such as "instinct." With Julian Jaynes, he reviewed literature on the effects of early experience on later behavior (1954); in another article (1945), he reviewed the information then available about play in animals.

Under the title "Locks and Beagles" (1969), Beach summarized his research on sexual behavior in dogs, whose copulatory pattern features a lock, or mechanical tie, between male and female. He found sexual behavior in dogs to be less closely tied to hormones than in rats. For example, individual preferences play a key role.

Early in his career, Beach expressed many of the masculine biases typical of his generation. However, as the culture changed, so did he, and he came to welcome and encourage women in his laboratory. He sensed that the study of reproductive behavior in mammals had been biased by a sexist perspective, and he realized that females often took a more active role in sex than had been recognized by many scientists. In a remarkable paper, "Sexual Attractivity, Proceptivity, and Receptivity in Female Mammals" (1976), Beach delineated three aspects of female sexual behavior: their attractiveness to males, their receptivity to sex, and, most importantly, their appetitive component in actively soliciting mating. The latter component referred to this active role and altered the emphasis in the field. The paper opened up the broad nature of sexuality in female mammals to more realistic investigation. Beach was always careful in categorizing behavior into functional classes, such as "sexual" or "aggressive." The same motor pattern might function in several different motivational contexts. He was equally cautious in generalizing both terminology and results back and forth between humans and other species.

Beach was less successful in "Hormonal Factors Controlling the Differentiation, Development, and Display of Copulatory Behavior in the Ramstergig and Related Species" (1971). This was published as research on the role of early hormones on adult mating patterns was coming into prevalence. The "ramstergig" was a hypothetical species satirically alleged to display characteristics of rats, hamsters, and guinea pigs. The prevailing interpretation, not yet supported by definitive evidence, was that the hormones organized the parts of the nervous system that controlled mating behavior. Although this proved to be largely accurate, and Beach misguided in his critique, his classic paper forced the reevaluation of the research and directed it toward the more satisfactory interpretations. These and other integrative articles both helped to coalesce developing trends and to direct research into productive areas.

Personally, Beach was an extroverted and friendly man; indeed, he has been called earthy. He was equally at home discussing the fine points of the English language and beating students in darts or pool. He was conservative in many ways, but he did not ask his students to follow him. This was especially apparent during the period of political activity on the Berkeley campus during the 1960s. Beach took federal funding reluctantly and preached the importance of responsible spending of such monies. He believed that scientists must communicate their findings in order to justify the work. His background as an English teacher made him both a persuasive author

and a tough, but effective, mentor on the writing styles of his students. His style was clear and straightforward. Sachs (1988) wrote that "lively debate was spiced by Frank's ample wit and rapier-like turns of phrase, which could, with a stroke, deflate pomposity or uncover poor preparation" (p. 312).

Beach was the embodiment of the scientist as a seeker of truth. He loved to discuss and debate scientific issues of the time. He rarely let his ego get in the way. He would applaud if an earlier finding of his was superceded by new and better research. However, Beach would insist that his work and conclusions were reasonable given the state of knowledge when it had been done. He was a firm believer in the importance of basic research. The job of the scientist, he thought, was to discover new knowledge. He left it up to the broader society to determine how to apply that knowledge. He had faith that it would be for human betterment.

Beach bemoaned the emphasis in psychology upon methodology. He believed that much research was conducted with first-rate methodology but without clear purpose. He believed that much of the research published in journals was worthless. He was fond of saying that if research is not worth doing, it is not worth doing well. He believed in progress in science—but only if research is conducted with clear purpose.

Frank Beach was among the very most important comparative and physiological psychologists of the twentieth century. He conducted groundbreaking research, helped to direct the field of psychobiology, and served as an effective mentor and sometime administrator.

BIBLIOGRAPHY

WORKS BY BEACH

"Central Nervous Mechanisms Involved in the Reproductive Behavior of Vertebrates." *Psychological Bulletin* 39 (1942): 200–226.

"Current Conceptions of Play in Animals." *American Naturalist* 79 (1945): 523–541.

"Evolutionary Changes in the Physiological Control of Mating Behavior in Mammals." *Psychological Review* 54 (1947): 297–315.

Hormones and Behavior. New York: Hoeber, 1948.

"The Snark Was a Boojum." *American Psychologist* 5 (1950): 115–124.

With Clellan Ford. *Patterns of Sexual Behavior*. New York: Harper, 1951.

With Julian Jaynes. "Effects of Early Experience upon the Behavior of Animals." *Psychological Bulletin* 51 (1954): 239–263.

"The Descent of Instinct." *Psychological Review* 62 (1955): 401–410.

"Experimental Investigations of Species-Specific Behavior."
American Psychologist 15 (1960): 1–18.

Sex and Behavior. New York: Wiley, 1965.

"Locks and Beagles." *American Psychologist* 24 (1969): 971–989.

"Hormonal Factors Controlling the Differentiation,
Development, and Display of Copulatory Behavior in the
Ramstergig and Related Species." In *Biopsychology of
Development*, edited by Lester R. Aronson and Ethel Tobach.
New York: Academic Press, 1971.

"Frank A. Beach." In *A History of Psychology in Autobiography*,
vol. 7, edited by Gardner Lindzey. Englewood Cliffs, NJ:
Prentice-Hall, 1974.

"Behavioral Endocrinology: An Emerging Discipline." *American
Scientist* 63 (1975): 178–187.

"Sexual Attractivity, Proceptivity, and Receptivity in Female
Mammals." *Hormones and Behavior* 7 (1976): 105–138.

Human Sexuality in Four Perspectives. Baltimore, MD: Johns
Hopkins University Press, 1977.

"Confessions of an Imposter." In *Pioneers in Neuroendocrinology*,
vol. 2, edited by J. Meites, B. T. Donovan, and S. M.
McCann. New York: Plenum, 1978.

"Historical Origins of Modern Research on Hormones and
Behavior." *Hormones and Behavior* 15 (1981): 325–376.

OTHER SOURCES

Dewsbury, Donald A. "Frank Ambrose Beach 1911–1988."
American Journal of Psychology 102 (1989): 414–420.

———. "Frank A. Beach." *Biographical Memoirs,* vol. 73.
Washington, DC: National Academy of Sciences, 1997.

———. "Frank A. Beach, Master Teacher." In *Portraits of
Pioneers in Psychology*, vol. 4, edited by Gregory A. Kimble
and Michael Wertheimer. Washington, DC: American
Psychological Association, 2000.

Fleming, Joyce D., and David Maxey. "The Drive of the Pure
Researcher: Pursuit of Intellectual Orgasm." *Psychology Today*
8, no. 10 (1975): 68–77.

Glickman, Stephen E., and Irving Zucker. "Frank A. Beach
(1911–1988)." *American Psychologist* 44 (1989): 1234–1235.

McGill, Thomas E., Donald A. Dewsbury, and Benjamin D.
Sachs, eds. *Sex and Behavior: Status and Prospectus*. New York:
Plenum, 1978.

Sachs, Benjamin D. "In Memoriam: Frank Ambrose Beach."
Psychobiology 16 (1988): 312–314.

Whalen, Richard E., et al. "In Memoriam Frank A. Beach (April
13, 1911–June 15, 1988)." *Hormones and Behavior* 22
(1988): 419–443. Eleven brief articles by various authors.

Donald Dewsbury

BEADLE, GEORGE WELLS (*b.* Wahoo,
Nebraska, 22 October 1903; *d.* Pomona, California, 9
June 1989), *classical genetics, molecular genetics, plant biology, academic administration.*

Beadle's principal scientific discovery, for which he
received the 1958 Nobel Prize in Physiology or Medicine,
was the demonstration in 1941 that the primary role of
genes is to specify the production of proteins. That
insight, which was initially termed one gene–one enzyme
(and came to be expressed as one gene–one polypeptide)
transformed genetics from its classical mode, the abstract
analysis of the patterns and mechanisms of inheritance,
into a molecular science concerned with how genes act to
create traits. He went on to become an effective science
administrator, a university president, and a key science
adviser to the federal government.

Early Life. A prominent sign posted on the road leading
to Wahoo, a small town in the southeastern part of
Nebraska, proclaims the names of five famous native sons:
Darryl Zanuck of movie-making fame; Sam Crawford,
elected to the Baseball Hall of Fame; C. W. Anderson,
painter and children's book author and illustrator;
Howard Hanson, composer and orchestra conductor; and
George W. Beadle, Nobel Prize–winning geneticist. While
their accomplishments could not have been more different, each in his own way reflected the history, culture, and
values of Wahoo in the early twentieth century. Wahoo's
citizens, and especially Beadle's father, adhered to notions
of independence, individual initiative, and hard work.

Beets (a nickname Beadle acquired as a boy and was
used by his friends and family throughout his life) was
born on a forty-acre family farm on the outskirts of
Wahoo. He was the family's second son and was followed
by a sister. The death of his mother in 1908 and his
brother in 1913 and the inadequate attention of surro-
gates imposed substantial responsibilities on Beets for
helping his father work the farm and raising his younger
sister. Throughout high school it was his and his father's
expectation that he would take over the family farm. But
it did not take long for a young high school science
teacher, Bess McDonald, to recognize Beadle's intelligence
and promise and to encourage him, against the wishes of
his father, to continue his education at the University of
Nebraska in nearby Lincoln.

Education. The Nebraska College of Agriculture had an
outstanding reputation in plant sciences and Beadle
thrived there, garnering academic honors and bachelor's
(1926) and master's (1927) degrees. More important for
his future, however, one of his professors, Franklin D.
Keim, engaged Beadle in research and then convinced
him to do graduate work at the College of Agriculture at
Cornell University. Becoming a scientist supplanted his
early aim to return to the family farm. Nevertheless, he
never abandoned a lifetime interest in agriculture and no
matter how busy his life he almost always had a garden.

Arriving in Ithaca in the fall of 1926, Beets soon demonstrated the independence and self-confidence that characterized his entire scientific career. He was dissatisfied with the arrangement Keim had made for him to work with a professor who was an ecologist and switched to the Department of Plant Breeding and Professor Rollins A. Emerson, one of the nation's leading maize geneticists. The individuals that composed Emerson's research group included brilliant young scientists such as Marcus Rhoades, Charles Burnham, and Barbara McClintock, and they were contributing to the steady advance of genetics in innovative ways. Using both classical genetic and novel cytogenetic techniques he learned from McClintock, Beadle investigated several sterile mutants of maize and demonstrated that mutations can affect chromosome behavior at different points during meiosis, the process that yields the sex cells, egg, and pollen. That work, embodied in fourteen published papers, was an original contribution showing that chromosomes themselves are under genetic control and formed the basis for his PhD degree (1930). In 1928, Beadle met and married Californian Marion Hill, a Cornell master's student in botany. Marion and George Beadle's son David was born in December 1931.

The Young Scientist. Beadle's achievements as a PhD student won him a coveted National Research Council Fellowship for postdoctoral work at the California Institute of Technology (1930). At Caltech, Beadle completed his studies of maize mutants and collaborated with his Cornell professors Emerson and Allan Cameron Fraser in a major compendium of maize chromosome maps. Most significantly, he came under the tutelage of Thomas Hunt Morgan's "fly group," which included Alfred Sturtevant, Calvin Bridges, Theodosius Dobzhansky, and Jack Schultz. Beadle mastered the essentials of *Drosophila* (fruit fly) genetics, in the course of which he made seminal observations on the mechanism of crossing-over in meiosis. The lessons Beadle learned from his mentors remained with him, becoming the foundation of his own approach to research and teaching and his relationships with his students, postdoctoral fellows, and colleagues.

While Beadle was still a research fellow at Caltech, his interests took off in a totally new direction: how genes determine the processes of embryonic development. To pursue that problem, he teamed up with Boris Ephrussi, a visiting French embryologist. Together they decided to examine the development of *Drosophila,* specifically its eye pigments. They set out to determine whether embryonic eye buds (called imaginal discs) taken from one larva could develop into eyes if they were transplanted into another larva. Working together in Paris, they produced adult flies with three eyes, two in the normal head position and one in the abdomen. Transplanting eye buds

George Beadle, 1958. © BETTMANN/CORBIS.

from mutants with various unusual eye colors into the abdomens of both mutant and normal flies, Beadle and Ephrussi then observed whether the transplanted eyes were of the normal or of the mutant color. These observations led them to conclude that each different mutation blocked a different step in the formation of eye pigment. Their experiments laid the groundwork for the idea that genes control the sequential order of chemical reactions within the cell.

The Professor. Beadle pursued the *Drosophila* eye color work for several years, first as an assistant professor at Harvard (1936–1937) and then as a tenured professor at Stanford. His hope was that this would lead to an understanding of how genes control particular metabolic reactions in a cell. But finally he concluded that *Drosophila* was not the optimal system for identifying the mechanisms through which genes exert their effect on a cell's chemical reactions. Another approach was needed.

In a flash of brilliant insight early in 1941, Beadle realized that instead of trying to identify the metabolic reactions affected by known mutations, he should better turn the problem around and seek the genes that affect already-known metabolic reactions. It was a bold idea but it needed testing. To pursue that goal he teamed up with Edward Tatum, an American biochemist who had joined

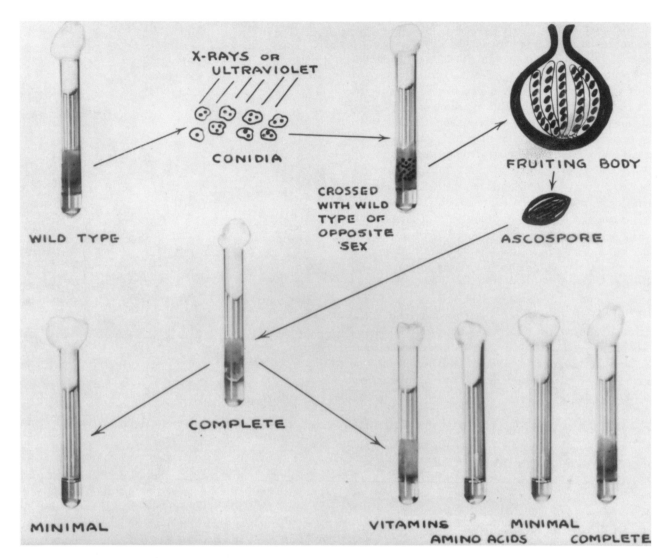

Neurospora drawing by George Beadle. *Beadle drawing illustrating the experiment that led to the 'one gene one enzyme' hypothesis. To obtain Neurospora mutants with nutritional deficiencies, irradiated wild-type spores were germinated and crossed with un-irradiated wild type organisms. The resulting spores were tested for growth on minimal and complete medium. Those that grew on complete but not on minimal medium were tested for growth with various supplements; in this example the mutant grows with a supplement of vitamins.* **COURTESY OF THE ARCHIVES, CALIFORNIA INSTITUTE OF TECHNOLOGY.**

his research group shortly after Beadle arrived at Stanford in 1937.

They decided that *Neurospora crassa*, a fungus that often covers rotting vegetation, was an ideal organism for testing the strategy. Its genetic system was well characterized, and it needed only minimal nutritional supplements to grow. The plan was to induce mutations in *Neurospora* spores and to determine if the sprouting cells were still able to grow in a minimal culture medium. Those isolates that were unable to grow were presumed to be deficient in their ability to make a required metabolite. To determine what function was affected, many normal metabolites were added first in groups and then singly to the minimal

culture medium to determine if they were able to restore cell growth. Within only a few months, Beadle and Tatum discovered and isolated many *Neurospora* strains bearing mutations affecting a single gene; each of the mutants required a single identified nutritional supplement for growth.

Over the ensuing years, Beadle and Tatum and a large cast of undergraduate and graduate students and postdoctoral fellows isolated many different single mutants, some requiring one or another amino acid, or a vitamin, or one of the constituents of nucleic acids. Based on these experimental findings, they surmised that each mutation affected the organism's ability to make the required amino acid, or the vitamin, or the nucleic acid precursor. Well aware that enzymes, protein catalysts, are responsible for the synthesis of all of these essential metabolites, Beadle and Tatum made the intellectual leap that each mutation affects the ability of a single enzyme to function as a catalyst, in their case to catalyze the formation of the required metabolite. This supposition came to be known as the *one gene–one enzyme hypothesis,* a truly transforming event in the field of genetics.

Initially, however, there was both skepticism and some serious criticism among biologists about the one gene–one enzyme concept. It was difficult for classical geneticists to accept that a mutation in a single gene affected only a single function. It took almost a decade to respond with additional experiments and, with the help of related and consistent observations, to convince the skeptics.

In time, Beadle and Tatum's one gene–one enzyme formulation evolved into one gene–one polypeptide, because many proteins consist of several polypeptides, each the product of a single gene. Lamentably, those scientists who daily depend on Beadle's one gene–one polypeptide formulation rarely know his name. Subsequently it became clear that genes are made of DNA and not proteins, as Beadle tended to believe. Also, it has become clear that many genes encode RNA as well as proteins.

Return to Caltech. In 1946, Beadle accepted the challenge of chairing the biology division at Caltech and abruptly ceased active research. The division needed rebuilding and Beadle's vision was to promote a blending of genetics and biochemistry, the natural extension of his own discovery. That implied a new discipline, chemical genetics or what came to be called molecular genetics. He put his own interests aside in the interests of science and Caltech. Linus Pauling, who chaired Caltech's chemistry division, shared this vision and supported Beadle's recruitment of scientists who would advance these ideas. Beadle's recruits would eventually garner five Nobel Prizes, in addition to his own. Outstanding students and postdoctoral fellows were trained at Caltech in the fifteen years of Beadle's leadership and took the excitement of molecular biology to many institutions throughout the United States.

The Beadles' marriage had grown increasingly troubled after their return to Caltech, and they were divorced in the summer of 1953. Soon after, he married widow Muriel McClure Barnett, the well-known editor of the Women's Section of the *Los Angeles Times,* and adopted Muriel's son, Redmond Barnett.

National Leadership. The 1950s generated many public issues concerning science and scientists. Scientists were sought out for advice and leadership on national policies for science, radioactive fallout, health, and technology.

George Beadle and Alfred Sturtevant at Caltech, 1951.
COURTESY OF THE ARCHIVES, CALIFORNIA INSTITUTE OF TECHNOLOGY.

Beadle, who had a reputation for being thoughtful, non-political, and wise, accepted a full load of these responsibilities. As an individual he also worked, in the early days of the Cold War, to counter the national paranoia concerning scientists who might sympathize with the U.S.S.R. Publicly and privately, he defended those he believed to be falsely accused of disloyalty to the nation, with special attention to close colleagues. When, in the face of such false accusations including a campaign by Senator Joseph McCarthy, the Caltech trustees called for Linus Pauling's dismissal, Beadle spoke up for his colleague. When the U.S. Public Health Service began to rescind grants to suspected communists without a hearing or other elements of due process, he led, with the support of Caltech's trustees, the faculty's successful challenge to the Public Health Service.

In 1955, as president of the American Association for the Advancement of Science, he urged the scientific community, in a strong editorial in *Science* magazine, to protect the integrity of science against government interference and unscientific propaganda. Beadle did believe that the nation's nuclear secrets required protection. However, he objected to government procedures for rooting out security risks and to restrictions on researchers doing unclassified work.

The academic pursuit of genetic research became of immediate public interest in the 1950s because of widespread concern regarding radioactive fallout from atmospheric testing of nuclear weapons. American geneticists were themselves worried when the official statements of the U.S. Atomic Energy Commission tried to calm public fear by claiming that the radiation from fallout was safe. The commission had disregarded or was ignorant of extensive work on the genetic effects of radiation.

Beadle joined a National Research Council study panel, funded by the Rockefeller Foundation, that was charged with explaining the genetic hazards. For five years, eventually as chairman, Beadle participated in this challenging task. The panel members, a who's who of genetics, included Alfred Sturtevant, Sewell Wright, Milislav Demerec, and Herman J. Muller, who had won a Nobel Prize for the discovery of the mutagenic effects of ionizing radiation. The panel's job was made more difficult by deep disagreements between Muller and Wright and by official secrecy concerning essential data.

Beadle's pragmatic and judicious views helped the group reach consensus over its final reports. The committee concluded, "that from a genetic point of view there appears to be no threshold level of exposure below which genetic damage does not occur" ("Genetic Effects," 1960). It recommended establishing a lifetime limit on the amount of radiation exposure to individuals, including medical x-rays, and proposed such a limit. It also described a research agenda that predicted the shape of biological research over the next decades.

With the Division of Biology now strong, Beadle was able to take a year's sabbatical and accept appointment as the George Eastman Visiting Professor at Oxford during the 1958–1959 academic year. Muriel Beadle's quaint and humorous account of that year's stay in Oxford appears in her book *These Ruins Are Inhabited*. While in England, he learned that he and Ed Tatum would share, with Joshua Lederberg, the 1958 Nobel Prize in Physiology or Medicine.

Later Years. Upon returning to Caltech in late summer of 1959, Beadle was appointed dean of the faculty. He had always traveled a great deal and was now often invited to speak on matters of science policy. Improving the relations between science and society was a major theme in these presentations. In 1961, Beadle accepted the presidency of the University of Chicago. The university had experienced a tumultuous and disruptive period since the end of World War II, and the trustees hoped he would restore the institution's former academic eminence as well as its finances. He succeeded on both scores and reestablished

civility and confidence between the faculty and administration. During the disruptive period of the 1960s, he coped judiciously, firmly, and fairly with the student opposition to the way the university responded to local civil rights issues and the encroachment of the war in Vietnam and the draft on the students' futures.

Beadle retired at the mandatory age of sixty-five and, after twenty years away from research, returned to experimental work. As a graduate student, he and Emerson had investigated the origin of maize, alone among common crop plants in having no obvious wild parent. As far as he was concerned, his last paper on the topic (in 1939) put the matter to rest: teosinte, a Mexican wild grass, was of the same species as maize and its immediate progenitor. In the intervening years, a competing concept was widely accepted. For more than a decade after his retirement, Beadle labored to prove his original conclusion. With the help of amateurs and professionals, he carried out classical genetic experiments on maize-teosinte hybrids, planting tens of thousand of plants in Mexico. These experiments confirmed that the two plants differed by no more than four to five genes. Finally, all the battling scientists had to agree that Beadle's forty-year-old proposal was correct.

By the age of eighty, Beadle had been diagnosed as suffering from Alzheimer's disease. The Beadles had moved to a retirement community in Pomona, California. As the disease took its toll, even the life-long pleasure he obtained from working in the garden was lost. Until his death, he was increasingly divorced from reality.

Beadle's Legacy. Beadle was an early articulate spokesman for the integration of biochemistry and genetics. Although not a biochemist, he assailed the barriers between biochemists and geneticists. He was prophetic in believing that the biochemist could not understand what goes on chemically in the organism without considering genes any more than the geneticist could fully appreciate the gene without taking account of what it is and what it does. He coined and consistently used the term *biochemical genetics,* seemingly preferring it to *molecular biology*, although the latter won out in the end.

Equally significant, his work on *Drosophila* eye pigments and on *Neurospora* established an experimental paradigm for analysis of complex biological processes such as the cell cycle, embryonic development, and memory. In the first step of this approach, a large number of mutant organisms affecting various stages of a particular biological process are isolated. Then, from the phenotypes of the mutants, the order of the various steps in the process can be determined. In the early twenty-first century, the affected genes can be identified and isolated and the corresponding gene products and their functions identified.

Beadle and his generation also demonstrated to future scientific generations the relevance of genetics to societal issues and the importance of an active role for scientists in fostering sound national policy. Altogether, this Nebraska farm boy left a profound scientific legacy.

BIBLIOGRAPHY

WORKS BY BEADLE

With Boris Ephrussi. "Transplantation in *Drosophila*." *Proceedings of the National Academy of Sciences of the United States of America* 21 (1935): 642–646.

With Rollins A. Emerson and Allan Cameron Fraser. *A Summary of Linkage Studies in Maize.* Cornell University Agricultural Experiment Station Memoir 180. Ithaca, NY: Cornell University, 1935. This paper was referred to in *Nature* in volume 436 (25 August 2005): 1119–1126.

With Boris Ephrussi. "The Differentiation of Eye Pigments in *Drosophila* as Studied by Transplantation." *Genetics* 21 (1936): 225–247.

"Teosinte and the Origin of Maize." *Journal of Heredity* 30 (1939): 245–247.

With Edward L. Tatum. "Genetic Control of Biochemical Reactions in *Neurospora*." *Proceedings of the National Academy of Sciences of the United States of America* 27 (1941): 499–505.

"Biochemical Genetics." *Chemical Reviews* 37 (1945): 15–96.

"The Genetic Control of Biochemical Reactions." *Harvey Lectures Series* 40 (1945): 179–194.

"H. J. Muller and the Geneva Conference." *Science* 122 (1955): 813.

"Genes and Chemical Reactions in *Neurospora*." 1958 Nobel Prize Lecture. In *Nobel Lectures, Physiology or Medicine 1942–1962.* Amsterdam: Elsevier Publishing Company, 1964. Also available from http://nobelprize.org/nobel_prizes/medicine/laureates/1958/beadle-lecture.html.

With others. "Genetic Effects." In *The Biological Effects of Radiation, Summary Reports.* Washington, DC: National Academy of Sciences–National Research Council, 1960. The report of the genetics panel regarding the effects of radiation fallout.

"Biochemical Genetics: Some Recollections." In *Phage and the Origins of Molecular Biology,* edited by John Cairns, Gunther S. Stent, and James D. Watson. Cold Spring Harbor, NY: Cold Spring Harbor Laboratory Press, 1966.

"Recollections." *Annual Review of Biochemistry* 43 (1974): 1–13.

OTHER SOURCES

Beadle, Muriel. *These Ruins Are Inhabited.* New York: Doubleday, 1961. A memoir of the Beadles' experiences at Oxford.

Berg, Paul, and Maxine Singer. *George Beadle, An Uncommon Farmer: The Emergence of Genetics in the 20th Century.* Cold Spring Harbor, NY: Cold Spring Harbor Laboratory Press, 2003. A full biography of Beadle.

Crow, James F. "Quarreling Geneticists and a Diplomat." *Genetics* 140 (1995): 421–426. A description, by a participant, of the genetics panel investigating the genetic effects of radiation fallout.

Doebley, John. "George Beadle's Other Hypothesis: One-Gene, One-Trait." *Genetics* 158 (2001): 487–493. The story of the determination of the relation between teosinte and maize.

Horowitz, Norman. H. "George Wells Beadle." In *National Academy of Sciences: Biographical Memoirs.* Vol. 59. Washington, DC: National Academy Press, 1990, pp. 26–53.

———, Paul Berg, Maxine Singer, et al. "A Centennial: George W. Beadle, 1903–1989." *Genetics* 166 (2004): 1–10.

Singer, Maxine, and Paul Berg. "George Beadle: From Genes to Proteins." *Nature Reviews Genetics* 5 (2004): 949–954. The present article is a modified version of this publication.

Maxine Singer
Paul Berg

BECHER, JOHANN JOACHIM (*b.* Speyer, Germany, 6 May 1635; *d.* London, England, October 1682), *chemistry, economics, reform, noble court, commerce.* For the original article on Becher see *DSB,* vol. 1.

Research in the history of science since the original *DSB* article has highlighted the importance of the patronage of the noble court in legitimating and shaping the investigation of nature in early modern Europe. Becher spent his life in the search for such patrons for his chemical and commercial projects. The demands of his patrons that he produce tangible and valuable products as a result of his investigation of nature, as well as the potential for reform that he saw in the new philosophy, shaped the emergence of science in the early modern period.

Johann Joachim Becher has been a familiar name in the history of chemistry since the Prussian physician and chemist Georg Ernst Stahl edited and republished Becher's major chemical work of 1669, the *Physica subterranea,* and took up Becher's idea of three earths that gave all metals and minerals their characteristics. In Stahl's hands, one of Becher's three earths, the *terra pinguis,* became the basis for Stahl's phlogiston theory. Becher himself, as Allen G. Debus makes clear in his splendid *DSB* article, had cobbled together various preexisting (al)chemical concepts in support of his thoroughgoing vitalistic theory of nature. In his alchemy and chemistry, Becher was less concerned with matter theory than with the kind of investigation that chemistry represented. It was a new philosophy that combined textual and manual work, and he believed its practice would help to bring about a new world of productive knowledge. The vitalism of Becher's matter theory was reflected in his view that (al)chemical investigation could be directed to discovering the productive capacities of nature. Moreover, Becher employed his vitalist ideas in his practical and product-oriented chemical and commercial schemes that he promulgated throughout Europe from the 1650s until his death in 1682.

Projects of Reform. Becher's importance in the history of science thus lies not in his theories, but instead in his use of the investigation of nature and natural knowledge—what in the early twenty-first century would be called science—as a central part of his efforts to reform his society. His reform involved the territorial states of the Holy Roman Empire of the German nation in which he lived, and thus he drew the investigation of nature into the realm of the central state. Although he was not the first to link natural knowledge and territorial wealth, his writings formed a massive project of reform that linked commercial and (al)chemical ideas and projects in a novel way that would be mined by others following in his footsteps.

Reform pervaded Becher's works, and nature had a new meaning in it. In the sixteenth century, nature and the knowledge of nature had been a source of millenarian hopes, as expressed, above all, in the (al)chemical work of Philippus Aureolus Theophrastus Bombast von Hohenheim, called Paracelsus. But in the seventeenth century, these millenarian hopes were transmuted into material ambitions, expressed in the commercial projects of such individuals as Johann Rudolf Glauber, Gottfried Wilhelm Leibniz, and Becher, who all employed the language and concepts of millenarian reformers, but turned their attention to reform in the material and temporal sphere. Becher's polymathic strivings—he published works on alchemy, medicine, chemistry, commerce, politics, universal language, perpetual motion, pedagogy, ethics, moral philosophy, and inventions; as well as carrying out practical projects such as establishing a house of manufacture, colonial trade companies, and many other schemes—can be viewed as part of the same effort at reform of the material realm by employing the power of natural knowledge and the vital generative properties of nature.

These vital principles were the basis of commercial productivity as well, an idea that comes across particularly well in Becher's 1669 colony project, when, in the service of Friedrich Casimir, Count of Hanau, Becher negotiated title to a colony in what is now French Guiana from the Dutch West India Company. The Dutch desired settlers to hold their New World possessions and thus were eager for the German colonists and their trade (the Dutch also profited from the transportation of commodities on Dutch ships and transshipment through Dutch ports). Although Becher's colony project eventually failed, his discussion of the uses to which the colony could be put tells much about the knowledge of nature in such a project. In a pamphlet published to defend his part in this scheme, he waxed enthusiastic about the promise of sugar cultivation in the colony. As every courtier like Becher knew, sugar was an important exotic delicacy at court, firmly associated with the riches—commercial and natural—of the New World.

Speaking as a natural philosopher and medical doctor, Becher could pronounce sugar a powerful medicament, one in which the spirit of generation and growth emanating directly from the heavens was particularly concentrated. The air of the tropics and the New World hung heavy with this universal spirit, it rained down on the land, and sugar plants drew up this essence, resulting in a plant that contained "the noblest and sweetest juice of the earth, digested and cooked through by the heat of the sunbeams, and thus a noble balsamic substance, most closely related to the human blood (1676, folio 10v.) Sugar was a powerful product of nature, but it also had a place in a new economic cycle: Becher explained that sugar was an agricultural product that was not difficult to turn into cash, unlike the traditional agricultural goods of the German territories. This cash would go directly into the colonial ruler's treasury as ordinary income, making no extraordinary tax burden on the ruler's subjects.

Becher emphasized the traditional agricultural advantages of the colony and sugar growth. He praised the West Indian land, which he claimed needed neither fertilization nor the plow, and he praised the system of slavery, which he said made the land inexpensive to work. Germans, he believed, would have the agricultural skills to cultivate this natural product of the land that produced commercial wealth. Sugar would thus bring monetary wealth into a territory, but within a traditional noble framework. It gave the prince more land and additional titles. Sugar cultivation depended on traditional landed power structures and on agricultural methods and skills, and it provided a source of income that mimicked the established ordinary income that flowed from a prince's hereditary lands. In Becher's pronouncements, sugar was a self-regenerating product of nature, one of the noblest, but one that also multiplied the artificial wealth of money.

Commerce, productive knowledge, and natural philosophy were intertwined for Becher, and an essential component of his commercial projects was the knowledge of nature, suitably controlled by the new philosopher. This comes across particularly in twin alchemical and commercial reports he presented to Emperor Leopold I in 1674, "Wie die Commercien…verschaffen seye," and "Gutachten über Herrn Daniels Marsaly Process zur Tinctur." In these reports, Becher's conception of generation and material productivity contained above in all his alchemical writings informed both the chemical and commercial projects put forward. As becomes clear in these reports, commerce and alchemy are both movable wealth that did not depend entirely upon the traditional land and landed wealth of the nobility. Becher attempted to draw the prince and the realm of government into the world of money wealth and commercial transaction, for he believed that the realm of the prince and his court could no longer subsist only on the land and the natural fruits of that land, but also had to participate in the world of the manufactured object and movable wealth. The proper activity of government and the prince was to be the creation of artificial wealth through the arts and inventions of manufacture and the movements of commerce.

Princes and city councils alike eagerly heeded Becher's proposed projects because they promised production of valuable knowledge, goods, and wealth through the study of nature. The view of nature as a source of wealth for commercial powers or would-be commercial powers, and the view that the arbiters of this natural knowledge were new philosophers of nature—of whom Francis Bacon had written—increasingly informed colonial powers and princely territorial governments throughout the seventeenth century and into the future. The projects of men such as Becher represent the beginnings of an increasingly close relationship between science and the state that would give unprecedented importance to the study and knowledge of nature.

Experimental Philosophy. Becher's writings also show a reassertion of a social and epistemic divide based on theory and practice, and the development of a new identity for the experimental philosopher of nature. In the sixteenth century, an exchange between vernacular and elite ways of knowing occurred, as humanists visited workshops, artisans published treatises on their working methods, and artists claimed their manual labor constituted practice of the liberal arts. Up through the middle of the sixteenth century, scholars and other individuals engaged in mind work (as opposed to manual work) exhibited openness to manual practice and to the handworkers who carried out such practice. This can be seen in humanist interest in workshop techniques, for example, and the collection of vernacular information and practices on the part of naturalists and others.

By the late seventeenth century, while many of the observational and empiricist practices of artisans had been incorporated into the new method of what Bacon had pronounced the "New, Active Science," there was a greater gap than ever between the new experimental philosophers of the institutionalized academies such as the Royal Society and artisan-practitioners. Becher began his career at the courts of the Holy Roman Empire as a projector and purveyor of choice secrets for perpetual motion and alchemical transmutation, moved on to become an intermediary between his princely patrons and tradespeople,

Johann Joachim Becher. THE LIBRARY OF CONGRESS.

practitioners, and mechanicals of all kinds. Around 1674, he began to articulate a new role for himself as a man of theory, a *Naturkündiger*, who could marshal, organize, and extract useful knowledge from the crowds of practitioners offering practical, productive schemes to the princes and city councils of Europe.

Alchemical Laboratory Plan. It has been seen that Becher spoke as a natural philosopher about the colony project. His hierarchical organization of the production of natural knowledge can be seen with clarity in his manufactory project. Becher's plan for an alchemical laboratory, at the heart of his house of manufacture on which he reported to Emperor Leopold I in his 1676 "Referat, oder gründliche Beschreibung was in dem Kunst- undt Werckhauss … gethan und operirt wirdt" provides an extraordinarily clear example of the way in which this distancing was envisioned in the production of natural knowledge and commercially valuable goods.

The aim of Becher's alchemical laboratory was the ennoblement of base natural materials by art into noble and useful objects, not just gold, but medicines and curiosities that mirrored the trade goods that were produced in the rest of the manufactory. As in his model polity, Becher's entire laboratory was overseen and regulated by the territorial prince. The prince's representative in the laboratory was a *Naturkündiger,* or "natural philosopher," called by Becher the *Consilarius Laboratorii,* the highest member of the laboratory, holding direct responsibility to the prince. These advisors were men of theory and practice who could transform a vernacular and sometimes oral recipe into a scholarly document to be tested in the laboratory. They were to collect recipes and techniques, scorning none no matter how mechanic the artist who proffered them, with the aim of ordering all into the written form of a *consilium.* The *Consilarius* was to bind all recipe sellers with a contract to hold these mechanics in the laboratory as long as possible in order to transform their tacit procedures into written recipes. Although the counselors were to collect and test all recipes gained orally and in writing, their stance was to be distant, maintaining an attitude at all times of proper skepticism toward the wild claims and loose living of hawkers of recipes.

The second class of worker in the laboratory was the *Dispensator Laboratorii,* who received instructions from the counselors for undertaking processes, based on the written *consilia.* Once the dispensators were given the process, they were not to "tinker with it or add anything to it, but should perform it as it is written down and annotated in the *consilium*" (1682/1974, p. 99). The real task of this second class of worker, as his title suggests, was to divide each process into its proper operations and delegate it to the different types of laborers beneath him. He was to report on the trials performed and write a report, which included quantitative information on the materials used and the outcome achieved.

Below the dispensator were three more groups of workers, each charged with one part of the physical and chemical techniques used in testing the recipes. These laborers were to be kept in ignorance of each other's part in the trials, and even of each other's existence. Indeed, they should be "rough, strong people who should understand nothing else" (1682/1974, p. 101) and who would ideally be unable to read and write. In any case, they were not to be allowed writing implements or paper. The laborers were not allowed to talk, eat, or drink together, and the materials they produced in the laboratory were to be taken quickly from them so they could not keep samples.

Organized in this manner, Becher believed that the laboratory would function philosophically. The elusive tacit knowledge by which nature was manipulated and known—the expertise of artisans—would be brought under the control of the natural philosopher, and the products of the laboratory would go to fill the coffers of the territorial ruler.

Becher's life was one of ceaseless activity in the search for (mostly) princely patronage that would lead to realization of his goals for reform. That Becher's claims to the knowledge of nature were at the heart of both his search for patronage and his plans for reform says much about the power and promise discerned in natural knowledge in the seventeenth century. Moreover, Becher's projects demonstrate the new type of authority asserted by the self-proclaimed new philosopher of nature and the novel hierarchy of knowledge-production that he was to oversee in the service of his prince.

SUPPLEMENTARY BIBLIOGRAPHY

WORKS BY BECHER

Nachlass. Mss. var. 1 (1), Mss. var. 1 (2), Mss. var. 1 (3), and Mss. var. 2. Rostock University Library. These four (not three) folio volumes are essential in reconstructing Becher's pre-1678 years, and attest particularly to his interest in mechanical schemes. Mss. var. 2 was not known to Herbert Hassinger.

Gründlicher Bericht von Beschaffenheit und Eigenschafft/ Cultivirung und Bewohnung ... dess in America ... Strich Landes.... Frankfurt, 1669. Here Becher laid out and defended his colony project.

"Doctor Johann Joachim Bechers ... Rath Gutachten über Herrn Daniels Marsaly Process zur Tincture." 11 May 1674, Hs. 11472, Handschriften-Abteilung, Österreichische Nationalbibliothek, Vienna.

"Doctor Johann Joachim Bechers Römischer Kayserl. Mayt. Commercien Raths Referat Wie die Commercien, auch gemeiner Handel und Wandel, gegenwärtig in Ihro Kayl. Mayt. Erblanden, verschaffen seye." 11 May 1674, Hs. 12467, Handschriften-Abteilung, Österreichische Nationalbibliothek, Vienna.

"Referat, oder gründliche Beschreibung was in dem Kunst- undt Werckhauss sambt beyliegenden Schmeltz- undt Glaßhütten, gethan und operirt wirdt, auch wie selbige angeordnet sey." 19 March 1676, Hs. 8046, Handschriften-Abteilung, Österreichische Nationalbibliothek, Vienna.

Chymischer Glücks-Hafen/ Oder Grosse Chymische Concordantz und Collection. Frankfurt, Germany: Georg Schiele, 1682. Facsimile reprint, Hildesheim, Germany: Georg Olms, 1974.

OTHER SOURCES

Debus, Allen G. *The Chemical Philosophy.* 2 vols. New York: Science History Publications, 1977.

Frühsorge, Gotthardt, and Gerhard F. Strasser, eds. *Johann Joachim Becher (1635–1682).* Wiesbaden, Germany: Otto Harrassowitz, 1993.

Smith, Pamela H. *The Business of Alchemy: Science and Culture in the Holy Roman Empire.* Princeton, NJ: Princeton University Press, 1994.

Teich, Mikulas. "Interdisciplinarity in J. J. Becher's Thought." *History of European Ideas* 9 (1988): 145–160.

Pamela H. Smith

BECKMAN, ARNOLD ORVILLE (*b.* Cullom, Illinois, 10 April 1900, *d.* La Jolla, California, 18 May 2004) *chemistry, business, civic leader, philanthropy.*

Beckman was a man of many parts, as the saying goes. He had really four distinct, albeit interrelated, careers: research scientist and educator; entrepreneur and businessman; civic leader, and philanthropist. His inventions, and the businesses he founded to commercialize them, represented the beginnings of the American chemical instrument industry.

Early Years. Beckman was the son of a blacksmith, George W. Beckman, and his wife Elizabeth. In addition to a younger sister, he had two elder half brothers, born to George Beckman's deceased first wife. His birthplace, Cullom, Illinois, was then, and still is, a small rural farming community with a population of about 500. Life was fairly austere, a fact for which Beckman later expressed a kind of gratitude; he was forced to improvise. When he was nine, Beckman discovered in the family's attic a copy of Steele's *Fourteen Weeks in Chemistry*, printed in 1861. The book contained instructions for carrying out simple experiments using ordinary household chemicals and other supplies that were commonly available. For his tenth birthday, his father built him a small shed, which became his chemistry laboratory, and Beckman decided at an early age that he would become a chemist. He recalled later that Cullom was lit at night by a few arc lights that burned carbon rods. He and his friends used the stubs of spent rods along with scrap zinc in attempts to form makeshift electric batteries.

Arnold also learned to play the piano in a half-dozen lessons, and before long he was playing as part of a village band. His mother died when he was twelve. After a time his father sold his blacksmith business to become a traveling salesman for a hardware company, moving the family to Bloomington, Illinois, so that his children could have a better education. For the first time, at age fourteen, Beckman lived in a house with indoor plumbing. Arnold won a scholarship to nearby University High School, associated with Illinois State Normal, a state teachers' college. There he was encouraged to pursue his interest in chemistry. By the time he completed high school he had shown a bent for business; he had started his own company, complete with business cards that read "Bloomington Research Labs," and had regular work doing analyses for the local gas company. He also became the regular pianist for the local silent movie house, and worked there nearly every night, often improvising to create a mood in keeping with the film being shown.

When Beckman graduated from high school in 1918, the United States was at war, and Beckman joined the U.S. Marine Corps. While temporarily stationed at the

Arnold Beckman. COURTESY OF THE ARCHIVES, CALIFORNIA INSTITUTE OF TECHNOLOGY.

Brooklyn Navy Yard, he met Mabel Meinzer, a local Red Cross volunteer, on Thanksgiving Day in 1918. It would be more than seven years before they were married, but even before then she changed his life in important ways. After being discharged from the Marines, he enrolled in chemistry at the University of Illinois, and focused his interests on physical chemistry. He obtained both bachelor's and master's degrees in four years, became engaged to Mabel, and set off for graduate school at the newly formed California Institute of Technology. However, his love for Mabel bested his enthusiasm for chemistry, and at the end of his first year he left graduate school for New York. He obtained employment at the Western Electric Laboratory, which became Bell Laboratories during his employment. Beckman became the first technical employee of Walter A. Shewhart, a pioneer of quality control and efficiency studies of manufacturing processes. Beckman also learned about vacuum tubes and electronic circuit design. The lessons he learned at Bell Labs would later serve him well.

A Life in Academic Science. Beckman's serious interest in research and chemical science resumed in 1926, after he and Mabel had been married for a year. Arthur A. Noyes, chairman of Caltech's chemistry department, visited Beckman in New York, and induced him to return to Caltech to complete his PhD work. He took up experimental work in photochemistry and carried out his thesis research under the direction of Roscoe Gilkey Dickinson. His thesis project involved study of the photodecomposition of gaseous hydrogen azide. At issue was whether the decomposition of an explosively unstable molecule such as hydrogen azide would follow a simple law of photochemistry, in which a single photon of incident light would give rise to the decomposition of a fixed and small number of molecules of hydrogen azide, the "quantum yield." His thesis research, in which he showed that the quantum yield for photodecomposition of hydrogen azide at low pressure is three, was a tour de force of experimental inventiveness and skill in execution, and it foreshadowed the career path that lay ahead.

One of Beckman's fellow graduate students, Linus Pauling, also studied with Roscoe Dickinson at about the same time. Upon completion of their PhD requirements, both Pauling and Beckman were invited to remain on the Caltech chemistry faculty. In that role, while continuing his researches in photochemistry, Beckman taught experimental design and instrumentation as well as a course in scientific glassblowing (there were few scientific glass supply houses in existence at that time). He clearly had an aptitude for experimental innovation. Even as a graduate student, in 1927, he had applied for and received a patent for a signaling device that would announce to the driver of a car when the car had attained a particular speed. In 1934, he invented a new, nonclogging ink for postal meters. Although the ink contained butyric acid, which has a rancid odor, it was sufficiently promising that Beckman began operating a small business in his spare time. In that same year a former classmate from Illinois who was working in the citrus industry approached Beckman for help in measuring the acidity of lemon juice. There was need for a rugged, accurate, and portable device that could be safely carried. The device that Beckman designed drew upon his experience with electronic circuitry at Bell Labs as well as his knowledge as a physical chemist. His device for measuring pH, or acidity, was revolutionary in two respects: It incorporated electronic amplification into a chemical measurement, and it integrated all the components involved in the measurement into a single compact and readily usable instrument. Using the facilities of the small company with which he was involved, National Technical Laboratories, Beckman and his assistants worked to refine their "acidimeter." A patent for the device was applied for in 1934 and granted in 1936. In 1935, he began selling the instrument through his small

company, after a market research trip with Mabel to scientific supply houses in the East. He was advised that the market could absorb perhaps 600 of the acidimeters, an estimate that in time proved extraordinarily short of the mark. Other patents followed, for example, for a factory-sealed glass electrode, an innovation that captured the glass-electrode market. At this time the Beckman family had become a foursome; when Arnold and Mabel found themselves unable to have children of their own, they adopted two children, Patricia Beckman in 1936 and Arnold Stone Beckman in 1937.

Inventor and Entrepreneur. The acidimeter, now referred to as the pH meter, was a huge success, so much so that in 1939 Beckman decided to resign his position at Caltech and assume the full-time presidency of National Technical Laboratories. With the advent of World War II, the demand for scientific instrumentation rose greatly. Beckman saw that there was a great need for new spectroscopic instrumentation. The model D quartz photoelectric spectrometer, introduced in 1941, followed the philosophy of incorporating all of the components—light source, optical system, and detection—into a single package with convenient controls. With the addition of an ultraviolet capability, the instrument's name was changed to "DU." It became one of the most celebrated scientific instruments ever produced. It was fast, accurate, precise, and affordable. When production was finally ended in the 1960s, some 21,000 units had been sold. Here and there a few continued in use in the early twenty-first century. The DU was an important tool in many wartime research efforts, including vitamin research. It was used by Erwin Chargaff in 1946 for the first complete analysis of DNA, providing the basis for Chargaff's rules. In 1942, Beckman agreed to build infrared spectrophotometers, needed for the American synthetic rubber program. The company eventually produced a long line of high performance infrared instruments to complement its array of ultraviolet-visible spectrophotometers.

A key component of the Beckman pH meters was the "Helipot," a Beckman-patented helical potentiometer that provided more precise and accurate settings than could be attained in other ways. The Helipot is in effect a precise variable resistor, wound into a helical form and with an accurate, reproducible contact along the wire. During the war a militarized version of the Helipot was needed in instruments such as radars. The demand for the Helipots was so great that a separate subsidiary corporation, with Beckman as owner, was established to produce them. Beckman thus became a manufacturer of electronics components.

Civic Contributions. In the postwar years, with his company (renamed Beckman Instruments, Incorporated, in 1950) growing steadily and expanding into new markets, Beckman gave more of his attention to civic matters. Smog had become a serious environmental problem in the Los Angeles basin, home to both Beckman Instruments and the Beckman family. The mayor of Los Angeles asked Beckman for help, and he in turn recruited Arie J. Haagen-Smit, a Caltech professor of chemistry, to work on the problem. In company with Beckman Instruments scientists, Haagen-Smit established that ozone was the offending pollutant, creating noxious peroxy compounds through oxidation of hydrocarbon emissions, a conclusion counter to the prevailing view that the offending substance was sulfur dioxide. California governor Goodwin J. Knight set up a Special Committee on Air Pollution, and Beckman was appointed as chair. Beckman also played a role in creating the not-for-profit Air Pollution Foundation to support research on solutions to the smog problem. At the same time, Beckman Instruments produced a variety of instruments for the measurement and analysis of atmospheric pollutants. Beckman became president of the Los Angeles Chamber of Commerce in 1956, and he used that position to further argue for measures that would control smog formation. His Chamber of Commerce connections garnered an invitation to accompany Vice President Richard M. Nixon on his trip to Moscow in 1959. He was thus present at the famous "Kitchen Debate" between Nixon and Soviet premier Nikita Khrushchev.

The Expanding World of Beckman Instruments. While William Shockley had been an undergraduate physics major at Caltech, graduating in 1932, he had occasion to seek Beckman's help with some experimental work. In 1955, Shockley asked Beckman to help him in forming a new company to manufacture semiconductor materials. In due course the Shockley Semiconductor Laboratories was formed in Palo Alto, California, as a subsidiary of Beckman Instruments. All the signs for success of the enterprise were propitious, made even more so by the 1956 Nobel Prize for invention of the transistor shared by Shockley, John Bardeen, and Walter H. Brattain. But it was not to be; Shockley proved to be an inept manager and director of people. Despite many signs of trouble, Beckman was reluctant, out of a sense of loyalty, to remove Shockley from his leadership role. When the needed changes did not occur, a group of eight leading researchers, including Gordon Moore and Robert Noyce, left the company to form Fairchild Semiconductor. The new company was soon successful in manufacturing integrated circuits on silicon-based semiconductors. Noyce and Moore later left Fairchild to form Intel. Shockley Semiconductor never achieved any measure of success,

and Beckman sold the subsidiary in 1960. It had not been a profitable investment, but Beckman had provided a major impetus for the explosive growth of Silicon Valley.

Beckman Instruments continued to grow in size and also in the range of its products. The company expanded into international markets. The first international subsidiary, Beckman Instruments GmbH, opened in Munich in 1953, as the first postwar U.S. business in Germany. Beckman expanded into new product lines through careful acquisitions. In 1955, he acquired Spinco, a producer of ultracentrifuges. The Beckman Spinco instruments came to dominate the market, proving to be of immense importance in much biological research. There followed a strong development of biological research tools such as amino acid analyzers and sequencers. In addition, the company produced an ever-expanding line of clinical medical instrumentation, such as the oxygen meter and glucose analyzer.

A New Career: Philanthropy. In 1965, at the age of sixty-five, with the company doing very well, Beckman stepped down as president of Beckman Instruments. It was the beginning of a new phase in his life. While he remained chairman of the board of Beckman Instruments, he had more time for other activities. One of those was chairmanship of the Board of Trustees of Caltech, a position he held until 1974. He and Mabel also launched a program of philanthropy, beginning with several major gifts to Caltech. He also became involved in politics; he was the major organizer of the Lincoln Club, which brought together Orange County, California, businesspeople to support conservative political causes. The activities of this group were key to Richard Nixon's win of California in the 1968 presidential campaign, which in turn was essential to his winning the election.

In 1981, Beckman agreed to sell his company to SmithKline Corporation, a Philadelphia-based pharmaceutical company. He and Mabel made a decision to disburse most of the very considerable wealth they had accumulated, largely through science-oriented philanthropy. They had created the Arnold and Mabel Beckman Foundation in 1977 as a vehicle for this endeavor. There followed a series of major gifts, beginning with $10 million to City of Hope National Medical Center to establish the Beckman Research Institute there. Following this, the Beckman Laser Institute was built in Irvine, California; it later became a part of the University of California, Irvine. In 1985, the Beckmans awarded the University of Illinois $40 million, contingent upon a $10 million match from the state, for construction of a large, broadly based, multidisciplinary research institute. The Arnold and Mabel Beckman Institute for Advanced Research and Technology held its inauguration in 1989 under the directorship of Theodore L. Brown. By the early 2000s it had become a world-renowned center for interdisciplinary research.

The Beckmans gave Stanford University $12.5 million toward the Arnold and Mabel Beckman Center for Molecular and Genetic Medicine. The Nobel Laureate, Paul Berg, was a leading figure in formulating the Stanford proposal and was the center's founding director. At Caltech, the Beckmans provided a total of $15 million toward a Laboratory of Chemical Synthesis, followed in 1986 by a $50 million gift to design, construct, and partially endow an interdisciplinary research center, named the Beckman Institute. The eminent chemist Harry B. Gray played a lead role in formulating the plan for the Caltech Beckman Institute and became its founding director. The Beckmans also gave $20 million to the National Academies of Science and Engineering to establish the Arnold and Mabel Beckman Center of the Academies in Irvine, California. Intended as a West Coast base for the Academies, it also serves as a home for the Beckman Foundation. Beyond these major gifts, the Beckman made many additional gifts to a wide range of institutions.

Mabel Beckman died on 1 June 1989; her death was a major blow for Arnold. The Beckmans had always worked as a team in their philanthropy. Although they had given away nearly $200 million during the 1980s, the foundation's assets were still very substantial. Beckman recast the foundation as a foundation in perpetuity and turned over its direction to a board. As of 2007 the Beckman Foundation supported important programs, such as the Beckman Young Investigator program, designed to assist newly appointed tenure-track faculty in chemistry and the life sciences get their research off to a good start, and the Beckman Scholars Program, which supported undergraduate research in chemistry and the life sciences. In addition, the foundation has funded an innovative $14 million program, Beckman@Science, which provides hands-on training and supplies for teaching science in elementary schools of Orange County, California.

Arnold Beckman lived a long, vigorous, and very productive life. At ninety-nine he still played piano quite well. The Nobel Laureate James D. Watson had this to say of him: "Arnold Beckman's contributions to science and to society came in part, from his rare talent for creating these new instruments and his decision to make them available to industry and science alike. It has been amplified by his unique philanthropic support of the same forward-looking research that his innovation furthered" (quoted in Arnold and Myers, 2000, p. x) The many recognitions Beckman received include the National Medal of Science (1989), the National Medal of Technology (1988), and the Lifetime Achievement Award of the National Inventor's Hall of Fame.

BIBLIOGRAPHY

There is a rich archive of Beckman memorabilia and papers in the Beckman Institute at the California Institute of Technology, Pasadena, California.

WORKS BY BECKMAN

"An Improved Quartz Fiber Manometer." *Journal of the Optical Society of America* 16 (1928): 276–277.

With Arthur A. Noyes. "The Structure of the Atoms as a Periodic Property and Its Relation to Valence and Ion-Formation." *Chemical Reviews* 5 (1928): 85–107.

With Roscoe G. Dickinson. "The Quantum Yield in the Photochemical Decomposition of Hydrogen Azide." *Journal of the American Chemical Society* 52 (1930): 124–132.

With Howard H. Cary. "A Quartz Photoelectric Spectrophotometer." *Journal of the Optical Society of America* 31 (1941): 682–689.

OTHER SOURCES

Stephens, Harrison. *Golden Past, Golden Future.* Claremont, CA: Claremont University Center, 1985.

Thackray, Arnold, and Minor Myers Jr. *Arnold Beckman: One Hundred Years of Excellence.* Philadelphia: Chemical Heritage Foundation, 2000.

Vischer, Ernest, and Ervin Chargaff. "The Separation and Characterization of Purines in Minute Amounts of Nucleic Acid Hydrolysates." *Journal of Biological Chemistry* 168 (1947): 781–782.

———. "The Separation and Quantitative Estimation of Purines and Pyrimidines in Minute Amounts." *Journal of Biological Chemistry* 176 (1948): 703–714.

Wex, Bridgette, and D. C. Neckers. "The Quantum Yield: An Historical Perspective." *The Spectrum* 18 (2005): 10–15, 26.

Theodore L. Brown

BELL, JOHN STEWART (*b.* Belfast, Northern Ireland, United Kingdom, 28 July 1928; *d.* Geneva, Switzerland, 1 October 1990), *physics, elementary particle theory, foundations of quantum mechanics, accelerator design.*

Bell was a physicist of extraordinary depth and scope. As a member of the Theoretical Division of the Conseil Européen pour la Recherche Nucléaire (CERN) he made many theoretical analyses of the experiments performed there and formulated important general ideas regarding elementary particles and quantum field theory. Most important of these is his discovery (with Roman Jackiw) of quantum mechanical symmetry breaking: the Bell-Jackiw-Adler anomaly. In addition he applied elegant mathematics to the design of accelerators.

He worked privately, outside of CERN, on hidden variables (HV) interpretations of quantum mechanics

(QM), on quantum nonlocality (which was authoritatively established by Bell's theorem and experiments inspired by it), and on the measurement problem. He is widely considered the most important investigator of these subjects in the latter half of the twentieth century and the person most responsible for reopening questions about these topics, which once were considered to have been settled by the founders of quantum mechanics.

Background and Career. The biographical information for the present article was largely drawn from an essay by Andrew Whitaker (2002) of Queen's University in Belfast, a Royal Society biographical memoir by Philip Burke and Ian Percival (1999), and an interview by Jeremy Bernstein (1991).

John Bell was the son of John and Annie Bell, both from working-class families, strongly Protestant but on friendly terms with Catholic neighbors. Although none of Bell's ancestors were academically distinguished, his parents valued education for practical reasons. Because secondary schooling in Belfast was not free and the family was poor, only John was educated beyond elementary school, but his brothers were self-taught and one became a professor of electrical engineering in a Canadian college and wrote several textbooks. John read avidly as a boy, expressed his intention at age eleven to become a scientist, and was called "the Prof" in his family. He won a scholarship to the Belfast Technical High School, where he did excellent work in academic and practical subjects.

Upon graduation in 1944 he was hired as a technician in the physics department of Queen's University of Belfast, being too young and impecunious to enter as a student. Karl Emeléus and Reader Richard Sloane recognized his ability, loaned him books, and allowed him to attend lectures. The following year he received a small grant from the Co-operative Society and entered the university as a student. He was able to take a BSc degree with first class honors in experimental physics in only three years, and in a fourth year took a BSc degree with first class honors in mathematical physics.

Bell's training in classical and atomic physics at Queen's University was excellent, and the emphasis on experimental physics undoubtedly influenced his later work as a theoretician. He was discontented, however, with Sloane's exposition of the principles of QM and challenged, sometimes angrily, Sloane's advocacy of the Copenhagen interpretation. In Bell's extra year as a student at Queen's University he was the beneficiary of the arrival of the great crystallographer Paul Peter Ewald, a refugee from Nazi Germany. Ewald was very open to discussions of matters of principle in physics and was undoubtedly more sophisticated about subtleties in quantum theory than Bell's other teachers.

For financial reasons Bell went from Queen's University into the Scientific Civil Service without a PhD. Following Ewald's advice he applied successfully to the Atomic Energy Research Establishment at Harwell, from which he was recruited by an accelerator design group at Malvern that was later incorporated into the Theoretical Physics Division back at Harwell. He was recognized as a brilliant solver of theoretical and practical problems of accelerator design.

At Harwell he met Mary Ross, a Scottish mathematical physicist also working on accelerator design, whom he married in 1951. Their collaboration on accelerators continued until the end of his life, and she also was an adviser in his research on the foundations of QM. The partnership of John and Mary Bell was exemplary in the history of science.

In 1953 and 1954 John Bell was granted a year's leave of absence to work in the Department of Mathematical Physics at the University of Birmingham. There he demonstrated the CTP theorem (invariance of physical processes under the combination of charge conjugation, time reversal, and space inversion) under the direction of Rudolf Peierls. This result was part of his PhD thesis, but was independently discovered by Gerhart Lüders (1954). The experience at Birmingham enabled Bell to do important research in quantum field theory and nuclear physics upon his return to Harwell. However, organizational changes at Harwell made it an unsuitable locus for the interests of both John and Mary Bell, and therefore in 1960 they resigned tenured positions there for untenured positions at CERN in Geneva, where they remained except for occasional leaves until the end of their careers.

At CERN John Bell worked on a wide variety of problems connected with nuclear and high-energy particle physics. He also continued work on accelerator design, often in collaboration with Mary Bell (1991). With Jon Magne Leinaas (1987) he demonstrated that a circular variant of the Unruh effect, which in its original version relates the linear acceleration of a charged particle to the effective temperature of the blackbody radiation that it encounters, is responsible for the depolarization of electrons circularly accelerated in storage rings—remarkably showing that a nuisance to experimentalists is actually a beautiful phenomenon in relativistic quantum field theory.

During Bell's sojourn at CERN his obsession with the principles of QM did not diminish, but it remained his "hobby" which he pursued in evenings and on holidays, since it was not part of his professional responsibilities. Josef Jauch at the University of Geneva was a knowledgeable and enthusiastic partner in discussions of the foundations of QM. John Bell was personally modest and seemed to be surprised by the recognition given to him by laymen as well as physicists. Bell's theorem and the experiments inspired by it, which seem unavoidably to imply the existence of nonlocal causal relations in nature, has intrigued philosophers, theologians, devotees of science fiction, and lovers of mysteries. Bell accepted this renown with good nature, amusement, and perhaps with some satisfaction.

Field Theory and Elementary Particle Physics. John Bell's public profession (also his employment) from the mid-1950s was that of a theoretical nuclear and later particle physicist, a progression that reflects the historical development of the subject. The framework within which he approached subatomic phenomena was always field theory, even when competing ideas such as S-matrix/Regge theory in the early years and string theory in later years became popular among particle theorists. (This section was largely drawn from the corresponding more detailed discussion in Jackiw and Shimony, 2002.)

His first paper in this area, "Time Reversal in Field Theory," published in 1955, followed five years of research in accelerator physics. Drawn from his doctoral thesis at Birmingham University, it established the CTP theorem, one of the most basic precepts of particle physics. For example, it can be utilized to show that particles and their antiparticles must have equal masses.

Unknown to Bell this result had already been shown the year before by Lüders using an argument markedly different from Bell's. Yet Bell was not often credited for his independent derivation, perhaps because he was not in the circle of formal field theorists (Wolfgang Pauli, Eugene Wigner, Julian Schwinger, Res Jost, etc.) who dominated this topic. However, today Bell's "elementary derivation" is more accessible than the formal field theoretic arguments.

The subject of time reversal remained an important theme in his subsequent research (1957), especially when it became clear that time inversion (T) (unaccompanied by space inversion and charge conjugation) is not a symmetry of nature, and neither is space inversion conjoined with charge conjugation (PC) (unaccompanied by time inversion). Together with his friend, the experimentalist Jack Steinberger, he wrote an influential review on the phenomenology of PC-violating experiments (1966), and with Perring (1964) proposed a "simple model" theory to explain that effect. Though speculative, the suggestion was truly physical, hence falsifiable, and it was soon ruled out by further experiments. Nevertheless, it remains a bold and beautiful idea that continues to intrigue theorists.

In 1960, Bell joined CERN and remained there to the end of his life. Although primarily a center for particle physics accelerator experiments, CERN houses Europe's preeminent particle theory group, and Bell became active in that field. Typically particle theorists are divided into phenomenologists—people who pay close

attention to experimental results and interact professionally with experimentalists—and formalists, who explore the mathematical and other properties of theoretical models, propose new ideas for model building, and usually are somewhat removed from the reality of the experiments. Although Bell's time-reversal paper belongs forcefully in the formalist category, at CERN he was very much also a particle physics phenomenologist, drawing on his previous experience with nuclear physics. Indeed, with characteristic conscientiousness, Bell felt an obligation to work on subjects related to the activities of the laboratory, such as the analysis of the first neutrino experiments performed there in 1963. But his readiness to discuss and study any topic in physics ensured that he would pursue highly theoretical and speculative issues as well.

In a crucial paper in 1967 Bell argued that weak interactions should be described using a gauge theory, a type of mathematical formalism that provides a unified framework in which to describe quantum field theories of electromagnetism. Theoretical understanding of particle physics at that time had been hampered by the absence of a single reliable model for the fundamental interactions of elementary particles, and competing models could not be assessed because of their extremely complicated dynamical equations. To overcome these difficulties, Murray Gell-Mann (1964) had proposed *current algebra,* which is a particle physics/quantum field theory reprise of an old technique of atomic physics: the Thomas-Reiche-Kuhn sum rule, and the Bethe energy loss sum rule (see Bethe and Jackiw, 1967).

Bell (1967a) contributed to the program of current algebra by demonstrating for a solvable model (Lee model) that using current algebra relations sometimes led to sum rules that disagreed with explicitly calculated amplitudes. To improve the situation, Bell (1967b, 1968) invoked the non-Abelian gauge principle, at the heart of Yang-Mills theory, to derive the desired current commutation relations. (For a review, see the section on field theory in Jackiw and Shimony, 2002.)

Bell found, however, some failures in his generally successful version of current algebra, notably that current algebra and PCAC (partially conserved axial-vector current) seemed to forbid the decay of the eta-meson into three pi-mesons; yet this process was seen experimentally (Bell and Sutherland, 1968). Investigating this failure led to Bell's most far-reaching contribution to particle physics: a novel method of symmetry breaking, in which symmetries of an unquantized theory do not survive quantization. This led to Bell's most famous field theory paper, coauthored with Roman Jackiw in 1969, in which is described what is now called the Bell-Jackiw-Adler anomaly (also known as the chiral anomaly): a mechanism that would explain physical phenomena such as neutral pion decay in terms of a so-called anomalous term. This work resolved the failures of current algebra and also provided important support for the color theory of quarks. (For details of the analysis and for applications see Bell and Jackiw, 1969; Treiman et al., 1985; Holstein, 1993; and Jackiw and Shimony, 2002.

Another investigation by Bell provides yet another example of his far ranging interests and research style. On a visit to India, R. Rajaraman told Bell about a peculiar effect seen in quantum field theory, according to which the number operator of an electron moving in the background of a topological soliton, such as that created by the domain wall of a solid-state substance, would be a fraction of an integer. It was alleged that this effect could be physically realized in a polymer. But is the observed fraction an expectation value, or a sharp observable without fluctuations? Only in the latter case would this represent a truly novel and unexpected phenomenon.

Bell doubted that the fraction could be a sharp observable. Nevertheless, he wanted to find out, and in two papers with Rajaraman (1982, 1983) he established that, perhaps somewhat counter to his intuition, the fractions were indeed eigenvalues of a number operator though one which implied a "somewhat sophisticated definition of charge." This last-mentioned work illustrates well John Bell's attitude to his research on fundamental physical questions. Rather than merely advancing new theoretical models, his publications are infused with the desire to know and explain existing structures, preferably in "simple terms", in a "simple model"—phrases that occur frequently in his papers.

Research on Foundations of Quantum Mechanics. As a student at Queen's University Bell sharply questioned Sloane, the reader who taught the course on QM, about Heisenberg's uncertainty principle and Bohr's quantum mechanical epistemology (Whitaker, 2002, pp. 14–15). Bell's skepticism about the justification of the "Copenhagen" interpretation of QM, and even the meaningfulness of Bohr's terms, such as "complementarity" (Bohr, 1958), continued in his later career (e.g., Bell, 1989, reprinted 2004).

Bell's skepticism regarding Bohr's rationalizations attracted him to the general program of *hidden variables* (HV), according to which the QM state of any system S describes it incompletely and only statistically, while a complete description of S would also require a specification of the HV. Bell's interest in HV was further stimulated by reading David Bohm's pair of papers of 1952, proposing a specific HV model that agreed with the statistical predictions of QM.

Bell first examined the demonstration in von Neumann (1955) of the impossibility of an HV interpretation

agreeing with all the predictions of QM. He realized that although von Neumann's theorem was mathematically rigorous, it was physically unconvincing because it depended upon the premise

$$\text{Exp}(A + B) = \text{Exp}(A) + \text{Exp}(B), \qquad (1)$$

where A and B are physical quantities of a system S—represented in QM by arbitrary self-adjoint operators on the Hilbert space associated with S—and "Exp" designates the expectation value calculated by means of a probability distribution over the space of HV. Equation (1) is evidently true in a theory obeying the standard logic of classical physics, and it is also true in QM. There is, however, no general reason for asserting its truth in HV if A and B are quantum mechanically represented by noncommuting operators, because then the procedures for measuring A and B cannot be combined into a single procedure (1966, reprinted 2004, pp. 4–5). Bell then constructed a counterexample to von Neumann's theorem in the case of Hilbert space of dimension two if equation (1) is assumed only for commuting A and B (1966, reprinted 2004, pp. 2–4).

Having undercut von Neumann's impossibility proof he turned around and gave a new physically definitive proof of the impossibility of a HV interpretation of QM for Hilbert spaces of dimension three or greater, assuming equation (1) only for commuting A and B (1966, reprinted 2004, pp. 7–8). Actually, this theorem is a corollary of a previous deep and difficult theorem published by Andrew Gleason (1957). (Bell remarked once that he realized he either had to understand Gleason's theorem or produce a simpler one of his own, and it was easier to do the latter.) It should be noted that essentially the same result as Bell's was proved independently and published somewhat later by Simon Kochen and Ernst P. Specker (1967).

Bell surprisingly introduced a new consideration which transformed the conceptual significance of all the results previously achieved by himself and others concerning HV: he broadened the conception of HV by arguing for the physical acceptability of *contextual* theories.

> That so much follows from such apparently innocent assumptions leads us to question their innocence. … It was tacitly assumed that measurement of an observable must yield the same value independently of what other measurements may be made simultaneously. … The result of an observation may reasonably depend not only on the state of the system (including hidden variables) but also on the complete disposition of the apparatus." (1966, p. 451, reprinted 2004, pp. 8–9).

There is a wonderful irony in Bell's innovation: he rescued the entire program of HV from Bohr's philosophical objections by insisting along with Bohr on the inseparability of a physical quantity of a system from the apparatus used to measure that quantity. In HV that are contextual (incidentally, not Bell's own terminology), the value of a quantity A of a physical system S has the functional dependence A(λ, B, C, ..., Z), where λ is a full specification of the HV, and B, C, ..., Z is a set of physical quantities of S which are measured together with A, thus constituting the context of the measurement.

Bell reflected on two peculiarities of Bohm's HV model: that it is contextual and also nonlocal, in that the trajectory assigned by the theory to a particle is instantaneously changed by varying the magnetic field in an arbitrarily distant region. Bell intensively studied variants of Bohm's model in order to remove this feature, which was undesirable because of its conflict with the locality of special relativity theory, but without success. This failure provided the heuristics for proving that nonlocality is necessary for agreement between HV interpretations and the predictions of QM concerning systems with spatially separated constituents, a proposition now referred to as *Bell's theorem*. The theorem marks a rare case of experimental metaphysics in that it allows the transformation of the famous thought experiment presented by Albert Einstein, Boris Podolsky, and Nathan Rosen (1935), known as EPR, and later elaborated on by Bohm (1951), into a definite setup—a setup that led to a series of experiments (the first carried out by Freedman and Clauser in 1972 and improved by Alain Aspect *et. al.* in 1981). The nonlocality it has exposed was at first considered a paradox, but in recent years, with the development of quantum information science, physicists regard it more as an important resource for outperforming classical information processing.

The original version of Bell's theorem (1964, reprinted 2004, pp. 15–19) focused on a pair of spin one-half particles, in the singlet quantum state ϕ. A($\mathbf{a}$) is the outcome of measurement of σ_1-$\mathbf{a}$, the component along $\mathbf{a}$ (a unit vector in Euclidean space) of the Pauli spin of particle 1 and B($\mathbf{b}$) is the analogous quantity for particle 2. The possible values of each of these two quantities are +1 and -1. The expectation value of the product of these two quantities in the quantum state ϕ is

$$E[\mathbf{a},\mathbf{b}|\phi] =_{\text{def}} E[A(\mathbf{a})B(\mathbf{b})| \phi] = -\cos \alpha , \quad (2)$$

where α is the angle between the $\mathbf{a}$ and $\mathbf{b}$ vectors. The HV expectation value of the same product when ρ is the distribution over the space of HV is

$$(\mathbf{a},\mathbf{b}) = \int d\lambda \rho(\lambda)\{A(\mathbf{a})B(\mathbf{b})[\lambda, \text{context}]\}. \quad (3)$$

In order to avoid the nonlocality exhibited by the Bohm model Bell assumed that the integrand satisfies the following factorization:

$$\{A(\mathbf{a})B(\mathbf{b})[\lambda, \text{context}]\} = A(\mathbf{a})[\lambda] \cdot B(\mathbf{b})[\lambda], \quad (4)$$

which asserts that A($\mathbf{a}$) does not depend on $\mathbf{b}$, a parameter of a quantity measured on the distant particle 2, and likewise B($\mathbf{b}$) does not depend on $\mathbf{a}$. Furthermore, the context for particle 1 contains no quantities of particle 1 other than A($\mathbf{a}$) itself (with the trivial exceptions of A(-$\mathbf{a}$) and scalar multiples of the identity operator, scalar multiples of A($\mathbf{a}$), and linear combinations thereof), since for a spin one-half particle no others commute with it; and likewise regarding the context of particle 2. Because the spins of particles 1 and 2 are strictly anticorrelated in the singlet state, the HV model can recover the statistical predictions of QM only if

$$A(\mathbf{a},\lambda) = -B(\mathbf{a},\lambda) \quad (5)$$

for all values of λ (except a set of measure zero). Straightforward reasoning from equations (3), (4), and (5) yields

$$1 + E(\mathbf{b}, \mathbf{c}) \geq |E(\mathbf{a},\mathbf{b}) - E(\mathbf{a},\mathbf{c})|. \quad (6)$$

Inequality (6) is the pioneering example of formulas called *Bell's inequalities*. It is easily checked that if the HV expectation values E($\mathbf{a},\mathbf{b}$), etc. agree with the expectation values of QM expressed in equation (2), then inequality (5) is violated for some choices of the unit vectors $\mathbf{a}$, $\mathbf{b}$, $\mathbf{c}$, for example $\mathbf{a}$ along the $\mathbf{x}$-axis, $\mathbf{c}$ along the $\mathbf{y}$-axis, and $\mathbf{b}$ in the $\mathbf{xy}$-plane at a 45° angle to both $\mathbf{x}$ and $\mathbf{y}$.

Hence no HV theory in which all quantities recognized by QM are assigned definite values, and which furthermore satisfies Bell's locality condition, can agree with all of the statistical predictions of QM. (Further comments on Bell's argument are given in Jackiw and Shimony, 2002.)

Bell (1971, reprinted 2004, pp. 37–38) strengthened his original result by considering a much wider class of HV (sometimes called "stochastic theories"), in which λ does not assign a definite value to each self-adjoint operator but rather assigns probabilities to all of the eigenvalues of the operator. He considered theories which are local in the sense that the probability of a specified outcome of a measurement on particle 1 is independent of the choice of a measurement on particle 2 and also of the outcome of this measurement (and likewise with 1 and 2 interchanged). He then demonstrated that no local stochastic HV theory can agree with all of the statistical predictions of QM.

A striking feature of Bell's theorem is the light it throws on of the thesis of the classical paper of Einstein, Podolsky, and Rosen (1935), hereafter referred to as EPR. These authors had maintained that hidden variables are needed in order to eliminate the apparent nonlocality in certain two-particle quantum correlations, but Bell

240

showed that nonlocality recurs in any HV theory agreeing with the quantum theory of correlated systems. Numerous experiments have been performed to test Bell's inequalities and are summarized in essays in the book edited by Bertlmann and Zeilinger (2002) and also in Shimony's "Bell's Theorem" (2004). Since these experiments overwhelmingly confirm the predictions of QM and violate Bell's Inequalities, the program of EPR of postulating HV to rescue relativistic locality from its conflict with QM does not seem to be salvageable.

Several authors (Eberhard, 1978; Ghirardi, Rimini, and Weber, 1980; Page, 1982) have tried to reconcile the apparent nonlocality of QM with the locality of special relativity by demonstrating that the nonlocal causal connections exhibited in certain quantum correlations cannot be used to send superluminal messages. It is not surprising that Bell, who throughout his career had insisted on a nonanthropocentric understanding of QM, rejected this attempt at reconciliation of the two great physical theories.

> Do we then have to fall back on "no signaling faster than light" as the expression of the fundamental causal structure of contemporary physics? That is hard for me to accept. For one thing we have lost the idea that correlations can be explained, or at least this idea awaits reformulation. More importantly, the "no signaling…" notion rests on concepts which are desperately vague, or vaguely applicable. (1990b, reprinted 2004, p. 245)

Because of the evidence against local HV one cannot accept EPR's initially attractive explanation of the measurement process, which would show how the physical part of a measurement can conclude with a definite value of the indexical quantity of the measuring apparatus. What are the alternative explanations of definite measurement results? Bell regrettably died before the flowering of the currently influential "consistent histories" interpretation of QM by Griffiths (2002), Omnès (1999), and Gell-Mann and Hartle (1990). However, it is reasonable to conjecture that he would assess their proposals as he did that of Kurt Gottfried (Bell, 1987, reprinted 2004, pp. 221–222), who claimed that the exact statistical operator ρ of a system plus apparatus can be replaced by a convenient ρ' by dropping interference terms involving pairs of macroscopically different states. Bell granted that for all practical purposes, for which he used the skeptical acronym FAPP, the interference between macroscopically different states is elusive. To go beyond practicality to true theoretical justification Bell clearly felt that an appropriate set of real physical attributes is essential.

> … to avoid the vague "microscopic" "macroscopic" distinction—again a shifty split—I think one would be led to introduce variables which

have values even on the smallest scale. If the exactness of the Schrödinger equation is maintained, I see this leading towards the picture of de Broglie and Bohm." (1987, reprinted 2004, pp. 224–225)

But note that this criticism of Gottfried, which plausibly would be directed also to the consistent history theorists, ends with a conditional: "if the exactness of the Schrödinger equation is maintained." In conjecturing about promising solutions to the measurement problem Bell was strongly attracted to a program in which that exactness is not maintained: that of GianCarlo Ghirardi, Alberto Rimini, and Tullio Weber (1986).

In the GRW project, the standard time evolution of the quantum state is modified on rare occasions and in small amounts by stochastic reductions: the wave function, which is the quantum state in the position representation, is truncated to a region of atomic size. The retention of the spread of the wave function in this small region has the effect of preserving quantum dynamics for atoms and their constituents, with all the richness of phenomenology that has been discovered in the twentieth century. But the truncation has the consequence of making pointer needles and other indexical entities have quite definite values on a human scale. Bell was enthusiastic about this program, even though it has so far not been confirmed experimentally (1987, reprinted 2004, pp 202–204).

John S. Bell died of a stroke at the age of sixty-two. He was still at the height of his powers. If physicists come in two types, those who try to read the book of nature and those who try to write it, Bell belonged to the first category. He was conservative when it came to speculative and unconventional suggestions: he would prefer that unexpected contradictions not arise, that ideas flow along clearly delineated channels. But this would not prevent him from establishing what exactly is the case and accepting, albeit reluctantly, even puzzling results. Even in his quantum mechanical investigations, Bell would have preferred to side with the rational and clearly spoken Einstein rather than with the murky pronouncements of Bohr. But once he convinced himself where the truth lies, he would not allow his investigations to be affected by his inclinations, even if he remained disturbed by their outcome. Such a commitment to "truth"—as he saw it—marked John Bell's activity in science and in life.

Bell was honored fairly early by election to the Royal Society in 1972. In the 1980s many more honors came his way including the Reality Foundation Prize (with John Clauser), the Dirac Medal, the Dannie Heineman Prize for Mathematical Physics and the Hughes Medal of the Royal Society.

BIBLIOGRAPHY

Reprints of Bell's major papers are given in Mary Bell et al., 1995, and in John Bell, 2004. A full bibliography is contained in Burke and Percival, 1999.

WORKS BY BELL

"Time Reversal in Field Theory." *Proceedings of the Royal Society of London, Series A, Mathematical and Physical Sciences* 231 (1955): 479–495.

"Time Reversal in Beta-Decay." *Proceedings of the Physical Society of London Section A* 70 (1957): 552–553.

"On the Einstein-Podolsky-Rosen Paradox." *Physics* 1 (1964): 195–200. Reprinted in Bell, 2004.

With J. K. Perring. "2π Decay of the K_2^0 Meson." *Physical Review Letters* 13 (1964): 348–349.

With J. Steinberger. "Weak Interactions of Kaons." In *Oxford International Conference on Elementary Particles, 19/25 September 1965, Proceedings*, pp. 195–222. Chilton, U.K.: Rutherford High Energy Laboratory, 1966.

"On the Problem of Hidden Variables in Quantum Mechanics." *Reviews of Modern Physics* 38 (1966): 447–452. Reprinted in Bell, 2004.

"Equal-Time Commutator in a Solvable Model." *Nuovo cimento A* 47 (1967a): 616–625.

"Current Algebra and Gauge Variance." *Nuovo cimento A* 50 (1967b): 129–134.

"Current and Density Algebra and Gauge Invariance." In *Selected Topics in Particle Physics*, edited by J. Steinberger. Società italiana di fisica, course 41. New York: Academic Press, 1968.

With D. G. Sutherland. "Current Algebra and $\eta\eta \to 3\pi$." *Nuclear Physics B* 4 (1968): 315–325.

With Roman Jackiw. "A PCAC Puzzle: $\pi^0 \to \gamma\gamma$ in the σ-Model." *Nuovo cimento della Società italiana di fisica A—Nuclei Particles and Fields* 60 (1969): 47–61.

"Introduction to the Hidden-Variable Question." In *Foundations of Quantum Mechanics*, edited by Bernard d'Espagnat, pp. 171–181. Società italiana di fisica, course 49. New York: Academic Press, 1971. Reprinted in Bell, 2004, pp. 28–39.

With R. Rajaraman. "On Solitons with Half Integral Charge." *Physics Letters B* 116 (1982): 151–154.

With R. Rajaraman. "On States, on a Lattice, with Half-Integral Charge." *Nuclear Physics B* 220 (1983): 1–12.

With Jon Magne Leinaas. "The Unruh Effect and Quantum Fluctuations of Electrons in Storage Rings." *Nuclear Physics B* 284 (1987): 488–508.

"Six Possible Worlds of Quantum Mechanics." In *Possible Worlds in Humanities, Arts, and Sciences: Proceedings of Nobel Symposium 65*, edited by Sture Allén. Berlin: W. de Gruyter, 1989. Reprinted in Bell, 2004.

"Against 'Measurement.'" In *Sixty-Two Years of Uncertainty*, edited by Arthur I. Miller. New York: Plenum, 1990a. Reprinted in Bell, 2004.

"La Nouvelle Cuisine." In *Between Science and Technology*, edited by Andries Sarlemijn and Peter Kroes, pp. 232–248. Amsterdam: Elsevier, 1990b. Reprinted in Bell, 2004.

With Mary Bell, Kurt Gottfried, Martinus Veltman, eds. *Quantum Mechanics, High Energy Physics and Accelerators: Selected Papers of John S. Bell, with Commentary*. Singapore: World Scientific, 1995. Represents John Bell's work in all of his fields of research, including some, like accelerators, which are scantly treated in the present article.

Speakable and Unspeakable in Quantum Mechanics: Collected Papers on Quantum Philosophy, first ed. Cambridge, U.K.: Cambridge University Press, 1987; revised ed., 2004. The revised edition is a collection of all of Bell's papers on the foundations of quantum mechanics, except for some near duplicates; it is referred to in the text as "Bell (2004)." The first edition does not contain his late papers "Against 'Measurement'" and "La Nouvelle Cuisine."

OTHER SOURCES

Aspect, Alain, Philippe Grangier, and Gérard Roger. "Experimental Tests of Realistic Local Theories via Bell's Theorem." *Physical Review Letters* 47 (1981): 460–463.

Bell, Mary. "John Bell and Accelerator Physics." *Europhysics News* 22 (1991): 72.

Bernstein, Jeremy. *Quantum Profiles*. Princeton, NJ: Princeton University Press, 1991.

Bertlmann, Reinhold A., and Anton Zeilinger, eds. *Quantum [Un]speakables: From Bell to Quantum Information*. Berlin: Springer, 2002.

Bethe, H. A., and R. Jackiw. *Intermediate Quantum mechanics*. 3rd ed. Reading, MA: Addison Wesley, 1997.

Bohm, David. *Quantum Theory*. Englewood Cliffs, NJ: Prentice-Hall, 1951.

———. "A Suggested Interpretation of the Quantum Theory in Terms of 'Hidden' Variables," parts I and II. *Physical Review* 85 (1952): 166–179, 180–193.

Bohr, Niels. *Atomic Physics and Human Knowledge*. New York: Wiley, 1958.

Burke, Philip G., and Ian C. Percival. "John Stewart Bell: 28 July 1928–1 October 1990." *Biographical Memoirs of Fellows of the Royal Society* 45 (November 1999): 2–17. Includes a full bibliography.

Eberhard, Philippe. "Bell's Theorem and Different Concepts of Locality." *Nuovo cimento della Società italiana di fisica B-General Physics Relativity Astronomy and Mathematical Physics and Methods* 46 (1978): 392–419.

Einstein, Albert, Boris Podolsky, and Nathan Rosen. "Can Quantum-Mechanical Description of Physical Reality Be Considered Complete?" *Physical Review* 47 (1935): 777–780.

Freedman, Stuart J., and John F. Clauser. "Experimental Test of Local Hidden Variable Theories." *Physical Review Letters* 28 (1972): 938–941.

Gell-Mann, Murray. "The Symmetry Group of Vector and Axial-Vector Currents." *Physics* 1 (1964): 63–75.

———, and J. Hartle. "Quantum Mechanics in the Light of Quantum Cosmology." In *Complexity, Entropy, and the Physics of Information*, edited by Wojciech Zurek. Redwood City, CA: Addison Wesley, 1990.

Ghirardi, Gian Carlo, A. Rimini, and T. Weber. "General Argument against Superluminal Transmission through the Quantum Mechanical Measurement Process." *Lettere al Nuovo cimento* 27 (1980): 293–298.

———, A. Rimini, and T. Weber. "Unified Dynamics for Microscopic and Macroscopic Systems." *Physical Review D* 34 (1986): 470–491.

Gleason, Andrew. "Measures on the Closed Subspaces of a Hilbert Space." *Journal of Mathematics and Mechanics* 6 (1957): 885–893.

Griffiths, Robert B. *Consistent Quantum Theory.* Cambridge, U.K.: Cambridge University Press, 2002.

Holstein, B. "Anomalies for Pedestrians." *American Journal of Physics* 61 (1993): 142–147.

Jackiw, Roman, and A. Shimony. "The Depth and Breadth of John Bell's Physics." *Physics in Perspective* 4 (2002): 78–116.

Kochen, Simon, and Ernst Specker. "The Problem of Hidden Variables in Quantum Mechanics." *Journal of Mathematics and Mechanics* 17 (1967): 59–88.

Lüders, Gerhart. "On the Equivalence of Invariance under Time Reversal and under Particle-Antiparticle Conjugation for Relativistic Field Theories." *Matematisk-fysiske meddelelser det Kongelige Danske videnskabernes selskab* 5 (1954): 1–17.

Omnès, Roland. *Quantum Philosophy.* Princeton, NJ: Princeton University Press, 1999). Translation by Arturo Sangalli of *Philosophie de la science contemporaine.* Paris: Gallimard, 1994.

Page, Don. "The Einstein-Podolsky-Rosen Physical Reality Is Completely Described by Quantum Mechanics." *Physics Letters A* 91 (1982): 57–60.

Shimony, Abner. "Bell's Theorem." Updated 2004. In *Stanford Encyclopedia of Philosophy (Fall 2006 Edition)*, edited by Edward N. Zalta. Available at http://plato.stanford.edu/archives/fall2006/entries/bell-theorem/.

Tielman, Sam, Roman Jackiw, Bruno Zumino, and Edward Witten. *Current Algebra and Anomalies.* Princeton, NJ: Princeton University Press, 1985.

von Neumann, John. *Mathematische Grundlagen der Quantenmechanik.* Berlin: Springer, 1932. English translation, *Mathematical Foundations of Quantum Mechanics.* Princeton, NJ: Princeton University Press, 1955.

Whitaker, Andrew. "John Bell and the Most Profound Discovery of Science." *Physics World* (December 1998). Available from http://physicsweb.org/articles/world/11/12/8.

———. "John Bell in Belfast: Education and Early Years." In Bertlmann and Zeilinger, 2002.

R. Jackiw
A. Shimony

BENIOFF, VICTOR HUGO (*b.* Los Angeles, California, 14 September 1899; *d.* Mendocino, California, 29 February 1968), *geology, seismology.*

Benioff, who used his middle name, played an important role in the development of seismology, first by creating instruments of greater sensitivity than had been used before, and second by developing ideas about the relationships between earthquakes, rock deformation, and tectonics.

Benioff was raised by his mother, Frieda (née Widerquist) after her brief marriage to Simon Benioff. Originally Hugo had planned to become an astronomer, and worked summers doing solar observing at Mt. Wilson Observatory while attending Pomona College, from which he graduated in 1921; he then did graduate study at the California Institute of Technology (Caltech) while working as an assistant at Lick Observatory. However, he found it impossible to observe at night and sleep during the day, and so abandoned this career in 1924 for the newly formed seismology program that the Carnegie Institution of Washington had begun in 1921 under the leadership of H. O. Wood. He remained there as the program merged with Caltech, becoming a member of the faculty there in 1937. He stayed at Caltech until his retirement in 1965, though he had little involvement with students, working primarily with the other scientists and engineering staff at the Seismological Laboratory a few miles from campus.

Development of Instruments. The initial assignment given to Benioff was to develop a system that would allow seismic signals recorded at different stations to be accurately timed to the nearest tenth of a second: not an easy task. To drive the recording drums, he developed a motor driven by a tuning fork, to give uniform speed; time marks were put on the records from marine chronometers driving relays, with the whole system checked by twice-daily radio time signals—all run automatically.

Benioff's next contribution, in 1930, was to design a seismometer of much higher sensitivity than any so far built—an activity he pursued in various ways over the next three decades. At the time the highest sensitivity came either from very large masses (up to 20 tons) driving mechanical systems, or from electromagnetic systems, in which the motion of a coil in a magnetic field generated a voltage to drive a galvanometer. The sensitivity of these systems was limited by the low field strength available from permanent magnets. Benioff adapted a transducer that used changes in the flux through a magnetic circuit with a variable air gap (termed the reluctance) to generate a higher voltage for a given motion. Applying this variable-reluctance sensor to vertical and horizontal seismometers gave magnifications at periods of around one second up to 100 times larger than had been available before, especially in the vertical component. These instruments were first installed at the stations of the southern California network, where they not only recorded local earthquakes but gave high-quality records of distant earthquakes, showing seismic waves not previously observed and providing especially good records of deep earthquakes.

Hugo Benioff. *Benioff kneeling next to his 60 ft. strain seismograph.* AP IMAGES.

With slight redesigns, these instruments remained one of the best available seismic sensors for many years; they were used in the World-Wide Standardized Seismic Network, which operated from 1961 into the 1980s.

The next application of the variable-reluctance transducer, in 1932, was to a strain seismograph, which used a steel rod attached to the ground at one end, with the other end using the transducer to measure the distance from the end of the rod to another attached point, so that the whole system measured the stretching of the ground from seismic waves. Originally designed to give good records at high frequencies, this turned out to be most useful at lower ones, especially for recording long-period surface waves from distant earthquakes.

After 1946 Benioff combined instrument development with studies of earthquake mechanism and the relationship between seismicity and tectonics. Using the recent results of his colleagues Beno Gutenberg and Charles F. Richter on the relationship between earthquake magnitude and energy in seismic waves, he equated this energy to the energy released by the elastic rebound of rocks around an earthquake fault, and from this derived the average strain in the earthquake region. For a series of earthquakes, plotting the cumulative strain against time showed patterns that could be related to experimental studies on the creep of rocks under stress. Benioff's first application of these ideas, in 1949, was to argue that the pattern of strain release for deep earthquakes in a particular area showed that they all occurred on a common structure, which he took to be a large inclined fault. In 1952 he extended this concept to zones of deep earthquakes all around the Pacific Ocean, making many geologists aware of these large and deep structures; when plate tectonics explained these regions of deep seismicity as locations of subduction, they came to be called Benioff zones. While Benioff used his strain-release methodology to display other patterns of earthquake occurrence, this approach was not much pursued by other seismologists.

Benioff, in his instrumental work in the 1950s, continued to pursue higher sensitivity at longer periods. One stimulus for this was the observation on the strainmeter, following a great earthquake in 1952, of signals with about a one-hour period, which could be interpreted as free vibrations of the whole Earth, a phenomenon known from theory but never observed. Benioff improved the performance of his strainmeter, and built new instruments in quieter locations in California and (as part of the International Geophysical Year in 1957–1958) in Peru. When the largest earthquake of the twentieth century occurred in Chile in 1960, these instruments gave clear records of free vibrations at many frequencies, inaugurating a new branch of seismology. For his accomplishments Benioff was elected to the National Academy of Sciences in 1953, and received two awards, the Arthur L. Day Medal of the Geological Society of America in 1957 and the William Bowie Medal of the American Geophysical Union in 1965.

Benioff had a lifelong interest in acoustics and music, which led him to develop novel musical instruments and to experiment with listening to sped-up seismograms to see what the ear might detect. He put this interest to more direct use during World War II, when he and his engineering staff worked on radar and acoustics for the Submarine Signal Company.

Benioff married Alice Silverman in 1929; they had three children and divorced in 1953, after which he married Mildred Lent, with whom he had one child.

BIBLIOGRAPHY

WORKS BY BENIOFF

"Seismic Evidence for the Fault Origin of Oceanic Deeps." *Bulletin of the Geological Society of America* 60 (1949): 1837–1856.

"Earthquakes and Rock Creep." *Bulletin of the Seismological Society of America* 41 (1951): 31–62.

"Earthquake Seismographs and Associated Instruments." In *Advances in Geophysics,* vol. 2. New York: Academic Press, 1955.

With Frank Press and Stewart W. Smith. "Excitation of the Free Oscillations of the Earth by Earthquakes." *Journal of Geophysical Research* 66 (1961): 605–619.

OTHER SOURCES

Goodstein, Judith R. "Waves in the Earth: Seismology Comes to Southern California." *Historical Studies in the Physical and Biological Sciences* 14 (1984): 201–230.

Press, Frank. "Victor Hugo Benioff." *Biographical Memoirs,* vol. 43. Washington, DC: National Academy of Sciences, 1978.

Duncan Carr Agnew

BERGERON, TOR HAROLD PERCIVAL

(*b.* Godstone, Surrey, England, 15 August 1891; *d.* Uppsala, Sweden, 13 June 1977), *synoptic meteorology, cloud and precipitation physics, weather forecasting.*

Bergeron was one of the principal scientists in the Bergen School of Meteorology, which transformed this science by introducing a new conceptual foundation for understanding and predicting weather. While developing innovative methods of forecasting, the Bergen scientists established the notion of weather fronts and elaborated a new model of extratropical cyclones that accounted for their birth, growth, and decay. Bergeron is credited with discovering the occlusion process, which marks the final stage in the life cycle of an extratropical cyclone. Bergeron also contributed to cloud physics, most notably the description of the Bergeron-Findeisen process by which precipitation forms inside a cloud containing both ice crystals and water droplets.

The Early Years. Bergeron was born in England to Swedish parents Armand Bergeron and Hilda Stawe. Much later, evidence came to light in Sweden that Bergeron was one of several illegitimate children born to a radical Stockholm intellectual couple who were also owners of a prominent newspaper. Bergeron, as with the other children, was given to a well-chosen family abroad, with money provided for his education in Sweden. His mother knew Nils Ekholm, director of the Swedish Meteorological Institute (SMI), which proved valuable for the young Bergeron. After receiving his BSc from the University of Stockholm in 1916, Bergeron spent the summers taking observations of visibility at different locations around Sweden and returning to SMI in Stockholm during the autumn to complete his research. He found that changes in visibility seemed to be related to wind-shift lines (what would be later called fronts). On 1 January 1919, Bergeron received the title of "extra assistant meteorologist" at the reorganized SMI, later called the Swedish Meteorological and Hydrological Institute (SMHI). Within a few months, the tiny core of the incipient Bergen School, father and son Vilhelm and Jacob Bjerknes and Halvor

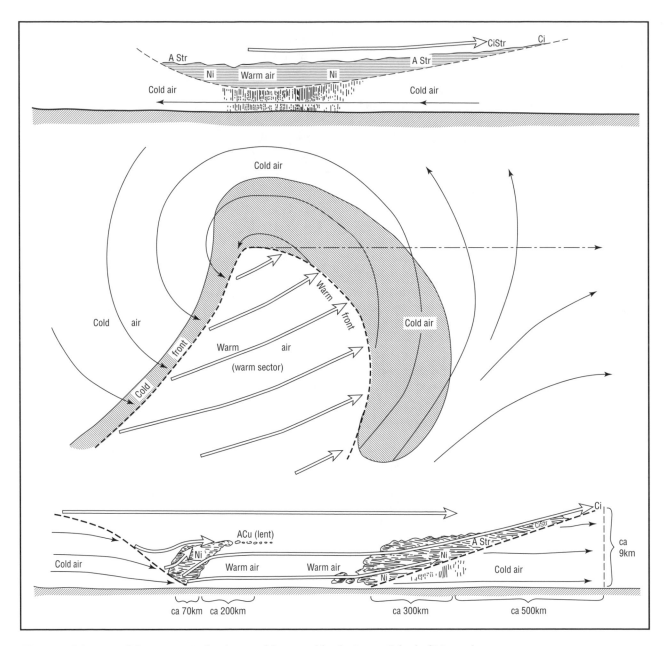

Figure 1. *Schematic of the extratropical cyclone model proposed by the Bergen School of Meteorology.*

Solberg, recruited Bergeron to Bergen, Norway, to join a new weather forecasting service.

The Bergen School and the Occlusion Process. In 1917, the Bergen Museum (precursor of Bergen University) called Vilhelm Bjerknes to a new professorship in meteorology. Bjerknes had been working in Leipzig on a research program for creating an exact physics of the atmosphere and ocean. In contrast, meteorologists at the time predicted weather primarily by often inaccurate empirical rules of thumb and statistical insight. Upon coming to Bergen in 1918, Bjerknes organized an experimental

weather prediction service, directing a number of enthusiastic young scientists in developing new forecasting practices based on insight into physical processes. The impact of the work performed in Bergen, combined with the incubation of several high-quality scientists, had an immense impact internationally on the burgeoning scientific field of meteorology.

Much of the earliest work in Bergen focused on understanding the structure of extratropical cyclones, storms outside the tropics responsible for most of the weather in the midlatitudes (not violent tropical storms like hurricanes). Based on the first summer's forecasting,

Jacob Bjerknes proposed in November 1918 a new model for these disturbances which accounted for their asymmetric distribution of precipitation (Figure 1). The basic structure was described as a counterclockwise swirl of air around the low-pressure center. Warm air advancing from the south rose up over cold air retreating northward on the east side of the low center. The boundary between the two was ultimately called a *warm front*. On the southwest side of the low center, dense cold air advancing from the north lifted the warm air, forming a boundary later called a *cold front*. The recently ended World War I inspired using the word *front* to describe battle lines of advancing and retreating air masses. Bergeron would later suggest the symbols that came to be used for cold and warm fronts (lines with filled triangles and semicircles, respectively) on a postcard to Jacob Bjerknes on 8 January 1924.

During the fall of 1919, Bergeron noticed that the cold front at times seemed to catch up to and overtake the warm front, what he dubbed *sammenklapping* (roughly "coming together" or "closing up"). He intuited that the cold front probably rode aloft over the warm front, but he remained puzzled over the nature and significance of this finding. It was not clear whether *sammenklapping* entailed an evolutionary component of extratropical cyclones or simply a local geographical effect. Furthermore, Jacob Bjerknes resisted changes to his model.

While in Stockholm and Bergen, Bergeron returned on occasion to this baffling phenomenon. International efforts to increase the amount and frequency of weather data enabled Bergeron to bring into clearer focus the cyclone's structure. He arrived at a convincing three-dimensional representation by which a cold front and warm front merged, resulting in the previously sandwiched warm air being lifted aloft. Without access to the warm air fueling the storm, such a cyclone would weaken. Eventually, Bergeron used the term *occlusion* for this process, and the resulting boundary between the two cold air masses was called an *occluded front*. By 1922, he convinced Jacob Bjerknes of the importance of this process to the evolution of extratropical cyclones. This discovery, along with Solberg's concept of cyclone families, changed the Bergen cyclone model from a static conceptualization (Figure 1) into one that featured the entire life cycle of birth, maturity, and death (Figure 2). Forecasters and theoreticians now had a model to help them understand the processes affecting storm intensification and decay.

Occlusion is a seminal feature of the classic 1922 paper by Jacob Bjerknes and Halvor Solberg, "Life Cycle of Cyclones and the Polar Front Theory of Atmospheric Circulation," yet Bergeron was not a coauthor. At the time, Bergeron was in Stockholm where he was preoccupied with other tasks, including preparation of a supplemental manuscript, which never was completed. Bergeron

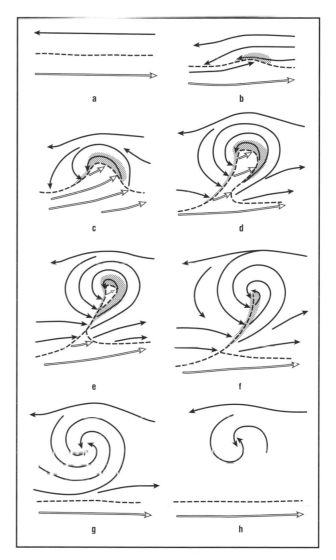

Figure 2. *Schematic life cycle of the extratropical cyclone model proposed by the Bergen School of Meteorology with Bergeron's occluded front shown in panels e and f. Dashed lines represent surface fronts; arrows represent streamlines of the flow.*

was a perfectionist, oftentimes not completing publications for want of further analysis. And whereas Solberg and the Bjerkneses accepted the need to simplify when presenting the new findings, Bergeron aimed to depict all the new insights in their full complexity. By temperament and principle, he could not easily collaborate with the others in writing what he considered a much too hastily prepared publication. Although he was not a coauthor, his Bergen colleagues always gave him full credit in discovering occlusion, the capstone of the Bergen school's early achievements.

Indirect Aerology and Air-Mass Analysis. To convince others of the reality and importance of fronts, the Bergen

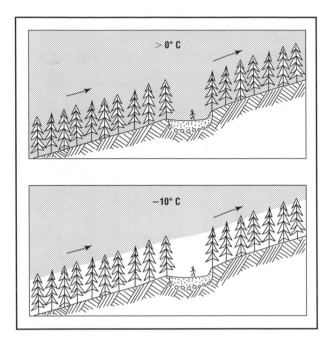

Figure 3. *Sketch of the conditions (top) not favoring and (bottom) favoring the Bergeron–Findeisen process. Dotted areas represent clouds composed of liquid water droplets.*

meteorologists needed to create systematic methods to reproduce them reliably in daily forecasting work. Although all members of the emerging Bergen school contributed towards this goal, Bergeron played a crucial role in establishing innovative forecasting practices.

Bergeron collaborated with Swede and close friend Ernst Calwagen to bring greater clarity to an ever-growing number of new but elusive phenomena emerging from the analysis of weather maps. To achieve this goal, they sought to refine and systematize the Bergen group's innovative methods for observing and analyzing weather. They brought to maturity a method of *indirect aerology*, to identify fronts and track the life history of large homogeneous bodies of air called air masses. At a time when direct measurement of the atmosphere through weather balloons and kites above the surface (aerology) was not available for daily forecasting, this method combined observation of the clouds and sky overhead with analyses of phenomena plotted on the weather map to envision the physical processes occurring in a three-dimensional atmosphere. With the help of the Norwegian military air forces Calwagen began to supplement the indirect aerological methods with direct vertical measurements in the atmosphere. While taking observations on 10 August 1925, Calwagen was killed along with the pilot after their airplane fell apart in midair. Calwagen's death deeply affected Bergeron—he never flew again. Bergeron took over his friend's work, integrated it with his own, and helped bring the

methods of air-mass analysis to maturity. Indirect aerology enabled the Bergen meteorologists to achieve more accurate and detailed predictions, as well as to gain insight into the nature of fronts, cyclones, and air masses. For Bergeron as well as other members of the Bergen school, synoptic meteorology, or the study of the state of the atmosphere at a specific moment in time on scales with a range of several hundred kilometers, was a legitimate means for winning new knowledge of the atmosphere, an equal partner to theoretical and mathematical study.

The Bergeron-Findeisen Process. When Bergeron returned to Bergen in 1922, he stopped for several weeks at a health resort at Voksenkollen, a hill north of Oslo often enclosed by fog. Bergeron noted that when the temperature was well below freezing the roads through the forest were clear of fog. When the temperature was above freezing, however, the fog would extend down to the ground. Bergeron recognized that the saturation water-vapor pressure over water is higher than that over ice at temperatures below freezing. Thus, he surmised that diffusion of water vapor from evaporating supercooled liquid-water droplets in the fog to frost growing on the trees might have been occurring to disperse the fog. Although Alfred Wegener had already argued in 1911 that such growth was possible in a cloud with both ice and water droplets, Bergeron was the first to recognize that this growth of the ice crystals to precipitation-sized particles at the expense of the supercooled liquid-water droplets could lead to precipitation. These ideas would be briefly developed in his doctoral thesis in 1928, and presented more fully in 1933. Coupled with experimental confirmation by the German Walter Findeisen in 1938, this process of forming precipitation in a cloud possessing both ice crystals and supercooled liquid-water droplets was eventually called the Bergeron-Findeisen process (sometimes called the Wegener-Bergeron-Findeisen process). This discovery promoted the subsequent growth of cloud physics as a vital subdiscipline, not the least by providing a means to dissipate fog and a physical mechanism for precipitation enhancement through cloud seeding.

Apostle of the Bergen School. More than any other member of the Bergen School, Bergeron conducted the detailed case studies, lectures, and travel needed to develop grassroots support abroad for the Bergen School concepts and methods. His role as apostle was facilitated by his linguistic talents: he spoke seven languages and knew some of three others.

While employed during the early and mid-1920s by the Norwegian Meteorological Institute, Bergeron spent time in Leipzig, working with Gustav Swoboda to demonstrate the applicability of the Bergen School concepts in an analysis of a weather event over Europe. "Wellen und Wirbel an einer quasistationären Grenzfläche über Europa" [Waves and vortices at a quasi-stationary frontal surface over Europe] (1924) was the first detailed publication to use the methods developed in Bergen. Bergeron wrote part 1 of his "Über die dreidimensional verknüpfende Wetteranalyse" [Three-dimensionally combining synoptic analysis] in 1928, for which he received a doctoral degree from the University of Oslo. That paper covered many disparate topics, including air-mass analysis and frontogenesis (the process of forming and strengthening a front). Bergeron recognized that fronts were found in regions where the horizontal flow was confluent. What had been considered an uninteresting singularity in the field of flow—the neutral point or col—held the key for understanding where and when fronts form. Bergeron showed that such flows tended to occur between the semipermanent highs and lows, explaining the climatological locations of fronts around the world.

After completing his doctorate, Bergeron traveled to Malta and the Soviet Union to lecture on the Bergen School methods. Part 2 of his doctoral thesis on fronts and their perturbations was published in Russian in 1934. But his overly critical demands prevented him from publishing his own research and completing several books. Still, he produced several texts that played critical roles in the diffusion of the Bergen meteorology. Although many of Bergeron's papers remained unpublished into the early 2000s, his popular lecture notes served as foundations of major textbooks on synoptic meteorology written by his colleagues in Russian, English, and German.

In 1935, Bergeron failed in his bid to be appointed professor of meteorology at Uppsala University. Bergeron and his many supporters from abroad could not overcome local bias against synoptic meteorology, which was considered inferior to laboratory-based research, as well as a long-standing resentment against Bjerknes and the "Norwegian" achievements with which he was intimately associated. Bergeron returned to Stockholm in 1936, initially as a meteorologist, but eventually as scientific chief of SMHI. He began giving lectures and conducting laboratory exercises in weather-map-analysis techniques based on the Bergen methods. These proved popular, although at times his perfectionist goals in map analysis and in the wording of predictions created tension between him and his meteorological colleagues working with him at SMHI. Legend has it that he insisted on the exclusive use of a particular brand of colored pencils if accurate weather maps were to be drawn. Within two years, however, the quality of Swedish forecasting had significantly improved. Often meteorologists came from abroad to Bergeron for training. During this time, Bergeron also served on the Commission of Synoptic Meteorology of the World Meteorological Organization and was influential in the development of the international terminology and classification of clouds and precipitation.

Uppsala University. By the time World War II ended, Sweden had a great shortage of meteorologists, especially for its rapidly growing aviation interests. Practical weather forecasting classes were not offered at the universities, and an official report indicated the need for a professorship in this subject. Although efforts were underway to create such a professorship for him in Stockholm, in 1947 Bergeron instead became professor and head of the Department of Synoptic Meteorology at Uppsala University. Despite Bergeron's reputation, finding students was difficult, especially after Carl-Gustaf Rossby established an active department at Stockholm. Nevertheless, Bergeron persisted in lecturing and writing on the principles of meteorology.

Slowly he returned to the topic of cloud physics. In 1949, Bergeron posited that ice crystals could fall from high-altitude clouds into liquid-water clouds below. Such a *seeder-feeder process* could enhance precipitation at the ground. He also wrote about the feasibility of artificially stimulating the production of precipitation from a synoptic and cloud-physics perspective.

In 1953, Bergeron started Project Pluvius, a research program designed to understand precipitation better by establishing high-resolution surface rainfall networks. Among its rich research results, Project Pluvius showed that a modest elevation of only 40 to 70 meters could produce orographic precipitation enhancement. During the last decades of his life, Bergeron wrote many articles and lectures on the history of meteorology. He seems in part to have been drawn to history after his unsuccessful bid for a professorship in Uppsala in the mid-1930s. History provided a way to set the record straight as to his own and others' contributions to the Bergen School, which is not always clear from the publications. He also sought to show what the Bergen School actually did accomplish, since the originality of its contributions was, in part, denied by some German, Austrian, and Swedish meteorologists. His most important contribution from this time, "Weather Forecasting: Methods in Scientific Weather Analysis and Forecasting. An Outline in the History of Ideas and Hints at a Program" (1959) offers a highly personal, but insightful, essay outlining the development of modern forecasting as the result of improvements in observations, analytical tools, and models of atmospheric structures. Bergeron retired in 1961, but continued to work on Project Pluvius, spending his time traveling and lecturing worldwide, including several trips to the United States. He died in 1977 of pancreatic cancer, the last of the original Bergen School meteorologists to do so.

BIBLIOGRAPHY

A complete bibliography for Bergeron can be found in Liljequist, 1981a. His correspondence and unpublished manuscripts are housed in the Department of Meteorology, Uppsala University.

WORKS BY BERGERON

"Wellen und Wirbel an einer quasistationären Grenzfläche über Europa.Analyse der Wetterepoche 9.–14. Oktober 1923." [Waves and vortices at a quasistationary frontal surface over Europe. Analysis of the Weather Epoch 9-14 October 1923.]. *Veröffentlichungen des Geophysikalischen Instituts der Universität Leipzig,* series 2, 3 (1924): 62–172.

Über die dreidimensional verknüpfende Wetteranalyse, I. Teil. (Three-dimensionally combining synoptic analysis, part 1.) Geofysiske Publikasjone 5. Oslo: Grøndahl & Sons boktrykkeri, I kommission hos Cammermeyers boghandel, 1928.

Trechmerno-Svjaznyj Sinopticeskij Analiz, I-II. (Three-Dimensionally Combining Synoptic Analysis.) Moscow, 1934.

"Methods in Scientific Weather Analysis and Forecasting: An Outline in the History of Ideas and Hints at a Program." In *The Atmosphere and the Sea in Motion: Scientific Contributions to the Rossby Memorial Volume,* edited by Bert Bolin. New York: Rockefeller Institute Press, 1959.

"Some Autobiographic Notes in Connection with the Ice Nucleus Theory of Precipitation Release." *Bulletin of the American Meteorological Society* 59 (April 1978): 390–392.

OTHER SOURCES

Blanchard, Duncan C. "Tor Bergeron and His 'Autobiographic Notes.'" *Bulletin of the American Meteorological Society* 59 (April 1978): 389–390.

Bjerknes, Jacob, and Halvor Solberg. "Meteorological Conditions for the Formation of Rain." *Geofysiske Publikasjoner* 2, no. 3 (1921): 3–60.

———. "Life Cycle of Cyclones and the Polar Front Theory of Atmospheric Circulation." *Geofysiske Publikasjoner* 3, no. 1 (1922): 3–18.

Eliassen, Arnt. "Tor Bergeron 1891–1977." *Bulletin of the American Meteorological Society* 59 (April 1978): 387–389.

Friedman, Robert Marc. *Appropriating the Weather: Vilhelm Bjerknes and the Construction of a Modern Meteorology.* Ithaca: Cornell University Press, 1989.

Liljequist, Gosta H. "Tor Bergeron: A Biography." *Pure and Applied Geophysics* 119 (1981a): 409–442.

Liljequist, Gosta H., ed. *Weather and Weather Maps: A Volume Dedicated to the Memory of Tor Bergeron (15.8.1891–13.6.1977).* Basel: Birkhäuser, 1981b.

Schwerdtfeger, Werner. "Comments on Tor Bergeron's Contributions to Synoptic Meteorology." *Pure and Applied Geophysics* 119 (1981): 501–509.

Robert Marc Friedman
David M. Schultz

BERGMANN, ERNST DAVID (*b.* Karlsruhe, Germany, 18 October 1903; *d.* Jerusalem, Israel, 6 April 1975), *organic chemistry, education, science policy in Israel.*

Bergmann, a German-Jewish chemist, was forced out of his position in Berlin under Nazi laws and emigrated to Mandate Palestine in 1934 to become the first director of what was later the Weizmann Institute of Science. He subsequently aided the British scientific effort during World War II. He is best known for leading the development of science in the fledgling State of Israel, including the inauguration of its nuclear research program. Bergmann typified the close involvement of scientists in Israel with political and defense matters. His research interests in organic chemistry were extensive. He introduced German-style chemical research and teaching at the Weizmann Institute of Science and then at the Hebrew University of Jerusalem.

Early Life in Berlin. Bergmann was born into a strongly Zionist-leaning German family. In 1908, his father, Rabbi Judah Bergmann, accepted a post in Berlin and moved there with his mother, Hedwig Rosenzweig Bergmann, and his brothers, Artur and Felix. Both brothers later held influential positions in Israel, the latter as a pharmacologist.

Ernst David studied chemistry at the University of Berlin, where in 1924 he began research for his doctoral degree under the supervision of Wilhelm Schlenk. His work involved investigations on polycyclic aromatic compounds, of great interest to the chemistry of synthetic dyestuffs and, increasingly, in cancer studies. In 1927, Bergmann was awarded his doctorate and in the following year was appointed *Privatdozent* (lecturer) at the university's chemical institute. In 1928, he married the chemist Ottilie Blum, a research assistant in the institute. By then, his outstanding scientific capabilities were widely recognized. In 1929, chemistry Nobel Laureate Richard Willstätter proposed that Bergmann become his successor to the chair of chemistry at the ETH (Eidgenössische Technische Hochschule, or Federal Institute of Technology) in Zurich; however, the more renowned Leopold Ruzicka was appointed instead. With Schlenk, Bergmann in 1932 published the first volume of a textbook on chemistry, *Ausführliches Lehrbuch der Organischen Chemie,* and was the leading candidate for a vacant chair at the Technische Hochschule in Berlin. Following passage of the anti-Semitic Law for the Restoration of the Professional Civil Service on 7 April 1933 under the Nazi regime, Bergmann was not appointed to the Berlin position. On the contrary, he was dismissed from his post as research assistant and lost his *venia legendi*—his right to teach at a German university.

Schlenk himself was reproached for remaining "alien to the [Nazi] movement" and for his contacts with Jews, which in some cases continued after 1933, including communication with Bergmann. Schlenk was forced to leave his post in Berlin and, in 1935, was transferred to Tübingen. He faced a difficult choice in 1939, when the manuscript for the second volume of the textbook written with Bergmann was ready. As he told Bergmann, he could either publish as sole author, since Bergmann's name could not appear on the cover or withdraw the manuscript from publication altogether. Schlenk chose the former option, despite Bergmann's strong protests.

The Daniel Sieff Institute. In 1933, Carl Neuberg, director of the Berlin's Kaiser Wilhelm Institute for Biochemistry, recommended Bergmann to the Zionist leader and organic chemist and microbiologist Chaim Weizmann, who at that time was working in London at the Featherstone Laboratories. Bergmann immediately moved to England to join Weizmann, whose reputation was based mainly on pure-strain fermentation studies, and especially his acetone process, which was important in the Allied war effort during 1914–1918. In 1933, Weizmann was in the process of establishing the Daniel Sieff Institute at Rehovot, in Mandate Palestine, after he became frustrated by differences with Albert Einstein over how the Hebrew University of Jerusalem, opened in 1925, was run, and also because of the poor quality of research at the university. He was looking for a head of the new Sieff Institute, dedicated to applied research, and offered Bergmann its directorship. Bergmann was also offered a post at Oxford by Sir Robert Robinson, which he declined in favor of Rehovot. The opportunity of participating in the scientific development of a Jewish homeland, despite the complete absence of facilities, held a stronger appeal to Bergmann than a position at a prestigious European university and the chance to be associated with Robinson, a world-renowned chemist. From London, Bergmann and Weizmann organized staff and equipment for Rehovot. On 1 January 1934, Bergmann arrived in Palestine, and soon after the institute was opened.

Research and Teaching. Among Bergmann's main fields of research at Rehovot were reactions of metals with aromatic compounds (a continuation of his work with Schlenk), which in 1935 and 1936 led to joint publications with Chaim Weizmann, Felix Bergmann, and Ernst David's wife, Ottilie Blum-Bergmann (who died in the mid-1930s). Another research area was the related arsenic-containing heterocyclic aromatic compounds, including analogs of dyestuffs such as methylene blue, and products originally used as chemical warfare agents during World War I, although when this work was published, the interest was probably in their pharmaceutical or pesticidal properties. Other fields were photochemistry and polycyclic aromatic compounds, again publishing with Weizmann (1938 and 1939) and with Felix and Ottilie (from 1937); syntheses of biochemical interest; and isolation and modification of natural products. The work on polycyclic compounds was, incidentally, also an extension of Weizmann's own earlier studies in the field of synthetic dyestuff chemistry, particularly in connection with derivatives used in the manufacture of indanthrene vat dyes.

Wartime Research. In 1939, the commencement of World War II brought Bergmann back to London to work on war-related research projects for the Ministry of Supply at the Grosvenor Laboratories, where Weizmann was an advisor. At the Manchester Oil Refinery in Manchester, England, Bergmann studied a process suggested by Weizmann for making aromatic compounds—in particular, toluene for high octane aviation fuel—from straight chain hydrocarbons (olefins) by high-temperature cracking in the presence of a catalyst. This was known as the catarole process. It offered the potential for large-scale production of aromatic compounds and reactive aliphatics from petroleum. In 1942, Weizmann and Bergmann traveled to the United States, where Bergmann worked with Commercial Solvents, at Terre Haute, Indiana, on the conversion of agricultural products into isoprene, the building block for synthetic rubber. This fermentation process was not adopted, according to Weizmann, because the oil lobby convinced the U.S. government to adopt exclusively petroleum-based synthetic rubber processes. (By contrast, in Germany coal-derived synthetic rubber processes were developed based on acetylene chemistry, another of Bergmann's interests.) Despite the setback, and possibly in part because of it, this and similar endeavors provided a thorough grounding in approaches to the supply of essential strategic materials that would be put to good use from 1946, when Bergmann returned to Palestine and the Daniel Sieff Institute. He also continued his research on polycyclic aromatic hydrocarbons, including hydrocarbons with two linearly annellated rings. At Rehovot, young people from the Science Corps (HEMED) of the Haganah, the military organization that later became the nucleus of the Israel Defence Forces, worked closely under Bergmann's guidance on weapons research.

Weizmann Institute and Hebrew University. The State of Israel was established in 1948, with Chaim Weizmann as its first president. One year later the Weizmann Institute of Science was founded (with the Daniel Sieff Institute becoming the Department of Organic Chemistry), and Bergmann was named as its scientific director. He began work on secret military projects and, significantly, grew close to David Ben-Gurion, Weizmann's rival in the

Zionist movement. Following on from his HEMED activities, Bergmann favored military-related work as a principal area of research at the institute. However, this met with strong opposition from Weizmann, despite the fact that he greatly admired Bergmann. Weizmann was adamant that he did not want the generals to decide on any aspect of the research policy at the Weizmann Institute, and he rejected any dependence on funding from the Ministry of Defence. It was mainly over these differences concerning the organization of national science, and Bergmann's work as scientific advisor to Ben-Gurion, that the previous father-and-son relationship between Weizmann and Bergmann eventually soured. The rift between the two men was aggravated by personal problems in which Mrs. Weizmann and the woman who would in 1952 become Bergmann's second wife, Hani Itin, were very much involved. In 1951, Bergmann left the Weizmann Institute and the following year was appointed professor at the Hebrew University of Jerusalem, where the Department of Organic Chemistry was divided into two sections, one now headed by Bergmann, the other by Max Frankel, who had emigrated from Austria in 1925. Bergmann spent the remainder of his scientific career at Hebrew University, where he also served with distinction as vice president.

Research in Israel. Bergmann's research activities had a significant impact in Israel, particularly his studies on cancer and aromaticity at Hebrew University; his supervision of research at the Technion, in Haifa, in the early 1950s; and during the 1950s and 1960s, his investigations into organofluorine chemistry at the University of Tel Aviv and into applied science in general. His research interests included acetylene chemistry, which held out great promise in the late 1940s and early 1950s for the production of commercial chemicals, based on the work of J. Walter Reppe at IG Farben, and, increasingly, areas of biological chemistry. He also returned to what his colleague David Ginsberg called his "first love," the study of polycyclic aromatic compounds, an endeavor that contributed to theoretical, physical, and organic chemistry; the chemistry of dyestuffs; and knowledge of biological activity, the latter emphasized in cancer studies carried out at both the Weizmann Institute and Hebrew University. During the 1960s, he also returned to the chemistry of insecticides. He authored or coauthored over five hundred scientific publications, as well as two books: *The Chemistry of Acetylene and Related Compounds* and *Isomerism and Isomerization of Organic Compounds*, both published in 1948. Important reviews included "Pentalene and Heptalene" in *Non-benzenoid Aromatic Compounds* and "The Michael Reaction" (co-author) in *Organic Reactions,* both published in 1959.

The Nuclear Program. While Bergmann helped science in Israel to become respected, his greatest contribution was, as Ephraim Katzir, chemist, molecular biologist, and later president of Israel, emphasized, not in science but mainly in politics and defense activities (Katzir, interview by Ute Deichmann, 27 May 1998). In *Israel and the Bomb* (1998), an analysis of the early history of Israel's nuclear program, Avner Cohen stresses Bergmann's decisive role in converting Ben-Gurion to the view that access to nuclear energy was essential for the survival and prosperity of Israel, since it could create unprecedented options for both civilian and military applications. Even at the end of the 1940s Bergmann believed that Israel should adopt a nuclear program, not only for military purposes but also to provide energy for the desalination of water. In 1952, Ben-Gurion founded the Israeli Atomic Energy Commission (IAEC) on Bergmann's recommendation and with the backing of Shimon Peres, a leading Labour Party politician and director-general of the Ministry of Defence. Bergmann was appointed the IAEC's first director. In common with Ben-Gurion, Bergmann was convinced that the tragic circumstances of the recent Nazi Holocaust fully justified Israel's taking all steps to ensure its survival by becoming a nuclear power. Peres has cited Bergmann as saying, "I am convinced that the State of Israel needs a defense research program of its own so that we shall never again be as lambs led to the slaughter" (Cohen, 1998, pp. 15–16).

Bergmann's wish to model Israel's nuclear program on French lines—as state-sponsored, project-oriented big science aimed primarily at the production of nuclear materials—met with strong opposition from the nuclear physicists in the IAEC. To them, nuclear research and teaching, not production, had the highest priority, and they wanted the IAEC primarily to support and coordinate academic research. Moreover, they considered Bergmann much too optimistic. In addition, Bergmann's authoritarian management style as chairman was highly resented, causing one of the IAEC's scientists, Zvi Lipkin, later to describe it as reminiscent of a "Russian or Prussian regime" (Cohen, "Before the Beginning," p. 130). Under Minister of Defence Pinhas Lavon, the physicists managed for several years to carry out nuclear research at the Weizmann Institute—independently of Bergmann's influence—at least until the budget was cut. Only after Ben-Gurion returned to power in 1955, first as minister of defense and then as prime minister, did Bergmann's and Peres's influence once more become important. French assistance was deemed essential, and in the aftermath of the Suez Crisis of 1956, the French became very receptive to Israel's nuclear needs and contributed essential expertise until the mid-1960s. At the end of the 1950s, Bergmann was instrumental in procuring heavy water for the nuclear program from Norway. He also played an important role in the development of Israel's chemical and biological warfare capabilities that from 1952 came under the aegis of the Institute of Biological Research. This work was considered essential for defense prior to the establishment of a nuclear capability.

Bergmann the Teacher. Bergmann's students, many colleagues, and politicians were impressed by his grasp of fundamental knowledge, his energy, and his talent for organization. Bergmann, in common with other scientists trained under the German system, brought with him a breadth of knowledge and tradition of thoroughness in teaching and research that has endured and influenced generations of chemists. This included long hours spent in the laboratory, combined with colloquia with the laboratory supervisor, who was frequently the professor himself. There was also the personal example set by the professor who visited the laboratory constantly, wearing his lab coat and even performing experiments. Ernst Bergmann would on occasion work overnight in the laboratory at Hebrew University, despite his many other commitments.

Chaim Gilon, professor of organic chemistry at Hebrew University, who was in close scientific contact with Bergmann, emphasized Bergmann's great knowledge in all fields of chemistry, which he taught in nine lectures given during the same period of time. "His lectures were brilliant," Gilon has said. "He was a very ambitious and a very capable man. Having an excellent memory, he could tell every student who asked him about organic syntheses the page number of the pertinent volume of a journal or book, which contained the answer" (Gilon, interview by Ute Deichmann, 14 December 1994).

According to Bergmann's former student, Mordecai Rabinovitz, also a professor of organic chemistry at Hebrew University, Bergmann's students sometimes had problems following lectures since, "while he was talking about one topic, he would already be drawing structural formulae for the next topic on the blackboard" (Rabinovitz, interview by Ute Deichmann and Anthony S. Travis, 4 December 2003). Joseph Klein, another professor of organic chemistry at Hebrew University, has recalled, "He was a good teacher for students who wanted to learn. His lectures were well prepared, but not interrupted by nice stories. He worked hard until the last day of his life" (Klein, interview by Ute Deichmann, 23 November 1994). Gilon emphasized Bergmann's role in science policy:

> He always saw the application side of science. Coming from a German origin, he never spent a wasted minute, and he embarked on many activities apart from his research. Thus he became scientific advisor to Ben Gurion, and it is due to Bergmann's influence that science in Israel became

highly respected and by that gained much more support financially than before. If Bergmann had concentrated his forces, he would presumably have achieved more in his own research. (Gilon, interview by Ute Deichmann, 14 December 1994)

Rabinovitz considers Bergmann a "lost star" for organic chemistry, because "as soon as he came to Israel, he dealt with many other things.... Bergmann was a man of vision" (Rabinovitz, interview by Ute Deichmann and Anthony S. Travis, 4 December 2003). The ability and readiness to look in many directions, political as well as scientific, reduced Bergmann's focus on organic chemistry and increased his commitment to politics and defense.

Bergmann transferred to Israel from Germany not only his fields of research but also stereotypical German characteristics, such as punctuality and the placing of high demands on himself and his students. But, as Gilon has recalled, he also changed certain of his attitudes. Thus, he was able to combine his sense of order with Israeli improvisation, and though he did not become close to his students, he treated them in a friendly way. This was also the experience of Rabinovitz, who opined that Bergmann was, at least outside of politics, a real gentleman, despite being very authoritarian.

Ernst David Bergmann transformed the study of organic chemistry in Mandate Palestine and Israel and was responsible for its high international standing. After 1948, Bergmann also played an important political role in influencing Israeli science and military research policy for decades. Bergmann and another young scientist, the Hungarian-born Ladislaus Farkas, a physical chemist, who was also forced to emigrate from Germany, together contributed greatly to the emergence of world-class scientific research in Israel. This was possible because Israeli political leaders considered science a decisive basis for the intellectual and economic development of the country and—despite many problems due to the weak economy and military threats—provided the necessary freedom and support. Bergmann's name is perpetuated through the Weizmann Institute's Ernst David Bergmann Prize.

BIBLIOGRAPHY

WORKS BY BERGMANN

With Wilhelm Schlenk. *Ausführliches Lehrbuch der Organischen Chemie.* Vol. 1. Leipzig, Poland, and Vienna: Beuticke, 1932. This was originally planned as a three-volume textbook, of which only two volumes appeared.

The Chemistry of Acetylene and Related Compounds. New York: Interscience, 1948.

Isomerism and Isomerization of Organic Compounds. New York: Interscience, 1948.

With Chaim Weizmann, Herbert Steiner, and Max Sulzbacher. "Production of Aromatic Hydrocarbons from Petroleum." *Journal of the Society of Chemical Industry* 67 (March 1948): 114–118.

With David Ginsburg and Raphael Pappo. "The Michael Reaction." In *Organic Reactions*. Vol. 10. New York: John Wiley, 1959, 199–555.

"Pentalene and Heptalene." In *Non-benzenoid Aromatic Compounds*, edited by David Ginsberg. New York: Interscience, 1959, 141–169.

OTHER SOURCES

Clar, E. *Polycyclic Hydrocarbons*. London; New York: Academic Press, 1964.

Cohen, Avner. "Before the Beginning: The Early History of Israel's Nuclear Project." *Israel Studies* 3 (1998): 112–139.

———. *Israel and the Bomb*. New York: Columbia University Press, 1998.

Deichmann, Ute. "The Expulsion of Jewish Chemists and Biochemists from Academia in Nazi Germany." *Perspectives on Science* 7 (1999): 1–86.

———, and Anthony S. Travis. "A German Influence on Science in Mandate Palestine and Israel: Chemistry and Biochemistry." *Israel Studies* 9 (2004): 34–70.

Ginsburg, David. "Ernst David Bergmann." *Israel Journal of Chemistry* 1 (1963): 323–350.

Michaelis, Anthony R. *Weizmann Centenary: His Living Memorial, The Institute Bearing His Name*. London, 1974.

Pinkus, Binyamin. "Atomic Power to Israel's Rescue: French-Israeli Nuclear Cooperation, 1949–1957." *Israel Studies* 7 (2002): 105–138.

Rose, Norman. *Chaim Weizmann: A Biography*. New York: Viking, 1986.

Seltzer, Richard J. "Israel Spurs Development in Industrial R&D." *Chemical and Engineering News* 58 (8 September 1980): 18–29.

Ute Deichmann
Anthony S. Travis

BERNOULLI, JAKOB (JACOB, JACQUES, JAMES) I (*b*. Basel, Switzerland, 27 December 1654; *d*. Basel, 16 August 1705), *mathematics, mechanics, astronomy*. For the original article on Bernoulli see *DSB*, vol. 2.

When the original *DSB* article was written, the collected works of Jakob Bernoulli were still in preparation, although volume 1 of *Die Werke von Jakob Bernoulli*, on astronomy and natural philosophy, actually appeared before volume 2 of the *DSB*. Work on the papers of the Bernoulli family had been underway for many years and the results were known to some scholars, but after 1970 many scholars, including especially the editors of *Die*

gesammelten Werke der Mathematiker und Physiker der Familie Bernoulli, published on the Bernoullis using a wealth of newly or more easily available evidence. The volumes of Jakob Bernoulli's *Werke* include not only his published books and journal articles but also passages from his meticulous research notebook and the hard-to-find pamphlets he had published in connection with lectures and disputations at the University of Basel. The introductions to and commentaries on the texts, as well as the work in editing previously unpublished materials, are of very high quality. Needless to say, materials that appeared in the *Werke* of Johann and Daniel Bernoulli are also important for understanding Jakob Bernoulli. Because J. E. Hofmann's article in the original *DSB* describes the main points of Jakob Bernoulli's mathematical and scientific work, this postscript will emphasize historiographic, social, and institutional factors.

The Multiple Bernoullis. Jakob Bernoulli was the first famous Bernoulli scientist or mathematician, but he was followed into science and mathematics first by his brother Johann and then by many later Bernoullis of the next generations, starting with their nephew Nikolaus and then Johann Bernoulli's sons. Because the family chose to repeat the same given names from generation to generation, and because these given names appear in many languages (so that Jakob in German may appear as Jacob in Latin, Jacques in French, James in English, and so forth), confusion between different Bernoullis is not infrequent. In order to create some order, it is standard to number the most famous Bernoullis, starting with Jakob I, the subject of this postscript, his brother Johann I, their nephew Nikolaus I, and so forth. A frequently repeated error is to say that the nephew, Nikolaus I Bernoulli (1687–1759), helped in the posthumous publication of *Ars Conjectandi* in 1713. When Jakob I Bernoulli died in 1705, there had been so much struggle between Jakob I and Johann I over their respective contributions to mathematics that Jakob's wife and son resolved to keep his unpublished papers out of the hands of other family members. After many years, Jakob's *son* Nikolaus (1687–1769, an artist and not a mathematician and therefore without a number, but sometimes labeled "Nikolaus the younger" to distinguish him from his uncle "Nikolaus the elder," 1662–1716, also a painter and the father of Nikolaus I) finally sent the manuscript of *Ars Conjectandi* to be printed. Only when the printing was nearly complete did Jakob's *nephew* Nikolaus I return from a long period of travel, compile one page of errata, and write a two-page introduction to the reader for the book.

Because Nikolaus I had been active in continuing his uncle's work in mathematical probability in the years between Jakob's death in 1705 and the publication of *Ars Conjectandi* in 1713, it is not unimportant to know that

Jakob Bernoulli. *Jakob Bernoulli with his brother and fellow mathematician Jacques.* © BETTMANN/CORBIS.

the book was published with no emendation by Nikolaus I beyond the one page of errata. Although one might wonder at Nikolaus I's extensive use of his uncle's unpublished work, first in his law dissertation *De Usu Artis Conjectandi in Jure* (1709) and then in extensive letters to Pierre Rémond de Montmort, published in the second edition of Montmort's *Essay d'analyse sur les jeux de hazard* (1713; just after *Ars Conjectandi*), many historians credit Nikolaus I with helping to establish and disseminate the new discipline of mathematical probability, particularly in its applications to law. Given that Johann I in correspondence repeatedly downplayed the importance of publishing *Ars Conjectandi*, Nikolaus I's promotion of that work, even while borrowing from it, was an important contribution. Nikolaus I helped spread Jakob's probability work not only to Montmort but also to Abraham De Moivre, who took the next giant steps in developing the mathematics of probability.

Although the very useful articles on the Bernoullis available from the St. Andrews MacTutor History of Mathematics Archive acknowledge their significant indebtedness to *DSB* articles, repeated copying of the MacTutor articles on other Web sites may lead to a cancerous spread of errors. As an example, the misinformation has proliferated that when Johann I left his professorship of mathematics in Groningen to return to

Basel in 1705, he was unaware that Jacob I had "died of tuberculosis." Tellingly, the idea that tuberculosis was the cause of Jakob I's death appears only in Web biographies of Johann I and not in those of Jakob I himself.

Conflict between Jakob and Johann. More seriously, the present popular image of Jakob Bernoulli is much distorted by being seen through the eyes of Johann I, who survived Jakob I and served as the professor of mathematics at Basel for more than forty years after Jakob's early death at age fifty in 1705. It is beyond doubt that the brothers spoke sharply about each other in print concerning their respective contributions to the development of the calculus of variations (see the *Streitschriften* listed below). Otto Mencke, editor of the *Acta Eruditorum*, at a certain point made a firm decision that the journal would publish no more articles in which the brothers attacked each other. The Académie Royale des Sciences at Paris admitted Jakob and Johann at the same time in 1699 *on the condition* that they make peace and end their mutual public vituperations, which were thought to give mathematicians a bad name. Gottfried Wilhelm Leibniz, Pierre Varignon, and others wrote to the brothers pleading with them to act in a more fraternal manner. Nevertheless, Johann I was probably more responsible for the falling out between the brothers than Jakob I, thirteen years his senior and Johann's most important mathematics teacher.

Although the evidence is incomplete, it seems likely that a huge source of tension between the brothers was that when Johann I traveled to France in the early 1690s, he signed a very lucrative contract with the Marquis de l'Hôpital stipulating that he would teach l'Hôpital Leibniz's new methods of calculus and provide l'Hôpital with new mathematical results, while keeping secret the extent of his contributions. Johann I wrote to l'Hôpital that Jakob I was jealous of the payment he was receiving from l'Hôpital, but it is clear that Jakob believed that some of the methods and results Johann I was providing to l'Hôpital secretly were Jakob's own intellectual property. No wonder that, whereas at first the brothers published each other's results, inserting such phrases as "when he saw my work, my brother suggested … ," Jakob began to try much more carefully to distinguish his own work from that of his brother. In an autobiography he wrote many years after Jakob's death, Johann claimed to be responsible for the introduction of the word "integral" for the operation opposite to differentiation, for issuing challenge problems that were in fact first published by Jakob, and much more. Thus began a confusion of credit between the brothers, which helped lead to the creation of, in Jeanne Peiffer's terms, the "chimera" of "the Bernoulli brothers." Writing of "the Bernoulli brothers" may be thought to finesse the problem of distributing credit between them and may help explain why inventions of or quotations from Jakob are often attributed to Johann and vice versa.

Relationship to their Father. It is commonly said that both Jakob I and Johann I studied mathematics secretly and against their father's will, while, following their father's dictates, Jakob I obtained a degree in theology and Johann in medicine. It is true that Jakob Bernoulli chose as his motto *Invito patre sidera verso* or "Against the will of my father, I turn [or disturb] the heavens." This should be understood, however, in connection with Bernoulli's emblem, which showed the mythical phaeton disastrously attempting to drive the chariot of his father, the sun-god Apollo. Jakob's contemporaries, moreover, would almost certainly have paired his phrase *invito patre* with the common phrase *invita Minerva*, meaning "against one's natural bent." The real point is that both Jakob and Johann became academic mathematicians because that was their natural bent and they strongly believed that one should follow one's talents, natural or God-given, in choosing a vocation, Jakob being the model for Johann in this regard. Their father was not necessarily opposed to mathematics—at one point he was named *Rechenherr*, something like an auditor, in the town government of Basel—so much as he wanted his sons to pursue educations leading to jobs (so-called *Brotstudia*) by which they could support

their families. The position of professor of mathematics at the university of Basel in the seventeenth and eighteenth centuries was not well paid (and there was only one such position), and both Jakob and Johann Bernoulli had to take on additional jobs or rent rooms in their houses to supplement their incomes. They were lucky to get the Basel chair of mathematics in turn, while most of the later Bernoullis had to find other jobs (Johann II Bernoulli succeeded his father in the chair of mathematics).

Thanks to the publications on Jakob Bernoulli after 1970, much more could be added to this postscript, but scholars had only just begun to profit from the publication of *Die gesammelten Werke der Mathematiker und Physiker der Familie Bernoulli*, which as of 2007 continued, so that researchers could expect continued growth in their knowledge of the contributions of the Bernoullis in the future.

SUPPLEMENTARY BIBLIOGRAPHY

WORKS BY BERNOULLI

Collected Works and Correspondence

Die Werke von Jakob Bernoulli. Vol. 1, *Astronomie: Philosophia naturalis*, edited by Joachim Otto Fleckenstein (1969); vol. 2, *Elementarmathematik*, edited by Clara Silvia Roero and Tulio Viola (1989); vol. 3, *Wahrscheinlichkeitsrechnung*, edited by Bartel Leendert van der Waerden (1975); vol. 4, *Reihentheorie*, edited by André Weil, (1993); vol. 5, *Differentialgeometrie*, edited by André Weil and Martin Mattmüller (1999). Basel, Switzerland: Birkhäuser. The last volume, which covers mechanics, had not appeared at this writing.

Die Streitschriften von Jacob und Johann Bernoulli. Edited by Herman H. Goldstine. Basel: Birkhäuser, 1991.

Der Briefwechsel von Jacob Bernoulli. Edited by André Weil, with contributions from Clifford Truesdell and Fritz Nagel. Basel: Birkhäuser, 1993. The previously unpublished correspondence of Jakob Bernoulli with his brother Johann (there are only four extant letters, all of which are from Johann to Jakob, the last written in the autumn of 1691 from Geneva) were included in *Der Briefwechsel von Johann Bernoulli*, vol. 1 (Basel: Birkhäuser, 1955). Because the correspondence of Jakob with l'Hôpital and with Varignon has been lost, it is important, for understanding the relationship of the brothers, to read the correspondence between Johann and l'Hôpital in this volume, as well as the correspondence between Johann and Varignon: part 1, 1692–1702, in vol. 2 (Basel: Birkhäuser, 1988) and part 2, 1702–1714, in vol. 3 (Basel: Birkhäuser, 1992). The correspondence with Varignon reveals the way in which Jakob and Johann were admitted at the same time to the Académie Royale des Sciences in Paris on the condition that they end their public quarrel. In the later correspondence, Varignon's efforts to supervise Jakob's son Nikolaus when he was in Paris studying painting are a repeated topic.

Translations of Ars Conjectandi

Jacques Bernoulli et l'Ars Conjectandi. Translated by Norbert Meusnier. Rouen, IREM, 1987. Includes a French translation of part 4.

Christian Huygens et Jacques Bernoulli: La première partie de l'Ars Conjectandi (1657–1713). Translated by Norbert Meusnier. Paris, CAMS, 1992. Includes a French translation of part 1, which consists of Christiaan Huygens, *De ratiociniis in ludo aleae,* together with Bernoulli's notes.

The Art of Conjecturing, together with Letter to a Friend on Sets in Court Tennis. English translation with an introduction and notes by Edith Dudley Sylla. Baltimore, MD: Johns Hopkins University Press, 2006.

OTHER SOURCES

Hess, Heinz-Jürgen, and Fritz Nagel. *Der Ausbau des Calculus durch Leibniz und die Brüder Bernoulli.* Symposion der Leibniz-Gesellschaft und der Bernoulli-Edition der Naturforschenden Gesellschaft in Basel, 15–17 June 1987. Studia Leibnitiana, Sonderheft 17. Stuttgart: Franz Steiner Verlag Wiesbaden GMBH, 1989. See especially Clara Silvia Roero, "The Passage from Descartes' Algebraic Geometry to Leibniz's Infinitesimal Calculus in the Writings of Jacob Bernoulli" and Heinz-Jürgen Hess, "Die Briefwechsel von Jacob Bernoulli und Leibniz: Eine Kurz-charakteristik."

Meusnier, Norbert. "Nicolas, neveu exemplaire." *Journal Electronique d'Histoire des Probabilités et de la Statistique* 2, no. 1 (June 2006). Available from http://www.jehps.net. See also other articles in this volume and in vol. 2, no. 2 (November 2006), resulting from a conference commemorating the three hundredth anniversary of Jacob Bernoulli's death.

Nagel, Fritz. "Jacob Bernoullis Vorschläge zur Universitätsreform während der Basler Unruhen von 1691." In *Der Briefwechsel von Jacob Bernoulli,* edited by André Weil. Basel: Birkhäuser, 1993.

O'Connor, J. J., and E. F. Robertson. "Jacob (Jacques) Bernoulli." MacTutor History of Mathematics Archive. Available from http://turnbull.mcs.st and.ac.uk/history/. A convenient starting point but should be used with caution.

Peiffer, Jeanne. "Jacob Bernoulli, Teacher and Rival of His Brother Johann." *Journal Electronique d'Histoire des Probabilités et de la Statistique* 2, no. 2 (November 2006). Available from http://www.jehps.net.

Roero, Carla Silvia. "Jacob Bernoulli attento studioso delle opere di Archimede: Le note marginali all'edizione de Barrow del 1675." *Bollettino di Storia delle Scienze Matematiche* 3, no. 1 (1983): 77–125. Reprinted in *Die Werke von Jakob Bernoulli,* vol. 2, *Elementarmathematik,* edited by Clara Silvia Roero and Tulio Viola. Basel: Birkhäuser, 1989.

Sylla, Edith Dudley. Introduction to *The Art of Conjecturing together with Letter to a Friend on Sets in Court Tennis* by Jacob Bernoulli. Baltimore: Johns Hopkins University Press, 2006. Contains much more detail about Jakob's work in probability mathematics and its context.

Truesdell, Clifford. *The Rational Mechanics of Flexible or Elastic Bodies, 1638–1788. Leonhardi Euleri Opera Omnia,* Series 2. Vol. 11, part 2. Zürich: Orell Füssli, 1960. Contains the detailed examination of texts supporting Truesdell's praise of Jakob Bernoulli in the following article.

———. "A Program toward Rediscovering the Rational Mechanics of the Age of Reason." *Archive for History of Exact Sciences* 1 (1975): 1–36. Truesdell states (p. 14) that "the creation of rational mechanics is due as much to James Bernoulli as to Newton, though James Bernoulli's work nowadays is little known." He goes on to say that Jakob's paper of 1703 (sent in parts to the Académie Royale des Sciences) was "second only to the *Principia* itself in its influence on the later growth of the discipline."

———. "Mechanics, Especially Elasticity, in the Correspondence of Jacob Bernoulli and Leibniz." In *Der Briefwechsel von Jacob Bernoulli,* edited by André Weil. Basel: Birkhäuser, 1993.

Yushkevich, Adolf P. "Nicholas Bernoulli and the Publication of James Bernoulli's *Ars Conjectandi.*" *Theory of Probability and Its Applications* 31, no. 2 (1987): 286–303.

Edith Dudley Sylla

BERNSTEIN, RICHARD BARRY (*b.* New York, New York, 31 October 1923; *d.* Helsinki, Finland, 8 July 1990), *chemistry.*

Bernstein was born to an immigrant family that attached great importance to education. His father, Simon Bernstein, was a lawyer and businessman; his mother, Stella Grossman Bernstein, owned a small dress shop and, after her children had grown, became a psychologist. A gifted pianist, Bernstein considered a career in music but decided instead to pursue science. He graduated from high school at the age of fifteen and enrolled at Columbia University, where he studied chemistry and mathematics. In 1942, Bernstein began work in the Synthetic Alloy Materials (SAM) Laboratory at Columbia, a part of the Manhattan Project. The laboratory, which was supervised by Harold C. Urey, carried out studies of isotope separation by gaseous diffusion and centrifugation. After receiving his AB with honors in 1943, Bernstein was inducted into the U.S. Army Corps of Engineers; he was first assigned to Oak Ridge, Tennessee, and then was posted back to Columbia in 1945. Before leaving the army in 1946, he was a participant in the first tests of fission weapons at Bikini Atoll.

Bernstein received an MS degree from Columbia in 1946 and began to carry out doctoral research with T. I. Taylor on gas-phase processes for isotopic separation. He was awarded a PhD in physical chemistry in 1948 and accepted a position in Chicago as assistant professor of chemistry at the Illinois Institute of Technology (IIT). In the same year he married Norma Olivier; they had three daughters and a son.

While at IIT, Bernstein carried out research on gas-phase spectroscopy and chemical kinetics. In 1953, he moved to the Department of Chemistry at the University of Michigan. This was the first of his many moves. He once jokingly noted that he changed positions every ten years. In fact, on average, he moved more frequently.

Early Studies of Molecular Beams. It was at Michigan that he began his research on molecular beams, which brought him fame and which would occupy him for the rest of his life. Scattering techniques had been employed as a tool in nuclear and atomic physics for many years, but the applications in chemistry that require crossing two molecular beams did not begin until the mid-1950s. In the address that he presented when he received the Robert A. Welch Foundation Award in 1988, Bernstein recounted that in 1953–1954 he became aware of the progress that his friend Sheldon Datz had made in studying chemical reactions with molecular beams. (Datz had also worked at the SAM in Columbia.) Earlier attempts at using beams in chemistry had been unsuccessful, largely because of the lack of sensitive detection, but ionization detectors could be employed to examine reactions involving alkali metals. Bernstein decided to begin a molecular beam program in Michigan early in 1955 and set out to measure the systematics of total collision cross sections for the interactions of atoms with molecules. His first paper (with Edward W. Rothe) applying beam techniques appeared in 1959.

At this time Bernstein and several others recognized that beam experiments offered an opportunity to provide a molecular-scale understanding of the kinetics of chemical reactions. He reasoned, however, that before one could understand reactive scattering (the result of collisions between molecules that can react with each other) it was necessary to understand nonreactive collisions. He therefore began with both experimental and theoretical examinations of elastic scattering. It was nearly a decade later, in 1965, that his first study of reactive scattering was published. By that time he had been at the University of Wisconsin for two years, where he was named W. W. Daniels Professor of Chemistry in 1967.

The path of his research with molecular beams, which he followed until his death, led through appointments at the University of Texas as W. T. Doherty Professor of Chemistry and Physics; to Columbia, where he returned in 1977 as Higgins Professor of Natural Science; and to the position of senior vice-president of the Occidental Research Corporation in Irvine, California, in 1983. Two years after Bernstein's arrival, the company decided to reduce its commitment to fundamental research, and he joined the faculty in chemistry at the University of California, Los Angeles (UCLA). His career

path also traced the refinements in the technique—velocity and state selection, alignment and laser pump and probe—that made it possible to examine in detail the molecular nature of chemical reactivity.

Chemical Reactions at the Molecular Scale. In the early 2000s, even biochemical processes were being probed at the molecular level. But until the mid-twentieth century, there was mostly indirect evidence for how molecules interact and react. Matter was studied in the bulk, and from observing the macroscopic properties and their rate of change, inferences were made about the underlying molecular-level mechanism. Because only bulk averages could be studied—not the truly elementary events—there was always the possibility that the assumed mechanism was consistent with the rate as observed but was not, in fact, correct. Scattering techniques seek to undo the averaging inherent in bulk chemical kinetics.

An example and an experiment that brought Dick Bernstein worldwide recognition is the direct demonstration of the steric effect in chemical reactions. The understanding that chemical forces have a strong directional character goes all the way back to Jacobus van't Hoff. Molecules therefore have a shape, and how they react must depend on their relative orientation as they approach one another. During the first part of the twentieth century, organic chemists provided compelling but indirect evidence for the importance of steric requirements of chemical reactions. The three-dimensional, shape-selective nature of chemical processes is inherent in the proposed "lock and key" mechanism for enzyme selectivity that takes the steric requirements as a key concept. When the reaction takes place in the bulk, all orientations of the approaching reactants are possible. The steric requirements mean that not all collisions are fruitful; those that are not do not have a favorable orientation. Bernstein took it upon himself to provide a direct experimental demonstration of the validity of the concept that chemical reactions have steric requirements. The story is well known. It is described in Bernstein's own words in his Welch lecture (1989), and the experimental and conceptual progress built upon his pioneering effort is well represented by the proceedings of an international conference held a short time after his death and dedicated to his memory (Levine, Zewail, and El-Sayed, 1991).

The Mechanics of Molecular Collisions. At the beginning of his lifelong study of elementary chemical reactions, Bernstein decided to start with the simplest questions and build from there. So his earliest experiments dealt not with chemical reactivity but with a prerequisite. In order for two molecules to react, they need to come together and collide. Bernstein's early experiments dealt with the rate of collisions of molecules, regardless of whether these collisions resulted in a reaction. Such experiments determine the total collision cross section ("total" because all possible outcomes are counted). Curiously, classical and quantum mechanics differ in what they regard as the allowed outcomes. In classical mechanics, any time a force acts between two molecules, it may be said that a collision took place. By Newton's first law, a collision takes place whenever the molecules deviate from a straight-line motion. But in quantum mechanics, very tiny deflections cannot be detected in principle because such detection violates the uncertainty principle. (For the same wave-diffraction reason, a shadow is never absolutely sharp.)

Bernstein was fascinated by these essentially quantal features and showed how their experimental observation provides a signature of the attraction that is always present between any two atoms or molecules. By these early experiments, which lasted throughout the first decade of his foray into the new field, Bernstein established the insights and detail that the scattering technique can provide. With the perception provided by several decades of hindsight, it was in the early 2000s possible to suggest on the one hand that with this careful setting of the stage, he delayed his exploration of the more chemical questions and left some key issues to be ably addressed by others and later comers such as Dudley Herschbach. On the other hand, these early pioneers, who styled themselves the "lunatic fringe," had the entire field of chemical reactivity, a field that many regard as the *sine qua non* of chemistry, to explore. There were plenty of fundamental questions for all; one remarkable aspect of the emerging field of molecular reaction dynamics is the friendly and collegial relations between its participants. By 1974, the field was sufficiently well mapped that Levine and Bernstein could write a primer for it (*Molecular Reaction Dynamics*, 1974). By the beginning of the twenty-first century, almost all textbooks of physical chemistry had a chapter (or more) on reaction dynamics.

From physics and Newton's first law, the small molecular beams community took the idea of the change in the direction of the velocity, the deflection, as a probe of the collision. What is more characteristic of chemical physics is the change in the magnitude of the velocity. For molecular collisions the velocity can change in an essentially continuous manner; this occurs because the total energy is conserved. After the collision is over, the total energy is the sum of the internal energy of the products and of the kinetic energy of their motion. Strictly speaking, the internal energy is quantized, and so it can only assume discrete values. But as compared to the kinetic energy, the energy spacings between different internal energy states are typically small. So the final kinetic energy of the motion of the collision products can take a continuous range of values.

Analyzing the velocity with which the products recede from the collision was pioneered by Bernstein in the study of inelastic collisions (collisions in which the chemical identity is maintained but the internal state is changed). It was, however, in the study of chemical reactions, where Bernstein and his coworkers determined both the direction and the magnitude of the velocity of the products, that the real benefits were reaped. Contour maps of the final velocity are a polar coordinate representation where the polar angle is the angle of deflection and the radius is the magnitude of the velocity. Polar maps from Bernstein's laboratory can be found in the early 2000s in textbooks of chemical kinetics and even in introductory textbooks of physical chemistry. An overview of the set of tools that he pioneered and perfected can be found in his Hinshelwood Lectures at Oxford (published as *Chemical Dynamics via Molecular Beam and Laser Techniques*, 1982).

Bernstein regarded theory as part of the tools that experimentalists must have at their command; to this end, he edited a handbook, *Atom-Molecule Collision Theory: A Guide for the Experimentalist* (1979). It is interesting to note that this ability to be equally at home in experiment and theory is common to many other pioneers of the field of reaction dynamics.

Lasers as a Probe of the Transition between Reactants and Products. Very early on, Bernstein added another experimental technique that was to revolutionize the field: lasers as both promoters of the chemical change and probes of the products. In 1990, he spent a sabbatical leave as a Sherman Fairchild Distinguished Scholar at the California Institute of Technology, where he collaborated with Ahmed Zewail to devise ways of using lasers to probe the "transition state," the transitory configuration leading from reactants to products of a chemical reaction. At the same time he continued to lead his group at UCLA through a rather active period of looking at the steric effect of processes happening at the interface of a solid. Later that year, while on a scientific visit to Moscow, he suffered a heart attack. He was airlifted to a hospital in Finland but did not recover from the secondary attack.

Richard Bernstein would publish experimental results only if he had been present in the laboratory while the experiment was carried out. The scientific community celebrated his integrity, seriousness of purpose, innovation of scientific questions, the novelty of experimental design, and the quality of the results with many awards and honors. Principal among them are his early elections to membership in the National Academy of Sciences in 1968 and as a fellow of the American Academy of Arts and Sciences in 1970. He received the American Chemical Society's Peter Debye Award in Physical Chemistry in 1981, the National Academy of Sciences Award in the Chemical

Sciences in 1985, and the American Chemical Society's Irving Langmuir Award in Chemical Physics in 1986, as well as an honorary doctorate in science from the University of Chicago. In 1988, he was the recipient of the Robert A. Welch Award in Chemistry, the American Chemical Society's Willard Gibbs Medal, and the National Medal of Science. With his wife Norma at his side he also edited the journal *Chemical Physics Letters* for more than a decade.

BIBLIOGRAPHY

A complete bibliography is included in the Journal of Physical Chemistry, *R. B. Bernstein Memorial Issue (see last citation below).*

WORKS BY BERNSTEIN

With Edward W. Rothe. "Total Collision Cross Sections for the Interaction of Atomic Beam of Alkali Metals with Gases." *Journal of Chemical Physics* 31 (1959): 1619–1627.

With Hans U. Hostettler. "Observation of Quantum Effects in the Scattering of a Monoenergetic Li Beam by a Crossed Hg Beam. *Physical Review Letters* 5 (1960): 318.

"Extrema in Velocity Dependence of Total Elastic Cross Sections for Atomic Beam Scattering: Relations to Di-atom Bound States." *Journal of Chemical Physics* 37 (1962): 1880–1881.

With Arthur E. Grosser and Anthony R. Blythe. "Internal Energy of Reaction Products by Velocity Analysis. I. Scattered Br from the Crossed Molecular Beam Reactions K + Br." *Journal of Chemical Physics* 42 (1965): 1268–1273.

"Quantum Effects in Elastic Molecular Scattering." In *Advances in Chemical Physics,* edited by Ilya Prigogine, vol. 10, p. 75. New York: Wiley-Interscience, 1966.

With R. J. Beuler and K. H. Kramer. "Observation of the Reactive Asymmetry of Methyl Iodide. Crossed-beam Study of the Reaction of Rubidium with Oriented Methyl Iodide Molecules." *Journal of the American Chemical Society* 88 (1966): 5331–5332.

With Raphael D. Levine, B. R. Johnson, and J. T. Muckerman. "Computational Investigation of Internal Excitation in Nonreactive Molecular Collisions: Resonances in Rotational Excitation." *Journal of Chemical Physics* 49 (1968): 56–64.

With Robert J. LeRoy. "Dissociation Energy and Long-range Potential of Diatomic Molecules from Vibrational Spacings of Higher Levels." *Journal of Chemical Physics* 52 (1970): 3869–3879.

With Keith T. Gillen and Alan M. Rulis. "Molecular Beam Study of the K + I_2 Reaction: Differential Cross Section and Energy Dependence." *Journal of Chemical Physics* 54 (1971): 2831–2851.

With Alan M. Rulis. "Translational Energy Dependence of Product Energy and Angular Distribution for the K + CH_3I Reaction." *Faraday Special Discussions of the Chemical Society* 55 (1973): 293.

With Raphael D. Levine. *Molecular Reaction Dynamics.* Oxford: Clarendon Press, 1974.

———. "Energy Disposal and Energy Consumption in Elementary Chemical Reactions: The Information Theoretic Approach." *Accounts of Chemical Research* 7 (1974): 393–400.

With S. Stolte and A. E. Proctor. "Translational Energy Dependence of the Branching Fraction and Cross Sections for the Decay of Collision Complexes: K + CsF, RbF." *Journal of Chemical Physics* 65 (1976): 4990–5008.

As editor. *Atom-Molecule Collision Theory: A Guide for the Experimentalist.* New York: Plenum Press, 1979.

With Richard N. Zare. "State-to-State Reaction Dynamics." *Physics Today* 33 (1980): 43.

Chemical Dynamics via Molecular Beam and Laser Techniques. London: Oxford University Press, 1982.

"Systematic of Multiphoton Ionization-Fragmentation of Polyatomic Molecules." *Journal of Physical Chemistry* 86 (1982): 1178–1184.

With Raphael D. Levine. *Molecular Reaction Dynamics and Chemical Reactivity.* London: Oxford University Press, 1987.

With N. F. Scherer, L. R. Khundakar, and Ahmed H. Zewail. "Real-Time Picosecond Clocking of the Collision Complex in a Bimolecular Reaction. The Birth of OH from H + CO_2." *Journal of Chemical Physics* 87 (1987): 1451–1453.

With Dudly R. Herschbach and Raphael D. Levine. "Dynamical Aspects of Stereochemistry." *Journal of Physical Chemistry* 91 (1987): 5365–5377.

"Selectivity in Elementary Chemical Reactions." Presented at the Selectivity in Chemical Reactions: NATO Advanced Research Workshop, Sept. 1987, Browness-on-Windermere, U.K.

With Ahmed H. Zewail. "Real-Time Laser Femtochemistry: Viewing the Transition from Reagents to Products." *Chemical Engineering News* 66 (1988): 24–43.

"Molecular Beams in Chemistry: A Subjective Account." In *Welch Conference on Chemical Research XXXII: Valency,* pp. 157–197. Houston: Robert A. Welch Foundation, 1989.

With D. H. Parker. "Oriented Molecule Beams via the Electrostatic Hexapole: Preparation, Characterization and Reactive Scattering." *Annual Review of Physical Chemistry* 40 (1989): 561.

OTHER SOURCE

Levine, Raphael D., Ahmed H. Zewail, and Mostafa A. El-Sayed, eds. *Journal of Physical Chemistry* (R. B. Bernstein Memorial Issue) 95 (1991): 7961–8421.

Raphael Levine
Charles Knobler

BERS, LIPMAN (*b.* Riga, Latvia, 22 May 1914; *d.* New Rochelle, New York, 29 October 1993), *mathematics, complex analysis, partial differential equations.*

The central theme of Bers's work was the theory of complex analytic functions, which are essentially infinitely long complex polynomials. In his early work he most often used complex analytic techniques, in the guise of partial differential equations, to study physical problems. Later, in the body of work he assessed as his most important, he and Lars Ahlfors further developed the theory of quasiconformal mappings and related areas. They then used these mappings and the spaces they define to solve Riemann's problem of moduli, initiated the modern theory of Kleinian groups, and participated in the foundational work on iterations of rational functions.

Family and Early Life. The members of Bers's immediate family were all intellectuals. Both his parents were educators in the Yiddish language school system in Riga, Latvia. His wife, Mary Kagan Bers, taught disabled children. In the early 2000s their daughter, Ruth, was a psychoanalyst and professor emeritus of psychology at the City University of New York; and their son, Victor, was a professor of classics at Yale University.

Bers, known informally to all as Lipa, spent his early years in Petrograd during the Russian Revolution and was raised in Riga and Berlin between the world wars. Even from his youth, he mixed his love for mathematics with political and social involvement. After a short period of study at the University of Zurich in Switzerland, he returned to Riga. His political activism—Latvia was ruled by a right-wing dictator—led to an arrest warrant. He fled to Prague, Czechoslovakia, where he continued his graduate studies under the direction of Charles Loewner. His dissertation was submitted, in some haste, to Charles University in Prague in 1938; he then moved to France just ahead of the Nazi takeover of Czechoslovakia. His dissertation was never published. In Paris, he worked on Green's functions and integral representations.

From Europe to America. He and Mary left Paris in 1940 ahead of the German invasion of France and, after a stay in the unoccupied part of that country, departed war-torn Europe for New York City. There, they were welcomed by his mother, then a psychoanalyst, and his stepfather, Benno Tumarin, later a theatrical director and teacher at the Julliard School in Manhattan.

After a period of living as a refugee in New York, Bers joined the Advanced Research and Instruction in Applied Mathematics Program at Brown University, in Providence, Rhode Island, during 1942. At Brown he was involved in war-related research; in particular, he started his work on two-dimensional subsonic fluid flow—to laypersons, the study of what allows planes to fly. With respect to a suitable choice of coordinates, the potential u for the flow is the real part of a complex function $f = u + iv$. The equations satisfied by u and v are generalizations of the Cauchy-Riemann equations that characterize complex analytic functions. A direct outgrowth of this work

Lipman Bers. COURTESY OF THE UNIVERSITY ARCHIVES, COLUMBIA UNIVERSITY IN THE CITY OF NEW YORK.

was the development, paralleled by Ilia Vekua in the Soviet Union, of the theory of classes of pseudo-analytic functions. Each class is defined by replacing the numbers 1 and i, in the definition of f given above, by suitable functions. There is a Cauchy theory for these classes. Much of Bers's work during World War II was not published immediately and appeared, if at all, after the end of the war.

Minimal Surfaces and Quasiconformality. In 1945, Bers moved to Syracuse University in New York State. About that time, he started to work on removability of singularities of the solutions to nonlinear elliptic partial differential equations. In particular, he worked on the minimal surface equation. These are the equations satisfied by a soap film or bubble, although there are other types of solutions. Bers's first widely recognized scientific result was the proof that the equation has no isolated singularities. One physical interpretation of the nonexistence of singularities is that a pinprick will destroy a soap bubble. The technique used in the proof is to continually reparamatrize the surface so that the singularity becomes removable. This is the same technique later used in particle physics to "gauge away singularities." This work led to his first address to the International Congress of Mathematicians in 1950 at Cambridge, Massachusetts.

While he was staying at the Institute for Advanced Study from 1949 to 1951, his interests started to move from partial differential equations to geometric analysis—the area of overlap between geometry and such analytic techniques as partial differential equations and complex analysis. His interest quickly settled on the study of quasiconformal mappings of surfaces and, in particular, of planar regions. These are mappings that do not distort shape too much; they take infinitesimal circles into infinitesimal ellipses of uniformly bounded eccentricity. The basic notion of a quasiconformal map was first given by Helmut Grötzsch. He proved that, among all maps of a rectangle onto another which sends vertices to corresponding vertices, the "best" map is the affine stretching of the first rectangle to fit over the second without overlap.

Around 1940, Oswald Teichmüller extended the result of Grötzsch to more general Riemann surfaces, such as donuts and pretzels. He showed that one could piece together affine stretchings to achieve a map between almost any two (topologically finite) Riemann surfaces which may be distorted one onto the other. The restriction is that punctures (that is, missing points) cannot be stretched into holes, which are not punctures, and vice versa. Indeed, he showed that the piecewise affine stretches are the best maps between two given surfaces. He also showed that the best maps are unique. These two results are known as Teichmüller's existence and uniqueness theorems. The proofs were not widely accepted until Ahlfors produced technically formidable proofs in 1954. At roughly the same time, Bers's work on quasiconformal mappings began appearing.

Teichmüller Theory and Moduli. It was, however, the proof of the Teichmüller theorems produced by Bers in 1958 that led directly to the later theory. In the late 1950s, Ahlfors and Bers worked in close contact on problems related to the geometric implications of quasiconformal mappings in both surface theory and complex analysis. In their only joint paper, entitled "Riemann's mapping theorem for variable metrics," which appeared in the *Annals of Mathematics* in 1960, they gave a new proof of (as it later became known) the measurable Riemann mapping theorem, or, in the original terminology, the Riemann mapping theorem for variable metrics. In his 1958 lecture at the International Congress of Mathematicians in Edinburgh, Scotland, Bers announced that work and many of its consequences—including the solution to Riemann's problem of moduli. A short description, of

both the moduli problem and the Ahlfors-Bers solution, follows.

Much of Riemann's early work was devoted to the study of solution sets of algebraic equations in two variables, i.e. the pairs of points (z,w) at which a given polynomial $P(z,w) = 0$. That solution set is called the Riemann surface of the algebraic function P. Without focusing on details here, it is important to note that Riemann gave an interesting count of the dimension of the space of Riemann surfaces S that are topologically equivalent to S but are not the same (holomorphically equivalent) as S. Justifying that count is called "Riemann's problem of moduli."

Planar sets may be described as those that may be globally parametrized using the complex variables z and $\bar{z}$ On an infinitesimal level, arc length may be measured as

$$ds = \Lambda(z)\left|dz + \mu(z)\,d\bar{z}\right|.$$

The quantity, or more precisely the form, ds^2 is called a Riemannian metric. The Euclidean metric is simply $|dz|^2$.

The function, more precisely the form, $\Lambda(z)$, is a pointwise rescaling of the metric and does not, on the infinitesimal level, distort Euclidean circles. Any distortion of such circles, arising by changing the metric, is carried by the form $\mu(z)$, which is called a Beltrami coefficient. A mapping of plane domains or Riemann surfaces is effected by a quasiconformal mapping that satisfies the differential equation

$$w_{\bar{z}} = \mu(z)\,w_z.$$

This is called the Beltrami equation. The existence of solutions of this equation, under successively weaker conditions on μ, goes back to Carl Friedrich Gauss. The key contribution of Ahlfors and Bers was to show that, if μ depends on parameters, then so does w—indeed, w depends on the parameters to the best extent possible—and to realize the implications of this fact.

Bers used the solution of the Beltrami equation to prove the Teichmüller theorems. In a one and one-half page paper, entitled "Correction to Spaces of Riemann Surfaces as Bounded Domains" which appeared in the Bulletin of the American Mathematical Society in 1962 Bers—correcting an earlier error—produced what he considered to be his finest work. He embedded Teichmüller's space of deformations of Riemann surfaces into N-dimensional complex space $\boldsymbol{C}^N$. The embedding uses the solution of the Beltrami equation together with classical notions from complex analysis such as Schwarzian derivatives and quadratic differentials and gives an elegant solution to the moduli problem of Riemann.

Later Research and Academic Positions. In 1951, Bers became a professor at the Courant Institute of New York

University in New York City. He was considered one of the legendary teachers of mathematics. His lecture notes, informally published by that institute, helped set the direction of modern partial differential equations and the study of complex analysis on surfaces and in several variables.

In 1964, Bers moved to Columbia University, also in New York City, and then started working on Kleinian groups, the groups of motions of hyperbolic 3-space H^3. Again, his methods were complex analytic—he studied the groups through their action on the sphere at infinity for H^3. He did some of the earliest work on the Eichler cohomology for Kleinian groups and found sharp bounds on the area of the conformal boundary of hyperbolic 3-orbifolds. He gave an analytic proof of the Nielsen-Thurston classification of homeomorphisms of surfaces. Late in his career, he worked on both Kleinian groups and the parallel theory of iteration of rational functions and studied their common roots. After retiring from Columbia in 1984, he was Distinguished Professor at the Graduate Center of the City University of New York. During Bers's career he supervised forty-eight PhD dissertations, and many of his students carried forward his mathematical legacy.

Personality, Vision, and Commitments. Throughout much of his career, Bers was in gentlemanly collaboration and competition with Ahlfors—a typical contest, at a given conference, might have been who had the most students in attendance.

Bers had a broad knowledge and vision of mathematics—it just seemed to come naturally to him. Marc Kac wrote of a fascinating technical question:

> I first heard the problem posed this way some ten years ago from Professor Bochner. Much more recently, when I mentioned it to Professor Bers, he said, almost at once: "You mean, if you had perfect pitch could you find the shape of a drum." (Kac, p. 3)

His was an active presence in defining the societal role of scientists, in particular, mathematicians. Among his other activities in the mathematics community, he was active in the American Mathematical Society from 1957 and was its president in 1975–1976. He expressed his pride at being elected to the American Philosophical Society—he took great delight in that select group especially since it had been founded by Benjamin Franklin, whom he much admired. He was the 1971 Colloquium Lecturer for the American Mathematical Society as well as the first G. H. Hardy Lecturer of the Royal Society in 1967.

It is not only as a researcher that Bers is renowned. He was deeply committed to human rights, helping to found the National Academy of Sciences (U.S.A.) Committee on Human Rights and the American Mathematical Society's Committee on Human Rights of Mathematicians.

BIBLIOGRAPHY

WORKS BY BERS

With Ahfors, L.V. "Riemann's mapping theorem for variable metrics," Annals of Math. 72 (1960): 345–404.

"Correction to 'Spaces of Riemann surfaces as Bounded Domains." *Bulletin of the American Mathematical Society* 67 (1961): 465–466.

Kra, Irwin, and Bernard Maskit, eds. *Selected Works of Lipman Bers: Papers on Complex Analysis.* 2 vols. Providence, RI: American Mathematical Society, 1998. This is a collection of Bers's papers on complex analysis that Bers asked Kra and Maskit to edit. Additionally, it contains a list of his students and the texts of articles by Kra and Maskit, William Abikoff, and Frederick Gardiner and Linda Keen.

OTHER SOURCES

Abikoff, William. "Remembering Lipman Bers." *Notices of the American Mathematical Society* 42 (1995): 8–25. This obituary includes contributions by Cathleen S. Morawetz, Carol Corillon and Irwin Kra, Tilla Weinstein, and Jane Gilman. It also contains a bibliography listing videotapes of some of Bers's lectures as well as interviews with him and his survey articles about his work.

Bass, Hyman, and Irwin Kra. "Lipman Bers: May 22, 1914 October 29, 1933. A Biographical Memoir." *Proceedings of the American Philosophical Society* 140 (1966): 206–219.

Kac, Marc. "Can one hear the shape of a drum?" *American Mathematical Monthly* 73:4 (1966): 1–23.

Keen, Linda. "Lipman Bers: A Mathematical Mentor." *AWM* [Association for Women in Mathematics] *Newsletter*, July 1984.

O'Connor, J. J., and E. F. Robertson. "Lipman Bers." Available from http://www-groups.dcs.st-and.ac.uk/~history/Printonly/Bers.html.

William Abikoff

BERTHOLLET, CLAUDE LOUIS (*b.* Talloires, near Annecy, Savoy, 9 December 1748; *d.* Arcueil, France, 6 November 1822), *pure and applied chemistry.* For the original article on Berthollet see *DSB,* vol. 2.

Berthollet was one of the leading French chemists in the late eighteenth century. He became a close associate of Antoine Lavoisier. As the founder of the Society of Arcueil in the opening years of the nineteenth century he began a further career, not only with his own ideas on chemical reactions, but also as the patron and friend of a group of

Claude-Louis Berthollet. © STEFANO BIANCHETTI/CORBIS.

talented young scientists. Some areas of Berthollet's life and work previously unexamined are: (1) his association with Lavoisier; (2) his activities during the French Revolution; (3) his founding of the Society of Arcueil and his friendship with Pierre-Simon Laplace; and (4) his influence.

Life. Berthollet was broad in build, amiable, and even homely in disposition, a character quite different from most of his scientific colleagues. He was the first major convert to Lavoisier's oxygen theory (1785) despite justifiable disagreement on the idea of oxygen as the principle of acidity. Only slightly junior, Berthollet worked closely together with Lavoisier. His importance in the Lavoisier school is suggested by the inclusion of his name on the title page of the collaborative *Méthode de nomenclature chimique* (Paris, 1787), despite the fact that successive chapters of the book appear only under the names of his colleagues Lavoisier, Louis-Bernard Guyton de Morveau, and Antoine Fourcroy. Again when the key chemical journal the *Annales de chimie* began publication in 1789 Berthollet's name appeared on the title page as a founding member of the editorial board. He was active in soliciting contributions to the journal. When finally it had reached nearly its hundredth volume in 1815 it was he who organ-

ized a new series with his protégés Louis-Joseph Gay-Lussac and François Arago as editors.

All "the big four" (authors of the *Méthode*) were appointed to different major positions of responsibility during the momentous revolutionary period, with the tragic death of one (Lavoisier, 1794) and Berthollet as the last survivor (d. 1822). In 1791 Berthollet was appointed successively as commissioner of the mint and member of the Bureau de Consultation des Arts et Métiers, concerned with rewarding artisans for their inventions. He joined the Bureau of Weights and Measures in 1793 at a time when several members had been arbitrarily excluded as politically unreliable. (Berthollet prudently avoided all political association.) Also in 1793 he became a member of the Commission des Arts, where his duties included making an inventory of the contents of the laboratory of the unfortunate Lavoisier. In 1794 he was appointed to the Commission for Agriculture.

Yet all these posts were arguably less important than those involving the direct application of chemistry to the war effort. In September 1793 he and two others were ordered by the minister for war to write a booklet to explain the manufacture of iron and steel. As the discoverer of potassium chlorate and its dangerous explosive properties (1787), probably his main contribution to the war effort was in the manufacture of gunpowder and the extraction of its main constituent saltpeter (potassium nitrate). For example, in December 1793 he was put in charge of a new refinery of saltpeter. In 1794, together with Guyton and Fourcroy, he taught a crash course to prospective gunners on the manufacture of gunpowder.

A more constructive period followed after the fall of Maximilien Robespierre (July 1794), when many educational plans were made. November 1794 saw the foundation of the École Normale, where Berthollet was appointed as professor of chemistry. Yet the students were an astonishingly mixed crowd and Berthollet was a poor teacher. He had a little more success as professor at the École Polytechnique (September 1795), where its students had been selected by examination.

Yet Berthollet's role as professor was to be interrupted in May 1796, when he was sent to Italy as a member of a commission to confiscate art treasures in the territory newly conquered by General Napoléon Bonaparte. Contact with the future emperor was to affect Berthollet's future. The chemist was chosen again in May 1798 to accompany Bonaparte to Egypt. Bonaparte returned suddenly to Paris in November 1799, leaving the army behind but taking with him Berthollet and his friend Gaspard Monge.

The turn of the next century was to find Berthollet at Arcueil, then a village a few miles south of Paris. He bought a country house, built a chemistry laboratory, and invited Gay-Lussac, a promising young graduate from the École Polytechnique, to join him as an assistant. This was to lead to the foundation of the private Society of Arcueil that announced its existence to the world by the publication of its first volume of *Mémoires* in 1807. Berthollet had recently been joined by the distinguished mathematician Laplace, who had bought a neighboring house at Arcueil, a summer retreat away from the noise and pollution of Paris. They assembled a small group of outstanding young men of science whom they advised and encouraged, even helping several to become members of the first class of the institute, which now replaced the former Royal Academy of Sciences.

In 1803 Bonaparte had made Berthollet a senator, a position which carried a large income. Yet the chemist did not handle his fortune well and by 1807 was in some difficulty. Laplace, also a friend of the head of state, wrote to Napoléon, mentioning the plight of his friend. The emperor immediately authorized payment of a substantial sum for the man he once called "his chemist."

In 1783 Berthollet had met Charles Blagden, very soon to be appointed secretary to the Royal Society of London, then on one of his many visits to Paris. They soon became great friends, reinforced by their common early medical careers, and they kept up a correspondence for the next forty years. The letters were of great importance in conveying scientific news between the two capitals. In 1784 Blagden was appointed as one of the official correspondents of the Academy of Sciences. Berthollet was also to correspond with many other foreign men of science, including Martin van Marum, Joseph Proust, and Jöns Jakob Berzelius.

Work. The close association of Berthollet with Laplace in the Arcueil period was based on more than personal friendship. They shared a common interest in the legacy of Isaac Newton's theory of gravitational attraction. This had played a prominent part in Laplace's previous astronomical work, but in the early 1800s he became interested in attraction on the microscale, that is, the short-range attraction between particles of matter. Having explained satisfactorily capillary attraction, he directed his ambition towards a theory of "the identity of the attractive forces governing capillarity with those responsible for [chemical] affinities" (see also Crosland, 2006). He tried unsuccessfully for some time but eventually realized that his equations would have to take into consideration the size and the shape of the ultimate particles—an impossible task.

Of course chemical affinity was one of Berthollet's great interests since his visit to Egypt, where he had discovered that large masses of reactants could overwhelm normal affinities. Thus he had set out to study what he called

"chemical statics," as in the title of his book. He even introduced the term *chemical mass* (1803, vol. 1, p. 16).

Although John Dalton published his atomic theory only in 1808, it had been described in Thomas Thomson's textbook of 1807. Thomson sent Berthollet a copy and Berthollet had it translated into French (9 volumes, 1809). Berthollet wrote a long introduction and, although he was critical, describing Dalton's atoms as "an ingenious hypothesis," it was often through this book that, in time of war, Dalton's theory was known on the continent of Europe.

The defeat of Napoléon marked the effective end of the Society of Arcueil but Berthollet decided to work on a second edition of his *Essai,* taking into account recent research. In particular he was able to comment on the work of Dalton, William Wollaston, and Berzelius. He was still critical of Proust's theory of definite proportions despite growing evidence in its favor but he allowed for its possibility in certain cases. The new edition of the *Essai* was never published but the manuscript has recently been found and analyzed. Although the Society of Arcueil was no longer in existence, Berthollet managed in 1817 to bring out a final volume of its *Mémoires,* consisting of papers by some of its former members.

Influence. The person on whom Berthollet had the greatest immediate influence was Gay-Lussac who, for example, suspected that "oxymuriatic acid" (chlorine) was a simple substance but said that "it appeared so extraordinary that M. Berthollet prevailed upon us to state it with the greatest reserve" (1814, p. 97). It was Berthollet who had discovered the bleaching action of "oxymuriatic acid," which was simply and logically explained as oxidation due to its oxygen content. Thus the French chemists lost any claim to the discovery of the elementary nature of chlorine, which went to Humphry Davy. Even after Berthollet's death Gay-Lussac admitted that he still felt the influence of his mentor in the interpretation of chemical phenomena. In 1823 Jean-Baptiste Dumas, the young aspiring chemist from Geneva, had hoped to study under Berthollet, whose works he had studied, but when he arrived in Paris he found that the great chemist had died in the previous year. After this Berthollet's work seems to have been largely forgotten until the time of Cato Maximilian Guldberg and Peter Waage with their law of mass action (1867). They referred to Berthollet's work but he had not gone far enough with the question of mass for them. When Wilhelm Ostwald in 1896 republished Berthollet's *Essai* in his series of science classics, he remarked that the book was often praised but seldom read.

SUPPLEMENTARY BIBLIOGRAPHY

WORK BY BERTHOLLET

Essai de statique chimique. 2 vols. Paris, 1803.

OTHER SOURCES

Crosland, Maurice. Introduction to reprint of *Essai de statique chimique* [1803], by Claude Louis Berthollet. 2 vols. New York: Johnson Reprint Corp., 1952.

———. *The Society of Arcueil: A View of French Science at the Time of Napoleon I.* London: Heineman, 1967.

———. "A Science Empire in Napoleonic France." *History of Science* 44 (2006): 29–48.

Cuvier, Georges. "Eloge historique de M. le comte Berthollet." In *Recueil des éloges historiques,* vol. 3. Paris, 1827.

Gay-Lussac, Joseph-Louis. Mémoire sur l'iode." *Annales de Chimie* (31 July 1814): 5–160.

Grapí, Pere. "The Marginalization of Berthollet's Chemical Affinities in the French Textbook Tradition at the Beginning of the Nineteenth Century." *Annals of Science* 58 (2001): 111–135.

Laplace, Pierre-Simon. *Mécanique céleste,* vol. 4, *Supplément à la théorie de l'action capillaire.* Paris, 1807.

Sadoun-Goupil, Michelle. *Le chimiste Claude-Louis Berthollet, 1748–1822: Sa vie, son œuvre.* Paris: J. Vrin, 1977. This includes correspondence and a full bibliography of Berthollet's publications.

———, ed. *Revue de l'Essai de statique chimique,* by Claude Louis Berthollet. Paris: École Polytechnique, 1980.

———. *Du flou au clair? Histoire de l'affinité chimique.* Paris: Editions du Comité des Travaux historiques et scientifiques, 1991.

Thomson, Thomas. *Système de chimie.* Translated by Jean Riffault. 9 vols. Paris, 1809. With an introduction by Berthollet.

Maurice Crosland

BERZELIUS, JÖNS JACOB (*b.* Väversunda, near Linköping, Sweden, 20 August 1779; *d.* Stockholm, 7 August 1848), *chemistry.* For the original article on Berzelius see *DSB,* vol. 2.

A man of immense learning and energy, one of the most brilliant experimentalists of his century, and a creative and influential theorist, Berzelius was the dominating European figure in the science of chemistry during most of the first half of the nineteenth century. He was also a prominent authority in such cognate areas as geology, mineralogy, and physiology. Always sociable, witty, and amiable in private conversation, he could be blunt or even harsh in his letters and published critiques. But whatever his views, they always attracted attention and respect.

Literature on Berzelius prior to 1970. At the time of Henry Leicester's *DSB* article on Berzelius, the literature on this illustrious scientist was sparse. There existed a detailed three-volume biography—Henrik Gustaf Söderbaum's *Jac. Berzelius Levnadsteckning* (Uppsala, 1929–1931)—but this work has never been translated from the Swedish, which has limited its impact. Söderbaum had earlier published a short version of part of this biography in German, titled *Berzelius' Werden und Wachsen, 1779–1821* (Leipzig: Barth, 1899). There existed a good short biography in English (Johan Erik Jorpes's *Jac. Berzelius, His Life and Work* [Stockholm: Almqvist & Wiksell, 1966]), Berzelius's own autobiography in Swedish and English, and a handful of more derivative biographies, obituaries, and articles in the secondary literature. There was also a good edition of much of Berzelius's surviving correspondence, printed in original languages and edited by Söderbaum, *Jac. Berzelius Bref,* 6 vols. and supplements (Uppsala: Almqvist & Wiksell, 1912–1961), separate editions of his correspondence with Friedrich Wöhler and with Justus von Liebig in German, and a definitive bibliography edited by Arne Holmberg, *Bibliografi över J. J. Berzelius,* 5 vols. (Stockholm, 1933–1953). A generation after Leicester's article, the literature on Berzelius is incomparably larger, and much has been learned in the intervening years.

Early Career. It is now understood that Berzelius was not quite the complete autodidact he has been portrayed (an image he himself wished to cultivate). Although his relations with the elderly phlogistonist professor Johan Afzelius were uneven at best, Berzelius's studies at Uppsala benefited from the up-to-date teaching of Afzelius's younger brother Pehr and of Johan's capable assistant Anders Ekeberg. Swedish chemistry had suffered recent losses in the deaths of Torbern Bergman and Carl Scheele, but Ekeberg in particular had been influential in introducing Antoine-Laurent Lavoisier's antiphlogistic chemistry to Sweden. From an early age Berzelius also avidly read the French, German, and English chemical literatures. He consorted with progressive circles at the university, imbibing many of the materialist, empiricist, rationalist, and utilitarian values typical of the late Enlightenment. These values coexisted comfortably with the liberal religious faith that he unreservedly shared with his Lutheran forebears, several of whom were pastors. His MD degree was awarded in May 1802, under the direction of Pehr Afzelius. In the same year, he was appointed unpaid assistant to the professor of medicine and pharmacy at the Stockholm School of Surgery while simultaneously serving as physician to the poor. Almost immediately he also began electrochemical experiments in collaboration with a wealthy friend, Wilhelm Hisinger, an investigation that resulted in a major discovery, that of a new element which Berzelius named cerium.

Influence and Writings. In 1807 Berzelius succeeded to the professorship of medicine and pharmacy. He spent his entire career in Stockholm rather than in the university city of Uppsala, teaching at the School of Surgery, renamed the Karolinska Institutet in 1810. This activity may have played a role in keeping his attention focused on the practical and empirical sides of chemistry, consistent with his inclinations. In the late 1820s Berzelius attempted to elevate his institution to official university status and fought for more utilitarian and modernist curricula across Sweden. He despised what he viewed as the metaphysical obfuscations of G. W. F. Hegel, Friedrich Schelling, and the *Naturphilosophen*. His was an increasingly influential voice: in 1810 he served a term as president of the Swedish Royal Academy of Sciences and in 1818 was elected its permanent secretary, a remunerative as well as an honorific post.

Berzelius's influence abroad was promoted by his personal travels, by the few but highly select foreign students who spent time in his Stockholm laboratory, by his prolific publications, and by his massive private correspondence. His first visit abroad was to Great Britain, for four months in the late summer of 1812. In 1818–1819 he spent a year abroad, mostly in France although he visited Germany as well. Between 1822 and 1845 he made six more trips to Germany, which country became his principal foreign redoubt. His authority there was enormous, especially in the 1820s and 1830s, partly because of personal influence with such former students as C. G. Gmelin, Eilhard Mitscherlich, Heinrich and Gustav Rose, Gustav Magnus, and above all the great Göttingen chemist Friedrich Wöhler. In addition, he powerfully influenced Justus von Liebig, Robert Bunsen, Hermann Kolbe, and many others. Wöhler was the only one of these men whose regard for Berzelius extended so far as to master the Swedish language. For little financial reward, he translated thousands of pages of Berzelius's massive textbook editions into German, and thousands of additional pages of Berzelius's annual reports. Berzelius's *Lärbok i kemien* (Textbook of chemistry) went through five German editions, four French editions, and editions in Spanish, Italian, and Dutch—though never in English. It was perhaps the last time that a single textbook author purported to treat the entire science in total detail. From portions of the second edition on (1825), each new authorized German edition came out simultaneously with the Swedish and can be regarded equally as editio princeps, due to Wöhler's superb and prompt translations from the Swedish manuscript supplied by his older friend.

Jöns Jacob Berzelius. © BETTMANN/CORBIS.

Starting in 1821, two months of every spring in Berzelius's life was devoted to writing a detailed critical summary for the Swedish Royal Academy of chemical papers and books published during the preceding calendar year. These book-length *Årsberättelser om vetenskapernas framsteg*, or in Wöhler's skilled translation the *Jahresberichte über die Fortschritte der physischen Wissenschaften*, immediately assumed enormous authority. Each year the book was anxiously awaited by European chemists, not only for the useful summaries of the international literature but for the sometimes sharply expressed judgments contained therein. In this manner Berzelius became known as the supreme authority in the science, whose favorable testimony could make a scientific career or whose severe criticism could lame one.

Initial Research. As a researcher, Berzelius's earliest passion was physiological ("animal") chemistry, and this was the subject of his first book (*Föreläsningar i djurkemien*, 2 vols., Stockholm, 1806–1808). This pioneering work, which has never been translated from the Swedish, summarized what was known on the subject, added much new empirical information, and proclaimed an essentially materialist philosophy of biology. Berzelius's underlying program apparently was to demonstrate that materials derived from animals were not indeterminate generic mixtures but analyzable combinations of well-defined chemical substances. An adequate understanding of these fluids in this purely chemical sense would open the door, he thought, to rapid progress in the science of physiology, leading to knowledge that would have important new practical applications.

Chemical Atomic Theory. Berzelius retained a lifelong interest in physiological chemistry, but he was soon diverted into inorganic chemistry and mineralogy. This happened as the result of a careful literature review he conducted in 1807 in preparation for writing his general textbook of chemistry, the first volume of which was published in Swedish the following year. He encountered some of the early research on elemental combining proportions (stoichiometry), then early in 1809 learned secondhand about John Dalton's atomic theory. He immediately understood the deep significance of chemical atomism and resolved to pursue the subject himself. In 1810 (in Swedish) and 1811–1812 (in German) he published a book-length stoichiometric study, reporting on, and experimentally repeating, essentially all of the determinations of elemental combining proportions in the literature. By the end of 1812 he had read Dalton in the original and had personally met with Humphry Davy and William Wollaston, both of whom were engaged with the same subject. Up until this time he had refrained from all theoretical interpretations of the emerging laws of stoichiometry. Now he began to offer a theory that, he said, was "analogous" to Dalton's, namely the "volume theory." In this context he introduced an early version of the formula notational system still used today, in an installment of an English-language essay published in November 1813, in which Latin letters represent unit-combining "volumes" of elements (what Dalton had called "atoms").

Berzelius's influential development of the chemical atomic theory has been carefully studied by Evan Melhado, Anders Lundgren, Alan Rocke, and Ursula Klein, and these scholars' approaches differ somewhat. Melhado portrays Berzelius as profoundly original, rather than a mere consolidator of earlier work, in that he successfully sought to understand the specific level of precisely characterized compounds rather than the generic level of property-bearing principles. Lundgren emphasizes Berzelius's only partial acceptance of Dalton's theory and characterizes his attitude toward atoms as more instrumental than realist, while Rocke argues that there was more in common between Berzelius and Dalton than may initially appear. Klein has demonstrated the extraordinary power of Berzelius's formula notation, especially when it

began to be used in an aggressively productive way from around 1830.

All these scholars recognize the enormous labor and thought that went into Berzelius's final revision of atomic weights and molecular formulas, accomplished in 1826. Berzelius was almost unique at this time in his insistence on applying all possible approaches, physical as well as chemical, to the problem of the determination of weights and formulas, as well as creatively developing novel experiments, ingenious hypotheses, and useful conventions. Although it would be another generation before most European chemists agreed on a single system of atomic weights and molecular formulas, only minor modifications ultimately proved necessary to transform the Berzelian system of 1826 into that which provided the basis for modern chemistry.

Organic Chemistry. Berzelius's profound influence extended also into organic chemistry, of which he must be considered one of the principal founders. From about 1811 he and Joseph-Louis Gay-Lussac semi-independently developed the combustion method of elemental organic analysis that was further improved by Liebig some few years later. In 1814 Berzelius published analyses of thirteen organic compounds, together with proposed atomistic formulas for their molecules, the first time this had ever been done for organic substances. As Melhado has argued, this development demonstrates again Berzelius's strong interest in providing a means to get to the specific level of well-defined homogeneous chemical compounds, in this case for organic nature. Although it would be others who would develop organic chemistry further, led especially by Liebig and Jean-Baptiste Dumas, they did so on this Berzelian foundation.

For Berzelius, all molecules, organic as well as inorganic, were thought to be held together by the coulombic attraction of oppositely charged components (atoms or radicals). This "electrochemical-dualist" theory of chemical combination worked well in the inorganic and mineral realm but proved to be less satisfactory for organic compounds, because in such substances it was soon found that electrochemically dissimilar elements could substitute for each other indiscriminately. Berzelius's heated opposition to substitutionist "type" theories during the last twenty years of his life has damaged his subsequent reputation, for those newer ideas led eventually to modern theories of atomic valence and molecular structure. John Brooke has argued persuasively, by contrast, that Berzelius's opposition was neither unreasonable nor unproductive if one views the history in a more sympathetic, philosophical, and contextual fashion.

The Vitalism Issue. Berzelius has also sometimes been castigated for continuing the tradition of vitalist thought, which posited a special force that creates the properties of living creatures and which denies the possibility of artificial synthesis of organic compounds. In fact, recent historical research has suggested that Berzelius had a much more complex stance toward these issues. Many of his pronouncements, enunciated in his first book on animal chemistry and repeated occasionally throughout his life, suggest in fact that he had ardent materialist convictions and denied anything approaching a conventional vital force. But other statements, such as those in later editions of his textbook, appear to proclaim a pure and untroubled vitalist faith. There are in fact ways to understand how both of these convictions could coexist in Berzelius's mind. His sincere religious faith made atheistic or reductionistic materialism repugnant, but his ardent commitment to Enlightenment values honored naturalism, empirical methods, and a materialist metaphysics. The result appears to have been a middle-ground position, which affirmed that there was indeed something unique in the circumstances of organic nature but that those circumstances were produced by the same scientific laws that reigned in the inorganic realm. These mysteries, Berzelius thought, may ever remain veiled to human understanding.

SUPPLEMENTARY BIBLIOGRAPHY

Berhhard, Carl Gustaf. *Through France with Berzelius: Live Scholars and Dead Volcanoes.* Oxford: Pergamon, 1985.

Brooke, John. *Thinking about Matter: Studies in the History of Chemical Philosophy.* Aldershot, U.K.: Ashgate, 1995.

Dunsch, Lothar. *Jöns Jacob Berzelius.* Leipzig, Germany: Teubner, 1986.

Klein, Ursula. *Experiments, Models, Paper Tools: Cultures of Organic Chemistry in the Nineteenth Century.* Stanford, CA: Stanford University Press, 2003.

Lundgren, Anders. *Berzelius och den kemiska atomteorin* [Berzelius and the chemical atomic theory]. Uppsala, Sweden: Almqvist & Wiksell, 1979.

Melhado, Evan M. *Jacob Berzelius: The Emergence of His Chemical System.* Madison: University of Wisconsin Press, 1981.

Melhado, Evan M., and Tore Frängsmyr, eds. *Enlightenment Science in the Romantic Era: The Chemistry of Berzelius and Its Cultural Setting.* Cambridge, U.K., and New York: Cambridge University Press, 1992.

Rocke, Alan J. *Chemical Atomism in the Nineteenth Century: From Dalton to Cannizzaro.* Columbus: Ohio State University Press, 1984.

Alan J. Rocke

BETHE, HANS ALBRECHT (*b.* 2 July 1906, Strassburg, Alsace; *d.* 6 March 2006, Ithaca, New York), *theoretical physics, quantum mechanics.*

Bethe was one of the great physicists of the twentieth century. After the advent of quantum mechanics, in two classic articles published in 1933 in the *Handbuch der Physik* he detailed the applications of the new quantum theory to atomic and solid state physics. After the discovery of the neutron in 1932 in a series of articles in the *Reviews of Modern Physics,* he did the same for nuclear physics. In 1938 he formulated the nuclear physics responsible for energy production in stars. During World War II he contributed importantly to the development of radar and of atomic weapons. Because of his involvement in making A- and H-bombs possible, he subsequently devoted considerable efforts in limiting further developments of atomic weaponry and bringing about international agreements for the reduction of extant nuclear weapons and the curtailment of their production and design. He made Cornell University, his base of operation from 1935 until his death, an outstanding center of theoretical physics and a model research community in all branches of physics.

Youth and Education. Hans Bethe was born on 2 July 1906 in Strassburg, when Alsace was part of the Wilhelminian empire. His father, Albrecht Julius Bethe, obtained a PhD in zoology at the University of Munich with Richard Hertwig in 1895, and thereafter went to Strassburg to study physiology. He became a Privatdozent there and also acquired a medical degree. In 1912 Hans's father accepted the chair in physiology at the University of Kiel, and three years later a professorship in the newly established Frankfurt University. Albrecht Bethe became a world renowned physiologist specializing in comparative studies of the nervous system of animals and of animal behavior. Hans's mother, née Anna Kuhn, was born in Strassburg, where her father was a professor of medicine specializing in diseases of the ear, nose, and throat. Bethe was an only child. He grew up in a Christian household, but one in which religion did not play an important role. His father was Protestant; his mother had been Jewish but had converted and became a Lutheran before she had met Hans's father. She was a talented and accomplished musician who became a successful author of children's plays. A year or two before World War I her hearing was impaired as a result of contracting influenza. The illness left psychological scars. She became prone to what was diagnosed at the time as bouts of "nervous exhaustion," extended periods of depression. The marriage suffered under the strain and Hans's parents eventually divorced in 1927. From the mid-1920s on, it was Hans who looked after his mother's welfare and wellbeing.

Bethe started reading at the age of four and began writing at about the same age. His numerical and mathematical abilities manifested themselves early. At age fourteen he taught himself calculus. At age eighteen he published his first scientific paper: a joint publication with his father on diffusion and fluid flow in living organisms. His mathematics teacher at the Goethe Gymnasium he attended in Frankfurt recognized his exceptional mathematical talents and encouraged him to continue studies in mathematics and the physical sciences. By the time he finished gymnasium in the spring of 1924 he knew he wanted to be a physicist. In the fall of 1924 he enrolled in the University of Frankfurt and took courses in physics with Walther Gerlach, and in mathematics with Carl Ludwig Siegel. After completing two years of studies at the University in Frankfurt, he was advised by one of his teachers there, the spectroscopist Karl Meissner, to go to Munich and study with Arnold Sommerfeld, who at the time was the outstanding university physics teacher in Germany. In the summer of 1926 Bethe joined Sommerfeld's seminar.

Gregor Wentzel was Sommerfeld's assistant at the time and helped make the seminar, together with Niels Bohr's Institute in Copenhagen and Max Born and James Frank's Physics Institute in Göttingen, the pivotal centers in the development of the new quantum mechanics. Sommerfeld's seminar attracted many American postdoctoral fellows, and it was in Munich that Bethe first met Edward Condon, Carl Eckart, William Houston, Philip Morse, Linus Pauling, Isador Rabi, and Lloyd P. Smith. In 1927, Rudolf Peierls, a young German physics student a year younger than Bethe, joined Sommerfeld's seminar. Bethe and Peierls then cemented a very close intellectual bond and personal friendship that lasted until Peierls's death in 1995. Sommerfeld's seminar met weekly. In contrast to the usual practice at the other German universities where only invited guests spoke, Sommerfeld had his *Doktoranden* and *Assistents* make presentations in his seminar. Bethe arrived in Munich just as Erwin Schrödinger's papers on wave mechanics were being published in the *Annalen der Physik* and his first presentation in the fall of 1926 was on the perturbative methods that Schrödinger had developed.

It was in Munich that Bethe discovered his remarkable talents and proficiency in physics and anchored his self-confidence. Sommerfeld indicated to him that he was among the very best students who had studied with him, and these had included among others, Max von Laue, Paul Ewald, Wolfgang Pauli, and Werner Heisenberg. From Sommerfeld Bethe learned to analyze masses of experimental data, go to the main points of a problem, assimilate the salient features of the data and of the problem into a mathematical model, express the model in appropriate mathematical equations, and then fearlessly use every available mathematical tool to solve the equations quantitatively as exactly as possible.

Early Career. Bethe obtained his doctorate—summa cum laude—in 1928 with a thesis that analyzed and explained the results that Clinton Joseph Davisson and Lester Germer had obtained in their experiments on electron diffraction by nickel crystals. When the de Broglie wave length of electrons is comparable to the lattice spacings of a crystal they diffract in a manner similar to x-rays. Bethe made use of the methods that von Laue and Ewald had formulated for x-ray diffraction by crystals and found that their results could readily and successfully be adapted to the electron case.

During Sommerfeld's travel around the world in 1928–1929, Bethe spent a semester in Frankfurt as Erwin Madelung's *Assistent*, and another semester in Stuttgart as Paul Ewald's. Upon Sommerfeld's return Bethe went back to Munich and undertook his *Habilitation*.

In the fall of 1929 Sommerfeld recommended Bethe for a Rockefeller Foundation fellowship. And so during 1930 Bethe spent a semester in Cambridge under the aegis of Ralph Fowler, and a semester in Rome working with Enrico Fermi. Though only five years older than Bethe, Fermi became the other great formative influence on him. Fermi helped Bethe free himself from the mathematically rigorous and exhaustive approach that was the hallmark of Sommerfeld. For Fermi a mathematical solution served as corroboration and confirmation of his physical understanding of a problem. From Fermi, Bethe learned to reason qualitatively, to obtain insights from back-of-envelopes calculations, and to find the easiest way to solve a problem. Bethe's craftsmanship became an amalgam of what he learned from these two great physicists and teachers, combining the best of both: the thoroughness and rigor of Sommerfeld's approach to problems with the clarity and simplicity of Fermi's. Fermi and Sommerfeld both believed that science is also communication and both were also superb lecturers. Bethe followed in their footsteps and honed his skilled in communication. Bethe's lectures became masterpieces of organization and exposition. Like Fermi and Sommerfeld, Bethe made no concession to expediency when lecturing on a difficult subject, but presented it in a clear, concise, and insightful manner. However, it was difficult at times to reconstruct his lectures, as what was clear and simple to him was not necessarily so for his audiences.

Bethe's craftsmanship was displayed in full force in the many "reviews" that he wrote. His two book-length "reviews" in volume 24 of the 1933 *Handbuch der Physik*—the first the result of Sommerfeld asking him to collaborate in the writing of his entry on the *Elektronentheorie der Metalle*, and the second on the quantum theory of one- and two-electron systems—exhibited his remarkable powers of synthesis and became classics as soon as they were published. Together with the one on nuclear physics in the *Reviews of Modern Physics 1936-1937*—written in collaboration with his colleagues at Cornell, Robert Bacher and Stanley Livingston and known as the "Bethe Bible"—they are merely the most famous. All of Bethe's reviews were syntheses of the fields under review, giving them coherence and unity, charting the paths to be taken in addressing new problems. They usually contained much that was new, materials that Bethe had worked out in the preparation of his essay.

In the fall of 1932 Bethe obtained an appointment in Tübingen as an acting assistant professor of theoretical physics. In April 1933, after Hitler's accession to power, he was dismissed from his position because he had two Jewish grandparents. Sommerfeld was able to help him by awarding him a fellowship in his institute for the summer 1933 and got William Lawrence Bragg to invite him to Manchester. The appointment in Manchester was for a year's duration and thus the question of what would happen the following year came up early on. There then occurred a confluence of events that determined Bethe's subsequent life. The physics department at Cornell University was looking for a theorist, and on its faculty was the young theorist Lloyd P. Smith, who had studied with Bethe in Munich and who recommended him strongly. At that very same time Bragg was visiting Cornell for the spring semester and could corroborate Smith's assessment of Bethe. In the fall of 1934 Bethe accepted a position at Cornell University. But as he had received an offer of a yearlong fellowship in Bristol with Neville Mott, he asked and obtained permission from Cornell to assume his duties there in the spring term rather than at the beginning of the academic year. He went to Bristol during the fall semester of the academic year 1934–1935 and arrived in Ithaca, New York, in February 1935. He stayed there for the rest of his life.

Problems of Stellar Energy. Bethe arrived in the United States at a time when the American physics community was undergoing enormous growth. The influence of the émigré scientists who had come from Nazi Germany was particularly noticeable at the many theoretical conferences that were being organized to assimilate the insights that quantum mechanics was giving to many fields, especially molecular physics and the emerging field of nuclear physics. The annual Washington Conferences on Theoretical Physics, initiated in 1935 and jointly sponsored by the Carnegie Institution and George Washington University, were paradigmatic of such meetings. Their intellectual agenda was set by George Gamow and by Bethe's friend, Edward Teller. Their purpose was to evolve in the United States something similar to Niels Bohr's Copenhagen Conferences, in which a small number of theoretical physicists working on related problems would assemble to discuss in an informal way their research. The conferences proved to be extremely influential and seminal, partly because they were restricted to theory and partly because their size was strictly regulated so that they would remain "working" meetings. Bethe attended the 1935 and 1937 Washington Conferences but when invited to the 1938 meeting first declined because he was not interested in the problem of stellar energy generation, the topic for that year that had been chosen by Gamow, who recently had turned his attention to the problem. It was only after Teller's repeated urgings that Bethe agreed to come.

The opening lecture was given by the Danish astrophysicist Bengt Strömberg, who had just written a seventy-page paper that critically reviewed all that was known about stellar structure and the evolution of stars. In his presentation Strömberg focused on the problem of the temperature and density distribution in the interior of stars. He indicated that spectroscopic data suggested that the most reasonable model for the Sun was for hydrogen to be the prevalent element in its composition. He noted that a model of the Sun with a central temperature of 19 million degrees, a central density of 76 g/cm3, and a hydrogen content of 35 percent by weight would result in its generating 2 erg/g sec. The challenge he posed to the physicists in the audience was to find the thermonuclear reactions that would give rise to the observed luminosities of the Sun and other main sequence stars. In the subsequent discussion Bethe was critical of any theory, such as Gamow's and Carl Friedrich von Weizsäcker's, that proposed a chain of nuclear reactions that would simultaneously generate energy and account for the building up of heavy elements in stars; this because of the instability of He^5 and of Be^6. Thus there was no obvious way to create elements heavier than helium. It seemed more likely to Bethe, given the great abundance of hydrogen in the Sun, that von Weizsäcker's suggestion that the fusion of two protons to form a deuteron, a positron, and a neutrino,

$$p + p \longrightarrow D + e^+ + \nu \qquad (1)$$

as the first step in proton reactions that led to the formation of helium was a more likely source of stellar energy. In fact Charles Critchfield, a graduate student of Teller's, had for some months tried to persuade Gamow and Teller to help him investigate this (weak interaction induced) reaction. Upon hearing of Critchfield's interest in the reaction Bethe proposed that they collaborate. Before the conference's end they were able to report that the reaction (1) together with the chain of reactions

$$D + p \longrightarrow He^3 + \gamma \qquad (2)$$

$$He^3 + He^3 \longrightarrow He^4 + p + p \qquad (3)$$

$$He^3 + He^4 \longrightarrow Be^7 + \gamma \qquad (4)$$

$$Be^7 \longrightarrow Li^7 + + e^+ + \nu \qquad (5)$$

$$Li^7 + p \longrightarrow 2\ He^4 \qquad (6)$$

—the end result of which is the combination of four protons into one α-particle and thus the release of a large amount of energy—accounted for the energy production of the Sun, but not of other heavier bright stars. From astronomical observations one could show that core temperature of stars increases slowly with increasing mass, but the amount of observed radiation, that is, their luminosity, increases very rapidly. This left unsolved the problem of energy production in larger stars because the proton-proton (pp) reaction could not explain this. Upon his return to Cornell from the conference Bethe started investigating reactions involving heavier nuclei that would explain energy production in massive stars. Lithium, beryllium and boron could be ruled out because of their comparative scarcity in stellar interiors. The next element was carbon. The detailed investigation of the reaction of carbon with protons yielded a positive result:

$$C^{12} + p \longrightarrow Ni^{13} + \gamma \qquad (7)$$

$$Ni^{13} \longrightarrow C^{13} + e^+ + \nu \qquad (8)$$

$$C^{13} + p \longrightarrow Ni^{14} + \gamma \qquad (9)$$

$$Ni^{14} + p \longrightarrow O^{15} + \gamma \qquad (10)$$

$$O^{15} \longrightarrow Ni^{15} + e^+ + \nu \qquad (11)$$

$$Ni^{15} + p \longrightarrow C^{12} + He^4 \qquad (12)$$

At the end of the cycle the C^{12} nucleus is recovered and four protons have been combined into an α-particle. The C^{12} nucleus thus acts as a catalyst for the reaction and hence the relatively low abundance of carbon nuclei could still allow the reaction to proceed frequently. Under the same condition as the rates calculated for the pp cycle, and with a concentration of N^{14} of 10 percent, Bethe calculated an energy production of about 25 ergs/g sec. The reaction is extremely sensitive to temperature (a dependence of T^{18}), and thus accounted for the sharp increase in luminosity with slight increases in core temperature. Bethe could exclude on various grounds almost all other reactions besides the pp and carbon-nitrogen (CN) cycles by detailed investigations of their properties. He was thus able to explain why stars like the Sun and heavier ones burn for billions of years at the rate that they do. His conclusions were rapidly accepted by the astrophysical community. In 1967 he was awarded the Nobel Prize for this work.

Research Style. Bethe's scientific output during the 1930s was remarkable. More than half of the papers that he characterized as particularly meaningful to him and that he included in his *Selected Works* were from the 1930s. He was one of the founding fathers of solid state theory. He was one of the first theorists to apply group theoretical methods to quantum mechanical calculations. His theory of energy loss of charged particles in their passage through matter became the basis of the extraction of quantitative information from cloud chamber tracks and later from nuclear emulsions. His calculations of the cross-sections for the production of electron-positron pairs and for *bremsstrahlung* (the emission of radiation when charged particles are deflected in their collisions with other charged particles) became classics and important elements in understanding cosmic ray showers. His refinement of the Bragg-Williams method offered important insights into long-range correlations near the phase transition point in alloys—and thus into phase transitions in general. With Rudolf Peierls he laid the foundations for understanding the structure of the deuteron, its photo disintegration, and neutron-proton and proton-proton scattering. The so-called Bethe Bible summarized what was known and understood in nuclear structure and nuclear reactions, and his paper on the energy generation in stars solved that problem and created the field of nuclear astrophysics.

Bethe early on recognized his limitations, and in particular, that his forte was not in the formulation of what Einstein had called principle theories, that is, empirical generalizations such as the first and second laws of thermodynamics, or the principles that specify the special theory of relativity and its domain of validity, or the principles of quantum mechanics. His strength lay in the formulation of constructive theories that offer constructive models for the description of the phenomena under consideration, which, as Einstein had formulated it, "attempt to build up a picture of the more complex phenomena out of the materials of a relatively simple formal scheme from which they start out." An example of a constructive theory would be the application of non-relativistic quantum mechanics to the Rutherford model of atoms to explain the Mendeleev table of the chemical elements.

From his first acquaintance with quantum mechanics, Bethe immediately recognized its amazing robustness. It was clear to him that the revolutionary achievements of quantum mechanics stemmed from the confluence of a theoretical understanding: the quantum mechanical representation of the kinematics and dynamics of microscopic particles, *and* the apperception of an approximately stable ontology—electrons and nuclei. Approximately stable meant that these entities, the electrons and nuclei—the building blocks of the atoms, molecules, simple solids that populated the domain that was being carved out—could be treated as *ahistoric* objects, whose physical characteristics were independent of their mode of production and whose lifetimes could be considered infinite. At the available energies these entities could be assumed to be essentially point-like objects that were specified by their mass, their spin, and their electromagnetic properties such as their charge and magnetic moment. Furthermore they were indistinguishable: all electrons were identical; all protons were identical; all He^4, Li^6, and other nuclei in their ground state were identical and by virtue of their indistinguishability obeyed characteristic statistics: Einstein-Bose if their spins were integral multiples of $h/2\pi$ or zero; Fermi-Dirac, if half integer multiples.

Thus it was only after the discovery of the neutron by James Chadwick in 1932 that Bethe believed that an adequate particle ontology for the description of nuclear structure was at hand—neutrons and protons—and that quantum mechanical models could be introduced. He thereafter began to intensively study developments in the field.

Turn to Quantum Mechanics. With his *Handbuch* articles Bethe mastered the principles of quantum mechanics, its models and its explanations of various systems and explorations of various domains in atomic, molecular, and solid state physics; for example, the properties and behavior of hydrogen and helium atoms in external electric and magnetic fields, the Thomas-Fermi and Hartree-Fock methods for the calculation of the properties of atoms, the elastical and inelastic scattering cross-section for charged particles interacting with atoms, the Born-Oppenheimer method in the description of molecules, the Heitler-London model to account for covalent bonding in molecules, the various models of and approximations to the motion of electrons in solids, the quantitative explanation of the thermal properties of solids and of their electrical conductivity, and so forth. What is characteristic of these articles—in fact, of all of Bethe's scientific papers—is the detailed comparison of theoretical predictions with experimental data. Agreement was the criterion used for gauging the validity of the model, discrepancies the criterion for changing the model to include further relevant physical interactions or, if the disagreement was substantial enough, to abandon the model and the theory.

Bethe's conception of physics was that it is an experimental science. It is concerned with those statements which can be verified by experiments. Knowledge in physics accretes because it is reproducible. The purpose of theory is to provide a classification, systematization, and unification of the reproducible experimental results. Theories are mathematical, quantitative, informative compactifications that can explain and predict new phenomena. And in view of the enormity of the available reproducible data, in order to grasp and comprehend the regularities discerned in experiments it is necessary that theories be in some sense simple: They must describe and represent the maximum amount of experimental information with a minimum of concepts.

As experiments yielded information about the higher energy interactions of electrons and photons in the 1930s,

Bethe helped develop the tools to describe the observed phenomena. Thus after Dirac devised his equation to describe quantum mechanically relativistic electrons and formulated its hole theoretic interpretation to accommodate the existence of negative energy solutions and of positrons, Bethe—together with Walter Heitler—used hole theory to calculate the cross-section for the production of electron-positron pairs by γ-rays in the (screened) Coulomb field of an atom. For Bethe, the calculation was also performed in order to gauge the limit of validity of quantum electrodynamics (QED). The interaction between the electromagnetic field and charged particles, when these were assumed point-like, resulted in arbitrarily high energy photons being involved and this gave rise to divergences in higher order perturbative calculations. The divergences reflected explicit incorrect assumptions about the way the short distance interactions were being described by the theory.

What is most remarkable about Bethe's approach to this and other problems in physics was the way he consistently handled the experimentally inaccessible aspects of the phenomena being investigated. Thus in 1949 when he analyzed very low energy nucleon-nucleon scattering, he was aware that the short-distance nature of the nucleon-nucleon interaction potential was not being probed in the scattering. He devised a method to effectively parametrize this unknown aspect of the interaction by introducing two experimentally determined parameters, the "scattering length" at zero energy and the "effective range." The energy dependence of low energy scattering is then completely and accurately quantum mechanically described in terms of these two parameters. These insights were further generalized after 1955, in work with Geoffrey Goldstone, to handle the effects of the details of the repulsion between nucleons at very small distances in the theory of nuclear matter.

Bethe's concern with the limits of validity of theories and how to parametrize unknown aspects of the description was similarly manifested in his non-relativistic, quantum electrodynamic calculation of the Lamb shift in hydrogen. At the Shelter Island conference in June 1947, Willis Lamb had reported on his experimental finding that contrary to the prediction of the Dirac equation describing the motion of an electron in a Coulomb field, the 2s and 2p states of a hydrogen atom were not degenerate: the 2s state lay some 1000 MHz higher than the 2p state. At the conference Hendrik Kramers had indicated that the parameter m_0 that is introduced as the mass of the electron in the equations of quantum electrodynamics is not the experimentally observed mass, m, of the electron. The parameter m_0 must be "renormalized" to the value of the "experimental" mass as the corrections to the inertia of the electron by virtue of its self interaction are taken into account. Bethe believed the shift was of quantum electrodynamic origin. On a train ride after the conference, he investigated the simple possible model in which the electron in the Coulomb field of the proton is described quantum mechanically but non-relativistically, and the radiation field and the interaction between the electron and the radiation field is treated quantum field theoretically. Bethe then introduced a cutoff which limited the latter interaction to a non-relativistic domain of validity: No photons of energy greater than mc^2 were to enter in the description. At energies greater than mc^2 a relativistic field theoretic description of electrons and photons was to be used. Bethe followed Kramers's prescription and somewhat to his surprise the model accounted for most of the observed shift. Subsequent fully relativistic quantum field theoretic calculations, making use of the recently formulated notions of mass and charge renormalization, verified that indeed Bethe's calculation accounted for most of the Lamb shift and that the quantum electrodynamic explanation of the Lamb shift was correct.

Wartime Work. In 1941 Bethe was naturalized as a U.S. citizen. During World War II he first worked on problems in armor penetration, then worked on radar and spent a year at the Radiation Laboratory at MIT, and in 1943 he joined the Los Alamos Laboratory and became the head of its theoretical division. He and his division made crucial contributions to the feasibility and design of both the uranium and the plutonium bomb. It was at Los Alamos that there occurred the first rift between Bethe and Teller, who had been Bethe's closest friend during the 1930s. Teller had aspired to be the head of the theoretical division, but Oppenheimer appointed Bethe instead. It was also at Los Alamos that Bethe first met Richard Feynman. After the war Feynam joined the Cornell physics department and Bethe was instrumental in helping Feynman develop his approach to quantum field theory and thereafter to disseminate it.

The years at Los Alamos changed Bethe's life. On 14 September 1939 Bethe had married Rose Ewald and their two children were born at Los Alamos. At the professional level his wartime work introduced him to applied and engineering physics, and in particular to the challenges of combining knowledge in very different fields. The design of the plutonium bomb was based on the idea that the best way to bring a critical mass together was to compress a spherical shell of plutonium by the simultaneous detonation of a surrounding spherical shell of high explosives. The detonation of the explosives would ignite a converging ingoing shock wave that would almost instantaneously implode the plutonium into a compact sphere well beyond the critical mass, with a density well beyond that of the normal plutonium metal. In order to calculate the evolution of the explosions—chemical and nuclear—it was necessary to determine the equation of state of pluto-

nium at the very high pressures, density and temperature that were created by the initial shock wave of a few million atmosphere, and thereafter to calculate how the plutonium would move and react. All this involved hydrodynamics, statistical mechanics, shock wave theory, nuclear physics, metallurgy, and immense, extremely complicated calculations on primitive IBM computers. Bethe continued working on such applied problems, combining many disciplines, after the war by becoming a consultant at Los Alamos, Oak Ridge, General Electric, Detroit Edison, and AVCO. The problems he addressed ranged from the design of nuclear reactors and their shielding, and the choice of materials for the heat shields of rockets and space vehicles, to the design of lasers, for which he obtained several patents.

Bethe's researches in interdisciplinary areas of science gave him much satisfaction. It gave proof of the effectiveness and usefulness of science. And at a deeper level, particularly in his work in astrophysics, the result of the theorizing and its confrontation with the observational data gave proof of the consistency of the web of interconnections. Physics thus says something which, to an impressive accuracy and thus with a high probability, is true of the world.

In the aftermath of the wartime development of fission weapons, Bethe became deeply involved with investigating the feasibility of developing fusion bombs, hoping to prove that no terrestrial mechanism could accomplish the task. He believed their development to be immoral. When in 1951 the Ulam-Teller mechanism for igniting a fusion reaction was advanced and hence the possibility of an H-bomb became a reality, Bethe helped design such a weapon. He believed that the Soviets would likewise be able to build one and that only a balance of terror would prevent the use of these genocidal weapons. The political and military issues surrounding the development of the hydrogen bomb were important factors in the revocation of Oppenheimer's clearance in 1954. Bethe was one of Oppenheimer's staunchest supporter at his trial. In 1955, as a consultant for AVCO Corporation, he devised a general theory of ablation that was applied to the construction of warheads that could withstand the searing heat of reentry through the Earth's atmosphere. His idea helped design an effective intercontinental ballistic missile.

Political Physics. After World War II Bethe became deeply involved in what he called "political physics," the attempt to educate the public and politicians about the consequences of the existence of nuclear weapons. He became a relentless champion of nuclear arms control. He also became deeply committed to making the peaceful applications of nuclear power economical and safe. Throughout his life he was a staunch advocate of nuclear power, defending it as an answer to the inevitable fossil-fuel shortages. Bethe served on numerous advisory committees to the government, including PSAC, the President's Science Advisory Committee. As a member of PSAC, he helped persuade President Eisenhower to commit the United States to a ban on atmospheric nuclear tests, and such a partial nuclear test ban treaty was ratified in 1963. In 1972 Bethe's arguments against the use of antiballistic missile systems helped to prevent their deployment. He was an influential opponent of President Ronald Reagan's Strategic Defense Initiative, the missile defense system popularly known as Star Wars, arguing that it would involve impossible tasks to make lasers of unheard-of power and thereafter to deploy them on satellites in space. By virtue of all these activities Bethe became the science community's liberal conscience.

Throughout the political activism that marked his life after World War II, Bethe never abandoned his scientific researches. As noted earlier, in 1947 he made a crucial calculation which explained the discrepancy between the predictions of Dirac's relativistic quantum mechanical equation for the level structure of the hydrogen atom and the observed spectrum determined by Willis Lamb and Robert Retherford. From the mid-1950s until the early 1970s he was an important contributor to the understanding of the properties of nuclear matter. Well into his nineties, from the 1970s until a few years before his death, Bethe remained an extremely productive scientist, making important contributions at the frontiers of physics and astrophysics. He helped elucidate the nature of neutrinos and explain the observed rate of neutrinos emission by the sun. And with Gerald Brown he worked to understand why massive old stars can suddenly become supernovae, exploding with the brilliance of an entire galaxy. To this problem he brought to bear all he had learned at Los Alamos about shock waves and explosions.

It was indicative of Bethe's constant grappling with moral issues that at age eighty-eight, on the occasion of the fiftieth anniversary of Hiroshima, he went to Los Alamos and called on "all scientists in all countries to cease and desist from work creating, developing, improving and manufacturing further nuclear weapons—and, for that matter, other weapons of potential mass destruction such as chemical and biological weapons."

Hans Bethe died of congestive heart failure on 6 March 2005 in his retirement community home in Cayuga Heights, New York. He was one of the greatest of the theoretical physicists of the twentieth century. He was an outstanding teacher: Among his PhD students and post-doctoral fellows were many of the best theoretical physicists of the second half of the twentieth century. At Cornell University he endowed the physics department and the Newman Laboratory, the center for high energy

Hans Bethe. *Presiding at physicists press conference, Hans Bethe declares total secrecy for the H bomb.* **RALPH MORSE/TIME LIFE PICTURES/GETTY IMAGES.**

physics he helped create there after World War II, with the qualities and norms to which he was committed: honesty, integrity, and a deep commitment to science and to the institution. Physics at Cornell became a model of a communicative community: one that exists under the constraint of cooperation, trust, and truthfulness, one that is uncoerced in setting its goals and agenda. For Bethe such a community was the guarantor that one of the most exalted of human aspirations—the desire to be a member of a society which is free but not anarchical—could indeed be achieved.

BIBLIOGRAPHY

WORKS BY BETHE

"Quantummechanik der ein und zwei-Electronenprobleme." *Hanbuch der Physik*, Part I. Berlin: Springer Verlag, 1933.

With Arnold Sommerfeld. "Elektrotheorie der Metalle." *Hanbuch der Physik*, Part II. Berlin: Springer Verlag, 1933.

With Edwin E. Salpeter. *Quantum Mechanics of One- and Two-Electron Atoms.* New York: Plenum, 1977.

With Robert F. Bacher and M. Stanley Livingston. *Basic Bethe: Seminal Articles on Nuclear Physics, 1936–1937.* New York: American Institute of Physics, 1986. (A republication of the Bethe Bible.)

The Road from Los Alamos. New York: American Institute of Physics, 1991.

With Roman Jackiw. *Intermediate Quantum Mechanics.* 3rd ed. Reading, MA: Addison Wesley, 1997.

A Life in Science. Told to Sam Schweber. London: Science Archive Limited, 1997. A transcript of a videotape.

Selected Works of Hans A. Bethe: With Commentary. Singapore: World Scientific, 1997. Contains a bibliography of 290 of Bethe's publications (1928–1996) and reproduces 28 of his papers with brief introductory comments by Bethe.

With Gerald E. Brown and Chang-Hwan Lee. *Formation and Evolution of Black Holes in the Galaxy: Selected Papers with Commentaries.* Singapore and River Edge, NJ: World Scientific, 2003. Includes many of the papers that Bethe wrote with Gerald E. Brown and others dealing with astrophysical subjects, giving commentaries on how the ideas came up and the papers came to be written.

OTHER SOURCES

Bahcall, John N. and Edwin E. Salpeter. "Stellar Energy Generation and Solar Neutrinos." *Physics Today* 58 (October 2005): 44–47. (Special issue on Hans Bethe.)

Bernstein, Jeremy. *Hans Bethe: Prophet of Energy.* New York: Basic Books, 1980.

Brown, Gerald E. "Hans Bethe and Astrophysical Theory." *Physics Today* 58 (October 2005): 62–65. (Special issue on Hans Bethe.)

———, and Chang-Hwan Lee, eds. *Hans Bethe and his Physics.* Singapore: World Scientific, 2003. Gives a survey of Bethe's accomplishments by outstanding members of the physics community.

Dyson, Freeman. "Hans Bethe and Quantum Electrodynamics." *Physics Today* 58 (October 2005): 48–50. (Special issue on Hans Bethe.)

Garwin, Richard L., and Kurt Gottfried. "Hans in War and Peace." *Physics Today* 58 (October 2005): 52–57. (Special issue on Hans Bethe.)

Marshak, Robert E., ed. *Perspectives in Modern Physics: Essays in Honor of Hans A. Bethe on the Occasion of his 60th Birthday.* New York: Interscience Publishers, 1966. Describes Bethe's life and work.

Negele, John W. "Hans Bethe and the Theory of Nuclear Matter." *Physics Today* 58 (October 2005): 5861. (Special issue on Hans Bethe.)

Schweber, Silvan S. "The Happy Thirties." *Physics Today* 58 (October 2005): 38–43. (Special issue on Hans Bethe.)

———. *In the Shadow of the Bomb: Bethe and Oppenheimer and the Moral Responsibility of the Scientist.* Princeton, NJ: Princeton University Press, 2000.

Silvan Schweber

BIERMANN, LUDWIG FRANZ BENEDIKT (*b.* Hamm, Westfalen, Germany, 13 March 1907; *d.* Göttingen, Germany, 12 January 1986), *comets, convection, interstellar medium, plasmas, stellar interiors, Sun.*

Biermann was a German theoretical astrophysicist who conducted important research in the areas of convection in gases, stellar interiors, the Sun and its granulation and sunspots, comet tails as driven by the solar wind, comet nuclei and envelopes, the interplanetary medium, magnetic fields in the interstellar medium, and plasma physics. He was also the director of the Astrophysics Section of the Max Planck Institute for Astrophysics in Göttingen (1947–1958) and then in Munich (1958–1972). In those capacities he was one of the most influential German astronomers of the mid-twentieth century.

Biography. Biermann's parents were Franz and Thea (née Schulte) Biermann. He was a student at the University of Munich in 1925–1927 and the University of Freiburg in 1927–1928. In 1932 he received a PhD from the University of Göttingen with a thesis on the topic of convection in stellar interiors. He married Ilse Wandel on 3 January 1942 and they had three children: Peter, Christine, and Sabine. Son Peter L. Biermann, following his father into the astronomy profession, became a productive observational radio astronomer at the Max Planck Institute for Radio Astronomy in Bonn, Germany. Ludwig Biermann died in 1986 at age seventy-eight.

Biographies in English can be found in Helmut A. Abt (1967) and Thomas G. Cowling and Louise Mestel (1986); biographies in German include those by Rudolf Kippenhahn, Arnulf Schlüter, Walter F. Huebner, and Heinz Billing, all collected by Biermann's successor Gerd Buschhorn (1988).

Positions. Biermann held positions as an exchange scholar at the University of Edinburgh (1933–1934), lecturer in physics at the University of Jena (1934–1937), lecturer at Universität Sternwarte Berlin und Babelsberg (1937–1945), and lecturer at the University of Berlin (1938–1945). He was a professor at the University of Hamburg (1945–1947) and at the University of Göttingen (1948). Between 1947 and 1958 he was director of the Astrophysics Section of the Max Planck Institute for Astrophysics at the University of Göttingen. With the establishment of the Max Planck Institute for Physics and Astrophysics in Munich in 1958, he became director of its Institute of Astrophysics while R. Heinz F. Lüst was director of its Institute of Extraterrestrial Physics and Werner Heisenberg was simultaneously both director of its Institute of Physics and director of the entire Max Planck Institute. Biermann was also a visiting professor at the

California Institute of Technology, Haverford College, and Princeton University in 1955 and 1961; at the University of California in Berkeley in 1959–1960; in Sydney and Canberra, Australia, in 1960; and at the Joint Institute for Laboratory Astrophysics in Boulder, Colorado, in 1966–1967.

Research on Stellar Interiors. Biermann's (1932) first published research concerned stellar interiors. That was at a time before the energy source for a star was known, but it was generally thought to be some sort of subatomic process. He used the usual equations for stellar interiors, except that of the unknown energy generation, and therefore obtained an infinite central temperature. He realized that the gas in the core of the star might be degenerate, that is, in a physical state in which the energy states are filled so that the gas does not behave in a classical manner in which the pressure increases when the temperature or density increases.

Biermann (1935, 1938) continued to work on convection in stars. The energy at any level in a star can be transported by radiation from one ion to another or by mass motion of globs of gas. Which process predominates depends on the local conditions. Cool stars tend to be convective throughout, particularly those that are still contracting, while hot stars are partly in radiation equilibrium. He discovered that an extensive zone below the photosphere of the Sun was in convection equilibrium. That research was partly done through lengthy correspondence (by letter) with Thomas G. Cowling in England before World War II. Biermann suggested (1938b) that the granulation in the solar atmosphere—the rice-grain pattern of bright and less-bright areas seen in high-resolution photographs—is due to convection. That explanation is still regarded as valid. Later work (Biermann et al., 1959) extended that explanation.

Convection in a nonrotating star is one thing, but if a star is rotating rapidly there are meridional (i.e., along one meridian of a star, carrying material from the core to the surface and back again) currents that interfere with the convection. Biermann (1948) analyzed that complex situation. With certain radial zones being convective (well mixed) and others radiative (not mixed), there is the possibility of different zones having different compositions as the core changes from being composed nearly totally of hydrogen to being composed mostly of helium. This led Biermann (1943) to consider the composition of the Sun. This proved to be premature because the lack of knowledge about the opacities of gases at temperatures of millions of degrees inhibited a careful comparison with astronomical data. He calculated ionizations and opacities of such material.

Biermann (1938c) computed solar spectra and wondered whether it is possible to see the absorption edges for various metals. However, that was before Rupert Wildt (1939) discovered that the main source of opacity in the stellar atmosphere was H⁻, the negative hydrogen ion. The predominance of that source made it unlikely that any absorption edges would be seen. Nevertheless, Biermann computed, often with students, the oscillator strengths (line strengths) for many ions of interest in the solar interior to compute the opacities within stars. This work was published in a half-dozen papers.

Biermann also investigated whether a totally convective star would be dynamically stable to unlimited expansion. Cowling (1938) proved that such a star would be stable because a star would always radiate as much energy as it produces inside, which provides an extra boundary condition that always makes it stable. That was later substantiated in a joint paper by Biermann and Cowling (1940).

One application of Biermann's thinking of convection was his application to the nova phenomenon. Novas are stars that suddenly become brighter by a factor of 100,000 in a couple of days. Biermann wondered (1939) whether a star could suddenly change from being in radiative to convective equilibrium, thereby causing such an outburst. However, in 1964 Robert P. Kraft proved that all novae are in binaries, consisting of an expanding cool star that dumps material upon a white dwarf companion. They have orbital periods around one day. The hydrogen-rich material ignites, much like throwing gasoline on the fire, in the white dwarf atmosphere, provoking a violent outburst.

In 1961, simultaneously with but independently of Martin Schwarzschild, Biermann suggested that waves in the outer convection zone of the Sun just below the atmosphere caused acoustic waves that heated the chromosphere and corona. That would mean that other late-type stars, later than spectral type F2, would also have hot coronas. That was confirmed later with the detection of x-rays from most late-type stars, stellar winds and mass loss, low rotational velocities, and calcium emission lines.

Studies of the big bang were very successful in predicting the abundance of helium in the early universe, and studies of stellar interiors, particularly by E. Margaret Burbidge et al. (1957), explained many of the abundance characteristics in most normal stars. However, there is a class of peculiar A-type stars (Ap) that have drastically different atmospheric abundances, for example, stars with 10^6 times the normal mercury abundance. William A. Fowler and others (1965) proposed that some nuclear reactions were occurring in subsurface regions initiated by strong magnetic fields (>1,000 gauss). That proposal was later replaced when Georges Michaud (1970) showed that a more natural and successful explanation was in diffusion. Ap stars have a still radiative zone between two outer convective zones just below the photosphere. In the quiet zone, heavy ions that exhibit few spectral lines will fall inward while light elements with rich spectra will be pushed outward by radiation pressure. To date that explanation has been accepted for the extreme Ap stars and the less extreme metallic-line (Am) stars that also have over-abundances by factors of 10 and underabundances of helium, calcium, and scandium.

Comets. Sidney Chapman (1929), occasionally working with V. C. A. Ferraro (Chapman & Ferraro, 1930), proposed that a solar wind of neutral particles caused magnetic and electrical disturbances in Earth's atmosphere and auroras during magnetic storms. Biermann (1951) wondered whether the same particles could be deflecting the gaseous tails of comets. Comets often have two tails: one of particles that trail behind due to the motion of the comet in its orbit, and a gaseous tail that points generally away from the Sun. He measured the structure in the tail of Whipple-Fedtke (1943 I) and computed the density and speed of the wind, getting 600 particles per cm^3 and speeds of 500–1000 km sec^{-1}. Those numbers agreed with results from whistlers. (Whistlers are radio signals of audio frequencies heard at random times.) The explanation for them is that if lightning strokes occur at one place on Earth (e.g., in Annapolis, Maryland), at the other end of a geomagnetic line (Cape Horn, South Africa) a whistler or click occurs. The event can pass back and forth with one, three, five, or even seven passages between the two points. However, those numbers for the density and speed of the solar wind later had to be revised substantially downward because of a lack of consideration of the effects of magnetic fields. Biermann was the first to realize that the solar wind was acting continuously in time, not just during magnetic storms on Earth.

Biermann and Eleonore Trefftz (1964) speculated that comets should have extensive envelopes, up to 10,000 kilometers or more in diameter. Those should consist of neutral hydrogen and various molecules. These are the result of evaporation from Fred Whipple's (1950) "icy conglomerate model." Later observations from spacecraft in Lα (Lyman alpha at 1,216 angstroms) in the far ultraviolet region of the spectrum confirmed the presence of envelopes in Comet Bennett and other comets.

Biermann joined other astronomers in investigating the composition of the molecules in cometary nuclei. The physical conditions within the nuclei are not sufficient to produce the observed molecular abundances. Biermann and K. W. Michel (1978) considered whether the composition of cometary nuclei originated in the presolar nebula, the gaseous disk from which the Sun, its planets,

asteroids, comets, and other constituents formed. Biermann and others (1982), working at Los Alamos National Laboratory in New Mexico, found that by suggesting a cometary origin in interstellar matter, the molecular abundances were consistent with observations.

The Interplanetary Medium. In 1968 Biermann delivered a series of lectures in the Department of Aerospace Engineering Sciences at the University of Colorado on the interplanetary medium that was reproduced in a book coauthored with Evry Schatzman, *Cosmic Gas Dynamics* (1974). This is a comprehensive and highly mathematical review, starting with the hydrodynamics and kinematics of the solar corona and solar wind, continuing through the magnetic fields and turbulence of the interplanetary medium, and concluding with the termination of the solar wind at the heliosphere, where it joins the interstellar medium.

The Interstellar Magnetic Field. Together with Leverett Davis Jr. (1960), Biermann calculated the magnetic fields that needed to be present in the halo and disk of Earth's own galactic system in order to explain the in situ cosmic ray measurements in balloons by C. L. Critchfield and others (1952). That is, Biermann and Davis proposed that magnetic fields store the relativistic electrons produced by cosmic rays. For this to happen the magnetic fields must be greater than 5 x 10^{-6} gauss in the halo and 2 x 10^{-5} gauss in the disk. These values are consistent with the idea that the magnetic fields, cosmic rays, thermal pressure (pressure due to the gas temperature), and kinetic energy (due to the motions in the gas) are just able to counteract the inward force of gravity. These values are also consistent with other estimates on the interstellar magnetic field strengths.

Administrative Work. As noted above, Biermann was director of the Astrophysics Section of the Max Planck Institute in Göttingen from 1947 to 1958 and in Munich from 1958 to 1972. At both places he gathered around himself an outstanding group that was interested in cosmical electrodynamics and plasma physics in areas such as the solar chromosphere and corona, the solar wind, sunspots and flares, the interplanetary medium, stellar interiors, and the interstellar medium. He collaborated with Arnulf Schlüter, Eleonore Trefftz, Reimar and Rhea Lüst, Rudolf Kippenhahn, Friedrich Meyer, and Stefan Temesvary. He helped establish the parallel institutes of plasma physics and extraterrestrial physics. Together these made the Max Planck combined institute in Munich the outstanding theoretical astronomical center in continental Europe in the second half of the twentieth century.

Honors. Biermann was the recipient of the Copernicus Prize in 1943, member of the Bavarian Academy of Sciences and Humanities and of the International Academy of Astronautics, corresponding member of the Société Royale des Sciences de Liège, member of the Akademie der Naturforscher Leopoldina in Halle (East Germany), foreign associate of the National Academy of Sciences (United States), recipient of the C. W. Bruce Gold Medal of the Astronomical Society of the Pacific (United States) in 1967, associate of the Royal Astronomical Society (England) in 1964, and recipient of the Gold Medal of the same society in 1974. He was a member of the Astronomische Gesellschaft (Germany) and a German delegate to EURATOM.

BIBLIOGRAPHY

WORKS BY BIERMANN

"Untersuchungen über den inneren Aufbau der Sterne, IV. Konvektionzonen im Innern der Sterne." *Zeitschrift für Astrophysik* 5 (1932): 117–139.

"Konvektion im Innern der Sterne." *Astronomische Nachrichten* 257 (1935): 269–294.

"Konvektion im Innern der Sterne (II)." *Astronomische Nachrichten* 264 (1938a): 361–395.

"Zur Theorie der Granulation und der Wasserstoffkonvektionszone der Sonne." *Astronomische Nachrichten* 264 (1938b): 395–398.

Über die Möglichkeit des Auftretens von Metallabsorptionskanten im Spektrum der Sonne und der Sterne." *Zeitschrift für Astrophysik* 16 (1938c): 291–296.

"Über die dem Novaphänomen zugrunde liegenden physikalischen Vorgänge." *Zeitschrift für Astrophysik* 18 (1939): 344–361.

With Thomas G. Cowling. "Chemische Zusammensetzung und dynamische Stabilität der Sterne, II." *Zeitschrift für Astrophysik* 19 (1940): 1–10.

Über die chemische Zusammensetzung der Sonne." *Zeitschrift für Astrophysik* 22 (1943): 244–264.

"Konvektion in rotierenden Sternen." *Zeitschrift für Astrophysik* 25 (1948): 135–144.

"Kometenschweife und solare Korpuskularstrahlung." *Zeitschrfit für Astrophysik* 29 (1951): 274–286.

With Rudolf Kippenhahn, Rhea Lüst, and Stefan Temesvary. "Beiträge zur Theorie der Sonnengranulation." *Zeitschrift für Astrophysik* 48 (1959): 172–188.

With Leverett Davis Jr. "Considerations Bearing on the Structure of the Galaxy." *Zeitschrift für Astrophysik* 51 (1960): 19–31.

With Eleonore Trefftz. "Über die Mechanismen der Ionisation und der Anregung in Kometenatmosphären." *Zeitschrift für Astrophysik* 59 (1964): 1–28.

With Evry Schatzman. *Cosmic Gas Dynamics.* Edited by Mahinder S. Uberoi. New York: Wiley, 1974.

With K. W. Michel. "On the Origin of Cometary Nuclei in the Presolar Nebula." *Moon and the Planets* 18 (1978): 447–464.

With Paul T. Giguere and Walter F. Huebner. "A Model of a Comet Coma with Interstellar Molecules in the Nucleus." *Astronomy & Astrophysics* 108 (1982): 221–226.

OTHER WORKS

Abt, Helmut A. "Award of the Bruce Gold Medal to Professor Ludwig Biermann." *Publications of the Astronomical Society of the Pacific* 79 (1967): 197–200.

Burbidge, E. Margaret, et al. "Synthesis of the Elements in Stars." *Reviews of Modern Physics* 29 (1957): 547–650.

Buschhorn, Gerd. "Ludwig Biermann, 1907–1986." *Max-Planck-Gesellschaft Berichte und Mitteilungen* 2 (1988): 5–80.

Chapman, Sidney. "Solar Streams of Corpuscles: Their Geometry, Absorption of Light, and Penetration." *Monthly Notices of the Royal Astronomical Society* 89 (1929): 456–470.

Chapman, Sidney, and Vincent C. A. Ferraro. "A New Theory of Magnetic Storms." *Nature* 126 (1930): 129–130.

Cowling, Thomas G. "The Stability of Convective Stars." *Monthly Notices of the Royal Astronomical Society* 98 (1938): 528–535.

Cowling, Thomas G., and Louise Mestel. "Ludwig Franz Benedict Biermann." *Quarterly Journal of the Royal Astronomical Society* 27 (1986): 698–700.

Critchfield, Charles L., Edward P. Ney, and Sophie Oleksa. "Soft Radiation at Balloon Altitudes." *Physical Review* 85 (1952): 461–467.

Fowler, William A., et al. "The Synthesis and Destruction of Elements in Peculiar Stars of Types A and B." *Astrophysical Journal* 142 (1965): 423–450.

Michaud, Georges. "Diffusion Processes in Peculiar A Stars." *Astrophysical Journal* 160 (1970): 641–658.

Whipple, Fred L. "A Comet Model I: The Acceleration of Comet Encke." *Astrophysical Journal* 111 (1950): 375–394.

Wildt, Rupert. "Negative Ions of Hydrogen and the Opacity of Stellar Atmospheres." *Astrophysical Journal* 90 (1939): 611–620.

Helmut A. Abt

BIJVOET, JOHANNES MARTIN (*b.* Amsterdam, Netherlands, 23 January 1892; *d.* Winterswijk, Netherlands, 4 March 1980), *x-ray crystallography, physical chemistry.*

Bijvoet was an x-ray crystallographer who developed a new technique, based on the so-called anomalous scattering of x-rays, that permitted a direct determination of the configuration of molecules and crystals with x-rays alone. In 1950 he was the first scientist to determine the absolute spatial configuration of an optically active organic molecule (sodium rubidium tartrate). Through this crucial experiment, Bijvoet was able to prove that the geometries of the L- and D- structures of an organic molecule with a center of asymmetry, which had been proposed arbitrarily by Emil Fischer around 1900, corresponded to reality. Later Bijvoet developed his method into a more general technique to determine the spatial configuration of optical antipodes. Bijvoet was reader of crystallography and thermodynamics at the University of Amsterdam from 1929 to 1939, and professor of general and inorganic chemistry at Utrecht University from 1939 to 1962. In 1951 he succeeded Sir W. Lawrence Bragg as president of the International Union of Crystallography.

Childhood and Education. Jo Bijvoet was born in Amsterdam on 23 January 1892, the third son of Willem Frederik Bijvoet, a paint manufacturer and trader of tar products, and Barendina Margaretha Bijvoet (née Rüfer). His father was a partner in the firm of A. Pleging and Company, but only the fourth son, Frederik, decided to enter the business. All the other sons studied at university, and there was undoubtedly an intellectual and artistic atmosphere in the family; Jo studied music from an early age, and loved to listen to Mozart and other classical composers all his life. His eldest brother, Willem Frederik, Jr., was a gynecologist; his second brother, Bernard, became a well-known modern architect, who also designed the cover of Bijvoet's textbook on crystallography. From 1902 to 1908 his father was a member of the municipal council of Amsterdam.

In 1903 Bijvoet entered the Hogere Burgerschool (a modern secondary school) at the Keizersgracht in Amsterdam, where he had an inspiring teacher of chemistry, H. Hemmes. In 1908 Bijvoet decided to study chemistry at university. In those years a knowledge of classical languages was required for Dutch university degrees, and therefore from 1908 to 1910 he studied Latin and Greek and spent many hours on his passion for music. Bijvoet studied chemistry at the University of Amsterdam from 1910 to 1914, and from 1918 to 1919. He was slightly disappointed by his chemistry courses, but he became enthusiastic about the field of physics. In the second year of his studies he wrote a publication, together with Remmelt Sissingh, professor of experimental physics, about an optical experiment he had done during the physics course. In 1914 he did his *kandidaats* examination (bachelor's degree) cum laude.

In August 1914 World War I broke out, and Bijvoet was called to military service. Although the Netherlands remained neutral during the war, Bijvoet had to stay in the army from 1914 to 1918. He was stationed at Fortress Abcoude, about 9 miles (15 km) south of Amsterdam, and he spent most of his time studying the theories of Josiah Willard Gibbs as well as other works on his favorite topics, thermodynamics and statistic mechanics. After the end of the war, in 1918, he studied physical chemistry at the laboratory of professor Andreas Smits, followed the

lectures on statistical mechanics given by J. D. van der Waals, Jr., the son of the Nobel laureate, and did his *doktoraal* examination (master's degree), again cum laude, in 1919.

X-Ray Crystallography. After his graduation, Bijvoet became an assistant to Andreas Smits in the department of general and inorganic chemistry in Amsterdam. In those years the recent X-ray studies of William and W. Lawrence Bragg were hotly debated at the Amsterdam laboratory. The Braggs had concluded that crystals of sodium chloride (NaCl), and similar salts, were regular lattices of sodium and chloride ions. Bijvoet agreed, but his supervisor Smits strongly opposed that view; according to Smits, well-defined molecules, such as NaCl, were the cornerstone of inorganic chemistry. Smits decided to begin x-ray experiments at Amsterdam, and asked his students Bijvoet and Albert Karssen to introduce that new technique to his laboratory.

After the discovery of x-ray diffraction by Walter Friedrich, Paul Knipping, and Max von Laue in 1912, and the first determination of crystal structures by William and W. Lawrence Bragg in 1913, several Dutch scientists had quickly entered the new field. Peter Debye at Utrecht and Hendrik A. Lorentz at Leiden made important contributions to the theory of x-ray diffraction. At the University of Groningen, Frans M. Jaeger, professor of inorganic and physical chemistry, started experimental work in 1913, which was the beginning of the Groningen chemical-mineralogical crystallographic school. Later, also in the physics department at Groningen, important research was conducted by Dirk Coster, Frits Zernike, and their colleagues. In 1917 Willem H. Keesom, who had studied with Heike Kamerlingh Onnes and Hendrik A. Lorentz at Leiden, became professor of physics and physical chemistry at the Veterinary School at Utrecht. This was the same school where Jacobus Hendricus (Henry) van 't Hoff had worked in the 1870s, when he developed his important ideas on the carbon tetrahedron. In 1918 the Veterinary School became part of Utrecht University. Immediately after his appointment, Keesom, together with the physicist Nicolaas H. Kolkmeijer, began experimental x-ray analysis of crystals, in close collaboration with Ernst Cohen, professor of inorganic and physical chemistry at the university.

In 1919 the University of Amsterdam lagged behind, and Bijvoet and Karssen decided to go to Keesom's laboratory at Utrecht in order to master the new technique. Their three months of work with Keesom and, especially, Kolkmeijer, initiated a long period of intense collaboration between the crystallographic groups of Utrecht and Amsterdam. After their return to Amsterdam in 1920, Bijvoet and Karssen received grants for the acquisition of

x ray equipment and started working on their dissertations. In 1923 Bijvoet obtained his PhD with his dissertation, which was published as *X-Ray Investigation of the
Crystal Structure of Lithium and Lithiumhydride*. The fact
that it was in English was quite unusual at that time.

The same year, Bijvoet became Andreas Smits's "first
assistant," a post that he held until 1929. From 1924 to
1929 he also taught chemistry at the municipal gymnasium (grammar school) of Hilversum, and from 1925 he
also taught "special topics from physical chemistry" at the
University of Amsterdam as a personal lecturer (*Privat-
Dozent*). Meanwhile, he continued his research on x-ray
crystallography of simple salts, which resulted in several
joint publications with Kolkmeijer and Karssen. In 1926
Bijvoet and Karssen worked for a few months in the laboratory of Sir W. Lawrence Bragg at Manchester, which
was one of the international centers of chemical crystallography research. In 1928 Kolkmeijer, Bijvoet, and
Karssen published the first Dutch textbook on x-ray crystallography, *Röntgen-analyse van kristallen*. The book went
through revised editions in 1938 and 1948, was translated
into German in 1940, and was published in English in
1951. As with all Bijvoet's textbooks, it was extremely
well-structured and clear, and was considered by Paul
Ewald, the doyen of German crystallography, to be the
best introduction to the field.

Building on his stimulating international experience
at Manchester, Bijvoet soon became one of the leading x
ray crystallographers of the Netherlands. In addition to
his diligence, he was open to new developments, and he
one of the first Dutch chemists—as contrasted to physicists—who thoroughly studied quantum mechanics. In
1928 Bijvoet was the first Dutch x-ray crystallographer to
apply Fourier analysis to the determination of crystal
structures, shortly after it had been introduced to crystal
analysis by Bragg, following theoretical studies in 1924 by
P. S. Epstein and Paul Ehrenfest (at Leiden University).
Together with Anton E. van Arkel at Leiden University
and Jan de Boer at the Philips company, Bijvoet belonged
to a small group of "modern" physical chemists and crystallographers in the Netherlands who deviated from the
classical thermodynamics and phase rule school—of
which Andreas Smits and Ernst Cohen were typical examples—that dominated university research.

Reader at the University of Amsterdam. In 1928, after
the retirement of Eugène Dubois—the discover of the
Pithecanthropus erectus (or *Homo erectus*), the "missing
link" between man and ape—as professor of geology, mineralogy, crystallography, and paleontology, the municipal
council of Amsterdam decided to completely reorganize
and expand the geology department of the University.
Hendrik A. Brouwer, younger brother of the renowned

mathematician L. E. J. Brouwer, was appointed professor
of general and practical geology, with the task of establishing a large new geological institute. When in 1932 an
impressive new laboratory was opened, Brouwer succeeded in attracting two more professors, a reader, and a
number of assistants. The reader was Bijvoet, who in February 1929 was given the task of teaching crystallography,
general and propaedeutic descriptive mineralogy, thermodynamics, and their applications to chemical problems. It
was quite a hybrid position; attached to the geological
institute, Bijvoet was supposed to lecture not only to the
geology students, but also to students of chemistry and
other natural sciences. His economic position secured,
Bijvoet in April 1930 married the pharmacist Marie
Hardenberg, who had been among his students five years
earlier. They had three sons and one daughter.

In his new position, Bijvoet had hoped to expand
considerably his research in x-ray crystallography. He met
with strong opposition, however, from Brouwer, who
doubted the relevance of x-ray work for mineralogy, and
who wanted Bijvoet to limit himself to classical, descriptive crystallography and mineralogy. A deep, long-lasting
conflict resulted. When the new geology laboratory was
opened in 1932, there were no facilities for crystal analysis with x-rays, no budget for Bijvoet, and an injunction
by Brouwer that students of chemistry would not be
allowed to work at the institute. Therefore, Bijvoet continued to work in the chemical laboratory of Andreas
Smits, almost without any funding. In the course of the
1930s the professors of physics informally gave part of
their budget to Bijvoet, convinced as they were of the
importance of his research. They also decided that all students of physics should follow Bijvoet's lectures on x-ray
crystallography.

Despite these difficult circumstances, Bijvoet became
a successful and widely admired lecturer. He taught x-ray
analysis of crystals to undergraduates, and for advanced
students he introduced a new course on "chemical thermodynamics," which was at that time unique in the
Netherlands. In addition to these courses for large audiences, he organized informal study groups on Saturday
afternoons on Linus Pauling's books *Introduction to
Quantum Mechanics* and *The Nature of the Chemical Bond*,
on statistical mechanics, and on the so-called "dynamical
theories" of x-ray and electron diffraction proposed by
Paul Ewald, Max von Laue, and Hans Bethe.

In his research during the early 1930s, Bijvoet continued the x-ray analysis of relatively simple inorganic crystals. He focused on halides and dihalides such as $HgBr_2$,
$PbBr_2$, $PbFBr$, $PbFCl$, Ag_2HgI_4, AlF_3, and $Hg(NH_3)_2Cl_2$.
Along with Bijvoet's technician Bram Kreuger, a small,
enthusiastic group of PhD students and assistants did
most of the practical research: Herman J. Verweel (PhD

1931), Willem Nieuwenkamp (1932), Jan Ketelaar (1933), Caroline (Lien) MacGillavry (1937), and Eelko Wiebenga (1940) and Gerard Rieck (1945), who finished their dissertations with Bijvoet after he left Amsterdam. All of them (except Verweel, who died in 1937) became university professors of crystallography, or physical chemistry. In this way, the approach of the successful Amsterdam-Utrecht school spread to almost all other Dutch universities.

The Phase Problem. Apart from tedious calculations, which were typical of x-ray crystallography in those years, Bijvoet and his students were confronted with several scientific problems during their investigations of the (di)halides, which presented great challenges: polymorphy, molecular rotation, irregular occupation of lattice vacancies, and so-called "twin formation" of crystals. Initially, the crystal structures were solved by the trial-and-error method: on the basis of chemical and thermodynamic considerations, a plausible structure was proposed, the x-ray diagram associated with that structure was calculated, and it was then compared to the x-ray reflections that had been measured. Differences between the experimental data and the calculations led to new assumptions about the specific crystal structure, and new calculations were made. This procedure was repeated until an almost prefect agreement between experiment and calculated intensities was reached.

For complicated molecules, this approach was in most cases impossible. The introduction of the mathematical technique of Fourier synthesis in the late 1920s was a great step forward. In principle, if the amplitudes and phases of all the Fourier density waves, belonging to a certain structure, were known, then that crystal structure could be calculated deductively from these data. In practice, however, only the intensities (amplitudes) can be measured by x-ray analysis. This fact definitely put the so-called "phase problem" on the research agenda of crystallographers. Bijvoet started to become fascinated by the phase problem during the 1930s, and it occupied him for the rest of his career. He had been the first in the Netherlands to use the Fourier method, and he also was an early adopter of new methods with which the phase problem could be circumvented, or (partly) solved. In 1934 a great advance was made by the physicist A. Lindo Patterson in the group of quantum physicist John C. Slater at the Massachusetts Institute of Technology (MIT), with the help of the mathematician Norbert Wiener. Patterson developed an adapted Fourier function—the Patterson function—that circumvented the phase problem by proposing a mathematical series of quadratic Fourier density functions, in which only the intensities of the x-ray reflections played a role. Two years later, J. Monteath Robertson, working in the group of Sir William Bragg at the

Royal Institution in London, developed the so-called isomorphic replacement method that was applicable to structures in which an atom could be replaced by a "heavy atom"—for instance, Cl by Br; or S by Se; or H by Ni, or by Pt—without disturbing the original structure. From a comparison of the X-ray diagrams of crystals with and without the heavy atoms, Robertson and his assistant Ida Woodward in 1936 succeeded in solving the Fourier synthesis of phthalocyanin ($C_{32}H_{18}N_8$), a complex centrosymmetric molecule governed by sixty independent parameters for the carbon and nitrogen atoms. It was the first organic structure deduced directly from x-ray data, without any previously chemical assumptions. According to the crystallographer Dorothy Crowfoot Hodgkin, the Nobel laureate, it was "the first purely physical demonstration of the truth of organic chemistry" (quoted by Krom, 1946, p. 13). Bijvoet was delighted by Robertson's research and used it as a paradigmatic example of the power of x-ray analysis in his lectures and textbooks.

The new ideas of Patterson and Robertson were soon used by Bijvoet in his own research. In 1936 Bijvoet and his students and colleagues Verweel, MacGillavry, and Rieck determined the structure of succinic acid with the help of Fourier and Patterson synthesis. It was the first organic substance investigated by his group, and the first time that the Patterson method was applied in the Netherlands. From then on, Bijvoet shifted his attention increasingly to the x-ray analysis of organic molecules, and he asked his student Wiebenga to study a number of urea compounds. This research was continued at Utrecht University, where Bijvoet was appointed to a full professorship in 1939. In 1941, after Andreas Smits's retirement in 1940, Smits and Bijvoet were succeeded by Bijvoet's students Jan Ketelaar, who took over his lectures on chemical thermodynamics, and Lien MacGillavry, who very successfully continued the x-ray research at Amsterdam.

Professor at Utrecht University. After the retirement of Ernst Cohen in 1939, Bijvoet succeeded him as professor of general and inorganic chemistry at Utrecht. He had a high teaching load, up to ten lectures a week, and he was responsible for all lectures on physical chemistry, with the exception of those on colloid chemistry and electrochemistry, which were taught by his colleague Hugo Kruyt (and later, Theo Overbeek). Bijvoet's and Kruyt's research groups each occupied a floor in the so-called Van 't Hoff Laboratory of Utrecht University. Jacobus Henricus (Henry) van 't Hoff was one of Bijvoet's great heroes, and on several occasions he noted the ways in which he was following in Van 't Hoff's footsteps: studying with Van 't Hoff's successors at Amsterdam, learning the x-ray techniques in the Veterinary School, working in the laboratory named after Van 't Hoff, and, eventually, determining the absolute geometrical configuration of non-symmetrical organic substances with the help of x-rays.

In his inaugural lecture of November 1939, Bijvoet gave a broad overview of his future research and teaching. He paid attention not only to x-ray analysis, but also to quantum theory, statistical mechanics, chemical thermodynamics, and reaction rate theory. And indeed, in the years to come, Bijvoet would modernize the chemistry curriculum at Utrecht completely. He introduced new courses on atomic theory, crystal chemistry, chemical thermodynamics, statistical thermodynamics, theory of the chemical bond, and the Debye-Hückel theory of electrolytic solutions. His lectures were delivered enthusiastically, though the material presented was difficult. As one of the premier science professors in the country, he tried to stimulate dialogue with his lecture audiences, and he organized small-sized classes around the solution of practical problems in x-ray analysis and thermodynamics. Like his textbook on the x-ray analysis of crystals, his textbook on chemical thermodynamics was well received and went through numerous editions.

Bijvoet stayed at Utrecht University until his retirement in 1962. During the years at Utrecht he created a productive crystallographic school and supervised numerous dissertations. In 1952 Bijvoet's group left the Van 't Hoff Laboratory and moved to a converted large villa the Laboratory for Crystal Chemistry, called the "Crystal Palace" by the students. Bijvoet's private home was part of that building. Four years earlier, in 1948, Bijvoet and Wiebenga, who in 1946 had become professor at Groningen University, had founded the organization Fundamenteel Onderzoek der Materie met Röntgen- en Electronenstralen (FOMRE; Fundamental Research of Matter with the Help of X-rays and Electron-rays), which, under the auspices of the Dutch national foundation for pure scientific research, donated funding for x-ray equipment and computers to the Dutch crystallographic research groups. Computers were introduced into Dutch crystallographic research only at the end of the 1950s, but by 1956 Adriaan J. van Bommel in Bijvoet's laboratory used an "I.B.M. calculating punch type 604" for the time-consuming Fourier additions. It replaced the use of Beever-Lipson strips for these calculations, which had been introduced in 1936. As in Amsterdam, several of his research students at Utrecht became professors of crystallography, inorganic chemistry, or physical chemistry. In the 1970s almost all chairs of chemical crystallography in the Netherlands, and three chairs at universities in Belgium, were occupied by Bijvoet's students.

Anomalous Scattering and the Absolute Configuration of Molecules. At Utrecht, Bijvoet continued the search for the development and improvement of so-called "direct methods" of x-ray analysis, which he had begun at Amsterdam. The ultimate goal was the deduction by means of Fourier synthesis of the structures of molecules and crystals directly from the experimental x-ray data, without the help of chemical considerations or trial-and-error procedures. Robertson had only been able to determine the structure of phthalocyanin because of the fact that the molecule was centrosymmetric, with the heavy atom at its center. In 1940 Bijvoet developed the important insight that by combining the Patterson synthesis with the heavy atom and isomorphic replacement methods of Robertson, it would be possible to also determine the structures of molecules in which the heavy atom was in an arbitrary position. With Patterson's method it would be possible to determine the position of the heavy atom, and by comparing the intensities of isomorphic molecules with and without a heavy atom, the phases could be calculated from intensity differences, and the rest of the molecular structure could be unveiled. Together with his assistant Wiebenga, who had followed him to Utrecht, and his PhD student Cornelis J. Krom, Bijvoet applied this new method successfully for the first time in the structure determination of three isomorphic camphor derivatives: α-Br-, α-Cl- and α-CN-camphor. Although teaching at the Dutch universities almost came to a halt in 1943, university research continued during World War II. In January 1944 Bijvoet and Wiebenga published their new method in a German journal. Full details were presented in Krom's dissertation of 1946.

After this first success, Bijvoet decided to embark on the structure determination of the far more complex molecule strychnine, a molecule without a center of symmetry. This "attack" of non-centrosymmetric molecules with the help of x-ray techniques was partly inspired by Bijvoet's colleague Fritz Kögl, professor of organic chemistry at Utrecht, who held the view that the stereochemistry of, for instance, amino acids played a role in the development of cancer tumors. In a "neck-to-neck race with the organic chemists" Robert Robinson and Robert B. Woodward, Bijvoet and his students Cornelis Bokhoven and Jean C. Schoone in 1947 obtained a first rough Fourier synthesis of the sulphate and the selenate (W. L. Bragg in Ewald, 1962, p. 131). In the following years they succeeded in making a complete determination of the structure of strychnine by constructing a Fourier series that contained a double number of terms, namely those of the strychnine molecule and its mirror image. With the help of geometrical considerations and tedious calculations, Bijvoet and his team arrived at the correct stereochemical structure. Their result was confirmed by the research of Sir Robert Robinson.

Bijvoet and his team were the first to determine a non-centrosymmetrical molecular structure with the help of x-ray diffraction. This was a great success, but the methods had been complicated, and Bijvoet was not completely satisfied because non-x-ray, geometrical considerations had played a role. In 1948 he suddenly realized that anomalous scattering of x-rays could possibly provide a method for distinguishing between a non-centrosymmetrical molecule and its mirror image by means of x-ray analysis alone. It was this idea that would bring him world fame among the x-ray crystallographers.

Many crystallographers held the view that Friedel's law, formulated in 1913, made any attempt to distinguish between a molecular structure and its mirror image by x-rays alone an illusion. Georges Friedel's law says that the reflection of the front side of a plane in a crystal lattice is identical to the reflection of its back side. As early as the 1920s Nicolaas Kolkmeijer and Bijvoet were among a small number of crystallographers—including Max von Laue—who doubted the general nature of this law. In 1930 the physicist Dirk Coster at Groningen University showed with the help of anomalous scattering that crystals of zinc blende (ZnS) gave different reflections in one direction, and its opposite. This was an important result, which meant that Friedel's law does not apply in the case of anomalous scattering on non-symmetrical structures (in the case of ZnS there are successive Zn and S planes, so one side of the crystal has a Zn plane facing outward, and the other side an S plane). Anomalous scattering takes place when the energy of x-ray radiation comes close to the energy difference between two electron orbitals in a molecule. In those cases the x-rays are not only reflected by the electrons, but also excite the electrons to a higher orbital, with the end result that a phase shift occurs between the reflection at the front side of a plane, and the reflection from its back side. "Now x-ray analysis not only detects a difference," Bijvoet commented on Coster's research, "but it concludes—and this is, of course, completely impossible to the human eye—that it is the dull plane that has the Zn side facing outward: for the dull plane is found to give the weakest reflection and, as has been argued, the weakest reflection is that of the Zn plane" (Bijvoet, 1955, p. 76).

In 1948 the results of Coster's experiments were largely forgotten, but Bijvoet remembered them, and realized that there was an analogy between the non-symmetrical zinc blende crystals and the non-symmetrical carbon atoms that occur in many natural organic products. The following year he published a short notice stating that anomalous scattering could solve the phase problem in x-ray analysis. The different intensities between a reflection and its opposite—later called "Bijvoet differences"—made it possible to calculate the phase of a reflection. During the next year Bijvoet and his students Antonius (Ton) Peerdeman and Adriaan J. van Bommel tried to find experimental proof for this idea. They chose a substance, the sodium rubidium salt of tartaric acid, whose structure

was known, apart from its left- or right-handedness. Tartaric acid had played a role in Van 't Hoff's seminal publication of 1874 on stereochemistry, and Emil Fischer had given natural tartaric acid the so-called D-configuration by convention. There was only a 50 percent chance that Fischer's convention corresponded to reality.

In 1950, after complicated experiments that required up to 230 hours of continuous measurements, supervised day and night, because of the great losses of intensity inside the zirconium x-ray tube, Bijvoet and his team finally succeeded in establishing the expected effect. In Bijvoet's own words: "Exciting also was our first record with anomalous scattering, which required a continuously watched exposure of some hundreds of hours. It had to be successful in view of an intended journey, and was daily threatened with failure because of the improvised Zr-tube and the freakishness of a pump that had been hurriedly put back into use. Twenty-four hours before the time of departure half of the Weissenberg (deflection 0/180°) was developed and revealed nothing, the next day the further exposed other half (0/-180°) showed the effect looked for" (Bijvoet, 1962b, p. 530).

Early in 1951 these results were published, and they were recognized as a great step forward. It appeared that the Fischer convention, purely by accident, had been correct. The fact that Bijvoet was the first to prove this result experimentally made his name also well known outside the world of crystallography. Nevertheless, it would take several years before anomalous scattering was generally applied in x-ray analysis. During the 1950s Bijvoet and his team worked hard on an improvement of the new method. In 1955 S. W. Peterson, in Bijvoet's laboratory, succeeded in determining the spatial configuration of the HCl and HBr salts of the amino acid tyrosine, solely by using anomalous scattering and the isomorphic replacement method. This was the first determination of a previously unknown structure by direct Fourier synthesis and anomalous scattering. The following year, Bijvoet and Peerdeman—who in the meantime had found that conventional copper tubes could replace the zirconium tubes in these experiments, a fact that greatly improved the precision of their results—succeeded in determining the structure of a non-centrosymmetrical crystal, without using the replacement method. This was again a great step forward, because in principle any single structure could now determined with this technique. In 1955 Ray Pepinski and his group in Auburn, Alabama, devised an adapted Patterson function of the anomalous differences, which proved to be an important tool in making the use of anomalous diffraction more popular. In the 1960s the structures of important proteins, such as hemoglobin, were determined with an array of techniques, including anomalous scattering. And in the 1970s and 1980s anomalous scattering became part of the standard repertoire of x-ray crystallography (Blow, 2003).

For his work on the structural determination of organic molecules, by anomalous scattering in particular, Bijvoet received many honors and distinctions. He was elected a member of the Royal Netherlands Academy of Sciences in 1946, and a foreign member of the Royal Belgium Academy of Sciences and Arts in 1945, of the Royal Society of London in 1972, and of the Royal Swedish Academy of Sciences. In 1954 he was award the Cresner Peny Prize of the Société Chimique Belge. He received honorary doctorates from the Technical University of Delft (1967), the ETH Zürich (1970), and the University of Bristol (1971).

The International Union of Crystallography. In 1946, at a conference in London, Sir W. Lawrence Bragg, Paul Ewald, and some other crystallographers took the initiative to found an international organization on crystallography. Bijvoet became a member of the organizing committee that prepared the establishment of the International Union of Crystallography (IUCr) in 1948. It was also decided that the Union would publish a journal, the *Acta Crystallography*, together with Cambridge University Press. At the first congress of the Union, in 1948 at Harvard, Bragg was elected as its first president. In 1951, at the second congress, in Stockholm, Bijvoet was elected as its second president. During his term, held until 1954, he helped to give the Union a solid financial basis. Starting in 1950, Bijvoet was also a member of the committee that edited the *Structure Reports* on behalf of the IUCr. He personally edited nine volumes of the reference work with great care.

After his retirement in 1962, Bijvoet taught chemical thermodynamics for one year at Eindhoven University of Technology, before he started to live in the countryside, in the eastern part of the Netherlands. Every few weeks he visited his old laboratory at Utrecht, discussed their work, and read the latest literature in the library. The topics he studied he discussed in colloquium with students of nearby Twente University, who visited him at home, together with their professor, Dirk Feil, who had been a student of his.

Together with Willy Burgers and Gunnar Hägg, Bijvoet in 1969 and 1970 edited two volumes for the IUCr with *Early Papers on Diffraction of X-rays by Crystals*. It was an enormous enterprise to select almost 200 papers from the literature up to 1935, and then to select parts of these texts. The two volumes "were the outcome of his original and cherished idea that welding together appropriate parts of these papers into a continuous story made far better reading than a textbook" (Groenewegen and Peerdeman, 1983, p. 37). As was the case with all of Bijvoet's books, this work is very well structured and clear. Not surprisingly, it also contained large parts of Friedel's and Coster's original papers.

Bijvoet kept an active interest in x-ray crystallography until an advanced age, despite the deterioration of his physical health. He passed away on 4 March 1980, at the age of eighty-eight.

BIBLIOGRAPHY

Many sources on the history of crystallography, including the book edited by Paul P. Ewald, mentioned below, can be found on the Web site of the International Union of Crystallography, available from http://www.iucr.org/. For the genealogy of the Bijvoet family, and for additional sources, see: http://www.bijvoet.org/. For a bibliography of Bijvoet's publications, see M. P. Groenewege and A. F. Peerdeman in Biographical Memoirs of Fellows of the Royal Society. *Bijvoet's published papers are kept at the former Laboratorium voor Kristalchemie of Utrecht University, now called the Bijvoet Center for Biomolecular Research (see http://www.bijvoet-center.nl).*

WORKS BY BIJVOET

X-Ray Investigation of the Crystal Structure of Lithium and Lithiumhydride. Leiden: Sijthoff, 1923.

With N. H. Kolkmeijer and A. Karssen. *Voordrachten over röntgen-analyse van kristallen.* Amsterdam: Centen, 1928. Later editions of this textbook appeared in 1938 and 1948, with the title *Röntgen-analyse van kristallen.*

Wegen, meten, tellen. Amsterdam: Centen, 1939. Inaugural lecture at University of Utrecht, on 27 November 1939.

With E. H. Wiebenga. "Eine direkte röntgenographische Molekülstrukturbestimmung durch Vergleich isomorpher Kristallstrukturen." *Die Naturwissenschaften* 32 (1944): 45–46.

"Crystallography and X-ray Analysis of Crystals." In *Chemistry in Wartime in the Netherlands: A Review of the Scientific Work Done by Dutch Chemists in the Years 1940–1945.* Amsterdam: Centen, 1947.

"Phase Determination in Direct Fourier-Synthesis of Crystal Structures." *Proceedings of the Section of Sciences, Koninklijke Akademie van Wetenschappen te Amsterdam* 52 (1949): 313–314.

With A. F. Peerdeman and A. J. van Bommel. "Determination of Absolute Configuration of Optical Active Compounds by Means of X-Rays." *Nature* 168 (1951a): 271–272.

With C. Bokhoven and J. C. Schoone. "The Fourier Synthesis of the Crystal Structure of Strychnine Sulphate Pentahydrate." *Acta Crystallographica* 4 (1951b): 275–280.

With N. H. Kolkmeyer and Caroline H. MacGillavry. *X-ray Analysis of Crystals.* London: Butterworth, 1951c. The English translation of the third edition of *Röntgen-analyse van kristallen* (1948).

"Determination of the Absolute Configuration of Optical Antipodes." *Endeavour* 14 (1955): 71–77.

"Anomalous Scattering in the Determination of Phase and of Absolute Configuration." In *Beiträge zur Physik und Chemie des 20. Jahrhunderts: Lise Meitner, Otto Hahn, Max von Laue zum 80. Geburtstag,* edited by O. R. Frisch et al. Braunschweig: Vieweg, 1959.

"The Netherlands." In *Fifty Years of X-Ray Diffraction: Dedicated to the International Union of Crystallography on the Occasion of the Commemorative Meeting in Munich, July 1962,* edited by Paul P. Ewald. Utrecht: Oosthoek, 1962a.

"Reminiscences." In *Fifty Years of X-Ray Diffraction: Dedicated to the International Union of Crystallography on the Occasion of the Commemorative Meeting in Munich, July 1962,* edited by Paul P. Ewald. Utrecht: Oosthoek, 1962b.

As editor, with W. G. Burgers and G. Hägg. *Early Papers on Diffraction of X-rays by Crystals.* 2 vols. Utrecht: Oosthoek, 1969–1972. Contains selected text fragments from almost 200 important papers up to 1935.

OTHER SOURCES

Blow, D. M. "How Bijvoet Made the Difference: The Growing Power of Anomalous Scattering." *Methods in Enzymology* 374 (2003): 3–22. On the impact of Bijvoet's anomalous scattering methods on X-ray crystallography up to 2003.

Coster, Dirk, K. S. Knol, and J. A. Prins. "Unterschiede in der Intensität der Röntgenstrahlenreflextion an den beiden 111-Flächen der Zinkblende." *Zeitschrift für Physik* 63 (1930): 345–369.

Ewald, Paul P., ed. *Fifty Years of X-Ray Diffraction: Dedicated to the International Union of Crystallography on the Occasion of the Commemorative Meeting in Munich, July 1962.* Utrecht: Oosthoek, 1962.

Groenewege, M. P., A. F. Peerdeman, and H. F. van Sprang. "In memoriam Prof. Bijvoet: Markante, onvermoeibare en veeleisende leermeester." *Chemisch Weekblad* (20 March 1980): 126–127.

———, and A. F. Peerdeman. "Johannes Martin Bijvoet. 23 January 1892–4 March 1980. Elected For. Mem. R. S. 1972." *Biographical Memoirs of Fellows of the Royal Society* 29 (1983): 27–41. With a bibliography of Bijvoet's publications.

Knegtmans, Peter Jan. *Een kwetsbaar centrum van de geest. De Universiteit van Amsterdam tussen 1935 en 1950.* Amsterdam: Amsterdam University Press, 1998.

Krom, Cornelis Jan. *Röntgenanalyse langs directen weg. Onderzoek van α-Br-, α-Cl- en α-CN-kamfer.* PhD diss., University of Utrecht, 3 July 1946.

Le Pair, C., and J. Volger, eds. *Physics in the Netherlands: A Selection of Dutch Contributions to Physics in the First Thirty Years after the Second World War.* 2 vols. Utrecht: FOM, 1982.

Looijenga-Vos, Aafje, and Jan Kroon. "J. M. Bijvoet's Discovery: A Landmark in the Structure Elucidation of Natural Products." *Proceedings Koninklijke Nederlandse Akademie van Wetenschappen* 100, no. 3–4 (1995): 45–56.

MacGillavry, Caroline H., and A. F. Peerdeman. "Johannes Martin Bijvoet, 23 January 1892–4 March 1980." *Acta Crystallographica,* Section A 36, no. 6 (1980): 837–838.

Peerdeman, Antonius Franciscus. *Determination of the Absolute Configuration of Optically Active Compounds by Means of X-Rays.* PhD diss., University of Utrecht, 19 December 1955.

Schenk, Henk. "Kristallografie." In *De geschiedenis van de scheikunde in Nederland 3: De ontwikkeling van de chemie van*

1945 tot het begin van de jaren tachtig, edited by Ernst Homburg and Lodewijk Palm. Delft: Delft University Press, 2004.

Snelders, Harry A. M. *De geschiedenis van de scheikunde in Nederland 2: De ontwikkeling van chemie en chemische technologie in de eerste helft van de twintigste eeuw.* Delft: Delft University Press, 1997. On the history of Dutch chemistry, 1900–1950.

Werken aan scheikunde. 24 memoires van hen die de Nederlandse chemie deze eeuw groot hebben gemaakt. Delft: Delft University Press, 1993. This book contains the personal reminiscences of Bijvoet's students and colleagues Caroline H. MacGillavry, Jan A. A. Ketelaar, Eelko H. Wiebenga, and Aafje Looijenga-Vos.

Wiebenga, E. H. "Bijvoet: ongelooflijke interesse en werkkracht." *Chemisch Weekblad* (20 March 1980): 127.

Ernst Homburg

BIRKHOFF, GARRETT

BIRKHOFF, GARRETT (*b.* Princeton, New Jersey, 10 January 1911; *d.* Water Mill, New York, 22 November 1996), *abstract algebra, computing.*

Birkhoff was the son of mathematician George David Birkhoff and Margaret Grafius Birkhoff. George Birkhoff, the father, was the first American mathematician to gain wide respect in Europe. Garrett Birkhoff is more remembered for promoting new conceptions than specific theorems. His most important single result was a theorem that instituted a conception, the *Birkhoff variety theorem,* originating modern universal algebra. He showed the power of deceptively simple algebraic properties and the feasibility of more complex and realistic applied mathematics, and he was among the first mathematicians to rely heavily on computers.

Lattices and Universal Algebra. Entering Harvard College in 1928, Birkhoff aimed at mathematical physics. Physics led him to partial differential equations, which in turn led to more abstract ideas, including Lebesgue theory and point-set topology. Curiosity led him to finite groups. After graduating in 1932, he went to Cambridge University for physics. That July, though, he visited Munich and met Constantin Carathéodory, who pointed him towards algebra and especially van der Waerden's great new textbook *Moderne Algebra* (Berlin: Springer, 1930). Back in Cambridge he switched to algebra with group theorist Philip Hall.

Birkhoff turned the study of subgroups, subrings, and so on into two branches of mathematics. The intersection $H \ni K$ of subgroups of a single group G is also a subgroup of G. The union $H(K)$ of subgroups of G is generally not a subgroup because an element of H and another of K may combine to give one that is in neither. Yet *H* and *K* will generate a subgroup *H/K* which is called their *join*, defined as the smallest subgroup of *G* that contains both *H* and *K*, and so is generally larger than the set theoretic union. This suggests a dual definition: the *meet H–K* is the largest subgroup of *G* contained in both *H* and *K*. In fact, the meet of subgroups is their intersection, but other structures than groups can have meets that are smaller than intersections. In England Birkhoff organized and generalized the study of such order relations into *lattice theory*. He also characterized a wide array of structures whose substructures form lattices and organized their study as *universal algebra*. Each subject had precedents, notably in the work of Richard Dedekind and Emmy Noether, but Birkhoff established them as subjects.

Birkhoff enjoyed the unity and economy of the abstract idea of an *order relation* on a set. That is any relation $x\mathrm{B}y$ on the elements of the set such that: 1) $x\mathrm{B}x$ for all elements *x* of the set; 2) for any elements x,y,z, if $x\mathrm{B}y$ and $y\mathrm{B}z$ then $x\mathrm{B}z$; and 3) for any elements x,y, if $x\mathrm{B}y$ and $y\mathrm{B}x$ then $x = y$. The relation $x\mathrm{B}y$ is usually read "*x* is less than or equal to *y*" although it may have nothing to do with magnitude. He gave the example of logical propositions with $x\mathrm{B}y$ defined to mean *x* implies *y*, and $x = y$ defined to mean that *x* is logically equivalent to *y*. He defined a *lattice* as an ordered set where every two elements x,y have a join x/y defined as the smallest element greater than or equal to both *x* and *y*, and a meet $x–y$ defined as the largest element less than or equal to both *x* and *y*, with a few further properties. Logical propositions form a lattice where the join x/y of propositions is their disjunction "*x* or *y*," and their meet $x–y$ is the conjunction "*x* and *y*." The subgroups of a group *G* form a lattice when $H\mathrm{B}K$ is defined to mean *H* is contained in *K*. The notion of lattice is wide enough to include many examples yet specific enough to yield many theorems. Birkhoff also found further abstract conditions characterizing various kinds of lattice. His 1940 book *Lattice Theory* is still in print, with new concepts and results tripling its original length.

Not all mathematical structures are as tidy as groups. The substructures of a given structure do not always form a lattice. So, which ones do? Birkhoff found an elegant sufficient condition.

A *Birkhoff variety* is a class containing all the structures defined by a given set of operators and equations. For example, a *commutative ring* is a set *R* with a selected zero element *0* and unit element *1* and addition, subtraction, and multiplication $+,-,\cdot$ satisfying equations familiar from arithmetic, such as the zero law $x+ 0 = x$ and the commutative law for addition $x+ y = y + x$. These equations are understood to hold for all elements x,y of *R*. A *field* is a commutative ring *R* meeting a further more com-

plex condition, not an unrestricted equation but a conditional equation: If $x \neq 0$ then *x* has an *inverse*, an element *y* in *R* with $x \cdot y = 1$. A *variety* is a class of structures definable purely by operators and equations, as shown above for the class of commutative rings and not for the class of fields.

Varieties enjoy very special properties compared to other classes of structures. For example, any two rings *R,S* have a *product R×S*. An element of *R×S* is an ordered pair x,u with *x* and element of *R* and *u* and element of *T*. The zero element of *R×S* is the pair of zeros *0,0*, the unit is the pair of units *1,1*. The operations are defined componentwise, which for addition means $x,u+ y,v = x+y,u+v$.

The analogues hold for subtraction and multiplication, and *R×S* satisfies all the ring equations since it satisfies them all in each component. The same does not work for fields. Even if *R* and *S* are both fields, *R×S* is not. Its element *1,0* is not zero because the first component is not the zero of *R* but it has no inverse either because the second component has no inverse in *S*.

The *Birkhoff variety theorem* lists a few constructions such as products, and proves that a class of structures is a variety if, and only if, it is closed under these operations. Given any class of structures, no matter how it was originally defined: it can be defined purely by equations if, and only if, these listed constructions apply to it and always yield results in that class. Because fields do not have products there cannot be any way to characterize fields purely by equations. These constructions imply that the substructures of any structure in a variety form a lattice. The theorem created modern *universal algebra* defined as the study of *Birkhoff varieties*. Earlier more sweeping universal theories of algebra were not so productive as Birkhoff's.

A Career at Harvard. In 1933, Birkhoff returned to Harvard as a member of the Society of Fellows, and in 1936 he joined the mathematics department. He never earned a doctorate. He married Ruth Collins in 1938 and eventually had two daughters and a son (Ruth, John, and Nancy). He began teaching the new abstract algebra, which Saunders Mac Lane also taught there. Their 1941 *Survey of Modern Algebra* was the first effective English language introduction to the material of van der Waerden's *Moderne Algebra* and was an immediate success. It was augmented by the 1967 *Algebra* with the order of the authors' names reversed and more emphasis on category theory. These two books had a huge impact on mathematics students for fifty years and continued to shape the standard U.S. algebra curriculum in the early twenty-first century.

During World War II, Birkhoff worked on fluid dynamics, including the explosion of bazooka charges and problems of air-launched missiles entering water. Chapters of his 1950 book *Hydrodynamics: A Study in Logic, Fact, and Similitude* were named for various "paradoxes" where either the models idealize phenomena in unrealistic ways or basically plausible models give some bizarre results. Birkhoff emphasized group theory for handling symmetries in hydrodynamics, although one paradox was the breakdown of symmetries in some realistic hydrodynamic situations. He urged innovative numerical methods and his later more specialized hydrodynamics relied more heavily on computing.

He consulted on reactor design for the Bettis Atomic Power Laboratory from 1955 to 1961, working on numerical solutions for partial differential equations by repeatedly improving successive approximations. Starting in 1959 he consulted for General Motors on numerical description of surfaces, to guide numerically controlled machinery cutting the dies used to stamp out automobile body parts. This led him to major contributions to "spline" methods fitting segments of cubic polynomials to data points.

Birkhoff was elected to the American Academy of Arts & Sciences in 1945, the American Philosophical Society in 1960, and the National Academy of Sciences in 1968. He received honorary degrees from the National University of Mexico, the University of Lille, and Case Institute of Technology.

BIBLIOGRAPHY

WORKS BY BIRKHOFF

"On the Combination of Subalgebras." *Proceedings of the Cambridge Philosophical Society* 29 (1933): 441–464.

Lattice Theory. New York: American Mathematical Society, 1940. Third edition, greatly expanded, 1967.

With Saunders Mac Lane. *A Survey of Modern Algebra.* New York: Macmillan, 1941.

Hydrodynamics: A Study in Logic, Fact, and Similitude. Princeton, NJ: Princeton University Press, 1950.

With Gian-Carlo Rota. *Ordinary Differential Equations.* Boston: Ginn, 1962.

Mac Lane, Saunders, and Garrett Birkhoff. *Algebra.* New York: Macmillan, 1967.

The Numerical Solution of Elliptic Equations. Philadelphia: Society for Industrial and Applied Mathematics, 1971.

"Current Trends in Algebra." *The American Mathematical Monthly* 80 (1973): 760–782.

With Gerald L. Alexanderson and Carroll Wilde, "A Conversation with Garrett Birkhoff." *The Two-Year College Mathematics Journal* 14 (1983): 126–145.

OTHER SOURCES

Corry, Leo. *Modern Algebra and the Rise of Mathematical Structures.* Basel and Boston, MA: Birkhäuser, 1996.

Describes the history and influence of Birkhoff's lattice theory and universal algebra in several places; see the index.

Mac Lane, Saunders. "Garrett Birkhoff (10 January 1911–22 November 1996)." *Proceedings of the American Philosophical Society* 142 (1998): 646–649.

Young, David. "Garrett Birkhoff and Applied Mathematics." *Notices of the American Mathematical Society* 44 (1997): 1446–1450.

Colin McLarty

BJERKNES, VILHELM (*b.* Christiania, Norway, 14 March 1862; *d.* Oslo, Norway, 9 April 1951), *meteorology.* For the original article on Bjerknes see *DSB,* vol. 2.

Frequently called the father of modern meteorology, Bjerknes reluctantly devoted himself to atmospheric science. His scientific career, beginning in the 1890s, reveals an astute scientist willing to overcome professional marginalization by developing skills as a disciplinary entrepreneur. Beginning as a theoretical physicist devoted to a mechanical worldview, he hesitantly turned to creating a physics of the atmosphere and oceans. In 1897 he elaborated a hydrodynamic equation for circulation in fluids in which density could depend upon several variables. He soon understood that motions in the atmosphere and oceans could be comprehended through this theorem: He ultimately developed a physical hydrodynamics that became a basis for dynamic meteorology and oceanography. The capstone of his career, the creation of the so-called Bergen School of meteorology, established a new conceptual foundation for the science while creating innovative predictive practices that enabled greater integration of weather as a resource for agriculture, aviation, and fishery.

Career Strategies. Bjerknes's professional options in physics were limited by both his disposition and his circumstances. Bjerknes hoped to achieve a mechanical depiction of the ether, which would vindicate his father Carl Anton's hydrodynamic analogies to electromagnetism and serve as an illustration of the contiguous-action physics proposed by Heinrich Hertz. He thought this research would remain central to European physics and could be his vehicle to prestige and authority, but he was mistaken. He felt helpless in the early 1900s when, to his mind, German-speaking theoretical physicists in a state of mass psychosis abandoned the mechanical worldview for electromagnetic alternatives. In Sweden there was little sympathy for theoretical physics, and as a Norwegian working in Stockholm at a time of tensions between the two nations, he found his options limited.

Bjerknes took a calculated risk and transferred his mechanical physics to the atmosphere and less directly to the oceans. Stockholm colleagues helped Bjerknes understand that his generalized circulation theorem, derived theoretically within his work on hydrodynamic analogies, actually held great promise to comprehend motions in the atmosphere and ocean. Although he and his students achieved some notable early successes in applying the circulation theorem, Bjerknes was well aware that "a physicist who goes into meteorology is lost," as Berlin physicist Friedrich Kohlrausch had informed him. Even after publishing in 1904 his now classic program for pre-calculating changes of state of the atmosphere, Bjerknes remained hesitant about devoting himself to meteorology. Bjerknes was first willing to focus his professional energies on creating an exact physics of the atmosphere (and oceans) once he understood that the growing "conquest of the air" by aeronautics would make possible a transformation of atmospheric science and would bestow cultural and social value on such a science.

His idea of a physics of the atmosphere was informed by his desire to maintain a mechanical worldview and by his understanding that aeronautics would make possible and require three-dimensional diagnoses and prognoses of conditions in the atmosphere. Bjerknes elaborated a program for creating analytic methods by which physical theory could be applied to depict the state of the atmosphere at a given time and rationally pre-calculate changes several hours later. Bjerknes's program aimed at providing graphical methods that could be applied in practice immediately even while working towards a distant goal of establishing an exact physics of the atmosphere and oceans.

Move to Leipzig. Bjerknes soon realized he needed data for his project that only the international community of aerologists could provide. His difficulties in influencing this rapidly growing subdiscipline, which aimed at exploring the atmosphere well above the ground, to adopt rational units of measurements led him in turn to realize the necessity of producing a new generation of aerologists to shape the profession. To obtain resources for this task, he accepted a call in 1912 to Leipzig University. The new geophysical institute and the choice of Bjerknes as director were linked with a desire of Leipzig physicist Otto Wiener and the Saxony government to create a rigorous atmospheric science that could serve the budding German commercial and military airship activity. Bjerknes understood that if he did not accept the position, the vast resources of the institute would fall to someone else. Amply supported in Leipzig, Bjerknes began to claim great authority for himself, his project, and his institute. Then came the war. Although Bjerknes had little sympathy for German militarism, he and his work were of significance for the rapidly growing use of weather

information in strategic operations, not the least for aerial and gas warfare. German military weather services recruited his students and publications; his institute came to a near standstill. With no end of the war in sight and suffering from malnutrition, he accepted in 1917 a call to the Bergen Museum, where Bjørn Helland-Hansen was establishing a geophysical institute as part of a plan to create a new university for west Norway.

The Bergen Project. To continue his project in Bergen, Bjerknes had to adapt once more to local conditions. He tried to capitalize on wartime exigencies by proposing first a field weather service for neutral Norway's air defense and then an emergency weather service to assist agriculture, in both cases with an eye toward the opportunities that commercial aviation would create for advancing meteorology at war's end. During the summer 1918 experiment, Bjerknes's son, Jacob, continued the work begun in Leipzig by identifying lines of convergence in the horizontal wind field and pre-calculating their movement. These lines were associated with hazardous conditions for flying, such as squall lines, as well as with areas of rain. Although the attempt to put theory directly to practice proved vexing, under his father's guidance and encouragement Jacob gradually came to realize through the daily forecasting that two such lines of convergence seemed to be a fundamental feature of extra-tropical cyclones (low-pressure systems). Moreover, a tangent to where the front-most line (steering line; later, warm front) meets the other line (squall line; later, cold front) indicates the direction of the cyclone, while the regions of precipitation within the cyclone could be localized to the two lines.

Local conditions again forced a strategy change after the war. The new university was not to be built. Vilhelm Bjerknes saw that his best chance now lay in establishing a permanent practical forecasting service and defining new predictive methods. He set out to integrate an academic research program into a weather bureau. Toward this end, he sought indirect methods of applying physics to practical forecasting as a means to gain new insight, while simultaneously addressing the concerns of aviators, farmers, and fishermen. Although not actually engaged in the daily predictive practices, Bjerknes supervised and discussed regularly with his assistants the insights and problems arising from the forecasting work. In 1919 he and his young assistants abandoned an earlier mode of conceptualizing based on kinematics of the wind flow and instead considered three-dimensional air masses and the physical boundaries separating them, which they called fronts. Using an analogy with wartime skirmishes and stalemates along the fronts separating enemy armies, they gradually articulated a new model of the extra-tropical cyclone based on air masses and fronts. The Bergen scientists extended their cyclone model to hemispheric dimensions by postulating a polar front, upon which cyclones develop as one or the other air mass pushes into the other's territory. While his younger disciples refined the models and provided practical advice to aviators and seamen through forecasting work, Bjerknes attempted to reproduce the models in theory.

Bjerknes and his school managed to combine the search to know with a need to serve the public interest. Conceptual change and new insight resulted from demands on, and transformation in, practice. New knowledge arose through changes in the practice of weather forecasting. Criteria for using weather in commerce played a role in how meteorologists perceived weather phenomena and conceptualized atmospheric systems. In spite of theoretical and empirical "precursors," the concept of the front could be articulated and integrated into meteorology only after an overhaul in the observational and predictive practices as international meteorology geared up to satisfy regular commercial flight.

The Bergen group hoped the weather service could continue to serve as a hothouse for deeper inquiry into and understanding of atmospheric processes, but maintaining a balance over time proved difficult. The Bergen School's claim that its methods and conceptual breakthroughs were derived from physical theory, and in direct contact with theoretical inquiry, contributed to meteorology's more general claim to greater legitimacy as an academic science.

SUPPLEMENTARY BIBLIOGRAPHY

A complete bibliography can be found in Geofysiske publikasjoner, *24 (1962): "In Memory of Vilhelm Bjerknes on the 100th Anniversary of His Birth," pp. 26–37. Vilhelm Bjerknes's unpublished papers and correspondence are deposited at the National Library (formerly University Library) in Oslo.*

OTHER SOURCES

Friedman, Robert Marc. "Constituting the Polar Front, 1919–20." *Isis* 73 (1982): 343–362.

———. *Appropriating the Weather: Vilhelm Bjerknes and the Construction of a Modern Meteorology.* Ithaca, NY, and London: Cornell University Press, 1989.

Grønås, Sigbjørn and Shapiro, Melvyn, eds. *The Life Cycles of Extratropical Cyclones.* Boston: American Meteorological Society, 1999

Robert Marc Friedman

BLACKETT, PATRICK MAYNARD STUART (Baron Blackett of Chelsea) (*b.* Kensington, London, 18 November 1897; *d.* London, 13 July

1974), *nuclear physics, cosmic-ray physics, cloud-chamber physics, geomagnetism and geophysics, operational research.*

Blackett was one of the most versatile experimental physicists of his generation. He received the Nobel Prize in Physics in 1948 for his development in the 1920s and 1930s of new methods for using C. T. R. Wilson's cloud chamber and for his discoveries which included pair production of electrons and positrons in cosmic radiation. During the 1950s, Blackett undertook magnetic research that provided evidence from paleomagnetism in sedimentary rocks for the much-debated theory of continental drift. Blackett pioneered operational research during the Second World War, and he was an influential voice in government circles from the 1930s to the 1970s on matters of science and technology policy, science education, nuclear armaments, and British technical aid to India.

Nuclear Physics and the Cloud Chamber. Blackett entered Osborne Royal Naval College in 1910 and matriculated with other cadets to Dartmouth Royal Naval College in 1912. At these two schools, Blackett received what was probably the most intensive physical science and engineering secondary education available in England at the time. When war broke out in August 1914, Blackett and his fellow students were immediately sent into action. He fought in the Battle of Falkland Islands in 1914 and the Battle of Jutland in 1916, emerging from the war with the rank of lieutenant. In January 1919, the Admiralty sent him to Cambridge along with other officers whose study had been interrupted in 1914. Once he had settled into Magdalene College and visited the Cavendish Laboratory at Cambridge, Blackett found the prospect of studying mathematics and physics so appealing that he resigned from the navy in February 1919.

After earning his undergraduate degree in 1921 and gaining election to a Bye-Fellowship at Magdalene College, Blackett became a research postgraduate student under Ernest Rutherford in the autumn of 1921 at the Cavendish Laboratory. Assigned by Rutherford to modify an automatic cloud chamber for the study of alpha particles bombarding targets, Blackett worked diligently to perfect the instrument in the face of Rutherford's impatience for results. When the volume of a cloud chamber suddenly expands, the temperature decreases and water droplets form on charged particles in the chamber. Blackett perfected a spring action linking the sudden expansion to a camera shutter so that a photograph is taken just as the expansion is completed. Peter Kapitza collaborated with him briefly in developing a powerful magnetic field around the chamber. At last, in the summer of 1924, Blackett obtained eight tracks (from twenty-three thousand photographs) showing the capture of an incident alpha particle by a nitrogen nucleus, creating an isotope of oxygen, and the path of a hydrogen ion (proton) ejected from the recoiling oxygen nucleus. These photographs were widely reprinted after that, and they made Blackett's reputation at the age of twenty-seven.

In March 1924, Blackett married Costanza Bayon, a student of modern languages at Newnham College, Cambridge. Their daughter Giovanna was briefly a photographer before her marriage and their son Nicolas followed a career in medical physics, studying the effect of radiation on biological cells. Patrick Blackett spent the 1924–1925 academic year with the physicist James Franck in Göttingen and returned to Germany in 1930 for a summer in Berlin. There he met Bruno Rossi, who was thinking of ways to use the Geiger-Müller counter to detect charged particles in cosmic radiation, and Rossi suggested that Giuseppe P. S. Occhialini join Blackett in Cambridge to learn cloud-chamber techniques.

Blackett and Occhialini soon devised a counter-controlled cloud chamber in which the passage of charged particles through the plane of the cloud chamber triggered expansion of the chamber. While they were accumulating data and discussing its theoretical implications with Cambridge theoretical physicist Paul Dirac in the autumn of 1932, Carl Anderson at the California Institute of Technology announced his discovery, using a cloud chamber, of a positively charged electron and characterized this particle's production as a rare event. In contrast, Blackett and Occhialini in a paper in February 1933 used their data explicitly to link this antielectron, or positron, to Dirac's relativistic electrodynamics, a theoretical insight that had not occurred to Anderson. Blackett and Occhialini also demonstrated the existence of showers of positive and negative electrons in cosmic radiation. This was called the phenomenon of pair production. They further confirmed the reverse process, or annihilation, of electrons and positrons upon their collision with one another, in confirmation of Dirac's theory of the electron. British newspapers attributed a revolutionary discovery to the Cavendish physicists, dubbing the new, tiny positive particle a "googlie" electron because, like a cricket ball, it breaks the wrong way. Although Blackett and Occhialini immediately received nominations for a Nobel Prize, it was Anderson who received part of the Nobel Prize in Physics in 1936, for discovery of the positron, sharing the award with Viktor Hess who had established the existence of cosmic radiation.

Blackett was a Fellow of King's College from 1923 until 1933, when he moved to Birkbeck College in London to head the physics department and his own laboratory. In 1937, he succeeded William Lawrence Bragg in the physics chair at Manchester, a position that previously had been held by Rutherford. During the mid and late 1930s, Blackett's research groups gathered additional evidence for

Patrick Maynard Stuart Blackett, 1963. COURTESY OF GIOVANNA BLACKETT BLOOR AND MARY JO NYE.

the cosmic-ray cascade or shower effect. Lively debate occurred in the mid-1930s over the identity of a particle that Anderson and Seth Neddermeyer called a mesotron or heavy electron, which Robert Serber and Robert Oppenheimer suggested was the theoretical particle predicted by Hideki Yukawa in 1935, even though the mesotron's mass was lower than Yukawa's prediction. Blackett initially questioned the interpretation of the mesotron, which later was renamed the mu-meson and eventually often shortened to muon. In 1947, Cecil Powell and his colleagues at Bristol found Yukawa's particle and demonstrated that it (the pi-meson) decays into the mu-meson and a single neutral particle which they soon hypothesized to be a neutrino. In the same year, at Blackett's laboratory in Manchester, George Rochester and Clifford Butler announced discovery of another new particle, evidenced by a V-shaped track, which they followed Blackett in interpreting as the product of decay of a heavy neutral ("strange") particle.

The Second World War and Operational Research. In late 1934, Harry Wimperis, who was director of Scientific Research in the Air Ministry, joined others in setting up a Committee for the Scientific Survey of Air Defense, chaired by the chemist and rector of Imperial College, Henry T. Tizard. Blackett joined the committee, which advised the Air Ministry to give high priority to the development of radar for defense against future air attack. This argument prevailed over the objections of Oxford physics professor Frederick A. Lindemann (Lord Cherwell), who favored other kinds of defense technologies and who was to become Winston Churchill's scientific advisor in 1939.

At the outbreak of the war in 1940, Blackett joined the instrument section of the Royal Aircraft Establishment, where he worked with Henry John James Braddick on the design of the Mark 14 bombsight, which eliminated the need for a level bombing run at the time of bomb release. In August 1940, Blackett became scientific advisor to General Frederick A. Pile in the Army's antiaircraft command, organizing a group of scientists to study the operational use of radar sets, guns, and mechanical calculators for antiaircraft fire. Joining the Royal Air Force's Coastal Command in March 1941, Blackett headed a group that recalculated the depth settings for antisubmarine explosives and applied mathematical techniques, such as the Poisson distribution, to settle tactical and strategic arguments within the command. At the Admiralty, from January 1942 to the summer of 1945, Blackett and "Blackett's circus," as it became known, brought about significant improvement in the use of airborne radar for finding German submarines that were sinking merchant ships in the Atlantic. This work often is credited as a turning point in the war during the summer of 1943, so that U.S. supplies and troops could reach England for the invasion of Europe.

Two reports that Blackett drafted in 1941 on the organization and methodology of operational research enjoyed broad circulation in Great Britain and the United States, earning Blackett the reputation as a founder of operational research. However, by the late 1950s, Blackett was expressing misgivings about the teaching of operational research as an academic specialty divorced from intimate everyday contact with military officers. He considered nuclear-war game theory inadequate on practical grounds and reprehensible on moral grounds. In addition, and more controversially, Blackett made public at the war's end the arguments against saturation bombing of German cities that he had pressed in government circles during wartime. These arguments brought him into conflict during wartime and afterwards with Churchill's scientific advisor Frederick Lindemann, who had favored large-scale bombing of German cities as a means of undermining German morale, although John Desmond Bernal and other scientists had data disputing the claim that British citizens' morale was undermined following the Germans' bombing of Hull and Birmingham.

In 1948, Blackett published the book *The Military and Political Consequences of Atomic Energy,* which appeared in slightly revised form in 1949 in the United States as a book-club choice under the title *Fear, War and the Bomb.* In this book Blackett criticized Lindemann's strategy which, Blackett noted, had escalated from the

incendiary bombing of Hamburg and Dresden to the nuclear bombing of Hiroshima and Nagasaki. He further debunked claims that bombs and the air force alone can win a war, whether with traditional bombs or nuclear bombs. Blackett also offered the then novel interpretation that the decision to use nuclear bombs in Japan owed more to fears in the United States of Soviet ambitions in Asia and Europe than to conviction that Japan would not otherwise surrender. He opposed the development of atomic weapons in Great Britain, bringing him into conflict with the policy of his own Labour Party under Clement Attlee. These views led some of Blackett's opponents to characterize him as a Soviet sympathizer and communist fellow traveler.

The Earth's Magnetism and Continental Drift. After the war, new fields of study opened up for Blackett and his collaborators in the Manchester physics department. With Blackett's support, Bernard Lovell located a radar facility at Jodrell Bank, twenty miles south of Manchester, and turned it into an observatory for radio astronomy that would become world famous. While some of his Manchester colleagues, including Rochester and Butler, continued cosmic-ray studies, Blackett became enthusiastic for a program of research that revived the hypothesis that the magnetic fields of the Sun, stars, and the Earth are fundamental properties of their rotating masses. His presentation at the Royal Society in May 1947 of a simple equation, including Newton's constant of universal gravitation and the speed of light, led journalists to compare his new work with Einstein's theory of relativity.

In 1952, in a tour-de-force paper titled "A Negative Experiment Relating to Magnetism and the Earth's Rotation," Blackett announced that he had failed to confirm this rotational theory of magnetism, following a series of experiments using a magnetometer which he had designed to detect minuscule magnetic effects in a rotating cylinder. He noted the suitability of his magnetometer for investigating remanent magnetism (paleomagnetism) in sedimentary rocks, a research program that resulted in a new kind of evidence for Alfred Wegener's 1912 hypothesis of continental drift, which had largely languished in the previous few decades. Stanley Keith Runcorn, Edward A. Irving, and John A. Clegg were among those who subsequently worked with Blackett's magnetometer or its successor instruments to gather data that converged in the 1960s with evidence leading to a theory of plate tectonics for explaining the continents' past and present motions. Blackett's work was important in convincing many skeptics that continental drift was a conjecture that could be tested. His group's researches on paleomagnetism, along with his enthusiastic support of empirical studies of paleolatitudes (or the locations of the latitudes of land masses in ancient times) and paleoclimates, played a huge role in the revival of the theory.

Leadership and Politics. In 1954, Blackett left Manchester for Imperial College in London, where he implemented a new strategy of a multiprofessorial department as he aimed to create an urban scientific educational and research institution that would equal the old universities of Cambridge and Oxford. In that year he declined to be a candidate to succeed Bragg as director of the Cavendish Laboratory. Throughout the 1940s and 1950s, Blackett was a forceful advocate of university expansion and government funding of research and development as a member of the Barlow Committee (1945–1946), the council and the research-grants committee of the Department of Scientific and Industrial Research (1956–1960), and the National Research and Development Corporation (1949–1964). He was dean of the Faculty of Science (1948–1950) and pro-vice-chancellor (1950–1952) at Manchester; and then dean of the Royal College of Science (1955–1960) and pro-rector (1961–1964) in London. Formally retiring from Imperial College and the University of London in September 1965, he served as president of the Royal Society from 1965 to 1970.

Blackett had Fabian and socialist political allegiances dating from his undergraduate years, and he was strongly associated publicly with the views of J. D. Bernal and others who advocated the social responsibility of the scientist and strong government support of science, although Blackett was himself not a Marxist. He was an active member and president (1943–1946) of the trade unionist British Association of Scientific Workers. From 1953 to 1963, he met with a group of scientists, including Bernal and Charles Percy Snow, that advised Hugh Gaitskell, when Gaitskell was leader of the Labour Party, and then advised the future prime minister Harold Wilson and his Shadow Minister for Education Richard H. S. Crossman. Under Wilson's Labour Party government, Blackett was science advisor in the Ministry of Technology from 1964 to 1969.

Blackett's maternal grandfather Charles Maynard had served in India at the time of the Indian mutiny in 1857, and his uncle William Maynard had been a tea planter in India. After Blackett first traveled to India in 1947, he became increasingly concerned with the gap between rich and poor and with the need to improve conditions in poorer countries through applications of science and technology. Blackett stirred up considerable protest when he put forward these ideas in his presidential address at the Dublin meeting of the British Association for the Advancement of Science in 1957. Blackett was a close friend of the Cambridge-educated Indian physicist Homi

Bhabha, and he became a military and scientific advisor to Jawaharlal Nehru's Indian government.

Blackett never took a PhD. He held twenty honorary degrees and was an member of academic or other institutions in eleven countries, including the Soviet Union and China. In 1956, he was appointed to the Order of the Companions of Honour and in 1967 to the Order of Merit. In 1969, while President of the Royal Society, he received a life peerage, an honor that he had declined five years earlier. In an obituary essay in *Nature,* Sir Edward Bullard recalled Blackett's quip that, at any rate, he had remained Mr. Blackett until after he retired. Tall and slim, always described as handsome, Blackett was said to be both formidable and charming. The grandson of a vicar on his father's side, Blackett respected religious observances that were established social customs, but described himself as agnostic or atheist.

In the official presentation speech of the Nobel Prize in Physics to Blackett in 1948, the experimental physicist Gustaf Ising noted that the prize may be awarded for discovery or invention and that the award to Blackett was motivated on both grounds. At the Nobel banquet in 1948, Gustaf Hellström spoke of Blackett's active part in two world wars and of his dedication to scientific discovery following each war. Blackett replied by discussing the paradoxes faced by scientists who pursue pure science, only to find that their discoveries make possible terrible catastrophes. Faithful to the principles that he maintained throughout his scientific career, Blackett challenged his Stockholm audience to recognize that it is the task of scientists and citizens to insure that scientific knowledge is used for the good of humanity and not its destruction. After becoming Baron Blackett of Chelsea in 1969, Blackett spoke four times in the House of Lords, using this new forum to warn against the widening gap between rich and poor. Frail in the last two years of life, Blackett died in hospital in July 1974.

BIBLIOGRAPHY

WORKS BY BLACKETT

With Giuseppe P. S. Occhialini. "The Ejection of Protons from Nitrogen Nuclei, Photographed by the Wilson Method." *Proceedings of the Royal Society,* Series A, 107 (1925): 349–360.

"Some Photographs of the Tracks of Penetrating Radiation." *Proceedings of the Royal Society,* Series A, 139 (1933): 699–726.

"The Craft of Experimental Physics." In *University Studies,* edited by Harold Wright. London: I. Nicholson & Watson, 1933.

The Military and Political Consequences of Atomic Energy. London: Turnstile Press, 1948. Revised as *Fear, War and the Bomb: Military and Political Consequences of Atomic Energy.* New York: Whittlesey House, 1949.

"A Negative Experiment Relating to Magnetism and the Earth's Rotation." *Philosophical Transactions of the Royal Society,* series A, 245 (1952): 309–370.

"Comparison of Ancient Climates with the Ancient Latitudes Deduced from Rock Magnetic Data." *Proceedings of the Royal Society,* Series A, 263 (1961): 1–30.

Studies of War: Nuclear and Conventional. Edinburgh: Oliver and Boyd, 1962.

OTHER SOURCES

Bullard, Sir Edward C. "Patrick Blackett … An Appreciation." *Nature* 250 (1974): 370.

Bustamante, Martha Cecilia. "Blackett's Experimental Researches on the Energy of Cosmic Rays." *Archives Internationales d'Histoire des Sciences,* 47 (1997): 108-141.

Butler, Clifford. "Recollections of Patrick Blackett, 1945–1970." *Notes and Records of the Royal Society of London* 53 (1999): 143-156.

Hore, Peter, ed. *P. M. S. Blackett: Sailor, Scientist, Socialist.* London: Frank Cass, 2003.

Lovell, [Sir] Bernard. "Patrick Maynard Stuart Blackett, Baron Blackett, of Chelsea." *Biographical Memoirs of Fellows of the Royal Society* 21 (1975): 1-113. Includes bibliography of Blackett's publications.

"The Nobel Prize in Physics 1948." Available from http://nobelprize.org/physics. Includes presentation and banquet remarks.

Nye, Mary Jo. *Blackett: Physics, War, and Politics in the Twentieth Century.* Cambridge, MA: Harvard University Press, 2004.

Rau, Erik P. "Technological Systems, Expertise, and Policy Making: The British Origins of Operational Research." In *Technologies of Power: Essays in Honor of Thomas Park Hughes and Agatha Chipley Hughes,* edited by Michael Thad Allen and Gabrielle Hecht. Cambridge, MA: MIT Press, 2001: 215-252.

Mary Jo Nye

BLAIR, ROBERT (*b.* Murchiston [near Edinburgh], Scotland, 1748; *d.* Westlock, Berwickshire, Scotland, 22 December 1828), *optics, maker of optical instruments.*

Blair was an expert in optics and a maker of optical instruments. His main contributions were twofold. First, throughout his adult life he improved the performance of achromatic prisms and lenses. Second, he wrote an important paper on the classical relativistic optics of moving bodies. The manuscript was never published, but it provides an essential demonstration of the application of Newton's dynamics to light and a most interesting foreword to Einstein's relativity. In this context, after John Michell (on whose work he based his efforts), he discov-

ered what sixty years later would be named the Doppler effect.

Career. Robert Blair was the son of Archibald Blair, a minister in Garvald, Scotland, and his wife, Janet Barclay. Robert was born at Murchiston, near Edinburgh. After studying medicine at Edinburgh University, he was apprenticed as a naval surgeon and served in the West Indies, where he became interested in navigation and its instruments.

In 1785 Blair was appointed the first professor of practical astronomy at the University of Edinburgh. He was awarded the degree of master of divinity. His chair at Edinburgh, a regius one, was created for him by the Edinburgh Town Council for "the great advantages which Navigation … derive from the cultivation of Practical Astronomy" (Brück, 1983, p. 11). In 1786 he became a fellow of the Royal Society of Edinburgh. At the university, Blair "enjoyed forty two years of endowed leisure": he refused to give lectures on the ground that he had neither apparatus nor observatory and did not attend meetings of the university senate (Grant, 1884, 2, p. 362). He resided for eight years in London working with his son Archibald, also an optician. After 1793, Blair held the appointment of first commissioner of the board for the care of sick seamen. He was instrumental in banishing scurvy from the navy by introducing the use of lime juice. After a long illness he died at Westlock, Berwickshire, on 22 December 1828.

Blair published few articles: one on Hadley's quadrant, one on optics, and another on the construction of achromatic telescopes. In 1786 he wrote a paper that would remain unpublished. (The manuscript was read on 6 April 1786 at the Royal Society. It was communicated by Alexander Aubert (1730-1805), fellow of the Royal Society and director of the London Assurance company.) In it he gave a systematic treatment of the Newtonian kinematics of light, taking into account in the absolute space of Newton the motion of the light source, that of the observer, and the velocity of the corpuscles of light.

Later he published two books, *Essays on Scientific Subjects* (1818) and *Scientific Aphorisms* (1827). He was well known for his work on achromatism and one of those who contributed through research to the Newtonian optics of moving bodies.

A Doppler Effect. Blair's most important contribution to the optics of moving bodies follows from a deep understanding of how Newton's dynamics were applied to light at the end of the eighteenth century. At the time it was not clear that the velocity of light was a constant; in fact, because of Galileo's kinematics it could not be constant. Newton's *Principia* (1687) proposed a dynamics of particles whose application to gravitation was highly successful. But its application to light—the corpuscular theory of light—is also of interest.

It consists of a short range of dynamics of light that essentially implied the sinus law of refraction. Blair was to follow John Michell's analysis of the corpuscular theory of light and took seriously what Michell called then his method, using a prism as a tool to measure the velocity of light. The following result stems from a simple argument in the refraction model of the corpuscular theory: the greater the velocity of an incident light corpuscle on a crystal, the smaller is its angle of refraction. Thus, a measure of the refraction angle is a measure of the incident velocity of the light corpuscle. But from Galileo's kinematics, which then had of necessity to apply to a light corpuscle, the incident velocity of a light corpuscle should be the sum of the emission's velocity (supposed to be a constant) and the relative velocity between the source and the observer. Thus, from a measure of the refraction suffered by a light ray emitted by a moving body, one gets a measure of the velocity of the body relative to the observer. From such an analysis, Blair reasonably thought that he would be able to determine "the motion with which any planet, Comet or fixed star however remote, is approaching toward, or receding from the observer" (Blair, 1786, p. 10). This is precisely the essence of what has come to be called the Doppler effect. Blair constructed an instrument in order to make such measures, but for different reasons (he used twelve achromatic prisms and absorption was far too important due to the number of prisms), he was unable to make any measurement. Blair's proposal is at the root of François Arago's well-known experiments from 1806 into the 1810s on the velocity of light, whose influence on the acceptance of Augustin-Jean Fresnel's undulatory theory of light has been so important. Most probably Arago never read Blair's manuscript but he heard of it through an article written by John Robison. (John Robison, "On the Motion of Light, as affected by Refractiong and Reflecting Substances, which are also in motion," *Royal Society of Edinburgh. Transactions* 2 (1790): 83–111, p. 98, which is quoted in Arago's article).

Moreover, in the context of the undulatory theory of light, Blair proposed an experiment to determine the absolute motion of the Earth, laying the basis for the famous experiment performed by Albert Michelson one hundred years later. Actually Blair's unpublished manuscript contains the very basic questions of light relativity and the roots of spectroscopy. It addresses precisely the problems that would be hotly debated in the nineteenth century, only to be solved by Albert Einstein in 1905.

Achromatism. In his *Opticks* (1704), Newton had erroneously asserted that chromatic aberration could not be corrected by combining two lenses of differing refracting indices. The quest for achromatism is well known; in the eighteenth century chromatic aberration was much reduced by John Dollond and many others.

At the turn of the nineteenth century, the insufficient quality of flint glass was one of the most serious problems facing opticians. While at Edinburgh, Blair sought to improve the performance of refracting telescopes and hoped to substitute a dense fluid for flint glass. The most satisfactory system was a solution of antimony of mercury in hydrochloric acid sealed between two crown glass lenses, a system he called *aplanetic,* meaning free from aberration.

In 1791 Blair reported his work at two meetings of the Royal Society of Edinburgh and published a paper, "Experiments and Observations on the Unequal Refrangibility of Light," in its *Transactions* in 1794. In it he detailed alternative methods of constructing achromatic telescopes. He combined two oils with very different dispersive powers. The *secundary spectrum* (a term Blair coined) was greatly reduced but still appeared. Blair's work was the origin of the technology of liquid-lens telescopes, which David Brewer, Archibald Blair, and Peter Barlow developed in the 1820s in response to Joseph von Fraunhofer's superior achromatic telescopes. For Great Britain, it was one of the attempts made to regain world hegemony in optical lenses.

BIBLIOGRAPHY

Blair's unpublished manuscript, "A Proposal for Ascertaining by Experiments whether the Velocity of Light Be Affected by the Motion of the Body from Which it is Emitted or Reflected," Royal Society Manuscript, L & P, 8, 182, 1786, is housed in the Royal Society in London.

WORKS BY BLAIR

"A Description of an Accurate and Simple Method of Adjusting Hadley's Quadrant for the Back Observation." In *Nautical Almanac.* London: William Richardson, 1788).

"Experiments and Observations on the Unequal Refrangibility of Light." *Royal Society of Edinburgh, Transactions* 3 (1794): 3–76.

"The Principles and Application of a New Method of Constructing Achromatic Telescopes." *Journal of Natural Philosophy* 1 (1797): 1–13.

"Beschreibung einer neuen Art von achromatischen Fernröhren, oder der sogenannten aplanetischen Teleskope, und Entwickelung der Gründe, vorauf sie beruhen." *Annalen der Physik* 6 (1800): 129 148.

Essays on Scientific Subjects. Edinburgh, UK: Macredie, 1818.

Scientific Aphorisms, Being an Outline of an Attempt to Establish Fixed Principle of Science. Edinburgh, UK: n.p., 1827.

OTHER SOURCES

Brewster, David. "Observations on the Superiority of Achromatic Telescopes with Fluid Object-Glasses, as Constructed by Dr. Blair." *Edinburgh Journal of Science* 5 (1826): 105–111.

Brück, Hermann A. *The Story of Astronomy in Edinburgh from its Beginnings until 1975.* Edinburgh, U.K. Edinburgh University Press, 1983.

Cantor, Geoffrey N. *Optics after Newton: Theories of Light in Britain and Ireland, 1704–1840.* Manchester, U.K. Manchester University Press, 1983.

Eisenstaedt, Jean. *Avant Einstein : Relativité, lumière, gravitation.* Paris: Seuil, 2005.

———. "Light and Relativity, a Previously Unknown Eighteenth-Century Manuscript by Robert Blair (1748–1828)." *Annals of Science* 62 (2005): 347–376.

Grant, Alexander. *The Story of the University of Edinburgh during Its First Three Hundred Years.* 2 vols. London: Longmans, Green, 1884.

Jackson, Myles W. *Spectrum of Belief: Joseph von Fraunhofer and the Craft of Precision Optics.* Cambridge, MA: MIT Press, 2000.

Jean Eisenstaedt

BLASIUS OF PARMA (*b.* Costamezzana, Parma, Italy, *ca.* 1345; *d.* Parma, 1416), *natural philosophy.* For the original article on Blasius of Parma see *DSB,* vol. 2.

The recent critical edition of some of the most important of Blasius's works has allowed for a more complete acquaintance with his thought, as well as a more informed appreciation of his great importance in the history of science and philosophy of the later Middle Ages, particularly in terms of the European dissemination of debates that occurred at the University of Paris and at Oxford.

Blasius of Parma's importance in medieval scientific thought can be found in his promotion, in Italian universities, of the outcome of fourteenth-century Parisian and English debates on logic and natural philosophy (John Buridan, Albert of Saxony, Thomas Bradwardine). The great importance of the University of Pavia in the fifteenth century as a center where the Parisian and, above all, the English works on natural philosophy were commented on (with Giovanni Marliani as a prominent master) is at least partly due to Blasius's presence as a master there. Blasius's works, even those not originating from his university teaching, are addressed to an academic audience, with the exceptions of two *astrological iudicia* given in 1386 (Padua) and 1405.

Natural Philosophy. In addition to Aristotle's natural philosophy (*Physics, On the Heavens, On Becoming and Passing Away, Metereologics, On the Soul*) Blasius wrote commentaries on two of the most common university manuals: some parts of Peter of Spain's *Tractatus logicales* and John of Holywood's *On the sphere.* His strong interests in natural philosophy, as well as in relying on the new languages of proportions and intension and remission, occasioned an original way of introducing and dealing with physical problems in his lectures on logical works and even in his commentaries on Aristotle. In particular, he tackled explicitly the problem of the relationship between the point and the line in his commentary on Peter of Spain's *Tractatus* (III, 10 "whether points are in the line" [*utrum puncta sint in linea*], presenting one of the topic arguments against indivisibles), and introduced a way of treating limits (*incipit/desinit*) in discussions about the quality of categorical propositions (I, 16).

In discussing contrariety he openly declared a preference for analysing the problem physically rather than logically, which led him to cursorily introduce the problem of intension and remission (III, 3), discussed in a lengthier form in III, 16. In his commentaries on Aristotle's physical works Blasius included some of the relevant topics of fourteenth century Parisian and English natural philosophy: in *On the Soul* the way in which to measure the perfection of a form (II, 6 "whether the essential perfection in living substances is to be measured by the proximity to the highest degree" ["*utrum in latitudine viventium sit essentialis perfectio penes accessum ad summum attendenda*"]). In the *Physics* commentary the intension and remission of qualities is discussed in the last question of the fifth book (V, 10), whereas in the questions on the seventh book he dealt with the way of calculating the speed ("*penes quid attendenda est velocitas*") in the three different Aristotelian motions (local motion, alteration, and augmentation/diminution: VII, 6–8), the way of calculating the speed considering the ratios of the speed and those of the movers (VII, 9 "*utrum in motibus proportio velocitatum sit sicut proportio causarum*") and the limits of natural agents as well (VII, 10 "*utrum agens naturale sit limitatum*").

Role of Mathematics. Blasius maintained, following Aristotle, the primacy of mathematics as far as certitude is concerned. The main problem, however, was the abstract character typical of mathematical and geometrical notions, which made them unfit for physical research. Blasius's reductionist attitude in ontology did not let him consider proportions, points, lines, and surfaces as real objects. It was very urgent, therefore, to solve this semantic problem if one wanted to take advantage from the clear and cogent procedures of mathematics. Blasius relied on logic in order to solve this problem and to enable the application of mathematics in dealing with natural philosophy problems. He maintained that geometrical and mathematical notions are very useful tools, because they are the outcome of complex operations of human reason, which need not denote specific objects, but rather relations between real objects. He relied explicitly on the semantic theory of *appellatio rationis*, as did many late medieval thinkers, John Buridan included. He did not uphold the theory according to which propositions denote something different from the subject term. Truth and falsehood, moreover, do not refer to true or false propositions, as for the main part of the terminists taking their lead from William Ockham. They are rather the two ways of referring of propositions.

Blasius was resolute in his reliance on the new fourteenth-century tools of analysis. So much so that in question eight of his commentary on Bradwardine's *Treatise on Proportions* he blended proportions, latitudes of forms, and a special topics like reaction (*reactio*) in discussing whether the power of the agent has always to be greater than that of the patient in order to produce an effect ("*utrum a proportione equalitatis vel minoris inequalitatis proveniat vel provenire posit aliquis effectus; vel sic: utrum in omni motu potentia motoris debeat excedere potentiam rei mote vel equari ei*"). Blasius did not accept Bradwardine's solution concerning speed: Taking into consideration time, speed depends on the ratio between power and resistance, whereas considering the outcome (*effectus productus*) only the agent must be considered (q. 10, 2). This solution was coherent with his ontological convictions, according to which proportions are nothing more than the outcome of the comparing soul (and in this sense one can rely on mathematics in comparing times, power, and resistances). If one takes speed for the final result, the only element to be considered is the power of the agent ("*proportio velocitatum, id est effectuum productorum vel producibilium, insequitur proportionem agentium absolute*", q. 10, 2). The different ways of attaining the speed, respectively in rectilinear local (speed can be attained through the linear space obtained by the fastest point in a given time) and in downward motion (speed can be attained through the distance from the center of the world), rest upon such ontological commitments.

Ideas on Qualities. In his question *On Intension and Remission of Forms* (*De intensione et remissione formarum*) Blasius denied the existence of *species* in order to explain vision, following his reductionist agenda. Also knowledge, even scientific knowledge, was for him nothing different than the knowing soul. No quality, moreover, could be inherent to the soul without having an infinite degree of intensity, being soul in-extended. In the first part of the question (*articulus I*) Blasius had a wider project: to limit ontology only to substances, refusing the existence of

every kind of accidental qualities. In order to do that concerning the accidental category of quality (admitted by William Ockham), Blasius relied upon the theory of intension and remission in analysing the presence of contrary qualities in natural substances. In particular, he felt himself entitled to refuse the existence of coldness on the basis that it could be considered hotness in a lower degree (the last conclusion of the *articulus I*: "*frigiditas non est aliud quam remissa caliditas*"). Between the two contrary qualities, therefore, there is no specific distinction. He rejected, moreover, qualities's power to produce, in their highest degree, the substantial form, a theory defended by Walter Burley in his *On Intension and Remissiom of Forms*. For example hot in its highest degree can produce fire. According to his reductionist attitude, Blasius upheld the solution according to which intension and remission concern the natural being, the bearer of the quality, rather than quality itself. This solution permitted Blasius to take into consideration two dimensions of the changing quality: intension of the quality properly and the extension of the quality in the subject. In this way Blasius was able to deal with the topic introducing a way of representing quality's changes through geometrical figures.

In this question, moreover, Blasius blended some topics of fourteenth-century English and Parisian natural philosophy, as he did in his commentary on Bradwardine's *Treatise on Proportions*. In addition to intension and remission, he discussed the ways of attaining speed in local motion and alteration, problems concerning limits (first/last instant, *primum/ultimum instans*) and reaction (*reactio*). On this last topic he granted the position of Parisian masters, according to which there is a difference between the power of acting and that of resisting in every quality.

SUPPLEMENTARY BIBLIOGRAPHY

A complete bibliography of Blasius's works, listing the known manuscripts, has been prepared by Graziella Federici Vescovini in the "Appendix" to Federici Vescovini, Graziella and Barocelli, Francesco, eds., Filosofia, scienza e astrologia nel Trecento Europeo. Biagio Pelacani Parmense, *a cura di con un intervento di Raymond. Klibansky. Padova: Il Poligrafo 1992: 181–216.*

WORKS BY BLASIUS OF PARMA

Quaestiones super de anima: Federici Vescovini, Graziella, *Le 'Quaestiones de anima' di Biagio Pelacani da Parma.* Firenze: Leo S, Olschki, 1974 (based on two mss.: Città del Vaticano, ms. Chig. 0.IV,41; Napoli, Biblioteca Nazionale Vittorio Emanuele III, ms. VIII, G., 74). Italian translation: Biagio Pelacani da Parma, *Quaestiones de anima. Alle origini del libertinismo,* a cura di Valeria Sorge. Napoli: Morano, 1955.

Quaestiones de musica discovered by John E. Murdoch in the ms. Paris: Bibliothèque Nationals, lat. 7372, ff. 1r–72r, published as Murdoch, John, E. "Music and Natural Philosophy:

Hitherto unnoticed " Quaestiones" by Blasius of Parma (?)", *Manuscripta*, XX (1976): 119–136. The author maintains that this text cannot be surely attributed to Blasius.

Questio de intensione et remissione formarum: Federici Vescovini, Graziella, "La *Quaestio de intensione et remissione formarum* di Biagio Pelacani da Parma", *Physis*, XXXI (1994): 433–535 from the ms. Venice, Biblioteca Marciana, ms. VI, 62 (2549).

Questiones super Tractaus logice Magistri Petri Hispani. Edited by Joël Biard and Graziella Federici Vescovini, avec la coll. de Orsola Rignani et Valeria Sorge. Paris: J. Vrin, 2001.

Questiones circa Tractatum proportionum Magistri Thome Braduardini. Edited by Joël Biard et Sabine Rommevaux. Paris: J. Vrin, 2005.

OTHER SOURCES

Biard, Joël. "L'être et la mesure dans l'intension et la rémission des formes (Jean Buridan, Blaise de Parme)." *Medioevo* 27 (2002): 415–447.

———. "Le système des senses dans la philosophie naturelle du XIVe siècle (Jean de Jandun, Jean Buridan, Blaise de Parme)." *Micrologus* 10 (2002): 335–354.

———. "Mathématique et philosophie dans les 'Questions' de Blaise de Parme sur le 'Traité des rapports' de Thomas Bradwardine." *Revue d'Histoire des Sciences* 56 (2003): 383–400.

Buzzetti, Dino. "Blasius Pelacani, the Paradoxes of Implication and the Notion of Logical Consequence." In *Medieval and Renaissance Logic in Spain. Acts of the 12th European Symposium on Medieval Logic and Semantics held at the University of Navarra (Pamplona 26-30 May 1997)*, edited by Ignacio Angelelli and Perez Ilarbe, 97–135. Paloma, Spain: Olms, 1998.

Federici Vescovini, Graziella. "Biagio Pelacani: filosofia, astrologia e scienza agli inizi dell'età moderna." In *Filosofia, scienza e astrologia nel Trecento Europeo. Biagio Pelacani Parmense*, edited by Graziella Federici Vescovini and Barocelli, Francesco, 39–52. A cura di con un intervento di Raymond. Klibansky. Padova: Il Poligrafo, 1992.

Rommevaux, Sabine. "*L'irrationalité de la diagonale et du côté d'un même carré dans les 'Questions' de Blaise de Parme sur le 'Traité des rapports' de Bradwardine.*" *Revue d'Histoire des Sciences* 56 (2003): 401–418.

Sorge, Valeria. "'Contra communiter philosophantes': a proposito della fisiologia della visione in Biagio Pelacani da Parma." *Atti dell'Accademia di scienze morali e politiche della Società nazionale di scienze, lettere e arti di Napoli* 106 (1996): 299–322, 455–474.

———."L'influenza di Alhazen sulla dottrina della visione in Biagio Pelacani da Parma." In *Filosofia e scienza classica, arabo-latina medievale e l'età moderna*, edited by Graziella Federici Vescovini, 113–127. Louvain-La-Neuve: FIDEM, 1999.

Stefano Caroti

BLAU, MARIETTA

BLAU, MARIETTA (*b.* Vienna, Austria, 29 April 1894; *d.* Vienna, 27 January 1970), *physics, radioactivity, method of nuclear photographic emulsions, photomultiplier technology.*

Blau developed the method of photographic emulsions that enabled the recording of tracks of atomic particles and became known for the discovery of "contamination stars," explosions of atomic nuclei produced by high-energy cosmic-ray particles. She elaborated a theory on the effect of x-rays on biological objects. Using photomultipliers, she designed the first electrically modified scintillation counter and several user-friendly medical instruments for radioactive measurements. She was nominated twice for the Nobel Prize. Blau received the Schrödinger Prize and the Ignaz Lieben Prize of the Austrian Academy of Sciences.

Blau was born in fin de siècle Vienna as the third child of an upper-class Jewish family. Her father, Markus Blau, was a lawyer in the kaiser's courts and an important music publisher. Her mother, Florentine Goldenzweig, was the sister of Josef Weinberger, the main publisher of Gustav Mahler's works in Europe. During her childhood, Blau attended some of the best Viennese schools and in 1905 was sent to the private Mädchen Obergymnasium, the only school with official state recognition to prepare women for academic studies. In 1914, when the young men were drafted and women had more access to education, Blau enrolled at the University of Vienna to study physics and mathematics. During the last year of her studies she conducted her *Praktikum* (practical training) at the Institute for Radium Research, one of the four most important radioactivity research centers in Europe. In 1918, Blau submitted her dissertation on the absorption of diverging gamma rays, and her first paper appeared both in the annual bulletin of the Radium Institute and in the *Sitzungsberichte* of the Austrian Academy of Sciences.

Blau's research topic turned out to be important for clinical treatments of cancer. Discovered by a French physicist, Paul Villard, gamma rays had occupied the interest of the radioactivity community since 1900. Because of their penetrating power, which is much higher than that of x-rays, gamma rays proved to be crucial in killing cancerous cells. Eventually, that research topic led Blau to medical physics and to the Laboratory for Medical Radiology at Guido Holzknecht's clinic in Vienna where she worked as a research assistant after defending her thesis in 1919.

Blau hovered at the boundary of medicine and physics for the rest of her career. In 1921, she left Vienna to accept a position as a physicist in Eppens and Co., which manufactured x-ray tubes in Fürstenau, Germany. A year later she moved to the Institute of Medical Physics in Frankfurt am Main, where she worked as a research assistant. For more than a year Blau instructed doctors in radiobiology, while she conceived and elaborated a theory on the effect of x-rays on biological objects. At that time the Frankfurt Institute was the epicenter of target theory in Germany, which described the impinging of radiation on living tissues as particles hitting a target. The theory's aim was to use radiation to probe the structure of the organic world. Blau played an instrumental role in developing the statistical analysis of biophysical processes that constituted "hits," which was the main research project of Friedrich Dessauer, the director of the institute (Beyler, 1997, pp. 39–46). Working with Kamillo Altenburger, she studied the number of "hits" that were entailed in order for a biological process to occur. Her research career in Germany was interrupted abruptly in the fall of 1923 when her mother became ill and she had to return to Vienna. Although she left Dessauer's laboratory, Blau retained her ties. Later she contributed a piece on photographic investigations of radioactive rays in a multiauthored volume edited by Dessauer on the boundary between physics and medicine (Blau, 1931).

Photographic Emulsions. Between 1923 and 1938, Blau's research was centered at the Radium Institute in Vienna. Still, when she attempted to obtain a position as *Dozentin* (instructor) at the University of Vienna, the response was astounding; "You are a woman and a Jew and together this is too much" (Halpern, 1997, p. 197). In the 1920s, the Radium Institute was less conservative than the university, hosting an astonishing number of women researchers and welcoming Jews. During this time, thanks to the Swedish physicist Hans Pettersson, the institute proved to be a major participant in a serious controversy over the artificial disintegration of light elements. The second participant was Rutherford's laboratory in Cambridge, England. Blau joined Pettersson's group in Vienna, and with her expertise on the use of photography in radioactivity, she was immediately assigned to develop a new method for tracking charged nuclear particles, that of photographic emulsions.

Rutherford's discovery of the phenomenon of artificial disintegration by alpha particles prompted the need for more sensitive tools to detect and measure the emitted protons, a need that became urgent during the Vienna-Cambridge controversy. The method of photographic emulsions had been already used by S. Kinoshita and Maximilian Reinganum in the beginning of the 1910s to identify trajectories of alpha particles through emulsions. In early 1924, Blau was assigned by Pettersson to use the same method to observe recoil protons produced by alpha particles in paraffin. With weak radioactive sources she could observe the lower-energy particles, but the accuracy of the measurement was limited. The only strong source available was polonium. To prevent darkening of the plate by gamma radiation, Blau worked with polonium, which

was prepared in highly concentrated preparations by Elizabeth Rona, an experienced experimenter at the Institute.

In 1925, Blau detected for the first time the trajectories of slow protons. As the grain thickness of proton tracks was appreciably smaller than that of alpha tracks, it was evident to her that the photographic conditions (emulsion characteristics and development conditions) would have to be improved if high-energy protons—with smaller ionization thickness—were to be observed. In the following years, the method was applied to the disintegration of various atoms and detected the tracks of faster protons. Blau also improved the quality of the processing techniques and emulsions and was able to increase the thickness of the emulsion layers. However, what proved to be decisive for Blau's career and for the success of her method was the exposure of the emulsions to cosmic radiation. In this achievement, Blau's collaborator was Hertha Wambacher.

Nine years younger than Blau, Wambacher entered the institute as a *Praktikum* student, having Blau as her main but informal advisor in her dissertation on the impact of photographic desensitizers on the imprints of alpha, beta, and gamma rays on photographic plates. As Wambacher proved, a major desensitizer of photographic emulsions was the organic dye pinakryptol yellow. In June 1932, the two women coauthored their first paper. Just five months after James Chadwick's discovery of the neutron, Blau and Wambacher were able to detect photographically protons liberated by unseen neutrons. These protons did not leave an imprint unless the photographic plates were desensitized by means of pinakryptol yellow. As a consequence of this first success in photographically detecting the ionization protons and explaining the effect of desensitization, Blau was invited by the German photographic giant Agfa, "as their guest of honor," and a medal was bestowed upon her by the Photographic Association (Blau, curriculum vitae). Additionally, in the fall of 1932, Blau received a scholarship from the Association of Austrian Academic Women to spend six months at Robert Pohl's physics institute in Göttingen and the rest of her stipendium time at Marie Curie's Institut du Radium in Paris. But during Blau's absence from her home institute, Wambacher teamed with Gerhard Kirsch—a Viennese physicist, a Nazi, and Pettersson's main collaborator—on an investigation of neutrons from beryllium, using Blau's photographic method. On Blau's return in 1934, both the institute and Vienna had changed, affected profoundly by the political upheavals of 1933.

Political Unrest. In the context of the wider European political crisis and Hitler's rise to power in Germany, the political situation in Vienna became increasingly unstable. The socialists lost power and control of the city in 1934,

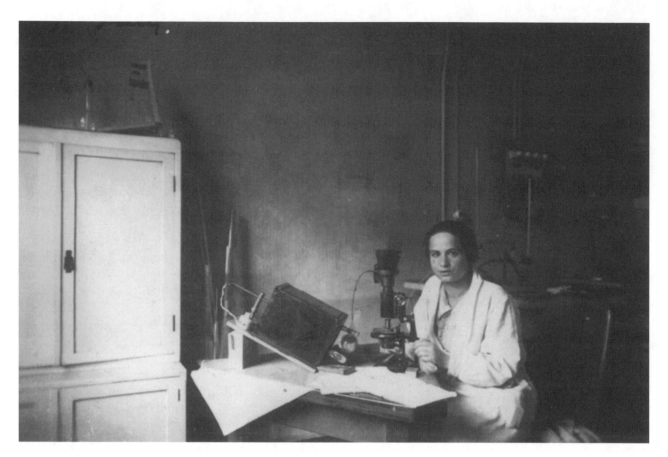

Marietta Blau. AGNES RHODE PERSONAL PAPERS.

giving rise to Austrian fascists and to the Nazis consequently. After her return from Paris, Blau continued her
collaboration with Wambacher under an obvious political
tension within the institute.

The two women worked on two fronts. First, they
improved the emulsion technique by thickening the photographic plates to allow a better deposit of the particle
tracks. Ilford, the English photographic company, offered
to produce sufficiently thick plates, and Blau suggested
that new development methods had to be created. Second, while still struggling to alter their apparatus to suit
their experimental needs, Blau and Wambacher applied
the photographic technique to neutron studies. Their collaboration turned out to be threatening for Blau's existence at the institute. In June 1934, Wambacher joined
the National Socialist Party and around that time became
intimately involved with an ardent Nazi, Georg Stetter,
assistant at the Second Physics Institute of Vienna and
member of Pettersson's group.

Continuing their cooperation, in 1936 the two
women exposed their emulsions on the Haferlekar, a
mountain near Innsbruck, for four months in order to
secure high-intensity radiation. Their research project
consisted in determining the existence of heavy particles
such as protons, neutrons, and alpha particles in cosmic
rays, which at the time was considered quite doubtful.
Upon first examination of the plates, they observed proton tracks longer than anyone else had at that time. Yet, to
their surprise, Blau and Wambacher observed in the emulsion a "contamination star" (several tracks emanating
from a point) that could neither be explained by irregular-
ities in the emulsion nor by unknown radioactive products during the handling and storage of the plates in the
laboratory. The assumption was that the large "stars" originated from the disintegration of heavy particles, probably
bromine or silver, and that the smaller ones originated
perhaps from light elements in the gelatin. Given the theoretical limitations of nuclear physics of the time, the two
women could not determine the nature of the primary
particle and the exact process of the disintegration. These
impressive results, which American historian Peter Galison considers the first "golden event" using emulsions,
provoked the interest of the scientific community (1997,
p. 44). In 1937, on the basis of their discovery, Blau and

Wambacher were awarded the Ignaz Lieben Prize of the Austrian Academy of Sciences.

While the two women were preparing a publication, Stetter approached Blau. He accused her of being unfair to Wambacher and expected her to change the order of the names on their publication since Wambacher was, after all, he argued, the first to look into the microscope and find the star. Blau refused. In the midst of the world's serious political upheavals and Blau's tenuous position, Ellen Gleditsch, a Norwegian expert on radioactivity, took a personal interest in her situation and offered her a temporary position as a research assistant in her laboratory in Oslo. Under the enormous pressure from her own ex-advisee and Stetter, Blau rushed to arrange research matters with Wambacher, an arrangement which was a total defeat for her.

As the agreement went, Wambacher, in collaboration with Gustav Ortner, another Nazi at the institute, were going to investigate the relation of the grain and density of the tracks recorded on the photographic emulsions to the energy of the particles produced by them. By measuring the grain thickness of the tracks one could even estimate the energy of the particles that were not brought to rest in the emulsion but passed through. This process had the potential of identifying the particles and the total energy released in the process, the two key points of Blau's and Wambacher's earlier work. Blau agreed to continue the absorption experiments, a less promising and more tiresome task. Luckily, she left Vienna on a 7:00 a.m. train to Oslo a day before the Germans paraded triumphantly into Austria on 12 March 1938.

Exile. While Blau knew that she could only remain in Oslo for a limited time, Berta Karlik, a young colleague then and later director of the Radium Institute, encouraged Pettersson to reclaim the instruments he brought to Vienna in the early 1920s. Given the simplicity of the photographic emulsions method and its tabletop scale, portable objectives and microscopes could, at least temporarily, ensure Blau's research prospects.

In November 1938, after Albert Einstein's recommendation, Blau left Norway to accept a position at the Polytechnic School in Mexico City. On her way to Mexico the Gestapo confiscated her scientific notebooks, forcing her zeppelin down in Hamburg. She later speculated that those ended up at the hands of her Nazi colleagues in Vienna. However, with or without Blau's scientific notebooks, Wambacher continued to use the experimental facilities of the Radium Institute. Within two weeks of the *Anschluss,* she was promoted to the position of assistant at the First and Second Physics Institutes. Publications in major German journals accompanied her rapid promotion in the university ranks. On the contrary, from 1940

to 1944, Blau centered her work in Mexico, deeply frustrated by the lack of research opportunities and by the teaching overload. Only through the efforts of the Jewish community in Mexico, was she able to enter the United States in May 1944.

Photomultipliers and Scintillation Counters. Blau was one of the first to suggest the use of a photomultiplier in combination with a scintillation counter. The original scintillation counter consisted of a thin glass plate spread with an equally thin layer of zinc sulfide. When the plate was struck by charged particles, the screen produced light flashes that were observed through a microscope specifically designed to increase their brightness. The instrument had extensively been used at the Radium Institute during the Cambridge-Vienna controversy. Working for competitive industrial corporations after the Second World War, Blau sought possibilities for professional existence by saving and modifying an old-familiar technique; her past secured her present.

In the physics department of the International Rare Metals Refinery, her first position in the United States, Blau teamed up with B. Dreyfus in combining the use of a photomultiplier tube to a scintillation screen for the measurement of alpha ray sources (Blau and Dreyfus, 1945). Putting together a fluorescent screen with the photomultiplier, which took a very small amount of light and converted it into an amplified electrical signal, and using strong polonium sources, Blau and Dreyfus had in fact described the first electrically modified scintillation counter. As the references to Elizabeth Kara-Michailova's and Berta Karlik's work show, both colleagues in Vienna, Blau was the driving force in designing the device. In 1933, after abandoning the ordinary scintillation counter, Karlik had worked on the determination of alpha particle ranges utilizing a photoelectric cell, a sensitive electric device for the detection of the scintillations that replaced the fragile and unreliable human optical system. Karlik's method, however, was seldom used, as Blau explained, given the limited range of measurements of the ordinary photocells and the lack of adequate and constant alpha-sources. Thanks to the multiplier phototube, Blau overcame the earlier difficulties.

Through her hybrid instrument Blau sought to merge the competing prewar and postwar cultures in physics research. The shift from the ordinary photocells to photomultipliers, in Blau's experimental practice, was not just a simple replacement of two pieces in an instrument. The transformation was a deeper, conceptual one for both the experimenter and the instrument. From a research-oriented position in the Radium Institute in Vienna, Blau's occupation shifted to industrial physics in the postwar United States. The corporations that she worked for

1944 to 1948 were deeply involved in the manufacture of nuclear weapons, the commerce of uranium and radium, and the industrial uses of radium. In the beginning of 1948, Blau moved to the Gibbs Manufacturing and Research Corporation and with J. R. Carlin she worked on industrial applications of radioactivity. Her creative time and efforts were taken up by a number of radioactive devices such as resistors, electrostatic voltmeters, leveling systems, and micrometers.

In her effort to find a decent research position, Blau moved again within the next few months, this time to the Canadian Radium and Uranium Corporation. Carrying over her knowledge in medical physics to the Radium Corporation, Blau designed a photomultiplier scintillation counter for medical use. Designed for "persons not very familiar with radioactive measurements," Blau's scintillation counter was a convenient and practical instrument for wide use in hospitals and medical laboratories (Blau and Smith, 1948, p. 68). Despite the fact that she was the first to design and suggest medical applications of the photomultiplier scintillation counter, Blau remained peripheral and isolated in the competitive world of industrial physics.

In 1950, she moved to the Brookhaven National Laboratory where she had restricted access to the high-energy physics facilities. Remaining faithful to the experimental tradition of the 1930s, Blau was unable to continue her research in the new settings of big science. Although Erwin Schrödinger nominated Blau and Wambacher for a Nobel Prize based on their pioneer work on photographic emulsions in this same year, the Nobel Prize committee almost unanimously intended to give the prize to someone who was doing follow-up work to the previous year's prize winner, Hideki Yukawa, on the existence of mesons. While the committee recognized the importance of Blau's contributions, the prize was eventually awarded to the physicist Cecil Powell, who had adapted Blau's method to his industry-like laboratory in Bristol and turned it to a powerful tool for making "foundational discoveries concerning mesons and their properties" (Nobel Committee Report, 1950).

Return to Vienna. Because of prolonged exposure to radioactivity, in the late 1950s, Blau developed cataracts, requiring an operation. In the dusk of her life facing financial and health problems, Vienna seemed the most suitable destination. She finally returned in 1960. A number of old colleagues tried to gather funds for her and Schrödinger put her up for the Schrödinger Prize, which she received in 1962. Poor, disconnected from any major scientific network, and bitter about several members of the Radium Institute for reaccepting the Nazi Stetter as one of the heads of the Physics Institute after the end of the war, Blau distanced herself from serious research and from old

friends such as Karlik. She died on 27 January 1970, in the intensive care ward of the Lainz hospital, lonely and unknown to the international physics community.

BIBLIOGRAPHY

WORKS BY BLAU

"Über die Absorption divergenter-Strahlung." *Sitzungsberichte der Kaiserlichen Akademie der Wissenschaften in Wien, Mathematisch-naturwissenschaftliche Klasse,* Abteilung 2a, 127 (1918): 1253–1279.

With Kamillo Altenburger. "Über einige Wirkungen von Strahlen." *Zeitschrift für Physik* 12 (1922): 315–329.

"Über photographische Untersuchungen mit radioaktiven Strahlungen." In *Zehn Jahre Forschung auf dem physikalisch-medizinischen Grenzgebiet,* edited by Friedrich Dessauer. Leipzig, Germany: Georg Thieme, 1931.

With Hertha Wambacher. "Disintegration Processes by Cosmic Rays with the Simultaneous Emission of Several Heavy Particles." *Nature* 140 (1937): 585.

Curriculum Vitae. 1941 (unpublished). Grenander Department of Special Collections and Archives, State University of New York at Albany.

With B. Dreyfus. "The Multiplier Photo-Tube in Radioactive Measurements." *The Review of Scientific Instruments* 16 (1945): 245–248.

With J. R. Carlin. "Industrial Applications of Radioactivity." *Electronics* 21 (April 1948): 78–82.

With J. E. Smith. "Beta-Ray Measurements and Units." *Nucleonics* 2 (June 1948): 67–74.

OTHER SOURCES

Beyler, Richard. "'Imagine a Cube Filled with Biological Material': Reconceptualizing the Organic in German Biophysics, 1918–1945." In *Fundamental Changes in Cellular Biology in the 20th Century,* edited by Charles Galperin, Scott F. Gilbert, and Brigitte Hoppe. Proceedings of the 20th International Congress of History of Science, Liège, Belgium 20–26 July 1997. Turnhout, Belgium: Brepols, 1999.

Galison, Peter. "Marietta Blau: Between Nazis and Nuclei." *Physics Today* 50 (1997): 42–48.

Halpern, Leopold. "Marietta Blau: Discoverer of the Cosmic Ray 'Stars.'" In *A Devotion to Their Science: Pioneer Women in Radioactivity,* edited by M. Rayner-Canham and G. Rayner-Canham. London: McGill-Queen's University Press, 1997.

Lindh, Axel. "Nobel Committee Report on Marietta Blau and Hertha Wambacher." Uppsala 1 July 1950 (unpublished). Nobel Archive of the Center for History of Science, The Royal Swedish Academy of Sciences. Stockholm.

Rentetzi, Maria. "Gender, Politics, and Radioactivity Research in Interwar Vienna: The Case of the Institute for Radium Research." *Isis* 95 (2004): 359–393.

Rosner, Robert, and Brigitte Strohmaier, eds. *Marietta Blau— Sterne der Zetrümmerung.* Wien: Böhlau Verlag, 2003. Includes a complete list of Blau's publications.

Maria Rentetzi

BLOCH, FELIX (*b.* Zürich, Switzerland, 23 October 1905; *d.* Zürich, 10 September 1983), *theoretical and experimental physics, solid-state physics, superconductivity.*

Bloch is considered one of the founders of solid-state physics. He made particularly significant contributions to the quantum theory of metals and solids, he worked on the magnetic scattering of neutrons and, together with Luis Alvarez, he experimentally measured the magnetic moment of the neutron. His discovery of nuclear magnetic resonance won him the Nobel Prize in Physics for 1952, which he shared with Edward Mills Purcell.

Early Years and Education. Felix Bloch was born in Zürich on 23 October 1905. His father Gustav Bloch was a wholesale grain dealer in Zürich. His mother Agnes Meyer was from Vienna. Both parents were Jews. His father moved to Zürich in 1890 to take a position in his uncle's business and became a Swiss citizen. Gustav and Agnes had a daughter in 1902.

In his primary school years Felix had difficulties relating to other children, and the teachers were not particularly encouraging. But this changed when he moved to another school where they used the Pestalozzi method. In the spring of 1918, he entered the gymnasium run by the Canton of Zürich, which had a six-year curriculum preparing students for the university. He seemed to like mathematics; he applied elementary mathematics to astronomy and could successfully calculate the length of daylight in Zürich at various times of the year. In the fall of 1924, he entered the Federal Institute of Technology (ETH) in Zürich, planning to study engineering. The next year he decided to study physics, despite the initial discouragement by Hermann Weyl. One of the persons who had made a lasting impression on him was his teacher at the ETH, Peter Debye. Years later, in 1976, Felix Bloch still remembered the acute manner by which Debye was assessing the early developments in quantum mechanics and how his comments were rather catalytic in the development of the wave equation by Schrödinger:

> Once at the end of a colloquium I heard Debye saying something like: "Schrödinger, you are not working right now on very important problems anyway. Why don't you tell us some time about that thesis of de Broglie, which seems to have attracted some attention?" ... Schrödinger gave a beautifully clear account of how de Broglie associated a wave with a particle and how he could obtain the quantization rules of Niels Bohr and Sommerfeld by demanding that an integer number of waves should be fitted along a stationary orbit. When he had finished, Debye casually remarked that this way of talking was rather childish. As a student of Sommerfeld he had learned that, to deal properly with waves, one had to have

a wave equation. It sounded quite trivial and did not seem to make a great impression, but Schrödinger evidently thought a bit more about the idea afterwards. Just a few weeks later he gave another talk in the colloquium which he started by saying: "My colleague Debye suggested that one should have a wave equation; well I have found one!" (Bloch, 1976, pp. 23–24)

In 1927, Debye accepted an appointment at the University of Leipzig. Bloch followed him there and started to work for his doctorate with the twenty-six-year-old Werner Heisenberg, who had just been appointed professor of theoretical physics at the university. Heisenberg asked his first graduate student to examine the problems related to the conductivity of metals with the new quantum mechanics. There had been some semiclassical treatments which gave satisfactory agreements with the experimental results. Wolfgang Pauli had assumed that the conduction electrons behaved as if they were an ideal gas, obeying Fermi statistics, and was able to derive the temperature independence of the paramagnetism of metals. With Arnold Sommerfeld, Pauli derived the relationship between electrical and thermal conductivity. Still, physicists could not comprehend why the conduction electrons should be treated as an ideal gas of free electrons.

Research on Theory of Metals and Collective Phenomena. Felix Bloch proposed a satisfactory electron theory of conduction on the basis of quantum mechanics in his doctoral thesis, "Über die Quantenmechanik der Elektronen in Kristallgittern" (The quantum mechanics of electrons in crystal lattices), which was published in the *Zeitschrift für Physik* (1928). The electrons in a metal were considered to be uncoupled, though the field in which any one electron moved was found by an averaging process over the other electrons. If the metal was at absolute zero, its lattice determined a periodic potential field for the electronic motions, and the electrical resistance by the immobile lattice was zero. An electron could move freely through a perfect crystal and a finite free path could only be due to the imperfections in the lattice. In general the imperfections were caused predominantly by the thermal motion of the atoms and were strongly temperature dependent, increasing with increasing temperature. Impurities, however, also scattered the electrons, but in this case the free path would not vary appreciably with temperature. The resistance, therefore, consisted of the "impurity resistance" and the resistance due to the thermal motion of the atoms. According to Bloch's analysis of the motion of an electron in a perfect lattice, all the electrons in a metal could be considered to be "free," but it did not necessarily follow that they were all conduction electrons. This theory accounted for metals, semiconductors, and insulators but not for superconductors.

But even though in 1928 there was a successful theory of electrical conductivity, superconductivity regarded as a phenomenon of infinite conductivity was still not understood. Bloch, after a suggestion by Wolfgang Pauli, started working on superconductivity while he spent the year 1928–1929 as Pauli's assistant in Zürich. Though the phenomenon had been discovered by Heike Kamerlingh Onnes in 1911, there was no satisfactory theory. Such a theory could not be derived in any straightforward manner from the calculations of Bloch's thesis, since his approach using single electrons in order to derive the resistance of metals in low temperatures could not give rise to superconductivity. It appeared that something radically new was needed for the theoretical explanation of the phenomenon. His interpretation was suggested through analogy with ferromagnetism. He showed that the most stable state of a conductor, in the absence of an external magnetic field, was a state with no currents. And since superconductivity was a stable state displaying persistent currents without external fields, it was difficult to see how a theory for superconductivity could be constructed. "This brought me to the facetious statement that all theories of superconductivity can be disproved, later quoted in the more radical form of 'Bloch's theorem': 'Superconductivity is impossible'" (Bloch, 1966, p. 27).

At the beginning of November 1933, there appeared a short letter in *Naturwissenschaften* by Meissner and Ochsenfeld that presented strong evidence that, contrary to every expectation and belief of the past twenty years, a superconductor expelled the magnetic field. Superconductors were found to be diamagnetic. The assumption that there was a perfect shielding of the superconductors by their persistent currents ceased to be valid. In the experiment by Meissner and Ochsenfeld, it appeared that the magnetic field was pushed out after the transition to the superconducting state and the magnetic flux became zero. The phenomenon of transition to the superconducting state turned out to be a reversible phenomenon.

By the end of September 1934, Fritz and Heinz London had formulated the phenomenological theory of the electrodynamics of a superconductor. They had assumed that the diamagnetism must be taken to be an intrinsic property of an ideal superconductor, and not merely a consequence of perfect conductivity. They proposed that superconductivity demanded an entirely new relation in which the current was connected not with the electric, but with the magnetic field.

In a letter, London had stated that

> The progress I claim is mainly a logical one: by a new and more cautious interpretation of the facts I tried to avoid a fundamental difficulty (the so called theorem of Bloch) which stood in the way of explaining superconductivity by the customary

theory of electrons in metals and which could not be overcome as long as one has considered this phenomenon as a limiting case of ordinary conductivity. (London to McLennan 21 June 1935, in Gavroglu, 1995, p. 129)

Another significant contribution Bloch made while he was in Zürich was his improvement of Heisenberg's theory of ferromagnetism, where the exchange interaction of electrons played a dominant role. Bloch was able to show that the zero-point energy of the electrons figured importantly in determining whether a metal would be ferromagnetic. He spent the academic year 1929–1930 in Utrecht, where Hendrik Anthony Kramers was. There he developed the concept of spin-waves, examining their connection with ferromagnetism and derived the dependence of the magnetic moment on the absolute temperature in the low-temperature region.

After spending the academic year 1930–1931 with Heisenberg in Leipzig, Bloch wrote his Leipziger Habilitationsschrift. In this work, he systematically studied exchange-interaction problems and residual magnetization in ferromagnets and, at the same time, developed much of the formalism which has been used ever since in condensed-matter theory and problems of collective phenomena. Beyond its contribution to the theory of domain walls, this work serves as a bridge between the quantum theory of ferromagnetism in the 1930s and present theories of many-particle systems (see Hoddeson et al.). Bloch was also able to work out the thickness and structure of the boundary walls, and the wall structure became known as the *Bloch wall*. Richard Becker was experimentally studying the domain structure and how it varied as magnetization proceeded. In a space of a few hundred angstroms magnetization could reverse direction within the thickness of the wall, and this was shown to be energetically more favorable than a complete reversal at the boundary.

In 1932, Bloch returned to Leipzig as a Privatdozent (instructor), where he completed the calculations on stopping power he had already started after Bohr's instigation in Copenhagen where he had spent the previous year. In 1933, Bloch proved that the Dirac-Fock-Podolsky theory with the relativistically covariant formulation of quantum electrodynamics was equivalent to the Heisenberg-Pauli theory. He had a continuous interest in the problems of quantum theory. When Robert Hofstadter, at a later date, expressed his belief that Einstein's view on determinism in quantum mechanics would ultimately prevail, Bloch was rather unconvinced; "anyone who takes that view doesn't understand quantum mechanics" he answered (Hofstadter 1994, 50).

Physics of the Neutron. In March 1933, with the Nazis already in power, Bloch left Germany with a Rockefeller

Fellowship. He was planning to start working in the fall with Fermi's group in Rome. In the meantime he traveled to Paris, Utrecht, and Copenhagen, and a short while before going to Rome, he was contacted by the Physics Department of Stanford University to be offered a position there. He took the position as acting associate professor in April 1934. While in Stanford, he had the opportunity to organize seminars in theoretical physics, jointly with Robert Oppenheimer, who was at Berkeley. In the summer of 1935, he combined a trip he took to Switzerland with a trip to Copenhagen. Bohr thought that Bloch's experience with problems of ferromagnetism would be useful for thinking about the physics of the newly discovered neutron. Since the magnetic moment of neutron had already been discovered, Bloch started considering the possibilities of polarized neutrons in ferromagnetic materials. In a letter to the *Physical Review* Bloch submitted in 1936, he outlined his theory of magnetic scattering of neutrons. It was also shown that the scattering could lead to a beam of polarized neutrons and how temperature variations of the ferromagnet could be used to separate the atomic scattering from the nuclear scattering.

Bloch returned to his considerations about neutrons and, together with experimentalists like Norris. E. Bradbury at Stanford, built a low-voltage neutron source. The neutrons were produced by the deuteron-deuteron reaction and were used to find the scattering cross section of neutrons on cobalt. This work showed that the anomalously large cross sections for iron and nickel do not depend on their ferromagnetism, because cobalt, which is also ferromagnetic, has a normal cross section.

After Fermi's summer visit to Stanford in 1937, Bloch started thinking about experiments using a polarized beam of neutrons. Isidor I. Rabi was also involved with experiments with such beams. Berkeley had a 37-inch cyclotron which produced a rather intense source of neutrons, and Ernest Lawrence at Berkeley suggested to Bloch that he collaborate with Luis Alvarez about the experiments he was contemplating.

Bloch and Alvarez developed the resonance method, through the use of a beam of polarized neutrons resulting from the passing of the unpolarized neutron beam from the cyclotron through a very strongly saturated plate of magnetized iron. A strongly magnetized analyzer iron plate was used to measure the fractional depolarization of the neutron beam. Between the two plates there was a constant strong magnetic field together with a weak oscillating magnetic field, normal to the constant field and of variable frequency. The transmitted beam, depending on the frequency of the oscillating field, would pass through a resonance at the Larmor precessional frequency corresponding to the value of the magnetic moment in the constant magnetic field. When there was resonance, the

Felix Bloch. *Felix Bloch with a nuclear induction spectrometer, used in determining properties of atomic nuclei.* © BETTMANN/CORBIS.

polarization of the incident beam was changed, and the scattering of the beam in the second plate could be detected. In this way they were able to determine the value of the neutron magnetic moment. They found it to be equal to 1.935 ± 0.02 nuclear magnetons, and the sign was negative with respect to the proton's moment.

Rabi with his team had already found the values of the magnetic moments of the proton and the deuteron. Further improvements led to measurements of the magnetic moment of neutron in absolute units and, of course, with ever higher precision. Eventually, Bloch was able to measure the precise values of the magnetic moment of the neutron, proton, deuteron, and triton, as well as the spin of the triton. This provided the possibility of applying the method for measuring the moments of any nucleus and such measurements helped to clarify a number of problems related with the nucleon-nucleon interactions. Because all these measurements were performed at Berkeley, it was decided to build a cyclotron at Stanford. Bloch was helped by Hans Staub and William Stephens to build the 20-inch cyclotron, and with Morton Hamermesh and

Hans Staub, he was able to establish rather high percentages of polarization effects.

In 1940, Bloch married Lore Misch, an x-ray crystallographer who had received her doctorate with Victor Moritz Goldschmidt in 1935 in Göttingen. She had left Germany in 1936, spent two years as assistant in physics at the University of Geneva, Switzerland, and in 1938 went to the United States, taking a post of research associate at MIT. They had four children, three boys and a girl.

After Oppenheimer's invitation, Bloch got involved with the Manhattan Project in 1942. Under Bethe's supervision, Bloch used the cyclotron to measure the energy distribution of the neutrons emitted during fission. The results were classified, and they showed that the energy was well above the expected value of 2 million electron volts. After completing this work, he moved to Los Alamos, where he worked on the implosion method suggested by Seth Neddermeyer. He stayed there a few months, then decided to join the Radio Research Laboratory at Harvard and worked in John Van Vleck's group on reflectivity of materials to waves used in radar research.

Nuclear Magnetic Resonance and the Nobel Prize. After the war, Bloch devised a method for measuring atomic magnetic moments. This method he called *nuclear induction*. When the atomic nuclei were placed in a constant magnetic field, then their magnetic moments would be aligned. If a weak oscillating magnetic field is superposed on the constant field in a direction which is perpendicular to the constant magnetic field, then, as the Larmor frequency is approached, the original rotating polarization vector will be forced nearer the plane perpendicular to the constant magnetic field. The rotating horizontal component of the polarization vector will induce a signal in a pickup coil whose axis is perpendicular to the weak oscillating field. The exact value of the frequency that gives the maximum signal can then be used, as in the Larmor resonance formula, to calculate the magnetic moment. Using this method, the proton moment was measured and found to be in close agreement with the value that had been already determined by Rabi in his experiments with molecular beams. Bloch's collaborators in the experiments were William. W. Hansen and a graduate student, Martin Packard.

In December of 1945, Bloch and E. M. Purcell of Harvard met at the annual meeting of the American Physical Society and realized that they were working on similar problems. They decided that Bloch would continue his researches and investigate liquids, whereas Purcell would concentrate on crystals. The results of Henry. C. Torrey, E. M. Purcell, and Robert. V. Pound at Harvard, who used a similar resonance method involving energy absorp-

tion of radiation in a cavity, appeared at the same time as Bloch's measurements. Both methods came to be known as *nuclear magnetic resonance*. Bloch and Purcell shared the Nobel Prize in Physics in 1952 for the development of new methods for the exact measurement of nuclear magnetism and for the discoveries made in the development of these methods. This was Stanford's first Nobel Prize.

In developing his magnetic resonance technique, Bloch introduced two parameters, known as T_1 (longitudinal) and T_2 (transverse) relaxation times, which relate to the interaction of the nuclear magnetic moment with the surrounding atomic or molecular environment. The behavior of these parameters was related to chemical bonding or biological processes in the material examined. Subsequently he, in collaboration with Roald. K. Wangsness, worked out a theoretical understanding of the nuclear inductive process including T_1 and T_2, leading to what are still known as the *Bloch equations*. The technique started to be extensively used for the measurement of many nuclear magnetic moments, and, most importantly, it was found to have applications in chemistry and biology. Eventually, magnetic resonance became the predominant spectroscopic tool used in structural and dynamic studies in chemistry. In 1971, Paul. C. Lauterbur and others developed a method for producing images of tissues, based on Bloch's techniques. Magnetic resonance imaging has come to be one of the most effective and extensively used tools in medicine.

Bloch had started his career among the very best theoreticians. He continued as a theoretician and at the same time got involved in rather ingenious experimental work, where a substantial part of the setup was of his own design. By the end of World War II, he, together with almost all of his colleagues, had to make decisions concerning the dramatic changes and the challenging choices faced by the physics community. Defense Department contracts, funding agencies, progressively closer ties with engineers, and involvement of industry were defining the new framework within which the universities, and especially their physics departments, were being forced to function. Bloch in 1943 wrote to David Webster who, as chairman of the Physics Department at Stanford, had offered a position to Bloch in 1933, "I snobbishly maintained the principle of 'l'art pour l'art' for physicists ... right now I am gladly using 'l'art pour the war'" (Gailson 1997, p. 277).

Despite his reservations about the role of large accelerators, in 1954 Bloch accepted the post of director general of CERN in Geneva. He stayed for only a year, returning to Stanford. And though he abhorred the administrative chores and the involvement with all kinds of bureaucratic dealings in building "Project M" (M for Monster), upon his return to Stanford in the fall of 1955, he acquiesced and joined other colleagues to building what was later called the Stanford Linear Accelerator Center.

After the discovery of magnetic flux quantization in 1961, Bloch worked again on problems superconductivity, such as the Josephson effect and the possibilities offered by a charged Bose-Einstein gas to reproduce some of the features of superconductivity. In 1961, he was appointed as Max Stein Professor of Physics at Stanford University.

He was elected president of the American Physical Society in 1965. He was also a member of the National Academy of Sciences, the American Academy of Arts and Sciences, the American Philosophical Society, and the German honor society known as Pour le Mérite. He was appointed an honorary member of the Swiss Physical Society and received honorary degrees from Grenoble University, Oxford University, the University of Jerusalem, and the University of Zürich. He was, also, a member of the American Professors for Peace in the Middle East, the Committee for U.N. Integrity, the Committee of Concerned Scientists, the Universities' National Anti-war Fund, and Scientists and Engineers for Secure Energy. He was not able to finish his book on statistical mechanics; after his death, John Dirk Walecka reworked Bloch's notes and the *Fundamentals of Statistical Mechanics* appeared in 1989.

BIBLIOGRAPHY

The Bloch (Felix) Papers can be found in the Department of Special Collections and University Archives, Stanford University. Online finding aid available at Online Archive of California, *http://www.oac.cdlib.org/.*

WORKS BY BLOCH

"Über die Quantenmechanik der Elektronen in Kristallgittern." *Zeitschrift für Physik* 52 (1928): 555–600. Bloch's doctoral dissertation.

"Bemerkung zur Elektronentheorie des Ferromagnetismus und der electrische Leitfähigkeit." *Zeitschrift für Physik* 57 (1929): 545–555.

"Zur Theorie des Ferromagnetismus." *Zeitschrift für Physik* 61 (1930): 206–219. Bloch's Habilitationsschrift.

"On the Magnetic Scattering of Neutrons." *Physical Review* 50 (1936): 259–260.

"On the Magnetic Scattering of Neutrons II." *Physical Review* 51 (1937): 994.

With Luis Alvarez. "A Quantitative Determination of the Neutron Moment in Absolute Nuclear Magnetons." *Physical Review* 57 (1940): 111–122.

With Morton Hamermesh and Hans Staub. "Neutron Polarization and Ferromagnetic Saturation." *Physical Review* 64 (1943): 47–56.

With Isidor I. Rabi. "Atoms in Variable Magnetic Fields." *Reviews of Modern Physics* 17 (1945): 237–244.

With William W. Hansen and Martin Packard. "Nuclear Induction." *Physical Review* 69 (1946): 127.

With William W. Hansen and Martin Packard. "The Nuclear Induction Experiment." *Physical Review* 70 (1946): 474–485.

With David Nicodemus and Hans Staub. "A Quantitative Determination of the Magnetic Moment of the Neutron in Units of the Proton Moment." *Physical Review* 74 (1948): 1025–1045.

With Carson D. Jeffries. "A Direct Determination of the Magnetic Moment of the Proton in Nuclear Magnetons." *Physical Review* 80 (1950): 305.

"Nuclear Induction." *Physica* 17 (1951): 272.

With Roald K. Wangsness. "The Dynamical Theory of Nuclear Induction." *Physical Review* 89 (1953): 728–739.

"Nuclear Magnetism." *American Scientist* 43 (1955): 48–62.

"Dynamical Theory of Nuclear Induction. II." *Physical Review* 102 (1956): 104–135.

"Generalized Theory of Relaxation." *Physical Review* 105 (1957): 1206.

"Some Remarks on the Theory of Superconductivity." *Physics Today* 19, no. 5 (1966): 27.

"Josephson Effect in a Superconducting Ring." *Physical Review B* 2 (1970): 109–121.

"Superfluidity in a Ring." *Physical Review A* 7 (1973): 2187–2191.

"Heisenberg and the Early Days of Quantum Mechanics." *Physics Today* 29 (December 1976): 23–27.

"Memories of Electrons in Crystals." *Proceedings of the Royal Society of London, Series A,* 371 (1980): 24–27.

"Past, Present and Future of Nuclear Magnetic Resonance." In *New Directions in Physics: The Los Alamos 40th Anniversary Volume,* edited by Nicholas Metropolis, Donald M Kerr, and Gian-Carlo Rota. Boston: Academic Press, 1987.

With John Dirk Walecka. *Fundamentals of Statistical Mechanics.* Stanford, CA: Stanford University Press, 1989.

Bloch's Nobel speech in *Nobel Lectures, Physics, 1942–1962,* editors Bengt Samuelson, Michael Sohlman. Singapore: World Scientific, 1998.

OTHER SOURCES

Galison, Peter. *Image and Logic: A Material Culture of Microphysics.* Chicago: University of Chicago Press, 1997.

Gavroglu, Kostas. *Fritz London: A Scientific Biography.* Cambridge, U.K.: Cambridge University Press, 1995.

Hoddeson, Lillian, Gordon Baym, and Michael Eckert. "The Development of the Quantum Mechanical Electron Theory of Metals, 1926–1933." In *Out of the Crystal Maze: Chapters from the History of Solid-State Physics,* edited by Lillian Hoddeson, Ernest Braun, Jürgen Teichmann, et al. Oxford: Oxford University Press, 1992.

Hofstadter, Robert "Felix Bloch." In *Biographical Memoirs,* vol. 64, 34–71, Washington, DC: National Academy of Sciences, 1994.

Krige, John. "Felix Bloch and the Creation of a 'Scientific Spirit' at CERN." *Historical Studies in the Physical and Biological Sciences* 32 (2001): 57–69.

Kuhn, Thomas, John Heilbron, Paul Forman, and Lini Allen, eds. *Sources for History of Quantum Physics*. Philadelphia: American Philosophical Society, 1967. Interview with Bloch by T. S. Kuhn on May 14, 1964. Information available online at http://www.amphilsoc.org/library/guides/ahqp/.

Kostas Gavroglu

BODENSTEIN, ADAM OF (*b*. Kemberg/
Saxony-Anhalt, Germany, 1528; *d*. Basel, Switzerland, March 1577), *medicine, alchemy, natural history*. For the original article on Bodenstein see *DSB*, vol. 2.

Research since 1970 has resulted in new information and insights about Bodenstein's life and publications. Programmatic dedications and other texts by Bodenstein in numerous Paracelsian printed works have undergone additional editing and annotation. This subsequent research confirms Bodenstein's central position in the field of early German Paracelsianism.

Life. The son of the theologian Andreas Bodenstein (A. Carolostadius/Karlstadt; 1486–1541) spent his youth in Basel, which had been his father's workplace since 1534. He obtained his baccalaureate at the local university in 1546 and MA degree in 1548, then continued his studies in Freiburg, Leipzig, Mainz, and Ferrara, Italy, where he received his doctorate in medicine in 1550. In 1547 Bodenstein married Esther Wyss, who died in Basel in 1564. One year later he married Maria Jakobea Schenck zu Schweinsberg, who died in 1618 at Sinnershausen near Meiningen.

Following a stay in Vienna (1551) Bodenstein was, at least until 1559, in the service of Count Palatinate Ottheinrich (1502–1559; elector since 1556), a sovereign favorably disposed toward alchemical Paracelsianism. He appointed Bodenstein in 1553 to the position of "servant by order of the house" (not to the position of "court physician" [Trevor-Roper, 1990, p. 82] or "personal physician" and "colleague" of Thomas Erastus [Nutton, 1995, p. 112]), and "admonished" him several times around 1556 to read Paracelsus. In part because of certain successful therapies with Paracelsian medicine in Basel (1556), Bodenstein became, about this time, receptive to the *medicina nova* of Theophrastus Bombastus von Hohenheim (Paracelsus). Whether he was already disseminating "Paracelsian thinking and writings" in the "1550s" (Nutton, 1995, p. 112) remains uncertain; there are no testimonies or proofs of documents. However, undoubtedly Bodenstein's "Paracelsian turn" combined with an orientation toward *alchemia transmutatoria metallorum* (transmutational alchemy). Encouraged by an itinerant alchemist

(possibly Denis Zecaire) and two friends from Basel, the councillor of the margrave Ludwig Wolfgang of Habsburg and the university mathematician Johannes Acronius. Bodenstein made himself out to be an expert on the philosopher's stone (1559–1560) and published Paracelsian writings from 1560 until his death.

Bodenstein was a professed follower of John Calvin and Théodore de Bèze (Geneva); he participated in religious-confessional controversies in Basel and accused Sebastian Castellio (1515–1563) of heresy ("Pelagianism") and of a "libertinism" dangerous to youth (1563). At about the same time, Bodenstein's editions of Paracelsus brought him into serious conflict with the Basel-based Consilium Facultatis Medicae (Council of the Faculty of Medicine), to which he had belonged since November 1558. Because he was apparently adhering to Hohenheim's "false doctrines," on 27 January 1564 Bodenstein was excluded from the university faculty and the consilium owing to the decisive influence exerted by Theodor Zwinger (1533–1588). The claim that Bodenstein had been teaching "iatrochemistry at the University of Basel" (Walton, 2000, p. 319) lacks any firm basis.

By the 1560s many members of the *res publica medica* viewed Bodenstein as a leading figure of the Theophrastians that were gradually forming at the time. He combined his medical practice with the preparation of iatrochemical medications and spent time on the laboratory-based production of gold (around 1570 in collaboration with Pierre de Grantrye, the French royal envoy in Rhaetia), but he first devoted himself to an extensive publishing effort relating to Paracelsian writings.

Bodenstein was among the well-known personalities of early modern Basel. The number of his dedications to secular grandees (including Emperor Maximilian II, Archduke Ferdinand II, and Cosimo de' Medici) and members of the urban elites—though not to the representatives of the humanistic educational elites at postsecondary schools—testify to Bodenstein's wide-ranging network of connections extending beyond the German-speaking cultural area as far as Italy and France. In the course of both his pro-Paracelsian publishing offensive and his iatrochemical practice, Bodenstein supported such famous Paracelsians as Michael Toxites, Gerhard Dorn, and Georg Forberger, as well as Samuel Schlegel, the personal physician of Georg Friedrich, Margrave of Brandenburg-Ansbach, and other medical practitioners. After Bodenstein's death (on Palm Sunday, 1577), Theodor Zwinger (then no longer an opponent but a sponsor of the Paracelsians) formulated a highly appreciative epitaph for his fellow traveler: "Adamus a Bodenstein, Theophrasti Paracelsi ut primus sic fidus scitusque et opere et ore interpres, palmam victoriae suae regi triumphanti oblaturus" (Adam of Bodenstein, about to offer the palm of his victory to the triumphant king, as the first and so faithful and wise interpreter of Theophrastus Paracelsus, both in deed and in speech.)

Work. During his literary beginnings Bodenstein dealt with Heinrich Cornelius Agrippa of Nettesheim's *De occulta philosophia*, Book 3 (translation and commentary, produced before 1556; subsequently lost). He then entered the publishing market as a Galenic physician: Bodenstein increased the plethora of German-speaking prognostics with a translation of a *practica* for the year 1557 written by Luca Gaurico (*Weyssagung Sibylle Tyburtine*, 1557) as well as contributing to the literature on podagra (gout) and on astro-medicine (*Wie sich meniglich vor dem Cyperlin … waffnen solle. Vnnd bericht diser kreüter / So den himmelischen zeichen Zodiaci zügeachtet*, 1557). Soon, however, he emerged as an adherent of the pre-Paracelsian *alchemia transmutatoria metallorum*, believing himself to possess the deepest secrets of the philosopher's stone (*Isagoge* to the *Rosarium chymicum* [Ps.-]) by Pseudo-Arnald of Villanova, 1559; with an *Epistola* to Anton, Johann Jacob, Georg, and Ulrich [Huldricus] Fugger). With the exception of a *Philosophischer rhatschlag* (a philosophical counsel on how to fight the plague, 1577), all of the writings Bodenstein published from 1560 onward were related to Paracelsian topics.

In terms of the history of science, Bodenstein gained significance as a publicizing herald of Hohenheim's teachings. To foster understanding of Paracelsian technical terms, he compiled an *Onomasticon* (Strasbourg, 1566; Basel 1575, a revised separate edition), marking the beginning of printed lexicography on Paracelsus, and completed more than forty editions of Paracelsian writings. They reveal Bodenstein as a harsh opponent of the Aristotelian-Galenic natural history and medicine, who lent strong impulses to the Paracelsian revival by adopting the *prisca-sapientia* idea and further Neoplatonic didactic material, critically examining the basic concepts of the Aristotelian-academic philosophy of nature. In conjunction with the Paracelsus editions by M. Toxites, G. Dorn, and G. Forberger (partly supported by Bodenstein), his work played a crucial role in fostering the emergence and further development of European Paracelsianism. Certainly some of Bodenstein's tracts are testimony, as Pearl Kibre wrote in the original *DSB*, to "the strength of tradition in both medicine and alchemy in the sixteenth century." However, viewed as a whole, the subversive, pro-Paracelsian fundamentals of his publishing efforts, having an eroding effect on tradition, ensure Bodenstein's standing in the history of science.

SUPPLEMENTARY BIBLIOGRAPHY

Bodenstein's main literary achievements are the well over forty Paracelsian editions appearing between 1560 and 1576. These editions were recorded by Sudhoff, 1894 (standard); see also Jüttner, 1985. Numerous Paracelsian printed works offer programmatic dedications and other supplementary texts by Bodenstein. The bulk of these early testimonials of European Paracelsianism have undergone editing and annotation; see Corpus Paracelsisticum, edited by Wilhelm Kühlmann and Joachim Telle, 2001, nos. 6–30, pp. 104–544.

WORKS BY BODENSTEIN

Weyssagung Sibylle Tyburtine … aussgelegt RECTE: außgelegt für das 1557 jar, by Luca Gaurico. Translated into German and edited by A. von Bodenstein, without place name (probably Basel), 1557.

Wie sich meniglich vor dem Cyperlin Podagra genennet waffnen solle. Vnnd bericht diser kreüter / So den himmelischen zeichen Zodiaci zügeachtet. Basel, Bartholomäus Stähelin, 1557; Amberg, Michael Forster 1611. The statement in Kibre's *DSB* article that this tract has not been "identified or located" in modern times is not correct.

Isagoge in excellentissimi philosophi Arnoldi de Villa Nova, Rosarium chymicum, per Adamum à Bodenstein … paraphraststicè et magna diligentia tradita. With *Epistola … ad dominos Fuggeros, in qua argumenta Alchymiam infirmantia et confirmantia adducuntur, quibus et eam artem esse certissimam demonstratur, lapisque uerè inuentus ostenditur.* Basel, Gabriel Ringysen, 1559.

Onomasticon: Theophrasti Paracelsi eigne aussslegung RECTE: außlegung etlicher seiner wörter vnd preparierungen. Basel, Pietro Perna 1575. Not an independent first version. In *Paracelsus, opus chyrugicum.* Strasbourg: Paul Messerschmidt 1566.

Herrlicher Philosophischer rhatschlag zu curirn Pestilentz / Brustgeschwer / Carfunckl. Without place name (Basel), 1577.

OTHER SOURCES

Jüttner, Guido. "Adam von Bodenstein." In *Die Deutsche Literatur: Biographisches und bibliographisches Lexikon.* Reihe 2: *Die Deutsche Literatur zwischen 1450 und 1620*, edited by Hans-Gert Roloff. Vol. 1, no. 43, part A, pp. 135–156; part B, p. 33. Bern: Peter Lang 1985.

Kühlmann, Wilhelm, and Joachim Telle, eds. *Corpus Paracelsisticum.* Vol. 1, *Der Frühparacelsismus: Erster Teil.* Early Modern Period, vol. 59, pp. 104–544. Tübingen: Niemeyer, 2001. Includes a biography and further readings.

Nutton, Vivian. "Der Luther der Medizin: Ein paracelsisches Paradoxon." In *Paracelsus: Das Werk, die Rezeption*, edited by Volker Zimmermann. Stuttgart: Franz Steiner Verlag, 1995.

Perifano, Alfredo. "Considérations autour de la question du Paracelsisme en Italie au XVIe siècle: Les dédicaces d'Adam de Bodenstein au Doge de Venise et à Côme Ier de Medicis." *Bibliothèque d'Humanisme et Renaissance* 62 (2000): 49–61.

Sudhoff, Karl. "Ein Beitrag zur Bibliographie der Paracelsisten." *Centralblatt für Bibliothekswesen* 10 (1893): 317–320; 11 (1894): 170.

———. *Versuch einer Kritik der Echtheit der Paracelsischen Schriften. I. Theil: Die unter Hohenheim's Namen erschienenen Druckschriften.* Berlin: Georg Riemer, 1894. Reprographic reprint under the title *Bibliographia Paracelsica: Besprechung der unter Theophrast von Hohenheims Namen 1527–1893 erschienenen Druckschriften.* Graz, Austria: Akademische Druck- und Verlagsanstalt, 1958.

Telle, Joachim. "Adam von Bodenstein." In *Literaturlexikon*, edited by Walther Killy. Vol. 2. Gütersloh and Munich: Bertelsmann Lexikon Verlag, 1989.

Trevor-Roper, Hugh. "The Court Physician and Paracelsianism." In *Medicine at the Courts of Europe, 1500–1837*, edited by Vivian Nutton, 79–94. London and New York: Routledge, 1990.

Walton, Michal T. "Iatrochemistry." In *Encyclopedia of the Scientific Revolution: From Copernicus to Newton*, edited by Wilbur Applebaum. New York: Garland, 2000.

Joachim Telle

BOER, JAN HENDRIK DE (*b.* Ruinen, Netherlands, 19 March 1899; *d.* The Hague, Netherlands, 26 April 1971), *inorganic chemistry, physical chemistry, industrial chemistry, catalysis, nuclear energy.*

De Boer was a prominent industrial chemist who combined a career in the management of industrial research, with scientific research of a high academic level. During the first half of the twentieth century he was considered one of the leading Dutch physical chemists. Together with Irving Langmuir of General Electric, de Boer belonged to a small group of chemists who contributed significantly both to solid state chemistry and to heterogeneous catalysis. As an all-round materials scientist he also became an important advisor to the Dutch government in the field of nuclear energy.

De Boer's most significant contributions to science are the development of a process for the separation and purification of transition metals such as hafnium, zirconium, and titanium (the so-called Van Arkel–de Boer process), the formulation of a theory (the de Boer–Mott model) on the so-called color centers (F-centers) in semiconductors, and the development of an improved method for the determination of the surface area and pore distribution of catalysts (the de Boer-t-curve). Together with Anton E. van Arkel, de Boer wrote an influential theoretical treatise on the structure of molecules and crystals, based on Walther Kossel's electrostatic theory. His theoretical work on Van der Waals–London forces and the role of electric "double layers" in colloids prepared the road for the DLVO theory (Derjaguin, Landau, Verwey, Overbeek) on the stability of colloids.

De Boer's scientific work stands out as a result of his ability to construct relatively simple theoretical models—often grounded in more advanced theories—with a great heuristic value for industrial and academic research. As research leader at three multinational corporations—Philips, Unilever, and DSM (Dutch State Mines)—de Boer contributed creatively to such diverse fields as solid state electronics, food research, and the ammonia synthesis for fertilizer production. "I have never met an investigator," Philips' research director Evert Verwey wrote in 1970, "who found his way so easily between experimental facts and simple theoretical concepts in his attempts to open new roads in science and technology. In the five years that I worked with him I was repeatedly struck by his flexible mind. No discouraging experiment could defeat him; on the contrary, an unexpected result or a new theoretical concept was always immediately incorporated in his arsenal and used successfully. He showed continually that he combined the typical traits of an inventor and of a scientist, a mixture rarely met in such high concentration, in a single person" (Verwey, 1970, p. xvi). De Boer published about 300 scientific papers and filed more than 150 original patents.

Childhood and Education. Jan Hendrik de Boer was born in Ruinen near Assen, in the northern part of the Netherlands, on 19 March 1899, the son of Jan de Boer, head of a primary school, and Jantina de Boer (née Somer). From 1912 to 1917 he went to the Hogere Burgerschool (a modern secondary school) in Assen. De Boer studied chemistry at the University of Groningen from 1917 to 1922. A year later, on 25 April 1923, he obtained the doctorate at Groningen with a dissertation on the synthesis and separation of the optical isomers of alpha-sulfobutyric acid.

De Boer from 1919 to 1921 became the assistant of Frans M. Jaeger, the professor of inorganic and physical chemistry at Groningen, who engaged him in the recovery of the metal ruthenium from waste products. De Boer also worked as a teacher of chemistry at a modern secondary school at Hoogezand, near Groningen. From 1921 to 1923 he was assistant to Hilmar J. Backer, the professor of organic chemistry at Groningen. He developed a keen interest in physical chemistry. Although his dissertation was on organic chemistry, it had a strong physical-chemical orientation. In November 1923 de Boer married Grietje Hilbrands. They had two daughters.

Research Chemist at Philips. In June 1923 de Boer was engaged as research chemist at the Natuurkundig Laboratorium (Physics Laboratory) of the N. V. Philips' Gloeilampenfabrieken (Philips' Incandescent Lamps Factories) at Eindhoven. This research laboratory, founded in 1914, was led by the physicist Gilles Holst. In 1922, just before de Boer's arrival, the Nat Lab, as the laboratory was commonly called, was still a modest research laboratory, with thirty-three employees, of which twelve were academics. In the following years, however, the laboratory expanded considerably. By 1940 there were 174 academic scientists among a total staff of 516.

One of the fields of expansion initiated by Holst was materials research. In 1921 Van Arkel had become the first chemist engaged by Holst for that purpose. Van Arkel tackled the purification of tungsten, the crucial metal in lamp filaments, and in 1923 discovered a process in which tungsten was purified via a (cyclical) sublimation process of tungsten hexachloride (WCl_6), followed by deposition of tungsten on a glowing tungsten wire. This followed research done by Irving Langmuir at General Electric and by F. Koref at Osram.

In 1923 the element hafnium was discovered in zirconium ores in the Copenhagen laboratory of Niels Bohr by the Hungarian chemist Georg (György) von Hevesy and the Dutch physicist Dirk Coster. Holst immediately decided to investigate the possibilities of zirconium and hafnium as filaments in incandescent lamps, instead of tungsten. At the advice of Wander J. de Haas, professor of physics at Groningen, who knew Holst from their student days in Leiden, Holst engaged de Boer for that purpose. De Haas had been on de Boer's dissertation committee and was impressed by the ingenuity of the latter to separate the optical isomers of alpha-sulfobutyric acid. Although this separation was very different from the problem of separating hafnium and zirconium, de Boer, together with Van Arkel, in 1924 developed a complicated, multistep, fractional crystallization process for the separation of the two metals.

The next target was their purification. De Boer first tried a process similar to the one invented by Van Arkel for the purification of tungsten, but the route via the chlorides did not work. De Boer then had the idea to try the tetra-iodides, in an autoclave at temperatures of about 800 centigrade, and that worked very well (Van Arkel and de Boer, 1925). Between 1926 and 1930, together with his research assistant Johan D. Fast, he successfully developed a large-scale, cyclical thermal process for the production of very pure, and ductile, hafnium, zirconium, titanium, thorium, vanadium, and other metals. Later, this so-called "Van Arkel–de Boer" process proved to be of great significance for the production of pure transition metals for the electronic industries, the aircraft industry, and the nuclear power industry.

During this same period, Holst and the theoretical physicist Paul Ehrenfest, who was research advisor to the Nat Lab, encouraged De Boer and Van Arkel to write a synthetic monograph on the chemical research on the structure of atoms, molecules, and crystals, thereby using the electrostatic theory developed by Kossel in 1916. The monograph *Chemische binding als electrostatisch verschijnsel* (Chemical Bonding as an Electrostatic Phenomenon), published by these two industrial chemists in 1930, had a long-lasting influence on academic inorganic and physical chemistry, both in the Netherlands and abroad. A German edition came out in 1931, and a French one in 1936. It showed the inorganic chemists that their field was more than a disparate collection of facts. Van Arkel and de Boer presented a theoretical framework that could make sense of a great number of chemical properties. And it showed the physical chemists that their work—then dominated in the Netherlands by thermodynamics and the phase rule —could be understood fruitfully in terms of intermolecular forces.

During the next decade the electrostatic theory showed its great power and heuristic value in the research at the Nat Lab. De Boer incorporated the ideas on crystal defects, formulated around 1930 by Adolph Smekal ("Locker-stellen"), Walter Schottky (vacancies), and Yakov Frenkel (interstitials), into the crystal models that Van Arkel and he had formulated. That helped him, together with Verwey, in 1936 to understand the electrical and magnetic properties of spinel type oxides, such as Fe_3O_4, Co_3O_4, and Mn_3O_4. These insights played a role in the research on magnetic ferrites at Philips, which proved of crucial strategic importance after World War II, when Philips exchanged its patent portfolio on ferrites with the transistor patents of Bell Labs. Building on the notion of crystal defects, de Boer also developed a model for understanding the luminescence of so called light-emitting "phosphors" such as potassium chloride, which found application in the production of x-ray screens and television screens. In 1937 Schottky's ideas helped de Boer in the formulation of his theory on color centers in semiconductors, which the next year was put into a more sophisticated form by the English physicist Nevill F. Mott. De Boer thus laid the foundations for a whole new area of research—"defect chemistry"—at Philips, which after World War II was developed successfully by chemists such as F.A. Kröger and Henny Vink.

From Photochemistry to Catalysis. In the meantime, de Boer's attention shifted increasingly to surface phenomena and colloid chemistry. Among the nine research groups at the Nat Lab in 1931, there were two groups on chemistry: Chemistry A, headed by Van Arkel, on solid state chemistry, and Chemistry B, headed by de Boer, on photochemistry. After Van Arkel left Philips in 1934 to become professor of inorganic and physical chemistry at Leiden, de Boer became the head of all the chemistry research at Philips. Although his work on photochemistry also included the emission of electrons and photons from inside the crystals (see above: phosphors; F-centers), many effects took place at the surface, or in layers of substances adsorbed at crystal surfaces. When the British surface chemist and catalysis expert Eric Rideal visited the Philips Nat Lab in March 1933, he invited de Boer to write a monograph for his *Cambridge Series on Physical Chemistry*, which would show how new insights on adsorption could be gained from the study of electron emission. Two years later de Boer's book *Electron Emission and Adsorption Phenomena* was published. It was a wide-ranging book with great relevance to the electronic industries, but also to parts of the chemical industries. It was soon translated into German, with a preface by Schottky of Siemens, and also into Russian. De Boer, by again using the electrostatic theory, was among the first to show how adsorption could be understood with the help of the same interatomic and intermolecular forces that were crucial to understanding the structures of crystals and molecules. With the help of potential energy diagrams, de Boer succeeded in giving insight into a great number of surface phenomena. Although the word *catalysis* does not appear in the index of the book, the theoretical insights on adsorption developed by de Boer had a relevance for that emerging field, and led in time to the setting up of the "Dutch School of Catalysis."

De Boer's work thus constituted a unique link between research within the electronic industries and research done by companies in the process industries. The same is true for several other of his pre-war contributions to surface chemistry and colloid science: theoretical work, together with H. C. Hamaker, on the non-isotropic nature of Van der Waals–London forces, and the electrical double layers of colloids (1936; 1937); the organization of a symposium (1936) on natural and artificial rubber, for which he cooperated with Dutch rubber scientists such as Johan R. Katz and Roel Houwink; the organization of a symposium on the dynamics of hydrophobic suspensions and emulsions (1937); and the organization of a symposium on proteins (1939).

At the eve of World War II, de Boer was the undisputed leader of chemical research at Philips and one of the leading physical chemists of the country. During his years at the Nat Lab he had published more than 140 scientific books and papers, and filed about 150 patents, by far the majority of those he would ever file. In 1940 he was elected an ordinary member of the Royal Netherlands Academy of Sciences. Moreover, he was the intended successor to Gilles Holst, as the leader of all research at Philips. Then, in September 1939, the war broke out and de Boer's career took a completely different turn.

War Years in London and Brussels. Because of the threat of war, the Dutch government in 1939 decided to create

the function of "officer-chemist" and to establish a Central Laboratory of the Supreme Command of the Army and the Navy, based inside the inorganic and organic laboratories of the University of Leiden. Jan de Boer was asked to become its director. He stayed in the employ of Philips, but was detached to the defense organization, with the rank of captain. In 1939 he set up a research team of "officer chemists" at Leiden who started research on the protection against chemical war gases by means of adsorption to active carbon and other materials.

On 10 May 1940 German forces crossed the Dutch border, and the Netherlands entered the war. After Rotterdam had been destroyed by the German Luftwaffe on 14 May, Queen Wilhelmina and the Dutch government left the country and went to London. The next day the Dutch commander in chief capitulated. On the same day, 15 May 1940, de Boer managed to escape with a fishing boat to England, together with one of his collaborators, J. van Ormondt, carrying all the technical papers and documents of the Central Laboratory.

After his arrival in London, de Boer succeeded in obtaining laboratory space in Imperial College in South Kensington. He led a small research team of Dutch chemists, which grew gradually during the war. They did chemical work for the Dutch government in exile, translated technical military papers into English, and did research for the British Ministry of Supply. Although a foreigner, de Boer was asked to become a member of the Chemical Warfare Board of the Ministry of Supply.

From 1942 onward he also was a member of the Buitengewone Raad van Advies (the Extraordinary Advisory Council) to the Dutch government in exile, which was set up as a kind of small parliament, under the pressure of industrialists such as Paul Rijkens, member of the board of Unilever. As a lieutenant-colonel, later colonel, de Boer in 1944 became head of the section on repatriation of the so-called Militair Gezag (Military Authority), a body created to govern the liberated parts of the Netherlands during the military operations in the country. It had the task of preparing the transition of the country from German occupation to a free democracy. In September 1944 de Boer arrived on the continent and was attached to the headquarters of the Military Authority in Brussels. He returned to London after German capitulation in May 1945, and stayed in the service of the military until 1946. In England, de Boer also met his second wife, Evangeline A. Malcolm Swanson, whom he married in March 1946, after a divorce from his first wife earlier that year. The second marriage was childless.

Research Leader at Unilever. In 1946 Gilles Holst retired as leader of the Nat Lab and of all corporate research and development at Philips. He was succeeded by a triumvirate: Henk Casimir (physics), Evert Verwey (chemistry), and Herre Rinia (electronics), but not by de Boer, who had decided for personal reasons, related to his divorce and second marriage, not to return to Eindhoven (report of a phone call of DSM director Jan van Aken with Gilles Holst, on 21 January 1950. Personal papers de Boer, DSM Archives; cf. de Boer, 1969, pp. 8–9). With the help of Unilever director Paul Rijkens, whom he knew well from their joint meetings within the Buitengewone Raad van Advies, de Boer succeeded in obtaining a leading research position at the British-Dutch multinational Unilever.

In 1946 de Boer started as manager of scientific research at the Unilever research laboratory at Port Sunlight, near Liverpool, with the specific task of setting up a Food Research Department for the company. This second British research center of Unilever was established in 1947 in Colworth House (Bedfordshire). De Boer had expected to become the director of the new research institute, but as a result of a conflict between the Dutch and the British members of the board of Unilever, he was not appointed. De Boer's views on industrial research played a crucial role in this conflict. He wanted to set up a research organization similar to the one created by Holst at Philips: with a true academic atmosphere, in which work of high scientific value was done, and in which publication in scientific journals was encouraged. This approach was unacceptable to the British board members, who preferred a greater degree of secrecy (report of a phone call of J. L. Poelhekke of DSM with Professor Hein Waterman of Delft, on 17 September 1949. Personal papers de Boer, DSM Archives).

As a result, de Boer decided to leave Unilever. He stayed in Colworth House from 1948 until 1950, and wrote a textbook on adsorption during this period (see below). In the meantime, he tried to secure a new research position elsewhere. With the help of his friend and colleague Hein Waterman, professor of chemical technology at Delft, de Boer succeeded in finding a new job at Staatsmijnen (DSM; Dutch State Mines) in March 1950.

Professor of Catalysis at Delft. In 1946 Waterman had already offered de Boer a part-time professorship of chemical technology at the Technological University at Delft. After consultation with Unilever, de Boer accepted the offer. As a result, he traveled every month for two days to Delft, acted the next day as an advisor of the Unilever research laboratory at Zwijndrecht, near Rotterdam, and went on Saturday to the monthly meeting of the Royal Netherlands Academy of Sciences, at Amsterdam.

De Boer decided to focus his research and teaching at Delft on catalysis, a field that was not represented at any of the Dutch universities. In his inaugural lecture of 23

May 1946 on *Monomoleculaire lagen in de chemische industrie* (Monomolecular layers in the chemical industry) he presented a broad picture of the role of surface phenomena in industry: in separation processes; in mixing and adhesion; and in chemical processes, such as photochemical and catalytic processes. Adsorption and Van der Waals forces were the focus of this lecture, and their investigation would occupy de Boer during the next twenty-three years as a part-time professor at Delft.

The monthly lectures that he gave during the first years of his professorship "were very popular as they gave lucid and vivid explanations of the fundamentals, avoiding unneeded bookishness, instead using straightforward models and examples" (Steggerda, 1994, p. 84). They resulted in a review paper on "Atomic Forces and Adsorption" for *Advances in Colloid Science* (1950), and a textbook called *The Dynamical Character of Adsorption* which was written during de Boer's stay at Unilever but published in 1953. That book shows de Boer's didactic qualities at their best: It is lucidly written, well structured, and clear. With the help of the kinetic theory of gases, de Boer succeeded in creating "a picture of adsorption" that would stay in the minds of his students. He visualized the phenomena as an imaginary "gas of super bees," and structured the content of his book in terms of a small number of crucial parameters: the number of molecules striking a unit area of surface in a unit time; the time of adsorption; and the amount of adsorbed molecules per unit area (de Boer, 1953, pp. v, 1–3).

After his return to Holland in 1950, de Boer started to build a research team at Delft. He supervised at least twenty-six doctoral dissertations. Several of his students later became university professors themselves: Piet Mars, Jacques Coenen, John Geus, and Jos Scholten in catalysis, Jan Steggerda in inorganic chemistry, and Jan Fortuin in chemical engineering. Others, such as Hans Linsen of Unilever, became research leaders in industry. Before 1960 the research was somewhat hampered by the poor equipment of the Delft laboratory, but even though de Boer visited the laboratory only a few days a months, and left his PhD students finding their own way most of the time, he succeeded in creating a true research spirit in which new results on adsorption on, especially, alumina, silica, and Ni-silica catalysts could be obtained with simple means.

The trademark of the Dutch School of Catalysis, as shaped by de Boer, was its focus on the investigation of the structure and texture of catalysts. Together with his students, and partly in his other roles, described below, de Boer again published about 150 scientific papers between 1946 and his untimely death in 1971. The phase transitions of alumina were studied, which were important for the understanding of the activation process of alumina supported catalysts. The research done on nitrogen adsorption isotherms that were used for the determination of the surface areas of catalysts was also important. De Boer succeeded in finding a better alternative for the popular BET-equation (Brunauer, Emmett, and Teller), and with the help of theoretical studies on the two-dimensional Van der Waals equation, on two-dimensional phase transitions, and on the entropy of adsorption, he developed the so-called t-method that is still used in the early twenty-first century. In this way, he offered a theoretical foundation to the experimental result—studied in detail by his students Ben Lippens and Hans Linsen between 1961 and 1964—that the volume of adsorbed nitrogen plotted as a function of the relative pressure follows a common t-curve for a great variety of adsorbents and catalysts. In the course of the 1960s, de Boer and his students Hans Broekhoff and Linsen succeeded in developing this t-curve method not only for the determination of the surface areas, but also for the pore size distribution of catalysts. This gave a better understanding of the chemical activity of catalysts.

De Boer had a large network of international contacts, and he organized several national and international conferences, such as the symposium on "The Mechanism of Heterogeneous Catalysis" in 1959, and one on "Reactivity of Solids" in 1960. In 1956 he received an honorary doctorate from the Technological University of Hannover.

Scientific Advisor at DSM. When de Boer started to work for Staatsmijnen (DSM), on 1 March 1950, the Central Laboratory of that company had a staff of 420 persons, with about fifty academics among them. The day-to-day research work was supervised by Dick van Krevelen, who created an academic atmosphere in the laboratory, following the example of the Philips Nat Lab. The overall supervision of all research and development at DSM was in the hands of Gé Berkhoff. Therefore, there was no clear position available for de Boer within the hierarchy of the DSM research organization, and it was decided to give him an independent role as scientific advisor to board member Jan van Aken, who was responsible for the chemical division of the company, as well as for research.

De Boer must have felt at home in the academic atmosphere of the laboratory, which he had helped to shape himself in the 1930s, when DSM board member F. K. Th. van Iterson had visited him frequently at home on Sunday mornings to get advice on the creation of a research laboratory at DSM (de Boer, 1969, pp. 9–10). He encouraged fundamental research on the mechanism of the ammonia synthesis at DSM, within the physical chemistry group, headed by Henk de Bruijn, and later by Cor van Heerden. The catalyst used for that process was made by the reduction of the iron oxide Fe_3O_4 (magnetite), a material that de Boer knew very well from his research at Philips. At the first Dutch conference on catalysis, organized by de Boer in 1951, he gave an opening lecture on theoretical ideas on the mechanism of the catalytic synthesis of ammonia. Four years later his collaborators wrote an extensive review article on the "Research on Ammonia Synthesis since 1940." In 1959 three of his coworkers again reviewed the mechanism of the ammonia synthesis (Mars, Scholten, and Zwietering, in de Boer, 1960, pp. 66–89).

Apart from this fundamental research on catalysis, de Boer mainly acted as a go-between for academia and industry. He liaised with the external academic advisors to DSM, and was a member of numerous advisory bodies and committees. From 1953 to 1955 he was president of the Koninklijke Nederlandse Chemische Vereniging (Royal Dutch Chemical Society), and from that position he founded the Dutch research organization for fundamental chemical research, Scheikundig Onderzoek Nederland (SON), which acted as a national funding agency from 1956 onward. In September 1961 the Dutch government asked de Boer to become the chairman of the newly established Wetenschappelijke Raad voor de Kernenergie (WRK; Scientific Council for Nuclear Energy). This was an almost full-time position. De Boer left DSM, and until his retirement in 1969 he chaired this important advisory body.

Nuclear Energy. De Boer's involvement with nuclear energy had started in 1950, almost immediately after his return to his home country. Already on 17 March, his friend and successor at Philips Nat Lab, Evert Verwey, asked his advice about the technical purification of a large stock of uranium oxide, bought by Dutch government in 1939 on the advice of Wander J. de Haas, and hidden from the Germans during World War II. Later that year The Netherlands and Norway agreed to collaborate in building a nuclear research reactor at Kjeller, Norway. Together, both countries had the essential ingredients: Holland had its stock of uranium, and Norway was in the possession of heavy water. A Joint Committee was coordinating the effort, and de Boer became one of its deputy members. At the end of 1950 the national physics research organization, Fundamenteel Onderzoek der Materie (FOM; Fundamental Research of Matter), established a Reactor Committee, of which de Boer became a member. His knowledge of materials science, of metals especially, was of great value to the Dutch-Norwegian project. He solved several problems, and also send de Bruijn and other DSM chemists to Norway to investigate radiochemical issues that played a role during the construction of the reactor.

In 1955 the Dutch government decided to build a nuclear research reactor in the Netherlands and founded the Reactor-Centrum Nederland (RCN). The same year, de Boer became chairman of the Wetenschappelijke Advies Raad (WAR; Scientific Advisory Council) of RCN, and from then on he played a key role in science policy with respect to nuclear research. Between 1955 and 1969 he was involved in almost all major decisions about nuclear energy, cooperating closely with the research leaders of Shell, Philips, Werkspoor, and the other companies that were participating in the Dutch nuclear energy effort. Already during the 1950s, together with his collaborators de Bruijn and Jan Houtman, he had cooperated closely with scientists of KEMA, the research organization of the Dutch electricity companies, in the construction of a so-called suspension reactor. He also encouraged the initiative to develop on an industrial scale the ideas of the physicist Jaap Kistemaker on uranium enrichment by ultracentrifuges. This ultimately led, in 1971, to the founding of the Dutch-German-British company Urenco (Uranium Enrichment Corporation) in 1971, which has produced enriched uranium in the Netherlands since 1976.

In 1958 he chaired the Dutch delegation at the Second International United Nations Conference on the Peaceful Applications of Nuclear Energy in Geneva. Given his multiple roles in this field, his appointment to chairman of the WRK was no surprise. Between 1962 and 1969 de Boer and his Council wrote about 135 advisory reports on all aspects related to nuclear research, from medical applications to radioactive waste. From 1963 to 1969 he also chaired the Centrale Raad voor de Kernenergie (Central Advisory Council on Nuclear Energy), which coordinated the industrial and scientific efforts. Although undoubtedly *the* spider in the Dutch nuclear web of the 1960s, his multiple roles also caused problems. After a conflict with the board of directors of RCN, he resigned as chairman of the WAR in 1967.

On 26 April 1971, Jan de Boer suddenly passed away. Those who knew him were impressed by his flexible mind, which had involved him in so many different fields, although sometimes the critique was voiced that, without being pedantic, de Boer was too often a "schoolmaster." Clearly his father's profession had left its stamp on him.

BIBLIOGRAPHY

Museum Boerhaave, Bibliotheek, Leiden, the Netherlands, houses a set of offprints of de Boer's scientific papers, 1920–1972. At Teyler's Museum, Haarlem, are physical artifacts produced by De Boer, such as a zirconium rod and lamps with zirconium filaments. The Regionaal Historisch Centrum Limburg, Maastricht, the Netherlands, houses the archive of the DSM company, including the personal files of J. H. de Boer (with a full list of his publications until 1949).

WORKS BY DE BOER

With A. E. Van Arkel. "Darstellung von reinem Titanium-, Zirkonium-, Hafnium- und Thoriummetall." *Zeitschrift für Anorganische und Allgemeine Chemie* 148 (1925): 345–350.

———. *Chemische binding als electrostatisch verschijnsel.* Amsterdam: D.B. Centen, 1930, and *Supplement van "Chemische Binding."* Amsterdam: D.B. Centen, 1937.

———. *Chemische Bindung als elektrostatische Erscheinung.* Leipzig: Hirzel, 1931.

Electron Emission and Adsorption Phenomena. Cambridge: Cambridge University Press, 1935.

Monomoleculaire lagen in de chemische industrie. Delft: Technische Hoogeschool, 1946.

The Dynamical Character of Adsorption. Oxford: Clarendon Press, 1953.

As editor. *Proceedings of the Symposium on the Mechanism of Heterogeneous Catalysis, 12–13 November 1959, Amsterdam (The Netherlands).* Amsterdam, London, and New York: Elsevier, 1960.

Van het Een komt het Ander. Afscheidscollege gehouden op 26 juni 1969. Delft: Waltman, 1969. This is a brief and selective autobiography.

OTHER SOURCES

Andriesse, C. D. *De Republiek der Kerngeleerden.* Bergen, NH: Beta Text, 2000. On the history of nuclear energy research in the Netherlands, 1962–1984.

Boersma, Kees. *Inventing Structures for Industrial Research: A History of the Philips Nat Lab, 1914–1946.* Amsterdam. Aksant, 2002.

Bokhoven, C.; C. van Heerden; R. Westrik; and P. Zwietering. "Research on Ammonia Synthesis since 1940." In *Catalysis.* Vol. III: *Hydrogenation and Dehydrogenation,* edited by Paul H. Emmett, 265–348. New York: Reinhold, 1955.

Burgers, Willy C. "Een persoonlijke herinnering aan prof. dr. J. H. de Boer." *Chemische Weekblad* 67 (11 June 1971): 17–18.

De Vries, Marc J., with contributions by Kees Boersma. *Eighty Years of Research at the Philips Natuurkundig Laboratorium (1914–1994). The Role of the Nat Lab at Philips.* Amsterdam: Pallas Publications, 2005.

Goedkoop, Jaap A. *Een kernreactor bouwen. Geschiedenis van de Stichting Energieonderzoek Centrum Nederland. Deel 1: Periode 1945–1962.* Bergen, NH: Beta Text, 1995. On the history of nuclear energy research in the Netherlands until 1962.

Le Pair, C., and J. Volger, eds. *Physics in the Netherlands: A Selection of Dutch Contributions to Physics in the First Thirty Years after the Second World War.* 2 vols. Utrecht: FOM, 1982.

Linsen, B. G.; J. M. H. Fortuin; C. Okkerse; and J. J. Steggerda, eds. *Physical and Chemical Aspects of Adsorbents and Catalysts, Dedicated to J. H. de Boer on the Occasion of His Retirement from the Technological University Delft, The Netherlands.* London and New York: Academic Press, 1970.

Scholten, Jos J. F. "Heterogene katalyse: de moeizame weg naar wetenschappelijk inzicht." In *De geschiedenis van de scheikunde in Nederland 3: De ontwikkeling van de chemie van 1945 tot het begin van de jaren tachtig,* edited by Ernst

Homburg and Lodewijk Palm, 193–211. Delft: Delft University Press, 2004.

———, ed. *A Short History of the Dutch School of Catalysis.* The Hague: Royal Netherlands Chemical Society, May 1994.

Schuit, George C. A. "J. H. de Boer and Heterogeneous Catalysis. The Period after 1945." In *Physical and Chemical Aspects of Adsorbents and Catalysts*, edited by B.G. Linsen et al., pp. xix–xxiv. London and New York: Academic Press, 1970.

Snelders, Harry A. M. "Boer, Jan Hendrik de." In *Biografisch woordenboek van Nederland*, volume 4, edited by J. Charité and A. J. C. M. Gabriëls, pp. 45–47. 's-Gravenhage: Instituut voor Nederlandse Geschiedenis, 1994.

———. *De geschiedenis van de scheikunde in Nederland 2: De ontwikkeling van chemie en chemische technologie in de eerste helft van de twintigste eeuw.* Delft: Delft University Press, 1997. On the history of Dutch chemistry, 1900–1950.

Steggerda, Jan J. "The Delft School of Catalysis of J. H. de Boer (1946–1969). In *A Short History of the Dutch School of Catalysis*, edited by Jos J. F. Scholten, pp. 83–86. The Hague: Royal Netherlands Chemical Society, 1994.

Verwey, Evert J. W. "Dr. J. H. de Boer." *Chemisch Weekblad* 37 (1940): 311.

———. "J. H. de Boer and the Inorganic and Physical Chemistry. The Period 1923–1940." In *Physical and Chemical Aspects of Adsorbents and Catalysts*, edited by B.G. Linsen et al., pp. xiii–xvii. London and New York: Academic Press, 1970.

———. "Levensbericht van Jan Hendrik de Boer (19 maart 1899–25 april 1971 [sic])." *Jaarboek 1971 der Koninklijke Nederlandse Akademie van Wetenschappen*, pp. 88–93. Amsterdam: Noord-Hollandsche Uitgevers Maatschappij, 1972.

Ernst Homburg

BOGOLUBOV, NIKOLAI NIKO-LAEVICH (*b.* Nizhny Novgorod, Russia, 21 [old style 8] August 1909; *d.* Moscow, Russia, 13 February 1992), *mathematics, theoretical physics.*

Bogolubov (the name can also be spelled Bogolyubov or Bogoliubov) was a prominent Russian and Ukrainian mathematician and mathematical physicist, one of the founders of non-linear mechanics and the quantum theory of many-body systems. Bogolubov also developed fundamental mathematical methods in kinetic theory, quantum statistics, quantum field theory, and the theories of superfluidity and superconductivity.

In Lieu of Education. Bogolubov descended from a family line of Russian Orthodox priests. His father, Nikolai Mikhailovich, taught philosophy and theology at a seminary in Nizhny Novgorod, and later at Kiev University; his mother, Olga Nikolayevna, gave music lessons. Nikolai was the oldest of the family's three sons, all of whom eventually became prominent scientists. The boy's childhood coincided with the turbulent period of the Russian revolution. He was mainly self-taught and received little formal education, other than a certificate from a seven-year secondary school in a Ukrainian village, where the family survived during the years of the Civil War, 1919–1921, and where his father served as a parish priest after his university chair of theology was closed by revolutionary authorities. During those village years, family friends and relatives aroused Nikolai's interest in mathematics and noticed his exceptional aptitude for the subject.

In 1921 the Bogolubov family returned to Kiev, where the father accepted another parish. With the help of old faculty acquaintances, he obtained permission for his thirteen-year-old son to start attending an advanced university seminar in mathematics. There Nikolai's talents came to the attention of a senior mathematician, Nikolai Mitrofanovich Krylov (1879-1955), who held the chair of mathematical physics at the recently organized Ukrainian Academy of Sciences. Krylov took the boy under his informal patronage and tutelage, and also offered him room and board at his house in 1925, after the rest of the Bogolubov family left Kiev and returned to Nizhny Novgorod following the father's new church appointment. The same year Krylov obtained for Nikolai status at the Academy of Sciences as an *aspirant*, which was a junior academic position similar to that of graduate student. Because of Bogolubov's "phenomenal talents" and advanced knowledge of mathematics, an exception was made to his minor age and lack of university courses. The Soviet educational system, in general, allowed much flexibility in the early post-revolutionary period: It was undergoing many different reforms and often permitted young students to skip certain formal stages and degrees in their scientific education.

At the age of fifteen Bogolubov published his first research paper. Many of his early works were authored together with Krylov in the latter's fields of specialization: variational calculus, differential equations, approximate solutions. Sometimes they published their important results only in Ukrainian, sometimes in Russian, English, or French. Some papers appeared in established international journals with wide circulation, others in small and rare local publications. In 1930 the Bologna Academy of Sciences recognized one of Bogolubov's early accomplishments with its special prize. Earlier that year the twenty-one-year-old completed his graduate studies and received from the Ukrainian Academy of Sciences the degree of Doctor of Mathematics. He continued working under Krylov's supervision as research associate at the Academy.

Non-linear Mechanics. Starting around 1932, Bogolubov and Krylov extended their joint research from well established branches of mathematics to a new and practically unexplored area. In the course of the crash industrialization campaign in the Soviet Union, scientists came under increased pressure to turn their research work toward practical goals and produce immediately applicable results. Krylov, a mining engineer by initial education, was well prepared for the challenge, which led him and Bogolubov to a new class of mathematical problems, the theory of non-linear oscillations.

Some non-linear differential equations had previously been studied by Henri Poincaré in celestial mechanics, in the case of conservative systems. Krylov engaged in collaboration with the Institute of the Mechanics of Buildings and some other industrial research sites in Ukraine concerned with construction of power stations and aviation. In all these unrelated branches of industry he and Bogolubov encountered phenomena and practical problems that involved non-linear oscillations in essentially non-conservative systems. In the practically unlimited range of important cases, the oscillation process was close enough to the linear, harmonic one, whereas the non-linear part could be regarded as a small perturbation, resulting in the dependence of the period of oscillation upon the amplitude.

Krylov and Bogolubov developed methods of asymptotic integration for large classes of corresponding non linear differential equations with a small parameter, extending the methods of perturbation theory onto non-conservative systems in general. They studied invariant manifolds in phase space and developed methods for direct computation and approximations of periodic solutions. The results were important not only for fundamental mathematics, but also for solving practical problems in various fields of engineering. Their method of describing function (quasi-linearization), in particular, proved essential for the new field of non-linear control engineering developed since World War II.

At about the same time, starting 1930, and for analogous reasons, another group of Soviet researchers around Leonid I. Mandelstam and Aleksandr A. Andronov in Moscow and Nizhny Novgorod attacked similar problems with non-linear equations and oscillations arising from the tasks of radio engineering and communications. Combined, their work and the work of the Kiev group around Krylov and Bogolubov established a new research community and a subdiscipline within mathematical sciences, which they called non-linear mechanics. Krylov and Bogolubov summarized their main contributions to the field in a 1937 book, *Introduction to Non-Linear Mechanics*, translated into English by Solomon Lefschetz in 1943.

Recognition amidst Troubled Times. During the height of the Soviet anti-religious campaign around 1930, Bogolubov's father was imprisoned for almost three years. Bogolubov reportedly sought advice of the Russian Church leader and would-be patriarch Metropolitan Sergius and requested an appointment with the head of the Soviet state police, Vyacheslav S. Menzhinsky, which eventually won his father's release from prison. By accounts of those who knew him well, Bogolubov held deep and sincere religious beliefs throughout his entire life. At the same time, he also operated perfectly smoothly within the avowedly and often militantly atheistic Soviet polity, so that his absolute political loyalty could never be doubted. How exactly he justified to himself the apparent contradiction and managed the situation is hard to answer, because he kept his thoughts on the matter largely to himself.

His academic rise, in any case, was fast and steady. From 1936 onward, while holding a research position at the Ukrainian Academy, Bogolubov also taught as professor at Kiev University. He traveled abroad to conferences in France and Belgium in the years preceding World War II, when the Soviet Union already severely restricted its citizens' foreign contacts and granted permission for foreign travel only on very rare exceptions. Bogolubov married Yevgeniya Aleksandrovna Pirashkova in 1937 and in 1939 was elected to the Ukrainian Academy of Sciences as a corresponding member. After the 1939 Soviet annexation of Bukowina, the formerly Austrian part of western Ukraine that had belonged to Romania since World War I, he was commissioned to visit the University of Chernivtsi to help reorganize and modernize the university curriculum along the Soviet pattern.

Fleeing Hitler's 1941 attack on the Soviet Union and the occupation of Ukraine by German troops, most academic institutions were evacuated from Kiev to the east. In 1941–1943 Krylov and Bogolubov worked and lived in poor conditions in Ufa near the Ural mountains. They applied their computational methods to new problems in war production, in particular to non-linear resonance in aviation engines. They also responded to criticism by some mathematicians regarding the difficult problem of divergence of approximate solutions by upgrading non-linear mechanics to a much higher level of generality. Their related investigations extended into the general abstract theory of dynamical systems, in particular the qualitative analysis of equations in non-linear mechanics, introduction of ergodic sets, and the Krylov-Bogolubov theorem proving the existence of invariant measure.

As the war fortunes reversed, Bogolubov returned from the evacuation, at first to Moscow in 1943, and in 1944 to the recently liberated Kiev. As the Dean of the Department of Mathematics and Mechanics, he handled the difficult tasks of the postwar and post-occupation reconstruction of Kiev University. Bogolubov applied his new methods of perturbation theory also to the problems of statistical mechanics. Already in 1939, together with Krylov, he published a paper on the Fokker-Planck equation and the emergence of stochastic regularities in dynamical systems, followed by a series of investigations on the theory of stochastic differential equations and chains. Bogolubov's idea of the hierarchy of times in non-stationary statistical physics, in particular, became crucially important for the subsequent development of the statistical theory of irreversible processes. In the classic 1946 monograph, *Problems of Dynamical Theory in Statistical Physics,* Bogolubov developed the method of chains of equations for the distribution functions in both equilibrium and non-equilibrium statistical mechanics and derived kinetic equations for systems with various types of interactions (short-range, and long-range Coulomb forces). The book laid foundations for the subsequent development of non-equilibrium statistical mechanics. In 1947 Bogolubov was elected to the USSR Academy of Sciences as corresponding member, and the following year the Ukrainian Academy promoted him to full member.

Theoretical Physics and Many-Body Systems. In the postwar years Bogolubov's research style and interests changed. Up until 1941 he published mostly in collaboration with Krylov, a teacher and colleague many years his senior. After the war, Krylov's advanced age and increasingly poor eyesight hampered his research activities. Bogolubov, now in his mid-thirties, became a widely recognized scholar leading independent new programs of investigations often in collaboration with junior students and research associates. Together with Yuri Alekseyevich Mitropolsky, Bogolubov continued developing non-linear mechanics and asymptotic methods of mathematical physics, including the method of quick convergence, but more and more of his time was devoted to theoretical physics, where he used his superior powers as a mathematician to help attack some of the most central and difficult problems in the field.

One such problem, generally considered insoluble in both classical and quantum theory, concerns the treatment of many-particle systems with interactions. Even when the forces and the laws of movement governing individual particles are known exactly, the situation when several such particles mutually and simultaneously influence one another cannot be resolved mathematically. Only when such interactions could be considered severely limited, such as in the model of ideal gas where particles are rare, classical physics was able to develop extremely powerful mathematical descriptions and methods. Such descriptions could also be modified to the case of quantum—but still non-interacting—particles, in the model of

an ideal quantum gas. While enormously successful in their proper domain, ideal-gas descriptions were hard to apply realistically in the cases of many real-life systems when constituent particles are packed together closely and strongly interact with each other, such as in liquids, solids, and condensed matter in general.

One promising strategy of circumventing insurmountable mathematical difficulties had been initiated by Soviet theorists Yakov Il'ich Frenkel and Lev Davidovich Landau. They suggested treating particles in condensed matter collectivistically rather than individually and proposed models of so-called "collectivized particles" or "elementary excitations," which were the quanta of collective movement of many constituent particles at once. With the help of such assumptions, Landau in 1941 explained the strange property of superfluidity in liquid helium. Despite successful applications, some basic ideas behind the collectivist approach were intuitive rather than rigorous, and in the absence of solid proof, aroused controversy. In 1947 Bogolubov refuted such doubts by demonstrating mathematically how collective excitations, which he called "quasiparticles," arise naturally in the model of an ideal gas, when one adds a weak interaction between its particles. The solution could be found if the interaction was sufficiently small, but already in this case it reproduced the main features of the collective excitation model and helped to justify the general approach.

Bogolubov's paper proved enormously influential internationally, as it established the quasiparticle concept on a solid mathematical foundation and essentially transformed it into a universally accepted method, the basic tool of contemporary quantum physics of condensed matter. In the case of a non-ideal Bose gas, his microscopic theory of 1947 justified and somewhat corrected Landau's more phenomenological theory of superfluidity. In the case of a non-ideal Fermi gas, Bogolubov with collaborators in 1958 developed some earlier ideas of Herbert Fröhlich and Leon N. Cooper into a consistent quantum theory of superconductivity. Their theory appeared practically simultaneously and independently of a similar microscopic explanation of superconductivity achieved by a different method by John Bardeen in collaboration with Cooper and J. Robert Schrieffer (the BCS theory of superconductivity). The same year Bogolubov also applied the quasiparticle approach to the treatment of atomic nucleus predicting nuclear superfluidity.

Quantum Field Theory and the "Bogolubov School." Like many leading Soviet physicists of the immediate postwar period, Bogolubov was invited to participate in the atomic project and in 1948 joined a classified research group at the Institute for Chemical Physics in Moscow. He never fully abandoned connections to Kiev and Ukraine, but started teaching part-time at Moscow University, spending increasing amounts of time in the capital, for several years maintaining two residences, and eventually relocating to Moscow. Although Bogolubov did not play a central role in the development of atomic weapons, in 1950–1953 he lived and worked in a secret location, later known as Arzamas-16, where the Soviet analog of the Manhattan Project's Los Alamos laboratory operated (the town's original historic name, Sarov, was restored to it only during the post-Soviet era). After the successful test of the first hydrogen bomb in 1953, Bogolubov returned to civilian research. That same year he became a full member of the Soviet Academy of Sciences, the highest rank in the country's academic hierarchy.

From 1950 on Bogolubov's interests extended to quantum field theory, where he could apply successfully his already developed mathematical treatments of many-body systems, as well as new methods. He founded his approach on Heisenberg's S-matrix formalism with the goal of achieving a more rigorous and consistent representation of renormalization procedures. On the basis of the "Bogolubov microcausality condition," in 1956 he provided a rigorous proof of dispersion relations, the line of research that eventually led Bogolubov to the so-called axiomatic formulation of quantum field theory. Together with Dmitry V. Shirkov, he also proposed in 1955 the renormalization group method, an extremely useful tool in practical calculations in quantum electrodynamics. In 1961–1963 Bogolubov suggested the mathematical idea of quasi-averages in statistical physics, which proved instrumental for the development of the general concept of broken symmetry and the modern theory of phase transitions. The 1964–1965 papers by Bogolubov and coauthors analyzed the symmetry properties of quark models in strong interactions and introduced a new quantum number for quarks, which subsequently became known as quark's color.

As one of the country's top-ranked scientists, Bogolubov accepted an increasing number of administrative appointments at various academic and research institutions. From 1949 on he directed the theoretical physics department at the V.A. Steklov Mathematical Institute of the USSR Academy of Sciences, and from 1953 headed the chair of theoretical physics at Moscow State University. In 1956 Bogolubov organized the theoretical physics laboratory at the Joint Institute for Nuclear Research in Dubna near Moscow and led it until 1965, when he was elected director of the entire institute. In 1966 he successfully lobbied for the creation of the Institute of Theoretical Physics at the Ukrainian Academy of Sciences in Kiev and became its first director. In all this academic entrepreneurship, Bogolubov proved extremely capable of working and manipulating the bureaucratic labyrinths of the Soviet political and administrative system. But he never became a Communist Party member, which in the late Soviet period was typically expected of an administrator at such high rank. The expanding number of institutions he and his associates controlled served as the seats for the flourishing "Bogolubov school of theoretical physics."

The clustering of the academic community into "research schools," clan-like groups around top-ranked scientists, became a common social phenomenon in late Soviet science. Scientific schools cultivated high esprit de corps and educated and nurtured their members from the late college years onward. They maintained distinctive research programs and styles, and a researcher often remained associated with a chosen school for his or her entire academic career. Typically scientific schools did not mix, and their members tended to work together in the same or friendly institutions. Soviet scientists often perceived the existence of such schools as a natural and necessary feature of science itself, universal and beneficial for the very progress of knowledge. Administrative leaders of Soviet science were expected to establish and maintain their own schools in the institutions they headed, and as their associates matured, if an opportunity availed itself, branch out and occupy or establish new institutes and laboratories. During the late Soviet period in the discipline of theoretical physics, two scientific schools were particularly successful in pursuing such a strategy—one associated with Bogolubov, the other with Landau. They respected each other's accomplishments and often profited from each other's ideas, but also developed a strong sense of institutional rivalry and competition for resources, positions, national and international reputation. To a significant degree, the school identities and rivalries survived the death of their founders and continued well into the post-Soviet era.

Bogolubov's ideas and methods spread to become classical, working, and indispensable tools in numerous branches of the exact sciences. He received almost every possible recognition—national as well as international—except the Nobel Prize, which somehow avoided him even though more than one of his accomplishments could have deserved it. By the time he retired from most of his administrative duties in 1989 at the age of eighty, the society around him was in a state of utter turmoil. Mikhail Gorbachev's perestroika unleashed social forces that would ultimately destroy the Soviet Union and, along with it, much of the scientific empire, infrastructure, and research community Bogolubov so carefully created as a result of many laborious years. Scholars do not quite know how he perceived and lived with this new contradiction in life, but in his last public statement he welcomed the news of the restoration and reopening to believers of the church in Nizhny Novgorod where his father once served as a priest.

Nikolai Bogolubov. *Bogolubov at CERN, Geneva, in 1966.* **CERN/SCIENCE PHOTO LIBRARY/PHOTO RESEARCHERS, INC.**

BIBLIOGRAPHY

WORKS BY BOGOLUBOV

With Nikolai M. Krylov. "Sur les equations de Focker-Planck déduites dans la théorie des perturbations à l'aide dune méthode basée sur les propriétés spectrales de l'hamiltonien perturbateur." *Zapiski kafedri matematichnoi fiziki AN URSR* 4 (1939): 5– 157.

With Nikolai M. Kryloff. *Introduction to Non-Linear Mechanics,* translated by Solomon Lefschetz. Princeton, NJ: Princeton University Press, 1943. Russian originals published in 1934 and 1937.

Problems of a Dynamical Theory in Statistical Physics. Cambridge, MA: Harvard University Press, 1959. Russian original, 1946.

"On the Theory of Superfluidity." *Journal of Physics* 11 (1947): 23–32.

Lectures on Quantum Statistics. Edited by Lewis Klein and Solomon Glass. London: Macdonald, 1968. Ukrainian original, 1949.

With Yuri A. Mitropolsky. *Asymptotic Methods in the Theory of Non-Linear Oscillations.* New York: Gordon and Breach, 1961. Russian original, 1955.

With Dmitrii V. Shirkov. "Charge Renormalization Group in Quantum Field Theory." *Nuovo Cimento* 3 (1956): 845–863.

With Dmitrii V. Shirkov. *Introduction to the Theory of Quantized Fields,* translated by G.M. Volkoff. New York: Interscience, 1959. Russian original, 1957.

With Vladimir V. Tolmachev and Dmitrii V. Shirkov. *A New Method in the Theory of Superconductivity.* New York: Consultants Bureau, 1959. Russian original, 1958.

With Anatoli A. Logunov and Ivan T. Todorov. *Introduction to Axiomatic Quantum Field Theory.* Reading, MA: W.A. Benjamin, 1975. Russian original, 1969.

Selected Works, 4 vols. Edited by A.M. Kurbatov. New York: Gordon and Breach, 1990–1995. Published in Russian in 3 volumes (Kiev, 1969–1971). A twelve-volume Russian edition of *Collected Works* is being prepared, with several volumes already published as of 2007.

OTHER SOURCES

Nikolai Nikolaevich Bogoliubov: Matematik, Mekhanik, Fizik. Dubna, Russia: Ob'edinennyi institut iadernykh issledovanii, 1994. A volume of recollections and essays by Bogolubov's students and coworkers.

Nikolai Nikolaevich Bogoliubov. Dubna, Russia: Ob'edinennyi institut iadernykh issledovanii, 1989; updated edition, 2004. Edited by Dmitrii V. Shirkov and Alexei N. Sisakian. The full bibliography, plus a biographical essay and a review of major works.

Alexei Kojevnikov

BOHM, DAVID JOSEPH (*b.* Wilkes-Barre, Pennsylvania, 20 December 1917; *d.* London, United Kingdom, 27 October 1992), *theoretical physics, quantum mechanics, philosophy of physics.*

Among the first generation of American physicists to receive his advanced training in the United States, Bohm initially distinguished himself with his work in plasma physics. It is, however, his work in quantum physics and his attempt to develop an alternative to the standard interpretation of quantum mechanics for which he is most remembered in the early twenty-first century. His work on more esoteric philosophical matters, beginning in the 1960s, attracted a substantial group of admirers for whom the details of his work in physics were of lesser importance.

Early Years and Education. David Joseph Bohm was born on 20 December 1917, the eldest child of Eastern European Jewish immigrants, Samuel and Frieda Bohm, in the Pennsylvania mining town of Wilkes-Barre. Although Samuel enjoyed success as a small businessman and the family was secure financially, David's childhood was not ideal. His mother suffered from mental instability, which rendered her largely incapable of taking care of her children. His father's focus on the social and more practical aspects of life led to conflict with a son who was shy, socially awkward, and more interested in science fiction. In spite of David's early interest Samuel discouraged a scientific career as impractical.

During his high school years David began to take an interest in the more political and societal aspects of the world around him. Growing up in a mining town during the Great Depression, he witnessed the socially disruptive effects of economic instability. Furthermore, as a Jew with many relatives still living in Central and Eastern Europe, he became increasingly concerned with the rise of European fascism. These events were influential in the shaping of Bohm's left-wing politics, which later played an important role in his professional career.

It was also in high school that he began to display an aptitude for solving math and science problems in a creative way. This emphasis on creativity and alternative ways to approach physics remained characteristic of Bohm's work throughout his life. In spite of his father's misgivings, his interest in science continued, and Samuel eventually agreed to pay his son's way through college. In the spring of 1939 Bohm received his degree in physics from Pennsylvania State College and entered graduate school at the California Institute of Technology (CalTech) that fall. He began the trip to California on the same day war was declared in Europe.

California and Political Activity. Bohm quickly soured on CalTech. Whereas he had envisioned his time as being filled with discussing physics with other students and professors and with his own research, he found extensive coursework, competitive colleagues, and frequent examinations that required little more than the ability to perform calculations. By the beginning of his second year he resolved to transfer. In the fall of 1940 Bohm contacted J. Robert Oppenheimer, the most distinguished American theoretical physicist of the time, who helped him transfer to the University of California–Berkeley in the spring of 1941.

At Berkeley Bohm found a more favorable environment. In Oppenheimer, a man whose intellectual interests went far beyond physics, he found an advisor with whom he approached physics as more than a series of calculations. In his fellow graduate students he found colleagues with whom he could discuss physics, philosophy, politics, and music. Increasingly, the topic of conversation turned to the war and the fate of European Jewry, as Bohm's closest friends were themselves the children of recent Jewish immigrants from East and Central Europe. This interest in politics was initially reinforced by Oppenheimer, whom Bohm—although less than some of his fellow students—saw more as a mentor than as simply a physics advisor.

Against the increasingly tumultuous backdrop of world affairs, Bohm continued his work in physics and established himself as one of, if not the, most promising of Oppenheimer's students. At his advisor's suggestion, he began research on the phenomenon of proton-deuteron collisions, a deuteron being a proton-neutron packet. Whereas his research was known at the time to address issues in elementary particle physics and stellar fusion, it later proved relevant in the far more earthly realm of hydrogen weapons. In the course of his graduate career two other concerns emerged that largely shaped his physics and philosophy. First, Bohm began to sense an almost mystical interconnectedness of objects. Beginning two decades later, he began to explore this feeling more directly and in so doing attracted a number of admirers unaware of his technical work in plasma and quantum physics. Second, he developed doubts about the Copenhagen interpretation of quantum mechanics. This approach to atomic phenomena was the standard view by the early 1940s, but Bohm found its probabilistic and acausal account of atomic physics troubling. An attempt to develop an alternative was the dominant theme of his technical work from 1951 until his death more than four decades later.

As Bohm's scientific work progressed, so did his politics. Although his initial activity consisted primarily of attending talks by various speakers associated with left-wing causes, this involvement changed dramatically with the advent of the Manhattan Project in 1942 and the naming of Oppenheimer as its scientific director that autumn. It was at the same time that Bohm made the decision to join the Communist Party. Although he remained a member for only approximately nine months, this decision would later have far-reaching consequences. While completing his dissertation in early 1943 Bohm joined Berkeley's Radiation Laboratory, Rad Lab, directed by Nobel Laureate Ernest Lawrence, to work on the separation of uranium isotopes as part of the Manhattan Project. During his time there he, along with other graduate students, sought to form a union at the Rad Lab. Although the union did come into existence, it was soon disbanded under intense pressure from the army and the White House. Such activity only heightened the concern of security officials in the FBI and military intelligence as to Bohm's suitability on the project. By spring 1943 Bohm's status as a security risk began to affect his life. When he completed his dissertation that semester, his scattering calculations were recognized as having weapons applications and immediately classified. Lacking the necessary clearance, he was denied access to his own work and thus unable to defend his dissertation. He

received his doctorate only after Oppenheimer assured the Berkeley physics department that Bohm's work was worthy of the degree. In spite of his security issues, he continued to work on the Manhattan Project throughout 1943. After leaving the project he remained at Berkeley through 1946 as a post-doc.

Princeton, Quantum Physics, and HUAC. Bohm's status as one of the most promising young theorists in America was cemented in June 1947 when he attended the prestigious Shelter Island Conference. Invited physicists included Albert Einstein, J. Robert Oppenheimer, Hans Bethe, and numerous Nobel Laureates. The following autumn he began his new position on the faculty of Princeton University and published a number of articles on plasma physics. Over the next three and a half years, Bohm's focus increasingly shifted from plasma physics and toward quantum mechanics, culminating in the publication of a well-received textbook, *Quantum Theory*, in spring 1951. Whereas the textbook focused on the orthodox view known as the Copenhagen Interpretation, which suggests that atomic phenomena are acausal and probabilistic, it was different from other texts in that it explored not only the technical aspects that could be addressed in equations but also the theory's more philosophical and conceptual aspects.

Concurrent with Bohm's changing interests in physics was a change in status at Princeton. Although departmental evaluations suggested that he was succeeding both as a researcher and as a teacher, the growing sentiment of anti-communism began to affect his career. Bohm's political activity while at the Rad Lab led to his being called before the House Committee on Un-American Activities in May and June 1949. Asserting his Fifth Amendment rights, he refused to answer questions about his political past as well as those of his friends. Although the university initially supported him, its president, Harold Dodds, was among the most outspoken supporters of anti-communism in higher education, and having a former communist on the faculty was noxious to numerous alumni.

On 4 December 1950 Bohm was indicted on the charge of contempt of Congress and arrested. Princeton immediately suspended him and barred him from using any university facilities, including the library, effectively ending his tenure at Princeton. In May 1951 Bohm was acquitted of the contempt charge, and he was reinstated at Princeton in the first week of June. Bohm's contract however was not renewed, and he left the university permanently when it expired on 30 June 1951.

Hidden Variables. It was also in June 1951 that Bohm submitted a pair of articles published on 15 January 1952 in the leading physics journal in the United States if not the world, *Physical Review*, titled, "A Suggested Interpretation of the Quantum Theory in Terms of 'Hidden' Variables." In these articles Bohm argued that the standard view, although consistent, simply assumes that the most complete explanation of a system involves probabilities and that this assumption cannot be tested experimentally. For him, the only way to investigate the truth of this assumption was by trying to find some other interpretation of the quantum theory in terms of hidden variables, which in principle determine the precise behavior of an individual system, but which are in practice averaged over in the measurements that could be carried out at the time. In supporting his claim that physicists ought to consider this alternative, Bohm demonstrated that his interpretation led to precisely the same results for all physical processes as did the usual one. He believed the benefit of the hidden variables interpretation was that it provided a broader conceptual framework than the usual interpretation, in that it made possible a precise and continuous description of all processes even at the quantum level. This broader framework allowed for more general mathematical formulations of the theory than those allowed by the usual interpretation. In putting forth this argument, Bohm suggested that the mere possibility of such an interpretation proved that it was not necessary to give up a precise, rational, and objective description of individual systems at a quantum level of accuracy.

The initial response to Bohm's work from physicists was silence. Worse than disagreeing with his work, many scientists, including key figures such as Niels Bohr, Werner Heisenberg, and Wolfgang Pauli, did not feel that Bohm's challenge merited a response. For most working physicists at the time, his alternative did not seem worth considering because it did not yield new results, but simply offered a different explanation than the standard view. Because physicists were already familiar with the Copenhagen approach, they found little or nothing to be gained from adopting the hidden variables interpretation. With respect to the issues that Bohm sought to raise, most in the physics community saw the subject as closed.

The supremacy of the Copenhagen Interpretation had been firmly established by the late 1920s, and had been highlighted at the 1927 Solvay Congress by Pauli's challenge of Louis de Broglie's interpretation of atomic motion in terms of particles being guided by pilot-waves. As a result of Pauli's attack, de Broglie himself abandoned his pilot-wave approach. It was not until Bohm's work that another scientist picked up de Broglie's line of thought, and, as a result, this work is sometimes subsumed under the title of "de Broglie-Bohm theory of motion."

The esteemed mathematician John von Neumann moved the physics community further away from a hidden-variables approach when in 1932 he published what was seen as a mathematical proof for the non-existence of hidden variables. In spite of the work of Pauli and von Neumann in critiquing non-Copenhagen approaches, some physicists, most notably Einstein, continued to question the orthodox view by arguing that it was incomplete. Einstein's concerns resulted in a 1935 *Physical Review* paper entitled, "Can Quantum-Mechanical Description of Physical Reality Be Considered Complete?" which he co-authored with Boris Podolsky and Nathan Rosen—the paper became known as the EPR paper. Bohr's successful refutation of Einstein's challenge effectively ended the debate over the primacy of Copenhagen. Even Einstein, in spite of his reservations concerning the standard view, was critical of Bohm's approach because it suggested the possible existence of superluminal signals, i.e. signals that could travel faster than the speed of light. For Einstein the notion that anything could travel faster than light was unacceptable.

Brazil and Israel. Although Bohm had submitted the articles while still at Princeton, by the time they were published he was teaching at the University of São Paulo (USP) in Brazil. After his contract had expired at Princeton, he was unable to obtain another position in the United States due to the political climate of the time. With the help of two Brazilian physics graduate students who were at Princeton prior to his departure, Bohm began working at USP in autumn 1951 and thus was able to maintain a physics career in spite of the dislocation. Leaving the country, however, did not put an end to Bohm's political problems. In late October 1951 Bohm was called to the U.S. Consulate in São Paulo, at which time his passport was seized and was returned to him marked as being good only for return to the United States. Afraid to return to the United States because of the chance of being arrested and unable to travel elsewhere, Bohm remained in Brazil until January 1955 when he moved to Israel and began teaching at the Technion in Haifa. His movement to Israel was made possible with the help of Einstein and only after Bohm took the drastic step in 1954 of giving up his U.S. passport and obtaining a Brazilian one.

Although not near the level of Princeton, the Technion did offer better resources for Bohm's research than did Brazil. It also offered greater interaction with other physicists from the United States and Europe, including David Fox, whom Bohm first met as a fellow graduate student at Berkeley, and Nathan Rosen, one of the co-authors of the EPR paper. On a personal level the move to Israel was significant in that it was there that Bohm met Saral Woolfson, a young Englishwoman living in Israel. The two married on 14 March 1956 in Haifa and remained married until his death in 1992. The Bohms had no children.

Bristol and Birkbeck. While the Technion offered more scientific interaction with others, Bohm still felt the need for increased stimulation and so in late summer 1957 he and his wife left Israel for England, where he had accepted a position as a research associate at Bristol University. Although he found Bristol far from ideal, his time there did yield his best received work in quantum mechanics—the 1959 discovery of the Aharonov-Bohm effect, which he co-discovered with the graduate student Yakir Aharonov. The effect, which resulted in Bohm's receiving numerous awards, contradicted the belief, dating back to the nineteenth-century work of James Clerk Maxwell on electricity and magnetism, that a vector potential was simply a mathematical convenience. Bohm and Aharonov demonstrated that on the quantum level, vector potentials, like electric and magnetic fields, had a physical effect. The discovery arose when Aharonov first noticed that even when electrons did not pass through a magnetic field, their interference properties could be changed simply by the field. Unlike the hidden variables interpretation, the Aharonov-Bohm effect became a standard topic in advanced quantum mechanics courses.

In 1961 Bohm was offered and accepted the chair for theoretical physics at Birkbeck College in London. Although the historically working-class school had limited resources, Bohm saw the move as one step closer to obtaining a position at a more prestigious university. Birkbeck, however, proved to be his final position, as he remained there until his retirement in 1983. Throughout his time in London Bohm collaborated extensively with Basil Hiley.

Philosophy/Physics in London. In spite of its poor reception in the 1950s, by the 1990s Bohm's hidden variables approach enjoyed a renaissance as numerous philosophers of science began to reexamine the question of whether or not his approach did help resolve problems involving quantum measurement. Although working physicists did not make use of Bohm's work at the end of the twentieth century, it became the subject of many books and articles more than forty years after it first appeared in print.

During his early years in London, however, the causal interpretation played only a minor role in the work he pursued. At Birkbeck, while much of Bohm's work remained technical, his interest in the philosophical aspects of science began to play a more prominent role than ever. He focused not simply on finding new equations of motion, but on reexamining the basic categories that were used. For example, Bohm and Hiley explored existing notions of order, space and time, causality and

David Bohm. *Theoretical physicist Dr. David J. Bohm at a symposium in London, 1971.* **HULTON ARCHIVE/GETTY IMAGES.**

chance—a topic he first explored at length in his 1957 work *Causality and Chance in Modern Physics*—and other related topics. Rather than simply exploring particle and fields as they interacted, Bohm focused increasingly on notions of process. Seeking to move away from viewing these concepts as a mere matter of making measurements, Bohm emphasized topology and how phenomena such as small-scale fluctuations expected in quantum gravity could result in a drastic alteration of traditional notions of the structure of spacetime. This reexamination of categories led Bohm to incorporate numerous other fields such as philosophy, biology, linguistics, and art and culminated in the 1987 work *Science, Order, and Creativity,* which he co-authored with David Peat.

During the first decade at Birkbeck, Bohm, like Niels Bohr before him, became increasingly interested in the role of communication and language. It was also during this period that Bohm thought extensively about questions of order and its deeply entwined constitutive and descriptive aspects, especially as they applied to quantum processes. In 1971 Bohm proposed the notion of implicate and explicate order. In doing so he suggested that it is not possible to display all aspects of a quantum process together at one time. In that one can have only a partial view at any given time, some aspects must remain implicit in any single display. Displaying a view explicates one aspect of the process at the expense of a complementary aspect that cannot be displayed at the same time. The implicit aspect can be explicated only by changing the display, making some of the original aspects implicit. Although initially treating questions of quantum process, the goal of implicate and explicate order was to provide a more coherent framework for exploring the question of wholeness and the relationship between objects.

Wholeness and Nonlocality. This notion of wholeness led Bohm to revisit questions of non-separability and nonlocality in nature, which had first emerged with his hidden variables interpretation and posited the possibility of superluminal signals. Since 1964 the question of nonlocality had been the subject of significant interest in the physics community due to the work of John S. Bell and his famous inequalities. Using simple math Bell was able to show that the notion of locality (i.e., that physical effects propagate at a finite speed) was inconsistent with quantum mechanics' description of nature. For Bell, the EPR critique assumed local realism and such an assumption led to certain requirements, mathematically resulting in inequalities which had to be satisfied. These inequalities were violated by quantum mechanical predictions; neither Bohm's theory nor Copenhagen satisfied them. Although Bell's work undermined the viability of Bohm's hidden variables approach as well, by the mid-1970s the causal approach, though different from its 1950s form and shaped in part by his work on explicate and implicate order, was once again at the center of Bohm's thoughts. The late 1970s and early 1980s produced several attempts at physically investigating Bell's inequalities, culminating in the work published by French physicist Alain Aspect in 1981 and 1982, which showed experimentally that Bell's inequalities were, indeed, violated.

The final development in Bohm's work was the development of the quantum potential. Whereas many scientists had criticized Bohm's 1952 papers as a return to mechanistic and causal principles that had dominated classical physics prior to the quantum revolution, a similar charge could not be leveled against the quantum potential. According to Bohm the quantum potential guided the electron in a nonmechanical way with its influence being a result of its form and not its strength. It was a concept that had no antecedent in physics.

Beyond his technical work in physics, Bohm was known to many of his admirers solely through his work on questions of interconnectedness/wholeness and the nature of thought, all of which were explored during his time with the Indian philosopher and teacher Jiddu Krishnamurti, with whom he maintained a close friendship from 1961 to 1984. For many, Bohm was not simply a great physicist but a great thinker on important esoteric subjects. On 27 October 1992, Bohm died of a heart attack on the steps of his home in suburban London.

BIBLIOGRAPHY

Bohm's Papers, 1953–1996, are held at the University of London, Birkbeck College Library.

WORKS BY BOHM

Quantum Theory. New York: Prentice-Hall, 1951.

"A Suggested Interpretation of the Quantum Theory in Terms of Hidden Variables. I." *Physical Review* 85 (1952): 166–179.

"A Suggested Interpretation of the Quantum Theory in Terms of Hidden Variables. II" *Physical Review* 85 (1952): 180–193.

Causality and Chance in Modern Physics. Foreword by Louis De Broglie. London, Routledge and Paul, 1957.

With Yakir Aharonov. "Significance of Electromagnetic Potentials in the Quantum Theory." *Physical Review Series II* (1959): 485–491.

The Special Theory of Relativity. New York: W. A. Benjamin, 1965.

Wholeness and the Implicate Order. Boston: Routledge & Kegan Paul, 1981.

With David Peat. *Science, Order, and Creativity* New York: Bantam Books, 1987.

On Dialogue. Edited by Lee Nichol. New York: Routledge, 1996.

On Creativity. Edited by Lee Nichol. New York: Routledge, 1998.

OTHER SOURCES

Cushing, James T. *Quantum Mechanics: Historical Contingency and the Copenhagen Hegemony.* Chicago: University of Chicago Press, 1994.

———. Arthur Fine, and Sheldon Goldstein, eds. *Bohmian Mechanics and Quantum Theory: An Appraisal.* Dordrecht, Holland: Kluwer, 1996.

Freire, Olival, Jr. "Science and Exile: David Bohm, the Cold War, and a New Interpretation of Quantum Mechanics." *Historical Studies in the Physical and Biological Sciences* 36:1 (2005): 1–34.

Holland, Peter. R. *The Quantum Theory of Motion: An Account of the de Broglie-Bohm Causal Interpretation of Quantum Mechanics.* Cambridge, MA: Cambridge University Press, 1993.

Kojevnikov, Alexei. "David Bohm and the Collective Movement." *Historical Studies in the Physical and Biological Sciences* 33:1 (2002): 161–192.

Olwell, Russell. "Physical Isolation and Marginalization in Physics: David Bohm's Cold War Exile." *Isis* 90 (December 1999): 738–756.

Peat, F. David. *Infinite Potential: The Life and Times of David Bohm*. Reading, MA: Addison-Wesley, 1997.

Shawn Mullet

BOHR, NIELS HENRIK DAVID (*b.* Copenhagen, Denmark, 7 October 1885; *d.* Copenhagen, 18 November 1962), *atomic and nuclear physics, chemistry, epistemology, philosophy of physics.* For the original article on Bohr see *DSB*, vol. 2.

Bohr's legacy to physics and its interpretation is a controversial one. He contributed decisively to the development of atomic and nuclear physics in many ways (especially to quantum theory from 1913 to 1925), and he is widely recognized as possessing remarkable insight into the nature of physical problems. Yet his theoretical approach and interpretive outlook sometimes have been questioned as vague, unclear, or inconsistent. Scholarship from 1970 to 2007 emphasized both the radical successes and some of the interpretive challenges of Bohr's work.

Influences on Bohr's Work. Much attention has been paid to possible philosophical influences on Bohr's thought, especially, it seems, because his work is both groundbreaking and strangely conservative and is not easily made sense of via traditional analyses of the trajectory of the physics of his time. Thus some have looked to influences such as Immanuel Kant, Søren Kierkegaard, and William James (especially as conveyed to Bohr by his teacher, Harald Høffding) to account for his willingness to use incomplete and non-causal models or for his apparent views on the role of observation in quantum phenomena. However, although the influence of various well-known philosophical views of the time should be acknowledged, at least on the way Bohr described his ideas and probably on his methods, Bohr's work is best explained by focusing on the close attention he paid to specific issues in physics, the particulars of his methods, and his interactions with other physicists.

Correspondence Principle. It has become increasingly clear that Bohr's much-misunderstood correspondence principle, a critical component of his work from at least 1918 to 1925, was internally motivated and more robust than the loose heuristic it has often been made out to be. Bohr relied on it for epistemological reasons concerning our ability to infer atomic properties from empirical phenomena such as spectra. His emphasis on this empirical

approach over simple hypothesizing can be seen in his justification for his 1913 model via the application of the frequency relation $E=h\nu$ to the Balmer formula for the hydrogen spectrum. But that method justified claims only about stationary states and transitions between them. To allow investigation of other atomic properties, Bohr looked to mathematical limiting relations in order to set up some sort of correspondence between those properties and the properties of observable emitted radiation. He then used the classical limit as a guide to indicate how observable emitted radiation corresponded to presumed electron motion.

This sense of correspondence is precisely the idea that led to both the unusual Bohr-Kramers-Slater theory and Werner Heisenberg's quantum mechanics, and it influenced much of Bohr's later work. The success of classical electrodynamics, especially in spectroscopy, convinced Bohr that something must be vibrating long enough to emit (and therefore correspond to) electromagnetic radiation at precise frequencies. But that meant that the oscillators and radiation were not independently detectable (thus dubbed "virtual"), and that they conserved energy only statistically. When energy conservation was shown to hold strictly, Bohr questioned the reality of the oscillators, which helped lay the foundation for Heisenberg's purely formal use of the classical mechanics of oscillatory motion.

Copenhagen Interpretation. Previous orthodoxy accepted the idea that Bohr and Heisenberg shared a Copenhagen interpretation (often conflated with John von Neumann's collapse interpretation) of Heisenberg's new quantum mechanics. But in fact there were significant differences. It has become well known that Heisenberg wrote his 1927 paper on the indeterminacy relations independently of Bohr and waited to show it to him until he had it completed. Upon reading the paper, Bohr corrected a fault with Heisenberg's microscope thought experiment and pushed Heisenberg to explain indeterminacy in a wider context, especially in terms of Bohr's developing conception of complementarity, which he thought was a better way to conceive of indeterminacy than Heisenberg's formal derivation and disturbance interpretation. Heisenberg relented only by conceding Bohr's point in an endnote.

Albert Einstein was one of the more visible critics of the Copenhagen approach, and the discussions between Bohr and Einstein regarding the status and interpretation of the newly developed quantum mechanics looms large in legend. For some time, conventional wisdom had been that Bohr won the friendly debates. That view changed somewhat in the late twentieth century, during which time scholars began to question the clarity of Bohr's work, especially his response to the 1935 Einstein-

Niels Bohr. © CORBIS.

Podolsky-Rosen paper regarding whether quantum mechanics is complete. Bohr's response contained such confusing but crucial language as that expressing the claim that there exists a non-mechanical, at-a-distance "influence on the very conditions which define the possible types of predictions" of remote particles (1935, p. 700). Bohr's language was always chosen with almost obsessive attention to the nuances of the way things were expressed, yet the reasoning behind the language often got lost in the end result. In particular, in that response Bohr apparently did have specific formal and philosophical arguments in mind. Bohr's interpretive views of quantum mechanics never really invoked disturbance by observation, but were more focused on the recognition of the apparent holism of quantum phenomena of entangled systems, which he recognized in an early way even in 1925.

Interactions with Colleagues Some scholarship has suggested that Bohr won his converts not through the cogency and successes of his theories but from the forcefulness of his attempts to forge forge consensus. It is true that some

of Bohr's work, especially his methods and interpretation of the developing physics, was not convincing to those who were looking for more rigorous foundations or were concerned primarily with mathematical formalism. However, Bohr's intuition and ability to see through problems were widely appreciated, and his influence spread in virtue of his decisive and well-recognized successes. Those were achieved through his collaborative methods, which involved much discussion, reworking of solutions, and repeated dictation and feedback from those around him.

Another legendary aspect of Bohr's life concerns his meeting with Heisenberg in 1941, during which they apparently discussed prospects for a German atomic bomb. Heisenberg later indicated that he had told Bohr he had been trying to undermine those prospects. While what was said at that meeting is a matter of much speculation (and became the subject of a play by Michael Frayn), in 2002 the Niels Bohr Archive released drafts of letters Bohr had written, but never sent, to Heisenberg. In those letters, Bohr gently expressed his dismay that Heisenberg would try, perhaps not entirely consciously, to make it seem as if he (Heisenberg) had expressed anything other than support for the German cause at the time. The strain that issue placed on the relationship between Heisenberg and the man who from 1943 on had pushed for the peaceful, open sharing of all science and technology was clear.

SUPPLEMENTARY BIBLIOGRAPHY

WORKS BY BOHR

"Can Quantum-Mechanical Description of Physical Reality Be Considered Complete?" *Physical Review* 48 (1935): 696–702. Bohr's response to EPR.

Niels Bohr Collected Works, 12 vols. Edited by Léon Rosenfeld and Erik Rüdinger. Amsterdam: North-Holland, 1972–2006. Comprehensive, with excellent introductions.

The Philosophical Writings of Niels Bohr, 4 vols. Woodbridge, CT: Ox Bow Press, 1987–1998. New editions of the popular collections of Bohr's essays.

"Documents relating to 1941 Bohr-Heisenberg meeting." Niels Bohr Archive. Available from http://www.nba.nbi.dk.

OTHER SOURCES

Beller, Mara. *Quantum Dialogue: The Making of a Revolution.* Chicago: University of Chicago Press, 1999. Critical of Bohr and his influence.

Blædel, Niels. *Harmony and Unity: The Life of Niels Bohr.* Madison, WI: Science Tech, 1988. Contains insights into Bohr's personal history.

Einstein, Albert, Boris Podolsky, and Nathan Rosen. "Can Quantum-Mechanical Description of Physical Reality Be Considered Complete?" *Physical Review* 47 (1935): 777–780. Written mostly by Podolsky and not entirely representative of Einstein's views.

Favrholdt, David. *Niels Bohr's Philosophical Background*, Vol. 63, *Historisk-Filosofiske Meddelelser.* Copenhagen: Munksgaard, 1992.

Faye, Jan, and Henry J. Folse, eds. *Niels Bohr and Contemporary Philosophy*, Vol. 153, *Boston Studies in the Philosophy of Science.* Dordrecht: Kluwer Academic, 1994.

Frayn, Michael. *Copenhagen.* New York: Anchor Books, 2000. Play about the Bohr-Heisenberg meeting.

French, Anthony P., and P. J. Kennedy, eds. *Niels Bohr: A Centenary Volume.* Cambridge, MA: Harvard University Press, 1985.

Jammer, Max. *The Conceptual Development of Quantum Mechanics.* New York: McGraw-Hill, 1966. Claims influence on Bohr from Kierkegaard and James.

Mehra, Jagdish, and Helmut Rechenberg. *The Historical Development of Quantum Theory*, 6 vols. New York: Springer-Verlag, 1982–2001.

Pais, Abraham. *Niels Bohr's Times: In Physics, Philosophy, and Polity.* Oxford, U.K.: Clarendon Press, 1991.

Rozental, Stefan, ed. *Niels Bohr: His Life and Work as Seen by His Friends and Colleagues.* Amsterdam: North-Holland, 1985.

Scott Tanona

BOK, BARTHOLOMEUS (BART) JAN (*b.* Hoorn, Holland, 28 April 1906; *d.* Tucson, Arizona, 5 August 1983), *astronomy and astrophysics, studies of the spiral shape of the Milky Way and of the formation of stars.*

Bok was an essential figure in twentieth-century understanding of the Milky Way. Through a two-tracked research career, he offered a visualization of this galaxy both by helping determine its shape as a spiral galaxy and by his work on the nature of how stars are formed in it. With Edith Reilly he discovered that very small, dense dark nebulae, later called Bok globules, are really the cocoons of nascent stars. As assistant director of Harvard College Observatory and director of Mount Stromlo Observatory in Australia and Steward Observatory in Arizona, he contributed to the evolution of modern astronomy through his designs of new telescopes and observatory structures in both these places.

Early Life. In a land famous for its astronomical contributions, including the first use of the telescope almost three hundred years earlier, Bartholomeus Jan Bok was born on 28 April 1906. (His long first name was legally changed to Bart when he became a U.S. citizen in 1938.) The family lived in Hoorn for only nine months before his father, Jan Bok, a sergeant-major in the Dutch army, was transferred to Haarlem, a town near Amsterdam and less than five miles from the shore of the North Sea. The young Bok attended Nassau Laan, a small primary school. The coming of peace after World War I meant another move for the Bok family just as he was starting high school. After he had just one year at City High School in Haarlem, his father was transferred to The Hague, where the Waldeck-Pyrmont Kade School had first-rate mathematicians and physicists, some of whom had doctorates.

It was in The Hague that Bok, at age twelve, joined the Boy Scouts and his interest in astronomy got its start on a clear evening when he found that he could not identify a single star. As he delved deeper into astronomy, he learned of the work of Harlow Shapley, a famous American astronomer who had used Cepheid variable stars to show that our solar system was not at the center of the Milky Way galaxy, but somewhere near its edge.

With this new-found passion, in 1924, Bok entered the University of Leiden as an undergraduate where he decided to do whatever he could to build upon Shapley's work. In the fall of 1927, Bok began graduate studies at Groningen University with a study of the structure of the Milky Way galaxy. He also enthusiastically joined in the planning for the major event that would come with the summer of 1928, the triennial Congress of the International Astronomical Union (IAU) in Leiden. The two people Bok met at that congress changed the direction of his life. Shapley, of course, was one; he offered Bok a position at Harvard. The other was the young astronomer Priscilla Fairfield. The IAU general assembly lasted ten days, which was plenty of time for Bart to declare that he wanted to marry Priscilla.

A year later Bok left for the United States to marry Priscilla and accept his new position at Harvard. As Bok studied the galaxy, he suspected that its dark clouds contained precious clues about how stars are formed. He became interested in these clouds while writing his doctoral thesis on Eta Carinae, a star surrounded by nebulosity. "The grand sweep of the swirling gases" (as he described the nebula) was even more interesting to him than the star itself. Over the course of their lives Bok and his wife spent time under the southern hemisphere sky observing, photographing, and studying this beautiful area. In early years Shapley teased Bok about this passion, suggesting that his dissertation should be entitled "Miscellaneous Nonsense Vaguely Related to Eta Carinae." It was a joke: Shapley had suggested Eta Carinae to Bok as a thesis subject in the first place. He always supported Bok's interest in the star that first attracted attention in 1677 when Edmond Halley noticed its brightening to fourth magnitude. In 1827, it rose to the first magnitude, faded a bit, and then in 1843, it tied with Sirius for being the brightest star in the sky. Bok's dissertation began as a study of the distribution of stars in the region of Eta Carinae, but through that distribution Bok was hoping to shed some light on the structure and rotation of the Milky Way. He would later expand his thesis to work with problems involving the stability of the galaxy's open clusters and how they disintegrate over time as stars leave their nests.

How Stars Are Distributed in Space. As Bok's interests deepened into the dynamics of open star clusters, he investigated how such aggregations of stars evolve, how long they last, and what process makes them fall apart. He was particularly concerned with the more loosely concentrated clusters that might disintegrate more quickly as the forces of the rotating galaxy tear them apart. Our Sun, in fact, might once have been a member of an open cluster, which has long since dissociated, its members now spread out all over the galaxy. In the brief history of these clusters might lie a clue to understanding the Milky Way and the fact that it rotates over a certain period of time. If this galaxy does rotate, Bok reasoned, its gravity would produce massive tidal disruptions that could cause the loose open clusters to fall apart. Tides occur when two bodies interact; the Moon with some help from the sun causes tides in Earth's oceans that can exceed 50 feet. Stars close to each other can affect their paths, causing them to spread apart.

Bartholomeus Jan Bok. © CORBIS.

As Bok's interest in the distribution of stars and the structure of the galaxy continued to grow, in the summer of 1936, he gave a series of lectures at Yerkes Observatory about his research. In the audience was his friend Otto Struve of Yerkes. As an editor of the *Astrophysical Monographs,* Struve suggested that Bok write the series' opening book about this subject. Bok was well prepared for the task; he had a summary of each lecture he had given and had even taken the trouble—as he would do throughout his career—to photograph the notes he had written on the blackboard. By early 1937, Bok had begun work on *The Distribution of the Stars in Space,* and the first draft went quickly. But on the Memorial Day weekend of 1937, as Bok was completing the final stages of *Distribution* from his home in Lexington, he suffered an attack of polio, which left him no permanent disability save for a somewhat disfigured right thumb. When Bok completed the 124-page *Distribution* in 1937, he was only thirty-one years old. It is a remarkable book, written with a prescience and understanding of the subject not shared by most of his peers.

Dark Nebulae. From the time of his doctoral dissertation, Bok always had an interest in the Milky Way's dark clouds. In *The Distribution of the Stars in Space,* he described in detail the numbers, sizes, and studies of the then-known dark nebulae in the Milky Way. Around 1947, Edith Reilly, a technical assistant suffering from multiple sclerosis, began work at the Harvard College Observatory. One afternoon Reilly asked Bok if she could study dark nebulae with him. Realizing that Reilly's multiple sclerosis would prevent her from handling Harvard's heavy 8-by-10-inch photographic plates, Bok asked her to examine the catalogs of dark nebulae kept decades earlier by the famous American astronomer Edward Emerson Barnard, to select candidates for further study. As work progressed, Reilly noted a particular kind of small, round, and unusually dense nebula. Bok began photographing these nebulae, and in 1947, a preliminary paper discussed their work on these "small dark nebulae"—typically roundish, from three to five arc minutes wide (about one-sixth the apparent diameter of the Moon) and located in regions of the Milky Way with no bright nebulae or unusual stars nearby. Through a telescope, Bok later described, "you would come to the leading edge of one of these things and suddenly the stars would just disappear. And then you would push the telescope's slow motion button a bit and bloop! the stars come back." (Bok, interview by David Levy, 1983).

Bok and Reilly found about two hundred of these dark objects within the relatively close distance of some 500 parsecs (somewhat more than 1,500 light-years) outside the solar system, the best examples being in the constellations Taurus and Ophiuchus. These tiny nebulae were optically extremely thick, with possibly thirty magnitudes of extinction; if one could, for example, cover a first magnitude star with one of these clouds, it would become invisible even through the Hubble Space Telescope. Bok thought that these nebulae marked the birthplaces of new stars. As their dark gases move about slowly, he reasoned, they begin a slow collapse under their own gravity that intensifies until stellar fusion starts. In 1956, a search of two prints of the newly completed Palomar Sky Survey revealed seventeen thousand new dark objects. When astronomers began using radio telescopes to study these objects around the same time, the nature of these small dark nebulae as star precursors became much more credible.

Radio Astronomy and Discovery of Spiral Structure. In the early 1950s, Bok embraced the new idea of studying the Milky Way at radio wavelengths. On the horizon was a new 21-centimeter radio telescope whose penetrating ear would soon hear into the galaxy's heart. This completely new approach was only part of the story of how the Milky Way's spiral structure was actually found. The discovery was a long process involving both optical and radio telescopes. Although Bok was not the one to make the discovery, his approach to the problem certainly helped point

the way. As the acknowledged master of statistical studies of the structure of the galaxy and its interstellar material, Bok's work on galactic structure had concentrated on the analysis of counts of stars; however his results did not go far enough to indicate the concentrations of matter necessary to establish the existence of spiral arms.

In 1951, William W. Morgan, Stewart Sharpless, and Donald Osterbrock, all of Yerkes Observatory, detected evidence of two spiral arms, which they called the Orion and Perseus arms, plus part of a third called the Sagittarius arm. The same year, using a small pyramid-shaped horn antenna mounted on a roof of Harvard's Civics Building, Harvard physicists Harold I. Ewen and Edward M. Purcell detected radiation from neutral hydrogen atoms at the 21-centimeter wavelength, as a radio signal from the Milky Way. Before the advent of radio telescopes, the galaxy's shape lay hidden behind a dark veil of interstellar dust that optical telescopes cannot penetrate. But radio telescopes "see" a different wavelength of sky, and through it, the Milky Way's spiral shape could be mapped. The spiral arms are traceable by observing where hydrogen is especially concentrated. Not only could the Orion and Perseus arms be confirmed, but the arms could also be extended much further out, beyond the dark matter that blocks the view of the optical telescopes. It was possible to complete a 21-centimeter map of the galaxy. Intrigued by these developments, Bok arranged for the construction of a radio telescope at Harvard. The telescope was dedicated on 28 April 1956, on Bok's fiftieth birthday. In a few short years Bok had so honed his skills with radio telescopes that he had become one of the country's top radio astronomers. He later helped select the site for the National Radio Astronomy Observatory in a valley near Green Bank, West Virginia.

International Efforts and the McCarthy Era. During the Second World War, Bok understood that communications among astronomers were at considerable risk. Accordingly he launched what he described as "a quiet international newsletter" designed to keep scientists throughout Europe in touch with scientific progress of the day. After the war that operation metamorphosed into the United Nations Educational and Cultural Organization (UNECO). It would go without saying that Bok strongly supported the idea that "there should be an 'S' in UNECO." Other scientists agreed: the Science Commission of the Conference of Allied Ministers of Education (CAME) proposed that the term "Scientific" be added to UNECO. On 2 September 1945, the same day that the *New York Times* reported the surrender of Japan, Bok coauthored a letter to the *New York Times* formally proposing the idea. It is to some extent because of Bok's efforts that the organization became known as the United Nations Educational, Scientific, and Cultural Organization (UNESCO).

This effort had a negative side, for an FBI agent claimed to him that his "premature interest" in the founding of the United Nations made him suspected of being a communist. By 1954, Senator Joseph R. McCarthy's investigation was nearing its zenith. In addition to the House Committee on Un-American Activities, several states formed their own committees. The Massachusetts variant was the "Educational Sub-Committee of the Commonwealth Commission to Study Communism, Subversive, and Related Activities." Bok was subpoenaed to appear before this committee. On Friday afternoon, 19 February 1954, Bok answered its summons in a forty-minute interview. Their discussion centered around his wartime interest in the American Association of Scientific Workers. After the questions, Bok commented on the subcommittee's central agenda and methods. He testified to his belief that there was little risk of communist infiltration of voluntary liberal organizations. However, he added this caveat that "excessive protective legislation" would discourage young scientists from participation in social issues. "Already there is a premium on the wearing of blinders," he added, "by anyone of the younger generation of scientists" (Bok, interview with David Levy, 1982; Bok, personal letter to Arthur Sutherland and McGeorge Bundy, 23 February 1954).

Australian Years. Although Bok's own testimony before a state committee was not harmful to him, his friendship and steadfast support of Harlow Shapley was. Senator McCarthy accused Shapley of being a communist, and he was forced to testify before the House Committee on Un-American Activities as well as, in absentia, a Senate foreign relations subcommittee. This political atmosphere was ultimately poisonous to Bok, and in 1956 he decided to resign from Harvard. He accepted a position as director of the Australian National Observatory's Mount Stromlo Observatory.

As ANU's first full professor of astronomy, Bok intended to establish a graduate school as good as the one he had left at Harvard. Of all his achievements in Australia, Bok considered his establishment of the graduate school at the Australian National University his most significant. His predecessor had started a few regular courses but nothing on the scale Bok foresaw. The top caliber students Bok attracted strengthened the work on Mount Stromlo, and Bok's supportive and outgoing personality fed this constructive loop.

A few months after his arrival in Australia, the Soviet Union launched its artificial satellite on 4 October 1957. So exciting—and ominous—was *Sputnik* that Bok was invited to address both houses of the Australian parliament about it. Concerned about this evidence of Soviet military strength, the senators and representatives listened

closely as Bok explained the consequences of the new technology. Although satellites were far from Bok's specialty, he did expound on the possibilities of communications satellites. After Bok finished his talk, Sir Alister McMullin, the house speaker, inquired if it would be possible for some of the audience to go out and see the satellite. The speaker appointed a group of six to go outdoors and watch for it at the time calculated for its next appearance. Bok was a bit uneasy about the prediction but he need not have worried, for the satellite appeared right on schedule. By the end of that evening Bok had befriended the lawmakers, and his reputation as a salesman for astronomy in Australia was ensured. That evening also led to the start of a friendship with Australia's prime minister Robert Menzies.

During Bok's first years at Stromlo, *The Milky Way* came out in its third edition, its first appearance since 1945 and a major rewriting effort from the first two versions. Completed in his last year at Harvard, the new text reflected a better understood Milky Way than the ones of 1941 and 1945. Its leading changes reflected the new work on spiral structure and the role played by radio astronomy. For all but the fifth edition, Priscilla Bok acted as coauthor and editor.

Bok saw that radio telescopes were less useful than optical telescopes for determining distances of objects. Partly because of this weakness, he felt strongly that a healthy approach to galactic studies needed to coordinate both optical and radio astronomy. He strongly urged his students not to consider themselves as either radio astronomers or optical astronomers, but just astronomers. This approach was far reaching and vitally important in a time of great change for astronomy.

By 1958, radio studies had painted a complex picture of a galaxy with a nucleus that seemed to be relatively smaller than those in some other spiral galaxies. However, the Milky Way appeared to be surrounded by a huge swath of at least three spiral arms, one in the direction of Orion, another toward Perseus, and a third toward Sagittarius.

Bok was troubled by a discrepancy between the spiral structure as revealed by the radio observations and the optical data. Morgan's canonical map showed the spiral arms as elliptical, but radio studies at the 21-centimeter wavelength revealed them to be more circular, like those in other galaxies. Because of obscuring matter between the stars, it was still hard to tell whether a feature was a major arm, or simply a small spur of a larger and hidden arm. The problem is similar to trying to map the shape of a forest from a thicket of trees near the edge; the cartographer knows the nearby trees but has only a vague view of the rest of the woods. With radio telescopes, astronomers can search for the dark clouds of hydrogen between the stars, and for clouds which populate spiral arms in other galaxies, and they can trace the presence of spiral arms in The Milky Way. With optical telescopes, certain types of stars populate the spiral arms and help astronomers trace the extent of a spiral arm. But the arms are so large and extensive that it is difficult to determine what constitutes a complete arm and what is just a spur off another arm. Bok suspected that the arms were tightly wound up "like the spring of a watch." And in one of these arms, about 27,000 light-years from the galaxy's center, is our Sun.

Final Years. In 1966, Bok returned to the United States to direct the Steward Observatory at the University of Arizona, a position he held until his retirement in 1973. In December 1976, Bok published *Objections to Astrology*, a book that remained in print into the early 2000s. "Every ten years," he reminisced, "I decide to do something about astrology." Two years earlier, a fourth edition of his classic *The Milky Way* appeared, to be followed in 1981 by a fifth and final edition, this one dedicated to Priscilla's memory.

A few days before her death in 1975, Priscilla and Bart attended the opening of the Flandrau Planetarium in Tucson. Priscilla stopped at the picture of their beloved Eta Carinae. "Bart," she said, "when I die, this is where I want to be. I will be watching you from here." Priscilla died just four days later, and Bart died in 1983. Whenever people look at the Eta Carinae nebula, they can appreciate the Boks, who did so much to increase appreciation of the Milky Way.

BIBLIOGRAPHY

WORKS BY BOK

A Study of the Eta Carinae Region. Groningen: Hoitsema Brothers, 1932.

The Distribution of the Stars in Space. Astrophysical Monographs. Chicago: University of Chicago Press, 1937.

With I. Amdur. Letter to the editor. *New York Times*, 2 Sept 1945.

With Priscilla Bok. *The Milky Way.* Philadelphia, Blakiston Co., 1941. 2nd ed. Philadelphia: Blakiston Co., 1945. 3rd ed. Cambridge: Harvard University Press, 1957. 4th ed. Cambridge: Harvard University Press, 1974. 5th ed. Cambridge: Harvard University Press, 1981.

With Edith F. Reilly. "Small Dark Nebulae." *Astrophysical Journal* 105 (1947): 255–257.

"Radio Studies of Interstellar Hydrogen." *Sky and Telescope* 13 (1954): 408–412.

Objections to Astrology. Amherst: Prometheus Books, 1975.

OTHER SOURCES

Gascoigne, S. C. B. "Bart Bok at Mount Stromlo." *Mercury* 13, no. 2 (1984): 45–47.

Levy, David H. *The Man Who Sold the Milky Way.* Tucson: University of Arizona Press, 1993

"Spiral Arms of the Galaxy" *Sky and Telescope* 11 (1952): 138–139. This "American Astronomer's Report" is apparently the original announcement of William Morgan's work.

Struve, Otto. "Galactic Exploration by Radio." *Sky and Telescope* 11 (1952): 214–217.

White, Raymond E. "Bart J. Bok (1906-83: A Personal memoir from a 'Grandson')" *Sky and Telescope* (October 1983): 303–306.

David Levy

BOLTON, JOHN GATENBY (*b.* Sheffield, England, 25 June 1922; *d.* Buderim, Australia, 6 July 1993), *radio astronomy, "radio stars," Caltech, Owens Valley Radio Observatory, Parkes Radio Telescope, radio source identifications, quasars.*

Bolton was one of the early founders of radio astronomy. He was responsible for the discovery and identification of many of the earliest "radio stars," carried out important early surveys of discrete sources, established the radio astronomy program at the California Institute of Technology (Caltech) and the Owens Valley Radio Observatory, and was the first director of the Parkes Radio Telescope. Later in his career, he developed new techniques that led to the location and identification of more than one thousand quasars. For his pioneering research in radio astronomy Bolton received many honors, including the Bruce Medal of the Astronomical Society of the Pacific, the Edgeworth David Medal of the Royal Society of New South Wales, the Encyclopaedia Britannica Gold Medal and Prize for Science, the American Astronomical Society's Henry Norris Russell Lectureship, and the Gold Medal of the Royal Astronomical Society. He was a Fellow of the Royal Society, a Commander of the Order of the British Empire, a Fellow of the American Academy of Arts and Sciences, a foreign associate of the U.S. National Academy of Sciences, an Honorary Fellow of the Indian Academy of Sciences, and a Fellow of the Australian Academy of Science.

Early Years. John Gatenby Bolton was born in Sheffield, England, on 25 June 1922, to John and Ethel Bolton, both of whom were schoolteachers. After graduating from King Edward VII Grammar School, he entered Trinity College, Cambridge, and a few days after completing his final exams in May 1942 he enlisted in the Royal Navy. After a brief introduction to electronics, he began designing and testing airborne radar units. In 1944 he joined the aircraft carrier HMS *Unicorn* as a radar officer. At the end of the war he left the ship in Sydney, Australia, and on the basis of his radar background secured a research post with the Commonwealth Scientific and Industrial Research Organization's (CSIRO) Division of Radiophysics, where he was assigned to the radio astronomy group.

The Radio Source Surveys. Radio astronomy was in its infancy at this time. Following the pioneering efforts of Karl Jansky and Grote Reber in the United States during the 1930s and early 1940s, radio astronomy blossomed in the late 1940s and early 1950s, largely as a consequence of developments associated with radar during the war. In the late 1940s, Britain and Australia emerged as the two leading nations in this new branch of astronomy, with much of the Australian development taking place through the CSIRO's Division of Radiophysics. Bolton went to work at the Division's Dover Heights field station, which was located at a former World War II radar station, 5 kilometers to the south of the entrance of Sydney Harbor. It was sited on top of a 79-meter coastal cliff, which offered special advantages for radio astronomy research.

Bolton teamed up with Bruce Slee, and in November 1946 they began studying radio emission from the Sun. In 1947 Bolton, Slee, and Gordon Stanley investigated the enigmatic radio star in the constellation of Cygnus, which had just been reported by British radio astronomers. By March 1948 Bolton's team had not only confirmed the existence of the Cygnus A radio source but had also discovered five others, including Taurus A, Centaurus A, and Virgo A. The equipment used for these searches was primitive by twenty-first century standards and comprised simple Yagi antennas operating at frequencies of 60, 100, and 200 megahertz that were used to determine the first radio source spectra. These Yagi antennas, similar to modern TV antennas, were positioned on the roof of a World War II concrete blockhouse at Dover Heights, close to the cliff edge.

The search was now on to solve the mystery of the radio stars, and the first thing to do was obtain their precise positions so that photographs of these regions could be examined to see if there were any optical counterparts. Unfortunately, the positions of the sources obtained in Sydney were imprecise, as they relied solely on the rise-time of the sources as they appeared above the eastern horizon. This technique became known as sea interferometry, but what was needed was a site that also allowed the radio astronomers to track the setting times of these sources over the western horizon. However, the only relatively nearby locations that permitted this were in New Zealand, 2,000 kilometers to the east of Sydney.

Between June and September 1948 Bolton and Stanley observed the radio stars Cygnus A, Taurus A, Centaurus A, and Virgo A from 300-meter high coastal cliffs at Leigh and Piha to the northeast and west of Auckland, while Slee continued parallel observations from Dover

Heights. This strategy was a resounding success, for precise positions were obtained for all four sources and when photographs of the relevant sections of sky were examined, the Sydney radio astronomers were able to associate the Taurus A radio source with the Crab Nebula (the remains of a supernova that was widely observed in 1054 CE), Centaurus A with a galaxy crossed by a distinctive dark dust lane, and Virgo A with a galaxy known to contain a peculiar jet. These identifications were published in *Nature* and the *Australian Journal of Scientific Research* and created a major impact, for they showed that these sources were in no sense radio stars but were associated with the remnants of galactic supernova, as well as with distant galaxies. The realization that these so-called radio galaxies were the most energetic objects known in the universe attracted the attention of astronomers around the world and ushered in the modern era of radio astronomy.

In 1949 a nine-element Yagi antenna was set up on the roof of the blockhouse, and was used to discover fourteen new sources, including the powerful radio galaxies Hydra A, Hercules A, Fornax A, and Pictor A. Early in 1952 Bolton, Stanley, and Slee completed a new twelve-element Yagi array, and this was used to detect a total of 122 sources. This was the most complete radio survey carried out worldwide at that time, and the apparent excess of weak sources in their catalog opened a long-standing debate about the cosmological implications of radio source population statistics.

Bolton, Stanley, and Slee wanted to construct a much larger radio telescope at Dover Heights, but with many competing innovative projects from Division of Radiophysics colleagues and limited funding from the government, their bid was unsuccessful. Their ingenious response was to build a new radio telescope themselves—as a lunchtime project. Over a three-month period in 1951 they used shovels and a wheelbarrow to excavate a dish-shaped depression in the sand 150 yards north of the blockhouse. After constructing a 72-foot diameter dish and testing out the system, they expanded this to 80 feet, and when this was furnished with an antenna mast and dipole it fed radio signals from directly overhead through to equipment in a mobile laboratory. At the time, this was one of the largest radio telescopes in the world, but the disadvantage was that it was fixed, so it could not move and point to selected areas of sky. Instead, different areas of sky passed through the beam of this novel radio telescope as Earth rotated, but it was possible to expand the survey area slightly by tilting the mast that supported the dipole antenna. Fortunately, at the latitude of Sydney, the plane of Earth's galaxy passes almost directly overhead, so for the first time, the Dover Heights radio astronomers were able to investigate the radio emission from this vital central part of Earth's galaxy. They were excited to discover a strong new radio source located at the very center

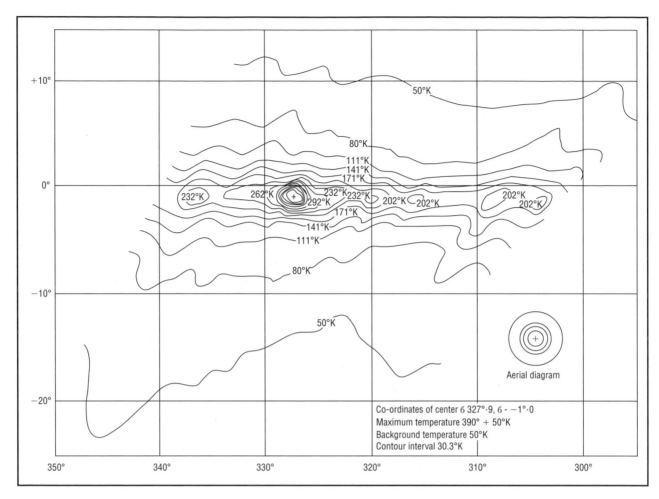

Figure 1. *400 MHz contours obtained with the 80-ft. "hole-in-the-ground" antenna, clearly showing the Galactic Center source, Sgr A.*

of this galaxy, and named this Sagittarius A. 'This is the distinctive source with celestial coordinates of 328 degrees (longitude) and -01 degree (latitude) shown in Figure 1. Several years later, the International Astronomical Union adopted the position of Sagittarius A as the official center for a new international system of galactic coordinates (equivalent to latitude and longitude here on Earth).

In 1953, when it appeared that the Radiophysics Laboratory could not fulfill his ambitious plans to build an even larger radio telescope at Dover Heights, Bolton temporarily left radio astronomy to work with the laboratory's cloud physics group. Until his departure for Caltech in 1955, he pursued a variety of cloud-seeding experiments designed to bring rain to Australian farmers.

During the seven years he spent at Radiophysics, Bolton was involved in forefront research that led to discoveries that would change the nature of astronomical research. Through this work he became well known and

highly respected in the international astronomical community, even though his education and experience were in physics and electronics.

The Caltech Interlude. Although the first pioneering observations in radio astronomy had been made in the United States, by the 1950s the United States had fallen far behind Australia and the United Kingdom in this important, new, and rapidly developing field. With the support of the Radiophysics chief, Taffy Bowen, Bolton went to Caltech to exploit the opportunity of complementing radio observations with those made with the large optical telescopes at the Mount Wilson and Palomar observatories. Funding was readily acquired from the U.S. Office of Naval Research for a new radio observatory, with strong support from Caltech and private donors.

Bolton, who was joined by Stanley, located a suitable site for Caltech's planned new radio observatory in the

John Bolton. COURTESY OF CALTECH ARCHIVES.

remote Owens Valley, about 200 miles north of the Caltech Pasadena headquarters, and they began the construction of a two-element interferometer. At this time, radio telescopes fell into two main categories: those operating at meter wavelengths, which used wire arrays, often in the form of interferometers; and those working at the shorter decimeter and centimeter wavelengths, which used single parabolic dishes. Bolton, Stanley, and Caltech's chief engineer, Bruce Rule, designed the first radio interferometer operating at decimeter wavelengths by using a pair of large 90-foot (27.4-meter) parabolic dishes mounted on wheels

and capable of being positioned at stations along a 1,600-foot (487.7-meter) railway track. While the interferometer was under construction at Owens Valley, Bolton, Stanley, and Harris (1958) used a 24-foot antenna on Mount Palomar to do hydrogen-line studies at 21 centimeters. This was followed by the observation of an occultation of Taurus A by the solar corona using a 25 Megahertz array, which they built at Owens Valley. In this study, they were able to establish the existence of scattering by the solar corona out to much greater distances than had hitherto been determined by other workers operating at higher frequencies.

The Owens Valley interferometer quickly became one of the premier radio telescopes in the world and was used initially to determine radio source coordinates with unprecedented accuracy. In collaboration with astronomers from Caltech and the Mount Wilson and Palomar observatories, the program of the Owens Valley Radio Observatory led to the identification of radio galaxies at ever-increasing redshifts and ultimately to the discovery of quasars. Other programs were aimed at determining the two-dimensional brightness distribution of radio galaxies, radio source spectra and polarization, the study of planetary atmospheres and surfaces including Jupiter's unique radiation belts, interstellar hydrogen clouds, and the first high-frequency galactic plane survey. Most of the work was published by his students and postdoctoral fellows, but Bolton provided the inspiration, and much of the hard labor of observing, reducing the data, designing and building the radio telescopes, and preparing the papers for publication.

Director of the Parkes Radio Telescope. In 1961 Bolton returned to Australia to supervise the completion of the new 210-foot (64-meter) radio telescope near Parkes, New South Wales, and to become the first director of the radio telescope, which was the largest in the Southern Hemisphere. One of the first observing programs at Parkes was the initiation of a Southern Hemisphere sky survey. Under Bolton's leadership more than two thousand radio sources were detected, and accurate positions and flux densities were measured at three wavelengths, 11, 20, and 75 centimeters. Bolton and a series of colleagues and students went on to refine the survey, and they made more sensitive observations at additional wavelengths in order to determine the spectra of the various radio sources and establish more accurate positions. Later they extended the survey itself to 11 centimeters, and more than eight thousand sources were cataloged in fourteen publications over a period of nearly a decade of painstaking work.

By the late 1960s Bolton's research was almost entirely involved in optical work in collaboration with a series of students and postdoctoral associates such as Margaret Clarke, Jennifer Ekers, Jasper Wall, Jet Merkelijn, and Ann Savage. Optical identifications were made for nearly one thousand sources and were reported in a series of more than forty research papers published between 1965 and 1982. During this period, Bolton returned frequently to Caltech to inspect the original Palomar Sky Survey plates and to observe at the Palomar and Lick observatories. He also took part in the planning and commissioning of the new 3.9-meter Anglo Australian Telescope (AAT) at Siding Spring and became the first chairman of its time allocation committee. He urged the

use of an altazimuth mount for the AAT, but optical astronomers were not yet ready to depart from the traditional equatorial mount. Based on his experience at Parkes and Caltech, Bolton argued for a strong, relatively large observatory staff on the mountaintop to support the complex operations of a modern observatory, but again he ran into opposition from the "traditionalist" astronomers at Australia's Mount Stromlo Observatory.

Bolton designed and built a blink machine capable of simultaneously examining pairs of plates from the 48-inch UK Schmidt Telescope in two colors. It differed from conventional blink machines of the 1970s in that the plates were viewed with TV cameras, which could present the images side by side or coincidentally with the signal from one reversed. Bolton's machine was a great success not only for research, but for teaching as well, because several people could view the monitor with up to a hundred times magnification. Everyone who saw the prototype wanted one, and over time he built three machines. Later modifications included interfacing with a computer. The optical identifications provided a grid of accurately known positions in the southern radio sky, which was used to better calibrate the pointing of the Parkes Radio Telescope.

In July 1979 Bolton suffered a severe heart attack. Although he was no longer capable of long nighttime hours at the telescope, he spent the next eighteen months with his associates finishing the analysis of data already in hand, archiving thirteen years of data from the Parkes 11-centimeter catalog, and bringing the catalog up to date in computer-readable form. He and Letty, his wife of thirty-three years, then retired to Buderim on the Queensland coast in 1981, and enjoyed the next decade surfing in the warm Pacific Ocean and playing golf. He died at his home on 6 July 1993.

John Bolton was known to have strong opinions, and had little tolerance for people and ideas that did not coincide with his own. Nor did he have any patience for bureaucracy or authority. But he was generous with his students and young colleagues, often refusing to be included as a coauthor for works that he had initiated and directed. Many of his students and postdoctoral associates went on to productive careers in radio astronomy: one (Robert Woodrow Wilson) was a future Nobel Prize winner, and six others later became directors of observatories or research institutes. He was survived by Letty and her two children from a previous marriage, Brian and Peter (whom he had adopted).

BIBLIOGRAPHY

WORKS BY BOLTON

"Discrete Sources of Galactic Radio Noise." *Nature* 162 (1948): 141–142.

With G. J. Stanley and O. B. Slee. "Positions of Three Discrete Sources of Galactic Radio Frequency Radiation." *Nature* 164 (1949): 101–102.

With K. C. Westfold. "Structure of the Galaxy and the Sense of Rotation of Spiral Nebulae." *Nature* 165 (1950): 487–488.

With G. J. Stanley and O. B. Slee. "Galactic Radiation at Radio Frequencies VIII." *Australian Journal of Physics* 7 (1954): 110–129.

With N. A. Qureshi. "The Effects of Air Temperature and Pressure on the Decay of Silver Iodide." *Bulletin of the American Meteorological Society* 35 (1954): 395–399.

With G. J. Stanley and B. G. Clark. "A Solar Occultation of the Crab Nebula at a Wavelength of 12 Meters." *Publications of the Astronomical Society of the Pacific* 70 (1958): 594–597.

With G. J. Stanley and D. Harris. "A 21-Cm Survey for Galactic Longitudes 294° to 328°, Latitudes +/-8°." *Publications of the Astronomical Society of the Pacific* 70 (1958): 544–555.

With V. Radhakrishnan. "21-Cm Absorption Studies of Galactic Radio Sources." *Astronomical Journal* 65 (1960): 498.

With R. W. Wilson. "A Survey of Galactic Radiation at 960 Mc/s." *Publications of the Astronomical Society of the Pacific* 72 (1960): 331–341.

With others. "The Parkes 2700-MHZ Survey: Part Fourteen; Catalogue and New Optical Identifications." *Australian Journal of Physics* 46 (1979): 1–14.

"Radio Astronomy at Dover Heights." *Astronomical Society of Australia, Proceedings* 4 (1982): 349–358.

"The Fortieth Anniversary of Extragalactic Radio Astronomy: Radiophysics in Exile." *Astronomical Society of Australia, Proceedings* 8 (1990): 381–383.

OTHER SOURCES

Goddard, Dorothy E., Raymond F. Haynes, and R. P. Robertson, eds. "Pioneering a New Astronomy: Papers Presented at the John G. Bolton Memorial Symposium, Dec. 1993." Special issue, *Australian Journal of Physics* 47, no. 5 (1994): 495–680.

Kellermann, K. I. "John Bolton." *Physics Today* 47 (1994): 73–74.

———. "John Gatenby Bolton (1922–1993)." *Publications of the Astronomical Society of the Pacific* 108 (1996): 729–737.

Murdin, Paul. "John Gatenby Bolton." In *Encyclopedia of Astronomy and Astrophysics,* edited by Paul Murdin. Philadelphia: Institute of Physics Publishing; London and New York: Nature Publishing Group, 2001.

Wild, J. P. "John Bolton (1922–1993)." *Quarterly Journal of the Royal Astronomical Society* 35 (1994): 225–226.

Wild, J. P., and V. Radhakrishnan. "John Gatenby Bolton." *Biographical Memoirs of Fellows of the Royal Society* 41 (1995): 72–86.

———. "John Gatenby Bolton, 1922–1993." *Historical Records of Australian Science* 10 (1996): 381–391.

Wayne Orchiston
Kenneth I. Kellermann

BOLTZMANN, LUDWIG EDUARD

(*b.* Vienna, Austria, 20 February 1844; *d.* Duino, near Trieste, 5 September 1906), *physics, thermodynamics, statistical mechanics.* For the original article on Boltzmann see *DSB,* vol. 2.

After the original *DSB* article, historical research focused on the study of specific aspects of Boltzmann's work, particularly the application of mechanics to thermodynamic systems, the role of the ergodic hypothesis, the analysis of the statistical arguments, and his contribution to the philosophical debate at the end of the nineteenth century. Furthermore, the publication of a large section of Boltzmann's scientific and personal correspondence has contributed to the shedding of light upon the historical and philosophical context (see Fasol-Boltzmann, 1990; Höflechner, 1994; Blackmore, 1995). This postscript provides a picture of the most interesting elements of this critical work.

Mechanics and Thermodynamics. Throughout the 1850s and early 1860s, Rudolf Clausius's and James Clerk Maxwell's works made clear that the study of thermodynamic properties was closely related to the mechanical analysis of systems with many degrees of freedom. On the basis of this relation, during the 1860–1885 period a number of attempts were made to obtain mechanical analogies of thermodynamic laws, that is, expressions which were formally identical to the latter, but which contained mechanical quantities only (see Klein, 1974; Bierhalter, 1992). The most important among these analogies concerned the second law of thermodynamics.

Ludwig Boltzmann was the first, as early as 1866, to use tools of the Lagrangian analytical mechanics to investigate this issue. In his paper "Über die mechanische Bedeutung des zweiten Hauptsatzes der Wärmetheorie," he showed that if the quantity of heat provided to the system is interpreted as mechanical energy, and the temperature is interpreted as the average kinetic energy of the particles, the principle of least action leads to an equation that is formally identical with the second law. In 1871 Clausius (who was especially concerned with finding a mechanical interpretation for the disgregation function) and the Hungarian physicist Kálmán Szily arrived independently at a similar result. However, Boltzmann considered the mechanical analogy as the starting point of a more ambitious program: to specify the conditions that a mechanical system has to satisfy in order to represent thermodynamic behaviors.

Indeed, to obtain the mechanical analogy of the second law, the action integral for a system trajectory must be solved. In general, the solution depends on the initial and the final states, which are not knowable because of the extreme complexity of the system. However, if some

Ludwig Boltzmann. © CORBIS.

special conditions are met, this requirement can be neglected. Boltzmann realized that the kinetic theory needed an additional particular assumption about the long-term behavior of the system. This assumption was as of 2007 known as the ergodic hypothesis: a mechanical system tends to pass through all the states allowed by its general constraints; in other words, its trajectory fills all the allowed phase space.

From Boltzmann's point of view, the ergodic hypothesis is closely connected with thermodynamic behaviors such as the dependence on general constraints, irreversible evolution towards equilibrium, and so on. Hence, Boltzmann devoted some sections of his papers of 1871 ("Einige allgemeine Sätze über Wärmegleichgewicht") and of 1877 ("Bemerkungen über einige Probleme der mechanischen Wärmetheorie") to the study of mechanical trajectories in order to characterize the features of the ergodic kind of motion. In 1879, Maxwell also recognized the importance of the ergodic hypothesis, although his version of this assumption differs significatively from Boltzmann's (see von Plato, 1991).

Role of Statistical Arguments The ergodic hypothesis was important also for the statistical understanding of thermodynamic phenomena and the application of statistical

arguments. In fact, if the trajectory of the system covers the entire phase space, then a description of such a trajectory can be obtained by means of a combinatorial calculation of the possible configurations in the phase space itself. Accordingly, the statistical arguments of which Boltzmann made use after his 1868 paper "Studien über das Gleichgewicht der lebendigen Kraft zwischen bewegten materiellen Punkten" are not simply a generalization of Maxwell's; on the contrary, they played a constructive part in Boltzmann's general approach to thermodynamics.

Research in the 1990s revealed interesting differences between the arguments used in 1868 and in the 1877 paper "Über die Beziehung zwischen dem zweiten Hauptsatze der mechanischen Wärmetheorie und der Wahrscheinlichkeitsrechnung respektive den Sätzen über das Wärmegleichgewicht" (see Bach, 1990; Costantini and Garibaldi, 1997; Costantini and Garibaldi, 1998). In 1868 Boltzmann calculated the marginal distribution of energy for a molecule, that is, the probability that a molecule has a certain energy independent of the energy distribution of the other molecules. To perform his calculation, Boltzmann assumed that the energy was divided in many intervals of equal dimension and defined probability in a classical way as the ratio between favorable cases and total cases. It is worth noting that Boltzmann's marginal argument is probabilistically exact, because it uses classical probability rather than relative frequencies. In 1927 a similar procedure was used by Louis Brillouin in his important paper on quantum statistics. Furthermore, a deep analysis shows that Boltzmann was able to derive and to apply statistical distributions that would be studied by professional statisticians only many years later, notably the Polya bivariate distribution, the Beta distribution, and the Gamma distribution (see Costantini and Garibaldi, 1997).

In 1877, Boltzmann had to resort again to statistical arguments to answer the paradox of reversibility raised by Josef Loschmidt, but the procedure he adopted is remarkably different from that of 1868. First, Boltzmann considered *packets* of energy instead of intervals in order to apply his famous urn model. While an interval is defined by two values of energy, a packet is defined by one value only; this fact changes the number of statistical predicates and the form of the normalization factor. Second, he calculated the equilibrium distribution by means of the maximization of the state probability. Third, he understood the probability as relative frequency and made use of the Stirling approximation.

These developments notwithstanding, the role of statistical arguments in Boltzmann's approach to thermodynamics remained not completely clear. The difficulty was partly due to ambiguities and inconsistencies in Boltzmann's papers. For instance, the issue of what kind of statistics Boltzmann actually used is not settled. In the 1990s, interpreters have hypothesized that Boltzmann assumed the equiprobability not for the individual configurations, but for the distributions of the occupation numbers (how many molecules were in each energy cell). This assumption would imply that Boltzmann used the Bose-Einstein statistics rather than the classical Maxwell-Boltzmann statistics (see Bach, 1990).

Boltzmann's popular and philosophical writings were also the subject of detailed analysis from the 1970s through the 1990s. Scholars agree that Boltzmann's methodology and epistemology evolved over time, but there was wide disagreement in interpreting the direction of this evolution. Lakatosian writers claimed that Boltzmann started from realism and in his late years moved to the positivistic side (see Elkana, 1974; Clark, 1976). According to other interpretations, Boltzmann's late position is, rather, a more tolerant form of realism coupled with a pluralistic methodology of evolutionistic flavor (see Hiebert, 1981; de Regt, 1996). However, this issue, as well as the relation between Boltzmann's philosophical view and his scientific work, remained as of 2007 an open question.

SUPPLEMENTARY BIBLIOGRAPHY

WORKS BY BOLTZMANN

Fasol-Boltzmann, Ilse M., ed., *Principien der Naturfilosofi: Lectures on Natural Philosophy, 1903–1906.* Berlin-Heidelberg: Springer Verlag, 1990. Boltzmann's philosophical lectures at the University of Vienna.

McGuinness, Brian, ed. *Theoretical Physics and Philosophical Problems: Selected Writings / Ludwig Boltzmann.* Dordrecht, Holland and Boston: Reidel, 1974. An English translation of Boltzmann's popular papers.

OTHER SOURCES

Bach, Alexander. "Boltzmann's Probability Distribution of 1877." *Archive for History of Exact Sciences* 41 (1990): 1–40. An interpretation of Boltzmann's statistical arguments in terms of Bose-Einstein statistics.

Battimelli, Gianni, Maria Grazia Ianniello, and Otto Kresten, eds. *Proceedings of the International Symposium on Ludwig Boltzmann.* Vienna: Verlag der Österreichischen Akademie der Wissenschaften, 1993.

Bierhalter, Günther. "Von L. Boltzmann bis J. J. Thomson: die Versuche einer mechanischen Grundlegung der Thermodynamik (1866–1890)." *Archive for History of Exact Sciences* 44 (1992): 25–75. A survey on the problem of the mechanical analogy of the second law.

Blackmore, John, ed. *Ludwig Boltzmann, His Later Life and Philosophy, 1900–1906.* Dordrecht, Holland and Boston: Kluwer, 1995.

Brush, Stephen. *Statistical Physics and the Atomic Theory of Matter.* Princeton, NJ: Princeton University Press, 1983.

Clark, Peter. "Atomismus versus Thermodynamics." In *Method and Appraisal in the Physical Sciences: The Critical Background to Modern Science, 1800–1905,* edited by Colin Howson. Cambridge, U.K.: Cambridge University Press, 1976. A Lakatosian interpretation of Boltzmann's scientific work.

Costantini, Domenico, and Ublado Garibaldi. "A Probabilistic Foundation of Elementary Particle Statistics. Part I." *Studies in History and Philosophy of Modern Physics* 28 (1997): 483–506.

———. "A Probabilistic Foundation of Elementary Particle Statistics. Part II." *Studies in History and Philosophy of Modern Physics* 29 1 (1998): 37–59. A deep analysis of Boltzmann's statistical argument in modern terminology.

De Regt, Hank W. "Philosophy and the Kinetic Theory of Gases." *British Journal for the Philosophy of Science* 47 (1996): 31–62.

Elkana, Yehuda. "Boltzmann's Scientific Research Programme and Its Alternatives." In *The Interaction between Science and Philosophy,* edited by Yehuda Elkana. Atlantic Highlands, NJ: Humanities Press, 1974.

Hiebert, Erwin N. "Boltzmann's Conception of Theory Construction: The Promotion of Pluralism, Provisionalism and Pragmatic Realism." In *Proceedings of the 1978 Pisa Conference on the History and Philosophy of Science.* Vol. II, edited by Jakko Hintikka, David Gruender, and Evandro Agazzi. Dordrecht, Holland and Boston: Reidel, 1981.

Höflechner, Walter, ed. *Ludwig Boltzmann. Leben und Briefe.* Graz: Akademische Druck und Verlaganstalt, 1994. Boltzmann's scientific correspondence with comments and a biography.

Klein, Martin J. "Boltzmann, Monocycles and Mechanical Explanation." In *Philosophical Foundations of Science: Proceedings of Section L, 1969, American Association for the Advancement of Science,* edited by Raymond J. Seeger and Robert S. Cohen. Dordrecht, Holland and Boston: Reidel, 1974.

Von Plato, Jan. "Boltzmann's Ergodic Hypothesis." *Archive for History of Exact Sciences* 42 (1991): 71–89.

De Regt, Hank W. "Philosophy and the Kinetic Theory of Gases." *British Journal for the Philosophy of Science* 47 (1996): 31–62.

Massimiliano Badino

BONDI, HERMANN (*b.* Vienna, Austria, 1 November 1919; *d.* Cambridge, United Kingdom, 10 September 2005), *relativity theory, cosmology, astrophysics, science policy.*

Bondi, an atheist Jewish Anglo-Austrian, was an eminent mathematical physicist, astronomer, and cosmologist. He is probably best known as one of the chief architects of the steady state model of the universe, which he defended between 1948 and the mid-1960s when it was disproved by observations. However, it would be unfair to identify his scientific work with the steady state theory. From 1947 to the 1990s, Bondi contributed to a variety of problems in astrophysics and relativity theory, and he was a central figure in the renaissance of general relativity, roughly the 1955–1975 period.

Bondi's interest in and contributions to science were far from limited to theoretical physics and astronomy. More than able as an organizer and administrator, from the late 1960s, Bondi got increasingly involved in science policy, internationally as well as on the government level. He was instrumental in the establishment of the European Space Research Organization, served as chief scientific advisor to the British government, and from 1983 to 1990, he was master of Churchill College, University of Cambridge. He served as secretary of the Royal Astronomical Society 1956–1964. Bondi received many honors for his contributions to science and science policy. He became a Fellow of the Royal Society in 1959, and was awarded the Einstein Society Gold Medal in 1983, the Gold Medal of the Institute of Mathematics and its Applications in 1988, the Planetary Award in 1993, and the Gold Medal of the Royal Astronomical Society in 2001. He was knighted (Knight Commander of the Order of Bath) in 1973.

In 1947, Bondi married Christine Stockman, an astrophysics research student supervised by Fred Hoyle. Together with her husband, Christine Bondi published several papers on stellar structure. The couple had five children, two sons and three daughters. His wife and children survived him.

Education and Early Career. Bondi belonged to a nonreligious Jewish family that had moved from Germany to Vienna in 1884. He attended a *Realgymnasium* (secondary school focused on science, rather than traditional classical education), where he demonstrated a remarkable talent for mathematics and physics. When Arthur Eddington happened to be in Vienna in 1936, the sixteen-year-old schoolboy managed to meet him, which fueled his ambitions of following a career in science. With the help of Abraham Frankel, his great-uncle and an eminent mathematician at the Hebrew University in Jerusalem, Bondi succeeded in being admitted as a foreign student at Trinity College, Cambridge, where he arrived in the fall of 1937, not yet eighteen years old. This was half a year before Austria became part of the Third Reich and adopted Hitler's racial laws against the Jewish population. However, young Bondi's decision to leave Austria were not politically motivated, but due to his wish to study in Cambridge.

Bondi had not been long in Cambridge as an undergraduate student of mathematics when Germany invaded Poland; Britain and France declared war on Germany a couple of days later. In a letter of recommendation, Eddington described Bondi as "a mathematical student of great brilliance and promise," but it did not prevent him from being interned in May 1940. He was, after all, a citizen of a nation with which England was at war. Bondi spent most of the time until August 1941 in an internment camp in Quebec, Canada, where he happened to meet another Austrian internee, Thomas Gold, who studied engineering at Cambridge University. Bondi and Gold became close friends and used much of their time in the camp to discuss questions of physics. After returning to England, Bondi took up his studies in theoretical physics under the supervision of the distinguished mathematician and geophysicist Harold Jeffreys. He made his debut in the world of pure research in 1942 with a publication in the *Proceedings of the Royal Society* on the wind generation of waves on shallow water. But there was a war going on, and Bondi was subsequently drawn into military research, working for the admiralty on the theory of the magnetron, the kind of vacuum tube which was a central component in the radar sender.

Together with Gold, who in the summer of 1942 had been hired by Fred Hoyle's radar group, Bondi rented a three-bedroom house in Dunsfold, near Witley. Hoyle frequently stayed in the house, with the result that the three young physicists established a lasting friendship based on their common conceptions of the situation in physics and astronomy. Unlike Bondi and Gold, Hoyle was already deeply interested in astrophysics and astronomy, subjects which were part of their long discussions. When Bondi returned to Cambridge in the summer of 1945, he was appointed assistant lecturer by the faculty of mathematics. Three years later he advanced to the permanent position as university lecturer. In 1946, he (as well as Gold) became a British subject. The following year, after he was married, he and his wife moved to a flat near Trinity College. The young couple continued to be in close contact with Hoyle and Gold.

By about 1945, Bondi had become interested in the general theory of relativity, a subject which was far from fashionable at the time but appealed to a few mathematically inclined physicists such as Bondi. He was asked by the Royal Astronomical Society to prepare a review report on cosmology and accepted the offer in spite of having only a superficial knowledge of the field. After having acquired the necessary background knowledge, he produced a masterly report on the state of cosmology, which was published in the Royal Astronomical Society's *Monthly Notices* in early 1948. Although Bondi did not, at this stage, advocate a particular cosmological theory, his review paper reflected the same methodological commitments which shortly later were made explicit in the steady state theory. For example, he was quite critical towards the "extrapolatory" approach of relativistic cosmology, which he contrasted with the "deductive" approach of Edward A. Milne's kinematic cosmology. In the first approach, the physicist extrapolates laboratory physics to form a comprehensive theory, which is then assumed to be valid for the entire universe; the alternative, which Bondi preferred, is to start from a small number of cosmological postulates and from these to deduce the corresponding physical theories. Bondi emphasized that, whatever the approach, any cosmological theory had to account for the repeatability of experiments, a claim that would be highlighted in the version of steady state theory that he and Gold published a few months later.

The Steady State Theory of the Universe. To the extent that there existed a standard cosmology in the late 1940s, it was the evolutionary universe based on Einstein's field equations of 1917, either in the big bang version or the ever-expanding but no-bang Lemaître-Eddington version. In their discussions of 1946 and 1947, Hoyle, Gold, and Bondi agreed that an evolutionary universe governed by general relativity was unsatisfactory in whatever version. They concluded that an unchanging yet expanding universe was preferable, and for this reason they postulated continual creation of matter to occur throughout space at such a rate that it compensated for the expansion and left the average density of matter constant (the idea came from Gold). In early 1948, Gold and Bondi and, independently, Hoyle worked out their two formulations of the steady state universe.

The theory presented in the 1948 Bondi-Gold paper was deductively founded on what they called the perfect cosmological principle, the postulate that the universe is uniform not only spatially but temporally as well: it has always looked the same. This principle, they claimed, was a fundamental axiom from which physical results should be deduced; if theoretical extrapolations from experiments conflicted with the principle, such as did the law of energy conservation, they had to be rejected. Bondi and Gold consequently denied that the universe could be described by the energy-conserving theory of general relativity. Moreover, they objected that relativistic cosmology was "utterly unsatisfactory" because it covered so many models and was based on so many free parameters that as a whole it could not be falsified observationally. In spite of the qualitative and philosophical flavor of their paper, Bondi and Gold could prove that their theory led to a number of definite predictions, including a specific rate of matter creation of about 10^{-43} g/s/cm^3. It also followed from their theory that the metric of the steady state universe had to be of the De Sitter type, a flat space expanding exponentially. Whereas the Hubble parameter was a measure of the age of the universe in the relativistic theories, according to Bondi and Gold it was a true constant.

Hermann Bondi. NICK SINCLAIR/SCIENCE PHOTO LIBRARY/PHOTO RESEARCHERS, INC.

The Bondi-Gold theory differed methodologically from Hoyle's version of steady state cosmology, but the two versions led to the same physics and were generally known as one theory. It was met with stiff resistance by critics who argued that it was contradicted by observations and also that it was methodologically flawed because it relied on the perfect cosmological principle. During the heated debate in the 1950s, Bondi defended the theory skillfully and largely successfully. For example, observations from 1948 indicated an excess reddening in the spectra of distant galaxies which seemed to contradict the steady state theory. Big bang cosmologists used this so-called Stebbins-Whitford effect to discredit the steady state theory, but in a critical review of the data Bondi, Gold, and Dennis Sciama showed in 1954 that the effect was spurious. Together with Raymond Lyttleton, Bondi suggested in 1959 a new "electrical cosmology" in conformity with the steady state theory and based on the hypothesis that the numerical charge of an electron differed slightly from the proton's charge. The ingenious theory was short lived, for it quickly turned out that the predicted charge excess disagreed with experiments.

When it came to defending steady state cosmology from a methodological and philosophical point of view,

Bondi was the theory's leading spokesman. Inspired by Karl Popper's falsificationist philosophy of science, he argued that the steady state theory was methodologically superior to the relativistic evolution theories because of its unique predictions. However, when the steady state theory ran into serious trouble in the early 1960s, first when confronted with radio astronomical data, Bondi did not act as a Popperian falsificationist. Rather than admitting that the steady state theory had been proved wrong, he questioned the reliability of the observations and preferred to suspend his judgment on the matter. Earlier criticisms of the steady state theory by some radio astronomers had proven to be based on bad data, and so it is perhaps not surprising that Bondi did not quickly reject the steady state theory when other attacks followed later. Neither did he follow Hoyle in inventing new versions of the steady state theory, and by 1965 (when the cosmic microwave background was discovered), he had quietly left cosmology as a research field.

Works in Relativity and Astrophysics. Bondi's work in astrophysics started in the mid-1940s when he, inspired by Hoyle, got interested in how a star in a gas cloud accretes interstellar matter by way of gravitational attraction. His work in this area, in part done in collaboration with Hoyle and Lyttleton, continued for several years and led to concepts named after him, such as *Bondi accretion* and *Bondi mass*. In 1952, he collaborated with Edwin Salpeter in a study of thermonuclear reactions in stars, his only work in nuclear astrophysics.

Although Bondi denied that the universe was fully governed by general relativity, he had great confidence in Einstein's gravitation theory and did much to revitalize it during the 1950s and 1960s. He made his entry in general relativity in 1947, when he examined the solution of the Einstein equations in the case of a spherically symmetric, inhomogeneous universe. This work was an extension of a theory put forward by Richard Tolman in 1934 which again relied on an investigation by Georges Lemaître from the previous year. The solution is generally known as the *Tolman-Bondi model*, although from a historical point of view *Lemaître-Tolman model* would be more appropriate. Bondi's paper anticipated future developments in the field of inhomogeneous models and was considered of such importance that it was reprinted in 1999. In a paper of 1957, he analyzed the concept of negative mass in general relativity by constructing a solution to the Einstein equations in terms of hypothetical matter with repulsive gravitation.

Gravitational radiation was a subject that occupied Bondi for about thirty years. His papers in this area "are still canonical reading," the relativist Andrzej Krasinski wrote in 1999 (p. 1778). In a series of papers between 1959 and 1988, some of them coauthored by Felix Pirani, Bondi conclusively showed that general relativity theory predicts gravitational waves and that these are not a coordinate effect but should be observable. He was particularly interested in plane waves, which he studied in great detail. He found that such waves could produce a relative acceleration in free test particles, from which he inferred that the waves transport energy. In one of his last scientific papers, published in 1988 with Pirani, he studied a mechanism for the conversion of gravitational energy into electromagnetic energy. In a couple of works (1967–1969), Bondi examined the radial motion of uniform spheres in general relativity, concluding that in certain cases the system would "bounce," i.e., reverse its radial motion.

Among the books that Bondi wrote during his long scientific career, *Cosmology* (1952) was an excellent introduction to and survey of the contemporary state of cosmology, including relativistic cosmology as well as steady state theory and Edward A. Milne's kinematic relativity. Reprinted in 1960, it was for a long time the standard textbook on the subject. In the early 1960s, he wrote two popular books, *The Universe at Large* (1961) and *Relativity and Common Sense* (1964), and in 1968, he published *Assumption and Myth in Physical Science*. His autobiography, focusing more on his administrative and political work than on his scientific contributions, appeared in 1990 under the title *Science, Churchill & Me*.

Statesman of Science. In spite of his scientific work being highly theoretical, Bondi was far from an ivory-tower scientist. As early as 1953, while deeply engaged in the cosmological controversy, he wrote a report on the floods that devastated parts of eastern England that year. It was largely as a result of Bondi's report that the London Barrier was built a few years later. After he left King's College, London, he began a parallel career in public service, first from 1967 to 1971 as director general for the European Space Research Organization, ESRO, the predecessor of ESA, the European Space Agency. From 1971 to 1984, Bondi worked as a high-level public servant, first as chief scientific advisor for the Ministry of Defense and subsequently as chief scientist in the Department of Energy, where he laid the groundwork for Britain's first long-term energy policy. During the 1980–1984 period he served as chairman and chief executive of the Natural Environment Research Council. Remarkably, during these busy years in public service, he continued doing work in pure physics.

Bondi's views on science and society were in line with the ideals of the Enlightenment era. He strongly believed in the social value of science and the social responsibility of scientists, including educational reforms based on science. He was active in the scientific education of the public and published several articles in the journal *Physics*

Education. Philosophically, he was a follower of Popper, whom he greatly admired and in 1992 characterized as "the philosopher for science." (When Popper died in 1994, Bondi wrote his obituary in *Nature.*) Since his childhood in Vienna Bondi had been an atheist, developing from an early age a view on religion that associated it with repression and intolerance. This view, which he shared with Hoyle, never left him. On several occasions he spoke out on behalf of freethinking, so-called, and became early on active in British atheist or "humanist" circles. From 1982 to 1999, he was president of the British Humanist Association, and he also served as president of the Rationalist Press Association of United Kingdom.

BIBLIOGRAPHY

Janus Project. "The Papers of Sir Hermann Bondi." Bondi's papers, contained in 109 archive boxes, are deposited at Churchill Archives Centre, Cambridge, England. Finding aid: http://janus.lib.cam.ac.uk.

WORKS BY BONDI

"On the generation of waves on shallow water by wind." *Proceedings of the Royal Society* 181 (1942): 67–71.

"Spherical Symmetrical Models in General Relativity." *Monthly Notices of the Royal Astronomical Society* 107 (1947): 410–425.

"Review of Cosmology." *Monthly Notices of the Royal Astronomical Society* 108 (1948): 104–120.

With Thomas Gold. "The Steady-State Theory of the Expanding Universe." *Monthly Notices of the Royal Astronomical Society* 108 (1948): 252–270.

"On Spherically Symmetrical Accretion." *Monthly Notices of the Royal Astronomical Society* 112 (1952): 195–204.

Cosmology. Cambridge, U.K.: Cambridge University Press, 1952.

"Fact and Inference in Theory and Observation." *Vistas in Astronomy* 1 (1955): 155–162.

"Negative Mass In General Relativity." *Reviews of Modern Physics* 29 (1957): 423–428.

"Some Philosophical Problems in Cosmology." In *British Philosophy in the Mid-Century,* edited by Cecil Alec Mace. London: Allen and Unwin, 1957.

With Felix Pirani and Ivor Robinson. "Gravitational Waves in General Relativity. III. Exact Plane Waves." *Proceedings of the Royal Society of London A* 251 (1959): 519–533.

Assumption and Myth in Physical Science. Cambridge: Cambridge University Press, 1967.

Oral History Interview by David DeVorkin. 20 March 1978. Available at http://www.aip.org/history.

"A Non-Believer Looks at Physics." *Physics Education* 22 (1987): 280–283.

"The Cosmological Scene 1945–1952." In *Modern Cosmology in Retrospect,* edited by Bruno Bertotti et al. Cambridge, U.K.: Cambridge University Press, 1990.

Science, Churchill & Me. The Autobiography of Hermann Bondi. London: Pergamon, 1990.

OTHER SOURCES

Kragh, Helge. *Cosmology and Controversy. The Historical Development of Two Theories of the Universe.* Princeton, NJ: Princeton University Press, 1996.

Krasinski, Andrzej. "Editor's Note: Spherically Symmetrical Models in General Relativity." *General Relativity and Gravitation* 31 (1999): 1777–1781.

Mestel, Leon. "Obituary: Hermann Bondi (1919–2005)." *Nature* 437 (2005): 828.

Helge Kragh

BOREL, ARMAND (*b.* la Chaux-de-Fonds, Switzerland, 21 May 1923; *d.* Princeton, New Jersey, 11 August 2003), *mathematics, Lie groups, algebraic groups, arithmetic groups, topology.*

Lie groups and linear algebraic groups played a central role in Borel's work. His exploration of these was basic in important trends in pure mathematics in the second half of the twentieth century, for example in the development of the theory of modular forms.

Biography. Borel grew up in the French-speaking part of Switzerland. After finishing his secondary school education in Geneva, he entered the Eidgenössische Technische Hochschule (ETH) in Zürich in 1942, studying mathematics and physics. He graduated in 1947, having also fulfilled his obligatory military service. Distinguished mathematicians were teaching at the ETH, including Heinz Hopf, who introduced Borel to topology, and Eduard Stiefel, who taught him the arcana of the theory of Lie groups. After two years as an assistant at the ETH, Borel spent the academic year of 1949–1950 in Paris with a grant from the Centre National de Recherches Scientifiques. There he came in contact with French mathematicians of his generation (notably Jean-Pierre Serre). He studied the work of Jean Leray in topology, being one of the first to become familiar with that work. After fulfilling a temporary teaching position at the University of Geneva, he obtained his doctoral degree (Doctorat ès Sciences Mathématiques) in 1952 in Paris, under the aegis of Leray. Also in 1952 Borel married Gabrielle (Gaby) Aline Pittet. They had two daughters.

Borel spent the academic years of 1952–1954 at the Institute for Advanced Study in Princeton, New Jersey. The period was crucial for the broadening of his mathematical interests. The next academic year (1954–1955) he was a visiting lecturer at the University of Chicago, where André Weil stimulated his interests in algebraic geometry and number theory. In 1955 Borel returned to Switzerland to take up a professorship at the ETH in Zürich. He then accepted, in 1957, a professorship at the Institute for Advanced Study in Princeton. This remained his base, although over the years he had many visiting positions elsewhere. An institution frequently visited was the Tata Institute of Fundamental Research in Bombay (Mumbai), of which he was an honorary fellow. In 1983–1986 he also held a professorship at the ETH in Zürich.

Borel retired from the Institute for Advanced Study in 1993, but he remained vigorous and active until the very end of his life. In 1999–2001 he was engaged in a program on Lie groups at the University of Hong Kong. Shortly after his eightieth birthday he was struck by cancer. He died a few months later.

Almost all of Borel's published papers can be found in the four volumes of his *Oeuvres* (Collected Papers). The fourth volume contains a list of all publications, including seventeen books. The numbering of that list is used below (numbers in square brackets).

The theory of Lie groups is central in Borel's work. Many of its aspects are explored. The work is of great depth and reveals not only a profound insight but also a remarkable clarity in the presentation of difficult material.

Borel had a somewhat reserved personality and at first sight could seem unapproachable. But once one knew him a little better he turned out to be a very friendly person, with a good sense of humor. Many mathematicians were helped or stimulated by him. Frequently, mathematical contacts with him resulted in collaborations, in which he freely shared his ideas. His mathematical erudition was extraordinary. Outside mathematics, his interests and knowledge were also impressive. He traveled widely and he was very knowledgeable about the culture of the countries he and his wife had visited. A particular interest of Borel's was Carnatic (South Indian) classical music, of which he had expert knowledge.

He received several honors, including an honorary doctorate of the University of Geneva and memberships in the French Académie des Sciences and of the National Academy of Sciences. In 1992 he received the Balzan Prize for mathematics.

Lie Groups and Topology. Lie groups embody the continuous symmetries in mathematics and physics. Their theory was started in the nineteenth century by the Norwegian mathematician Sophus Lie. At first the notion of a Lie group was "localized," which led to the theory of Lie algebras. But in the beginning of the twentieth century, for example in the work of Élie Cartan and Hermann Weyl, "global" aspects came into play, involving the geometry of the Lie group viewed as a geometric entity. A little later, in the 1940s, Borel's teacher Heinz Hopf made important contributions to the study of the topology of Lie groups. A fundamental problem in that study is the

determination of the homology groups or better, of the cohomology ring, of compact Lie group. Borel in his thesis [23] uses a new approach to the problem.

This approach is based on the ideas developed by Jean Leray (during his internment as a prisoner of war, 1940–1945). His ideas led to the cohomology theory of sheaves. Also, he devised a technical tool called "spectral sequence," which has become a standard ingredient in homological algebra. Leray lectured about these new and unusual matters in Paris around 1950. Borel attended the lectures, digested Leray's ideas, contributed to them, and gave a course on Leray's work at the ETH (which led to the lecture notes [18]).

To elucidate, let G be a compact connected Lie group. In his thesis Borel introduces a "universal space" E_G for G, an acyclic principal fiber space with fiber G (actually, finite dimensional approximations to E_G are used). The basis B_G of the fiber space is a *classifying space* for G. A central object in Borel's thesis is the Leray spectral sequence associated to the map $E_G \rightarrow B_G$. A difficult algebraic result gives, in good situations, a connection between the graded cohomology algebras $H^*(G, F)$ and $H^*(B_G, F)$ over a field F, say. The first one will be a graded exterior algebra with generators of odd degrees say $2d_1 - 1, 2d_2 - 1, \dots 2d_l - 1$, and the second one a graded polynomial algebra with generators of degrees $2d_1, 2d_2, \dots, 2d_l$, with an explicit connection between the respective generators (involving the Leray spectral sequence). The result is quite powerful and Borel exploits it, for example to study the cohomology of homogeneous spaces G/U, where U is a closed subgroup of G. In subsequent publications Borel studied several aspects of the cohomology of G. One of these is its torsion. In [53] the torsion primes p, the prime numbers for which $H^*(G, Z)$ has p-torsion, are described in terms of the root system of G. These primes turned up later in seemingly unrelated questions in the theory of algebraic groups.

In connection with the universal space of G, mention should be made of the "Borel construction," which is somewhat hidden in the seminar notes [52]. Let X be a space with a G-action. The universal space E_G has a free G-action. The Borel construction associates to X the quotient $_GX = G \backslash (E_G \times X)$ of $X \times E_G$ relative to the diagonal G-action. Then $H^*(_GX, F)$ is the *equivariant cohomology* of X over F. It has become an important tool of algebraic topology.

During his stay at the Institute for Advanced Study in 1952–1954, Borel started a collaboration with Friedrich Hirzebruch on the algebraic topology of homogeneous spaces of Lie groups. The collaboration led to the three influential papers [43, 45, 47]. A spin-off of the work with Hirzebruch was the "Borel-Weil theorem" (obtained in 1953, but unpublished at the time, see [30]). It describes a realization of the irreducible representations of a compact Lie group by sections of certain line bundles, a description that has become methodically important. The joint paper [49] with John C. Moore is a contribution to algebraic topology, introducing the much used "Borel-Moore homology."

Linear Algebraic Groups. Around 1960, topics related to the theory of linear algebraic groups became paramount in Borel's work. Linear algebraic groups are algebraic versions of Lie groups. They had already occurred in the nineteenth century. A linear algebraic group is a subgroup G of a group $GL_n(k)$ of invertible $n \times n$-matrices, where k is an algebraically closed field, such that the elements of G are the solutions of a set of polynomial equations in the matrix coordinates (an orthogonal group is an example). If $k = C$, the field of complex numbers, G can be made into a Lie group.

The theory of Lie groups uses analytic and local methods, unavailable for algebraic groups. Their theory requires tools from algebraic geometry, which had become available by the middle of the twentieth century. Borel took up the theory of linear algebraic groups during his stay in Chicago in 1954–1955. The foundations of the theory were laid in Borel's paper [39]. A linear algebraic group G over the algebraically closed field k is an affine algebraic variety and as such is provided with a topology, the Zariski topology. There is an analogy with the theory of Lie groups.

Borel discovered an elementary but quite fundamental result, whose analogue in the theory of Lie groups is not true, the "orbit lemma." It states that if G acts on an algebraic variety X (in the sense of algebraic geometry), then G has a Zariski-closed orbit in X. The lemma is an ingredient of the proof of the "Borel fixed point theorem." This asserts that if the connected, solvable, linear algebraic group G acts on a complete variety X, then G fixes a point of X.

Borel showed the importance of the maximal closed, connected, solvable, subgroups B of G (soon after called *Borel subgroups*). Two Borel subgroups of G are conjugate in G. Moreover, a quotient G / B is a projective algebraic variety.

An (algebraic) *torus* is a linear algebraic group isomorphic to a group of diagonal matrices in some $GL_n(k)$. Another fundamental result of Borel's paper (an analogue of a basic result about compact Lie groups) is the conjugacy of maximal tori of G. The theory of linear algebraic groups over algebraically closed fields was completed soon after the appearance of [39] by Claude Chevalley. He introduced in the theory of algebraic groups the combinatorial ingredients of the theory of Lie groups (root system, Weyl group). His work culminated in the classification of simple algebraic groups. The work was published in the seminar notes [Chev].

Borel next turned to the "relative" theory of linear algebraic groups, over a field F, which is not necessarily algebraically closed. His interest in the relative theory was certainly motivated by applications to arithmetical questions. Let G be a linear algebraic group over the algebraically closed extension k of F. Then G is *defined over F* if G and the group operations are defined over F in the sense of algebraic geometry. If F is a field of characteristic zero, this means that G is a subgroup of some $GL_n(k)$ defined by polynomial equations with coefficients in F. If G is defined over F one has the subgroup $G(F)$ of elements of G with coordinates in F.

An early publication on the relative theory is the joint paper [64] with Jean-Pierre Serre on Galois cohomology. Much of it has become standard material (see, e.g., Serre's book [Ser]). Fundamental for the relative theory is the joint paper [66] on reductive groups with Jacques Tits. A reductive group is a linear algebraic group whose radical (the maximal closed, connected, normal, solvable subgroup) is a torus. The theory of reductive groups over k resembles the theory of compact Lie groups.

The object of study of [66] is a connected, reductive group G, which is defined over F. Important in the theory are the parabolic subgroups of G, that is, the closed subgroups of G containing a Borel group. They are introduced and studied in this work.

G need not have Borel groups which are defined over F. Instead, one considers parabolic subgroups that are defined over F, and in particular the minimal ones. It is shown that two minimal groups are conjugate by an element of $G(F)$. This is the "relative" version of the conjugacy of Borel groups. G is said to be *isotropic* over F if there exist proper parabolic subgroups over F. If this is the case, Borel and Tits introduce a relative root system and a relative Weyl group. Of Borel's later work pertaining to the general theory of algebraic groups, there is another joint paper [97] with J. Tits. This work studies the group-theoretical homomorphisms between groups of the type $G(F)$, where G is a simple linear algebraic group defined over F. The paper brings the subject to a certain close. Borel's last publication on the general theory of linear algebraic groups is the joint paper [158] with Frédéric Bien and János Kollár on rational connectedness of homogeneous spaces of algebraic groups. It is methodologically interesting, applying new insights of algebraic geometry to algebraic groups.

Arithmetic Groups. Let $GL_n(C) \ni G$ be a linear algebraic group that is defined over the field of rational numbers Q. The group $G(R)$ of real-valued points of G is a Lie group. $G(Z)$ denotes the subgroup of integral-valued points of

$G(R)$. A subgroup Γ of $G(R)$ is *arithmetic* if the intersection $\Gamma \cap G(Z)$ has finite index in both Γ and $G(Z)$.

Fundamental for all arithmetical applications is the joint paper [58] with Harish-Chandra. It brought a conceptual approach to arithmetical questions in group theory that so far had been handled by ad hoc methods, and it lays the foundations of the modern theory of automorphic forms. Let G be defined over Q and assume G to be semisimple (i.e., with trivial radical). Let Γ be an arithmetic subgroup of $G(R)$. Borel and Harish-Chandra construct an open subset U of $G(R)$ with $G(R) = \Gamma.U$, having good properties (a "fundamental subset"). These imply that Γ is finitely generated and that the quotient space $G(R)/\Gamma$ has finite volume (relative to a natural measure). It is compact if and only if G is not isotropic over Q.

The study of the (infinite-dimensional) representation of the Lie group $G(R)$ in the Hilbert space $L^2(G(R)/\Gamma)$ leads into the theory of automorphic forms. In the subsequent paper [60] Borel gave an "adelic" version, also basic for the theory of automorphic forms, of his work with Harish-Chandra. Maintaining the previous notations, let K be a maximal compact subgroup of $G(R)$. The quotient $X = K \backslash G(R)$ is the symmetric space associated to the Lie group $G(R)$. An arithmetic group Γ acts on it and the quotient space X/Γ is an image of $G(R)/\Gamma$.

Borel and Walter L. Baily, Jr., in [69] studied the case that X is hermitian symmetric, that is, has an invariant complex structure. Then $V = X/\Gamma$ is a normal analytic variety. In this work a "compactification" is constructed, that is, a compact analytic variety V^*, containing V as an open subvariety. (Actually, V^* is a projective algebraic variety.) The boundary V^*-V is a union of pieces, each related to classes of parabolic subgroups of G that are defined over Q. Here the relative theory of algebraic groups is crucial. Embeddings of V^* in complex projective spaces are constructed using automorphic forms.

For arbitrary semisimple G a compactification of the space V was constructed by Borel and Serre [98]. Now the compactification V^* is a real manifold with corners.

Much of Borel's later work deals with the cohomology of arithmetic groups. Let Γ be as before and let E be a Γ-module. To study the Eilenberg-MacLane cohomology groups $H^*(\Gamma, E)$ the space V is brought into the picture. One shows that $H^*(\Gamma, E)$ is isomorphic to a relative Lie algebra cohomology group, with coefficients in a vector space related to functions on V. In Borel's talk [101] at the 1974 International Congress in Vancouver he gave a brief review.

The case $E = R$ is discussed in [100], using the Borel-Serre compactification. A beautiful result, important in algebraic K-theory, is the determination of the stable

cohomology of groups like $H^*(SL_n(\mathbf{o}), R)$, where $\mathbf{o}$ is the ring of integers of an algebraic number field. Borel's article [108] gives further arithmetical applications.

In Borel's book [172] with Nolan R. Wallach the connection with relative Lie algebra cohomology is thoroughly explored. Later Borel gave various refinements of his previous work, for example in [125]. One of the refinements is the study of the L^2-cohomology of V, basic results about which are established in the joint paper [126] with W. Casselman. Of a somewhat different nature is the work with Gopal Prasad on finiteness results for arithmetic subgroups of semisimple groups (see [139]).

Other Publications. Borel's publications include seventeen books. Several are based on lectures given by him, about various subjects related to his interests, for instance, the widely used textbook *Linear Algebraic Groups* [142]. At the Institute for Advanced Study, he organized seminars on current topics of research, and he was involved with the publication of notes of these seminars, such as [52] (on "Transformation Groups," 1960), [Ind] (on the "Index Theorem," 1965), and [Sem] (on "Algebraic Groups and Related Finite Groups," 1970). Similar publications, outgrowths of seminars held in Switzerland, are [IC] (on "Intersection Cohomology," 1984) and [DM] (on "Algebraic D-modules," 1987).

Borel was a co-organizer of two Summer Research Institutes of the American Mathematical Society, on "Algebraic Groups and Discontinuous Subgroups" (Boulder, 1966) and on "Automorphic Forms, Representations, and L-functions" (Corvallis, 1977). An aim of the conferences was to present and explain new developments. The conference proceedings ([Proc 9] and [Proc 23]), containing several contributions by Borel himself, have been very influential.

Borel was an outstanding expositor. He gave several talks about the work of others, for example in talks at the Séminaire Bourbaki in Paris. An important expository paper is the report [44] written with J.-P. Serre on Grothendieck's Riemann-Roch theorem. It remains the most accessible description of Grothendieck's work. Borel was a member of the Bourbaki group of mathematicians (see [165]). Originally, their goal was to write textbooks for large parts of mathematics. Some of the published books have become standard references. The group was most influential around the middle of the twentieth century. Borel was involved with the preparation of several Bourbaki books.

In the last ten years of his life he made several contributions to the history of twentieth-century mathematics, for example in reminiscences about other mathematicians. Borel's book *Essays on the Theory of Lie Groups and Algebraic Groups* (American Mathematical Society, 2001) is unique: a historical study of mathematical research in the twentieth century written by one of the leading researchers.

BIBLIOGRAPHY

The Borel archive is kept in Geneva, in the Bibliothèque Publique et Universitaire de Genève.
Borel's four-volume Oeuvres *(Collected Papers) lists almost all of his published papers. The fourth volume contains a list of all publications, including seventeen books. The numbering of that list is used below.*

WORKS BY BOREL

Oeuvres: Collected Papers. Berlin: Springer-Verlag, vol. I, II, III, 1983; vol. IV, 2001.

18. *Cohomologie des espaces localement compacts d'après J. Leray. Lecture Notes in Mathematics* vol. 2. Berlin: Springer-Verlag, 1961.

23. "Sur la cohomologie des espaces fibrés principaux et des espaces homogènes de groupes de Lie compacts." *Annals of Mathematics* 57 (1951): 115–207.

30. "Représentations linéaires et espaces homogènes kähleriens des groupes simplement connexes compacts." (1954, unpublished at the time).

39. "Groupes linéaires algébriques." *Annals of Mathematics* 64 (1956): 20–82.

43, 45, 47. With Friedrich Hirzebruch. "Characteristic Classes and Homogeneous Spaces, I." *American Journal of Mathematics* 80 (1958): 458–538; II, ibid. 81 (1959). 315–382, III, ibid. 82 (1960): 491–504.

44. With Jean-Pierre Serre. "Le théorème de Riemann-Roch, d'après Grothendieck." *Bulletin Société Mathématique de France* 86 (1958): 97–136.

49. With John C. Moore. "Homology Theory for Locally Compact Spaces." *Michigan Mathematical Journal* 7 (1960): 137–159.

52. "Seminar on Transformation Groups." *Annals of Mathematical Studies* 46. Princeton, NJ. Princeton University Press, 1961.

53. "Sous-groupes commutatifs et torsion des groupes de Lie compacts connexes." *Tôhoku Mathematical Journal* 13 (1961): 216–240.

58. With Harish-Chandra. "Arithmetic Subgroups of Algebraic Groups." *Annals of Mathematics* 75 (1962): 485–535.

60. "Some Finiteness Properties of Adele Groups over Number Fields." *Publications Mathématiques de l'Institut des Hautes Études Scientifiques* 16 (1963): 5–30.

64. With Jean-Pierre Serre. "Théorèmes de finitude en cohomologie galoisienne." *Commentarii Mathematici Helvetici* 39 (1964): 111–164.

66. With Jacques Tits. "Groupes réductifs." *Publications Mathématiques de l'Institut des Hautes Études Scientifiques* 27 (1965): 55–150.

"Seminar on the Index Theorem." *Annals of Mathematical Studies* no. 57. Princeton, NJ: Princeton University Press, 1965. [Ind.]

With George D. Mostow, eds. "Algebraic Groups and Discontinuous Subgroups." *Proceedings of Symposia in Pure Mathematics* no. 9, American Mathematical Society (1966). [Proc. 9]

69. With Walter L. Baily, Jr. "Compactification of Arithmetic Quotients of Bounded Symmetric Domains." *Annals of Mathematics* 84 (1966): 442–528.

"Seminar on Algebraic Groups and Related Finite Groups." *Lecture Notes in Mathematics* no. 131. Berlin: Springer-Verlag, 1970. [Sem.]

97. With Jacques Tits. "Homomorphismes 'abstraits' de groupes algébriques simples." *Annals of Mathematics* 97 (1973): 499–571.

98. With Jean-Pierre Serre. "Corners and Arithmetic Groups." *Commentarii Mathematici Helvetici* 48 (1973): 436–491.

100. "Stable Real Cohomology of Arithmetic Groups." *Annales Scientifiques Ecole Normale Supérieure* 7 (1974): 235–272.

101. "Cohomology of Arithmetic Groups." *Proceedings International Congress of Mathematicians, Vancouver, 1974,* I (1975): 435–442.

108. "Cohomologie de SL_n et valeurs de fonctions zeta aux points entiers." *Annali Scientifici Scuola Normale Superiore Pisa* 4 (1977): 613–636; Correction, ibid. 7 (1980): 373.

With William Casselman, eds. "Automorphic Forms, Representations and *L*-functions." *Proceedings of Symposia in Pure Mathematics* no. 23 (2 vols.), American Mathematical Society (1979). [Proc. 23]

125. "Regularization Theorems in Lie Algebra Cohomology." *Duke Mathematical Journal* 50 (1983): 605–623.

126. With William Casselman. "L-cohomology of Locally Symmetric Manifolds of Finite Volume." *Duke Mathematical Journal* 50 (1983): 625–647.

Intersection Cohomology, Progress in Mathematics, no. 50. Boston: Birkhäuser, 1984. [IC]

Algebraic D-modules. Perspectives in Mathematics. Boston: Academic Press, 1987. [DM]

139. With Gopal Prasad. "Finiteness Theorems for Discrete Subgroups of Bounded Covolume in Semisimple Groups." *Publications Mathématiques de l'Institut des Hautes Études Scientifiques* 69 (1989): 119–171; Addendum, ibid. 71 (1990): 173–177.

142. *Linear Algebraic Groups.* 2nd ed. Graduate texts in Mathematics, no. 126. New York: Springer-Verlag, 1991.

158. With Frédéric Bien and János Kollár. "Rationally Connected Homogeneous Spaces." *Inventiones Mathematicae* 124 (1996): 103–127.

"Twenty-five years with Nicolas Bourbaki, 1949–1973." *Notices of the American Mathematical Society* 45 (1998): 373–380.

172. With Nolan R. Wallach. "Continuous Cohomology, Discrete Subgroups and Representations of Reductive Groups." *Annals of Mathematical Studies* 94. Princeton, NJ: Princeton University Press, 1980; 2nd ed., American Mathematical Society, 1999.

OTHER SOURCES

Arthur, James, et al. "Armand Borel (1923–2003)." *Notices of the American Mathematical Society* 51 (2004): 498–524. [AMS]

Chevalley, Claude. "Classification des groupes algébriques semi-simples" (The Classification of Semi-simple Algebraic Groups). *Collected Works of Claude Chevalley*, vol. 3. Edited by Pierre Cartier. New York: Springer-Verlag, 2005.

Serre, Jean-Pierre. "Cohomologie galoisienne." *Lecture Notes in Mathematics* no. 5, 5th ed. Berlin: Springer-Verlag, 1994. English translation, "Galois Cohomology." Berlin: Springer-Verlag, 1997. [Ser.]

T. A. Springer

BORELLI, GIOVANNI ALFONSO (*b.* Naples, Italy, January 1608; *d.* Rome, Italy, 31 December 1679), *astronomy, epidemiology, mathematics, physiology (iatromechanics), physics, volcanology.* For the original article on Borelli see *DSB,* vol. 2.

During the last forty years some notable work has been made on subjects connected with Borelli's life and achievements: his Sicilian context during the years 1636-1657 and 1667-1672; the ideas and works of some of his least known pupils in Pisa, and their later relations with him; the scientific ideas of some of his friends or adversaries in Tuscany (Famiano Michelini, Antonio Oliva, Carlo Rinaldini); the Roman circles to which he was connected during his last Roman period (1673-1679); his library, and, especially Christina's of Sweden academy and the students in the Piarists' school and professed house of S. Pantaleo. A more detailed intellectual biography of Borelli is becoming possible because a substantial amount of his letters has been published, described, or simply uncovered. In particular, his first period in Messina is now better understood, both in terms of his personal relations and in those of the structuring of his mathematical competence. Some substantial progress, however, is still to be made concerning two focal points: first, his formative years until 1636 and the nature and extent of his intellectual relations with Tommaso Campanella; second, the concrete political activities he performed in Messina during years 1670 to 1672 and their extension through his French connections in Rome.

Borelli's Life until about 1635. According to a late seventeenth-century Neapolitan source, Borelli's family lived in one of the castles in which Tommaso Campanella was detained, and Borelli's mother was believed to have had a love affair with the philosopher. Some even supposed that Giovanni Alfonso was his son although Campanella was not in that castle when Giovanni Alfonso was conceived. Borelli's link with the prisoner seems to be confirmed by a manuscript of Campanella's *Medicinalium libri* that was in his possession and is now in Rome's Biblioteca Nazionale (ms. S. Pantaleo 82). At the end of the text he still used his father's name ("ad usum Ioannis Alonsii Borelli"), so he received the copy when still very young. After 1630 he always named himself Giovanni Alfonso. Perhaps this provided some ground for the rumors about his being a pupil of Campanella and explains his later interest in medical-physiological subjects (a study of medicine at Naples University has not been proven).

It is uncertain if he followed Campanella to Rome in 1626 or arrived later. Perhaps his mathematics studies under Benedetto Castelli did not coincide with those of Evangelista Torricelli, who was a pupil of Castelli's before 1632, because the latter seems to have met Borelli only in 1642. In any case, before September 1636 Borelli went to Sicily. It is likely the master had obtained for him the mathematics chair at Messina's university as his name appears in the registers in 1639. His activity in the three preceding years is uncertain.

After leaving Rome, Borelli detached himself from Campanella (no trace exists of relations with him or even with his brother Filippo, the philosopher's secretary, after 1634) and from his ideas and style of thought: The Galilean influence absorbed through Castelli left no trace of any previous relationship. Already in the Sicilian period this was proven by his *Delle cagioni delle febbri maligne* ("On the causes of the malignant fevers", Cosenza 1649). A section of it, regarding astrological explanations of a plague occurring in Sicily from 1647 to 1648, was the most destructive attack to the very foundations of natural astrology produced in Italy until late seventeenth century.

Borelli's Early Mathematical Works. While travelling in Italy during the years 1642 and 1643 Borelli probably stopped in Naples, because some of the mathematics books he owned in a later period came from the library of Giovanni Camillo Gloriosi, Galileo's successor at Padua's university. Gloriosi returned to Naples and died there in 1643. One of those books, Marino Ghetaldi's *De resolutione et compositione mathematica* (Rome 1630), has many annotations in his hand, showing a careful study. This is notable, because that work was one of those marking the passage from François Viète's algebra to Cartesian geometry, although Borelli's published mathematical writings were purely geometrical.

When again in Messina, Borelli took a role in a project to print some of Francesco Maurolico's unpublished works. According to some sources he edited Maurolico's *Emendatio et restitutio Conicorum Apollonii Pergaei* (Messina 1654), and this is confirmed by the draft of a contract signed by him and the printer, recently found in one of his books (Moscheo 1988, 94-107; Baldini 1996; 197). When again in Messina after the Tuscan years (1656–1667), he also prepared an edition of Maurolico's recension of Archimedes's works; owing to the political trouble in the town and Borelli's flight from it in 1672, it was completed by others and published only in 1685 in Palermo (*Admirandi Archimedis Syracusani monumenta omnia mathematica quae extant ex traditione Maurolyci*). Borelli also owned copies of other unpublished works by the Messina mathematician, now in Rome, Biblioteca Nazionale (mss. S. Pantaleo 115–117).

The Research Program on Animal Motion. *Delle cagioni delle febbri maligne* partially attempted to apply Galilean concepts and methods to medical-biological subjects, but not to animal motion. Borelli's works and known letters never hint at this theme before the years 1657 to 1658 (that is, one or two years after his transfer to Pisa) and nothing proves that he had known in Sicily the works concerning that theme he used later. So, unless new evidence is found, it must be assumed that his interest in the field originated in a Tuscan context. Borelli certainly read while in Messina Galileo's *Discorsi e dimostrazioni matematiche* (1638), treating the relationship among a bone's volume, its weight, and its resistance to fracture, but his treatment of animal motion almost abstracts from this relationship. This is notable because, although it is often considered as the founding work of biomechanics (a word, like "iatromathematics," he never used, at least to denote something more specific than a quantitative study of physiological phenomena), *De motu animalium* studied the phenomenology of walking, running, flying, and swimming and the mechanics of it (the statics involved and the work performed, in terms of suspended weights) taking into almost no account the tensions imposed by those motions on the bones, and the effects of the relationships between volumes, weights, and rupture limits on the dimensions of animals moving on the earth's surface, in water or in air. Because this aspect, considered by Galileo in *Discorsi* and some of his some unpublished notes, is most important in modern biomechanics, *De motu animalium* cannot be seen as the origin of the whole range of subjects now encompassed by it. This is true although it fixed a disciplinary paradigm including many of these subjects existed before in a fragmentary form (as shown by a comparison between Borelli's work and those of predecessors like Girolamo Fabrici, Jacob Müller, Pierre Gassendi, Walter Charleton, William Croone, and others). Whatever Galileo's influence on Borelli was in other matters, it was not primary in this. At the same time, Borelli's mechanical approach to organic phenomena was entirely distinct from the Cartesian (which he criticized harshly), and founded—in principle at least—on detailed observations and measures.

Borelli and the Mathematics of the Galilean School. Borelli's work in pure mathematics dealt with some minor, old fashioned geometrical problems (those he dis-

Giovanni Alfonso Borelli. SPL/PHOTO RESEARCHERS, INC.

cussed in Sicily), with the logical ordering of traditional geometry (mainly from a didactical point of view: *Euclides restitutus*), or with exegetical-philological questions (the editions of Maurolico and the translation of Apollonius). Whatever the historical interest and the influence of these works on contemporary discussions, he cannot be placed on a same level with Bonaventura Cavalieri, Torricelli, and even Vincenzio Viviani. His geometry was inferior to theirs also in the sense that, having been detached from the school's centers for twenty years, he never got fully acquainted with the method of indivisibles, remaining mainly a user of the classical (synthetic) method. In addition, he gave algebra almost no place—at least in published works. As a mathematician, he was attacked even from such Galileans as Viviani and a minor figure such as Cosimo Noferi (*Disceptatio pro Euclide, et Torricellio, in qua proportionum Theoriae per methodum Multiplicium defenduntur et confirmantur contra Euclidem restitutum à Io. Alphonso Borellio*, Urbania, Bibl. Comunale, ms. 44). He was mainly interested in the applications, not only in astronomy and pure mechanics, but also in engineering and technological questions. Submarine navigation was one of them. This remains perhaps the least studied part of his scientific work.

Relations with the Royal Society. Attempts to establish a contact with Borelli were made by Henry Oldenburg beginning in July 1666. In the years 1667, 1668, and 1669 the Royal Society's secretary collected information on the Italian scientist from Marcello Malpighi, John Downes, and John Wallis, and on 18 May 1669 wrote a letter to him, asking for information about an ongoing eruption of Mount Etna. Borelli's answer was *Historia et meteorologia incendii Aetnei* (Reggio Calabria 1670, received by Oldenburg in August 1671). After collecting other information on Borelli by such correspondants as Malpighi and Wallis in 1670, the Secretary wrote him again, starting an exchange of scientific books (perhaps the most notable between England and Italy in those years, because it included works by Isaac Barrow, John Wallis, Robert Boyle, René François Walter de Sluse, Malachi Thruston and perhaps others by Thomas Willis, Thomas Hobbes, Robert Hooke, James Gregory, and Walter Needham, in additon to Gottfried Leibniz's *Hypothesis physica nova*: Borelli was perhaps the first Italian scientist to know the mechanical ideas of the German philosopher). Oldenburg's last letter to Borelli (1676) was apparently lost and Borelli probably did not answer. Other letters to Malpighi and different Roman correspondants expressed his concern about the Italian's project *de motu animalium*.

Political Vicissitudes and the Late Roman Years. Borelli's ideology and his religious and political ideas have not been clarified entirely, even if some points seem established. In a very cautious way, he opposed scholasticism and the religious orders defending it (mainly the Jesuits), while being always on good terms with the Piarists (an almost not doctrinal order, already supported by Campanella). He was linked with individuals and parties opposing the Spanish rule in southern Italy and had some reserved contacts with Italian partisans of the French monarchy. Probably considering it the means to subvert that rule and, also probably, not in view of a united Italian or south Italian state, but of a republican government in Messina and its countryside. It has to be supposed that in 1672 the friends he had in the upper Sicilian nobility informed him promptly that the Spanish authorities looked at him as the strategist of the town's upheaval because he left Messina, taking all his belongings and books with him. He first hid himself in a village in the Calabrian coast along the Ionian Sea. Then in late spring or early summer of 1673, he went to Rome. He possibly considered it a provisory refuge, because he addressed the Medici for a new position in the Tuscan state. Their answer (for political but, perhaps, also personal reasons) was negative. He had to remain in Rome and rely on his own resources while trying to obtain the patronage of both Queen Christina of Sweden (who had retired to Rome after her abdication and conversion to Catholicism) and Louis XIV, who was interested in him through the royal astronomer Giandomenico Cassini. Cassini was an acquaintance of Borelli's beginning in the Tuscan years. None of them, however, offered him a stable and remunerated position, so from 1676 or 1677 until his death he had to live poorly in the Piarists's house. Christina admitted him to her academy and granted the money to print *De motu animalium*.

SUPPLEMENTARY BIBLIOGRAPHY

Many unpublished works and letters remain in the "Collezione galileiana" of Florence's Biblioteca Nazionale and in other libraries and archives, not only in Italy. Two short writings on the mechanics of the helm and of walking on an ice surface are in Stefano Gradi's papers in the Vatican Library (ms. Vat. Lat. 6921); copies of letters and unpublished dissertations (mostly read in Queen Christina's academy in Rome) are in Vancouver, Woodward Library, ms. Q 113 B 6, I-II; the Roman archive of the Piarists has the original of the first part of De motu animalium *(ms. 90).*

Baldini, Ugo. "Animal Motion before Borelli: 1600–1680." In *Marcello Malpighi Anatomist and Physician,* edited by Domenico Bertoloni Meli. Florence: Olschki, 1997.

———. "Borelli, Giovanni Alfonso." *Dizionario Biografico degli Italiani* 12 (1970): 543–551.

———. *Un libertino accademico del Cimento. Antonio Oliva.* Florence, Italy, Olschki, 1977.

———. "Galileismo e politica: il caso borelliano." *Annali dell'Istituto e Museo di storia della scienza di Firenze* 3 (1978): 81–93.

———. "Giovanni Alfonso Borelli e la rivoluzione scientifica." *Physis* 16 (1974): 97–128.

———. "Giovanni Alfonso Borelli biologo e fisico negli studi recenti." *Physis* 16 (1974): 234–266.

———. "Libri appartenuti a Giovanni Alfonso Borelli." In *Filosofia e Scienze nella Sicilia dei Secoli XVI e XVII,* edited by Corrado Dollo. Catania, Italy: Università di Catania-Regione Sicilia, 1996.

Breimer, Lars, and Patrick Sourander. "Alphonso Borelli and Christina: The Father of Kinesiology and the Queen of Sweden." *Clio Medica* 18 (1983): 155–165.

Conforti, Maria. "Testes alterum cerebrum. Succo nerveo e succo seminale nella macchina del vivente di Giovanni Alfonso Borelli." *Medicina nei secoli* 13 (2001): 577–595.

Des Chene, Dennis. "Mechanisms of Life in the Seventeenth Century: Borelli, Perrault, Regis." *Studies in History and Philosophy of Science* 36 (2005): 245–260.

Galluzzi, Paolo. "Lettere di Giovanni Alfonso Borelli ad Antonio Magliabechi." *Physis* 12 (1970): 267-298.

———, and Maurizio Torrini, eds. *Le opere dei Discepoli di Galileo Galilei. Carteggio 1642–1648. Volume primo.* Florence, Italy: Giunti-Barbera, 1975.

Guerrini, Luigi. "Due lettere inedite di Tommaso Frosini a Francesco Redi sul *De motu animalium* di Giovanni Alfonso Borelli." *Nuncius* 13 (1998): 193–208.

———. "Matematica ed erudizione. Giovanni Alfonso Borelli e l'edizione fiorentina dei libri V, VI e VII delle Coniche di Apollonio di Perga." *Nuncius* 14 (1999): 505–523.

Guglielmo Righini, and Thomas B. Settle. "Giovanni Alfonso Borelli e la visibilità di Venere." *Annali dell'Istituto e Museo di storia della scienza di Firenze* 1 (1976): 37–56.

Hall, Alfred Rupert, and Marie Boas Hall, eds. *The Correspondence of Henry Oldenburg.* Madison: University of Wisconsin Press, 1965–1986. Volumes 3, 5, 6, 7, 8, 9, 10, and 13 contain correspondence with Borelli.

Kirsanov, V.S., and S.S. Demidov. "On the History of Aeromechanics in the 17th Century." *XIVth International Congress of the History of Science. Proceedings*, No. 2. (1975): 114–117.

Meli, Domenico Bertoloni. "The Neoterics and Political Power in Spanish Italy: Giovanni Alfonso Borelli and His Circle." *History of Science* 34 (1996): 57–89.

———. "Shadows and Deception: From Borelli's *Theoricae* to the *Saggi* of the Cimento." *British Journal for the History of Science* 31 (1998): 383–402.

Middleton, William E. Knowles. "Borelli and the eruption of Etna in 1669: Some Unpublished papers." *Physis* 15 (1973): 111–130.

———. "Giovanni Alfonso Borelli on the Construction of Galleys." *Mariner's Mirror* 59 (1973): 3–8.

———. "Giovanni Alfonso Borelli and the Invention of the Heliostat." *Archive for History of Exact Sciences* 10 (1973): 329–341.

———. "The 1669 Eruption of Mount Etna: Francesco d'Arezzo on the Vitreous Nature of lava." *Archives of Natural History* 11 (1982): 92–102.

———. "Some Unpublished Correspondence of Giovanni Alfonso Borelli." *Annali dell'Istituto e Museo di Storia della Scienza di Firenze* 9 (1984): 99–132.

———. "Texts and documents: An Unpublished Letter from Marcello Malpighi." *Bulletin of the History of Medicine* 59 (1985): 105–108.

Moscheo, Rosario. *Francesco Maurolico tra Rinascimento e scienza galileiana. Materiali e ricerche.* Messina, Italy: Società Messinese di Storia Patria, 1988.

———. "Galileans in Sicily: A Hitherto Unpublished Correspondence of Daniele Spinola with Domenico Catalana in Messina (1650–1652)," In *The Light of Nature. Essays in the History and Philosophy of Science Presented to A.C. Crombie*, edited by J.D. North, J.J. Roche, et. al., 237–264. Dordrecht, Netherlands: M. Nijhoff, 1985.

Nastasi, Pietro. "Una polemica giovanile di Giovanni Alfonso Borelli." *Physis* 26 (1984): 215–247.

Palladino, Franco. "Sulla teoria delle proporzioni nel Seicento: due 'macchinazioni' notevoli: le sezioni dei razionali del galileiano G.A. Borelli–Le classi di misure del Gesuita A. Tacquet." *Nuncius* 6 (1991): 33–81.

Quondam, Amedeo, and Michele Rak, eds. *Lettere dal Regno ad Antonio Magliabechi.* Naples, Italy: Guida, 1978.

Rigaud, Stephen Jordan. *Correspondence of Scientific Men of the Seventeenth Century*, vols. I–II. Oxford: Oxford University Press, 1841. Contains letters documenting Borelli's relations with the English scientists

Scorsone, A. *Giovanni Alfonso Borelli: ricerche e considerazioni sulla vita e sulle opere.* Palermo, Italy: Brotto, 1993.

Yokoyama, Masahiko. "G.A. Borelli and the Demonstration of the Times-Squared Law of Fall Based on the Graphic Method." *Kagakusi Kenkyu* 15 (1976): 167–170. In Japanese.

Ugo Baldini

BORESKOV, GEORGIĬ KONSTAN-TINOVICH

(*b.* Omsk, Russia, 20 April 1907; *d.* Novosibirsk, Russia, 12 August 1984), *physical chemistry, catalysis, chemical technology.*

Boreskov enriched contemporary science by developing catalysts for important chemical processes, some of which are fundamental for industry. He also developed the theoretical foundations for predicting catalytic action and scientifically selecting active catalysts. Together with Mikhail Gavrilovich Slin'ko, he forged a new direction in science: the mathematical modeling of catalytic processes. Moreover, he founded the Institute of Catalysis in Novosibirsk, one of the first scientific establishments in this sphere in the world, and in 2006 also one of largest, with branches in Omsk and St. Petersburg.

Georgiĭ Konstantinovich Boreskov was born into a good family with a strong engineering tradition. His grandfather, Mikhail Matveevich Boreskov, a lieutenant-general in the Russian Army, was a famous military engineer with a number of inventions in the sphere of mine works. His father, Konstantin Mikhaĭlovich Boreskov, was one of the first military aviators in Russia (after the October Revolution of 1917 he emigrated to Belgium). His mother, Ida Petrovna Dombren, was the daughter of a teacher at a gymnasium (secondary school). In 1916 his parents separated, and his mother left with the two children for Odessa, where she soon married another military engineer, Aleksandr Nikolaevich Paton, a colonel in the czarist army. After the start of the revolution of 1917, the stepfather joined the Red Army. Later, in 1937, he was repressed.

Odessa, Moscow, and Sulfuric Acid Catalysis. Boreskov received his education in Odessa. In 1924 he graduated from a professional secondary school there. From 1924 to 1929 he studied chemical technology at the Odessa Chemical Institute. After graduating from this institute he started working in the Odessa Chemical and Radiological Institute as a researcher in the catalysis laboratory, headed at that time by Ivan Evgrafovich Adadurov, who was famous for his work on the preparation of catalysts. In 1932 Boreskov was appointed head of the catalysis laboratory at the institute. Around that time (1930–1937) he held the Chair of Processes and Apparatuses of the Odessa Institute of Chemical Technology, where he taught courses on processes and apparatuses of chemical technology and also on kinetics and catalysis.

Boreskov began nonacademic work during the first five-year plan (in accordance with Stalin's program for developing the country, the first five-year plan was started in October 1928). The major energies of this program were aimed at industrialization, and in particular at the development of heavy industry, for which immensely high goals were set. With respect to the chemical industry the largest capacity was allocated to the production of sulfuric acid. As it was a basis for many other chemical syntheses, production of sulfuric acid demanded highest priority. Boreskov's work on sulfuric acid catalysis, which started in 1929 and was dedicated to these goals, succeeded in the development of a new catalyst and a new process.

The basic reaction in the industrial production of sulfuric acid is the oxidation of sulfurous anhydride. For this process a platinum catalyst was used in the 1920s and early 1930s, but it was quite expensive and sensitive to "poisoning" of the catalyst by contaminations. These drawbacks limited growth in production of this important chemical reagent. Perhaps following the example of Monsanto (USA), where vanadium-based catalysts had been introduced in 1925, Boreskov created two new highly effective composite catalysts named BOV (barium-tin-vanadium) and BAV (barium-alumino-vanadium), which had better operational qualities than previous catalysts. These catalysts revolutionized the production of sulfuric acid. Cheap vanadium catalysts have high catalytic activity and are quite robust with respect to catalyst poisons, and thus took the place of platinum catalysts. Already by the end of the 1930s all plants in the Soviet Union were using the BAV catalyst. They gave rise to a whole generation of effective catalysts for a number of industrial oxidation processes.

In 1937 Boreskov received a master's degree in chemical science without defending a thesis. The Ministry of Industry ordered the laboratory of catalysis to be moved to Moscow and placed under the Research Institute of Fertilizers, Insecticides, and Fungicides, where Boreskov continued to work as head of this laboratory until 1946. At the research institute work that was started in Odessa, work on vanadium catalysts for the production of sulfuric acid continued. For his research on sulfuric acid catalysis, Boreskov was given the title of USSR State Prize Laureate (1942) and was awarded the Prize of Honor (1944). This work is summarized in *Kataliz v proizvodstve sernoĭ kisloty*

(Catalysis in the production of sulfuric acid, 1954), in which Boreskov explained the basics of his approach to developing catalysts for industrial application.

Boreskov married three times. He was married to his first wife, Zemenkova Ekaterina Petrovna, for ten years (1934–1944), and to Professor Nadezhda Petrovna Keêer from 1959 to 1973. His last wife, also a chemist, was Marina Vasil'evna Chaĭkina. Boreskov had four children: a daughter, Elena (1935); and three sons, Konstantin (1943), Vadim (1947), and Iuriiu (1961).

The Theory of Catalytic Action. In 1946, after Boreskov was granted the degree of doctor of chemical science for his thesis "Teoriia sernokislotnogo cataliza" (Theory of sulfuric acid catalysis), he was made head of the laboratory of technical catalysis in the Karpov Scientific Research Institute of Physics and Chemistry (Moscow), a position he served in from 1946 to 1959. Here Boreskov launched research on the development of the scientific basis for selecting and preparing catalysts and developing new catalytic processes. For this work Boreskov was granted a second USSR State Prize (1953), and in the same year he was given the Labor Red Flag Award.

In the course of detailed investigations of specific catalytic processes (oxidation of ammonia, hydrolysis of chlorobenzene, and others), the conditions of their realization, their reaction kinetics, and the chemical nature of the catalysts used, Boreskov formulated the task of defining the optimal characteristics of a catalyst—its internal structure, its form, and the size of its particles—as a major objective for increasing catalytic activity and the selectiveness of its action in various chemical reactions. "For increasing catalyst activity," he wrote in "Mekhanism deĭstviia tverdykh katalizatorov" (The mechanism of action of solid catalysts, 1953), "it is necessary not simply to increase the internal surface, but also to create a certain cavernous structure of the catalyst's particles to provide speedy input of reacting substances to the internal surface most remote from the particle's periphery parts and speedy diffusion of reaction products from this site. For each catalytic process, depending on the process conditions, its kinetic behavior and the specific activity of the catalyst, an optimal porous structure can be established, that providesthe highest reaction rate" (1997 edition, p. 290). The choice of catalyst supports, the necessary thermal consistency for the catalyst, the distribution of active components, the preparation of the catalyst, and a number of other characteristics determined by the conditions of preparation—Boreskov reviewed all these aspects in developing a theoretic basis for preparing active catalysts, work that occupied him from 1950 to 1955. (These issues are covered in detail in Boreskov 1958a and 1964.)

Boreskov considered all his investigations in catalysis as a basis for solving the problem of predicting a substance's catalytic action, because to his mind this was an important theoretical goal of this science.

The 1950s should be regarded as a turning point in the development of a science of catalysis. During these years, catalysis was transformed into a large independent area of science: In a number of countries, specialized institutes were organized, specialized journals were established, and regular international congresses on catalysis were held. During this time Boreskov's views of the essence of catalytic action were being formed. As early as 1953 he presented a programmatic statement of his views on this issue at the All-Union Meeting on Heterogeneous Catalysis in the Chemical Industry (Moscow).

Boreskov first of all supported a chemical approach to catalysis, according to which the mechanism of catalytic action lies in the intermediate chemical interaction of catalyst with reacting substances. His research related mostly to heterogeneous catalysis, but it also played an important role in the development of the science of catalysis in general.

As is well known, in homogeneous catalysis the catalyst and reacting substances occur in one common phase, usually a liquid, in which catalyst and reacting substances are dissolved. In heterogeneous catalysis, the reaction takes place at the interface of two phases (the catalyst is in the solid state, but the reaction mixture is a gas or liquid). Because of the nature of heterogeneous catalysis, the discovery of the character of the intermediary chemical interaction in heterogeneous catalysis was quite complicated. A simple transfer of the concepts of homogeneous catalysis, which was often done in the study of heterogeneous catalysis, led to a situation where for a long time even quite famous scientists were of the opinion that the intermediary compounds represented a separate phase (such as oxides in the case of catalytic oxidation on metals). Boreskov proved this idea of an intermediary phase transition in heterogeneous catalysis to be false. He pointed to the role of intermediary compounds on the surface, in a so-called chemisorbed state (where absorption of a substance by a surface of some body occurs with the formation of a link between the substance's molecules and the adsorbent).

In developing his theory of catalysis, Boreskov formulated a number of important determining factors of catalytic action. Fisrt, he allocated an important role to the chemical structure of the catalyst. The main task of catalysis theory is to establish a quantitative link between the chemical composition of a catalyst and its catalytic activity in some definite reaction. The catalytic activity of solid catalysts is measured by the rate of the reaction per unit volume or total catalyst mass. But as catalytic reactions usually proceed at the catalyst's surface, in early 1940

Boreskov proposed using the notion of specific catalytic activity, determined by the rate of a catalytic reaction per unit of catalyst surface. This characteristic measure, determined mostly by the chemical composition of the catalyst allows the researcher to quantitatively describe a catalyst's activity. In the early twenty-first century, specific catalytic activity is a common characteristic of catalysts without which quantitative description of their activity cannot be imagined.

Research from 1945 to 1953 showed that specific catalytic activity is relatively constant at different surface sizes and crystal sizes, and does not depend on the conditions of preparation of catalysts. This discovery was quite unexpected in the scientific community, but it played a decisive role in establishing new concepts of catalysis. The principle of constant specific catalytic activity entered into the science of catalysis as Boreskov's rule (1953), for Boreskov had clearly defined the scope of its application. Practice has shown that for most industrial catalytic reactions proceeding at high temperatures, Boreskov's rule can serve as a good basis for choosing catalysts. This discovery also established a new view of catalysis according to which catalysts and reacting substances are regarded as an integrated chemical system in which not only reagents but also the catalyst itself change.

Boreskov's experiments showed that in catalytic reactions, surface atoms can shift in catalysts and also the ratio of catalytic components can change because of the interaction with reagents. This discovery, the so-called "principle of the influence of the reaction medium on the catalyst" was extensively proven (Boreskov, 1958b). In the 1960s Boreskov and his colleagues confirmed the effect of the reaction environment on the catalyst in numerous works. They established, that in the course of reactions, specific mechanisms of change in catalysts occurred relating either to changes of composition of the surface layer or to its structural reconstruction.

Much of Boreskov's work in this direction from 1950 into the 1970s was connected also with the role of the bond energy of the reagents with the catalyst. Boreskov assumed that for separate groups of reactions, a limited number of links, or one link, of a reagent with a catalyst can have a decisive importance. In the course of examining concrete catalytic oxidation reactions, he chose the oxygen link to the catalytic surface as defining a class of reactions, and later (1971) he investigated the dependence between catalytic activity and the durability of this link in a number of reaction systems. He proved that there was a correlation between the catalytic activity and the energy of the oxygen link, not only for simple oxides but also for more complex compounds such as spinels, salts such as vanadates and molybdates, and mixed oxides. These established regularities were successfully used for choosing specific catalysts for a number of industrial processes.

This research also included Boreskov's investigations of stages in the mechanisms of heterogeneous catalytic reactions. Does catalytic oxidation, for instance, occur through chemical conversion of the reagents (the so-called associative mechanism), or does it involve oxidation and reduction of the catalyst (which would mean an extra stage in the mechanism)? In the course of sophisticated and laborious experiments, it was shown that at high temperatures in most oxidation reactions, a multi-step mechanism predominates, but if the temperature is decreased, the associative mechanism prevails. Boreskov examined these regularities in detail in the late 1960s by looking at the example of the reaction of carbon monoxide with steam. Over an iron oxide catalyst the reaction followed a multi-step mechanism, yet at low temperatures with a cupric catalyst the mechanism became associative. These results were of fundamental importance for establishing the basic forms of catalytic action (Boreskov, 1973).

Use of tracer elements played an important role in Boreskov's creation of the theory of catalytic action. For eleven years (1949–1960) Boreskov occupied the Chair of Isotope Separation and Application in the Mendeleev Moscow Institute of Chemistry and Technology. Here Boreskov (together with A. I. Gorbunov, V. V. Popovskiĭ, Vitaly S. Muzykantov, and others) started work on clarifying catalytic reaction mechanisms and the reactivity of catalyst surfaces using hydrogen, oxygen, and nitrogen isotopes. The research was later continued within limits at the Institute of Catalysis founded by Boreskov. The tracer method itself was noticeably developed by this work.

A separate place in Boreskov's scientific work belongs to the paper "Sootnoshenie mezhdu molekuliarnost'iu i ėnergiiami aktivatsii v priamom i obratnom napravleniiakh" (Correlations between Molecularity and Energies of Reaction Activation in Forward and Reverse Directions, 1945). Twenty-first-century kinetics of complex reactions cannot be imagined without this short, but fundamental work. The Horiuchi-Boreskov correlations deduced in this paper establish a connection between kinetic and thermodynamic characteristics of equilibrium reactions. Such correlations are widely used in the early 2000s in kinetic-research calculations.

Kinetic Research and Chemical Reactor Theory. According to Boreskov, the reaction mixture influences the rate of the catalytic reaction in two ways: first is its interaction with the surface of the catalyst, and second is its effect in changing the properties of the catalyst. Yet processes resulting from the influence of the reaction mixture upon the catalyst will not necessarily be stages in the catalytic reaction mechanism. It is also important that the dura-

tions of these two processes (the effects on the surface of the catalyst and on the properties of the catalyst) can substantially differ. Boreskov proposed a formula for calculating the rate of the catalytic reaction that took into consideration the contribution of both processes to the kinetics of the reaction (Boreskov, 1959). His kinetic equation (the 1960 variant of which bears the name "Boreskov-Ivanov equation") is successfully used by technologists in their calculations.

Boreskov's view, taking into account the interaction between the reaction environment and the catalyst, leads inevitably to the consequence that the kinetics of a heterogeneous catalytic reaction depends on the rate with which the catalyst's surface is refreshed. Issues of nonstationary technology (where processes are conducted in conditions of varying flow rates, concentrations of reaction mixture, temperatures, etc.) were developed by Boreskov together with Yuri Shaevich Matros in the last years of his life (1977). During 1979 and 1980 he discovered, and for the first time realized, the oxidation of SO_2 to SO_3 in a nonstationary catalytic process in the production of sulfuric acid. In the 1990s in Russia there were six large plants using this type of process.

Boreskov's kinetic researches were always aimed at solving two problems at once: revealing the mechanisms of catalytic processes and calculating the characteristics of the chemical reactors. As Boreskov wrote, "To prepare an active catalyst is half the work; the second half, which may be the most important, is to create a real chemical apparatus, a chemical reactor, in which this catalyst works" (1997, pp. 400–401). In the late 1950s and early 1960s Boreskov and Michail G. Slin'ko stepped forth as pioneers in the development of a new direction in science: mathematical modeling of chemical processes and reactors (Boreskov, 1961). This issue had already been briefly formulated (Boreskov, 1935), but realization of such mathematical modeling proved possible only after the appearance of analog and digital computers. The formation of this direction in the science of catalysis took place in an atmosphere of lively discussion. Boreskov and Slin'ko clearly brought out the impossibility of applying traditional methods of "similarity theory" for describing chemical processes.

The initial aim of mathematical modeling in catalysis was to facilitate the transition from laboratory research on reactions to the creation of industrial reactors. This approach based on equations describing chemical transformations, together with the equations for heat and mass transfer, gives a description of the process that is independent of the size of the system. A whole sequence of strict mathematical models (a kinetic model, a model of the catalyst's particles, a model of the catalyst's layer, a model of the contact apparatus, etc.) was worked out, and in accordance with it an industrial system was calculated. Solutions of the mathematical equations were obtained by computer. Applications of Boreskov's methods in this direction turned out to be of substantial importance for understanding conditions for catalytic reactors to operate stably.

Heading the Institute of Catalysis. In 1957 the Soviet government decided to develop science in Siberia. A large scientific center was organized in Novosibirsk, the Siberian branch of the USSR Academy of Sciences, under which the Institute of Catalysis was established in 1958. Its founder and director was Boreskov, who served in the latter capacity from 1958 to 1984. At almost the same time (1959), Novosibirsk State University was founded. Its main task was to prepare specialists for the scientific center. Boreskov organized and served as chair of the Department of Catalysis and Absorption in the university from 1960 to 1984. In 1958 he was elected corresponding member of the Academy of Sciences, and in 1966 a full member. In 1967 Boreskov was given the title of Hero of Socialist Labor for his outstanding achievements in the development of chemical science and industry and for his active participation in the creation of the Siberian Branch of the Academy of Sciences. Over the next two decades he was given the State Prize of the Ukrainian Soviet Socialist Republic (1970) and two Lenin Prizes (1975, 1982).

Within the framework of the institute, Boreskov managed to broaden considerably the practical scope of his work. He created catalysts for obtaining acrylonitrile (a monomer for production of synthetic fibers), as well as for the production of acrylic acid and acrolein from propylene, for converting carbon monoxide, and for obtaining formaldehyde, monomers of synthetic rubber, and other substances. An important direction was his development of catalytic methods of cleaning the exhaust gasses of industrial processes, and for waste water purification. At Boreskov's initiative, the specialized engineering firm, called Siberia, was created in 1970 with a pilot-plant facilities for a quick transfer of the institute's results to industry.

Boreskov was interested in nontrivial approaches to catalysis and technology. He was the first in the world (1931) to propose a method of carrying out catalytic processes in a fluidized bed. In the early twenty-first century fluidization is a method for realizing large-capacity catalytic processes. As a promising new approach to catalysis, Boreskov considered the application of fluidization in processes of burning fuel (at lower temperatures). In 1980–1982 the institute, under Boreskov's supervision, developed catalytic heat generators (with an efficiency factor of 80%–90%) in which coal is burned with catalysts in conditions of fluidization.

Boreskov was elected a foreign member of East German Academy of Science and an honorary member of New York Academy of Science. He also received honorary degrees from some foreign universities. From 1972 to 1976 he was the president of International Catalysis Congress. In 1993 the Institute of Catalysis was renamed the Boreskov Institute of Catalysis.

BIBLIOGRAPHY

WORKS BY BORESKOV

"Fisiko-khimicheskiĭ raschët kontaktnykh apparatov" [Physicochemical calculation of catalytic reactors]. In *Sbornik trudov Ukrainskogo nauchno-issledovatel'skogo khimicheskogo instituta tresta "Ukrkhim" v Odesse.* Collected Works of the Ukrainian Chemical Scientific Research Institute of the "Ukrkhim" Trust in Odessa, vol. 1: *Tekhnologiia sernoĭ kisloty* [Technology of sulfuric acid], 8–48. Odessa, Russia: 1935.

"Sootnoshenie mezhdu molekuliarnost'iu i ênergiiami aktivatsii v priamom i obratnom napravleniiakh" [Correlations between molecularity and energies of reaction activation in forward and reverse directions]. *Zhurnal fizicheskoĭ khimii* 19, no. 1–2 (1945): 92–95.

"Mekhanism deĭstviia tverdykh katalizatorov" [The mechanism of action of solid catalysts]. In *Akademik Georgiĭ Konstantinovich Boreskov: Ocherki, materialy, vospominaniia,* edited by Valentin N. Parmon. Novosibirsk, Russia: Institut kataliza SO RAN, 1997. Originally published in 1953.

Kataliz v proizvodstve sernoĭ kisloty [Catalysis in the production of sulfuric acid]. Moscow: Goskhimizdat, 1954.

"Nekotorye voprosy teorii podbora katalizatorov" [Some theoretical issues in choosing catalysts]. In *Problemy fizicheskoĭ khimii,* vol. 1: *Trudy Nauchno-issledovatel'skogo fiziko-khimicheskogo instituta im. L. Ia. Karpova.* Moscow: Goskhimizdat, 1958a.

"Vzaimodeĭstviie katalizatora i reaktsionnoĭ sistemy" [Interactions of catalyst and reaction systems]. *Zhurnal fizicheskoĭ khimii* 32, no. 12 (1958b): 2739–2747.

"Vliianie vzaomodeĭstviia reaktsionnoĭ sistemy i katalizatora na kinetiku kataliticheskikh reaktsiĭ" [The influence of the interaction between the reaction system and catalyst on the kinetics of catalytic reactions]. *Zhurnal fizicheskoĭ khimii* 33, no. 9 (1959): 1969–1975.

With M. G. Slin'ko. "Modelirovanie kataliticheskikh protsessov" [Modeling catalytic processes]. *Vestnik AN SSSR* 10 (1961): 29–35.

"Nauchnye osnovy podbora i prigotovleniia katalizatorov" [The scientific basis of the choice and preparation of catalysts]. In *Nauchnye osnovy podbora i proizvodstva katalizatorov,* edited by N. P. Keĭer. Novosibirsk, Russia: Redaktsionno-izdatel'skiĭ otdel Sibirskogo otd-niia AN SSSR, 1964.

With V. V. Popovskiĭ and V. A. Sazonov. "The Correlation between the Catalytic Activity of Oxide Catalysts and Oxygen Bond Energy." In *Proceedings of the Fourth International Congress on Catalysis, Moscow, USSR, 23–29 June 1968,* vol. 1. Budapest, Hungary: Akadémiai Kiadó 1971.

"Stadiĭnye mekhanizmy v kataliticheskikh reaktsiiakh okisleniia" [Stages in the mechanisms of catalytic oxidation reactions]. *Problemy kinetiki i kataliza* 15 (1973): 27–39.

"Associative Mechanism of Oxidation Reactions on Oxide Catalysts." In *The Second Japan-Soviet Catalysis Seminar: New Approach to Catalysis, Oct. 1–3, 1973*. Tokyo: 1973.

With Yuri Shaevich Matros, O. V. Kiselev, and G. A. Bunimovich. "Osushchestvlenie geterogennogo kataliticheskogo protsessa v nestatsionarnom rezhime" [Conducting a heterogeneous catalytic process in a transitional regime]. *Doklady AN SSSR* 237, no. 1 (1977): 160–163.

"O katalize i Institute kataliza: Itogi i perspektivy" [About catalysis and the institute of catalysis: Results and perspectives]. In *Akademik Georgiĭ Konstantinovich Boreskov: Ocherki, materialy, vospominaniia*, edited by Valentin N. Parmon. Novosibirsk, Russia: Institut kataliza SO RAN, 1997.

Geterogennyĭ kataliz [Heterogeneous catalysis]. Edited by K. I. Zamaraev. Moscow: Nauka, 1986. Completed by his associates.

Kataliz: Voprosy teorii i praktiki [Catalysis: Issues of theory and practice]. Edited by G. I. Panov. Novosibirsk, Russia: Nauka, 1987. A collection of selected works of Boreskov.

OTHER SOURCES

Bebikh, I. G., V. S. Muzykantov, et al. *Georgiĭ Konstantinovich Boreskov*. Materialy k biobibliografii uchenykh SSSR, vyp. 70 [Materials for bibliographies of USSR scientists, vol. 70]. Moscow: Nauka, 1982. Basic aspects of his scientific career are reviewed in detail. Includes a bibliography to 1981 of Boreskov's more than 800 articles and discoveries.

Hall, Homer J. "Soviet Research in Catalysis: Lack of Consumer Demand Is Major Drawback to Development of Industrial Catalysis in USSR." *Industrial and Engineering Chemistry* 62, no. 3 (1970): 33–40.

Kal'ner, Veniamin D., ed. *Iz istorii kataliza: liudi, sobytiia, shkoly* [From a history of catalysis: People, events, schools]. Moscow: Kalvis, 2005.

Parmon, Valentin N., ed. *Akademik Georgiĭ Konstantinovich Boreskov: Ocherki, materialy, vospominaniia* [Academician Georgiĭ Konstantinovich Boreskov: Articles, materials, reminiscences]. Novosibirsk, Russia: Institut kataliza SO RAN, 1997. Contains Boreskov's autobiography and essays and reminiscences of scholars, employees, journalists, and close relatives. Also includes a list of publications with Boreskov's name that appeared after his death (1985–1989).

Turkevich, John. "Boreskov Georgii Konstantinovich." In *Soviet Men of Science: Academicians and Corresponding Members of the Academy of Sciences of the USSR*. Princeton, NJ: Van Nostrand, 1963.

———. "Boreskov Georgii Konstantinovich." In *Chemistry in the Soviet Union*. Princeton, NJ: Van Nostrand, 1965.

Zaitseva, Elena A., and Ernst Homburg. "Catalytic Chemistry under Stalin. Science and Scientists in Times of Repression." *Ambix* 52 (2005): 45–65.

Elena Zaitseva

BORING, EDWIN GARRIGUES (*b.* Philadelphia, Pennsylvania, 23 October, 1886; *d.* 1 July, 1968, Cambridge, Massachusetts), *psychology, history of psychology, psychology of scientific creativity and progress, visual illusions.*

From the 1920s to the 1960s Boring, known as "Mr. Psychology," was a leading figure in academic psychology. He was a tireless builder of the discipline. In his writings and his administrative work he helped achieve the formal separation of psychology from philosophy and helped secure experimentation as the dominant form of inquiry for psychologists. He was the leading historian of psychology and promoted the careful examination of scientific change and scientific creativity.

Early Life and Education. Boring was a lonely and insecure child from a matriarchal family. His father, Edwin McCurdy Boring, a druggist, was a member of the Moravian Church. His mother, Elizabeth Garrigues, was raised in a Quaker family. The young Boring attended a Moravian Church but an Orthodox Quaker school. He credited his religious background with instilling an "ever-present sense of right and duty." Throughout his career he was known for his eighty-hour work week, fifty-week work year, and rigid administrative style.

After graduating from the George School, a Quaker coeducational high school, Boring entered Cornell University to study electrical engineering, which he later admitted that he never liked. For one of his two electives he chose introductory psychology with Edward B. Titchener, a leading figure in the "new experimental psychology" from Germany and the founder of the Society of Experimental Psychologists. Boring found Titchener's lectures "magic" and his praise highly motivating. Receiving an ME degree in 1908, he took a position as an electrician with Bethlehem Steel. He resigned after one year when offered a promotion, to prevent himself from being lured into a permanent career in the steel industry. Before taking a position teaching science at the Moravian Parochial School in Bethlehem, Pennsylvania, he returned to Cornell for summer school and took a laboratory course in psychology with Madison Bentley. After a rather unsuccessful year of teaching, Boring again returned to Cornell in 1910 to pursue an AM degree in physics, with plans to continue teaching science. However, Bentley provided more financial and intellectual encouragement than the physicists, and Boring switched to psychology. He became a devoted student of E. B. Titchener and a member of Titchener's laboratory, one of the most important of its time. Boring's future wife, Lucy M. Day, was also a member of the group and received a PhD in 1912.

Titchener was paternalistic and authoritarian, demanding complete loyalty from his students and controlling all aspects of their lives. Boring was in awe of Titchener's intellect and erudition and generally submitted to his mentor's control, including written instruction on what day to return from his honeymoon. However, Boring managed to broaden his background by studying animal behavior. He also worked with Shepherd Ivory Franz on studies of learning in dementia praecox patients, resulting in three publications in 1913. For his dissertation Boring studied a topic assigned by Titchener, sensory processes in the alimentary tract. After receiving a PhD in 1914 he spent four additional years as an instructor at Cornell. Boring and Lucy Day were married in 1914, shortly after he received his degree. They had four children.

Early Career. In 1917 the psychologist Robert M. Yerkes organized his colleagues to contribute to the war effort. He asked Boring to help with the World War I army intelligence testing program, in which 1.75 million recruits were examined. Although he had no involvement in the development of the tests, Boring became chief psychological examiner at Camp Upton, Long Island, a major center for new recruits. Boring's critical contribution came at the end of the war, when Yerkes asked him to analyze and summarize the enormous body of data and help prepare the 890-page report on the army testing program, published in 1921. Boring sometimes defended the use of intelligence tests but was critical of their interpretation. He did not accept the conclusions on purported hereditary racial differences that some of his colleagues drew from the army data. Boring's training in engineering never quite left him, and he suggested in the *New Republic* in 1923 and again in 1926 with Helen Peak, that "intelligence is like 'power' as the physicist uses the word: the amount of work that can be done in a given time" (p. 37). His work on the army intelligence testing brought Boring into contact with Lewis Madison Terman, and they remained close friends until Terman died in 1956.

In 1919 Clark University president G. Stanley Hall offered Boring a position as professor of experimental psychology at Clark to replace J. W. Baird. Although Clark added undergraduates in 1902, it remained an important center for psychological research and graduate training. At Clark, Boring was able to enhance his reputation as a careful scientist and a thoughtful writer, but he produced no notable discoveries. Wallace W. Atwood, who succeeded the psychologist Hall as the university's president, was a geographer, and in Boring's view Atwood downgraded research and the central place of psychology at Clark. In 1923, during the Red Scare, President Atwood became convinced that Boring was part of a secret Bolshevik underground promoting radicalism at Clark, a charge without foundation. Harvard had been interested in Boring since 1919, and now in 1923 made an offer less finan-

cially rewarding than a simultaneous offer from Stanford but more enticing for the challenges it presented.

Boring at Harvard. Boring accepted an associate professorship at Harvard, a move that began inauspiciously with a fractured skull and concussion from an automobile accident. When he recovered in the late fall, he began the task of "rescuing" psychology at Harvard from the philosophers. He became the director of the Psychological Laboratory in 1924, making him the de facto chair of the psychology "department," which was still part of the Department of Philosophy and Psychology. Boring faced serious challenges in building experimental psychology at Harvard. Funds for the laboratory were extremely tight, and Boring often used his own money to pay his secretary. The growing popularity of applied psychology during the early 1920s was an additional challenge for establishing "pure" experimental work as the premier form of the discipline. With the departures of Herbert Langfeld in 1924 and William McDougall in 1926, Boring carried the entire administrative burden for the development of psychology at Harvard along with a heavy responsibility for graduate teaching and supervision. He performed these duties with fierce dedication and compulsive attention to detail, while also serving as secretary of the Ninth International Congress of Psychology in 1929, secretary of the American Psychological Association from 1920 to 1922, a member of its governing council from 1920 to 1925, and president of the APA in 1928. Although he published on a variety of experimental and methodological topics, he developed no major findings or research programs.

In 1924 Boring began work on the book that made him well known to subsequent generations of psychologists: his *History of Experimental Psychology* (1929). Using a highly detailed, biographical approach, he traced the development of the new psychology that emerged in the late 1900s out of the disparate strands of philosophy and physiology. Each chapter contained an extended, rather informal "notes" section, with useful suggestions, sources, and expansions. Heavy emphasis was placed on the German origins of psychology, and especially on the Wundt-Titchener line of descent. Although criticized for neglecting or shortchanging applied, animal, abnormal, and social psychology, the book was praised for its readability and became the classic statement of the discipline's history. Starting in the 1970s, Boring's *HEP*, as it was known, was blamed for creating a whiggish, Titchenerian version of Wilhelm Wundt, overemphasizing Wundt's *Physiologische Psychologie* while downplaying the importance of his *Völkerpsychologie* and his antipositivist voluntarism. There is no doubt that *HEP* shaped the way in which psychologists viewed their emerging science and the aims of experimentation. Boring planned his complete history as three volumes, but he did not publish the second, *Sensation and Perception in the History of Experimental Psychology* until 1942 and never produced the third. A substantially revised second edition of the *HEP* was published in 1950 and was widely used through the 1970s. It continued to be used, cautiously, in the early 2000s as a reference work.

Perhaps Boring's most important contribution was his analysis of scientific progress, and he interwove his discussions of history of psychology and the "science of science" throughout his career. He addressed the problem of originality in 1927 in the *American Journal of Psychology*, concluding that progress may be due to the "unusual originality" of an individual but is "more likely to be the result of previous converging tendencies, which render a 'discovery' the next natural step in the process" (pp. 88–89). He continued this theme, including the problem of "founders," in his 1928 APA presidential address, "The Psychology of Controversy," in which he outlined the necessity of conflict for scientific progress. With explicit reference to Hegel but without Hegelian idealism, he argued that the history of science consisted of a long series of theses, antitheses, and syntheses. In the last chapter of *Sensation and Perception in the History of Experimental Psychology*, Boring introduced psychologists to the concept of *Zeitgeist*, and although William James and G. Stanley Hall had occasionally used the term, there is no doubt that Boring transformed and popularized its use by psychologists as the key concept for understanding history. In later publications Boring noted Johann Wolfgang von Goethe rather than Johann Gottfried von Herder as his source of the term, as he believed Goethe's formulation to be closer to his own. Given that German idealism and romanticism were unsuitable intellectual systems for Boring, he transformed Zeitgeist into "the total body of knowledge and opinion"of a particular time, thereby creating a concept that was acceptable within Boring's monism and the positivist Zeitgeist of mid-twentieth-century psychology. Boring outlined a view of history of science that reconciled "Great Man" notions with Zeitgeist explanations of scientific change. By adding "erudition," love of the unexpected, visualization, alertness, and efficient thinking as psychological attributes, he hoped to provide a naturalistic explanation of "scientific genius."

Boring as Analysand. The daunting administrative responsibilities at Harvard, combined with Boring's compulsive style, severely limited his time for research. He very rarely took credit or second authorship for his students' work. If asked to give feedback on a manuscript, his comments might exceed the original in length. He worried over all details, including who should or should not have a key to Harvard's Emerson Hall. Despite the success of the *HEP* and the respect accorded his 1933 book *The Physical Dimensions of Consciousness*, Boring was deeply

critical of himself, his level of productivity, and his perceived failure as a laboratory scientist. By 1933 his feelings of insecurity and depression and his desire for the admiration of his peers became overwhelming. At the urging of friends he entered psychoanalysis with Hans Sachs, one of Freud's original committee, who had fled the Nazis to Boston.

In hopes of a personality change and a return to productivity, Boring had 168 sessions with Sachs, five per week from September 1934 to June 1935, at considerable personal expense. Although Sachs reminded Boring of Titchener, and Boring cried and threw things, the analysis was not successful, a point on which Boring and Sachs agreed when both wrote about the analysis four years later in the *Journal of Abnormal and Social Psychology*. Despite this period of despair, Boring collaborated with Harry Weld and Herbert Langfeld on a 1935 introductory psychology textbook that went through several revisions and was reasonably successful. At Harvard he guided psychology through its initial separation from philosophy in 1934 and to its status as a fully independent department in 1936, but he took no credit for this accomplishment, believing that it would have come about without him. He published a careful critique of Gestalt psychology. The PsycINFO database shows eighteen publications of one sort or another between 1934 and 1938, but these publications did not represent important achievements to Boring. The change in his scholarly work that he hoped psychoanalysis would produce did not come about until 1939, when he finally developed a program of research on visual phenomena.

Boring's Other Contributions. Boring's one specific and lasting contribution to the experimental literature was a series of well-known experiments on size constancy in visual perception and on the Moon illusion, published between 1940 and 1943 with Alfred H. Holway and Donald W. Taylor. The size constancy studies required the observers to adjust the size of a disk of light until it matched a standard, and showed how the elimination of depth cues changed the perceived size. The studies of the Moon illusion, the apparent increase in size when the Moon is at the horizon, also used an adjustable stimulus for matching. With a clever series of mirrors on adjustable arms positioned on the roof of Emerson Hall, Boring showed that the illusion depended in part on the position of the eyes in the skull. With the head in a fixed position, the illusion increased as the Moon (on the mirror) ascended in the sky. If the Moon was viewed while lying down, the illusion disappeared, and the effect was also eliminated under certain conditions of monocular vision. Boring was not able to develop a suitable theory to explain these effects. The role of angle of regard in the Moon illusion remained under dispute, and Boring's findings were replicated as recently as 1998.

Less well recognized by psychologists is Boring's contribution to the mind-body problem. After the death of his domineering mentor, E. B. Titchener, in 1927, Boring was finally able to express fundamental disagreement with Titchener and reformulate Titchener's dualism. Boring's 1933 *Physical Dimensions of Consciousness* attempted to transcend Titchener by using monistic physicalism as a guiding principle. This physicalism was conceptually related to operationism, but in 1933 Boring had not yet read the physicist Percy Bridgman's 1927 *The Logic of Modern Physics*, in which Bridgman outlined the operational viewpoint. Retrospectively, Boring described operationism as a modern form of physicalism, in that consciousness was reduced to the operations by which consciousness was known to scientists. He was able to "save" Titchener's work by translating "intensity" and Titchener's other dimensions of consciousness into physicalist terms. Boring's position rejected both ontological and epistemological dualism as well as mind-body parallelism, but he did not consider himself a behaviorist. Consciousness was to be understood in terms of neural systems, in a position he called "psychoneural isomorphism" or the "identity theory" of mind.

Boring's writings on experimental control, measurement, and statistics provided an analysis of basic methodological and theoretical constructs in historical context. Of his concerns with scientific method, his promotion of operationism was the most significant. Boring credited his most talented student, Stanley Smith Stevens, with introducing the concept to psychology, although Boring had hinted at some features of operationism in his writings of the 1920s on the stimulus error and intelligence testing. In the mid-1930s Stevens and Boring began active promotion of their interpretation of Percy Bridgman's concept, possibly under the influence of Herbert Feigl. Despite the disunity over operationism evident at the famous symposium held in 1945, Boring continued to argue that operations could converge and provide a foundation for the advancement of knowledge, thus revealing his essentially positivist faith. In his obituary for Boring, Stevens outlined the very extensive way in which Boring had shaped and refined Stevens's ideas on operationism.

Although known as the guardian of pure experimentation, Boring was eager to assist in the application of psychology in World War II, as he had done in World War I. This time he used the premier skill that he had developed for his entire career: editing the work of others. A mass-market textbook of psychology for the average soldier was created by Boring and the science writer Marjorie van de Water from chapters written by fifty-nine specialists. Although the book explained the basics of personnel selec-

tion, vision and hearing, propaganda, and psychological warfare, the focus was on practical information for the soldier on morale, food, sex, neurosis, panic, and personal adjustment. Priced at 25 cents, the 450-page *Psychology for the Fighting Man* was published in 1943. Approximately 400,000 copies were sold. Shortly thereafter, Boring tried his hand at producing a more academic tome, *Psychology for the Armed Services*, designed as a military textbook.

Boring's war efforts, and those of his colleagues, helped to change his view of applied psychology and professional practice as problematic for the discipline. He now saw that those he termed "biotropes," psychologists drawn to the traditional experimental topics of sensation, psychophysics, perception, learning, and physiology, could also do important applied work, as in the case of S. S. Stevens's research on soundproofing at the Harvard Acoustical Laboratory. "Sociotropes" such as Henry Murray and Gordon Allport, interested primarily in personality, culture, individual differences, social psychology, and clinical problems, could do basic research and were of more value to society than Boring had previously allowed. In his 1950 revision of *The History of Experimental Psychology*, Boring suggested that the schism of experimental psychology and mental testing was partially healed and that testing, especially ability testing for selection, was working well. Although he was forced to adapt to the 1946 splitting off of the sociotropes into Harvard's Department of Social Relations, he was no longer their adversary, and both biotropes and sociotropes were part of his broadened vision for psychology.

Boring as Gatekeeper: The Jewish Problem and the Woman Problem. From the 1920s to the 1950s Boring served a leading role as a gatekeeper for those seeking to enter academic psychology. His recommendations and evaluations were actively sought, and he referred to his files as his "employment agency." His letters of reference were highly detailed, often ranking a number of candidates. Not all Harvard students were helped by these letters. Boring followed the common practice in academia of identifying which students were Jews and whether they showed the "unpleasant personal characteristics" thought to be likely in the Jewish "race." He felt obliged to do so, even though it meant that the candidate might therefore be rejected. Although he wielded substantial power within the discipline and believed himself fiercely devoted to principles of fairness, he never challenged these practices.

Boring also did little to support the growing feminist movement within psychology. He had never made it easy for women graduate students at Harvard in the 1920s and 1930s, but when he discovered that the psychologist Alice Bryan was correct in her challenge that women were underrepresented in APA offices, he invited her to collaborate in 1943 on a study of the role of women in psychology, resulting in three jointly authored articles. They surveyed women's positions, salaries, and opportunities. But their conclusions were tepid, and Boring insisted that culture and biology were the explanation, not discrimination. He repeated this conclusion on his own in the *American Psychologist* in 1951 in an article he titled "The Woman Problem." Again, Boring did not use his considerable influence to bring about change, even though his own wife had been unable to pursue a career in psychology. In the case of both Jewish students and women, Boring was unable to see himself as part of a system of discrimination, and it would have been intolerable for him to think of himself as having been unfair.

Boring's Later Years and General Influence. In his late fifties and sixties, Boring continued his tireless efforts to organize and promote the discipline of psychology. He played a key role in the reorganization of the American Psychological Association and the unification of the APA with other psychological organizations in 1945. He was the principal founder and the first editor of the APA journal of book reviews, *Contemporary Psychology*, and set high standards for the intellectual tone and quality of the reviews. Boring was one of the first to present a psychology course on public television, as the 1957 Harvard Lowell Television Lecturer. He was made Edgar Pierce Professor of Psychology in 1956, and he officially retired from Harvard in 1957. He continued active publication on history and other topics until two years before his death in 1968 from multiple myeloma.

In 1959 the American Psychological Foundation awarded Boring a Gold Medal for his achievements as an experimentalist, teacher, critic, theorist, administrator, popularizer, and editor. Inspired in part by Boring, psychologists developed journals and organizations specifically devoted to the history of their discipline and made the study of history a part of the discipline. All who subsequently taught or studied the history of psychology began with Boring's fundamental conception of naturalistic versus personalistic interpretations, the role of the Zeitgeist, and the dangers of eponyms. This creation of historical self-consciousness in a scientific discipline is certainly a more enduring legacy than the often transitory findings of the laboratory.

BIBLIOGRAPHY

WORKS BY BORING

"The Stimulus Error." *American Journal of Psychology* 32 (1921): 449–471.

"Intelligence as the Tests Test It." *New Republic* 34 (1923): 34–37.

"The Problem of Originality in Science." *American Journal of Psychology* 39 (1927): 70–90.

A History of Experimental Psychology. New York: Appleton-Century-Crofts, 1929.

The Physical Dimensions of Consciousness. New York: Century, 1933.

With Herbert Sidney Langfeld and Harry Porter Weld. *Psychology: A Factual Textbook.* New York: Wiley, 1935.

"A Psychological Function Is the Relation of Successive Differentiations of Events in the Organism." *Psychological Review* 44 (1937): 445–461.

Sensation and Perception in the History of Experimental Psychology. New York: Appleton-Century-Crofts, 1942.

"The Moon Illusion." *American Journal of Physics* 11 (1943): 55–60.

As coeditor with M. Van de Water. *Psychology for the Fighting Man.* Washington, DC: Infantry Journal, 1943.

As editor. *Psychology for the Armed Services.* Washington, DC: Infantry Journal, 1945.

"The Use of Operational Definitions in Science." *Psychological Review* 52 (1945): 243–245.

"Mind and Mechanism." *American Journal of Psychology* 59 (1946): 173–192.

"Great Men and Scientific Progress." *Proceedings of the American Philosophical Society* 94 (1950): 339–351.

The History of Experimental Psychology. 2nd ed. New York: Appleton-Century-Crofts, 1950.

"The Woman Problem." *American Psychologist* 6 (1951): 679–682.

"The Nature and History of Experimental Control." *American Journal of Psychology* 67 (1954): 573–589.

Psychologist at Large: An Autobiography and Selected Essays. New York: Basic Books, 1961. Includes an autobiographical sketch expanded from *History of Psychology in Autobiography*, Worcester, MA: Clark University Press, 1952, vol. 4, pp. 27–52.

History, Psychology, and Science: Selected Papers of E. G. Boring. Edited by Donald T. Campbell and Robert I. Watson. New York: Wiley: 1963.

"Eponym as Placebo." In *History, Psychology, and Science: Selected Papers of E. G. Boring*, edited by Donald T. Campbell and Robert I. Watson. New York: Wiley: 1963.

OTHER SOURCES

Capshew, James H. *Psychologists on the March: Science, Practice, and Professional Identity in America, 1929–1969.* New York: Cambridge University Press, 1999.

Cerullo, John. "E. G. Boring: Reflections on a Discipline Builder." *American Journal of Psychology* 101 (1988): 561–575.

Jaynes, Julian. "Edwin Garrigues Boring: 1889–1968." *Journal of the History of the Behavioral Sciences* 5 (1969): 99–112.

Kelly, Barry N. "Inventing Psychology's Past: E. G. Boring's Historiography in Relation to the Psychology of His Time." *Journal of Mind and Behavior* 2 (1981): 229–241.

O'Donnell, John. "The Crisis of Experimentalism in the 1920s: E. G. Boring and His Uses of History." *American Psychologist* 34 (1979): 289–295.

Rosenzweig, Saul. "E. G. Boring and the Zeitgeist: *Eruditione gesta beavit.*" *Journal of Psychology* 75 (1970): 59–71.

Stevens, S. S. "Edwin Garrigues Boring: 1886–1968." *American Journal of Psychology* 81 (1968): 589–606.

Winston, Andrew S. " 'The Defects of His Race …' E. G. Boring and Antisemitism in American Psychology, 1923–1953." *History of Psychology* 1 (1998): 27–51.

Andrew S. Winston

BORRO, GIROLAMO (also known as Borri, Girolamo; Borrius, Hieronymus) (*b.* Arezzo, Italy, 1512; *d.* Perugia, Italy, 26 August 1592), *natural philosophy, medicine, methodology of science.* For the original article on Borro see *DSB,* vol. 15.

After the publication of Charles Schmitt's article in *DSB,* scholars have paid very little attention to the figure of Girolamo Borro. Regarded as typical outcomes of the most conformist Aristotelianism, Borro's works have been scarcely studied in recent years, not least because their prolix (and often boring) prose does not facilitate their reading.

Nevertheless, it would not be without interest to go deeper into Borro's thought, because he seems to share with other natural philosophers of the Tuscan scene (such as, for instance, Andrea Cesalpino and Francesco Buonamici) a remarkable refusal to resort to occult and theological causes in the explanation of natural phenomena. This genuinely naturalistic approach might have exerted some influence on the young Galileo Galilei, who could also have profited from the notable experimental vein that marked the debate on motion developed by the Pisan professors of philosophy (among which Borro was a prominent figure) at the end of the sixteenth century.

Professor of philosophy at the University of Pisa when Galileo was a student there, Girolomo Borro is the author of several works, including two relevant treatises on natural philosophy—an intriguing dialogue on tides (*Dialogo del flusso e reflusso del mare,* 1561, with further revised editions printed in 1577 and 1582), and a book on the motion of heavy and light bodies (*De motu gravium et levium,* 1575). Borro's works are important for a deeper appreciation of the Renaissance Aristotelian natural philosophy; they also provide valuable clues to reconstruct Galileo's scientific training. Indeed, the above-mentioned books on tides and on motion were both owned by Galileo, who should have read them carefully. Thus, Borro's theory of tides is discussed in the Fourth

Day of the *Dialogue concerning the Two Chief World Systems,* whereas the *De motu gravium et levium* is explicitly cited in Galileo's youthful writings on motion (*De motu antiquiora*), and proved to be an influential source for a few remarkable aspects of his early dynamics.

Relationship to Aristotle. Born in Arezzo in 1512 and dying in Perugia eighty years after (for his biography see Charles Schmitt's article in *DSB*), Borro has been pictured as the typical exponent of the most conservative Aristotelianism. Actually, his allegiance to Aristotle was indefectible: "Aristotle, the true guide of philosophers,"—he wrote in the preface to the *De motu gravium et levium*—"was given us as a divine gift; the whole posterity learnt more, and in a easier, better and sooner way, from him alone than from all antecedents " (*De motu gravium et levium,* Florence: Marescotti, 1575, *Preface:* p. 2n).

Nevertheless, Borro's Aristotelianism cannot be properly defined scholastic. With the exception of Albertus Magnus and Witelo (cited in his book on tides), Borro did not mention any Christian authors, his sources mostly consisted of Greek and Hellenistic philosophers, and, among the medievals, of Arab thinkers (Averroës, Avicenna, Avempace, and al-Ghazālī).

This absence of references to Christian authors was not by chance, as it reflects Borro's antitheological attitude. The Pisan professor was imprisoned twice by the Roman Inquisition (in 1551 and in 1583), while, in 1567, he was implicated in the third heresy trial of Pietro Carnesecchi. Moreover, like his colleague Buonamici, Borro maintained that God contemplated only himself, without bothering about human matters: "The life of God consists in a perpetual activity of conceiving and loving himself," he wrote in *De motu gravium et levium* (1575, p. 59), and in his treatise on tides he explained that God could not turn his mind to inferior entities, because, in doing so, "he would fail in being divine" (*Del flusso e reflusso del mare,* 1577, p. 56). Hence, the Pisan professor did reject any interference of the divinity in ordinary course of nature, claiming that miracles had to be considered as results of ignorance: "Whoever knows the way by which the nature generates the springs"—he stated in denying that a source in Tuscan countryside could be deemed miraculous because of the great amount of water gushing from it—"can easily understand the cause of the effects produced by that spring" (ibid., p. 240).

Thus, like other exponents of the Tuscan Aristotelianism of the age (Buonamici, Cesalpino, Flaminio Nobili, and Francesco Piccolomini), Borro adopted a resolute naturalistic approach, marked by a drastic refusal to introduce theological arguments within the framework of natural phenomena's inquiry. According to this approach, always "processes and effects of nature originate from the natural form of their causes" (ibid., p. 42).

Also in explaining sea tides Borro resorted to a natural cause, because he viewed the raising of seas as produced by a rarefaction of waters due to the moonlight's heat. In fact, "the heat entering humid bodies makes them more rarefied and inflates them ...; hence, the sea will swell and begin to raise the more the moon will be out from its oblique horizon [i.e., the more the moon will be higher in the sky]" (ibid., pp. 125–126).

In defending such a theory (already held by several authors in Middle Ages), Borro openly rejected the role of astrological influences, strongly denying their existence. According to him, the discovery of the natural cause of a phenomenon "gets rid of influences, and this is especially true in the case of sea tides, in which they do not play (nor they could not play), any part, because they do not exist at all" (ibid., p. 47).

De motu. The most interesting of Borro's works is perhaps the *De motu gravium et levium,* published in 1575. The problem of the motion of heavy and light bodies was a very controversial issue among the renaissance Aristotelians. As Borro claimed at the beginning of his book: "There is nothing that philosophers debate as much over, and nearly come to blows over, as this motion [of heavy and light bodies]" (*De motu gravium et levium,* p. 2).

Even if its pages do not include any explicit reference to such a circumstance, Borro's book was very likely connected to a quarrel on the matter aroused among Pisan professors. At that time, it was usual for philosophers not to mention their adversaries by name, and this custom may account for the silence kept by Borro on his opponents. Anyway, his main rival in the quarrel should have been his colleague Buonamici, whose *De motu,* published in 1591, holds views directly opposed to those defended by Borro.

In contrast with Buonamici's allegiance to Greek Aristotle's commentators, Borro held a strict Averroist position. In particular, he maintained the typical Averroist thesis that the elements (whose dynamical tendencies determined, according to Aristotelian physics, the motion of terrestrial bodies) were not true substances, but intermediate entities between substance and accident. On this ground, Borro also argued that each element had a peculiar motion, being directly and entirely moved by its form. Borro's firm Averroist stance was underlined by Galileo (see *Opere di Galileo Galilei,* Ediz. Naz., I, p. 333), who also remarked that the philosopher from Arezzo treated the subject of motion "most thoroughly" (*exactissime;* ibid., p. 367).

In his early writings on motion Galileo might have drawn inspiration from Borro's *De motu gravium et levium*

in order to defend his theory of extrusion as cause of the motion upward. Replying to the objection according to which, if bodies moving upward were truly extruded by the medium, then, because their motion was enforced, they should move more slowly at the end (which did not occur), Galileo claimed that when the mover (*motor*) is joined (*coniunctus*) to the body—as in the case of bodies extruded by the medium—it is not necessary for speed to decrease (see ibid., p. 365). The notion of *motor coniunctus* may have been suggested to Galileo by Borro's treatment of those natural motions in which the speed of the body increases by virtue of the action of the medium (antiperistaltic acceleration). In these kind of motions, "the mover is always joined [*coniunctus*] to the body, therefore it always moves and, in moving, acquires a greater power, by which the motion becomes swifter at the end" (*De motu gravium et levium,* p. 235). According to this explanation, it was thus possible to posit a natural motion in which the medium played an active role. Even if Galileo used the concept of *motor coniunctus* in a very different context, there are several clues that he took inspiration from Borro's *De motu gravium et levium* (see Camerota and Helbing, pp. 346–357).

Experiment. A noteworthy aspect of Borro's book concerns the report of an experiment of fall. In a chapter of his book, titled "What Themistius Claimed against Aristotle and Averroes Claimed against Themistius on the Weight of Air," Borro recounted how he and some friends dropped pieces of wood and lead of about the same weight from a high window, in order to settle the question of whom (between Averroës and Themistius) were right (see Schmitt's article in *DSB*). Borro's conclusion emphasized the significance of the test:

> Compelled by the results of the experiment, all [those present] came to adhere to our opinion. Therefore, by reason, experiment and authority, it is appropriate to conclude that air has some weight in its own place, so that a piece of wood, which contains a greater part of air than a piece of lead of equal weight, descends more swiftly in air. (*De motu gravium et levium,* 1575, p. 215)

This experiment paralleled similar ones described by Buonamici and by Galileo. Each of them (Borro, Buonamici, and Galileo) relied heavily on experience, invoking experimental evidence to confirm their views. It seems, therefore, that the Pisan debate on motion of the last decades of the sixteenth century was marked by a strong experimental vein (see Camerota and Helbing, pp. 334–345). Hence, the famous "leaning tower experiment," allegedly performed by Galileo during his years in Pisa, turns out to be much less imaginative than many historians of science have been willing to acknowledge.

SUPPLEMENTARY BIBLIOGRAPHY

WORKS BY BORRO

Dialogo del flusso e reflusso del mare d'Alseforo Talascopio. Con un ragionamento di Telifilo Filogenio della perfettione delle donne. Lucca, Italy: Busdragho, 1561. Also available from http://archimedes.mpiwg-berlin.mpg.de.

De motu gravium et levium. Florence, Italy: Marescotti, 1575 (reprinted 1576). Also available from http://archimedes.mpiwg-berlin.mpg.de.

Del flusso e reflusso del mare, et dell'inondatione del Nilo. Florence, Italy: Marescotti, 1577 (rev. ed. 1582; reprint 1583). Also available from http://archimedes.mpiwg-berlin.mpg.de.

De peripatetica docendi atque addiscendi methodo. Florence, Italy: Semartelli, 1584.

Lettere scritte a Pietro Aretino. Edited by Teodorico Landoni. Bologna, Italy: Romagnoli, 1873–1875, vol. 2.1, pp. 182–193. These are several letters to Pietro Aretino.

Multae sunt nostrarum ignorationum causae. Biblioteca Apostolica Vaticana, Ms. Ross. 1009, published in Schmitt, 1976 (see below).

Vita magni Cosmi Medicis Etruscorum imperatoris invictissimi. Florence, Italy: Biblioteca Nazionale Centrale. Ms. II. IV. 15, published in Menchini, 2005 (see below).

De constructione syllogismorum. Dedicated to Iacopo Salviati. Florence, Italy: Biblioteca Nazionale Centrale, Magl. V. 24, ff. 1r–9r.

Preface to the *De motu gravium et levium.* Not published because of the death of the recipient of the dedication, the Grand Duke Cosimo I (died in April 1574). Florence, Italy. Biblioteca Nazionale Centrale, Magl. XI. 9, ff. 1r–5r.

Letters to Lorenzo Giacomini Tebalducci, Florence, Italy: Biblioteca Riccardiana, Ms. 2438.

Letters, Siena, Biblioteca Comunale, Ms. D. V. 12.

Multae sunt nostrarum ignorationum causae. Biblioteca Apostolica Vaticana, Ross. 1009, ff. 20r–25r (published in Schmitt, 1976).

Vita magni Cosmi Medicis Etruscorum imperatoris invictissimi. Florence, Italy: Biblioteca Nazionale Centrale 2,4,15 (published in Menchini, 2005).

OTHER SOURCES

Camerota, Michele, and Mario Helbing. "Galileo and Pisan Aristotelianism. Galileo's *De motu antiquiora* and the *Quaestiones de motu elementorum* of the Pisan Professors." *Early Science and Medicine* 5 (2000): 319–365.

Conti, Lino. "Girolamo Borro: cardiocentrismo e 'perfettione delle donne.'" In *Medicina e biologia nella rivoluzione scientifica,* edited by Lino Conti, 65–106. Assisi, Italy: Porziuncola, 1990.

Cox, Virginia. "The Single Self: Feminist Thought and the Marriage Market in Early Modern Venice." *Renaissance Quarterly* 48 (1995): 513–581. On page 518 is a brief comment on Borro's dialogue on "women's perfection" (*Della perfetione delle donne*), enclosed in the 1561 edition of his *Del flusso e reflusso del mare.*

De Pace, Anna. "Galileo lettore di Girolamo Borri nel *De motu.*" In *De motu. Studi di storia del pensiero su Galileo, Hegel, Huygens e Gilbert.* Milan, Italy: Cisalpino, 1990, 3–69.

Galluzzi, Paolo. *Momento. Studi galileiani.* Rome: Edizioni dell'Ateneo & Bizzarri, 1979, 113–114, 147, 169, 178.

Helbing, Mario Otto. *La filosofia di Francesco Buonamici.* Pisa, Italy: Nistri-Lischi, 1989.

Ioffrida, Manlio. *La filosofia e la medicina (1543–1737).* In *Storia dell'Università di Pisa,* vol. I.1: 239–338 (296–301). Pisa, Italy: Pacini, 1993.

Malpezzi Price, Paola. *Moderata Fonte: Women and Life in Sixteenth-Century Venice.* Madison, NJ: Fairleigh Dickinson University Press, 2003, 128–131. On Borro's dialogue on "women's perfection" (*Della perfetione delle donne*).

Menchini, Carmen. *Panegirici e vite di Cosimo I de' Medici: tra storia e propaganda.* Florence, Italy: Olschki, 2005.

Schmitt, Charles B. "Girolamo Borro's 'Multae sunt nostrarum ignorationum causae' (Ms. Vat. Ross. 1009)." In *Philosophy and Humanism. Renaissance Essays in Honor of Paul Oskar Kristeller,* edited by Edward P. Mahoney, 462–476. Leiden, Netherlands: Brill, 1976.

Schmitt, Charles B. and Quentin Skinner, eds. *The Cambridge History of Renaissance Philosophy.* Cambridge, U.K.: Cambridge University Press, pp. 205, 218, 222, 223, 810.

Settle, Thomas B. "Galileo and Early Experimentation." In *Springs of Scientific Creativity: Essays on Founders of Modern Science.* edited by Rutherford Aris, H. Ted Davis, and Roger H. Stuewer, 3–20. Minneapolis: University of Minnesota Press, 1983.

Thurot, Charles. "Recherches historiques sur le principe d'Archimède." *Revue archéologique* (1869): 284–299 (295–297). The first source that mentioned Borro's experiment on fall, with a French translation of the passage from the *De motu gravium et levium.*

Michele Camerota

BOURBAKI, NICOLAS, *mathematics.* For the original article on Bourbaki see *DSB,* vol. 2.

Bourbaki was a pseudonym adopted in 1934 by a group of young French mathematicians for their joint activities, which led to the publication of a highly influential collection of books on several fields of mathematics, including analysis, algebra, and topology, among others. The group was active for several decades thereafter (exactly how long is unknown) and shaped mathematical activity in many countries across the world, especially in France, through research, teaching, publishing, career building, and resource allocation. The name of Nicolas Bourbaki and the kind of associations it typically raises in mathematicians' minds play a unique role in the history of twentieth-century mathematics. The very inclusion of an article about a group of mathematicians under the name of an individual in the first edition of the *Dictionary of Scientific Biography*, and the fact that the article spoke about Bourbaki mostly in the third-person singular (following a practice well-entrenched among mathematicians), indicate the force of the myth surrounding the group's activities; at the same time, this history illuminates the difficulties that have been faced in attempts to produce serious historical accounts of the group's actual contribution to mathematics.

Early Years. The would-be members of Bourbaki met for the first time to discuss the project at the end of 1934 in a Parisian café. They stated as the goal of their joint undertaking "to define for twenty-five years the syllabus for the certificate in differential and integral calculus by writing, collectively, a treatise on analysis. Of course, this treatise will be as modern as possible" (Beaulieu, 1993, p. 28). They were motivated by an increasing dissatisfaction with the texts then traditionally used in their country for analysis courses. These were based on the university lectures of the old French masters: Jacques Hadamard, Emile Picard, and Edouard Goursat. They also felt that French mathematical research was lagging far behind that of other countries, especially Germany, and they sought to provide a fresh perspective from which to reinvigorate local mathematical activity.

The founding members of the group included Henri Cartan, Claude Chevalley, Jean Coulomb, Jean Delsarte, Jean Dieudonné, Charles Ehresmann, Szolem Mandelbrojt, René de Possel, and André Weil. Cartan, Chevalley, Delsarte, Dieudonné, and Weil, all former students of the École Normale Supérieure, remained the most influential and active force within the group for decades. Jean Leray and Paul Dubreil had attended the Paris meeting but did not join the group. Over the years, many younger, prominent mathematicians joined the group, while the elder members were supposed to quit at the age of fifty. Among later-generation Bourbaki members, the most prominent include: Samuel Eilenberg (one of the few who were not French), Alexander Grothendieck, Pierre Samuel, Laurent Schwartz, Jean-Pierre Serre, Serge Lang, and Armand Borel. All members were among the most prominent mathematicians of their generation, actively pursuing separately their own individual research in different specialties, while the activities of Bourbaki absorbed a part of their time and effort.

Beginning in 1935, and except for a break during the war years, the group met three times per year in different places around France for one or two weeks. At each meeting, individual members were commissioned to produce drafts of the different chapters. The drafts were then subjected to harsh criticism by the other members and then were reassigned for revision. Only after several drafts had been written and criticized was the final document ready for publication. What was initially projected as a modern textbook for a course of analysis eventually evolved into a multivolume treatise entitled *Eléments de mathématique*, each volume of which was meant to contain a comprehensive exposition of a different mathematical subdiscipline. Every chapter and every volume of Bourbaki's treatise was the outcome of arduous collective work, and the spirit and point of view of the person or persons who had written it were hardly recognizable.

The first chapters of Bourbaki's book on topology, for instance, were published in 1940, following almost four years of the usual procedure of drafting and criticism. The book was meant to provide the conceptual basis needed for discussing convergence and continuity in real and complex analysis. Bourbaki's early debates on topology were gradually dominated by a tendency to define this conceptual basis in the most general framework possible, avoiding whenever possible the need to rely on traditional, intuitive concepts such as sequences and their limits. This effort helped the understanding of, among other concepts, the centrality of compactness in general topology. It also yielded a thorough analysis of the various alternative ways to define general topological spaces and their central characteristic concepts: open and closed sets, neighborhoods, and uniform spaces. Moreover, an important by-product of Bourbaki's discussions was the introduction of filters and ultrafilters as a basis for defining convergence while avoiding reliance on countable sequences. Bourbaki, however, rather than including these latter concepts in the treatise, encouraged Henri Cartan to publish them, while elaborating on their relation to topological concepts, under his own name.

Over the next years, alternative approaches to questions of continuity and convergence were developed by other mathematicians, based on concepts such as directed systems and nets. The equivalence of the various alternative systems and those of Bourbaki was proven in 1955. Thus, the history of the development of topology, at least from 1935 to 1955, cannot be told without considering in detail the role played in it by both Bourbaki as a group and its individual members.

Bourbaki's Influence. In the decades following the founding of the group, Bourbaki's books became classics in many areas of pure mathematics in which the concepts and main problems, the nomenclature, and the peculiar style introduced by Bourbaki were adopted as standard. The branches upon which Bourbaki exerted the deepest influence were algebra, topology, and functional analysis. Notations such the symbol (for the empty set, and terms such as *injective*, *surjective*, and *bijective* owe their widespread use to their adoption in the *Eléments de mathématique*.

Disciplines such as logic, probability, and most fields of applied mathematics were not within the scope of interests of Bourbaki, and they were therefore hardly represented in the many places in the world where Bourbaki's influence was more strongly felt. This was the case for many French and several American universities at various times between 1940 and 1970. In addition, disciplines such as group theory and number theory, in spite of being strong points for some of the members (notably Weil for number theory) would not be treated in the *Eléments*, mainly because their character as mathematical disciplines was less amenable to the kind of systematic, comprehensive treatment typical of the other disciplines in the collection. As part of a basic estrangement of pictorial or intuitive elements in mathematics, geometry was completely left out of the Bourbakian picture of mathematics, except for what could be reduced to linear algebra.

Bourbaki's *Eléments* came to comprise a large collection of more than seven thousand pages. The first chapter appeared in 1935, and new ones continued to appear until the early 1980s. In its final form it comprised the following: I. Theory of Sets; II. Algebra; III. General Topology; IV. Functions of a Real Variable; V. Topological Vector Spaces; VI. Integration; Lie Groups and Lie Algebras; Commutative Algebra; Spectral Theories; Differential and Analytic Manifolds (which is essentially no more than a summary of results).

Bourbaki's austere and idiosyncratic presentation of the topics discussed in each of the chapters—from which diagrams and external motivations were expressly excluded—became a hallmark of the group's style and a manifestation of its thorough influence. Also the widespread adoption of approaches to specific questions, concepts, and nomenclature promoted in the books of the series indicate the breadth of this influence. Concepts and theories were presented in a thoroughly axiomatic way and were systematically discussed, always proceeding from the more general to the particular and never generalizing a particular result. A curious consequence of this approach was that the real numbers could only be introduced well into the treatise and not before a very heavy machinery of algebra and topology had been prepared in advance.

The Hierarchy of Structures. Underlying all of Bourbaki's presentation of mathematics is the conception of the discipline as a hierarchy of structures. In the more reduced framework of algebra alone, this idea had reached maturity in 1930 as it appeared in the famous book by Bartel L. van der Waerden, *Moderne Algebra*. The discipline appeared in this book as the investigation, from a unified point of view, of several concepts that were defined in similar, abstract terms: groups, rings, ideals, modules, fields, and hypercomplex systems. All of them comprised a set

on which one or more operations were defined that satisfied certain properties defined in advance and prescribed in the form of abstract axioms. The kinds of questions asked about each of them were similar and so were the tools used to investigate them. Each of them was an individual manifestation of a more general idea, that of an algebraic structure.

In Bourbaki's presentation of mathematics, different mathematical branches, such as algebra, topology, and functional analysis, appeared as individual materializations of one and the same underlying, general idea, that is, the idea of a mathematical structure. Bourbaki attempted to present a unified and comprehensive picture of what they saw as the main core of mathematics, using a standard system of notation, addressing similar questions in the various fields investigated, and using similar conceptual tools and methods across apparently distant mathematical domains.

In 1950, Dieudonné published, under the name of Bourbaki, an article that came to be identified as the group's manifesto, "The Architecture of Mathematics." Dieudonné raised the question of the unity of mathematics, given the unprecedented growth and diversification of knowledge in this discipline over the preceding decades. Mathematics is a strongly unified branch of knowledge in spite of appearances, he claimed, and the basis of this unity is the use of the axiomatic method. Mathematics should be seen, he added, as a hierarchy of structures at the heart of which lie the so-called "mother structures":

> At the center of our universe are found the great types of structures ... they might be called the mother structures. ... Beyond this first nucleus, appear the structures which might be called multiple structures. They involve two or more of the great mother-structures not in simple juxtaposition (which would not produce anything new) but combined organically by one or more axioms which set up a connection between them. ... Farther along we come finally to the theories properly called particular. In these the elements of the sets under consideration, which in the general structures have remained entirely indeterminate, obtain a more definitely characterized individuality. (Bourbaki 1948 [1950], pp. 228–229)

While van der Waerden had left the idea at the implicit level, the centrality of the hierarchy of structures became explicit and constitutive for Bourbaki. Moreover, Bourbaki wanted, in addition, a formally defined concept of *structure* that would provide a conceptual foundation on which the whole edifice of mathematics as presented in the *Eléments* could supposedly be built. This concept was introduced in the fourth chapter of the book on set theory. In the opening chapters of the books on specific branches, for example, algebra and topology, some sections were devoted to show how the specific branch can be formally connected with the concept of *structure* that had been defined. This connection, however, was rather feeble and amounted to not much more than a formal exercise.

The central notion of structure, then, had a double meaning in Bourbaki's mathematical discourse. On the one hand, it suggested a general organizational scheme of the entire discipline, which turned out to be very influential. On the other hand, it comprised a formal concept that was meant to provide the underlying formal unity but was of no mathematical value whatsoever either within Bourbaki's own treatise or outside it.

In 1945, Saunders Mac Lane and Samuel Eilenberg introduced the concepts of category and functor that were to become central as a unifying tool and language for mathematical disciplines that followed the structural approach developed in the various books of Bourbaki. Groethendieck and Serre were among the mathematicians who made a most impressive use of this new theory in their own research starting in the early 1950s. Grothendieck attempted to introduce these concepts, together with some topics that were yet to be treated, into the Bourbakian agenda, but he succeeded only partially. A curious situation ensued in which a theory that could have fitted nicely into the overall picture of mathematics promoted by Bourbaki was not adopted, partly because that would have meant reformulating considerable parts of the already existing texts in order to make them fit the new approach. In Bourbaki's book on homological algebra, published in 1980, this tension reached a noticeable peak. While the categorical approach has become widespread and indeed the standard one in this mathematical discipline, Bourbaki's presentation could not rely on it, because category theory had not been developed in the treatise. Using it here would go against the most basic architectonic principles that had guided the enterprise since its inception. Thus, while Bourbaki's treatment of a field such as general topology had embodied in the 1940s a truly innovative approach that many others were to follow, this would hardly be the case with homological algebra in the 1980s.

SUPPLEMENTARY BIBLIOGRAPHY

WORKS BY BOURBAKI

Eléments de mathématiques. 10 vols. Paris: Hermann, 1939–1988.

"L'architecture des Mathématiques." In *Les grands courants de la pensée mathématique*, edited by F. Le Lionnais. Paris: Caguers du Sud, 1948. Translated by Arnold Dresden in *American Mathematics Monthly* 57 (1950), 221–232.

OTHER SOURCES

Beaulieu, Liliane. "A Parisian Café and Ten Proto-Bourbaki Meetings (1934–35)." *Mathematical Intelligencer* 15 (1993), 27–35.

Chouchan, Michéle. *Nicolas Bourbaki: Faits et legendes.* AgrenteuilCedex: Editions du Choix, 1995.

Corry, Leo "The Origins of Eternal Truth in Modern Mathematics: Hilbert to Bourbaki and Beyond." *Science in Context* 12 (1998), 137–183.

———. *Modern Algebra and the Rise of Mathematical Structures.* 2nd rev. ed. Basel; Boston: Birkhäuser, 2004.

Krömer, Ralf. "La 'machine de Grothendieck,' se fonde-t-elle seulement sur des vocables métamathématiques? Bourbaki et les catégories au cours des années cinquante." *Revue d'Histoire des Mathématiques* 12 (2006): 119–162.

Schwartz, Laurent. *A Mathematician Grappling with His Century.* Translated by Leila Schneps. Basel; Boston: Birkhauser, 2001. Originally published as *Un mathématicien aux prises avec le siècle.* Paris: O. Jacob, 1997.

Weil, André. *The Apprenticeship of a Mathematician.* Translated by Jennifer Gage. Basel; Boston: Birkhauser Verlag, 1992.

Leo Corry

BOWDICH, SARAH

SEE **Lee, Sarah Eglonton Wallis Bowdich**.

BOWMAN, JULIA

SEE **Robinson, Julia**.

BOYLE, ROBERT

(*b.* Lismore, Ireland, 25 January 1627; *d.* London, England, 30 December 1691), *natural philosophy, physics, chemistry.* For the original article on Boyle see *DSB,* vol. 2.

The landscape of the history of science has changed dramatically in the years since the original *DSB* was published, and Boyle has been at the center of a seismic shift resulting from a new emphasis on intellectual traditions formerly written off as marginal and on broader social and cultural factors once dismissed as irrelevant to the growth of scientific ideas. Marie Boas Hall's article is succinct and at times brilliant; it was a model account of Boyle according to the terms of reference that prevailed when it was written. Much of its content still stands and need not be recapitulated here, including its account of Boyle's pneumatics, his appetite for the experimental vindication of the mechanical philosophy against the prevailing Aristotelian orthodoxy, and his empirical investigations of colors, salts, and the like. At the same time, the article needs to be significantly supplemented on aspects of Boyle's ideas and milieu that it neglected, and the result is to give a markedly different overall picture of Boyle.

Sources. In Boyle's case, revaluation is also required because the materials on which studies of him are based have radically changed since 1970. Boyle's massive archive at the Royal Society was cataloged for the first time in the 1980s and has since been fully exploited, with the result that a number of studies and editions have appeared based on hitherto unknown material in it. In addition, a new edition of Boyle's *Works,* published in 1999–2000, has replaced the eighteenth-century edition by Thomas Birch on which Hall was dependent. This offers a more accurate text of Boyle's published writings, with a full apparatus lacking from Birch's edition that describes the history of the composition and publication of each book, including the Latin translations that Boyle had made to ensure that his ideas reached an international audience. In addition, it makes available for the first time a number of previously unpublished texts by Boyle, some of the most important of these dating from his early life and hence illustrating the formative period of his career as a writer. These early writings have received intensive scrutiny, resulting in an awareness of a period of Boyle's life when he saw his role as that of a moralist and attempted to write in the style of the French romances by which he was strongly influenced. Only in about 1650, it appears, did he turn to science, and even when he did so his earlier moralistic concerns and literary aspirations left a significant legacy.

The new edition of Boyle's *Works* is accompanied by a complete edition of his *Correspondence,* superseding the selection of letters included by Birch in his edition, and this too gives a somewhat different view of Boyle from that available hitherto, not least because of its inclusion of many letters on alchemical and other topics that Birch omitted; other letters reveal the teeming underworld of minor virtuosi with whom Boyle interacted, giving more of a sense of the texture of the science of the day than was evident from Birch's rather partial selection. Indeed, it turns out that even more such material once survived but has been lost, in at least some cases because of the disdain of Birch and his collaborator, Henry Miles, whose idealized view of Boyle has influenced evaluations of him ever since.

Alchemy and Speculative Science. Undoubtedly the most dramatic element in the revaluation of Boyle by comparison with the image of him presented in the original *DSB* concerns his interest in alchemy. This goes back to the earliest phase of Boyle's scientific activity in the early 1650s, when he was mentored by the American alchemist George Starkey, who introduced him to the ideas of the Flemish iatrochemist Joan Baptista van Helmont, a figure whose crucial influence on Boyle and his contemporaries is now clear, although ignored in more traditional histories of science. In Boyle's case, Starkey seems to have introduced Boyle to Helmontian practices of quantification and compositional analysis as key elements in his chemical method, while he also showed him how to make the Helmontian drug *Ens veneris* and a philosophical mercury. The latter remained of absorbing interest to Boyle throughout his career, during which it is clear that he engaged in alchemical activities of quite an arcane kind and sought contact with other practicing alchemists to a much greater extent than had hitherto been acknowledged. In fact, far from the antipathy to "mystical" writers implied by Hall in her article, Boyle had a great respect for adepts whose penetration of the secrets of nature he hoped to emulate; it was only for "vulgar chymists" of the textbook tradition that he showed disdain in his *Sceptical Chymist* (1661). Though Boyle's alchemical interests mainly have to be reconstructed from manuscript sources, he brought out two publications on such topics in the late 1670s, his article in *Philosophical Transactions* on the incalescence of mercury and his tract on the "degradation" of gold published in 1678.

Other published writings also show an interest in aspects of "chymistry" that might at one time have seemed inappropriate in a figure such as Boyle, including his *Producibleness of Chymical Principles* of 1680, and Hall's own insight that Boyle was a chemist before he was a physicist can now be taken much further, in that it seems likely that he considered that corpuscles were endowed with chemical, as against strictly mechanical, principles, and that the texture of bodies might vary regardless of the shape and size of the corpuscles that they comprised. Also revealing are some of the shorter treatises that Boyle published in the early 1670s, in which he divulged speculative ideas that had often been merely the subject of asides in the more substantial and better-known works of the 1660s on which Hall's account mainly focused. Thus Boyle considered the possibility that the universe might contain "cosmical qualities" that transcended purely mechanistic laws, or that there were "seminal principles" in the plant, animal, and mineral kingdoms.

Other notions that were to prove influential included his view of the potency of "effluvia" emanating from the earth that affected health and other aspects of human life; his interest in the life-giving properties of salts; and his speculations on such topics as the nature of the seabed and the temperature of the subterranean regions. Such writings were often based on information he learned from travelers and others, of which he kept extensive notes in his "workdiaries," compendia in which such data rubbed shoulders with experimental findings; these also included accounts of "supernatural" phenomena, on which he

Robert Boyle. © BETTMANN/CORBIS.

explicitly solicited information in order to vindicate the reality of divine or other spiritual interventions in the world. Such activities, as much as his alchemical concerns, reveal the need for a nuanced view of Boyle and an awareness of the extent to which his adherence to the mechanical philosophy was tempered by a wish to do justice to the complexities that the world might contain.

Natural History and Utility. Nevertheless, Boyle was himself at pains to distinguish between the more speculative elements in his corpus and the foundation of natural historical data, which, following Francis Bacon, he saw at once as crucial to the growth of science and as his own chief legacy to posterity. Indeed, Boyle's Baconian methodology is a further aspect of his science that requires greater emphasis than Hall gave it. (Her main claim for

Bacon's influence on Boyle related to the supposed significance of Bacon's particulate matter theory; her assertion of Bacon's influence on Boyle in this respect was in fact almost certainly exaggerated.) A sophisticated form of Baconianism seems to have come to the fore slightly later in Boyle's career than might have been expected, in the 1660s rather than the 1650s, but once Boyle had awoken to the full potential of Bacon's prescriptions he showed the zeal of a convert in adopting and seeking to exemplify this methodology. Up to a point this is encapsulated in his appeal to "matters of fact" in controversy, his wish to separate issues susceptible to empirical proof on which people could agree from those which were matters of hypothesis. But he also took to heart the Baconian method of organizing data by "heads" or "titles," and he devised a sophisticated "design" for the pursuit of natural history in which he laid out an agenda for collecting data and the procedures that needed to be implemented so that researchers were aware of but not "prepossessed" by theories as they investigated nature. In addition, the Baconian ethos encouraged Boyle to explore a variety of novel forms of publication as a means of divulging his findings, if necessary in provisional form, including journal articles and volumes made up of disparate "tracts." Indeed, such strategies go far toward explaining the apparently chaotic nature of a number of Boyle's books which scholars have often found puzzling.

A further aspect of Boyle's science that is strangely absent from the original *DSB* article is his concern for the application of science, as exemplified in his *The Usefulness of Natural Philosophy,* largely written in the late 1650s and published in 1663 and 1671 (with supplementary material included in the *Works* in 2000). Boyle's aspiration to utility worked at various levels. One, divulged in part 1 of the work, was the significance of science in religious terms, as a source for understanding a theistic cosmos. But equally important was the utility of natural knowledge to human life, the subject matter of part 2, which aimed to show that practical inventions and technical improvements were grounded in more theoretical developments which were worth encouraging for just this reason. This was exemplified by a plethora of instances of the spin-offs of scientific investigation for practical affairs, ranging from diving bells to improved methods for fertilizing land. In connection with this, Boyle also stressed the value for scientists of taking an interest in the activities of practitioners of trades and other "mechanical disciplines."

The largest single section of *Usefulness* dealt with medicine, in which Boyle argued for the value of natural philosophy in understanding and improving human health. This was a major preoccupation for Boyle throughout his career, and it was a field where he was particularly anxious to vindicate the practical benefits of an improved understanding of nature. Though he abandoned the outright assault on orthodox medical practice that he planned and partially wrote by way of developing the more cautious remarks that he included in *Usefulness,* in his later years he brought out a number of treatises devoted to the significance of what might be called the medical sciences, including his *Memoirs for the Natural History of Human Blood* (1684) and his *Medicina Hydrostatica* (1690). He also collected and tested medical recipes with a view to making the best of them more widely available, a project that he started to implement in his later years, although inhibited by an anxiety that the publication of such material might be beneath his dignity as a natural philosopher.

Religious and Other Contexts. Boyle shared his ambition to make science useful with other contemporaries, notably the circle of Samuel Hartlib in the 1650s and the Royal Society after the Restoration, and this aim of achieving a wider social role for the study of the natural world is undoubtedly a significant theme in the history of science in the period, even if opinions differ as to the effectiveness of many of the projects that resulted: a case in point is the scheme for desalinizing water with which Boyle and various colleagues were involved in the 1680s, which seems to have met with rather mixed success. However, the claims that have been made for Boyle's involvement in broader, political objectives in his pursuit of science—not least in connection with his controversy with Thomas Hobbes— have been less convincing. These claims have focused on the perceived need to control subversion in the aftermath of the English civil war and to overcome the fragmentation of intellectual authority associated with that by capitalizing on the consensual nature of experimental activity, especially as represented by the Royal Society.

In fact, though certainly active in such debates, Boyle turns out to have been a less establishmentarian figure than such views have often implied, and the reason for this is his strong religious commitment, the dominant force in his entire life. Indeed, it could be argued that without a proper understanding of this it is impossible to do justice either to Boyle's intellectual ambitions and achievements or to his life as a whole. Boyle's personal piety was strong to the extent of being tortured; this gave him an obsessiveness that is in evidence in many facets of his life, not least his intense experimental practice. (Hall could not have been more wrong in asserting that "fortunately, he experienced no conflicts of conscience," even if she was here thinking of a potential science-religion tension from which Boyle was certainly immune, rather than the acute scruples on moral and other issues from which it is known that he suffered.) Boyle's own deep piety also gave him considerable respect for others whom he considered comparable recipients of religious insight, even if they were opposed to the powers that be. His commit-

ment to his Christian duty also made him sympathetic to the plight of the poor to an extent that set him at odds with the Restoration establishment, and his enthusiasm for missionary work did not always go down well with the colonial interests of the day.

More publicly, it seems clear that Boyle's ongoing controversy with Hobbes owed less to political motives than to religious ones, in that he explicitly stated in his *Examen* of Hobbes (1662) that it was because of the pernicious effect of Hobbes's principles on religion and morality that he felt obliged to oppose his views in natural philosophy. Earlier, it appears that Boyle initially came to espouse experiment not least because he believed that such knowledge would offset what he saw as the damaging religious implications of the prevailing Aristotelianism of the day. Moreover, he was unswerving in his conviction that a proper understanding of the natural world could make a crucial contribution to the comprehension and worship of God, a topic to which he devoted various treatises in his later years. He even devoted an entire book to a discussion of the final causes of natural things, arguing that it was appropriate for the naturalist to speculate about these, even if it was not his task to be primarily concerned with them. This is the background to the foundation of the Boyle Lectures through one of the provisions of his will, as described by Hall in her article.

Yet Boyle was not a complacent rationalist like some of his eighteenth-century successors. His deep sense of the limitations of human reason in comparison with the power and inscrutability of God led to a stress on the need for intellectual humility that goes beyond a simple avoidance of dogmatism. Indeed, he was convinced that there were "things beyond reason" both in natural philosophy and in divinity, and the true profundity of his views on such matters is now better understood. Just as in theology he believed that things might seem contradictory or incomprehensible to inferior humans but not to God, so in his natural philosophy his empiricism was accompanied by a stress on the extent to which God could have created the world differently had he wished, and to which even the laws of nature were contingent by virtue of being expressive of the divine will. Hence, the "new" Boyle that has emerged is not exclusive of the figure presented in the original *DSB* but is a more complex and in many ways a more interesting one—more at home in his seventeenth-century context and perhaps more sympathetic to the twenty-first.

SUPPLEMENTARY BIBLIOGRAPHY

WORKS BY BOYLE

The Early Essays and Ethics of Robert Boyle. Edited by John T. Harwood. Carbondale and Edwardsville: Southern Illinois University Press, 1991.

The Works of Robert Boyle. 14 vols. Edited by Michael Hunter and Edward B. Davis. London: Pickering & Chatto, 1999–2000.

The Correspondence of Robert Boyle. 6 vols. Edited by Michael Hunter, Antonio Clericuzio, and Lawrence M. Principe. London: Pickering & Chatto, 2001.

The Workdiaries of Robert Boyle. Available from http://www.livesandletters.ac.uk/wd.

OTHER SOURCES

Anstey, Peter R. *The Philosophy of Robert Boyle.* London and New York: Routledge, 2000.

———. "Boyle on Seminal Principles." *Studies in History and Philosophy of Biological and Biomedical Sciences* 33 (2002): 597–630.

Chalmers, Alan. "The Lack of Excellency of Boyle's Mechanical Philosophy." *Studies in the History and Philosophy of Science* 24 (1993): 541–564.

Clericuzio, Antonio. "A Redefinition of Boyle's Chemistry and Corpuscular Philosophy." *Annals of Science* 47 (1990): 561–589.

Frank, Robert G., Jr. *Harvey and the Oxford Physiologists: Scientific Ideas and Social Interaction.* Berkeley and Los Angeles: University of California Press, 1980.

Hunter, Michael, ed. *Robert Boyle Reconsidered.* Cambridge, U.K.: Cambridge University Press, 1994.

———. *Robert Boyle, 1627–91: Scrupulosity and Science.* Woodbridge, U.K.: Boydell Press, 2000.

———. "Robert Boyle and the Early Royal Society: A Reciprocal Exchange in the Making of Baconian Science." *British Journal for the History of Science* 40 (2007): 1–23.

Hunter, Michael, et al. *The Boyle Papers: Understanding the Manuscripts of Robert Boyle.* Aldershot, U.K.: Ashgate, 2007. Includes a revised version of the catalog of the Boyle archive referred to above.

Jacob, James R. *Robert Boyle and the English Revolution: A Study in Social and Intellectual Change.* New York: Burtt Franklin, 1977.

Kaplan, Barbara Beigun. *Divulging of Useful Truths in Physick: The Medical Agenda of Robert Boyle.* Baltimore, MD: Johns Hopkins University Press, 1993.

Knight, Harriet. "Organising Natural Knowledge in the Seventeenth Century: The Works of Robert Boyle." PhD diss., University of London, 2003.

Newman, William R., and Lawrence M. Principe. *Alchemy Tried in the Fire: Starkey, Boyle, and the Fate of Helmontian Chymistry.* Chicago: University of Chicago Press, 2002.

Principe, Lawrence M. "Virtuous Romance and Romantic Virtuoso: The Shaping of Robert Boyle's Literary Style." *Journal of the History of Ideas* 56 (1995): 377–397.

———. *The Aspiring Adept: Robert Boyle and His Alchemical Quest.* Princeton, NJ: Princeton University Press, 1998.

Sargent, Rose-Mary. *The Diffident Naturalist: Robert Boyle and the Philosophy of Experiment.* Chicago: University of Chicago Press, 1995.

Shapin, Steven. *A Social History of Truth: Civility and Science in Seventeenth-Century England.* Chicago: University of Chicago Press, 1994.

Shapin, Steven, and Simon Schaffer. *Leviathan and the Air-Pump: Hobbes, Boyle, and the Experimental Life.* Princeton, NJ: Princeton University Press, 1985.

Webster, Charles. *The Great Instauration: Science, Medicine, and Reform 1626–1660.* London: Duckworth, 1975; reissued with new introduction, Oxford and New York: Peter Lang, 2002.

Wojcik, Jan W. *Robert Boyle and the Limits of Reason.* Cambridge, U.K.: Cambridge University Press, 1997.

Michael Hunter

BRACHET, JEAN LOUIS

BRACHET, JEAN LOUIS (*b.* Etterbeek, Belgium, 19 March 1909; *d.* Braine-l'Alleud, Belgium, 8 February 1988), *embryology, cytology, molecular biology.*

In the course of the 1930s, Brachet established that RNA and DNA are both universal constituents of both animal and plant cells. During the two following decades, Brachet, Raymond Jeener, Hubert Chantrenne and colleagues decisively demonstrated that a specific RNA fraction, the *messenger RNA* (mRNA), enables the transfer of genetic information from the nucleus to cytoplasmic microsomes, where the synthesis of protein occurs.

Biographical Sketch. The youngest of the two sons of the Belgian embryologist Albert Brachet and Marguerite Guchez, one of the first Belgian women to have undertaken medical studies (though interrupted after the fifth year, as she fell in love with her teacher), Jean Brachet grew up and started his career during a period darkened by the two world wars. In August 1914, as Albert Brachet was working at the marine station of Roscoff (France), the Brachet family was surprised by the German invasion and stayed in France until the end of World War I. As his father was teaching at the Collège de France and at the School of Medicine, the five-year-old Jean Brachet learned to read and write in Paris.

Back in Belgium after the war, Brachet pursued his studies in Brussels, graduating in medicine in 1934 at the University of Brussels. Fascinated by the histology course of Pol Gerard and surprised by the fact that the role of the nucleus in the cell was so poorly understood, Brachet decided to study this problem. He approached Albert Dalcq about working in his laboratory; Dalcq proposed several areas of research, and Brachet selected the problem of the localization of thymonucleic acid (now called DNA) at different stages of egg formation. Performed in tandem with medical studies, his researches led to the publication of his first paper in 1929. This early start prefigured a long series of more than 400 articles dealing with various molecular aspects of embryonic development during sixty years of intensive scientific activity.

After his graduation, Brachet became an assistant professor at the Faculty of Medicine and pursued his scientific work in parallel with teaching duties. In 1934 Brachet married Françoise de Barcy, an excellent musician, with whom he had three children: Etienne, who became a physician and also taught at the University of Brussels; Lise, a dentist and talented painter; and Philippe, who was a successful researcher in molecular biology at the Centre national de la recherche scientifique (CNRS) in France. Brachet's wife took care of most daily domestic aspects, enabling him to fully devote himself to scientific research.

A member of the international brigades, Brachet's older brother Pierre was killed in 1936, a loss that deeply affected his parents, who were barely recovering from the loss of Albert Brachet in 1930.

In 1937 Brachet obtained a grant from the Rockefeller Foundation, which enabled him to work at Princeton University as well as at the Marine Biological Laboratory of Woods Hole, where he met the best American embryologists and cell biologists of the time. Brachet was deeply influenced by the pervasive pragmatism and open attitude of American researchers, which contrasted with continental European traditions.

Back in Brussels, Brachet joined the Faculty of Science to teach animal morphology in the context of the undergraduate program of zoology, and soon also taught general biology to chemistry students. At this point, Brachet joined efforts with Raymond Jeener, who was teaching physiology and who was also attracted by biochemical approaches. This partnership was the seed of a quickly growing interdisciplinary research group, ultimately leading to the founding of the first department of molecular biology in Belgium.

However, in July 1942, the promising researches of Brachet and Jeener were brutally interrupted, as the University of Brussels closed down in protest against the Germans' expulsion of all Jewish professors. Jeener and Brachet then pursued their research in the laboratories of colleagues from other Belgian institutions. Brachet was arrested in December 1942 and detained as a hostage together with other intellectuals. Liberated in 1943 but prevented from pursuing his experimental researches until the end of the war, Brachet focused on writing a book. Titled *Embryologie Chimique* and published in 1944, this book is devoted to a critical synthesis of what was known about the biochemistry of embryonic development, pointing to unsolved issues and delineating specific strategies to address them. This book stimulated the interest of the young French-speaking scientists who regularly visited

Jean Brachet. Jean Brachet circa 1980. COURTESY OF THE ARCHIVES DE L'UNIVERSITE LIBRE DE BRUXELLES.

Brachet and Jeener's laboratory settlement at the outskirts of Brussels from the end of World War II.

At that time, most opponents to the German invasion were affiliated with the Communist Party, which was the most efficient resistance organization. Brachet remained a member of the Communist Party until 1949, when he was asked to support the accomplishments of Trophim Lyssenko in the Soviet Union. After visiting Moscow and talking with several Russian scientists, including Lyssenko himself, Brachet realized that their claims relied much more on ideology than on scientific analysis. His public critical account angered Belgian communist leaders. Threatened with expulsion, Brachet offered and was finally authorized to resign from his party membership to avoid open conflict.

This relatively brief episode as a member of the Belgian Communist Party had long-term detrimental effects on Brachet's scientific carrier, in particular by complicating access to a U.S. visa until his retirement. However, this did not preclude Brachet and his colleagues from

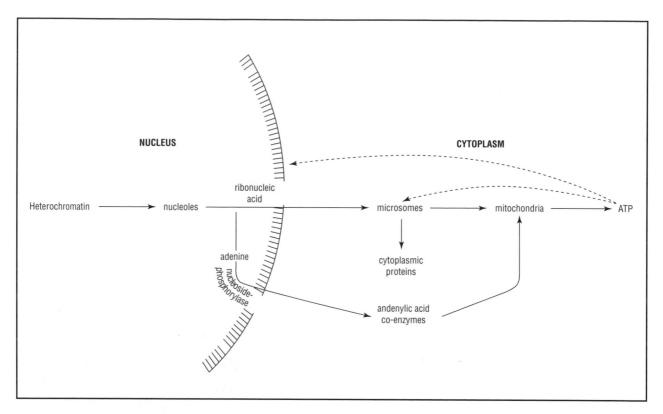

Figure 1. *Jean Brachet's schematic synthesis of the biochemical fluxes between nucleus and cytoplasm (1952).*

obtaining several grants from the Rockefeller Foundation, which enabled them to equip their laboratory with the analytical instruments (centrifuge, spectrophotometer, and the like) needed to remain at the forefront of molecular biology research.

From the 1960s on, Brachet spent several months each year in Italy, first in the International Laboratory of Genetics and Biophysics headed by Adriano Buzzati Traverso in Naples, and later in the laboratory of Molecular Embryology directed by Alberto Monroy, located nearby in Arco Felice. Together with his Italian colleagues Brachet also regularly worked at the Anton Dorhn Zoological Station, renowned among embryologists for the availability of fresh marine material, as well as for its friendly atmosphere. After his retirement in 1977, Brachet split his time between Brussels and the Naples area. During this period he remained extremely active, pursuing experimental embryological research and giving regular scientific presentations.

From Experimental to Chemical and Molecular Embryology. At the beginning of the twentieth century, experimental embryology was well established in most academic centers of western Europe. At the Free University of Brussels, Albert Brachet pioneered experimental studies of vertebrate development. He called his approach *Causal*

Embryology, also the title of one of his major books. Jean Brachet learned embryology with his father's academic heir, Dalcq, whose studies initially focused on the cytological analysis of spermatogenesis, parthenogenesis, and mitosis. During the 1930s Dalcq turned his attention to the first steps of embryonic development, from fecundation to gastrulation. His experimental studies were synthesized and contextualized in a book, *Form and Causality in Early Development* (1938).

In parallel, Joseph Needham at Cambridge was developing extensive chemical analyses of the developing eggs, focusing in particular on respiratory metabolism. Published in 1931, Needham's monumental *Chemical Embryology* compiled most contemporary data on the chemical constitution of eggs and embryos, and discussed the main directions of a research program aiming at providing chemical bases to major concepts of experimental embryology such as gradient, morphogenetic field, induction, and organizer.

Deeply influenced by Needham, Brachet embraced his general attempt to explain embryonic development in terms of chemical processes, and titled his first book *Embryologie Chimique* (1944, translated into English in 1950). In 1934–1935 Brachet spent a year in Needham's laboratory and participated in the hunt for the illusive organizer molecule, which would explain the phenomenon of neural induction uncovered during the early 1920s by Hilde Mangold and Hans Spemann. Conrad H. Waddington, Brachet, and collaborators observed that even artificial substances such as methylene blue could provoke neural induction, leading them to postulate an inherent neural potency, which could be stimulated by various means (Waddington referred to these stimulants as "evocators").

It is in this context that Brachet initiated his studies on the characterization of nucleic acids in eggs and developing embryos. At that time, two classes of nucleic acids where distinguished. On the one hand, thymonucleic acids (later called DNA) were found in large quantities in thymus of animals. The use of a specific staining technique developed by Robert Feulgen revealed a spatial and quantitative correlation of DNA with chromosomes across cell divisions. On the other hand, zymonucleic acids (later called RNA) were initially isolated from yeast cultures and wrongly considered to be plant specific.

Two main theories were then advanced. According to Jacques Loeb, nucleic acids would be synthesized de novo from elementary constituents (phosphoric acid, sugar, purine and pyrimidine bases). In contrast, the embryologist Emile Godlewski thought that the cytoplasm of the egg would contain a reserve of nucleic acids, which would progressively migrate into nuclei, where chromosomes were known to be located. Experimental results at the time were confusing. On the one hand, purine or phosphoric acid dosages suggested a global conservation of nucleic acids. On the other hand, the quantification of deoxyribose suggested a net synthesis of deoxyribonucleic acids.

To solve this contradiction, Brachet hypothesized the presence of ribonucleic acids in animal eggs. To test this hypothesis, he developed a novel cytochemical technique to estimate cellular contents in DNA and RNA. This technique, known as the Unna-Brachet method combines two stains (pyronine and methyl green) revealing RNA in pink, DNA in green. The use of ribonuclease permitted double-checking whether stained material was RNA or not, as this enzyme removed the color where RNA was present. Comparison with parallel Feulgen staining provided further cross-checking of the proportion of staining really due to DNA.

This sophisticated protocol resulted in a considerable increase in spatial and temporal sensitivity and enabled Brachet to demonstrate the presence of RNA in all organisms tested, first in sea urchin eggs and soon in many different animal and plant cell types. Brachet further established that DNA remained present at all stages of egg and embryo formation, with notable DNA synthesis during cell duplications.

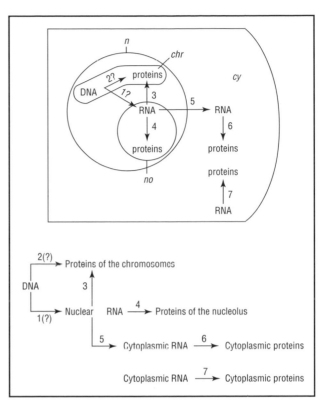

Figure 2. *Diagrams describing the relationships between DNA, RNA and proteins. According to the original legend, "chr" stands for chromosomes, "cy" for cytoplasm, "n" for nucleus, and "no" for nucleolus. Brachet had numbered the different steps for discussion in the text, with question marks denoting the steps considered as dubious or still lacking direct experimental support.*

The comparative analysis of RNA and DNA contents of various animal and plant cell types soon led Brachet to emphasize another correlation, which later proved to be of primary importance. Indeed, in parallel with the group of Torbjörn Oskar Caspersson in Sweden, Brachet realized that the DNA content per cell is roughly conserved in the diverse cell types of a given organism, whereas RNA content varies much more widely and is particularly high in cells strongly involved in protein synthesis.

Molecular Explorations at the Rouge-Cloître. During the 1940s the blending of various biological, chemical, and physical approaches, accompanied by the development of novel instruments such as the ultracentrifuge and the electron microscope, as well as by novel experimental protocols, led to a profound transformation of biology. In this respect, several Belgian scientists notably contributed to the progressive delineation of cellular ultra-structures. At the Free University of Brussels, the physicist Émile Henriot invented an ultracentrifuge prototype propelled and supported by compressed air. Beckman later commercialized a modified version of this centrifuge. Henriot also contributed to the development of electron microscopy and to its adaptation to biological purposes. Independently from Ernst Ruska, Henriot's assistant Lucien Marton built a transmission electronic microscope in Brussels, which was later developed for the RCA Company. However, the proper biological exploitation of this transmission electronic microscope would have to wait until the development of novel techniques to prepare very thin slices of biological tissues, notably by Albert Claude and Keith Robert Porter at the Rockefeller Institute for Medical Research in New York.

These two novel analytic instruments enabled Claude, George Emil Palade, and Christian De Duve to progressively uncover the structural and functional organization of cells, progressively separating mitochondria, lysosomes, ribosomes, and other constituents from the cytoplasm. These achievements earned them the 1974 Nobel Prize in Physiology and Medicine.

Inspired by Claude's results, and despite German occupation and the consequent practical difficulties, Jeener, Brachet, and a young doctoral student in biochemistry, Hubert Chantrenne, took advantage of Henriot's centrifuge to isolate small cytoplasmic particles, and demonstrated that almost the totality of RNA in adult cells was located in macromolecular granules (soon called microsomes), in association with hydrolytic or respiratory enzymes. Together with the established correlation between RNA and protein synthesis, this observation led Brachet, Jeener, and Chantrenne to propose that the microsomes constituted the site of protein synthesis.

After the end of the war, the trio, soon joined by Maurice Errera and René Thomas, would pursue this lead, refining centrifuge-based partitions and their chemical characterization, further consolidating the connection between microsome, RNA, and protein synthesis.

At this point, radioactive isotopes started to be used by biochemists to track molecular processes in living cells. The use of radioactive labeling was at the basis of the famous blender experiment by Alfred Hershey (1908–1997) and Martha Chase (1927–2003), which established that DNA (and not proteins) constituted the hereditary material in bacteriophages in 1952.

As radioactive compounds were barely available in post-war Belgium, Jeener produced radioactive phosphorus (^{32}P) in a lead-protected container located in the laboratory garden, using radium and beryllium salts obtained from the Union Minière company as a neutron source. Using self-prepared ^{32}P as tracer, Jeener, Brachet, and collaborators engaged in an analytical study of the metabolism of ribonucleic acid and soon showed that ^{32}P was incorporated at very different rates into the various ribonucleic fractions of the cell. Jeener also noticed that a depletion of Uracil, a nucleic acid base that is specifically needed for RNA synthesis, caused a concomitant arrest in cell growth.

Independently from Heinz Frankel-Conrad, Gerhard Schramm, and Alfred Gierer, Jeener further demonstrated that the genetic material of tobacco mosaic virus is constituted of RNA. He was then one of the very few researchers to use analogs of nucleic acid bases to analyze their necessity for viral growth. Another collaborator of Brachet and Jeener, Adrienne Ficq, developed a novel auto-radiographic technique to localize tritium (^{3}H) and radioactive Carbon (^{14}C) in histological preparations, thereby completing the current array of nucleic acid and protein in situ visualization techniques.

Focusing on DNA, Thomas, a doctoral student of Brachet, measured and compared the ultraviolet absorption spectrum of native DNA to a theoretical spectrum computed on the basis of the spectra of single nucleotides. Thomas observed a discrepancy that vanished following mild DNA treatments, without effects on covalent bounds. This strongly suggested the establishment of weak bonds between DNA molecules and the formation of a secondary structure, an hypothesis which would find independent confirmation in the DNA double helix model proposed by James Watson and Francis Crick in 1953.

The publication of the double-helix model in *Nature* in 1953 had a high impact on the scientific community but gave little clue about the detailed mechanisms of DNA replication and protein synthesis. The following decade witnessed an intensive hunt for the mechanisms of protein synthesis. Guidelines were provided by Crick in his landmark paper "On Protein Synthesis," presented at the 1957 annual meeting of the Society of Experimental Biology (published in 1958). Indeed, in this paper, Crick crisply stated the problem of protein synthesis in terms of the specification of the linear amino-acid sequence of proteins by the linear sequence of nucleotides in DNA, stressing the need for (yet to identified) adapter molecules. The solution of the genetic code from studies using in vitro

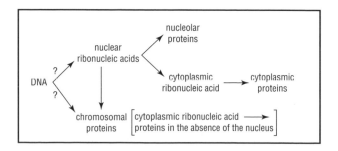

Figure 3. *Diagram describing the relationships between DNA, RNA, and proteins.*

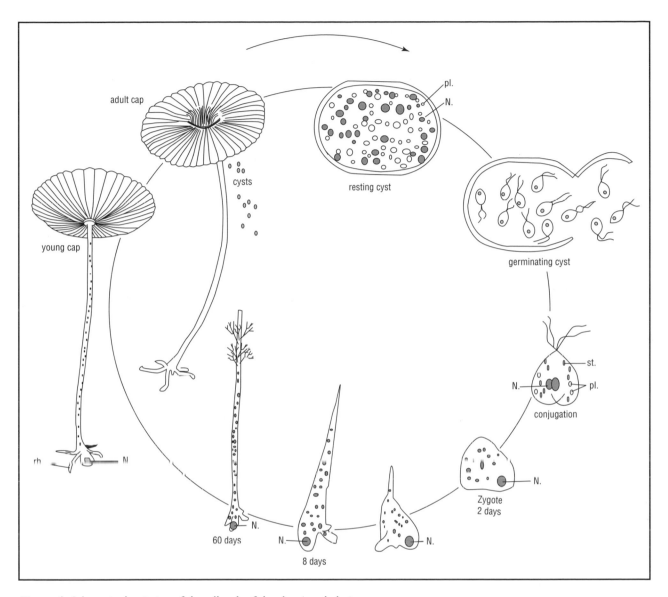

Figure 4. *Schematic description of the cell cycle of the alga Acetabularia.*

protein synthesis systems, with notable contributions from Har Gobind Khorana, Marshall W. Nirenberg, and Robert W. Holley, who shared the 1968 Nobel Prize of Physiology and Medicine.

Although Brachet and collaborators did not directly contribute to deciphering the genetic code, their work certainly played a role in the pervasive implication of RNA in the synthesis of proteins. For example, working with large unicellular organisms (in particular the giant Acetabularia alga), Brachet and Chantrenne demonstrated that protein synthesis can persist for days in enucleated cells, and even undergo substantial morphogenetic events (for example, the generation of a cap). They further established that this protein synthesis remains dependant on the presence of RNA in the cytoplasm. The role of RNA

in protein synthesis found a spectacular confirmation in the work of François Jacob, Jacques Monod and collaborators, who delineated the main properties of the bacterial messenger RNA around 1960.

The Golden Age of Molecular Biology at the University of Brussels. From the 1950s, Brachet's small unit could secure equipment with the support of the Rockefeller Foundation and was frequently visited by researchers from United States, England, Italy, and France. This boosted the scientific research activities of Brachet and his colleagues, which can only be partially mentioned here.

Pursuing the mRNA thread, Chantrenne set out to isolate genuine eucaryote mRNA. Under Chantrenne's direction, Arsène Burny, Gérard Marbaix, and Georges

Huez succeeded in extracting, purifying, and characterizing the mRNA coding for hemoglobin from rabbit reticulocytes (red blood cell precursors, devoid of nucleus but nevertheless synthesizing large amounts of hemoglobin). This series of delicate biochemical and biophysical experiments culminated in 1971 with the demonstration by John Gurdon and Marbaix that the injection of rabbit hemoglobin mRNA in frog enucleated oocytes indeed results in the production of rabbit hemoglobin protein.

Taking advantage of two postdoctoral training stays in genetics with Harriet Ephrussi-Taylor in 1953–1954 and with Alfred Hershey in 1957–1958, René Thomas launched a novel research program in bacterial genetics, which led him to uncover one of first cases of positive genetic regulation (trans-activation of most prophage genes by hetero-immune superinfection), and later to develop an original method to model and analyze the behavior of complex regulatory networks, using a logical algebra.

Around the mid-1960s, the multidisciplinary group was so renowned that it was selected by the European Atomic Energy Community (Euratom) as one of the four European centers for the training of biologists, in the context of a European project to study the effects of radiations on living organisms. This led the Free University of Brussels to build new research and teaching facilities on the periphery of Brussels, at Rhode-Saint-Genèse. Inaugurated in 1965, this institute was large enough to host the different units burgeoning from the original little group, spanning diverse biological fields such as microbiology, biochemistry, genetics, embryology, electronic microscopy, virology, parasitology, and immunology.

The mid-1960s were also the time of harsh linguistic conflicts in Belgium, leading to the split of several Belgian universities into autonomous French- and Dutch-speaking entities. In the case of the Free University of Brussels, both resulting entities collaborated in the development of the new molecular biology campus in Rhode-Saint-Genèse and shared several facilities, including a library and a restaurant.

By then Brachet's scientific accomplishment and international recognition earned him a continuous flow of academic honors, including many affiliations with foreign academies (Denmark, Boston, Edinburgh, Washington, Milan, London, Bologna, and Rome), a wealth of scientific prizes (including the Belgian Franqui Prize, the Schleiden Medal, and the Heineken Prize), nine Honoris Causa doctorates, as well as several prestigious Belgian decorations.

Under the leadership of Brachet and his colleagues, the new Department of Molecular Biology (DBM) quickly grew in size and reputation during the 1970s and 1980s, hosting more than three hundred researchers, technicians, and students. This department has played a crucial role in the development of molecular biology in Belgium, contributing to the formation of many outstanding scientists such as Jeff Schell and Marc Van Montagu, who promoted the development of a large and successful department of plant molecular biology in Ghent.

Brachet and his colleagues were actively involved in the discussions about the building of international bodies and laboratories to foster the development of molecular biology in Europe, ultimately resulting in the foundation of the European Molecular Biology Laboratory (EMBL) and that of the European Molecular Biology Organisation (EMBO).

BIBLIOGRAPHY

The Archives of the Université Libre de Bruxelles house the papers of Brachet, including notes from his Chemical Embryology, *a collection of reprints, and some of his correspondence.*

WORKS BY BRACHET

"Recherche sur le comportement de l'acide thymonucléique au cours de l'oogénèse chez les diverses espèces animales." *Archives de Biologie* 39 (1929): 677–697.

With Conrad H. Waddington and Joseph Needham. "Studies on the Nature of the Amphibian Organization Center: III. The Activation of the Evocator." *Proceedings of the Royal Society B* 120 (1936): 173–198.

"Étude histochimique des protéines au cours du développement embryonnaire des Poissons, de Amphibiens, et des Oiseaux." *Archives de Biologie* 51 (1940): 167–202.

"La détection histochimique et le microdosage des acides pentosenucléiques." *Enzymologia* 10 (1941): 87–96.

"La localisation des acides pentosenucléiques dans les tissus animaux et les oeufs d'Amphibiens en voie de développement." *Archives de Biologie* 53 (1942): 207–257.

With Raymond Jeener. "Recherches sur des particules cytoplasmiques de dimensions macromoléculaires riches en acides pentosenucléique." *Enzymologia* 11 (1943): 196.

Embryologie chimique. Paris: Masson & Liège, 1944. 2nd ed., 1945. Published as *Chemical Embryology.* Translated by Lester G. Barth. New York: Interscience, 1950a.

"The Metabolism of Nucleic Acids during Embryonic Development." *Cold Spring Harbor Symposia on Quantitative Biology* 12 (1947a): 18–27.

"Nucleic Acids in the Cell and the Embryo." *Symposia of the Society for Experimental Biology* 1 (1947b): 207–224.

"The Localization and the Role of Ribonucleic Acid in the Cell." *Annals of the New York Academy of Sciences* 50 (1950b): 861–869.

With Hubert Chantrenne. "Protein Dynthesis in Nucleated and Non-Nucleated Halves of *Acetabularia mediterranea* Studied with Carbon-14 Dioxide." *Nature* 168 (1951): 950.

Le rôle des acides nucléiques dans la vie de la cellule et de l'embryon. Paris: Masson, 1952.

Biochemical Cytology. New York: Academic Press, 1957.

The Biochemistry of Development. London: Pergamon Press, 1960a.

The Biological Role of Ribonucleic Acids. Amsterdam: Elsevier, 1960b.

"Ribonucleic Acids and the Synthesis of Cellular Proteins." *Nature* 186 (1960c): 198.

Introduction to Molecular Embryology. New York: Springer Verlag, 1974.

"From Chemical to Molecular Sea Urchin Embryology." *American Zoologist* 15 (1975): 485–491.

With Henri Alexandre. *Introduction to Molecular Embryology,* revised and enlarged ed. Berlin: Springer Verlag, 1985a.

Molecular Cytology, 2 vols. New York: Academic Press, 1985b.

"Reminiscences about Nucleic Acid Cytochemistry and Biochemistry." *Trends in the Biochemical Sciences* 12 (1987): 244–246.

"Recollections on the Origins of Molecular Biology." *Biochimica et Biophysica Acta* 1000 (1989): 1–5.

OTHER SOURCES

Académie Royale de Belgique. *Florilège des Sciences en Belgique.* Brussels: Author, 1968–1980.

Alexandre, Henri. "Jean Brachet and His School." *International Journal of Developmental Biology* 36 (1992): 29–41.

Bechtel, William. *Discovering Cell Mechanisms. The Creation of Modern Cell Biology.* Cambridge, U.K.: Cambridge University Press, 2005.

Brachet, Albert. *Traité d'Embryologie des Vertébrés.* Paris: Masson, 1921.

Brachet, Lise. *Le Professeur Jean Brachet, Mon Père.* Paris: L'Harmattan, 2004. A short biography of Jean Brachet by his daughter, with a collection of testimonies from colleagues, in French.

Burian, Richard M. "Underappreciated Pathways toward Molecular Genetics as Illustrated by Jean Brachet's Chemical Embryology." In *The Philosophy and History of Molecular Biology: New Perspectives,* edited by Sahotra Sarkar. Dordrecht: Kluwer, 1996.

———, and Denis Thieffry, eds. *History and Philosophy of the Life Science,* Vol. 19: *Research Programs of the Rouge-Cloître Group.* Brussels: University of Brussels Press, 1997. A collection of essays on the work of Jean Brachet and colleagues at the University of Brussels.

Chantrenne, Hubert. *The Biosynthesis of Proteins.* New York: Pergamon Press, 1961.

———, Arsène Burny, and Gérard Marbaix. "The Search for the Messenger RNA of Hemoglobin." In *Progress in Nucleic Acid Research and Molecular Biology,* Vol. 7. New York: Academic Press, 1967.

———. "J. Brachet (1909–1988)." In *Selected Topics in the History of Biochemistry: Personal Recollections, III,* ed. G. Sameness and R. Jaenicke. Amsterdam: Elsevier, 1990a.

———. "Notice sur J. Brachet." *Annuaire 1990 de l'Académie Royale de Belgique* (1990b): 3–87. The most complete biographical notice on Brachet, including a comprehensive list of Brachet's writings, in French.

Daly, Albert. *Form and Causality in Early Development.* Cambridge, U.K.: Cambridge University Press, 1938.

Gurdon, John B., Charles D. Lane, Hugh R. Woodland, et al. "Use of Frog Eggs and Oocytes for the Study of Messenger RNA and its Translation in Living Cells." *Nature* 233 (1971): 177–182.

Halleux, Robert; Jan Vandersmissen; Andrée Despy-Meyer; and Geert Vanpaemel, eds. *Histoire des sciences en Belgique,* 2 vol. Brussels: La renaissance du Livre (Dexia), 2001.

Jeener, Raymond, and D. Szafartz. "Relations between the Rate of Renewal and the Intracellular Localization of Ribonucleic Acid." *Archives of Biochemistry* 26 (1950): 54–67.

———, and J. Rossels. "Incorporation of 2-Thiouracil-35S in the ribose nucleic acid of tobacco mosaic virus." *Biochimica et Biophysica Acta* 11 (1953): 438.

———, and Paul Lemoine. "Occurrence in Plant Infected with Tobacco Mosaic Virus of a Crystallizable Antigen Devoid of Ribonucleic Acid." *Nature* 171 (1953): 935–937.

Judson, Horace Freeland. *The Eighth Day of Creation: Makers of the Revolution in Biology,* 2nd ed. Plainview, NY: Cold Spring Harbor Laboratory Press, 1996.

Morange, Michel. *The History of Molecular Biology.* Translated by Matthew Cobb. Cambridge, MA: Harvard University Press, 1998.

Mulnard, Jacques G. "The Brussels School of Embryology." *International Journal of Developmental Biology* 36 (1992): 17–24.

Rheinberger, Hans-Jörg. *Toward a History of Epistemic Things: Synthesizing Proteins in the Test Tube.* Stanford, CA: Stanford University Press, 1997.

Thieffry, Denis, and Richard Burian. "Jean Brachet's Alternative Scheme for Protein Synthesis." *Trends in Biochemical Sciences* 26, no. 3 (1996): 114–117.

Thomas, René. "Bacteriophage λ: transactivation, positive control and other odd findings." *BioEssays* 15 (1973): 285–289.

———. "Molecular Genetics under an Embryologist's Microscope: Jean Brachet, 1909–1988." *Genetics* 131 (1992): 515–518.

Denis Thieffry

BRADWARDINE, THOMAS. (*b.* England, c. 1300; *d.* Lambeth, England, 26 August 1349), *mathematics, natural philosophy, theology.* For the original article on Bradwardine see *DSB,* vol. 2.

Much has been published on Bradwardine since the original *DSB* article was written. New editions of several of Bradwardine's works have appeared. In comparison to the original article, Bradwardine's tentative birth date is here set at 1300, rather than left open within the range 1290 to 1300. This fits with his listing as a bachelor of arts in a Balliol College document of August 1321, before he moved to Merton College about 1323.

Scholarly Career Path. Although researchers still have no proof that Thomas Bradwardine's works on mathematics and philosophy were not written early in his career, some of them at least were written after he began his theological studies. His *Tractatus de proportionibus*, for instance, appeared in 1328, while he was bachelor of the *Sentences* from 1332 to 1333. Bachelor lectures on the *Sentences* ordinarily came after seven years of theological study, so that he might have begun to study theology about 1325 to 1326. Like his *De proportionibus*, his *De continuo* (On the continuum), an unabashedly multidisciplinary work, running through all the main arts disciplines as well as optics and medicine to prove that no continuum is composed of indivisibles, was also written when he had already begun his studies of theology. However, Lauge Olaf Nielsen, the editor of Bradwardine's *De incipit et desinit* (On beginning and ceasing), argues that William of Ockham changed his position on the exposition of propositions involving the words "to begin" and "to cease" between what he argued in Part I of his *Summa logicae* and what he argued in Part II, and this as a result of Bradwardine's explicit arguments against what Ockham said in Part I. If this is the case, then Bradwardine must have composed his *De incipit et desinit* before 1323 when Ockham completed his *Summa logicae*.

In his theological works, including his question on future contingents, now recognized to have been part of his bachelor lectures on Peter Lombard's *Sentences* (delivered about 1332–1333), as well as in his *De causa Dei* (completed about 1344), Bradwardine makes clear use of his philosophical training. He argued that God knows the future just as God knows the past. In the 876 printed folio pages of *De causa Dei*, Bradwardine argues against those he calls Pelagians (who argue that by their actions humans can earn salvation) that no one is saved without grace, that God is immutable and does not "change his mind," and yet, somehow, predetermination with respect to God is not incompatible with human free will. For a full understanding of Bradwardine's positions, it is advisable to examine his theological, as well as his philosophical and mathematical works.

Some of the logical works attributed to Bradwardine have now been published. He likely composed his *De insolubilibus* as a young teacher in the arts faculty at Oxford. Whereas this work on logical paradoxes, such as the statement "What I am saying is false," belongs to a tradition of works in the same genre, Stephen Read argued in a 2002 article that Bradwardine's ideas concerning the liar paradox form "arguably a genuine and original solution" (p. 190).

On Beginning and Ceasing. More obviously related to the history of science, although also in a logical framework, is Bradwardine's *De incipit et desinit*, on beginning and ceasing. The historiography of the thirteenth and fourteenth centuries development of ideas on beginning and ceasing, or on first and last instants, is still in flux. This is, in part, because of the uncertain status of the work of Peter of Spain on the subject. Both the identity of the author and the original content of Peter of Spain's work, before modifications in later centuries, have been opened to doubt. Nevertheless, Bradwardine's view that neither successive entities such as motion nor permanent things such as animals have a last instant of existence was widely held.

Scholarly focus on the issue of first and last instants might have arisen both within natural philosophy and within logic (especially in view of so-called supposition theory. Aristotle had argued in the *Physics* that in a change from one permanent state to another, the instant of transition should always be assigned to the later state. So, for instance, if water is heated until it becomes air (a different permanent substance), there will be no last instant of being water, but only a first instant of being air (when the temperature has become so high that it is incompatible with the continued existence of water).

Within logic, there was a long tradition of analyzing the truth or falsity of propositions in terms of the supposition (Lat. *suppositio*) of their terms, either for things in the world, approximately corresponding to the later concept of the reference of terms, or for concepts in the mind or for the actual words (as the phrase "what I am saying" in the proposition "What I am saying is false" might be said to supposit for or refer to the verbal expression itself). Whereas some words in propositions were supposed to have supposition for things in the world, other terms, called syncategoremata, were supposed not to have supposition themselves, but to affect the supposition of other terms in the proposition. The terms *incipit* (begin) and *desinit* (cease) were considered to be syncategorematic terms. It was often said that propositions containing syncategorematic terms must be unpacked (expounded) into other propositions in order to check their truth or falsity. Thus the proposition "Air begins to be present" would be expounded into the compound proposition "Air is now present and immediately before this it did not exist." This exposition fits with the fact that permanent things such as air have a first instant of existing.

But what about propositions containing terms referring to so-called successive entities such as motion and time? What exposition should be given for the proposition "Socrates begins to run"? According to Bradwardine and most other fourteenth-century logicians, running, like other successive entities, does not have a first instant of existence. When a person is standing still and then begins to move, there is no first instant when he has moved. Thus the proper exposition would be "Socrates is not now running and immediately after this he will be running."

By the 1320s, scholars were well aware that William of Ockham and others had said that in the outside world there are no "successive entities" (*res successivae*). There are only permanent entities, such as Socrates. What is meant by saying "Socrates is running" is that Socrates is now in a given location, immediately before now he was in a different location, and immediately after now he will be in a different location. Bradwardine begins *De incipit et desinit* with suppositions and distinctions and then turns to conclusions, objections against each conclusion, and replies. He distinguishes between permanent things, such as "animal," and "white," as opposed to successives, such as "motion," "time," and "to traverse." But although Bradwardine uses the term *successive thing*, he recognizes the ontological minimalism of thinkers such as William of Ockham, when he explains that terms are said to be of permanent things, not because they do not signify successive things, but because they can signify these things even though they are not moved. Likewise terms are said to be of successive things, not because they do not signify permanent things, but because they do not signify these permanent things unless these things are moved (p. 48). At one point Bradwardine, in a way atypical for fourteenth-century authors, even calls Ockham by name, calling him "a modern thinker, brother William of Ockham" (Bradwardine/Nielsen, 1982, p. 74).

Although Bradwardine's *De incipit et desinit* had far less influence than his *Tractatus de proportionibus*, it was, nevertheless, a work very typical of Oxford University at this time, particularly in the objections that Bradwardine listed after every conclusion and his replies. A typical objection runs as follows: if no motion has a last instant of being, then if a body is in motion at any given instant, it necessarily continues to move after that instant (Bradwardine/Nielsen, 1982, p. 54). This makes a future contingent necessary. Bradwardine solves this problem by distinguishing between two kinds of future contingents: first, there are those that in no way can be false, and second there are future contingents that for the same instant at which they could be true could also be false. Thus, from the proposition "Socrates eats," the future contingent "Socrates will eat" could be true or false. From the present proposition "Socrates is moving," however, the future contingent "Socrates will move" is necessarily true in the first way and cannot be false (pp. 55–56). Besides future contingents, Bradwardine uses his discussion of beginning and ceasing to give his students practice in analyzing the relations of indivisibles and continua and in using many other logical tools favored in fourteenth-century universities.

Bradwardine's *Tractatus de proportionibus* was already well-known at the time the original *DSB* article was written. Successive attempts to explain Bradwardine's use of mathematics in formulating his dynamical rule may be found in the supplementary bibliography below. Developments in thinking about Bradwardine's *De continuo* can also be found in the bibliography, although a printed version of the text itself continues to be available only in John Murdoch's 1957 dissertation. George Molland's edition of the *Geometria speculativa* appeared in 1989 and his expert analysis already in earlier articles is listed below.

SUPPLEMENTARY BIBLIOGRAPHY

WORKS BY BRADWARDINE

De incipit et desinit. In "Thomas Bradwardine's Treatise on 'incipit' and 'desinit.' Edition and Introduction," edited by Lauge Olaf Nielsen. *Cahiers de l'Institute du moyen âge grec et latin* 42 (1982): 1–83. The same volume includes a logical work on Ockham's doctrine of consequences and a work *Opus Artis Logicae*, both sometimes attributed to Bradwardine. See Jan Pinborg. "A Logical Treatise Ascribed to Bradwardine." In *Studi sul XIV secolo in memoria di Anneliese Maier,* edited by Alfonso Maierù and Agostino Paravicini Bagliani, 27–55. Rome: Edizioni di Storia et Letteratura, 1981.

De insolubilibus. In "La problématique des propositions insolubles du XIII siècle et du début du XIV, suivie de l'édition des traités de William Shyreswood, Walter Burleigh et Thomas Bradwardine," edited by M. L. Roure. *Archives d'histoire doctrinale et littéraire du moyen âge* 27 (1970): 205–326. A new edition of the *De insolubilibus* is scheduled to appear in early 2008: Stephen Read, ed., *Thomas Bradwardine's* Insolubilia: *A New Edition from the Manuscripts, with English Translation and Substantial Introduction.* Dallas: Medieval Texts and Translations; and Louvain: Peeters.

De continuo. In *Geometry and the Continuum in the Fourteenth Century: A Philosophical Analysis of Thomas Bradwardine's 'Tractatus de Continuo,'* edited by John E. Murdoch. PhD diss., University of Wisconsin, 1957. The microfilm of this dissertation from University Microfilms currently remains the best source for this text.

Arithmetica Speculativa. H. L. L. Busard attempts to identify which, if any, work by this name should be ascribed to Bradwardine in "Zwei mittelalterliche Texte zur theoretischen Mathematik: Die *Arithmetica speculativa* von Thomas Bradwardine und die *Theorica numerorum* von Wigandus Durnheimer." *Archive for History of Exact Sciences* 53 (1998): 97–124.

Geometria Speculativa. In *Thomas Bradwardine: Geometria Speculativa,* edited and translated by A. George Molland. Stuttgart, Germany: Franz Steiner Verlag Wiesbaden, 1989. Based on Molland's 1967 Cambridge dissertation, this includes an introduction, English translation, and commentary. For a fuller analysis, see Molland's 1978 article listed below.

Tractatus de futuris contingentibus. Edited by Jean-François Genest. *Recherches augustiniennes* 14 (1979): 249–336.

De memoria artificiali. Selections from this work are published in *The Medieval Craft of Memory: An Anthology of Texts and Pictures,* edited by Mary Carruthers and Jan M. Ziolkowski. Philadelphia: University of Pennsylvania Press, 2002. Latin text in Mary Carruthers, ed., "Thomas Bradwardine: 'De memoria artificiali adquirenda.'" *Journal of Medieval Latin* 2 (1992): 25–43. Although James Weisheipl doubted the ascription of this work to Bradwardine, Bradwardine appears as author in the two existing manuscripts. Mary Carruthers argues that the work is by Bradwardine and that it was written soon after Edward III's victory at Berwick on 20 July 1333. See Mary Carruthers, *The Book of Memory: A Study of Memory in Medieval Culture.* Cambridge, U.K.: Cambridge University Press, 1990.

OTHER SOURCES

Dolnikowski, Edith Wilks. *Thomas Bradwardine: A View of Time and a Vision of Eternity in Fourteenth-Century Thought.* Leiden, Germany: Brill, 1995. Considers Bradwardine's view of time as it appears in his mathematical, philosophical, and theological works.

Genest, Jean-François. *Prédétermination et Liberté Crée à Oxford au XIV Siècle. Buckingham contra Bradwardine.* Paris: Vrin, 1992. Includes the text of Buckingham, *Determinatio de contingentia futurorum.*

Genest, Jean-François and Katherine H. Tachau. "Le lecture the Thomas Bradwardine sur les Sentences." *Archives d'histoire doctrinale et littéraire du moyen âge* 56 (1990): 301–306. Some fragments of Bradwardine's commentary on the *Sentences,* previously thought to be lost, including the question on future contingents, that had been known as a separate text.

Kaluza, Zénon. "La prétendue discussion parisienne de Thomas Bradwardine avec Thomas de Buckingham. Témoignage de Thomas de Cracovie." *Recherches de théologie ancienne et médiévale* 42 (1976): 219–236. Shows that, contrary to an often repeated story, the text in MS Paris BNF 16409 does not refer to a live *disputatio in aula* at Paris between Bradwardine and Buckingham, but instead consists of notes by a later scholar taken from written texts.

Molland, A. George. "An Examination of Bradwardine's Geometry." *Archive for History of Exact Sciences* 19 (1978): 113–175. Reprinted in A. George Molland, *Mathematics and the Medieval Ancestry of Physics.* Aldershot, U.K.: Variorum, 1995. Also in the same volume is a reprint of Molland's "The Geometrical Background to the 'Merton School,'" first published in *British Journal for the History of Science* 4 (1968): 108–125.

———. "Addressing Ancient Authority: Thomas Bradwardine and Prisca Sapientia." *Annals of Science* 53 (1996): 213–233.

Murdoch, John Emery. "Thomas Bradwardine: Mathematics and Continuity in the Fourteenth Century." In *Mathematics and Its Applications to Science and Natural Philosophy in the Middle Age: Essays in Honor of Marshall Clagett,* 103–137. Cambridge, U.K.: Cambridge University Press, 1987. This includes the Latin text of the propositions of *De continuo.*

Read, Stephen. "The Liar Paradox from John Buridan Back to Thomas Bradwardine." *Vivarium* 40, no. 2 (2002): 189–218. Argues that Bradwardine's solution to the liar paradox was genuine and original and that it has not been appreciated in

part because the adaptation of it by John Buridan and Albert of Saxony seriously weakens it.

Sbrozi, Marco. "Metodo matematico e pensiero teologico nel 'De causa Dei' di Thomas Bradwardine." *Studi medievali* 31 no. 3 (1990): 143–191.

Spade, Paul Vincent. "Insolubles." *Stanford Encyclopedia of Philosophy.* Available from http://plato.stanford.edu/entries/insolubles (2005). Puts Bradwardine's theory of insolubles into context and states that it was "enormously influential on later authors."

Sylla, Edith Dudley. "Medieval Concepts of the Latitude of Forms: The Oxford Calculators." *Archives d'Histoire Doctrinale et Littéraire du Moyen Age* 40 (1973): 223–283. Describes John Dumbleton's use of latitudes of proportion to express Bradwardine's rule.

———. "Compounding Ratios: Bradwardine, Oresme, and the First Edition of Newton's *Principia.*" In *Transformation and Tradition in the Sciences: Essays in Honor of I. Bernard Cohen,* edited by Everett Mendelsohn, 11–43. Cambridge, U.K.: Cambridge University Press, 1984.

———. "Thomas Bradwardine's *De continuo* and the Structure of Fourteenth-Century Learning." In *Texts and Contexts in Ancient and Medieval Science: Studies on the Occasion of John E. Murdoch's Seventieth Birthday,* edited by Edith Sylla and Michael McVaugh, 148–186. Leiden, Germany: Brill, 1997.

———. "The Origin and Fate of Thomas Bradwardine's *De proportionibus velocitatum in motibus* in Relation to the History of Mathematics." In *Mechanics and Natural Philosophy before the Scientific Revolution,* edited by Walter Roy Laird and Sophie Roux. Boston Studies in the Philosophy of Science, vol. 254. New York: Springer Verlag, 2007. Explains how Bradwardine's rule for the proportions relating forces, resistances, and velocities takes advantage of the methods of compounding ratios found in works on music and in Latin translations of Euclid's *Elements* such as that of Campanus, which was used by Bradwardine.

Edith Dudley Sylla

BRAHE, TYCHO (*b.* Skåne, Denmark [later in Sweden], 14 December 1546; *d.* Prague, Czech Republic, 24 October 1601), *astronomy.* For the original article on Brahe see *DSB,* vol. 2.

Brahe's contribution to the history of European science and culture appears far richer in the early 2000s than it did in 1970. Victor E. Thoren's 1990 biography established a new starting point for understanding Tycho's astronomy, whereas Peter Zeeberg showed how deeply Tycho was embedded in the humanist culture of the late Renaissance, and J. R. Christianson examined his patronage of scientists, technicians, artists, and natural philosophers who participated in his large-scale research and cultural projects. Many other scholars have presented new understandings of Tycho's astronomy, cosmology, and natural philosophy. Tycho Brahe was a generous, courtly, but demanding aristocrat who was a theoretical astronomer of the first rank and founder of the first modern research institute, as well as the inventor of fundamental methods of observational science.

Humanist Influence. During the decade 1559 to 1570 that Tycho spent as a university student, studies that bore the imprint of the humanist reformer, Philipp Melanchthon shaped his outlook. In the Philippist curriculum of the Lutheran universities Tycho attended, students acquired an awareness of divine law by studying the laws placed by God in nature, because the "manifest footprints of God in nature" led onward to religious faith. Arithmetic, geometry, astronomy, astrology, geography (including cartography and chorography), anatomy, and botany were parts of this plan of study. The Philippist curriculum channeled Tycho Brahe's strong personal interests in astronomy and astrology, and it resonated with his attraction to Paracelsian medicine. The urge to return *ad fontes*—to the sources of wisdom that lay within the natural world itself—energized these approaches. Lutheran theology, Hermetic philosophy, and millenial astrology all taught Tycho to strive for the instauration of a lost golden age, and he came to believe that active natural philosophy could help to achieve it. By the age of sixteen, he was convinced that the sources of wisdom in astronomy and astrology lay not in books but in the heavens themselves and that only precise observation could recover them. At the same time, he believed that knowledge of God's laws discovered in nature must harmonize with the divine wisdom of the Bible.

Tycho Brahe had grown up in the circle of the Danish court. He returned to his native Denmark from studies abroad in 1570 and became a courtier in 1572. Around the same time, he fell in love with Kirsten Jørgensdatter (sometimes erroneously called Kristine Barbara). She was probably the daughter of a Lutheran pastor, but because she did not share his noble birth she was not acceptable at court. A wedding between an aristocrat and a commoner was illegal in sixteenth-century Denmark, but a common-law marriage was not. Tycho and Kirsten began living together in 1572, and the first of their eight children was born in September of 1573. They enjoyed a warm, harmonious marriage that lasted a lifetime.

Tycho was still a courtier when he observed the supernova of 1572. He discussed it with others at court, including the royal physician, Petrus Severinus; the French ambassador, Charles de Danzay; and his powerful uncle, Steward of the Realm Peder Oxe. They urged him to publish it, and he did so in 1573. Aristotelian physics denied that change could occur in the celestial spheres, but Severinus had just published a book on Paracelsus's

theory of *semina,* spiritual principles throughout the universe that give birth in their appointed times. This could explain how the birth of a new star might take place far beyond the Moon in the region of the stars. Tycho reported on the star's astrological implications to King Frederik II. That winter, he lectured on astronomy in Copenhagen University, using Copernicus as his textbook—one of the first at any university to do so.

King Frederik was building "Hamlet's Castle" at Kronborg in Elsinore to proclaim the power and splendor of the Danish realm at the very entrance to the Baltic Sea. Tycho traveled throughout Germany, Switzerland, and northern Italy in 1575. When he returned, he recommended various artists and artisans in Augsburg, Nürnberg, Hesse, and the Veneto for the Kronborg project. Landgrave William IV of Hesse-Cassel, whom Tycho had visited during his travels, sent a message to King Frederik, urging him to promote Tycho Brahe's astronomy and natural philosophy for the benefit of humanity and the glory of the kingdom of Denmark. With this in mind, King Frederik on 11 February 1576 proposed to Tycho that he establish a royal Danish research center within sight of Elsinore on the island of Hven. The king intended it to be a place that would complement Kronborg Castle in contributing to the prestige of the kingdom. Tycho was astonished by the offer and accepted.

For the next twenty-one years, Tycho was given a free hand and extraordinary financial support to carry out research in astronomy, Paracelsian chemistry, and related subjects. The same artists and artisans who embellished Kronborg were also employed to make Uraniborg into a place of splendor. At Uraniborg, Tycho Brahe found innovative ways to integrate into an aristocratic lifestyle his far-ranging interests in astronomy, astrology, meteorology, mathematics, cosmology, cartography, chemistry, medicine, geodetic triangular surveying, hydraulic engineering, and a host of other fields including architecture, poetry, music, history, theology, and philosophy. Tycho's collections of *naturalia,* scientific instruments, books, manuscripts, paintings, animated "Vitruvian" statues and other sculpture, his printing press and paper mill, botanical gardens and aviaries, the music and spirited conversation that filled his house, and his open-handed hospitality in entertaining kings, queens, princes, ambassadors, nobles, scholars, and artists from many lands became legendary. Tycho was a fine stylist of Latin poetry and prose who admired Ovid and Augustan classicism. His learned sister, Sophie Brahe, a genealogist, astrologer, and Paracelsian chemist, was a frequent guest.

Zeeberg has compared Tycho's Uraniborg with Castiglione's Urbino, the Platonic Academy of Medici Florence, and the circle of Erasmus and Thomas More in England as one of the most brilliant expressions of

Renaissance culture. In short, Uraniborg fully achieved the aims of King Frederik when he commissioned Tycho Brahe to establish it.

Astronomical Instruments. Tycho's instrumentation had been rather rudimentary when the supernova of 1572 appeared. By the time he saw his first comet in 1577, however, he could observe its altitude and azimuth with a quadrant that was a landmark because of its innovative features. Tycho fitted a large steel sextant with the same innovations and used it, as well as a cross-staff, to observe distances between the comet and nearby stars, frequently repeating the same observation with two instruments in order to compare results. In his persistent search for observational precision, Tycho Brahe gradually invented the modern rules of empirical evidence. As Thoren put it, nobody before Tycho

> even catered to the ordinary rules of evidence, whereby several determinations of result would be deemed to provide more credibility than one or (rarely) two did. The problem with such redundancy, no doubt, was that it required concomitantly modern attitudes toward empirical data. The willingness to acknowledge error and the capacity to analyze its origins were the crux of Tycho's concern for and success in the construction of instruments, so it is not surprising to see these attributes manifested in his handling of data. (Thoren, 1990, p. 137)

Tycho's observations located both the supernova of 1572 and the comet of 1577 in celestial space above the Moon. This was contrary to Aristotelian physics, so Tycho and many of his contemporaries were compelled to reconsider the shape of the cosmos as a whole. In 1578, Tycho wrote a manuscript in German on the comet, not for publication but as a secret report to King Frederik II in his capacity as royal astrologer. He laid out the political effects that the comet foretold on Earth and included his astronomical and cosmological analysis as background. Tycho determined that the comet was located somewhere between the Moon and Venus and concluded that a separate cometary sphere occupied that space. He theorized that Mercury, Venus, and the comet revolved around the Sun, which in turn revolved around the Earth. When another comet appeared in 1580, Tycho assigned it to the same cometary sphere. That year, Paul Wittich visited Uraniborg and inspired Tycho to rethink his cosmology. In 1582, Tycho set out to observe Mars in opposition as a way to judge between the Copernican and Ptolemaic systems, repeating these observations in 1585 and 1587 with superior instruments in Uraniborg and his new Stjerneborg observatory. He located the comet of 1585 very close to the Sun. This finally led Tycho to reject the

Tycho Brahe. *Detail from a map of Tycho Brahe's system of planet orbits.* © **STAPLETON COLLECTION/CORBIS.**

theory of solid celestial spheres, although he continued to believe that the celestial medium, aether, was a different element than terrestrial air. Once the spheres were out of the way, however, Tycho felt able to propound a new planetary theory in which orbits intersected, with all comets, planets, and the Moon revolving around the Sun, which in turn revolved around a stationary earth. Scholars still debate the role played in the development of Tycho's theory by his competition with Nicolas Reimers Ursus and his exchanges with Paul Wittich and Christopher Rothmann.

Tycho Brahe's innovative skill as a theoretical astronomer was clearly demonstrated by Thoren's analysis of his three major contributions to lunar theory. Thoren noted that Tycho's discovery of the variation was "the first new astronomical phenomenon to be discovered since Ptolemy's time." Tycho went on to discover nutation, and finally, he deduced the existence of nodal oscillation. The "theoretical prediction of the existence of a previously unnoticed phenomenon," Thoren noted, was "completely unprecedented" (Thoren, 1990, pp. 327, 333). He showed that Tycho's solar theory was equally innovative, whereas Owen Gingerich and James Voelkel emphasized the importance of Mars in Tycho's mature program of observation. These Mars observations later played an indispensible part in Kepler's discovery of his laws of planetary motion.

Tycho Brahe's organization of research on a large scale, involving centrally directed teams of scientists and technicians, scientific expeditions to gather data from distant locations, and collaboration with numerous other researchers across the face of Europe, was largely unprecedented. He used his aristocratic wealth, leadership ability, and social panache to solve classic problems in unprecedented ways with whole teams of scholars and technicians. As part of this process, Tycho personally taught his methods of observation and data reduction to numerous younger astronomers, including Johannes Kepler, Willebrord Snel, Paul Wittich, Simon Marius (Mayr), Duncan Liddel, David Fabricius of Resterhave (father of Johannes Fabricius), Johannes Müller of Berlin, Christian Sørensen Longomontanus, Adriaan Metius, and Christopher Rothmann. Leading seventeenth-century cartographers, Willem Janszoon Blaeu and Arnold Floris van Langren, also worked as his assistants, and Tycho prepared the first Scandinavian map based on geodetic triangular surveying. Tycho corresponded with astronomers and princes across Europe and sent them copies of his published works.

Tycho was a lifelong proponent of aristocratic constitutional government, and this put him at odds with the absolutist ambitions of King Christian IV, who was crowned in 1596. Moreover, a powerful clique at Copenhagen University resented Tycho's attracting their best students, and orthodox theologians opposed his Lutheran Philippism. These forces combined to drive Tycho into the voluntary exile from Denmark that eventually led to the court of Emperor Rudolf II and to his contact with Johannes Kepler.

Analysis of hairs preserved from Tycho's beard revealed high levels of mercury, which probably stemmed from plague medicine that he administered to himself and may have contributed to his death. Unsubstantiated speculation that he was poisoned proved to be without credibility.

SUPPLEMENTARY BIBLIOGRAPHY

WORKS BY BRAHE

Christianson, John Robert. "Tycho Brahe's Facts of Life." *Fund og Forskning i det kongelige biblioteks samlinger* 17 (1970): 21–28.

———. "Addenda to Tycho Brahe Opera Omnia tomus XIV." *Centaurus* 16 (1972): 231–247.

Zeeberg, Peter. *Tycho Brahes "Urania Titani: " Et digt om Sophie Brahe.* Copenhagen: Museum Tusculanum, 1994. Tycho Brahe's major Latin poem and the Renaissance culture of Uraniborg.

Hadravová, Alena, Petr Hadrava, and Jole R. Shackelford, trans. and eds. *Tycho Brahe: Instruments of the Renewed Astronomy.* Prague: Konaisch Latin Press, 1996.

Zeeberg, Peter. "The Inscriptions of Tycho Brahe's Uraniborg." In *A History of Nordic Neo-Latin Literature.* Edited by Minna Skafte Jensen. Odense, Denmark: Odense Universitetsforlag, 1996.

OTHER SOURCES

Blair, Ann. "Tycho Brahe's Critique of Copernicus and the Copernican System." *Isis* 51 (1990): 355–377.

Brosseder, Claudia. "The Writing in the Wittenberg Sky: Astrology in Sixteenth-Century Germany." *Journal of the History of Ideas* 66 (2005): 557–576.

Christianson, John R. "Tycho Brahe's German Treatise on the Comet of 1577: A Study in Science and Politics." *Isis* 70 (1979): 110–140.

———. "Tycho Brahe in Scandinavian Scholarship." *History of Science* 36 (1998): 467–484.

———. *On Tycho's Island: Tycho Brahe and His Assistants, 1570–1601.* Cambridge, U.K.: Cambridge, 2000. The abridged paperback edition (2003) has the subtitle, *Tycho Brahe, Science, and Culture in the Sixteenth Century.*

———. "The Legacy of Tycho Brahe." *Centaurus* 44 (2002): 228–247.

Christianson, John Robert, Alena Hadravová, Petr Hadrava, et al., eds. *Tycho Brahe and Prague: Crossroads of European Science,* vol. 16, *Acta Historica Astronomiae.* Frankfurt am Main: Harri Deutsch, 2002. Twenty-six articles on Tycho

Danneskiold-Samsøe, J. F. C. *Muses and Patrons: Cultures of Natural Philosophy in Seventeenth-Century Scandinavia,* vol. 10, *Ugglan Minervaserien.* Lund, Sweden: Lunds Universitet, 2004.

Daussy, Hugues. "Un diplomat protestant au service d'un roi catholique: Charles de Danzay, ambassadeur de France au Danemark (1515–1589)." In *Élites et notables de l'Ouest, XVIe-XXe siècle: Entre conservatisme et modernité,* edited by Frédérique Pitou. Rennes, France: Presses Universitaires, 2004.

Frank, Günther, and Stefan Rhein, eds. *Melanchthon und die Naturwissenschaften seiner Zeit.* Sigmaringen, Germany: Jan Thorbecke Verlag, 1998.

Gingerich, Owen. "Tycho Brahe and the Great Comet of 1577." *Sky and Telescope* 54 (1977): 452–458.

———, and Robert S. Westman. *The Wittich Connection: Conflict and Priority in Late Sixteenth-Century Cosmology.* Philadelphia: The American Philosophical Society, 1988. Tycho's relationship with Paul Wittich.

———, and James R. Voelkel. "Tycho Brahe's Copernican Campaign." *Journal for the History of Astronomy* 29 (1998): 1–34.

Granada, Miguel A. "Did Tycho Eliminate the Celestial Spheres Before 1586?" *Journal for the History of Astronomy* 37 (2006): 125–145. Includes references to other literature on celestial spheres.

Grant, Edward. *Planets, Stars, and Orbs: The Medieval Cosmos, 1200–1687.* Cambridge, U.K.: Cambridge, 1994.

Håkansson, Håkan. "Tycho the Apocalyptic: History, Prophecy and the Meaning of Natural Phenomena." In *Science in Contact at the Beginning of the Scientific Revolution,* edited by Jitka Zamrzlová. Prague: National Technical Museum, 2004.

———, ed. *Tycho Brahe och Renässansen: Att låta själen flyga mellan himlens tinnar.* Stockholm: Atlantis, 2006.

Haasbroek, N. D. *Gemma Frisius, Tycho Brahe and Snellius and Their Triangulations.* Delft, The Netherlands: Rijkscommissie voor Geodesie, 1968.

Hannaway, Owen. "Laboratory Design and the Aim of Science: Andreas Libavius versus Tycho Brahe." *Isis* 77 (1986): 585–610.

———. "Johan Gregor van der Schardt: Sculptor—and Architect." *Hafnia: Copenhagen Papers in the History of Art* 10 (1985): 147–164.

Honnens de Lichtenberg, Hanne. *Johan Gregor van der Schardt: Bildhauer bei Kaiser Maximillian II, am dänischen Hof und bei Tycho Brahe.* Translated from Danish by Georg Albrecht Mai. Copenhagen: Museum Tusculanum, 1991.

———. "Tycho Brahe als Mäzen." In *Europa in Scandinavia: Kulturelle und soziale Dialoge in der frühen Neuzeit,* vol. 2, *Studia septemtrionalia,* edited by Robert Bohn, 91–97. Frankfurt am Main: Peter Lang 1994.

Howell, Kenneth J. *God's Two Books: Copernican Cosmology and Biblical Interpretation in Early Modern Science.* South Bend, IN: University of Notre Dame, 2002.

Jacobsen, Aase R., and Lars Petersen. "How Tycho Brahe Really Died." *Planetarium* 30 (2001): 9–10.

Jardine, Nicholas. *The Birth of History and Philosophy of Science: Kepler's* A Defense of Tycho Against Ursus *with Essays on Its Provenance and Significance.* New York: Cambridge University Press, 1984.

Jardine, Nicholas, Dieter Launert, Alain Segonds, et al. "Tycho *v.* Ursus: The Build-Up to a Trial, Part 1." *Journal for the History of Astronomy* 36 (2005): 81–106.

Jarrell, Richard A. "The Contemporaries of Tycho Brahe." In *The General History of Astronomy,* vol. 2, *Planetary Astronomy from the Renaissance to the Rise of Astrophysics, Part A: Tycho Brahe to Newton,* edited by René Taton and Curtis Wilson. New York: Cambridge University Press, 1989.

Jones, Michael. "Tycho Brahe, Cartography and Landscape in 16th Century Scandinavia." In *European Rural Landscapes: Persistence and Change in a Globalising Environment,* edited by Hannes Palang, Helen Soovāli, Marc Antorp, et al. Boston: Kluwer Academic Publishers, 2004.

Kæmpe, Bent, Claus Thykier, and N. A. Pedersen. "The Cause of Death of Tycho Brahe in 1601." *Proceedings of the XXXI Congress of the The International Association of Forensic Toxicologists (TIAFT), 15–20 August 1993 in Leipzig* (1993), 1–7.

Kongsted, Ole. *Kronborg-Brunnen und Kronborg-Mottetten,* vol. 43, *Schriften des Gesellschaft für Flensburger Stadtgeschichte.* Copenhagen: Det kongelige Bibliotek, 1991.

Kusukawa, Sachiko. *The Transformation of Natural Philosophy: The Case of Philip Melanchthon.* Cambridge, U.K.: Cambridge University Press, 1995.

Lundquist, Kjell. "The plant material in the Renaissance garden of Tycho Brahe at Uraniborg (1581-1597) on the island of Ven—A restoration project in progress." *Museologica scientifica* 14 (1998), suppl.: 223–235.

———. "Reconstruction of the Planting in Uraniborg, Tycho Brahe's (1546–1601) Renaissance Garden on the Island of Ven." *Garden History: Journal of the Garden History Society* 32 (2004): 152–166.

Methuen, Charlotte. "The Role of the Heavens in the Thought of Philip Melanchthon." *Journal of the History of Ideas* 57 (1996): 385–403.

Moesgaard, Kristian Peder. "Copernican Influence on Tycho Brahe." In *The Reception of Copernicus' Heliocentric Theory,* vol. 1, *Colloquia Copernicana,* edited by Jerzy Dobrzycki. Dortrecht, Netherlands: D. Reidel, 1972.

———. "How Copernicanism Took Root in Denmark and Norway." In *The Reception of Copernicus' Heliocentric Theory,* vol. 1, *Colloquia Copernicana,* edited by Jerzy Dobrzycki. Dortrecht, Netherlands: D. Reidel, 1972.

———. "Tychonian Observations, Perfect Numbers, and the Date of Creation: Longomontanus's Solar and Precessional Theories." *Journal for the History of Astronomy* 6 (1975): 84–99.

———. "Cosmology in the Wake of Tycho Brahe's Astronomy." In *Cosmology, History, and Theory,* edited by Wolfgang Yourgrau and Allen D. Breck. New York: Plenum Press, 1977.

Moran, Bruce T. "Christoph Rothmann, the Copernican Theory, and Institutional and Technical Influence on the Criticism of Aristotelean Cosmology." *Sixteenth Century Journal* 13 (1982): 85–108.

———. *Distilling Knowledge: Alchemy, Chemistry, and the Scientific Revolution.* Cambridge, MA: Harvard University Press, 2005.

———, ed. *Patronage and Institutions: Science, Technology and Medicine at the European Court 1500–1750.* Rochester, NY: Boydell Press, 1991.

Mosley, Adam, Nicholas Jardine, and Karin Tybjerg. "Epistolary Culture, Editorial Practices, and the Propriety of Tycho's Astronomical Letters." *Journal for the History of Astronomy* 34 (2003): 421–451.

———. *Bearing the Heavens: Tycho Brahe and the Astronomical Community of the Late Sixteenth Century.* Cambridge, U.K.: Cambridge University Press, 2007.

Norlind, Wilhelm. *Tycho Brahe: En levnadsteckning.* Lund, Sweden: C. W. K. Gleerup, 1970. Tycho's life, works, and library, with a German summary.

Rosen, Edward. *Three Imperial Mathematicians: Kepler Trapped Between Tycho Brahe and Ursus.* New York: Abaris Books, 1986.

Schofield, Christine Jones. *Tychonic and Semi-Tychonic World Systems.* New York: Arno Press, 1981.

Schofield, Christine. "The Tychonic and Semi-Tychonic World Systems." In *The General History of Astronomy,* vol. 2, *Planetary Astronomy from the Renaissance to the Rise of Astrophysics, Part A: Tycho Brahe to Newton,* edited by René Taton and Curtis Wilson. New York: Cambridge University Press, 1989.

Shackelford, Jole. "Paracelsianism and Patronage in Early Modern Denmark." In *Patronage and Institutions: Science,*

Technology, and Medicine at the European Court 1500–1750, edited by Bruce Moran. Rochester, NY: Boydell Press, 1991.

———. "Tycho Brahe, Laboratory Design, and the Aim of Science: Reading Plans in Context." *Isis* 84 (1993): 211–230.

———. "Early Reception of Paracelsian Theory: Severinus and Erastus," *Sixteenth Century Journal* 26 (1995): 123–135.

———. "Rosicrucianism, Lutheran Orthodoxy, and the Rejection of Paracelsianism in Early Seventeenth-Century Denmark," *Bulletin of the History of Medicine* 70 (1996): 181–204.

———. "Seeds with a Mechanical Purpose: Severinus' Semina and Seventeenth-Century Matter Theory." *Sixteenth Century Essays and Studies* 41 (1998): 15–44.

———. "Unification and the Chemistry of the Reformation." *Sixteenth Century Essays and Studies* 40 (1998): 291–312. Tycho's assistant, Cort Aslakssøn.

———. *A Philosophical Path for Paracelsian Medicine: The Ideas, Intellectual Context, and Influence of Petrus Severinus (1540/2–1602).* Copenhagen: Museum Tusculanum Press University of Copenhagen, 2004.

Skovgaard-Petersen, Karen, and Peter Zeeberg. "Recent Work on Nordic Neo-Latin Literature (1992–1996). *Symbolae Osloenses,* 72 (1997): 172–184.

———. "Recent Work on Nordic Neo-Latin Literature (1997–2000). *Symbolae Osloenses,* 76 (2001): 201–210.

———. "Recent Work on Nordic Neo-Latin Literature (2001–2004)." *Symbolae Osloenses,* 79 (2004): 179–189.

Thoren, Victor E. "An Early Instance of Deductive Discovery: Tycho Brahe's Lunar Theory." *Isis* 58 (1967): 19–36.

———. "Tycho Brahe's Discovery of the Variation." *Centaurus* 12 (1967): 151–166.

———. "An 'Unpublished' Version of Tycho Brahe's Lunar Theory." *Centaurus* 16 (1972): 203–230.

———. "New Light on Tycho's Instruments," *Journal for the History of Astronomy* 4 (1973): 25–45.

———. "Tycho Brahe as the Dean of a Renaissance Research Institute." In *Religion, Science, and Worldview,* edited by Margaret J. Osler and Paul Lawrence Farber. Cambridge, U.K.: Cambridge University Press, 1985.

———. "Tycho Brahe." In *The General History of Astronomy,* vol. 2, *Planetary Astronomy from the Renaissance to the Rise of Astrophysics, Part A: Tycho Brahe to Newton,* edited by René Taton and Curtis Wilson. New York: Cambridge University Press, 1989.

———, with contributions by John Robert Christianson. *The Lord of Uraniborg: A Biography of Tycho Brahe.* Cambridge, U.K.: Cambridge University Press, 1990. The standard biography.

Thykier, Claus. "Dødsårsagen." *Skalk* no. 1 (2001): 12–14.

Vanden Broecke, Steven. "Teratology and the Publication of Tycho Brahe's New World System (1588)." *Journal for the History of Astronomy* 37 (2006): 1–17.

Voelkel, James R. "Publish or Perish: Legal Contingencies and the Publication of Kepler's *Astronomia nova.*" *Science in Context,* 12 (1999): 33–59.

Warner, Deborah Jean. *The Sky Explored: Celestial Cartography 1500–1800.* New York: Alan R. Liss, 1979.

Webster, Charles. *From Paracelsus to Newton: Magic and the Making of Modern Science.* Cambridge, U.K.: Cambridge University Press, 1982.

Wesley, Walter. G. "The Accuracy of Tycho Brahe's Instruments." *Journal for the History of Astronomy* 9 (1978): 42–53.

———. "Tycho Brahe's Solar Observations." *Journal for the History of Astronomy* 10 (1979): 96–101.

———. "The Melanchthon Circle, Rheticus, and the Wittenberg Interpretation of the Copernican Theory." *Isis* 66 (1975): 165–193.

Westman, Robert S. "The Astronomer's Role in the Sixteenth Century: A Preliminary Study." *History of Science,* 18 (1980): 105–147.

———, ed. *The Copernican Achievement.* Berkeley: University of California, 1975.

Zamrzlová, Jitka, ed. *Science in Contact at the Beginning of the Scientific Revolution,* new ser. vol. 8, *Prague Studies in the History of Science and Technology.* Prague: National Technical Museum, 2004. Six articles on Tycho Brahe, including Håkansson above.

———. "Science versus Secular Life: A Central Theme in the Latin Poems of Tycho Brahe." In *Acta Conventus Neo-Latini Torontonensis,* edited by Alexander Dalzell, Charles Fantazzi, and Richard J. Schoeck. Binghamton, NY: Center for Medieval and Early Renaissance Studies, 1991.

Zeeberg, Peter. "Alchemy, Astrology, and Ovid—A Love Poem by Tycho Brahe." In *Acta Conventus Neo-Latini Hafniensis,* edited by Ann Moss et al. Binghamton, NY : Center for Medieval and Early Renaissance Studies, 1994.

———. "Neo-Latin Poetry in Its Social Context. Some Statistics and Some Examples from Sixteenth-Century Denmark." In *Mari Balticum—Mari Nostrum: Latin in the Countries of the Baltic Sea (1500-1800),* series B, no. 274, *Annales Academiæ Scientiarum Fennicæ,* edited by Outi Merisalo and Raija Sarasti-Wilenius. Helsinki: Academia Scientiarum Fennica, 1994.

John Robert Christianson

BRAUN-BLANQUET, JOSIAS (*b.* Coire, Switzerland, 3 August 1884; *d.* Montpellier, France, 20 September 1980), *plant sociology, ecology, botany.*

Braun-Blanquet founded the Zürich-Montpellier school of plant sociology (or *phytosociology*). The school was so named because Braun-Blanquet studied at Zürich University in Switzerland, but carried out most of his research in the French city of Montpellier. The school spread rapidly in south and central Europe and became the dominant European approach to phytosociology (alongside the Physionomic-Ecological, Uppsala, and Russian Schools). It identified adaptations to environmental factors not brought to light by traditional methods, thus playing an important part in the history of ecology. In 1930 Braun-Blanquet established the "Station Internationale de Géobotanique Méditerranéenne et Alpine" (SIGMA, International station for Mediterranean and Alpine geobotany). This school of phytosociology also became known by the neologism *sigmatism*. In 1974 Braun-Blanquet was awarded the Gold Medal of the Linnean Society of London.

Background and Education. Born Josias Braun in Switzerland in Coire (Chur in Alemannic dialect), the regional capital of the Grisons canton, the scientist came from a humble background: His father, Jakob, was a state employee and his mother, Elizabeth Kindschi, was a housewife. After business studies he began his own study of botany in the Swiss Alps before studying the subject at Zurich University, where he was taught by the renowned Helvetian botanists Eduard Rübel (1876–1960) and Carl Schroeter (1855–1939). In Geneva, where he stayed in 1907 and 1908, he was taught by Casimir de Candolle (1836–1918), son of Alphonse de Candolle (1806–1893) and grandson of Augustin-Pyramus de Candolle (1778–1841), and by John Briquet (1870–1931), then director of the Geneva Botanical Conservatory and Gardens. Briquet was also behind the adoption of the botanical nomenclature international rules. This interest in systematics was consistent with Braun-Blanquet's subsequent studies on plant community taxonomy. It had long been of interest to ecologists. The general appearance of a plant community is the outcome of the particular look of each plant. It is therefore related to the growth-forms of plants that compose vegetation. Now, as growth-forms represent the state of the adapted plants, any physionomical classification of plant communities takes on an ecological significance more or less evident, according to the advancement of biological forms studies.

Birth of Plant Community Study. In 1805, in his *Essai sur la géographie des plantes*, Alexander von Humboldt (1769–1859) had described Calluna heath vegetation in the following way: "Heathers, this association of *Erica vulgaris, Erica tetralix, Icmadophila* and *Hoematomma* lichens, spread between the most northern extremity of Jutland up to 52° N, through Holstein and Luneberg" (p. 17). This reasoning amounted to defining a plant community by its main floristic components. Humboldt also geographically localized the extension of this "association" (in contemporary terms, "plant formation") in relation to climate. In 1822, the Danish botanist Joakim Frederik Schouw (1789–1852) proposed a method for defining associations: He recommended adding the suffix *-etum* to the root of the dominant plant's name. Thus, *Fagetum* denoted an association of which the dominant species is the beech (*Fagus sylvatica*), and *Quercetum* an association where the oak (*Quercus*) is dominant. According to this method, the dominant species provides the name of the association, but this does not imply an exhaustive floristic survey of the community.

In 1863, the Austrian botanist Anton Kerner von Marilaün (1831–1898) reversed the traditional relationship between plant communities and environment. Instead of starting from environmental factors in order to define communities, he described communities according to their own characteristics of physionomy and floristic composition. This reasoning provided a foundation for modern plant sociology, as it made possible discovery of adaptations to environmental factors previously obscured by communities classed according to environmental criteria. Until then, plant communities had been described on the basis of their appearance, or physiognomy, and therefore in terms of one or several dominant species, as stated in the historical definition by the Göttingen botanist A. H. R. Grisebach (1814–1879) in "Ueber den Einfluss des Climas auf die Begränzung der Natürlichen Floren" [On the influence of climates on the discontinuities of natural floras]:

> I would name phytogeographical formation a group of plants with a definite physionomic character like a meadow, a forest, etc. It is sometimes composed of an only species, sometimes of a complex of dominant species belonging to the same family, sometimes finally of a species aggregate which, although different, take on some common particularity in their organization; thus alpine meadows are almost exclusively composed of perennial grasses. (*Linnea* 12, p. 160)

This definition dates back to 1838, and would encourage research and controversies lasting almost a century. Indeed, being both rich and imprecise, it paradoxically played an important part in the evolution of plant community study, as plant sociology was born in the 1910s out of this work and scholarly confrontations. It is rich because it is derived from both the physionomic tradition that dates back to Humboldt's geobotany, and the floristic tradition, in which plant groups are defined in terms of their floristic composition. If the formation had an essentially physionomical value for Grisebach, it was characterized by the dominant species, which does not necessarily determine the physionomy of the community, thus requiring a thorough floristic survey. Because of this very duality, Grisebach's definition is also imprecise. Juxtaposing physionomy and floristics, it discouraged accurate distinction between formations (physionomical criteria) and associations (criteria gradually becoming floristic). To establish this distinction became more and more urgent during the nineteenth century as vegetation studies advanced. It was indeed most important to go beyond physionomical criteria, as they did not allow botanists to decisively distinguish between formations physionomically identical but floristically different—such as the tropical rain forests of Amazonia, Nigeria, and Malaysia.

The Importance of Characteristic Plants. In 1913 Josias Braun studied in Montpellier, attracted by the teaching of the renowned botanist-forester Charles Flahault (1852–1935). Braun had already published several scientific papers, including a contribution to the *Flora des Graubündens* (1904) and a study of the nival-level vegetation in Rhetic Alps—a massif of the Central Alps spreading over Switzerland (Grisons), Italy (Lombardia and Alto Adige), and Austria (Tyrol). He then, under Flahault's supervision, began to write a doctoral thesis in which he studied the plant groups of southern Cévennes, in the south of France. But in this same year, he transformed the study of plant communities with publication of "Remarques sur l'étude des groupements de plantes" [Remarks on the study of plant groups], authored with another advanced student, Ernst Furrer (1888–1976) in the *Bulletin de la Société Languedocienne de Géographie.*

The authors broke the impasse between physiognomic and floristic approaches by stressing not only the importance of the complete floristic inventory of an association (an approach that had not yet been systematically explored), but also and above all the importance of the "character species." Returning to a definition first proposed by Flahault and Schröter at the Third International Congress of Botany (Brussels, Belgium, 1910), and according to which "The association … is a plant group with a definite floristic composition and a uniform physionomy, growing in homogeneous station conditions" (*Actes du III.e Congrès International de Botanique*, p. 152), they added: "and possessing one or several character species," which are "species almost exclusively localized in a given association" (*Remarques sur l'étude des groupements de plantes*, p. 21). Braun and Furrer acknowledged the limits of their point of view, as botanists are not able to distinguish all associations solely by means of character species when they are in the presence of mixed groups or associations. Therefore, they followed Flahault, who had recommended since 1900 that the study of the association include a complete floristic inventory. These "Remarques sur l'étude des groupements de plantes" had great repercussions, including the origin of the Zürich-Montpellier school.

Braun met Gabrielle Blanquet in Flahault's laboratory where she was also studying botany. He married her in 1915, bearing from then on the name of Braun-Blanquet in accordance with a Swiss onomastic custom, in order to associate his spouse to his scientific activities. Back in Zürich in 1916, he became assistant to Eduard Rübel, then lecturer at the University of Zürich (1922–1926).

Although World War I had ruined botanical research in Europe, by 1925 a revised edition of the *Vocabulaire de sociologie végétale* (Plant sociology glossary) was published. The authors were Jules Pavillard (1868–1961), who was about to replace Flahault, and Braun-Blanquet. The first edition had been very rapidly translated into English, Polish, and Russian, illustrating its international reception. This publication was of interest historically as it expressed pedagogic intentions, a tangible sign of success in the development of a scientific theory.

Yet by 1926 conflicting opinions were evident. Leonid Grigorievitch Ramensky (1884–1953) and Henry Allen Gleason (1882–1975) linked the individuality of associations to the single plants that compose them, and particularly to seed scattering: Fortuitous but constant, scattering introduces species that should not be "normally" found in these associations. Hence, they considered heterogeneousness in the pattern of an association to be a coincidence; it was not to be considered a phenomenon inherent to natural vegetation dynamics, but the outcome of accidents or external environmental circumstances.

Between 1923 and 1927 Braun-Blanquet was *Privat Dozent* (a professor authorized to deliver free lectures) at the École Polytechnique Fédérale de Zürich. When he resigned from his post, Pavillard, who had replaced Flahault in 1927, immediately offered him the position of head of a laboratory in the Institute of Botany. In 1928, on Pavillard's recommendation, the Faculty of Sciences Council granted him the right to teach in the University.

The Zürich-Montpellier School. In 1928, Braun-Blanquet published in Berlin his magnum opus: *Pflanzensoziologie*. The book was translated into English by 1932 and has been republished many times. Ecologists still refer to this comprehensive survey of theory and method. An important topic of the book was precisely the question of vegetation discontinuity, and focused on the minimal area, the area beyond which the number of new species met ceases to increase rapidly. Delimitation of the minimal area, through appropriate sampling methods, provides an objective basis for identifying a vegetation discontinuity: When the number of new species met again increases rapidly, the phytosociologist is in the presence of a new community.

The reasoning is schematically the following: The minimal area being far smaller than the analyzed community, the phytosociologist establishes floristic sample plots at least equal to the minimal area. Then he or she carries out, through various statistical methods, a floristic comparison of the samples from the community at issue. Certain species are found in every sample: This identifies them as *constant* species. Others show lower degrees of presence. When one compares samples belonging to different communities, one observes that certain species have a strong preference for particular groups. Such selective species are of great diagnostic value for the characterization of a community, and so are called "character species" (Becking, 1957, p. 444) because of their *fidelity*. This method is based on analysis of the entire species composition of a plant group.

The phytosociologist is then faced with the problem of their designation. Braun-Blanquet rejected the dominant species criterion, as the dominants are too often ubiquitous, and hence their presence is not ecologically informative. Moreover, as dominance is not necessarily linked with abundance, the criterion was considered too subjective, being physionomical in the final analysis. Braun-Blanquet finally chose the fidelity criterion. The association was therefore named after the character species (*Charakterpflanzen*), generally the most constant in a community. Following Schouw, the associations were named by the suffix *-etum* appended to the gender name of the character species, while the species name was written in the genitive: thus, the association characterized by the yellow flatsedge *Cyperus flavescens L.* was named *Cyperetum flavescentis*. The associations were grouped together in higher or lower taxa—that is, alliances, orders, and subassociations.

Braun-Blanquet's system was quickly recognized in countries where it was hytogeographically suitable. The Cracow school developed on Zürich-Montpellier basis: Worked out in the Alps, the system could also be applied in the Tatras mountains. Within three decades the same phenomenon occurred in Hungary, Bulgaria, Czechoslovakia, Austria, the Netherlands, and Belgium. Indeed, in Europe—apart from Soviet ecologist Vladimir Nicolayevich Sukachev (1880–1967), who, like the Americans Henry Chandler Cowles (1869–1939) and Frederic Edward Clements (1874–1945), linked closely the slow variation of the Russian forest communities with gradual transitions in environmental factors—only the school of the Uppsala (Sweden) botanist Gustav Einar Du Rietz (1895–1967) developed an alternative approach to that of Braun-Blanquet. As Scandinavian and Arctic vegetation is relatively poor in species for a Zürich-Montpellier analysis, Uppsala phytosociologists elaborated a complex system founded on the analysis of a layered vegetation. Such an approach proved to be also appropriate in the uniform vegetation of the tropics. At the very beginning, Du Rietz defined the association as a vegetal society endowed with definite constant plants and physiognomy. This perspective was adapted to this terrain: In regions richer in species than Scandinavia, it would have revealed too many communities. It is indeed plausible that, at the time, numerous theoretical confrontations between schools of phytosociology were caused by the fact that researchers worked on different ground covers.

Foundation of SIGMA. How can historians of ecology assess the importance of Braun-Blanquet's plant sociology in the elaboration of a systematic conception of plant communities? On the one hand, phytosociological groups have a significant ecological value: Through vegetation analysis and cartography, ecologists are able to pursue ever more accurate research on environmental factors. On the other hand, certain communities can be interpreted as indicators (sometimes of environmental gradients), and this was significant in ecological and agroecological researches during the interwar years. This is true of all phytosociological systems, but the success of the Zurich-Montpellier school has, if not overshadowed, at least relegated other systems to the background.

By 1929 Braun-Blanquet's influence and activities were such that his laboratory had become obviously inadequate. The Scottish biologist and sociologist Sir Patrick Geddes (1854–1932) untangled the situation. He offered to Braun-Blanquet, for a symbolic rent, an entire floor of the Collège des Ecossais (Scots College), an international school for traveling scholars he had founded in Montpellier. This was the first headquarters of the Station Internationale de Géobotanique Méditerranéenne et Alpine (SIGMA), which eventually become known throughout the world among botanists. SIGMA was founded in 1930 by the Dutch botanist W. C. de Leeuw (1881–1964) and Raoul Combes (1893–1964), teacher of plant physiology at the Sorbonne (Paris). Braun-Blanquet was appointed director. It was financed by indirect international subsidies: Certain countries rented in the SIGMA space for their doctoral students or researchers and subscribed to the institution's numerous scientific publications. After the death of Geddes, the rental lease could not be extended and the SIGMA had to be transferred to another site, acquired thanks to the generosity of another sponsor, Fritz Alleman von Albertini (1895–1971). Braun-Blanquet remained in charge of the SIGMA until he reached the age limit. After the death of his wife in 1966, his daughter, Mireille Braun-Blanquet, teacher at the Montpellier Faculty of Medicine, resumed the institution's tradition of hospitality. The founder of the Zürich-Montpellier school died in 1980 at the age of ninety-six.

BIBLIOGRAPHY

WORKS BY BRAUN-BLANQUET

With Ernst Furrer. "Remarques sur l'étude des groupements de plantes." *Bulletin de la Société languedocienne de Géographie* (1913).

With Jules Pavillard. *Vocabulaire de sociologie végétale.* Montpellier, 1922.

Pflanzensoziologie. Berlin: Springer, 1928.

Plant sociology. Translated and edited by Henry S. Conard and George D. Fuller. New York: McGraw-Hill, 1932.

With L. Emberger and R. Molinier. *Instructions pour l'établissement de la carte des groupements végétaux.* Montpellier, 1947.

La végétation alpine des Pyrénées-Orientales. Etude de phytosociologie comparée. Barcelona: La Estación de Estudios Pirenaices y del Instituto Español de Edafologia, Ecologia y Fisiologia Vegetal, 1948.

"Essai sur la végétation du Mont Lozère comparée à celle de l'Aigoual." *Bulletin de la Societe botanique de France*, 80ᵉ sess. extr. S.I.G.M.A., Com. 127, Tom. 100 (1953): 47–59.

Pflanzensoziologie, 3rd ed. Vienna: Springer Verlag, 1964.

OTHER SOURCES

Becking, Rudy W. "The Zürich-Montpellier School of Phytosociology." *The Botanical Review* 23(7) (1957): 411–488. An essential reading.

Gleason, Henry Allan. "Braun-Blanquet's Plant Sociology." *Ecology* 14(1) (1933): 70–74. A rather critical look at the Zürich-Montpellier school of phytosociology.

Guinochet, Marcel. "Josias Braun-Blanquet (1884–1980)." *Bulletin de la Societe botanique de France* 129 (1982): 73–76.

Pascal Acot

BRAUN, WERNHER VON
SEE **von Braun, Wernher**.

BREIT, GREGORY (*b*. Nikolayev, Russia, 14 July 1899; *d*. Salem, Oregon, 11 September 1981), *physics.*

Breit was one of the most prolific members of the U.S. physics community for nearly fifty years. Equally active in experimental and theoretical physics, he left his mark in geophysics (upper-air studies), radio, ballistic, and accelerator technology, experimental nuclear physics, and, above all, in nuclear theory—with his seminal contributions to nucleon-nucleon scattering and nuclear reactions. His wartime contributions included neutron studies, ship degaussing, the proximity fuse, and various ordnance problems. Reflecting the breadth of his interests, and despite a difficult personality, he left a large school of appreciative students, colleagues, and collaborators—the "Breit group," as it was called—attested to by the many notable speakers at a symposium in his honor at Yale in 1968.

Yet Breit was hardly known at all in the early twenty-first century. As emphasized by John Wheeler, one of his close colleagues, "Anyone in the United States who before

World War II contributed more importantly to more fields of physics than Gregory Breit would be difficult to name." However, oddly enough, continues Wheeler, "Insufficiently appreciated in the 1930s, [Breit] is today the most unappreciated physicist in America" (1979, p. 234). Part of this lack of recognition can probably be blamed on Breit's legendary irascibility. This in spite of Breit's devotion to the development of his students, a trait McAllister Hull treats as "equally legendary" (p. 34).

Background. Breit's parents, Alfred and Alexandra Smirnova Breit Schneider, operated a textbook business in Nikolayev, some 100 kilometers northeast of Odessa on the Black Sea. When Alexandra died in 1911, the business was sold, and the next year Alfred emigrated to the United States, leaving Gregory and his sister Lubov in the charge of a governess. In 1915, Alfred insisted that his children follow him to the United States, and with their governess they traveled by train to Arkhangelsk, and thence by steamer to New York. They joined their father, Alfred Breit, having dropped "Schneider" from the family name, in Baltimore where he had settled.

In addition to his sister Lubov, Gregory had an older brother, Leo, who had avoided recruitment in the tsar's army by fleeing through Turkey; he, too, wound up in Maryland where he practiced medicine—still sought by the tsar's agents as a deserter. Gregory, by contrast, approached Russian recruiters in 1918, eager for service in the Russian army. Turned down on physical grounds, he continued his higher education, begun at the School of Emperor Alexander in Nikolayev, by enrolling at Johns Hopkins University in Baltimore. There he earned his AB in 1918, the MA in 1920, and the PhD in 1921, all three degrees in electrical engineering. His dissertation, under the advice of Joseph Sweetman Ames, was on the distributed capacity of inductive coils. This work, with both calculations and measurements, Breit carried out while he was an apprentice in the Radio Section of the Bureau of Standards. A man of great reputation, the motto of "Joe Ames" was that "no matter what it is, everybody who is anybody at Hopkins goes to work on something that deeply interests him"—an admonition that suited Gregory, only twenty-two in 1921, to a tee (Wheeler, 1979, p. 219).

Career. With his doctorate in hand, Gregory Breit served a postdoctoral stint as a National Research Council fellow at the University of Leiden (1921–1922). There, in his own words, he "was exposed to the influence of Ehrenfest in theory and of Kamerlingh Onnes in experiment." Kamerlingh Onnes's influence on his career would prove to have "been salutory," and "being with Ehrenfest was also an unforgettable experience" (Bromley et al, 1970, p.

192). He held a subsequent fellowship at Harvard University (1922–1923), after which he began his professional career as an assistant professor of physics at the University of Minnesota (1923–1924). From there he went on to the Carnegie Institution of Washington, DC, where he held a staff position as a mathematical physicist from 1924 to 1929, with a residency at the Eidgenössische Technische Hochschule (ETH), Zürich, in 1928. Breit would remain associated with the ETH as a research associate until 1944. For the next five years (1929–1934), he was professor of physics at New York University, followed by a professorship at the University of Wisconsin in Madison from 1934 to 1947. The latter appointment was interrupted by a two-year residency at the Institute for Advanced Study at Princeton (1935–1936), and his wartime work. He worked in the Naval Ordnance Laboratory during 1940 and 1941, at the Metallurgical Laboratory, University of Chicago, in 1942, became a member of the Applied Physics Laboratory, Johns Hopkins University (1942–1943), and headed physics at the Ballistic Laboratory, Aberdeen Proving Grounds (1943–1945). (His brief service with the fledgling Manhattan Project below.)

Breit's postwar stay on the Madison campus was cut short by his acceptance of a professorship at Yale University in 1947. He remained at Yale, the last ten years as the first Donner chair, until he reached Yale's mandatory retirement age of sixty-eight in 1968. He completed his professional career as distinguished professor of physics at the State University of New York at Buffalo, from which he retired to private life in Oregon in 1973.

Honors. Breit was elected to the National Academy of Sciences in 1939, and to the American Academy of Arts and Sciences in 1951. He was a fellow of the American Physical Society, Physical Society of London, Institute of Radio Engineers, and the American Association for the Advancement of Science. He was a member of the American Mathematical Society, American Geophysical Union, Washington Academy of Science, The Army Ordnance Association, Sigma Xi, and Phi Beta Kappa. He was awarded an honorary doctorate of science by the University of Wisconsin in 1954, the Benjamin Franklin Medal in 1964, and the National Medal of Science in 1968. He served, at various times in his career, as associate editor of *Physical Review, Proceedings of the National Academy of Sciences,* and *Il Nuovo Cimento.*

Breit married Marjory Elizabeth McDill on 30 December 1927, in Washington, DC, and acquired a stepson, Ralph Wycoff, from Marjory's previous marriage. When he retired from the State University of New York (SUNY) Buffalo, he and Marjory moved into a retirement home near Salem, Oregon, where Marjory could be near her son and daughter-in-law. His health had begun

declining in Buffalo, and Breit died on 13 September 1981.

Early Work: Geophysics. Breit's first noteworthy item of research involved the experimental determination of the height of the "conducting" or "Kennelly-Heaviside" layer in the upper atmosphere. This ionospheric layer was inferred, nearly simultaneously in 1902 by Arthur Edwin Kennelly in the United States and Oliver Heaviside in the United Kingdom, to account for the long-distance propagation of very long wavelength radio waves. The auroras and magnetic storms pointed toward the circulation of large electrical currents in high regions of the atmosphere—a subject obviously within the province of the Carnegie's Department of Terrestrial Magnetism (DTM). Breit's partner in this effort was Merle Antony Tuve, whom he met in the summer of 1923 while at Minnesota, when he assisted Tuve on his MA thesis on UHF oscillator tubes. The tubes were experimental components in a project involving short radio waves, vacuum tubes, and related phenomena, including the Kennelly-Heaviside layer. Breit's own MA thesis, at Johns Hopkins in 1920, had been on the transmission of electromagnetic waves in wireless telegraphy. Tuve's interest in radio stemmed from his childhood in Canton, South Dakota, where he and his pal across the street, Ernest Orlando Lawrence, communicated in Morse code via home-crafted radio transmitters and receivers.

On joining the DTM in July of 1924, Breit began to plan a program for an in-depth study of the Kennelly-Heaviside layer; he was joined by Merle Tuve, who was then an instructor at Johns Hopkins while casting about for a PhD thesis topic. Breit's scheme involved beaming short radio waves upward on a slant, reflecting them from the Heaviside layer down to Baltimore, where Tuve was conveniently available as an observer. Tuve, however, was somewhat skeptical of the critical reflection coefficient for such short waves, suspecting the waves would pass right through the reflecting layer, and suggested instead using pulses of conventional-length radio waves in a radio-echo sounding method first proposed by the English physicist William Francis Gray Swann. Swann was a former DTM staff member, where he started the first U.S. work on what was later called cosmic rays. He had left the department for a professorship at Minnesota, where he discussed his method at a seminar in 1922 that Tuve had attended. The new scheme involved comparing two sets of signals, one arriving by the line-of-sight path from the transmitter and the other scattered via the ionosphere. The time difference between the two paths would afford a measure of the height of the conducting layer.

Breit believed a large parabolic reflector, perhaps forty feet in diameter, located at the Broad Branch Road

Campus of DTM, along with a much smaller receiving set in Baltimore, would be suitable for the attempt; however, funding limitations at DTM ruled that out. Instead, they availed themselves of a Naval Research Laboratory crystal-controlled transmitter located in Bellevue, Anacostia, a few miles from the DTM laboratory, which was modulated to transmit a series of short pulses. In June of 1925, they recorded pulse echoes at 4 MHz, received and recorded on the roof of the main building at DTM. In testing the apparatus, they noted occasional spurious signals, finally attributed to aircraft flying out of Washington's airport; in effect, they had unknowingly observed a radar signal.

On Breit's urging, Joseph Sweetman Ames accepted Tuve's contributions to the radio-echo project for his PhD dissertation in 1926, and, again on Breit's suggestion, Tuve joined Breit at the DTM on 1 July of that year. In 1927, he and Breit were joined by the Norwegian Odd Dahl in the ionospheric work. However, several developments soon steered them away from this project. In England, the energetic physicist Edward Victor Appleton (whom Breit met during his postdoctoral stint in Europe) and his students at King's College, London, were also working seriously on radio methods for investigating the ionosphere, but by a somewhat different method that would earn Appleton the Nobel Prize in Physics in 1947. At the same time, Breit's interest was turning towards the emerging field of quantum mechanics, which led to his extended trip to Europe in 1928. Finally, the ongoing nuclear studies by Ernest Rutherford and colleagues at Cambridge had captured the attention not only of Breit and Tuve, but of John Ambrose Fleming, the assistant director at DTM; after all, the structure of the atomic nucleus was surely the fundamental key to the secrets of terrestrial magnetism! Before long, goaded by Fleming, the study of nuclear structure would occupy most of the working hours of Breit, Tuve, and Dahl.

Nuclear Physics Experiments. The key to a successful attack on the atomic nucleus, as Rutherford himself had declared, and as Breit realized early on in the United States, was to replace the weak flux of alpha particles from a radioactive source, as utilized by Rutherford in 1919 while still at Manchester University, with a potent artificial source of alphas or other particles, preferably protons, accelerated through an electric potential of millions of volts in a vacuum tube. However, there were limited methods of producing a million volts or higher in 1927. About the only device available was the Tesla transformer, in which a resonant primary coil of a few turns induces high alternating voltages in a multiturn secondary coil. Very high voltages could thereby be produced, especially if operated in oil under high pressure—the method by which the DTM team coaxed the coil to more than five million volts. However, the oscillatory character of the output potential, with a very short duty cycle, soon ruled the Tesla coil out for nuclear disintegration experiments. What was needed for energizing the discharge tube was a steady DC voltage. Just as Breit left the DTM, Tuve and Dahl, now joined by Lawrence Hafstad, adopted the electrostatic generator devised by Robert Van de Graaff as a highly suitable accelerator for precision experiments in nuclear research.

Breit sailed for Europe in August of 1928, where he spent his time following up on some theoretical work by Wolfgang Pauli and Werner Heisenberg. However, he cut his year abroad short and returned to the United States in January 1929. In view what he saw as the untruthful nature of theoretical physics and the need for new data about the nucleus, Breit felt that it was more desirable to return to Washington to assist in obtaining this information through investigations into high-voltage developments.

However, back at DTM, Breit found himself in a situation less happy than it had been before his sojourn abroad. He had left DTM partly because his personal relations with his colleagues had reached an impasse. Now his relationship with Tuve was, if anything, more difficult, and Breit left DTM in August 1929 to accept a position at New York University. Curiously, in the years to come he cooperated closely with Tuve's nuclear physics team, offering sound theoretical knowledge and analysis of their experimental results via letters and occasional visits with Tuve in New York.

Theory. In New York, Breit, too, continued high voltage experiments with various collaborators on the ground floor of a large building at University Heights in the Bronx. However, increasingly his time was spent, at New York and later in Madison and New Haven, on theory and advising students and colleagues on proposed experiments and their results. Many have nostalgic memories of the joint Columbia–New York University theoretical seminar conducted by Isidor I. Rabi and Breit, in Room 831 in the Pupin Laboratory, often followed by a late evening discussion in Rabi's Riverside Drive apartment. Breit's range of contributions was sufficiently diverse that only a full-length biography could do them justice. For a starter, they encompassed fine and hyperfine structures, magnetic moments, and the nuclear isotope shift. Altogether, Breit published, alone and with colleagues, some 320 papers, according to McAllister Hull. His definitive work, carried out at Princeton with Eugene P. Wigner on the resonance theory of the capture of slow neutrons, appeared in 1936. The same year saw his famous paper, with Edward U. Condon and Richard D. Present, on the theory of the scattering of protons by protons—the original objective at

DTM as an experimental tool for probing the short-range attractive force between the constituents of atomic nuclei.

At Wisconsin, as in New York, Breit began his tenure with the construction of an accelerator, of the Cockcroft-Walton type pioneered in Cambridge, and this modest experimental program inspired the work of Ray Herb and colleagues in their classic Van de Graaff experiments on proton-proton scattering begun shortly before World War II and resumed after the war. His paper on evidence concerning the equality of neutron-neutron and proton-proton forces appeared in 1950. With McAllister H. Hull and Robert L. Gluckstern, he explored, in 1952, the possibility of heavy-ion bombardment in nuclear studies. With Gluckstern he studied Coulomb excitation in great detail, and Hull was his partner in nucleon-scattering studies over a number of years. At Yale he collaborated with his student Gerald E. Brown, who later rose to high prominence in theoretical nuclear physics. It might be added that Robert K. Adair, who knew Breit well at Yale, believed that once ensconced in New Haven, Breit's creativity declined somewhat in that he largely spent his time going over in increasing depth research that had gained his reputation in the earlier years. Be that as it may, Breit's last concern with accelerators was apparently at Yale in 1964, with the proposal for a "meson factory" as a source of an intense beam of pi-mesons for the study of light nuclei.

Wartime Contributions. It was Breit who proposed, at a National Research Council meeting in April 1940, after experiments in 1939 confirmed the military potentials of nuclear fission, the voluntary censorship of publications of uranium studies—a practice adhered to by most Allied scientists during Word War II. The same month, Breit was the second person to be appointed to the Advisory Committee on Uranium, chaired by Lyman Briggs of the Bureau of Standards, charged with the coordination of "Rapid Rupture": fast neutron bomb studies and overall evaluation of potential weapons problems. In January 1942, when Arthur Holly Compton organized the Metallurgical Laboratory in Chicago, he chose Breit to supervise bomb studies and lecture Met Lab staff on bomb theory that might guide plans for a plutonium bomb. When J. Robert Oppenheimer arrived, Compton made him a consultant, formally under Breit. However, Breit and Oppenheimer did not get along, with Breit's concern over bomb theory leaking out, and Oppenheimer's concern that the theory was not disseminated fast enough. Breit resigned, replaced by Oppenheimer, and left the fledgling Manhattan Project for ballistic research, as sketched earlier.

As for Breit versus Oppenheimer, John Wheeler had interesting things to say about the two leaders of theoretical nuclear physics in the United States. On receiving a National Research Council Fellowship for 1933–1934, he had to decide under whom to work, Oppenheimer or Breit. Having talked with both of them, he felt he could have worked with either.

> In personality they were utterly different. Oppenheimer saw things in black and white and was a quick decider. Breit worked in shades of gray and could be described in those words that Charles Darwin used in speaking of his own most important qualities: "The love of science—unbounded patience in long reflecting over any subject—industry in observing and collecting facts—and a fair share of invention ..." Being temperamentally uncomfortable with quick decisions, and attracted to issues that require long reflections, I chose to work with Breit. (Wheeler, 1979, p. 229)

Retirement Symposium. At the aforesaid symposium in honor of Breit's retirement at Yale in 1968, a multitude of his colleagues and former students from around the world filled the Yale Law School Auditorium. Chaired by Robert K. Adair and Robert Gluckstern, the symposium speakers were as follows: Hans Bethe, D. Allan Bromley, Gerald Brown, Ray Herb, Vernon Hughes, McAllister Hull, Merle Tuve, and Eugene Wigner. The talks are all reprinted in *Facets of Physics*, listed in the bibliography below. The banquet speakers included Henry Margenau, Isidor Rabi, Victor Weisskopf, and John Wheeler, the toastmaster. In his banquet remarks, Margenau recalled the waning of his own interest in nuclear physics due to imposed wartime secrecy:

> [M]y spirits rose when Gregory, having conceived of an important problem, offered me collaboration. I looked at it and it seemed intriguing. Closer study of what Gregory had already done and what would have been my task in bringing the calculations to a conclusion made it clear to me that nearly all the work had already been accomplished. The generosity involved in this offer was overwhelming, and I decided on what may have been an unwise surge of propriety or pride to decline the kind suggestion to share the honor of that publication.
>
> Thus I forfeited a chance to scientific stature by refusing the kind of bid from which many in this audience have profited; for collaboration with Gregory Breit was a road to distinction in physics, a road on which many have traveled, led by a master's hand. (*Facets of Physics*, p. 188)

Breit's response included recollections of a few "giants" of physics who "lived for essential ideas," including Einstein, Rutherford, Kamerlingh Onnes, Bohr, and especially Ehrenfest, whose "clarity of thought regarding essential steps in theoretical physics was of utmost importance to him" (pp. 193–194). The same year, 1968,

President Johnson presented Breit with a National Medal of Science for his contributions to the first atom smashers and ordnance developments.

BIBLIOGRAPHY

A selected bibliography is given by McAllister Hull in his biographical memoir (see below), the selection of which was "intended to note the [papers] that initiated a study [or] made a significant advance." Breit's geophysical papers, coauthored with Merle Tuve, are listed in the references of Gilmor's paper. A complete bibliography is found in Bromley and Hughes, eds., Facets of Physics.

WORKS BY BREIT

"The Distributed Capacity of Inductive Coils." *Physical Review* 17 (1921): 649–677.

With Merle Antony Tuve. "A Radio Method of Estimating the Height of the Conducting Layer." *Nature* 116 (1925): 357.

With Merle Antony Tuve. "Radio Evidence of the Existence of the Kennelly-Heaviside Layer." *Journal of the Washington Academy of Sciences* 16 (1926): 98.

With Merle Antony Tuve. "The Production and Application of High Voltage in the Laboratory." *Nature* 121 (1928): 535.

With Merle Antony Tuve and Odd Dahl. "Effective Heights of the Kennelly-Heaviside Layer." *Proceedings of the Institute of Radio Engineering* 16 (1928): 1236–1239.

"On the Possibility of Nuclear Disintegration by Artificial Sources." *Physical Review* 34 (1929): 817–818.

With Merle Antony Tuve and Lawrence R. Hafstad. "The Application of High Potentials to Vacuum Tubes." *Physical Review* 35 (1930): 66–71.

With F. L. Yost and John Archibald Wheeler. "Coulomb Wave-Functions in Repulsive Fields." *Physical Review* 49 (1936): 174–189.

With Eugene Wigner. "Capture of Slow Neutrons." *Physical Review* 49 (1936): 519–531.

With Edward Uhler Condon and Richard D. Present. "Theory of Scattering of Protons by Protons." *Physical Review* 50 (1936): 825–845.

With L. E. Hoisington, S. S. Share, and H. M. Thaxton. "The Approximate Equality of the Proton-Proton and Proton-Neutron Interactions for the Meson Potential." *Physical Review* 55 (1939): 1103.

"The interpretation of resonances in nuclear reactions." *Physical Review* 58 (1940): 506–537.

With Arthur A. Broyles and McAllister H. Hull, Jr. "Sensitivity of Proton-Proton Scattering to Potentials at Different Distances." *Physical Review* 73 (1948): 869–876.

With Gerald E. Brown. "Effect of Nuclear Motion on the Fine Structure of Hydrogen." *Physical Review* 74 (1948): 1278 1284.

"Evidence Concerning Equality of n-n and p-p Forces." *Physical Review* 80 (1950): 1110–1111.

With McAllister H. Hull Jr., and Robert L. Gluckstern. "Possibilities of Heavy Ion Bombardment in Nuclear Studies." *Physical Review* 87 (1952): 74–80.

With McAllister H. Hull Jr. "Advances in Knowledge of Nuclear Forces." *American Journal of Physics* 21 (1953): 184–220.

With Marvin E. Ebel. "Nucleon Tunneling in $N^{14} + N^{14}$ Reactions." *Physical Review* 103 (1956): 679–701.

With Robert L. Gluckstern and J. E. Russell. "Reorientation Effect in Coulomb Excitation." *Physical Review* 103 (1956): 727–738.

With McAllister H. Hull Jr., Kenneth E. Lassila, H. M. Ruppel, and F. A. McDonald. "Phase Parameter Representation of Neutron-Proton Scattering from 13.7 to 350 MeV. II." *Physical Review* 128 (1962): 830–832.

With McAllister H. Hull Jr., Kenneth E. Lassila, K. D. Pyatt Jr., and H. M. Ruppel. "Phase parameter representation of proton-proton scattering from 9.7 to 345 MeV. II." *Physical Review* 128 (1962): 826–830.

OTHER SOURCES.

Bromley, D. Allan, and Vernon W. Hughes, eds. *Facets of Physics.* New York: Academic Press, 1970.

Gilmor, C. Stewart. "The Big Story: Tuve, Breit, and Ionospheric Sounding, 1923–1928." In *The Earth, the Heavens and the Carnegie Institution of Washington,* edited by Gregory A. Good. History of Geophysics, vol. 5. Washington, DC : American Geophysical Union, 1994.

Hull, McAllister H., Jr. "Gregory Breit." *Physics Today* (October 1983): 102–104. Obituary.

———. "Gregory Breit: July 14, 1899–September 11, 1981." *Biographical Memoirs,* vol. 74. Washington, DC: National Academy of Sciences, 1998. The most extensive obituary notice and principal account of Breit's life and work.

Kihss, Peter. "Dr. Gregory Breit, Early Authority on Atom Weapons, Is Dead at 82." *New York Times,* 22 September 1981. A multicolumn obituary.

Wheeler, John. *Some Men and Moments in the History of Nuclear Physics.* Minneapolis: University of Minnesota Press, 1979.

Per F. Dahl

BRETZ, J HARLEN (*b.* Saranac, Michigan, 2 September 1882; *d.* Homewood, Illinois, 3 February 1981), *glacial geology, origin of limestone caves, Earth science education.*

J Harlen Bretz ("J" is his entire first name, not an abbreviation to be followed by a period) was the central figure in one of the most important controversies in the history of geology. In a series of papers in the 1920s and 1930s, Bretz formulated and defended the hypothesis that cataclysmic flooding during the last Ice Age produced the unusual landscape of the channeled scabland region of eastern Washington State. The controversy lasted until the 1960s and 1970s, by which time overwhelming field evidence combined with new understandings of flood mechanics, erosion, and sedimentation to convince most geologists that immense flooding was indeed the cause of the channeled scabland landscape.

Early Life. J Harlen Bretz was born on 2 September 1882, in Saranac, Michigan, to Oliver and Rhoda Bretz, on the family farm. His father dabbled in farming but worked mainly in a store (variety and furniture) and in an undertaking business, both of which he owned. The young J Harlen Bretz (his original given name was Harley) had intense interests in amateur astronomy and in exploring the natural environment around the family farm, including the nearby Grand River. He attended Albion College, where he studied biology and received an AB degree in 1905. At Albion he also met classmate Fanny Challis, who became his wife in 1906. Subsequently, as a high school teacher in Flint, Michigan, Bretz developed a strong amateur interest in glacial geology. He produced his first publication on the topic in 1907, and after later moving to Washington to teach at Seattle High School, Bretz's hobby evolved into his profession. He organized his mostly self-financed field studies of glacial geology in the Puget Sound region into a PhD dissertation, which was awarded summa cum laude from the University of Chicago in 1913. His thesis advisors at Chicago were the renowned glacial geologists Thomas Chrowder Chamberlin and Rollin D. Salisbury.

Bretz was appointed assistant professor of geology at the University of Washington for the 1913–1914 term. He was not happy at the university, complaining of his department's textbook and lecture methods and of the lack of attention paid to field studies. An urgent appeal from Salisbury to help with field-oriented teaching at the University of Chicago induced him to move there in 1915 at the starting rank of instructor, but by 1921 he had moved up to the tenured rank of associate professor. Bretz's work in teaching geology field courses, however, soon brought him back to the Northwest, initially to the Columbia River Gorge between Washington and Oregon. In 1922 his summer field course for advanced students initiated a study of the channeled scabland landscape in eastern Washington.

Flood Hypotheses. Bretz formally presented his famous hypothesis in a 1923 paper, "The Channeled Scablands of the Columbia Plateau," published in the *Journal of Geology*. He proposed that a huge late Pleistocene flood (now dated at about sixteen thousand years ago) emanated from the margins of the nearby Cordilleran Ice Sheet, which then covered much of western Canada, extending from Alaska down to Puget Sound and the northern parts of Washington State, Idaho, and Montana. Named the Spokane Flood for its then-presumed source area, this cataclysm neatly accounted for numerous interrelated aspects

of the channeled scabland landscape. The immense volumes of floodwater, up to 200 meters (about 660 feet) deep, were recorded by high-level spillways that developed when preflood valleys were inundated beyond their capacities, inducing the floodwater to spill over divides from one valley to another. Over a region of about 150 by 200 kilometers (about 490 to 660 feet) this process joined various preflood valleys into an anastomosing complex of dividing and rejoining channels. (*Anastomosing* refers to an interlacing network pattern of branching and reuniting channels.) This phenomenally deep floodwater was moving fast enough to produce an unusual form of erosion in the basalt bedrock, called "scabland" erosion because of its jagged appearance. Bretz also interpreted great mounds of fluvial gravel in the scabland channels to be subfluvial river bars, deposited in somewhat slower-moving portions of the floodwater. The name "channeled scabland" was applied to the entire complex of features. Farther downstream the flood passed through the Columbia Gorge, then formed a huge gravel delta at the location of present-day Portland, Oregon, and finally passed on into the Pacific Ocean.

All this proved too much for the geological community of the time. At the 12 January 1927 meeting of the Washington (D.C.) Academy of Sciences, Bretz was invited to defend his "outrageous" hypothesis before an audience of uniformly skeptical scientists. His oral presentation was followed by six other talks, all of which were sharply critical of the flood theory. For the next few decades, despite Bretz's continuing efforts, including twenty major papers on the topic, the geological community largely resisted the cataclysmic flood hypothesis. Among the many geologists who published papers opposing the Spokane Flood hypothesis, some of the best-known are Oscar E. Meinzer, Richard Foster Flint, James Gilluly, and William H. Hobbs.

Resolution of the controversy came gradually, initially with the recognition by Joseph Thomas Pardee of a plausible source for the huge amounts of floodwater. In the 1940s Pardee showed that the ice-dammed Pleistocene glacial Lake Missoula, holding about 2,500 cubic kilometers (600 cubic miles) of water, formed in northern Idaho and western Montana and subsequently drained very rapidly to the channeled scabland. Eventually, the accumulating field evidence became overwhelming, particularly when Bretz and others synthesized new data obtained by the Bureau of Reclamation during the development of the Columbia Basin Irrigation Project in the 1950s. Especially important for convincing the skeptics was the discovery that giant current ripples cap many of the scabland gravel mounds that Bretz had correctly interpreted in the 1920s to be river bars. Resembling the relatively tiny ripple marks that form along the sandy bottoms of active rivers, the giant scabland ripples occur in trains of twenty or

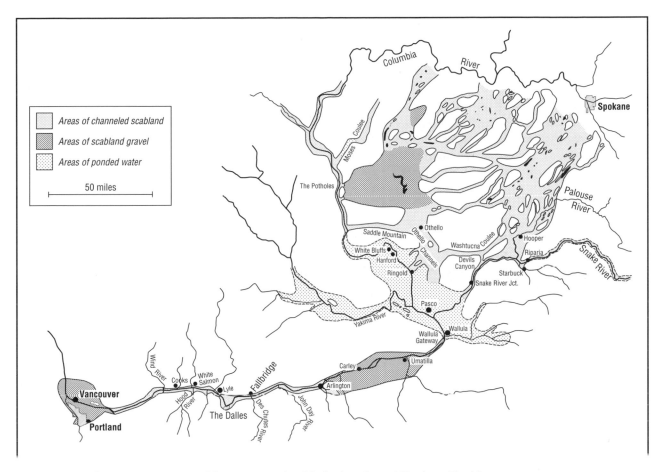

Figure 1. J Harlen Bretz's 1925 map of the region inundated by his hypothesized "Spokane Flood."

more, with individual ripples of up to 10 meters (some 33 feet) in height and 100 meters in spacing. Instead of sand, these ripples are composed of flood gravel and boulders up to a meter in diameter. By the 1960s and 1970s, as this evidence mounted and as advances occurred in the understanding of the physical processes of cataclysmic flooding, Bretz's bold hypothesis came to be almost universally accepted.

The debates of the 1920s and 1930s over the origin of the channeled scabland are important to geology for methodological reasons. The prolonged nature of the Spokane Flood controversy arose in part because of the adherence of many geologists to substantive and epistemological notions of uniformitarianism, a principle that was erroneously thought to underpin their science. According to the most common, mistaken applications of the uniformitarian principle, cataclysmic processes, such as those responsible for the origin of the channeled scabland, were considered to be unsuitable topics for scientific investigation. This doctrine had originally arisen with Charles Lyell (1797–1875), who used it to argue against proposals in the early 1800s that catastrophic processes

(some of them biblical) were important to consider in understanding Earth's history. To counter this presumption of uniformitarianism, Bretz could provide only meticulously described field evidence for those willing to seriously consider it. The eventual triumph of his hypothesis, against its initially antagonistic reception, set the stage for the resurgence of a new kind of geological catastrophism, which is most prominent in the new understanding of the role of impact cratering on Earth's history.

Work in Greenland. After a decade of near-continuous research on the channeled scabland, Bretz turned to other studies, beginning with participation in the Louise A. Boyd Expedition to East Greenland in 1933. Work on the surficial geology of the Chicago region led to two monographs. These outline ingenious analyses of the draining of Glacial Lake Chicago, a predecessor of modern Lake Michigan. From 1938 to 1961 much of Bretz's attention was devoted to studies of the origin of limestone caverns. He argued eloquently for the origin of many cave features by processes of groundwater circulation below the water table. His cave studies in seventeen U.S. states, Mexico, and Bermuda placed physical speleology on a firm scientific basis. Bretz's most extensive cave survey was his book, *Caves of Missouri,* published in 1956. His insights and energy were important to the late-twentieth-century resurgence of karst geomorphic and hydrologic studies in the United States.

While a faculty member at the University of Chicago from 1915 to 1947 and in subsequent semiretirement, Bretz supervised the field geology training of more than three hundred graduate students, including the future geological luminaries M. King Hubbert, William C. Krumbein, Francis P. Shepard, and Hakon A. Wadell. His teaching excellence, employing the Socratic method, was renowned among all the program's graduates and recognized in 1959 by the Neil Minor Award for teaching excellence from the National Association of Geology Teachers.

After his formal retirement from the University of Chicago, "Doc" Bretz (as he was known to students and colleagues) continued occasional work in association with the geological surveys of Illinois, Missouri, and Washington. With C. Leland Horberg in the 1940s and 1950s, Bretz published innovative research on the genesis of rocklike calcium carbonate encrustation in caliche soils. His 1965 monograph, "Geomorphic History of the Ozarks of Missouri," stands as classical analysis of landscapes. In the 1970s and 1980s, new discoveries of scablandlike landscapes in other parts of Earth and, surprisingly, on the planet Mars, all were being explained by cataclysmic flood processes, much in the same manner that Bretz had first outrageously proposed in 1923.

At age ninety-seven, in recognition of a lifetime of scientific achievements spanning more than seventy years, J Harlen Bretz was honored in 1979 with the Penrose Medal, the highest award of the Geological Society of America. In accepting the award Bretz gave the following assessment of his major research accomplishments: "Perhaps I can be credited with reviving and demystifying legendary catastrophism and challenging a too rigorous uniformitarianism" (1980, p. 1095).

BIBLIOGRAPHY

The J Harlen Bretz papers (25 boxes, 12.5 linear feet) are housed at the Special Collections Research Center, University of Chicago Library, 1100 East 57th Street, Chicago, Illinois 60637. The archive contains many of Bretz's writings from 1905 to 1977. There is no complete bibliography of all published works.

WORKS BY BRETZ

"Glaciation of the Puget Sound Region." *Washington Division of Mines and Geology Bulletin* 8 (1913): 1–244. The published version of Bretz's PhD dissertation.

"The Channeled Scablands of the Columbia Plateau." *Journal of Geology* 31 (1923): 617–649.

"Geology and Mineral Resources of the Kings Quadrangle." *Illinois State Geological Survey Bulletin* 43 (1923): 205–304.

"The Spokane Flood beyond the Channeled Scablands." *Journal of Geology* 33 (1925): 97–115, 236–259.

"The Channeled Scabland of Eastern Washington." *Geographical Review* 18 (1928): 446–477.

"The Grande Coulee." *American Geographical Society Special Publication* 15 (1932): 1–89.

"Physiographic Studies of East Greenland." In *The Fiord Region of East Greenland,* edited by Louise A. Boyd. New York: American Geographical Society, 1935.

"Geology of the Chicago Region: Part 1, General." *Illinois Geological Survey Bulletin* 65 (1939): 1–118.

"Vadose and Phreatic Features of Limestone Caves." *Journal of Geology* 50 (1942): 675–811.

"The Stages of Lake Chicago: Their Causes and Correlations." *American Journal of Science* 249 (1951): 401–429.

"Geology of the Chicago Region: Part 2, The Pleistocene." *Illinois Geological Survey Bulletin* 65 (1955): 1–132.

"Caves of Missouri." *Missouri Geological Survey and Water Resources Report* 39 (1956): 1–490.

With H. T. U. Smith and George Neff. "Channeled Scabland of Washington—New Data and Interpretations." *Geological Society of America Bulletin* 67 (1956): 957–1049.

"Washington's Channeled Scabland." *Washington Department of Conservation, Division of Mines and Geology Bulletin* 45 (1959): 1–57.

"Bermuda: A Partially Drowned, Late Mature Pleistocene Karst." *Geological Society of America Bulletin* 71 (1960): 1729–1754.

"Geomorphic History of the Ozarks of Missouri." *Missouri Division of Geological Survey and Water Resources Report* 41 (1965): 1–147.

"The Lake Missoula Floods and the Channeled Scabland." *Journal of Geology* 77 (1969): 505–543.

"Introduction." In *The Channeled Scabland: A Guide to the Geomorphology of the Columbia Basin,* edited by Victor R. Baker and Dag Nummedal. Washington, DC: National Aeronautics and Space Administration, 1978.

"Presentation of the Penrose Medal to J Harlen Bretz: Response." *Geological Society of America Bulletin,* Part II, 91 (1980): 1095.

OTHER SOURCES

Baker, Victor R. "The Spokane Flood Controversy and the Martian Outflow Channels." *Science* 202 (1978): 1249–1256.

_____, ed. *Catastrophic Flooding: The Origin of the Channeled Scabland.* Stroudsburg, PA: Dowden, Hutchinson and Ross, 1981. Editorial commentary and reprinted papers outline the Spokane Flood controversy, emphasizing Bretz's role and the relevant historical and scientific contexts.

———. "The Spokane Flood Debate and Its Legacy." In *Geomorphic Systems of North America,* edited by William L. Graf. Boulder, CO: Geological Society of America, 1987.

———. "Joseph Thomas Pardee and the Spokane Flood Controversy." *GSA Today* 5 (1995): 169–173.

Baker, Victor R. and R. C. Bunker. "Cataclysmic Late Pleistocene Flooding from Glacial Lake Missoula: A Review." *Quaternary Science Reviews* 4 (1985): 1–41.

Victor R. Baker

Robert Briggs. COURTESY OF INDIANA UNIVERSITY ARCHIVES.

BRIGGS, ROBERT W. (*b.* Watertown, Massachusetts, 10 December 1911; *d.* Indianapolis, Indiana, 4 March 1983), *developmental genetics, amphibian cloning, maternal gene products controlling embryogenesis.*

The research contributions of Robert W. (Bob) Briggs to developmental genetics extended over four decades. They included in chronological order four mains periods of studies in amphibian development, involving neoplasia, ploidy (even sets of chromosome number), nuclear transplantation (cloning), and maternal genes.

Early Life. Bob Briggs was the son of Robin J. Briggs and Bridget (née McGonagle) Briggs. When Bob was two years old, his mother and a younger brother (his only sibling) died of tuberculosis, and Bob was sent to his father's parents in Epping, New Hampshire. He learned how to play the piano from his aunt, and eventually he mastered the banjo, leading to a job as a banjo player in a small dance band that play two or three nights per week in southeastern New Hampshire towns. He developed an interest in classical music and later in life learned to play the recorder. Bob's interest in biology is also traceable to his early years, when he collected minnows, frogs, insects, and worms and studied them under magnifying glasses and a borrowed microscope.

Briggs went to Boston University from where he graduated in 1934 with a BS degree. He then moved to Harvard University and, under the sponsorship of Leigh Hoadley, studied the metabolic rate and density of the frog embryo during embryogenesis. In 1938 he received his PhD. His introduction to the amphibian embryo would guide his research interests for the rest of his life. Bob married Janet Bloch, who also held a PhD; they had two sons, Evan and Alexander, and one daughter, Meredith Briggs Skeath.

Neoplasia. After receiving his doctoral degree, Briggs became a Fellow in the Zoology Department at McGill University (1938–1942) in Montreal and characterized tumor growths in tadpoles of the frog, *Rana pipiens,* in order to study the behavior of tumors in the organization fields operative during development. He was the first to induce tumors in a developing system and did so with a carcinogenic agent. He transplanted fragments of the frog kidney adenocarcinoma to various sites of tadpoles and found that they grew well but regressed prior to metamorphosis, even in tadpoles prevented from entering metamorphosis. Briggs suggested that regression of this malignant tumor might be caused by the development of tissue specificity. Extension of this research can be found in many later studies by others who were concerned with the development of immunocompetence, tumor immunosurveillance, and attempts to normalize cancer cells in embryonic systems.

Ploidy (Chromosome Number). In 1942 Briggs joined the Lankenau Hospital Research Institute, later the Institute for Cancer Research, and now the basic science component of the Fox Chase Cancer Center in Philadelphia. There he became head of the Embryology Department. First, he compared the effect of changes in ploidy (even sets of chromosome number) on development with normal diploids. For those outside this field, that era of research predated knowledge of the DNA molecule. It was

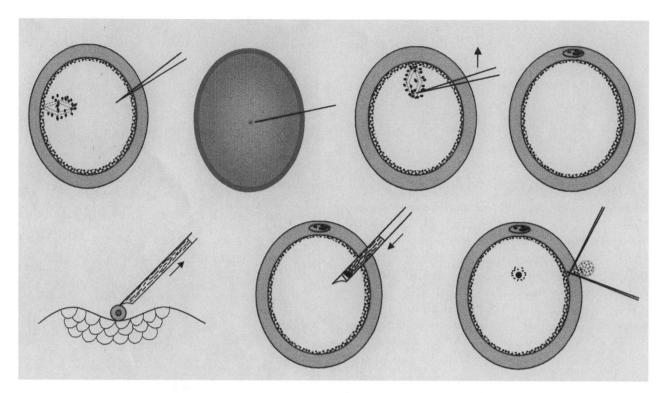

Nuclear transplantation. *The Briggs and King technique of nuclear transplantation (cloning) from Di Berardino,* Differentiation, *2001, p. 69.* REPRODUCED BY PERMISSION OF BASIL BLACKWELL LIMITED.

known that the nucleus was the bearer of heredity traits, but how it influenced development was unknown, so he focused on the nucleus and its organelles, the chromosomes. He developed a method for producing frog triploids by heat shocking fertilized eggs. This treatment prevented the egg from releasing the polar body (containing one set of chromosomes), and the embryo developed with an extra set of chromosomes. He found that triploid amphibians, unlike mammals, developed normally, except female gonads usually reversed to testes.

Next, Briggs characterized the development of haploid embryos containing only one set of chromosomes. Haploids were known previously to develop abnormally, and one interpretation for the cause of their abnormalities was that the nucleocytoplasmic ratio was abnormal. A serendipitous event permitted him to test this interpretation when he found a frog that produced very small eggs. Haploids from small eggs developed better than those from normal size eggs, but still they were not normal. He concluded that the nucleocytoplasmic ratio played a role but suggested that deleterious genes were mainly responsible for the haploid abnormalities, a suggestion verified later by others.

In his last ploidy studies, Briggs produced embryos lacking a functional nucleus (zero ploidy) but containing

a normal organelle for cell division. Such embryos developed for one day into partial blastulae. This study, predating the molecular biology of embryos, indicated that gene products (RNAs and proteins) produced during oocyte growth in amphibians are sufficient to support cell division after fertilization but that postblastula development required new gene products. As no chromosomes bearing genes were present in zero ploidy embryos, no gene products could be made and, therefore, the embryos ceased growing and eventually died. This information provided important directions for molecular biologists that later would analyze the RNAs and proteins in oocytes and embryos in order to explain how their gene products control normal embryonic development.

Nuclear Transplantation (Cloning). Beginning in 1952, Briggs and Thomas J. King pioneered a technique to determine whether or not nuclei of specialized cells remain equivalent to the nucleus of the fertilized egg in developmental potential, a question that had been posed by embryologists since the turn of the nineteenth century. Initially, they focused on cell nuclei from undetermined regions of the blastula and showed that after transplantation of nuclei singly into enucleated frog eggs (*R. pipiens*), many of the nuclei directed eggs to develop into normal tadpoles and, in a later study, into normal metamorphosed frogs. This result demonstrated that transplanted blastula nuclei were equivalent in developmental potential to nuclei at fertilization. This was the first time nuclear transplantation had been accomplished in multicellular organisms. Next, they tested nuclei from progressively older embryonic stages and found a decrease in the number of eggs that developed normally, indicating that most nuclei acquire restrictions concomitant with cell specialization. Their results were confirmed and extended by various laboratories around the world, especially by Marie A. Di Berardino and Robert G. McKinnell in the United States, John Gurdon in England, and Louis Gallien in France, and their respective colleagues.

In the early twenty-first century these classic studies are still consistent with the changing patterns of gene expression occurring during embryogenesis that are controlled by relatively stable alterations in chromosome proteins and DNA methylation. Although nuclear transplantation was developed principally to study nuclear differentiation, it had many applications, including but not limited to the biological analysis of haploidy, hybrid incompatibility, cancer, immunobiology, and cellular aging. It provided insight into the cytoplasmic control of nuclear and gene function, including nuclear reprogramming of nuclear and gene function.

Nuclear reprogramming is jargon among scientists to describe the significant changes that occur in the nucleus of the donor cell after it is transplanted into an egg. For example, even when the donor nucleus is taken from a nonembryonic cell, the chemicals in the egg change its function and those of its genes to behave like those from an embryonic cell. This reversal of nuclear and gene function is most significant, because when the chemicals are identified, it may be possible to reverse differentiated cells in the dish and then convert them with appropriate chemicals into differentiated cell types needed for the repair of human diseases. Most notably, nuclear transfer became the prototype for cloning multicellular organisms and was extended to insects, fish, and mammals.

A dramatic consequence of the research came in1996, when the clone Dolly was born. Dolly was derived from a nucleus of an adult sheep cell, the first clone ever derived from an adult cell. Subsequently, clones have been made from adult cells of other species, such as cats, cattle, horses, mice, pigs, rabbits, and sheep. Fifty years after the first tadpole clones were produced, the question of the totipotency of specialized cell nuclei was finally answered affirmatively in mice: sixteen fertile adults cloned from B-cell lymphocyte nuclei were produced, each carrying the rearranged DNA of immunoglobulin genes in all tissues. The presence of the rearranged DNA in the clones was proof that the injected nuclei were derived from a fully differentiated cell and not a progenitor or stem cell.

Some other applications stemming from cloning include the rescue of several endangered species and the production of transgenic animal clones producing human proteins. A transgenic animal clone derives from an egg receiving a transplanting nucleus into which an external gene was inserted into its DNA. For example, a human gene, producing a clotting factor to prevent hemophilia, was inserted into the DNA of fetal lamb cells, used as donor cells for cloning. The lamb Polly, the first transgenic clone, resulted and later produced milk containing the human clotting factor. This technique has been used to produce other transgenic farm animals secreting diverse human proteins in their milk. Testing of the human proteins for quality and safety from transgenic farm animals is in progress so that eventually human patients can be treated with these proteins.

Farm animal clones (cattle, sheep, goats, pigs) with uniform genetic backgrounds will be valuable for testing pharmaceutical drugs and vaccines, results that can be applied to humans, especially those from nonhuman primates (monkeys) when the latter can be routinely produced. Also, clones exhibiting exceptional growth rates, milk production, or beef quality could be produced faster than those emanating from selective breeding.

Maternal Genes. In 1956 Briggs became professor of zoology at Indiana University in Bloomington and initiated his fourth and last main research program, the effect of maternal genes on development in the salamander. In layperson's language the question was how the mother's genes affect the quality of her oocytes, from which the embryos develop after fertilization. Throughout his career, Briggs had focused on nucleocytoplasmic interactions during embryonic development, that is, how the nucleus interacts with the cytoplasm in directing embryogenesis.

To pursue this goal more specifically, he wanted to combine embryology with genetics. Available at that time were genetic lines of the salamander, the Mexican axoltol (*Ambystoma mexicanum*), developed by Professor Rufus Humphrey. Briggs recruited Humphrey and together they developed a research program in the developmental genetics of the axolotl. Among the various mutations available at that time in axolotl, he focused on mutations showing maternal effects that were expressed in the embryo. Such gene mutations synthesize abnormal RNAs and proteins during the growth of the oocyte that are stored in its nucleus or cytoplasm. After fertilization of the oocyte, those products modify the normal pattern of embryonic development.

For example, four mutations caused early arrest of development. One, the o$^+$ gene, produced a substance during oogenesis that is required for development beyond gastrulation, but embryos with the mutant gene failed to gastrulate. However, injections of cytoplasm or nucelo-plasm from the nuclei from normal oocytes corrected the abnormality, resulting in normal development. Eight other genes produced specific effects on embryonic organs, four others caused alterations in pigment cells, and four did so in nucleoli. Cytological, biochemical, embryological, molecular, and physiological studies performed by Briggs, Humphrey, students, and others explained how many of the mutant genes modified the embryos.

This last period of Briggs's research provided direction for the elegant molecular genetic experiments of others that followed in *Drosophila* (fruit fly), *Xenopus* (frog), zebrafish, chordates, and invertebrates, in which many genes contributing to pattern formation were identified and, in the best cases, their action was identified in a specific biochemical pathway. In 1995 Christiane Nüsslein-Volhard and Eric Wieschaus were awarded the Nobel Prize in Physiology or Medicine for explaining how the products of the maternal genes in the oocyte of the fruit fly *Drosophila* direct normal development of the embryo and why certain mutated maternal genes cause congenital abnormalities.

Briggs's Legacy. Although all his research was of pioneering quality, no doubt those outside his field will remember Briggs for his cloning studies, first performed more than fifty years ago with Thomas J. King. Much progress has been made with cloning based on their initial work on nuclear transplantation. For example, the U.S. Food and Drug Administration will soon release (as of 2007) a Draft Assessment on Animal Cloning reporting that meat and milk from cattle, swine, and goat clones and their progeny do not pose food safety risks for human consumption. Also, in the future, the production of human embryonic stem cells for the treatment of human diseases is envisioned, and one approach would be to use embryos cloned through nuclear transfer from the patient's own cells. This application is controversial because the technology currently involves the production of human embryos that have to be destroyed to produce embryonic stem cells. Although this has not yet been accomplished, some theorize that chemicals can be added to the culture medium to stimulate stem cells to differentiate into specialized cells that could be used to cure Parkinson's and heart diseases or alleviate stroke problems and other ailments. As the cells were derived from the same patient, they would not be rejected as foreign. This technology has not been accomplished, and may never be, but the possibility began with the nuclear transfer techniques developed first by Briggs and his collaborator, King, more than half a century ago.

Honors and Awards. Briggs was the recipient of various honors and awards, including election to the American Academy of Arts and Sciences (1960) and the National Academy of Sciences (1962) for his pioneering research on amphibian cloning. He was named research professor of zoology (1963) at Indiana University in Bloomington and Fellow of the International Institute of Embryology. Briggs also received honorary degrees from the Medical College of Pennsylvania (1971; now the Drexel University College of Medicine) and Indiana University (1983). For pathbreaking studies in amphibian nuclear transplantation, the French Académie des Sciences awarded him and his collaborator, Thomas J. King, the Charles-Leopold Mayer Prize (1973). They were the first Americans to receive this prize, the highest biology award of the French Académie. During his career he participated in many major symposia, served on editorial boards of leading journals, and provided intellectual leadership as chair of the Zoology Department (1969–1972) at Indiana University, Bloomington.

Personal Life. Briggs was not only an outstanding scientist and mentor of students, but also a generous and cordial person, one who laid the foundation for numerous research problems for others to pursue. In his personal life Briggs enjoyed numerous interests, including golfing, bowling, and listening to classical music and performing it with the piano and recorder. He owned an Austin-Healy beginning in the 1950s, later a Corvette, and then a BMW motorcycle and delighted in his motor excursions. In 1983, following more than four decades as a leading international scientist, Briggs succumbed to kidney cancer in the Krannert Pavilion of the Indiana University School of Medicine in Indianapolis. He was survived by his second wife, Francoise Briggs, his children, and Janet Bloch Briggs, the mother of his children.

BIBLIOGRAPHY

The complete peer-reviewed bibliography of Briggs is published in the National Academy of Sciences Bibliographical Memoirs, vol. 76, 1998: "Robert W. Briggs: December 10, 1911–March 4, 1983," by Marie A. Di Berardino. It is available from http://books.nap.edu/readingroom/books/biomems/rbriggs.html.

WORKS BY BRIGGS

"Tumour Induction in *Rana pipiens* Tadpoles." *Nature* 146 (1940): 29.

"Transplantation of Kidney Carcinoma from Adult Frogs to Tadpoles." *Cancer Research* 2 (1942): 309–323.

With R. Grant. "Growth and Regression of Frog Kidney Carcinoma Transplanted into the Tails of Permanent and Normal Tadpoles." *Cancer Research* 3 (1943): 613–620.

"The Experimental Production and Development of Triploid Frog Embryos." *Journal of Experimental Zoology* 106 (1947): 237–266.

"The Influence of Egg Volume on the Development of Haploid and Diploid Embryos of the Frog, *Rana pipiens*." *Journal of Experimental Zoology* 111 (1949): 255–294.

With Rufus R. Humphrey and G. Fankhauser. "Sex Differentiation in Triploid *Rana pipiens* Larvae and the Subsequent Reversal of Females to Males." *Journal of Experimental Zoology* 115 (1950): 399–428.

With E. U. Green and Thomas J. King. "An Investigation of the Capacity for Cleavage and Differentiation in *Rana pipiens* Eggs Lacking 'Functional' Chromosomes." *Journal of Experimental Zoology* 116 (1951): 455–499.

With Thomas J. King. "Transplantation of Living Nuclei from Blastula Cells into Enucleated Frogs' Eggs." *Proceedings of the National Academy Sciences of the United States of America* 38 (1952): 455–463. Reports the first successful cloning in multicellular animals.

With Thomas J. King. "Nuclear Transplantation Studies on the Early Gastrula (*Rana Pipiens*). I. Nuclei of Presumptive Endoderm." *Developmental Biology* 2 (1960): 252–270.

With Gloria Cassens. "Accumulation in the Oocyte Nucleus of a Gene Product Essential for Embryonic Development beyond Gastrulation." *Proceedings of the National Academy of Sciences of the United States of America* 55 (1966): 1103–1109.

"Developmental Genetics of the Axolotl." In *Genetic Mechanisms of Development*, edited by Frank H. Ruddle. New York: Academic Press, 1973. An excellent review of the effects of maternal gene products in the oocyte on embryonic development.

"Genetics of Cell Type Determination." In *Cell Interactions in Differentiation*, edited by Marketta Karkinen-Jaaskelainen, Lauri Saxen, and Leonard Weiss. New York: Academic Press, 1977. A good review of nuclear transplantation studies up to 1977.

OTHER SOURCES

Cibelli, Jose, Robert P. Lanza, Keith H. S. Campbell, et al. *Principles of Cloning*. Amsterdam and Boston: Academic Press, 2002. An extensive coverage of cloning diverse mammalian species.

Di Berardino, Marie A. *Genomic Potential of Differentiated Cells*. New York: Columbia University Press, 1997. Covers the origin and development of cloning in unicellular and multicellular animals from the late nineteenth century up to the birth of Dolly.

———. "Animal Cloning—The Route to New Genomics in Agriculture and Medicine." *Differentiation* 68 (2001): 67–83. Reviews the various applications of cloning.

Hoechedlinger, Konrad, and Rudolf Jaenisch. "Monoclonal Mice Generatedby Nuclear Transfer from Mature B and T Donor Cells." *Nature* 415 (2002): 1035–1038. This is the first report yielding normal clones from documented differentiated donor cell nuclei.

Rudenko, Larisa, John C. Matheson, and Stephen F. Sundlof. "Animal Cloning and the FDA—The Risk Assessment Paradigm under Public Scrutiny." *Nature Biotechnology* 25 (2007): 39–43.

Verma, Paul J., and Alan O. Trounson, eds. *Nuclear Transfer Protocols, Cell Reprogramming, and Transgenesis*. Totowa, NJ: Humana Press, 2006. Consists of recent protocols and reviews on cloning, nuclear reprogramming, transgenesis, embryonic stem cells, the rescue of endangered species by cloning, and other applications of animal cloning.

Wilmut, Ian, Angelika E. Schnieke, Jim McWhir, et al. "Viable Offspring Derived from Fetal and Adult Mammalian Cells." *Nature* 385 (1997): 810–813. Reports on Dolly the sheep, the first clone derived from an adult cell, born in 1996.

———. "Cloning for Medicine." *Scientific American* 279 (December 1998): 58–63. A good review for the general reader.

Marie A. Di Berardino

BROADBENT, DONALD ERIC (*b.* Birmingham, United Kingdom, 6 May 1926; *d.* Oxford, United Kingdom, 10 April 1993), *experimental psychology, attention and perception, decision making.*

Broadbent, often considered one of the founders of cognitive psychology, was best known for his experimental and theoretical work on attention and short-term memory. His "filter theory" of attention accounted for a wide range of phenomena, particularly in the auditory domain, and served to reawaken interest in the relation between attention and perception. His most influential work, *Perception and Communication* (1958), also served as a model of scientific method for the new orientation in psychology. It presented what may have been the first "flow chart" of a cognitive model. Among his many honors and awards, Broadbent was elected as a Fellow of the Royal Society in 1968 and a Foreign Associate of the U.S. National Academy of Sciences in 1971. He received the Distinguished Scientific Contribution Award from the American Psychological Association in 1975.

Origins and Education. Broadbent's father was a business executive whose success led to a brief period of family affluence that ended when his father lost his job and disappeared shortly before World War II. While Broadbent grew up in Wales (and always considered himself to be more Welsh than English), his mother insured that he was educated at Winchester, an exclusive English public (that is, private) school. Lack of funds, and the privations of wartime restrictions and rationing, made his school years grim in many respects, a factor he credited, perhaps whimsically, for his "dour and puritan" attitude toward psychology. A very private person, friends in fact described a "puritanical streak" in Broadbent, mixed with exceptional generosity toward friends and students and a deeply moral attitude toward public service. Pressured at school toward the humanities, he felt more affinity for the sciences, and his interest in "real world" problems led him toward the social sciences.

In 1944, Broadbent joined the Royal Air Force (RAF) and applied for pilot training. After completing a short course in engineering at Cambridge University, he was then sent to Florida, where RAF pilots were given flight training far from predatory Luftwaffe fighters. In the United States, Broadbent first became aware of psychology in the context of noticing the importance of psychological problems in practice:

> The AT6, which I was flying, carried two identical levers close together under the seat, one of which pulled up the flaps.... The other lever pulled up the wheels. With monotonous regularity, one or another of my colleagues would pull the wrong lever, drop an expensive airplane onto its belly … , and after a harrowing interview with our superior officer, disappear to England.... The technology was fine, but it seemed to be badly matched to human beings." (Broadbent, 1980 pp. 43–44)

Since psychology was widely taught in the United States (in contrast to the United Kingdom, where only a few programs were then in existence), Broadbent came to realize that psychology was a possible career choice, one that could combine his scientific affinities with social concerns. The end of the war meant a hasty return to England, and Broadbent, intrigued by the down-to-earth character and potential applications of psychological testing procedures, opted for a ground job with the RAF's personnel selection branch. Following the end of his military service in 1947, Broadbent applied to Cambridge University for undergraduate training in psychology where, as it turned out, Sir Frederic Bartlett was head of the Psychology Department. Bartlett was well-known for his work on constructive processes in perception and for the view that memory was reconstructive; both aspects heavily influenced Broadbent. In addition, the young Kenneth J. W. Craik, a Scottish experimental psychologist familiar with sophisticated engineering approaches, had been working closely with Bartlett. In spite of Craik's premature death in 1945, his influence on Bartlett's lab was immense, and he left behind a number of incomplete reports that sketched an agenda for research using a cybernetic approach to human behavior. Broadbent thus became part of an enthusiastic group of psychologists involved in extending such an approach. Beginning during Broadbent's school years, the advent of information theory, and subsequently the striking finding by William Edmunc Hick in 1952 that reaction time varied linearly

with the amount of information in bits led the Bartlett-Craik approach in the direction of what would later be called cognitive psychology. Broadbent was to be a major contributor to this development.

Career. Following graduation in 1949, Broadbent worked for the Royal Navy on the psychological effects of ambient noise, a project administered by the Medical Research Council. Broadbent carried out this research at Cambridge as a member of the Applied Psychology Unit (APU), where he remained until 1974. The APU, founded in 1944 as a result of Bartlett's efforts and initially led by Craik, provided advice and carried out research for government and military offices. When Craik died, Bartlett took over as director, assisted by Norman Mackworth, who became director in 1952, following Bartlett's retirement. At this point (and with a staff of more than twenty), the APU moved from the Department of Psychology to its own quarters away from campus.

Bartlett's research on noise led easily to an accommodation with the "vigilance" research of Mackworth and to Broadbent's focus upon the problems of attention, then a neglected topic in psychology. Concentrating during the 1950s on his laboratory work, which was closely tied to applied concerns, Broadbent's thinking increasingly involved problems of communication. New technology, especially in the form of tape recorders with separate channels for each ear, made possible experiments on the problems involved when one individual is receiving messages from several sources at one time. Watching flight controllers, studying aircraft landings on carriers at sea, conducting a communication experiment on the pilot while in-flight—such experiences led Broadbent to remark, "I could see human feats of perception, decision, and control that were clearly highly admirable, in which error might mean death, and yet that lay outside the view of human beings normally put forward by academics" (Broadbent, "Donald E. Broadbent," p. 55).

During these years, Broadbent enlarged his contacts with individuals in other disciplines, notably Colin Cherry of Imperial College and Peter Ladefoged of the University of Edinburgh. Exposure to the work of psychologists and others in the United States was slow and hampered by the expense of travel, but Broadbent gradually came to know of the work carried out at such nontraditional centers as the Harvard Psychoacoustic Laboratory and the Aviation Psychology Laboratory at Ohio State University, where, as at the APU, scientists from various disciplines worked on common problems. For Broadbent, such contacts confirmed the value of multidisciplinary approaches and revealed the limitations of what he saw as a frequently insular academic psychology.

By the mid-1950s, Broadbent was beginning to feel constrained by the narrow confines of the usual technical journal. To range more widely, he wrote *Perception and Communication* (1958), a book that remained his major achievement and that enhanced his already prominent reputation. In the same year, Mackworth left for a new position in the United States, and Broadbent became the director of the APU, a position he held until 1974. His work as director increasingly carried administrative duties, although he remained active as an experimenter and writer, publishing, besides many articles, the semi-popular work *Behaviour* in 1961; a major restatement and enlargement of his theories, *Decision and Stress* (1971); and a collection of lectures, *In Defence of Empirical Psychology* (1973). Moving in 1974 to Oxford University as a professor of experimental psychology provided more time for his own research. Retiring in 1991, Broadbent remained active until his sudden death from a stroke in 1993.

Research and Theoretical Contributions. Broadbent's "filter theory" of attention and perception, which receives notice in nearly every textbook of cognitive psychology, began as an attempt to understand certain curious results in his communication research. When multiple messages arrive at one time, how can a listener separate out the meaningful ones from those that are nonmeaningful? Broadbent's research on the problem, which began with studies of the effects of noise and of masking on speech (for example, his "The Role of Auditory Localization" in 1954), soon made clear that the difficulties of perception were not simply peripheral but were central as well. For example, ship operators sometimes appeared to be overloaded with information rather than hindered by purely sensory factors. Using the new technology of tape recording, separate messages could be delivered to each ear of a listener. Most ways of separating the messages spatially, even presenting stereo recordings with a message in each of the two channels, helped performance. Broadbent concluded that a selective mechanism was at work to reduce the information flow through a limited capacity perceiver.

In a 1957 paper, "A Mechanical Model for Human Attention and Immediate Memory," he analogized the selective mechanism to a Y-shaped tube with a hinge at the junction of three pipes. If incoming information is represented as a flow of balls being dropped into one of the tubes, then the first ball can push aside the hinge and reach the bottom pipe. The subsequent flow of balls in one pipe leaves the hinge pushed aside so that balls from the other pipe of the mechanism cannot pass the junction. Similarly, human attention to a selected message seemed to block out an unselected message. The story is too simple in this form, however, because it leaves out important aspects of the human mechanism, namely, the fact that the mechanism (unlike the simple hinge) can switch from

one channel to another, and also the fact that over time the balls in the unattended channel would be lost. Broadbent's initial model identified the switching with a central attentional process keyed to spatial location, and the loss (and the implied retention over short time intervals) to a memory mechanism, but one with very limited capacity. Invoking attention was a radical step, since the concept had disappeared almost entirely from experimental psychology for four decades. As Broadbent put it,

> The reason for its disappearance had been the lack of suitable terminology: common-sense language has great difficulty in discussing the problems of the air-traffic controller because, in one sense, he does more than one thing at the same time, and in another sense, his capacities are limited. But the new notions of information theory provided a suitable vocabulary. Instead of thinking of a "stimulus" in the outside world, which did or did not produce a response, one could speak of an event that produced some representation in the person. (1980 pp. 55–56)

Experimental studies by Broadbent and others showed that material that had gotten through the hinge initially could be recycled back to the original arm of the Y; it could be "rehearsed" and kept from being lost. In this respect, Broadbent's filter theory of attention requires a memory mechanism, a short-term store. In *Perception and Communication,* Broadbent dropped the mechanical analogy (which he had not represented as anything more than a mnemonic device in the first place) and emphasized instead the analogy between the flow of information and the function of attention and memory. Because information theory provided a metric for measuring the amount of information in "bits" (the logarithm of the number of alternatives, weighted by the probability of each alternative), quantitative studies became possible.

Broadbent's final representation of his filter model used a flow chart (Figure 1), that is, a figure showing "boxes" connected by arrows to indicate the separate processing stages and the flow of information from one stage to another. Note that the figure provides a short-term store preceding the selective filter mechanism, including also a feedback loop such that information could be recycled through the store ("rehearsed") as needed. Information in the short-term store could be held only for a short time (hence the need for a rehearsal mechanism). In addition, it appeared to have another unusual property, namely, it did not seem to have a limited capacity that could be defined in terms of information theory as such. It was not the number of bits of information in the technical sense that mattered. Rather, as Irwin Pollack, George Miller, and others had shown, its capacity was limited by

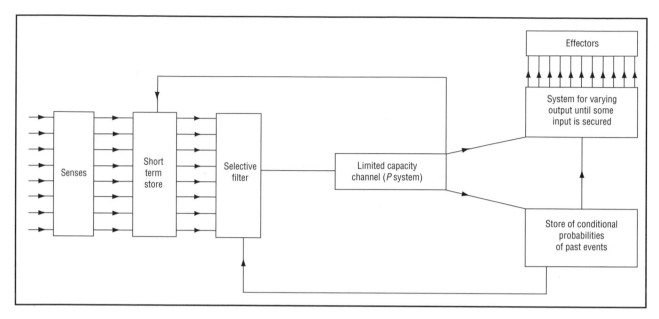

Figure 1. *Broadbent's flow chart, showing the filter model.*

the number of items in store—and each of the items could be a "packet" of very high information value.

In the late 1950s, experiments carried out by Anne Treisman at Oxford provoked Broadbent and Margaret Gregory (then his research assistant and later his second wife) to carry out a series of experiments that greatly modified the original filter theory. Treisman had found that in fact some information could get through an unattended channel. Thus, if a subject were asked to "shadow" (that is, repeat back out loud) words in the left ear channel while ignoring words in the right ear channel, and the shadowed message were then changed from left to right, subjects would often continue shadowing without pause, especially if the words in the unattended channel were a highly probable extension of the original message. Thus, some information, partial and fragmentary though it was, was getting through the unattended channel. Treisman's "double theory of attention" argued that incoming information was selected from something like a probabilistic "dictionary," as well as from a particular channel (left or right ear, say). Broadbent's filter theory was clearly disconfirmed by these results; "Attention does not simply switch off some sense organs and leave others switched on," he wrote (*In Defence of Empirical Psychology,* p. 137).

In revising his own account, Broadbent also credited Treisman for an important suggestion, namely, that in prolonged vigilance studies, some of the results could be due to changes in subject confidence about a percept rather than to changes in subjects' sensitivity to the incoming information. "Margaret and I," Broadbent recalled, "began to look at confidence ratings and, thus, to think about the theory of signal detection put forward by Spike Tanner and John Swets" ("Donald E. Broadbent," p. 66). Signal detection theory (SDT) was developed to analyze psychophysical changes in the threshold for detecting the presence or absence of a stimulus. By analyzing "hits," (correct detections, that is, "yes" responses when the stimulus is present or "no" responses when it is absent), "misses" (failures to detect when the stimulus is present), and "false alarms" ("yes" responses when no stimulus is present), the theory allowed changes in observer sensitivity to be separated from changes in the observer's criterion (or "bias") in reporting. Across a large number of tasks, Broadbent and Gregory were able to show that changes in error rate in complex tasks could be due to changes in bias, changes in sensitivity, or both. This resolved the apparent paradox presented by Treisman's results; a listener was not insensitive to information in the unattended channel but was in fact responding with greatly reduced bias toward that channel. When highly probable stimuli occurred in the unattended channel, this meant that the "bias setting" could change, thus changing the apparent "gain" in that channel. In this fashion, Broadbent's "filter" became instead a semi-permeable one, with two parameter settings, one for bias and one for sensitivity. Selective attention could then be understood as selection of the relevant parameter settings. Furthermore, Broadbent's new account in effect extended his model of attention and memory into a decision-making context. This further enhanced its ability to account for the effects of stress, noise, and the like on performance.

The new account required Broadbent to reassess completely all of the areas of research with which he had been associated. His *Decision and Stress* (1971) summarized the changes and widened the scope of his theory to include decision making, vigilance, and the choice of actions in voluntary behavior. In addition to SDT, Broadbent, like many others in the field of judgment and decision making, made extensive use of Bayesian formulations to understand how limited capacity organisms could function in probabilistic and uncertain environments. In 1973, he collected a series of lectures under the title *In Defence of Empirical Psychology,* which presented a simpler version of the new theory. This and *Decision and Stress,* however, enjoyed much less success than the 1958 book, *Perception and Communication.*

Views on Psychology and Science. Throughout his career, Broadbent's thinking centered on three principles of research, each of which he attributed to Bartlett's influence: (1) research problems should derive from real life whenever possible; (2) experimental situations should remain complex rather than be oversimplified; and (3) data should determine theory rather than the other way around. Ironically, he did not accept what has become Bartlett's most famous principle, that memory was organized in "schemas," organized complexes of stored information and templates for the generation and regeneration of specific recall, although Broadbent, like Bartlett, did rely heavily upon the overall notion of a dynamic perception and memory system.

In all of his books and many of his articles, Broadbent stressed his criticism of the hypothetico-deductive method, which he informally characterized as the "guess and test" approach. Drawing many of his illustrations from the work of Clark Hull, Broadbent felt that it was an ineffective scientific strategy to develop a formal theory (the "guess") and then assess it by drawing specific predictions and testing to see if the predictions were confirmed. Hull's system failed, in Broadbent's view, because of its excessive use of a priori theorems of great generality but little specificity; so much by way of ad hoc assumptions and theorems had to be added to the theory to make a specific prediction that the failure of a prediction told one essentially nothing about where the problem might lie; was it the theory itself or the ad hoc assumptions? And if the latter, which ones? Instead, he argued, science should begin with more narrowly construed theories based upon reliably observed phenomena. These should then be subject to as many alternative explanations as possible; experiments could then be designed that would rule out specific formulations. In this fashion, the theoretical side of psychology would not outrun the empirical side; "The proper road for psychology is ... by way of more modest theoriz-

ing," wrote Broadbent (*Perception and Communication,* p. 313).

In *Perception and Communication,* Broadbent illustrated his approach by beginning the book with extensive accounts of experiments, arranged in a compelling sequence of tests, alternative explanations, refined explanations, further tests, and so on. Only as these provided a base of reliable understandings of specific results did he seek extensions toward more general accounts. Thus, the famous flow chart that summarized his filter theory appears at the end of the book, on page 299, not at the beginning, as a theory to be "tested." In fact, read in the early 2000s, *Perception and Communication* remained a sterling example of an inductivist approach to experimental psychology.

Identified as one of the founders of cognitive psychology, Broadbent was never comfortable with all of the aspects of that designation. Giving full due to behavioral approaches (especially those of Ivan Pavlov and of Hull), Broadbent's invocation of unobservables was, he claimed, a natural development of those earlier systems, not a revolutionary new ideal. The unobservables he invoked were tied closely to observables, and he never lost the belief that behavior constituted an essential starting point for all of psychology and that the explanation of behavior was the ultimate goal of all of psychology. In critiquing a distributed memory model, for example, Broadbent argued in his paper, "A Question of Levels," that James L. McClelland and David E. Rumelhart's connectionist model had implications for a physiological level of explanation but not for a psychological level; for Broadbent, a neural network model is simply too far removed from the relevant behavioral data.

Broadbent's Influence. By bringing the problem of attention back into experimental psychology, Broadbent significantly changed the direction of that field, opening one of its most fruitful lines of inquiry in the cognitive era. Furthermore, his tireless efforts to enhance public perception of the new psychological results, and to extend their applications to real world problems, had a lasting influence on psychology, particularly in Britain. He was an important advocate and contributor at a time when British psychology moved from a marginal academic specialty to a thriving enterprise with connections to many aspects of British industry, government, academia, and public discourse. In contrast to American psychology, British psychology had never fully embraced behaviorism, retaining instead close ties to biological traditions of thought, especially those deriving from Darwinian influences. In this context, Broadbent extended the unique efforts of Bartlett and Craik to establish a purely psychological science, one tied closely to experiment and to real-world applications.

BIBLIOGRAPHY

L. Weiskrantz, *"Donald Eric Broadbent,"* Biographical
Memoirs of the Fellows of the Royal Society *40 (1994):
31–42, contains a microfiche with a complete bibliography of
Broadbent's published works.*

WORKS BY BROADBENT

"The Role of Auditory Localization in Attention and Memory
Span." *Journal of Experimental Psychology* 47 (1954):
191–196.

"A Mechanical Model for Human Attention and Immediate
Memory." *Psychological Review* 64 (1957): 205–215.

Perception and Communication. New York: Pergamon Press,
1958. His most influential and important work, a
sophisticated example of the power of experimentation, as
well as the basic exposition of his "filter theory."

Behaviour. New York: Basic Books, 1961.

"Attention and the Perception of Speech." *Scientific American*
206 (April 1962): 143–149. A good introduction for the
general reader.

Decision and Stress. London; New York: Academic Press, 1971.
The extensive revision of his 1958 theory along decision-
theoretic lines.

In Defence of Empirical Psychology. London: Methuen, 1973. The
substance of his William James Lectures at Harvard and
several others, including his critique of Noam Chomsky.

"Levels, Hierarchies, and the Locus of Control." *Quarterly
Journal of Experimental Psychology* 29 (1977): 181–201.

"Donald E. Broadbent." In *History of Psychology in
Autobiography,* edited by Gardner Lindzey. Vol. 7. San
Francisco: W. H. Freeman, 1980. Warm, witty, and
insightful, the best source for an appreciation of Broadbent as
a person, and for the major themes in his work.

"A Question of Levels: Comment on McClelland and
Rumelhart." *Journal of Experimental Psychology: General* 114
(1985): 189–192. Preceded by a paper of McClelland and
Rumelhart and followed by their rejoinder.

"Effective Decisions and Their Verbal Justification."
Philosophical Transactions of the Royal Society of London, series
B—Biological Sciences, 327 (1990): 493–502. Broadbent's
critique of the usefulness of verbal protocols in psychology.

OTHER WORKS

Baddeley, Alan, and Lawrence Weiskrantz, eds. *Attention:
Selection, Awareness, and Control, A Tribute to Donald
Broadbent.* Oxford; New York: Clarendon Press, 1993.
Published just after Broadbent's sudden death, this edited
collection of original papers by many of his students and
colleagues contains much information about his influence
and the direction of his ideas in the late twentieth century.

Berry, D. "Donald Broadbent." *The Psychologist* 15 (2002):
402–405. Also available from http://www.bps.org.uk. A
warm remembrance by a former student, with an account of
his work on implicit learning.

Lachter, J., K. I. Forster, and E. Ruthruff. "Forty-Five Years after
Broadbent: Still No Identification without Attention."
Psychological Review 111 (2004): 880–913. A revival of the
1958 filter model, with experiments suggesting that the
original model remained valid in some circumstances.

Weiskrantz, L. "Donald Eric Broadbent." In *Biographical
Memoirs of the Fellows of the Royal Society* 40 (1994): 31–42.
The fullest of several obituaries.

Ryan D. Tweney

BRODMANN, KORBINIAN (*b.* Liggers-
dorf in Hohenzollern, Württemberg, 17 November 1868,
d. Munich, Germany, 22 August 1918), *comparative neuroanatomy.*

Brodmann is best known for his advocacy of the view
that the mammalian cortex consists of six fundamental
layers and for his creation of neuroanatomical maps of the
mammalian brain. He took this structure to be fundamental in the sense that the cortices of all mammals are
supposed to be diverse modifications of this basic six-layer
structure. Further, insofar as these six layers differ over the
surface of the brain in a given species, they provide a neuroanatomical basis for dividing the brain of any given
species into a large number of distinct brain regions.
These regions are smaller than the frontal, parietal, temporal, and occipital lobes of the brain. Brodmann's division of the brain into distinct regions continued in wide
use in the early 2000s.

Like those of many neuroscientists of his day, Brodmann's career involved medical training, clinical practice,
and periods of scientific investigation. Brodmann received
his license to practice medicine in 1895, after study at the
Universities of Munich, Würzburg, Berlin, and Freiburg.
Practicing briefly in Munich, he contracted diphtheria.
Treatment for his illness led him into an appointment as
an assistant in the Neurological Clinic in Alexanderbad in
1896. At the clinic he devoted some time to the study of
hypnotherapy, eventually producing a literature summary
and two papers on hypnotic therapy for early volumes of
the *Journal of Hypnotism.* Seeing this work, the clinic
director, Oskar Vogt, encouraged Brodmann to abandon
plans for a medical practice in favor of further education
in preparation for a scientific career. Brodmann thus
turned to neurology and psychiatry in Berlin, then to
pathology in Leipzig where, in 1898, he received his medical doctorate with a dissertation on chronic ependymal
sclerosis.

For his residency, Brodmann worked at the University Psychiatric Clinic in Jena, under the direction of Otto
Binswanger, then at the Municipal Mental Asylum in
Frankfurt am Main. At Jena, Brodmann used measures of
blood flow as an indicator of brain volume when a person
falls asleep, sleeps, and wakes. Brodmann next took up a

suggestion by Alois Alzheimer to undertake microscopic investigations as a means of understanding the biological basis of psychiatric disorders. Using Weigert's glial stain to make cells visible to light microscopy, Brodmann studied a case of thalamic gliomas. These tumors to the supporting glial cells of the thalamus were associated with behavioral impairments ranging from changes in personality to dementia. In this study, he argued for the existence of an important class of glial cells, the astrocytes. In other work, Brodmann also used a light polarization microscope to study the structure of nerve fibers. This kind of technical work was excellent preparation for his future research.

During the time Brodmann was completing his doctoral degree and his residency, Oskar Vogt had moved to Berlin, where he founded his Neurobiological Laboratory in 1898. At the laboratory, Vogt and his wife Cécile were investigating, among other things, the myelinated fiber systems of the brain. This was the standard biological project of making an anatomical determination of the structure of an organ. What was distinctive was that the brain was not just any organ. It had long been recognized as the primary organ of the mind and implicated in psychological disturbances. In addition to the intrinsic interest of the brain, the work was an important response to the technical challenges to microscopy. For much of the nineteenth century, the delicacy of brain tissue and the translucence of its cells limited the quality and reliability of microscopic investigations. By applying stains that selectively colored the myelinated fibers of the brain, the Vogts hoped to overcome some of the obstacles facing previous investigators.

As the laboratory was developing nicely, the Vogts were able to recruit Brodmann to the laboratory to work on a complementary project. Brodmann was to fix brain sections in formalin, embed them in paraffin, then apply a cresyl violet staining technique developed a few years before by Franz Nissl. The relatively simple technique stains the RNA in the cytoplasm of neurons, thereby enabling an observer to determine the number, size, and form of nerve cells in the sample. This was the study of the cytoarchitectonics of the brain. Thus began the work for which Brodmann came to be best known. From 1901 to 1908, Brodmann produced a series of six papers on the structure of the cortex in distinct mammalian species. This comparative work spanned the mammalian orders of the primates, prosimians, chiropterans, insectivores, rodents, and marsupials. In some cases, such as with the rodents, several species within the order were investigated. The series culminated in his treatment of histological localization in the human cerebral cortex. These papers formed the basis for Brodmann's 1909 monograph on the comparative anatomy of the cerebral cortex in mammals.

Brodmann maintained that, in general, it is not possible to make reliable demarcations of distinct regions of the brain by exclusive reliance on the types of cells to be found in a region. In other words, "elemental localization" was not generally reliable. The one exception to this rule that Brodmann recognized was the existence of exceptionally large pyramidal cells found anterior to the central sulcus in the motor cortex. These so-called "Betz cells" were first reported in 1874 by Vladimir Betz . Brodmann also maintained that one could not rely exclusively on distinctive characteristics of particular layers to demarcate brain regions. This technique might work to delimit the early visual processing region of the brain with its stria of Gennari, but the method is not generally reliable. According to Brodmann, the most reliable method available at the time was topographic localization, in which a region is identified by a homogeneous intrinsic structure that is heterogeneous with respect to adjacent regions. A transition of this sort is marked with a small arrow in Figure 1. One can clearly see a number of features of this transition. For example, in moving from left to right across the transition, one finds that in layer I the number of darkly stained cells in the upper portion of the layer decreases dramatically, that layer III is greatly reduced in thickness, and that layer IV subdivides into layers IVA, IVB, and IVC.

Prior to Brodmann's research, the emerging view was that the cortex has a layered structure. Differences of opinion, however, remained concerning the number and location of the proposed layers. Some authors proposed only five layers, others as many as seven. All authors recognized the layers Brodmann identified as layers I and IV, with layer I being the closest to the surface of the brain and the other layers lying deeper. Other authors, however, either lumped or further subdivided the layers Brodmann identified as layers II and III and lumped or further subdivided what were to become Brodmann's layers V and VI. In particular, Brodmann's colleague Oskar Vogt faulted Brodmann for failing to recognize a seventh layer. Among those who contributed to the theory of laminar structure were Theodore Meynert, Bevan Lewis, Vladimir Betz, Santiago Ramon y Cajal, Alfred Walter Campbell, and Frederick Walker Mott. Based on developmental and comparative data, Brodmann proposed that, in mammals, the cerebral cortex is a modification of a basic six-layer structure. Brodmann maintained that the six-layer structure could be modified by having individual layers split, by having individual layers disappear with more or less completely (by fusion), and by having individual layers change in their thickness, cell density, cell size, and cell shape.

Brodmann informed his comparative anatomy with the theory of evolution in many ways. To justify his use of both comparative and developmental data to argue for the six basic layers of the cortex, he appealed to Ernst Haeckel's biogenetic law that embryological development (ontogeny) in a species represents an abbreviated recounting of the evolution of the species (phylogeny). Brodmann also maintained that valid comparisons of neuroanatomical features, such as layer thicknesses, cell sizes, and cell densities, in distinct species must be comparisons of homologous structures; that is, they must be comparisons of structures that are modifications of a single brain structure possessed by an ancestor common to the distinct species. This is not to say that Brodmann found simple applications of evolutionary theory to all he examined. In fact, he rejected many earlier hypotheses as simplistic, insufficiently well supported by observation, and at times contradictory. For example, it had been proposed both that the more evolutionarily advanced a species the thicker its cortex would be and that the more evolutionarily advanced a species the thinner its cortex would be. Brodmann maintained that neither such simple rule held true. Similarly it had been proposed both that the more evolutionarily advanced a species the greater its cell density would be and that the more evolutionarily advanced a species the lower its cell density would be. Again Brodmann argued that neither such simple rule was correct. Further, he maintained that even when comparing homologous cell types, such as the Betz cells, there is no simple relation between cell size and position on an evolutionary scale. Nor is there any simple relationship between cell size and such properties as an organism's body size, length of axon, or size of a dependent muscle.

Brodmann was consistent in the application of his general methodological principles to histopathology. He rejected earlier hypotheses that one could find modifications of individual neuronal elements corresponding to particular psychiatric or psychological problems. Instead he maintained that psychiatric and psychological disorders should be attributed to multiple changes in all the components of a given brain region, including the glial cells and vascular and connective tissue.

Brodmann also recognized one of the most fundamental features of brain mapping, namely, individual variation. Individual organisms of a given species differ, sometimes dramatically, in both intrinsic properties, such as the thickness and cell density of particular regions of the brain, and in extrinsic properties, such as the size, position, and shape. For example, in humans, there are regions of the brain that range in thickness from 1.5 to 4.5 millimeters, so that some individuals have cortices three times thicker than others. The need for methods for accurately representing this degree of variability in brain maps is part of Brodmann's legacy.

At the end of *Localisation,* Brodmann turned directly to the complex issue of the possible anatomical and phys-

iological localization of functions in the brain. When Brodmann wrote, the idea that distinct psychological functions might be performed by distinct regions of the brain had been around for about a century and had already been the subject of extensive debate. Despite the intense interest in the topic, experimental methods had largely been inadequate to the task of associating particular brain regions with particular psychological functions. One marked success had been achieved with the motor cortex, in which electrical stimulation of the exposed surface of animal brains enabled researchers to correlate regions of the brain with specific motor capacities. Among the leaders in this area were David Ferrier, Eduard Hitzig, Victor Horsley, and Herman Munk. Another success was the recognition of a role for the left parietal lobe in linguistic processing. This was spurred by Pierre Broca's discovery of correlations between brain damage in this region and particular language deficits. Brodmann believed that his neuroanatomical findings definitively established that there must be some form of functional localization in the brain. Anatomical differences in general imply functional differences; objects with different structures carry out different functions. Given this principle, the numerous anatomical differences among the many regions of the brain he had studied implied that there must be corresponding functional differences. What, therefore, remained to be done was to work out just exactly what those functions were.

During his time at Vogt's Neurobiological Laboratory, Brodmann was never appointed to a permanent university position, but was instead sustained by a series of grants and a heavy burden of clinical work in neurology. In addition, Brodmann assisted the Vogts in editing the *Journal für Psychologie und Neurologie,* which the Vogts had founded in 1902. The financial hardship on Brodmann was exacerbated when the faculty of medicine at the University of Berlin rejected his habilitation thesis on the cytoarchitectonics of the prosimians (a suborder of primates that includes the lorises, lemurs, and tarsiers). This thesis, over and above that written for his doctoral degree, was meant to certify Brodmann's ability to conduct independent scientific research and to prove his qualification to hold a more significant teaching appointment at the university. To all appearances, both Brodmann and Vogt remained quite bitter about this rejection for the remainder of their careers.

In search of greater economic security and more supportive colleagues, Brodmann moved to the University of Tübingen in 1910. By 1913, his habilitation thesis was accepted and Brodmann was given a professorial appointment where he taught courses on the significance of brain localization from anatomical, physiological, and clinical perspectives. In addition to his teaching and research obligations, Brodmann retained clinical responsibilities. He served as an assistant physician, then later chief physician, of the anatomical laboratory of the psychiatric clinic. This clinical work drew his attention to various cognitive deficits, including aphasia, agnosia, and apraxia. The outbreak of the First World War placed additional demands on Brodmann's time, which included his volunteering for work in a military hospital. In May of 1916, he assumed an appointment as the prosector at the Nietleben Mental Asylum in Halle an der Saale. Here he met the much younger Margarete Franeke, an assistant at the asylum, whom he married on 3 April 1917. Although Brodmann's personal life was much enriched, Germany's growing military losses in the war brought Brodmann's scientific work to a halt.

In 1917, Emil Kraepelin, one of the early leaders in German psychiatry, opened the German Research Center for Psychiatry in Munich. Kraepelin was interested in determining how anatomy could aid our understanding of neuropathology. To this end, Kraepelin recruited Franz Nissl and Walther Spielmeyer, both with an extensive research background in neuropathology. Kraepelin had also known Brodmann during Brodmann's years in Berlin and convinced him to move to the center to work with Nissl. For Brodmann, the prospects looked bright. He anticipated a happy family life, economic security, and a prestigious academic position. The Brodmanns' first child had been born in early 1918. He would also be able to focus on scientific research with Nissl, whose work he greatly respected. Yet Brodmann did not live to enjoy the fruits of his labors. In an era lacking in antibiotics, Brodmann succumbed to a massive infection on 22 August 1918.

BIBLIOGRAPHY

WORKS BY BRODMANN

"Beiträge zur histologischen Lokalisation der Grosshirnrinde. VI. Mitteilung: Die Cortexgliederung des Menschen." *Journal für Psychologie und Neurologie* 10 (1908): 231–246.

Vergleichende Lokalisationslehre der Grosshirnrinde in ihren Principien, dargestellt auf grund des Zellenbaues. Leipzig: Johann Ambrosius Barth Verlag, 1909. (2nd ed., 1925.) English translation, with biographical introduction and editorial notes, by Laurence J. Garey: *Brodmann's "Localisation in the Cerebral Cortex."* Smith-Gordon, 1994; Imperial College Press, 1999; 3rd ed. Springer Verlag, 2006.

OTHER SOURCES

Danek, A., and J. Rettig. "Korbinian Brodmann (1868–1918)." *Schweizer Archiv für Neurologie und Psychiatrie* 140 (1989): 555–566.

Vogt, Oskar. "Korbinian Brodmann." *Journal für Psychologie und Neurologie* 24 (1919): 1–10.

Ken Aizawa

BROGLIE, LOUIS (VICTOR PIERRE RAYMOND) DE (*b.* Dieppe, France, 15 August 1892; *d.* Louveciennes, France, 19 March 1987), *physics, quantum theory, wave mechanics.*

Louis de Broglie achieved a worldwide reputation for his discovery of the wave theory of matter, for which he received the Nobel Prize for physics in 1929. His work was extended into a full-fledged wave mechanics by Erwin Schrödinger and thus contributed to the creation of quantum mechanics. After an early attempt to propose a deterministic interpretation of his theory, de Broglie joined the Copenhagen school's mainstream noncausal interpretation of the quantum theory. Stimulated by David Bohm's revival of his views in 1952, however, de Broglie returned to his early interpretation. Throughout his career, de Broglie wrote an impressive number of specialized books, together with more general accounts aimed at popularizing modern twentieth-century physics and discussing its philosophical issues.

Early Life. Louis-Victor de Broglie was the son of Victor, duc de Broglie, and Pauline d'Armaillé; he was the younger of two brothers in a family of five children. His family, from a noble Italian (Piedmont) lineage, the Broglia, settled in France when Francesco Maria Broglia followed Cardinal Jules Mazarin in the seventeenth century. After that time, the family served the French kings and then the French state in military and diplomatic affairs. With the brothers Maurice and especially Louis, it added to its famous representatives (among them three state marshals) two world-rank physicists of the twentieth century.

In 1901, Louis's family moved to Paris where he studied at the Lycée Janson de Sailly. He entered the university La Sorbonne in 1909 and first studied history, obtaining his *licence ès lettres* in 1910 before briefly switching, apparently without much conviction, to law. Soon, however, deeply impressed by Henri Poincaré's writings, he changed his mind and enrolled in the Faculty of Sciences, studying physics and mathematics in the years 1911–1913. Louis did not have to try hard to convince his family of his choice: His elder brother, Maurice, himself a physicist, who had been in charge of supervising Louis's education since the death of their father in 1906, encouraged this decision. To supplement the somewhat conservative education dispensed at the Sorbonne, Louis caught up with the most recent theoretical research, independently reading the works of the leading theorists of his time, Paul Drude, Paul Langevin, Hendrik Lorentz, Max Planck, and Poincaré. He obtained his *Licence ès sciences* in 1913. This same year, he joined the army to complete his military service. Maurice, who served for a long time in the navy's wireless communications, arranged for him to fulfill his duties with the team at the Eiffel Tower's radiotelegraphy station.

The outbreak of World War I marked a pause in Louis's pursuit of strictly theoretical speculations. Instead of being released after the regular three years of service, he stayed in the army until 1919. Throughout the whole duration of the conflict, he remained on the team at the Eiffel Tower station. Though he was involved in rather innovative applied research (for instance, in collaboration with Leon Brillouin and his brother Maurice, he contributed to the development of wireless communication for allied submarines), he longed for more theoretical and fundamental work. When the war ended, Louis de Broglie resumed his studies and research work in physics. While attending the lectures of Langevin at the College de France, he also began to assist his brother with experimental investigations. At the time, Maurice was already an experimentalist with an international reputation. His private laboratory was renowned for pioneering research on x-ray spectra, and the young Louis there became familiar with the most advanced techniques of the field.

Scientific Career. During this time, de Broglie was already forming ideas which would eventually lead to his discovery of the wave nature of matter. In contrast to his more experimental research, on which he collaborated with other members of Maurice's laboratory, the theoretical ideas that would secure Louis's fame were developed in almost total isolation. After a series of three groundbreaking communications to the Paris Academy in 1923, where he outlined the basics of a wave theory of matter, he exposed his ideas in his PhD thesis *Recherches sur la théorie des quanta* (Researches on the quantum theory), which he defended in 1924. These works suggested that the idea of the dual nature of light (as both a localized particle and a wave extended in space) put forth by Albert Einstein in 1905 should be applied to matter as well. With the successful extension of de Broglie's results by Schrödinger, and then especially with the discovery of electron diffraction in crystals by Clinton Joseph Davisson and Lester Halbert Germer at Bell Labs in the United States in 1927, and by George Paget Thomson at the University of Aberdeen in Scotland in 1928, which demonstrated experimentally that material particles exhibited wavelike properties, de Broglie's ideas were spectacularly vindicated. In 1929 the Swedish Academy of Sciences conferred on him the Nobel Prize for Physics "for his discovery of the wave nature of electrons."

After two years of lecturing at the Sorbonne, Louis was appointed *maître de conferences* in 1928 to teach theoretical physics at the Institut Henri Poincaré, which had been just created in Paris and was devoted to mathematical and theoretical physics. He obtained the chair of phys-

ical theories at the Paris Faculty of Sciences in 1933 and taught there until his retirement in 1962. De Broglie led a rather withdrawn life and never married.

De Broglie was elected a member of the Academy of Sciences in 1933 (*section des sciences mécaniques*), and was elected its permanent secretary in 1942 (*division des sciences mathématiques;* he resigned this charge in 1975). In 1929 he was the first recipient of the Henri Poincaré Prize of the Académie des Sciences and in 1932, he was granted the Albert I of Monaco Prize. In 1952 he received the first Kalinga Prize of UNESCO for his efforts to explain aspects of modern physics to the layman. He was elected a member of the Académie Française in 1944, (one of the fellow academicians to greet his election was his brother Maurice, himself elected in 1934). In 1945 he became an advisor to the French Commissariat à l'Energie Atomique (CEA). In 1956 he received the gold medal of the Centre National de la Recherche Scientifique (CNRS) and in 1961 he was decorated with the Grand Cross of the Légion d'Honneur (1961).

He was elected Fellow of the Royal Society in 1953 and was an Officer of the Order of Leopold of Belgium. He was an honorary doctor of the universities of Warsaw, Bucharest, Athens, Lausanne, Quebec, and Brussels, and a member of eighteen foreign academies in Europe, India, and the United States.

Development of de Broglie's Theory. Louis's acquaintance with quanta went back at least to his reading of his brother's reports and notes from the first Solvay meeting in 1911, where Maurice served as scientific secretary. According to Louis's recollections, he was immediately caught by the puzzle of the quanta and promised himself that he would devote all of his energy to understanding it. His work in his brother's laboratory was instrumental in providing him with firsthand knowledge of some aspects of the new phenomenology, essentially those related to the study of x-ray absorption and of the x-ray-induced photoelectric effect. The context of this research was the further study of the atomic structure, where investigation of the inner energy levels was made possible using x-rays instead of visible light. Serving as a house-theoretician, Louis de Broglie had to learn the most up-to-date theories to be able to interpret the experimental results. Alone, with Maurice, or with his collaborator Alexandre Dauvillier, Louis published numerous observations on the inner atomic levels and their occupation numbers, on the relation between absorption intensities and the number of levels and of the electrons, and on the photoelectric effect. This enabled Louis to enter the restricted field of quantum researchers; however, his important work on the absorption intensities did not bring him only praise. In spite of the agreement of de Broglie's results with the data,

Niels Bohr's close followers from Copenhagen and Munich found his derivations rather unorthodox, if not simply inconsistent with the subtle usage of Bohr's correspondence principle. This principle—that any quantum behavior must reproduce successful classical predictions at the limit where quantum effects can be neglected—was one they felt only "insiders" could properly handle.

Besides Bohr's atomic theory, Louis became familiar with Albert Einstein's light quantum hypothesis, which, at the time, was still rejected by most researchers in the quantum community. The experimentation in Maurice's lab, especially the latter's study of the x-ray-induced photoelectric effect in 1921, was making this hypothesis seem quite natural, and offered renewed arguments for those who, like Maurice, were defending the corpuscular hypothesis against more conservative (purely Maxwellian) views. Although he was not successful in persuading his colleagues of the validity of Einstein's thesis at the Solvay 1921 congress, Maurice de Broglie did not renounce his ideas about the validity of the corpuscular structure of light, but went even further in advocating, in vaguer terms, a kind of general wave-corpuscle duality valid not only for light, but for electrons (matter) as well. As is known, these ideas did not really express a clear-cut ontological thesis; however, they definitely had an impact on Maurice's younger brother.

In the years following the end of the war, many of Louis's theoretical considerations, fueled by his brother dualistic ideas and the continuation of his own prewar meditations, were centered on the formal analogy between the geometry of light ray propagation and the classical mechanics of point particles. This analogy, which had been the starting point for William Rowan Hamilton's famous nineteenth-century formulation of mechanics, if not simply ignored by Louis's contemporaries, was at any rate not taken as having the slightest physical relevance. However, Louis soon felt that it could prove crucial for better understanding the Bohr-Sommerfeld quantization scheme, which selected, among a continuity of classical motions, only a discrete range of quantically allowed ones. As explained by historian Olivier Darrigol, there did exist at the time interpretations of the Bohr-Sommerfeld quantization conditions, and some might have helped Louis in reaching his own (specifically Marcel Brillouin's "hereditary field" mechanism, or Einstein's considerations of the multivaluedness of the action). However, Louis obtained his own interpretation within a much broader scheme of a general wave-particle duality, using relativity theory as a guide—a theory that he had ample time to ponder following Langevin's outstanding teaching of the topic in the years 1920–1922.

Wave Theory of Matter. The hypothesis of light quanta was the starting point in Louis's 1922 paper "Rayonnement noir et quanta de lumière" (received on January 26 by the *Journal de Physique*) devoted to the study of the black body radiation. This work marks the beginning of Louis's final progression toward the discovery of waves associated with matter. Aiming at deriving Planck's law from a purely corpuscular standpoint, de Broglie was eventually able to derive only its low-density approximation, Wien's law, because he did not take into account the only later-derived quantum Bose statistics. However, he introduced in his paper, most significantly, the idea of a light quantum with a very small, but nonvanishing, mass. Apparently, de Broglie was guided by his desire to interpret the continuously varying energies of the light quanta as corresponding to the various (sublight) velocities these quanta could then have. As such, his light quanta did not differ from ordinary matter particles, so that the stage was set for the final step. In 1923 Louis de Broglie, in a series of three short communications to the Paris Academy, extended the wave-particles duality of light through his bold hypothesis of waves associated with matter particles. His first communication, "Ondes et quanta," dated 10 September 1923, introduced the idea of a wave associated with a particle, making use of an important observation on the relativistic transformation properties of the frequency of a periodic process as viewed in the rest frame of the corpuscle and in the laboratory frame. To start with, an "internal" periodic process could be associated with a particle of rest mass m_0 if one defined its frequency v_0 by the Bohr quantum condition (where c is the speed of light, h the Planck constant)

$$E_0 = m_0 c^2 \equiv h\, v_0$$

But then, transforming to the laboratory frame, where the particle had a velocity defined as Bc (with $B > 1$), one ended up with two different frequencies, depending if one wanted to transform first the energy:

$$v = E / h = E_0 / h\sqrt{1-\beta^2} = v_0 / \sqrt{1-\beta^2}$$

or transform the rest frame frequency using the relativistic time dilation formula:

$$v_1 = v_0\sqrt{1-\beta^2}$$

Louis de Broglie, initially puzzled by this discrepancy, eventually realized that one could reconcile both results provided one set the speed of the wave propagating in the laboratory equal to c / B. Indeed, this condition ensured that the wave of frequency v was constantly in phase with the internal oscillating process of the particle. De Broglie readily used this condition to show how one could then

Louis de Broglie. © BETTMANN/CORBIS.

understand Bohr's quantization conditions in terms of the stationary character of the wave, obtained only when the electron was on one of its Bohr's orbits. In the second communication, "Quanta de lumière, diffraction et interférences," dated 24 September, de Broglie discussed the relationship between the propagation of the particle and that of its associated wave. According to Hamilton's analogy between ray optics and mechanics, the particle had to follow the trajectories of the rays normal to the phase wave fronts. De Broglie also considered the necessity of modifying the free dynamics of the particle, as the obstacles to the propagation of the wave could curve the trajectories of the particles. He identified this as a possible experimental effect that could corroborate his phase waves. The interplay between the propagation of the particle and of the waves could be expressed in more formal terms as an identity between the fundamental variational principles of Pierre de Fermat (rays), and Pierre Louis Maupertuis (particles) as de Broglie discussed it further in his last communication "Les quanta, la théorie cinétique des gaz et le principe de Fermat" (dated 8 October 1923). Therein he also considered some thermodynamic consequences of his generalized wave-particle duality. He

showed in particular how one could, using Lord Rayleigh's 1900 formula for the number of stationary modes for *phase* waves, obtain Planck's division of the mechanical phase space into quantum cells.

In the next months, already working on his doctoral dissertation, de Broglie generalized the relations between the particle velocity and the wave velocity for cases where there were external forces. He again used relativity as a guide. He promoted the energy-frequency relation $E = h\nu$ to a full, four-vector (relativistic) relation between a 4-dimensional wave vector and the 4-momentum of the particle. Equating their spatial parts, de Broglie obtained his celebrated relationship between the particle momentum and the wave-length:

$$p = h\frac{1}{\lambda}$$

The more detailed derivations of his results formed the core of his dissertation, which he successfully defended on 25 November 1924 in front of a perplexed audience.

In order to reach an audience wider than the limited readership of the *Comptes rendus,* de Broglie arranged the publication of a summary of his results in *Nature* (October 1923); and a fairly complete account of his three communications appeared in the *Philosophical Magazine* (February 1924). In Germany, a summary of his communications was published in the *Physikalische Berichte* (1924). These accounts did not stir up much reaction from the community. The situation changed when, in the summer of 1924, Langevin personally informed Einstein of Louis's ideas, which the latter embraced quite enthusiastically. Indeed, Einstein quickly recognized that they fit remarkably with his own research on quantum gases. His support made many key actors in quantum research focus on and take seriously de Broglie's ideas in the years 1924–1925. In particular, Schrödinger extended de Broglie's results in the winter of 1925–1926 into a genuine wave mechanics, working out the wave equation of the theory. However, Schrödinger, while extending and completing in an essential way the original framework, altered de Broglie's original picture, granting reality only to the waves and refusing wave-particle dualism. The ensuing events, which led rapidly to the final formulation of quantum mechanics in 1926–1927, did not include the active participation of Louis de Broglie. Although he saw his ideas extended and vindicated, his conception of the meaning of his research and how it should be continued was increasingly at odds with the views of his peers.

The Meaning of Wave Mechanics. In his communications of 1923, and later in his 1924 PhD thesis, de Broglie did not want to commit himself to any physical interpretation of the waves. He granted physical relevance only to these wave features which could be directly related to the particle motion, namely their phase, while eluding any questions pertaining to their amplitude and proper dynamics. They were, as he dubbed them, "fictitious." However, in the months following his PhD, de Broglie started to explore the consequences of his wave-particle model for the problem of the interaction of light with matter. He also considered the possibilities of more physically interpreting his particle-associated waves. Willing to acknowledge the reality of the particles, he tried to conceive them as embodied by the singularities of the waves. However, he had then to cope with the Schrödinger view, where only continuous matter waves were considered. He first attempted to save his dualism by conceiving Schrödinger's equation as actually admitting pairs of solutions characterized by a common phase. He thought of each pair as consisting of a singular solution, with the singularity identified with the particle, while the corresponding continuous regular solution (the only one considered by Schrödinger) was interpreted as conveying solely statistical information. In this approach, the probabilistic (Max Born's) interpretation of the continuous wave reflected the inherent neglect of the singularity (the particle). This so-called double-solution interpretation was hence a causal one, conceiving Schrödinger waves as conveying all the potential outcomes, while concealing the realities of the underlying particle dynamics. These dynamics were non-classical, owing to the fundamental fact that the particle was coupled to the wave via the guiding mechanism which related the particle's velocity to the gradient of the wave phase.

Louis de Broglie met substantial difficulties in justifying his ambitious proposal mathematically. At the Solvay congress of October 1927, feeling unable to defend his interpretation against the more orthodox views, he presented an intermediate position, which viewed the continuous wave as the sole undulatory entity: its role was to guide the particle, because it shared with the singular solution, now discarded, the same phase. This weakened position, called the "pilot wave" interpretation, was nonetheless heavily criticized by the Copenhagen orthodoxy, especially with respect to Bohr's views according to which quantum mechanics was rooted in the uncontrollable disturbance that the observation necessarily brings upon the observed system—which had been presented just weeks before.

Some time after this confrontation, de Broglie, discouraged, joined the orthodox Copenhagen position, which he then consistently defended for the next two decades. From 1930 until 1950, de Broglie turned to study of the various extensions of wave mechanics. He worked on Paul Dirac's electron theory and on the quantum theory of light, developed a general theory of spin

particles, and considered some applications of wave mechanics to nuclear physics. This work, however, did not receive as much attention as what he achieved in the early 1920s.

The early 1950s again witnessed a major change in de Broglie's views. Impressed by the nonlocal theory put forth by David Bohm in 1951, which reintroduced pilot-waves, de Broglie turned back to his first theoretical convictions. Surrounded by some faithful followers, de Broglie resumed his quest for a causal interpretation, this time supplementing his initial views with the idea of nonlinear dynamics for the singular wave. This was, however, increasingly perceived as a marginal research program, even in his own country, where quantum theoreticians preferred to stick to more mainstream physics, less fundamental and closer to the wealth of new experimental data emerging in the 1950s. Although revered as one of the fathers of quantum physics, de Broglie became an isolated icon.

BIBLIOGRAPHY

Louis de Broglie published more than 150 scientific papers, about thirty books, and many philosophical and historical studies as well as numerous popular accounts, biographical notes, and obituaries. A list of all his writings has been published in Annales de la Fondation Louis de Broglie *17 (1992): 1–21. Louis de Broglie's papers are deposited in the archive of the Académie des Sciences. On the Web site of the Fondation Louis de Broglie (http://www.ensmp.fr/aflb/) one can find an English translation of de Broglie's PhD dissertation. The Fondation Louis de Broglie, dedicated to the pursuit of the ideas of Louis de Broglie, has edited texts and books of various level of scholarship commenting different aspects of the contributions of de Broglie.*

WORKS BY DE BROGLIE

"Rayonnement noir et quanta de lumière." *Journal de Physique* 3 (1922): 422–428.

"Ondes et quanta." *Comptes rendus hebdomadaires des séances de l'Académie des sciences* 177 (1923): 507–510.

"Quanta de lumière, diffraction et interférences." *Comptes rendus hebdomadaires des séances de l'Académie des Sciences* 177 (1923): 548–550.

"Les quanta, la théorie cinétique des gaz et le principe de Fermat." *Comptes rendus hebdomadaires des séances de l'Académie des Sciences* 177 (1923): 630–632.

Recherches sur la théorie des quanta, PhD diss. Paris: Masson et Cie, 1924; also *Annales de Physique* 3 (1925): 22–128. The Fondation Louis-de-Broglie has published a facsimile of the *Annales* edition together with Langevin's report and the three 1923 academy communications: Paris: Louis-Jean, 1992.

Ondes et mouvements. Paris: Gauthier-Villars, 1926.

La mécanique ondulatoire. Paris: Gauthier-Villars, 1928.

Matter and Light; the New Physics. London: Allen & Unwin, 1939.

Perspectives nouvelles en microphysique. Paris: Albin Michel, 1956. English translation, *New Perspectives in Physics,* translated by A. J. Pomerans. New York: Basic Books, 1962.

Une tentative d'interprétation causale et non linéaire de la mécanique ondulatoire: la théorie de la double solution. Paris: Gauthier-Villars, 1956. English translation: *Non-linear Wave Mechanics: A Causal Interpretation,* translated by Arthur J. Knodel and Jack C. Miller. Amsterdam and New York: Elsevier, 1960.

Sur les sentiers de la science. Paris: Albin Michel, 1960.

Introduction à la nouvelle théorie des particules de M. Jean-Pierre Vigier et de ses collaborateurs. Paris: Gauthier-Villars, 1961. English translation: *Introduction to the Vigier Theory of Elementary Particles,* translated by Arthur J. Knodel. Amsterdam and New York: Elsevier, 1963.

Étude critique des bases de l'interprétation actuelle de la mécanique ondulatoire. Paris: Gauthier-Villars, 1963. English translation: *The Current Interpretation of Wave Mechanics: A Critical Study.* Amsterdam and New York: Elsevier, 1964.

Certitudes et incertitudes de la science. Paris: Albin Michel, 1966.

Recherches d'un demi-siècle. Paris: Albin Michel, 1976. Apart from a selection of his technical papers, it contains a representative choice of de Broglie's writings on science, philosophy of science, and science policy.

Heisenberg's Uncertainties and the Probabilistic Interpretation of Wave Mechanics. Dordrecht, Netherlands, and Boston: Kluwer, 1990.

OTHER SOURCES

Abragam, Anatole. "Louis Victor Pierre Raymond de Broglie, 15 August 1892–19 March 1987." *Biographical Memoirs of Fellows of the Royal Society* 34 (1988): 23–41.

———. "Louis de Broglie: la grandeur et la solitude." *La Recherche* 245 (1992): 918–923. A tribute with some hints at de Broglie's isolated position in post-war France.

Académie des Sciences. *La découverte des ondes de matière, Actes du Colloque Louis de Broglie, Paris, 16–17 juin 1992.* Paris: Lavoisier, 1994.

Barreau, Hervé. "Le rôle de la relativité dans la pensée de Louis de Broglie." In *La découverte des ondes de matière: colloque organisé à l'occasion du centenaire de la naissance de Louis de Broglie, 16–17 juin 1992,* edited by Académie des sciences, 93–102. Paris: Lavoisier, 1994.

Ben Dov, Yoav. "De Broglie's Causal Interpretations of Quantum Mechanics." *Annales de la Fondation Louis de Broglie* 14 (1989): 343–360.

———. "De Broglie's Conception of the Wave-Corpuscle Duality." In *La découverte des ondes de matière: colloque organisé à l'occasion du centenaire de la naissance de Louis de Broglie, 16–17 Juin 1992,* edited by Académie des sciences, 115–122 Paris: Lavoisier, 1994.

Cormier-Delanoue, Christian. *Louis de Broglie que nous avons connu.* Paris: Fondation Louis de Broglie, 1988.

Darrigol, Olivier. "Strangeness and Soundness in Louis de Broglie's Early Works." *Physis* 30 (1993): 303–372.

———. "Les premiers travaux de Louis de Broglie." In *La découverte des ondes de matière: colloque organisé à l'occasion du centenaire de la naissance de Louis de Broglie, 16–17 juin*

1992, edited by Académie des sciences, 41–52. Paris: Lavoisier, 1994.

Forman, Paul, and Raman, Varadaraja. "Why Was It Schrödinger Who Developed de Broglie's Ideas?" *Historical Studies in the Physical Sciences* 1 (1969): 291–314.

George, André. *Louis de Broglie: Physicien et penseur.* Paris: 1953.

Gerber, Johannes. "Geschichte der Wellenmechanik." *Archive for History of Exact Sciences* 5 (1969): 349–416.

Hanle, Paul A. "Erwin Schrödinger's Reaction to Louis de Broglie's Thesis on the Quantum Theory." *Isis* 68 (1977): 606–609.

Hund, Friedrich. *The History of Quantum Theory.* Translated by G. Reece. New York: Harper and Row, 1974.

Jammer, Max. *The Conceptual Development of Quantum Mechanics.* New York: McGraw-Hill, 1960. A classic account.

Klein, Martin J. "Einstein and the Wave-Particle Duality." *Natural Philosopher* 3 (1964): 3–49.

Kragh, Helge. "The Heritage of Louis de Broglie in the Works of Schrödinger and Other Theoreticians." In *La découverte des ondes de matière: colloque organisé à l'occasion du centenaire de la naissance de Louis de Broglie, 16–17 juin 1992,* edited by Académie des sciences, 65–78. Paris: Lavoisier, 1994.

Kubli, Fritz. "Louis de Broglie und die Entdeckung der Materiewellen." *Archive for History of Exact Sciences* 7 (1970): 26–68.

———. "Conversations avec Louis de Broglie au sujet de sa thèse." In *La découverte des ondes de matière: colloque organisé à l'occasion du centenaire de la naissance de Louis de Broglie, 16–17 Juin 1992,* edited by Académie des sciences, 53–64. Paris: Lavoisier, 1994.

Kuhn, Wilfried. "L'influence des images métaphysiques du monde sur le développement des idées fondamentales dans la physique, particulièrement chez Louis de Broglie." In *La découverte des ondes de matière: colloque organisé à l'occasion du centenaire de la naissance de Louis de Broglie, 16–17 juin 1992,* edited by Académie des sciences, 103–114. Paris: Lavoisier, 1994.

Lochak, Georges. *Louis de Broglie: un prince de la science.* Paris: Flammarion, 1992.

Medicus, Heinrich A. "Fifty Years of Matter Waves." *Physics Today* 27 (1974): 38–45.

Nye, Marie Jo. "Aristocratic Culture and the Pursuit of Science: The de Broglies in Modern France." *Isis* 88 (1997): 397–421.

Russo, Arturo. "La découverte des ondes de matière." In *La découverte des ondes de matière: colloque organisé à l'occasion du centenaire de la naissance de Louis de Broglie, 16–17 Juin 1992,* edited by Académie des sciences, 79–92. Paris: Lavoisier, 1994.

Taketani, Mituo. *The Formation and Logic of Quantum Mechanics.* Vol. 2, *The Way to Quantum Mechanics.* Translated by Masayuki Nagasaki. Singapore and River Edge, NJ: World Scientific, 2002.

Wheaton, Bruce R. *The Tiger and the Shark: Empirical Roots of Wave-Particle Dualism.* Cambridge, U.K.: Cambridge University Press, 1983.

———. "The Laboratory of Maurice de Broglie and the Empirical Foundations of Matter-Waves." In *La découverte des ondes de matière: colloque organisé à l'occasion du centenaire de la naissance de Louis de Broglie, 16–17 juin 1992,* edited by Académie des sciences, 25–40. Paris: Lavoisier, 1994.

Jan Lacki

BRONN, HEINRICH GEORG (*b.*
Ziegelhausen bei Heidelberg, Germany, 3 March 1800; *d.* Heidelberg, 5 July 1862), *paleontology, zoology, morphology, geology, Darwin reception.*

Bronn was a great compiler of reference works in zoology and paleontology, but recent scholarship emphasizes that he also broke new conceptual and methodological ground by situating fossil species in geological time, geographic space, and environmental conditions. By considering when, where, and how species lived, quantifying rates and patterns of species turnover and morphological progress, Bronn helped to establish paleontology as a modern scientific discipline at the interface between biology and geology. His reference works and his editorship of an important geological journal also provided practical support for the discipline's growth.

In the 1840s and 1850s, Bronn's explanations of paleontological change centered on the physical evolution of Earth and the continual adaptation of floras and faunas to prevailing conditions. As the planet's environments changed and diversified, obsolescent species became extinct, to be replaced by better-adapted and morphologically similar, but more advanced, ones. He left open the question of how the new species arose, sometimes suggesting that divine intervention was needed, and sometimes invoking a hypothetical "creative force," and focused instead on deriving the laws that any such force would have to obey. The provisional nature of this solution, along with his lifelong attention to adaptation and diversification, made him cautiously receptive to Charles Darwin's theory of evolution by natural selection, which he introduced to German readers in his own translation, with a critical commentary at the end.

Life, Education, and Career. Bronn was the fifth of seven children of Georg Ernst Bronn, a government forestry official, and Elisabeth Margarethe Bronn. He was raised a Catholic, attended elementary school in Ziegelhausen and gymnasium in Heidelberg, and began attending the University of Heidelberg in 1817. He studied cameralism and natural history, possibly with the intention of pursuing a civil-service career like his father's. This course of study contrasts with the medical training that was more usual for German morphologists, and it allowed Bronn to range more broadly into applied sciences such as forestry, mining, and plant and animal breeding. Bronn's most influential teacher at Heidelberg was probably the geologist Karl von Leonhard.

In 1821, after completing his habilitation in natural history and *Encyclopädie der Staatswissenschaften* (general sciences of the state), Bronn began to teach at Heidelberg at the rank of Privatdocent (lecturer; paid from student fees, not on the state payroll). In 1824 and 1827 Bronn traveled to Switzerland, southern France, Austria, and northern Italy for field research. In 1828, back at Heidelberg, he was promoted to *ausserordentlicher Professor* (extraordinary professor) for topics in commerce and natural history. From 1830 on, he coedited the *Jahrbuch* (after 1833, the *Neues Jahrbuch*) *für Mineralogie, Geognosie, Geologie, and Petrefaktenkunde* (New yearbook for mineralogy, geognosy, geology, and fossil studies), which von Leonhard had founded in 1806. In 1833, he took over the directorship of the zoological collection and responsibility for teaching zoology. Finally, in 1837, he received his promotion to *Ordinarius* (ordinary, or full professor) and became head of Heidelberg's first full-fledged institute of zoology, while also retaining responsibility for applied natural history. This places him among the first generation of zoologists to establish their field as a university-based discipline.

Bronn spent the rest of his career at Heidelberg. He rose to the rank of *Hofrat* (court councillor) in the civil service, and served as university *Prorektor* in 1859–1860. Bronn's work in paleontology was honored with a gold medal from the Dutch Scientific Society in Haarlem and a prize from the French Academy of Sciences in 1857. He was married to Luise Bronn, née Penzel, and they had five children. Bronn died suddenly in 1862, apparently of a heart attack.

Paleontological Works—Overview. Bronn made his international reputation as a geologist and paleontologist between 1824 and 1831 with systematic works on fossil shells and zoophytes, and reports on the geology, paleontology, and economy of Heidelberg and of the regions he visited on his scientific travels. From 1835 to 1838 he brought out his *Lethæa geognostica,* the most complete compendium of fossil species of its time. By organizing fossils first by geological time period, and then taxonomically and geographically within each period, it put the organisms into concrete historical contexts instead of arranging them on a timeless scale of nature or in an abstract system. The arrangement also facilitated the practice, already widespread, of dating geological strata by the fossil species they contained. Other reference works followed, which featured alphabetical indexing and continued to add species and eliminate synonyms.

Handbuch einer Geschichte der Natur. Bronn's three-volume *Handbuch einer Geschichte der Natur* (Handbook of a history of nature, 1841–1849) is not only a paleontological reference work, but also a general introduction to natural history and Bronn's major theoretical statement on the history of the organic world, the causes and laws of change, and the places of zoology and paleontology among the scientific disciplines. It stresses the unity of the sciences and the bearing of cosmology, geology, physics, and chemistry on the study of life. Beginning with the nebular hypothesis and the origin of Earth as a molten sphere, it argues that the gradually cooling Earth presented progressively more hospitable and diverse environments. Such geological progress, Bronn argued, together with the principle that species must always be adapted to their environments, explains the patterns (or "laws") of species succession that are documented in the rest of the book.

Based on a study of variation, both in geographic varieties and artificially bred ones, Bronn decided against the possibility of species transformation. If a new species appears suddenly at some point in the fossil record, it must have been produced then and there by some creative force or process. Although the nature and causes of the creative force were unknown, Bronn could describe its effects and discover the laws that governed it. His most fundamental law (*Grundgesetz*) was that new species always had to be adapted to the environmental conditions they would actually encounter. Other, less fundamental laws saw to it that new creations stayed within taxonomic types, but also pushed their boundaries to make them include higher percentages of modern species, more "perfect," and more diverse ones, and also to colonize a progression of environments, from the marine, to the freshwater, to the terrestrial.

Bronn's law of adaptation implied that each species was suited to life at a particular time and place, and would gradually become less-well adapted as Earth evolved. Eventually it would diminish in numbers, become extinct, and be replaced by one or more better-adapted and more-advanced species. Because of complex interdependencies among species and environments, each extinction, in turn, triggered further extinctions, then further creations, resulting in continual turnover and improvement of the fauna and flora.

This successional theory of Bronn's was one of several that were current in the decades before *The Origin of Species,* but it had several distinctive features. Against Louis Agassiz's catastrophism, which had envisioned periodic mass extinctions and wholesale fresh creations of more advanced forms, Bronn argued for asynchronous extinctions and gradual species turnover. His detailed tabulations of fossils and their relative ages provided strong evidence against mass, simultaneous extinctions. In contrast, Bronn opposed the steady state uniformitarianism of Charles Lyell, which had gradual species turnover, but no net geological or morphological progress. Bronn's data also allowed him to document and quantify various forms of advancement in the fossil record. In addition, Bronn also rejected the notion, associated with *Naturphilosophie* and idealistic morphology, that embryonic development could serve as the model for historical change. Bronn argued that the sequences of fossil forms did not run parallel to embryonic stages and that species did not have life cycles and predetermined life expectancies. Bronn viewed paleontology as a separate subdiscipline, with its own laws and its own data, and paleontologists were to explain organic change with reference to the changing external world, rather than internal, developmental processes.

Later Works on Zoology and Morphology. Bronn did not consider himself a narrow specialist on paleontology, but was also concerned with zoology as a whole and its emerging position among the academic disciplines. In the interest of providing zoology with a unifying conceptual framework, Bronn devoted his next major project to an encyclopedic *Allgemeine Zoologie* (General zoology). Here he outlined a view of the animal as a living whole, to which every subdiscipline contributed: anatomy, physiology, biochemistry, animal psychology, biogeography, paleontology, and systematics. The same unifying urge provided the impetus behind Bronn's well-known series *Klassen und Ordnungen des Thierreiches* (Classes and orders of the animal kingdom), which was intended to give a complete account of every major animal group. Bronn produced the first three volumes between 1859 and 1862, and it has been continued by many other authors.

Bronn's prizewinning *Untersuchungen über die Entwickelungs-Gesetze der organischen Welt während der Bildungs-Zeit unserer Erd-Oberfläche* (Investigations on the developmental laws of the organic world during the formative period of our Earth's surface), originally written in French in 1855, first appeared in print in an 1858 German version. In it Bronn restated and refined his theory of organic history from *Handbuch einer Geschichte der Natur.* It was still a successional theory, rather than an evolutionary one, but the laws of change were much simplified and it was strongly suggested that they were all ultimately reducible to the effects of adaptation to an evolving Earth. Morphological progress was also measured by some new yardsticks, such as increasing "physiological division of labor," a concept developed by Henri Milne-Edwards, who was one of the judges at the French Academy.

Also in 1858, Bronn published *Morphologische Studien über die Gestaltungs-Gesetze der Naturkörper überhaupt und der organischen insbesondere* (Morphological studies of the formative laws of natural bodies generally and organic ones in particular), an analysis of crystals, embryonic stages, and the diversity of adult forms. By publishing a separate book on this subject, Bronn underscored the distinction between the process of forming an animal body and the historical progression of forms in the fossil record. According to Bronn, embryonic and fossil sequences did indeed have many superficial similarities, because they both involved increasing complexity and division of labor, and they both had the same endpoints in present-day adult forms, but they were not to be equated. Because embryonic stages did not have to be adapted to historical environments, one should not expect them to run parallel to anything in the fossil record.

Bronn and Darwin. Despite its threat to overturn his own successional theory, Bronn responded constructively to the publication of *The Origin of Species* in 1859. He translated the second and third editions of Darwin's book into German in 1860 and 1863, respectively, and he appended his own critical commentary to both of those editions. Bronn also translated Darwin's book on orchids.

Bronn's translation of *The Origin* has often been criticized for rendering Darwin's new ideas in the language of an older German morphology, which spoke of natural selection leading to increasing "perfection" of form. Darwin's supporters also objected to Bronn's commentary, which gave at best an ambiguous endorsement of Darwinism. Still, it was the first translation on the market in any language, and it was instrumental in disseminating Darwin's theory and initiating discussion in Germany. Starting with the 1867 third German edition (based on Darwin's fourth), J. Victor Carus took over as Darwin's principal German translator, and he removed Bronn's commentary and modernized some of the terminology.

Bronn's own work had anticipated Darwin's emphasis on adaptation to changing environments and on the demise of the maladapted, and he was willing to reconsider the fixity of species and even the direction and purposefulness of historical progress. But in his commentary, he complained of Darwin's inability to explain the origin of the very first species. As long as Darwin still allowed for a mysterious creative force to produce even one species long ago, Bronn argued, he had not really rid science of such forces or ruled out theories such as Bronn's that relied solely on them. Bronn also raised the problem of orderliness in taxonomy, especially the distinctiveness of species. He thought that there was not, in fact, such a great chaos of unclassifiable species as Darwinian variation ought to produce. Bronn observed that nature had "lawlike means" of maintaining species' identities and eventually returning varieties to the norm if they were ever altered by environmental influences, hybridization, or artificial selection. In contrast, under Darwin's theory, such order had to be maintained by natural selection, which carved out recognizable species and higher groups. But Darwin had no direct historical evidence that it always did so and, worst of all, nothing like a law of nature requiring it. The whole scheme seemed to Bronn to be too capricious to be a proper scientific explanation of life. Bronn rejected the theory as it then stood, but predicted that the Darwinians would eventually gain acceptance.

BIBLIOGRAPHY

WORKS BY BRONN

System der Urweltlichen Konchylien. Heidelberg, Germany: J.C.B. Mohr, 1824.

System der Urweltlichen Pflanzenthiere. Heidelberg, Germany: J.C.B. Mohr, 1825.

Ergebnisse meiner naturhistorisch-ökonomischen Reisen. Heidelberg, Germany: Karl Groos, 1826.

Gæa Heidelbergensis: Oder, mineralogische Beschreibung der Gegend von Heidelberg. Heidelberg, Germany: Karl Groos, 1830.

Lethæa geognostica: Oder Abbildungen und Beschreibungen der für die Gebirgs-Formationen bezeichnendsten Versteinerungen. Stuttgart, Germany: E. Schweizerbart, 1835.

Handbuch einer Geschichte der Natur. 3 vols. and atlas. Stuttgart, Germany: E. Schweizerbart, 1841–1849.

Index palaeontologicus. Oder Übersicht der bis jetzt bekannten fossilen Organismen. Stuttgart, Germany: E. Schweizerbart, 1848.

Allgemeine Zoologie. Stuttgart, Germany, 1850.

Morphologische Studien über die Gestaltungs-Gesetze der Naturkörper überhaupt und der organischen insbesondere. Leipzig, Germany: C.F. Winter, 1858.

Untersuchungen über die Entwickelungs-Gesetze der organischen Welt während der Bildungs-Zeit unserer Erd-Oberfläche. Stuttgart, Germany: E. Schweizerbart, 1858.

Die Klassen und Ordnungen der formlosen Thiere (Amorphozoa). Vol. 1: *Wissenschaftlich dargestellt in Wort und Bild.* Leipzig, Germany: C.F. Winter, 1859.

Review of *On the Origin of Species by Means of Natural Selection, Or the Preservation of Favoured Races in the Struggle for Life,* by Charles Darwin (1859). *Neues Jahrbuch für Mineralogie, Geognosie, Geologie und Pertefaktenkunde* (1860): 112–116. Translated by David Hull as: "Review of the *Origin of Species.*" In *Darwin and His Critics: The Reception of Darwin's Theory of Evolution by the Scientific Community,* edited by David L. Hull. Cambridge, MA: Harvard University Press, 1973.

Die Klassen und Ordnungen der Strahlenthiere (Actinozoa). Vol. 2: *Wissenschaftlich dargestellt in Wort und Bild.* Leipzig, Germany: C.F. Winter, 1860.

Translator. *Über die Entstehung der Arten im Thier- und Pflanzen-Reich durch natürliche Züchtung, oder Erhaltung der vervollkommneten Rassen im Kampfe um's Daseyn.* 1st German ed. Stuttgart, Germany: E. Schweizerbart, 1860. Translation of the second English edition of *The Origin of Species* by Charles Darwin.

Essai d'une réponse à la question de prix proposée en 1850 par l'Académie des Sciences. Paris: Mallet-Bachelier, 1861.

Die Klassen und Ordnungen der Weichthiere (Malacozoa). Vol. 3, part 1: *Wissenschaftlich dargestellt in Wort und Bild*. Leipzig, Germany: C.F. Winter, 1862.

Translator. *Über die Entstehung der Arten im Thier- und Pflanzen-Reich durch natürliche Züchtung, oder Erhaltung der vervollkommneten Rassen im Kampfe ums Daseyn*. 2nd ed. Stuttgart, Germany: E. Schweizerbart'sche Verlagshandlung und Druckerei, 1863. Translation of the third English edition of *The Origin of Species* by Charles Darwin.

Neues Jahrbuch für Mineralogie, Geognosie, Geologie und Petrefaktenkunde. Stuttgart, Germany: E. Schweizerbart. Edited by Karl Cäsar von Leonhard and H. G. Bronn, this journal contains numerous research papers and reviews by Bronn.

OTHER SOURCES

Baron, Walter. "Zur Stellung von Heinrich Georg Bronn (1800–1862) in der Geschichte des Evolutionsgedankens." *Sudhoffs Archiv für Geschichte der Medizin und der Naturwissenschaften* 45 (1961): 97–109.

Gliboff, Sander. "H. G. Bronn and the History of Nature." *Journal of the History of Biology* (in press).

Gümbel. "Bronn: Heinrich Georg." In *Allgemeine Deutsche Biographie*. Leipzig, Germany: Duncker & Humblot, 1876.

Junker, Thomas. "Heinrich Georg Bronn und die *Entstehung der Arten*." *Sudhoffs Archiv für Geschichte der Medizin und der Naturwissenschaften* 75 (1991): 180–208.

Nyhart, Lynn K. *Biology Takes Form: Animal Morphology and the German Universities, 1800–1900*. Chicago: University of Chicago Press, 1995. Chapter 4 places Bronn within the history of morphology as an academic discipline.

Schumacher, Ingrid. "Die Entwicklungstheorie des Heidelberger Paläontologen und Zoologen Heinrich Georg Bronn (1800–1862)." Diss., Ruprecht-Karls-Universität, Heidelberg, Germany, 1975. Still the best overview of Bronn's life and work, with an emphasis on his contributions to theory.

Sander Gliboff

BROVARNIK, HERBERT CHARLES

SEE **Brown, Herbert Charles**.

BROWN, HERBERT CHARLES (*b.*

London, United Kingdom, 22 May 1912; *d.* Lafayette, Indiana, 19 December 2004), *organic chemistry, organoboron compounds*.

Brown is best known for his work with boron compounds, for which he was awarded the Nobel Prize in Chemistry in 1979. He was also widely recognized in the chemical community for his work on steric strain, his work on aromatic substitution, and his long battle with much of the chemical establishment regarding the nonclassical ion. In his extremely productive career, he published four books and more than one thousand scientific papers.

Early Life. Herbert Brown was born in England in 1912, the second of four children of Charles and Pearl (Gorinstein) Brovarnik. The family immigrated to the United States in 1914 and joined Herbert's paternal grandparents in Chicago, where the family name had already been anglicized to Brown. Brown's father was trained as a cabinetmaker, but there was little demand for his skills in Chicago, so he worked as a carpenter and eventually opened a small hardware store. After his death in 1926, Herbert was forced to drop out of high school and tend the store. He was adept at running the business but found it boring; he was much more interested in reading. He returned to high school in 1929 and graduated the next year.

The family having sold the store by this time, Brown went out and worked at several jobs. But it was the beginning of the Depression, and good work was hard to find. He went to Crane Junior College for one semester before Crane was forced to shut down. At Crane he became fascinated with chemistry and also met Sarah Baylen, whom he would later marry. Brown attended night courses at the Lewis Institute for a couple of semesters, took a correspondence course in qualitative analysis from the University of Chicago, and did some laboratory work at the home laboratory of Nicholas Cheronis, who had been one of the chemistry instructors at Crane. Brown and Sarah Baylen graduated from Wright Junior College in 1935, where Cheronis was in charge of the physical sciences, and with Cheronis's help and encouragement, they entered the University of Chicago. Brown demonstrated what was to be his lifelong propensity for hard work and his inexhaustible energy by taking a large number of courses (up to ten per quarter) and completing his junior and senior course work in one year. He graduated with a Bachelor of Science degree in 1936. Julius Stieglitz, who had chaired the Chicago chemistry department for many years, convinced him to stay on and do graduate work.

Sarah had given Herbert a copy of Alfred Stock's book *The Hydrides of Boron and Silicon* (1933) as a graduation present. He was sufficiently interested in the hydrides of boron that he took up graduate work under the guidance of Professor Hermann I. Schlesinger, who had an active program in boron chemistry. Sarah and Herbert were married in 1937, and he completed his graduate work in 1938, receiving a PhD.

At that time diborane, a gas, was made in only two laboratories in the world, those of Stock and Schlesinger, and in both laboratories, the process was difficult and the yields very low. Brown's thesis work involved the reduction of aldehydes, ketones, and esters with diborane (B_2H_6) and was certainly a precursor to the Brown-led revolution that eventually would take place in organic chemistry.

Early Research. After completing his graduate research, Brown could not find an industrial position, but Professor Morris Kharasch offered him an Eli Lilly postdoctoral fellowship. He was supposed to work on the isolation of the active principle from the pituitary gland, but the glands were slow in coming, so he began work on the possible chlorosulfonation of hydrocarbons with sulfuryl chloride, a reaction Kharasch hoped might be useful in the preparation of detergents. This alternate project turned out to be quite fruitful and resulted in ten papers from 1939 to 1942 on chlorination, chlorosulfonation, and chloroformylation of a variety of organic compounds, and some fundamental work on the stereochemistry and isomerization of free radicals. Brown later carried out additional free radical research at Wayne State and Purdue universities.

After his year with Kharasch, Brown was offered the position of research assistant to Professor Schlesinger, which carried the title of instructor. This post involved some teaching, working on Schlesinger's research problems, directing Schlesinger's research students, and if time and energy permitted, carrying out some independent research with master's students. It was during this period, as a result of wartime research projects, that Brown and his coworkers first synthesized sodium borohydride ($NaBH_4$). A few years later Schlesinger's group synthesized lithium aluminum hydride ($LiAlH_4$). These two compounds and the derivatives developed by Brown over the next thirty years had an enormous impact on organic synthesis. An additional result of the war research that was to prove extremely important was the discovery that diborane could be readily prepared in solution from boron trifluoride (BF_3) and lithium hydride (LiH) or lithium borohydride ($LiBH_4$).

After five years as an instructor and as Schlesinger's assistant, Brown was told there was no future for him at the University of Chicago, so he began looking for a new position. Neil Gordon, a former colleague of Morris Kharasch from the University of Maryland, was moving to Wayne University (as it was then called) in Detroit to chair the chemistry department and Kharasch recom-

Herbert Charles Brown. HULTON ARCHIVE/GETTY IMAGES.

mended Brown for a position. Brown was on the faculty at Wayne from 1943 to 1947, during which time he published eighteen papers, established a reputation in the organic community for creativity and productivity, and had a son, Charles Alan, who became a chemist.

In 1947, Brown accepted a position as professor of chemistry at Purdue University. In 1959, he became R. B. Wetherill Professor and, in 1960, R. B. Wetherill Research Professor. He retired as professor emeritus in 1978 but continued to do research and publish until his death in 2004. (Although Brown spent the bulk of his academic career at Purdue, he was a visiting professor at UCLA [1951]; Ohio State [1952]; University of California at Berkeley [1957], Santa Barbara [1967], and San Diego [1979]; University of Colorado (1958); and a number of other major institutions. He also gave a large number of named lectures at most of the major universities in the country, including Harvard, Columbia, Cornell, Johns Hopkins, and the University of Pennsylvania.)

Steric Effects. During his years as Schlesinger's assistant, Brown began a project in steric effects that would bring him considerable attention in the larger chemical community. This work was prompted in part by observations he

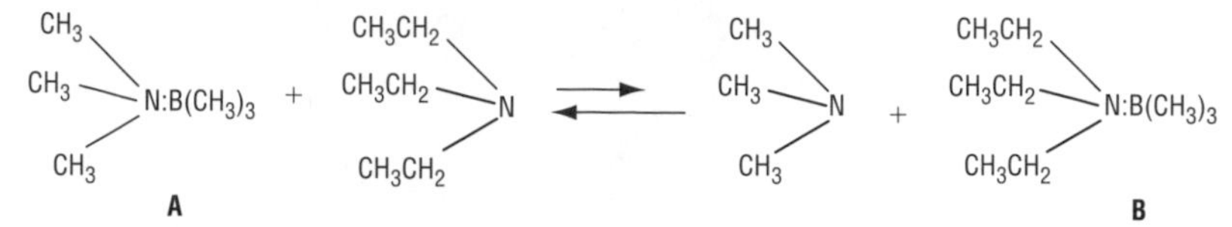

$$\text{(CH}_3)_3\text{N:B(CH}_3)_3 + \text{(CH}_3\text{CH}_2)_3\text{N} \rightleftharpoons \text{(CH}_3)_3\text{N} + \text{(CH}_3\text{CH}_2)_3\text{N:B(CH}_3)_3 \qquad (1)$$

A   B

Figure 1.

had made while a graduate student, and in part by what he considered a real neglect in the chemical literature of the part played by steric factors on chemical behavior. The work began with qualitative studies of the relative stabilities of a series of trialkylborane-alkylamine addition compounds.

Brown and his coworkers found that increasing the size of the groups attached to the nitrogen would cause instability in the addition compounds. For example, the trimethylamine-trimethylborane compound (A) shown in Figure 1 is more stable than the triethylamine-trimethylborane compound (B); that is, the equilibrium in the equation lies more to the left.

Brown then began a long-term quantitative study of the heats of formation of the amine-borane addition compounds and demonstrated the importance of steric effects in these systems and, by implication, in other areas of organic chemistry. He eventually identified three forms of steric strain, which are closely associated with his name: F(ront)-strain, B(ack)-strain, and I(nternal)-strain. Brown talked about these studies at the first Organic Reaction Mechanisms Conference at Notre Dame in 1946 and again at the third Organic Reaction Mechanisms Conference at Northwestern University in 1950. He summarized this work in a Centenary Lecture at Burlington House, London, before the Chemical Society (London) in 1955 and in a long article, "Chemical Effects of Steric Strains," in the *Journal of the Chemical Society* the following year.

Brown, who seldom shied from an argument when he felt the facts were on his side, engaged in a minor skirmish in the early 1950s with Christopher Ingold, one of the founding fathers of physical organic chemistry, over the relative importance of steric effects in the formation of alkenes during the unimolecular hydrolysis of tertiary alkyl halides. In a series of papers in 1948, Ingold and his coworkers maintained that steric effects were seldom important in determining the products of unimolecular reactions and that the dominating factor involved electronic effects. In a 1950 paper with Roslyn Fletcher, Brown challenged this view and offered the results of a number of experiments in support of his position. Ingold took issue with Brown in a 1953 paper titled "The Comparative Unimportance of Steric Strain in Unimolecular

Olefin Eliminations." This eventually evoked a five-paper response from Brown in 1955, culminating with a paper titled, "The Importance of Steric Strain in the Extent and Direction of Unimolecular Elimination." This argument with Ingold merely served as a preliminary bout for what was to become the most famous controversy of twentieth-century organic chemistry.

The Nonclassical Ion Problem. In the early 1930s, the concept of the carbocation, an organic ion with a positive charge on an electron-deficient carbon atom, was introduced. This new idea proved extremely useful in the development of organic theory, in particular in the detailed description of reaction pathways. Carbocations were proposed as intermediates in many reactions to explain rates, structural rearrangements, and steric consequences. In 1949, Winstein and Trifan suggested that some of their results could be better described by the introduction of a new reaction intermediate with unusual bonding. Intermediates of this type were eventually labeled "nonclassical ions."

Once introduced, the nonclassical ion was used by many others to explain, what appeared to be, anomalous results. Brown, whose basic philosophy was "nature is simple," challenged the concept of the nonclassical ion in a provocative paper titled "Strained Transition States" in 1962. He was following the principle of Occam's razor that is applied to all scientific models: one should not increase, beyond what is necessary, the number of entities required to explain anything. He essentially argued that all of the results for which the nonclassical ion was invoked, could as easily be explained using classical ions and, of course, steric effects.

The debate, with Brown on one side and the majority of the physical organic chemists on the other, continued for almost two decades and produced an enormous amount of research, much of it extremely inventive with respect to ideas and technology. Paul Bartlett, in his book, *Nonclassical Ions* (1965), wrote that the importance of the debate was: "(1) It has led to an extension of valence theory and has defined the meeting-ground of organic chemistry with the electron-deficient bonding principles as seen in boron compounds; (2) its study has provided new tools

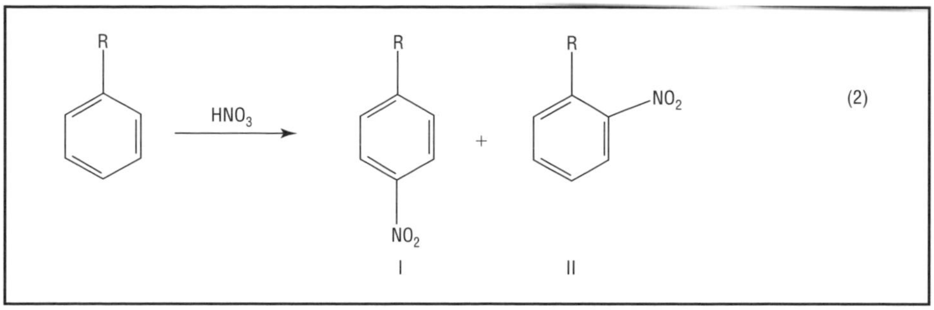

Figure 2.

and new insight relating to the ionization process in solution; (3) it has evolved some elegant methods of stereochemical study; ..." (p. v). Brown published a book, *The Nonclassical Ion Problem* (1977), and close to one hundred communications on the subject. Unfortunately, the dispute also produced some verbal abuse and considerable bitterness. The issue was never fully resolved to the satisfaction of all the parties, but the nonclassical ion remained a useful concept in the armament of the organic chemist.

Aromatic Substitution. As a further result of his interest in steric effects, Brown examined the electrophilic substitution of alkyl-substituted aromatic compounds (see Figure 2). Brown found that increasing the size of group R increased the ratio of I to II, demonstrating once more the profound effect that steric factors play in organic reactions.

Extending his interest to the general problem of electrophilic substitution, Brown and his coworkers developed a quantitative theory that could be used to predict the rates of a variety of reactions. In the process, he defined a new Hammett substituent constant, σ^+, thereby extending considerably the applicability of the Hammett equation, which was such a powerful predictive tool for chemists. Brown's work in this area was reviewed in detail in "A Quantitative Treatment of Directive Effects in Aromatic Substitution," a 1963 paper with L. M. Stock.

Return to the Boranes. In 1953, Brown published eleven articles describing the research on boron compounds that had been done at Chicago during the war. The series started with a paper titled "New Developments in the Chemistry of Diborane and Borohydrides. I. General Summary." He then initiated a research program in boron chemistry that eventually would lead to the Nobel Prize. It began with reductions of organic compounds using a variety of borohydrides, spread, as the result of an accidental observation, to the area of hydroboration, and finally led to the development of a large number of reactions using organoboranes.

Selective Reductions. In 1947, Schlesinger published "Lithium Aluminum Hydride, Aluminum Hydride and Lithium Gallium Hydride and Some of Their Applications in Organic and Inorganic Chemistry," which described the synthesis of lithium aluminum hydride, a compound that he and his coworkers had prepared during their war-related research. This solid reagent, which soon became commercially available, could easily reduce compounds containing carbonyl (C=O) groups to alcohols and compounds with carbon-nitrogen multiple bonds to amines. The procedure was relatively simple and the products could be isolated readily in very high yield. The major problem with the reagent was that it was highly reactive and thus unselective, and it reduced almost every compound that contained a carbon-oxygen or carbon-nitrogen multiple bond.

Weldon Brown at the University of Chicago worked with lithium aluminum hydride and collected data on its widespread use in organic synthesis. In 1951, he published "Reductions by Lithium Aluminum Hydride," an extensive review citing hundreds of examples of the use of the compound in the few short years that it had been available.

Sodium borohydride, which had been synthesized in 1942 in Schlesinger's laboratory but whose synthesis was not published until 1953, when Herb Brown finally found time to write up the war work, was a very mild and selective reducing agent and would only reduce aldehydes and ketones to the corresponding alcohols. After moving to Purdue University, Brown, who shared the patent with Schlesinger on the preparation of sodium borohydride, began a program designed to increase the reactivity of sodium borohydride and decrease the reactivity of lithium aluminum hydride. As in almost all his major research projects, Brown and his coworkers made systematic alterations to the two compounds, carefully observing and recording the effects of the changes. Over a period of thirty years, they developed a series of reducing agents that covered the entire spectrum of reactivity from the very selective sodium borohydride to the very reactive and unselective lithium aluminum hydride.

Hydroboration. While engaged in the reduction studies, one of Brown's postdoctoral fellows, B. C. Subba Rao, observed an anomalous result. During the reduction of an ester containing a carbon-carbon double bond, more diborane was consumed than was required for the ester alone. It turned out that the diborane not only reduced the ester to an alcohol but also added to the carbon-carbon double bond. Further investigation showed that diborane and other so-called hydroborating agents could be added to a carbon-carbon double bond easily and rapidly and that the resulting product could be oxidized to an alcohol. The addition of diborane was regiospecfic; that is, hydrogen and boron added to the double bond in only one of two possible ways (the hydrogen always added to the more substituted carbon of the double bond), and the addition took place with no rearrangement. The addition was also stereospecific; that is, the elements of hydrogen and boron added on the same side of the double bond, which was generally the least hindered side.

Brown pursued this new discovery very systematically, with energy and with considerable resources. This new reaction permitted Brown and his coworkers to synthesize a plethora of new organoboranes. The products were usually trialkylboranes (R_3B), but by careful selection of the starting alkene, they were able to synthesize a variety of monoalkylboranes (RBH_2) and dialkylboranes (R_2BH). The monoalkylboranes, RBH_2, and dialkylboranes, R_2BH, can also add to alkenes to produce mixed trialkyl boranes, RR'_2B and $R_2R'B$. Once Brown and his colleagues had perfected the synthesis of the organoboranes, they turned their attention to the use of these compounds.

Reactions of the Organoboranes. In addition to oxidizing the organoboranes to the corresponding alcohols, and in certain instances to the corresponding ketones, they found that the boron could be replaced by halogen, by an amino group, by hydrogen or deuterium, and by mercury. Furthermore, the organoboranes could be used to build more complex organic molecules by making new carbon-carbon bonds. The boranes can undergo coupling to form dimers, they can be utilized in the formation of cyclopropanes, and they can react with carbon monoxide and be converted to tertiary alcohols, secondary alcohols, ketones, and aldehydes. Organoboranes can also be used to extend carbon chains by two, three, or more carbon atoms by reactions with α,B-unsaturated aldehydes and ketones and α-halo esters and ketones. Utilizing well-chosen cyclic organic compounds containing multiple double bonds,

Brown was able to "stitch" with boron and "rivet" with carbon monoxide to make complex polycyclic systems.

The uses of the organoboranes in organic synthesis seem almost limitless, constrained only by the imagination and the technical skill of the researcher. In 1978, James Brewster, who has written several sketches of Brown and his research, wrote, "Organoborane chemistry was not just discovered, it was also the product of a high order of creative imagination—an artistic triumph as well as a scientific one" (p. 331).

Awards. Brown was the Centenary Lecturer of the Chemical Society of London in 1955 and the George Fisher Baker Non-Resident Lecturer at Cornell University in 1969. The Baker lectures formed the basis of his 1972 book, *Boranes in Organic Chemistry*. He was elected to the National Academy of Sciences in 1957 and the American Academy of Arts and Sciences in 1966. Brown was the recipient of the William H. Nichols Medal in 1959; the American Chemical Society Award for Creative Research in Synthetic Organic Chemistry in 1960; the Linus Pauling Medal in 1968; the National Medal of Science in 1969; the Roger Adams Medal in 1971; the Charles Frederick Chandler Medal in 1973; the Madison Marshall Award in 1975; the City College of New York Scientific Achievement Award Medal in 1976; the Ingold Memorial Lecturer and Medal and the Elliott Cresson Award, both in 1978; the Nobel Prize in 1979; the Priestly Medal in 1981; the Perkin Medal in 1982, the Gold Medal of the American Institute of Chemists in 1987; and the Emperor's Decoration (Japan): Order of the Rising Sun, Gold and Silver Star, in 1989.

BIBLIOGRAPHY

The Chemistry Department at Purdue University in West Lafayette, Indiana, is in possession of "Remembering HCB: Memoirs of Colleagues and Students of Herbert C. Brown." In addition to the memoirs, it also contains an essay by James Brewster on Brown's researches and Brown's bibliography through 1977. Purdue's Chemistry Department also holds "Herbert C. Brown: A Life in Chemistry," which honors Brown's Nobel Prize. It contains reprints of three articles covering his work with boranes, his Nobel lecture, an autobiographical extract from his book, Boranes in Organic Chemistry *(1972), and a biographical note by James Brewster. The Chemical Heritage Foundation in Philadelphia holds "Oral History with H. C. Brown," the transcript of an interview of Brown by Leon Gortler in 1982.*

WORKS BY BROWN

With Roslyn Silber Fletcher. "Chemical Effects of Steric Strain. II. The Effect of Structure on Olefin Formation in the Hydrolysis of Tertiary Aliphatic Chlorides." *Journal of the American Chemical Society* 72 (1950): 1223–1226.

With Hermann I. Schlesinger et al. "New Developments in the Chemistry of Diborane and the Borohydrides. I. General Summary." *Journal of the American Chemical Society* 75 (1953): 186–190.

With Hermann I. Schlesinger and Albert E. Finholt. "The Preparation of Sodium Borohydride by the High Temperature Reaction of Sodium Hydride with Borate Esters." *Journal of the American Chemical Society* 75 (1953): 205–209.

With Ichiro Moritani. "Steric Effects in Elimination Reactions. V. The Importance of Steric Strain in the Extent and Direction of Unimolecular Elimination. The Role of Steric Strains in the Reactions of Highly Branched Carbonium Ions." *Journal of the American Chemical Society* 77 (1955): 3623–3628.

"Chemical Effects of Steric Strains." *Journal of the Chemical Society* (1956): 1248–1268. A review of his work on steric effects.

Hydroboration. New York: W. A. Benjamin, 1962. Detailed description of the early work in hydroboration and the reactions of the organoboranes.

"Strained Transition States." In *The Transition State.* London: The Chemical Society, Special Publication No. 16, 1962: 140–158. First presented at a symposium in Sheffield, England, in April 1962.

With L. M. Stock. "A Quantitative Treatment of Directive Effects in Aromatic Substitution." In *Advances in Physical Organic Chemistry.* Vol. 1, edited by Victor Gold. London: Academic Press, 1963.

Boranes in Organic Chemistry. Ithaca, NY: Cornell University Press, 1972. A distillation of his Baker Lectures at Cornell University in 1969. Contains an autobiographical introduction and organized treatments of almost all of his research prior to 1970.

Organic Syntheses via Boranes. New York: John Wiley, 1975. Essentially a "how to" book for chemists, covering the formation and utilization of organoboranes. Contains short overviews of the synthesis and reactions of organoboranes and specific procedures for many syntheses.

The Nonclassical Ion Problem. New York: Plenum Press, 1977. Brown's view of the problem, with commentary and rebuttal by Paul von R. Schleyer.

"From Little Acorns to Tall Oaks—From Boranes through Organoboranes." Nobel Lecture, 8 December 1979. Available from http://nobelprize.org/chemistry/laureates/1979/brown-lecture.pdf

"The Nonclassical Ion Problem: Twenty Years Later." *Pure and Applied Chemistry* 54 (1982): 1783–1796.

OTHER SOURCES

Bartlett, Paul D., ed. *Nonclassical Ions: Reprints and Commentary.* New York: W. A. Benjamin, 1965. An overview of the nonclassical ion problem through a collection of literature reprints and commentary by Bartlett, one of the most important and most respected physical organic chemists.

Brewster, James H. "Herbert C. Brown—A Biographical Note." In *Aspects of Mechanism and Organometallic Chemistry: A*

Volume in Honor of Professor Herbert C. Brown, edited by James H. Brewster. New York: Plenum Press, 1978.

Brown, Weldon G. "Reductions by Lithium Aluminum Hydride." In *Organic Reactions,* edited by Roger Adams. Vol. 6. New York: John Wiley, 1951.

Cooper, K. A., E. D. Hughes, C. K. Ingold, and B. J. McNulty. "Mechanism of Elimination Reactions. Part VI. Introduction to a Group of Papers. Unimolecular Olefin Formation from *tert*-Butyl and *tert*-Amyl-sulfonium Salts." *Journal of the Chemical Society* (1948): 2038–2042. First of ten papers in this issue of the journal. Paper XVI, the final paper in this series, discusses the mechanisms of elimination reactions in great detail.

Finholt, Albert E., A. C. Bond Jr., and Hermann I. Schlesinger. "Lithium Aluminum Hydride, Aluminum Hydride and Lithium Gallium Hydride and Some of Their Applications in Organic and Inorganic Chemistry." *Journal of the American Chemical Society* 69 (1947): 1199–1203.

Hughes, Edward D., Christopher Kelk Ingold, and V. J. Shiner Jr. "Mechanism of Elimination Reactions. Part XVII. The Comparative Unimportance of Steric Strain in Unimolecular Olefin Eliminations." *Journal of the Chemical Society* (1953): 3827–3832.

Winstein, S., and Daniel S. Trifan. "The Structure of the Bicyclo[2,2,1]2-heptyl (Norbornyl) Carbonium Ion." *Journal of the American Chemical Society* 71 (1949): 2953.

Leon B. Gortler

BRUNO, GIORDANO

BRUNO, GIORDANO (*b.* Nola, Italy, 1548; *d.* Rome, Italy, 17 February 1600), *philosophy, physics, cosmology.* For the original article on Bruno see *DSB,* vol. 2.

Bruno was slow to gain recognition for his scientific contributions for two reasons. First, he was condemned to the stake for his heretical theological views, and this led to efforts to expunge all traces of his works from public memory (*damnatio memoriae*). Hence, his works tended to be forgotten. Second, his conception of Nature was not mechanistic. He even took an interest in natural magic as a way to understand Nature. These aspects of his thinking have led historians of science, who tend to view the development of science as the development of mechanistic philosophy, to consider Bruno as more philosopher and magus than scientist. Yet between 1584 and 1588–1591, Bruno was the first to propose a scientific theory of the relativity of motion, spatial lengths, and time intervals.

An Infinite Universe. Bruno assented to the Copernican world system, but he went beyond it. He eliminated all the celestial spheres, to which celestial bodies were considered bound. He gave a physical basis to the new astronomical system: His alternative to Aristotelian physics was the medieval theory of impetus. To this theory he added a

Giordano Bruno. *Giordano Bruno, circa 1590.* HULTON
ARCHIVE/GETTY IMAGES

atomistic physics and cosmology, and Tycho Brahe's new astronomical observations of comets. Bruno himself argued that the stars only seem fixed because of their distance from people on Earth, and hence that the fixity of the stars cannot be used to show that the universe is finite. He also argued that mathematical abstractions can never correspond to physical measures and to physical reality. He thus countered mathematical arguments for a finite universe.

Relativity of Motion. According to Bruno, the motions of celestial bodies are not really circular, but rather are completely free in infinite ethereal space. Each body has a dynamic consistency, determined by that body's own impetus, and is in motion in infinite space, as there are no bodies at rest. Moreover, there is no mathematical or physical center to the universe. Because no body is at rest, it is impossible to give an absolute measure of motion. Consequently, all motions are relative.

In *The Ash Wednesday Supper* (*La cena de le ceneri*, 1584, dialogue 3), Bruno sought to prove the Copernican system by arguing for the relativity of motion on a ship, an example already used in a simpler form by Jean Buridan, Nicole d'Oresme, Nicholas of Cusa, and Galileo Galilei. The relativity of motion considered by Bruno was based on the idea that everything belonging to a system participates in the motion of the system in such a way that any motion (uniform or nonuniform, rectilinear or curvilinear) without rotation does not modify any phenomenon. One cannot feel the Earth revolving around the Sun, because this motion does not affect phenomena. Rotations make a difference, but they are intrinsically relative motions among the different parts of the body. Bruno also argued that gravity is relative, giving a sort of principle of dynamic general relativity.

Galileo, in his *Dialogue Concerning the Two Chief World Systems, Ptolemaic and Copernican* (*Dialogo sopra i due massimi sistemi del mondo*, 1632), repeated some of Bruno's arguments, but he never quoted him because Bruno was condemned by the Inquisition. Hence, people must attribute the principle of the relativity of motion to Bruno, not Galileo.

Relativity of Time and Space. The relativity of time follows from an infinite universe, as Bruno discussed in *The Abruptly Ended Discourse in the College of France* (*Camoeracensis Acrotismus* 1588, XXXVIII) and *The Immense Universe, the Numberless and Figureless Worlds* (*De innumerabilibus, immenso et infigurabili* 1591, VII.7). According to Aristotelian and medieval definitions, time is physically and cosmically given by the motion of the eighth sphere of fixed stars, because this motion is perfectly uniform, continuous, and simple, as required by a

dynamic atomism. Atoms, or monads, are not purely material and inert, but have power and form, as Democritus asserted. The vacuum is not empty but full of ether.

Since the thirteenth century the Church had condemned many points of Aristotelian physics, and a Christian natural philosophy of a sort had tentatively been constructed. Christian theology progressively deconstructed Aristotelian physics and cosmology by arguing from the standpoint of God's absolute power (*de potentia Dei absoluta*). According to Bruno, the power of God's love is actually infinite, and so the creation must be actually infinite, that is, made of living worlds and atoms, full of powers, without limit. Atomism and Christian theology thus led Bruno to conceive of the universe as infinite.

After the Reform had destroyed the univocal Catholic interpretation of the Bible, Bruno argued that the Bible gives people only ethical indications and no scientific truth about the universe. Bruno also had scientific reasons for holding that the universe is infinite. These include his definition of time. If the universe is infinite, there are no spheres at all, and hence there is no privileged, perfectly uniform, continuous motion for the definition of time. The universe contains infinite motions, any one of which could be used for the definition of time. Since motion is used to measure time intervals, different motions define different, nonhomogeneous proper times. Motion affects time. Thus, the relativity of motion implies the relativity of time.

The relativity of space is already implicit in the notion that space is infinite and lacks a center, but for Bruno, spatial lengths and distances are also relative. He argued for this position in *Camoeracensis Acrotismus* (1588, XXVII, XXXII, XXXIV, XXXV, XXXVII), *De innumerabilibus, immenso et infigurabili* (1591, IV.6), and *The Threefold Minimum and the Measure* (*De triplici minimo et mensura* 1591, II.5). Bruno started from a radical epistemological critique of measurability: motion affects, and places limits on, exact measurements. Measurements of space under different conditions of motion imply different spatial lengths. Hence, lengths are relative.

Galileo followed only Bruno's idea that motion is relative, and only when motion is limited to uniform motion and relativity is considered as kinematic relativity, and not as dynamic relativity. Bruno's general dynamic relativity was followed only by Gottfried Wilhelm Leibniz. In different perspectives, Bruno's dynamic relativity was reconsidered, through Leibniz's influence, by Henri Poincaré in his special relativistic dynamics and, through the influence of Poincaré, Benedict de Spinoza, and Ernst Mach, by Albert Einstein in his theory of general relativity.

SUPPLEMENTARY BIBLIOGRAPHY

Italy's Instituto Nazionale di Studi sul Rinascimento has devoted a Web site to Giordano Bruno, available from http://giordanobruno.signum.sns.it/, that includes a bibliography of Bruno's work. A complete archive of Bruno's texts in Latin and in the vernacular, including indexes, is also available from this site, at http://giordanobruno.signum.sns.it/bibliotecaideale/.

Giannetto, Enrico R. A. "La relatività del moto e del tempo in Giordano Bruno." *Physis* 38 (2001): 305–336.

———. "Giordano Bruno and the Origins of Relativity." In *Albert Einstein, Chief Engineer of the Universe: One Hundred Authors for Einstein,* edited by J. Renn. New York: Wiley, 2005.

Enrico R. A. Giannetto

BUDKER, GERSH ITSKOVICH (*b.* Murafa, Vinitsk, Ukraine, 1 May 1918; *d.* Akadem-

gorodok, Novosibirsk, U.S.S.R., 4 July 1977), *high energy physics, plasma physics, controlled thermonuclear synthesis, particle accelerators.*

Budker was a leading specialist in high-energy physics whose colliding-beam accelerators revolutionized the efforts of experimentalists to understand subatomic structures and processes, and whose research institute at Akademgorodok, near Novosibirsk, Siberia, was a major center of nuclear physics.

Budker came from a poor rural Jewish family in the Vinitsk region of Ukraine, the son of an agricultural laborer who was shot by partisans during the civil war. Budker did not know his father, Itsak, who died a few months after he was born. He was raised by his mother, Rachel, and his grandmother. Budker was not very religious, but lived in and knew Jewish culture. He distinguished himself in school and as a ninth grader managed to complete his first scientific work under future Nobel laureate Igor Tamm at Moscow State University on the problem of the source of the energy-impulse tensor of an electromagnetic field in moving media. During his university entrance interview the 17-year-old was asked to explain the current food problems in the U.S.S.R. Always outspoken on a variety of issues, rather than hide his sentiments, he answered "collectivization" which had caused the deaths of millions of peasants in Ukraine due to famine. His entrance to the Physics Department was delayed by one year.

In the 1930s, Moscow State University was the site of ideological intrigues between scientists who accepted quantum mechanics and relativity theory, and those who questioned the epistemological issues raised by these fields of physics. They believed the new physics was incompatible with the Soviet philosophy of science, dialectical materialism. The intrigues led to the firing, arrest, and in some cases execution of scientists. Budker fortunately worked with Tamm, an active defender of the new physics.

Budker graduated in 1941, taking his last examination on 23 June, two days after the Germans had invaded the U.S.S.R. Budker immediately joined the army, and served in the Far East. After the war, Budker and other talented young scientists were conscripted into nuclear research. Budker joined Tamm and others connected with the theoretical department of Laboratory No. 2 (later the well-known Kurchatov Institute for Atomic Energy, and subsequently called the Russian Research Centre Kurchatov Institute), the lead institute in the atomic bomb project. Budker studied under Arkady B. Migdal. From the start Budker revealed a varied spectrum of interests. He undertook a series of studies on the theory of uranium-graphite lattices and other research important to the design of reactors. He conducted these experiments on the first Soviet reactor, the F-1.

VEP-1. *The first The first Soviet electron-electron storage ring, VEP-1. Construction started in Moscow, moved to Novosibirsk in 1962, and in 1965 was giving results on electron-electron scattering. There are two rings, each of 43 cm radius. The "equivalent energy" was 100 GeV.* **COURTESY OF BUDKER INSTITUTE OF NUCLEAR PHYSICS.**

Owing to plans for the construction of a massive new proton accelerator in Dubna on the Volga River (now the Joint Institute of Nuclear Research) under Vladimir Veksler, Budker grew interested in high-energy physics and finished a paper that provided a new way to generate a proton stream, for which he received a State Prize in 1949. He studied how to use the tracks left in bubble chambers to demonstrate the presence of various subatomic processes. He also began to consider the physics of relativistic plasmas, research important to accelerator technology and thermonuclear reactors that contributed to the development of so-called open "magnetic traps" as devices for controlled thermonuclear synthesis (fusion). Igor Kurchatov welcomed Budker's participation in work on the fusion problem. Only thirty years old, Budker had already distinguished himself as an outstanding, original thinker. Budker's work on relativistic plasmas of electrons and ions gained attention of the world scientific community at the Geneva Conference for the Peaceful Uses of Atomic Energy (1956).

At this time Stalinist policies directly interfered with Budker's career. In the late 1940s, Joseph Stalin apparently prepared for another major purge, in this case having singled out Jews. The secret police chief, Lavrenty Beria, claimed to have uncovered a plot by Jewish doctors to poison Kremlin leaders (the "Doctors' Plot"). All Jews came under suspicion in all walks of life. Anti-Semitism was rife. It had been a central feature of life in the empire under the tsars, and had been growing again since the early 1930s. Jews faced official and unofficial quotas that restricted their access to higher education. They had gravitated to mathematics and physics as two relatively new fields with greater opportunities for entry. But in the environment of the Doctors' Plot, Budker and a number of other promising young researchers were prohibited from working on secret nuclear topics. Beria suddenly dropped Budker from fusion research in 1951 or 1952. It was later claimed that Beria had Budker's dossier in his office safe, having it ready for the moment when he might arrest the physicist on trumped up charges but that Kurchatov had intervened personally to protect him.

Denied access to this research program, Budker instead used the opportunity to create his own group of theoreticians whose focus was the creation of a betatron-type accelerator that had the advantages of using direct current and producing a large stream of electrons. But Budker recognized that these machines also had significant limitations and eventually turned to the design of accelerators with colliding beams of charged particles. This led to the VEP-1 accelerator, built in the Siberian city of science, Akademgorodok, and a series of other more powerful colliding-beam accelerators that rivaled those in the west.

In order to understand the ultimate constituents of matter, physicists developed various machines – particle accelerators – to enable them to produce such charged particles as electrons, positrons, ions, protons and antiprotons moving at high energies. They used charged particles produced in bunches, utilizing electromagnetic forces to accelerate them. Initially, they smashed these particles into fixed targets to produce other smaller particles using such devises as cyclotrons, synchrotrons and betatrons. Later they turned to colliding beams of particles that they smashed into each other. One of Budker's major innovations was colliding beam accelerators. Along with such physicists as Austrian Bruno Touschek, who suggested injecting particles and antiparticles into a particle accelerator in different directions, then colliding them, Budker had advanced an idea to increase significantly the energy available for particle annihilations. Colliding beam machines had the advantage not only of higher interaction energies, but permitted experiments to be performed in extremely clean conditions. That is, observed interactions were not contaminated by the presence of secondary interactions as in the conventional fixed target machines.

Physicists produced particles in the accelerators in bunches. The goal in each machine was to increase "luminosity," that is, increase the number of ions in each bunch and the revolution frequency, and/or by decreasing the bunch area. There were several major problems that faced physicists as they strove to reach higher energies. One is the fact that when two bunches of charged particles collide there is a very low probability of a collision of two particles. In the late 1940s and early 1950s, scientists built "strong focusing" machines to increase luminosity. One of those machines was built in Dubna, Russia, under Vladimir Veksler. Veksler's work encouraged Budker's interest in high energy physics, especially after he was temporarily denied access to nuclear weapons research by Beria.

In 1956, at the suggestion of Igor Kurchatov, head of the Soviet atomic bomb project and Laboratory 2, the mathematician Mikhail Lavrentev asked Budker to move to a new, planned city of science, Akademgorodok. Soviet leader Nikita Khrushchev had triggered de-Stalinization reforms with a so-called "Secret Speech" at the Twentieth Communist Party Congress in 1956. The de-Stalinization reforms extended to the scientific establishment. They included an effort to give greater autonomy to specialists, improve their productivity by several measures, and restore the importance of basic research. The scientific establishment grew rapidly. Leading personnel of the Soviet Academy of Sciences pushed to create a series of new research centers or science cities outside Moscow, Leningrad, and Kiev, Ukraine, and also outside the military research establishment. The major such science city, Akademgorodok, located 35 kilometers south of Novosibirsk in Siberia, brought together scientists in over twenty new institutes built in what had been a pine forest. Lavrentev selected Budker to direct the Institute of Nuclear Physics.

Given the impediments to their research in bureaucracy and political interference, Soviet scientists were quite productive. Indeed they were leaders in a number of fields, such as fusion and high-energy physics, in which Budker worked. Another impediment to novel scientific research was that entire fields of Soviet science might be dominated by one or two scientists at one or two major institutes. Budker no doubt sensed that intellectually he might have difficulty in pursuing his research interests in Moscow where well-established scientists held great authority and had the power of the purse. The construction of modern accelerators, which Budker realized would require open spaces, would also be prohibited at the Kurchatov Institute. Finally, Budker was an impetuous, outspoken, and irreverent individual whose personality offended some of the more stodgy administrators and scientists in Moscow. Hence he had no doubts about the appropriateness of moving to Akademgorodok, where he might establish an institute where he had great latitude to set scientific directions, even though the institute would have to be built literally from scratch.

The Institute of Nuclear Physics was the leading institute in Akademgorodok in terms of size and authority. Massive even by Soviet standards, it covered several hundred hectares, had four particle accelerators, a foundry with cranes and other equipment, and several fusion devices. At its peak the institute had three thousand employees including thirty-five doctors of science and 130 candidates of science. Within a few years of its founding, in terms of publications, productivity, size, and reputation, it rivaled the other major nuclear research centers in the U.S.S.R.: the Leningrad Physical Technical Institute, the Ukrainian Physical Technical Institute in Kharkov, the Joint Center for Nuclear Research in Dubna, the Institute of High Energy Physics in Serpukhov south of Moscow, the Kurchatov Institute for Atomic Energy, and several military centers. In many respects it was the equivalent of a national laboratory in the United States or of CERN (Organisation Européenne Recherche Nucléaire) the major center in Europe.

Budker had three major foci of research (as did his institute). One was open thermonuclear systems. This research grew out of initial proposals of Tamm and Andrei Sakharov to create a toroidal magnetic thermonuclear reactor or tokamak. Budker suggested the idea of a direct axisymmetric magnetic system with enhanced magnetic fields at its ends (the "probkotron"). Although presented four years later because of secrecy restrictions, Budker's first paper on open traps (1954) made quite an impression at the second Geneva conference on Peaceful Uses of Atomic Energy (1958). The fusion of lighter particles, ions or atoms, say deuterium, into heavier particles, for example lithium, releases tremendous quantities of energy. Budker's theoretical and experimental investigations considered how to contain a plasma of the lighter particles in a reactor, fuse them into heavier ones, and transform the energy produced into electricity. Several experimental devices were built in Akademgorodok.

Since the Kurchatov and Ioffe institutes worked on tokamaks, other institutes focused on alternatives: the Physics Institute of the Academy of Sciences in Moscow, the Ukrainian Physical Technical Institute in Kharkov; and Budker's institute. Budker and his group focused on various open-trap, multicell, multimirror machines where the plasma is created by the injection of fast molecular ions into a chamber. Such physicists as Dmitrii Riutov, Eduard Krugliakov, and Roald Sagdeev developed the theoretical foundations for this work.

Budker's institute also worked on industrial applications for electron accelerators. The applications included improving insulating properties of polyethylene (with customers in the cable industry), production of artificial leather, disinfestation of grain, disinfection of waste water, and cutting and welding of metal. Along these lines institute workers built synchrotron radiation sources (storage rings of relativistic electrons) and detection equipment. Officials supported Budker's expansion of production facilities for these accelerators for they viewed them as a symbol of a healthy relationship between science and production, while Budker recognized the importance of the production facilities in generating income to build still larger accelerators. Applications resulted in x-ray metallography, holography, structural analysis, spectroscopy, microscopy, and in isomers and geology.

The major focus of Budker's work, and that which earned the institute's and his own reputation, was the construction, perfection, and operation of increasingly large and powerful colliding-beam accelerators that attracted researchers from around the nation. Budker's discoveries led to a Lenin Prize and other awards, however not the Nobel Prize. In 1976, Burton Richter (at Stanford) and Samuel C. C. Ting (at Brookhaven) shared the Nobel Prize for the use of colliding beams of high-energy electrons and positrons to discover the J/psi particle. Many Soviet—and western—physicists have argued that Budker ought to have shared in the prize for his pioneering work on accelerators using electron-positron colliding-beam experiments. Another important idea from Budker was electron cooling of proton beams, proposed in 1966, developed and tested in 1974 in his institute, and adopted and tested at such facilities as the European Center for Nuclear Research (CERN) and the Fermi National Accelerator Laboratory in Batavia, Illinois. In the early 2000s the Budker Institute continued to play a leading role in this research.

Budker claimed that western physicists would never have been able to perform in the environment of restrictions, secrecy, and bureaucratic impediments that faced Soviet physicists. He joked that the CERN accelerator, which straddles the boundary between Switzerland and France, would not operate in the U.S.S.R.: The charged particles going around the accelerator would have required a visa each time they crossed the border.

The revolutionary idea to use colliding beams of charged particles in accelerators was realized with some difficulty. The move from Moscow, the backwardness of industry, and bureaucracy slowed the efforts of Budker and his team. Yet in the twenty-five years that Budker was director, institute physicists made a number of important discoveries and measurements, including confirmation of quantum electrodynamics and more exact measurement of subatomic particles. The institute's first machine, the VEP-1, an electron-electron storage ring produced beams of particles in 1963 and electron-electron scatterings in 1964. The resulting particles produced in collisions, their energies and trajectories contributed to the creation of a theory called quantum electrodynamics, a quantum field theory of electromagnetic force, that explains how charged particles behave. Richard Feynman, Julian Schwinger, and Sin-itero Tomonaga developed this theory, for which they received a Nobel Prize in 1965.

Under Budker's direction, physicists next turned to electron-positron interactions, that were produced on the VEPP-2, on which physicists conducted the first experiments on elastic scattering of electrons at wide angles at energies of up to 700 MeV. and examined the instability of large currents in storage rings and accelerators based on the interaction of streams of particles. Electron-positron interactions were more difficult to produce, but given the zero charge of the reactions all energy and mass were devoted to the formation of new particles. VEPP-2 experiments on particle decay ran until 1970, when the accelerator was turned into an electron and positron booster for the VEPP-2M on which over fifteen years physicists have looked at processes occurring during electron-positron annihilation. While the VEPP-2M collider, the world's first electron-positron phi-Factory (1975), had the lowest energy range of among similar machines in the world, its luminosity enabled it to remain the main, if not only supplier of electron-positron physics results in the range of 150 to 700 MeV. Next was the VEPP-3 series of experiments at high-energy intervals and measurement of the cross section of the creation of charged particles. As with its predecessor, the VEPP-3 was adopted as a booster for the VEPP-4, a 360-meter circumference electron-positron collider with energy to 5.5 GeV.

High energy physics was an area of intense competition between teams of researchers in different countries to assert scientific priority in publications, recognition and even Nobel Prizes. For example, Budker and his colleagues were well aware of the work of Italian teams who built electron-positron colliders after the suggestions of Touschek in Frascati, Italy, at the National Institute of Nuclear Physics, first the Anello d-Accumulazione (AdA) and later the ADONE colliding beam accelerators, and were able to stay ahead in many stages of the race especially after funding levels for the Italian teams could not maintained.

In addition to research using beams of electrons and positrons, Budker and his team developed colliders using beams of such heavy particles as ions, protons, and antiprotons. While ultimately not an entirely successful endeavor in reaching energies of 10 GeV for protons, Budker set forth two important innovations. One was the charge-exchange method of injection of protons which stabilizes protons in an equilibrium orbit in the accelerator and facilitates the storage of the maximum proton current. The second was electron cooling. Budker and Alexander Skrinskii proposed the possibility of attaining high luminosity proton-antiproton collisions by electron cooling. Electron cooling forms and stores dense narrow beams of heavy charged particles.

Budker first proposed the idea of electron cooling in 1966 that he described as a "damping method of the synchrotron and betatron oscillations of heavy particles" based on the effect of a sharp rise of the cross sections of heavy particle interactions with electrons at small relative velocities that he suggested would help to compress and accumulate proton and anti-proton bunches, leading to higher luminosity. Physicists tested this technique of injecting a beam of "cool" electrons into a straight-section orbit of a heavy charged particle beam to introduce an effective friction in his institute in 1974; the first electron cooler had a cooling length of 1 m. The time required for

cooling, expected to be several seconds turned out to be 0.1 s. The electron beam moved with the same average velocity as the ion or proton beam, absorbing the kinetic energy of the heavy particles (ions or protons). This technique enabled shrinking ion beams of extremely high phase-space density. The main results of the Budker group were the discovery, explanation, and theory of super-fast and ultra-deep cooling; record results reached at the NAP-M cooler ring of cooling time and temperatures, and longitudinal ordering of deeply cooled proton beams and consequent suppression of intra-beam scattering. Many physicists were skeptical of Budker's idea of electron cooling. But he insisted upon following this possibility, even though it meant giving up his own project on a relativistic stabilized electron beam that was well advanced. Another way to increase luminosity by minimizing bunch area was to reduce the energy of the transverse motion or cooling, which requires some friction force. In electron-positron rings synchrotron radiation supplies the friction. For protons and ions, friction must be added. Simon van der Meer at CERN developed stochastic cooling for the SPS collider.

Many storage rings were built for synchrotron radiation. Budker saw an opportunity here to remove this radiation from machines especially for applications in biology because of its fine resolution, and in x-ray imaging for solid state physics and material science. Budker's institute then developed, designed and sold high power accelerators for technological applications, some of them in serial production, with ninety of them operating abroad including in Japan, German, Poland, China and Korea with power ranges from 20 kW to 100 kW, and energy from 0.7 MeV to 3 MeV.

The decision to use the VEPP-3 as a booster followed a pattern used in high energy research at accelerator facilities around the world. His colleagues at the institute claimed that Budker was fond of saying, "a physicist must also be an engineer." Second, Budker's institute encountered increasingly tight budgets as other institutes and teams of physicists embarked on research with expensive large-scale equipment. Scientists at Serpukhov, Gatchina (outside of Leningrad), Erevan (Armenia), and Kharkov (Ukraine) were building large accelerators, which made it more difficult to attract young talented physicists to the institute than it had been during its founding years. Third, teams of foreign scientists had moved beyond the parameters of the VEPP-3, so it made sense to move as quickly as possible to the VEPP-4. On the VEPP-4, researchers conducted experiments on mu, pi and v mesons and on symmetry nonconservation, and achieved results that reflected rapid progress in the field of high-energy physics at Stanford, DESY (the Deutsches Elektronen Synchrotron, outside of Hamburg), CERN, the French high-energy research facility Orsay, and elsewhere.

A democratic approach characterized Budker's administrative style. Much of the research and funding for Budker's institute came from the Ministry of Middle Machine Building, the ministry responsible for nuclear weapons. Budker hated the secrecy and bureaucracy of the ministry and sought another atmosphere. In all of the days of Budker's directorship, the institute had only one secretary and, unlike most Soviet scientific administrators, it was a simple matter to see Budker. One only had to drop in.

Budker was extremely hard working and openly critical. He offered penetrating analysis of other researchers' work on the spot, but meant nothing personal by it. He expected similar hard-hitting and open discussion within the walls of the Institute of Nuclear Physics. Every day at noon scientists gathered at the "round table" for a meeting of the academic council where they would hash out scientific, administrative, and other issues openly. In part, this openness was the essence of Akademgorodok, distant from Moscow and Leningrad and close scrutiny by Party officials of research activities and social issues both in physical and psychological senses. In Akademgorodok under the leadership of the physicists, scientists opened informal and formal social clubs where they discussed political issues, opened art exhibitions, and held festivals of folk singers that were impossible elsewhere in the country. Among the physicists who worked at or began their careers with Gersh Budker were Spartak T. Beliaev, Roald Z. Sagdeev, and Alexander N. Skrinsky.

In his last years, suffering from poor health, Budker declined to sign official Academy of Sciences condemnations of Andrei Sakharov for the latter's outspoken criticism of Soviet human rights violations. There were rumors that Budker would have been removed from directorship of his institute had not a heart attack killed him in 1977.

In addition to being a scientific leader and an administrator, Budker was also an educator who welcomed the opportunity to teach at Novosibirsk University. He taught at the university (created new along with Akademgorodok) from its first days. He participated in so-called Olympiads of school children created to identify the most promising students for entry into the university and then the institutes of Akademgorodok.

Budker was neither an experimentalist nor a theoretician, neither a scientist nor an administrator, but all four, and as such he oversaw the successful creation of a huge scientific enterprise with several directions of activity. Although budgetary problems buffeted the institute after the breakup of the U.S.S.R. in 1991, Budker's legacy persisted in the Budker Institute of Nuclear Physics which remained in the early twenty-first century one of the world's leading centers of high energy physics.

BIBLIOGRAPHY

WORK BY BUDKER

"Relativistic Self-Stabilized Electron Beam." [*in Russian*] Doctoral Thesis, Institute of Nuclear Physics, Akademgorodok, Novosibirsk, Siberia, 1958.

Proceedings of International Symposium on Electron and Positron Storage Rings. Saclay, France. (1966): Article II-1-1.

With G. Dimov and Vadim Dudnikov. *Proceedings of International Symposium on Electron and Positron Storage Rings,* Saclay, France. (1966): Article VIII-6-1.

"Effective Method of Damping of Particle Oscillations in Proton and Antiproton Accumulators." *Soviet Atomic Energy* 22 (1967): 346–348.

With G. Dimov and Vadim Dudnikov. "Experimental Investigation of the Intense Proton Beam Accumulation in Storage Ring by Charge-Exchange Injection Method." *Soviet Atomic Energy* 22 (1967): 384.

"Experimental Study of Electron Cooling." English from Russian paper IYaF-76-33. Upton, NY: Brookhaven National Laboratory, 1976.

With Alexander N. Skrinsky. "Electron Cooling and New Possibilities in Elementary Particle Physics." *Soviet Physics—Uspekhi* 21 (1978): 277–296.

OTHER SOURCES

Courant, Ernest David, Milton Stanley Livinston, H. S. Snyder. "The Strong-Focusing Synchrotron—A New High Energy Accelerator." *Physical Review* 88 (1952): 1190–196.

Dikansky, Nikolai S., Igor N. Meshkov, Alexander N. Skrinsky. "Electron Cooling and its Applications in Elementary Particle Physics." *Nature* 276 (21 December 1978): 763–767.

Josephson, Paul. *New Atlantis Revisited.* Princeton, NJ: Princeton University Press, 1997.

Parkhomchuk Vasily V., et al. "Electron Cooling: Physics and Prospective Applications." *Reports on Progress in Physics* 54, no. 7 (July 1991): 919–947.

Parkhomchuk, Vasily V., Alexander N. Skrinsky. "Electron Cooling: 35 Years of Development," *Soviet Physics—Uspekhi* 43, no. 5 (2000): 433–452.

Shafranov, V. D. "The Initial Period in the History of Nuclear Research at the Kurchatov Institute." *Physics–Uspekhi* 44, no. 8 (2001): 835–843.

Skrinsky, Alexander N., ed. *Akademik G. I. Budker. Ocherki. Vospominaniia.* Novosibirsk: Nauka, 1988. English version: *G. I. Budker: Reflections and Remembrances,* edited by Boris N. Breizman and James W. Van Dam. Woodbury, NY : AIP Press, 1994. Contains a list of Budker's publications and some of Budker's writings.

Zimmermann, Frank. "Review of Single Bunch Instabilities Driven by an Electron Cloud." *Physical Review Special Topics—Accelerators and Beams* 7 (2004): 124801 [36 pages].

Paul Josephson

BUFFON, GEORGES-LOUIS LE-CLERC, COMTE DE

(*b.* Montbard, France, 7 September 1707; *d.* Paris, France, 16 April 1788), *natural history, natural philosophy, probability theory, biogeography, Enlightenment philosophy.* For the original article on Buffon see *DSB,* vol. 2.

This article summarizes the new scholarship and new lines of interpretation that emerged since the original *DSB* article by Jacques Roger in 1970. In this period of time several major studies have appeared, a new recognition of Buffon's place in Enlightenment thought has been established, and the field of the history of natural history has developed considerably.

The author defines five defined areas of transformation in Buffon scholarship since the original article. Buffon has been repositioned as a major scientific figure of Enlightenment science. Strong arguments have been advanced for a deeper coherence and unity in Buffon's thought. A fuller contextualization of Buffon's thought within the institutions of late eighteenth-century French science and culture has taken place. A new level of understanding of Buffon's reception outside Parisian circles has been attained. Several interpretive issues provide opportunities for new research into the sources of his thought, the nature of his larger program in natural history and natural philosophy, and the reception of his work.

Reevaluating Buffon in Scientific History. Jacques Roger's original article appeared at a time when he was the leading interpreter of Buffon's thought. Pioneered by his massive critical study of the *Buffon: Les Époques de la nature* (1962, 1988), and followed shortly by his *Les sciences de la vie* (1963, 1993, 1997a), Roger's scholarship considerably advanced the reexamination of Buffon's work commenced by French scholars in the 1950s (Heim, 1952; Piveteau, 1954). Roger's work differed from this earlier scholarship through his development of several interpretive theses he continued to expand until his death in 1990. Culminating in a scientific biography that replaced others written since 1970 (Fellows and Milliken, 1972; Gascar, 1983), Roger presented a sustained argument for granting Buffon a major place in the history of science and in the French Enlightenment. Roger's Buffon is an intellectual force on the level of Baron de Montesquieu and Jean-Jacques Rousseau and a natural philosopher of major proportions in the class of Pierre-Louis Maupertuis, Alexis-Claude Clairaut, Leonhard Euler, Carolus Linnaeus, and Albrecht von Haller.

The success of Roger's repositioning of Buffon in the history of science depends, however, on the conception of science maintained by the historian. Buffon performed few experiments and those that he did had a long history of critique from commentators (Sloan, 1992a). Beginning almost immediately with his death, detractors preferred the detailed systematics of Linnaeus, the Jussieus, and Augustin-Pyrame deCandolle to the antitaxonomic approach of Buffon. In the historical sciences of Earth, the area where Roger placed the greatest emphasis, Buffon has still not been seen as equivalent in status to that of his younger contemporaries such as Jean-André De Luc, Horace-Bénédict de Saussure, and Abraham Gottlob Werner for the creation of the technical earth science of the nineteenth century (Taylor, 1992; Rudwick, 2005. The assessment of Buffon's early work in mathematics and probability theory has concluded that he was a minor, and not deeply original, contributor (Daston, 1988; Loveland, 2001a).

If Buffon is to warrant a substantial position in the history of science, careful consideration is required of his contributions to the sciences on an interpretive and theoretical level and of how these relate to the background of discussion on foundational questions. For Roger, Buffon was a primary creator of a new conceptual framework for the sciences of the earth, biogeography, anthropology, and comparative anatomy. This broke with the providentialism and design-argument natural theology that had long been associated with the natural-historical sciences. The foundations for this conceptual innovation remain, however, in need of further elaboration.

Roger emphasized through his works the claim that Buffon underwent a marked alteration in thought on many fundamental issues with the crucial transformation taking place in the mid-1760s. Prior to this period, Buffon was seen by Roger as still in search of some unifying principle of order. Roger also saw Buffon originally confined within a cyclical interpretation of history that discounted inquiry into origins. A newly developed appreciation for experiment, and an awareness of new empirical data is then seen as responsible for a marked development in Buffon's thought enabling him to step out in the 1760s into new conceptual territory. This new natural history was illustrated by the two *Vues de la nature* (1764–1765), the article "De la dégénération des animaux" (1766), and especially by the grand synthesis of *Buffon: Les Époques de la nature* of 1779. In the Roger interpretation, it was in this same period that Buffon broke with a cyclical view of history and embraced a linear historical view of natural history that extended the age of the earth in his private reflections to millions of years. This historical consciousness was also extended to the notion of the common historical origins of organic groups (Roger, 1992). A somewhat similar view of a major transformation in the 1760s has attributed this to Buffon's new appreciation of geography and his awareness of the irreversible theory of the earth's cooling. (Hodge, 1992). The thesis of a new historical consciousness in the later works has, however, been challenged (Eddy, 1994).

The Unity of Buffon's Program. Whereas the evidence for marked changes in Buffon's understanding of many issues in the 1760s is undeniable—the degeneration of species departs in dramatic ways from the claims of 1753 and the grand synthesis of the *Époques* is much more than a *Supplément* to the *Histoire et théorie de la terre* of 1749—the degree to which there is some deeper unity to Buffon's intellectual program requires careful analysis of the meaning of these evident changes. The author of this article has argued for such a unity, and a similar claim has been advanced in the recent detailed study of Buffon's philosophy by French scholar Thierry Hoquet (Hoquet, 2005b; Sloan, 1992b, 2006a). In contrast to the Roger thesis, these interpretations argue for the existence of continuity in Buffon's thought that dates from the 1740s. These foundations are seen as stable over time, but in creative interplay with an expanding body of empirical data. Buffon is seen on this interpretation to be developing a coherent project in the *Histoire naturelle* modeled on that of René Descartes: opening with a discourse on method and illustrating this method in action through specific empirical and theoretical studies. This program is expanded and developed through a long lifetime spent in working out the details of his system.

Such claims must, however, rest on some irreducible conjectures. Buffon unfortunately published no sustained arguments in support of a new theoretical program beyond the preliminary discourses to the *Histoire naturelle,* the *Histoire naturelle des oiseaux,* and the *Histoire naturelle des mineraux.* To this may be added occasional theoretical comments inserted into articles in the *Histoire naturelle,* with the theoretical treatises—*Essai d'arithmétique morale* (1777) and the *Époques of nature*—contained in the *Suppléments.* The absence of an illuminating archive of materials hampers efforts to move beyond these sources.

At least two issues require clarification. The first is that of Buffon's relation to the preexistent philosophical and scientific tradition at the time he began his move into natural history. Buffon's transition from an adjoint-*méchanicien* of the Académie, best known for his work on probability theory, to a major administrative position that made him a key figure in Enlightenment natural history can be viewed as a result of a political appointment within the complex patronage system of Bourbon France. But this migration also took place at a time when Buffon was wrestling with complex conceptual issues, particularly those surrounding the theoretical foundations of the calculus that occupied him during his translation of Isaac Newton's *Fluxions* (1740).

It is commonly claimed that Buffon can be located philosophically within the tradition of John Locke, Newton, and French sensationalism. But documentation of such affiliations is tenuous, and Buffon leaves few indications of his sources. The author of this article argued for the importance of the efforts to synthesize aspects of Newtonian and Wolffian philosophy by Buffon's acquaintances Maupertuis and especially by Gabrielle-Émilie de Bretueil, the Marquise du Châtelet-Lomont in the crucial period around 1740 (Sloan, 1992b; 2006a). This affiliation with French Leibnizianism illuminates several otherwise puzzling aspects of Buffon's original program. The eclecticism and the originality of Buffon's thought defies easy categorization or reduction to any one source of major derivation.

The second, related issue revolves around the meaning of his concept of physical truth in relation to his science. In the *Premi[è]er Discours* to the *Histoire naturelle* (1749), Buffon introduced his novel distinction of two orders of truth—*vérités mathématiques* and *vérités physiques.* He then proceeded to develop positions on epistemic questions that at least claimed to solve some of the pressing philosophical questions of mid-Enlightenment thought.

Buffon grounded his concept of physical truth on the succession of similar events that on repetition yielded an increasing degree of epistemic certainty. His arguments on this point seem to bear some fundamental connection to his exploration of probability theory commenced in the 1730s (Hanks, 1966; Sloan, 1987, 1992a; Loveland 2001a). This linkage between his explorations in the mathematics of probability to his notion of physical truth offers one way to understand the unity of Buffon's new approach to natural history. His theory of inductive probability, developed at length only in the *Essai d'arithmétique morale* in 1777, offered a quantitative means of estimating the link between past events and future occurrences. The author of this article claimed that a link between this theory and Buffon's emphasis after 1749 on the concept of physical truth provides a key to the understanding the meaning of his polemic against abstractions and his strong claims concerning the epistemic certitude of physical understanding of phenomena over that obtained through mathematical physics.

Assuming this as a theoretical foundation worked out in the early 1740s, the subsequent development of Buffon's program in natural history achieves some coherent unity. It allows for the changes of views on such issues as the interrelations among groups and even changes possible in time within physical species. It also gives a way of understanding his views on the interrelations of organisms and physical geography and the connection of the process of generation to the endurance of forms. Assuming this theoretical foundation also assists in understanding Buffon's realistic interpretation of Newtonian forces in relation to matter. It also can be related to his emphasis on the notions of relation and comparison, issues highlighted by Hoquet as the unifying theme of the *Histoire naturelle* (Hoquet, 2005b). But Buffon's failure to work out these claims in a sustained and systematic way leaves several uncertainties still to be resolved.

Buffon: Institutional Naturalist. Scholarship since 1970 has emphasized the issues of social role, institutions, and social context in the construction of science. The extension of such scholarship to the analysis of Buffon's position within the institutions of French science at the close of the ancien régime represents an important development. Roger Hahn's magisterial study of the Paris Académie royale des sciences (Hahn, 1971) supplied a detailed insight into the social history of one of the main scientific institutions with which Buffon was closely affiliated during his long intendancy of the Jardin du Roi. His social role has also been illuminated by several major studies (Corsi, 1988, 2001; Spary, 2000). The Revolutionary transformation of the Jardin into the *Muséum national d'histoire naturelle* in 1793, five years after Buffon's death, has been the focus of a major international symposium organized on the bicentennial of the Revolutionary period (Blanckaert et al., 1997). These studies permitted greater understanding of the continuities and differences between Buffon's approach to natural history and those of his successors—Bernard de Lacépède, Jean-Baptiste Lamarck, Georges Cuvier, Étienne Geoffroy Saint-Hilaire, Michel Adanson, Achilles Valenciennes, and the Jussieus. Buffon can now be situated within an institutional setting that helps explain some of his wide influence that also allows an understanding his intellectual independence from some of the defining traditions important within the Académie des sciences. This gives some historical explanation of the reasons why Buffon's natural history was markedly different from that practiced by his contemporaries within Parisian science affiliated more exclusively with the Académie des sciences.

Buffon's Reception. Reception studies since the 1960s considerably illuminated the understanding of the appropriation and reception of Buffon's works. Outside of Paris, the struggle between Buffonian and Linnaean natural history within France has been shown to have been more evenly matched than previously assumed (Duris, 1993). Studies by John Greene (Greene, 1992), Paul B. Wood (1987), and Jeff Loveland (2004a–b) illuminated primarily the Scottish and American receptions. Outside of Scotland, there still is a need for deeper understanding of the reasons which led to the failure to translate the *Premier discours* in any of the English editions of the *Natural History* (William Kenrick [London, 1775–1776]; William Smellie [Edinburgh, 1780–1785]; and J. S. Barr [London, 1797–1807], the reasons for the exclusion of Buffon's

George-Louis Buffon. *George-Louis Buffon, circa 1765.* HULTON ARCHIVE/GETTY IMAGES.

monumental *Buffon: Les Époques de la nature* from all English editions require further exploration.

Philosophically, the Germanies provided the most fertile home for Buffon's reflections, although more work is needed to develop this point. The translation of the *Histoire naturelle*, which commenced at Leipzig almost immediately, made this the only complete foreign translation of the first series of the *Histoire naturelle*, complete with the Louis-Jean-Marie Daubenton articles and plates in their original sequence. With the first two volumes prefaced by discourses by Buffon's great contemporary, Haller, Buffon was introduced to the German-speaking world through Haller's defense of the use of hypotheses in science. This situated Buffon's speculations in the first volumes on organic generation, the origins of the planetary system, and the causes of the varieties of human beings within a new conception of legitimate scientific reasoning. Concerning other German readings, Peter Reill detailed the importance of Buffon's reflections for the rise of historical thinking in the Germanies (Reill, 1992, 2005). The impact of Buffon's writings on Immanuel Kant's natural philosophy forms another area calling for additional work. Kant seems unique among Buffon's readers in his appreciation of Buffon's distinction between abstract and physical truth, and this distinction seems to be involved in Kant's important discrimination between the rival Linnaean and Buffonian programs of the description and history of nature (*Naturbeschreibung* and *Naturgeschichte*) (Sloan, 2006b). The impact of Buffon's *Époques* on Johann Herder's *Ideen zur Philosophie der Geschichte der Menscheit* and on Herder's formulation of a progressive history of nature and the history of humanity suggests Buffon's considerable importance for the rise of German historicism.

New Directions in Scholarship. The absence of a substantial manuscript and correspondence archive continues to hamper the development of the kind of historical scholarship that surrounds such figures as Galileo Galilei, Newton, and Charles Darwin. Primary Buffon scholarship must continue to depend largely on the analysis and interpretation of the printed sources. One expects no new perception of Buffon to emerge from intensive archival study similar to the revelations achieved from archival work on other major figures (Cohen, 1982).

The development of Buffon scholarship has resulted in inevitable subspecialization: Earth science (Taylor, 1992); anthropology (Blanckaert, 1992); systematics (Farber, 1982); biogeography (Larson, 1994); scientific rhetoric (Loveland, 2001b); and philosophy of science (Hoquet, 2005b; Grene and Depew, 2004). The Paris-Montbard-Dijon bicentennial commemoration of Buffon's death in France in 1988, organized under Jacques Roger's leadership, resulted in a major collection of interpretive studies on Buffon's importance that examined numerous aspects of his work. A new wave of commemorative scholarship will likely emerge from the tricentennial celebrations of Buffon's birth in 2007. The "*Other Buffon,*" which Jacques Roger sought to present to the public in 1970, has clearly achieved a new place in intellectual and scientific history.

SUPPLEMENTARY BIBLIOGRAPHY

A major Buffon Web site has been established at http://www.buffon.cnrs.fr under the auspices of the Centre national de la recherché scientifique (CNRS) in Paris under the direction of Pietro Corsi and Thierry Hoquet. This has made available a full electronically searchable text of the first edition of the Histoire naturelle, *including the* Histoire naturelle des oiseaux. *It is also a source of articles and discussions.*

WORKS BY BUFFON

The Natural History of Animals, Vegetables, and Minerals: With the Theory of the Earth in General. Translated by William Kenrick and John Murdoch. 6 vols. London: Bell, 1775–1776.

Buffon's Natural History: Containing a Theory of the Earth, a General History of Man, of the Brute Creation, and of Vegetables, Minerals, &c. &c. with Notes by the Translator. Translated by J. S. Barr. 10 vols. London: Symonds, 1797–1807.

Buffon: Oeuvres philosophiques. Edited by Jean Piveteau. Paris: Presses universitaires de France, 1954. This is a fundamental collection of primary texts.

Selections from Natural History, General and Particular. Translated by William Smellie. 2 vols. New York: Arno, 1977. These are reprints from the first Smellie translation of 1780–1785.

Un autre Buffon. Edited by Jacques-Louis Binet and Jacques Roger. Paris: Hermann, 1977. This is a short collection of primary texts, including the *Essai d'arithmétique morale,* the *Discours sur le style,* and other less commonly reprinted texts.

The Natural History, General and Particular. Translated William Smellie. 3rd ed., with an introduction by Aaron Garrett. 9 vols. Reprinted, London: Thoemmes Press, 2000. This is a reprinting of the final version of the Smellie translation of 1791.

OTHER SOURCES

Beaune, Jean-Claude, and Jean Gayon, eds. *Buffon 88: pour le bicentenaire de la mort de Buffon Actes du Colloque international Paris-Montbard-Dijon 14–22 juin 1988.* Paris: J. Vrin, 1992.

Blanckaert, Claude. "La valeur de l'homme: l'idée de la nature humaine chez Buffon." In *Buffon 88,* edited by Jean-Claude Beaune and Jean Gayon, 583–600. Paris: J. Vrin, 1992.

Blanckeart, Claude, Claudine Cohen, Pietro Corsi, et al., eds. *Le Muséum au premier siècle de son histoire.* Paris: Muséum national d'histoire naturelle, 1997.

Blanckeart, Claude, Jean-Louis Fischer, and Roselyne Rey, eds. "Bibliographie de Jacques Roger." In *Nature, Histoire, Société: Essais en hommage à Jacques Roger.* Paris: Klincksieck, 1995. A complete listing of all of Jacques Roger's writings, including his many articles and essays on Buffon.

Cohen, I. Bernard. "The Thrice-Revealed Newton." In *Editing Texts in the History of Science,* edited by Trevor Levere, 117–184. New York: Garland, 1982.

Corsi, Pietro. *The Age of Lamarck: Evolutionary Theories in France, 1790–1830.* Translated by Jonathan Mandelbaum. Berkeley: University of California Press, 1988. First published in Italian 1983. Revised French edition, *Lamarck: Genèse en enjeux du transformism: 1770–1830.* Paris: CNRS Éditions, 2001.

Daston, Lorraine. *Classical Probability in the Enlightenment.* Princeton, NJ: Princeton University Press, 1988.

Duris, Pierre. *Linné en France, 1750–1850.* Geneva: Droz, 1993.

Eddy, John H., Jr. "Buffon's *Histoire naturelle:* History? A Critique of Recent Interpretations." *Isis* 85 (1994): 644–661.

Farber, Paul L. *The Emergence of Ornithology as a Scientific Discipline: 1760–1850.* Dordrecht, Netherlands: Reidel, 1982.

Fellows, Otis, and Stephen Milliken. *Buffon.* New York: Twayne, 1972.

Gascar, Pierre. *Buffon.* Paris: Gallimard, 1983.

Genet-Varcin, Emilienne, and Jacques Roger. "Bibliographie de Buffon." In *Oeuvres philosophiques,* edited by Jean Piveteau in collaboration with Maurice Frechet and Charles Bruneau, 513–570. Paris: Presses universitaires de France, 1954. The fundamental beginning point for Buffon studies. Also available electronically from http://www.buffon.cnrs.fr/bibliographies

Greene, John. "Buffon en Amerique." In *Buffon 88*, edited by Jean-Claude Beaune and Jean Gayon, 681–688. Paris: J. Vrin, 1992.

Grene, Marjorie, and David Depew. *The Philosophy of Biology: An Episodic History.* Cambridge, U.K.: Cambridge University Press, 2004.

Hahn, Roger. *The Anatomy of a Scientific Institution: The Paris Academy of Sciences, 1666–1803.* Berkeley: University of California Press, 1971. Revised French edition, *L'anatomie d'une institution scientifique: l'Académie des sciences de Paris, 1666–1803.* Brussels, Belgium: Editions des Archives contemporaines, 1993.

Hanks, Lesley. *Buffon avant l'Histoire naturelle.* Paris: Presses universitaires de France, 1966.

Heim, Roger, ed. *Buffon.* Paris: Publications française, 1952.

Hodge, M. J. S. "Two Cosmogonies (Theory of the Earth and Theory of Generation) and the Unity of Buffon's Thought." In *Buffon 88*, edited by Jean-Claude Beaune and Jean Gayon, 241–254. Paris: J. Vrin, 1992.

Hoquet, Thierry. "Bibliographie." In *Buffon: histoire naturelle et philosophie.* Paris: Champion, 2005a, pp. 759–794. A valuable selective listing of major periodical articles, books, and other resources since 1860.

———. *Buffon: Histoire naturelle et philosophie.* Paris: Honoré Champion, 2005b.

Laron, Marie-Françoise. "Bibliographie de Buffon (1954–1991)." In *Buffon 88*, edited by Jean-Claude Beaune and Jean Gayon, 688–743. Paris: J. Vrin, 1992 An exhaustive listing of all new material since the Genet-Varcin-Roger bibliography until the publication of the 1992 commemorative volume.

Lanessan, Jean-Louis, ed. *Buffon: Correspondence générale.* 2 vols. Paris, 1885. Reprinted, Geneva: Slatkine, 1971.

Larson, James L. *Interpreting Nature: The Science of Living Nature from Linnaeus to Kant.* Baltimore, MD: Johns Hopkins University Press, 1994.

Loveland, Jeff. "Buffon, the Certainty of Sunrise, and the Probabilistic Reductio ad Absurdam." *Archive for the History of Exact Science* 55 (2001a): 465–477.

———. *Rhetoric and Natural History: Buffon in Polemical and Literary Context.* Oxford: Voltaire Foundation, 2001b.

———. "French Thought in William Smellie's Natural History: A Scottish Reception of Buffon and Condillac." In *Scotland and France in the Enlightenment*, edited by Deidre Dawson and Pierre, 192–217. Lewisburg, PA: Bucknell University Press, 2004a.

———. "George-Louis LeClerc de Buffon's *Histoire naturelle* in English, 1775–1815." *Archives of Natural History* 31 (2004b): 214–235.

Lyon, John, and Phillip R. Sloan, eds. *From Natural History to the History of Nature: Readings from Buffon and His Critics.* Notre Dame, IN: University of Notre Dame Press, 1981. A collection of translations of important articles from the early

volumes of the *Histoire naturelle,* reviews by contemporaries and other materials including the Haller prefaces.

Milliken, Stephen B. "Buffon and the British." PhD diss., Columbia University, 1965.

Reill, Peter H. "Buffon and Historical Thought in Germany and Great Britain." In *Buffon 88*, edited by Jean-Claude Beaune and Jean Gayon, 667–679. Paris: J. Vrin, 1992.

———. *Vitalizing Nature in the Enlightenment.* Berkeley: University of California Press, 2005.

Roger, Jacques, ed. *Buffon: Les Époques de la nature: Édition critique.* Memoires du muséum national d'historie naturelle, sciences de la terre 10. 1962. Reissued, Paris: Muséum national d'histoire naturelle, 1988.

———. *Les sciences de la vie dans la pensée française au xviiie siècle.* Paris: Colin, 1963. Reissued with a new historiographic essay by Roger, Paris: Albin Michel, 1993. Translated as *The Life Sciences in Eighteenth-Century French Thought.* Edited by Keith R. Benson and translated by Robert Ellrich. Stanford, CA: Stanford University Press, 1997a. This is a partial translation of Roger, 1963, lacking the final chapter on Diderot, but including the 1993 historiographic essay.

———. *Buffon: un philosophe au Jardin du roi.* Paris: Fayard, 1989. Published as *Buffon: A Life in Natural History,* translated by Sarah L. Bonnefoi. Ithaca, NY: Cornell University Press, 1997b.

———. "Buffon et l'introduction de l'histoire dans l'Histoire naturelle." In *Buffon 88*, edited by Jean-Claude Beaune and Jean Gayon, 193–205. Paris: J. Vrin, 1992.

Rudwick, Martin J. *Bursting the Limits of Time: The Reconstruction of Geohistory in the Age of Revolution.* Chicago: University of Chicago Press, 2005.

Sloan, Phillip R. "From Logical Universals to Historical Individuals: Buffon's Idea of Organic Species." In *Histoire du concept d'espèce dans les sciences de la vie*, edited by J.-L. Fischer and Jacques Roger, 101–140. Paris: Fondation Singer-Polignac, 1987.

———. "L'hypothétisme de Buffon: sa place dans la philosophie des sciences du dix-huitième siècle." In *Buffon 88*, edited by Jean-Claude Beaune and Jean Gayon, 207–222. Paris: J. Vrin, 1992a.

———. "Organic Molecules Revisited." In *Buffon 88*, edited by Jean-Claude Beaune and Jean Gayon, 415–438. Paris: J. Vrin, 1992b.

———. "Natural History." In *The Cambridge History of Eighteenth-Century Philosophy*, 2 vols, edited by Knud Haakonssen, 903–938. Cambridge, U.K.: Cambridge University Press, 2006a.

———. "Kant on the History of Nature: The Ambiguous Heritage of the Critical Philosophy for Natural History." *Studies in History and Philosophy of the Biological and Biomedical Sciences* 37 (2006b): 627 648.

Spary, Emma. *Utopia's Garden: French Natural History from Old Regime to Revolution.* Chicago: University of Chicago Press, 2000.

Taylor, Kenneth. "The Époques de la nature and Geology during Buffon's Later Years." In *Buffon 88*, edited by Jean-Claude Beaune and Jean Gayon, 371–385. Paris: J. Vrin, 1992.

Wood, Paul B. "Buffon's Reception in Scotland: The Aberdeen Connection." *Annals of Science* 44 (1987): 169–190.

Phillip R. Sloan

BULLOCK, THEODORE HOLMES

(*b.* Nanking, China, 16 May 1915; *d.* La Jolla, California, 19 December 2005), *comparative biology, neuroscience, neuroethology.*

Bullock had a career that spanned the development of twentieth-century neuroscience. Trained as a zoologist and comparative biologist, he was a key pioneer in the birth of the discipline of neuroethology—the study of the neural basis of naturally occurring animal behavior—as well as neuroscience more generally. Rather than being associated with a single scientific success, Bullock's contributions are as diverse as the biological world he studied. With a career that involved neurophysiological investigations into every taxonomic group of animals, he made important discoveries in nonhuman sensory physiology, created new tools and experimental techniques for neurophysiology, and expanded our understanding of how nerve cells communicate. But perhaps more than his role in generating this or that new datum point, Bullock was known throughout his career for his ability to synthesize what was currently understood and to set the agenda for future work. By presenting his fellow scientists with a clear and fair assessment of what is actually known and what was *not*, in fact, known—regardless of the prevailing *zeitgeist*—Bullock played a crucial role in the development of neuroscience and neuroethology.

Life and Times. One of four children of Presbyterian missionaries, Theodore ("Ted") Holmes Bullock was born in Nanking, China; and spent the first thirteen years of his life there before his family returned to Southern California in 1928, just prior to the Great Depression. He received his AB and his PhD (in zoology) from the University of California, Berkeley (in 1936 and 1940, respectively). His PhD work—on the nervous system of enteropneusts, also known as acorn worms, a group of organisms closely related to the chordates—was conducted under the supervision of S. F. Light. One benefit of his graduate stipend was finally feeling established enough to marry, and he did so, to Martha Runquist, who became his lifelong partner. After spending a number of years on the East Coast and in the Midwest, associated with both the Yale and University of Missouri Schools of Medicine and the Marine Biological Laboratory, he returned to the West Coast in 1946, joining the Zoology faculty at the University of California, Los Angeles

(UCLA). Finally, in 1966, he and Martha moved down the coast to the University of California, San Diego, to help Robert Livingston create the world's first Department of Neurosciences. It is with that department in the School of Medicine and with the Scripps Institution of Oceanography (where he directed the Neurobiology Unit) that he was associated for the final forty years of his research career. Although he had retired in 1982, Bullock was still actively publishing as an emeritus professor when he passed away of natural causes on 19 December 2005. He was survived by Martha, a son, a daughter, and five grandchildren.

Bullock had a long and rich research career that spanned seven decades. In the main, he was a comparative biologist who took neurophysiological phenomena as his traits of taxonomic comparison. Other comparative biologists take bone structure or, more recently, genetic markers, as their point of comparison across the different taxa. Bullock, however, was interested in what could be learned about evolution from the study of the diversity of nervous systems. This also led him into the field of neuroethology, with its comparative approach to the study of animal behavior and nervous systems.

His career was marked not by one or two significant discoveries or theoretical innovations, but by a large range of important work in the lab, in the field, in the classroom, and in the development of the discipline of neuroscience to which he was one of many midwives. However, there are highlights to his career that give one a flavor of his contributions to science.

Bullock, the Iconoclast. Bullock often embraced the role of heretic. For example, whereas the majority of those working in sensory physiology concentrated their attention on those senses enjoyed by humans, Bullock tackled senses of a nonhuman variety. During the 1950s at UCLA, Bullock, together with Friedrich Diecke and Raymond B. Cowles, investigated the pit organ of rattlesnakes, an organ located just below the eyes. Previous behavioral work had demonstrated that snakes with a pit organ were able to strike accurately at prey targets even when their eyes were covered. This behavior, together with previous anatomical discoveries, suggested the hypothesis that the pit organ mediated a unique modality of radiant heat perception independent of changes in ambient temperature; that is, that the pit organ was an infrared receptive sensory organ. Bullock and his colleagues confirmed this hypothesis by a careful study of the neurophysiology of pit organs of live rattlesnakes presented with a variety of controlled stimuli (Bullock and Cowles, 1952; Bullock and Diecke, 1956).

Bullock's love of the underappreciated or overlooked scientific hypothesis is also evident in his contributions to cellular neurophysiology. He challenged the ubiquity of the chemical synapse as the locus of communication between neurons. While he never denied the importance of the standard model of neural communication—whereby the arrival of an action potential at the axon terminal causes the release of neurotransmitter chemicals into the synaptic cleft leading to changes in the electrical state of the postsynaptic neuron—he incessantly urged his colleagues not to be blind to other potential means of communication between neurons. For example, while working with Bullock, Akira Watanabe discovered the existence of direct electrical connections between neurons in cardiac ganglion of lobsters (Bullock and Watanabe, 1960). (Bullock's lab was where Susumu Hagiwara had carried out the first intracellular recordings in these neurons a few years earlier.) Later work revealed that they had inadvertently discovered a significant means of neural communication: gap junctions, in which electrical activity travels directly between conjoined cells, without chemical mediation. Interestingly, while some see this work as pointing to the later discovery of gap junctions, Bullock himself believed that there is more going on in the cardiac ganglion preparation. In addition to the presence of electrical synapses there, he also held that work from his lab indicated the presence of lower frequency electrical connections—so called slow potentials (Bullock, 1996).

In addition, Bullock is generally credited, along with his colleague Hagiwara, with the first discovery of electroreceptive sensory cells in electric fish (Bullock and Chichibu, 1965; Bullock et al., 1961). These cells had been suspected at least since Hans Lissmann had proposed in the 1950s that these fish possess a nonhuman sense of electric fields, but Bullock and colleagues were the first to establish what cells were carrying out this function (and thereby establishing that the sense existed [Keeley, 1999; Bullock, 1974]). This work was later taken up by his former postdoctoral student, Walter Heiligenberg, who is credited with making the electrosensory system of the weakly electric fish, *Eigenmannia,* one of the best understood vertebrate sensorimotor system in neurobiology (Bullock and Heiligenberg, 1986; Bullock et al., 2005).

Bullock, the Synthesizer. One example of Bullock's contribution to the then nascent field of neuroscience is his influential review titled "Neuron Doctrine and Electrophysiology" (1959). This paper documents "a quiet but sweeping revolution" (p. 998) in neurobiology, as a result of developments specifically from neurophysiology. According to Bullock's review, Santiago Ramón y Cajal's *Neuron Theory or Reticular Theory?* (Ramón y Cajal, 1954) asserted that, "the nerve cell and its processes, together called the neuron, form the cellular units of the nervous system which are directly involved in nervous function" (Bullock, 1959, p. 997). As Bullock's review spells out,

whereas Ramón y Cajal's doctrine is largely structural or anatomical in nature, contemporary work on the physiology of the nervous system has spurred change in key aspects of the doctrine as a functional or neurophysiological one. (Bullock himself was a key innovator of techniques, experimental preparations, and methods in neurophysiology.) Bullock's review crystallized then nascent concepts such as that: the nerve impulse (now known as an "action potential") is a special property of neuronal axons, not the cell as a whole; impinging excitation does not become nerve impulse directly but spreads to special firing zones; distal dendrites may not affect firing of a given neuron, but may influence other neurons through local graded potentials (Watanabe's discovery in Bullock's lab, discussed above, motivated this proposal); and that multiple integrative zones within neurons provide evaluation actions. In sum, Bullock synthesized an understanding of the behavior of neurons in terms of the physiological contributions of different components that constitute them. He showed how neurophysiologists have developed an emerging theory of the dynamics of dendrites, cell body, and axon. This review, and the questions it posed, influenced the direction of neurophysiology for several decades afterward.

Another example of the "synthetic" role of Bullock in the development of twentieth-century neurobiology is his two-volume 1965 work, *Structure and Function in the Nervous Systems of Invertebrates* (cowritten with G. Adrian Horridge), which is still considered a landmark work of invertebrate neurobiology. Weighing in at over 1,700 pages, this work brings together much that had been learned by that date about the neuroanatomy and neurophysiology of spineless animals from the relatively primitive Protozoa and Porifora through the Deuterostomes (whose neural organization begins to resemble that of the vertebrates). They note that this "work is primarily for reference but it is not an encyclopedia or compendium. Rather, it attempts a synthetic, personal evaluation of the state of our information" (p. viii). This goal of synthesis is a hallmark of Bullock's career, in that he sees as his goal the creation of a coherent account of nature by extracting principles and regularities out of a bewildering array of evolved organisms: "If recognizing some of the gaps and pointing to the nearest relevant reports is a step forward, this work can pretend to be a contribution" (p. xi). This title exists in only a single edition, as the explosion of research that began in the 1960s made it impossible to publish ahead of the literature in this way again. The smaller, less comprehensive *Introduction to Nervous Systems* (Bullock, Orkand, and Grinnell, 1977) allowed him to bring some of the key developments up to date.

Bullock as Midwife and Honoree. In addition to his research contributions to neuroscience, Bullock also contributed to the birth and early development of two closely related contemporary disciplines: neuroscience and neuroethology. He also represented those fields in the larger world of science, as well as the larger world in general. He traveled widely and hosted innumerable foreign scientists in his laboratory. He served as president of the American Society of Zoologists (1965; now the Society for Integrative and Comparative Biology), the third president of the Society for Neuroscience (1973–1974) and was the first president of the Society for Neuroethology (1984–1987).

Bullock was awarded a number of honors during his career, most notably the Karl Spencer Lashley Prize from the American Philosophical Society (1968) and the Ralph W. Gerard Prize from the Society for Neuroscience (1984). He was inducted as a member of both the American Academy of Arts and Sciences (1961) and National Academy of Sciences, U.S.A. (1963). He was also named a Queen's Fellow in marine biology in Australia, and received honorary doctorates from the University of Frankfurt and the University of Loyola Chicago. His name also graces a building in Manaus, Brazil (one of the many place to which he made research field expeditions during his career): the Bullock-Heiligenberg Laboratory of Behavioral Physiology.

The Importance of Diversity. Finally, the key concept to understanding Bullock's approach to scientific inquiry is diversity. He brought to bear a diversity of techniques to study a diversity of biological phenomena in a diversity of organisms. He pioneered many new techniques in electrophysiology. Over his career, in addition to what has been described above, he published on topics as diverse the evolution of myelin, phylogenetic taxonomy, acclimation, and the measurement of metabolism, as well as ecological physiology. Nowhere is Bullock's love of scientific diversity more evident than in the wealth of organisms that he studied (in addition to those already mentioned): *Aplysia*, bats, catfish, corals, crabs, crayfish, cuttlefish, elephants, earthworms, frogs, hagfish, manatees, octopus, porpoises, rats, ratfish, rays, salamanders, sea lions, sea urchins, sharks, sloths, squid, starfish, tuna, turtles, not to mention humans. The point of this breadth is not a short attention span or perversity. The point is Bullock's conviction that taxonomic breadth and diversity of data form the single most important feature of evidence related to evolutionary hypotheses. Just as Charles Darwin did not just look only to domesticated pigeons to support his far-reaching theory about the biological world, Bullock saw that if we were to understand the evolution of nervous systems—and understand evolution via the study of nervous systems—it was incumbent on us to cast our net as widely as possible. For Bullock, this simply underlined the communal nature of science, as no one individual could collect

sufficient data about enough different species to evaluate appropriately hypotheses in comparative biology. Given the example he set over his career, one wonders whether Bullock himself was the exception to this rule.

BIBLIOGRAPHY

The personal and scientific papers of Theodore H. Bullock, comprising over 33 cubic feet of material from his entire career, can be found the Scripps Institution of Oceanography Archives located in the library of that institution. Starred references (*) below are reprinted in How Do Brains Work? Papers of a Comparative Neurophysiologist, Contemporary Neuroscientists. *Boston: Birkhauser, 1993.*

WORKS BY BULLOCK

*With Raymond B. Cowles. "Physiology of an Infrared Receptor: The Facial Pit of Pit Vipers." *Science* 115, no. 2994 (1952): 541–543.

With F. P. J. Diecke. "Properties of an Infra-red Receptor." *Journal of Physiology* 134 (1956): 47–87.

* "Neuron Doctrine and Electrophysiology." *Science* 129, no. 3355 (1959): 997–1002.

*With Akira Watanabe. "Modulation of Activity of One Neuron by Subthreshold Slow Potentials in Another in Lobster Cardiac Ganglion." *Journal of General Physiology* 43, no. 6 (1960): 1031–1045.

*With S. Hagiwara, K. Kusano, and K. Negishi. "Evidence for a Category of Electroreceptors in the Lateral Line of Gymnotid Fishes." *Science* 134 (1961): 1426–1427.

*With Shiko Chichibu. "Further Analysis of Sensory Coding in Electroreceptors of Electric Fish." *Proceedings of the National Academy of Sciences of the United States of America* 54, no. 2 (1965): 422–429.

With G. Adrian Horridge. *Structure and Function in the Nervous Systems of Invertebrates.* 2 vols. San Francisco: W.H. Freeman, 1965.

* "An Essay on the Discovery of Sensory Receptors and the Assignment of Their Functions Together with an Introduction to Electroreceptors." In *Handbook of Sensory Physiology,* edited by A. Fessard. Berlin: Springer-Verlag, 1974.

With Richard Orkand and Alan Grinnell. *Introduction to Nervous Systems.* San Francisco: W.H. Freeman, 1977.

With Walter F. Heiligenberg, eds. *Electroreception.* New York: John Wiley, 1986.

How Do Brains Work? Papers of a Comparative Neurophysiologist, Contemporary Neuroscientists. Boston: Birkhauser, 1993.

"Theodore H. Bullock." In *The History of Neuroscience in Autobiography,* edited by L. R. Squire. Washington, DC: Society for Neuroscience, 1996.

With Carl D. Hopkins, Arthur N. Popper, and Richard R. Fay, eds. *Electroreception.* Edited by R. R. Fay and A. N. Popper. *Springer Handbook of Auditory Research,* vol. 21, New York: Springer, 2005.

OTHER SOURCES

Josephson, Robert K. "Theodore Holmes Bullock (1915–2005)." *Biological Bulletin* 210 (2006): 169–170.

Keeley, Brian L. "Fixing Content and Function in Neurobiological Systems: The Neuroethology of Electroreception." *Biology & Philosophy* 14 (1999): 395–430.

Pearce, Jeremy. "Theodore H. Bullock, 90; Studied How Animals Function." *New York Times*, 9 January 2006, p. B7.

Ramón y Cajal, Santiago. *Neuron Theory or Reticular Theory? Objective Evidence of the Anatomical Unity of Nerve Cells.* Translated by M. Ubeda Purkiss and Clement A. Fox. Madrid: Consejo Superior de Investigaciones Cientificas, 1954.

Zupanc, G. K. "Obituary: Theodore H. Bullock (1915–2005)." *Nature* 439, no. 7074 (2006): 280.

Brian L. Keeley

Robert Wilhelm Eberhard Bunsen. © BETTMANN/CORBIS.

BUNSEN, ROBERT WILHELM EBERHARD

(*b.* Göttingen, Kingdom of Westphalia, 30 March 1811; *d.* Heidelberg, Germany, 26 August 1899), *chemistry, analytical chemistry, spectroscopy.* For the original article on Bunsen see *DSB,* vol. 2.

Bunsen is best remembered for inventing and teaching methods that were crucial to the development of nineteenth-century analytical chemistry—above all those on gasometry, photochemical induction, and spectral analysis. Furthermore, he made important improvements in instrumental techniques and had a sincere interest in geological matters. A good description of these topics is given in the original *DSB* article, though some of the dates are incorrect. Drawing on subsequent research, some of the stations of Bunsen's life and work are recapitulated. In addition, a fuller assessment of Bunsen's interdisciplinary research practices and his involvement in political matters are provided.

Career Path. Bunsen was born into a Protestant bourgeois family from the middle of what is modern day Germany. His father, at once professor of physical geography, rhetoric, Spanish, and Italian and sub-librarian at the University of Göttingen, worked hard to feed his family. But raising four sons and funding their studies (the eldest son, Carl, died in an accident when he was seventeen years old) left the finances running low. Unlike his brothers, Bunsen studied not law but sciences and mathematics. Among his teachers were such prominent scientists as Friedrich Stromeyer, Johann Friedrich Blumenbach, Wilhelm Weber, Johann Friedrich Ludwig Hausmann, and Bernhard Friedrich Thibaut.

When only twenty years old, Bunsen received his doctor's degree for a thesis originally written—and awarded—as an answer to the yearly announced *Preisfrage* (essay competition) of the philosophical faculty. His final exams

took place in September 1831. In May 1832 Bunsen departed on a fifteen-month grand tour through Germany, France, Switzerland, Tyrol, and Austria. Subsequently he started to work on ammonia cyano compounds for his *Habilitation* in January 1834. Together with the physician Arnold Adolph Berthold, he then began research on iron oxide as an antidote to arsenic acid, the first in a number of successful interdisciplinary projects. In April 1834 he took up a lectureship as a *Privatdozent* at the University of Göttingen. After Stromeyer's death in August 1835, he took over the main lecture until Friedrich Wöhler succeeded him. In return, in April 1836 Bunsen followed Wöhler as teacher at the vocational school (*Höhere Gewerbeschule*) in Kassel. Here he began to work on organo-arsenic compounds and continued this work, despite a bad accident in November 1836 which damaged his right eye, after being appointed professor of chemistry in Marburg in 1839.

Due to his increasing scientific reputation, built above all on his new gasometrical methods, Bunsen received a full professorship in 1841. Early in his career he developed an ongoing interest in technical-analytical

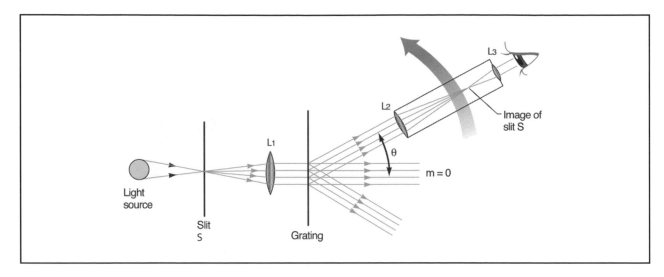

Figure 1. *Spectroscope diagram.*

questions, which was to play a significant role in linking his various research interests throughout his life.

In April 1851 Bunsen succeeded to Nikolaus Wolfgang Fischer's chair in Breslau. There he lectured on organic chemistry for the last time. In later years, his teaching focused on inorganic chemistry. Select parts of organic chemistry, however, were implemented in his experimental teaching. In the fall of 1852 he moved to Heidelberg as professor at the philosophical faculty and as director of the chemical laboratory. At the same time he received the title of *Hofrath*. Main achievements of his career in Heidelberg were the photochemical research undertaken with Henry Enfield Roscoe from 1853 onward, and the scientific foundation of spectral analysis together with Gustav Robert Kirchhoff in 1859–1860.

While the scientific and technical significance of Bunsen's work is generally accepted, the importance of interdisciplinary cooperation in it is frequently underestimated. Particularly the great inventions in photochemistry and spectroscopy would not have been possible, had he not been part of the well-developed experimental culture in Heidelberg at that time, the main features of which were the application of physical methods to chemical and physiological questions and the transfer of methods across disciplinary boundaries by means of scientific instruments.

Social Context. Subsequent research has shown that the emergence of this specific cultural setting was the result of both Baden's successful science policy, and Bunsen's own role in deliberately using academic employment policy for the creation of interdisciplinary networks. The nucleus of the Heidelberg network was built by Bunsen, Kirchhoff, Hermann von Helmholtz, Leo Königsberger, and, later on, Hermann Kopp. Their achievements, however,

depended on the services and know-how of a group of assistants, instrument makers, mechanics and draftsmen, for example, the famous Munich instrument maker Carl August von Steinheil, who supplied the lenses for the first spectrometer, or Heidelberg's university mechanic Peter Desaga, who provided Bunsen's laboratory with the famous burners and whose company, later on, specialized in *Bunsensche Apparate*, or the almost anonymous painter Friedrich Veith, whose pencil drawings of instruments were used for publications.

Little is known about Bunsen's political, and even less about his religious, position. But from his letters, from his actions and social relationships an antireactionary attitude can be inferred. Even though Bunsen played no active role in politics, Roscoe described him as a "staunch Liberal" (Roscoe, 1900, p. 552). While earlier research characterized Bunsen as apolitical, or, at best, hostile to Prussian politics, later research highlights his being part of a close network of liberal and politically active scholars such as Ludwig Häusser and Georg Gottfried Gervinus. Furthermore three of Bunsen's cousins, Gustav, Georg, and Karl Bunsen were active in the *Vormärz* era.

Bunsen's letters, especially those to his favorite pupil and friend Roscoe—in his later years a liberal member of Parliament for Manchester South—show him as a well-informed spectator of international politics who was well aware of the impact of political events upon university life and who knew how to interpret them for local purposes such as university politics. Thus it is by no means coincidental that Bunsen followed vocations from universities in more liberal states whenever the situation at his prior institution was worsening, a strategy that clearly demonstrates the close relationship between the careers of single scientists and science politics in the different territories of nineteenth-century Germany, which were competing for cultural excellence.

BIBLIOGRAPHY

Important archival resources lie in the Deutsches Museum Munich, Germany (foremost letters to colleagues), and the Universitätsbibliothek Heidelberg, Germany (a part of his literary remains, and some pupils' notes on Bunsen's lectures).

Boberlin, Ursula. *Photochemische Untersuchungen von R. Bunsen und H. Roscoe im Vergleich mit den Arbeiten J. W. Drapers und W. C. Wittwers. Die Anfänge der quantitativen Photochemie im 19. Jahrhundert.* Berlin: Köster, 1993.

Borscheid, Peter. *Naturwissenschaft, Staat und Industrie in Baden (1848–1914).* Stuttgart: Klett, 1976.

Hoß-Hitzel, Stephanie Brigitte. *"Es lebt sich himmlisch in Heidelberg." Robert Wilhelm Bunsen und seine Korrespondenz.* PhD diss., University of Heidelberg, 2003. Not in all aspects reliable.

James, Frank A. L. J. "Science as a Cultural Ornament: Bunsen, Kirchhoff and Helmholtz in Mid-Nineteenth-Century Baden." *Ambix* 42 (1995): pt. 1, 1–9.

Jungnickel, Christa, and Russell McCormmach. "Kirchhoff and Helmholtz at Heidelberg: Relations of Physics to Chemistry and Physiology." In *Intellectual Mastery of Nature: Theoretical Physics from Ohm to Einstein.* Volume 1: *The Torch of Mathematics, 1800–1870,* by Christa Jungnickel and Russell McCormmach. Chicago: University of Chicago Press, 1986.

Roscoe, Henry Enfield. *The Life & Experiences of Sir Henry Enfield Roscoe. Written by Himself.* London: Macmillan, 1906.

Roscoe, Henry Enfield. "Bunsen Memorial Lecture." *Journal of the Chemical Society* 77 (1900): pt. 1, 513–554.

Stock, Christine. *Robert Wilhelm Bunsens Korrespondenz vor dem Antritt der Heidelberger Professur (1852) – Kritische Edition.* PhD diss., University of Marburg, 2005. (To be published by Wissenschaftliche Verlagsgesellschaft mbH, Stuttgart, series "Quellen und Studien zur Geschichte der Pharmazie," in 2007.)

Tuchman, Arleen Marcia. *Science, Medicine, and the State in Germany. The Case of Baden, 1815–1871.* New York and Oxford: Oxford University Press, 1993.

Christine Nawa

BUONAMICI, FRANCESCO (*b.* Florence, Italy, 1533; *d.* Orticaia, in the municipality of Dicomano, Italy, 29 September 1603), *medicine, natural philosophy.* For the original article on Buonamici see *DSB,* vol. 2.

Since William Wallace's *DSB* article, scholars' knowledge of Buonamici's thought has been substantially extended by the valuable monograph of Mario Otto Helbing, *La filosofia di Francesco Buonamici, professore di Galileo Pisa* (1989). Relying on a careful study of Buon-

amici's huge treatise "On Motion" (*De Motu*), Helbing has changed the view of Buonamici as a very traditional and conservative Aristotelian, who was tightly linked to a scholastic philosophical background.

Indeed, thanks to his outstanding competence in reading Greek texts, Buonamici was familiar with a number of classical authors, whose theories he discussed, often in great detail, in his *De motu.* Furthermore, he took also into account some major achievements of the scientific debate of his age, examining, for example, such subjects as the Copernican system of the world and the renaissance of Archimedean hydrostatics. Thus, despite Buonamici's firm allegiance to Aristotle, his thought turns out to be richer and more complex than one could believe before Helbing's contribution.

Life. Buonamici was born in 1533, very likely in Florence, where his father served as a notary. He studied philosophy and medicine at the University of Pisa, and he was friend and disciple of two eminent philologists of the age, Pier Vettori and Ciriaco Strozzi, under whose guidance he gained an excellent competence in reading Greek texts. In 1565 Buonamici became assistant professor (*extraordinarius*) of philosophy at the University of Pisa. Then, in 1571, he became full professor (*ordinarius*) of natural philosophy, with the duty of teaching Aristotle's *De caelo, De Anima,* and *Physica* in three-year cycles. He stayed at the University of Pisa all his life, although after 1598 he was asked to succeed Francesco Piccolomini on the chair of natural philosophy in Padua. He died in his holding of Orticaia, a hamlet in the municipality of Dicomano (about 25 miles away from Florence), 29 September 1603.

Before his death, Buonamici published a book on nourishment and embryology, *De alimento,* printed in Florence in 1603. The book deals with the nature of food (*De alimenti essentia*), the first properties of food and excrements (*De primis affectionibus alimenti et excrementorum*), the external food and its appetite (*De alimento externo eiusque appetitu*), the making of the fetus (*De formatione foetus*), the development of the fetus (*De consequentibus foetus*).

De Motu. Buonamici's relevance for the history of science is mainly connected to his very thorough and detailed study of motion, carried out from an Aristotelian standpoint. His huge *De motu libri X* (1,011 pages plus 20 pages of index, *in folio*) covers the whole range of aspects of Aristotle's concept of motion, which is not limited only to local motion (*latio*), but encompasses all kinds of changes, be it alteration, increase and decrease, or coming into being and passing away (*generatio et corruptio*). Buonamici supplies a careful survey of the topic, with an extended discussion of the Aristotelian views as well as of the opinions of a number of ancient and early modern authors who played a major (sometimes innovative) role in philosophical debate of the sixteenth century. To cite only a few of them, one can mention Lucretius, Proclus, Plutarch, Pseudo-Aristotle, Pappus, John Philoponus, Theon, Archimedes, Nicolaus Copernicus, Pereira, Ludovico Boccadiferro, Christoph Clavius, Zabarella, and Toletus.

Buonamici's relationships with Galileo Galilei are well documented, though the link (originally suggested by Antonio Favaro) between Buonamici's *De motu* and Galileo's early writings on Aristotelian natural philosophy (the *Juvenilia*) has been in recent years shown to be groundless. Galileo studied at the University of Pisa under Buonamici, whose work he attacked in the *Discourse on Bodies in Water* (1612), explicitly referring to Buonamici's interpretation of Archimedes's hydrostatics. A reference to Buonamici's book can also be found in one of the notes Galileo wrote on Giulio Cesare Lagalla's *De phoenomenis in orbe lunae*. Furthermore, as noticed by Helbing (1989, pp. 64–71, 345–371), besides these explicit references, there are many implicit references to Buonamici's *De motu* in several of Galileo's later works. From these evidences it seems plausible to maintain that Galileo occasionally used Buonamici's long treatise on motion as a source for mastering Aristotelian natural philosophy.

Buonamici's major work remains the *De motu*, completed in 1587, but issued in 1591. The treatise is divided in ten books. In the first one, Buonamici establishes his method, giving the rules to be followed in natural research. The second book provides the definition of motion, touching the problems of its continuity and its relationship with quiet. The third and the fourth books discuss the motion of the elements, mainly surveying the role of the form in producing it, with interesting digressions on the motion in the void and on acceleration in free fall. In the fifth book, Buonamici, after discussing Copernican cosmology, examines the concepts of heaviness (*gravitas*) and lightness (*levitas*), expounding his views on the fall of heavy bodies. The next books till the eighth are devoted to aspects of *motus* different from the local motion, such as the substantial transformation, the generation, the increasing and decreasing, the condensation and rarefaction, the alteration, and the intension and remission of qualities. The last two books deal with the celestial circulation and its movers, the matter of heavens, the eternity and perfection of the world, and finally with God, who Buonamici, echoing Epicurus, outlines as an entity which eternally contemplates itself without any worry about human events.

Motion of Elements. A remarkable feature of the *De motu* concerns the reason that urged Buonamici to compose his bulky treatise. He explained that he wrote the book as a result of a controversy on the question of the motion of the elements, in which he quarrelled with other professors of the University of Pisa. Most likely, among Buonamici's opponents in the quarrel there was his colleague Girolamo Borro, a strong advocate of Averroës's views. By contrast, Buonamici mainly followed the Greek Aristotle's commentators. The quarrel must have arisen from the problem of the fall of light and heavy bodies (*quaestio de motu gravium et levium*), which was a very controversial issue among Renaissance Aristotelians. The *quaestio* concerned, in the first place, the local motion of the elements, and, by implication, also the motion of natural bodies. In accordance to Aristotelian physics, their motions depended on the dynamical tendency of the element predominant in their composition.

Several hundred pages of Buonamici's *De motu* are devoted to the rebuttal of Averroës's views on the motion of the elements and to support the theories of Alexander of Aphrodisias, Themistius, and Simplicius. Indeed, all along his huge treatise, Buonamici shows a rather hostile attitude toward medieval philosophers. As a pupil of the distinguished philologist Pier Vettori, he was a true admirer of classical antiquity, holding the medieval *Latini* in some contempt. Therefore, it seems not correct to portray him as follower of the scholastic philosophical trend (as Alexandre Koyré did in his *Études galiléennes*), or to define him as William Wallace does in his article in *DSB* as "an orthodox and traditional Aristotelian who cites the views of moderns (*iuniores*) mainly to refute them" (p. 590). Quite the contrary, even if Buonamici was a firm advocate of Aristotelian philosophy, his thought, permeated of classical influences and willing to take into account the opinions of modern authors, can more correctly be described as a product of the new renaissance learning.

Influence. Some of the main topics treated in the Pisan debate on motion resonate also in the pages of Galileo's early writings on dynamics, the *De motu antiquiora*. In particular, there are implicit references to Buonamici's work in the discussion of the questions of falling bodies and of Archimedean extrusion.

As for the first subject, Galileo, in chapter 22 of his treatise *De motu antiquiora,* discusses the problem of the fall of bodies of different matters (wood, lead, and iron), in direct reference to the accounts already provided by Buonamici and by his rival, Borro. All of them (Borro, Buonamici, and Galileo) resorted to experimental evidence as a way to corroborate their own theories. From this point of view the famous leaning tower experiment, allegedly performed by Galileo at the time in which he composed his early writings on dynamics, seems to be rooted in a tradition of experimental research shared also by Borro and Buonamici, as well as by other Pisan professors, such as Jacopo Mazzoni and Giorgio Coresio (see Michele Camerota and Helbing, 2000, pp. 334–345).

Furthermore, Buonamici's *De motu* developed a strong criticism of Archimedean extrusion. His arguments were explicitly directed against the mathematicians (*contra mathematicos*), and they were also devoted to reply to some modern authors (*neoterici*) who raised objections to the standard view of the motion of heavy bodies in media. In particular, Buonamici argued that the upward motion of bodies extruded by the medium would be decelerating, and not accelerating like all natural motion. Against this view, in several places of the *De motu antiquiora*, Galileo defended Archimedean extrusion, claiming that it was not necessary for the body to decelerate in upward motion, because the mover was joined to the body. It seems therefore that the question of extrusion must have been a subject discussed during the Pisan debate on the motion of the elements, and that Galileo's replies to the critics of Archimedean extrusion were mainly addressed to answer Buonamici's arguments (Camerota and Helbing, 2000, pp. 345–363).

A pupil of Buonamici, Scipione Aquilani, in a book on Greek pre-Aristotelian philosophy (*De placitis philosophorum qui ante Aristotelis tempora floruerunt*, Venice, 1620), portrayed his teacher as "the fiercest advocate of the Peripatetic doctrine." Despite Buonamici's reputation as *acerrimus Peripateticae doctrinae defensor*, his *De motu* can nevertheless be considered as a valuable source for the knowledge of renaissance natural philosophy as well as of the intellectual context in which Galileo matured his early theories on motion.

SUPPLEMENTARY BIBLIOGRAPHY

WORKS BY BUONAMICI

De motu libri X. Florence, Italy: Semartelli, 1591. Also available from http://archimedes.mpiwg-berlin.mpg.de.

Discorsi poetici nell'Accademia Fiorentina in difesa d'Aristotile. Florence, Italy: Marescotti, 1597. Also available from http://gallica.bnf.fr.

De alimento libri V ubi multae medicorum sententiae delibantur et cum Aristotele conferuntur. Florence, Italy: Semartelli, 1603.

Two letters to Pier Vettori published in Angelo Maria Bandini, *Clarorum Italorum et Germanorum epistolae ad Petrum Vettorium.* Florence, Italy: Praesidium facultate, 1758.

An mens sit forma assistens an informans. Biblioteca Nazionale Centrale of Florence: Magliab. 12: 40, ff. 2*r*–8*r*.

De logica ad Laelium Taurellum. Biblioteca Nazionale Centrale of Florence: Magliab. 8:49.

Lectiones super primo et secundo Meteororum. Biblioteca Nazionale Centrale of Florence: Magliab. 12: 29, ff. 45*r*–422*r*.

Letter to Benedetto Varchi. Biblioteca Nazionale Centrale of Florence: Magliab. 2. 4. 64. In Latin.

Letters to Lorenzo Giacomini. Florence, Italy: Biblio Riccardiana, 2438.

Letters to Giambattista Strozzi. Biblioteca Nazionale Centrale of Florence: Magliab. 8.1899.

Letters to Piero Strozzi. Biblioteca Nazionale Centrale of Florence, Magliab. 2. 5. 164, ff. 90*r*–91*v*.

Letters to Benedetto Varchi. Biblioteca Nazionale Centrale of Florence: Magliab. 2. 5. 164, f. 92*r*–*v*.

Letters to Baccio Valori. Biblioteca Nazionale Centrale of Florence: Rinucc. F 27.

Letters to Pier Vettori. London: British Library, 10, 264. In Italian.

Lettione dell'eccellentisimo filosofo Francesco Buonamici recitata nella felicissima Accademia Fiorentina (dated 1569). Biblioteca Nazionale Centrale of Florence: Magliab. 9. 125.

Porphyrii de abstinentia a esu carnium libri quattuor F. Buonamico interprete. Biblioteca Nazionale Centrale of Florence. Conv. Sopp. C.10.879. This is a Latin translation from the Greek of the work of Porphyry on the abstinence from eating meat.

Quaestio de primo cognito (dated 1565). Biblioteca Nazionale Centrale of Florence: Fondo Naz. 2. 5. 164.

OTHER SOURCES

Badaloni, Nicola. *Il periodo pisano nella formazione del pensiero di Galileo.* Florence, Italy: Off-print, 1965.

Camerota, Michele, and Mario Helbing. "Galileo and Pisan Aristotelianism. Galileo's *De motu antiquiora* and the *Quaestiones de motu elementorum* of the Pisan Professors." *Early Science and Medicine* 5 (2000): 319–365.

Galluzzi, Paolo. *Momento. Studi galileiani.* Rome: Edizioni dell'Ateneo & Bizzarri, 1979. 115–118, 147–148, 153, 197.

Garin, Eugenio. *Scienza e vita civile nel Rinascimento italiano.* Bari, Italy: Laterza, 1965, 109–146. Reprint, 1985.

Helbing, Mario Otto. "I problemi *De motu* tra meccanica e filosofia nel Cinquecento. G. B. Benedetti e F. Buonamici." In *Cultura, scienze e tecniche nella Venezia del Cinquecento: Atti del convegno internazionale di studio "Giovan Battista Benedetti e il suo tempo,"* 157–168. Venice, Italy: Istituto Veneto di Scienze, Lettere ed Arti, 1987.

———. *La filosofia di Francesco Buonamici.* Pisa, Italy: Nistri-Lischi, 1989. This is the most valuable study on Buonamici's thought.

———. "Mobilità della Terra e riferimenti a Copernico nelle opere dei professori dello Studio di Pisa." In *La diffusione del Copernicanesimo in Italia, 1543–1610,* edited by Massimo Bucciantini and Maurizio Torrini, 57–66. Florence, Italy: Olschki, 1997.

Ioffrida, Manlio. *La filosofia e la medicina (1543–1737).* In *Storia dell'Università di Pisa.* vol. 1.1, 239–338 (298–301). Pisa, Italy: Pacini, 1993.

Kraml, Hans. "Principle and Method: Francesco Buonamici's version of Renaissance Aristotelianism." In *Method and Order in Renaissance Philosophy of Nature: The Aristotle Commentary Tradition,* edited by Daniel A. Di Liscia, Eckhard Kessler, and Charlotte Methuen, 301–318. Aldershot, U.K.: Ashgate, 1997.

Lewis, Christopher. *The Merton Tradition and Kinematics in Late Sixteenth and Early Seventeenth Century Italy*. Padua, Italy: Antenore, 1980, 127–170.

Schmitt, Charles B. "The Faculty of Arts at Pisa at the Time of Galileo." *Physics* 14 (1972): 243–273 (265–267, 270).

———. "The University of Pisa in the Renaissance." *History of Education* 3 (1974): 3–17 (6–7, 12).

———. "Philoponus' Commentary on Aristotle's *Physics* in the Sixteenth Century." In *Philoponus and the Rejection of Aristotelian Science,* edited by Richard Sorabji, 210–230 (222–225). London: Duckworth, 1987.

Schmitt, Charles B., and Quentin Skinner, eds. *The Cambridge History of Renaissance Philosophy*. Cambridge, U.K.: Cambridge University Press, 1988.

Thurot, Charles. "Recherches historiques sur le principe d'Archimède." *Revue archéologique* (1869): 284–299 (297–299). This is an old, reliable account of Buonamici's discussion of Archimedean hydrostatics.

Michele Camerota

BURGERSDIJK, FRANK PIETERS-ZOON (in Latin, Burgersdicius, Franco Petri) (*b.* De Lier, near Delft, Netherlands, 3 May 1590; *d.* Leiden, Netherlands, 19 February 1635), *natural philosophy*. For the original article on Burgersdijk see *DSB,* vol. 2.

Burgersdijk's reputation in the seventeenth century rested on his systematic manuals. They derived their pedagogical significance from their efficient adaptation of the *Corpus Aristotelicum* to the standards of humanist method. Burgersdijk's neo-Aristotelianism is related to the Contra-Remonstrant movement in the Dutch republic.

Education. According to his biographer Meursius, Burgersdijk's father had some knowledge of Latin. His mother was a relative of Hugo Blotius, the librarian of the Roman emperor Rudolph II. Between 1606 and 1610 Burgersdijk attended the Latin school at Amersfoort and at Delft. In 1610 he went to Leiden University in order to study theology. In that center of humanist learning Burgersdijk received a complete humanist formation, attending lectures on Latin, Greek, Roman history, and rhetoric, besides the lectures of Gilbertus Jacchaeus on ethics and logic and of Bertius on physics. Due to his "deep affection towards philosophy" and his progress in that discipline, "the most learned people deemed him fit to obtain a doctorate in the liberal arts and philosophy." Burgersdijk took his degree on 29 March 1620, only two days before he delivered his inaugural address.

Since his matriculation, Burgersdijk had unwaveringly adhered to the Contra-Remonstrant or Gomarist faction. He attended the lectures of the theologians Fran-

ciscus Gomarus and Gijsbert Voet. The latter became the informal leader of strict Calvinism between 1640 and 1676, the year of his death. In 1614 Burgersdijk took part in a series of disputations *adversus Pontificos* organized by Festus Hommius, the later secretary of the National Synod of Dordt (1618–1619), which settled the fate of the Arminian party in the state and the church. In the same year 1614 he left Leiden in order to make a grand tour. After some months, however, he decided to stay at the Protestant Academy of Saumur, where he continued his studies of theology with Gomarus, who had left Leiden in 1611 because of the ascendancy of the more lenient party in the Reformed Church. After the five years in France spent "without the hope of office" in the Netherlands, as Burgersdijk observed in the preface of this *Idea philosophiae moralis* (An outline of moral philosophy), he returned to the republic, where he was appointed professor of logic at Leiden University in one of the vacancies caused by the purges after the Synod of Dordt. In November 1620, the month Jacchaeus received permission to resume his lectures on physics, ethics was added to Burgersdijk's teaching assignment. Some months afterward Burgersdijk became an ordinary professor of philosophy. In 1623 he completed his theological education by defending a disputation titled "The Clarity of the Bible and Its Interpretation."

Success as Philosophy Teacher. Notwithstanding his staunch Calvinism and his theological education, Burgersdijk's teaching contributed to raising the status of philosophy at the Dutch universities. Through his manuals covering the whole of philosophy he transformed the lingering propaedeutic discipline generally neglected by the students in the "higher faculties"—theology, law and medicine—into a discipline independent of theology and philology. It is therefore highly significant that only a month after the delivery of his inaugural address he presided over a disputation rejecting the doctrine of the double truth and defending the inalienable rights of philosophy with respect to theology. Burgersdijk adopted Thomas Aquinas's view of the relationship between these disciplines by observing that both sciences deal with the same object. The philosopher and the theologian, however, argue from different principles: the light of natural reason versus the light of revelation. The final conclusion of the disputation is neat: although theological dogma may exceed the limits of human reason, philosophy may be free from error. That is why the pagan Aristotle was the greatest philosopher. On this line of argument Burgersdijk fully acknowledged the authority of Iberian neo-Scholasticism and of other Roman Catholic philosophers. Therefore, the suggestion of Max Wundt (1939) and Paul Dibon (1954) that Burgersdijk attempted to create a Calvinist philosophy is to be rejected. The predominance of this attitude toward the discipline in the republic also facilitated the quick acceptance of Cartesianism. Apparently René Descartes's Catholicism formed no obstacle to the introduction of his ideas into the Reformed universities.

School Reform. The recommendations of the Synod of Dordt included the call for a reform of the Latin schools. In 1625 new regulations were promulgated. In final year some ethics, physics, and geography might be taught and Burgersdijk was asked to raise the medieval "barbaric" Latin of Johannes de Sacro Bosco's *De sphaera* to humanist standards by making "astronomy" perspicuous and easy to understand. This schoolbook commissioned by the states of Holland is not to be taken as an illustration of Burgersdijk's conservatism. Its aim was to make the pupils familiar with the "first principles" of the subject, which had to be dealt with more fully at the university, as is observed in the introduction of the compendium.

In 1628, after the death of Jacchaeus, Burgersdijk exchanged moral philosophy for physics, but well before that date he lectured on physics. In 1624 a first series of fifteen disputations dealing with the Aristotelian corpus of natural philosophy was held, and in 1627 the next series was organized. Although his funeral orator, Petrus Cunaeus, recorded that several of the deceased's friends were amazed by this step, for "moral philosophy conveyed by Socrates from heaven to earth is the most excellent part of philosophy," he noted the humanist ambition of Burgersdijk "to uncover the truth hidden in nature in such a manner that from the dark a clear light will radiate" (Cunaeus, 1640, p. 232). He therefore made the Aristotelian philosophy taught "by public authority" in the schools more perspicuous by clearing away "its obscurities," which were further augmented by later "scholastic" commentators such as Aquinas and John Duns Scotus. Hence, Burgersdijk's key notions are method and system, order being a necessary condition for a science.

Works on Physics. Physics is the focal point of Burgersdijk's entire philosophical undertaking. This discipline is its most noble part, because it leads humanity from the manifold things in nature that humans perceive by the senses to its hidden causes and finally to God. To physics Burgersdijk devoted two manuals. The *Idea*—his first manual published—is conceived as a "guide" to be used in disputation, presenting the subject matter of the course in natural philosophy in definitions and short theses. By referring only to the so-called new authorities such as Zabarella, Pereira, Toletus, and the commentators of Coimbra, Burgersdijk stated as his goal to open the debate on the "text of Aristotle." In the more extensive *Collegium* the same doctrinal tradition is elaborated in a synthetic

order. The first section of the series of thirty-four disputations deals with basic topics such as "the subject of the science": the natural body, its principles—matter, privation and form—and the final and efficient causes. This section continues with the properties of natural body— magnitude, place, motion—and time and reflects Aristotle's *Physics*. The second section deals with more specific and concrete topics, such as the heavens in disputation ten and the stars in disputation eleven. The *Collegium,* further, deals with the elements, the origin and destruction of things, the atmospheric phenomena and what we should now call chemistry and mineralogy. Here the corresponding parts of the *Corpus Aristotelicum* are *De Coelo* and the *Metereology*. With disputation twenty begins Burgersdijk's treatment of the soul, its functions and faculties: nutrition, generation, embryology, the senses, the intellect, and the will. These themes Aristotle dealt with briefly in his books on generation, parts of animals and the soul. In contrast with the *Idea,* which deals with "the world" after place and time, the *Collegium* ends with *De mundo,* because the world is the composition of all bodies and an insight into the more simple bodies is a prerequisite for understanding it.

It is obvious that the structure of Burgersdijk's manuals on physics is not simply a matter of didactic convenience, but mirrors the complexity of nature, which requires a study by means of the golden principles of Zabarellian method. These new ideas on the order of nature, however, conceal a framework of the traditional concepts of scholastic physics: motion arising from an internal principle, generation and corruption, the beginning and the end of motion, and locomotion, which was produced by the principles of the natural body. What is more, Burgersdijk did not take much notice of important discoveries such as the sine law of light's reflection made some years before by his colleague Willebrord Snellius, which prepared the way for the mathematical calculation of natural phenomena.

Burgersdijk, however, acknowledged a primitive form of the circulation of the blood discovered by William Harvey in 1628. Other examples of his readiness to accept new observations are his acknowledgment of the appearance of new stars, notwithstanding Aristotle's doctrine of the incorruptibility of the heavens, and his acceptance of the plausibility of the Copernican hypothesis. If the diurnal motion is attributed to the celestial bodies and not to the earth, the speed of the diurnal motion observed by his fellow Dutchman Philippus van Lansbergen would imply that Saturn in five minutes traverses more than 900 German miles and the fixed stars more than 643,000 miles. This is, according to Burgersdijk, hardly conceivable.

Burgersdijk never pondered the theoretical implications of these observations. Apparently he unconsciously realized that these new discoveries could not be readily integrated into the traditional Aristotelian framework of physics. Within a generation after his early death in 1635 the majority of Dutch scholars embraced Cartesianism. Other scholars, such as Martin Schoock (1614–1669) and Gisbert van Isendoorn (1601–1657), retained in their manuals the Aristotelian heritage. Reducing the significance of its concepts, however, they gradually turned toward empiricism.

SUPPLEMENTARY BIBLIOGRAPHY

WORK BY BURGERSDIJK

Problema utrum quod est verum in theologica possit esse falsum in philosophia aut vice versa. Edited by Petrus Doornyck. Leiden, Netherlands: Jacob Mark, 1620.

OTHER SOURCES

Bos, Egbert P., and H. A. Krop, eds. *Franco Burgersdijk (1590–1635): Neo-Aristotelianism in Leiden.* Amsterdam and Atlanta, GA: Rodopi, 1993. Lists the editions of his manuals.

Bunge, Wiep van. *From Stevin to Spinoza: An Essay on Philosophy in the Seventeeth-Century Dutch Republic,* 27–33. Leiden, Netherlands, and Boston: E.J. Brill, 2001.

Cunaeus, Petrus. "Oratio XVI habita in funere Franconis Burgersdicii." In *Orationes varii argumenti,* pp. 227–239. Leiden, Netherlands: Iaac Commelinus, 1640.

Dibon, Paul. *La philosophie néerlandaise au siècle d'or.* Vol. 1. Paris and New York: Elsevier, 1954.

Feingold, M. "The Ultimate Pedagogue: Franco Petri Burgersdijk and the English Speaking Academic Learning." In *Franco Burgersdijk (1590–1635): Neo-Aristotelianism in Leiden,* edited by Egbert P. Bos and H. A. Krop, 151–165. Amsterdam and Atlanta, GA: Rodopi, 1993.

Meursius, Johannes. *Athenae Batavae, sive de urbe Leidensi & Academia.* Leiden, Netherlands: Andries Clouck, Bonaventura and Abraham Elsevier, 1625, pp. 339–342.

Petry, M. J. "Burgersdijk's Physics." In *Franco Burgersdijk (1590–1635): Neo-Aristotelianism in Leiden,* edited by Egbert P. Bos and H. A. Krop, 83–118. Amsterdam and Atlanta, GA: Rodopi, 1993.

Ruestow, Edward G. *Physics at Seventeenth and Eighteenth-Century Leiden: Philosophy and the New Science in the University,* pp. 14–33. The Hague: M. Nijhoff, 1973.

Wundt, Max. *Die deutsch Schulmetaphysik des 17 Jahrhunderts.* Tübingen, Germany: Mohr (Siebeck), 1939.

Henri Krop

BURIDAN, JOHN (JEAN) (*b.* diocese of Arras, France, *ca.* 1295; *d.* Paris, France, *ca.* 1360), *philosophy, logic, physics.* For the original article on Buridan see *DSB,* vol. 2.

Since the appearence of the original *DSB*, considerable work has been done on the life of Buridan, on the edition of his works, and on their doctrinal interpretation.

Life. John Buridan originated from the diocese of Arras. This geographical origin made him belong to the Picard Nation, one of the four Nations into which the students and masters at the University of Paris were organized. The often-repeated tradition that he was born in the town of Béthune is spurious. The first clear information about him emerges in a document dated 9 February 1328, which mentions him as rector of the University of Paris. The usual term for a rector was three months. Since this position was only open to regent masters of arts, it is assumed that Buridan started his academic training around 1320. There are, however, no records which document his university education. During his training at the arts faculty, Buridan belonged to the Collège du Cardinal Lemoine, which provided him with housing and financial support. According to its statutes, he must have left the college as soon as he started to perform administrative functions at the university, such as proctor, rector and receptor (i.e., treasurer). He never was a member of the Collège de Navarre, as was incorrectly affirmed in the *DSB*. At some date before 1334, Buridan visited the papal court at Avignon. There is also evidence for a second visit, around 1345. During one of these trips (or possibly still other trips that are not documented), Buridan made the observations reported in his commentary on Aristotle's *Metheora* about the Cevennes and about the height of Mont Ventoux.

In early 1340 Buridan was elected rector of the university for a second time. The dating is crucial here, because in the older literature it has been assumed that he signed the so-called Ockhamist statute of 27 December 1340, which was issued by the masters of the faculty of arts. The statute prohibits six errors attributed in its rubric to the Ockhamists. The errors concern hermeneutics, in particular the failure to distinguish between the literal meaning of authoritative texts and the intention of their authors. As a matter of fact, however, Buridan was no longer rector at that time, and the statute was signed by his successor. Buridan's name is last mentioned in a university statute of 12 July 1358. As has now been established, he probably died around 11 October 1360, but no later than 12 June 1361, on which date one of his benefices had received a new owner. Buridan did not belong to a religious order, and never sought to obtain a degree in theology. For these reasons, he has been presented as an independent "real" philosopher. Independent, because he was not involved in any of the doctrinal disputes of the religious orders, and a philosopher, because he made philosophy into a career in itself, which lasted almost forty years.

Relationships with Contemporaries. Throughout the fifteenth and sixteenth centuries Buridan's writings had a huge impact on philosophical thought in Europe. The manuscripts and early printed editions of his works were disseminated in all corners of Europe and were read (*pronuntiata*), for instance, at the universities at Vienna, Prague, Kraków, Rostock, and Saint Andrews. In the older literature, it has been suggested that John Buridan had grouped around him a coherent inner circle of students and followers, such as Albert of Saxony and Nicole Oresme, the so-called Buridan school. It is certain, however, that neither of them studied under Buridan in any official way. It is more helpful to perceive them and Buridan as contemporary thinkers who were interested in a number of the same philosophical topics, and who at times were each other's opponents, as is clear from their texts. Other fourteenth-century opponents who are identifiable from Buridan's texts are Walter Burley, Nicholas of Autrecourt, Gregory of Rimini, Themon Judaeus, and the less well-known Giles of Feno and Michael de Montecalerio.

Buridan's name has often been linked with nominalism. This association is mainly due to sources from the fifteenth and sixteenth centuries, in which he is labeled a nominalist and a follower of William of Ockham. Literature in the early 2000s is much more cautious in viewing Buridan—and fourteenth-century philosophy in general—as "nominalist" because this terminology is marred with confusion. The precise relationship between Buridan's and Ockham's thought, and, by implication, the impact of Ockham's thought in fourteenth-century Paris, still needs further investigation. What Buridan and Ockham share, however, is that they use logic and semantics as a method in their natural philosophy, and in all other areas of philosophy, for that matter. This approach is, for instance, illustrated by their discussion of infinity and continuity, motion and time.

New Editions. Over the past decade, much work has been done in editing and studying John Buridan's works. From this work it emerges that Buridan was a prolific and important (natural) philosopher. Yet, many particular aspects of his thought are as yet unexamined. A relative or absolute dating of his works is still not possible. Buridan frequently produced two or three different versions of a set of lectures. The order of composition of the different versions usually is clear, but their dating is not, nor is the relative chronology of his works. Buridan's two most important works are the *Summulae de Dialectica*, a voluminous compendium of logic and semantics (presented as a commentary on the author's revised version of Peter of Spain's *Summulae*), and the *Questions on Aristotle's Physics* (*Quaestiones super libros Physicorum, secundum ultimam lecturam*). Certain parts of the *Summulae* are now dated around 1336 and 1340. Buridan's *Physics*, at least in its last

and ultimate version, originated sometime between 1352 and 1357. Interestingly, Buridan responds to views of Albert of Saxony, and not the other way around, as has often been assumed.

Buridan entertained a view on natural necessity that made him believe that one can achieve certain knowledge about the natural world, granted that it is running its common course. He attacks Nicholas of Autrecourt for his thesis that the only criterion of certitude is the principle of non-contradiction. According to Buridan, man can know many principles of scientific demonstrations without needing to derive them from the principle of noncontradiction, namely on the basis of the meaning of their terms, on the basis of sense perception, and experience. Buridan often refers to experiments in support of his theories, although one should be cautious in concluding that these were experiments that were actually conducted, rather than examples taken from tradition, or thought experiments. The importance of Buridan's impetus theory for the explanation of projectile motion has been mitigated. Its former context, as a significant step toward Galileo's dynamics, has been abolished. Instead, the focus has shifted to other aspects of Buridan's discussion of motion, such as its ontological status. Buridan was involved in the contemporary debate of whether motion was a thing distinct (*res distincta*) from, and added to, the mobile body. He refused to identify motion with the mobile body and its successive places, as Ockham did.

Buridan's *Questions on De generatione et corruptione* have only begun to be studied. It is clear that he was engaged in the fourteenth-century debates about the way in which the ingredients are present in a compound (*mixtum*), in particular the forms of the four elements, and also in the debate about *reactio*. This latter debate concerned the phenomenon that every agent in acting will undergo a reaction. For instance, the hot iron (*agens*) immersed into water will not only heat it, but will itself be cooled by the water (*patiens*). The process seemed to involve an action by the weaker resistive power upon the stronger agent, which was considered problematic in the fourteenth century.

SUPPLEMENTARY BIBLIOGRAPHY

A survey of Buridan's works and of most of the manuscript sources is provided in B. Michael, Johannes Buridan: Studien zu seinem Leben, seinen Werken und zur Rezeption seiner Theorien im Europa des späten Mittelalters, *2 vols., PhD dissertation, Freie Universität Berlin, 1985. This work is also crucial for Buridan's biography. See also O. Weijers,* Le travail intellectuel à la faculté des arts de Paris: Textes et maîtres (ca. 1200–1250), *vol. IV, Turnhout: Brepols, 2001, for a listing of Buridan's works and a bibliographical guide.*

WORKS BY BURIDAN

Sophisms on Meaning and Truth. Translated by Theodore Kermit Scott. New York: Appleton-Century-Crofts, 1966. A separate translation of treatise 9 of the *Summulae*, the so-called *Sophismata*.

Johannis Buridani Tractatus De Consequentiis. Edited by Hubert Hubien. Philosophes Médiévaux. Louvain: Publications Universitaires; Paris: Vander-Oyez, 1976.

Sophismata. Stuttgart-Bad Cannstatt: Frommann-Holzboog, 1977. Critical edition, with an introduction by Theodore Kermit Scott.

John Buridan on Self Reference. Chapter eight of Buridan's Sophismata. An Edition and a Translation with an Introduction and a Philosophical Commentary. Translated and edited by G. E. Hughes. Cambridge; London; New York: Cambridge University Press, 1982.

Quaestiones in Praedicamenta. Edited by Johannes Schneider. Munich: Verlag der Bayerische Akademie der Wissenschaft, 1983.

John Buridan's Tractatus de infinito, Quaestiones super libros Physicorum secundu ultimam lecturam, liber III, quaestiones 14–19. An Edition with an Introduction and Indexes. Edited and introduced by J. M. M. H. Thijssen. Nijmegen: Ingenium Publishers, 1991. A few parts of Buridan's voluminous *Questions on the Physics*, according to the final redaction (*secundum ultimam lecturam*).

Le traité de l'âme de Jean Buridan (de prima lectura). Édition, étude critique et doctrinale. Edited by Benoît Patar. Louvain-la-Neuve, Belgium; Longueil, Quebec: Éditions de l'Institut supérieur de philosophie; Éditions du Préambule, 1991. Allegedly the first redaction of Buridan's *Questions on De anima*.

Summulae. In Praedicamenta. Edited by E. P. Bos. Nijmegen: Ingenium, 1994.

Summulae. De praedicabilibus. Edited by L. M. de Rijk. Nijmegen: Ingenium, 1995.

Ioannis Buridani Expositio et Quaestiones in Aristotelis De Caelo. Édition, étude critique et doctrinale. Edited by Benoît Patar. Louvain-la-Neuve, Belgium; Paris: Éditions de l'Institut supérieur de philosophie; Peeters, 1996.

Summulae. De suppositionibus. Edited by Ria van der Lecq. Nijmegen: Ingenium, 1998.

John Buridan: Summulae de Dialectica. Translated by Gyula Klima. New Haven, CT; London: Yale University Press, 2001. The entire *Summulae de dialectica* has been translated here, though not based on its most recent critical edition.

Summulae. De demonstrationibus. Edited by L. M. de Rijk. Groningen: Ingenium, 2001.

De tijdfilosofie van Johannes Buridanus. Een historisch-wijsgerige studiemet editie van Buridanus' Quaestiones super octo libros Physicorum Aristotelis(secundum ultimam lecturam) IV, 12–16. Edited by D. J. Dekker. PhD diss., Radboud Universiteit Nijmegen, 2003. An edition of Book IV, pp. 12–16 (on Time).

Summulae. De practica sophismatum. Edited by Fabienne Pironet. Turnhout: Brepols, 2004.

Summulae. De propositionibus. Edited by Ria van der Lecq. Turnhout: Brepols, 2005.

OTHER SOURCES

Caroti, Stefano. "Da Buridano a Marsilio di Inghen: la tradizione parigina della discussione de reactione." *Medioevo* 15 (1989): 173–233.

Courtenay, William J. "Philosophy's Reward: The Ecclesiastical Income of Jean Buridan." *Recherches de théologie et philosophie médiévale* 68 (2001): 163–169.

———, ed. *John Buridan at the University of Paris.* Special issue of *Vivarium* 42 (2004).

Knuuttila, Simo. "Natural Necessity in John Buridan." In *Studies in Medieval Natural Philosophy*, edited by Stefano Caroti, 155–176. Florence: Leo Olschki, 1989.

Krieger, Gerhard. *Subjekt und Metaphysik. Die Metaphysik des Johannes Buridan.* Münster: Aschendorff, 2003.

Markowski, Mieczysław. "L'influence de Jean Buridan sur les universités d'Europe central." In *Preuve et raisons à l'université de Paris, Logique, ontologie et théologie au XIV siècle*, edited by Zénon Kaluza and Paul Vigneaux. Paris: 1984.

Pinborg, Jan, ed. *The Logic of John Buridan.* Copenhagen: Museum Tusculanum, 1976.

Rijk, L. M. de. "John Buridan on Universals." *Revue de Métaphysique et de Morale* 97 (1992): 35–59.

Saarinen, Risto. *The Weakness of the Will in Medieval Thought: From Augustine to Buridan.* Leiden and New York: Brill, 1994.

Schönberger, Rolf. *Relation als Vergleich. Die Relationstheorie des Johannes Buridan im Kontext seines Denkens und der Scholastik.* Leiden and New York and Cologne: E. J. Brill, 1994.

Thijssen, J. M. M. H. "Buridan on Mathematics." *Vivarium* 23 (1985): 55–77.

———. "John Buridan and Nicholas of Autrecourt on Causality andInduction." *Traditio* 43 (1987): 237–255.

———. 'The Buridan School Reassessed: John Buridan and Albert of Saxony." *Vivarium* 42 (2004): 1, 18–42.

———, and Jack Zupko, eds. *The Metaphysics and Natural Philosophy of John Buridan.* Leiden; Boston; Cologne: Brill, 2001.

Zupko, Jack. *John Buridan: Portrait of a Fourteenth-Century Arts Master.* Notre Dame, IN: University of Notre Dame Press, 2003. The best book-length study on aspects of Buridan's natural philosophy to date.

Johannes M. M. H. Thijssen

BURLEY, WALTER (*b.* England, c. 1275; *d.* c. 1345), *logic, natural philosophy.* For the original article on Burley see *DSB*, vol. 2.

Although Burley obtained his doctorate in theology from the University of Paris in the mid-1320s, and although he held numerous church livings, as well as serving both the English king and Richard de Bury, Bishop of Durham, he is unusual, among fourteenth-century scholars, for having continued to be active in natural philosophy and logic until his death, some time after 1344. Since he also began producing works on the subjects of the Faculty of Arts at Oxford as early as 1300, this means he had a career in philosophy of more than forty years.

Commentaries on Aristotle. Burley's commentaries on Aristotle's *Physics* may be taken as representative. His first commentary on the *Physics,* in the form of expositions of the text alternating with relatively long questions, is extant in MS Cambridge, Gonville and Caius 448/409. It most likely resulted from his teaching at Oxford before leaving for Paris to study theology, some time before 1310 and possibly as early as 1307. Besides this earliest work, which may be referred to as his *Expositio cum quaestionibus* on the *Physics,* there are several manuscripts that contain only *Quaestiones* on the *Physics* by Burley (and these only for certain books), without accompanying expositions. Although scholars have considered this a second work by Burley on the *Physics,* it is probably more accurate to understand it consisting of selected questions from the *Expositio cum quaestionibus* apart from the related expositions. And, finally, there is Burley's *Expositio in libros octo de phisico auditu,* compiled when he was in Paris and even later in the employ of Richard de Bury back in England, which was printed eleven times between 1476 and 1609. Book IV of this version, which includes revised versions of significant sections of Burley's Oxford *Expositio cum quaestionibus,* was finished at Paris in 1326. Books VII and VIII were revised ten years later, between 1334 and 1337, at the suggestion of Richard de Bury. In this final *Expositio* Burley on numerous occasions defends his views against the novel theories of William of Ockham. So, for instance, in response to Ockham, Burley inserted a long defense of the existence of indivisibles such as instants of time or geometric points into Book I of the final *Expositio,* something he had not thought it necessary to do in earlier versions, before Ockham and other ontological minimalists denied their reality.

Although much work has been done on Walter Burley since the original *DSB* article, he was so prolific, and his ideas may have developed from one period of his life to the next to such an extent, that it is still difficult to see his contribution as a whole and to place it within its fourteenth-century context, either at Oxford or on the Continent, where he is known to have lectured or disputed not only at Paris, but also at Toulouse and Bologna. In 1978 Agustin Uña Juarez published a large book devoted to Burley (see bibliography below). Uña Juarez discusses, for instance, Burley's relationships to Averroës, on the one hand, and to Ockham, on the other—both issues that scholars have continued to take up.

Relationship to Wylton. An issue yet to be resolved is Burley's relationship to Thomas Wylton. From remarks in Burley's *Tractatus Primus,* which derives from the *principia* or initial lectures on Peter Lombard's *Sentences* that Burley gave as a bachelor of the *Sentences* at Paris, it is probably safely concluded that it was Thomas Wylton who oversaw Burley's work in theology at Paris. But Wylton and Burley were also near contemporaries at Merton College in Oxford, and there are many passages in their works, such as their questions on Aristotle's *Physics,* that are so close as to be almost identical. Although this has been noticed, the explanation is unclear. Might Burley have first heard Wylton lecture on the *Physics* and then made use of Wylton's lectures when he came to teach the *Physics* himself? Would the source of the similarities have come from the men hearing each other lecture and dispute, or might one have had the manuscript of the other on hand while writing his own? At Burley's *principium* on Book IV of the *Sentences* at Paris, Wylton was very clearly in the room, raising objections orally. Was there also a live connection at Oxford? So far this remains an open question.

Relationship to Ockham. In the case of individuals from earlier times, such as Averroës, Thomas Aquinas, and Robert Grosseteste, Burley very clearly had manuscripts of each man's work in front of him as he wrote his own commentaries. He copied their opinions so exactly that his commentaries have been used in establishing editions of the others' works. The communication between Burley and Ockham is unclear, particularly if Ockham is supposed to have been living in the Franciscan house of studies in London for some time, where Burley, as a secular, would presumably not have been present. It has already been noted above that Burley reacted to Ockham's ontological parsimony in composing his final *Expositio* on the *Physics.* Did Burley become familiar with Ockham's views through Ockham's logical and natural philosophical works, or was he reacting to things that Ockham propounded in his commentary on the *Sentences*? In editing Ockham's *Quaestiones on the Physics,* Stephen Brown noted that several of Ockham's questions make wholesale use of Burley's *Tractatus Primus* (related to Burley's commentary on the *Sentences*) both in formulating questions and in proposing responses. Ockham comes sometimes to the same conclusion as Burley and sometimes to the opposing solution. There is little doubt in this case that Ockham was working from a manuscript of Burley's *Tractatus Primus,* so it is not necessary to conclude that Burley was involved in person in this transfer of ideas.

Ideas about Qualities. In his *De causis mirabilium,* Nicole d'Oresme cited Burley's opinion that contraries like hot and cold, white and black, and so forth belong to the same species—an opinion that Burley had argued for in his *Tractatus Primus*—no doubt distantly related at least to the qualities in the Eucharist, since the *Tractatus Primus* derived from Burley's *principium* on Book IV of Peter Lombard's *Sentences*. Oresme connected Burley's views on hot and cold and other qualities to the subjectivity of sensation—that what seems hot to one person may feel cold to another. Burley's influence on later authors seems to have derived primarily from the clarity and thoroughness of his writing, both in logic and in natural philosophy. His positions were established before William of Ockham electrified his contemporaries with his so-called nominalism or ontological minimalism. Although Burley is often characterized as Ockham's realist opponent, there are many similarities between the physical views of Burley and Ockham, particularly to the extent that both Burley and Ockham were influenced by the ideas of John Duns Scotus. The originality of the theory of beginning and ceasing expounded in Burley's *De primo et ultimo instanti* is becoming clearer to historians as it is realized that, unlike Burley, Peter of Spain in his earlier theory held that there is a last instant of permanent beings (this had been obscured because a fifteenth-century revision of Peter of Spain's *Tractatus syncategorematum* revised it along the lines of Burley's theory).

Burley's Logic. A great deal of the scholarship concerning Burley's work that has been done in recent decades concerns his logic, rather than his natural philosophy. Thus scholars have been interested in Burley's formulation of the logical exercise called "obligations," participation in which was required of late medieval university students. Although logic may normally be considered to fall outside the realm of "science," it would be a mistake to exclude contributions to logic from the history of medieval science, given that logic was as much the instrument of late medieval science as mathematics was to become the instrument of science par excellence in later periods. In the supplementary bibliography that follows are included a sample of recent articles on Burley's logical work. In his commentary on Aristotle's *Posterior Analytics*, and on Book I of the *Physics*, Burley argues that natural knowledge first derives from experience, following the pattern made famous by Robert Grosseteste of distinguishing knowledge of facts (*quia*) from knowledge of their causes (*propter quid*).

Institutional Context. As far as the institutional context of Walter Burley's work is concerned, his work first in the faculty of arts at Oxford and then in the faculty of theology at Paris falls into expected patterns. More intriguing is his continued participation, orally and in writing, in philosophical concerns after leaving the University of Paris about 1327. In part, Burley's continued scholarly activity

may be ascribed to his having been a member of the group of clerks with whom Richard de Bury surrounded himself, a group that included at different times Thomas Bradwardine, Richard Kilvington, and others. As Burley carried out diplomatic missions for Richard de Bury and for the king, he seems to have had occasion to communicate with other scholars—sometimes, perhaps, at the papal court in Avignon. Burley's peregrinations to Bologna and elsewhere, and the dedications of the revised versions of his works to Richard de Bury, found in several manuscripts, reveal a pattern of lifelong learning on the part of individuals outside universities or other educational institutions.

SUPPLEMENTARY BIBLIOGRAPHY

WORKS BY BURLEY

Obligationes. Introduction to the Logical Treatise 'De Obligationibus': with Critical Texts of William of Sherwood (?) *and Walter Burley*. Edited by Romuald Green. Louvain, Belgium: Université catholique, Institut Supérieur de Philosophie, 1963. Partial translation in *Logic and Philosophy of Language*. The Cambridge Translations of Medieval Philosophical Texts, vol. 1, edited by Norman Kretzmann and Eleonore Stump, 370–412. Cambridge, U.K., and New York: Cambridge University Press, 1988.

Insolubilia. Edited by Marie Louise Roure. "La Problématique des propositions insolubiles au XIIIe siècle et au début de XIVe, suivie de l'édition des traités de W. Shyreswood, W. Burley et Th. Bradwardine." *Archives d'histoire doctrinale et littéraire du moyen âge* 37 (1970): 262–284.

Tractatus de formis. Edited by Frederick J. D. Scott. Veröffentlichungen der Kommission für die Herausgabe ungedruckter Texte aus der mittelalterlichen Geisteswelt, Bd. 4. Munich, Germany: Verlag der Bayerischen Akademie der Wissenschaften, 1970.

Tractatus de suppositionibus. Edited by Stephen Brown. In "Walter Burleigh's Treatise *De suppositionibus* and Its influence on William of Ockham." *Franciscan Studies* 32 (1972): 15–64.

"Middle Commentary" on the *Perihermeneias*. Edited by Stephen Brown. "Walter Burley's Middle Commentary on Aristotle's Perihermeneias." *Franciscan Studies* 33 (1973): 42–134.

Quaestiones in Librum Perihermeneias. Edited by Stephen Brown. *Franciscan Studies* 34 (1974): 200–295.

De exclusivis. Edited by Lambertus M. de Rijk. In "Walter Burley's Tract *De exclusivis*: An Edition." *Vivarium* 23 (1985): 23–54.

De exceptivis. Edited by Lambertus M. de Rijk. In "Walter Burley's *De exceptivis*, an Edition." *Vivarium* 24 (1986): 22–49.

Utrum contradictio sit maxima oppositio. Edited by Lambertus M. de Rijk. In "Burley's So-Called 'Tractatus Primus,' with an edition of the additional questio 'Utrum contradictio sit maxima oppositio.'" *Vivarium* 34 (1996): 161–191.

With Adam Burley. *Questions on the De anima of Aristotle*. Edited by Edward A. Synan. Leiden, Netherlands, and New York: E.J. Brill, 1997. Krieger (see below) lists this as a doubtful or spurious work.

On the Purity of the Art of Logic: The Shorter and the Longer Treatises. Translated by Paul Vincent Spade. New Haven, CT: Yale University Press, 2000.

Quaestiones super librum Posteriorum. Edited by Mary Catherine Sommers. Studies and Texts 136. Toronto: Pontifical Institute of Mediaeval Studies, 2000.

OTHER SOURCES

Brown, Stephen. Notes. In Guillelmi de Ockham, *Brevis Summa Libri Physicorum; Summula Philosophiae Naturalis, et Quaestiones in libros Physicorum Aristoteles.* Opera Philosophica VI. St. Bonaventure, NY: St. Bonaventure University Press, 1984. 41ff. and 773ff. Notices Ockham's use of Burley's *Tractatus Primus* in his *Quaestiones in libros Physicorum.* If Ockham's *Quaestiones* date from 1323–1324, then the *Tractatus Primus* must have been available before that date.

Caroti, Stefano. "Da Walter Burley al 'Tractatus sex inconvenientium': la tradizioine inglese della discussione medievale 'De reactione.' " *Medioevo* 21 (1995): 257–374.

Dutilh Novaes, Catarina. "Medieval *Obligationes* as Logical Games of Consistency Maintenance." *Synthese* 145 (2005): 371–395. In the first section, surveys modern interpretations of the purposes of *obligationes* as university exercises, focusing on Walter Burley's treatise, and concluding with a bibliography of recent studies on *obligationes.*

Feltrin, Paola. "Il problema del primo e ultimo istante in Walter Burley." *Medievvo* 9 (1983): 137–178.

Grignaschi, Mario. "Lo pseudo Walter Burley e il 'Liber de vita et moribus philosophorum.' " *Medioevo* 16 (1990): 131–190. Calls Burley's authorship of the *Liber de vita et moribus philosophorum* into question.

Kretzmann, Norman, Anthony Kenny, and Jan Pinborg, eds. *The Cambridge History of Later Medieval Philosophy.* Cambridge, U.K.: Cambridge University Press, 1982. Covers the work of Walter Burley in many sections (see index under Walter Burley).

Krieger, Gerhard. "Studies on Walter Burley, 1989–1997." *Vivarium* 37 (1999): 94–100.

Lagerlund, Henrik, and Erik J. Olsson. "Disputation and Change of Belief—Burley's Theory of Obligationes as a Theory of Belief Revision." In *Medieval Formal Logic: Obligations, Insolubles and Consequences,* edited by Mikko Yrjönsuuri. Dordrecht, Netherlands, and Boston: Kluwer, 2001. An example of how Burley's views on logic are taken seriously, although the article involves modern theories of belief change as much as Burley's work on *obligationes.*

Lohr, Charles. "Medieval Latin Aristotle Commentaries." *Traditio* 24 (1968): 179–180. List of Burley's commentaries.

Ottman, Jennifer, and Rega Wood. "Walter Burley: His Life and Works." *Vivarium* 37 (1999): 1–23. This is the lead article in a volume also containing papers by Elizabeth Karger, Paul Vincent Spade, Risto Saarinen, Rega Wood, and Gerhard Krieger on Burley. Two of these articles are on logic and two others are on ethics.

Spade, Paul. "Three Theories of *Obligationes*: Burley, Kilvington and Swynesshed on Counterfactual Reasoning." *History and Philosophy of Logic* 3 (1982): 1–32.

———. "If Obligationes Were Counterfactuals." *Philosophical Topics* 20 (1992): 171–188. Retracts the theory of obligations as counterfactuals that he espoused in his 1982 article.

———. "How to Start and Stop: Walter Burley on the Instant of Transition." *Journal of Philosophical Research* 19 (1994): 193–221.

Stump, Eleonore. "The Logic of Disputation in Walter Burley's Treatise on Obligations." *Synthese* 63 (1985): 355–374.

Sylla, Edith Dudley. "The A Posteriori Foundations of Natural Science. Some Commentaries on Aristotle's *Physics,* Book I, Chapters 1 and 2." *Synthese* 40 (1979): 147–187. See pages 169–176 for Burley's commentaries and their relations to those of Thomas of Wylton and William of Ockham, as well as to the earlier commentaries of Averroës, Thomas Aquinas, and Robert Grosseteste.

———. "Walter Burley's *Tractatus Primus*: Evidence concerning the Relations of Disputations and Written Works." *Franciscan Studies* 44 (1984): 257–174.

———. *The Oxford Calculators and the Mathematics of Motion, 1320–1350. Physics and Measurement by Latitudes.* New York and London: Garland, 1991. Contains outlines of Burley's *Tractatus Primus* and *Tractatus Secundus,* as well as a discussion of his theory of latitudes and degrees.

———. "Walter Burley's Physics Commentaries and the Mathematics of Alteration." *Early Science and Medicine* 6 (2001): 149–184.

———. "Walter Burley's Practice as a Commentator on Aristotle's Physics," *Medioevo* 27 (2002): 301–372.

———. "The Status of Astronomy between Experience and Demonstration in the Commentaries on Aristotle's *Posterior Analytics* of Robert Grosseteste and Walter Burley." In *Erfahrung und Beweis: Die Wissenschaften von der Natur im 13. und 14. Jahrhundert,* edited by Alexander Fiodora and Matthias Lutz-Bachmann. Berlin: Akademie Verlag, 2007.

Trifogli, Cecilia. "The Reality of Time in the Commentary Tradition on the Physics: The Case of Wylton and Burley." In *Il Commento Filosofico nell'Occidente Latino, Secoli XIII–XV,* edited by Bianfranco Fioravanti, Claudio Leonardi, and Stefano Perfetti, 233–252. Turnhout, Belgium: Brepols, 2002.

Uña Juarez, Agustin. *La Filosofia del Siglo XIV. Contexto Cultural de Walter Burley.* Madrid: Biblioteca "La cuidad de Dios" Real Monasterio de el Escorial, 1978.

Weisheipl, James. "Repertorium Mertonense." *Mediaeval Studies* 31 (1969): 185–208.

Wood, Rega. "Walter Burley's *Physics* Commentaries." *Franciscan Studies* 44 (1984): 275–327. Burley's earliest *Physics* commentary, consisting of an exposition and questions, which Wood labels the "pre-1316 commentary," was probably written before Burley left Oxford for Paris, perhaps as early as Easter 1307 and in any case by 1310. From this earliest commentary are derived many if not all of the questions in Burley's separate *Questiones super libros Physicorum,* which Wood tentatively dates before 1322. Thus the separate questions might also have been completed at Oxford before 1310 or even 1307.

———. "Studies on Walter Burley, 1968–1988." *Bulletin de Philosophie Médiévale* 30 (1988): 233–250.

_____. "Walter Burley on Motion in a Vacuum." *Traditio* 45 (1989–1990): 191–217.

Edith Dudley Sylla

BURMEISTER, HERMANN KARL KONRAD

(*b.* Stralsund, Prussia, 15 January 1807; *d.* Buenos Aires, Argentina, 2 May 1892), *biology, entomology, paleontology.*

Burmeister spent the first half of his life in Germany and then worked as the director of the Museum of Buenos Aires and the Academy of Sciences of Córdoba, Argentina, in the second half of the nineteenth century, with modern and rigorous criteria of organization. His biological fixism (the belief that species are fixed) distanced him from the youngest scientists, and he did not gain disciples. However, his abundant work dramatically expanded knowledge of South American zoological systematics and paleontology.

Formation and First Steps. Hermann Burmeister was the son of Christian Hermann Burmeister, a civil servant in the Swedish customs service, and Wilhelmine Christine Burmeister. His father intended him to become a businessman, but his teachers at the gymnasium (secondary school) encouraged his ambition to study medicine and his interest in collecting insects. He studied in the universities of Greifwald and Halle, where he graduated as a medical and philosophical doctor in 1829, with a dissertation on entomology. He was a professor at the universities of Berlin and Halle, and director of the zoological museum of the latter. He had two sons between 1836 and 1840 from his marriage to Maria Elisabeth Sommer, which ended in divorce. In 1843 he published *History of the Creation*, a very widely read work and precursor of the *Kosmos* of Alexander von Humboldt, his friend and mentor.

In 1849–1850 Burmeister held a seat on his local city council as a member of the far left political party, but disappointed by the experience, he obtained a leave of absence from the university and a major subsidy from the Prussian state to travel around Brazil. He covered Brazil (1850–1852), Italy (1854–1855), and Uruguay and Argentina (1856–1859), obtaining abundant collections. He published scientific works, textbooks, and travel writings. When medical studies in Halle were reformed to omit zoology, he resigned from his professorship, separated from his first wife, and traveled to Buenos Aires, where he was designated director of the Public Museum in 1862. In 1865 he married Petrona Louise Tejeda in Argentina, where he had four sons, two of whom also became scientists.

In Argentina. When Burmeister returned to Buenos Aires in 1861, the direction of the Public Museum had just been rejected by the French naturalist Auguste Bravard, and Burmeister offered himself immediately for the position. He knew the museum, which was founded in 1812 but remained as a disorganized collection. He reorganized it in accordance with the German model characterized by the close relation between education and investigation. He divided the museum in three sections: artistic, historical and scientific, with natural history predominating. The museum bought and received donations of specimens and collections, among them the entomological collection of Burmeister and the fossil collection of Bravard. Its library also grew with the purchase of his personal library and exchange of the *Anales*, the journal he founded at the museum. The financing and the facilities of the museum were significantly extended. Burmeister did almost all the work, both of investigation and of public exhibition and publication, by himself. He published in the 1864–1874 and 1883–1892 periods eighteen installments of the *Anales del Museo Público de Buenos Aires*, later *Anales del Museo Nacional de Buenos Aires*, which allowed him to exchange with other similar publications of the world the spreading of his works and the defense of his theoretical positions. Also he gained the support of the Asociación de Amigos de la Historia Natural, then Sociedad Paleontológica de Buenos Aires (1866–1868), an ephemeral institution promoted by Burmeister to interest to the Buenosairean elite in the development of the museum and in the financing of the *Anales*. He sponsored policies of protection for the natural patrimony. Burmeister knew how to maintain his institutional independency from the University of Buenos Aires, even rejecting a university position, which caused him problems. Nevertheless, he was provided with the political and financial support from the Province of Buenos Aires for the publication of the *Anales* and of his personal works.

Between 1870 and 1872 Argentine president Domingo F. Sarmiento entrusted him with the organization of a Faculty of Mathematical and Physical Sciences in the University of Córdoba. By hiring several German naturalists, Burmeister constituted there an important scientific nucleus, but it failed as a center of scientific teaching, probably because of his authoritarian personality. This project was competing with the Department of Exact Sciences of the University of Buenos Aires, impelled by the rector Juan María Gutiérrez and supported with the hiring of Italian teachers. In 1873, finally, Burmeister was designated director of a National Academy of Sciences in Córdoba, but was opposed by the naturalists and contracted professors and resigned from his position in 1875.

His relation with organizations of promotion and education of the sciences—such as the Sociedad Científica Argentina founded in 1872 and in general with the activities of the Argentine young scientists, was problematic. Among them were Francisco P. Moreno, a teacher of zoology and creator of an own anthropological museum; Eduardo L. Holmberg, a student of medicine; and Florentino Ameghino, a notable paleontologist. The young naturalist Hendrix Weyenbergh, however, formed in Córdoba an Entomological Society, which became later the Zoological Society, which was fought by Burmeister for its open spirit and its adhesion to Darwinism. Holmberg in particular criticized the performance of Burmeister in the Museum of Buenos Aires, his ideological profile and his isolation from the local intellectual ambience. Ameghino, evolutionist and already known by his works in Europe, and Moreno, who began to adhere to Darwinism, also collided with his personality. Burmeister refrained from participation in academic affairs and formed no more disciples than his sons Carlos and Federico.

Between 1876 and 1886 Burmeister published, with the patronage of the Argentine State but in French, four volumes of a *Physical Description of the Argentina* that received an award in the Geographical Exhibition of Venice of 1891. In 1884, with the Argentine State definitively organized, the Public Museum became National Museum of Buenos Aires (at present Museo Argentino de Ciencias Naturales "Bernardino Rivadavia"). With other groups and rival institutions emerging, Burmeister concentrated on the enlargement of the museum and the defense of his scientific positions.

Work and Ideas. Burmeister's travel writings contain meticulous descriptions of many diverse objects, natural and social, although his specialities were entomology and paleontology. His bibliography registers almost three hundred titles on entomology, paleontology, mammalogy, geology, climatology, general zoology, ornithology, herpetology, carcinology, general natural history and trips. The majority were published in German, in specialized German, English and French reviews.

His work ranges between the synthetic tradition of the erudite naturalists and the modern tendency toward specialization. Burmeister's prestige was founded on international publication of original remarks and on recognition by the Argentine authorities. His performance as director of the Museum of Buenos Aires and his research positioned him as one of the main naturalists in South America.

The scientific ideas of Burmeister were based on idealism and the fixism of species. He conceived matter as eternal, not created, and considered living beings as materializations of ideal types, modifiable by abrupt changes or cataclysms. He admitted a paleontological progressive succession that would culminate in man, but he considered evolutionism a conjecture unacceptable from his strictly empiricist methodological standpoint. In entomology he was known especially for innovatively basing his classification scheme on variations in insect development.

BIBLIOGRAPHY

A fairly complete bibliography may be found in Taschenberg, Otto, "Karl Hermann Konrad Burmeister," Leopoldina 29 (1893): 43–46, 62–64, 78–82, 94–97.

WORKS BY BURMEISTER

Geschichte der Schöpfung [History of the creation]. *I Eine Darstellung des Entwickelungsganges der Erde und ihrer Bewohner. Für die Gebildeten aller Stände.* Leipzig: Otto Wigand, 1843. (7th edition, 1867.) Translated to Dutch (*Geschiedenis der schepping*), French (*Histoire de la Creation*) and Spanish (*Historia de la Creación*).

"La paleontología actual en sus tendencias y resultados." *Anales del Museo Público de Buenos Aires* 1, no. 1 (1864): 12–31.

"Fauna argentina. Primera parte: mamíferos fósiles. Introducción." *Anales del Museo Público de Buenos Aires* 1, no. 2 (1867): 87–120.

"Fauna argentina. Segunda parte: Mammifera pinnata argentina." *Anales del Museo Público de Buenos Aires* 1, no. 5 (1868): 301–311.

"Examen crítico de los Mamíferos y Reptiles fósiles denominados por D. Augusto Bravard y mencionados en su obra precedente." *Anales del Museo Nacional de Buenos Aires* 3, no. 2 (14) (1885): 95–174.

"Adiciones al examen crítico de los Mamíferos fósiles tratados en el 'Examen crítico de los Mamíferos y Reptiles fósiles denominados por D. Augusto Bravard'." *Anales del Museo Nacional de Buenos Aires* 3, no. 5 (17) (1891): 375–400.

"Continuación a las adiciones al examen crítico de los Mamíferos fósiles terciarios." *Anales del Museo Nacional de Buenos Aires* 3, no. 6 (1894): 401–461.

OTHER SOURCES

Asúa, Miguel de. "El apoyo oficial a la *Description Physique de la République Argentine* de H. Burmeister." *Quipu* 6, no. 3 (1989): 339–353.

Auza, Néstor T. "Germán Burmeister y la Sociedad Paleontológica, 1866–1868." *Investigaciones y Ensayos* (Academia Nacional de la Historia, Buenos Aires) 46 (1996): 137–155.

Birabén, Max. *Germán Burmeister: Su vida—su obra.* Buenos Aires: Ediciones Culturales Argentinas, 1968.

Lascano González, Antonio. *El Museo de Ciencias Naturales de Buenos Aires. Su historia.* Buenos Aires: Ediciones Culturales Argentinas, 1980.

Lopes, Maria Margaret. "Nobles rivales: estudios comparados entre el Museo Nacional de Río de Janeiro y el Museo Público de Buenos Aires." In *La ciencia en la Argentina entre siglos. Textos, contextos e instituciones*, edited by Marcelo Montserrat. Buenos Aires: Manantial, 2000.

Mantegari, Cristina. *Germán Burmeister. La institucionalización científica en la Argentina del siglo XIX.* Buenos Aires: Universidad Nacional de San Martín/Jorge Baudino, 2003.

Montserrat, Marcelo. "La mentalidad evolucionista: una ideología del progreso." In *La Argentina del Ochenta al Centenario*, edited by Gustavo Ferrari and Ezequiel Gallo. Buenos Aires: Sudamericana, 1980.

Navarro Floria, Pedro. "La mirada de la 'vanguardia capitalista' sobre la frontera pampeano-patagónica: Darwin (1833–1834), Mac Cann (1847), Burmeister (1857)." *Saber y Tiempo* (Buenos Aires) 10 (2000): 111–146.

———, Leonardo Salgado and Pablo Azar. "La invención de los ancestros: el 'patagón antiguo' y la construcción discursiva de un pasado nacional remoto para la Argentina (1870–1915)." *Revista de Indias* (Madrid) 64, no. 231 (2004): 405–424.

Salgado, Leonardo and Pedro Navarro Floria. "Germán Burmeister y su *Historia de la Creación*." *Episteme* (Porto Alegre) 13 (2001): 109–127. Available from http://www.ilea.ufrgs.br/episteme/portal/pdf/numero13/episteme13_artigo_salgado_floria.pdf.

Sheets-Pyenson, Susan. *Cathedrals of Science: The Development of Colonial Natural History Museums during the Late Nineteenth Century.* Kingston, Ontario and Montreal: McGill-Queen's University Press, 1988.

Taschenberg, Otto. "Karl Hermann Konrad Burmeister." *Leopoldina* 29 (1893): 43–46, 62–64, 78–82, 94–97.

Vera de Flachs, María Cristina. *La escuela científica alemana en la Universidad Nacional de Córdoba.* Córdoba: Junta Provincial de Historia, 1995.

Pedro Navarro Floria

BURNET, FRANK MACFARLANE

(*b.* Traralgon, Australia, 3 September 1899; *d.* Port Fairy, Australia, 31 August 1985), *virology, immunology, microbiology, tumor biology, gerontology.*

Burnet was a leading virologist and immunologist of the twentieth century. He contributed to the understanding of the complexity of host-parasite interactions through his studies of various microbial infections, including the bacteriophage phenomenon, Q fever, poliomyelitis, influenza, psittacosis, and herpes. With the insight gained from these studies, he proposed in 1949 the theory of the "self" and "not-self" distinction and immune "tolerance," which was confirmed by the team of British scientist Peter B. Medawar. For this achievement, Burnet and Medawar shared the Nobel Prize in Physiology or Medicine in 1960. Burnet's other major contribution to immunology was his clonal selection theory of 1957, which hypothesized that the antibody is produced through a Darwinian natural selection process among immunocompetent cells, which became one of the central doctrines of modern immunology.

Early Life and Education. Burnet was born in Traralgon, Australia, the second child of a family of Scottish descent. As a boy he was interested in beetle collecting, and in 1913, he entered Geelong College in Victoria, from which he graduated in 1916. He then enrolled in the University of Melbourne as a medical student, and successfully completed coursework in 1922, standing second in his class. Although he initially hoped to be a clinical neurologist after finishing his medical education, he eventually decided to pursue a career of laboratory research and entered the Walter and Eliza Hall Institute in Melbourne to study pathology and microbiology. In 1924, he received his MD from the University of Melbourne and published his first research papers on typhoid fever.

In 1925, a chance to broaden his perspective came when he went to the Lister Institute of Preventive Medicine in London as an assistant curator of the National Collection of Type Cultures. There he studied phage-bacterium interaction with leading British microbiologists and enrolled in the University of London for his graduate degree. His PhD dissertation (1928) interpreted the appearance of a specific strain of *Salmonella* in the presence of particular types of phages as the result of selective proliferation of the strain due to its resistance to the phages, rather than the transformation of the bacterium from one strain to another under their influence. In 1927, he returned to the Hall Institute as an assistant director, and in 1928, he married Edith Linda Marston Druce, an Australian he had met in 1923.

Host-Parasite Interaction and Infectious Disease. While staying at London, Burnet was influenced by his supervisors J. C. G. Ledingham and J. A. Arkwright, who studied bacterial variation and the problems of healthy carriers of infectious diseases. From them, Burnet learned a new direction in infectious diseases research, which began to depart from the previous paradigm established by the German bacteriologist Robert Koch and his colleagues. While Koch generally thought that a particular disease was caused by a specific germ strain, which—he assumed—hardly changed its character, Ledingham and Arkwright began to study the variation of bacteria and wrote a book on the healthy-carrier state, which showed that the occurrence of infectious diseases was dependent on numerous constitutional and environmental factors of the host that the earlier germ theorists had ignored. Healthy carriers were those who did not develop symptoms of disease due to these various factors, despite the presence of infectious agents in their body. Burnet's research after returning to Melbourne followed this new direction.

The first case Burnet investigated with the insight gained in London was "the Bundaberg tragedy," an incident involving the death of twelve children among the twenty-one who had been inoculated with diphtheria vaccine at Bundaberg, Queensland, in 1928. Although he found that the vaccine was contaminated with a strain of *Staphylococcus*, he did not attribute the cause of the tragedy to the mere presence of the bacterium within the body, because it was a common germ found on healthy human skin. How could such a normal bacterium cause death? For him, the real problem was that a large number of the bacteria had been suddenly injected into a blood vessel, which was not their natural habitat. Two factors, the number of the bacteria and their place within the body, were thus responsible for such an extreme and unnatural case of host-parasite interaction—the death of the twelve children.

Burnet's research on the bacteriophage led him to another example of the diversity of interactions between hosts and parasites. Although he studied various aspects of the bacteriophage, including its serological properties used for classification, his most pressing concern was its biological identity. On this issue, he was familiar with the controversy between the French-Canadian microbiologist Félix d'Herelle and the Belgian immunologist Jules Bordet. Burnet supported the former's view that the phage was a bacterial virus, rather than the latter's argument that it was merely a microbial metabolic product. Agreeing with d'Herelle, Burnet argued that lysogeny—a phenomenon that would later be known as a state in which a phage's genes were integrated into a bacterium's genome—was a sort of "symbiosis" between the bacterium and phage that had coevolved for a long time (Burnet, 1932, p. 859). In this respect, lysogeny was similar to the healthy-carrier states that his supervisors were studying, because in both cases, the parasite maintained a coexistence with its hosts, rather than destroying them. Burnet thus began to understand host-parasite interactions from an ecological and evolutionary viewpoint.

His study of psittacosis strengthened this view. During the 1930s, he found that many healthy-looking Australian parrots carried in their body the pathogen of psittacosis, which was assumed to be a kind of virus. They developed the symptoms of the disease only when they were kept in a stressful environment such as a cage, which disturbed the "equilibrium" between them and the pathogen. In the wild state, however, the host and parasite could maintain a harmonious cohabitation.

Burnet found another case of this cohabitation in his research on rickettsial diseases, particularly Q-fever. What was interesting in this case was the relationship between rickettsias and their "intermediate hosts," such as mites, ticks, and lice. While previous researchers had seldom asked why intermediate hosts did not develop diseases to which humans were susceptible, Burnet became interested in this question during his investigations into the Q-fever pathogen, especially its morphology, growth patterns, nat-

Frank Macfarlane Burnet. SCIENCE PHOTO LIBRARY/PHOTO RESEARCHERS, INC.

ural vectors, and relation to other rickettsial diseases. With these studies and others' research on similar subjects, he argued in 1942 that the rickettsia's intermediate hosts were actually its "natural" hosts that had maintained a peaceful relationship with it through their long coevolution, in which humans were not a part. The fever in human rickettsial infection was only an unnatural case of host-parasite interaction caused by the accidental invasion of humans into the peaceful world of the rickettsia and its natural hosts.

Burnet's poliovirus research during the 1930s led to a similar conclusion. Although his immediate concern was the experimental study of its properties such as serological differences between Australian and American strains, he was also interested in larger evolutionary issues. Through his experiments on the routes of poliovirus infection and other scholars' studies of its epidemiological changes in history, he found that the disease had originally been a mild infection affecting only the pharyngeal region till the early twentieth century. The severe poliomyelitis characterized by neuronal damage was caused by variant forms of the virus that had evolved in an overly improved hygienic environment of twentieth-century Western countries. While the virus tended to reduce its virulence to promote the survival of both hosts and parasites in its natural states, these developed countries blocked this usual pathway of the virus's evolution and made it search for other ways that promoted its survival at the cost of its host.

Self, Not-Self, and Tolerance. While Burnet had mainly been interested in virology and microbiology during the 1930s, after 1940 he began to investigate immunological problems as well. But one of his most important contributions to immunology, the theory of "self" and "tolerance," grew from his studies of host-parasite interactions. He was also influenced by the ecological and evolutionary view articulated in H. G. Wells, Julian Huxley, and G. P. Wells's *The Science of Life* (1929).

Burnet published his first account of "self" and "tolerance" in *Biological Aspects of Infectious Disease* (1940), in which he summarized contemporary knowledge on microbial diseases. In this book, he argued that every organism was both a predator and prey in the food chain and was able to maintain the boundary of its "self" during predation processes in the wild. Indeed, the predator could destroy its prey in digestive organs without sacrificing its own body. But the "prey" could also evade the predator's destruction system and eventually overwhelm it. If the prey was a microbe, it would then become an agent causing an infectious disease. As Burnet had observed in his previous research, however, the interaction between two organisms did not always bring about such a destructive consequence. Rather, continued infection of one organism by another during their evolution often resulted in mutual "tolerance," because it would benefit both species by allowing their survival and further proliferation.

Burnet maintained his biological view in his next book, *The Production of Antibodies* (1941). While criticizing contemporary chemical immunologists' "template theory" of antibody formation—which was the orthodox view at the time—he proposed that the antibody was produced by enzymes, which had lifelike characters such as adaptation and self-synthesis. This idea came from two sources. The first was his research following the Bundaberg tragedy on the antibody response against *Staphylococcus* toxoid, which led him to postulate that the logarithmic rise of antibody titer during the secondary contact with the toxoid could be explained by the "replication" of some cellular or subcellular entities responsible for antibody production after the first inoculation. The second source was the biochemical investigations at the Rockefeller Institute that showed the adaptability and self-synthesizing capacity of some enzymes.

Based on these sources, Burnet argued that antibodies were produced by the *adaptive enzymes,* which could proliferate in immune cells and modify their structure to the antigen. The antibody was the enzyme's "partial replica" released into the serum. This idea was different from that of chemical immunologists such as Friedrich Haurowitz and Stuart Mudd, who claimed that the antigen directly shaped the antibody by physically impressing it as its "template."

In this 1941 book, Burnet also discussed "tolerance." He cited James Murphy of the Rockefeller Institute and other researchers who observed that the embryonic animal body "tolerated" foreign cells and molecules without antibody response, although it rejected them as it became older. Burnet himself had begun to use the chick embryo to culture various viruses while he stayed at the National Institute of Medical Research in London from 1932 to 1933. He asked why these young animals did not show immune response to the foreign entity but did after becoming adults. He assumed that they could not do so when they were very young, because they then were immature animals without sufficient "training" in dealing with microbes (Burnet, 1941, p. 46).

Although this explanation was for him only a tentative hypothesis, it reveals that Burnet gradually became interested in the differential immune response of animals according to their age. Indeed, he emphasized that a host body's age, along with its sex, genetic constitution, and environmental conditions, was important for determining whether it developed a disease after contacting a microbe. While earlier scientists scarcely considered the importance of these various factors, he regarded them as crucial components in the pathogenesis of infectious disease.

Burnet observed a paradoxical phenomenon about age, which he called "the age-incidence of infectious disease" (Burnet, 1940, p. 199). While it had been often thought that younger animals and humans were more susceptible to infectious diseases than adults due to their weak and immature bodies, more recent investigations showed that their survival rates in many infections were higher. He explained this phenomenon by postulating that the overly strong immune response in the adult body could often overwhelm and destroy rather than defend it against germs. Children's immune response was less strong but quite adequate for protecting their body without threatening it. But the cases of infants and embryos were different, because their weak immune system might allow unrestrained proliferation of microbes in their body and cause disease and death. Yet the recent statistical data showed that even these very young organisms were better survivors in many infections than the adult. What, then, made them different? Since the peculiar characters of young animals' growing immune system seemed to be responsible for their higher chance of survival, Burnet recognized the need to know more about developmental processes in general in order to understand the growth of a young body's immunity from broader biological perspectives.

During the 1940s, cytoplasmic inheritance theories of enzymes offered a better explanation of embryogenesis and development than any other theories, especially those based on orthodox genetics. When mainline geneticists, particularly those in the United States, could not satisfactorily explain how nuclear genes directed cell differentiation in embryogenesis, the advocates of cytoplasmic inheritance, such as Tracy Sonneborn and Sol Spiegelman, could do so by postulating the existence of cytoplasmic entities—some of which were enzymes—that were inherited by descendent cells and adapted according to environmental conditions. These advocates thought that gradual hereditary changes of these entities guided cell differentiation during the developmental process as they were influenced by intercellular andintracellular environments.

Burnet began to use cytoplasmic inheritance theories after he returned from his wartime trip to the United States and became the new director of the Hall Institute and professor of experimental medicine at the University of Melbourne in 1944. For him, there were two reasons to use the theories. The first was that they were compatible with the self-replicating adaptive enzyme theory he had proposed in 1941. He wrote that the enzyme was located within the cytoplasm and its adaptation and replication occurred during embryogenesis like the hereditary entities Sonneborn and Spiegelman had proposed. The second and more important reason was that it helped him explain the differential response of the host toward microbes according to its age. Indeed, from the perspective of virology and bacteriology, the embryo of an animal, which cytoplasmic inheritance theorists aimed to understand, was only an extremely young host during whose growth diverse viruses and bacteria could gain entrance.

In the second edition of *The Production of Antibodies* (1949), Burnet proposed a new theory of "self" and "tolerance" based on his thoughts about the role of age and cytoplasmic inheritance in disease causation. Burnet cited two examples of "tolerance" developed in young animals, whose susceptibility to infectious disease was crucial for "the age-incidence of infectious disease": From 1936 to 1945, Erich Traub at the Rockefeller Institute and Ray Owen at the University of Wisconsin had observed that red cells with different blood types and viruses could be introduced into an embryonic animal that "tolerated" them even after it became an adult.

Burnet explained these observations with cytoplasmic inheritance. He thought that a "self-marker" that existed on every somatic cell was recognized by cytoplasmic adaptive enzymes within phagocytes during embryonic life. Through this recognition process, the adaptive enzymes' structure was modified according to the shape of the self-marker and inherited by descendant phagocytes till the end of the developmental phase. The adaptive enzymes could then "fit" with the marker on each somatic cell while phagocytes dealt with its normal death occurring in an adult animal.

But a foreign molecule that did not "fit" with the enzyme provoked antibody response by distorting the adaptive enzymes' shape and making them the "primary units," whose partial replicas were released as antibodies. Yet even such a "foreign" molecule could be recognized as a part of the organism's "self" and be "tolerated" thereafter, if it had been introduced during embryogenesis and modified the shape of adaptive enzymes that could thus remember its existence within the body. Hence Burnet argued that "the process by which self-pattern becomes recognizable takes place during the embryonic or immediately post-embryonic stages" (Burnet, 1949, p. 102). This argument was experimentally confirmed in 1953 by Medawar's British team.

The Influenza Virus. While Burnet's immunological research was mainly theoretical, his study of the influenza virus was mostly experimental. Although the latter did not make him as famous as the former did, many of his ideas gained from it were important for shaping his immunological theories as well as for the progress of animal virology in general.

Burnet began to be interested in the influenza virus when he saw its experimental pathogenesis during his stay in London in 1933. After returning to Australia, he started his own research and succeeded in culturing the virus within the chick embryo. He also developed the method of "pock counting" as a means of virus titration using the same embryo. Moreover, he attempted to develop during the Second World War a live influenza vaccine for Australians and their army, although it was not very successful.

In the 1940s, Burnet and his team studied viral hemagglutination—the phenomenon in which viruses clumped red blood cells—as a model of virus-cell interaction. Since the red cells treated with the viruses were agglutinated by the sera which had not clumped them before treatment, his team studied more detailed aspects of such an "enzyme-like character" of human influenza viruses and other pathogens with similar characters, such as the mumps virus, the Newcastle disease virus, and the swine influenza virus. Burnet's team noticed that after being agglutinated by one viral strain, the red cells were not agglutinated by certain other strains. His team also showed that the virus action on red cells could be emulated by cholera vibrio filtrates, which, he thought, contained the receptor-destroying enzyme (RDE) that acted upon the red cell's surface. But certain kinds of mucins and mucoids had an opposite capacity. They inhibited the activity of the virus, which in turn, along with RDE, could destroy this inhibitory function.

To interpret the results of his influenza virus research, Burnet used orthodox genetics rather than cytoplasmic inheritance theories. In 1943, Burnet wrote that the change of viral character during chick embryo passages was due to the "mutation" of viral genes. During the 1950s, he studied genetic recombination between two viral strains by mixed infections and argued that the influenza genome consisted of many distinct "linkage groups" that replicated independently. This argument, which was confirmed in the late 1960s, reveals his familiarity with and full acceptance of standard genetic theories.

The Clonal Selection Theory. Even though Burnet used orthodox genetics for his clonal selection theory in 1957, he had begun constructing this theory before abandoning cytoplasmic inheritance hypothesis. In the final part of *Production of Antibodies* (1949), Burnet postulated that there could be various kinds of "primary units"—which, he thought, were cytoplasmic hereditary entities—in an embryo, and some units that bound with "self" molecules were inactivated during development. The units that were not inactivated could then survive after fetal life and would be converted into antibodies when foreign molecules were introduced. But Burnet did not develop this idea further at the time. In *Enzyme, Antigen, and Virus* (1956), he still maintained his previous standpoint despite some changes of vocabulary.

Burnet's mature idea of clonal selection was proposed in 1957 after he read the Danish immunologist Niels K. Jerne's article, "The Natural-Selection Theory of Antibody Formation" (1955). According to Jerne, antibodies against the bodily components were eliminated during embryogenesis and then among the remaining ones those with an affinity to foreign molecules were selectively replicated to attack them.

Although Burnet did not immediately realize the implication of this idea, he eventually found that the antibody in Jerne's theory could be replaced with the antibody-producing cell, and somatic mutation during embryonic life could be suggested as a probable mechanism for expanding antibody diversity. In a paper published in 1957, Burnet wrote that randomization of antibody repertoire took place through somatic mutations during embryogenesis, and those cells producing antibodies against the body were removed. After the end of development, the remaining immune cells protected the organism from foreign antigens by being selectively stimulated to proliferate by the antigen. This was an application of "population genetics" rather than cytoplasmic

inheritance to the problem of antibody production, although an important part of his 1957 idea was already formed in 1949 using the latter theory (Burnet, 1957, p. 68). In 1959, Burnet stated, "Self-not-self recognition means simply that all those clones which would recognize … a self component have been eliminated in embryonic life" (p. 59). David W. Talmage at the University of Chicago independently proposed in 1957 that the replicating unit in Jerne's theory should be the cell.

Autoimmunity, Cancer, and Aging. In 1965, Burnet retired from the directorship of the Hall Institute and became a professor emeritus of the University of Melbourne. In 1942, he was elected a Fellow of the Royal Society and was knighted in 1951. He served as president of the Australian Academy of Science from 1965 to 1969, and was awarded numerous honors, such as the Copley Medal of the Royal Society (1959) and the Nobel Prize (1960). He also received honorary doctorates from many prestigious institutions, including Cambridge (1946), Harvard (1960), and Oxford (1968). After retirement, he worked for Australian science policy, public health, and education reform as a national scientific leader.

Meanwhile, Burnet kept writing about several important topics in biomedicine, including autoimmunity, aging, and cancer. In 1972, he argued that autoimmune disease was caused by the attack on "self" molecules by the "forbidden clones" of immunocytes that arose from somatic mutation or physiological changes. Aging was another problem that was explained by the failure of the immune system. In 1970, he argued that the weakening of the immune cells that approached the limit of proliferation caused the disturbance of other somatic cells and the senescence of the whole body. From 1973, however, he qualified this argument and claimed that aging resulted from accumulated somatic mutations engendered by the DNA polymerase, whose error rate was determined through evolution. The cause of cancer was similar. After 1957, like many other cancer researchers, he tried to understand how repeated mutations made a somatic cell cancerous, and attempted to conceptualize cancer in relation to immunity and aging. These active theoretical studies were discontinued only when he died of cancer at Port Fairy, Australia, in 1985.

BIBLIOGRAPHY

WORKS BY BURNET

"Bacteriophage Phenomena in Relation to the Antigenic Structure of Bacteria." PhD diss., University of London, 1928.

"Lysogenicity as a Normal Function of Certain Salmonella Strains." *Journal of Pathology and Bacteriology* 35 (1932): 851–863.

Biological Aspects of Infectious Disease. Cambridge, U.K.: Cambridge University Press, 1940.

With Mavis Freeman, A. V. Jackson, and Dora Lush. *The Production of Antibodies: A Review and a Theoretical Discussion.* Melbourne: Macmillan, 1941. 2nd ed. With Frank Fenner. *The Production of Antibodies.* Melbourne: Macmillan, 1949.

"The Rickettsial Diseases in Australia." *Medical Journal of Australia* 2 (1942): 129–134.

With D. R. Bull. "Changes in Influenza Virus Associated with Adaptation to Passage in the Chick Embryo." *Australian Journal of Experimental Biology and Medical Science* 21 (1943): 55–69.

Enzyme, Antigen, and Virus: A Study of Macromolecular Pattern in Action. Cambridge, U.K.: Cambridge University Press, 1956.

"Cancer—A Biological Approach." *British Medical Journal* 1 (1957): 779–847.

"A Modification of Jerne's Theory of Antibody Production Using the Concept of Clonal Selection." *Australian Journal of Science* 20 (1957): 67–69.

Clonal Selection Theory of Acquired Immunity. Nashville, TN: Vanderbilt University Press, 1959.

Changing Patterns: An Atypical Autobiography. Melbourne: William Heinemann, 1968.

"An Immunological Approach to Ageing." *Lancet* 2 (1970): 358–360.

Auto-immunity and Auto-immune Disease: A Survey for Physician or Biologist. Philadelphia, PA: F. A. Davis Company, 1972.

"A Genetic Interpretation of Ageing." *Lancet* 2 (1973): 480–483.

OTHER SOURCES

Billingham, R. E., L. Brent, and Peter B. Medawar. "'Actively Acquired Tolerance' of Foreign Cells." *Nature* 172 (1953): 603–606.

Crist, Eileen, and Alfred I. Tauber. "Selfhood, Immunity, and the Biological Imagination: The Thought of Frank Macfarlane Burnet." *Biology and Philosophy* 15 (2000): 509–533.

Fenner, Frank. *Sir Macfarlane Burnet: Scientist and Thinker.* St. Lucia: University of Queensland Press, 1988. A short description of Burnet's life and work by his close colleague.

Jerne, Niels K. "The Natural-Selection Theory of Antibody Formation." *Proceedings of the National Academy of Sciences of the United States of America* 41 (1955): 849–857.

Ledingham, J. C. G., and J. A. Arkwright. *The Carrier Problem in Infectious Diseases.* London: Edward Arnold, 1912.

Park, Hyung Wook. "Germs, Hosts, and the Origin of Frank Macfarlane Burnet's Theory of 'Self' and 'Tolerance,' 1936–1949." *Journal of the History of Medicine and Allied Sciences* 61 (2006): 492–534.

Podolsky, Scott H., and Alfred I. Tauber. *The Generation of Diversity: Clonal Selection Theory and the Rise of Molecular Immunology.* Cambridge, MA: Harvard University Press, 1997.

Sapp, Jan. *Beyond the Gene: Cytoplasmic Inheritance and the Struggle for Authority in Genetics.* New York: Oxford University Press, 1987.

Sexton, Christopher. *The Seeds of Time. The Life of Sir Macfarlane Burnet.* Oxford, U.K.: Oxford University Press, 1991. This biography includes Burnet's complete bibliography.

Talmage, David W. "Allergy and Immunology." *Annual Review of Medicine* 8 (1957): 239–256.

Tauber, Alfred I. *The Immune Self: Theory or Metaphor?* Cambridge, U.K.: Cambridge University Press, 1994. This philosophical monograph analyzes the nature and development of modern immunology, including Burnet's place in it.

Tauber, Alfred I., and Scott H. Podolsky. "Frank Macfarlane Burnet and the Immune Self." *Journal of the History of Biology* 27 (1994): 531–573. A good overview of Burnet's immunology and philosophy from the 1920s to 1959.

Wells, Herbert George, Julian S. Huxley, and George P. Wells. *The Science of Life: A Summary of Contemporary Knowledge about Life and Its Possibilities.* London: Amalgamated Press, 1929.

Hyung Wook Park

BUTENANDT, ADOLF FRIEDRICH JOHANN (*b.* Bremerhaven, Germany, 24 March 1903; *d.* Munich, Germany, 18 January 1995), *biochemistry, biotechnology, National Socialism.*

A successful figure in twentieth century science, Butenandt was a Nobel Prize winner, director of the most important biochemical research institute in pre- and post-war Germany, and was twice elected President of the Max Planck Gesellschaft in the 1960s. As a biochemist, he deciphered the chemical structure of steroid hormones of major importance, and was instrumental in the transition from chemical physiology to molecular biology. He was also a lifelong collaborator with the pharmaceutical industry, contributing to the transformation of steroids into powerful drugs. Contemporary scholars have viewed his trajectory as a typical example of the complex relationship prominent German scientists maintained with the Nazi regime in order to advance their careers and expertise.

Gifted (Bio)Chemist. Born in 1903 into the family of a local entrepreneur, Adolf Butenandt was the first among his kin to enter the academic world. Having completed a university curriculum in biology and chemistry, he joined the laboratory of the organic chemist Adolf Windaus in Göttingen to prepare his dissertation. The topic offered to him had been selected during one of Windaus's regular trips to the Swiss pharmaceutical firm Hoffmann La Roche: Butenandt was to study a white powder prepared at Hoffmann's laboratory that contained rotenone, a poison found in fish and insects. Butenandt completed his mission in less than one year, describing rotenone's molecular composition and molecular structure. Yet this was mere training in organic chemistry; the real challenge was launched when Windaus followed another industrial proposal, this time from the Berlin-based Schering AG: Butenandt was to work on the purification of the ovarian hormone, a biological entity whose isolation was already under way in several highly regarded laboratories.

The follicular hormone was not a purified chemical entity but a biological preparation. The raw material Butenandt received from Schering was an oily extract of placentas. To label it a female hormone was a pragmatic operation, based on physiological testing. Biological assays played an essential role in the development of hormone research during the first half of the twentieth century. They performed many functions, such as enabling the standardization of extracts, the concentration of active principles, as well as the quantification of their effects. In the case of the female hormone, the physiological change taken as a marker of its presence was the growth and differentiation of the mouse uterus. Imported from the United States, the procedure was implemented in Göttingen by Erika von Ziegner. She later married Butenandt, ultimately leaving biological research to take care of a rapidly growing family (the couple had seven children, five daughters and two sons).

In spite of its biological complexity and multiple effects, the female hormone was relatively easy to purify with organic solvents, giving Butenandt a crystallized powder sharing many features with cholesterol in fairly short order. Cholesterol was under close scrutiny in Windaus's laboratory, and was also the subject of a chemical controversy concerning its exact formula and structure. With his hormone, oestron, Butenandt extended Windaus's previous results in favor of a four-ring structure, which would later become typical of derivatives of cheolesterol and steroid in general. The general acceptance of this scheme brought Butenandt international recognition. In 1932, he was invited to join the committee for the standardization of hormones set up by the League of Nations.

Given the visibility of his work on oestron, Butenandt did not remain long as the assistant of Windaus. Soon after he defended his habilitation thesis in 1932, he was offered a professorship in the so-called free city of Danzig (present-day Gdansk in Poland). Although he did not enjoy the same financial and material resources as in Göttingen, Butenandt gathered a group whose main aim was to exploit the same strategy of purification and structural analysis with other hormones. In 1936, the group moved to Berlin where Butenandt had been called to become director of the Kaiser Wilhelm Institute for Biochemistry (KWIB). The sex steroids remained at the center of research activities. A male hormone, androsterone (which later became a metabolite of testosterone), was isolated; the physiological test then selected involved inducing the growth of a crest in castrated chickens. A third major steroid described by Butenandt in parallel with several other biochemists was the hormone of the corpus luteum (progesterone), obtained from pig ovaries and tested in rabbits.

Butenandt's way of analyzing the hormones was standard practice in organic chemistry at the time. He made extensive use of differential solubility in organic solvents as well as of reactions that led to changes of the steroid core structure, like the replacement of hydrogen by brome or chlorin atoms. The importance of his contribution to the isolation and characterization of the sex steroids, for which he was granted the Nobel Prize for chemistry in 1939, was not only in this application of chemical methods to natural substances of major physiological importance, but also in a structural approach to biological phenomena. This is best illustrated by Butenandt's vision of the polarity between male and female bodies. One remarkable achievement of the work done in Butenandt's laboratory was the combination of the then-emerging notion of a molecular continuum linking all sex steroids (with either male or female effects) with the prevailing approach of a reproductive biology stressing the incommensurability between the two sexes. During the 1930s, organic chemistry provided Butenandt's group with a whole range of molecules showing strong or weak male or female properties, as well as a few examples of "hermaphrodite" steroids. Considering the structural proximities between androsterone, testosterone, oestron, progesterone, and their derivatives, Butenandt's interpretation of their biosynthesis was based on two principles. Firstly, he was convinced that the laboratory reactions used to change the chemical groups attached to the core structure of the steroids had their counterpart in the cells of the sex glands. Secondly, he thought that the diverse sex steroids could be organized in natural biosynthetic series, such that the modification of peculiar lateral groups could be correlated with the acquisition of male or female potency, respectively (or, put another way, with the progressive acquisition of a unique sexual identity by the molecules).

Industrial Scientist. Butenandt called his female hormone Progynon, which was actually the brand name Schering had given to its commercial preparation made out of pregnant women's urine. Butenandt's choice was a vivid testimony to his debt to the pharmaceutical company, specifically for the biological material and the very basic possibility of conducting his research. Although Schering is often invisible in accounts of Butenandt's research, it was a key partner until the end of World War II. In exchange for its material support, the firm obtained the

Adolf Butenandt. *Adolf Butenandt posing next to an organic chemical model of a male hormone.* DAVID LEES/TIME LIFE PICTURES/GETTY IMAGES.

structure of the sex hormones and their purification protocols. These were patented, giving Schering exclusive intellectual property rights as well as considerable advances in the development of analogs and marketable derivates. As compensation, Butenandt obtained a significant percentage of the sales. Until the end of the war, these pharmaceutical revenues doubled the budget of the Institute.

The scientific consequences of this relationship were far from negligible. The question of steroid synthesis reveals the blurred boundary between industrial and laboratory practices that characterized biochemistry at the KWIB. In 1936, Butenandt reviewed and discussed the origins of the properties of the three families of natural and artificial sex steroids. He then proposed a unified scheme in which estrogens, progesterone, and male hormones could all be derived from cholesterol. Many of the intermediate molecules had been semi-synthesized at the bench, using natural steroids as starting material. The criteria ordering the reactions were simplicity of the reaction

path, structural homology between products and substrates, and yield at the bench. This economy of natural synthesis was the very same economy governing Schering's inquiries into the artificial production of such molecules out of cholesterol. In fact, many molecules the KWIB scientists used and eventually introduced in the natural pathways for steroid biosynthesis had first been elaborated by Schering's chemists in their attempts to obtain more potent or cheaper derivatives of the natural sex hormones. Governed by the same chemical order, the cell and the plant could be viewed as two sides of the same coin.

The emphasis Butenandt and Schering's scientists placed on the development of pathways and protocols was rooted in their shared interest for new steroids. It was also rooted in the political economy of the drug industry. In Germany, as in many European countries, drugs could not be patented until the 1960s. In practice, however, pharmaceutical companies protected production processes. The invention of processes thus became an essential part of the production and valorization of biochemical knowledge. During the 1930s, Butenandt's protocols thus eased the scaling up of Schering's hormone production, which in turn permitted wider uses. This dynamic deeply transformed reproductive medicine, resulting in new treatments—for female sterility, for male impotence—and more contested procedures like the medical handling of menopause.

Fellow Traveler of National Socialism. When Butenandt moved to Danzig to take his post, Adolf Hitler and the National Socialist party had seized power. The young professor was not an activist, but at the same time was far from non-political. During his Göttingen years Butenandt had become a member of a student fraternity opposed to the Versailles Treaty and the Weimar Republic. Butenandt hoped for a new order in Germany, although, in contrast to the National Socialists (Nazis), he did not look for a violent uprising. He did not join the Nazi Party in 1933, but rather later in 1936 in the context of intense negotiations about the succession of Carl Neuberg as head of the KWIB. Neuberg was forced into retirement because of his Jewish background. Butenandt was approached as a possible successor, but soon learned that his appointment was in jeopardy because of a report of "political unreliability" from the University of Göttingen. The application for membership in the Nazi Party was in effect a nomination passport. The move was not, however, purely opportunistic: as was the case for so many Germans, Butenandt's "move toward Hitler" was the product of an authoritarian culture, as well as an effect of what many Germans then considered the early international "successes" of the regime.

Butenandt did not become an active member of the Nazi elite but still came into close contact with the state power centers. He was not a public advocate of race research and race policy, but shared the basic prejudices against Jews that were commonplace at the time, and expressed these in private. Butenandt's vision of his duties toward the Reich was deeply imprinted by the traditions of the academic elite. His doubts about the Nazi revolution did not originate in the difficulties of the late war years, but surfaced somewhat earlier when he was denied the right to accept his Nobel Prize. After Carl von Ossietsky was granted the Nobel Peace Prize in 1935, the Nazi government had forbidden all German scientists to accept Nobel awards. In 1939, after three German scientists (Richard Kuhn for chemistry in 1938, Butenandt and Gerhard Domagk respectively for chemistry and physiology) were distinguished, Butenandt had hoped this policy would be softened. Although this event ruined the possibility of trust and ideological engagement, it did not annihilate opportunities for alliance, as Butenandt's relentless self-mobilization demonstrated.

In 1947 Butenandt was called to testify during the Nuremberg doctors' trial to answer questions about the work some of his collaborators had undertaken for the Luftwaffe. These links between the KWIB, forced medical experimentation, and race research have been much discussed in the recent historiography. Archives are incomplete and will remain incomplete. That said, enough is available to conclude that the connection was loose but real. Butenandt's institute became a major center of war-related research (*Kriegswichtige*). The label was widespread; it says little about the military relevance of the work, but testifies to the negotiations and agreements that were a precondition of funding.

The diversification of KWIB activities during the war was remarkable. Butenandt was not a passive director upon whom the military or health administration could simply impose research topics. He was instead an active and pragmatic source of ideas and proposals. By the end of the war, he was leading two dozen different projects, including research on viruses, hormones and cancer, blood cell formation, steroid synthesis, insect physiology, and antibacterial therapies. Some projects extended work begun during the war. Investigations on the carcinogenic power of steroids, for instance, started in 1936 after laboratory studies of mice demonstrated that estrogens could induce the formation of tumors, and continued after the question of medical uses of estrogens had been made more acute with the marketing of diethylstilbestrol (DES), a synthetic analog that was much cheaper than the existing "natural" preparations. During the war, in conjunction with Schering and its medical mode of practice, the KWIB biochemists completed systematic testing in mice to assess the carcinogenicity of sex steroids. In 1949 they concluded that DES as well as the biological hormones were safe if used in physiological dosage and under medical surveillance. Modeling did not solve all problems. The DES question surfaced again in the 1970s in a much more dramatic way, with thousands of cases of genital cancers in the daughters of women who had taken the drug to prevent spontaneous abortion.

Given Butenandt's strong industrial connections, it is not surprising that the majority of the KWIB war-related projects focused on the isolation, purification, and putative synthesis of biological agents. The skills developed with the study of sex steroids were thus incorporated in collaborative projects with Schering and (to a lesser extent) with IG Farben. War-time biopharmaceutical research at the KWIB targeted vitamins, a liver factor against anemia, a factor involved in resistance to tuberculosis, a hormone stimulating the formation of blood cells, penicillin and antibacterial secretions of molds, and plant viruses. The interest of these agents was rooted in far-reaching promises of use in military medicine. For instance, the work on the blood hormone (which would in time become erythropoietin) was sold to the Luftwaffe by Butenandt with the promise of increasing pilot resistance to low pressure, as well as being a potential agent in the etiology of epilepsy (insufficient intake of oxygen was considered a crisis factor).

Available records do not document any direct contribution by Butenandt to the development of biological weapons, although the preparation of highly purified viruses could be used both ways, on the one hand to develop protection systems (vaccines or biological protection of crops) and on the other to develop new arms. Nevertheless, a few projects did focus not only on the quest for new drugs, new food, or industrial ersatz but tied in with the criminal aspects of biomedical research in National-Socialist Germany. The putative connection of Butenandt's Dahlem institute to Auschwitz is the most typical example of this sort of gray zone: It linked on the one hand the world of basic laboratory experimentation and on the other hand the murderous technological world of the camps. The Kaiser Wilhelm Institute for Anthropology, Human Heredity and Eugenics played a critical role in the National Socialist system of research. After 1942 and under the leadership of Otmar von Verschuer, the institute included Josef Mengele, Auschwitz's chief physician, among its personnel. Conducting his own studies in the camp, Mengele simultaneously provided the Dahlem's institutes with human research material. Blood samples collected in Auschwitz under unknown conditions were for instance used to develop a biochemical system of race identification based on specific blood "enzymes" thought to be involved in resistance to foreign proteins. Butenandt did not invent the race-oriented project, but—following a request from Verschuer—provided technical assistance via one of his collaborators (Günther Hillmann), laboratory space, and tools. From Mengele to Verschuer to Hillman to Butenandt, the chain transferred samples and results. It also "purified" the inquiries. The existence of such mediations made it possible for Butenandt to speak about inheritance without any hints of racial policies, and to be aware of Verschuer's racial science without knowing too much about the camps. As a final testimony of his confidence and friendship, Butenandt remained loyal to von Verschuer. In the early 1950s, after the later's links to Auschwitz had become public knowledge, Butenandt helped von Verschuer resume an academic career.

Godfather of Molecular Biology. Butenandt does not belong to the long list of early "molecular biologists" the history has retained. Given his research topics during and after the war—gene physiological action, virus structure, hormonal control of the metabolism—one could in fact argue for quite the opposite. This absence is to some extent artificial, an effect of the emphasis the historiography of molecular biology has given to molecular genetics. However, the relationship of Butenandt's work to molecular biology was ambiguous.

On the one hand, the difference between his biochemistry and what would become molecular biology is obvious. It is best exemplified with his involvement in physiological genetics. In 1935, shortly before the move to Berlin-Dahlem, Alfred Kühn approached Butenandt asking for his help. Having found a mutation in the flour mite *Ephesia* that produced red instead of black eyes, Kühn thought that the mutants lacked a hormonal darkening factor. To follow the effects of the mutation, Kühn developed a system based on the transplantation of glandular tissues in mutant organisms. By the time he contacted Butenandt, he needed a biochemist to purify the active substance. Issues and techniques were in all respects similar to the work then being done by Boris Ephrussi and George Beadle on *Drosophila*, in Paris and Pasadena respectively. The contribution of Butenandt—or, more accurately, of his collaborator Ulrich Westphal—was preparing and testing candidate fractions. Given the size of *Ephesia*, the biochemist's skills, and the KWIB assay culture, the German teams won the race to identify the darkening factor. It proved to be kynurenin, a compound close to the amino acid tryptophan. In the United States, the study led to the "one gene, one enzyme" hypothesis, some version of which had been formulated by Kühn during the war. On the biochemist's side, however, the pursuit of gene action was transformed into a more biochemical analysis of pigment synthesis. The project was relocated within the KWIB and became the responsibility of another Butenandt student, Peter Karlson. After the war Karlson continued various studies of insect hormones. Silkworms were collected en masse to analyze the synthesis of eye pigments, the substances involved in sex attraction and the factors controlling metamorphosis. The ability to induce metamorphosis was tested in larvae from Calliphora. A ligature in the middle of the body isolated the head from the posterior segments of the body, thus forced to remain in a juvenile state. After inoculation, active substances would induce the formation of a pupa in the posterior half. In the 1950s, new methods of analysis including liquid chromatography and electrophoresis were introduced, facilitating the isolation of the metamorphosis hormone. Ecdysone, as it was named, was crystallized in 1954. During the following decade, Butenandt's collaborators' studies of its effects, for instance the control of chromosomal puffs in Drosophila, radically changed our understanding of cell differentiation and development, linking hormonal regulation and gene activity.

At the same time, the virus studies conducted during and after the war suggest that Butenandt and his KWIB have to be placed on the molecular biology landscape. In the 1930s, molecular biology was about genes and macromolecules rather than information, focusing on the uses of a new palette of physicochemical instruments including the ultracentrifuge, electrophoresis, and electron microscopy. The Rockefeller Foundation played an important role in this instrumental program. One of few German biologists invited by the Rockefeller Foundation to travel to the United States after 1933, Butenandt was well aware of these developments and rapidly followed up on them. In 1937, three directors of Kaiser Wilhelm Gesellschaft (KWG) institutes located in Dahlem, Kühn, Butenandt, and Fritz von Wettstein, discussed the creation of a common virus initiative. The idea was to work on the isolation, structure, and properties of viruses like the tobacco mosaic virus (TMV) that Wendell Stanley had recently crystallized. Industrial partners (IG Farben and Schering) and the KWG founded the project, which grew to the status of a full-fledged virus station in 1941 before being reincorporated within Butenandt's institute after the war. As with the laboratory output of the Rockefeller Foundation's 1930s investments in "molecular biology," the KWG viruses were products of the ultracentrifuge. The ultracentrifuge could be used both to prepare pure (eventually crystallized) viruses and to analyze their physical characteristics (weight, size). It was a perfect boundary-object, which linked the biological and the technical, botany and biochemistry, agriculture and medicine. Wartime research encompassed cancer and potato-virus studies as well as contributions to a decade-long discussion about the respective roles of proteins and nucleic acids in the control of TMV specificity and infectivity, a discussion that played a significant role in the identification of DNA as genetic material. After the war, the uses of the ultracentrifuge became ever more fundamental. Butenandt's former collaborators used TMV to pave their way into the second molecular biology, using studies of the plant virus to bring DNA structure and genetic information transfer to the fore. In 1954, on the basis of this work, they obtained the creation of an independent institute for virus research from the Max Planck Society, the postwar heir of the Kaiser Wilhelm Gesellschaft.

Reorganizer of German Biology. During the summer of 1944, Butenandt started to relocate his institute to Tübingen, well away from the dangers of a frequently bombed Berlin. When the Allies seized Tübingen, Butenandt was on a United States watch list because of his presumed participation in biological weapons research. However, the pressing need for German partners as well as a mounting cold war made Butenandt's case less and less suspicious. By 1947, he had been cleared of all accusations concerning his Nazi Party membership or his institutional successes. Moreover, having established new industrial connections and remained as the director of a major insti-

tute, he became a central figure in the reorganization of German science in general, and in the transition from the Kaiser Wilhelm Gesellschaft to the Max Planck Society in particular.

During the first postwar decade, Butenandt participated in the many decisions regarding the nominations of professors or the displacement, reorganization, and creation of laboratories making up the new West German biological landscape. His ideological role was no less minor. Butenandt contributed to a discourse of moral responsibility and denial of culpability, one that focused squarely on the value of pure science. Building on selective memories, he presented the KWG laboratories as centers of resistance against a Nazi dictatorship viewed as inherently hostile to science in light of the expulsion of good researchers and mandated technological work. Basing the reconstruction on this imagined tradition of fundamental research was all the more timely, as it echoed trends toward a massive governmental support of basic science then ascendant in the United States.

During the 1960s, while leading the Max Planck Institute for Biochemistry in Munich, Butenandt was a very active president of the Max Planck Society. Benefiting from large governmental funding for science, his presidency gave occasion for the development of a more fundamental and more molecular German biology, with the creation of institutes in molecular genetics and in biophysical chemistry. Butenandt advanced the collaboration between the Max Planck Gesellschaft institutes and German universities, but his reaction to the late 1960s student revolt was largely hostile. Although he accepted some "co-management" within the institutes (their reform gave the scientific collaborators new representation and protection), he viewed the Max Planck Society as a home for the defense of a productive and elite science against misplaced calls for the democratization of universities and the students' attacks against the generation of those who knew nothing and did nothing.

Adolf Butenandt died in 1995. His successful and problematic career blended biology, politics, and industry. As such he was a typical twentieth-century scientist.

BIBLIOGRAPHY

WORK BY BUTENANDT

Das Werk eines Lebens, 4 vols. Göttingen: Vandenhoeck & Rupprecht, 1981. Comprehensive collection of articles.

OTHER SOURCES

Brandt, Christina. *Metapher und Experiment: Von der Virusforschung zum genetischen Code.* Göttingen: Wallstein, 2004. Investigates the postwar development of virus research and the path toward molecular biology.

Ebbinghaus, Angelika, and Karl Heinz Roth. "Von der Rockefeller Foundation zur Kaiser-Wilhelm/Max-Planck-Gesellschaft: Adolf Butenandt als Biochemiker und Wissenschaftspolitiker des 20. Jahrhunderts." *Zeitschrift für Geschichtswissenschaft* 50 (2002): 389–418. Critical biography.

Gaudillière, Jean-Paul. "Better Prepared than Synthesized: Adolf Butenandt, Schering AG, and the Transformation of Sex Steroids into Drugs." *Studies in History and Philosophy of the Biological and the Biomedical Sciences* 36 (2005): 612–644. Analyzes the connection with industry.

Gausemeier, Bernd. *Natürliche Ordnungen und politische Allianzen: Biologische und biochemischen Forschung an Kaiser-Wilhelm-Instituten, 1933-1945.* Göttingen: Wallstein, 2005. Discusses Butenandt's research practices.

Karlson, Peter. *Adolf Butenandt: Biochemiker, Hormonforscher, Wissenschaftpoliker.* Stuttgart: Wissenschaftliche Verlaggesellschaft, 1990. Important but rather apologetic biography by former student. Includes a list of Butenandt's numerous publications.

Neubauer, Alfred. *Bittere Nobelpreise.* Berlin: Books on Demand, 2005. Analyzes refusal of the 1939 Nobel Prize.

Rheinberger, Hans-Jörg. "Virusforschung an den Kaiser-Wilhelm-Instituten für Biologie und Biochemie, 1937–1945." In *Epistemologie des Konkreten,* Frankfurt: Surkhamp, 2006.

Sachse, Carola, ed. *Die Verbindung nach Auschwitz. Biowissenschaften und Menschenversuche am Kaiser-Wilhelm Instituten.* Göttingen: Wallstein, 2003. Addresses the connection to Auschwitz.

Schieder, Wolfgang, and Achim Trunk, eds. *Adolf Butenandt und die Kaiser-Wilhelm-Gesellschaft, Wissenschaft, Industrie und Politik im Dritten Reich.* Göttingen: Walstein, 2004. Collection of studies of Butenandt's career; discusses the relation to Auschwitz.

Walker, Mark, and Carola Sachse, eds. *Politics and Science in Wartime: Comparative International Perspectives on the Kaiser Wilhelm Institutes.* Chicago: University of Chicago Press, 2004. An evaluation of the war-time mobilization of the Kaiser-Wilhelm institutes.

Jean-Paul Gaudillière

BUTLEROV, ALEKSANDR MIK-HAILOVICH

(b. Chistopol, Kazanskaya, Russia, 9 September 1828; d. Butlerovka, Kazanskaya, Russia, 17 August 1886), *chemistry, chemical structure, professionalization of Russian science.* For the original article on Butlerov see *DSB,* vol. 2.

Since G. V. Bykov's study of Butlerov appeared in the original *DSB,* relatively few works have been published that have examined Butlerov and his outstanding contributions to chemistry. The most important of these studies concern the nature of Butlerov's contribution to the the-ory of chemical structure, but others address topics including Butlerov's role in the professionalization of Russian chemistry, Butlerov's involvement with spiritual-ism, and his ultimately futile efforts to secure Dmitri Mendeleev a full membership in the St. Petersburg Acad-emy of Sciences.

The Theory of Chemical Structure. In his *DSB* study, Bykov forcefully argued that Butlerov was the originator of the concept of chemical structure. In doing so, he paid scant attention to Friedrich August Kekulé and other chemists who traditionally have been seen as the main contributors to the development of structure theory. Bykov's analyses in the *DSB* and elsewhere, as well as those of other Soviet historians of chemistry, were quite success-ful in bringing Butlerov's name to the attention of schol-ars outside of the Soviet Union, and some of these began to give Butlerov credit for the theory of chemical struc-ture. In the years since Bykov's *DSB* article, however, other very careful work has shifted the balance of attention back to Kekulé and other scientists for the formulation of the original concepts that comprised the structural theory in the years around 1858. Nevertheless, Butlerov played a seminal role in establishing a coherent theoretical frame-work for understanding these ideas, as well as in his exper-imental work elucidating various aspects of the structure theory.

Butlerov's interest in chemical structure undoubtedly arose during his first trip abroad in 1857–1858. Up to this time, he had focused his attention on teaching and finish-ing his master's and doctoral theses, neither of which con-tained significant experimental work. During his trip abroad, Butlerov met several times with Kekulé and Richard August Carl Emil Erlenmeyer, and later worked for several months in Charles Adolphe Wurtz's laboratory in Paris, conducting his first significant organic chemistry research there. It is clear that Butlerov's attention had shifted as a result of these conversations and meetings early in his trip, as his official plan for the trip written before he left Kazan included no provision for laboratory work at all and strongly hinted that the most important goal of the trip was to visit prominent vacation spots in Europe! While in Paris, Butlerov deepened his interest in the theory of chemical structure through discussions with Archibald Scott Couper, who shortly after Butlerov's departure published a paper that contained many of the essential features of Kekulé's theory, but which appeared slightly later. Butlerov, along with Couper, was one of the earliest members of the Société Chimique de Paris and presented an early version of his structure theory at a meeting of the society in 1858.

Butlerov returned to Russia following his trip abroad with a desire not only to transform chemistry in Russia

Aleksandr Mikhailovich Butlerov. SPL/PHOTO RESEARCHERS, INC.

but also to contribute to chemistry's general theoretical development. He continued the experiments he initiated in Paris and did not allow his geographical isolation in Kazan to isolate him from the chemical debates raging in western Europe, which often had happened to earlier Russian chemists when they returned from study abroad. When Butlerov next traveled abroad in 1861, he delivered a speech at the Speyer meeting of the Congress of German Naturalists and Physicians (Versammlung Deutscher Naturforscher und Aerzte), which Bykov took as the founding statement of the theory of chemical structure. However, Butlerov did not introduce any fundamentally new concepts in this speech. For example, while Butlerov insisted on the need to determine the chemical and not the actual physical arrangement of atoms in a compound, this distinction derived from a long line of his predecessors, including Jean Baptiste Dumas, Charles Frédéric Gerhardt, Auguste Laurent, Kekulé, Wurtz, and others. Moreover, Butlerov's call for chemists to search for "truly rational formulae" was not so different from Kekulé's use of formulas, even though the latter sometimes used differ-

ent formulae for the same substance in order to illustrate differing functions or reactions. Furthermore, Kekulé did not at this time begin "in despair to reject rational formulas" (in Bykov's phrase), but merely temporarily used empirical formulas in one paper because the substances he was addressing were too complicated for any other notational style to describe them simply. What *was* important about Butlerov's 1861 speech was that it clearly and convincingly argued that chemical structure could be determined through a consistent application of the theory of atomicity. Alan Rocke suggests that Butlerov's role here in the development of chemical structure was similar to the role Stanislao Cannizzaro had played only a few months earlier with respect to atomic and molecular magnitudes (1993). Finally, Butlerov himself in this speech disclaimed any priority to a new theory, but emphasized the need to consistently develop the existing theory of chemical structure.

In the years after 1861, Butlerov and his students conducted important experimental work that was designed to illustrate various aspects of the theory of chemical structure or its consequences. For example, Butlerov used structure theory to predict many different positional and structural isomers and he obtained many of them in the laboratory. One of the most famous of these was tertiary butyl alcohol, which Butlerov synthesized in 1863. The next year he was able to identify this compound as one predicted earlier by Hermann Kolbe. Butlerov and his students were able to synthesize and identify many homologues of this compound, greatly strengthening the structural theory. In the course of this work, Butlerov and his students formulated many different "rules" that showed how the specific structural environments of compounds help shape their chemical reactivity. Butlerov became, arguably, the most consistent and forceful advocate for the thorough use of the concepts of chemical structure. Butlerov himself never claimed to be the originator of the theory of chemical structure and did not deny Kekulé's role, but rather wanted his own role as a major developer of the theory to be acknowledged. Butlerov's goal was to clarify the confused and complex situation of organic chemistry by promoting a consistent use of standard terminology.

Professionalization of Russian Chemistry. Butlerov dramatically changed the style of his chemistry research after his trip abroad in 1857–1858, as well as its intellectual focus. Upon Butlerov's return from abroad, he expanded the chemistry laboratory and began to attract his first student "disciples." Of crucial significance for Russian science was his determination to professionalize chemistry at Kazan University by introducing various innovations that would put its teaching on the same basis as the most advanced university in Germany. First of all, this meant teaching chemistry through extensive laboratory exercises and practical work, including original research efforts, a pedagogical innovation of Justus Liebig and certain other German chemists of the 1830s and 1840s. Up to this time, chemistry laboratories at Russian universities largely were occupied with preparing items for lecture demonstrations, although a few students occasionally conducted some laboratory experiments, as did Butlerov when he was a student. Butlerov gradually persuaded the university to allocate more funds for the chemistry laboratory, which would permit all students to receive intensive practical training in the laboratory.

More importantly, Butlerov began to construct a stable pathway or career ladder for students who wished to pursue advanced training in chemistry. Over the course of several years, Butlerov obtained university funding to support a group of laboratory assistants who after several years of study and research work would be sent abroad to work for several years, usually in one of the best-known chemistry laboratories of western Europe. After returning to Kazan to finish their degrees, the young chemists would then be able to compete for a chemistry position at a higher educational institution in Russia. In spite of the relatively small number of chemistry students Butlerov was able to attract to his laboratory, he was spectacularly successful in producing future chemistry professors. His students became prominent chemists at Kazan, Moscow, and Warsaw Universities, among others. In addition, the tradition of excellence in chemistry continued at Kazan long after Butlerov's departure.

Other Aspects of Butlerov's Career. After Butlerov moved to St. Petersburg in 1868, he became heavily involved with spiritualism, an interest that lasted until his death. Until recently this aspect of Butlerov's career has not attracted much attention from scholars, and most historians of science tend to ignore or minimize any possible impact on or connection of spiritualism with his other more "scientific" activities. Butlerov was introduced to spiritualist phenomena by his cousin through marriage, Alexander N. Aksakov, a member of a very prominent cultural family in Russia at that time. Butlerov believed that spiritualist phenomena could be studied scientifically, but a scientific commission to investigate mediumistic phenomena organized by Mendeleev in 1875–1876 ended in mutual recriminations over deception and unfair practices. Bykov implies that this commission revealed the mediums as hoaxers and that the episode ended with a victory for the opponents of spiritualism. The verdict at the time, however, was not so clear-cut. The spiritualists claimed that Mendeleev and the commission had not followed the ground rules for séances, and so the results of their experiments were invalid; whether the spiritualists' objection was legitimate remains a matter of controversy.

While it is abundantly clear that Butlerov devoted considerable time and effort to spiritualism, the full extent of his activities and correspondence with other spiritualists likely will remain a mystery, as much of Butlerov's personal papers concerning spiritualism were destroyed after his death.

Perhaps surprisingly, considering Butlerov's clashes with Mendeleev over spiritualism, Butlerov took the lead only a few years later in trying to have Mendeleev elected to a full chair in the St. Petersburg Academy of Sciences. Butlerov had become involved with the Academy of Sciences shortly after his arrival in St. Petersburg and by 1874 had been elected to the highest (full chair) position in chemistry. Butlerov soon began to promote Mendeleev for an adjunct position at the Academy, but this failed in 1874, although a later vote for Mendeleev as a corresponding member in 1876 was successful. Soon after the death in 1880 of N. N. Zinin, a prominent chemist who held the chair of technology at the Academy, Butlerov proposed Mendeleev's candidacy for the vacant technology chair. However, the Academy declined to elect Mendeleev, despite Butlerov's vociferous advocacy. The result was a firestorm of protest in the media, which continued for months. Butlerov was convinced that an anti-Russian faction at the Academy was responsible for Mendeleev's rejection, although the situation was more complicated than only a conflict over nationalism. Butlerov continued to press for the election of Russians to the Academy until his death.

SUPPLEMENTARY BIBLIOGRAPHY

WORK BY BUTLEROV

Lektsii organicheskoi khimii, Nauchnoe nasledstvo 18, ed. O. D. Sterligov. Moscow: Nauka, 1990.

OTHER SOURCES

Brooks, Nathan M. "Alexander Butlerov and the Professionalization of Science in Russia." *Russian Review* 57 (1, 1998): 10–24.

Bykov, G. V. "K istoriografii teorii khimicheskogo stroeniia." *Voprosy istorii estestvoznaniia i tekhniki* 4 (1982): 121–130. A response to Rocke's 1981 article written shortly before Bykov's death.

Dmitriev, Igor S. "Skuchnaia istorii (o neizbranii D. I. Mendeleeva v Imperatorskuiu akademiiu nauk v 1880 g.)." *Voprosy istorii estestvoznaniia i tekhniki* 2 (2002): 231–280.

Gordin, Michael D. *A Well-Ordered Thing. Dmitrii Mendeleev and the Shadow of the Periodic Table.* New York: Basic Books, 2004. Includes information about Butlerov's involvement with spiritualism and his efforts to have Mendeleev elected to the Imperial Academy of Sciences in St. Petersburg.

Rocke, Alan J. "Kekulé, Butlerov, and the Historiography of the Theory of Chemical Structure." *British Journal for the History of Science* 14 (1981): 27–57. A detailed examination of the competing claims for Kekulé and Butlerov as the originator of the theory of chemical structure.

————. *The Quiet Revolution. Hermann Kolbe and the Science of Organic Chemistry.* Berkeley: University of California Press, 1993.

Nathan Brooks

BYERS, HORACE ROBERT (*b.* Seattle, Washington, 12 March 1906; *d.* Montecito, California, 22 May 1998), *meteorology, cloud physics, scientific administration.*

Byers was a leading educator and administrator in U.S. meteorology during the middle decades of the twentieth century. He worked to establish meteorology within American universities, built collaborations among schools, and wrote a widely used undergraduate textbook. As an officer of scientific societies and advisory committees, he guided the creation of institutions that structured government support for atmospheric science. As a researcher, he explored the physics of clouds and developed an influential model of thunderstorm dynamics.

Childhood and Education. Byers was the second of Charles H. and Harriet (Ensminger) Byers's four children. His father, a civil engineer, took a job with the Interstate Commerce Commission and moved the family to Berkeley, California, when Horace was nine years old. Byers grew up in a cultured home full of books where his mother often organized musical evenings. Byers developed a passion for journalism while in high school, editing the student newspaper and reporting for the *Berkeley Daily Gazette.* After a year working full-time for various papers around the San Francisco Bay Area, Byers enrolled at the University of California, Berkeley. While a student at Berkeley, Byers married Francis Isabel Clark in 1927. They remained together for the rest of Horace's life, over seventy-one years, and had one daughter, Henrietta.

Geography courses at Berkeley led Byers into meteorology. As a volunteer "cooperative observer" for the U.S. Weather Bureau, Byers took twice-daily weather observations in 1928. The Geography Department collected these observations and mailed them to several locations, including the Oakland airport. Through these observations, Carl-Gustaf Rossby found Byers and offered him a summer job helping to establish meteorological services supporting a model airway flying between Oakland and Los Angeles.

Early Career: "Backstop for a Genius." A summer job working for Rossby turned into a junior partnership that defined the first half of Byers's career. Partly through Byers's assistance, Rossby went on to become the most important figure in American meteorology in the twentieth century. In a 17 December 1956 article about Rossby titled "Man's Milieu," *Time* magazine described Byers as the "backstop for a genius." Between 1928 and Rossby's death in 1957, Byers often provided administrative and executive skills to support Rossby's ambitious plans for modernizing American meteorology.

During the summer of 1928, Rossby and Byers built a system to observe and forecast California weather. They put into practice the methods and theories of the Bergen School, originally developed by the Norwegian meteorologists working with Vilhelm and Jacob Bjerknes. This experimental arrangement became a model for later airline meteorological services. At the end of the summer, Rossby left to establish a teaching and research program in meteorology at the Massachusetts Institute of Technology (MIT). Byers returned to Berkeley, completing his AB degree in geography in 1929 and gathering data for his first research paper, "Summer Sea Fogs of the Central California Coast."

After receiving his bachelor's degree, Byers secured a fellowship from the Guggenheim Fund for the Promotion of Aeronautics to become Rossby's first graduate student. Rossby's teaching program focused on the relationship between synoptic meteorology (weather map analysis) and dynamic meteorology, the study of the physical laws that regulate the behavior of the atmosphere. He particularly focused on the weather models first developed in Bergen: air-mass analysis and the polar front. Rossby taught a few U.S. Navy "aerology" officers and civilians interested in working for the airlines, along with a handful of graduate students. Byers earned his MS from MIT in 1932 for a study of the characteristic weather phenomena of California.

During the Great Depression, meteorology had better job prospects than many professions. Byers first worked as a research assistant at the Scripps Institution of Oceanography under the direction of Harald Sverdrup, another Norwegian meteorologist and friend of Rossby. Later, Byers returned to work for the airline weather service he and Rossby had helped create. Now called Transcontinental and Western Airways and owned by the General Motors Corporation, TWA had Byers teach its pilots and flight dispatchers how to use Bergen techniques in daily operations. The teaching materials Byers developed became the core of his 1937 textbook, *Synoptic and Aeronautical Meteorology.* As an employee of a GM subsidiary, Byers became eligible for an Alfred Sloan fellowship, which supported his continued studies at MIT. Byers completed his doctoral degree in 1935, researching "The Changes in Air Masses during Lifting."

The disastrous crashes of two navy dirigibles, along with the general expansion of aviation during the 1920s, brought political attention to weather forecasting failures in 1933. After congressional hearings and a report by the newly founded Science Advisory Board, the Weather Bureau was directed to modernize its forecasting practices by incorporating the methods of the Bergen School. In June of 1935, the bureau appointed Byers to head a new Air Mass Analysis Section. For the next five years, Byers taught small groups of experienced forecasters the new methods. The bureau was a deeply conservative institution during the first half of the twentieth century, as a result of its public exposure and its insular organizational structure. As a twenty-nine-year-old outsider, hired to teach experienced older men new skills, Byers met a frosty reception. Reminiscing in 1976, Byers expressed considerable bitterness about the bureau's forecasters of this period.

Byers was detailed to Chicago to establish a new forecasting center in 1940. He left the Weather Bureau soon after, founding an Institute of Meteorology at the University of Chicago. Rossby, by this point the preeminent meteorologist in the United States, became the institute's official leader—despite his reputation for disregarding financial and administrative details. Over the next fifteen years, Byers worked behind the scenes to keep things running smoothly and ensure that Rossby had the people and resources he needed to build a world-class research and graduate program in dynamic meteorology.

The resources for building a premier program came primarily from the military. During World War II, Rossby and Byers worked through the University Meteorological Committee, a loose affiliation of the five university departments that offered graduate training in meteorology, to make Chicago a major center for training military weather officers. About seventeen hundred forecasters were trained there between 1940 and 1945. These trainees used Byers's *Synoptic and Aeronautical Meteorology* as a textbook, and after 1944 a much expanded version, *General Meteorology*. The teaching done by Byers and others during the war helped to secure the ideals of calculation, objectivity, and the primacy of research that characterized postwar weather forecasting. Byers also consulted for the armed forces, helping to set up airlift routes across South America and Africa during 1943–1944. Tropical forecasting challenges contributed to the creation of the Institute of Tropical Meteorology in Puerto Rico in 1943, associated with the University of Chicago. The Chicago department also issued a number of research publications during the war, including methods for single-station forecasting, operating mobile weather stations, and a 1942 report by Byers on *Non-Frontal Thunderstorms*.

Research: Thunderstorms and Weather Modification. Thunderstorms were a serious threat to aviation, especially as wartime needs often made it impossible to fly far around storms or stay on the ground. Byers's work on thunderstorms developed into a major investigation supported by the Weather Bureau, Army Air Force, Navy, National Advisory Committee on Aeronautics, and explicitly authorized by Congress. The Thunderstorm Project, designed and directed by Byers, was one of the first examples of post–World War II "big science" in meteorology. During the summers of 1946 in central Florida and 1947 in southern Ohio, Byers led sixty-six researchers and observers, supported by dozens of pilots and aircraft support crew. With a squadron of Army Air Force fighter planes at his disposal, Byers arranged for flights of five specially instrumented planes to penetrate storms simultaneously at different altitudes. Tracked by radar and film, the movements of the planes were recorded and later correlated with pilot balloon and surface measurements.

The project's final report (*The Thunderstorm*, 1949) proposed a model of thunderstorm behavior. The model posited that thunderstorms are composed of one or more convection cells, where each cell went through a three-stage life cycle. In the cell's cumulus stage, rising currents of warm, moist air produced strong updrafts, creating a tower of cumulus cloud. The mature stage was marked by side-by-side updrafts and downdrafts, and with water vapor condensing as it was pushed skyward by the updrafts. As water drops and ice crystals became larger in size, the warm air rushing upwards could no longer support them. Heavy rain fell from part of the cloud, dragging a strong downdraft of cold air with it. In the dissipating stage, the falling precipitation pulled in more of the cool, dry air surrounding the upper levels of the storm cloud. This extinguished the cell's convection and was accompanied by light rain and gentler downdrafts.

The Thunderstorm Project demonstrated the utility of radar for meteorological research and led to the development of airplane-mounted weather radars. The Thunderstorm Project also brought Byers into contact with Ted Fujita, a young Japanese severe-storm researcher whom Byers invited to the United States in 1951, enabling Fujita to establish a storied career in tornado research and aviation safety. More generally, the project demonstrated how academic-led experiments utilizing military equipment could benefit various parties, including commercial interests, scientists, the military, and civilian governments. Byers's next major research project followed patterns set by the Thunderstorm Project.

Weather modification became a central topic in meteorological research following the discovery of *cloud seeding* in late 1946 by Vincent Schaefer, a chemist working for General Electric. Schafer's boss, Nobel Laureate

Irving Langmuir, enthusiastically promoted this discovery and made increasingly extravagant claims about the capabilities of cloud seeding over the next decade. While dynamic meteorologists like Byers and Rossby utilized the funding and support for meteorology that came with new strategic importance of controlling the skies (many people compared weather modification to atomic energy), university meteorologists were generally skeptical of the large-scale effects claimed by cloud-seeding advocates such as Langmuir.

This skepticism was supported by the results of early weather modification experiments like the multi-agency Artificial Cloud Nucleation Project, conducted during 1953 and 1954. Byers led the University of Chicago portion. Again given World War II–surplus planes and military pilots to fly them, Byers tested cloud-seeding techniques over the Caribbean Sea and the American Midwest. The experiments produced extensive data on the physical properties of cumulus clouds and mechanisms of precipitation development; however, as Byers and his coauthors noted in their 1957 final report, "any effects from seeding these clouds were too small to be detected in the sample size obtained" (p. 47).

Cloud physics remained central to Byers's research until his retirement in 1974. While cloud physics research was primarily funded because of its connection to the possibilities of weather modification, Byers remained a "constructive critic" of weather modification, in the words of his colleagues Roscoe Braham and Thomas Malone (p. 45). Always concerned with education, Byers consolidated his research into a textbook, publishing *Elements of Cloud Physics* in 1965.

Organizing Atmospheric Science. Administrative work remained a central aspect of the second half of Byers's career. In the decades after World War II, Byers played key roles in organizing and structuring U.S. government support for atmospheric science research. Byers also spent the last ten years of his working career (1965–1974) as dean and then academic vice president at Texas Agriculture and Mining University, supervising the expansion of its geosciences programs.

Through his work with scientific societies and international organizations, Byers helped build professional identity among meteorologists, maintain standards of training and research behavior, and advocate for the interests of atmospheric science. Byers held policy-setting offices with the American Meteorological Society (AMS) and the American Geophysical Union, Section on Meteorology. Byers served as a councilor of the AMS from 1938 to 1950, and then president from 1951 to 1953. Between 1944 and 1950, he served as vice president and then president of the AGU, Section on Meteorology. Byers con-

tributed to the organization of the International Geophysical Year as vice president of the International Association of Meteorology and Atmospheric Physics between 1954 and 1960. He presided over the International Association from 1961 to 1963.

Byers's research and organizing work led to his election to the National Academy of Sciences in 1952. In 1956, Byers was appointed to the National Research Council's Committee on Meteorology, along with other eminent scientists, including Rossby, Lloyd Berkner, John von Neumann, and Edward Teller. When Rossby died in 1957, Byers was elevated to vice chairman. Charged with viewing "in broad perspective the present position and future requirements of meteorological research," the committee created two working groups, one on research, and a second led by Byers focusing on education (quoted in Braham and Malone, p. 37). Released in early 1958, the two groups' recommendations advocated the formation of an interuniversity committee to overcome challenges posed by the shortage of trained meteorologists and inadequate resources for research. According to Braham and Malone's biographical memoir, "Byers's distinctive contribution … was to pick up the telephone and call Henry Houghton [Meteorology Department chairman] at MIT and urge him to … [act] on the recommendation for a University Committee on Atmospheric Research" (pp. 39-40). Characteristically behind the scenes, Byers thus played a key role in creating UCAR, which became one of the most important organizations in U.S. atmospheric science in the twentieth century. More publicly, Byers served on UCAR's Board of Trustees, including three years as board chairman (1962–1965).

When Byers moved from the University of Chicago to Texas A&M in 1965, he became dean of the College of Geosciences. Elevated to academic vice president in 1968, he served until reaching mandatory retirement age in 1974. He and his wife returned to their native state, moving to Santa Barbara, California, where they lived for twenty-four more years, until their deaths a few months apart, in 1998.

BIBLIOGRAPHY

WORKS BY BYERS

"Summer Sea Fogs of the Central California Coast." *University of California Publications in Geography* 3 (1930): 291–338.

Characteristic Weather Phenomena of California. Massachusetts Institute of Technology Meteorological Papers, vol. 1, no. 2. Cambridge, MA: Massachusetts Institute of Technology, 1931.

"The Changes in Air Masses during Lifting." PhD diss., Massachusetts Institute of Technology, 1935.

Synoptic and Aeronautical Meteorology. New York: McGraw-Hill, 1937.

Non-Frontal Thunderstorms. University of Chicago Institute of Meteorology Miscellaneous Reports, no. 3. Chicago: University of Chicago Press, 1942.

General Meteorology. New York: McGraw-Hill, 1944.

With Roscoe Braham Jr. *The Thunderstorm.* Washington, DC: U.S. Department of Commerce, 1949.

With Roscoe Braham Jr. "Thunderstorm Structure and Dynamics." In *Thunderstorm Electricity*, edited by Horace Byers. Chicago: University of Chicago Press, 1953.

With Roscoe Braham Jr., and Louis Battan. "Artificial Nucleation of Cumulus Clouds." In *Cloud and Weather Modification: A Group of Field Experiments,* edited by Sverre Petterssen. Meteorological Monographs, vol. 2, no. 11. Boston: American Meteorological Society, 1957.

General Meteorology, Published Formerly under the Title Synoptic and Aeronautical Meteorology. 1st ed. New York: McGraw-Hill, 1944. *General Meteorology.* 3rd edition. New York: McGraw-Hill, 1959.

"Carl-Gustaf Arvid Rossby, the Organizer." In *The Atmosphere and the Sea in Motion: Scientific Contributions to the Rossby Memorial Volume,* edited by Bert Bolin. New York: Rockefeller Institute Press, 1959.

Elements of Cloud Physics. Chicago: University of Chicago Press, 1965.

"History of Weather Modification." In *Weather and Climate Modification,* edited by W. N. Hess. New York: John Wiley and Sons, 1974. A generally skeptical discussion of cloud-seeding-related events from 1946 to 1971.

"The Founding of the Institute of Meteorology at the University of Chicago." *Bulletin of the American Meteorological Society* 57

(1976): 1343–1345. Describes the institutions and attitudes of American meteorology around 1940.

Oral history interview by Earl Droessler. 3 August 1987. 1 sound cassette (2 hours). Archives. National Center for Atmospheric Research/University Corporation for Atmospheric Research, Boulder, CO 80307. Byers discusses early UCAR and NCAR development, the history of meteorology, and the history of the American Meteorological Society.

OTHER SOURCES

Braham, Roscoe Jr. "The Thunderstorm Project." *Bulletin of the American Meteorological Society* 77 (August 1996): 1835–1845. A published version of a lunchtime speech about Braham's and Byers's work on the project.

———. "Horace Robert Byers, 1906–1998." *Bulletin of the American Meteorological Society* 79 (December 1998): 2810–2813.

———, and Thomas F. Malone. "Horace Robert Byers." *Biographical Memoirs,* vol. 79. Washington, DC: National Academy of Sciences, 2001. Available from http://fermat.nap.edu/html/biomems/. Both Braham and Malone were close colleagues of Byers.

"Man's Milieu." *Time* (17 December 1956): 68–79. Mostly about Rossby, illustrates how Rossby's charisma often overshadowed Byers's contributions.

Roger Turner